MADISON
A History of the
Formative Years

To a special friend
Happy Birthday!

[signature]

1983

MADISON
A History of the Formative Years

David V. Mollenhoff

Kendall/Hunt Publishing Company
2460 Kerper Boulevard • Dubuque, Iowa

Graphic Credits

Graphics used in the book come from the Iconographic
Collections, Visual and Sound Archives, the State
Historical Society of Wisconsin; the University of
Wisconsin Archives; a variety of private collections; the
University of Wisconsin Cartographic Laboratory; and the
public domain. All graphics used in the first four categories
are attributed in the caption. All graphics provided by the
State Historical Society of Wisconsin will be designated by
the initials SHSW and the negative number, e.g., WHi
(X3)40531. All maps were prepared by the University of
Wisconsin Cartographic Laboratory.

To Leigh, Kristin, and Peter

Cover courtesy of Tom C. Pearson

Design, copy editing, and technical production assistance by
Warner Technical Services

This book was written with the help of grants from the following corporations, foundations, and individuals:

Publication and Library Distribution Grants

The Madison Rotary Foundation
United Madison Community Foundation

Research and Writing Grants

Patrons

American Family Insurance
Norman Basset Foundation
Garver Memorial Trust
Evjue Foundation
First Wisconsin National Bank of Madison
Oscar Mayer Foundation
Webcrafters-Frautschi Foundation, Inc.

Sponsors

Findorff Foundation
The Wisconsin State Journal
Verex Corporation

Supporters

Catherine H. Coleman
Jane and Reed Coleman
Dane County Title
Janet S. Ela
Hovde & Hovde, Inc.
Lydia Hendley Lunney Memorial Fund
Madison Gas and Electric Company
Marling Lumber Company
National Guardian Life Insurance Company
The Schroeder Funeral Home
The Stark Company
Bruce Thomas
Wisconsin Power and Light Company

Contents

Preface

In 1890 the U.S. census reported the close of a major era in American history. For the first time, there was no longer any frontier line. Americans had crossed and settled the continent. This fact, embodied in a famous 1893 essay by Frederick Jackson Turner, then a young history instructor at the University of Wisconsin, triggered a massive reinterpretation of American history focusing on the role of the frontier.

Then in 1920 the decennial census reported still another milestone development: for the first time more than half of all Americans lived in cities and towns. Like the demise of the frontier before it, the shift from farm to city prompted historians to examine the role of cities in American history. From the 1920s to the 1950s many scholars concentrated on developing a comprehensive and accommodating theory within whose confines productive research could be done. From the 1950s to the present most scholars concentrated on various components of urban history such as interurban rivalry, land use, social stratification, urban planning, and many others.

Curiously, amidst all the urban literature, there is one category that, with a few notable exceptions, has not received the attention it deserves, nor has it fulfilled its considerable potential. I refer to the urban biography, here defined as a book-length synthesis of forces that caused a city to develop in a particular way. This is not to say that large numbers of book-length community "histories" have not been published.

In fact, for many years such books have probably been the most popular form of local history. The point is that most of these books suffer from serious shortcomings. In 1972 and 1973 after I decided to write the history of Madison, but before I began my formal research, I examined about one hundred of these books. That experience produced a feeling of great promise but also of great disappointment. Many were little more than captioned photo albums. At the other extreme, there were three-volume tomes with almost no graphics. Most were antiquarian in tone, that is, they provided a chronicle of unrelated facts and little else. Most tended to romanticize the past. Indeed if one were to believe these sanitized versions, nearly all the early settlers were models of probity, enterprise and decorum, an interpretation the facts seldom sustain.

Madison, Wisconsin, like most other cities across the country has suffered from a lack of good local history. Although the city is 145 years old, the last reasonably comprehensive histories were published in 1874 and 1876. All other efforts to synthesize local history fall into such categories as tourists' guides, business anniversary editions, and civic primers.

This sampling of urban "histories" from various cities across the country and from Madison convinced me the time had come for a new type of urban biography that can enhance our understanding of cities, our culture, and ourselves. According to the 1980 census, more than seven out

of ten Americans live in urbanized areas. Therefore urban biographies can illuminate that stratum of history that touches the lives of most Americans most of the time. The urban biography is one of the very few sources from which we can obtain an *integrated* understanding of city development. This is not to say that monographs on this or that aspect of cities are not useful. They are. The problem with specialized studies is that they fail to provide what the more inclusive and interpretative urban biography can do better, namely, give meaning, coherence, perspective, a sense of place and even roots. The urban biography can allow contemporaries to see the drama of their town being born, growing into a village, and then maturing as a city. Indeed, who can read a good urban biography of their community and not despair at their predecessors' blindness, agonize about their problems, and admire their successes? The urban biography is also well suited to convey an appreciation of a fact now only dimly glimpsed by most citizens, viz, the exasperating difficulties inherent in building and rebuilding cities.

Fortunately, these benefits of the urban biography are beginning to be more widely appreciated. This fact in turn creates exciting opportunities for historians to write a new generation of urban biographies. This book is one effort in that direction.

But what, you ask, are the characteristics of this new generation? My research and reflection convinced me that the new urban biographies must have six key specifications. In the remainder of this preface I will illustrate these specifications with reference to *Madison: A History of the Formative Years.*

1. *They should serve the needs of a broad audience without abandoning the needs of more serious scholars.* This book was written for newcomers and natives, students, journalists, history buffs, community leaders, in short, anyone who wants to know how Madison got to be the way it is. To serve this broad audience I have tried to make the book rich in detail, nearly inclusive in coverage, consistently interpretive and, of course, readable. For those who may desire to do additional research in Madison history, I have provided ample assistance in notes at the back of the book.

2. *They should be inclusive and interdisciplinary.* Urban history is much like ecology in that everything is related in some way to almost everything else. Society is interwoven with politics, politics with economics, economics to geography, geography to sociology, sociology with religion, religion to politics, and on and on. Therefore the urban biographer is confronted with the formidable task of understanding these linkages. It is for this reason that the urban biographer must have a good grasp of geology, paleoecology, archeology, urban geography, political science, economics, literature, religion, sociology, demography, technology, and of course history insofar as they shed light on a particular community.

3. *They should recognize the reciprocal relationships between local, state, and national history.* The best urban biographies are those that portray local history in the context of state and national history. When properly used these two dimensions provide a backdrop against which local history can be seen with greater clarity. It is for this reason that I have tried to show these contextual relationships whenever appropriate. The rule I followed in determining whether to provide such a backdrop was straightforward: wherever state or national events have a significant impact on major local developments, I include them. Where they don't, I don't. For

example, when Andrew Jackson issued the famous Specie Circular in 1837 requiring all land sales to be transacted with gold, speculation in Madison-area lands collapsed and didn't recover for ten years. That was a significant local impact of a national policy.

4. *They should make effective use of graphics.* Graphics are one of the most valuable resources available to the urban biographer and yet few urban histories use them effectively. All graphics selected for use in this book were picked because they illustrate and supplement important points described in the text. Each is offered as evidence, not as ornamentation. Because they were selected for this reason, each graphic is located at the point where the subject is discussed in the text. Graphics have also been used to provide a better understanding of local geography. It was for this reason that several dozen maps were commissioned showing glacial characteristics, Indian features, presettlement vegetation patterns, postsettlement urban growth, locations of important buildings and events, and several others. It is my hope that taken together the more than three hundred graphics in this book will make Madison history richer, more vivid, more interesting and, most important of all, more understandable than what one could achieve with mere words.

5. *They should give the reader a feel for what it was like to live in the city.* Most urban biography readers are keenly interested in how people lived, how they played, what they wore, what role religion played in their lives, what irritants bedeviled them, and the like. This type of detail, often called social history, can in conjunction with key developments capture the all important community ethos, ambience, and personality as no other historical dimension can.

6. *They should offer a clear and compelling interpretive framework.* Probably no decisions faced by an urban biographer are more difficult and at the same time critical to the success of the book than those related to the interpretive framework. The sense of peril and risk that accompany this decision is heightened by the knowledge that

there are almost as many options as there are histories of cities. For this book I have selected an interpretive framework that, though experimental, offers great promise. More specifically I have emphasized public policies and the roles played by certain widely held values in shaping the city. My research convinced me that these two factors reveal more about a community more quickly and more coherently than any other framework and that they therefore provide one of the most effective means of charting the interrelated streams of life that flow through every community.

By "public policies" I mean the cumulative decisions affecting city character and development made by public or in some instances private bodies. In most cases these policies were products of debate although sometimes they were formulated by default. As I use the term I include a broad spectrum of elements ranging from minor "irritants," such as how to control rowdy behavior, to the more momentous questions about city destiny.

A public policy emphasis provides many advantages to the urban biographer. It enables a large amount of material to be effectively integrated. It allows one to compare the extent to which ideals and aspirations became reality. It keeps contemporaries mindful of the complexity of yesteryear's decisions. It puts the past in a frame of reference that can be readily compared to the present and in this respect offers a commodious bridge between past and present. Finally, the public policy emphasis can overcome one of the greatest bogies of the urban biography, namely, the ability to compare development among communities.

The emphasis upon values in this book is in part an attempt to compensate for their absence in most other urban biographies, but it is also an attempt to create a frame of reference that allows us to relate ourselves to our predecessors. I define values as those qualities thought to be good or bad by Madison residents that contributed to the character and direction of the city. At first glance one might conclude that such a definition is hopelessly broad—and there is a sense in which it is.

However, in practice the key values can be distilled into a mere handful. I will say more about this in a moment.

In researching this book I was struck by the way both public policy decisions and key values tended to cluster around three themes: (1) the clash of cultures; (2) the disagreement about Madison's destiny; and (3) the growth of local government power. I therefore decided to make this convergence of public policy and values around these three issues the core of my analysis. Let me briefly explain these themes.

Clash of Cultures. Madison like nearly all American cities provided a home for persons of many national and ethnic backgrounds. Sometimes these groups got along and sometimes they did not. The participants, particularly the Yankees and the Teutons, had very different concepts about the way the Sabbath should be observed, whether alcohol should be consumed, and how people should spend their leisure time. These conflicts, fueled by major value differences, produced running battles over important public policy questions such as the proper role and form of local government. An analysis of this theme reveals much about the distribution and use of power in Madison during this period.

Disagreement About Madison's Destiny. From earliest times, people considered Madison a special place. Because it was *the* state capital, Madison had to be a model, a city on a pedestal. As the home of the state university, Madison was expected to be a place of culture, a cerebral city, a magnet for distinguished, talented, and articulate people. As the proud possessor of an incomparable natural site, Madisonians felt compelled to enhance nature's gift with manmade beauty. But Madison also became the center of a nine-track railroad network linking the city with nearly every point on the compass—a fact that gave Madison great potential as a posh northern resort, as a regional commercial center, and even as a great manufacturing city. Like a gifted child with many obvious talents, Madison could become great and famous in many ways.

Like parents of a gifted child, Madison leaders possessed a fierce pride and intense love for their special city and wanted to do what was best for its future development. But, as they quickly discovered, they disagreed about what kind of city Madison should become. Once again this dispute was fueled by conflicting values. Smoke stacks (jobs) were pitted against beauty, and culture against commerce. Many argued that city population growth was an unalloyed good and a reflection of power to be sought for its own sake. Other Madisonians argued—and this was most unusual in American urban history—that growth was bad and should therefore be opposed. Predictably these differences were quickly transformed into public policy issues; seldom did the matter subside into consensus.

Growth of Local Government Power. During the early years of Madison's history nearly everyone agreed that the proper role for local government was to get out of the way and let private enterprise do what had to be done. If something was needed, someone would go around town raising money with a private subscription. But soon the serious consequences of this laissez faire policy became evident and led to a slow, reluctant, but inexorable growth in the scope and power of local government. Therefore the story of the abandonment of the laissez faire theory of government and the establishment of a more activist, interventionist progressive model represents one of the major developments of the formative years. In this instance expansion of local government was fueled by a strong belief in meliorism, that is, the belief that Madison could and should be improved. The changes in public policy resulting from this meliorism were particularly dramatic in the way people perceived the urban environment.

Another major decision relating to the interpretative framework was whether to organize the material topically or chronologically, or to blend the two elements. A pure topical approach can highlight single elements in brilliant detail, but usually at the price of subordinating context. A pure chronological approach can provide comfortable handrails through confusing events, but

can become Procrustean. Generally speaking, both approaches tend to smother the inherent drama of city building. I therefore decided to blend topical and chronological elements because such a blend better reveals the interrelatedness of forces that shaped Madison and at the same time, provides a better feeling about the quality of life in a particular period. It is for this reason that I organized the book into six *eras,* each of which became the subject of a chapter.

There is one final point on which I feel obligated to comment. Many will ask why I stopped at 1920. The answer is that by 1920 Madison had developed readily identifiable modern characteristics. The new (present) capital building had been completed, the auto was rapidly becoming the dominant mode of transportation, the first skyscrapers stood on the Capitol Square, the park system that was to serve the city so well for decades beyond 1920 had been acquired and developed, and central city housing quality was deteriorating, to name just a few. In short, these were the *formative* years when Madison's character, shape, and appearance were established.

Now, reader, you know the context in which this book was written, how it was organized and why. I hope you enjoy the book.

David V. Mollenhoff
Madison, Wisconsin
May 1982

Acknowledgments

No one can ever write a book like this without incurring many debts of gratitude. In this brief space I want to acknowledge those debts to the extent one can.

To the twenty-five individuals, foundations, and corporations listed on the donor page who provided generous financial assistance, I say thank you. Without their support this book would have remained a mere idea.

To Roth Schleck for his strong early interest in the book, for his invaluable help in fundraising, and for his persistent encouragement through a long gestation period, I say thank you.

To Carol Toussaint who played a key role in generating financial support and whose one-year leave of absence allowed me to work full-time on the book, I say thank you.

To Heidi Bollinger, Pat Butler, Mariann Goss, and Judy Woodward, four exceptionally able research assistants, I say thank you. Without their painstaking and resourceful research over five long years the book simply could not have been done.

To Margie Borgrud who for four years patiently, precisely, and cheerfully typed notecards, drafts, revisions, correspondence, more revisions, on and on, I say thank you. Lucky is the author who has someone like her. I also wish to thank Violet Lehmann, Catherine Ostlind, and Beverly Schrag who typed early portions of the manuscript.

To Merle Curti, Professor Emeritus of History, University of Wisconsin; Frank Custer, a devoted student of Madison history; Stanley K. Schultz, Professor of History, University of Wisconsin; William F. Thompson, Research Director, the State Historical Society of Wisconsin; and Elizabeth Uhr, a talented freelance editor, who read nearly all of the manuscript, I say thank you. Your astute and constructive comments greatly strengthened the manuscript.

I also want to thank Robert H. Dott, Jr., Professor of Geology, University of Wisconsin College of Letters and Science; Francis D. Hole, Professor of Soil Science, University of Wisconsin College of Agricultural and Life Sciences; David M. Michelson, Professor of Geology, University of Wisconsin College of Letters and Science; Phillip Salkin, Senior Archeologist, Archeology Consulting and Service Company; and Albert M. Swain, Assistant Scientist, University of Wisconsin Center for Climatic Research, for their helpful comments on those portions of the manuscript dealing with archeology, paleoecology, and geology in which I have no technical expertise.

To the good people at Kendall/Hunt who transformed a bulky manuscript into the book you hold in your hands, I say thank you. I particularly want to thank Tom Gantz, Kendall/Hunt Associate Editor, whose strong interest in the project buoyed up my spirits and whose continuing support greatly eased the transformation from manuscript to book.

To Marian Warner, Warner Technical Services, for her careful preparation of the long manuscript for the production stage, I say thank you. Under the best of conditions, this process is difficult and often exasperating, but Marian's expertise and wonderful personality made it a joy.

To Jerry Minnich who contributed much friendly counsel and his storehouse of book marketing expertise, I say thank you.

Finally, to my wife and children who tolerated long work hours, missed vacations, and too little time together, I say thank you and never again.

And now I come to that point at which all authors eventually arrive, that is, where I gulp and confess that in spite of all the outstanding assistance I have enjoyed from those named above—but in truth many more—I alone am responsible for all that follows. There, I said it!

MADISON
A History of the Formative Years

1 Foundations: Prehistory to 1846

Paleohistory

The Land

In early June, 1866, a group of well drillers assembled their equipment on the west lawn of the Capitol Park. The men had been hired by the State of Wisconsin to drill an eight-inch-diameter hole deep into the earth until they found a flowing (artesian) water supply that could protect the newly constructed capitol from fire. For two years the crews kept their drills spinning deeper and deeper into the earth until they reached a depth of 1,015 feet. But even at this great depth, one hundred feet below sea level, an artesian water source failed to appear. Why, no one could understand. The perplexed and frustrated drillers packed up their equipment and left.[1]

To the state officials and legislators who approved nearly nine thousand dollars to drill the hole, the enterprise was an embarrassing and expensive failure. But to a handful of early geologists who avidly examined the many layers of dark red, pink, green, yellow, black, and gray materials the drillers brought to the surface, the enterprise was a great success for it provided the first detailed record of Madison's geological history.[2] Indeed to this group of observers, the steam-powered machine that hammered steel bits deep into the earth was not merely a well-drilling rig. It was also a time machine capable of travelling great distances and revealing incredible stories.

In fact, that colorful pile of pulverized rock that drillers had discarded on the west lawn of the capitol contained a record going back one and one-half *billion* years.[3]

The first 125 feet were easy for the well drillers. Their bits moved quickly through the loose sand and gravel—materials that told the powerful and exciting climax of a long geological saga. Exactly when this last chapter began geologists cannot say for sure, but sometime between one and three million years ago the earth's climate began to cool. More and more snow fell and less and less melted. Snow falling in northern Canada accumulated to great depths. When it reached about twenty-five feet, the pressure of its own weight transformed the once soft and fluffy snowflakes into ice. When the snow accumulated to a depth of two hundred feet, an event of great moment occurred. A rock at the edge of the thickening ice sheet was nudged from its position. Like a pie crust spread by the pressure of a rolling pin, the ice began to spread outward. The ice mass had become a glacier. From a point centered around today's Hudson Bay the glacier crept forth, growing in thickness and size until it towered above all landforms and boasted continental proportions.[4]

As the continental ice mass entered what is now Upper Michigan, two bulges on its leading edge suggested that the glacier was about to unleash a great force. One bulge soon took the form of a peninsula and headed southwest at the speed of about one kilometer a year. Now known as the Green Bay lobe, it arrived in the place we now call Madison fourteen to twenty thousand years ago. The other bulge, now designated the Lake Michigan lobe, headed southwest toward a place later called Chicago.[5]

The great continental glaciers were the mightiest invaders ever loosed on the earth. By comparison, the wind was a feather duster, the water a mere rake. As the glacier advanced, it pried up bedrock, captured huge boulders, and pushed nearly everything out of its way. It pulverized, scraped, scoured, and bulldozed. Like a huge vacuum cleaner, it picked up massive amounts of dust, dirt, and debris. In northern Wisconsin the glacier reached a thickness of nearly two miles, and at the spot where the state Capitol now stands, the glacier towered sixteen hundred feet into the air—more than the combined height of five capitol buildings, the equivalent of a 160-story skyscraper![6]

Then, beginning about fourteen thousand years ago, the sun began to win its battle with the great continental glacier. Warmer, dryer weather shut off the source of motive power that had driven the massive ice machine in its thousand-mile advance from the north. Deprived of the cold and snow it needed to grow, the glacier ground to a halt just ten miles west of Capitol Hill. Each

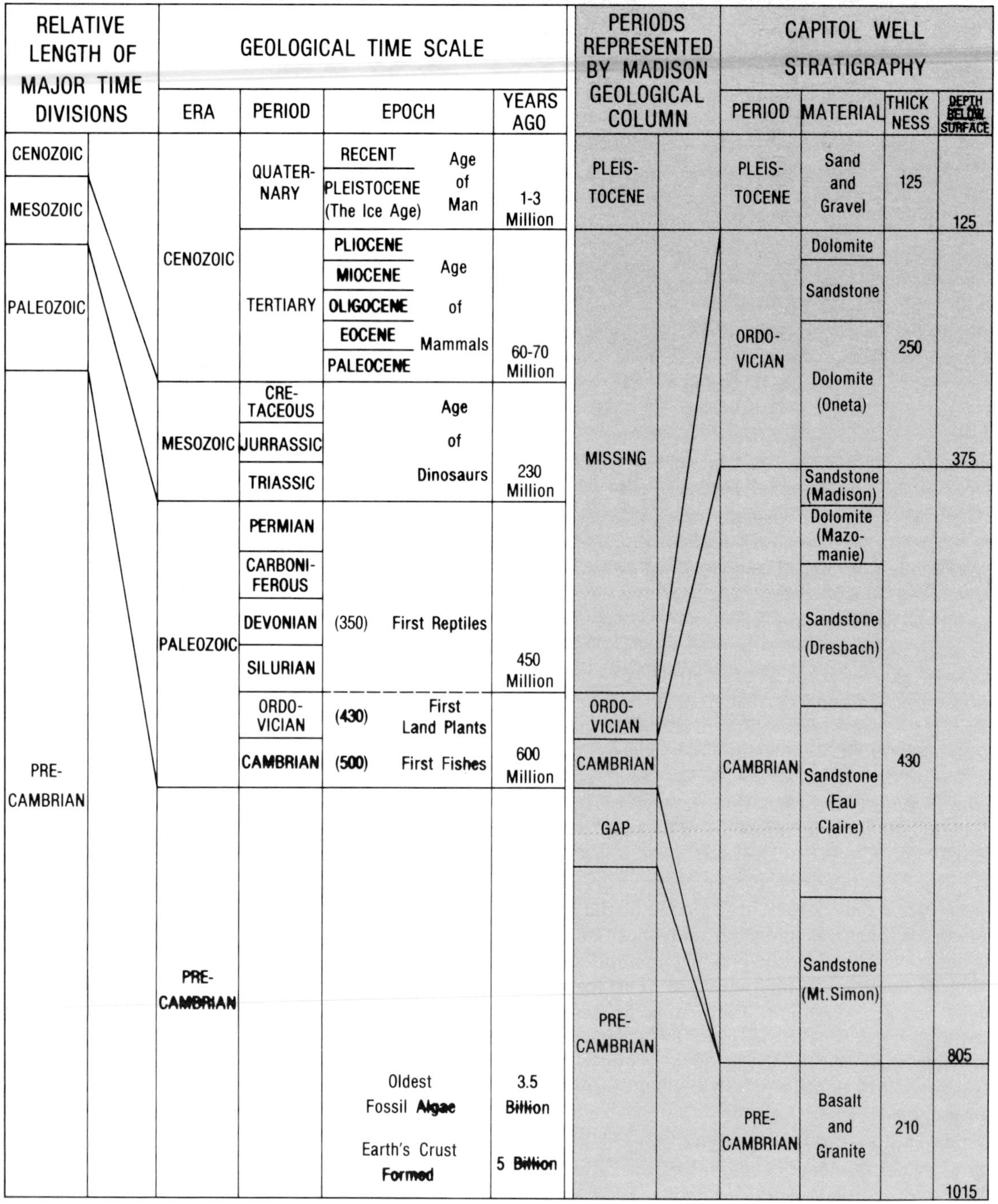

RELATIVE LENGTH OF MAJOR TIME DIVISIONS	GEOLOGICAL TIME SCALE				PERIODS REPRESENTED BY MADISON GEOLOGICAL COLUMN	CAPITOL WELL STRATIGRAPHY			
	ERA	PERIOD	EPOCH	YEARS AGO		PERIOD	MATERIAL	THICKNESS	DEPTH BELOW SURFACE
CENOZOIC	CENOZOIC	QUATERNARY	RECENT / PLEISTOCENE (The Ice Age) — Age of Man	1-3 Million	PLEISTOCENE	PLEISTOCENE	Sand and Gravel	125	125
MESOZOIC		TERTIARY	PLIOCENE / MIOCENE / OLIGOCENE / EOCENE / PALEOCENE — Age of Mammals	60-70 Million	MISSING	ORDOVICIAN	Dolomite / Sandstone / Dolomite (Oneta)	250	375
PALEOZOIC	MESOZOIC	CRETACEOUS / JURRASSIC / TRIASSIC	Age of Dinosaurs	230 Million		CAMBRIAN	Sandstone (Madison) / Dolomite (Mazomanie)		
	PALEOZOIC	PERMIAN / CARBONIFEROUS / DEVONIAN	(350) First Reptiles	450 Million	ORDOVICIAN	CAMBRIAN	Sandstone (Dresbach)	430	
		SILURIAN			CAMBRIAN		Sandstone (Eau Claire)		
PRE-CAMBRIAN		ORDOVICIAN	(430) First Land Plants	600 Million	GAP				
		CAMBRIAN	(500) First Fishes		PRE-CAMBRIAN		Sandstone (Mt. Simon)		805
	PRE-CAMBRIAN		Oldest Fossil Algae	3.5 Billion		PRE-CAMBRIAN	Basalt and Granite	210	
			Earth's Crust Formed	5 Billion					1015

FIGURE 1.1. MADISON IN GEOLOGICAL PERSPECTIVE. Materials taken from the 1866 Capitol Park and other area deep wells provide only a partial record of the earth's history. The geological column shows the relationships between the periods represented by Madison area drill cores and the many missing periods. (University of Wisconsin Cartographic Laboratory)

spring the brow of the great glacier began to glisten. Beads of water coalesced into tiny streams like nervous perspiration from a sentient being awaiting its imminent demise. The snout of the glacier began to drip.

During the heat of the summer the hungry sun and thirsty wind caused tiny streams to form atop the glacier. Soon they converged into rivers whose raging currents cut deep furrows in the top and the leading edge of the glacier. Between 12,000 and 9000 B.C. the once invincible glacier, its surface now deeply lined, beat a hasty retreat into Canada, melting at the rate of about one thousand feet per year.[7]

After thousands of years of icy oppression, the sun once again warmed the land. But the land it illuminated had been profoundly transformed by the Great Invader. Whenever the glacier paused in its retreat, fast flowing rivers of meltwater dumped huge piles of debris at the edge of the ice mass. Hilltops had been shaved off, and a blanket of glacial debris up to 372 feet deep covered the land around Madison. Some of this glacial debris blocked the path of the river we now call "Yahara" and formed four large lakes. Other glacial debris had been sculptured into oval-shaped hills. Not long after the glacier left, small bands of Indians whose ancestors had come from Asia sought shelter from the chill winter winds on the lee side of these hills. Then, thousands of years after the glacier had retreated, people whose ancestors had come from Europe eagerly sought these glacially formed hilltops for their fancy homes. A frontier promoter persuaded a group of lawmakers to erect the symbol of their new territory atop a pile of glacial rubble bordered by two lakes. A group of men who believed that well-educated minds could improve the human condition built a university atop another glacial legacy.

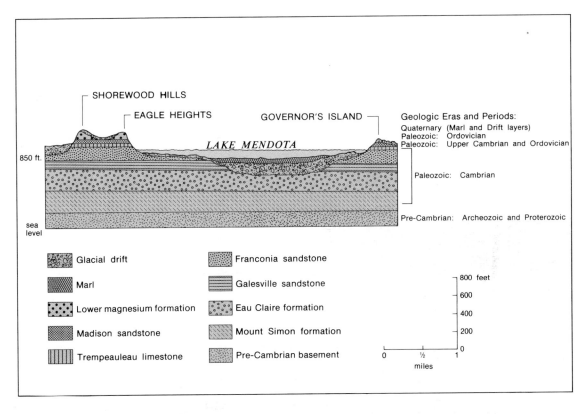

SHOREWOOD HILLS

EAGLE HEIGHTS   GOVERNOR'S ISLAND

Geologic Eras and Periods:
Quaternary (Marl and Drift layers)
Paleozoic: Ordovician
Paleozoic: Upper Cambrian and Ordovician

LAKE MENDOTA

850 ft.

Paleozoic: Cambrian

sea
level

Pre-Cambrian: Archeozoic and Proterozoic

Glacial drift   Franconia sandstone

Marl   Galesville sandstone   800 feet

Lower magnesium formation   Eau Claire formation   600

                                                                   400
Madison sandstone   Mount Simon formation
                                                                   200
Trempeauleau limestone   Pre-Cambrian basement   0
                                                  0   ½   1
                                                       miles

FIGURE 1.2. MADISON STRATIGRAPHY. Dozens of Madison area deep wells provide data about the thickness of sedimentary and glacial deposits. The cross section above shows the relative thickness of these layers in Lake Mendota between Shorewood Hills and Governor's Island. (Cartography by Stephanie and O. Brouwer)

On balance the glacier was a beneficent conqueror. In addition to picturesque hills and lakes, the glacier left other gifts. Somewhere along its thousand-mile march from Canada, the glacier snatched bits of gold, which it then dropped during its retreat. In 1905 a Madison man found a two-inch lump of the precious metal while digging a basement for a new home. Though less dramatic than gold and yet more important to a later civilization, the glacier left huge seams of sand, gravel, and clay. The sand found its way into cement and the gravel into roads, whereas the clay emerged from Madison kilns as yellow and red brick, which can still be seen in old homes around the city.[8]

The drills bit into the first bed of tough sedimentary rock in the Capitol Park well at about 125 feet below the surface. The drills had perforated the deepest footprint of the glacier and had come to another era. But wait: The rock was 475 million years older than the glacial debris. What had happened during those intervening years? Elsewhere in North America, coal fields were forming, dinosaurs were lumbering over the land, and mammals were making their slow but triumphant ascent. Did these things happen in Madison, too? Geologists cannot say for sure, because the wind, the rain, and a tiny stream—the

ancestor of the Yahara River—patiently removed hundreds of feet of surface rock layers—evidence geologists would require to give a definitive opinion.[9]

The sedimentary rock immediately under the glacial sand was deposited between 475 and 600 million years ago when the spot we now call Madison lay under or at the edge of an ancient tropical sea. At the time, the North Pole was somewhere in the Pacific Ocean, the equator ran along a line stretched between Minneapolis and El Paso, and Madison lay four hundred miles *south* of this familiar dividing line. Five times between 475 and 600 million years ago, Madison was completely covered by the sea; five times the land rose above the sea. As the land and sea alternately rose and fell, Madison sometimes lay two hundred feet under an open sea, sometimes under a shallow tropical lagoon, sometimes beside a coral reef. At still other times Madison was a beach pounded by tropical waves. Fossils later found in the Madison area showed that trilobites, worms, clams, and snails found food in these warm, salty waters.[10]

As the waves from these ancient seas crashed against rocky shores, they ground rocks into pebbles and pebbles into sand. Rivers that drained the land cut deep gorges in the rock and fierce winds added their abrasive forces. Eventually the awesome combination of wind and water produced thick sand deposits in and around Madison. The accumulating weight of this sand and the presence of certain minerals in the water cemented the grains into a rock called sandstone. One layer of this sandstone, a fine-grained, yellow, calcium-rich material formed 485 million years ago, was at one time Madison's most prestigious building material. The first Capitol and several University of Wisconsin buildings were made from it, as were dozens of the finest homes and most expensive commercial structures. In turn, some of the sand was broken down into silt and clay, which when deposited on the sea bottom formed shale. When tiny calcium-laden marine organisms died, their skeletons, too, accu-

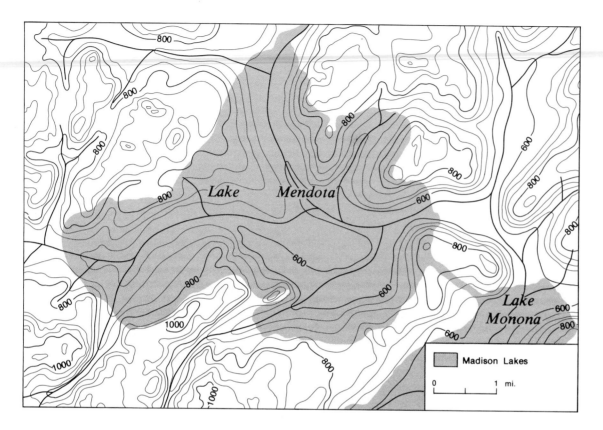

FIGURE 1.3. MADISON BEFORE THE GLACIER. Present day topography of the Madison area was mostly shaped by stream erosion and glaciation. The map shows the preglacial drainage pattern of the ancestor of today's Yahara River. The power of this little stream must not be underestimated. At the close of the Ordovician age about five hundred million years ago when Madison rose above the sea for the last time, the Madison area was covered by a layer of sedimentary rock nearly one thousand feet *above* today's hilltops. Today traces of this sedimentary layer appear only at a few places, such as at the top of the West Blue Mound in Iowa County. All the rest has been worn away—some by the wind and rain, but mostly by streams like the Yahara River working over millions of years.

Before the glacier reshaped the contours of the land, the Madison area looked much more rugged, very similar in fact to the unglaciated region in southwest Wisconsin. For example, if you had stood on Observatory Drive on the U.W. campus looking north, you would have seen Picnic Point as a castellated butte towering at least 250 feet above the preglacial University Bay Creek below. By the same token, if a group of persons in the vicinity of today's Shorewood Drive had wanted to go down into the stream valley carved by the preglacial Middleton River, they would have encountered an abrupt, rocky four-hundred-foot descent. (Cartography by Stephanie and O. Brouwer)

mulated on the sea bottom and formed limestone or dolomite, depending on where they were deposited. For 150 million years, grains of sand, powderlike particles of silt and clay, and tiny marine organisms accumulated on the ocean bottoms and beaches to a depth of nearly seven hundred feet.[11]

Eight hundred feet below the Capitol lawn, the well drillers encountered a new kind of rock, a rock much harder than any previously found, a rock with a very different history. It was one-and-one-half billion-year-old red granite. The granite was nine hundred million years older than the deepest sedimentary rock immediately above it, a gap geologists still do not fully understand. This red granite, later designated the state rock, was a remnant of the period when the earth's crust was cooling and forming "the basement of the earth." These once molten rocks tell us about a time when immense forces wrinkled the earth's crust as easily as your hand can crumple paper: A time when the great oceans formed, when volcanoes erupted, and glaciers rumbled across the earth. A time when primitive life began in the seas, and plants began producing oxygen. A time so vast that majestic mountain ranges were thrust into the air across the land we now call Wisconsin and then were levelled by the persistent but devastating forces of wind and water.[12]

Perhaps if the well drillers had realized that the pulverized rock they brought up from their shaft had witnessed these momentous events, they would have been less angry about their failure to find water. But of course one cannot be sure.

Could the well drillers have imagined a 1,600-foot-high continental glacier towering over the spot where they were standing? Could they understand that the lakes just a few blocks away and the isthmus on which they had been working had been carved by an icy bulldozer twenty thousand years ago? Would they believe that Madison once lay under a tropical lagoon four hundred miles south of the equator? Surely they would have leaned on their shovels and enjoyed a hearty laugh.[13]

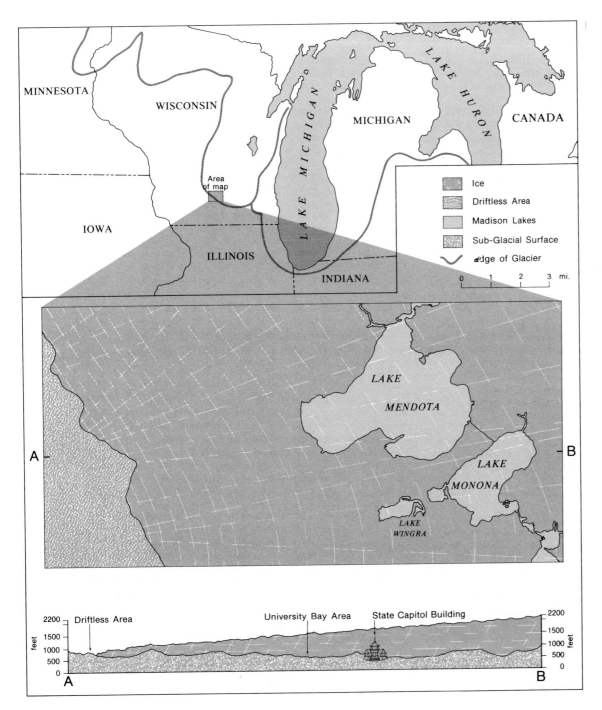

FIGURE 1.4. MADISON DURING THE MAXIMUM GLACIAL ADVANCE. Whether Madison was covered by all four glacial advances during the Pleistocene Epoch is not known since each succeeding glacier obliterated evidence from earlier glaciers. It is known that the Green Bay Lobe *(top)* arrived in Madison somewhere between 14,000 and 20,000 years ago and left about 13,000 years ago. A cutaway *(bottom)* shows the tapered thickness of the glacier. (Cartography by Stephanie and O. Brouwer)

The People

During the last part of the Wisconsin Ice Age, so much water was frozen in glaciers all over the world that the level of the oceans dropped by three hundred feet. This drop opened a land bridge up to eleven hundred miles wide in the area now known as the Bering Strait. Ocean currents warmed this land bridge and probably kept it glacier free. Sometime between twenty-five thousand to fifteen thousand years ago small bands of Asians made their way across this isthmus, probably pursuing mammoths, caribou, musk oxen, and bison—the same large mammals they had hunted in the tundras of Siberia.

Once they came into what is today Alaska, the Asians could go no further because their path to the south and east was blocked by huge ice sheets. However, a warming trend underway at the time caused the glaciers to melt, not only along their southern perimeters, but also at points where they had fused together late in the Wisconsin Ice Age. One such fusion point lay between the Alaskan Yukon and Montana, where an ice sheet straddling the Rocky Mountain spine had joined another sheet covering the western Canadian plains. The warming climate caused an early opening of this fusion point and created a convenient entrance to the ice-free south. Once through this corridor, a huge continent lay before them.[14]

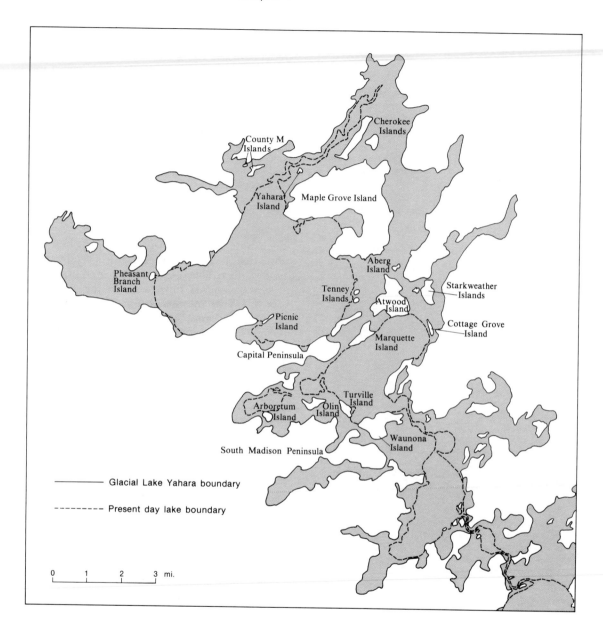

County M
Islands

Cherokee
Islands

Yahara
Island   Maple Grove Island

Pheasant
Branch
Island

Aberg
Island

Tenney
Islands

Starkweather
Islands

Atwood
Island

Picnic
Island

Cottage Grove
Island

Marquette
Island

Capital Peninsula

Turville
Island

Arboretum
Island   Olin
Island

Waunona
Island

South Madison Peninsula

—————— Glacial Lake Yahara boundary

---------- Present day lake boundary

0   1   2   3 mi.

FIGURE 1.5. GLACIAL LAKE YAHARA. When the glacier began receding, large volumes of meltwater flowed from its southwestern edge. At first this water flowed down the Sugar River and Black Earth Creek. However, as the glacier melted in the Yahara Valley, a basin was created between the edge of the ice mass and the high ground west of Madison. Glacial Lake Yahara *(left)* was the result. Lake Yahara stood about twelve feet above the current level of Lake Mendota and covered 26,112 acres, 100 percent larger than Lakes Mendota, Monona, and Wingra combined. The additional depth made the Madison area into one huge island-studded lake. Fanciful island and peninsula names are based on familiar current designations for these areas. Beaches from this lake can still be seen along steep slopes at Olin Park on Lake Monona. Eventually, water from Lake Yahara found an opening to the south and formed the modern bed of the Yahara River. As the river cut its way into glacial debris that had dammed the valley, the water level in Glacial Lake Yahara gradually dropped to present levels and created the three Madison lakes, Mendota, Monona, and Wingra. Current lake outlines are shown with a dotted line. (This map was based upon *Glacial Geology of Dane County* by D. M. Mickelson and M. C. McCartney 1979 published by the Wisconsin Geological and Natural History Survey.)

FIGURE 1.6. GLACIAL TOPOGRAPHIC FEATURES. In the process of passing over what is now the city of Madison and then stopping just a few miles to the southwest, the glacier left a distinctive set of "footprint" landforms. They are as follows:

End Moraines: Ridges composed of material deposited by the ice at the terminal zone of the glacier. The surface of these ridges is often bumpy and littered with boulders and sometimes contains slight depressions called "kettles."

Ground Moraine: A relatively flat or rolling surface containing unstratified clay, sand, and gravel created along the base of the glacier.

Drumlins: An elongated often oval hill created at the base of the glacier by moving ice. The axis of the elongated dimension is always parallel to the movement of the ice.

Ice-Contract Stratified Deposits: Sand and gravel deposited by a moving glacier.

Pitted Outwash Plain: A gradually sloping plain containing depressions called "kettles." Kettles are formed by melting ice blocks.

Lacustrine Plain: A nearly flat poorly drained surface composed of fine grained silt and clay marking the bottom of a former glacial lake.

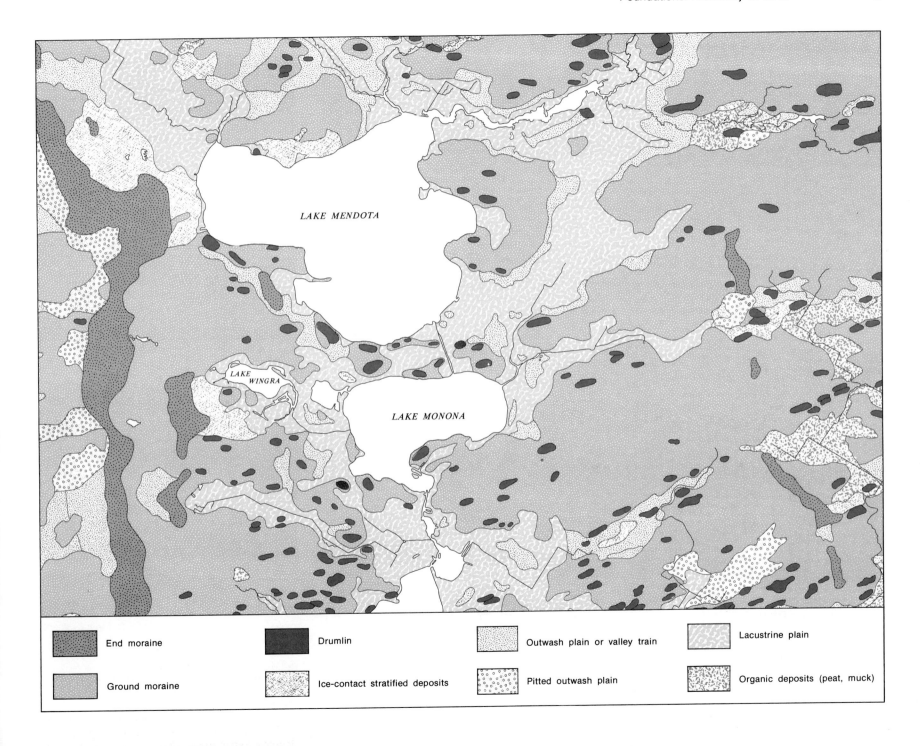

LAKE MENDOTA

LAKE WINGRA

LAKE MONONA

End moraine

Ground moraine

Drumlin

Ice-contact stratified deposits

Outwash plain or valley train

Pitted outwash plain

Lacustrine plain

Organic deposits (peat, muck)

1

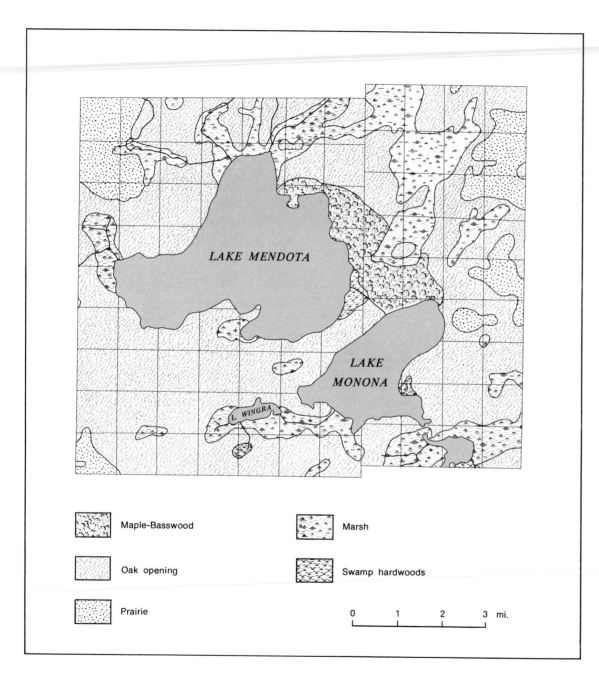

2

3

4

	Maple-Basswood			Marsh
	Oak opening			Swamp hardwoods
	Prairie			

LAKE MENDOTA

LAKE MONONA

L. WINGRA

0   1   2   3   mi.

FIGURE 1.7. 1834 PLANT COMMUNITIES. In December 1834, a team of five U.S. government surveyors walked back and forth along east-west and north-south lines in the area we now call Madison. At every mile interval, they established a section corner point so that later buyers could locate their land. Each of these section corners was located in relation to trees and other natural features and then entered in small notebooks they could stick in their pockets. From careful analysis of these notebooks, 1834 vegetation patterns can be established. The map shown on the left is based upon an analysis of Dane County surveyor notebooks by Robert Scott Ellerson (1949). His analysis showed that plant communities fell into five categories: oak openings, prairie, maple-basswood forests, marshland and swamp hardwoods. Photographs and descriptions of the four most common categories are shown here. The relatively rare swamp hardwoods were limited in the Madison area to what is now called Tenney Park. There surveyors found a "black ash swamp" plus willows and cottonwoods.

1. *Oak Opening:* The most common plant community in the Madison area was the "oak opening." Surveyors called these areas "thinly timbered," later settlers thought they resembled "ancient orchards," and one English visitor said they looked like well-manicured (English) parks. To the botanist an oak opening is defined as a collection of oak trees whose shade at noon in midsummer covers no more than fifty percent of the ground. Contrary to popular belief, the dominant species of the oak opening is not the oak tree, but rather a mixture of prairie grasses and forest herbs.

Unlike other plant communities, the oak openings is "artificial" in the sense that it was a direct result of nearly annual fires set by Indians each fall, apparently to increase the ease with which they could hunt. The annual burnings killed off nearly all trees except the white and burr oaks, which had a thick corklike layer under the bark that prevented the flames from damaging the life-sustaining cambium layer. The fires also prevented the development of undergrowth and, in conjunction with the dominant grasses, gave the openings their manicured parklike quality.

2. *Prairie:* When the French fur traders first encountered the large treeless areas dominated by grasses, they called them "prairies," meaning meadow. The term stuck and was used by the Americans who ultimately settled the area. For a people accustomed to the forested East, the prairie was a curious anomaly. At first it was thought that prairie soils were infertile because they could support no trees, but a few experiments quickly showed this theory to be untrue. Surveyors of the Madison area generally described the prairies as "first rate" farmland. Not only did the prairies provide some of the richest soils, but they also provided scenes of extraordinary beauty. Descriptions of the prairires by early Madison settlers were written with great feeling and frequent superlatives.

Relatively small amounts of prairie land lay within the current boundaries of the city. The largest prairies—the Arlington, Sun, and Rock prairies—lay north and south of Madison.

Most botanists believe that the prairies were originally forests that were burned. If the forest contained maples and other fire-vulnerable species, a treeless prairie resulted; if the forest contained fire-resistant oaks, an oak opening resulted.

3. *Maple-Basswood Forest:* Mature maple-basswood forests appeared only in widely scattered areas across Southern Wisconsin. The largest stand in Dane County lay north west of the Yahara River roughly between Elmside Boulevard and Governor's Island. Here they were protected by the Yahara River and the lakes from prairie fires most commonly propelled by westerly winds. Because of their relatively thin bark the trees in this plant community could not survive such fires.

Because of their high reproduction rates, tolerance for shade and long life, the sugar maples dominated these forests. Then came the basswood, a distant second, followed by a long list of species which gained a toehold and little more. They included the butternut, hickory, slippery elm, beech, black walnut, and black, white and red oaks. The magnificent maple forest in the Maple Bluff area, often called a "sugar bush" by early settlers, contained hundreds of trees two feet in diameter, more than two hundred years old, and growing so closely together that a wagon could not be driven through them.

4. *Marshland.* What the surveyors called "marshland," botanists today call a sedge meadow. The key characteristic is wet soil dominated by tall grasslike plants called sedges. As the soil gets wetter, sedge meadows become cattail or reed marshes. Early in Madison's history the sedge meadows provided marsh hay, which was used for mattress stuffing for early capital workers. (This map was prepared by the University of Wisconsin Cartographic Laboratory based upon a map provided by the Wisconsin Academy of Sciences Arts and Letters. Photographs courtesy of the University of Wisconsin Press)

The hardy people who made this trek, known by archeologists as Paleo-Indians, had learned to make three- to six-inch long flaked stone spearpoints, sharpened on both sides with a flute or channel down the center, where they were attached to wooden spear shafts. In the hands of Paleo-Indians, these sharp spearpoints could inflict mortal wounds to the largest mammals. Archeological evidence shows that Paleo-Indians were killing large animals with these weapons in the Western United States by 13,000 B.C.[15] Thousands of these distinctive spearpoints have been found in the United States. Over one hundred have been found in southern and central Wisconsin, including fifteen at Madison-area sites.[16]

Like their counterparts elsewhere around the country, Madison-area Paleo-Indians probably used their spearpoints to hunt a variety of game including now extinct ice age megafauna such as mastodons and the giant bison, plus deer, elk, caribou, and smaller game.[17] Little is known about the Paleo-Indian lifestyle except that they probably lived in small mobile bands. Wisconsin archeologists believe the Paleo-Indians arrived in the Madison area about 10,000 B.C.[18]

To the Paleo-Indians, Madison looked very different than it does today. Mounds of glacial deposits blocked the flow of what is now called the Yahara River and created the 26,112-acre glacial lake, two times larger than Lakes Mendota, Monona, and Wingra combined. The cool, damp climate greatly favored such trees as the spruce, fir, and birch. Like an army of tall sentinels, they quickly occupied the land once covered by the glacier and converted the Madison area into a fragrant boreal forest.[19]

Sometime around 9000 B.C. to 8000 B.C., for reasons not fully understood, the ice age megafauna died out. Madison-area Paleo-Indians therefore shifted to deer and caribou and fished in the postglacial lakes such as glacial Lake Yahara. Artifacts from this group of Indians dated between 8000 B.C. and 4500 B.C. have been found at the point where the Beltline highway crosses the Yahara River and at several other sites.[20]

Sometime after 8000 B.C. a warming climate caused the more heat tolerant pines to replace boreal species. Indian population in the Madison area may well have declined during this period because a pine forest provides very little bushy understory needed to support brousing animals.

About 5000 B.C. continued climatic warming caused hardwood forests to displace the pine as the dominant plant community—a change that had enormous implications for Madison area Indians. Not only did the hardwood forests support very large animal populations, but they also provided foods such as nuts and berries. Consequently the Madison area Indian population began to rise. About the time this shift occurred, a new group of Indians belonging to what archeologists call the Archaic stage (ca. 8000–1000 B.C.), learned to exploit this rich new hunting and gathering environment. Like their counterparts elsewhere in the country, Madison area archaic Indians learned to make axes and other tools from ground stone, and spearpoints, knives, and other tools from hammered copper.[21] The collection of regularly available resources such as nuts, berries, and shellfish allowed Archaic Indians to remain in one place for longer periods of time, although seasonal food-gathering movements may have been common.

Judging from the relatively large number of sites between 3000 B.C. and 1000 B.C., the Madison area archaic Indian population must have reached relatively high levels. By this time the oaks and prairie grasses had become codominants and the water level in glacial Lake Yahara had fallen perhaps ten feet so that the boundaries of the Madison lakes had assumed a near-modern configuration. The combination of oak-prairie environment and the shallow edges of Madison lakes and marshes constituted ideal environments for the Archaic hunter-gatherers.[22] The relatively large number of Archaic sites in the Madison-area coupled with the long span of time for this stage provide compelling testimony to the efficient and enduring partnership with nature these Indians had achieved.

About 1000 B.C. Indians in the eastern United States began to adopt a series of lifestyle changes that were gradually incorporated by many tribes to the west. These changes included the use of pottery, horticulture, village life, and the construction of mounds and earth works. This period continued until 1640 A.D. and is known by archeologists as the Woodland stage.[23]

Artifacts found at various Madison area camp and grave sites show that local Indians adopted the more sophisticated "woodland" lifestyle changes. Indeed, it was during this period that Madison became a "flourishing center" of Indian life.[24] For example, between 1000 B.C. and A.D. 400, Madison Indians began to build conical mounds and acquired trade goods such as Atlantic and Gulf coast seashells, then associated with a sophisticated Indian culture centered along the Ohio-Illinois border. Although Madison area Indians were influenced by such Indian cultures, perhaps the most significant characteristic of Madison Indians between 1000 B.C. and A.D. 400 was their disinterest in adopting the more advanced technologies and lifestyles enjoyed by these Eastern tribes. Quite possibly, their adaptations to the supportive Madison area environment was so good, they felt no compelling need to adopt these eastern ways.[25]

Around A.D. 400 Indians in the eastern United States began to adopt still other important lifestyle and technology changes, which gradually spread westward. These included an increase in the cultivation of corn, beans, and squash, the development of more complex village life, and the widespread use of the bow and arrow. An important Wisconsin manifestation of this period was the intriguing Effigy Mound Tradition.[26] From the time these mounds were first encountered in the 1820s and 1830s by explorers, U.S. government surveyors, and Wisconsin lead region map makers, they have fascinated thousands. Leading Wisconsin scientists and nationally known investigators from prestigious eastern institutions came to Madison to inspect the curiosities and gather data for articles and books.[27] Most of the mounds were under one hundred feet in length and four

feet in height. A few were much larger. The famous bird mound on the lawn of the Mendota State Hospital, for example, has a wingspread of 624 feet and is now recognized as the largest effigy mound in the state. Many are shaped like animals such as birds, panthers, buffalos, and turtles, but many others have geometrical forms such as lines, cones, and ovals. Most but not all of the mounds were used for burial purposes. Since not everyone could possibly have been buried in the mounds, their use was probably reserved for high-status persons. Various dating procedures show that most mounds were built between A.D. 300 and A.D. 1300.

Clearly, the Madison area was an attractive and special place to the effigy mound builders.[28] According to one scholar, ninety-eight percent of all effigy mounds lie within the boundaries of Wisconsin. County-by-county archeological surveys show that within Wisconsin, Dane County has the greatest concentration of mounds and that within Dane County, the largest concentration of effigy mounds lie around present day Madison. By 1937 Charles E. Brown, a Madison archeologist, had counted over one thousand mounds in the Four Lakes area, with 668 around Lakes Mendota, Monona, and Wingra alone.

Not until recently have archeologists known much about the way the mound builders lived. This was because from the time the mounds were first seriously studied in the 1850s until about 1950, archeologists were preoccupied with the excavation of mounds. Their presumption was that artifacts buried in the mounds would provide clues to mound builder lifestyles. Unfortunately, mound builders, unlike some other groups, buried very few artifacts in the mounds.

Only in the last thirty years since archeologists shifted to the excavation of effigy village sites has a more detailed portrait of their lifestyle emerged. One site that revealed much about effigy lifestyle was a camp adjacent to the pond on the Odana Golf Course, just north of the west Beltline highway, which was excavated in 1955. Known as the Dietz site after its long-time owner, it was shown to be an effigy mound village—one

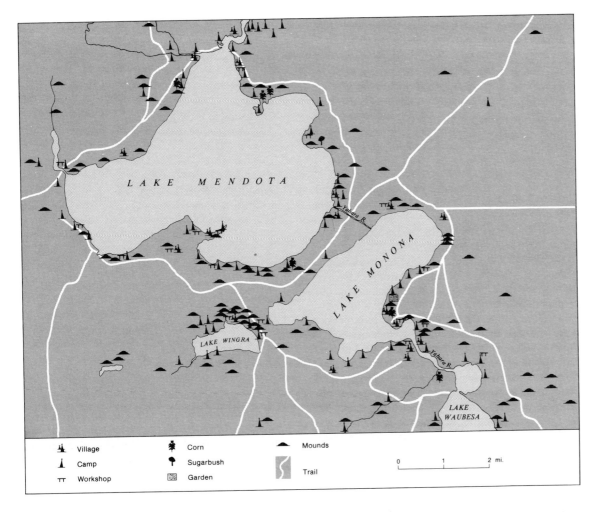

🪵	Village	🌲	Corn	◣	Mounds
⊥	Camp	🍄	Sugarbush		
⊤⊤	Workshop	▦	Garden		Trail

0   1   2 mi.

FIGURE 1.8. INDIAN FEATURES.   This map showing trails, camp and village sites, mounds, cornfields, and other Indian-created features is based upon a compilation done by Charles E. Brown, a well-known student of Madison-area Indian life. The map is a compelling visual reminder that for thousands of years, Indians found Madison a good place to live.

of the first in the state ever systematically excavated. Particularly instructive were contents of food and garbage pits, which revealed what village residents had been eating. The pits yielded hickory nuts, bones of deer, elk, and fish, and most interesting of all, a corn cob—the first instance of Indian corn raising in prehistoric Wisconsin.

Radioactive carbon tests showed the site was used between A.D. 1120 and 1170. Excavations of other effigy mound village sites around the state showed that these Indians erected semipermanent villages, lived in wigwams, smoked, and probably grew tobacco. Their pottery and stone tools were technically undistinguishable.[29]

Although knowledge of the effigy mound builders has grown, no one has been able to satisfactorily answer two questions posed by U.W. Professor H. B. Lathrop in July 1910, when he gave the dedication speech for the plaque commemorating the bear mound in the Vilas Avenue Oval. To his small crowd of early-day preservationists Lathrop asked: "What is the meaning of this heap of earth? With what thoughts was it built?" Some archeologists speculate that the mounds were clan symbols and that persons buried in them were members of that clan.[30] But no one knows for sure. Exactly what happened to the mound builders is not known either. Some archeologists believe they may have been the predecessors of the Winnebago, but compelling evidence is lacking.[31]

Nor is it known what tribe occupied the Madison area when the first French explorers came through the state since none of them passed through the Madison area. However, by 1650 the expansion of the Iroquois in the East were forcing the Sauks, Foxes, Ottawas, Chippewas, and Pottawatomis into what is now Wisconsin where they were forced to interact—sometimes violently—with indigenous tribes including the Winnebago. It is possible that the Sauks and Foxes may have controlled the Four Lakes area during the middle and late 1700s since they had villages at what is now Prairie du Sac and Blue Mounds.[32]

On the other hand, Winnebago occupation of the Madison area may have been continuous beginning in the seventeenth century. By the time the first Americans explored the Madison area, Winnebago control was undisputed. In fact, the 1832 treaty ceding the Madison area to the United States government was signed by Winnebago Chief White Crow whose major village lay on the shore of Lake Mendota near Fox Bluff. Other Winnebago villages of this period were located on the south shore of Lake Monona at Winnequah and Frost Woods, on the north shore of Lake Mendota at the point where Pheasant Branch Creek empties into Lake Mendota, at the outlet of Lake Mendota near Tenney Park, in the vicinity of St. Mary's Hospital, at Picnic Point, and at dozens of other locations.[33]

The Winnebagoes harvested wild rice that grew in the margins of the lakes, caught fish, and cultivated corn, potatoes, pumpkins, squashes, watermelons, and some tobacco. Major Winnebago cornfields were located along Pinckney Street between Gilman Street and East Washington Avenue, at Vilas Park, in the Squaw Bay area near Winnequah, on a hill west of the Mendota State Hospital near the mouth of the Yahara River, near a point where Pheasant Branch Creek empties into Lake Mendota, and at Camp Indianola (now a Dane County Park). An Indian fur trader who worked the Madison area between 1831 and 1833 estimated that Winnebagoes raised not less than three thousand bushels of corn each year at their Four Lakes villages.[34] Early settlers reported that the Winnebagoes, who dressed in deerskin and lived in wigwams shaped like haystacks, were extraordinarily good shots with bows and arrows and could make their lightweight birchbark canoes skim across the water at surprising speeds. They loved to run footraces and wrestle and then bet muskrat pelts on the outcome.[35]

From this fascinating but fragmentary composite portrait that can be assembled from archeological studies and early settlers' accounts, one unequivocal fact stands out above all others: for twelve thousand years Indians found the Madison area a good place to live.[36] Its richly supportive water-marsh-woodland environment provided fish, shellfish, water fowl, fur-bearing animals, nuts, berries, tubers, wild rice, and maple sugar plus fertile soil for their crops and clay for pottery—a cornucopia of life-sustaining elements—and beauty for the spirit besides. Hundreds of camp and village sites found in the Madison area show that there is hardly a Madison neighborhood that was not first enjoyed by Indians. Marquette, Mansion Hill, Tenney Park,

Winnequah, Maple Bluff, Shorewood, Nakoma, Vilas, the Arboretum, and Odana are just a few contemporary neighborhoods whose charms were long ago evident to Indians.[37]

Preparing the Way: Traders, Soldiers, and Surveyors

French and British Regimes

Whether French fur traders visited the Four Lakes area during their regime in Wisconsin from 1673 until 1763 is not known. What is known is that beginning in 1673, when Marquette and Joliet made their epic voyage across Wisconsin on the Fox and Wisconsin Rivers, French influence throughout the state increased dramatically. Although the desire to save souls was one motive for exploration and control, a more compelling reason was fur. In Europe furs were needed to make felt, and the demand for this stylish new commodity was running far ahead of supply. The best felt was made from beaver furs captured in New France, an area lying between Montreal and Minneapolis. French desire for pelts was matched in most instances by Indian desire for European products including knives, hatchets, cloth, beads and, later, liquor. In a few years the fur trade dominated Indian life.[1]

French effectiveness in harvesting the lucrative wilderness crop was based upon a policy of encouraging its fur traders—called *voyageurs* (licensed traders) and *coureurs de bois* (woods rangers)—to live with the Indians, learn their languages and marry their women. Over the years this policy produced a highly trained work force that enjoyed the respect of the Indian trappers.[2]

During the last three decades of the seventeenth century, pelts were taken from Wisconsin in considerable quantities, mostly from Fort La Baye at Green Bay. Beginning in the eighteenth century, however, the inevitable occurred. Years of relentless hunting had decimated the beaver population in many collection areas. With demand still high, the French traders expanded their collection network into southern Wisconsin.[3]

FIGURE 1.9. THE VOYAGUER CANOE. Some time before the capitol workmen arrived in June 1837, the Pecks found an abandoned forty-foot-long voyaguer canoe similar to the one shown above. Although it is not clear from Rosaline Peck's account, the context of her story suggests that the canoe was found in the Squaw Bay area. The Pecks equipped the huge craft with a primitive sail and derived many hours of pleasure from its use until it was taken over by the capitol workmen and ruined.

How the canoe's owners, presumably *coureurs de bois,* got the craft here and how they had used it is a mystery. The huge craft were known to be built in just two areas, Grand Portage on the Minnesota-Canada border and Montreal. Fur trade historians say the craft were used only on the Great Lakes to transport furs from wilderness collection areas to Montreal. The six-hundred-pound canoes could carry up to ten thousand pounds of cargo and commonly had ten to fourteen paddlers. Under adverse conditions four to six miles per hour was possible; with favorable wind plus a small sail, ten miles per hour could be attained. (Courtesy of the Chicago Field Museum of Natural History)

The French regime in Wisconsin officially ended in 1763 with the signing of the Treaty of Paris, which ceded to Great Britain a large area, including Wisconsin. To the French traders in Wisconsin, however, the change had little meaning. Britain had gained control of the Montreal "front office," but in the Wisconsin wilderness the French traders continued to exchange cheap trinkets and whiskey for the mother lode of the wilderness. Some worked directly for licensed British traders whereas others formed partnerships with them.[4]

Assertion of American Power

The assertion of American control of Wisconsin following the War of 1812 meant still another change at the "front office" to French traders. In 1817, just one year after an American fort had been constructed at Prairie du Chien and the same year a fort was built at Green Bay, John Jacob Astor's American Fur Company began systematic fur collection efforts in Wisconsin.[5] Like the British before him, Astor depended upon the French *coureurs* for field collection. Astor's agent for the Four Lakes area was Pierre Paquette, a product of a French-Winnebago marriage. Paquette, a six-foot, two-hundred-pound man, was well known to Indians and white traders over much of the state.[6] The success of Astor's collection system can be deduced from the fact that the beaver was nearly extinct in southern Wisconsin by 1825. From that time forward, the muskrat was the principal prey.[7]

American control of the Madison area cannot be said to have begun until after the construction of Fort Winnebago at Portage in the fall of 1828. The Fort was a direct response to the Winnebago "uprising" of 1827, in which Chief Red Bird and several others scalped a child in Prairie du Chien. Another direct response was the Indian cession of southwestern Wisconsin in 1829, which cleared that area of Indian title and made it safer for lead miners who were then pouring in.[8]

Under the new American regime, responsibility for regulating the fur trade fell to John Kinzie, U.S. Indian agent at Fort Winnebago. To Madison area Indians this change had little apparent meaning; Kinzie was merely the latest boss of their French-speaking traders. Thus when Kinzie passed through the Madison area on his way to Chicago on March 3, 1833, Winnebago Indians scattered along the banks of Lake Mendota greeted him with the cry "Bon jour, bon jour."[9]

But the assertion of American power had much greater meaning than the Indians and the French fur traders realized. To Americans cascading across the Alleghenies, southern Wisconsin was sought for lead mines and farms, not as a wilderness home for fur-bearing animals. The pick and the plow symbolized the American vision for southern Wisconsin and both were inimical to the fur trade and Indians.

The last systematic large scale fur collection efforts around Madison were made between 1829 and 1835 by four traders, two of whom were Americans. Frontiersman Wallace Rowan set up his trading operation on the north shore of Lake Mendota near Pheasant Branch Creek about 1830. His log cabin was the earliest known permanent habitation in the Madison area, and his wife was the first white woman known to have ventured into the area. In 1832 Rowan moved to a site on the eastern shore of Lake Monona later known as Winnequah.[10]

The other American trader, Kentucky-born Abel Rasdall, set up a trading post on the shore of Lake Kegonsa in 1831. Like the French *coureurs* before him, he married a Winnebago woman and at Indian camps around the Four Lakes exchanged cheap cloth, calico, beads, and whiskey for furs. At one time he also had a trading post on the block now occupied by the First Wisconsin Plaza.[11]

The two French traders working the Madison area at the time of American settlement were Michael St. Cyr and Oliver Armel. St. Cyr, his Winnebago wife and their four children took over Wallace Rowan's cabin on the north shore of Lake Mendota in 1833. In addition to exchanging whiskey and tobacco for Indian furs, St. Cyr raised corn, oats, potatoes, and a few vegetables on an eight-acre plot. The Frenchman reportedly exercised a commanding influence over the Winnebagoes with whom he traded.[12]

The French trader with the largest Madison area business (at the time of American settlement) was probably Oliver Armel, a *coureur* of the old school. According to one eye-witness account, in October 1832, over five hundred Indians camped in the vicinity of today's Monona Avenue, while they exchanged furs for Armel's whiskey and trinkets. Armel's "half brush and half canvas" trading shanty was located near the intersection of Johnson Street and Wisconsin Avenue[13] and was viewed by some as the first Madison business. This distinction, however, did not please one early historian. "In some cities, the first thing built has been a temple, or altar, or palace, or hospital, or fort, but *our* first building," he lamented, "was a grog shop."[14]

The French *coureurs* did not stay long in Madison after American settlement began. They were wilderness people whose livelihood was jeopardized by Indian land cessions, sawmills, roads, federal surveys, and farmers. However, the speed with which settlement occurred in the Madison area found several French traders caught "behind the lines" of the rapidly moving American frontier. During this period, several of the *coureurs* played minor but significant roles by providing labor, shelter, food, and drink to explorers, surveyors, and settlers.[15] By 1838 all the *coureurs* who had played bit parts in Madison's early settlement had gone west with the Indians, in most cases following them to their new but temporary hunting grounds in Iowa.[16]

While fur traders were gathering the last fur harvests, other Americans found reasons to explore the site now occupied by Madison. The first was a Blue Mounds lead miner, Ebenezer Brigham, and at least two other companions, who in the summer or fall of 1828 passed through Madison on their way to Fort Winnebago. Brigham thought it would be easier to get his supplies there than go all the way to Galena. He camped for a night on what is now the King Street corner of Capital Park and was so impressed by the beauty of the spot, he predicted that a city would grow up there.[17]

Three other groups of Americans are known to have passed through the isthmus in the summer of 1829. From the perspective of Madison settlement, most significant group was a party of three attorneys led by James Duane Doty, a Michigan territorial judge serving that portion of the Michigan territory now known as Wisconsin. Doty held court in Green Bay and Prairie du Chien, the two state population centers at the time. Normally the judge made the trip between these two places by canoe along the Fox–Wisconsin waterway. In May 1829, however, he decided to make the trip by land and expand his already extensive knowledge of the state.[18]

Another 1829 summer visitor was Jefferson Davis, later president of the Confederate States of America. Davis, a recent West Point graduate, had been sent to help build Fort Winnebago in 1828. In October 1829, his company of soldiers passed through Madison looking for deserters.[19] In the same month another lead miner rode through the isthmus looking for a stolen horse and was told where to find it by fur trader Oliver Armel.[20]

Thus by the fall of 1829, the Madison area was no longer an unopened book to Americans, but few had read its pages.

The Black Hawk War and Indian Removal

From the fall of 1829 until the spring of 1832 the record is nearly devoid of American visitors to the Madison area. But in the summer of 1832, an event of national interest caused eighteen hundred persons to pass through the Madison isthmus in a twenty-four-hour period. The reason for the presence of this large number of people was not exploration, though some of that was done, nor the collection of furs, for there was no time. About eight hundred U.S. soldiers were making a desperate attempt to catch Chief Black Hawk and his party of one thousand men, women, and children who were making an equally desperate attempt to escape.[21]

The seeds of the Black Hawk War—the last Indian war in the state—were sown in St. Louis, Missouri, on November 3, 1804, when William Henry Harrison signed a treaty with representatives of the Sauk and Fox tribe in which the Indians ceded approximately fifty million acres of land in what is now northern Illinois and

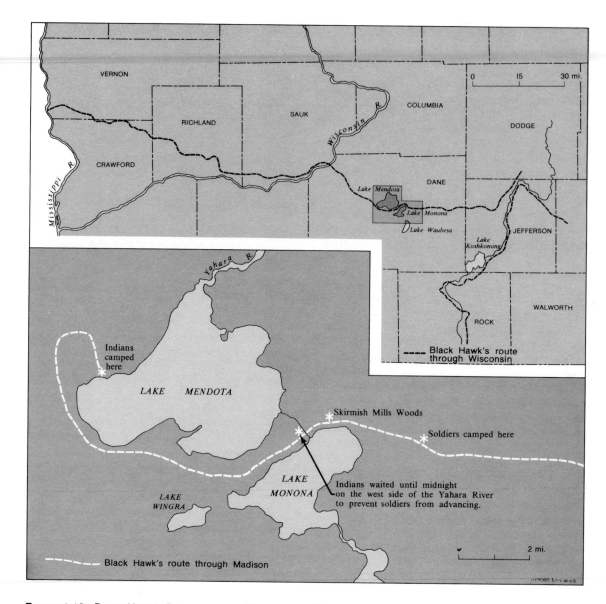

FIGURE 1.10. BLACK HAWK'S ROUTE THROUGH WISCONSIN.   These maps show the path taken by the retreating Black Hawk and his band in their attempt to elude capture by General Atkinson's troops. (University of Wisconsin Cartographic Laboratory)

southern Wisconsin. The treaty allowed the Indians to remain on their land until it was actually sold by the government to settlers. For nearly twenty years the Indians enjoyed undisputed possession of the area, but by the mid-1820s white settlers began to encroach on the main Indian village of Saukenuk located near the present site of Rock Island, Illinois. This growing number of incursions angered the Indians and produced a tribal schism. One group, led by the widely respected Keokuk, agreed to settle on an Iowa reservation in the spring of 1831. The other faction, led by sixty-five-year-old Black Hawk, returned to Saukenuk to raise another crop of corn on the rich Mississippi bottom lands. Not surprisingly Black Hawk's return was viewed as an invasion of Illinois and was blocked by the Illinois militia. Black Hawk agreed never to return to his ancestral home.[22]

In April 1832, however, ignoring the agreement of the previous spring, Black Hawk's band, buoyed by vague hopes of forming an alliance with disgruntled Winnebago, Kickapoo, and Pottawatomis, once again crossed the river, this time heading for their summer village on the Rock River where they intended to plant corn. But once again they were met by military force, this time consisting of both regulars and militia. Black Hawk, sick at heart about the failure of other tribes to give him the aid he had expected, decided to surrender and sent messengers to a battalion of militiamen camped just above what is now Dixon, Illinois. Unfortunately, just after the arrival of Black Hawk's messengers, another band of Indians arrived at the camp, causing the undisciplined militia to think they were being attacked. In the confusion that followed, one of Black Hawk's messengers was killed before the others in the party could escape. The frustrated and angry Sauks decided to sell their lives dearly. The Indians launched a series of lightning attacks on frontier outposts. Settlers retreated, militia companies were hastily formed, and army regulars were called in. The Black Hawk War had begun.

Recognizing that Winnebagos in the Four Lakes area might become involved in the war, Colonel Henry Dodge, a respected leader from the lead mining area, held a council with the Winnebagos on May 26, 1832, near the Wallace-St. Cyr cabin on the north shore of Lake Mendota. Perhaps intimidated by Dodge's fifty armed horsemen, the Winnebagos promised to remain neutral in the impending contest.[23] The importance of this meeting cannot be underestimated because at the time, an estimated five thousand Winnebagos lived in the southern and central Wisconsin area. If they had enlisted in the Black Hawk cause, American forces would surely have been defeated.[24]

The charge of putting down the insurgent Sauks fell to General Henry Atkinson. During the early months of the war, however, Atkinson could not find Black Hawk in spite of the fact that three thousand troops had been placed under his command. To conceal his band of about one thousand from the mounted soldiers, Black Hawk was forced to hide in marshy lowlands. Although they provided sanctuary, the marshes prevented the Indians from securing adequate food. By May, the rigors of their grass, root, and bark diet had caused several deaths of the more elderly Indians.

At first the Indians followed a northerly path up the Rock River to the vicinity of today's Watertown. There, almost by accident, one of the General's scouts discovered a fresh trail showing that the fleeing band was heading for the Mississippi. After weeks of an exasperating search, General Atkinson's troops were at last close behind the fleeing band. Indian possessions lay strewn across the trail and an occasional straggler awaited death. Sensing their advantage and the importance of rapid movement, Atkinson's officers decided to leave the heavy supply wagons behind.

The mounted soldiers reached the north end of Lake Monona just after sundown on July 20. The commanding officer called a halt and asked their French-Indian guide, Peter Pauquette, what

FIGURE 1.11. BLACK HAWK. "The poor, dethroned monarch, old Black Hawk . . . looked an object of pity," artist George Catlin wrote about the defeated Sauk chief in his *Letters and Notes on the Manners, Customs, and Conditions of the North American Indians.* The foremost painter of American Indians got the sixty-five-year-old Black Hawk to sit for this portrait in the late summer of 1832, shortly after Black Hawk had been taken prisoner. Black Hawk sat for the painting at the Jefferson Barracks, about ten miles from St. Louis, where he was imprisoned with some of his followers. Released the following year, Black Hawk spent most of his remaining days, until his death on October 3, 1838, on a small reservation set apart for him and his personal followers on the Des Moines River in Davis County, Iowa. (Courtesy of National Museum of American Art, Smithsonian Institution, gift of Mrs. Sarah Harrison.)

kind of country they were approaching. He informed them that the dense underbrush on the isthmus was so thick "one man could not see another ten steps away."[25] Because these circumstances greatly favored Indians, the decision was made to stop for the night. One of the soldiers recalled later that they camped "about a quarter mile north of the northeast end of Monona . . . and about one mile northeast" of the present Williamson-Winnebago bridge, roughly in the vicinity of today's Olbrich Park.[26] While the main body of soldiers made camp, another group was sent ahead to see if they could ascertain the Indians' location. The men returned in a very short time explaining that they had overtaken Black Hawk's rear guard in the thick timbered area between the Yahara River and what is now Elmside Boulevard. In the brief encounter one Sauk was wounded but "crept away . . . and hid himself in the thick willows and alders" near the point where the Yahara enters into Lake Monona, "where he died."[27]

From a Winnebago Indian, the troops later learned that about one-half of the Sauk warriors had taken a post near the west side of the Yahara River where the Williamson Street bridge is today located, with the intention of attacking the troops if they tried to cross the river that night. However, the soldiers chose to remain in their camp, so the Indians left about midnight to join the main body of the fleeing band, which camped that night just east of Pheasant Branch Creek.[28]

On July 21, a cool Saturday, the bugle sounded at the break of day, and the men, after gulping a quick breakfast, mounted their horses and commenced their pursuit. A group of scouts including Abel Rasdall was sent ahead of the main body. The troops followed and discovered that Pauquette had not exaggerated his description of the thicket. One member of the party recalled, "we could turn neither to the right nor left, but were compelled to follow the trail the Indians made, and that, for a great distance was at the edge of the water of the lake."[29] It seems clear that the soldiers were at this point walking along Lake Monona between Welch Avenue and Schiller Street.

Crossing the Yahara at the ford, some soldiers followed the Indian trail roughly along Williamson Street, while others fanned out along Third Lake Ridge. In their march through the isthmus the bloodthirsty soldiers left a barbaric and gory trail. Somewhere along the Monona shore of today's Marquette neighborhood the scouts came upon an elderly Indian huddling in a thicket. A Galena newspaper editor-physician turned soldier "popped him on the spot," grabbed the Indian's own knife and attempted to scalp the Sauk. Unfortunately the knife was dull and required a strenuous effort to wrench the scalp loose. The old Indian screamed in pain. Other troops crowded round in time to hear the editor say, "If you don't like being scalped with a dull knife, why don't you keep a better one?" The remark quickly became the *bon mot* of the campaign.[30]

Twelve days after the warring parties had passed through the Madison isthmus, the Black Hawk War ended following the bloody Battle of the Bad Axe. There 950 of Black Hawk's band of 1,000 were slaughtered. Tragically, just a few days before the Bad Axe slaughter, Black Hawk once again attempted to surrender at the Battle of Wisconsin Heights near present-day Sauk City, but the soldiers interpreted the effort as a delaying tactic.[31] More Indians died than settlers and soldiers, but the toll upon the settlers and soldiers was great also. At least 250 whites were killed.[32] The Black Hawk War left a legacy of hatred and distrust for Indians, a feeling that persisted for many years.

Just one month after the bloody finish of the Black Hawk War, all southern Wisconsin Winnebago chiefs, some of whom had allegedly encouraged and aided Black Hawk, were summoned to Fort Armstrong (Rock Island, Illinois) where authorities demanded the cession of all Winnebago lands lying roughly south of the Wisconsin River and north of the Rock River. Within this cession lay what is now Madison. Under the terms of the Rock Island Treaty, no Winnebago was to reside there after June 1, 1833.[33]

The future of Winnebagos living in the Four Lakes area was anything but bright. Not only did

they have to move either to Iowa or the area north of the Wisconsin River, but they had no corn for the winter. The conduct of the war during the summer had prevented them from planting and harvesting their usual crops. Moreover, during the winter of 1832–33 game was scarce and many Indians starved and froze to death.[34]

When spring came, the tribe, still in a state of semistarvation, pleaded with Indian agents to allow them to return one last time to their ancestral homes where they would plant and harvest corn and then leave without trouble. But the memories of the war were too fresh in the minds of the authorities to allow any such generous impulse. To work out the details for the removal activity, Colonel Henry Dodge called a meeting with the principal chiefs at the old council grounds on the north shore of Lake Mendota.[35]

On April 28, 1833, Colonel Dodge and the two area Indian agents, Gratiot and Kinzie, arrived at the hillside on Lake Mendota. The principal chiefs of the Yahara River area, including Whirling Thunder, White Crow, Little Priest, Little Black, Spotted Arm, and White Breast, attended. Dodge peremptorily rejected their plea to remain in the ceded territory until they had harvested their corn, but he did agree to have several wagonloads of corn brought to the council site on May 15, 1833 and to provide wagons and oxen to transport Indian belongings to the Wisconsin River.[36]

To superintend the distribution of rations and escort the Indians to the Wisconsin River, Dodge enlisted the services of two companies of dragoons who built a camp just west of the council grounds near a great spring, dubbed Camp Belle Fontaine.[37] By May 15, about 300 Winnebagos gathered at the council grounds ready for the trip.[38] The previous November, the Indian agent had taken a census that showed 163 Winnebagos camped around Lake Monona and 155 camped around Mendota.[39] On the evening before their departure the Indians held a grand medicine dance somewhere near the present city of Madison. At the conclusion of the ceremony they extinguished their camp fires and then kindled a new one, which they "hoped would burn clear and make them happy." The Indian agent then gave them a few presents, after which their canoes, wigwams, and effects, already brought up the chain of the Four Lakes, were loaded onto the wagons and transported to the shore of the Wisconsin River at Sauk Prairie.[40] The Indians were not eager to leave, and some didn't make the deadline imposed by the Rock Island Treaty. Not until five months later had the dragoons cleared the area of stragglers and holdouts.

Swift and dramatic though the Indian removal operation had been, it results proved both incomplete and temporary. In June 1835, two years after the mass removal, some twelve hundred to fourteen hundred Winnebagos were reportedly camped in the country between Lakes Mendota and Koshkonong."[41] Some had escaped the dragoon round up, and many had returned following their deportation. Clearly they liked the Four Lakes area. In at least one instance the Winnebagos were encouraged to remain in the area by French Indian traders so they could continue gathering furs.[42]

The Federal Land Survey
and the Military Road

For the eight hundred soldiers, mostly Illinois farm boys who pursued Black Hawk and his band across southern Wisconsin, the war served as an unplanned but intriguing geography lesson. On his way through Madison one soldier gave the future city site a very mixed review. "If," he said, "these lakes were anywhere else except in the country where they are, they would be considered among the wonders of the world. But the country they are situated in is not fit for any civilized nation of people to inhabit. It appears that the Almighty intended it for the children of the forest."[43] Such a negative impression was hardly surprising; Black Hawk in a very deliberate attempt to elude the soldiers forced them to pass through some of the swampiest land in what are now Jefferson and Dane Counties.

Yet for every soldier who had unflattering things to say about the country around present-day Madison, many more were pleasantly surprised to discover its extensive, fertile prairies and beautiful oak openings. Rare was the eastern newspaper that in the months immediately after the war did not carry at least one florid description of the parklike beauty and rich farmland in the Four Lake area.[44]

Preparation for settlement could be delayed no longer. Between 1833 and 1835 federal surveyors imposed Euclidan order on southern Wisconsin. Just a few days before Christmas, 1834, Orson Lyon and his four-man crew completed the survey of Town 7, Range 9 East, later named the Town of Madison and out of which "Madison City" would soon be carved. The surveyors described the isthmus as "second rate" land but said much of the land outside the isthmus was "first rate" farmland.[45] Speculators immediately studied surveyor notes and maps for desirable tracts.

In August 1835, just eight months after the Town of Madison had been surveyed, the first road across southern Wisconsin was completed. Connecting Fort Crawford (Prairie du Chien) with Fort Winnebago (Portage) the road nearly touched the northern shore of Lake Mendota.

The road was a monument to the lobbying ability of James Duane Doty, the Michigan territory judge who had visited the Madison area in May 1829. Beginning in 1829 Doty argued that Fort Winnebago could not be supplied, much less protected, unless it was connected to Fort Crawford (Prairie du Chien) and Ford Howard (Green Bay) by a military road. Besides, Doty argued—and a very big besides it was—such a road was a prerequisite for territorial settlement. Congress not only agreed with the idea and appropriated the money but made Doty one of two commissioners charged with laying out the road. After Doty had designated the route, U.S. soldiers were given the job of building it. In command of the section between Prairie du Chien and Portage was Zachary Taylor, who thirteen years later was elected president of the United States. The completed road was nothing fancy, just a thirty-foot-wide clearing in most places, but it was a vast

improvement over the two-foot-wide meandering Indian trails.[46]

Thus by the end of 1835, the Indians in southern Wisconsin had been subdued if not completely removed, the land had been surveyed, and a military road had been built just north of Lake Mendota linking the Four Lakes area to the two major territorial population centers. The stage was nearly ready for American settlement.

Madison City Wins the Territorial Sweepstakes

Doty Buys the Isthmus

When the townships in and around Madison were first placed on sale in Green Bay on August 1, 1835, business was brisk. The government price was just $1.25 per acre. A customer could buy an unlimited amount of land, but no less than a quarter section. Most of the purchasers, however, were not the sturdy yeomen of Jefferson's arcadian dream, but rather wealthy investors whose interests were strictly speculative. Everywhere people believed that land speculation was the road to riches, and for many it was. Appreciation of one hundred to seven hundred percent in just twelve to eighteen months was commonplace for those making astute purchases.[1]

Curiously, after five months of land office business in Green Bay, no one bought the isthmus between Third and Fourth Lakes! Only two persons had even dabbled in the area. One was Francis Tillou, a wealthy eastern speculator, who bought land around the point where the Yahara River flowed into Lake Monona. The other was James Duane Doty, the former territorial judge, active Wisconsin promoter in the Michigan territorial legislature, attorney, explorer, and, most recently, western land agent for wealthy and influential eastern clients. Doty was one of the best known men in the territory and was widely regarded as one of the smartest. In his typically shrewd manner Doty bought a ninety-nine-acre piece on both sides of the Yahara River between

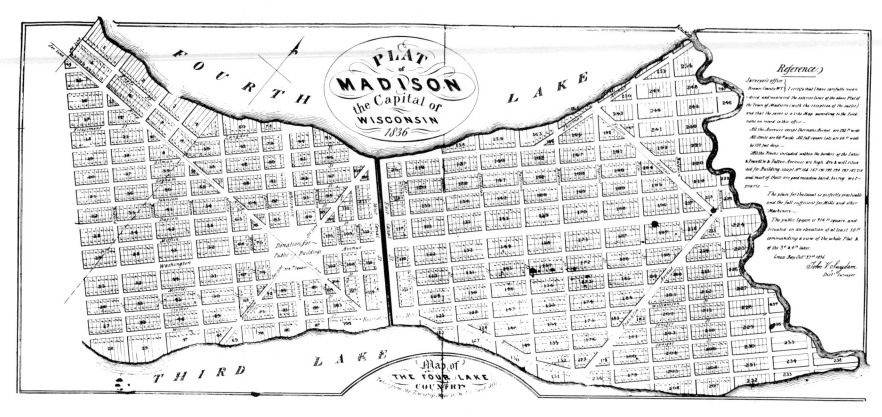

FIGURE 1.12. DOTY PLAT. The original plat of Madison shown here was not a model of surveying precision. Laid out in just forty-eight hours by Doty and his Green Bay surveyor, J. V. Suydam, on their way to Belmont, the plat spawned a legacy of legal problems.

Later surveys showed that some blocks along Lake Mendota were only half as deep on the survey as they were in fact; similarly the block on which National Guardian Life now stands was not even divided into lots because Doty's survey showed it was too shallow. Along Lake Monona, some lots were bought and sold that lay entirely under water!

Several claims made by Suydam on the plat legend are suspect. For example, the surveyor said that the canal location at the narrowest point of the isthmus was "perfectly practical." In fact to cut a canal through the isthmus at this point would have required cutting a gorge through a hill forty feet high at Main and Franklin Streets.

Suydam's second questionable contention was that everything inside of Franklin and Fulton Streets and between the lakes was high and dry with the exception of a handful of blocks that were "wet prairie." Later eyewitness accounts suggest that what was "wet prairie" in October when the survey was made was a shallow lake in the spring and in places covered by water at all times.

The most striking characteristic of the Madison plat was its use of the baroque radial street concept. The briefest examination of the plat shows the extent to which the concept was suggested by section lines established by the federal surveyors. Note, too, the attempt to create a second major focal point where Franklin and Fulton Avenues converged on East Washington. Noticeably missing from the Doty plat is open space, both along and away from the lakeshore. The only land along the lakeshores reserved for the public were street ends and the canal inlet on Lake Mendota. Inland the only open space in the plat apart from streets was the Capitol Park. Although Doty offered relatively little public space, his 66 × 132-foot lots were quite large by contemporary standards. (SHSW Map Collection WHi(X32)8775)

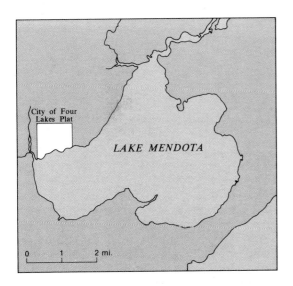

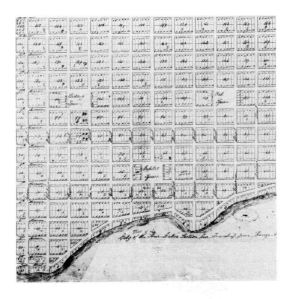

FIGURE 1.13. CITY OF THE FOUR LAKES. Until late November 1836, the City of the Four Lakes and at least twenty other paper towns and tiny villages throughout the state had high hopes of being selected territorial capital. Madison's victory made losers out of twenty aspirants. What happened to the losers is poignantly revealed by the brief history of the City of the Four Lakes shown here.

The site was officially purchased in August 1835, soon after the land office was opened by Colonel William B. Slaughter, a native of Culpepper, Virginia, and the Register at the Green Bay land office. On December 20, 1835, Slaughter conveyed an undivided interest to Judge Doty with the understanding that Doty would have the town laid out as a prospective capital site. Doty then hired John Bannister, a Green Bay surveyor, who laid out the town in the summer of 1836. The plat is dated July 7, 1836—one suspicious week *after* the date on Doty's plat of Madison City. Note the streets named for territorial officers and the square reserved for the Capitol.

From the beginning the town attracted considerable interest among astute investors like Lucius Lyon, who had purchased twenty thousand acres of Wisconsin land when it went on sale in Green Bay, much of it around the Four Lakes. Unfortunately the lobbyist that the City of the Four Lakes investors hired failed to appear at the Belmont session. Even so, the paper town was officially nominated in the House but lost by one vote—six ayes, seven nays.

The failure to get the territorial capital designation did not entirely discourage the City of the Four Lakes investors. They argued that their townsite could not fail to do well since it was situated right across the lake from the Capitol, near a contemplated canal connecting the Rock and Wisconsin Rivers, and beside the recently constructed Military Road connecting Prairie du Chien and Portage. Some investors, including several from the East, bought lots and built homes. As added insurance, the paper town owners sought another prize the territorial legislature could bestow. During the 1837–38 legislative session held in Burlington, Iowa, a bill was introduced to establish the University of the Territory of Wisconsin at the City of the Four Lakes. Unfortunately for the City of the Four Lakes the bill was amended to read "in the vicinity of Madison." With this language change the paper town suffered a serious setback. On April 5, 1843, the history of the once promising city was quietly closed by a legislative act saying the land within the town plat was to be taxed as farmland. (SHSW WHi(X3)33271).

the Tenney Park locks and East Washington Avenue. Unlike many speculators, Doty did not buy huge parcels, but rather concentrated his attention on the choice ones. Doty doubtless viewed his isthmus acquisition as a choice canal and water power site.[2]

The failure of anyone to buy the Madison isthmus did not go unnoticed for long. Among those who noticed the omission were the twelve Wisconsin members of the Michigan territorial legislature who held a rump session in Green Bay in January 1836, to work out details for the separation of the Wisconsin and Michigan territories. With this group Doty discussed the commercial advantages of the isthmus as a townsite. The group informally agreed to inspect the tract, form a company, and purchase the tract. In March, two of the men, Levi Sterling of Mineral Point and Ebeneezer Brigham of Blue Mounds, inspected the site.[3] Whether these two scouts reported their findings to Doty is not known.

In April, Doty left for New York on business. On the way he stopped at Detroit to see his old friend Steven T. Mason, who had recently been elected governor of Michigan Territory. Mason inquired about good land investments in Wisconsin, and Doty suggested the isthmus site. The two agreed to purchase the tract in equal shares with the understanding that a joint stock company would be formed. On April 6, 1836, Mason and Doty paid fifteen hundred dollars for about one thousand acres, the center of which was the spot where the capitol now stands (see fig 1.). On May 28, 1836, Mason gave Doty the power of attorney to "divide lay off and dispose of the property 'jointly' owned by the two. Operating under this authority, Doty organized on June 1 the Four Lakes Company . . ."[4] with a capital stock of twenty-four hundred dollars in twenty-four equal shares. At some point during this period Francis Tillou decided to include his land in the Four Lakes Company. On June 1, Mason and Tillou affixed their signatures to a deed conveying to Doty as trustee for the Four Lakes Company about 1,360 acres. From this point forward Doty enjoyed unquestioned clear title and nearly absolute control over the tract. He could therefore make decisions and wheel and deal on lot prices without having to get approval from anybody—a position enjoyed by few other townsite promoters.[5]

Showdown at Belmont

According to the Organic Act creating the Wisconsin Territory, President Andrew Jackson appointed the territorial officers and the people elected the legislature. Jackson's choice for governor, General Henry Dodge, a hero of the Black Hawk War, was easily confirmed by the Senate and took office on July 4, 1836. The Organic Act required Dodge to direct a territorial census, apportion members of the two legislative houses, the Council and the House, order an election, and then pick a time and place for the first meeting of that body. Following a census in August, Dodge divided the Wisconsin Territory, then five times larger than present day Wisconsin, into six huge counties and apportioned delegates in proportion to population. He then ordered elections for territorial delegates on October 10 and directed the winners to convene on October 25 in Belmont.[6]

Since the Green Bay rump session in January, competition for the capital site had grown intense. The selection of the seat of government was, after all, the principal question facing legislators at that first session. The reason for the speculation in townsites was simple enough: winning this coveted governmental prize was a sure way to get rich quick. Not surprisingly, the townsite promoters bearing beautiful maps of prospective cities threatened to outnumber the thirty-nine legislators who gathered at a barren prairie knoll called Belmont[7] where the momentous decision was to be made.

Into this highly charged atmosphere went James Duane Doty. He arrived about November 2, one week after the session opened, with John V. Suydam, his Green Bay surveyor who, on the way to Belmont, had measured the exterior lines of the paper town.[8] Immediately after arriving, Doty began giving Suydam "minute instructions" on how to lay out the town.[9] At the same time Suydam put the finishing touches on the "Madison City" town, Doty began to lobby on its behalf. Only one of the Belmont legislators, Ebeneezer Brigham, had even seen the site.[10] Doty had a difficult job before him.

Eight days after Doty's arrival, a bill was introduced in the Council calling for Madison to be the seat of government, but floor debate was deferred until November 23.

Beginning at 3:00 P.M. on that date, amendments calling for the deletion of Madison and the substitution of Dubuque, Cassville, Mineral Point, Milwaukee, Fond du Lac, Portage, Helena, Racine, Belmont, Platteville, Astor (now Green Bay), Belleview (Iowa), Koshkonong, Wisconsinapolis, and Wisconsin City were made. Fourteen failed by a vote of six to seven, and one—Dubuque—failed by a vote of five to eight. Finally, late in the afternoon, the upper house voted seven to six to give Madison the prize.[11]

Action then moved to the House of Representatives. In a marathon session on November 28, Madison won the sweepstakes over eighteen paper towns and fledgling villages.[12]

Why Madison Won

Although the complete story of how Madison was selected territorial capital can never be known, there can be no doubt that Doty played a large and influential role. Early commentators have not been charitable in their interpretation of Doty's success at Belmont. Some accused Doty of using underhanded if not illegal techniques, such as giving choice corner lots to undecided legislators.[13] A close look at the record, however, neither vindicates Doty nor fully supports his critics. Clearly many anti-Doty comments must be attributed to the fact that there were eighteen losing townsites, each of which had many promoters and few of which were inclined to be charitable to the winner of the Belmont prize.[14]

Doty critics must also concede that his success went far beyond the popular corner-lot explanation. His weapons included a well-located, thoughtfully designed "product" over which he could exercise complete control, a thorough understanding of territorial politics and the friendship of several delegates, an unrivaled knowledge of the territory, a superb grasp of human nature, and a network of influential friends in Washington, D.C.

Madison as a Product

Consider the characteristics of Doty's product. First, "Madison City" was located in the right part of the territory from the point of view of many delegates. One must remember that in 1836 the Wisconsin territory included all of what is now Iowa and Minnesota and the eastern half of the Dakotas. One must also remember that the August territorial census showed that nearly half of the total territorial population lived west of the Mississippi. These "western" delegates were keenly aware that several additional states would one day be carved out of the territory west of the Mississippi and were therefore interested in voting for a "Wisconsin" capital whose location would create no economic rivalry for fledgling towns in those envisioned states. Thus, sites on or near the Mississippi were not popular with the western delegates. Madison's location lying just half way between the Mississippi and Lake Michigan could not have been better from this point of view.[15] It was no accident that all of the Des Moines County delegates representing what is now much of the state of Iowa consistently voted for Madison and against all substitutions. The fact that Des Moines County was the most populous of the six "super" counties then constituting Wisconsin meant that it had the largest number of votes to throw behind its choice.[16] Doty knew these circumstances and used them to his advantage.

The fact that Madison lay in the center range of townships in the southern part of the future state was also a compelling argument. Not only was the site centrally and conveniently located, but its selection would encourage settlement of the rich undeveloped agricultural land in southern Wisconsin.

Second, Doty also draped his paper town in appealing political plumage. A revered president, James Madison, had died just five months before the Belmont session. Doty wisely capitalized upon sentimental feelings throughout the country and selected "Madison" as the name for his paper town. To add to the town's patriotic appeal, he named all the streets after signers of the Constitution and, of course, gave Washington's name to the principal thoroughfare.[17]

Third, Doty's town layout provided a vivid contrast to the almost exclusive dependence upon the grid system of his competition. Doty, an experienced town planner with towns like Fond du Lac, Astor (now Green Bay) and several others to his credit, had shown a willingness in some of his other towns to depart from the monotonous grid system in various ways, but in none had he gone as far as "Madison City." For the territorial capital, Doty borrowed heavily from baroque town planning ideas employed by L'Enfant, the designer of Washington, D.C. The key concept that Doty borrowed was the radial street plan in accord with which streets followed cardinal points of the compass and which led like spokes on a wheel to a central, usually symmetrical open space. Under this concept, street width reflected the relative importance of a street. Thus, streets like Washington, Wisconsin, and Monona were given the highest status at 132 feet wide.[18]

Fourth, Doty threw in two timely features designed to appeal to the rough-hewn Belmont legislators. One was a canal across the isthmus looking on the map like a small section of the magnificent and much imitated Erie Canal, then in its heyday. Few ideas were so uncritically supported in that era as canals.[19] However, railroads were already becoming a part of the expected future, and so, obligingly, Doty threw in a railroad, too. His idea was to send a railroad linking Milwaukee and the Mississippi right up the middle of East Washington Avenue, and so it was shown on the original plat. (How the tiny, puffing engines of the era were supposed to climb the steep hill leading up to the Capitol, or where the tracks were supposed to go after they reached Capitol Square, Doty did not say.)

Finally, the site was just plain beautiful. No other site was in the same league, lying on a narrow isthmus between two lakes. One can almost hear the proud promoter's smooth flow of superlatives.

Doty, Promoter Extraordinaire

Having a well-designed and well-located paper town, though a prerequisite, was hardly a guarantee of winning. A site needed an effective promoter, and James Duane Doty was the best in the territory. This "genial," "tall, good looking gentleman" with a "handshake for everybody"[20] was widely known and respected and generally regarded as one of the smartest men in the state. As a result of frequent trips around the state, Doty had acquired an unsurpassed knowledge of Wisconsin geography. Few Belmont delegates had seen more than one or two of the prospective sites on which they voted. Doty, by contrast, had either laid out or visited thirteen of the nineteen townsites placed in nomination for the seat of government![21]

Clearly, Doty knew how to make himself appreciated by the Belmont decision makers. While others complained about the crude accommodations and the shortage of fire wood, Doty dispatched a man to Dubuque for a wagonload of buffalo robes, which he then distributed to the shivering and grateful legislators.[22]

But of all the things that Doty did at Belmont to influence the seat of government vote, none drew more criticism than his alleged liberal dispensation of choice corner lots to undecided legislators. Unfortunately, for those who like crisp, unequivocal verdicts, the charge can neither be fully confirmed nor denied. What is known is that between December 2 and 10—*after* the final Madison vote—sixteen out of thirty-nine legislators *purchased* 175 lots at prices ranging from ten cents to one hundred dollars apiece. Among these sixteen purchasers were four who voted against the site, including one gentleman to whom Doty sold ten lots for a dime apiece.[23] Whether these purchases were arranged *prior* to the vote is not known. Nor can we know whether the sale prices stated on the transfer documents were actually paid. It is entirely possible that some lots were exchanged without cost, or that some lots were sold far below the going rate. Whether the lots were in fact "choice corner lots" can be determined by studying the buyers' names that Doty penned on the original plat. Although the names of some buyers are not legible, it would appear that thirty-three of the 175 lots (nineteen percent) purchased by legislators were corner lots. Of this number only seven lay within three blocks of the Square—surely a widely accepted definition of "choice"—and only two actually fronted on the square.[24]

Even after Madison City had been selected, Doty knew he could not rest on his laurels. He astutely recognized that backers of losing townsites would try to get Congress to nullify the Belmont decision, and so he moved quickly on two fronts. First, he sold town lots to as many influential persons as he could so that each had a financial interest in seeing the seat of government remain in Madison. Among territorial dignitaries to whom, Doty sold lots were Augustus Dodge, Governor Dodge's son Charles Dunn, Chief Justice of the Wisconsin Supreme Count, and Hercules Dousman, a wealthy Prairie du Chien fur trader. Doty also sold dozens of lots to men of national prominence. For example, John Jacob Astor, the well-known owner of the American Fur Company, bought two dozen lots.[25] Doty was so successful in selling lots to dignitaries that Governor Dodge wrote a letter to Wisconsin congressional delegate George W. Jones to bitterly complain about this practice. Doty, Dodge argued, "thinks (interested money) is the great *Lever* that governs and regulates the actions of all mankind, (and) that . . . all have their prices. . . ."[26] Unfortunately for Dodge, Doty had already sold Jones about thirty-six town lots—an act Dodge acknowledged and criticized in his letter.[27]

SHSW WHi(X3)35112

James Duane Doty: Frontier Promoter

When eighteen-year-old James Duane Doty said goodbye in 1818 to his family in Martinsburg, New York, a tiny community in upper New York state, he intended to go to St. Louis. However, when he reached Cleveland, he boarded a schooner sailing for Detroit. In that tiny seven-hundred-person community occupying a place of great strategic importance for the northwest, the tall good looking youth (here shown at about age fifty) met the Michigan Territory attorney general. The official was impressed by Doty's intellect and offered the youth a job as his clerk. Doty accepted. One year after his arrival he was admitted to the bar and appointed clerk of the Michigan supreme court and secretary

of the City of Detroit. Two years after his arrival, Michigan Governor Cass selected Doty to accompany him and several scientists on what is now called the Schoolcraft expedition, a 4,200-mile canoe voyage through the Upper Great Lakes, down the Mississippi and up the Fox and Wisconsin Rivers. The trip laid an early foundation for Doty's unsurpassed knowledge of the Wisconsin territory.

In 1821 the ambitious twenty-three-year-old Doty had decided the time had come to make his move. In that year Doty made two trips to Washington, D.C., one in January when he was admitted to practice before the Supreme Court and another in October when he began to promote the creation of a judgeship in the area now known as Wisconsin—a move he and others saw as a method of establishing civil law in the area. On February 17, 1823, President James Monroe officially appointed Doty as the circuit judge of the Western Michigan Territory. Doty's jurisdiction included all of the present day Wisconsin, Iowa, Minnesota, and part of the Dakotas—a weighty and impressive position for a young man just twenty-five years old. On the way back to Detroit from Washington, D.C., where he had received his judicial appointment, Doty stopped in Martinsburg, New York, long enough to marry his childhood sweetheart, Sarah Collins.

For nine years Doty was on the public payroll as the "additional judge" for the Michigan Territory. Each year he made a 1,360-mile circuit between Prairie du Chien, Green Bay, and Mackinac by canoe. During most of this period Doty lived in Green Bay where he built two homes including the first brick residence in the Wisconsin Territory. He also founded the Episcopal Church there—the first non-Catholic church west of Lake Michigan. He studied French, Sioux, Winnebago, and Chippewa and assembled what he called the "native code." The latter, a system of laws based upon Indian rather than American values, was an early expression of life-long sympathy for Indians. In 1823 Doty drafted the first bill for a separate territorial government in what is now Wisconsin. He popularized

the name "Wisconsin" for the area but argued that the correct spelling was "Wiskonsin."

By 1830 Doty began to complain in letters to friends about his "twelve years in exile" and "being buried in the wilderness." He tried but failed to get himself appointed as chief of the Bureau of Indian Affairs in Washington based on his "native code" and other legal work with Indians.

When Andrew Jackson appointed someone else to the circuit judgeship of Western Michigan in 1832, Doty plunged back into the private practice of law. However, during this interlude he used his connections with his friend, former Michigan Governor Louis Cass, then Secretary of War, to secure a commission to lay out the first military road in Wisconsin connecting Ft. Crawford (Prairie du Chien) with Ft. Howard (Green Bay) via Ft. Winnebago (Portage). In 1835 he used the same connection to get the commission to lay out a military road connecting Ft. Howard with Ft. Dearborn (Chicago). Doty felt the roads were critically important not only for the defense of the area but also for later settlement.

In January 1834 Doty was elected to a two-year term in the Michigan territorial legislature where he led a faction of the Democratic Party, which created the Wisconsin Territory. In a letter to a friend he called it the "greatest triumph he ever had."

During his two-year term in the Michigan legislature, Doty became the Wisconsin land agent for one of the richest men in the country, John Jacob Astor, a prestigious and practical connection the young legislator fully exploited. On behalf of the American Fur Company executive, Doty laid out Astor, now downtown Green Bay, and drew on the Astor account to pay for shares in various other land development schemes. The young dynamo peppered the aging Astor with requests to build hotels, construct dams, and buy steamboats, many of which Astor agreed to do. Independently, Doty purchased thirty-five-hundred acres at the southern tip of Lake Winnebago where he laid out Fond du Lac. By the summer of 1836 when he laid out Madison City, Doty was hardly a novice at city building.

Just one year after Madison was selected as the seat of government, the Panic of 1837 sent the country into a depression. Doty's land investments and nearly everyone else's were victims of that depression. In 1840 Doty wrote a plaintive letter to Astor asking the investor to save him from financial ruin. At the time an Astor subordinate estimated Doty's lands to be worth between $100,000 and $200,000, that is, if they could be sold. Astor gave Doty the money he needed and took back a mortgage sufficient to secure the loan. Doty's "thin" financial condition during the 1837 depression prevented him from becoming what he easily might have been—a Wisconsin land baron.

But the 1837 financial crisis was in many ways the easiest problem for Doty to solve. More damaging were several investigations launched by the 1838 territorial legislature. The first centered on how Doty had spent $40,000 in federal funds entrusted to his care for the erection of the capitol. In 1841 Doty accounted for all but $1,758 and promptly sent payment for this amount to the state.

Doty's second problem was the validity of his title to his Madison land. Moses Strong, a Mineral Point attorney, persuaded Steven T. Mason, Doty's partner on the Madison venture, that Doty did not have clear title to sell Madison lots. Though the matter was settled in Doty's favor in 1841, the title dispute adversely affected Madison lot sales during these critical formative years.

A third problem stemmed from Doty's deep involvement in two banks chartered by the Michigan legislature in 1835: the Bank of Wisconsin and the Bank of Mineral Point. Both banks were victims of the 1837 depression, but their demise was also brought on by questionable if not illegal underwriting and poor financial management. Contemporary investigators never were able to figure out what had happened. People did understand, however, that Doty was deeply involved in both, and again, he suffered from the association.

In 1838, in the midst of charges stemming from these investigations, Doty conducted a vigorous statewide horseback campaign to urge voters to send him to Congress as territorial delegate. The voters were apparently persuaded by his charming personality, his impressive appearance, and his forceful presentation of his side of the case because Doty was elected and in January 1839 took his seat in Congress. Doty enjoyed the Washington, D.C., life, lived in the same boarding house with Henry Clay, but did little to earn a good rating as a representative.

In 1841 Doty returned to Madison, bought a house on Doty Street and served two terms as territorial governor. Probably few years of Doty's life were filled with as much strife and villification as these. Although Doty made the required appearances as governor, he spent relatively little time in Madison, probably because he was subjected to fierce partisan charges stemming from his earlier controversies.

After leaving the governor's chair, Doty retired to a four-hundred-acre island, between Neenah-Menasha, where the Fox River flows out of Lake Winnebago. There he built a huge home called the Grand Loggery where he lived until 1861. During this period he and his son, Charles, became real estate dealers and laid out Menasha.

In 1846 Doty resumed public life as a representative to the ill-fated 1846 Wisconsin Constitutional Convention. In that same year Doty sought but failed to achieve his long-sought goal of being elected to the U.S. Senate. He settled for two terms in the House of Representatives (1849–1853) where he promoted a network of federally assisted canals and railroads. Had he been willing to abandon his maverick qualities and become a party man, he might have left more significant legislative accomplishments. But he did not. Doty could not overcome his lifelong tendency to march to his own music.

When Doty turned sixty-two in 1861, an age when most men are content to enjoy retirement, Doty left the comfortable, well-furnished Grand Loggery, his books, and friends and set his face once again to the west. President Lincoln appointed Doty to be Superintendent of Indian Affairs at Salt Lake City, Utah Territory. But at age sixty-two, going west was not the same as it had been as an eighteen-year-old young man. By this time Doty was crippled so badly from rheumatism that he had to be lifted onto his stagecoach at St. Joseph, Missouri, for the twelve-hundred-mile trip.

At first Doty did not seem to like the territory and before the end of his first year applied for a transfer to Southern California. When the request was denied, he satisfied his insatiable curiosity by traveling to San Francisco and Los Angeles as a part of a business trip to neighboring Nevada. In a letter to his daughter he wrote enthusiastically about the climate and tropical fruits. Doty probably would have settled in California had not Lincoln appointed him governor of the Utah Territory in 1863. As governor of the hostile Mormon community, Doty demonstrated great sensitivity and skill and won begrudging respect from his most severe critics. Had Doty completed his gubernatorial duties and had Lincoln not been assassinated, Doty probably would have been able to get a choice appointment in California. But as fate would have it, neither condition materialized. Doty died on June 13, 1865, after a short illness, and Lincoln was assassinated on April 14, 1865.

Because of his prominent role in the development of Wisconsin, Doty was often asked to write his recollections, but he always paried the request. "Perhaps I have been too much engaged in the making of history of this country to write it fairly, . . ." he said. In fact, Doty's bias was only part of the problem. He was a man of action, not reflection. Indeed, any man who in the compass of a single lifetime had been a farmer, a lawyer, a real estate agent, a judge, an explorer, a developer of cities including Madison, Fond du Lac, Menasha, and Green Bay, a railroad and canal promoter, a state territorial legislator, a two-term governor of the Wisconsin territory, a two-term congressman, a Superintendent of Indian Affairs, and governor of Utah would scarcely have had time for much else. No wonder his wife in an 1843 letter said "Mr. D. is always going or gone."

Doty also asked his influential friends in Congress to help. One congressman who received a steady stream of Doty letters before, during, and after the Belmont session was Aaron Vanderpoel, a New York Representative who at Doty's suggestion had purchased a quarter section of land on the western edge of Madison on which the University of Wisconsin was eventually built. In a letter dated November 26, 1836, just three days after the Wisconsin Territorial Council had selected Madison as the seat of government, but before the House had acted upon the bill, Doty warned Vanderpoel that an "application . . . may be made to Congress to reverse the decision there. . . ." and asked for his assistance should such an effort be necessary. Doty explained that Michigan Governor Mason and four other congressmen were also financially interested in doing what they could to keep the capital at Madison. In his correspondence, Doty reminded Vanderpoel that his quarter section would be worth ten thousand dollars, but only if Congress ratified the Belmont decision. In still another letter just a few days later, Doty bluntly told Vanderpoel that "If the (U.S.) government lets us alone, we can make a handsome spec(ulation) out of this."[28]

Whether one liked or despised the thirty-seven-year-old promoter, nearly everyone had to acknowledge his effectiveness. Indeed the highest compliments for his Belmont victory came from those who favored other sites for the seat of government. In their words: Doty was "the shrewdest, most subtle, suave and insinuating lobbyist who attended the first session"[29] and a "formidable opponent."[30]

To the Victor, Profit

From the time Madison City was officially selected, Doty enjoyed the proverbial land office business in town lots. By December 10, just twelve days after the final vote, the record showed that legislators had purchased lots worth $6,700, whereas nonlegislators bought lots worth $28,810,

for total sales of $35,510.[31] Taking the indicated sales prices at face value, the stockholders of the Four Lakes Company had received nearly a twenty-four hundred percent return on their eight-month-old investment. No wonder the competition for the capital site had been so keen!

Pecks Lead the Way

Establishing a Public House
in the Wilderness

After the Belmont session adjourned on December 9, 1836, several Green Bay men who had attended stopped at a Blue Mounds "tavern stand" run by Eben and Rosaline Peck and told them that Madison had been selected the territorial capital. Hearing this, the Pecks decided to open a public house there to accommodate visitors and workmen. On December 26 they purchased two lots at one hundred dollars each on which to build their public house.[1]

Mr. Peck made arrangements with a French *coureur,* Abraham Wood, then living at a spot later called Winnequah, to build two log cabins on their Madison property.[2]

The next job was getting ready for business at Madison, and that meant going to Mineral Point for supplies. There Peck bought one hundred dollars worth of groceries, including barrels of pork, flour, crackers, sugar, dried fruit, tea, and "as good a sack of coffee as was ever brought into the state."[3] These supplies plus some of Rosaline's own pickles, butter, jars of plums and cranberries, and several sacks of potatoes were loaded onto the wagon.

On Thursday afternoon, April 13, 1837, Eben, Rosaline, then four months pregnant, and their ten-year-old son Victor left Blue Mound in their loaded wagon. On Friday, with the help of warm sunny weather, they travelled to the area now known as Nakoma, where they camped for the night. At three in the morning the Pecks were "awakened to a tremendous windstorm and howling of wolves and found snow five or six

inches deep . . ."[4] on the ground. So there they were, said Rosaline, twenty-five miles from the Blue Mounds and nearly one hundred miles from Milwaukee, "sitting in a wagon under a tree, with a bed quilt thrown over my own and little boy's heads, in a tremendous storm of snow and sleet. . . ." At dawn they rode into Madison to their cabins.

An inspection of the two side-by-side 18-by-24-foot log cabins built for them the preceding month revealed that neither had a floor or had they been plastered and limed (painted). A proud and immaculate housekeeper, twenty-nine-year-old Rosaline refused to begin housekeeping with a dirt floor and unpainted walls. She thereupon had Eben build her an 18-by-24-foot lean-to behind and between the twenty-four-foot space separating the two cabins. There Rosaline moved in her stove and temporarily set up housekeeping.[5] (See fig 1.14 for more detail of the Peck cabin.)

For two weeks, until about the first of May 1837, the Pecks had the place to themselves. Then fifteen Milwaukee men arrived whose job it was to blaze a trail for capitol workmen who would soon follow. For their first customers the Pecks set tables for the men "under the broad canopy of heaven" and stuffed bed ticks with marsh hay.[6] Some of the men stayed a few days to hunt and fish while the others returned to Milwaukee. After three or four days all the men went on to Mineral Point but were soon back, this time accompanied by Judge Doty, Ebeneezer Brigham, and others. During their brief stay everybody helped the Pecks finish work on their cabins.

Around 9:00 P.M. on May 30 the Pecks had an unexpected visitor, a distinguished English geologist named George W. Featherstonaugh (pronounced Fan-show). His importance to Madison history lies in the fact that he wrote a jaundiced but informative account of his visit to the Pecks in a book published in London in 1847 (see excerpt on page 28).[7] When Rosaline Peck ten years later read that portion of Featherstonaugh's book describing his Madison visit, she was so incensed at his distortions, errors, and lies that she prepared a lively article without which the early history of Madison would be seriously anemic.

SHSW WHi(C7)6560

Rosaline Peck: Frontier Innkeeper

Twenty years before this photo was taken in 1857, Rosaline Peck was a twenty-nine-year-old coproprietor with her thirty-three-year-old husband of Madison's first public house. After one year of exhausting and onerous innkeeper duties—in Mrs. Peck's words, "being a slave to everybody"—the Pecks sold their "tavern stand" and bought an eighty-acre farmsite from James Doty one mile from Madison. After the backbreaking work of clearing the land, cutting the sod, and fencing their fields, the Pecks were told by Doty that he had deeded them the wrong piece of land.

Sick at heart, the Pecks moved to Baraboo in the fall of 1840, where they claimed, fenced, and improved a piece of farmland. Soon thereafter Mr. Peck left Rosaline under the pretense of going to Oregon, but it appears he went to Texas to marry another woman. Shortly after he left, a speculator entered the Peck's Baraboo cabin and with the aid of a drunk, literally threw Rosaline, her two children, and their possessions out into the cold.

About this time, history-minded Madisonians persuaded Mrs. Peck to come to Madison for a "sitting." Even that experience turned out badly. The roads were terrible, and the rented four-dollar-per-day rig got stuck several times and broke down. Three days after leaving Baraboo, Mrs. Peck arrived in Madison. While waiting for her picture to be taken, she picked up a copy of the recently published 1855 Madison business directory. The directory's local history rendition enraged Rosaline by portraying her role in Madison as a mere fiddler entertaining the early population with her toe-tapping music. "Bah," said Rosaline, "did you ever hear such trash." Perhaps these things explain her stern, almost defiant countenance. Going home she got stuck twice in mud up to the axle, and the axletree broke. Her trip expenses totalled nearly fifty dollars. Said Rosaline, "So much for gratifying the public with my face."

In her later years, she became quite bitter about life in general and particularly about her Madison years, especially after Featherstonaugh wrote a disparaging account of her in his book. Sometime around 1870 she penned a poem capturing those sentiments:

Ho Madison

And its once starved and hungry crew,
    With stomachs expanded so wide,
Who now, in their pride, can gulp down their stew,
    And Oysters, and turkeys beside.

They should

Look back a few years and remember their mother,
    Who perspired to give them relief
and have charity more for sister and brother
    Whilst gorging their pie, cakes and beef.

Rosaline died in Baraboo on October 20, 1899, at the age of ninety-two. On the day of her funeral, the flag atop City Hall was flown at half mast.

Rosaline gives the distinct impression that she was irritated not so much by his description of the leaky cabin, the unusually low door frame on which Featherstonaugh bumped his head, the lack of fresh meat, and the hard bed—all of which, according to Rosaline, were perfectly false. Nor was she overly indignant about his reference to her funny hat, her pregnant condition, and the absence of a husband. What really made Rosaline Peck mad was Featherstonaugh's charge that she made bad coffee![8]

Saturday, June 10, 1837, was an important day in Madison's history. Rising early from their camp in the vicinity of today's Union Corners, thirty men, four women, and six yoke of oxen under the direction of A. A. Bird, recently selected Capital Commissioner, began the last leg of their journey to Madison. In the party were mechanics hired to build the capitol, several farmers who intended to settle in the vicinity, and the Pierce family, with their three grown daughters. Their trip to Madison required ten days and the weather could not have been worse. Just once did the sun shine on their westward odyssey, and that was on the ninth day when they passed through a prairie ten miles northeast of Madison.

An Englishman Visits Madison

George W. Featherstonaugh was ostensibly touring the American West to collect interesting geological artifacts, but like several other cultured English gentlemen, he seemed more interested in writing a disapproving account of frontier life. Several with whom he came into contact during his tour felt he was "opinionated, ill-tempered, and given to exaggeration." The excerpt below from his book, *Voyages Up the Minnie-Sotor* (London, 1847) describes the geologist's two-day stay in Madison on May 30 and 31, 1837. The account begins with a description of the countryside just west of Madison.

Pursuing our journey, we soon afterwards got into one of the most exquisitely beautiful regions I have ever seen in any part of the world. In whatever direction our eyes were turned, the most pleasing irregularities of surface presented themselves. But that which crowned the perfection of the view, and imparted an indescribable charm to the whole scene, from the knoll where we stood to the most distant point where the alternate hills and vales blended with the horizon, was the inimitable grace with which the picturesque clumps of trees, that sometimes enlarged themselves into woods, embellished this rural landscape from the hand of Nature. Nature might be said to speak to you in a voice that must be listened to, and to tell you that she had here surpassed the most polished efforts of English park scenery, the most difficult of all her achievements. America will justly boast of this unrivalled spectacle when it becomes known, for certainly it is formed of elements that no magic could enable all Europe to bring together upon so grand a scale. At length we came to a belt of open trees, and, passing through it, we reached the flat, marshy shores of the largest of the four lakes: we could see almost entirely around it, and much did we look; but alas! no vestige of human dwelling was in sight.

This considerably changed the current of our thoughts, and materially impaired the beauty of the prospect. Not being disposed to express all we felt, we reluctantly took to the woods again, along the margin of the lake, in the hope to stumble upon some one or other. Night was gradually drawing her veil over everything, and it became rather doubtful whether we should not have—in the language of backwoodsmen—to camp out. Groping our way, and occasionally jolting over the fallen trees, we, at the end of an hour and a half, got to the shore of the third lake, having somehow or other missed the second lake, where Madison City was supposed to be. We now changed our course again, and keeping to the north-west, and meandering, and wondering, and shouting for my companion, who had got out of the wagon to follow a small trail he thought he had discovered, I at length gave up the attempt to proceed any further, and, selecting a dry tree as a proper place to bivouac near, had already stopped the wagon, when, hearing my companion's voice shouting for me in a tone that augured something new to be in the wind, I pushed on in that direction, and at length found him standing at the door of a hastily-patched-up long hut, consisting of one room about twelve feet square. Not another dwelling was there in the whole country, and this wretched contrivance had only been put up within the last four weeks. Having secured our horses, we entered the grand and principal entrance to the house, against the top of which my head got a severe blow, it not being more than five feet high from the ground. The room was lumbered up with barrels, boxes, and all manner of things. Amongst other things was a bustling little woman, about as high as the door, with an astounding high cap on, named Mrs. Peck. No male Peck was on the ground, but from very prominent symptoms that went before her, another half-bushel seemed to be expected.

My first inquiry was, whether she had any fresh fish in the house. The answer was "No!" Inflexible and unwelcome word. No fresh fish! no large, delicious catfish, of twenty pounds' weight, to be fried with pork, and placed before the voracious traveller in quantities sufficient to calm those apprehensions that so often arise in Indian lands, of there not being enough for him to eat until he falls fast asleep. "Why, then," exclaimed my alarmed companion, "what's to be done?" "I calculate I've got some salt pork," rejoined our little hostess. "Then, Madam, you must fry it without the fish," I replied. So to the old business we went, of bolting square pieces of fat pork, an amusement I had so often indulged in, that I sometimes felt as if I ought to be shamed to look a live pig in the face. Our landlady, however, was a very active and obliging person; she said she would make us as comfortable as it was possible for her to do, and "she guessed" she had a little coffee, and would make us a cup of it. Whether it was acorns, or what it was, puzzled me not a little; it certainly deserved to be thought tincture of myrrh, and, as we drank and grimaced, dear Mrs. Peck, in her sweetest manner, expressed her regret, that she had no other sugar for our coffee, they having "somehow or another, not brought any with them."

Whilst we were at this repast, the thunderstorm broke over us, and a deluge of rain came down, streaming through the roof in various places. In the midst of the confusion two other vagabonds came in; one of them a ruffian-looking fellow, who said he was a miner, on his way across the Indian country from Milwaukee; the other, a stupid, boorish, dirty-looking animal, said he had not tasted anything for two days, having lost his way on the prairie; and, having been overtaken the preceding night by a very heavy rain, whilst making his way up a coulee or vale, had been afraid to lie on the ground, and had passed the whole night sitting on a fallen tree. Fortunately, there was pork enough for us all, and when our landlady had put the frying-pan to bed, she did the same to us by the act of blowing the candle out. Where she stowed herself was her own secret. Choosing a place between two barrels, I lay down, and drew my cloak over me; of sleep there was very little to be had, for it rained in torrents almost the whole night, and, not having pitched my camp skillfully, it poured upon me from the unfinished roof as I lay.

May 31. With the first ray of light I jumped up from my uncomfortable berth, and, having procured some dry clothes from my carpet-bag, strode over the two hang-gallows-looking fellows that were snoring near me, and gained the door.

Having now fully made up my mind that I was in an Indian country as wild and unsettled as any I had yet visited, I hastened to the shore of the lake to espy what truly turned out to be the nakedness of the land, not a vestige of any human being or habitation being to be discerned. Rambling, however, along the lake-shore, . . . I came upon a wigwam inhabited by a squaw of the Winnebago tribe, and learnt from her that her mate was a French Canadian, and was fishing from a canoe a little lower down. Thither I hied, and having found him, engaged him, with the assistance of his squaw, to procure us a mess of sunfish. This being accomplished, I sent them to Mrs. Peck, and following my messenger to Madison City, requested her to prepare them for our breakfast. No time was lost in doing this, and we made a very hearty meal without putting her to the trouble of preparing us any coffee. Sallying out again, I walked across a tongue of land which separated this from the fourth lake, and soon reached its shore, from whence I had a view of an extremely beautiful sheet of water.

Advancing along, I found more signs of humanity: two men were cutting some poles down; the one a Canadian, the other a somewhat desperado-looking young American, with cropped hair. Near to the lake I observed other poles laid aslant upon a fallen tree, forming a sort of shed, and looking beneath, beheld a youthful Winnebago squaw lying down on a filthy blanket, thoroughly drenched with the rain of the preceding night. She was pursy and immensely fat, but had some good features. Near to her was a bower

of a similar character, containing an elderly squaw, with only one eye, as hideously wrinkled and frowsy as she could well be. Whilst I was standing near to these creatures, the men came up, and I soon saw that the young American was the cavaliero of the fat squaw, and that the couch where she was lying was their bower of bliss. This fellow, having a canoe, agreed, for a dollar, to take me out upon the lake, and down a channel that connects the fourth with the third lake, and thence to Madison City. Accordingly, getting into a badly-constructed log canoe with his fat beauty, we paddled off.

After visiting various parts of the lake, and being more than once nearly upset from the awkward management of this youth, at whom the squaw laughed heartily, we entered the channel which connects the two lakes. It was about three miles and a half long and about forty feet in breadth, and we found where a part of the band of Winnebagoes had their wigwams. Three horrible-looking frowsy she-savages were eviscerating fish, which they were curing by fire on some stakes. Their matted, coarse, black locks stood out at right angles, like the strands of a mop when it is twirled; scarce any thing was to be discerned in their lineaments that was human, and more loathsome and disgusting objects I never beheld. Every thing about the wigwams was in keeping with their revolting and odious persons; ordure and dead fish in the last stage of corruption made a perfect pestilence around, amidst which they moved in the most contented and philosophic manner. Establishing themselves where fish is plentiful, they never change the site of their wigwam, at the entrances to which they thrown down the entrails and offal of their fish. They have thus become notorious amongst the other Indians for the filthy existence they lead. Alecto, Megara, and Tisiphone, the far-famed furies, must have been beauties compared to these hags. I just stayed long enough to purchase from them a fine alligator gar *(Esox ossens)* for the sake of its skeleton, and then came away. Just as we were

starting, one of these she-devils, wanting to visit the one-eyed squaw we had left behind, strode into our canoe, and a pretty inside passenger we had of her. The canoe itself was a wretched, teetering affair, imperfectly hollowed out of a small log, and wabbled about in such a doubtful manner that we had been several times near upsetting in crossing the lake.

In this "dugout"—for that is the expressive name they go by—I had taken my seat on the bottom near the prow, with my face towards the stern, holding the sides with my hands; thus situated, this she-monster, clapping herself immediately in front of me, and seizing a paddle, of which she seemed a perfect mistress, most vigorously began to ply it. At first I was amused by her motions; but, alas! my satisfaction was of short duration, for warming with the exercise, every time she raised her brawny fins to propel the canoe, she at each stroke almost bobbed a particular part of her person into contact with my nose, when such lots of unknown odors came from her that I soon became wretchedly sick at my stomach, and was delighted when we arrived at dear little Mrs. Peck's paradise. I learnt from our hostess that the young Adonis, in whose canoe I had been, had deserted from the American garrison at Fort Winnebago, had been apprehended, flogged, his head shaved and then drummed out of the fort to choose his own mode of life. He had wandered about until he fell in with this band of Indians, and, rejected by his own race, had found refuge and a mistress amongst the savages.

As soon as we had taken a good reconnaissance of the country around, and packed up the unios, and other fresh-water shells I had collected, we bade adieu to the little inhabitant of Madison City and turned our faces to the prairie again.

FIGURE 1.14. PECK CABIN. The first occupied log cabin in Madison was not a single cabin, but rather a group of four connected cabins, three of which are shown in this idealized lithograph. The fourth was a lean-to kitchen directly behind the middle section. The "T"-shaped building was parallel to and close to the intersection of Butler and King Streets, where the General Executive Facility #2 stands today.

The two main cabins were built in March 1837, by three French coureurs who lived in the Madison area, Abraham Wood, Joe Pellkie, and a Mr. Lavec, but they were not floored, daubed, and limed until mid-May. Each was 18 X 24 feet and one and one-half stories high. When the capitol workmen arrived in June, they built the frame section between the two main cabins, the upper story of which was designed for a dormitory.

A workman who stayed at the Peck's Tavern Stand in the summer and fall of 1837 reported that he was among "50 or so" persons who boarded there. The bedroom cabin was lined with double and triple deck beds made out of small oak trees.

For one year, the Pecks admirably performed the duties that fell to them as owners of a public house in the wilderness. But then tiring of the long hours and the seemingly endless chores that fell upon them, the Pecks sold their "Tavern Stand" in June 1838 to Robert L. Reams and took up farming on an eighty-acre farm near Madison. The Reams named the establishment the "Madison House." (SHSW WHi(X32)5870)

FIGURE 1.15. THE FIRST MADISON CAPITOL BUILDING.
In nearly all early Madison descriptions, the capitol received generous and flattering coverage. Typically, accounts included references to its "splendid yellow stone," "lofty, spacious halls, wide corridors," and the shiny tin-covered dome "glancing like silver in the sun's rays." Some accounts, however, were not so kind. One said the building was too small and low and another said it looked like a toad squatting in the grass. Still another said its tin dome looked like an inverted washbowl—a characteristic that led some to call the controversial building "Doty's dome."

Unlike its replacements, the capitol was much more than a center for official state business. During the early years the building served as a dance hall, a forum for public lectures, a theater, a church, a meeting room, and even a funeral parlor. (SHSW WHi(X3)2920)

For this welcome relief of their soggy trip, the spot was named "Sun Prairie." But now on the morning of June 10 the hardships of constructing makeshift roads, traversing marshes, fording rivers, and getting drenched nearly nightly were all behind them. At last they stood on the heights outside Madison and exalted in their view of the lakes. As they came closer they could see the smoke from Indian wigwams ascending around the shores of the lakes. ". . . There reposed before us," said one of the men, "was the object of our toils—a beautiful elevation upon which the capital was to be built, surrounded by nature's most enchanting adornments, the lakes of liquid silver. . . ."[9] When they arrived on Capitol Hill about 9 A.M., they shouted for joy, shook hands, waved their handkerchiefs, and threw their "caps as high as vigorous hands could hurl them."[10]

Later that afternoon twenty-seven-year-old Simeon Mills, a man destined to play a large role in Madison history, arrived at the outlet of Lake Monona, after following Indian trails and surveyor markers from Chicago. There he found two Indian boys fishing. Mills could speak no Winnebago and they could speak no English. Finally, with the aid of Winnebago-speaking *coureur* Abraham Wood, then living at Winnequah, and two half-dollars, the boys were persuaded to take Mills and his carpetbag across the lake in a birch bark canoe. They landed him about sunset at the foot of Blair Street. "This," said Mills, "shall be my life-long home." And, as history would have it, it was.[11]

Sunday, June 11, dawned bright and clear. Everyone was up early, eager to solve the most pressing community problem: forty people and one finished log cabin. At once the men began building a log cabin boarding house for the Pierce family at the corner of Butler and Wilson Streets and a 24-by-24-foot log dormitory in Capital Park near the King Street corner, and helped to finish the Peck Tavern Stand. With these additions to the housing inventory, most of the workmen had a roof over their heads. However, some of the workmen, rather than pay rent to the Pecks or

the Pierces, erected their own cabins at the foot of King Street near Lake Monona.[12] Enterprising Simeon Mills erected a 14-by-16-foot log structure, Madison's first store, at the corner of Webster and Main where GEF I is now located.[13]

Madison's log cabin era lasted only a few months, because by December a steam-powered saw mill at the foot of Butler Street on Lake Mendota was placed in operation. Even before the steam mill, a large amount of lumber had been sawn by hand with the whipsaw. So great was the demand for lumber during these early days that the steam mill "was kept running day and night for about two years."[14]

As if things were not hectic enough for Rosaline with all her chores, Doty appeared some time in late June and said, "Madam, prepare yourself for company on the Fourth (of July), as a large number from Milwaukee, Mineral Point, Fort Winnebago, and Galena have concluded to meet here for the purpose of viewing the place and celebrating the day."

"Why, what shall I do?," asked Rosaline. Now seven months pregnant, she could not see how she could handle such an influx. Her husband, Eben, had been temporarily blinded by an eye inflamation, their center cabin was unfinished, and there were no provisions for such a large group. "Pshaw, talk about the times that try men's souls," bitterly commented Rosaline several years later "just as if a woman had none. . . ." Doty understood her dilemma and said, "Just constitute me your agent and I will contract for whatever you want. . . ." So Doty ordered the necessary lumber, wines, liquors, bed-ticking, bedding, table fixtures, and the like and dispatched teams to Mineral Point to haul the items back to Madison.[15]

As luck would have it, on the morning of July 2, a herd of cattle from Illinois were driven through Madison on their way to Green Bay. Rosaline took advantage of the opportunity to buy several animals so the expected guests would have something beside salt pork to eat.

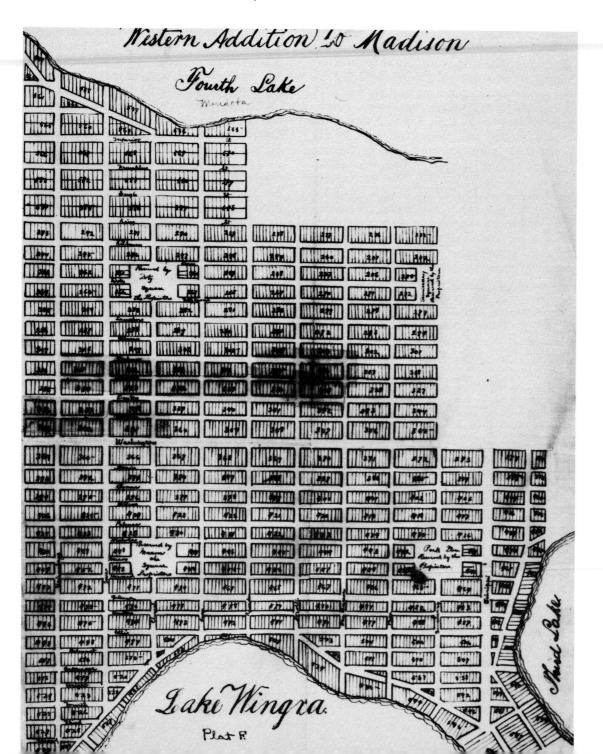

Western Addition to Madison

Fourth Lake

Lake Wingra.

Plat F.

FIGURE 1.16. WESTERN ADDITION. Two months after Madison was selected territorial capital and one month before the Peck cabins were erected, surveyors were laying out Madison's first suburb. Called the Western Addition, it contained about nine-hundred acres, almost two-thirds as much land as the original plat. The Western Addition was owned by a group of investors including James D. Doty, Stevens T. Mason, governor of Michigan, and Josiah Noonan, later editor of the *Wisconsin Enquirer*, the first newspaper published in Madison.

Doty's involvement is everywhere apparent on the plat. The main street connecting two of the plat's three squares is called Doty Street and one of the squares is modestly designated "Doty Square."

The reservation of "Seminary Square" on the eastern edge of the plat shows that Doty and his partners were already scheming to locate the University of the Territory of Wisconsin on the western edge of the village. In 1838 a bill was introduced into the legislature calling for the territorial university to be located at the City of the Four Lakes. However, the bill was amended to read "at or near Madison," a more inclusive phrase that allowed the City of the Four Lakes backers to think they still had a chance of getting the plum while opening up the possibility for other sites.

The Western Addition proved much too ambitious for a depression period. In 1838 steps were taken to abolish the plat. Although the plat was a failure to its owners, it helped establish the idea that the university should be located on the western edge of Madison. Beginning in 1838 people began calling the area just east of "Seminary Square" "College Hill," and in 1848 the first regents bought this spot for the university campus. (SHSW WHi(X3)33289)

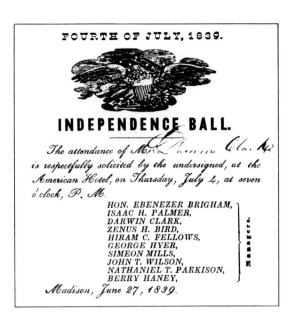

FOURTH OF JULY, 1839.

INDEPENDENCE BALL.

The attendance of Mr... Clark
is respectfully solicited by the undersigned, at the
American Hotel, on Thursday, July 4, at seven
o'clock, P. M.

HON. EBENEZER BRIGHAM,
ISAAC H. PALMER,
DARWIN CLARK,
ZENUS H. BIRD,
HIRAM C. FELLOWS,
GEORGE HYER,
SIMEON MILLS,
JOHN T. WILSON,
NATHANIEL T. PARKISON,
BERRY HANEY,

Managers.

Madison, June 27, 1839.

FIGURE 1.17. JULY 4, 1839, INDEPENDENCE BALL INVITATION. Accounts of the 4th of July celebration in 1839 help explain why so few attended the Independence Ball described in the invitation shown above. The real party was planned and carried out by Uncle Ab Nichols, the accommodating proprietor of a popular watering and gambling spot known as the ''Worser,'' located where the Tenney Building is today. To get provisions for his party, Nichols took his wagon to Galena where he bought several kegs of Peckatonica and Rock River whiskey and a steer. On his way back into Madison on the afternoon of July 3, he decided that he had better hide his beefsteak on the hoof where it would not tempt the men, so he tied it to a tree in a thicket near the intersection of State, Fairchild, and Doty Streets. Barely had Uncle Ab emerged from the thicket with his whiskey-laden wagon than he was spotted by the capitol workmen. The men decided that they would start their celebration right then and there. And so the whiskey kegs were tapped.

The following day the celebrants marched around the Square to the martial music of two squeaky fiddles and flute, men at the head of the line, women at the rear. The town dignitaries read the Declaration of Independence, gave spread eagle orations and prayed, after which everybody promptly marched back to the Worser where they drank whiskey, ate bacon and fish, and, according to the accounts, ''were right merry.'' It was not until three days later when Uncle Ab's whiskey ran out did anyone remember the poor steer tied to the tree.

The following year (1840), the Fourth of July was celebrated with more decorum. The County Temperance Society used the occasion to secure signatures to a temperance pledge. (SHSW WHi(X3)33257)

On the morning of the third the items arrived from Mineral Point, but the lumber did not come until about seven o'clock that evening. Working late that night, the workmen finally laid the floors in the Peck cabins. From Abel Rasdall, a local fur trader, Mrs. Peck purchased three hundred pounds of feathers so that the beds were spread by daylight on the morning of the Fourth. ". . . By 1:00 P.M. on the Fourth," Rosaline reports, "the dining room table (was) built and dinner set, and between that hour and sundown some two or three hundred persons bolted something besides pork."[16] Rosaline appears to have exaggerated the number of visitors, but just the same it was a lot of people to serve under the conditions. The participants included the capitol workmen, a sprinkling of territorial dignitaries, and Winnebago Chief Little Dandy and his band who, according to one account, outnumbered the whites. Focal point of the day was the laying of the capitol cornerstone. In the words of one participant, "The celebration was quite a spirited affair and lasted several days until the spirits gave out."[17] The only known casualties of the event were Rosaline's two pet crows. In the ardor of the celebration somebody shot them.[18]

With the exception of one Indian killing another, the rest of the summer and fall of 1837 was quiet.[19] Rosaline Peck had a baby girl in September, the first child born in Madison of white American parents.[20] Judge Doty suggested the name "Wisconsiana," and Simeon Mills suggested "Victoria" after the new British Queen. The Pecks compromised, took both suggestions and named their daughter Victoria Wisconsiana Peck. Simeon Mill's combination store-saloon-post office became a popular lounging place for the workmen. Mail came on horseback "only once or twice a week" from Green Bay and Mineral Point.[21] For recreation the workmen wrestled, ran foot races, and shot targets with the Indians who came over from their camps around the lake to spend the day, returning at night.[22] But mostly everybody just worked: shingling, digging, chopping, hewing, sawing, and joining—building an outpost of civilization in the wilderness.

After November, when construction on the capitol halted, the population of Madison plummeted. Most of the workmen returned to Milwaukee, leaving only four families, a few workmen, and two or three shopkeepers and officials, maybe thirty-five people altogether. One visitor coming to Madison in December 1837 with the thought of settling concluded that the place was not at all promising and left for the lead mining regions. Indeed, who could argue with that impression?[23]

Civilization, Such as It Is, Arrives

Bedding, Boarding, Amusing, and
Persuading the Legislature

In early November 1838, legislators and state officials converged on Madison for the first session ever held in the new capital. Some rode Indian ponies and others shuffled through the fallen leaves on foot. Nearly all the men wore homespun clothes, carried their own blankets and packed guns. When they arrived in Madison they found about thirty modest frame and log buildings on a stump strewn hillside centered along King Street. Among those buildings were three specifically built for legislators. The Peck Tavern Stand, now owned by the Reams and renamed the Madison House, had two rooms to rent. The Madison Hotel, a cheap frame structure had two more rooms. The third, the brand new two-and-one-half-story American Hotel had eight rooms and an attic. Together these three Madison hostelries offered twelve rooms to incoming legislators and officials. A few additional rooms were available in private homes.[1]

That the accommodations were primitive and expensive surprised no one, for Madison was little more than a raw frontier crossroads. For twelve cents a night a legislator could buy a two-by-six-foot space on the floor in the log bedroom of the Madison House. There, early legislators spread their blankets, used their saddles for pillows, and did what they could to induce sleep.[2] At the American House, the fanciest hotel in town, guests were offered seven-by-eight-foot rooms with a double bed or a space in the attic marked off by cracks in the floor. The legislators best off were those who found places in private homes "where four men might find two beds in a cold room ten or twelve feet square."[3] The term "strange bedfellows" had real meaning to that first group of legislators.

Rare was the legislator who, during winter evenings, was content to sit quietly in his small, cold, crowded bedroom. Many sought the two popular hard liquor and gambling emporiums known as the Worser and the Tiger. The Worser, "a partly completed framed building"[4] that stood where the Tenney Building now is, got its name because the proprietor was refused a cheap tavern license and was told to buy an expensive liquor license. This made the proprietor mad and he replied, "Okay, if you won't sell me a tavern license, then I'll keep 'something worser' in the basement"—a gambling establishment. And that is exactly what he did. His competitor, the Tiger, located where Carmen's is today, was a two-story frame structure that was built in 1838. For years it was operated "as a gambling house and was kept open to the public without fear of law."[5]

To establish an edge on the competition, the Worser's proprietor advertised that he had "procured a splendid billiard table so all who are desirous of driving the cue could have the opportunity." "My bar," he continued, "will at all times be furnished with wines, liquors, cigars, etc. Gentlemen annoyed by the crowd of the 'Tiger' can find comfortable quarters at the Worser."[6]

One 1840 legislator was shocked by these places. To him it seemed that all the wickedness in the territory was concentrated at Madison. "While the legislature was in session gambling, dancing and profanity ran rampant" and sharpers tried to 'skin Uncle Sam' for all they could get," he complained.[7] Finally, in 1841, several earnest and energetic ladies decided to stomp out sin in their sylvan settlement. A public meeting

at the capital drew a large crowd where the ladies blamed dissolute legislators for the town's ills. All sides were represented, including several people whose inebriation prevented them from being better spokesmen for the wet cause. But alas, the forces of sin were too entrenched and the meeting produced no results.[8]

If the hotels and saloons were nothing to brag about, neither was the capitol building. According to the agreement made at Belmont, the 1837–38 Territorial Legislature was supposed to meet at Burlington, Iowa, while the Madison Capitol was completed. When the time came to decide whether to meet another year at Burlington or try the new capitol, construction was moving along well. Therefore the decision was made to convene the third session of the Wisconsin Territorial Legislature at Madison on November 26, 1838. Unfortunately when the legislature arrived, the capitol wasn't ready, and so the first sessions were held in the basement of the American Hotel. After weeks of meeting at the hotel, a committee reported the capitol legislative chambers ready for use. On what basis the committee made their decision, no one could quite figure out. "The floors were laid with green oak boards, full of ice; the walls of the room were iced over; green oak seats, and desks made of rough boards; one fireplace, and one small stove. In a few days the flooring near the stove and fireplace had so shrunk, on account of the heat, that a person could run his hands between the boards. The weather was cold, the halls were cold, our ink would freeze—so that when we could stand it no longer, we passed a joint resolution to adjourn for twenty days," until the halls could be made more habitable.[9]

When the legislature resumed, the hall was in better condition, but contractor Morrison's pigs had moved into the unfinished basement directly under the legislative chambers. This situation provided one imaginative legislator with an irresistable opportunity to relieve the tedium of long-winded speeches. On several occasions when he got bored, he would slip from his seat, get a pole, go into the cellar, and stir up the pigs, who raised "a pandemonium of noise and confusion. The

New Line of
MAIL STAGES
FROM
Madison to Milwaukee.

THE undersigned would respectfully announce to the public that they have just put in operation a

Tri-Weekly Line of Stages, from Madison to Milwaukee,

via. of Cottage Grove, Lake Mills, Aztalan, Summit and Prairieville.

intersecting Starke's Line from Milwaukee to Watertown.

Passengers by the above line will leave Milwaukee and Madison every Tuesday, Thursday and Saturday, at 4 o'clock A. M. Stages from Milwaukee will stop at Aztalan over night.—Fare through, $4.00.

C. GENUNG, & CO.

Sept. 1844.   n7tf

FIGURE 1.18. SLOW MAIL. One of the irritants that early Madisonians had to endure was the irregularity and undependability of the mails. For newspaper editors who were dependent upon the mail for news, the problem was often embarrassing. For example, on September 2, 1840, an editor apologized for the "bareness" of a paper, explaining that no mail had been received . . . "for the past eight days." In this case, rain-swollen streams between Madison and Milwaukee could not be forded by stage coaches. When the mail did come, the news it brought was hardly fresh. In August 1840, an editor boasted getting a letter from Washington, D.C., in "only six weeks." Perhaps this was what an emigrant guide meant when it urged settlers "to feel perfectly patient with . . . the world even if (it) does not move quite as rapid(ly) as (you) desire."

The burgeoning volume of mail coming into Madison because of the legislature's presence necessitated the development of better mail arrangements, including the stage line shown above. The stage lines helped but did not entirely solve the problem. In 1852 an irritated citizen satirically reported that "a man just arrived from the East with a drove of hogs and reports that he passed the Milwaukee mail stage this side of Lake Mills and that it may be expected here in the course of a day or two at the farthest."

speaker's voice would become completely drowned, and he would be compelled to stop, not, however, without giving his squealing disturbers a sample of his swearing ability."[10]

The legislature continued to meet in the building in spite of its crude, unfinished condition. In fact, it was not really finished until 1844. It cost twice as much to build as it was supposed to—a fact that led to a major scandal—and when it was finished the roof leaked![11]

Only gradually were refinements added to the crude frontier capitol. In 1846 the enterprising capitol superintendent converted the basement from a hog house to legislator offices and built a gothic brick out-house in the trees just west of the capitol. The privy was built despite its eight hundred dollar price tag, a fact which caused some lawmakers to strenuously oppose its construction. The superintendent also took it upon himself to add a little beauty to the bleak grounds by planting one hundred fifty dollars worth of trees and found that his initiative was met by curses and growls. Although these public works projects were modest in scale, they were consistently opposed by a block of legislators who were eager to move the capital somewhere else and who felt such investments would make such a move harder.[12]

Unhealed wounds from the Belmont capital site decision, coupled with complaints of the primitive lodgings and legislative conditions, prompted legislators almost annually to introduce bills providing for the removal of the capital to another spot, usually Milwaukee. Each year these efforts were beaten down, but not without considerable effort by hardworking Madison innkeepers and newspaper editors. Headquarters for the keep-the-capital-in-Madison movement was the Madison Hotel owned by A. A. Bird. Here wavering legislators received at the expense of the proprietor free champagne, free room, free board, and just about unlimited credit providing, of course, the legislator became a Madison backer.[13] During times of high prices and an almost no-cash economy, such methods no doubt had considerable effect upon legislative decisions.

The editors of the *Wiskonsin Enquirer,* a state-wide paper published in Madison, launched a vigorous keep-it-in-Madison campaign of their own, which took the form of a test for candidates. The first question was: Is the candidate honest? The second question and one that "should be propounded in reference to every candidate in the state was: Will he oppose any and every measure having for its object the temporary or permanent removal of the seat of government?" If the answer to these two questions was not a resounding and unequivocal "no," the editor concluded that the man was obviously not fit for office.[14]

Churches, Schools, and Newspapers

To the cultured Easterner or foreigner, the American frontier was often a repugnant spectacle. One Englishman who visited the tiny hamlet in 1842 was overwhelmed by a siege of drab rainy weather, the sight of drunks lying in the mud beside the road, coarse language, crude accommodations, and a monotonous and often revolting menu. On his way out of town he exclaimed to his companion, "If you tell anybody I was in Madison, by God I will kill you!"[15]

If Madison was still a frontier village, it was not, at the end of its first decade, without improvements that folks called civilization. In fact, by 1846 Madison could boast one church, one small red schoolhouse and three newspapers.

That the Methodists won the distinction of providing the first formal religious service in Madison should come as no surprise, because it was their practice during this period to follow new settlers almost as fast as they could kindle their campfires. During the summer of 1837 an Illinois Methodist minister rode into town one Saturday afternoon and offered to preach a sermon. People seemed eager to inaugurate religion in Madison, and so the following day nearly everyone crowded into the dining room of a log boarding house at the intersection of Butler and Wilson Streets and heard a sermon on the theme "I was a stranger

and He took me in." After the service the boarding house owner passed the hat and turned up twenty dollars for the itinerant reverend. That was not all he took out of Madison. Just before the Sunday service, his horse suddenly turned lame. A prominent citizen, who though the lameness a temporary malady, offered to trade horses with the minister and give him fifteen dollars to boot. The minister accepted the offer and rode out of town on the new horse immediately after the service. Three days later the minister's lame horse died, and many folks wondered if the man really was a Methodist minister. All they knew was that he left town with a healthy horse and thirty-five dollars—the equivalent of two weeks' wages for one of the capitol workmen.[16]

Religion in Madison during the first decade was almost entirely provided by circuit riders, missionaries, and church officials attempting to organize churches. Because Madison was the capital of the territory, it was declared an official mission outpost of the American Home Missionary Society, a national organization whose purpose was to establish and maintain a Christian west. A corresponding national society, the American Board for Foreign Missions, provided a similar service to Asia, Africa, and the American Indian![17] Among the missionaries the Home Missionary Society sent to Madison was Reverend Slingerland, who presided at the founding of the First Congregational Church on October 4, 1840. Because the village was so tiny and poor, Slingerland's salary had to be paid almost entirely from Home Missionary funds.[18] Not until 1852 did the church become self-sustaining. A similar process occurred for the Episcopalians who, after declaring Madison a mission station, sent a man to superintend the formation of a church. On March 4, 1840 he succeeded in establishing Grace Episcopal Church.[19] At the time of their organization, the Congregationalists (1840) had just nine members, the Baptists (1847) twenty, Episcopalians (1839) sixteen, Catholics (1845) ten, and the Presbyterians (1845) six.[20]

Lacking formal church buildings, the communicants met in homes, halls, stores, and the various rooms of the capitol. The most popular, the capitol, was the spawning ground and nursery for many religious organizations. Most denominations held services there at one time or another for lengthy periods, and some held their organizational meetings there, too.

In church activities women played the dominant role. When the Congregational Church was formed, petitioners consisted of seven women and two men.[21] At the end of a full decade of work (1840 to 1850), the rolls carred thirty-nine females and nineteen males.[22] An Episcopal church organizer lamented in 1839 that he did not have a single male communicant in Madison.[23] One of the major reasons why so few men were members was the then heavy emphasis in the churches on temperence—a cause championed by women and avoided by men.[24]

Finally after several years of intermittent religious services and itinerant preachers, Madison in 1846 got its first church building, an austere 27-by-64-foot frame structure on Webster Street (where GEF I is now located), the proud property of the First Congregational Church.[25]

Like institutional religion, public education had to struggle against frontier conditions. Public education in Madison began with a dozen kids in the front room of a log cabin where Badger Furniture is now located (King-Doty corner). The school term was a student's dream—just three months long (March to May, 1838). To their twenty-two-year-old "schoolmarm" earning just two dollars per week, half of which had to go for boarding expenses, the situation was perhaps not so good. Sometime during the term a band of Indians surrounded the house shouting, screeching, hopping around, and banging pots. What the terrified scholars and their school marm did not know was that the Winnebagos were begging for whiskey, tobacco, and bread more or less in that order. They went away when a local citizen familiar with their language took charge.[26]

In 1839 Madison got its first regular school house, an eighteen-by-twenty-foot frame building covered by oak shakes. Located near the corner of East Johnson and Pinckney in a thicket, it was accessible only from a few foot paths. Its seventy dollar cost was raised by private subscription. At first the building served its purpose well, but by the winter of 1844–45, fifty students were crowded inside. To alleviate crowding, a special mezzanine for the smaller children was constructed over the front entrance. Desks and benches consisted of slabs of oak (rough side down and pegs inserted) freshly cut at the steam saw mill at the foot of North Hamilton Street.[27]

The outgrown school was replaced in the fall of 1845 with a substantial twenty-by-forty-foot brick building located at the corner of East Washington and Butler. Funded by a newly established county school tax, the building cost twelve hundred dollars and was the pride of all citizens. Unfortunately, it, too, was almost immediately outgrown. When it opened sixty students enrolled, but by the spring of 1846 enrollment had grown to one hundred, far too many for the school's two rooms.

Supplementing public education were several private or "select" schools generally designed for older girls and giving them instruction in the "upper branches of learning," plus music and drawing. Unable to charge much in such a poor village, none of the private schools lasted long and all had to meet wherever space was available. Among their makeshift classrooms were homes, hotels, and even the twelve-by-sixteen-foot capital tool shed.[28]

The printing press arrived in Madison with the first meeting of the Legislature in November, 1838. Its first product was a weekly four-page sheet called the *Wiskonsin Enquirer.* Like most papers of this vintage, page one carried literary works and moralistic editorials, page two, more editorials and news stories mostly copied from other papers, page three, legal notices and leftovers from pages one and two, and page four, advertising. At first the newspapers were about the

size of today's Sunday supplement, but gradually they increased in size until they were about the same size as today's papers.[29]

In 1839 Madison's second paper and progenitor of the *Wisconsin State Journal,* the *Wisconsin Express,* appeared. The *Express* was soon joined by two other papers and the *Wisconsin Enquirer* dropped out, leaving three newspapers in the village in 1846. The *Express* took a very doctrinaire Whig line, and the other two papers aligned themselves at various points along the Democratic partisan spectrum. Each week editors engaged in no-holds-barred editorial battles with rival editors. Passions ran high, income ran low, and the toll on editors was great. During the five-year life of the *Enquirer,* no less than seven editors guided its destiny.[30]

Off to a Slow Start

One of the most widely respected newspapers of the day, the *National Intelligencer,* carried a story on Madison in September 1837 that said: "We understand from sources upon which the utmost reliance can be placed" that 150 buildings will be built in Madison by October 1838.[31] In fact, Madison by October 1838, could boast a few more than thirty buildings![32] The failure to meet great expectations was hardly limited to Madison's first year. It was the most salient characteristic during the entire first decade.

The failure to get off to a fast start was the result of a confluence of six factors.

1. *Distance from the Farmers' Frontier.* Settlement of southern Wisconsin occurred first along lands bordering Lake Michigan and in the lead mining area, and last in the area centering around the Four Lakes. Between Madison and the first-settled areas were huge fertile tracts that had to be filled up before the advancing settlement line converged on Madison. Madison may have been the capital of Wisconsin, but it was still in the middle

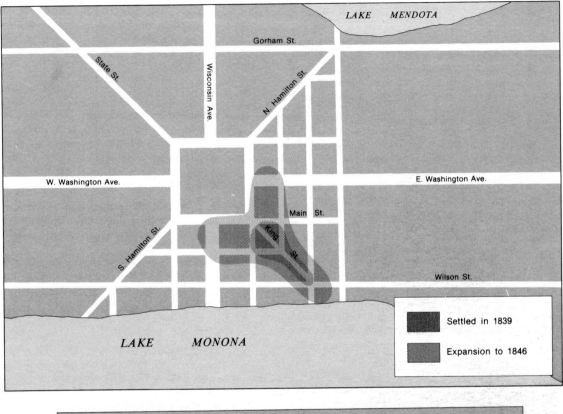

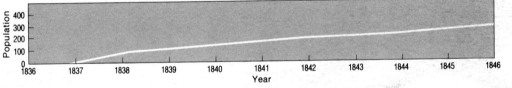

FIGURE 1.19. SETTLEMENT PATTERNS AND POPULATION GROWTH.   One of the most striking characteristics of Madison's first decade was its slow growth. The territorial census of 1842 showed just 172 people, a gain of only 26 over the 1840 census. Two years later only 44 more residents were counted. Between 1844 and 1846 the gain was only 63 persons. In 1845 on the eve of its incorporation as a village, less than 300 persons lived in the shaggy frontier outpost.

During this period Madison's population was predominantly young, Yankee, and male. In 1840 the editors of the *Wisconsin Enquirer* applauded the arrival of "the right kind" of immigrants, namely "hardy, industrial and enterprising farmers," the code phrase for Yankees. By 1843, with so embarrassingly little growth to brag about, the editor of the same paper said he was "happy" to see the arrival of Irish families. Better to have foreigners than stagnation, the editor reasoned.

Settlement in 1839 consisted of about twenty-four buildings clustered around the upper and lower ends of King Street. By 1846 nearly all buildings were still along King Street, with a few creeping about the edges of the Capitol Square. King Street, the only defined street, was stump-filled and still almost unbroken sod. (University of Wisconsin Cartographic Laboratory)

of a vast wilderness accessible only by poor roads and far from markets. For the farmer there was little incentive to locate in the Madison area and then haul his grain one-hundred miles to Milwaukee.

2. *Speculation.* Almost immediately after Madison was selected as the capital, a rush was made to buy up the land for many miles around. Unfortunately for those hoping to see Madison grow quickly, most of this land was purchased by speculators who bid up the cost of the land to such high levels that few settlers could afford it. Within the newly platted city a similar problem prevailed. Doty tried to compensate for this problem by selling city lots only to settlers who agreed to erect buildings by a certain date.[33] Not until 1840 and 1841 did local newspapers begin to report that the "fever of speculation" was broken and that speculators were willing to sell their lands at more reasonable prices.[34] By 1843 sixty percent of all lots still were owned by absentee owners.[35]

3. *Economic Depression.* Six months after Madison was certified as capital of the territory, President Jackson issued his famous Specie Circular requiring payment for all public lands in gold and silver. The decision was welcome in many circles because until that time payment for public lands was being made with often worthless paper money issued by state banks. The Specie Circular was a severe blow to all desiring to buy land, and for a time land sales almost stopped. The clamor for specie (gold and silver) was so great that in May 1837 banks were forced to suspend payments. The Panic of 1837 triggered a depression that lasted until the middle 1840s.

The economic shock waves from these national events were soon evident in Madison. By December 1838, Doty found that he was unable to make any cash sales in lots.[36] During the construction season of 1837 the stone cutters working at the Maple Bluff quarry went on strike—not for higher wages but for payment in specie. The federal government had deposited hard money (gold or silver) for capital construction costs in a Green Bay bank. However, the men were paid with paper money issued by the Green Bay bank worth much less than the $2.25 per day they had been promised by the commissioners. The men went back to work because they recognized that if they refused to complete their contract, they would be subjected to an even larger financial penalty.[37]

4. *Uncertainty about the Capital's Permanence in Madison.* The almost annual introduction of bills to move the capital somewhere else made many investors understandably reluctant to risk much money in a place whose future was primarily dependent upon the continued presence of the seat of government. Probably at no time in its history was Madison's future so vulnerable to political caprice. The uncertainty of Madison's future also affected the sale of nearby farmland. Why buy a farm outside a possible ghost town?

5. *Town Title Problems.* Not long after the founding of Madison, its two principal proprietors had a falling out. Stevens T. Mason called Doty a "liar, a caluminator and a swindler,"[38] and Doty reciprocated in kind. The issue was who had title to the land. On June 20, 1839, Mason placed a notice in Madison newspapers saying "persons who are indebted to J. D. Doty for part of the purchase price of lots they may have bought of him are cautioned against making any further payments to him as they are assured he had no title to them and no authority to sell."[39] Such notices had a chilling effect upon those who might be contemplating an investment in Madison and certainly for those who already had purchased lots.

Finally in June 1841, after a protracted legal procedure, the matter was resolved.[40] A deed from Mason to Doty made Doty the sole agent of the Four Lakes Company. The editors of the day took the occasion to hope "the settlement of the title question will considerably enhance the value of property and we may now calculate with some certainty on great improvements being made in the town. . . ."[41]

6. *Pioneering Rigors.* One of the most widely read emigrant's guides prepared settlers for the rigors of pioneering by telling them what to expect. ". . . Above all," it said euphemistically, "(emigrants) should take it for granted that there are difficulties to be encountered. . . ."[42] For early Madison settlers this meant sickness, mosquitoes, wolves, prairie fires, Indians, poor roads, high prices, labor shortages, and quicksand.

   a. *Sickness.*—Madison like other frontier communities had its share of frontier sicknesses. According to one expert, a malarial epidemic that swept through Madison in 1844–45 was caused by "the turning of the soil."[43] H. A. Tenney, who arrived in Madison in 1845, caught the disease and suffered fever, loss of energy, and chills for a full decade![44] Several cases of typhoid fever are also recorded in early Madison annals.[45] In the very early years, the nearest doctor was twenty-five miles away at Fort Winnebago.[46]

   b. *Mosquitoes.* "If the truth (were) known," said Simeon Mills in his otherwise sanguine account of his arrival in 1837, "there probably never was a place on this broad earth worse infested . . ." with mosquitoes, than Madison, Wisconsin.[47] A stonecutter who stayed in Peck's Tavern Stand during the 1837 construction season told how the mosquitoes were so bad in the "bedroom" cabin that "the men made a fire on the floor to smoke them out."[48] A traveler who rented a pony in Madison for a trip to Fort Winnebago discovered that his poor animal had been so badly bitten by mosquitoes "that the blood oozed from his skin."[49] An Englishman visiting Madison in 1839 found he was not able to hunt on the outskirts of Madison because mosquitoes were so bad. Said the thwarted hunter, "some of them marched down my back and another went to meet them up my inexpressibles." An Episcopal bishop who took a refreshing dip in Lake Monona in the summer of 1838 reported that he was attacked by hordes of the pesky insects.[50]

   c. *Wolves.*—The affinity between wolves and pigs was no children's story to settlers of the 1830s and 1840s. In 1839 Mr. Ream imported the first pigs and put them in a pen beside his public house, where the GEF III state office building now stands. Every last one of the pigs was carried off by prairie wolves.[51] Persons camping in Dane County not far from Madison had to keep log fires burning all night to keep the wolves away.[52] One of the first actions taken by the Board of (Dane) County Commissioners (the predecessor of the county board) was to establish a three-dollar bounty on wolf scalps. However, the wolves were so plentiful, and the hunters so eager and accurate, that the board was forced to lower the bounty to one dollar just three days later for fear the treasury would be exhausted![53] With the help of professional wolf hunters, traps, and strychnine, wolves were gradually killed off.[54]

   d. *Prairie Fires.* Of the many perils associated with frontier living, the one that caused the greatest dread was the wind-driven prairie fire. This fear was anything but idle. Accounts as late as 1845 describe prairie fires roaring across the isthmus. At night their "lurid glare" could sometimes be seen on the horizon twenty miles away.[55]

e. *Indians*—Although Indians were officially banished, many Winnebagos continued to live in the Four Lakes area. One early settler explained that the resulting close contact with Indians "removed every spark of romance and poetry with which they had in our imaginations been surrounded from reading Cooper's novels. . . ."[56] Indeed to nearly all settlers, Indians were regarded as shiftless, dirty, smelly and worst of all thieves. "If they remain with us, they will steal as usual and the settlers will shoot and the consequence will be an 'Indian War.' " It was or for this reason that early Madisonians demanded that Indians be deported, "forceably" if necessary. The prevailing view was this "this country was ceded to whites many years ago and the Indians have no right here whatsoever."[57]

f. *Poor Roads.*—An improved road in early Madison was generally considered to be one where the stumps and large boulders had been removed. The primitive condition of Madison steets can be gleaned from the suggestion of one citizen that people secure firewood in the public streets. The writer was not referring to stacked cordwood, but to standing trees.[58] The condition of the streets in wet weather can also be inferred from an amendment offered by a legislator who, with tongue only slightly in check, wanted to outlaw construction on King Street between the Capital Park and Lake Monona because they would keep the fish from coming up the street into the park.[59] As late as 1845 King Street

was "covered with an almost unbroken sod filled with stumps of trees. . . ."[60]

g. *High prices.*—Prices for food, general merchandise, and building materials in Madison were extraordinarily high during the first decade because nearly everything had to be shipped in from Milwaukee, Mineral Point, or Galena. In 1839 potatoes were $1 a bushel, eggs 37½–75 cents per dozen, butter 37½ to 62 cents a pound, and oats 75 cents a bushel. A workman had to pay $5 a week just for board. Nails were about 45 cents a pound and candles $1.00.[61]

h. *Labor shortage.*—A tiny village with only a few dozen men cannot be expected to offer a skilled labor pool. For example, the only shingle makers in Madison for many years were two alcoholics living in the area now known as Maple Bluff. Short of making the shingles themselves, early Madisonians often had to wait until the shinglemakers' whiskey or credit was exhausted. Then the two men would make a few more shingles.[62]

i. *Quicksand.*—If all these irritants were not sufficient, several others, like quicksand, could be thrown in for good measure. When innmaster Ream went out on the Great Central Marsh between Blair and the Yahara River on each side of East Washington Avenue to get marsh hay for bed ticks, his oxen and horses were nearly lost in the quicksand. Ream overcame this difficulty by improvising snowshoe-like devices on his boots so that weight was spread over a large area.[63]

Given all these difficulties, one might well inquire how Madison managed to attract 283 persons after only ten years!

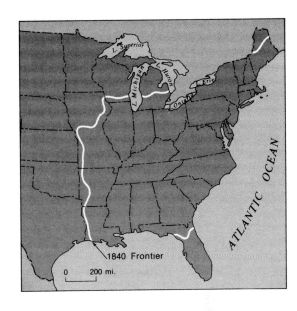

FIGURE 1.20. 1840 U.S. FRONTIER. From 1800 until 1890 the U.S. census chronicled the westward movement of the frontier. As shown on the above 1840 map, the frontier line practically ran through Madison. The frontier was defined as an area where there were between two and six persons per square mile. (This map was prepared by the University of Wisconsin Cartographic Laboratory based upon a map provided courtesy of Harcourt Brace Jonanovich, Inc.)

Puffery and Reality

Madison's lack of progress during her first decade was a source of enormous frustration to its citizens. The problem was especially difficult for newspaper editors whose role and constituency posed a cruel dilemma. Early Madison journalists felt compelled to criticize what they saw, but they were also committed to booming and boosting the town. What complicated their lives was the fact that wounds from the capital selection were still unhealed, and almost everywhere around the state anti-Madison feelings were rampant! Out-of-town newspaper editors therefore relished the opportunity to print something bad about Madison, the victor at Belmont. Thus, for a Madison editor to write something critical about Madison was almost a guarantee that it would be picked up by editors all over the state and devilishly embroidered.

For a time local editors refrained from criticism and relied instead on polite "puffery." For example, they might say "The prospects of Madison were never more encouraging,"[64] or population is "rapidly increasing,"[65] or "our beautiful village is rapidly improving its appearance."[66] In a sense these were all true, but their understandable emphasis was upon the future. Someday we'll get there, they said, someday.

With little progress to report, Madison editors emphasized the natural beauty of the area—a theme ampified by several earlytaveler' andemigrants' guides. The 1839 *Western Tourist and Emigrant's Guide* said that Madison had "the most beautiful and healthy townsite in the west."[67] In 1838 an easterner taking what was called the "grand western tour" said "no situation can be conceived more beautiful than the shores of (Lake Mendota) . . . The whole of this lovely shore is studded and adorned with woods and thick groves, giving the idea of park scenery in England, or the rich views of Italy; and more beautiful than either. . . ."[68] However, by 1840 editors recognized the natural beauty theme was "getting threadbare"[69] and that something else was needed.

Finally, editors decided to abandon the slick talk of the prospectus in favor of candor and hard-hitting criticism. Better, they reasoned, to give anti-Madison forces some ammunition and prod Madisonians to progress than to allow the fledgling community to stagnate. One of the first areas where candor was essential was the fact that land around Madison was expensive and required hard work to make it pay. The editors recognized that the future of Madison was dependent upon settlement of the surrounding countryside. Without farms there would be no grain to grind in the projected mills, no wagons for the planned roads, no customers for the anticipated stores. "Those

who come here expecting cheap land and abundant crops . . . without plowing and sowing where roasted pigs run around with forks sticking in their backs crying 'come eat me, come eat me!' will not find it here," said one editor, "and we are willing to have every person know this."[70]

Editors took every opportunity to puncture what they saw as glassy-eyed complacency. "Can you imagine," wrote one indignant editor in 1842, "we find . . . intelligent men who will yawn and stare and tell us that the time has not yet come (for railroads). . . . The world is going by steam and he who would not be run over must get out of the way."[71] In 1844 the really hard slugging began. "Why is it that we citizens of this industrious capital are so woefully deficient in energy and enterprise? . . . Why . . . are we so sluggish? Can we expect the mere name of 'Capital of Wisconsin' will cause houses to spring up on our lots, our streets to fill with busy throngs that pile dollars into our patrons. . . . No, a town will never be built but by exertion and enterprise."[72]

On Being First: Glimpses of Nature and Society

Twenty-seven year old Simeon Mills arrived in Madison on June 10, 1837, the same day the capitol construction crew arrived from Milwaukee. Mills was one of a handful of people who came at the beginning of the city's history, who stayed the rest of their lives and who saw a wilderness transformed into a city of 16,000 persons complete with railroads, telephones, lightbulbs, streetcars, factories, fine homes, a densely built up business district and a large university. The experience of this small fraternity of men and women who went out to build a city in the wilderness was in their words "wild," "wierd," "unique" and "an extraordinary privilege." Unlike all other Madison residents they could walk around the town and with a sweep of their hand say, "all this happened during my sojourn." They watched an idea once limited to the mind of a

single man become a bustling, sprawling but imperfect reality. They saw the before, the wilderness, and the after, the city.[73]

Fortunately, Mills and several other pioneers who witnessed this transformation anticipated the intense interest later residents would have about this period, particularly the appearance of the isthmus in its natural state and what people were like when society was simple.

Nature

The earliest written description of Madison came from Ebenezer Brigham who camped near the King Street entrance to the Capitol Square in May 1829. At that time Brigham said the Capital Park "was . . . an open prairie on which grew a few dwarf oaks. . . ."[74] His nephew Jerome visited the same site in 1839 and said the area "had the look of a well kept lawn, shaded by fine white oak and bur oak trees. . . ."[75] The rest of Capitol Hill and what is now called Mansion Hill was covered by a dense oak forest, whereas Third and Fourth Lake Ridges were covered by a "moderately heavy" oak forest.[76]

The cessation of prairie fires in the 1840s allowed dense undergrowth to spread through these forested areas—a fact that appears in nearly all pioneer accounts.[77] The area around the present day Milwaukee Road depot was a "dense thicket of poplar, crabapple and plum trees."[78] College Hill was described as a "blackberry bramble."[79] Between Starkweather Creek and the Yahara River lay an area of "dense woodland."[80] Unlike other isthmus forests, this area was protected from prairie fires by the Yahara River. Therefore it contained "very dense" underbrush and trees that were not prairie fire-resistant such as maple, elm, and basswood.[81]

An estimated twenty-five percent of the original plat was marshy.[82] The largest marshy area lay between Third and Fourth Lake Ridge and occupied 172 acres. Much of this area "was covered with water, especially during the spring of the year when the lakes were full. At such times fishermen in boats would move out into the marshes and make huge catches in its shallow waters with spears. Other parts of the marsh were a wet meadow that furnished the village with a generous supply of marsh hay."[83] The 35-acre area to the north of lower West Washington Avenue "was for a time covered more or less with water, and in some portions, was impassable at all times."[84] A small pond surrounded by marshland lay at the intersection of State and Lake Streets,[85] and the area near the intersection of Johnson and Wisconsin Avenue was said to be "low, wet and marshy."[86] The area around Tenney Park was described as a "dense black and white ash swamp."[87]

Early settlers fondly recalled the fragrant fringe of red cedar that grew along steep rocky shores and miles of broad white pebble beaches that ringed most of the shoreline of Lakes Mendota and Monona.[88]

"Game was profusely abundant"[89] when H. A. Tenney arrived in Madison in 1845. Tenney "repeatedly shot prairie chickens on the Capitol Square and the hunting of quail there was common."[90] Other early settlers described the lakes as "fairly black in places with flocks of ducks and geese."[91] Rosaline Peck told how she stood for hours at her cabin door watching flights of passenger pigeons.[92] The lakes abounded in "pickerel, bass, suckers, mellots, rock fish, catfish, muscalung, pike, perch, and sunfish."[93] Accounts of thirty-pound fish were common.

Larger game was plentiful too. In September 1844, a newspaper reported that twenty bears had been seen in and around Madison during the preceding weeks. "Scarcely a day passes," the account continued, "but one or more are seen within a few miles and on Monday morning last, three were seen about one-half mile from the capitol."[94] Deer were common within the town boundaries until about 1847, and even in that year a large buck was shot just beyond the spot where Bascom Hall now stands.[95]

The appearance of Madison in its wilderness state left vivid and indelible impressions in the minds of early arrivals. "Were it in my power I would describe the feelings and impressions that thrilled my very existence as I wandered over the landscape . . ." said Simeon Mills, recalling his walk into Madison in June, 1837.[96] "But language cannot paint the intoxicating beauty of this garden of the world before it was touched by the utilizing hand of civilization." Fortunately, however, the inadequacy of language to describe such surpassing beauty did not prevent Mills and others from recording their impressions.

A Walk into Madison, June, 1837

The land was "a vast rolling prairie, broken here and there with groves and openings and every hill and valley was radiant with the glossy foliage and the gayly variegated wild flowers of June. It was a paradise of loveliness, a veritable garden of Eden. At every step, at every turn, new and startling beauties came into view. The bur oaks stood out upon the hillsides like old orchards, while longing eyes peered beyond to catch a glimpse of the plowman at his work, or the smoke ascending from his dwelling. But none was there. . . . These fair and fertile fields studded with mirrored lakes and coursed with silvery streams covered with a carpet of mellow-green, figures with wild roses and crimsoned with ripening strawberries, there undulating meadows as they lay spread out and laughing in the midday sun revealed a country ready for use. Reader you who never behold the world you inhabit, except for the fitful glances through the narrow confines of a (railroad) car window, how do you like the picture?"

A description of the land
just south of Madison by
Simeon Mills

Reminiscences, 1880

When Darwin Clark, one of the members of the construction crew, arrived in June, 1837, he was "charmed" and "enchanted" by the view from atop Capitol Hill. "Not a ripple was to be seen on the surface of the lake. It lay gleaming in the sun like a vast resplendent mirror. . . . The scene was most fascinating to behold. It felt as if I was under the influence of some invisible alien power impressing me that this was to be my lifelong home and thus it has been."[97]

Madison was still a near wilderness in 1845 when H. A. Tenney first glimpsed the isthmus from the top of a knoll east of Lake Monona.

The spectacle was a vision so glorious, that it painted itself on my memory with a vividness that has never left it. Just previous to reaching the elevation I had been overtaken by a gentleman also bound for Madison, and when we reached the summit, both stopped our horses in involuntary surprise. Four Lakes lay spread out before us, brought out in strong relief by the declining sun just sinking in the west, shining like burnished mirrors. On all sides forest and prairie swept down in lines and patches unobstructed to their shores. Except the village, magnified a thousand fold as a central figure, there was no break in the scene— not a mark of human improvement. As this line of white beach sand glowing in the sunset stood in contrast with the dark, green foliage that encompassed it, while plain and level, precipice and peninsula, bay and gulf, were clothed in a brilliancy of outline, and a beauty beyond the power of description. Half an hour of twilight passed before our interest in the golden vision was satisfied.[98]

Permeating these accounts was a strong awareness of the wilderness beauty they were privileged to see. Some of this feeling must be attributed to nostalgia, for they were writing their impressions many years later. But lurking in their minds were mixed feelings about the propriety of the profound wilderness-to-city transformation each lived to see. "I sometimes wonder," said one Madison pioneer writing in 1878, "whether Madison of today eclipses that old picture that memory paints—when noble forests that surrounded the village were untouched and the view from the old capitol revealed scattered white houses nestled amid native woods; when the business (area) was confined to King Street and when Mendota had a long, clean white sand beach. . . , No one," he concluded, "can deny the charms of the modern 'Belle,' but we who knew the 'Indian princess' cannot forget her wondrous beauty."[99]

Society

In his reflections on pioneer characteristics, Simeon Mills observed that most writers paint the pioneer in glowing colors, always emphasizing their noble character and goodness of heart. The implication of such an interpretation, said Mills, was that "none but good men and women migrated to the new country."[100] Mills disagreed with that notion and argued that pioneer virtues were really pioneer necessities.[101] Nearly isolated from the outside world, impoverished by a depression and faced by frontier rigors, few felt they could say to another: your end of the boat is sinking. People had to cooperate to survive, much less prevail. Mills theorized that the real difference between pioneers and those they left behind was that the pioneer "inherited a trifle more energy, and a little more pluck or dare-devil spirit"—an essential characteristic of those who "elbow back the dusty savage and make possible the production of a more advanced civilization."[102]

Whatever the reason, Madison pioneers agreed that society in the tiny frontier community had many idyllic qualities, which were quickly lost as the community became larger and more complex. The simplicity of Madison society in 1845 can be deduced from the fact that H. A. Tenney met all seven state and local dignitaries just a few minutes after he arrived.[103] Tenney described Madison, then under three hundred persons, as "almost a pure democracy, bound together by every tie of sympathy and friendship. Almost every social gathering was in common. . . . Kind,

generous and neighborly acts were taken as a matter of course. None were so poor or lowly as not to receive necessary aid and attention."[104] ". . . None of the modern clap trap, little affectations, small jealousies and party dignity troubled us," he continued. "We lived lives of activity and usefulness—putting away sham, and looking only for substance."[105] Another early settler, John Catlin, said that in the early years "all were friendly and good will prevailed. The almighty dollar had not then taken possession of (our) souls to the exclusion of the milk of human kindness for each other. . . . The absence of fashion and the chilling influence of wealth had not yet appeared," he reported.[106]

Most early Madisonians were young and hailed from New England and New York. Simeon Mills, the first storekeeper was twenty-seven when he arrived in Madison from Connecticut.[107] Darwin Clark, a member of the capitol construction crew was twenty-five and hailed from New York.[108] Rosaline and Eben Peck were twenty-nine and thirty-three respectively when they opened their public house in the wilderness. Both were born in Vermont.[109] John Catlin, another Vermonter and Madison's first postmaster, was thirty-five when he arrived.[110] Pennsylvania-born Robert L. Ream was twenty-nine when he took over Peck's Tavern Stand.[111] New York-born James Duane Doty was just thirty-seven when he persuaded the Belmont Legislature to select Madison as the seat of government.[112] Joseph Knapp, editor and proprietor of the *Wiskonsin Enquirer,* also hailed from New York and was thirty-four when he arrived in Madison.[113] Vermont-born A. A. Bird, Madison's second mayor, was a capital commissioner when he arrived in Madison at the age of thirty-five.[114]

Though social relationships were nearly all supportive and constructive, antisocial behavior was not a stranger to Madison's early years. The most spectacular crime committed during Madison's first decade was the 1842 murder of Charles C. P. Arndt, a Green Bay legislator who was shot by another legislator, James R. Vinyard. Contrary to what one might expect, the crime did not

occur in a saloon but rather on the floor of the council, the upper house of the territorial legislature. The tragic incident caught the attention of Charles Dickens who was then touring America. In his widely read *American Notes* (1842), Dickens attributed the incident to a proclivity toward violence common in the "slave districts" of America.[115] Less spectacular but far more common were persons who stole horses and cut down timber on somebody elses property.[116] One resident indignantly reported that "some Rapscallion" had been milking his cow in the early morning before he got up.[117]

Food was abundant and wholesome but monotonous. Earliest settlers just about lived on fish, not because they liked it so well, but because they were free and easy to catch. Some bought fish from Corvalle, a French-Indian fisherman, who each night stretched a net across the outlet of Lake Mendota and caught ten to twenty pickerel weighing from twenty to forty pounds.[118] Early residents reported that an Indian pony could be loaded down with game by going no farther than College Hill or the Yahara River.[119] With flour at twenty-five dollars per barrel, some early Madisonians shaved ears of corn with a jackplane to obtain meal for cornbread. Boiled wheat after it was dried and run through a grinder was regarded as a coffee substitute.[120] The American Hotel owner raised tomatoes which in season were served for every occasion. At breakfast hotel guests ate "tomatoes with milk; at lunch tomatoes in pies and patties, mashed in side dishes, then dried in the sun like figs; at tea tomato conserves. . . ."[121] Among the few luxuries in which pioneers indulged were wild fruits including crabapples, choke cherries, sour grapes, and wild plums.[122]

In spite of long winters and their isolation from the rest of the world, Madison pioneers found much real "happiness and enjoyment" according to John Catlin, an 1837 arrival.[123] Twice a week a dance school was held in the twelve-by-twenty-four-foot Peck "ballroom." Fortunately there were two good fiddlers, Rosaline Peck and her brother-in-law, Luther.[124] Even more fortunate

was the presence of enough females to dance co-
tillions three sets at a time. Normally in a frontier settlement females were rather scarce, the
ratio for the territory at the time being about three
men to every woman.[125] In addition to the dancing school, the first residents held turtle soup suppers, euchre parties, a Christmas and a two-day
New Year's celebration.[126] Until the Indians were
rounded up in 1839 Madison boys found Indian
boys to be great playmates. Together they fashioned a winter version of the slalom ski by tying
a rope to the front of a tapered board. They would
then grab the rope in their hand, step onto the
board with both feet and swoop down hills with
lightening speed.[127]

Still another method of driving away winter
ennui and at the same time satisfying the deep-
seated Yankee desire to improve the mind was
the Madison Lyceum, begun by Darwin Clark
soon after he arrived in 1837. Under the auspices
of this fragile outpost of intellectual life in the
middle of the wilderness, Madison pioneers debated whether the credit system was injurious to
the community, whether capital punishment
should be abolished, and whether virtue or vice
had the greatest influence over mankind in the
natural state.[128]

The Village Incorporates

Following its designation as territorial capital in
1837, Madison was governed by Dane County's
three commissioners.[129] However, with twelve
hundred square miles of county territory under
their jurisdiction, the three part-time commissioners could hardly afford to give the fledgling
capital much of their time or scarce tax money.
Nevertheless Madison had grown to the point
where it needed laws governing health, sanitation
and rubbish disposal plus money for relatively
expensive fire suppression equipment, schools,
roads, sidewalks, and much more.[130] Several
community leaders concluded that their needs
could only be met by securing a village charter.

At first the proposal to move from county to
village government provoked howls of protest.
Critics charged that village government would
only lead to increased taxes and a long list of
onerous laws including but not limited to the requirement that citizens fence in their cows and
pigs. They insisted that money for community
improvements should continue to be raised by the
voluntary subscription system and not coerced
from property taxes. Under the subscription system, improvement proponents would go around
securing pledges called subscriptions. If enough
money were raised the project would go ahead; if
not, it would be dropped. For example, Madison's first public school, a seventy-dollar-frame
structure, had been built with the subscription
system. Very significantly, however, Madison's
second school, a two-room brick facility, cost
twelve-hundred dollars and was paid for with
county taxes.[131] Clearly, the handwriting was on
the wall. The subscription and the frontier individualism it reflected was rapidly drawing to a
close.

Finally, in December 1845 citizens met to discuss the need for more government and directed
a committee of prominent persons to draft a bill
suitable for introduction to the legislature. In
February 1846, the legislature approved the new
village charter, Madison officially became a village, and for the first time since its founding
Madison leaders received the power to make its
own laws and raise its own taxes.[132] Now came
the more difficult test: would village government
supply the laws and money that the village
needed? Time would tell and hopes were high.

2 The Village Decade: 1847 to 1856

Introduction

No period in Madison's history produced greater changes than the decade 1846 to 1856. Early in the decade cows pastured in the streets and found shelter under shade trees, groups of skinny pigs called "prairie racers"[1] feasted on garbage and acorns, and roving flocks of domestic ducks and geese declared Madison to be a tiny country hamlet. Beginning with only 625 persons in 1846, the village by the end of the decade had increased its population fourteen times to nine thousand people.[2] Not only had the population increased dramatically, but its composition had changed profoundly. In 1848 Madison had a nearly homogeneous Yankee and Eastern "native" population. By 1856 more than half of Madison residents were foreign born. More than any other period in Madison's history, this decade enjoyed a heady, almost uncontrollable prosperity. During the decade, Madison's accomplishments included a railroad, water power, one of the finest hotels in the entire state, elegant private homes, suburban developments, church and commercial buildings, gas lights, factories, bookstores, bands, visiting circuses, literary societies, fancy carriages and fast horses, street marking signs, pleasure boats for hire, taxis, omnibuses and yachting regattas.

As if these accomplishments were not enough, Madison ran off with three of the choicest prizes

state government could award. In 1848 immediately after Wisconsin became a state, Madison was made state capital (thereby ending a big question mark about the city's future) *and* made the home of the University of Wisconsin. In 1852 the State Insane Asylum was located just north of the city. To other cities all these government plums seemed like a triple coup.

At the same time Madisonians were bragging about city features, they were complaining about city problems including muddy, dusty, manure-filled, potholed streets, cluttered sidewalks, manmade ugliness of all kinds, an acute shortage of space to house and educate the living and bury the dead, uncontrollable ruffians, dog packs, wagon-train collisions, speeding horses, and even an energy crisis.

By 1856, Madison had passed through its municipal molting period, officially exchanging its incorporated village status for a full-fledged city charter. If by 1856 Madison did not possess the full style and dignity of a city, it was rapidly moving in that direction.

The Farwell Boom

Someone once said, "one man who believes in a town can make a town believe in itself." For Madison that man was Leonard James Farwell, a successful Milwaukee hardware merchant who,

at the age of twenty-eight, purchased for five hundred dollars cash all the unsold land originally belonging to James D. Doty.[1] The year of Farwell's purchase was 1847, and just about everybody made a good *theoretical* case for Madison. It lay in the center of a large fertile area with no competing towns for miles around, was the territorial capital, and possessed what was widely considered to be the most beautiful townsite in the West. In spite of this impressive argument, Madison's potential was unrealized and, according to some, unrealizable. By 1847 though, several trends suggested that Madison's hour might be at hand, and Farwell was willing to gamble on that future. The two agricultural frontiers, one moving west from Milwaukee, the other moving east from the Mississippi, were at last converging on Madison. After a long period of slow land sales due in part to speculation, land prices began to fall to a point where land in and around Madison became more attractive to the settler-farmer. Then in 1848, an event of great importance for Madison occurred. Wisconsin became a state, and Madison was made the permanent capital and home of the University of Wisconsin.

During the next eight years Farwell led the town from a state of near stagnation to unprecedented economic prosperity, by systematically promoting settlement and developing his land. Immediately after taking up residence in Madison in late 1848, after a year-long sojourn in Europe, Farwell worked through immigration agents

SHSW WHi(X3)2590

Leonard J. Farwell: Believer and Doer

The maestro of Madison's greatest boom, here shown at age thirty-four, in his first year as governor, was born in Watertown, New York, in 1819. Orphaned at eleven, he became an apprentice tinsmith. At age nineteen he went west to Lockport, Illinois, where he built a successful hardware business. In 1840 Farwell moved to Milwaukee where he started his own firm. Several years later the L. J. Farwell & Company advertised itself as the largest hardware house in the West.

Having made a fortune in a short period of time and eager for a new challenge, Farwell decided to try land development in Madison. By 1847, Farwell was convinced that economic and political conditions would soon cause Madison's great potential to be realized and so he bought a large number of lots and land on the eastern edge of the city. And then as if to allow his new investment to ripen, Farwell took an extended trip to Europe, Asia, and Africa. Immediately after his return in late 1848 he sold his Milwaukee business and moved to Madison. During his absence Wisconsin became a state and Madison was designated not only the permanent capital but also the home of the University of Wisconsin.

In 1852 at the age of thirty-three, Farwell became Wisconsin's youngest governor. During his two-year term (January 1852 to January 1854) Farwell established the state geological survey, abolished the death penalty, built the Institute for the Education of the Deaf and Dumb at Delavan, created the state banking system, reorganized the State Historical Society of Wisconsin, and built the Insane Asylum, now known as Mendota Mental Health Institute. Interestingly, Farwell sold the state the land on which the Insane Asylum was built while he was governor. But perhaps the achievement in which Farwell took the most pride was the creation of the State Commission of Immigration whose purpose was to actively encourage migrating Europeans to settle in Wisconsin. So good was Farwell's idea that it was copied by several other states. These accomplishments are all the more impressive when Farwell's youthfulness and precarious political position are taken into account. At the time, Farwell was an antislavery Whig and both houses of the legislature were solidly Democratic.

In 1857 three years after his second term had ended, Farwell decided to get back into electoral politics by running for alderman in what is now the Sixth District. Unfortunately, Farwell was defeated by just nine votes—surely a disappointing rebuke for a man who seemed to live for Madison.

Also in 1857 Farwell put his fortune on the line to secure a second railroad for Madison, the Watertown and Madison line. Not only did he invest thousands of his own dollars, but he extensively endorsed the notes of other investors. When the 1857 panic hit, railroad securities became practically worthless, and the value of Farwell's real estate dropped below its encumbrances. He had no choice, but to divide his holdings among his creditors.

After losing his Madison real estate he lived in the home he had built for his wife (and put in her name) on the north shore of Lake Mendota next to the Insane Asylum. While living there he won one term in the state assembly (1859–1861) representing the Towns of Dane, Vienna, Springfield, Middleton, and Westport.

In 1863 President Lincoln appointed Farwell as an assistant examiner in the Patent Office in Washington, and three months later to the post of Principal Examiner of Inventions. Interestingly, Farwell was present at Ford's Theater that fateful night Lincoln was assassinated. Thinking that the assassination might also include an attempt on Vice-President Johnson's life, Farwell had the presence of mind to rush to Johnson's hotel room to warn the Vice-President of possible danger and spent several hours with him until the danger had apparently passed. In gratitude for this gesture Johnson later offered Farwell his choice of government posts but Farwell declined.

In 1870, two years after his wife died, Farwell resigned his Washington position and moved to Chicago to start a patent-counseling office. Unfortunately that office, its contents, and his business hopes were destroyed in the Chicago fire of 1871. Farwell then moved to Grant City, Missouri, a tiny country crossroads in northwest Missouri where he hoped to duplicate his Madison achievements. There he opened a banking and real estate firm, and within a few years had given the community a high school, a courthouse, a brick store, and railroad connections. He died in Grant City in 1889 at the age of seventy.

Not until 1897 was Farwell's extraordinary contribution to Madison acknowledged in any enduring form and then in a very modest way. In that year the Madison Park and Pleasure Drive Association decided to name the new drive through Maple Bluff "Farwell Drive." However, the vote on the board was close; "Sunset Drive" nearly won.

HOMESTEADS
FOR SALE,
COMPRISING A LARGE NUMBER OF VERY DESIRABLE
VILLAGE LOTS,
Well located for Business purposes, or
PRIVATE RESIDENCES,
SITUATED IN THE
Village of Madison,
WISCONSIN.

Also, One Hundred and Fifty
FIVE and TEN ACRE LOTS, adjoining the Corporation limits, within a few rods of the
Madison Mills and Water Power;
Possessing a FERTILE SOIL—fronting on HANDSOMELY LAID-OUT AVENUES—well supplied with
WOOD, WATER, &c.
Surrounded by beautiful LAKE SCENERY, and affording a fine View of the
VILLAGE AND STATE CAPITOL.

TERMS AND CONDITIONS OF SALE.
Actual residence and immediate improvement, credit from one to ten years, to suit purchasers, and a PERFECT TITLE given.
For particulars enquire of
L. J. FARWELL,
Office, Bank Building, Pinkney st., Madison, Wis.

Choice Lake Shore Lots For Sale
ON LAKE MENDOTA,
Three Minutes Walk from Capitol.

A RARE OPPORTUNITY is offered for those wishing to get a LAKE SHORE LOTS for residence, near to to Town, and overlooking the City. The Lots are about Twelve Rods deep to the Lake Shore, and afford a fine opportunity for docking out for Boat and Bath Houses, Fishing, &c. The Lots will be sold in THIRTY FOOT FRONTS if desired, so as to enable people of small means to have a beautiful Lake Shore Residence.
au28d1m L. J. FARWELL.

FIGURE 2.1. FAREWELL'S LAND PROMOTION. In addition to actively promoting the sale of his real estate through Eastern and European publications, Farwell used local sources like business directories and the local papers. Two examples of Farwell's local promotions are shown here. The advertisement for thirty-foot lots on Lake Mendota appeared in the *Wisconsin State Journal* during August 1856. The five- to ten-acre lot ads appeared in the first (1855) city directory.

An examination of 1853 and 1856 city assessment rolls showed that Farwell owned more Madison lots than any other person. In 1853 Farwell owned nearly thirty percent of all the lots in Madison and in 1856 nearly twenty-eight percent. In value these lots constituted seven percent of the city's 1853 total, whereas in 1856 this figure had increased to nearly nine percent.

in the East to direct German immigrants to Madison. This effort was quickly followed by the preparation of tracts, maps, and pamphlets and their distribution all over the East and Europe. Throughout these materials Farwell emphasized business advantages and beauty to be enjoyed *only* in Madison.[2] Characteristically, Farwell did not limit his evangelizing to distant agents and the public mails. On several occasions he successfully applied his charming and forceful personality to buttonhole settlers passing through Madison with another western destination in mind.[3]

One of his most successful promotional efforts grew out of a visit in 1854 by Horace Greeley, editor of the *New York Tribune* and one of the best-known and most respected men in the country. In his newspaper account of his Madison visit, Greeley showered the area with superlatives.

> Madison has the most magnificent site of any inland town I ever saw. . . . The University crowns a beautiful eminence a mile west of the Capitol with a main street connecting them a la Pennsylvania Avenue. There are more comfortable private mansions now in progress in Madison than in any other place I have visited. . . . Madison has a glorious career before her.[4]

Farwell promptly hired Greeley to print ten thousand copies of a map showing the attractiveness of the area for settlement and prominently displaying the Greeley name, of course. Instead of designating the lakes as "Third Lake" or "Fourth Lake"—the order in which government surveyors had come upon them in 1834—Farwell selected more romantic names reminiscent of the recent Indian habitation. Frank Hudson, a surveyor and student of Indian lore, suggested "Mendota," which he said meant "great," and "Monona" meaning "beautiful." Lyman Draper, the young secretary of the State Historical Society of Wisconsin, suggested Waubesa ("swan") and Kegonsa ("fish") for the two other lakes and Yahara ("catfish") for the river connecting the lakes. All were three syllables and euphonious. To make the christening official, the names were incorporated in an act of the legislature signed into law on February 14, 1855.[5] With these and other efforts Farwell literally put Madison on the map. Madison, Wisconsin, if not exactly a household word, was no longer an unknown crossroads in the wilderness.

At the same time he was promoting, Farwell was also making improvements to his own extensive holdings. In this category his first and most important task was to harness the water power of Lake Mendota so its energy could turn lathes, grind farmers' wheat into flour and saw logs into lumber.[6] But harnessing Mendota proved to be much more difficult than anyone imagined.[7] The primary difficulty arose from Doty's decision to cut the mill race through the isthmus between Hancock and Franklin Streets, then called East and West Canal Streets. While the canal was located at the narrowest and most logical point on the isthmus, the site required extensive cuts through hills forty feet above lake level. A recent engineering estimate showed that the volume of excavation material this site would have required would have been sufficient to fill the Tenney Building thirty-five times![8] But Farwell had a better idea. Rather than build the canal across the waistline of the isthmus, he decided to make his attempt in the low marshy land where the Yahara meandered from lake to lake about one and one-half miles from the capitol.

To create the greatest possible water power, Farwell had to raise the water level of Mendota and lower Monona. Therefore in early 1849 he built a damn at the outlet where the Tenney Park Lock is today located[9] and cleared out debris from the outlet of Lake Monona.[10] Together these actions created a "head" or a difference of about four feet between the two lakes.

After cutting a new channel for the Yahara and increasing lake level differences, Farwell put the water power to work by constructing a large mill containing machinery of all kinds. Construction of "Madison Mills," as they were known, was begun in the spring of 1850 and completed in the fall of 1851. The water power proved "vastly superior"[11] to what had been anticipated.

As if the construction of the mill was not enough to keep Farwell busy, during the 1850 construction season his crews opened Williamson Street and the (Fort) Winnebago and Milwaukee Road, now Winnebago Street. During 1851 Farwell's major "public works" projects were draining portions of the immense marsh east of the village roughly bounded by Blount, Williamson, East Johnson Streets, and the Yahara River, and laying out miles of streets there.[12]

In addition to his developmental activities, Farwell became active in local politics, simultaneously serving as chairman of the Dane County Board of Supervisors and as a village trustee. His energetic entrepreneurial and civic activities caused politicos to view him as a most attractive candidate for governor, but Farwell, "an antislavery Whig,"[13] was not at all interested. Nevertheless, his undeterred backers nominated him, and Farwell fled town. As fate would have it, his political admirers found his horse in the barn of his hostess and insisted that she yield up her prize. Farwell reluctantly returned to Madison where he stood for election and narrowly defeated his Democratic rival in the November election. One

FIGURE 2.2. MADISON MILLS (1851). Farwell's Madison Mills were one of several developments that greatly stimulated Madison's economy in the early 1850s. In the words of a local reporter, the "merry clatter" of its grist mills, turning lathes ,and buzz saws had "a very agreeable effect on the minds of our citizens." The reason is not hard to find. The Mills, for years the only flour mill, made Madison the focal point for a growing agricultural economy. Farwell's business was so good the mill was operated twenty-four hours a day. For a short time Farwell kept a couple of pet bears on the premises and played with them "as familiarly as kittens." Eventually, however, the bears became "troublesome" and ended up at a local meat market.

This advertisement appeared as a full page ad in the Farwell-promoted 1851 Business Directory. The Mills partly straddled the Yahara River where the Tenney Park lock is now located. The main part was five stories high and built of stout oak timbers.

MADISON MILLS.

Erected at the outlet of the Fourth Lake; 50 by 130 feet on the ground and five stories high, with eight run of Burrs. and abundant supply of water. Capacity for storing Thirty Thousand bushels of grain. All the latest

IMPROVEMENTS IN MILLING,

Have been introduced into these Mills, and designed for both custom and merchant work. A

SAW MILL ATTACHED.

WHEAT, FLOUR, SHORTS, BRAN, CORN, MEAL, OATS, ETC., ETC., Constantly on hand, at wholesale or retail.

L. J. FARWELL.   JAMES FARWELL.

The subscriber, one of the proprietors of the village of Madison offers rare opportunities for investments in

Water Power,

For Mills and Machinery. Buildings for rent. &c.

To persons coming West for the purpose of making a permanent settlement, he can offer the most satisfactory inducements in the way of locations for residences.

FARMING LANDS,

and COUNTRY SEATS. Will take pleasure in affording any information desired relative to advantages for selections of locations, Free of Charge.

Madison, June, 1851.   L. J. FARWELL.

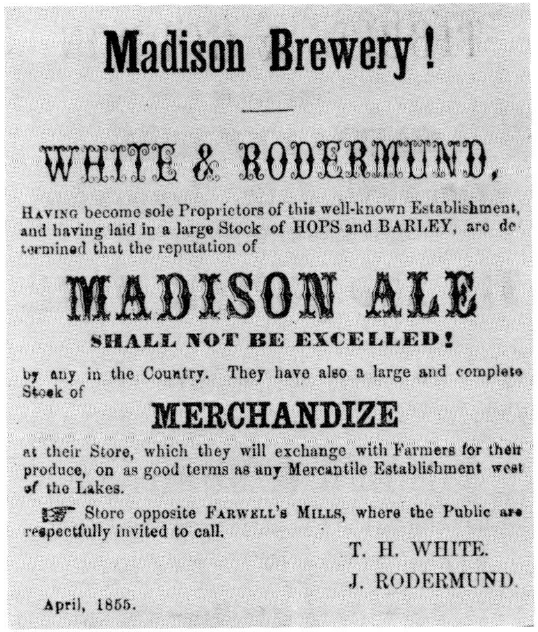

Madison Brewery !

___

WHITE & RODERMUND,

HAVING become sole Proprietors of this well-known Establishment, and having laid in a large Stock of HOPS and BARLEY, are determined that the reputation of

MADISON ALE

SHALL NOT BE EXCELLED !

by any in the Country. They have also a large and complete Stock of

MERCHANDIZE

at their Store, which they will exchange with Farmers for their produce, on as good terms as any Mercantile Establishment west of the Lakes.

☞ Store opposite FARWELL's MILLS, where the Public are respectfully invited to call.

T. H. WHITE.
J. RODERMUND.

April, 1855.

FIGURE 2.3. MADISON ALE.   One of the businesses that grew up next to Farwell's Mills was the White and Rodermund Brewery (1850), later known as the Rodermund Brewery. Its specialty, Madison ale, was described in the 1855 advertisement shown above. Rodermund was one of many Germans who were successfully persuaded by Farwell's literature and personal overture to settle in Madison. In this case, one cannot help but suspect that Farwell made a special deal with Rodermund because a brewery and general store was an ideal business to have next door, especially for farmers who had to sit around a good part of the day while they had their grain ground at Farwell's mill. The Rodermund Brewery was purchased by the Hausmann Brewery, another Madison brewery, in 1888 and the buildings of that operation stood until they were torn down to make way for the former CUNA Filene House.

man who knew Farwell said that after taking office in January 1852, he manifested little interest in the affairs of state but had the good sense to hire a man capable of attending to those details. His name was Harlow S. Orton, later a Madison mayor and Supreme Court justice. Orton Park on Madison's near East Side was named for him.[14]

With Orton performing many of the gubernatorial duties, Farwell was able to continue his first love—developing Madison. During the construction seasons of 1852–1853, Farwell set sixty hands to work filling, ditching, and grading East Washington Avenue from about Blount Street to the Yahara River. Then he laid a double plank road, Madison's first form of paving, and planted six thousand soft maple and cottonwood trees along its sides.[15]

During the same period Farwell spearheaded investment groups that put up the Capital House (see fig. 2.13) one of the fanciest hotels in the state at the time, and the Bruen Block, a large, prestigious commercial building where the First Wisconsin Plaza now stands (see fig. 2.14). He was also a major financial backer of the Dane County Bank, the forerunner of the First Wisconsin.[16]

After his term as governor (January 1852–January 1854), Farwell continued his Madison development activities, becoming a financial backer of the Water Cure (1854) and the Madison Gas and Light Company. He also continued his commitment to religious, governmental and educational matters. Between 1855 and 1857 Farwell was a leader of the Grace Episcopal Church. In 1855 he served a second term as Village Trustee and during the same year was elected to Madison's first Board of Education.[17]

Farwell's energetic entrepreneurial activities produced countless public conveniences, created hundreds of jobs, and greatly stimulated settlement. Farwell's contemporaries were awed that for none of his public improvements did he request a single cent from the public purse.[18]

But, above all, Farwell's aggressive investment and development activities inspired confidence in Madison's future.

Although there can be little doubt that Farwell's activities got Madison moving, the arrival of the first railroad in 1854 assured continuation and even acceleration of the Farwell momentum. To have a railroad pass through town was regarded as a prerequisite for urban success. Already the limits of canals were evident. Ordinary roads were undependable and impassable during much of the year.[19] Plank (toll) roads were only slightly more reliable and often cost too much for farmers. But a railroad—paragon of power and progress, glory of the age—*that* was something else. Its relatively fast, cheap, all-weather service would stimulate commerce as nothing else could.

Typically, fledgling cities had to compete for a railroad's attentions with great vigor. Money, usually in the form of stocks but not uncommonly in the form of bribes, played a paramount role in many railroad locational decisions. But because Madison was the capital of the state, the county seat, the home of the University of Wisconsin, and the center of a rich agricultural area, it did not have to sell its soul and mortgage the future to get its *first* railroad. At the same time, Madison residents—in spite of their community's railroad appeal—could not sit back and wait for the first engine to steam through town. There was railroad stock to buy and land to donate for depots and rights-of-way. To generate the necessary capital, railroad "rallies" were held in Madison on a regular basis from the middle 1840s on. Sentiment was nearly always unanimous and enthusiastic in favor of the railroad. Typically the question came down to this: Farmers of Dane, Citizens of Madison, etc., "how much stock do you stand ready to subscribe to this great enterprise the moment the papers are placed before you?"[20]

For a time there was some confusion about which railroad would reach Madison first and hence which stock to buy, but by the early 1850s it was evident that the Milwaukee and Mississippi Railroad, the ancestor of the Chicago, Milwaukee, and St. Paul system, was going to be the first. John Catlin, president of the Milwaukee and Mississippi Railroad, wrote a letter to the village

RAIL ROAD MAP.

WISCONSIN

IOWA

ILLINOIS

MICHIGAN

LAKE

LA CROSSE.   BARABOO.
FORT WINNEBAGO.
SHEBOYGAN.
WATERTOWN.
MADISON.
PRAIRIE DU CHIEN.
MILWAUKEE.
MINERAL POINT.
MILTON.   WHITEWATER.
JANESVILLE.   RACINE.
POTOSI.   KENOSHA.
BELOIT.
DU BUQUE.
GALENA.
Chicago & Galena Railroad
BELVIDERE.
CHICAGO.
LYONS.

NAMES OF THE DIFFERENT RAILROADS.

No. 1. Milwaukie and Mississippi.	No. 4. Madison and Watertown.	No. 7. Madison and St. Croix.
" 2 Madison and Beloit.	" 5. Madison and Sheboygan.	" 8. Madison and Potosi.
" 3. Wisconsin and Illinois.	" 6. Madison and Fort Winnebago.	" 9. Milwaukie and La Crosse.

This Diagram shows the large number of railroads in Wisconsin centering at Madison, which is also the centre of a magnificent farming region of more than 40 miles in all directions, the physical peculiarities of which are such as will admit of nothing like a rival town within that entire circuit; embracing a highly productive agricultural territory equal to a New-England state, the vast products of which this must ever be the grand Entrepot.

FIGURE 2.4. RAILROAD MAP (1854). Few maps inspired as much confidence in Madison's future as this "spider web" published in June 1854, just two months after the arrival of Madison's first railroad, the Milwaukee and Mississippi. To the common man the map dramatized the "inevitability" of Madison's economic prosperity. Indeed, what other conclusion could any reasonable person have drawn from being in the center of a rich agricultural region as large as Rhode Island? Although Madison eventually got its network of nine railroads, it required thirty-three years.

Railroad Meeting.

To the Inhabitants of Dane County

The undersigned, appointed a committee at a public meeting held at the Court House, in Madison, on the 19th inst., to call a public meeting of the citizens of Dane County, to take into consideration such measures as will advance the speedy completion of the Milwaukee & Mississippi Railroad to Madison, solicit a general attendance of the citizens of Dane County, at the Court House, in Madison, on Saturday the 20th of December next, at 2 o'clock P. M., to discuss the measures that shall be then proposed to advance the completion of said Railroad

JOHN CATLIN,
N. J. TOMPKINS,   } Committee.
A. L. COLLINS,
Madison, Nov. 21, 1851.

FIGURE 2.5. RAILROAD MEETING. Throughout this period of railroad courting, local papers were filled with announcements for "railroad meetings," an example of which is shown here. Really little more than pep rallies for marketing and selling railroad stocks, they were nevertheless an essential part of the railroad-building procedure. Also shown is a Milwaukee and Mississippi Railroad schedule for 1854.

1854] Summer Arrangement. [1854

Mil. & Miss. Rail Road.

Now in operation from Milwaukee to Madison, about 100 miles.

ON and after Monday, May 29th, THE TRAINS will run as follows, (Sundays excepted)

GOING WESTWARD.

A **Passenger Train** will leave Milwaukee at 7.30 A. M.,—arrive at Janesville at 11 A. M.—at Madison the capital of the state, at 12.40 P. M.

A **Passenger Train** will also leave Milwaukee at 5.15 P. M., on the arrival of the Boat from Chicago, and arrive at Janesville and Madison the same evening.

GOING EASTWARD.

A **Passenger Train** will leave Madison for the present at 3 A. M., and Janesville at 5 A. M., and arrive at Milwaukee at 8.30 A. M., in time for the morning Boat for Chicago.

A **Passenger Train** will also leave Madison at 1.30 P. M., and Janesville at 3.30 P. M., and arrive in Milwaukee at 7 P. M., in time to connect with the Evening Boat for Chicago, which will commence running on or before June 30th.

FREIGHT TRAINS RUN EACH WAY EVERY DAY, THE ENTIRE LENGTH OF ROAD.

Stages run in connection with the Cars, to and from the Forest House and Whitewater to Watertown, Fort Winnebago, Fond du Lac, Beaver Dam, Horicon, Waupun and Berlin.

Also from Janesville and Madison to Sauk, Baraboo, Dodgeville, Mineral Point, Florence, Galena and Dubuque and to various other portions of the state.

Passengers are ticketed to and from Madison to Chicago at $5.00, and to and from Janesville to Chicago at $3.60.

N. B.—The price from Milwaukee to all Eastern points is the same as from Chicago, which makes the Milwaukee route the cheapest by several dollars.

EDWARD H. BRODHEAD,
je23dw1y   Superintendent and Engineer.

trustees saying that his railroad would want depot grounds "as near to the center of business as possible" and ". . . rights of way through the streets of said village passing to and from the depot . . . plus rights of way through either Bedford or Bassett Streets." Just one day after getting the letter, the village trustees voted unanimously to give land to the railroad, only slightly departing from Catlin's request.[21] Thus, after years of citizen hopping and waiting, Madison got its first railroad (see insert p. 51).

The beneficent effects of the railroad were immediately evident. Just days after the line opened, twenty-five to thirty-car trains carried Madison area wheat to Milwaukee. Travel through the town doubled during the summer of 1854. Housing starts dramatically increased.[22] An entire "village" including warehouses, taverns, and other businesses, grew up around the depot grounds where just a few months before had been a dense thicket of poplar, crab and plum trees. Actually businesses were not the only thing that grew up around the depot. So did rats, brought to Madison aboard one of the first trains.[23]

Unfortunately the railroad was not very reliable at first because the tracks into town kept sinking. In their search for level ground and lowest construction costs, railroad engineers commonly laid tracks through marshes. This strategy

The Triumphal Entry of the First Railroad

Never was the day more auspicious. The heavens were cloudless, the air warm, but not sultry. . . . By ten in the morning the streets were filled with teams and the sidewalks crowded with people. Great numbers of them were men who had settled in the country at an early day and had never seen a locomotive or railroad.

. . . By one o'clock in the afternoon the grounds about the Depot were thronged with people anxiously obeying the injunction so common along railroads and looking out for the "engine." We should judge that at least two thousand people from the country were about the Depot, and at the end of the bridge where the railroad crosses the bay. . . . Bright colored parasols ranged in groups along the shore lent liveliness to the scene.

At length the unmistakable whistle of the engine was heard, and the long train with two locomotives at its head, swept grandly into sight—thirty-two cars, crowded with people. . . . At the rear of the train were several racks occupied by the Milwaukee Fire Companies in their gay red uniforms with their glistening engines. A fine band of music attended them, and, at intervals as they slowly moved across the bridge the piece of artillery brought along by the firemen was discharged. It was a grand but strange spectacle to see this monster train, like some huge unheard of thing of life with a breath of smoke and flame, emerging from the green openings—scenes of pastoral beauty and quietude—across the Third Lake. . . . It was estimated that at least two thousand were on board.

Wisconsin State Journal[24]
May 24, 1854

usually worked, but not around Madison. On a single day in June, 1854, the track sank five feet just south of Monona Bay.[25] Recent soil borings in this area have shown subsoil to consist of thirty feet of peat and marl, which when used for railroad purposes behaves like geological silly putty.[26]

Under the spell of the Farwell boom, population doubled between 1849 and 1851 and then nearly doubled again between 1851 and 1853.[27] In 1850 a new resident reported that immigrants were "pouring in like a deluge" and that the streets were filled with covered wagons and droves of cattle.[28] Some of course were on their way to northwestern Wisconsin, Iowa, or Minnesota, but many came to stay.

Madison, during the Farwell boom, was a paradise for builders. A new courthouse was begun in 1849, North Hall (the first university dormitory) in 1851, South Hall in 1855, large fancy business blocks like the Bruen Block (1853), the Water Cure (1854), dozens of elegant mansions for men like Farwell, Nathaniel Dean, Jairus Fairchild, and hundreds of ordinary homes. "Go where you will," said one account, "visit whichever part of town you may, and you see on all sides, in every nook and corner, apparently upon every lot, the most busy-bustle preparations for building. You pass an untouched vacant lot in the morning and at night you will find it strewn with building materials, a foundation laid, frame raised for a good sized house, nearly clapboarded, and partly painted."[29] A village paper proudly reported that one thousand new buildings had been erected between 1847 and 1854![30] A large number of these were inexpensive, almost temporary homes designed to generate income. Demand for housing was so great and building costs so low, "homes to let" were sometimes paid for in just a single year.[31] Newspapers touted the brick and stone buildings because they represented achievement, dignity, wealth, and—most of all—permanence, an understandable contrast with the more common "cheapest kind of buildings."[32]

No sector of society was more caught up in the building boom than the churches. Ballooning population made rented halls harder to get and increasingly inadequate. Even the capitol, the most popular temporary house of worship in Madison's history, had to be scheduled in shifts, with the Episcopalians preaching at 10:30 A.M., the Baptists at 2:30 P.M. and the Presbyterians at 4:00 P.M. One by one the denominations felt it imperative to begin their own churches, the Methodists in 1849, the Presbyterians in 1852, the Baptists and Catholics in 1853, and the Episcopalians in 1855. Since the Congregationalists already had their church (1846), they did not join in the great construction binge. However, in the spirit of one upsmanship, they did contribute the first church bell in 1848. Villagers were so proud of the bell, visitors called it the "Madison Idol."[33]

Aiding the building boom was the increasing availability of relatively inexpensive, locally produced construction materials. Steam and water-powered saws and planing mills produced dimensional lumber, quarries yielded the cream-colored Madison sandstone, and brickyard ovens converted clay to red and cream colored bricks.[34]

Property values commonly increased one, two, and three hundred percent in just one or two years.[35] Sales were brisk and rents were sometimes enormous.

At the same time construction was booming and property values were soaring, a quiet revolution had occurred in the ownership of Madison real estate. In 1846 about seventy percent of all Madison lots were owned by nonresidents. Many of these nonresidents had purchased the lots in 1837 during the speculative fever immediately after Madison was named territorial capital. However, the Panic of 1837 and several local conditions left the Madison real estate market depressed for a decade. Not until the Farwell boom did prices rise to a point where many of the speculators felt they should sell the lots and minimize their losses. By 1853 seventy-five percent of all Madison lot owners lived in Madison. In just seven years, Madison had become "home owned."[36]

Propelled by the heady atmosphere of the Farwell boom and ecstatic reports from eastern correspondents, Madisonians began to view their town as a marvelous resort. One reporter from the Worcester, Massachusetts, *Express* was convinced that Madison's hunting, fishing, boating, and sightseeing bill of fare easily surpassed the posh traditional eastern resorts like Saratoga, Newport, Lake George, and others. "In the same day," he exclaimed, "the lover of field sports may fill his game bag with fish and duck from the lake, grouse from the marshes, quails and prairie chickens from the prairie, and all without going two miles from his hotel. Fishing, boating, and bathing in lakes where you can see the drifts of white sand far down to the transparent depths. . . . Driving you can see over the prairies with the same unfenced freedom as upon the water . . . watching the long grass as it twines around your wheels . . . leaning from the seat to gather from the tall flowers, bouquets for the nose. . . . Picnicking on the lakesides, refrigerating your excited system with ice cream and cold duck internally applied, horseback excursions, but it is useless to attempt to enumerate the routine of enjoyments in the loveliest climate in this latitude."[37]

Hoping to capitalize on this resort boomlet, two Madison developers, George P. Delaplaine and Elisha Burdick, built in 1854 a $40,000 resort-spa called the Water Cure. In the same year an enterprising mariner launched in Lake Mendota the first steamboat and announced himself "in readiness to take out parties for fishing excursions and pleasure rides. . . ."[38]

Stimulated by waves of new residents and the pace of construction and growing confidence in the town's future, business flourished as never before. During the 1856 construction season twenty-five *new* stores were opened.[39] Seven Madison banks were begun within four years of the state's first banking law in 1852.[40] Newspapers received so much advertising they sometimes had to cut news to make room. Bumper crops and demand-inflated prices made boom times for farmers too. Times were so good on the farm that farmers' daughters, normally sent to town to earn a wage as servant girls, stayed on the farm, and the townfolk complained about the unavailability of

FIGURE 2.6. THE FARWELL MANSION. The most elegant private mansion erected in Madison during the 1850s boom was the home of Leonard J. Farwell. Begun in 1852 and completed in 1854 while Farwell was still governor, its opening constituted "the greatest social event Madison had ever seen." The huge home was octagonal (25 feet on a side, 200 feet in circumference), three stories high, contained nearly 9,000 square feet of interior space, boasted an octagonal barn with a circumference of 160 feet, and stood on an entire block bounded by Spaight, Brearly, and Lake Monona. The building was crowned by a cupola from which Farwell enjoyed unrivaled views. A dramatic circular staircase extended up all four stories.

This photograph was taken sometime after 1871 when a parochial school was built to the east of the home. The wing visible on the left was added during the Civil War when the home served as a hospital for wounded veterans, but the original elegance of the structure is still evident. After serving as a soldiers' orphan's home, the distinguished building was used as a Norwegian Lutheran Seminary. For a brief period Thorstein Veblen, the originator of the term "conspicuous consumption" and author of *Theory of the Leisure Class,* taught at the seminary. When the Lutherans sold the home it nearly became the UW medical school, but the regents opposed the move on the ground that the state did not need a medical school and if it did, it should be in Milwaukee.

The Farwell mansion was the first of two octagonal houses erected in Madison. (The other, a much more modest home at 121 West Wilson, known as the Jarvis home, burned in 1977.) The Farwell home was probably the largest and most elegant octagonal home ever built in the state. If ever there was a landmark worth preserving, this was it. Unfortunately, the eminent old structure was razed in 1895 and the land subdivided into lots. (SHSW WHi(D31)587)

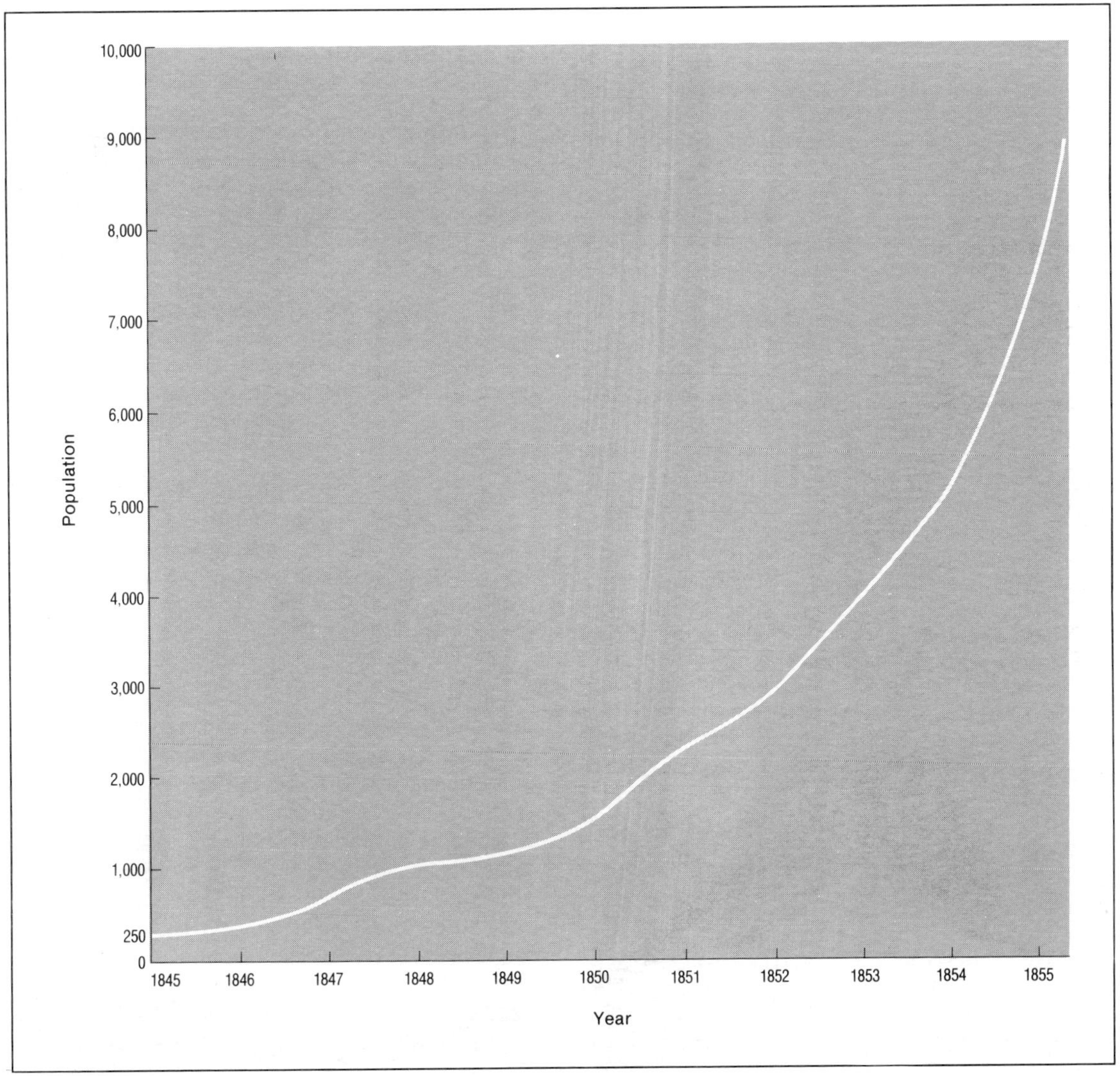

FIGURE 2.7. THE POPULATION BOOM. The Farwell boom had two stages: a period of steady growth from 1845 to 1850, averaging fifty-five percent per year, and a period of almost explosive growth from 1850 to 1855, averaging eighty-seven percent per year.

servants.[41] Madison boosters were elated: "It is truly gratifying to witness such indisputable evidences of prosperity,"[42] said one. "Crowds of teams are jammed in the streets constantly. People are rich and prosperous and times are glorious,"[43] said another.

Madisonians were aware that their community was at last achieving the critical mass needed to warrant the more prestigious designation "city." One by one major urban amenities were being added. Newspaper editors, knowing their squibs would often be picked up by other editors around the country, relished reporting the arrival of the latest urban amenity. The Capital Hotel was "the best hotel in the state"[44] and the fancy carriages and fast horses were "luxuries heretofore considered Eastern."[45] The telegraph brought Madison "within speaking distance of New York, Washington and nearly all the principal cities in the country. . . ."[46] The first hacks and cabs in the streets were viewed as "regular city institutions,"[47] and the gas street lights "cast a brilliant light . . . about the Capitol Park."[48] These things, the boosters were saying, don't happen in quiet hamlets, but rather in flourishing cities.

Madisonians held an almost uncritical confidence in their future. And why not? The sounds of construction were stilled only by nightfall and bad weather. Estimates of a village population of twenty thousand by 1860 appeared in a scholarly pamphlet.[49] Optimism begat optimism and nowhere was the rollicking booming mentality more clearly reflected than in the newspapers of the time. Cascading through their columns was indomitable bravado in quantities to embarrass the timid, shock the profane, and bore the cynic. At every opportunity editors laced sentences with bold adjectives, vigorous verbs, sparkling adverbs, and, curiously enough, concluded them not by an exclamation point, but by a mere period! It was the language of the times, a dialect still spoken, but never so unabashedly as in the Great Farwell Boom.

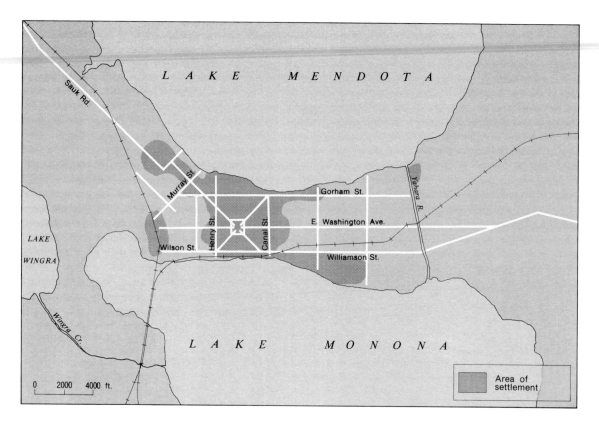

FIGURE 2.8. 1856 SETTLEMENT PATTERNS. Until 1846 settlement in Madison was concentrated on the southeast side of Capitol Hill. However, by 1856 settlement covered all of Capitol Hill and Madison became a city upon four hills: Capitol Hill; what is now often called "Mansion Hill"; Fourth Lake Ridge; and Third Lake Ridge. Until the Farwell boom, spatial growth of the city had been quite slow, particularly on the west side of the village. When H. A. Tenney erected his two-story frame home in 1847 where the Loraine Building (123 W. Washington Avenue) now stands, it was the *only* home southwest of the Capitol Square. When J. T. Clark built a home in 1846 where National Guardian Life is today, it was the first improvement made in that part of town and almost the first on the northwest side of the Capitol Park. Even after he completed the home, his friends asked him how he enjoyed the "country life" and whether he had any difficulty finding his way back and forth. West Washington Avenue was not opened until 1854.

Generally, residential growth was limited to reasonable walking distance. Ads appearing in newspapers of the 1850s commonly stipulatd that the home be within twenty minutes' walking distance or no more than three-fourths of a mile from the Capitol.

One of the most curious characteristics of growth during the 1846–1856 decade was the lack of interest in lake property. In 1855 the Mendota lakeshore from Farwell's Mills (Tenney Park Lock) to the university grounds was vacant with very few exceptions. When two of the wealthiest men in town, Levi B. Vilas and J. T. Marston, selected lots on which to build their fancy homes, both chose "inland" corner lots.

Growth Pains: Problems Amidst Prosperity

"We have grown fast, and done much within a short time, in this little burgh," said a letter to the editor of the *Wisconsin State Journal* in December, 1853. "But," the writer continued, "Madison cannot be pronounced finished just yet."[1] Indeed, it could not. While the prosperity was a source of immense pride and satisfaction, it was not without problems. No urban area can multiply its population fourteen times in just ten years and not expect growing pains.

Schools

Of all the growth-related problems of the village decade, none was more talked about than public school inadequacies. The problem was too many school children and not enough schoolhouses and teachers. It was with great pride that the village in 1846 built the twenty-by-forty-foot brick schoolhouse with a capacity of maybe sixty children. But ten years later, the "little brick" schoolhouse was *still* the only school in a city with 1,602 school-age children, only 450 of whom were attending the Madison public schools.[2] Those who couldn't be squeezed into the "little brick" were squeezed into churches, a part of a carriage factory, and sundry other places. To make matters worse, only three to four teachers were available, yielding a teacher-pupil ratio of something like one to 125. Probably 150 children from well-heeled families were attending private schools, but that still left nearly one thousand kids in the streets.[3] No wonder the superintendent complained of "great irregularity" in attendance and "habitual tardiness."[4] Teachers were grossly underpaid, or when village finances were especially meager, simply not paid at all.[5] Editorials and letters to the editors were saturated with righteous indignation. "We have plenty of saloons, groceries and tippling shops—a class of schools pretty well attended. . . ."[6] but no regular

VIEW of MADISON the CAPITAL of WISCONSIN.
TAKEN FROM THE WATER CURE,
SOUTH SIDE OF LAKE MENONA, 1855.

FIGURE 2.9. CURRIER SKYLINE. In early 1855 the editor of still another Eastern newspaper decided to tour the rapidly growing American West. In March of that year the editor visited Madison and, in a dispatch to his paper, said the city" had the most beautiful townsite in the West." Under most circumstances the comment would have been forgotten, but in this case it was not because the writer was Horace Greeley, the nationally famous editor of the prestigious *New York Tribune*.

Greeley's article was probably the basis for the Currier lithograph shown here, which appeared just a few months after Greeley returned to New York. Greeley knew well the Currier brothers, Nathaniel and Charles, and often visited them in their shop just a few blocks from his newspaper. The Currier brothers were always looking for an event or a statement that piqued people's curiosity and that, if embodied in one of their lithographs, would sell well. Greeley's superlative-laden account of Madison was one of those occasions. What did the most beautiful townsite in the West look like?

Charles Currier decided to exploit the opportunity. To do the sketch he commissioned Samuel Hunter Donnell, a prominent Madison architect, then in partnership with August Kutzbock. The 9 by 12-inch lithograph originally sold for fifteen cents and was one of about one hundred prints published by Charles Currier. (Charles Currier, although not a partner in the Currier and Ives firm, was an active participant and had full access to its equipment and staff. It seems likely that Nathaniel, after whom the firm was named, rejected the Madison print as a regular Currier and Ives production because it would not enjoy a large national market. Today collectors make no distinction between which brother published the lithographs; all prints are listed and priced together. The Madison print is valued at $150.)

The lithograph contains a number of distortions and errors, all no doubt intended to enchance Madison's beauty. For example, the railroad is shown as going around Monona Bay rather than across it by trestle, and the tall spire dominating the skyline belongs to St. Raphael's Catholic Church, but was not built until more than twelve years later. (SHSW WHi(X3)2314)

FIGURE 2.10. HOEFFLER'S STATE STREET (1852). This sketch of Madison from College Hill was done in 1852 by a German artist, Adolph Hoeffler. The main street in the center is State Street and the Greek columned building in the top right is the new (1850) courthouse (where the Dane County Ramp is now located.) (SHSW WHi(X31)384)

schools. "We have some fine churches, a Court House and a costly jail—but have not a common school house large enough to accommodate one-eighth of the youth of the place."[7] Characteristically, the modest village educational accomplishments were viewed as a great deterrent to settlement and hence "a serious detriment to the prosperity of the town. . . ."[8]

One cause for the lack of progress was shifting responsibility for the schools. In 1847 the village had formed its own school district but soon discovered that state financial aids for schools went directly to the Town of Madison, of which the Village of Madison was a part, and not to the village school district. On the assumption that the Town of Madison would channel its state financial aids to the village if the township were given the responsibility, the village trustees in 1850 dissolved the Village of Madison school district and transferred all its educational powers to the Town of Madison board. Unfortunately, the town board took little interest in village schools. Then in 1855, in response to a new state enabling law, a separate, more powerful Board of Education for the

Village of Madison was established. In its enabling act the board was empowered to determine the *levels* of school expenditures, and the village trustees were authorized to raise the money through a tax levy. Theoretically this tandem arrangement would end the eight-year do-nothing period. The board of education decided it needed $10,000 for new schools and passed along this request to the village trustees. Unhappily the village trustees refused to approve the loan.[9]

A second cause for the lack of educational progress was the fact that the majority of parents and citizens were not clamoring for more school buildings because this meant higher taxes. Yankee public school advocates and editorial writers aside, many residents had come to Madison for pecuniary reasons alone; and for them education was a frill. For these reasons, no public schools were built during the village decade.

FIGURE 2.11. HOEFFLER'S N. HAMILTON STREET (1852). Another Hoeffler sketch done in 1852 looks down North Hamilton Street from the Capitol. Note the rutted, irregular street and the sparse development. (SHSW (X31)387)

FIGURE 2.12. WENGLER'S KING STREET (1851). Johann Baptist Wengler (1815–1899), an Austrian artist, toured America in 1851 and left this fine water color. The drawing shows King Street, the heart of the Madison "business district." On the left side of the street was the well-known Madison Hotel (about where the Majestic Theater is today). Built in 1838, the building stood until 1863, when it was destroyed by fire. During the early years it was a stage depot and focal point of state politics, particularly for those forces who lobbied to keep the capitol in Madison. Note the board sidewalks common during this era. (SHSW WHi(X3)30106)

Streets and Sidewalks

In 1846, at the beginning of the village period, only King Street, State Street, and a part of Main Street had been cleared of stumps and opened for travel,[10] and nearly all of those streets were still unbroken sod.[11] Promotional tracts described these roads as "always in passable order,"[12] but in truth, they were far from it. During rainy weather, teams and wagons transformed the streets into deeply rutted, muddy mucilage. During dry weather the streets were a "moving body of dirt" making the "air about as pleasant to breathe as sandpaper."[13] One correspondent described potholes in Madison streets as "the greatest opening for settlers in all Wisconsin."[14] The

streets were viewed as free storage places for debris, boxes, barrels, piles of wood, lumber, coal, hay, straw, ashes, and rubbish of all kinds. No wonder people regarded the streets as "detestable without one redeeming quality."[15] The wood or gravel sidewalks were similarly detestable. At first private property owners were responsible for building them, but they seldom built them except in the business sections of town where they were viewed as outdoor merchandise showcases. Faced by mounting cries for sidewalks, village trustees began constructing sidewalks. By 1855 sidewalks became the largest single item in the village budget, eclipsing streets by a five-to-one margin.[16]

Public Sanitation and Disease

Residents during the village period, like their counterparts elsewhere around the country, were not fastidious about public sanitation. Garbage and slops were commonly dumped into the streets, dead animals were allowed to decay wherever they dropped, and offal from slaughterhouses was sometimes thrown into the lakes. Added to these problems were prodigious quantities of horse manure and urine constituting a major street-cleaning problem as well as a health hazard. All of these practices poisoned the air "with an insufferable stench." Citizens who complained were sometimes "invited to go to hell."[17] Every now and then an enterprising citizen would take matters into his own hands and submit a bill to the village trustees for "burying one dead hog," or the like and hope the trustees would reimburse him.

Private and public response to these conditions depended almost entirely upon the prevalence of human disease. If disease rates were low, little if anything was done; if high, a few cosmetic efforts were made. The two most troublesome diseases of this period were malaria and cholera. Malaria sapped strength but rarely killed and was considered an inevitable part of the frontier life. Cholera, by contrast, was almost always a killer and a quick one at that. One day a man would be seen on the street in robust health; the next day his death would be reported.[19] Although the causes of these diseases were not precisely known, there was general agreement that cleanliness and swamp draining were the best defenses.

Cholera's epidemic years in Madison were 1849, 1852, and 1854. In the wake of the 1849 epidemic, "masses of filth" were collected and burned in the streets and several marshes were drained.[20] In response to the 1852 epidemic, the village committee on health distributed large quantities of lime to purify yards and streets.[21] In 1854 the board of health, in addition to removing filth and distributing lime, established a quarantine house,[22] inaugurated a get-tough policy again those who failed to clean up their premises, declared all slaughterhouses a public nuisance, and drained more marshes.[23]

Another response to the cholera epidemics was increasing agitation for a piped water system. For nearly twenty years householders had provided their own water and sewage systems by digging wells and privies in their backyards. Many feared that wells in built up areas of the city would be permanently ruined by sub-soil seepage from the privies. But even with this compelling justification, backers of a private piped system, known as the Madison Hydraulic Company, failed to secure adequate financial backing.[24] Not until nearly thirty years later was running water a reality in Madison.

Because Madison editors recognized that the presence of cholera would deter settlement and slow or even jeopardize the boom, they seldom mentioned the disease and when they did, used benign terms. Typically, the appearance of the first case brought denials. "A rumor was current yesterday that the cholera has made its appearance in this town and that a woman had died with it the night before. We have made diligent inquiry and have been unable to obtain any authentic information on any such case. The salubrity and healthfulness of our locality precludes any serious apprehensions from this scourge. . . ." said one newspaper account.[25] Such protestations aside, cholera *was* present in Madison. Reminders of its sojourn can be found in the oldest section of Forest Hill Cemetery. There, written on tiny tilting pieces of marble, are the names of children, recently arrived immigrants, and robust pioneers who were its victims.

The Village Cemetery

Perhaps no other block in Madison generated so much controversy during the village decade as Block 180. Known today as Orton Park, to the villagers it was "the burial ground." In 1847, just after its formal designation as village cemetery, the block was laid off into 256 burial lots, and efforts were begun to have the grounds dignified with a handsome fence. Unfortunately, this early momentum seems to have been lost, and between 1847 and 1852 the condition of the village cemetery was a simmering local scandal. The problem, according to indignant newspaper accounts, was the failure of the village trustees to properly enclose "this most sacred spot on earth"[26] with a fence. In other words, pasturing cows were desecrating the graves of dear departed citizens. Part of the problem was the awkward fact that the trustees never acquired clear title to the graveyard until 1850—a convenient and even compelling excuse for doing nothing. The other part of the problem was a disagreement on how scarce village funds should be spent.[27]

No sooner had the cows been fenced out in 1852 than it dawned on the village trustees that the 3.5 acre cemetery was inadequate for future needs. By 1853, due to cholera epidemics and a burgeoning population, only 117 burial lots out of the original 256 remained.[28] At once a search for a new, bigger cemetery was begun.

In 1856, soon after the city charter went into effect, the common council formally selected the Forest Hill site. By 1877 all the bodies at the Orton site—all, that is, except one pauper stolen by U.W. medical students—had been disinterred and reburied at the new cemetery.[29] In 1879 the village cemetery was turned into a park, thereby becoming one of a handful of instances in the entire country where this occurred.

Fire Protection

Fire protection during the village period was ridiculously inadequate. Like so many village efforts, the trustees got off to a creditable start but did little after that. In 1846, the trustees issued an order requiring all buildings to keep filled firebuckets in a convenient public place and appointed two fire wardens for supervising extinguishment efforts.[30] Ten years later the Madison fire department consisted of "one wagon, two ladders, one whole pole and one broken one, and 11 buckets."[31] Even more remarkable was the fact that during much of this period Madison had no fire company capable of using what little equipment existed. Because buildings in the business section of town began using common walls early in the 1850s, a fire in one building could easily have spread to adjoining buildings if wind conditions had been just right and produced the Madison equivalent of the 1871 Great Chicago Fire. According to the *Wisconsin State Journal,* Madison was "the luckiest town in the whole state in escaping fires."[32]

FIGURE 2.13. CAPITAL HOUSE. "Among the absolute wants of our town," wrote the editor of the *Daily Democrat* on May 1, 1852, "is a first class hotel. There are two German and five American hotels in town, all of which are as well kept as circumstances will permit and very well supported; but none of them have the means or convenience as a suitable lodging . . . for a large class of individuals whose buisness or pleasures lead them to visit the town." That "large class of individuals" mentioned by the editor were wealthier visitors who, because of their inability to secure fine hotel accommodations, were sometimes "prejudiced against the place." This need did not go unnoticed for long. In 1852 a joint stock company was formed consisting of L. J. Farwell, L. B. Vilas, G. C. Fairchild, Simeon Mills, E. B. Dean, and others. The objective of their venture, the Capital House, was opened in late 1853 and did a flourishing business for decades. In 1865 L. B. Vilas bought out the other stockholders and changed the name to Vilas House. The building continued as a hotel until it was converted to an office, building called the Pioneer Block.

From the beginning the hotel enjoyed an unequalled reputation in Madison and for a time was considered to be one of the finest hotels in the entire state. The five-story hotel boasted one hundred twenty large, airy rooms furnished "in the style of the best eastern hotels" and an observatory with a commanding view of the lakes and prairie. The hotel also had its own omnibus, shown in the front left, to take guests to and from the railroad station. (SHSW WHi(X3)6260)

FIGURE 2.14. BRUEN BLOCK.   During the 1850s large business buildings called "blocks" were cited as unmistakable evidence of town's advance. During the village decade many of these business "blocks" were built, but none was more prestigious or more widely copied than the Bruen Block (1852) shown here, located on the corner of East Washington Avenue and South Pinckney Street. Prime tenants included L. J. Farwell, the Wisconsin State Journal, and the James Richardson and Company, a forerunner of the First Wisconsin National Bank. The building was named after W. D. Bruen, a wealthy Philadelphian who helped finance the venture. Farwell also invested in the building and superintended its construction. The lithograph appeared in a national magazine known as *Gleason's Pictorial Drawing Room Companion* in April 1854. (SHSW WHi(X3)2053)

What was needed was a fire engine, a fire station, and water reservoirs costing about fifteen-hundred dollars. To get this money either an amendment to the charter had to be obtained (to authorize a special tax) or an existing tax had to be earmarked for this purpose. The trustees took the more expedient tack and earmarked revenues from liquor licenses for fire equipment. Unfortunately this revenue source proved insufficient, and the village went without adequate fire equipment for the entire decade. In 1853, about $250,000 worth of property was being jeopardized for the lack of about fifteen hundred dollars worth of apparatus.[33]

Roving Animals

Few problems proved as irksome to village residents as pigs and dogs running at large.[34] Although they had the power to control the problem, village trustees did not choose to exercise that power in any significant sense until 1855. The first feeble effort to control pigs came in 1849 when an antipig ordinance provided for a pig pound and a pound master (pig catcher). Enforcement appears to have been sporadic until the spring of 1855, when handbills posted about the village warned pig owners a pig roundup was about to occur. Any pigs caught would be kept for two days and then sold to the highest bidder.[35] The owner could retrieve an impounded pig only after paying a fine of fifty cents per pig plus daily care charges.

Like the pig problem, the dog problem was not effectively confronted until 1855, when a very stiff antidog ordinance was passed *and* enforced.[36] Among its provisions was a section giving the village marshall power to kill any dog found running at large. Before this Draconian law was promulgated, however, dogs ran in packs through the streets, greatly annoying citizens, especially with their nocturnal activities. (See insert, p. 63.)

FIGURE 2.15. 1856 DAGUERROTYPE, CAPITOL SQUARE (PINCKNEY STREET).   This 1856 daguerrotype shows the south end of the block now occupied by the First Wisconsin Plaza. On the extreme right and only partially in the picture is the United States Hotel, today occupied by the Tenney Building. Entirely out of the photograph on the left is the Bruen Block (shown in figure 2.14). Leonard Farwell's new octagonal mansion in the 900 block of Spaight Street just beyond B. B. Clarke beach dominates the top center of the photograph. Note how the young trees planted just outside the capitol fence are enclosed by wooden frames to protect them from hungry horses. Unfortunately, many other young shade trees set out along other village streets were not so well protected and were commonly killed by horses when their owners, described as "stupid" and "senseless vandals" by the editor of the *Daily Argus and Democrat,* used them as hitching posts.

Visible in the foreground are a number of young trees set out the previous summer to replace the native oaks, which were "beginning to die out." Among the replacements were the elms, "the noblest of our native forest trees," maples, lindens, and hackberries. (SHSW WHi(X3)11101)

Night Warblers

Messrs. Editors:

Amongst all the notices of public entertainments with which the Madison papers abound, I have seen none of the splendid canine concerts which greet the ears of all who have ears, every night, Sundays not excepted. Whole nights have I lain and listened to these "night warblers," without the possibility of so much as a single snooze until dog bed-time, which seems to be fixed, by some law of the canine race, at precisely three o'clock A.M. . . . You can no more bribe them than you can bribe the fates, and stones and brick bats only serve as sharps and flats injudiciously thrown in, producing irregular modulations, to the positive detriment of harmony.

Do you say you never hear them? Well, I can sleep in a sawmill, a railroad car, or a nail factory, but I should as soon think of sleeping through one of Handel's Oratorios with a dozen imps punching my ribs with sharp sticks, as with a dozen indefatigable yelpers within pistol shot of my window, and extended ad infinitum. A good pointer is a respectable animal and worthy of a place amongst village gentlemen, if kept close at night; but of what possible use are the swarms of curs which infest our town except to make the night hideous with their insupportable din and drive sleep to a hopeless distance from all who are so unfortunate as to have ears and nerves. Should men or boys make half the disturbance that our army of village dogs are wont to, they would be arrested and put in jails as disturbers of the peace; and I know not why dogs should have more liberty, in this respect, than their masters.

I am fond of music, very; that is, some kinds of music; but our Canine Concerts have become a nuisance, an intolerable nuisance, and must be abated in some way. It is an unpleasant alternative to be obliged to spend whole nights in feverish wakefulness, or go out with a gun and make war upon the neighbors' dogs; but as the boy said when lightning struck the tree, "Something must be done." If our villagers who keep dogs and think they must keep them, will not shut them into their cellars or hang them down their wells overnight, where their music will be softened a trifle to the ears of outsiders, will not our City Fathers try their wits at devising a remedy?

Signed,
AUDITOR
Wisconsin State Journal
June 21, 1854

Eyesores

Everyone understood that mess and clutter were natural components of a construction boom. What bothered many of the townfolk, particularly the "opinion leaders," was the lack of concern evidenced by residents for the slummy appearance of their homes. Editors refrained from calling attention to such unsightliness for fear of scaring away settlers, but every now and then they would drop their public relations posturing and lay it on the line. One writer began gingerly, "dwelling houses . . . should be surrounded by a fence and a yard and a garden. It matters now how small (the houses) may be; if they look *neat and tidy* they can greatly add to the looks of the place."[37] But then his tone became stern and righteous. ". . . Nothing can be more disgusting than a shabby house with two or three fence posts in front, a few remnants of boards or rails giving the outline of a lot, some of the aquatic races sporting in a frog pond under the front window, and a long-shanked porker snoozing on the doorstep. Such a specimen of domestic felicity," he exclaimed, "passes all our comprehension. . . ."[38]

Shifting to a more constructive mode, he exhorted his fellow townsmen to "PAINT, PAINT, PAINT. If you are unable to do this, then by all means whitewash your houses and fences. This will cost but a few shillings and a little labor will add 50 percent to the value of almost every place it is applied."[39] Unfortunately to such early-day beautifiers, such exhortations failed to motivate many. Hundreds of cheap, hastily built "homes to let" rented to a very mobile, uncaring population produced a limited concern for such niceties. Nevertheless, local editors continued their clean-up-paint-up-gravel-your-walks campaign each time the crocuses popped through the freshly thawed earth.

Village Society and Leisure: Pluralism, Ruffianism, and Leisure

Those who lived in Madison during the entire village decade (1846–1856) witnessed profound demographic changes. A heterogeneous, rapidly growing and foreign population was replacing a smaller, homogeneous and Yankee population. In 1850 two out of three Madisonians were "native born." By 1855, however, one out of every two Madisonians was either born in a foreign country or born of parents who were born in a foreign country.[1]

A recent settler provided a biased but colorful description of this population mix in 1852. "The effect is very picturesque," he said, "when we see in one group the sturdy white haired and blue coated and capped German, the red haired and ugly-mouthed Irishman, the swarthy half-breed, copper-colored cosmopolitan Yankees and native 'Badgers' all with beards, some with kossuth hats with feathers and many with firearms and hunting gear."[2]

These profound demographic changes evoked cool to hostile responses from the "native born."

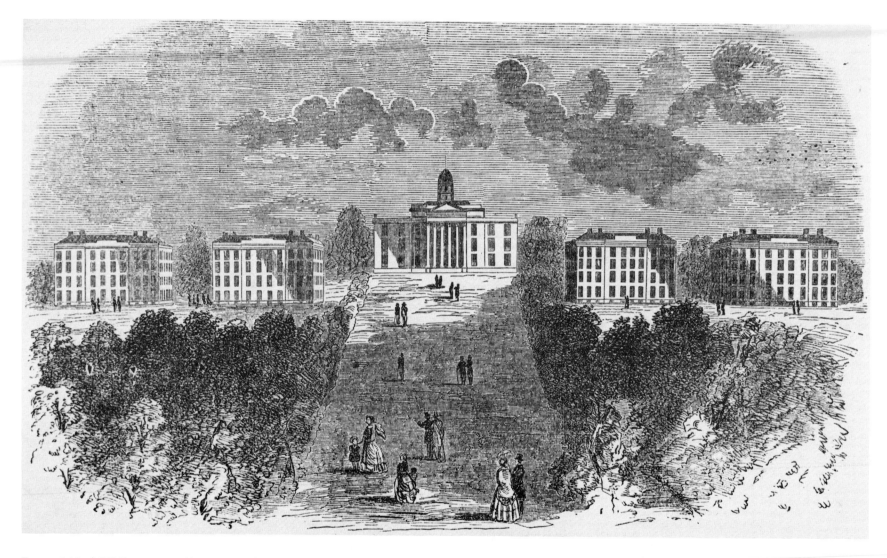

FIGURE 2.16. 1850 PLAN FOR THE UNIVERSITY OF WISCONSIN. Another reassuring visual reminder of Madison's glorious future was this 1854 engraving based upon an 1850 master plan for the University of Wisconsin. Done by an accomplished Milwaukee architect, J. F. Rague, the plan envisioned a central classroom building and four dormitories providing a total of 123 rooms for 256 students—the maximum anticipated enrollment. All the buildings were to cluster alongside a 240-foot-wide avenue flanked by carriage ways. Rague recommended that the area between the carriage way and Lake Mendota and between the carriage way and what is now University Avenue be subdivided into lots for professors' houses. The original campus consisted of a fifty-five acre "park" in the center of which was an "eminence" one hundred feet above Lake Mendota. At the time this engraving appeared in 1854, only North Hall was finished, but South Hall was well along. (University of Wisconsin Archives)

Nationally, the foreign "deluge" threatened "establishment" powers and took the form of the Nativist or Know-Nothing movement, manifestations of which were visible in Madison.[3] The newspapers commonly carried condescending and even impudent accounts involving foreigners. When several Dane County Norwegian families packed up their wagons and headed west, the *Wisconsin State Journal* said the county was "losing nothing by their departure unless it be the removal of so many cattle and sheep where there are not enough in the county now."[4] About half the Germans and nearly all the Irish were suspected of "popery" because they were Catholics. One version of "tolerance" called for giving the newly constructed St. Raphael's Church good marks for architecture but degrading the religion inside. For example, at a cornerstone-laying ceremony at St. Raphael's in May 1854, the religious portions of the event were described by the leading newspaper as "absurd and puerile . . . and suggestive of a semi-civilized state of society."[5]

The *Wisconsin State Journal* approvingly described a technique used during the election on November 7, 1854. On that date, "native sons" stationed themselves at the polls to intercept "sons of Erin" with this technique:

> "Wait a minute friend, Are you a voter?"
> "A voter? an' sure an' hav'nt I voted this five year in the state of New Yorrick? Away wid ye that wad deprive an honest man of his vote in this fray country!"
> "But have you lived in the State six months?" (knowing the residency requirement was one year).
> "Ah, be Jasus, an' that I have. It'll be siven months that I lived here, Monday week. Do ye mind that now?"

At this point the board would interfere and inform Patrick that the law required a residence of *one year* in the state before a native born or naturalized citizen was allowed to vote.[6]

An organized counterresponse to the Madison cold shoulder quickly developed. During the 1850s the foreign press mushroomed and Madison streets were filled with German and Norwegian papers like *Wisconsin Staats-Zeitung* (1854), *Madison Demokrat* (1858), *Emigranten* (1852), *Nordsternen* (1858). With these papers, the Norwegians and Germans fought for effective participation in politics and against the nativist movements. Organizations such as the St. George Society and the Turnverein offered emigrants from England and Germany fellowship in good times and assistance in the bad.[7]

Although "native sons" felt strong personal aversion to the foreign invasion, merchants sought their dollars and politicians sought their votes. Nearly all the Capitol Square stores made strong bids for the foreign trade and therefore had to deal freely in whiskey. A candidate in a local judgeship election in 1854 accused his opponent of being a "nativist" and provided free liquor to those who agreed to vote for him, particularly the Irish. For added insurance some of his intoxicated supporters surrounded polling places, making it impossible for opposition voters to vote without being insulted and jostled. Not surprisigly, the man courting the foreign vote won.[8]

The most frequent friction point between Yankees and foreigners was over what one should and should not do on Sundays. Yankees believed the Lord's Day should be spent going to church, reading the Bible, and little else. This attitude was illustrated by an incident described by Swedish novelist Fredericka Bremer, who visited Madison in 1850 and stayed with one of the staunch Yankee families. After church on a sunny October day when the leaves were at their peak of color, Bremer suggested the afternoon might be a fine time for an excursion around the lake. "But it is Sunday," she was told with a smile, "and on Sundays people must not amuse themselves, not even in God's beautiful scenery."[9]

Unlike the refugees from New England's stony hills, German immigrants practiced what was called the "Continental Sunday" in which having fun with friends was the central idea. To the Germans, the ideal way to spend a Sunday afternoon was at a beer garden talking with friends, listening to band music, playing ten pins on the grass, dancing, and, of course, drinking lager and smoking the weed of Virginia.

Yankee response to the Continental Sunday was uniformly censorious at first, but gradually apologists and even advocates for the idea appeared in the Madison Yankee press. One apologist, trying to extend the olive branch without falling off his pietistic perch, argued that they do it "not because they are sinners, but because they are Germans."[10] In Beriah Brown, editor of the *Daily Argue and Democrat,* the Germans finally found a champion. "There are many of the social habits of our adopted citizens," he suggested in an 1852 article, "that would be profitable for us to imitate."[11] "Americans seem to enter upon every undertaking with so much gravity that they make their holidays dull affairs."[12] "We make everything sedate and gloomy. Our leisure time is not used for any purpose of enjoyment. Our men say they have no time for play and our children put on old looks and ape the habits of their fathers. It is unmanly to roll a ball, to pull an oar, to dance on the green or join a party for woods ramble. . . . Why should bowling alleys . . . be given up to 'fast men'? Why should rowing matches, fishing and shooting be any more a privilege of the 'world' than the church?"[13]

Editor Brown even defended German beer drinking. "A Yankee," he argued, "cannot be made to understand beer drinking. He runs down a pint in haste, deposits his half dime in payment, and vanishes in pursuit of business. The German . . . sets his beer before him on the table, drinks a few swallows at a time . . . with a proper interval between each. He indulges at his leisure. His thoughts are on what he is about, not on a real estate speculation at Windville. . . . We do not look upon beer drinking as the worse of vices. It seldom or never ruins anybody whose ruin was not already certain. . . . Let us not disturb its free enjoyment."[14]

While the predilections of Madison's German citizens were gradually accepted, the immigrant group that won the warmest and most immediate support from the native born were the English. They spoke the same language, were Protestants, and generally practiced the work ethic. Probably the most popular non-English-speaking foreign group were the Norwegians, whose Protestantism, belief in hard work and little drinking made them similar to the Yankee model. Though English speaking, the Irish tended to be viewed with condescension for their menial jobs, drinking habits, and Catholicism.

Public treatment of Blacks was sometimes less than cordial during this period. The village charter limited voting to "all free white males" and few Madisonians seemed interested in changing this policy. One attempted lynching was recorded, and there may have been more.[15] An abolitionist visiting the city in September 1848 was ridiculed in the press as "a great farce."[16] According to the accounts, the speaker smelled of eggs and tar from his recent labors, and his main message was "let the nigger go."[17] When Frederick Douglass, the distinguished "orator of color," appeared before a very crowded audience at the courthouse in 1854, *The Daily Democrat* described him as "an orator among niggers, and a nigger among orators."[18] Nevertheless, antislavery sentiment was growing. Two years later two thousand persons (in a village of just eight thousand) gathered in Capitol Park on June 5, 1856, to hear an abolitionist speak.[19]

From time to time anti-Jewish sentiment emerged. Referring to a well-known Jewish merchant and the first Jew in Madison, Samuel Klauber, an ad of a competing merchant read: "A Bold Stand, Fifty Percent Saved by not Buying Clothing of the Jews."[20]

Ruffianism

Madison's remote location and rapid growth combined to attract a very rough class of people whose drinking, gambling, fighting, brawling, and swearing were notorious. An 1851 editorial warned readers ". . . that haunts of vice, dens of iniquity and grog shops of various sizes and dimensions have been on the increase . . . to an almost alarming extent this past year."[21] A settler arriving in 1852 wrote a friend back east that "drunkenness is a terrible vice . . . , few are safe from its insinuations and the best men in the state are sots."[22] Horace Greeley, lecturing in Madison in March 1855, wrote in his *New York Herald* that Madison had a glorious future "*if* she can speedily and thoroughly rid herself of some barnacles that have fastened upon her—gamblers and like such vermin. . . ."[23] An English doctor who settled in Madison in 1850 "was astonished at the frequent use of profanity . . ." he heard.[24] This was not exactly the kind of publicity Madison needed, but it was all deserved. When village trustees completed their first saloon census in 1853, they discovered no fewer than forty-three—or one saloon for every ninety residents.[25] In addition to these "groggeries and rum holes,"[26] there were three "tigers or gambling rooms in operation."[27]

An accusing finger was sometimes pointed at legislators and judges. "It is deplorable that members of the legislature, generally men of ordinary moral character at home, should contribute to this moral pestilence, while acting in an official capacity. . . . What kind of laws can Wisconsin except from legislators who have such an extensive practice at the 'bar,' the billiard table, the gambling room . . . and the tiger?"[28] asked one critic. One reputable observer witnessed "two of the Judges of the Supreme Court in a saloon engaged in a game of billiards and a group of rowdies looking on and commenting on their skill."[29] But in truth these leaders were little more than convenient scapegoats.

More troublesome than the sheer number of gambling and drinking establishments was the behavior they tended to cause. As early as 1853 a lead editorial denounced the "spirit of ruffianism"[30] that had recently descended upon the village. Said one account, "It is not uncommon for the people of our village to be disturbed in their quiet repose by rowdies who traverse the streets making all manner of unearthly noises by ringing bells, blowing tin horns, drumming on tin pans, etc."[31] "Our streets have been made to ring with boisterous obscenity, supercilious drunken wit, midnight carouses and the unearthly howlings of the inebriated and reckless street brawlers."[32] University officials were attacked for turning out "a pack of howling rioters to make the night hideous and shock the ears of our citizens with blasphemy and vile songs. . . ."[33]

The solution to rowdy behavior short of relocating the capital and university—a solution suggested by one newspaper[31]—was shutting down the liquor stands. This was the objective of the Madison Sons of Temperance, established in 1847.[34] Before the Sons of Temperance could mount their campaign, the trustees in April 1846, in one of their first official actions, dried up the village by establishing a heavy fine on anyone who sold liquor. Apparently the outcry against a dry Madison must have been great because just one year later the state required a binding referendum on the wet-dry issue, and in Madison the wets won three to one. Thus after one noble year Madison's first dalliance with prohibition came to an end.[35]

Leisure-Time Activities

In spite of ten-hour days, the absence of labor-saving devices, and the rigors of settling the West, Madisonians during the village decade had surprisingly generous amounts of leisure time. In overall popularity, the year-round favorite was horse racing. At first, races were held on a one-mile stretch of Williamson Street between Blount Street and the Yahara River. Usually the horse races were run in the afternoon, but not infrequently saloon arguments would produce a little impromptu midnight competition. A correspondent for the *Boston Chronicle* was astounded to discover that in Madison horseracing was not a disreputable thing ". . . as it is considered to be in the East; on the contrary, it is visited by many 'very respectable' men."[36]

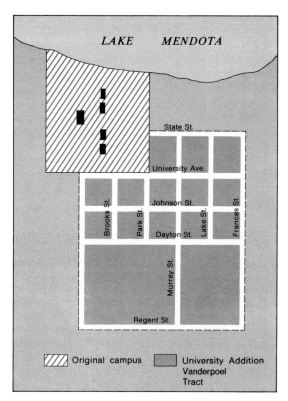

FIGURE 2.17. "AT OR NEAR MADISON": THE UNIVERSITY SELECTS A SITE. Immediately after Madison was selected territorial capital at the fateful 1837 Belmont session, a bill was passed establishing a territorial university at Belmont. The bill was probably a sop to the host community of that first legislative session whose bid to become territorial capital had been rejected. There is no evidence that the governing board of the proposed university ever met or had any intention of meeting. Even if they had, they would have discovered that the hastily drated bill provided no means of financial support.

The second territorial legislature, by contrast, was more serious about starting a university. A bill was passed that changed the location to a point "at or near Madison" and asked Congress for two townships of land, the sale of which was expected to pay for the institution. Congress quickly authorized the designation of two townships and in December 1838, a Board of Visitors committee was appointed to examine the suitability of a tract of land just west of the village limits (see map). The principal owner, Aaron Vanderpool, was a wealthy New York congressman and western land speculator whose Wisconsin agent was James Duane Doty. (The other site owner was Josiah Noonan, the editor of the *Wisconsin Enquirer,* the first newspaper to be published in Madison.) Vanderpoel said he was willing to donate his land to the University. The Board of Visitors committee said they found the land "most eligible."

Meanwhile, another Board of Visitors committee requested the legislature to select the university lands which Congress had authorized, but the legislature took no action. One reason offered for inaction was the fact that the sale of the university lands was contingent upon the territory becoming a state, and few legislators saw any immediate prospect of this change in status.

Though no action was taken to launch the university until nearly a decade later, the idea was implanted that the land lying at the end of State Street would become the site of the university. From 1838 on, it was known as College Hill.

Not until the Constitutional Convention of 1847 did the university idea again receive serious attention. That body made specific provision for the establishment of a state university "at or near the seat of government," established a university fund, and set forth a procedure for governance headed by a Board of Regents. In the nine years that had elapsed since the ill-fated 1838 legislative action, the idea of locating the university at the capital had become widely accepted, and College Hill seems to have been the preferred—even presumed—location. The 1847 constitution was ratified by Wisconsin voters in March, 1848; in May, 1848, Wisconsin was admitted as the thirtieth state.

In October 1848, at the first Board of Regents meeting, a committee was appointed to negotiate the purchase of College Hill. However Vanderpoel was no longer willing to donate his land; he now wanted fifteen dollars an acre and was willing to sell only if the entire 157 1/2 acre tract was purchased by the regents. In early 1849 the legislature approved the purchase of this land.

The new university policy makers were eager to get their new institution started. Unfortunately, they had no money. The regents recognized that it would be some time before the legislature selected the townships, the

FIGURE 2.17—*Continued*

proceeds of which were to go to the university, and that it would be some time after the lands were selected before the income from their sale would actually begin. Neither student fees nor tuition could be expected to pay more than a tiny fraction of annual operating costs. Therefore, the regents had a choice of waiting for money from the university fund or finding another source of start-up money.

The regents selected the latter alternative. More specifically they decided to get into the land development business and become a beneficiary of the Farwell boom, then beginning to gather momentum. They owned 157 1/2 acres of choice land on the western edge of the village, only a small portion of which was needed for a university campus. The regents' contribution to village booming, the 188-lot University Addition was the result.

Then a discrepancy surfaced. The seventeen acres specifically selected as the UW site in the Vanderpoel tract did not include all of College Hill (see map)—a fact that was acknowledged in 1850 without apparent embarrassment. Fortunately, the regents were able to secure the rest of College Hill including the choice Mendota frontage, by giving other College Hill owners valuable village lots in the University Addition—probably in accord with some prearranged deal.

From the ease with which the rest of College Hill was secured and the obvious need for start-up money, the conclusion seems inescapable that the regents had purchased the Vanderpoel site as a means of generating start-up revenue. The regents' land subdivision produced nearly $7,700 profit, even after the initial price for the land was deducted.

Based upon anticipated revenue from the sale of University Addition lots, the regents hired John Sterling in 1849 to head up the preparatory department of the university, a glorified high school designed to prepare students for University entrance. The citizens of Madison, also eager to get the university started, contributed one floor of the red brick building (see p. 67) known as the Madison Female Seminary. Located on the southwest corner of Wisconsin Avenue and Johnson Street, the building was the only "university" building from 1849 to 1851, when North Hall was completed. (From 1860 to 1873 the building was used as the Madison High School. The sketch was made by a university student in 1873 shortly before the building was torn down for a new high school.) On February 5, 1849, when the Preparatory Department opened its doors, seventeen boys from Madison and the surrounding area enrolled. (SHSW WHi(X32)3831)

Gradually the boys with the "fast stock" got organized and in 1855 formed the Wisconsin Sporting Association. The association gave great impetus to the sport by increasing prize money and with it the quality of horses. The association's first big race, held in March 1855 on the Williamson Street track, was *the* big event of the winter. "Every horse in town, every sleigh, cutter, pung and jumper . . . were out"[37] filled with spectators. So great was the interest in the event that even the legislature adjourned. One of the first actions taken by the Wisconsin Sporting Association was the grading of a one-mile oval track called the "Prairie Course" located where Orchard Ridge is today.[38] From that time forward the association's four-day annual races were considered the finest display of speed in the entire state. In the winter sleigh races on Lake Monona were popular, and twenty to thirty sleighs racing each day after supper were common.[39]

Hunting and fishing were also popular. In June 1855, one of the local newspapers reported: "The woods are full of (passenger) pigeons, many of which are young and all of which are fat and juicy. It is no trick at all to bag four or five dozen in a couple of hours. Our 'good eaters' live on little besides pigeons and rock bass now."[40] Hunters did not even have to leave the village. In the fall of 1852 a newspaper reported: "The boys about town have had a fine sport . . . shooting quail on the Capitol Park. Hundreds of these lovable little creatures have been slain upon the village plat. They may be seen almost any day running about our streets like domestic fowl. It is a great convenience for those who enjoy sports and are too lazy to travel." Many "sportsmen" preferred shooting at live turkeys secured to the top of a box one hundred feet distant. Each marksman paid ten cents for a shot at the bird and the rivalry was keen.[41] And the fishing? Well, they were "only waiting for a chance to bite. . . ."[42] said one account. Pickerel, pike, and bass and "occasionally a mammoth musquelaunge"[43] were especially prized.

Popular summer pastimes were band concerts two nights a week in the Capitol Park and periodic rowing and sailing regattas.[44] In the winter, skating races on Lake Monona attracted as many as one hundred fifty spectators.[45] Sleigh rides, too, were a source of great entertainment, especially in the spring, when a hundred sleighs and cutters were not an uncommon sight on Lake Monona.[46]

On New Year's Day, making house calls was looked upon as a duty and made the streets lively with callers. "Every house that could be entered would be visited and generally the tables of the ladies would be bountifully spread. . . . This custom of calling was well observed to the advantage of all, as it enabled people to become acquainted with each other and produced a most excellent feeling among all classes."[47]

The more cerebral leisure-time activities were largely provided by the Madison Institute, which in 1854 began bringing nationally prominent lecturers to Madison, men like Horace Greeley, Ralph Waldo Emerson, James Russell Lowell, and Bayard Taylor. The institute also operated a lending library with a thousand books and a reading room featuring newspapers and periodicals of the day available to anyone who paid the $1 membership fee.[48] Some twenty years later books collected by the Madison Institute became the basis for the Madison Public Library.

In 1850, several variety companies began to make Madison a regular stop. Madison had no regular theaters at the time, but it did have a number of converted halls where stage performances were commonly given. Especially popular were "variety" companies featuring songs, dances, magicians, tricks, comedians, clowns, gymnasts, and trained canaries. The first full-fledged circus arrived in the summer of 1853—none other than P. T. Barnum's "grand colossal museum and menagerie."[49] Another popular form of entertainment was the two-dimensional "pictorial theater" consisting of single frames painted on canvas and requiring two hours to unroll. One of the favorite scrolls was a panorama of Milton's *Paradise Lost* that gave viewers a livelier idea of death and damnation than they had had before.[50]

WINES.

MADEIRA.

Blackburn's Table, old	$2 00
South Side	2 00
Page's London Particular	2 00
Old Madeira	2 00
Wedding Madeira	2 50
Dry Madeira	2 00
Leacock's Old East India	2 50
Howard, March & Co.	3 00

CHAMPAGNE.

Heidsick, Piper & Co., quarts	2 00
Do. do., pints	1 25
Mumm, quarts	2 50
Do. pints	1 25
Piacet, quarts	2 00
Do. pints	1 25
Charles Heidsick, quarts	2 00
Do. do. pints	1 25
Creme de Bouzee, quarts	2 00
Do. do. pints	1 25

NATIVE WINE.

Longworth's Sparkling Cataw- ba, quarts,	2 00
Do. do. do. pints	1 25
Corneau's Still Catawba	1 00

PORT.

Old Port	2 00
London	2 00
Queen's	2 00

HOCK.

Sparkling Hock	2 00
Hockheimer, 1846	2 00
Rudesheimer	2 00

BILL OF FARE.

Sunday, December 2, 1855.

SOUP.
French White.

FISH.
Boiled Mackinaw, White Fish—Anchovy sauce.

BOILED DISHES.	ROAST DISHES.
Corned Beef and Cabbage,	Sirloin of Beef,
Leg of Mutton, Turnip Sauce,	Loin of Mutton,
Beef's Tongue,	Rib of Beef,
Pig's Jole, with Cabbage,	Spring Lamb,
Turkeys, with stuet sauce.	Spare Rib of Pork, with Apple sauce-
	Young Pig—stuffed
	Turkeys, Liver sauce

Cold Pressed Corned Beef, spiced.

GAME.
Rabbits Roasted

SIDE DISHES.
Haricot of Turkeys Wings garnished with Vegetables—ancient style
Giblet Pie—according to Gunter.
Beef Kidneys, stewed with champaigne sauce, John Bull fashion.
Mutton Chops, broiled—with Mushroom catsup for sauce.
Tenderloin of Beef, with sauce a la Meurice, and potatoe border.
Spring Chickens fricasseed, with salt pork, and garnishrd with Rice.
Turkeys' Livers, with salt pork, breaded and broiled, sauce Marsellaise
Forms of Maccaroni, with cheese. a la Hippolita.
Rabbits broiled on Toast.
Vermicelli Cake baked, flavored with lemon sand smothered in sugar

RELISHES.

Pickled Beets,	Pickled Cucumbers,	Pickles,	Cold Slaugh,

VEGETABLES.

New Potatoes,	Rice with Cream,	Onions,
Hot Slaugh,	Boiled Cabbage,	Potatoes Mashed,
Potatoe Balls Baked,	Boiled Rice,	Turnips Mashed,
Onions browned whole,		Beets sliced and stewed,
Carrots,	Summer Squash.	Parsnips browned.

PASTRY AND PUDDINGS.

English Plum Pudding, Brandy sauce,	Variety Pie.
	Bird's Nest Pudding, Cold sauce.
Peach Pie.	Green Apple Pie.
Mince Pie.	Apple Pie.
Yankee Squash Pie,	Pumpkin Pie,	Frosted Pie.

DESSERT

Ginger Snaps,	Ladies' Kisses	Vanities,
Plain Cake,	Follies,	Jelly Cake	Sponge Cake,
Queen Cakes,	Almonds,	Raisins.
	Apples,	Fruit.

Jamaica rum jelly, Maderia Wine jelly, Rose jelly, Port wine jelly

NOTICE
Gentlemen having friends to dine, will please give notice at the Office.
Meals, Lunches, or Fruit sent to rooms, or carried from the table by guests, will be charged extra.
Children occupying seats at the first table, will be charged full price.
Waiters are furnished with Wine cards and pencils.

HOURS FOR MEALS—by Office Time.
Breakfast from 7½ to 9 o'clk – Dinner at 1 o'clk—Tea from 6 to 8.

SUNDAYS.
Breakfast from 8 to 10 o'clk—Dinner at 1½ o'clk—Tea from 6 to 8

Argus & Democrat print, Madison.

WINES.

SHERRY.

Queen Victoria	2 00
Yriarte	3 00
Pale Delicate	2 00
Harmony	2 00
Amontillado	2 00
Golden, 1845	2 50
Brown	2 00
Imperial Pale	2 50
Old Brown, Duff Gordon & Co.	3 00

CLARET

St. Julien Este	1 00
La Rose	1 00
Leoville	1 00
St. Emelien	1 00
St. Julien Medoc	1 50
Chateau Margaux	2 50

BRANDY

United Vineyard Proprietors	2 00
Martell	2 00
Old London Dock	2 50
Old Hennessey	2 00
Page & Sons London Particular	2 00
Thomas Hines & Co.	2 00
Otard, Dupuy & Co.	2 00
Pints of the above	1 25
Q, very old and fine	3 00
Corneau's Catawba	2 00

PORTER.

London Brown Stout, quarts	0 75
Do. do. pints	0 40
Byas do.	
Guinness do.	

SCOTCH ALE.

Younger s, quarts	0 75
Do. pints	0 40
Reynold's	
Byron's	

CAPITAL HOUSE,

NELSON & RUSSELL.

Breakfast Bill of Fare.

BEVERAGES.

Coffee,	Chocolate,	Black Tea,	Green Tea,

COLD

Ham,	Roast Beef,	Corned Beef,	Roast Pork.

BROILED. / FRIED.

BROILED.		FRIED.	
Beef Steak,	Mutton Chops,	Calf's Liver with Salt Pork,	
Pork Steak,	Ham,	Mush,	Ham,
Veal Cutlets,	Chickens, Tripe,	Sausages,	Kidneys.

HASH.

Meat Hash,	Stewed,	Beef's Kidney.

FISH.

Broiled Mackerel	Minced Fish,	Pickerel,
Codfish Balls,	Lake Trout,	Pike.

EGGS.

Omeletes,	Fried,	Boiled,	Poached,	Scrambled.

PIGS' FEET. / FRICASEE CHICKENS.

POTATOES.

Fried,	Stewed,	Mashed,	Baked,	Hashed.

BREAD.

Hot Corn Bread	Graham Rolls,	Boston Crackers	Dry Toast.
Hot Wheat Rolls	Graham Bread,	Soda Crackers	Milk Toast,
Brown Bread,	Wheat Bread,	Griddle Cakes,	Butter Toast.

HOURS FOR MEALS.
(BY OFFICE TIME.)

BREAKFAST.	DINNER	TEA.
From 7 to 9 o'clock,	At 1 o'clock	At 6 o'clock
Sunday, 8 to 10 o'clock,	Sunday, 1 o'clock,	Sunday, 6 o'clock

Children occupying seats at the first Table, will be charged full price.
Meals or lunches carried to rooms will be charged extra.

Argus & Democrat print, Madison, Wisconsin.

FIGURE 2.18. CAPITAL HOUSE MENU. These menus were placed before guests dining at the Capital House Hotel on Sunday, December 2, 1855. With the exception of rabbit, all the meat was domestic, thereby coming closer to the coveted "Eastern" adjective. Cheaper hotels and many common folk, however, depended heavily upon wild game for their larder, especially ducks, pheasants, rabbits, deer, quail, and fish. In the colder months deer were brought into Madison by the sleigh load, frozen stiff "in their natural vestments" sans entrails, and sold for four to six cents per pound. (SHSW WHi(X3)34307 and WHi(X3)38332)

Two Irish actors trained on the stages of London and Broadway, Messrs. Langerishe and Atwater, booked about twenty-seven plays each year during the twelve-week season always designed to coincide with the legislative session. Their effort developed a strong constituency for serious theater. The popular duo also organized a very capable amateur repertory company.[51]

All these leisure-time activities were viewed as a fine thing by almost everyone except the sober Yankee, to whom leisure was suspect if not used for moral uplift and spiritual enlightenment. Yankee opinion makers therefore reserved the highest marks for the lecture. "Our young men," explained the *Wisconsin State Journal* in a typical laudatory editorial, "are prone to go somewhere—the confinement of their business pursuits during the day, unfix them for sitting in quiet study when evening comes—and they sally out for amusement. Places of temptation to evil meet them at every corner, and they are very liable to be led astray."[52] Lectures by contrast "would have a tendency to draw them away from these tempting places, will be the means of directing their attention to literary pursuits and they may thereby save a young person from ruin and start him successfully on the road to honor and fame."[53]

A New Charter

Soon after the Village of Madison charter was enacted in 1846, its shortcomings became evident. One of its most serious limitations was a ceiling on property tax rates of five dollars per thousand dollars of assessed value. (Today's tax rates by contrast hover around twenty dollars per one thousand dollars of assessed value.) Even if all other revenue sources such as liquor licenses, fines, special assessments and even private subscriptions had been used to the maximum possible extent, the yield could not have begun to pay for fire engines, school houses, a new cemetery,

roads, sidewalks, and all the other expensive needs of the rapidly growing village. Clearly the village needed the power to levy higher taxes upon its citizens.[1]

A second problem stemming from the village charter was a series of jurisdictional disputes. For example, both the Town of Madison and the Village of Madison claimed the exclusive right to levy and collect liquor license fees within village boundaries. The disagreement was significant because liquor taxes were one of the largest sources of village revenue. Until the matter was resolved, tavern owners tended to get their licenses from the government offering the lower rate.[2]

A third problem was a series of tax and representational inequities. The Village of Madison generated eighty-four percent of all Town of Madison revenues, but got only twenty percent back from the town for projects within the village. Representation on the county board under the village system was also grossly unfair. Madison with a population in early 1853 of thirty-five hundred persons had the same number of representatives on the county board as a town with seventy-five people.[3]

To correct these and many similar problems village authorities had to request the legislature to make changes nearly every year to the charter. By 1852 the size of the amendment section nearly exceeded the original charter.

Village leaders concluded that the only way to surmount these problems was to request a *city* charter, which by definition and usage would dramatically increase the taxing, borrowing and general powers of local government officials. An effort to secure a city charter was begun in 1852 but came to naught.[4] Not until January 1856 was another concerted effort made and this time it was led by village trustee and former Governor Farwell. With the backing of a citizen petition he persuaded the village board to draw up a new charter and submit it to the legislature for approval. The board moved quickly on the matter and so did the legislature. The governor signed the bill into law on March 7, 1856.[5]

The forty-eight page document officially went into effect on April 7, 1856, when the first mayor and twelve aldermen (three from each of its four new wards) met at 10:00 A.M. in the county courthouse to organize the new government. The new charter overcame the structural and financial problems of the village period and gave city officials the power they needed to govern the then very rapidly growing city. Thus the question became: how would the new city officials use these greatly increased powers?

3 Prosperity, Depression, and War: 1857 to 1865

Great Western Expectations

Swaggering Western Optimism

"We commence our city under most favorable circumstances," said Mayor Jairus C. Fairchild in his inaugural address to the first common council on April 7, 1856. "Our growth has been most extraordinary; our population doubling in period of short duration. We can fix no limit to our growth and we challenge the world to produce a location for a city whose position embraces so many practical advantages. . . ."[1]

One year later Fairchild's successor, A. A. Bird, expressed even more unbounded confidence in Madison's future. "In 1850," Bird began,

> "the population of Madison stood at 1500. At the present time we number about 12,000 souls, an increase unparalleled even in the history of other inland Western towns. When I look back six or eight years and see the collection of wooden tenements called Madison, and compare it with the Madison of today, I almost doubt the reality. . . . No town of the western world can boast of having better buildings than Madison." Suffice it to say that Madison will be the greatest centering and diverging point for Railways in the West. . . . These roads will develop the trade and manufactures of Madison to an inconceivable extent, enhancing the value of real estate. Travelers to and from all parts of the globe will make their calculations to stop at Madison a few days to rest and refresh themselves, recruit their tired and

weary frames preparatory to resuming their journey to any portion of the world. Such are our railroad advantages. When all the roads are completed and in successful operation . . . we can form an adequate conception of the immense trade, traffic and travel which must necessarily center at Madison; and I am not setting the figures too high when I say that the population of Madison in 1860 will be 25,000 souls."[2]

Local newspapers of the period echoed this untrammeled optimism. One frequently reprinted article gave no less than seventeen reasons to expect Madison's population to be between thirty and forty thousand by 1866, just ten years away. Another considered a ten percent annual growth rate "very low" for a Western city.[3]

Then, turning to the more conservative members of the community, Bird added, "Perhaps there are some who are so bound down by old fogyism as to object to the rapid strides which our city is making toward opulence and power reiterating the old eternal bugbear taxes. To those persons I would say that as the taxes raised for the erection of public structures increase, so does the valuation of their real and personal property increase in the same ratio. Be warned gents," the ebullient Bird concluded, "he who attempts to dog the wheel of young America is sure to be run over."[4]

Flexing New Fiscal Muscles

The One-Hundred-Thousand-Dollar Bond Issue

If contemporary accounts are any indication, few attempted to dog the wheels of Madison progress. Certainly not the Common Council. Like the first two mayors, early aldermen took great delight in the prospect of quickly creating a city replete with luxuries and conveniences that took older eastern communities generations to develop. Like the mayor, they viewed themselves as "Western men endowed with Western energy and enterprise and understanding."[5] To them the rapid pace of Madison's progress was not a source of anxiety, but rather a source of genuine exhilaration.

Just days after the charter went into effect, the Common Council directed the Finance Committee to estimate the "probable wants" of the community and prepare the first budget. The need for fire-fighting equipment, for example, could hardly have been more compelling. The inventory of fire equipment bequeathed to the City of Madison by the village consisted of one ladder wagon, one eighteen-foot ladder and eleven leather buckets—not exactly adequate for protecting two million dollars worth of property.[6] The need for school houses also seemed beyond dispute. There were over sixteen hundred school age children in Madison, only three hundred of which could be crammed into grossly inadequate facilities.[7] Then,

FIGURE 3.1. STATE STREET, 1858. This delightful panorama appeared in the November 20, 1858, issue of a popular nationally distributed weekly publication, *Frank Leslie's Illustrated Newspaper*. Framed by North and South halls on University Hill, is State Street, then sparsely developed. (SHSW WHi(X31)17434)

too, there were some things that, although not essentials in the strict sense, were perceived as needed to achieve respect and status. For example, Mayor Fairchild had forcefully argued in his inaugural address that "no city can be complete without some convenient and capacious hall for public use."[8] The list of "needs" was long and expensive.

In addition to recommending $36,000 for the first year's operating expenses, the Finance Committee suggested the following permanent improvements: four school houses ($16,000); two fire stations, two fire engines, and a network of public cisterns ($7,000); one cemetery ($5,000); one city hospital ($7,000); one city hall ($25,000); and two wood weighing scales ($1,000). Then, without the

least hesitation, the committee recommended that the city issue $100,000 in bonds to cover these costs.[9] To some, this amount was an extraordinarily large amount of money for a community whose elected leaders just one year earlier had refused to go in debt $10,000 to build schoolhouses because it was felt this was a larger debt than Madison should incur.[10] But that was during the village decade before elected officials became caught up in the feeling of great power and wealth of western cities.

Local papers were quick to applaud the Finance Committee for the "great care" and "sound common sense" embodied in its recommendations.[11] The fact that the Finance Committee was chaired by conservative bank president Napoleon Bonaparte Van Slyke added great credence to its

work. Because the property tax base and population were rapidly rising, Van Slyke felt that the loan could be paid off easily and that Madison would avoid the tendency among "young and ambitious cities" to make "extravagant expenditures."[12]

Two weeks after hearing the one-hundred-thousand-dollar loan recommendation for the first time, the Council endorsed the measure by a six-to-one vote.[13] The loan was at once an expression of unbounded confidence in the future, a manifestation of the western desire to build a city in a day, and a reflection of pentup demands from the village era.

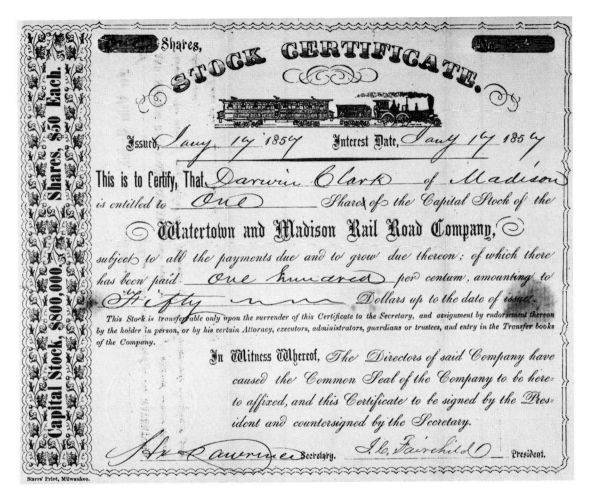

Consequently the road was completed from Milwaukee to Watertown, a distance of forty-three miles. Where to get the money for the remaining thirty-four miles into Madison was a serious problem facing the directors. Confronted with extremely tight money in the fall and spring of 1856, its directors hit upon an ingenious solution—namely, getting cities along the line to lend the railroad their credit. Under this scheme a city would issue bonds and make the proceeds available to the railroad. The railroad would then make regular payments of principal and interest until the bonds were paid off.[15]

Momentum behind the city railroad loan began in February 1856, when Madison newspapers reported that the City of Watertown had loaned its credit to the railroad in the amount of two hundred thousand dollars. This action put the pressure on Madison and other towns along the projected route to follow suit. The request was in full accord with the charter, which allowed the city to loan up to one hundred thousand dollars to each of three railroads.[16] Local newspapers immediately jumped on the bandwagon, urging Madison to follow Watertown's example and berated certain property owners called "croakers" who opposed the move.[17] Support for loaning the credit of the city to the railroad even became a campaign issue in the municipal election in March 1856, when at least one ward caucus vigorously discussed a proposition that would have denied nomination to any person opposing the railroad bond issue.[18]

Sometime in December 1856, Watertown and Madison railroad officials formally requested the city to loan its credit by issuing one hundred thousand dollars in city bonds. So eager were members of the Common Council to respond to this request, they dropped their regular agenda and held a special meeting.[19] One reason the city was eager to act was that the railroad was controlled by Madison men, many of whom were personally familiar to the aldermen. Mayor Jairus C. Fairchild, for example, was elected president of the line at the stockholder's meeting in November. Other directors included former

FIGURE 3.2. RAILROAD BOND. Bonds for the ill-fated Watertown and Madison Railroad were issued on these certificates and signed by the railroad president and mayor of Madison, Jairus C. Fairchild. (SHSW WHi(X3)34545)

The One-Hundred-Thousand-Dollar Railroad Loan

Buoyed by the continuing economic and population boom, the City of Madison went another one hundred thousand dollars into debt in January 1857. This time the objective was to secure a second railroad for Madison, the Watertown and Madison Railway. From the time the Milwaukee and Mississippi Railroad was completed into Madison in 1854, users had been increasingly unhappy with the fares charged and treatment they received. By 1856 the M&M was widely considered a "soulless monopoly" to whom tribute had been paid for too long.[14] The Watertown & Madison Railroad promised shippers relief through competitive rates, but—as in so many early railroads—its original promoters had underestimated its initial capital requirements.

Governor Leonard Farwell, B. F. Hopkins, head of the Madison Gas and Light Company, Nathaniel W. Dean, and H. K. Lawrence.[20] "The directors of the line," said the *Daily Patriot,* "are sound to the core—thorough going businessmen, perfectly reliable in all things. . . ."[21]

Immediately after the council approved a referendum on January 12, 1857, the drum beating began. The line was expected to reduce freight and passenger bills by twenty-five thousand dollars per month, advance property value "no less than 50 percent," shorten the distance to Milwaukee by twenty miles and cut the cost of living in Madison.[22] The people apparently needed little convincing. Two-thirds of all eligible voters turned out at the special election and ninety-eight percent of all voters approved the measure.[23]

The rest was routine. An ordinance was passed authorizing the railroad to use East Mifflin Street coming into town from the Catfish River to Patterson Street, whereupon it was to cut south to Blair and along the lakeshore to link up with the Milwaukee and Mississippi at Murray Street.[24] A huge champagne banquet for railroad officials was given by the mayor and Common Council to celebrate the new city-railroad partnership.[25] No one seemed to mind that the president of the line was also the mayor of Madison. Many felt this was the kind of partnership required for progress. Soon after the banquet Mayor Fairchild, Leonard Farwell, and another Madison man went to New York to convert the city bonds into cash and came back "eminently successful."[26]

At the same time the drum beaters were whipping up enthusiasm for loaning the city's credit, railroad promoters were raising additional construction money from city businessmen using a clever mortgage technique. Under this scheme a landowner bought a fully paid share of Watertown and Madison stock with a dividend rate of ten percent. To secure the purchase the landowner gave the railroad a ten-year personal note at eight percent secured by a mortgage on his land. These personal notes were then used as security for an eight percent bond, which the railroad sold to investors. The genius of the system

was that the landowner had no cash outlay and a "sure" gain of two percent. The *Daily Patriot,* for example, said the Watertown and Madison Railroad "like all Western roads, . . . must be a handsomely paying stock."[27] The kicker was that if the company defaulted on its payment of principal or interest, the bondholder could foreclose on the land. That prospect, however, seemed extremely unlikely to most observers.[28]

Promoters of the mortgage scheme included some of the most prominent people in town. Years later, a Westport girl recalled that the editor of one of the Madison newspapers, probably the *Patriot,* visited her farmhome in his carriage to persuade her father to buy Watertown and Madison Railroad stock.[29] Lucius Fairchild, son the mayor, future war hero and three-term governor, also took to the hustings to persuade farmers along the proposed route to convert farm equities to railroad stock.[30] Prominent city business people generously contributed mortgages totalling ninety thousand dollars. Farwell alone gave a twenty-five-thousand-dollar mortgage.[31]

In these ways the City of Madison and Madison business people raised over one hundred ninety thousand dollars for the completion of the Watertown and Madison Road. On May 2, 1857, the railroad contractor began work at the Madison end of the line.

The Fifty-Thousand-Dollar Capitol Loan

Two months after approving the one-hundred-thousand-dollar loan to the Watertown and Madison Railroad, Madison once again demonstrated its western liberality. The object of its third major bond issue in just ten months, this time for fifty thousand dollars, was to help pay for a much-needed enlargement of the capitol and thus assure its continuation in Madison. The bond issue was prompted by Governor Coles Bashford's January 15, 1857 message to the legislature in which he expressed concern about the absence of fireproof storage facilities in the capitol for valuable state records. The governor suggested the problem could be corrected in one of

two ways: either the capitol could be enlarged at the present site or a new capitol could be built somewhere else.[32] The words sent a cold chill down the spines of Madison legislators and property owners. The threat was immediate and real. Not only did the old 1837 capitol have inadequate fireproof storage facilities, but it was widely recognized as "too crowded for convenience" and architecturally unimpressive—certainly less grand than a rapidly growing and proud young state ought to have. Not since 1848, when the legislature agreed to convert Madison from territorial to state capital, had the future of the greatest of all state plums been in such jeopardy.

Madison leaders and legislators moved quickly to keep the capitol in Madison. Fortunately, H. A. Tenney, a prominent Madison businessman, was chairman of the Assembly Committee on State Affairs to whom the matter was referred. Still, Tenney and other Madison supporters had a tough job. Although they could muster good arguments on why the capital ought to remain in Madison, they recognized that some kind of scheme with an obvious and compelling financial incentive would be required—something that would require a minimum of state taxation. Two weeks after the governor's message, Tenney's committee unanimously reported out a bill calling for a huge new one-hundred-thousand-dollar wing on the capitol—but costing the state just twenty-five thousand in actual cash. ". . . The Committee," reported a proud Tenney, "had met with the most liberal spirit by the citizens and Common Council of the City of Madison."[33] The city, he explained, was willing to give the state fifty thousand dollars in city bonds as an outright grant if approved by a referendum. Another twelve to twenty thousand dollars could be realized by selling ten sections of land given to the state by the federal government, the proceeds of which were to be used for the "completion of public buildings."[34] Thus, the only direct appropriation the state needed to make was an estimated twenty-five thousand dollars. This was an offer the state could hardly refuse. Both the senate and assembly quickly passed the bill by overwhelming margins.[35]

FIGURE 3.3. CITY HALL. When City Hall was first opened
in the spring of 1858, Mayor Smith no doubt spoke for
most Madisonians when he said "we (now) have an edifice which is an ornament to the city . . . and an object
of public pride." At the grand opening newspapers paid
particular attention to the "spacious and splendid" third
floor auditorium capable of seating nine hundred persons. Over one hundred feet long and fifty feet wide, the
room featured twenty-four-foot-high ceilings, huge windows with over four hundred panes of glass, one hundred
fifty gas burners, and two large twelve-burner chandeliers for illumination. This photograph, taken in the 1890s
after utility lines had been strung, best reveals the building's interesting architecture. The building stood at the
intersection of Mifflin Street and Wisconsin Avenue, just
opposite the former Manchester store.

Although an ornament and object of pride, the building was not without its problems. The building was supposed to have cost $22,300 but actually cost $40,117,
an eighty percent cost overrun. Softening this overrun
somewhat was the fact that contractors and their men
got paid in a form of city script, which effectively discounted their remuneration by twenty-five percent. Three
months after the building was completed, it had to be
mortgaged to its full value to provide collateral for $50,000
in bonds used to aid in the capitol enlargement. Worst
of all, the city found it could not afford to use the office
space expressly designed for its use. Therefore, it rented
the space to the state.

The effects of the depression-emptied coffers were
evident just one year after the building opened. When
two hundred persons gathered in the great hall for a theatrical performance on a cold evening in October 1859,
they found the hall woefully neglected. Dust reportedly a
quarter of an inch deep (doubtless an exaggeration)
covered the seats, none of the stoves had any fire in
them, and the cold was streaming into the room through
several broken windows. Then some structural problems
appeared and serious leaks plagued the building for
years, causing some of the roof timbers to rot. During
the Civil War the great hall was used by soldier companies for drill practices, and the shaking caused by the
marching men caused the plaster to fall off the ceiling of
the floor below.

Then, too, from the year of its opening through the
Civil War, few years went by without the building being
everywhere embellished by obscenities. If the building
were preserved in its present form, said one writer in
1860, and "some searcher of antiquarian novelties should
chance to hit on that building, surely . . . Madisonians
would be thought to be very vulgar . . ." he concluded.
(SHSW WHi(X3)29954)

Two days after the bill was signed into law the
Madison Common Council suspended its rules,
read the bill three times, and unanimously agreed
to hold a referendum on 14 March.[36] On that date
property owners voted 266 to 1 to approve the
$50,000 bond issue.[37] With just one exception
property owners saw the intimate connection between property values and keeping the capital in
Madison.[38]

Governor Bashford quickly hired Madison architects August Kutzbock and Samuel Donnell
to design the "enlargement", and construction got
underway in July 1857.[39] Madison leaders congratulated themselves for their "business tact"[40]
and the legislature for its "sound judgment."[41]
Once again the capital location seemed secure.

FIGURE 3.4. PINCKNEY STREET, 1859. This 1859 daguerreotype looking north on Pinckney Street shows two problems prevalent in Madison during this period. On busy days farmers had a hard time finding a space to hitch their wagons. The problem was exacerbated by men with wagons and carriages for hire who monopolized long stretches of choice curb space in front of the busiest stores. Finally in 1860, in response to merchant and shopper complaints, an ordinance was passed requiring persons with hacks and wagons for hire to park in more out-of-the-way places. This was among the first of a long series of ordinances designed to make downtown shopping more convenient.

The other problem was street litter. As evident in the lower right-hand corner, the public streets were commonly viewed as dumping grounds.

The block face on the right of the photograph is now occupied by the First Wisconsin Plaza. The large building at the corner of East Washington and Pinckney, known as the Bruen Block, is illustrated in fig. 2.14. Visible in the distance at the right end of Pinckney Street, on what is now called "Mansion Hill," is the 1857 towered Italianate mansion that is now a Madison landmark known as the Bashford House. (SHSW WHi(X3)2595)

The Ten-Thousand-Dollar
Cemetery Bond Issue

Still another big ticket item that Madison's first Common Council felt obligated to purchase for posterity was a cemetery. Back in 1846, soon after Madison became incorporated as a village, the village trustees after much controversy acquired the city block where Orton Park is presently located for the village cemetery. However, by the mid-1850s nearly all the cemetery lots at this site had been sold and most used. Consequently the search began for something more commodious. For a time during 1856 it appeared as if a private corporation known as The Wildwood Cemetery Company would secure an exclusive franchise for an eighty-acre east side tract centered around the present location of Elmside Boulevard.[42] When this private enterprise solution failed, the Common Council voted in early 1857 to buy a different eighty-acre tract on the west side now known as Forest Hills. In payment thereof the city issued ten thousand-dollar bonds in addition to the one-hundred-thousand-dollar bond issue.[43]

Two Hundred and Sixty Thousand
Dollars in Debt

Counting the $100,000 city loan, the $100,000 Madison and Watertown Railroad loan, the $50,000 capitol enlargement grant and the $10,000 cemetery loan, the City of Madison incurred a staggering debt load of $260,000 in just eleven months. Even more amazing, nobody seemed to care. Everybody seemed imbued with uncritical confidence in Madison's future and enamored by the bounteous, booming economy. However, the first crack in this beatific scene occurred when several "irregularities" suddenly erupted into a lip-pursing scandal.

Disillusionment, Depression, and Reform

The One-Hundred-Thousand-Dollar Loan Scandal

Beginning in late 1856 major local news stories were so peppered with references to "thieves," "swindlers," "plunderers," "rogues," and "scoundrels" that a casual reader might reasonably have assumed that the city was beseiged by an extraordinarily effective and elusive band of criminals. But the journalists were not describing garden variety masked bandits, petty thieves, or con artists. They were referring to several members of Madison's first Common Council Finance Committee. Although the epithets may seem harsh to the modern reader, they clearly revealed the intensity of contemporary newsmen's feelings about a loan scandal that erupted in late 1856 and colored city politics for a decade.[1]

The focal point of the controversy quickly became thirty-four-year-old Napoleon Bonaparte Van Slyke, a major stockholder and cashier of the Dane County Bank, a private bank that in 1863 became the First National Bank. Van Slyke had tried farming and manufacturing in New York before he came to Madison in 1853 and became a banker and a builder of fancy residences. After being elected alderman from the Second Ward, the ambitious Van Slyke played a large and dominant role in city affairs.[2] Because of his banking experience he was elected chairman of the Finance Committee that made the initial recommendation to secure the one-hundred-thousand-dollar city loan. In addition, in May of 1856 he was appointed chairman and special agent of the loan commissioners, to whom the council had delegated broad responsibility for negotiating and selling the bonds "to the best of his ability taking such measures and incurring such reasonable expenses as his discretion might deem expedient. . . ."[3] In addition to his job as special bond agent for the city, the council gave Van Slyke authority to buy two fire engines. Consequently Van

Slyke spent three months at city expense traveling around the East in the spring and early summer of 1856 shopping for fire engines and selling bonds.

In his report to the council on August 20, 1856, Van Slyke reported that he was able to net only $78,731 from the sale of the $100,000 bonds and that, although this amount fell short of what he had hoped to get, it was the best he could do.[4] Most of the bonds, he explained, had been sold for eighty cents on the dollar because the city's credit was not yet established. Then there were expenses attendant to selling the bonds, such as commissions, legal opinions, and travel expenses.[5] Van Slyke's report was more than disappointing; to many it was downright disconcerting. The more city leaders thought about it, the more irregular and illogical it seemed. On 5 September, several aldermen introduced a resolution calling for a complete investigation. Their major question was, "If we only netted $79,000 out of $100,000, what happened to the other $21,000?"[6]

The soothing majority report of the investigating committee said the entire matter had been "well and honorably transacted and as economically as was possible under the circumstances. . . ." The incendiary minority report, by contrast, said the entire matter was handled in a manner "most unbusinesslike and improper" and was "in fact wholly unwarrantable and illegal. . . ."[7]

The minority report levelled six charges against Van Slyke:

First, that Van Slyke had tried to conceal his "exorbitant" twenty-five-hundred-dollar commission for negotiating the loan by claiming only one thousand dollars in cash. The balance was to be paid by allowing Van Slyke to put the loan proceeds in his bank so he could loan it out at interest.

Second, that the loan commissioners had no authority to pay Van Slyke a penny because any fee would had to have been authorized by the council and signed by the mayor.

Third, that the loan commissioners had no authority to put the money in the Dane County Bank at zero interest and that this action was illegal.

Fourth, that after putting the loan proceeds in his bank vault, Van Slyke got himself appointed chairman of a newly created special Building Committee giving him control over expenditures for the City Hall, ward schools, and other projects for which loan proceeds were earmarked. From this powerful vantage point Van Slyke allegedly refused to make timely payments to the contractors and deliberately thwarted efforts to finish the school buildings so that the money could stay in his bank longer and earn more interest.

Fifth, that Van Slyke had charged twenty-five hundred dollars for selling the bonds when, in fact, a bond firm in New York had done so for a commission of $777, but which was represented by Van Slyke as a "Discount"—a blatant case of "double dipping" and willful misrepresentation.[8]

The minority report charges, although devastating, were just the beginning of many additional charges that quickly followed. The *Daily Patriot* suggested that Van Slyke had used the proceeds from the city to underwrite a new bank venture in Stevens Point.[9] Under loose banking laws at the time, it was possible to start a bank and withdraw initial capital once the bank got started. Since Van Slyke had control of a large amount of city capital in his bank under his complete control, suspicions were naturally rampant that the shrewd financeer used city money to prime the pump of the new bank.

Van Slyke replied that the allegations made against him were "false in fact and malicious in design."[10] The thrust of Van Slyke's defense was that "everything he had done was done with the complete unanimity of the loan commissioners," that the council's acceptance of his report should be construed as council sanction, and that his actions were completely within his delegated authority.[11]

The *Argus and Democrat* and the *Wisconsin State Journal* generally supported Van Slyke, but the *Patriot* sustained a vigorous, almost vicious vendetta against Van Slyke. In response to the

Patriot's vituperation Van Slyke got a friendly local judge to slap a twenty-thousand-dollar libel judgment on that newspaper.[12]

Van Slyke's six month "trial" by newspaper provided great drama for readers during late 1856, pitting a shrewd "villain" against naive city officials. Or was it an honest businessman taking reasonable steps under difficult circumstances being pilloried by a vengeful editor? People were clearly polarized on Van Slyke's culpability. Some urged more businesslike, agreed-upon-in-advance methods of conducting city business, yet no one sought to implement such methods. After all, business was splendid and Madison was rapidly becoming a rich metropolis. In the minds of most Madisonians, the loan scandal quickly receded to an unfortunate but affordable episode in the life of a booming city. Significantly, Van Slyke's silk stocking constituency did not seem sufficiently concerned about their alderman's alleged malfeasance to turn him out of office. On the contrary, in April 1857, they gave him a strong vote of confidence in the form of a second aldermanic term.

The 1857–1860 Depression

1857: Great Expectations

"At no time within the recollection of our citizens have the merchants made such extensive arrangements as this spring for an increase of business," boasted the *Daily Patriot* in March, 1857.[13] ". . . With the absolute certainty of fast accessions to our population and an immense amount of building going on in every part of the city, our merchants will limit their purchases only by the dimensions of their stores and warehouses. We can see no reason why Madison should not have this season the most prosperous times known in our history," the editor concluded.[14] One month later that marvelous spring trade appeared as predicted, and the streets adjacent to the Capitol Park were described as "so thronged with teams from the country that it is difficult to pass through them."[15]

Madisonians remained unabashedly bullish about their future. The *Argus* published a plea for two thousand workmen so that ambitious public and private construction plans could proceed.[16] A journalist from a Buffalo, New York, newspaper said Madisonians, "like residents of any other western city or village, were all crazy about corner lot speculations."[17] Former Governor Leonard Farwell held spectacular parties for five-hundred guests in his splendidly furnished, nine-thousand-square-foot mansion on Spaight Street. Attending were not only only the "beauty and fashion of Madison,"[18] but also many distinguished guests from all over the state. Farwell's guests dined at tables loaded with everything an epicure could desire and danced until the wee hours of the morning.[19]

In May 1857, the building boom demolished Madison's premier landmark, the Peck Tavern Stand—the first log cabin, first hotel, first dance hall, and for a time the major building in the raw frontier village. Gone was this mute witness to a decade of stagnation, and then another decade of dizzy prosperity. Ironically, that same month the first acrid economic winds blew in from the East.[20]

Madison editors were faced by a dilemma. On the one hand they did not want to play the alarmist and "frighten everybody out of their commercial wits." On the other they did not want to "lull the business world into a fatal feeling of security when there *are* actual breakers ahead."[21] The editor of the *Daily Patriot* delivered a brief discourse on American economics to his readers. "It is among the peculiar characteristics of the American people to get up a panic at least once in five years and a commercial *crisis* as often as fifteen or twenty years. It is in fact a constitutional disease with mankind the world over wherever men live by commerce." Concluded the editor, "We think we can clearly see from the hundreds of exchanges we get daily, and from other sources, the rapid and certain approach of a financial whirlpool such as this country has never witnessed since the crash of '37."[22]

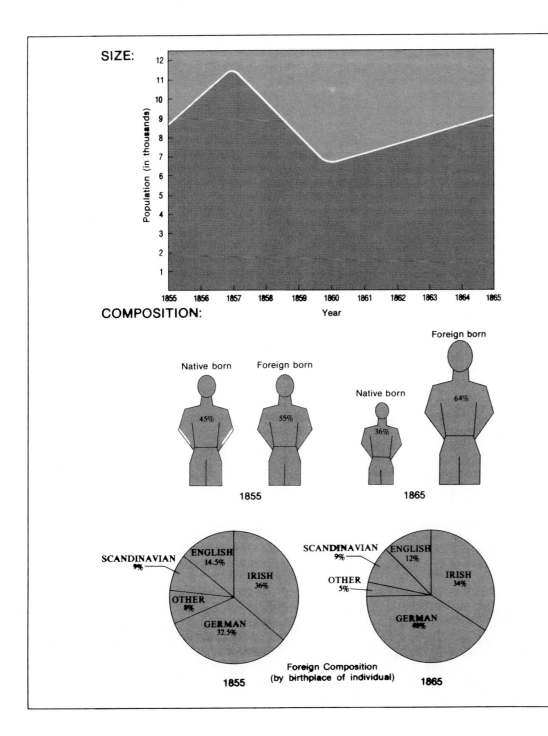

SIZE:

COMPOSITION:

Native born   Foreign born

Native born

Foreign born

45%   55%   36%   64%

1855   1865

SCANDINAVIAN 9%   ENGLISH 14.5%   IRISH 36%   OTHER 8%   GERMAN 32.5%

SCANDINAVIAN 9%   ENGLISH 12%   IRISH 34%   OTHER 5%   GERMAN 40%

Foreign Composition
(by birthplace of individual)

1855   1865

FIGURE 3.5. 1855–1865 DEMOGRAPHICS. Never in Madison's history did the population curve take on such roller coaster proportions as it did during the 1855 to 1865 decade. After an entire decade Madison's net gain was just four hundred persons. The number of Madisonians either born in a foreign country or born in the United States of foreign parents continued to increase relative to the native-born groups. Within the foreign population, the Germans displaced the Irish as the numerically dominant group.

Patriot editors argued that the crash was being precipitated by the "vast expansion of credit," especially for purposes of buying real estate.[23] "It is safe to say that nine-tenths of western capital is invested in non-producing real estate which, unless it rises in value rapidly, and finds a market, is a dead loss to the owner." It was with considerable frustration that the *Patriot* editor tried to get his readers to see that "some business must be respectable beside land agencies, and men must be contented to be more than six months acquiring a fortune."[24] Subsequent events in 1857 proved the editor entirely correct in his diagnosis.

By September of that year the newspapers carried lists of the "oldest and most responsible" banks in the East going under—banks whose portfolios were full of real estate notes.

That, as a result of the sharp loss of confidence in the economic future, were reduced to a tiny fraction of their original value. In a matter of days many Wisconsin banks succumbed to the same disease and a panic engulfed the state as speculators, hoping to salvage something, simultaneously dumped their properties on the market.[25] But the more they dumped, the lower prices fell.

In October, the *Wisconsin State Journal* jauntily predicted that "within six weeks . . . everybody will be out of their financial pinch . . . ,"[26] but this expression of confidence proved premature. In fact, ". . . the depression following the Panic of 1857 was to go deeper and last longer in Wisconsin than in most other states."[27]

In November 1857 a long legal notice quietly announced the financial demise of Madison's most prominent citizen, Leonard J. Farwell.[28] Like others heavily invested in Madison real estate, Farwell was unable to raise enough cash from the sale of his property to stave off creditors. The nearly overnight collapse of this very wealthy man sent a great shock wave through the community.[29]

Although the depression hit hardest those who were making their fortunes by real estate speculation,[30] a great many Madison merchants were swept up in the financial revulsion as well.[31] Many other merchants avoided foreclosure only by the forebearance of their creditors. Brokers and auctioneers reaped a great harvest selling merchandise from bankrupt stores.[32] Many businesses adopted a strictly cash system but then found in the absence of cash that a barter system based upon wheat, oats, barley, corn, and other grains and produce had to be used.[33] A forty to fifty percent drop in the price of the 1857 wheat crop drastically reduced farmer buying power, on whose trade Madison merchants were heavily dependent.[34] Mr. J. E. Moseley, bookseller and stationer, said the period between 1857 to 1861 were the "hardest times Madison merchants ever saw."[35]

Nearly everybody had great difficulty paying taxes, and the newspapers were filled with legal notices announcing tax sales, bankruptcies, dissolutions, and other economic casualties. One formerly well-to-do-attorney sent a letter to the Common Council acknowledging his inability to pay his taxes and offered to do all the legal work for the city in exchange for remission of his taxes,[36] but the council denied the request.

Another casualty of the depression was the Madison and Watertown Railroad, which, assisted by a one-hundred-thousand-dollar city loan, had been completed only to Waterloo, Wisconsin, when the depression hit. Not until 1859 under the direction of its new owner, wealthy eastern capitalist Russell Sage, was the line completed to Sun Prairie.[37] Disappointment over the failure of this railroad to reach Madison was intensified by hatred for the Milwaukee and Mississippi Railroad. That feeling was so intense that many

Madisonians regularly took the stage coach to Sun Prairie, and rode the Madison and Watertown to Milwaukee, rather than patronize Madison's only railroad.[38]

As the stain of depression worked its way into the fabric of the Madison economy, hundreds of mechanics and day laborers were thrown out of work.[39] The ranks of the unemployed were swelled by men released by the Watertown and Madison Railroad.[40] As early as the summer of 1857, ward and city "poormasters" were appointed to distribute relief to those whose future was singularly unpromising.[41] Funds for their support came from the city license fund, the principal source of which were liquor licences.[42] Supplementing city efforts to fight poverty was the Ladies Benevolent Association, a group of "Samaritan ladies" who raised money and supplies by holding "calico balls" and "plain suppers."[43] Although most relied on public and private charity, a few still-employed Madison workers, notably the journeymen shoemakers, went on strike for higher wages and won a satisfactory agreement from their employers.[44]

Efforts made by the city to cut back its expenses were comprehensive, immediate, and impressive. Plans to construct six and one-half miles of wooden sidewalks were cancelled.[45] Street im7provements dropped from $17,237 in 1856 to a miniscule $1,184 in 1860.[46] City employee salaries were cut back a whopping sixty percent.[47] Assessed valuation of all personal and real property was reduced an average of twelve percent citywide. Even the police force was cut back, and one alderman urged that the city police force be abolished and temporary policemen be used if necessary.[48] Plans to build two ward schoolhouses were scrapped.[49]

As the depression deepened, additional steps were taken. The jobs of Chief of Police and the Superintendent of Streets were combined in 1860.[50] Lacking any tax money for street maintenance, the City of Madison worked out an arrangement with the Dane County jailer to have prisoners make repairs to the streets.[51] Because

street lights were relatively expensive and dispensable, all street lights except six in the main part of town were shut off in 1858.[52] In 1860 the council went a step further and shut off all the street lights except when the legislature was in session.[53] Even the Common Council cut back on its lawmaking activities, in one instance going nine months without passing a single ordinance.[54]

Of all the consequences of the 1857 depression, the great exodus of population was surely one of the most difficult to accept. In 1855 the state census showed Madison to have 8,664 persons, but the 1860 federal census counted only 6,611 persons, a reduction of twenty-four percent. But the decline in population was really greater than the census figures revealed because the city population did not peak until 1857 when it reached eleven thousand. Although there were no census figures for that year, other methods of calculating population suggest that Madison's population was somewhere between ten and twelve thousand persons.[55] Assuming a peak population of eleven thousand in early 1857, in just three years (1857–1860), Madison's population plummeted by a whopping forty percent. Two out of five persons left Madison—a massive expression of no confidence in its future. Not until 1883—twenty-five years later—did Madison's population reach 1857 levels again.

Taxpayer Revolt and Reform

> Whereas many citizens feel themselves aggrieved with the extravagant taxes levied upon the city, and the continual unjust appropriations being made from time to time, all who feel themselves thus aggrieved hereby will meet in the Courthouse, tomorrow, Saturday evening at 7 o'clock to see what can be done to remedy the evil.

This announcement appearing in the *Wisconsin State Journal* on December 19, 1857 was hardly unusual. Dozens of similar announcements had appeared at various times in Madison's twenty-year history to express indignation over high taxes, but seldom with any consequence. Typically politicians accepted these indignation meetings as a part of the job much like the common cold is a part of winter—a momentary discomfort requiring few changes in the conduct of life. This time, however, was different. Never had so many been united against such a well-defined problem and with such good reasons. New economic casualties of the 1857 depression were appearing in newspapers daily and already included Madison's most prominent and possibly wealthiest man, Leonard Farwell, hundreds of workmen, and dozens of businessmen. At the same time property values were plummeting, city expenditures were skyrocketing. Moreover, Madison taxpayers had just received word that their taxes for 1857 would be at least as high as those of the preceding year. The explanation was simple enough. The council had not kept track of how much money they were spending. Not only did they spend all the proceeds of the city loan and twenty thousand more generated by the tax levy, but they also spent twenty-five thousand beyond all this. It was this amount that had to be carried over into 1857. So many bad things were happening to Madison so quickly. So much needed to be done. The question was not how Madison got into its predicament, but rather how it could possibly get out.

After berating the extravagant, unscrupulous, reckless, rapacious, and dissolute manner in which city business had been conducted, the huge crowd passed a resolution saying that more money had been "lost, misapplied and squandered by the City Council in just 18 months than had ever been destroyed by fire, seized by burglars or abstracted by pickpockets in 20 years." A Committee of twenty was directed to prepare written recommendations on how the citizens could prevent "being further plunderd by city officials," to see what could possibly be done to pay off the two-hundred-fifty-thousand-dollar public debt and whether the taxes had been illegally levied.[56]

Just eight days later the Committee of Twenty issued a tightly argued and devastating portrait of abuses.[57]

1. That city records had been so badly kept that it was impossible to precisely determine what was spent for what purpose and by whom.[58]
2. That charter prohibitions against aldermen receiving pay for performing city duties were widely and willfully ignored.[59]
3. That aldermen voted to give themselves city contracts inside of gross conflicts of interest.[60]
4. That numerous street and sidewalk improvements were made whose primary value was to enhance the value of private property, often belonging to council members.
5. That property in the various wards was assessed at different rates and that some property was grossly underassessed.[61]
6. That aldermen received kickbacks on land sold to the city.
7. That the prudent expenditure of half as much money as the council actually spent could have produced the same results. (One wonders how much additional street work might have been done if something as simple as a low bidder requirement had been in effect.)
8. That the Common Council president when the mayor was out of town signed into law legislation that had been vetoed by the mayor.

Unlike nearly all earlier taxpayer indignation meetings, the December 1857 meeting produced significant reforms—and quickly. On February 8, 1858, barely more than one month after the scathing indictment by the Committee of Twenty was first released, Governor Randall signed into law a chapter amendment designed to remedy the recently identified abuses.[62] The bill bristled with prohibitions, onerous state mandates, and fines for noncompliance. More specifically the new charter: prohibited any situation where an alderman either directly or indirectly might receive any compensation of benefit arising from aldermanic service and inflicted a fine of up to one hundred dollars or one hundred days in jail for violators;

replaced the friendly ward assessor system with a single citywide assessor who could be more objective about property values across ward lines; established a citywide Superintendent of Streets who was to perform nearly all work previously done by the senior aldermen (street commissioners)[63]; and placed a limit of eight thousand dollars on what the city could levy for general city purposes such as fire, police, streets, and lighting. The bill also put an annual ceiling of six thousand dollars for school operational costs plus four thousand dollars for each ward school house. Very importantly, the amendment placed no limit on how much interest the city could pay on its debt, but did require the city to use every penny of rent taken in from the City Hall to be used for debt service. The city was prohobited from any additional borrowing it could not repay using the eight-thousand-dollar annual fund. Since this was barely adequate for operating expenses, it was assumed that the city could not go on any new spending sprees.

There is no question that the charter amendment was a heavy-handed unilateral top-down action, but the likelihood of those reforms being imposed by the city seemed very remote.[64] Mayor Bird complained that the eight-thousand-dollar levy limit for general city purposes would barely be enough to pay annual operating costs and would be insufficient to make any capital improvements. But that of course was exactly what the framers of the amendment had in mind.[65]

It is easy for the modern reader to underestimate the intensity of people's feelings about these early abuses—abuses that were greatly curtailed but hardly stopped by the 1858 charter amendments—but it would be a mistake to do so. Like Watergate in the early 1970s, these abuses became a common frame of reference and a staple in local political campaigns for years. Even in 1861, three years after the charter amendment had been placed in effect, Mayor Levi P. Vilas could refer in his inaugural address to the fact that "the people have been swindled so often, and so much by those elected to fill official positions

. . . that it is not surprising that taxes have become odious, and that some are beginning to look at government as a means by which a few can rob the many. . . ."[66] This reform-minded mayor's sense of indignation was so great that he recommended that the incoming council launch an investigation seeking restitution of old monies aldermen had illegally received primarily between 1856 and 1858, but also up to 1862 if necessary.[67] Based upon contemporary responses to these points, it seems clear that Vilas had struck a very popular note.

Settling the Bonded Debtedness,
1857 to 1864

Of all the difficult problems Madison faced after the onset of the depression, none was more exasperating and seemingly intractable than how to pay off the two hundred sixty thousand dollars in bonded indebtedness. Mayor George B. Smith in his 1858 inaugural correctly recognized that the first step of an enduring solution was to establish a constructive atmosphere in which the incredibly difficult problem could be handled. He insisted that it was useless "to indulge in regrets for the past or recrimination of those who were merely the agents for the people incurring those large expenditures."[68] The Finance Committee, still headed by N. B. Van Slyke, was quick to concur with the magnanimous mayor. Referring to the one-hundred-thousand-dollar city loan, it reminded Madisonians that "no act of the Council was ever so highly approved—so emphatically endorsed—and no vote has proved so extremely unfortunate and unprofitable."[69] The mayor and the Finance Committee were also united in their opposition to any notion of repudiating the bonds—a practice so commonplace around the state during this period that among eastern financial circles "Wisconsin" became a term almost synonymous with dishonor and moral turpitude.[70]

Mayor Smith quickly moved from soothing words to constructive action when he secured council approval to appoint a Committee of Three to investigate the financial affairs of the city from the first meeting of the Common Council. Unfortunately the committee's report issued four months later was only able to report that the city books had been so "unsystematically and improperly kept" that a precise determination of Madison's financial situation was impossible. Still, this report was the most rigorous accounting of city finances ever done. If the path to the present was unclear, at least everyone had a better idea of where they stood than ever before. Even more disappointing was the committee's failure to provide a hoped-for handrail out of the morass. At least the committee was candid when it threw up its hands saying the solution "was beyond their knowledge and comprehension."[71]

Meanwhile two developments further complicated the already difficult situation. Bondholders began filing lawsuits against the city, and seven of the city's largest property taxpayers began legal proceedings that allowed them to withhold payment of all property taxes until the court had ruled on their case.[72] Together they controlled about twenty-five percent of city property.[73] In addition to the large property taxpayers who were legally withholding their taxes pending the court action, there were a very large number of delinquent properties on the tax rolls owned in nearly all cases by persons who simply couldn't pay. The effect of these two types of "withholdings" was to place an extremely heavy and unfair burden upon remaining taxpayers.

Charges levelled by the big property taxpayers were both serious and numerous. Clearly the most disconcerting were that the one hundred thousand dollars in city and cemetery bonds had been improperly and illegally issued and were therefore invalid.[74] In April 1859, Dane County Circuit Judge Hood upheld the contention of Simeon Mills, one of the seven plaintiffs, and thereby put a serious cloud over the legal status of the one-hundred-thousand-dollar city bonds.[75]

City leaders found themselves in a classic lose-lose dilemma. If they failed to pay interest on the city bonds, the bondholders would sue the city; if the city tried to collect taxes from taxpayers to pay the bondholders, the taxpayers could sue the city.

Judge Hood recognized the seriousness of the dilemma and commended the case to the Wisconsin Supreme Court, which did not rule until fifteen months later. At that time the high court reversed the Dane County Circuit Court, saying that the city had recognized the bonds by paying interest on them and that the gentlemen whose taxes had heretofore been enjoined by the court action had to pay up.[76] Meanwhile, for two years the city had been unable to assess taxes for payment of interest and principal on city bonds pending the resolution of litigation, and so many lawsuits were coming in from irate bondholders that the city attorney had to do a special study so the aldermen could keep track of them all.[77]

Immediately after the Supreme Court decision upholding the legality of all bonds, The mayor charged the Finance Committee with the tough but imperative job of formulating detailed plans to resolve the bonded indebtedness problem. In December 1860 the Finance Committee issued one of the most candid, incisive, and persuasive reports ever prepared by a Madison public body. Using incontrovertible facts and syllogistic reasoning, its authors sought to win concessions from eastern bondholders.

Briefly, the committee's report stated: "The Truth is as a city, we have been swindled and robbed and the state prison for life would be none too good for the men who have done this." It pointed out, "We are bankrupt for the present, bankrupt for the future, bankrupt forever, unless we can effect a reasonable compromise." The property values shown on tax rolls were terribly inflated, a holdover the committee said from the "wild speculative prices of 1857." To meet general city expenses a thirty-mill tax rate would be necessary, and fifty mills if interest and principal on debt were to be met. Since half of Madison real estate consisted of vacant, unproductive land,

John Muir: The Madison Years
1860–1863

On a September day in 1860, a bearded twenty-two-year-old John Muir left his family farm near Portage for Madison. There he hoped to find work in a machine shop so that he could earn money for medical school. His plan to secure that job was as unconventional as the man himself. Instead of going directly to machine shops and asking for jobs, Muir expected his employers to come to him.

When he got off the train at Madison he struggled under the weight of two wooden handmade clocks, which he had invented and which he planned to display at the state fair. When the fairgrounds gatekeeper saw the mysterious contraptions, he allowed Muir into the grounds without a ticket and told him to set up an exhibit in the Fine Arts Hall. There the clocks delighted spectators and newspaper reporters who called the shirt-sleeved farmer a "genius" and his inventions "prodigies in the art of whittling."

What happened next far exceeded Muir's wildest expectations. Not only did a Prairie du Chien inventor offer Muir a job, which he accepted, but the state fair officials awarded the Scot immigrant a fifteen-dollar prize.

After working for the inventor for a few months, Muir returned to Madison in early 1861, lusting for an education but thinking himself too poor to pay for it. One day he chanced to meet a university student who recognized him from the fair. Expressing envy that the man could afford schooling, Muir learned that many students lived on a dollar a week. Heartened by this news, Muir presented himself to Professor John Sterling, then acting president of the University of Wisconsin, and explained that although he hadn't been to school since he left Scotland at age eleven, he had taught himself arithmetic, algebra, geometry, trigonometry, and grammar. Impressed with the youth's determination and love of learning, Sterling welcomed him to the preparatory department, from which Muir quickly graduated into the freshman class.

Muir's room in the northeast corner of the first floor of North Dormitory, now North Hall, became a campus showplace as the young man continued to invent mechanical contrivances. Having perfected a clock-controlled tipping bed that ejected the sleeper at a set hour, Muir invented another early-riser bed controlled by sunbeams. Perhaps his most outstanding creation was an elaborate clock mechanism that raised and opened books according to a predetermined schedule of study. This remarkable invention may be seen at the State Historical Society.

Then during Muir's second term came a chance encounter that profoundly affected his career. A fellow student, Milton Griswold, snatched a bud from a locust tree and explained the relationship between the locust and the pea families. Muir was so intrigued by this botany lesson that he began exploring the woods and meadows around Madison with unrestrained enthusiasm, gathering plant specimens and keeping them fresh in a bucket to study at night after his homework was completed. Each night after a day in the field, he would return to his room in North Hall to analyze the bucket of plant specimens. From this point forward Muir became a student of the natural world.

Muir was a frequent guest of Professor Ezra Slocum Carr and his wife Jeanne. Mrs. Carr shared Muir's love of botany and instructed him in the humanities. Muir described the Carr's sandstone house (still standing at 114 West Gilman Street) as "filled with books, peace, kindliness, and patience."

Muir decided to leave the university in the spring of 1863 to study medicine at the University of Michigan. Before he embarked for Michigan, he took a trip down the Wisconsin River where the urge to gather, examine, and classify botanical and geological specimens overcame him. He returned to Madison to bid farewell to his friends and then left the University of Wisconsin for what he called the "University of the Wilderness." Thereafter, when not exploring the wilds, Muir made his home in the Yosemite and the then Alhambra Valley in California.

Just a few days before leaving Madison in April 1863, the twenty-five-year-old Muir cut his shaggy hair and beard and had his photograph taken by a local photographer. Some years later Muir examined the photograph shown here and said, "I do look kind of innocent."

For more than fifty years after he left Madison, Muir continued his love affair with the wonders of nature. He discovered glaciers in California, classified plants and insects, and led an effort to establish national parks and forest reservations. Even today his pleas for the preservation of "the pure wilderness" are among the most eloquent ever written.

the committee estimated that the burden on productive—improved—real estate would equal one hundred mills, or ten percent a year. "We might as well expect a blade of corn to grow up through an anvil as expect a town to grow under such circumstances." To repay the debt, productive property must be kept productive by maintaining an endurable tax level, and since, the committee surmised, most productive Madison property produced a return of ten percent per year, to reduce its return to five percent with a fifty-mill rate would be to sound a death knell for the city. "No man would be foolish enough to invest capital on ground subject to an annual tax of five percent." The only way Madison could possibly extricate itself from its predicament was to compromise on the value of the bonds. The only other alternative was repudiation.

Therefore, said the committee, we are able to pay city and cemetery bondholders fifty cents on the dollar and railroad bond holders thirty cents on the dollar. The council then unaminously approved the measure and appointed one of its members, Alderman John Y. Smith, to contact the bondholders and secure their agreement.[78]

Alderman Smith quickly learned that a New York banker who controlled most of the city bonds wanted eighty cents on the dollar. Holders of railroad bonds told Smith they wanted to wait until city bonds had been settled, reasoning that they would come out better by pegging the rate at the city bond level.[79] There the matter rested for nearly two years while the city fathers were preoccupied by Civil War problems.[80]

Not until 1863, when Mayor William T. Leitch urged resolution of the problem in his inaugural message, did the matter again receive public and decision-maker attention. Said Leitch in his speech to the incoming council in April 1863: "Now in justice to our creditors . . . how much longer shall this state of affairs continue and the business of the city be conducted in so careless a manner? . . . If in the transaction of our own private affairs we would resort to such measures, we would be considered by our neighbors a very poor business man, if not downright

dishonest."[81] Almost as if to prove the wisdom and timeliness of the mayor's exhortation, an angry bondholder secured a Wisconsin Supreme Court writ of mandamus requiring the city to levy a tax to cover bond coupons to which he was entitled. It was the largest settlement yet paid and forced the council to stop dillydallying.[82]

Finally, nearly three years after making the first settlement offer, the Common Council on October 12, 1863, agreed to pay 66⅔ cents on the dollar for all city and cemetery bonds and thirty-three cents on the dollar for the railroad bonds. Equally important, the council directed a prominent local attorney to visit all known bondholders to secure their agreement to the compromise.[83] In November, after an exhaustive round of meetings with eastern bondholders, the attorney returned to report that the city bond holders would settle for seventy cents on the dollar and the railroad bondholders would settle for thirty-three cents on the dollar.[84] Formal council agreement with the bondholders' counteroffer was ratified in March 1864.[85]

The compromise scheme cut Madison's outstanding indebtedness from two-hundred sixty thousand to one hundred sixty thousand dollars, a reduction of just over sixty percent.[86] Solving the bonded indebtedness problem had hardly been easy. Most of the seven-year delay can be attributed to political buck passing and a flurry of crosscutting court actions that reflected a fundamental disagreement about whether the bonds should be repudiated or compromised, and if compromised, under what terms.[87] Some of the delay must be attributed to a general preoccupation with Civil War problems and much to the intrinsic difficulty of the job itself. The settlement hardly guaranteed a trouble-free fiscal future, but it did mean that at last Madisonians could afford the past. The ongoing financial burden imposed by this early episode of profligate spending also explains why Madison was prevented from borrowing money for general city purposes until 1893, twenty-seven years after the compromise settlement.[88]

The 1858 Capital Removal Scheme

While coping with the serious, sudden economic depression, Madison leaders were forced to deal with another concerted attempt to remove the capital from Madison. The move began because construction on the "enlargement" had gone so slowly during the winter of 1857–58 that Governor Randall felt obligated to call this fact to the attention of the legislature.[89] The matter was referred to the Senate Committee on State Affairs, but this time there was only one Madisonian on the committee, Andrew Proudfit, and he was not the chairman. Without consulting Senator Proudfit, the other committee members called upon two architects, a contractor, and a bondsman to criticize the enlargement plans prepared by Madison architects Kutzbach and Donnell. These experts, it turned out, had compelling reasons to collaborate with the legislators. One was the bondsman of the contractor who wanted to get out of the contract, two were architects whose proposals for the job had been rejected, and the fourth was an architect who disliked all plans not done by himself.[90] Not surprisingly, these men found serious structural errors and deficiencies in the enlargement plans. Even more important was the discovery by the senators that the "enlargement" was really the first of a five-phase plan that would have produced an entirely new capitol over a period of years at a cost of a half million dollars.[91] They charged that enlargement proponents had used "cunningly drawn" plans to make the remaining four phases all but certain.[92]

The *Milwaukee Sentinel* charged that the plan was a "botch and a humbug" and recommended scrapping the whole thing and starting over.[93] Instead of getting a "new, elegant and stately structure . . ." the *Sentinel* editors said the state would be getting an enlarged capitol that would look like a "pair of twin pumpkins on their native vines."[94]

Such criticisms led to the introduction of a bill calling for the "temporary" removal of the capital to Milwaukee while a more suitable building could be designed and built. Although the assumption was that the capital would stay in

Madison, Madison leaders were concerned that the temporary move would turn out to be permanent, particularly if agreement on the design of the new capitol could not be reached. To make the temporary Milwaukee interlude even more attractive, Milwaukee officials promised to provide "free rooms and apartments" suitable to accommodate the legislative, executive, and judicial branches.[95] Five days later, Madison offered the state the use of its newly completed City Hall, free of charge of course.[96] For a city on the verge of bankruptcy, this offer must be viewed as a desperate act designed to keep the city's most important institution. This is particularly true in light of a charter amendment passed on February 1, 1858, four months before the free offer was made, which *required* all rents collected from City Hall to be used to pay off the bonded indebtedness of the city.[97] Meanwhile, a group of resourceful Madison businessmen tried to counter the charge that the new enlargement was structurally unsound by offering to give the state a large indemnity bond.[98]

During the debate on relocation certain state newspapers jumped on the editorial bandwagon to get the capital out of Madison. For example, the *Fox Lake Gazette* said "it is a notorious fact that Madison is not the place for (the capital). Everything that is bad is concentrated at that point. Even its own papers cannot get along without abusing everybody and everything."[99] Madison editors retaliated to such charges by saying that "if Madison has more gambling dens, more grog shops, more houses of infamy in proportion to its population than most other cities in the state, it is because the people send representatives here who patronize and encourage such things."[100]

On the day the "temporary" relocation bill was voted upon in the assembly, the galleries were packed with persons who desired to keep the capital in Madison. Madison legislators denounced Milwaukee interests and corruption, but according to Milwaukee reporters, Madison legislators did not "hesitate themselves to make use of all sorts of arts and appliances to influence the vote."[101] Finally, late in the morning, the matter came to a vote. Forty-one voted to move the capital to Milwaukee and thirty-eight voted to keep it in Madison. Immediately a Janesville representative moved to reconsider the vote. By the slimmest majority—thirty-nine to thirty-eight—his motion prevailed and once again the bill was before the assembly. However, for some reason, twenty-eight representatives had wandered out of the chamber so a call of the house was made. This time the vote was a tie, forty-one to forty-one. There being no majority in favor of removal, the seat of government remained in Madison. Loud cheers and applause erupted from the gallery, but the speaker, who had voted to move the capital to Milwaukee, banged his gavel until order was restored and then ordered the gallery cleared of the Madison claque.[102]

Once more Madison had managed to keep its major institution, but the ease with which removal votes could be mustered was profoundly disconcerting to leaders of the financially embarrassed town. Paying off its huge indebtedness with capital in the city was one thing; without the capital, it was inconceivable. Proponents of the Milwaukee move may well have been correct when they claimed that if the bill had come up earlier in the session before fifteen legislators had to leave for their homes, the Milwaukee bill would have passed.[103]

Immediately after the legislature voted to keep the capital in Madison, the City of Madison withdrew its offer of free rent for state use of City Hall. In its financial embarrassment, the city needed every extra dollar it could get. Ironically, two months after the free rent offer was withdrawn, the newly completed City Hall was mortgaged for its full value to provide collateral for holders of the capitol expansion bonds.[104] For many years, the state rented the entire building, supplementing Madison's treasury in the process. Thus Madison leaders kept the capital, and they also used City Hall rents to reduce the bonded indebtedness.[105]

Depression Bright Spots

Although the effects of the depression were devastating to some and difficult for most, the 1857–1860 period was not without its bright spots. Relatively large amounts of state construction, including the Insane Asylum (1857–1860), Bascom Hall (1857–59), and the Capitol Enlargement (1857–1859), kept many Madison workmen employed. Private construction was limited to individiuals who had not concentrated money in speculative real estate. Several wealthy businessmen whose fortunes were only mildly affected by the depression took advantage of the lowered building costs to erect lavish mansions. In fact, the area now known as "Mansion Hill" became Madison's new prestige neighborhood during this period. Among landmarks constructed there during the depression were the Pierce House (1857), the Keenan House (1858), the Bashford House (1857), the Van Slyke House (1857), and the Hoyt House (1858).[106]

The other exception was theaters. In 1858 two private theaters and one public theater began operation. The public theater was the "splendid and spacious" third floor of City Hall boasting twenty-four-foot high ceilings, two large chandeliers, and space for nine hundred persons. The most distinguished private theater was the remodelled Van Bergan Hall at the corner of Doty and Pinckney. Like the city auditorium, it could seat about nine hundred persons, but, unlike the city facility, it boasted a "theater saloon" just one floor below the hall so the boys could bolt a quick one between acts. The third theater that made its appearance in 1858 was Turner Hall.[107]

The smaller-than-expected proceeds from the one-hundred-thousand-dollar loan were responsible for nearly all the important city improvements. One benefactor of these funds was the fire department. Two hand-operated fire engines were purchased and in April 1857 turned over to the two Madison volunteer fire companies.[108] In December of that year a fire district was created which required exterior walls of all downtown buildings to be made of brick or stone.[109] Fire-houses for the new engines and cisterns were also constructed, giving Madison its best fire protection in its short history. The only dissonant note was that the specially designed large capacity fire cisterns leaked badly—a fact that jeopardized the entire fire-fighting system.[110] Unfortunately, the city was too poor to remedy this problem for years. City loan proceeds were also used to buy the Forest Hill Cemetery and build two new school houses.[111]

Food was both abundant and cheap. Newspapers described rows of rabbits, chickens, turkeys, geese, and partridges dangling in front of Capital Square stores and huge freshly speared pickeral from the lakes and baskets of sweet honey in the marketplace. Best of all, there was free lunch at the finer saloons beginning at 10:30 A.M., and all drinks except brandy were a nickel.[112]

The depression also witnessed the reopening of Water Cure, a large hotel-spa facility where Olin Park is located today. However, instead of offering guests spartan forty-day water diets, hot and cold baths, and other forms of hydrptherapy as their bankrupt predecessors had done, the new proprietor provided booze, billiards, and bowling. Although the enterprise was cut short by the depression, it set a precedent for later chapters in Madison's resort industry.[113]

Then, too, there were those satisfactions that even a serious economic depression could not snatch away: the rich, sweet fragrance of newly mown hay in the Capitol Park wafting through the hot, dusty July air; the spectacular sound of a moving waterfall in the sky issued by huge flocks of passenger pigeons flying over the city;[114] the thrill of flushing a covey of quail from the tall grass in Capitol Park; a cool swim in the crystal clear lakes on a hot August day; and ice skating on a crisp December moonlit night.[115] These things were free for all to enjoy.

The Civil War Era

The Gathering Storm

Most Madisonians probably considered the issue of slavery settled by the Missouri Compromise of 1850, which said that slavery could not be extended to any new territories admitted to the Union. However, the Kansas-Nebraska Act of 1854 reopened that debate by declaring the 1850 Compromise void and leaving slavery up to the people and their elected officials. Almost overnight Kansas became a battleground for abolitionist and proslavery forces.

Meanwhile an event in Racine brought the slavery issue home to Wisconsin. In March 1854, federal marshals acting under the orders of a Missouri slave owner arrested Joshua Glover, an escaped slave, in a hut on the outskirts of Racine. Glover was immediately taken to Milwaukee, where he was to be tried under the Fugitive Slave Act of 1850. The day after his arrival in Milwaukee, a local abolitionist editor, Sherman Booth, was outraged to learn that a free and open trial was not extended to escaped slaves under the Fugitive Slave Act. He galloped through the streets of Milwaukee exhorting his fellow citizens to attend a meeting at the Courthouse to adopt a resolution demanding Glover's release. Later in the day a mob responding to Booth's appeal, but not under his control, stormed the Milwaukee jail, freed the captured slave, and sent him on his way to Canada. Booth was arrested and quickly became a *cause celebre* among those who wished to free Wisconsin from any association with slavery.

The Republican party in Wisconsin was formed in direct response to this incident. Its leaders concentrated on the single issue of slavery largely because it was the only issue on which they could agree. But theirs was a coalition of great potential appeal, as the history of the state and nation was about to reveal. On the afternoon of July 13, 1854, the fledgling party held its first large meeting on the lawn of the capitol. There

those present passed a resolution saying that the issue of slavery had been forced upon them by a slave power and in "the defense of freedom (we) will cooperate and be known as Republicans."[1]

From this time forward Madison newspapers became lively forums for debating the slavery issue, black suffrage, and black equality. The Democratic *Patriot* early staked out its position on what it came to call the "nigger question."[2] "Every particle of history . . . goes to show that the African race is by nature inferior to the white. Man could not alter this fact if he would. . . . The African is a race distinct from the white and we do not believe that the God of our being ever contemplated that the black and white races should live together with equal franchises and privileges."[3] The Republican *Wisconsin State Journal* under the vigorous pen of Horace Rublee took a strong, consistent but unpopular antislavery stand.[4] Its pages were full of articles describing the horrible conditions of slavery in the south.[5] The *Patriot* editor took obvious delight in tormenting the *Wisconsin State Journal* for its support of black suffrage and abolition of slavery.[6] These editorial fusillades continued until the fall of 1857 when a state-wide referendum on the issue of black suffrage was ordered. When the results were tallied, state voters rejected the black suffrage by a five-to-one margin whereas Madison voters rejected it three to one.[7] Clearly black suffrage was an idea whose time had not yet come.

War Fever

This resounding defeat failed to silence Rublee and his radical Republican supporters, but it did force them to play a waiting game until December 20, 1860, when the seccession of South Carolina provided a fresh opportunity. The most dramatic Madison response to this news came on January 5, 1861 when D. K. Tenney, the only Republican alderman on the Common Council, introduced a sensational resolution to petition the legislature to supply the president with fifty thousand armed men and put down the rebellion.[8] Although the measure was defeated by Democratic alderman, it showed the eagerness of local "fire eaters," the Democrat's name for pro-war Republicans. One day later the *State Journal* urged the state to raise ten thousand troops at a cost of one million dollars.[9] The Governor's Guard and the Madison Guards, companies of local militiamen, quickly tendered their services to the governor.[10] The most stirring words on the South Carolina action came from Governor Randall himself. In his annual msssage to the legislature on January 10, he said "secession is revolution, revolution is war and war against the government of the United States is treason."[11]

To the Republicans the die was cast. The irrepressible conflict had begun. To the Democrats the future was not so inevitable. The *Patriot* argued that the irrepressible scenario was valid only for those who insisted on the abolition of slavery. The true objective was the preservation of the Union with slavery. The *Patriot* favored a return to the Missouri Compromise of 1850 allowing slavery in those states which had it then,[12] but opposed allowing new slave states. In the words of the *Patriot* editor they were "for the Union as it was and must be under the Constitution."[13] During the next three months the editorial pages of the Madison papers were seldom silent on this volatile issue.

At 4:30 A.M. Friday morning, April 12, 1861, Confederate batteries began firing upon Fort Sumter, a fortress in the Charleston, South Carolina, harbor occupied by federal troops. Word of this action appeared in Madison newspapers Friday evening,[14] although at this point there was no indication that the attack meant war. Realizing the extreme seriousness of this action, three Madison newspapers printed extras on Saturday morning with the latest dispatches from Charleston, but telegraph dispatches contained frustrating repetitions. When the telegraph office closed Saturday night it was announced that the office would be open Sunday evening at 7:00 P.M.

On Sunday evening, April 14, a large crowd gathered below the second story balcony near the corner of Main and Pinckney Streets to hear the telegraph operator read the latest dispatches. When the assembled Madisonians heard that Sumter had been surrendered, they stood in stunned silence, then left quietly for their homes. It was hard for the people to believe "that the regular army of the United States had been forced to lower its colors."[15]

By Monday the mood in Madison had changed from numbed disbelief to aggressive indignation. "The most intense feeling prevails here," reported the *Wisconsin State Journal*. "The only subject of conversation is war and the news of the taking of Sumter."[16] At 2:00 o'clock in the afternoon a large assembly of people watched the young American Coronet Band resplendent in new scarlet caps and coats lead militiamen of the Governor's Guard and the Madison Guards in a parade around the Capitol Square. Voluntary militia Captain J. P. Atwood then lined up the men in front of the east portico of the capitol. Captain Atwood made a brief speech to the Governor on behalf of the men, saying it was not the duty of soldiers "to anticipate the orders of their commander," but "that they would always be found ready to execute with alacrity his commands."[17] The governor replied with a stirring speech and was loudly applauded.[18] The militiamen then "marched around the city, their plumes and strains of martial music creating quite a war spirit."[19] That evening the German Turnverein met to formally place their organization in support of the struggle. A passerby heard a spirited rendition of the Star Spangled Banner coming from Turner Hall *in English*.[20]

Meanwhile the governor had received a telegram from President Lincoln asking for one regiment of militia totalling 780 men for service for ninety days. On Tuesday, April 16, Governor Randall issued a proclamation asking citizens to unite and saying that enlistments in militia companies would be offered immediately.[21]

The proclamation suddenly thrust Madison's two militia companies to front center stage. Once taunted for their "childish delight" in "playing soldier," they were now viewed as heroes as they prepared to respond quickly to the President's call.[22] However, in the absence of a pressing military justification for their existence, the Madison units became known for their fancy dress balls and uniforms and had allowed membership to drop below the authorized strength of seventy-eight men.[23] To get their companies up to full strength, militia members took to the streets looking for recruits. Proudly attired in blue uniforms with guilt buttons and gold epaulets, they announced their presence with a loud beating drum and proclaimed their purpose with a huge American flag. New recruits sported red, white, and blue ribbons or rosettes in their buttonholes.[24] By Thursday evening, April 18, the Governor's Guard had recruited enough men to bring their unit to seventy-eight men and by noon on Friday the Madison Guard had done the same.[25] The problem, according to the *Wisconsin State Journal* was not finding recruits but rather in deciding "who shall be compelled to remain at home."[26] Both the Governor's Guard and the Madison Guard offered their services in January shortly after the secession of South Carolina, but the Governor's Guard was the first to have its services accepted.[27]

During the first few weeks after the surrender of Sumter, support for the war grew in an almost breathtaking crescendo. One day excitement was described "at fever heat."[28] The next day it was described "indescribably intense."[29] Even the minister of the First Methodist Church who served as the senate chaplain was swept up by the martial spirit. In a prayer to the senate on Tuesday morning, April 17, in reference to the southern secessionists, he said: "Oh God . . . the conviction is forced upon our minds . . . that these men who have thus turned traitors against their country ought to be hung in this world and damned in the world to come." At this point those present in the chamber interrupted with "a slight and respectful demonstration of applause."[30]

THE MADISON ZOUAVES
FOR
THE WAR!

TH NION MUST AND   SHALL B PRESERVED!

This Co. which has been organized and in active Drill
FOR MORE THAN A YEAR, HAS ENLISTED FOR THE WAR!

Under the recent call by the President of the United States. For the purpose of filling the ranks to the required number, a commission has been specially issued by the Governor to the undersigned, the Captain of the Company. The

ARMORY OF THE COMPANY, IN THE CITY HALL AT MADISON,
IS NOW OPENED AS THE RECRUITING OFFICE.

All the advantages of enlisting in connection with a *well drilled Company*, and of enlisting for a new regiment, are here presented together. The

HIGHEST BOUNTY & PAY!

given to volunteers, will be given to the men of this Company. The undersigned was a member of the Old Governor's Guard from its earliest orgnaization until called, in 1861, to command the Madison Zouaves ; and can satisfy any applicant as to his competency as a military officer.

The ranks of the Company will be filled by volunteer enlistments by the 15th of August, or after that date   ☞DRAFTING WILL BEGIN!☜

The Drafted Soldier gets $11 a month only,& no Bounty!
The Volunteer gets the full Pay and all Bounties!!

☞The pay of Volunteers will begin from the time of enlistment at full rates. What able-bodied man will desert his country in her hour of peril? Where is the coward who will shrink from the contest for the maintenance of our institutions and the preservation of our Constitution! Where the poltroon who will see our flag trampled by rebels and traitors, without a blow!! Rally Men of Dane County! Fill the ranks of our armies with brave hearts and strong hands! for the rescue of the Union!!

[Wisconsin State Journal Print, Madison.]   **WM. F. VILAS, Recruiting Officer.**

FIGURE 3.6. MADISON ZOUAVE POSTER. These twelve-by-eighteen-inch posters appeared on Madison billboards and buildings in August 1862 amidst frenzied efforts to raise men to satisfy Madison's 124-man portion of Lincoln's recent 300,000-man call. The poster emphasized the financial advantages of volunteering versus being drafted. Although not stated in the poster, a Madison volunteer was entitled to a total of one hundred fifty dollars in bounties—one hundred dollars from the federal government and fifty dollars from the City of Madison volunteer fund—in addition to regular monthly base pay of eleven dollars. At the time unskilled workmen were earning only about one dollar per day, so the bonus was the equivalent of a half-year's pay.

The Zouaves were modelled after flashy French fighting units known for their bright colored uniforms. Organized in October 1861, the Madison group at first consisted of young men who had not yet reached the age of eighteen and could therefore not volunteer. Their plan was to organize and drill so that when they became of age they would be well prepared. At the time of their formation the *Wisconsin State Journal* commended the young men for their patriotism and for their plan to meet for weekly drill sessions. ". . . Drill affords an invigorating exercise," said the *Journal,* "and the time devoted to it is much better employed than when spent in billiard rooms and drinking saloons."

The Zouave recruiting officer William F. Vilas, the twenty-one-year-old son of Mayor Levi P. Vilas, had just returned to Madison in 1860 after receiving a law degree from a New York law school. In 1858 Vilas had graduated from the University of Wisconsin at the age of eighteen. After a brief military career in the Civil War, Vilas had a brilliant legal and political career, ultimately serving as Grover Cleveland's Secretary of the Interior and Postmaster General (1885–1889) and then U.S. Senator (1891–1897). (SHSW WHi(X3)18004)

Meanwhile the beating of recruiting drums was heard from morning to night. Overnight "plowmen have left their plows, artisans their benches, and clerks their stores to take part . . . in grim visaged war."[31] All over the city large crowds of citizens congregated on street corners and in the saloons reading the extra editions of the newspapers.[32] Even the hypercritical *Patriot* stated its unwavering support for the Union. "We now stand by the Government—right or wrong," said the *Patriot*.[33]

Perhaps the greatest outpouring of martial spirit during that first week was a mass meeting in the Assembly Chambers on Thursday evening, April 18, to raise money for the support of volunteers' families. Between one thousand and fifteen hundred persons attended. After a short business meeting, leading business and professional men began to make pledges almost in the spirit of an auction. The owner of the Madison Gas Light and Coke Company began the "bidding": "I will give $200 to the fund to maintain the families of volunteers." (Cheers.) The president of the State Bank, who happened to be a Quaker, gave five hundred dollars. (Three hearty cheers.) Soon the band and members of the Governor's Guard made a dramatic entrance and were received with enthusiastic applause. A member of the company advanced to the speaker's stand and was greeted by a "tempest of applause." "Fellow citizens," he began, ". . . I thank God that Madison is loyal, and that Wisconsin is loyal (cheers). If there was ever a holy war, this is one (great applause). . . . And boys (turning to the volunteers) I tell you all—if any one of you shall fall upon the field of battle, or die of disease in this campaign, Madison will not forget you. (Tumultuous applause.) Fired with enthusiasm, the audience rose and sang the national anthem. A few moments later Captain Lucius Fairchild strode to the front of the room and cried, "I will give $50 *and* myself!" (Great applause.) The editor of the *Wisconsin State Journal* gave one hundred dollars; a rich businessman, fifty dollars a month, so long as the war would last. Gradually mechanics and others announced

their more modest contributions of five and ten dollars: A farmer gave one hundred bushels of wheat. By 11:00 P.M. an impressive seventy-five hundred dollars had been subscribed. Once more the Star Spangled Banner was sung and the participants emerged emotionally spent into the cool spring night.[34]

Enthusiasm for the war, although intense and growing during the first week of the war, was not uniformly shared by all segments of the population. A Madison hostess who had a party Monday evening, April 15, 1861, said her guests became "quite warlike" and had a "war of words" when they discussed the impending conflict.[35] Harlow Orton, a prominent Madison attorney and captain of the Dane County Cavalry, a Madison based militia unit, refused to call a meeting of his company on Thursday, April 18, on the grounds that his men "lived in the country and could not meet in time." When the company did meet two days later the men voted twenty-seven to twelve not to answer the call.[36] Orton felt that sending a vessel to Fort Sumter with provisions was a "pretense" concocted by the Lincoln administration to force the South Carolinians to attack.[37] In a letter dated April 29 to his brother, Orton said he "fully disapproved of the Administration's decision to fight the South and he planned to go with his law practice and not get caught up in the whole affair."[38] Orton was later appointed to the Wisconsin Supreme Court.

Around noon on Wednesday, April 24, 1861, just nine days after President Lincoln issued his call for one regiment from Wisconsin, a large procession gathered on the Capitol Square. Present were Mayor Vilas, Governor Randall, all the aldermen, and many local leaders. Interspersed among the dozens of dignitary carriages was the Young America Coronet Band, the two fire engine companies, and the Madison Turners—all in uniform. But the featured elements were two full strength militia companies, the Governor's Guard and the Madison Guard. They were about to participate in a spectacle few ever expected to witness and all wanted to avoid. They were leaving the city to fight fellow Americans in a civil war.

According to newspaper accounts, the whole town turned out to say good bye.[39] "The street leading to the depot was thronged with pedestrians and a long line of carriages. The two companies marched with bayonets fixed in rifles and as they passed with erect gait and soldierly tred, they enjoyed admiring gazes from the thousands that looked at them." The governor, the mayor, and others gave brief speeches from the verandah of a hotel on West Washington Avenue adjacent to the depot. "Then came the farewells, the clasping of hands, the 'God bless you's,' the faces of strong men wet with tears, women sobbing, and all those affecting incidents which . . . this generation has never before witnessed."[40] As the train pulled away from the depot, a "deafening cheer" arose from the huge crowd. In the terse words of the last entry in the Governor's Guard record book, the men were "off for the Wars."[41]

For her contribution of two full strength companies to Wisconsin's first regiment, Madisonians could be justifiably proud. On the basis of population Madison had turned out more than three times as many men as Milwaukee, almost twice as many as Fond du Lac, about twenty percent more than Kenosha and Beloit. Moreover, there were cities much larger than Madison, such as Racine and Janesville, that did not turn out a single company at this early stage of the war. "Of all the towns in the state," said the *Milwaukee News,* "Madison takes the palm for patriotism."[42]

Raising Soldiers for the Union

Military developments during the summer of 1861 were not encouraging for the North. The administration, desirous of a quick victory using ninety-day militia troops, decided it could best secure that goal by capturing Richmond, Virginia, the new capital of the Confederacy. Toward this end thirty-five thousand Union troops were sent across the Potomac, including Wisconsin's Second Regiment of which Madison's Randall Guard were a part. The march was uneventful until it reached a sluggish stream named Bull Run just thirty miles southwest of Washington, D.C. There Union forces met a humiliating and decisive defeat in spite of their superior numbers. Wisconsin's Second Regiment, for example, lost one-third of its men.[43] The defeat was a profound shock to the people of the North and certainly to Madisonians. The cherished hope for the quick victory was dashed and the wisdom of calling three-year troops, which Lincoln did in May, now seemed clear.

Facing a war of unknown length, Madisonian soldier families confronted a pressing problem. Just four months after the splendidly successful meeting on April 18, 1861, where seventy-five hundred dollars had been raised by private subscription for ths support of volunteers' families, it became clear that this fund would soon be exhausted. The problem was that Madison had turned out a very large number of volunteers for a city of its size. In its special session the legislature, anticipating the need to earmark tax resources for money for volunteers, passed a law that allowed local governments to add a two-mill levy on the property tax if approved by a referendum.[44] The Madison Common Council unanimously decided to use this procedure and laid the matter before the voters on September 30, 1861. Only twelve percent of the citizens who had voted in the spring bothered to go to the polls, but of those who did, four approved the measure to every one who did not.[45] Money from this source first became available in 1862 and was distributed by senior aldermen to deserving soldiers' families.[46] Most families received four to five dollars a month—barely a subsistence stipend.[47]

In the fall of 1861 prospects for the Union army began looking up. Several beachheads had been secured along the Southern coast from which an effective blockade could be maintained. Major battles in the spring of 1862 in Missouri, Kentucky, and Tennessee had also gone well for Union

forces. New Orleans was occupied by federal troops, and the entire length of the Mississippi came under the control of the Union army. There were 632,000 men in the Union army, surely enough, most thought, to quell the rebellion. So confident were federal authorities that the war would soon be won that recruiting stations were closed April 30, 1862.

But developments during the summer and fall of 1862 produced a very different outlook. The Union offensive in the West faltered just when it might have produced victory. The march on Richmond was repulsed by the dazzling offensive maneuvers of General Stonewall Jackson. General Lee recaptured nearly all of Virginia and boldly crossed the Potomac River into Pennsylvania. By fall, 1862, the future of the Confederacy looked bright indeed.[48]

Once again Lincoln had to ask governors to provide the necessary troops. Under the President's call of July 2, 1862, Wisconsin had to provide 11,904 men willing to serve for three years. Madison's quota under this call was quite small, just fifty-three men,[49] because so many had volunteered under the 1861 calls. Nevertheless, response to this call, according to the alarmed editors of the *Wisconsin State Journal*, was "utter torpor." "Will Madison, the Capitol of the state, manifest less zeal and less ardor of patriotism than the other cities of the Commonwealth? Let us have a public meeting called at once and revive the enthusiasm of the past. Our people," the editors concluded, "want a stirring up."[50] This journalistic cheerleading aside, earlier enthusiasm of the war had been profoundly dampened by the growing prospect of a long and bloody war and the lengthy casualty lists. The easy gallantry and bravado of 1861 had given way to a much more calculating attitude among Madison's young men.

The need for a "stirring up" was even more evident when a few days later, August 4, 1862, Lincoln issued still another call for another three-hundred thousand men who would agree to serve for nine months. Madison's quota under this call was reported to be 124 men,[51] but the ground rules

for this call had changed. As a result of the passage of the Militia Act of July 17, 1862, the federal government was empowered for the first time in history to use the draft *if* the states could not meet their quotas. As if to underline this new federal muscle, the governors were ordered to meet their quotas by August 15.[52]

That the use of the draft in Madison would forever tarnish the city's reputation was widely and intensely felt. To secure the needed men and avoid the disgraceful draft, spirited rallies were held on August 12, 13, and 14 at the capitol. To help insure their success, businesses closed at 6:00 P.M. on Monday, 4:00 P.M. on Tuesday, and 1:00 P.M. on Wednesday so that all businessmen could take to the streets and round up recruits before the evening meetings. Unfortunately after three days of frenzy, church bell ringing, cannon firing, martial band music, spread-eagle rhetoric by the city's finest orators, moving testimonials, and great crowds, the yield of recruits fell short of the quota.[53]

Already the depth of local commitment to the war was being tested and found wanting. Willingness to volunteer was found to be very much dependent upon financial incentives. In 1861 the federal government had established a one-hundred-dollar bounty for any recruit, but leaders of the Madison war rallies recognized that would have to be supplemented by *local* bounty. Although the war rallies had not produced enough volunteers, they had produced thirteen thousand dollars, so each Madison volunteer would be able to have a fifty-dollar local bounty. Thus by combining the federal and local bounties and base pay, a Madison volunteer could receive $271 (one hundred dollars in federal bounty, fifty dollars in local bounties, plus regular base pay for the term of enlistment). Volunteering had always been regarded as a noble and patriotic act, but gradually it became profitable too.[54]

Meanwhile Madison's inability to meet its quota was relieved when the governor received permission from federal authorities to postpone the draft until November. By mid-September,

"Rally Round the Flag, Boys!
Rally Once Again!"

SOLDIERS WANTED!

FOR THE TERM OF

One Hundred Days!

TO ENABLE OUR GALLANT
veterans to go immediately to the front.

Clothing, Rations and Pay, the same as for other volunteers, to commence from the date of enrollment.

The undersigned is authorized by the Governor, to raise a Company for the above.

He has been in active service in the field for over two years, both as Private and Lieutenant, and knows how to treat soldiers, as they deserve to be treated.

For further information please call at his Recruiting Headquarters on King street, near the Bank of Madison.   CHAS. H. BARTON.

Madison, May 4, 1864.   d1w

FIGURE 3.7 ONE-HUNDRED-DAY MEN. War rallies held in Madison in the spring of 1864 aroused little enthusiasm. Employers stayed away from the meeting in droves, recognizing that if they attended they would be pressured into allowing employees to go and then guarantee them a job when they got back. The meetings were therefore pronounced a "magnificent failure."

Patriots trying to arouse enthusiasm for this war elsewhere around the country were encountering a similar problem. As a partial response to that problem, Lincoln issued a special call for volunteers to serve just one hundred days. The call came in May 1864, just five weeks before seniors were scheduled to graduate from the University of Wisconsin. Caught up in a paroxysm of patriotism the UW seniors decided to respond to the call rather than graduate. Seniors immediately went on a recruiting expedition and got over one hundred fifty men to serve in the University Guards captained by a professor. Said one of the seniors, "Nearly the whole school enlisted. None but copperheads and cripples were left. . . ." With only one member left in the senior class of 1864, commencement was cancelled that year.

The men were put into the Fortieth Regiment and went directly to Memphis, where, as railroad guards, they were involved in several skirmishes. Their presence freed up veteran troops for what became the very successful 1864 summer campaigns. They were mustered out on September 16, 1864, almost in time to register for the fall term.

with the help of the local bounty and the extension, Madison was able to make its quota and avoid the draft.[55]

With a draft hanging over the heads of all healthy men between eighteen and forty-five years of age, draft exemptions became topics of household discussions. Because one of the most widely used and accepted exemptions was joining a local fire company, the *Patriot* on August 6 noted a sudden "great desire to become firemen." Madison draft records show that three local fire companies applied *en masse* for their exemptions and got them.[56] Unfortunately for new fire company applicants, several months were required for new firemen to be accepted by a company, so few escaped the draft in this way. Interestingly, one Madison company ran against the trend of hiding behind fireman status. The Madison Sack Company felt "denied the privilege of enlistment" and asked the Common Council to exempt them from the exemption so they could "exhibit their love of country." The council denied their request.[57]

The bitter irony of the frenzied 1862 recruiting efforts was that Madison should have had no quota at all. Draft authorities had failed to give Madison credit for all her volunteers under the 1861 calls.[58] This error was matter-of-factly noted on October 24, 1862, when the *Daily Patriot* announced that Madison had raised 186 men over he quota, nine men above the 177 raised to satisfy the July and August 1862 quotas! As if to add insult to injury, draft authorities had credited Madison's overage to various Dane County townships. Even here the normally hypercritical *Patriot* reserved judgment and expressed faith in the authorities. "Should there be another call, the 186 men will undoubtedly be placed to the credit of the city, for not to do so would be manifestly unjust to the citizens who have exerted themselves and spent time and money in raising men."[59]

From a military point of view, 1863 was quite successful. Union forces captured Vicksburg and Chattanooga and won an impressive but costly victory at Gettysburg. But once again, while the Northern future looked brighter, the army required massive infusions of manpower to replace casualties and men being mustered out of the service and to expand the size of the army. In July Lincoln issued calls for three-hundred thousand men who would serve three years. Madison's share of that call was reported to be 117 men.[60] The state militia system had proved to be woefully inadequate to raise manpower, and even the federal-state system reflected in the Federal Militia Act of 1862 had proved disappointing. In March 1863, Congress passed the National Conscription Act, which not only contained strong draft provisions but placed the draft entirely in the hands of the federal government. This meant that power had shifted from local and state governments to Washington, D.C., and that was a cause for great anxiety among Madisonians.

The most pressing question for local officials to resolve was whether full and proper credit would be given to the city for its excess enlistments under earlier state calls. Mayor Leitch conferred with the State Adjutant General and learned that up to the end of 1862 Madison had exceeded all its previous quotas by one hundred fifty percent, or more than two hundred men.[61] The mayor appointed a committee to meet with "his excellency" the governor and all appropriate military authorities to get Madison credit for these overages. They returned with bad news. Draft officials refused to honor any geographical unit smaller than a congressional district—the basic draft unit under the 1863 Military Conscription Act.[62] Madison therefore faced the draft. In spite of this manifest inequality, remarkably little grumbling surfaced—that is, at first.

In June 1863 federal enrolling officers began formally entering the names of all men between the ages of twenty and forty-five.[63] When the list of draftees was published in late August 1863, a furor broke loose. Leading the criticism was the *Daily Patriot*. "It would seem hardly possible that so many errors should have been committed innocently . . . ," they said.[64] This was particularly evident to a group of six young men who got together with the draft list to compare notes. The

FIGURE 3.8. WANTED: SUBSTITUTES. This ad, appearing in the Madison newspapers in February 1865, offered to pay one hundred dollars for soldier substitutes. Together with five to six hundred dollars in federal and local bounties, a man responding to this ad could have received seven hundred dollars for enlisting under Lincoln's last call. Reports of substitutes receiving a total of eight hundred dollars in bounties and substitute fees circulated in Madison in late August 1864.

name of one of the six boys was missing entirely, two others were put in the wrong class, and another was spelled so erroneously as to be scarcely recognizable.[65] A careful investigation showed that one out of three eligible men in the first ward had been omitted, one out of four in the third ward, and one out of ten in the second and fourth.[66] This did little to inspire confidence in the federal draft process.

Even after the lists were corrected, there was so much suspicion of the federal draft that the Common Council sent one of its own members to Janesville to observe the name drawing process on November 13.[67] Although 117 men drew "prizes,"[68] including one alderman, one priest, and the editor of the *Wisconsin State Journal*, who also happened to be the chairman of the powerful Republican State Committee.[69]

Madison community leaders were deeply embarrassed by the fact that the draft had to be used and, to many, Madison's image as a loyal city had been disgracefully defiled. More than anything else, the 1863 draft rudely reminded leaders that an even more generous financial incentive was going to be necessary to avoid another draft. Explained one account, ". . . where labor is in such good demand and pays so well, it is hardly necessary to expect men to be in haste to volunteer, unless better pecuniary rewards are offered."[70] The threat was immediate because another draft was expected in January 1864, to cover a call Lincoln had made in October 1863. After an unsuccessful attempt to raise a two hundred dollar local bounty by private subscription, the decision was made to use the public purse.[71] Under a law passed by the legislature earlier in the year, local governments were authorized to raise bounty money by taxing property *providing* the measure was approved by citizens at a referendum.[72] Billed as an election to "free the city from the draft,"[73] a referendum held two days before Christmas 1863, approved the $19,000 measure by a nine-to-one margin.[74] Coupled with the increased federal bounties, now in the three- to four-hundred dollar range with the new local bounties, a man enlisting in Madison during this period could get

between five and six-hundred dollars in bounties for enlisting, enough to buy a good farm.[75] Ads began appearing in the newspapers for "acceptable substitutes . . . to whom a liberal amount will be paid."[76]

Two months after passing the bounty measure, city officials received good news from the local draft director. He explained that the decision had been made to give Madison credit for the 202 excess men raised under previous calls and that the city was "handsomely clear of the draft."[77]

The respite, though welcome, lasted just six months. The largest single call for Civil War soldiers was made on July 18, 1864, when President Lincoln asked for five hundred thousand more men. Madison's quota after taking the earlier credits into account was estimated at 125 men. The day after the President's call, the Common Council formed a committee to determine how this number could be raised without resorting to the draft.[78] The question really became quite simple: How much would the city have to put up as a bounty to buy the men? There is no evidence to suggest that the Madison Common Council would have refused to authorize another bounty election, but events moved too quickly for such time-consuming deliberations. Under a new state law, a local bounty election could be called by just five property owners *without* council approval.[79] Just two days after Lincoln's call, five property owners signed the necessary petition, and the clerk called an election for July 30.[80] Once again the people supported the measure—this time sufficient to provide a two-hundred-dollar bounty, by a nine-to-one margin.[81]

But even with the two-hundred-dollar local bounty and the three- to four-hundred-dollar federal bounty—both at all-time high levels, volunteers were slow to sign up. By this time, volunteers had learned that they could get another one or two hundred dollars if they found someone who agreed to pay them to be their substitutes. In an open letter to Madison citizens, the district draft officer urged citizens to bring in recruits to his office even if they came from other towns.

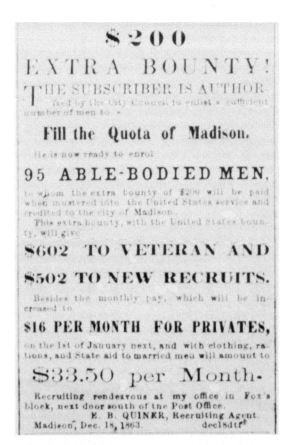

$200

EXTRA BOUNTY!

THE SUBSCRIBER IS AUTHOR-
ized by the City Council to enlist a sufficient
number of men to —

Fill the Quota of Madison.

He is now ready to enrol

95 ABLE-BODIED MEN,

to whom the extra bounty of $200 will be paid
when mustered into the United States service and
credited to the city of Madison.

This extra bounty, with the United States bounty, will give

$602 TO VETERAN AND

$502 TO NEW RECRUITS.

Besides the monthly pay, which will be increased to

$16 PER MONTH FOR PRIVATES,

on the 1st of January next, and with clothing, rations, and State aid to married men will amount to

$33.50 per Month.

Recruiting rendezvous at my office in Fox's
block, next door south of the Post Office.

E. B. QUINER, Recruiting Agent.
Madison, Dec. 18, 1863.   dec18dtf

FIGURE 3.9. CITY BOUNTY AD. A few days before the city bounty election on December 23, 1863, the Madison recruiting officer was authorized by the Common Council to place this ad trumpeting the availability of the $200 city bounty.

Federal draft officials had ruled that the men would be credited to the place where they were enrolled and not to their place of residence.[82] At least one vagrant picked up by police during this period became a candidate for glory when given a choice by Madison magistrates of staying in jail until the war was over or volunteering.[83]

With combined local and federal bounties now in the range of six to seven hundred dollars per volunteer, Madison could now easily outbid surrounding townships and municipalities. Naturally this circumstance encouraged residents of nearby communities to enlist in wealthier communities like Madison, but it severely strained smaller communities by reducing their pool of draftable men without reducing their quotas. Finally, the legislature stopped this bounty competition by imposing a maximum local bounty of two hundred dollars. The effect of this ceiling was to cause Madison and other communities to use schemes such as the "municipal insurance program."[84] Under this scheme all draftable men were required to contribute thirty dollars into a fund that was then given to actual volunteers. Exactly how much money was raised in this process is not clear, but it appears that an additional one hundred dollars per volunteer was raised from this source.[85] By the end of August 1864, after about one month of recruiting and the payment of liberal bounties, the newspapers reported that the city quota was full and that the city was out of the draft.[86]

The competition for "volunteers" was hardly limited to intercommunity rivalry, however. Toward the end of the war Wisconsin was forced to pit its recruit "buying power" against neighboring states, particularly Illinois. In March 1865, thirty Madison-area men a day reportedly enlisted in Illinois to get the richer bounties available there.[87]

The question posed by Lincoln's last call in December 1864, for three hundred thousand men, or 121 more Madison men, was whether to tax for the local bounty or simply let the draft handle the matter. Once again the matter was put to the voters, and on January 4, 1865, an overwhelming ninety-five percent of the voters approved another tax supported bounty issue of twenty-five thousand dollars, enough for two hundred dollars per volunteer.[88] As a result of a series of public meetings, the decision was again made to supplement the local bounty with the "municipal insurance program." While only about sixty percent

of the men in the draftable pool ever paid the required thirty dollars, enough actually contributed to constitute a one-hundred-dollar bonus for the volunteers.[89] Thus, Madison was able to buy its way out of the draft for the fourth and last time. Though such procedures had become commonplace, there were many who condemned the replacement of patriotism with pecuniary motives. Such high-minded individuals as H. A. Tenney were disgusted that the recruiting process had become a commercial transaction where poor brave men sold themselves to wealthy cowards.[90]

Supporting the War Effort at Home

The job of helping soldier families and providing for the special needs of soldiers fell largely to the women of Madison, who formed ladies aid societies and the Ladies Union League to perform these tasks. Early in the war, soldier pay was not only very low, but very irregular, and this caused great hardship among many soldier families— particularly to the many who had no savings. The ladies' systematic collection and distribution of food, clothing, and wood to needy families was generously supported and was said to be a great morale booster among the soldiers. Madison women also organized to make soldier uniforms and scrape lint from cloth to be used as a cotton substitute for bandages. Beginning in 1863 the women led local efforts to raise onions and other vegetables, which were then rushed to Chicago where they were distributed to soldiers to combat scurvy.[91]

Madisonians avidly followed military activities during the war and staged great celebrations whenever Union armies won significant victories. When word was received that Vicksburg had been taken, full salutes were fired in the Capitol Park, stores closed early, and enthusiastic crowds gathered in saloons and the streets to celebrate the good news.[92] When Sherman captured Savannah the "air rang with hurrahs," flags went up all over town, and people staged spirited celebrations.[93]

FIGURE 3.10. THE HARVEY HOSPITAL. This primitive sketch shows the Harvey U.S. Army Hospital located in the block bounded by Spaight, Brearly, and Lake Monona. Originally built as a home for Leonard J. Farwell in 1854, it had been vacant and in the hands of a receiver since Farwell's financial reverses in 1858. Indeed, the huge 9,000-square-foot mansion might well have continued vacant if it had not been for the extraordinary work of Cordelia Harvey, widow of Governor Louis P. Harvey. Governor Harvey was accidentally drowned while visiting Wisconsin soldiers in southern Illinois in April 1862.

After her husband's death, Cordelia continued her intense concern for Wisconsin soldiers, especially the treatment of the sick and wounded. Soon after being appointed state sanitary agent by Acting Governor Salomon, Mrs. Harvey began a whirlwind tour of Union hospitals from New Orleans to St. Louis, where she visited Wisconsin soldiers. During these trips she became convinced that sick and wounded Wisconsin soldiers would more quickly recover in northern hospitals. In a letter to Governor Salomon written from Memphis in March 1863, Mrs. Harvey explained her views more completely. "Oh, how we feel the necessity of Northern hospitals now," she said. "Could the 'Water Cure' at Madison have been fitted up by the Government for a military hospital, many a valuable life might have been spared to Wisconsin. . . . How our dying ones look with longing eyes and outstretched arms northward, and with their last breath ask, 'Can't we go home?' "

Acting Governor Salomon agreed with Mrs. Harvey on the efficacy of northern hospitals and in 1862, along with several other governors, he urged the national government to establish a network of northern recovery hospitals. Washington military officials, however, turned down the request, fearing that soldiers would never return to their units after their recovery. Their decision was largely based upon the failure of an earlier system, which provided furloughs to injured soldiers. Unfortunately, many men failed to return to their units after their recovery and fighting ability of several armies was virtually destroyed. In response to the abused furlough system, a policy had been established whereby all wounded soldiers were to be kept in military hospitals as near the front as possible.

Undeterred by this official turn-down, Mrs. Harvey resolved to go to the top and had Wisconsin's Senator Doolittle arrange an audience for her with President Lincoln. Mrs. Harvey took with her a petition bearing the signatures of eight thousand Wisconsin voters. Her lively account of her three meetings with the President in September 1863, which appeared in the *Wisconsin Magazine of History* (1917, pp. 232–255), reveals both the determination of Mrs. Harvey and a very human portrait of a frustrated and fitful Lincoln.

Soon after her visit with the president, Mrs. Harvey received a letter from Secretary of War Edward M. Stanton explaining that he had ordered the establishment of the Harvey Hospital at the Farwell House at Madison. Later that year two other hospitals were established at Milwaukee and Prairie du Chien.

When the Harvey hospital opened in early October 1863, 106 patients were in residence. In February, 1864, a large three-hundred-foot-long wing (shown on the right in the sketch) was added and capacity went up to about six hundred patients. So many men were being sent to the Harvey Hospital that two hundred men had to be accommodated at the Camp Randall hospital. By September 1865, all the men had left and the furnishings were sold. Today all that remains is a little-noticed marble stone at the corner of Spaight and Brearly Streets, placed there to commemorate the spot by Madison school children in 1908. (National Archives 165-C-697)

By the same token there were periods of the war when Union prospects looked very bleak, especially between July 1862, and July 1863, when many Madisonians dreaded to read the newspapers for fear there might no longer be a country to love and honor.[94]

In spite of spirited celebrations of military victories and the widespread support for soldier and soldier family assistance efforts, a nagging and fundamental disagreement about the purpose of the war lurked below the surface. Nearly all Madisonians wanted to preserve the Union; the question was—under what conditions. The local Republican Party; the *Wisconsin State Journal;* the Union League, an uncompromising patriotic loyalty organization; and the Freedmen's Society, a freed slave welfare organization—all insisted on preservation of the Union but with the *abolition* of slavery, whersas the local Democratic party and the *Daily Patriot* warmly embraced preservation of the Union *with* slavery.

The role of slavery in the future of the Union became clearer after Lincoln issued his emancipation proclamation in January 1863. Steven D. Carpenter, editor of the *Daily Patriot,* ridiculed Lincoln's decision to "fix the price of niggers at $300" (the compensated emancipation proposal) by noting that this was the same price the administration was willing to pay in the form of a bounty to a white soldier conscript. "Thus we have it by abolition legislation," continued Carpenter, "that the liberty of one negro is worth just as much as the life of one white man. The nation ought to feel grateful to the abolition party for settling this matter. Heretofore there had been some doubt on the subject,"[95] he added sarcastically. During the 1864 campaign the *Daily Patriot* carried a long, fervent editorial arguing that "disguise is no longer possible. The object for which the war is being prosecuted is the liberation of the black. Credulous, indeed, must that man be who honestly thinks that the administration is now governed by a desire to preserve the Union or reestablish constitutional government over the

rebel states. No peace without the overthrow of slavery is now the rallying cry of the party in power."[96]

The *State Journal* took the position that to be for the Union *with* slavery was to be disloyal and did all it could to pillory the *Patriot* and Democrats for this form of high treason. However, when the votes were counted in heavily Democratic Madison, Lincoln got forty-seven percent, whereas McClellan, who appeared to favor a negotiated reunion with the South, received fifty-three percent.[97] Certainly there was no shortage of reasons to vote against Lincoln without having to pick his emancipation proclamation. His difficulty in finding a winning general, being soft on the South at certain critical junctures, his conscription program, and many more no doubt caused many to vote against Lincoln's program. But mixed into the overwhelming majority of votes rolled up for McClellan in Madison in 1864 were many who strongly opposed Lincoln's "Negro policy."

Disagreements about slavery and the role of Negroes were also evident elsewhere in the community. From city pulpits, both prior to and after the outbreak of hostilities, ministers made fervent arguments both for and against slavery, with the Baptists and Presbyterians generally for slavery and the Methodists against.[98] In 1864 a member of the Madison school board offered a resolution prohibiting "persons of African descent" from being admitted to the public schools. The resolution also offered to make "adequate provision for their education" providing this could be done "without detriment to the education of white children." Although the motion was tabled by the board, one must wonder how many Madisonians would have supported it.[99] Madison's black population in 1860 was a miniscule half of one percent (thirty-two persons). The threat of numbers can hardly be seen as the basis for the request. Perhaps it was based upon the fear that emancipated slaves would come streaming into Madison after the war was over, a common fear in the North at the time. Certainly there is little evidence of generosity of spirit toward blacks in Madison. A black man who came to Madison in

April 1864, with a white woman—possibly his wife—was turned away from all of Madison's hotels.[100] Even the *Wisconsin State Journal* used pejorative terms like "sambo" and "nigger" in referring to blacks.[101] What the future held for blacks in Madison was far from settled.

Madison's War Record

Even before the war ended, Madison's impressive contribution was evident.[102] Following the departure of men who volunteered for Lincoln's last call in the spring of 1865, the *Wisconsin State Journal* calculated that there could not be more than six hundred able-bodied men between the ages of twenty and forty-five left in town.[103] This meant that about two out of every three men in this age group were no longer in the city. Most were fighting for the Union.[104]

Madison's disproportionate contribution of men was confirmed after the war by the 1865 report of the Wisconsin Adjutant General, which compared the record of Wisconsin cities. Measured in soldiers produced per total 1860 population, Madison ranked number one.[105] Among the ten largest cities in the state, Madison had not only produced more soldiers on a proportionate basis, but also lost more men than the state average. Statewide about fifteen percent died, whereas twenty-four percent of men credited to Madison died in service.[106]

One need only examine where these Madison men died to see how extensively they participated in the bloody war. They were killed in the famous battles of Bull Run, Virginia, and Gettysburg, Pennsylvania. They fell capturing cities like Vicksburg, Mississippi; Memphis, Tennessee; Mobile, Alabama; Little Rock, Arkansas; and Atlanta, Georgia. They died at the infamous Andersonville prison in Georgia and of war related diseases and accidents. There is no question that surviving Madison soldiers could have written a remarkably complete military history of the war.[107]

An examination of Wisconsin units composed largely of Madison men showed that one unit, the Governors Guard, had produced an unusually large number of high ranking officers. From that original seventy-eight-man company composed of professionals and businessmen, which left Madison in April 1861, came one brigadier general, nine colonels, six lieutenant colonels, five majors, ten captains, twelve lieutenants, and nine noncommissioned officers and privates. An early Madison historian asked: "Can any military organization in the United States of its own age and numbers show a better record? . . . If not, we claim the championship for the Governor's Guard of Madison."[108]

The amount of direct public and private support given by Madisonians for bounties and soldier family welfare was equally impressive. Something in the vicinity of $133,000 can be documented.[109] The contributions came from a city almost hopelessly in debt, whose citizens were also paying a steep war-time income tax.

Rowdies in Blue: Madison as
a Civil War Camp Town

A few days after the surrender of Fort Sumter, Governor Alexander Randall called upon one of his administration appointees, Horace A. Tenney, who was at work in his garden. He told the prominent attorney, editor, and long-time Madison booster to do all work necessary to convert the thirty-acre state fair grounds into a military camp for the reception and training of volunteers, who would arrive in about two weeks.[110]

Randall and many others thought the rebellion would be put down quickly and that an elaborate camp would not be needed. They were wrong. By 1864 the State Agricultural Society's fairgrounds had become Wisconsin's largest and most important military training complex, containing ninety-four buildings capable of accommodating five thousand men at a time. By the end of the war seventy thousand men—eighty-five percent of all Wisconsin soldiers who served in the Grand Army of the Republic—had received their basic military training there. The presence of seventy thousand young men, mostly between eighteen and thirty-five years of age, had a dramatic and predictable effect upon the staid little city of about sixty-six hundred persons: they transformed Madison into a rough and lively military camp town.[111]

On May 1, 1861, the first group of soldiers, the Second Wisconsin Regiment, arrived. Their commanding officer named this place Camp Randall in honor of the governor. Tenney's small army of carpenters had only been at work for three days when the men arrived. Consequently little work had been done except enclosing the cattlesheds around the perimeter of the grounds so they could be used for temporary soldier barracks. Until the conversion from fairgrounds to military camp grounds could be completed, some of the soldiers were forced to stay in local hotels. The Randall Guards, for example, stayed at a popular farmer's hotel, the Jaquish House, now a residence at the corner of Jenifer and Patterson Streets. From this location the men marched back and forth to camp in military style. Those who stayed at the unfinished camp were forced to sleep on wet, straw-filled bunks because the roofs on the old cattlesheds leaked. When it rained, the bread became soggy and the coffee diluted because the cook shack had no walls. Still, the enthusiastic volunteers complained remarkably little and many boasted of their ability to endure hardship.[112]

A camp routine was quickly established: For enlisted men the schedule called for reveille and roll call at 5:00 A.M., breakfast at 6:30, liberty until 10:00, then two hours of drill between 10:00 and 12:00. At noon the men dined on beans, corned beef, bread and butter, with soup every other day. Following lunch the men were at liberty until 2:00 P.M., when all would assemble for two hours of batallion drills and regimental parades. Supper was at 5:30. Most had nothing to do after supper and nearly all complained bitterly about the 9:00 P.M., bedtime for grown men."[113]

The townfolk took a strong, immediate interest in the camp. Large numbers turned out to watch the colorful and impressive afternoon drills. At first it was common for nearly all the members of the legislature to attend. Newspaper accounts described the "evolutions" in great detail. Madison women provided boxes of delicacies and put on fancy dinners and special parties for the men.[114]

To the soldiers and townfolk the first month was new, exciting, inspiring and hopeful—a mutual great adventure. The townfolk were thrilled to have the brave volunteers in their midst and eager to do all they could to increase their physical comforts and reinforce their patriotism. The soldiers deeply appreciated the large local audiences at their drills and the tasty supplements to their meager menus. But the first month turned out to be a brief honeymoon before a tempestuous relationship that was marked by intense and mutual ambivalence.

Although the camp remained an exciting place to the townfolk, it quickly became boring to the men. According to contemporary military theory, drilling taught discipline and discipline made men ready for war. Basic military training for the Camp Randall soldier, therefore, consisted primarily of drilling. Incredible as it may seem, rifles were often not issued until the day before departure from the camp. Practice with the weapons therefore had to wait until the battlefield. So to the men it was eat and drill, drill and eat, drill, drill, drill.[115]

Getting ready for the war was, of course, deadly serious business, but with drill only occupying three to four hours a day, the men had a lot of time on their hands. Letters and diaries reflected a wide variety of leisure-time interests. One man looked around his barracks one evening and wrote his family that there were "six games of cards going, four or five writing letters, five or six singing psalms, and some singing something of a good deal worse character, Charlie Franklin is playing the fiddle, Bartholomew the tambourine and someone is dancing the jig. Two or three are eating and another group are just organizing a debating lyceum."[116]

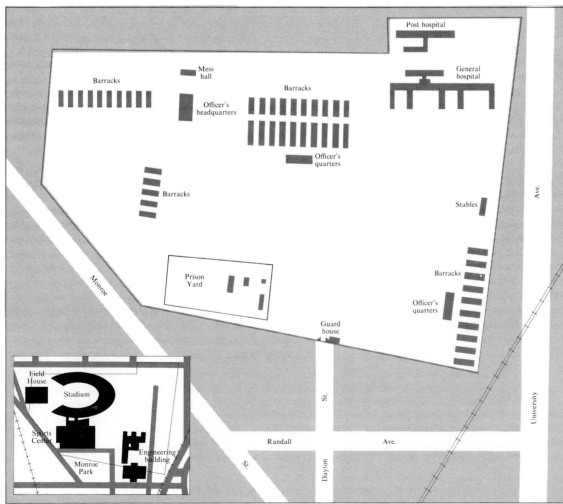

FIGURE 3.11. CAMP RANDALL LITHOGRAPH AND SITE PLAN. This busy military scene shows Camp Randall in May 1864, just after a major building program had been completed. To capture this scene, the enterprising Moseley brothers hired a Milwaukee lithographer who apparently sat atop Bascom Hall to obtain this view. The scene was no doubt popular as a souvenir for soldiers and relatives who at that time were pouring through the camp. The soldiers in the foreground are marching along University Avenue, and the Milwaukee and Prairie du Chien troop train is running along the same right of way used today by the Milwaukee Road. The road extending into the horizon on the upper left is Randall Avenue.

The site plan shows the camp in January 1865. Major buildings are identified and can be easily related to the buildings on the lithograph. The inset shows camp boundaries in relation to existing streets and buildings. (SHSW WHi(X32)8764).

What the letter writer did not say was that some of his buddies had gone uptown. Uptown Madison to a bored and lonely soldier was a far more attractive place to be than a dank converted cattleshed. Uptown there were billiard halls, bowling alleys, lager beer gardens, saloons, cigars, card games, cameraderie, and much more. The problem was that a soldier had to have a pass to get out of camp, and passes were sometimes tough to get. Consequently a lot of Camp Randall soldiers indulged in what must have been an exceptionally popular pastime, namely, jumping the eight-foot-high board fence surrounding the camp and going uptown. Much of the time the camp officers didn't know the men were gone.

The citizens of Madison, by contrast, caught on very quickly. Just four days after the first regiment arrived in camp the newspapers reported a melee at one of the local watering spots. The camp commander insisted the brawlers were not soldiers, but camp hangers-on. For a time everyone seemed satisfied by this explanation. No one wanted to believe that brave and patriotic volunteers were capable of such rowdy conduct. Even the police treated the rioters with great deference, thinking they were members of the revered Second Regiment.[117]

Gradually, however, townfolk realized that thousands of young men gathered together in a military camp are not likely to exercise decorum and restraint all the time. The *State Journal* put it this way: "The behavior of the men gathered here as soldiers has been on the whole commendable, but among so many it could hardly fail that there should be some of the 'baser sort.' A few rowdies have been cutting up some rascally pranks. . . ."[118]

For the first month most Madisonians had been tolerant and understanding of the "rascally pranks." But a "scandalous outrage" on the evening of June 10, 1861, provided an unceremonious introduction to the perils of being a military camp town. On that evening three or four hundred men were given furloughs after being mustered into the army. Typically, the men went home for

a few days before returning to Madison to go south, but for some reason the men were turned loose between 9:00 and 10:00 P.M. One group of soldiers allegedly killed a German woman in a "base and brutal manner." At 3:00 A.M. the following morning another group of drunken soldiers tried to break into Voigt's brewery at the intersection of State and Gorham Streets. When the irate Mr. Voigt ordered them to leave, they refused. He fired a warning shot over their heads. The men then began to lay seige to the brewery, discharging their pistols in the direction of Mr. Voigt and breaking his windows with stones. Several citizens opened fire on the men and they retreated, but not until one of the soldiers had been hit.[119]

Response to the incident was "intense indignation." Citizens wanted immediate answers. How does it happen that volunteers are permitted to roam around the streets of a peaceable city armed with revolvers? What can be done without the "totally inadequate" police force? Perhaps the question that perplexed people the most, though, was how soldiers engaged in such a noble cause could be involved in such sordid affairs?[120]

The following evening an excited crowd jammed the courthouse to consider measures for the better protection of citizens. Mayor Vilas called the meeting to order. Governor Randall attempted to quiet the storm of indignation but was jeered for several minutes by the hostile crowd. Some thirty to forty Germans armed with guns threatened to shoot one speaker. Finally order was restored and the crowd instructed the mayor "to take such steps as necessary to insure the peace and quiet of the city."[121]

Mayor Vilas met with Colonel Coon, commanding officer of the Second Regiment, after which the colonel made a surprise check of the sentinels guarding the camp fence. To his chagrin, he found three guards asleep. Coon immediately established a better guard system and allowed men to leave the camp only in the custody of a responsible officer. The reforms were undertaken with mixed feelings by Camp Randall officers and men. Coon felt his men had been

unfairly maligned, and in the course of the investigation the men became so angered at the bad press they were receiving, they vowed to attack the newspaper office if their officers would give them the word.[122]

In spite of precautions on both sides, the year after the June 1861 "outrage" was full of incidents. Accounts of merchants being beaten and robbed and households having chickens and turkeys stolen were very common. Several attempted rapes were reported.[123] In October 1861, a group of two hundred men who had just received orders to ship out openly defied camp authorities, charged the fence, and headed uptown for the saloons and one last fling. Fortunately the chief of police received word of the break. With the help of military patrols all the fence jumpers were rounded up, except for one determined group that was found the following morning serenading a house of ill repute.

To some Madisonians these continued incidents proved the futility of trying to induce better behavior by promulgating regulations. The real solution, they argued, required a sincere change of heart. Numerous officers who also felt there was great hope in internal moral reform marched their troops to Madison churches to attend Sunday services.[124] One group of ladies therefore brought their hymn books and Sunday School right into the barracks. Another group held a revival. Still another group sought pledges to abstain from alcohol. None seemed conspicuously successful, however. The teetotalers, for example, only secured 363 abstinence pledges during the entire war.

In spite of strained town-camp relations resulting from these incidents, there were also circumstances that generated close bonds between citizens and soldiers. Certainly the huge turnouts for the early regiment departures, the presence of many townfolk at regimental parades and drills, and the fund-raising benefits helped. But the single most effective generator of good feeling from the soldier point of view was the home-cooked food, especially dinners and desserts provided by the local ladies. It was no accident that immediately after one such dinner a soldier wrote that his regiment would always have a warm spot in their hearts for the people of Madison.[125]

Madisonians were again aroused to the boiling point by a brutal and unprovoked attack on a farmer in January 1862. "Have we no police regulations," asked one fed-up observer, "that can be brought to bear upon the drunken rowdies that infest our streets at almost all hours of the day and night making it unsafe for a lady to step outside her own dwelling unless attended by a guard? A man cannot even walk or drive his team along the public avenues after nightfall without being insulted and beaten by a rowdy soldier."[126]

This time relief was sought from the legislature. Camp Randall officers argued that it was impossible to control the men with liquor and beer so readily available. Nearly every other house between Camp Randall and the capitol sold spirits, said one soldier's letter with pardonable exaggeration. Thus by the time the men got into town they were "full to running over." Adding credence to the officers' alarm was the fact that between 1860 and 1865 the number of Madison saloon and tavern licenses tripled. The senate responded in early February 1862, by passing a bill prohibiting the sale of liquor to any soldier within three miles of the camp. The measure was backed by a heavy fine, with one-half of the money going to the informers. Unfortunately for the officers and townfolk, the assembly killed the bill.[127]

With legislative relief out of the picture, citizens became much more militant and banded together whenever called upon to do so. In one instance "two or three lawyers and other civilians" used pitchforks and sled sticks to prostrate a band of soldiers who had just assaulted a citizen.[128]

Camp officers took several corrective steps, including the imposition of earlier curfews, stricter punishments, street patrols, and very limited pass privileges. One colonel required any soldier involved in rowdyism to carry an eighty-pound bag of sand on his back for an entire day with a guard watching so the delinquent could not rest. Not all

the officers, however, felt the blame lay entirely with the soldier. Some felt "poisons" in cheap liquor sold by Madison grog dealers were responsible.[129]

It didn't take long for townfolk to find causes for the soldier misbehavior. Officers were blamed for not being able to control their men. This deficiency is not as surprising as it seems when one understands that the men held the right to elect their own officers; in this respect the officers held power at the sufferance of their men. Moreover, very few officers knew any more about drilling than their men. To correct this problem, special drill sessions were held for the officers during weekday mornings at Camp Randall. It was not at all unusual for the rank and file to pause to debate an order. During the summer of 1861 one group of harrassed officers were forced to reach into their own pockets and buy twenty kegs of beer simply to maintain control of men who couldn't stand the camp food. Clearly the men did not view officers and military discipline as ordained on high. Symptomatic of this mind-set were criticisms made by the *Daily Patriot* of the new style of giving orders in a "gruff forbidding voice" instead of "kindly and courteously." The writer argued that the new rough, domineering style was appropriate for "dumb brutes" but not "educated men."[130]

Another factor that encouraged soldier misbehavior was that the Madison police force was so pathetically small. During most of the war it consisted of a handful of officers, and during the early part of the war they were being pushed by Mayor Vilas to spend their time impounding itinerant animals.[131]

Poor camp conditions were also a contributing factor. Complaints about sour bread, stinky meat, lice in clothing, and vermin in bedding were staples of soldier letters. Leaky roofs in the old converted cattlesheds made wet bunks commonplace, and the sheds were intolerably cold. Once when the thermometer fell to below zero, some of the older buildings were torn down so their wood could be used for fuel. Even this was insufficient to keep the men warm, and so they were given

furloughs so they could fend for themselves in local hotels and friends' homes. Riots and disturbances protesting the poor conditions were an integral part of Camp Randall throughout its history.[132]

Apparently the soldiers were not exaggerating camp conditions. A senate select committee investigating Camp Randall conditions in late 1862 and early 1863 found the cattlesheds "wholly unfit for any human being to live in," the bread "sour, dank, and not well baked," the beans ". . . in a state of decay and entirely unfit for use," the meat "composed of hogs heads and neck pieces . . . of poor beef much of which had been killed too long ago to be palatable," and the coffee "a villainous . . . execrable counterfeit so unsavory and deleterious as to be beyond use." Camp officials contended things were not as bad as the senators said but agreed they were not as good as they should have been. They argued they had tried hard to correct known problems. For example, one man who had a contract to supply food to the camp said he had tried nearly all bakeries in Madison in an effort to get a decent bread—but without real success. Perhaps the most telling fact of the investigation was that numerous improvements were immediately ordered.[133]

The men were outraged they should receive such treatment in the capital of their state. Curse upon curse was heaped upon the contractors, many of whom were Madison businessmen, for their poor quality food and supplies. Some felt the camp superintendent, H. A. Tenney, was getting rich putting up cheap barracks for the men.[134] At best some Madison people seemed intent upon exploiting the soldiers.

Nor is it difficult to see how easily anti-Camp Randall feelings became widely shared among Madisonians. After eighteen months of first hand observation, many were disillusioned and angered by the assaults, rapes, thievery, swearing, and general misbehavior of the soldiers. No longer did the townfolk persist in portraying the men in blue in rosy hues. At the same time, some Madison residents acknowledged that some regiments were better behaved than others. Still, with so many units coming and going it was difficult to keep the good and bad units straight.[135]

Accompanying this disillusionment was a steady decline of interest in Camp Randall activities all through 1862. Drills became dull and send offs routine. Even the solicitous Ladies Aid Society discontinued its practice of providing lavish dinners for the men and giving them boxes of delicacies. Instead they sent occasional pies and cakes and practical items such as jelly, ink, magazines, and newspapers. Camp Randall has definitely become passé.[136]

The year 1863 was a quiet interlude in the stormy town-camp relationship. Secretary of War Stanton's decision to discontinue recruiting in April 1862 caused the flow of new regiments through Camp Randall to stop by January 1863. Although they did not know how long it would last, most Madisonians were surely pleased about a respite from military "liveliness."

Left in charge of the camp was the Thirtieth Regiment, whose primary responsibility was enforcement of the draft law in the state. Unlike other military units, the thirtieth became a part of the community. Because they knew they would be based in Madison for some time, some of the married men made arrangements for their wives to stay in town. The unmarried men also seemed to find ample female companionship. By attending the Methodist church one bachelor found three girls happy to do his laundry. Another bachelor simultaneously dated three town girls. The men lived relatively comfortably in newly constructed barracks and had light duty at the camp, such as picking weeds from the parade grounds. Because they were a relatively well-behaved unit, passes were generously distributed. The men used their passes to attend church, lectures and theater, go fishing, play baseball, take in circuses, participate in picnics and just about all the things the townfolk were doing. To the townfolk the idyllic period with the Thirtieth Regiment helped brighten the tarnished image of the Camp Randall soldier.[137]

Meanwhile the quick crusade to restore the Union had become a long, costly, and increasingly unpopular war. Fewer and fewer volunteers responded to the calls. No longer would men fight only for love of country or because the cause was just; they wanted money. Even the substitute provisions and high bounties were not producing soldiers. To satisfy manpower requirements, Lincoln issued calls for six hundred thousand men in 1863 and added a full-blown federal draft system to insure results.

Because it took several months to set up and implement the draft, the first Wisconsin draftees did not begin pouring into Camp Randall until February 1864. Their arrival further strained town-camp relations. The townfolk were about to learn that the behavior of reasonably inspired volunteers was one thing; the behavior of reluctant draftees was something else. Madisonians held their breath and hoped for the best. By late April, camp population soared to three thousand soldiers, nearly one soldier for every three citizens. Mayor Leitch took the initiative and got camp military authorities to field street patrols. Their job was to promptly take to the guard house anyone involved in disorderly conduct. One reporter said there were so many patrols on Madison street corners the city looked like it was under "marshall law." Marked improvement was observed as a result of this night guard, and great hope was held out for the day guards because they might reduce the increasingly frequent "swearing scenes." "Every man is interested, or should be," said an indignant *Journal* editorial, "in having the ears of his wife or daughter protected from foul language while traveling the streets." Judging from soldier letters, local newspaper articles, and camp visitor accounts, swearing seemed to come with a uniform and was especially common among draftees. Typical of visitor reaction was the response of John Muir, then a student at the UW, who visited a hometown friend at camp. "Dear! such conversation," he later wrote a friend, "you have no idea how abominable it was. And yet when I expressed my abhorrence of such language, Bryan laughingly said, 'Why John this is

not a beginning of what you would hear in other camps. This is one of the best in the regiment.' "[138]

In spite of the strict rules for getting out of camp, the resourceful soldiers found loopholes. One of the few acceptable reasons for getting a pass out of camp was to go to church. Instead of going to church, however, the soldiers would visit grog shops, which remained open in violation of the law. Apparently it wasn't hard to find a place to take this form of communion. The men also learned that they could extend the number of days on their passes by adding an extra digit where appropriate. To get more men out, they would hand the pass back through the fence. The problem of getting back in was easy. "Civilians" were rarely questioned when they passed through the gate. While soldiers schemed to get out of camp, Madison officials used every possible technique to keep the soldiers in there. Thus when a circus came to town two performances were arranged: one for Madisonians, another for the soldiers *inside* Camp Randall.[139]

The first outbreak of serious violence from the new influx of draftees was on May 13, 1864, when soldiers visited the Sprecher brewery at the intersection of Blount and Williamson Streets and demanded beer. Brewery workers had to arm themselves with iron pipe to repel the soldiers. Shots were fired, but no one was injured except a soldier whose neck was grazed by a ball and a brewery worker whose skull was bashed in.[140]

Then on June 12, 1864, came the first killing. A saloon keeper got into a fight with a soldier over a woman of "questionable character" and was shot by the soldier. Just two months later another murder was committed in Madison. A "respected citizen from Cottage Grove" was stabbed in the neck by a soldier wielding a butcher knife. This second murder triggered a fierce political battle swirling around the fact that the dead man was a "copperhead," the Republican designation for a Democrat. Said the *Patriot,* a staunch Democratic paper, "If Democrats are to be shot down in the streets because they are . . . Copperheads as the Abolitionists are pleased to call them, there will be shooting and mobbing on both sides and woe unto those who shall inaugurate a reign of terror." The strong feelings engendered by the long war had worn down the veneer of civilization to a thin brittle covering.[141]

In the summer and fall of 1864 things once again seemed to be veering out of control. By September camp population had risen to thirty-four hundred, an all-time high.[142] Unprovoked assault and battery and robbery once again became everyday occurrences. Citizens were urged to secure arms to protect themselves from "these brutal attacks from the rowdies in blue." Some residents in the four hundred block of West Main Street had to post guards in front of their houses as protection against soldiers who would come to the windows, knock down fences, and worse. Respectable women would seldom be seen on the streets. The ladies of the evening reportedly did right well in the Capitol Park, especially after the soldiers had been paid. Some enterprising madams had houses of ill-repute built within convenient walking distance of the camp. In the words of one commentator, "girls and chickens strayed from their yards at their own peril." So boisterous were the soldiers in camp that their shouting could be heard for miles.[143]

Neither military nor civilian authorities seemed able to curtail this behavior. Mayor Leitch delivered a special message to the Common Council in which he said that "murder and highway robbery and riot have been with impunity committed against us." He pleaded with aldermen to petition the legislature to remove the onerous and punitive levy limit inflicted on the city by the legislature for its improvident spending eight years before. Until that limit was removed, the mayor said the city could not possibly raise the money to hire the policemen needed to protect citizens.[144]

Suddenly in April 1865, at an obscure town in southern Virginia the great war ended. Almost overnight the attitude of the townfolk toward Camp Randall lost its tense, brittle qualities. Now the feeling was forgiving, understanding—even

generous. With the war over and the Union preserved, the townfolk found it easier to establish a sense of perspective about Camp Randall and the boys in blue. The fact was most of the soldiers behaved remarkably well most of the time under some very trying conditions. Still, as the recipients of so many soldier depredations during the war, many townspeople had trouble keeping this in mind. The misbehavior of the few predictably received the most attention. In the end Madisonians endured the soldiers, and the soldiers endured Camp Randall.

The Local Economy: Civil War Developments

Wisconsin's economy had barely recovered from the Panic of 1857 when the secession of southern states placed great strains on state banks. Banks of that period were able to issue their own money providing they were backed by acceptable bonds and three-fourths of Wisconsin banks backed their currency with Southern bonds. As the likelihood of recession increased, the value dropped steadily. By the time hostilities began, the value of many of these bonds had dropped to just one-fourth of their prewar value.[145] Banks that relied most on the Southern bonds found they were unable to compensate for the declining value of the underlying collateral bonds. By the end of 1861 nearly one out of three of Wisconsin banks had failed.[146] The problem was relieved but not solved when representatives of Wisconsin's stronger banks agreed not to accept the notes of the weaker Wisconsin banks at any price.

Fortunately all of Madison's banks were a part of this strong bank pact, so Madisonians were spared the financial devastation suffered by many around the state. However, this did not mean that Madisonians were spared the chaotic currency conditions that characterized the state during the early war years. A University of Wisconsin student discovered when he tried to make some purchases at a Madison store that many of his bills

had been declared worthless by the Wisconsin Bankers Association.[147] A leading merchant had to close down for an hour until he could consult with his banker on which bills were "current."[148] The customer then had the problem of determining what bills to accept as change.[149]

The Madison papers began featuring daily monetary news columns telling readers which bills were worth what amount. Many customers paid for goods with gold or silver coins or—lacking these—with bushels of wheat. Things got so bad in 1862 that Congress made stamps a legal medium of exchange—probably the worst medium ever known in the U.S. Imagine trying to hand the stage driver his fare of two three-cent stamps on a rainy day.[150] Not until 1863, when a new federal currency known as "greenbacks" was issued in massive quantities, did the country achieve a stable monetary system.

As if the chaotic currency and financial conditions were not enough, Wisconsin farmers were forced to endure an unusually severe drought in 1858 and 1859. Not only was the wheat crop negligible, but "grass and hay were deficient, and potatoes and root crops were all failures." Fortunately, better times were around the corner. According to one observer, "the winter of 1859–60 was, however, mercifully mild, open, and terminated by an unprecedented early spring. There had been practically no snow to relieve the drought, and when farmers began sowing wheat in March, it was with the but faint hope of a harvest. The sown grain . . . lay in the dust dry soil for a month without sprouting. Then came the rains, steady, continuous, abundant and the crop was made."[151] It was a crop as Wisconsin had never seen, even in the palmy days of the pioneers.

The 1860 bumper wheat crop was largely responsible for a sharp recovery of the Madison economy in late 1860 and 1861. In that boom year, Dane County's billowing wheat fields yielded over three million bushels—a record never surpassed.[152] Beginning in 1860 and continuing until 1930 Dane County led the state in the number of acres devoted to farming. In 1860 nearly half of Dane County's total acres were devoted to crops, mostly wheat.[153] For the agriculturally based Madison economy, these conditions produced a strong infusion of wheat prosperity.

Beginning in the spring of 1861, farmers once again had money in their pockets. That money flowed into Madison in substantial quantities. Like the halcyon days of the Farwell boom, the streets around Capitol Square were once again full of teams and business was brisk.[154] Madison grain buyers did a flourishing business with farmers, many of whom did not sell their crop until 1861. Large numbers of costly and substantial homes were started and rental housing was becoming scarce— "a sure sign of prosperity."[155] Said the *Wisconsin State Journal,* "mechanics and laborers have found plenty of employment, and our people may be considered as prosperous and happy."[156] Business was brisk, too, at Camp Randall, where more than sixteen businessmen had set up shops to do business with the soldiers right on the grounds.[157]

Business seemed to be moving along to everyone's satisfaction until the spring of 1862, when the spring trade failed to appear. A meeting was held to inquire into the cause of "The Great Falling Off of Business."[158] Newspaper coverage of the problem revealed clear agreement. Madison was "becoming a second rate marketing town,"[159] because Madison's only railroad, the Milwaukee and Prairie du Chien, was charging outrageously high freight rates to ship wheat from Madison to Milwaukee. Instead of coming to Madison, farmers were taking their wheat to Sun Prairie, the new terminus of the Watertown and Madison Railroad, because that line offered cheaper rates to Milwaukee. On a typical day Sun Prairie was allegedly getting seven times more wheat than Madison.[160] With only slight exaggeration, one observer noted that wheat teams on their way to Sun Prairie kept the grass down on Madison's major streets.[161] The bitter irony was that Madison had loaned the Madison and Watertown railroad one hundred thousand dollars to get that railroad into Madison, but the 1857 crash halted

constructed at Sun Prairie. The City of Madison had unintentionally helped Sun Prairie become a successful rival.

Everyone agreed the city desperately needed a second railroad. The *Journal* argued that "a crisis had . . . arrived in the history of our town and we must either meet it like practical men or consent to sink into a fourth-rate country village—a way station on the Milwaukee and Prairie du Chien Road—our business confined to a little peanut trade at the depot in the summer, and wooing and washing the Legislature in the winter."[162]

In 1862 Madison's dream of becoming a railroad center was so tantalizingly close to being realized that one could almost smell the smoke of the engines. Just twelve miles separated Madison from Sun Prairie, the terminus of the Watertown and Madison railroad, the critically important alternative route to Milwaukee. Just twenty-three miles separated Madison from Footville, Wisconsin, the terminus of the Beloit and Madison Railroad, Madison's first direct line to Chicago. Just thirty-three miles separated Madison from Portage and connections to Green Bay and the pineries to the north. Thus, just sixty-eight additional miles of railroad could have given Madison three new lines. Unfortunately none of the railroads could secure enough money to complete the lines.

Many Madisonians felt the company most likely to liberate their city from the railroad monopoly was the Madison and Portage Railroad. Backers believed that if this railroad were completed, it would force the other two railroads to complete their lines into Madison. One reason the Madison and Portage line was being pushed was that Simeon Mills, a very prominent, active businessman and former village trustee had been elected president of the line in January 1862 and enjoyed the complete confidence of Madisonians.[163] At a railroad subscription rally in mid-May, fifteen thousand dollars were raised, mostly by workingmen and mechanics, for the completion of the line.[164] Although some grading was

done with the funds raised by subscription, the money was insufficient to complete the line into Madison.

Meanwhile, Simeon Mills, wearing another hat as a director of the Beloit and Madison Road, was moving to raise ten thousand dollars to complete that line from Footville and give Madison a direct line to Chicago. Mills moved quickly to get the Common Council to give him a right-of-way along Johnson Street between Francis and Blair Streets.[165] Johnson Street might well have become a railroad corridor if wealthy and influential property owners had not intervened. Former Mayor Levi B. Vilas, who lived just one block from the proposed railroad track, was joined by many others to prevent the neighborhood from being violated by a noisy, dirty railroad. The council upheld the residents of this newly fashionable neighborhood and said that no "respectable street" should be used for a railroad track. Instead, the council recommended that a lakeshore route be used.[166] Three months later the council gave the lakeshore to the railroad. Finally on September 7, 1864, the long-awaited second railroad began serving Madison. By the time it arrived the road had been consolidated with the rapidly growing Chicago and Northwestern Railroad.[167]

While the Beloit and Madison was the second railroad to reach Madison, some might argue that another railroad deserves that distinction. The line had no name, was only seven blocks long, and was built without the help of any subscription rallies, city loans, stock, bonds, or speeches. Its builder was Alexander A. McDonnell, the contractor of the capitol extension, and its purpose was to haul stone from Prairie du Chien right into Capitol Park. Built in July and August 1858, the road passed along Mifflin Street from the Milwaukee and Prairie du Chien depot to a point just before the intersection of Wisconsin Avenue, where it curved into the Capitol Park. The railroad was especially popular with boys who would jump on and make the run down to the depot. After all, the price was reasonable, and a steam train was a pretty exciting contrivance for boys of that era.[168]

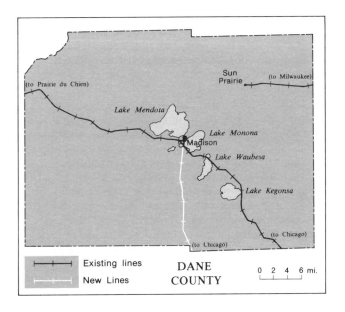

FIGURE 3.12. BELOIT AND MADISON RAILROAD. The 1864 Common Council decision to use the lakeshore as a railroad right-of-way profoundly affected Madison's land use patterns. Property owners on the lake side of Wilson Street between Bedford and Blair found their lots much less desirable for residential purposes when their lakeyards had to be shared with noisy soot-belching locomotives.

In 1952, after serving eighty years as a railroad corridor, city officials found it easy to expand this transportation corridor into a four-lane highway for automobiles.

To make the connection between the south shore of Monona Bay and the lakeshore right-of-way, the railroad had to cross the Mississippi and Prairie du Chien tracks in the middle of Monona Bay. Thus, the Beloit and Madison right-of-way ordinance may have made Madison the only city in the world where two railroad tracks cross in the middle of a lake.

By the time the first Beloit and Madison train arrived in Madison on September 7, 1864, the railroad was acquired by the Chicago and Northwestern Railway, then in a period of rapid growth. Their first schedule published in September 1864 is shown here.

The last two years of the Civil War witnessed a strong upturn in Madison business activity. The number of new homes, churches, and business buildings started in the spring of 1863 in Madison was unusually large.[169] Many of Madison's prominent businessmen took advantage of the favorable building conditions to erect fancy mansions, many of which are landmarks today.[170] Both the German Jews and the Methodists launched building programs.[171] Ads for real property began reappearing in the newspapers, and by early 1864

some were already talking about another real estate boom.[172] Wheat prices, although not reaching the highs of 1861, assured farmers a large share of the accelerating economy.[173] Reputable Madison businessmen were quoted in early 1864 as saying that business and manufacturing interests in the city had doubled since 1862.[174] A growing number of Madison businessmen found ways to make small fortunes tailoring uniforms, baking bread, churning butter, providing coffee, and butchering cattle and pigs for the Camp

Randall soldiers. A local purchasing agent put an ad in the papers for one thousand cavalry horses.[175]

During the Civil War Madison and several other inland railroad towns secured a toe-hold in manufacturing, nearly all of which was concentrated in agricultural implements. The industry grew up in response to a very rapid expansion in the number of acres devoted to wheat in the late 1850s and early 1860s, the relatively simple construction of many essential implement parts, many of which could be fabricated with readily available hardwoods, and, finally, to the scarcity of manpower due to the war. By 1864, agricultural implements were the number one manufacturing industry in Madison based on volume.[176]

Madison's leading manufacturer was E. W. Skinner Company, which concentrated in reapers and mowers. Other Madison businessmen chose not to manufacture agricultural implements and instead got lucrative franchises to distribute agricultural equipment throughout the entire northwest.[177]

Madison's nascent manufacturing was also encouraged by the sudden absence of southern crops such as cotton and sugar. Dane County acreage devoted to sheep raising and flax—both substitutes for cotton—increased dramatically between 1860 and 1865.[178] In 1863 the old Farwell water-powered mill was converted into a woolen mill turning out large amounts of cloth, much of it used for soldier uniforms.[179] In 1864 clothing manufacturing, mostly military uniforms, was the second biggest industry in Madison after agricultural implements.[180]

During the Civil War Madison became the center of the state sorghum industry. Madison manufacturer E. W. Skinner began making sorghum mills for grinding the pulp into syrup in 1861. By 1863 this manufacturer was producing one hundred mills a year, and by 1865 about five hundred were produced each year at his large factory located on Lake Mendota at the foot of Lake Street.[181] Between 1863 and 1866 Madison hosted annual conventions of sorghum raisers and

equipment manufacturers. A short-lived industry periodical, the *Northwestern Sorgho Journal,* was published in Madison in 1865.[182] In spite
of great enthusiasm and energy among sorghum
promoters, it was impossible to escape the fact
that Wisconsin summers simply did not allow
enough time for the sugar substitute to ripen. Said
one knowledgeable observer, all we have ever been
able to "extort from the bastard cane called
sorghum" was a "miserable pumpkin molas-
ses."[183] Even a handsome prize offered by the state
agricultural society for powdered dry sorghum
sugar proved insufficient to overcome the short
northern growing season.[184]

In addition to being buffeted by major shifts
in the economic cycle, Madisonians were hard hit
by inflation. Although some Madisonians were
accumulating great fortunes, most business and
professional people found that when inflation was
taken into account they were making less money
than before the war.[185] Low income persons and
households with husbands off fighting found
themselves in particularly severe financial straits.
To make matters worse, the rich were creating
invidious contrasts by building huge new mansions, traveling in posh carriages, draping themselves in silk, lace, and fur, and indulging
themselves at lavish parties.[186]

Although Madison stores were well stocked
with general merchandise, many Madisonians
found they could not afford to buy staples. Between late 1862 and early 1864 butter went from
ten cents to fifty cents a pound, pork from three
and one-half cents to twenty cents per pound,
boots and shoes doubled in price, cotton products
quadrupled, and coffee got so expensive that most
people began using coffee substitutes.[187] Some of
these increases in such staples as butter, meat,
and shoes were caused in part by strong Camp
Randall-generated demand. Other cost increases
in commodities such as cotton were due to the
sudden cutoffs of southern products.

During the war prices throughout the state increased about one hundred percent, whereas
wages went up only sixty to seventy-five percent.[188] This disparity between wages and prices

provided strong impetus for skilled labor to organize into trade unions, but results were very
limited. In Madison only the seamstresses—faced
with pitifully inadequate wages—organized in the
spring of 1864.[189]

Clearly one of the most frustrating cost increases that Madisonians were called upon to endure was the price of fire wood. Until 1861 wood
costs had been kept relatively low because large
amounts of timber were being brought onto the
market by farmers converting forests to wheat
fields. However, by 1861 this conversion process
slowed dramatically; this fact and the rapidly rising demand from Camp Randall caused wood
prices to quadruple from a low of $2.50 when the
war began to $10.00 in the spring of 1864. By
1864 about one thousand wagon loads of wood
had to be hauled into the city each week to meet
energy needs. During the same year, between
seventeen hundred and two thousand acres of
timber were required to satisfy Madison energy
demands.[190] It was during the Civil War years
that conveniently located University Heights was
deforested to satisfy Camp Randall fuel needs. A
similar fate awaited the huge maple forest in
Maple Bluff, a magnificent vestige of primeval
forest whose three- to four-hundred-year-old trees
measured two and one-half to three feet in diameter, stood sixty to sighty feet high, and grew
so closely together that a wagon could scarcely
be driven through them.[191]

As the cost of fire wood went up, the quality
went down from hard maple, generally considered the best firewood, to oak and finally to green
basswood.[192] A new ordinance bristling with stiff
fines had to be passed in 1863 to prevent wood
sellers from cheating customers.[193]

Madisonians shivered and did what they could.
During the winter of 1864–65 one of the hottest
selling items was a damper for stove pipes that
would conserve fuel.[194] Capitalists were urged to
use new extraction equipment to exploit the vast
peat beds discovered in the 1850s in the Middleton area, then known as Peatville. The great hope
bordering on a panacea was cheap coal from Illinois, but this required lower freight rates and

more direct lines to the coal fields. Unfortunately, both cheap coal from Illinois and cheap
peat from Middleton eluded attempts by entrepreneurs to make them available in Madison. The
high cost of energy simply had to be endured.[195]

Society and Leisure

The Beginnings of Madison's Educational Systsm

In April 1854, Damon Kilgore, a twenty-seven-
year-old Massachusetts man, arrived in Madison
with his family. Kilgore was a Methodist minister, but he was not looking for a church. As a result of preaching for ninety successive nights and
three times on Sunday, Kilgore had ruined his
throat; he therefore wanted a new career less demanding on his vocal chords. In Madison he found
that career. One week after arriving, he signed a
one-year contract to teach in the Madison public
schools. The shift to teaching was natural enough
for Kilgore. Prior to entering the ministry, he had
taught in some of the better New England schools
and had become a disciple of Horace Mann—the
champion of the public school.[1]

Kilgore was shocked when he found Madison,
a community of five thousand persons and fifteen
hundred school-aged children, with just one
twenty-by-forty-foot schoolhouse, suitable for
maybe forty children. About eighty children were
jammed into this tiny building and another two
hundred twenty were housed in makeshift accommodations around the city, such as the basement of the Methodist Church. Another three
hundred went to various private schools, whereas
nine hundred children—sixty percent of the total
child population—did not attend school at all.[2]

The recent arrival was at once "indignant and
eager" to do something about Madison's educational inadequacies. As fate would have it, he
boarded in a house with the chairmen of both the
assembly and the senate committees on education. Kilgore used this circumstance to get the

legislature to pass a bill that established a Madison Board of Education. For this initiative the enterprising educator was rewarded by being appointed as the first superintendent of schools.[3] From this position, Superintendent Kilgore launched a vigorous campaign to sell Madison citizens on education in general and the Horace

Apathy about Public Schools

In spite of regular appeals in the newspapers, very few parents during the Civil War period took enough interest in the Madison public schools to visit them. To combat this problem, an early-day supporter of public education wrote the following catchy verses. They were sung to the tune of "Oh dear, what can the matter be, Johnny's so long at the fair." The parody was printed in the *Wisconsin State Journal* on March 1, 1864.

O, dear, what can the matter be.
Dear, Oh dear, what can the matter be;
O, dear, what can the matter be,
    Parents don't visit the school.

They visit the circus, they visit their neighbors;
They visit their flocks and the servant who labors;
They visit the soldiers with murderous sabres.
    Now, why don't they visit the school?
        O, dear, what can the matter be, etc.

(Chorus)
They care for their horses, they care for their dollars,
They care for their parties and fancy fine collars,
But little, we think, do they care for their scholars,
    Because they don't visit the school.
        O, dear, what can the matter be, etc.

We know we from hunger and cold are protected,
In virtue and knowledge our minds are directed,
But still we do think we are sadly neglected
    Because they don't visit the school.
        O, dear, what can the matter be, etc.

Mann version in particular. For this purpose Kilgore held weekly meetings for parents and other interested persons in which he led discussions, read essays, delivered lectures upon school topics, and thus created a lively public sentiment in every measure calculated to advance the interest of the public schools.[4] Parents, he quickly discovered, were not particularly interested in their children's education. He pleaded with parents to visit the school, to view the school "as a common temple for intellectual development"[5] and to recognize that teachers were holders of the "most momentous and responsible job on earth."[6] To help fan his glowing educational coals, Kilgore was instrumental in bringing Horace Mann to Madison for a spirited lecture on the evils of ignorance ("education is the only remedy against corrupt government") and began the Madison Public School Association to lobby for better public schools.[7]

The young superintendent held parents responsible for the "great irregularity" of attendance and chided them for withdrawing their children from school for frivolous reasons such as taking lessons from an itinerant singer.[8] He warned parents who furnished easy excuses for their children's tardiness that they may cause their children to be "late for success when they become men and women."[9]

Kilgore reserved some of his most pungent comments for the strong preference he found among Madisonians for the pernicious elitist private school—a predilection he fought publicly and privately to the best of his ability.[10] To those parents who worried about the physical or moral contamination of mixing "sons and daughters of poverty" with "children of the wealthy and refined," Kilgore said that "an aristocracy of wealth is the least reliable and to instill its notions into the mind of the child is unpardonable."[11] Besides, he added, the rich and poor will come into contact in later life anyway. "How much better to have the influence of refinement and virtue exerted upon the uncouth and vicious at an age when evil habits will be corrected."[12] Corporal punishment was strongly discouraged, and children who

were not clean and neatly dressed were sent home.[13] To those parents who worried about the mixing of the sexes, Kilgore said such separation was "obviously unnatural" and that daily meetings of the sexes would produce both "moral restraint and intellectual excitement."[14] To those parents who preferred private sectarian schools, the former minister had an ascerbic response: "to fill the minds of children with metaphysical speculation on religion which even mature minds do not comprehend, is absolutely and forever injurious."[15]

While he was holding weekly meetings with parents and citizens, Kilgore was meeting every Saturday morning with his growing coterie of teachers to improve their methods of instruction. For these early versions of "inservice training" he would bring different grades into a classroom for the teachers to practice upon. After the class had retired from the school room, each teacher, who had been looking on with pencil in hand, was called upon to criticize the teacher who had conducted the exercise.[16] Nearly all of Kilgore's teachers were women, whom he regarded as "the only natural and proper educators of the young."[17]

At the same time Kilgore was proselytizing for the public school, he was working to get decision makers to earmark money for school buildings and equipment. That Madison desperately needed schoolhouses was painfully obvious. During Kilgore's first year he had 267 children enrolled under his supervision in a single makeshift classroom in the basement of the Methodist church.[18] He first tried to get the village board to borrow ten thousand dollars to correct Madison's "shameful lack of school-house accomodations,"[19] but the board refused, saying it would be too large a debt. Momentarily stopped on the building front, he ordered modern school desks from Boston, but he was told by the city's more substantial citizens that such desks were an extravagance and that wooden slabs were good enough.[20] These rebuffs forced Kilgore to recognize that most of Madison's citizens were more interested in keeping down the tax rate and speculating in village lots than spending money for public schools.[21] Finally in 1856, when Madison became a city, Kilgore persuaded the first Common Council to earmark twenty-four thousand dollars of the one-hundred-thousand-dollar bond issue for four school houses, one for each ward. Unfortunately, smaller than expected proceeds from the bond issue coupled with strong disagreements between the Board of Education and Common Council members resulted in just two school houses being started during 1856—and then only after a needless lawsuit against the Common Council for withholding money. (The school board won the lawsuit.) Then in quick succession came the one-hundred-thousand-dollar loan scandal and the 1857 depression, making the prospect of any additional money for buildings almost out of the question. Only two of the four schools were completed.

The extreme financial predicament in which Madison found itself in 1857–58 forced Madison teachers to take their already meager pay in a form of script called "city orders" to be discounted up to sixty percent of face value. This de facto salary reduction quickly produced financial disaster for Kilgore, who was providing room and board to many of Madison's teachers at below market rates. The drastic cut in income from his teacher-roomers made it impossible for Kilgore to make his mortgage payments and so he lost his house.[22]

In spite of almost impossible financial conditions, Kilgore pushed for more school buildings and won. In August 1858, the Board of Education purchased its high school, the Madison Female Academy, a formerly excellent private school that went bankrupt, at the corner of Wisconsin Avenue and Johnson Street. This eventually became Madison's Central High School and then the Madison Area Vocational School. Kilgore also succeeded in starting schools in rented facilities for citizens in the outlying areas.[23]

Who Do You Want, Lincoln or McClellan?

Who do you want? This was the question that confronted Madison voters in the 1864 presidential election between Abraham Lincoln and George B. McClellan. The contrast between the two men that appears below was provided by the *Daily Patriot* on September 6, 1864. At the time the *Patriot* reflected the dominant Democratic partisan line. In November Lincoln got only forty-seven percent of the Madison vote.

Vote for Lincoln

Do you want high taxes?
Vote for Lincoln.
Do you want four years more of war?
Vote for Lincoln.
Do you want the Constitution utterly destroyed?
Vote for Lincoln.
Do you want civil liberty laid prostrate?
Vote for Lincoln
Do you want freedom of speech and of the press destroyed?
Vote for Lincoln.
Do you want the land flooded with a depreciated, worthless currency?
Vote for Lincoln.
Do you want a national debt too enormous for calculation?
Vote for Lincoln.
Do you want bankruptcy?
Vote for Lincoln.
Do you want gold and silver coin go up to five hundred per cent?
Vote for Lincoln.
Do you want to pay two dollars a yard for calico?
Vote for Lincoln.
Do you want everything you eat, wear, use—all the necessaries and luxuries of life so high that none but the richest can buy?
Vote for Lincoln.
Do you want the degraded negroes made your social and political equal?
Vote for Lincoln.

Vote for McClellan

Do you want peace and Union?
Vote for McClellan.
Do you want the Constitution reestablished?
Vote for McClellan.
Do you want a government of laws?
Vote for McClellan.
Do you want your taxes reduced?
Vote for McClellan.
Do you want your liberty protected by law?
Vote for McClellan.
Do you want a safe, sound national currency, redeemable in gold?
Vote for McClellan.
Do you want the necessaries of life brought within the reach of the poorest?
Vote for McClellan.
Do you want a pure and incorrupt Administration?
Vote for McClellan.
Do you want the enormous expenses which war brings with it, stopped?
Vote for McClellan.
Do you want the expenses of the Government reduced from more than one thousand millions annually to less than one hundred millions?
Vote for McClellan.
Do you want the writ of *habeas corpus* restored to you?
Vote for McClellan.
Do you want a Government which will secure the rights of the citizen at home, and command respect abroad?
Vote for McClellan.

Vote for Lincoln

Do you want the Union of your fathers forever destroyed?

Vote for Lincoln.

Do you want to be arrested and confined in loathsome dungeons without process of law and without hope of release?

Do you want a government which uses its powers in persecuting and imprisoning women?

Vote for Lincoln.

Do you want the rights of the destroyed?

Vote for Lincoln.

Do you want a Depotism?

Vote for Lincoln.

Do you want Conscription?

Vote for Lincoln.

Do you want a fresh call for five hundred thousand men to fill the armies every six months?

Vote for Lincoln.

Do you want hundreds of millions of your money squandered yearly for the purpose of enriching Court favorites, and Loyal shoddy contractors?

Vote for Lincoln.

Do you want corruption the most shameless to run riot in the councils of the nation?

Vote for Lincoln.

Do you want Provost Marshals, and thousands upon thousands of other new officials unknown to our laws dispersed through the land to fatten upon the fruits of your toil?

Vote for Lincoln.

Do you want a man for President without ability, without statesmanship, without dignity, and whose vacilating mind is controlled by events?

Vote for Lincoln.

Vote for McClellan

Do you want the Commissaries, the Contractors, the Provost Marshals, and all that vast multitude of officials created by Lincoln to be discharged?

Vote for McClellan.

Do you want that terrible corruption which now prevails in the government checked?

Vote for McClellan.

Do you want all the blessings which must flow upon the land when Peace and Union are established?

Vote for McClellan.

Do you want a man for President of spotless purity, of distinguished patriotism, a ripe scholar, of exalted talent, of glorious repute, of solid understanding, and of dignified demeanor?

Vote for GEORGE B. McCLELLAN.

When Damon Kilgore left Madison in 1860 after six frustrating but fruitful years, he left a legacy of two new elementary schools, a city high school, a graded school system with an advanced curriculum including singing and exercise, a corps of trained teachers and, most important of all, strong and growing support for the public schools—very impressive accomplishments for a period marked by severe depression and a very limited commitment to education. Clearly Kilgore deserves to be called the "father of Madison's educational system."[24]

Between Kilgore's departure and the end of the Civil War, the superintendency was a veritable revolving door, with some incumbents staying only a few days and few staying an entire year. All were apparently discouraged by the dismal prospects. In 1861 the city budget became so tight that the high school had to be closed until 1863 and some elementary schools were periodically closed or cut back. Schools continued to be crowded; new or additional rented schools were out of the question. In 1863, out of about twenty-five hundred school-aged children, fifteen hundred never set foot inside a public school door; and of the eight hundred who enrolled, only four hundred completed the term. The Civil War was not a good time for the Madison public schools.[25]

During the 1855–1865 decade the link between the Madison public schools and the University of Wisconsin continued to be close.[26] An analysis of the 1856 UW enrollment showed that forty percent of the entire student body was from the city of Madison.[27] In an era when travel was relatively difficult, Madison students not only had an overwhelming proximity advantage over "outstate" students, but they sometimes had the advantage of special college preparatory courses offered as a part of the high school curriculum—a program rarely offered elsewhere around the state and one which made a disproportionately large number of Madison students academically qualified to enter the University.[28] No wonder many around the state complained that the University of Wisconsin was "merely a Madison high school."[29] Significantly, Madison dominance of the UW went beyond student numerical superiority. Of the more than sixty regents who served between the founding of the University and 1865, one-third were Madison residents.[30]

Carriages, Bonfires, and Lager Beer: Local Politics between 1856 and 1865

Madison became a city just two years after the Republican party was founded. Strong partisan alignments extended to the local level and evoked intense and sometimes uninhibited expression at election time. Not only were the mayor and aldermen elected under partisan labels, but so were the city treasurer, ward constables, and ward assessors. The only point on which the parties seemed to agree was that the "best men" should be nominated.[31] But even here partisan differences crept in, with the Republicans insisting that "efficient businessmen" were best.[32]

The heart of the local political system was the ward nominating caucus, not always known for its decorum. In February 1858, for example, American and German Democrats in the First Ward fought a knock-down, drag-out battle against Irish Democrats.[33]

Partisan city conventions composed of persons elected at ward caucuses nominated candidates for city-wide offices. Campaigns were always unapologetically partisan, yet party leaders felt no obligation to define party differences. A mayoral candidate, for example, might be advanced first because he was a Democrat, but also because he had lived in the city a long time and was interested in the city's prosperity.[34] Nor did candidates themselves proffer platforms to dispel the confusion. Newspaper editors seemed to feel they had done their duty by urging readers to "vote the ticket."

Most election days "passed off quietly," which meant that the city charter prohibition against selling alcoholic beverages on election days kept partisan spirits within bounds.[35] The Republicans had another explanation for elections passing off quietly: "With the Democracy having about a five hundred majority in the city . . . there is no special excitement about the election. . . ."[36] In the absence of alcohol, election days were enlivened by bands, handbills, and, for the Democrats, free carriage rides to the polls. Spirited celebrations were nearly always reserved for the day after elections because it took time to count the votes by hand and the results usually were not announced until the following day anyway. The winners built huge bonfires in the streets, most commonly at the interesection of Main and Pinckney, and drank "copious effusions of lager."[37]

Just about all the celebrating was done by Democrats, since they won nearly all the elections. During Madison's first decade as a city, only one Republican mayor received a plurality from Madison voters, and he was swept into office by the crest of pro-Union sentiment at the end of the Civil War. Except for the Second Ward, all wards were strongly Democratic. With the exception of 1862 every council had Democratic majorities. During the same period, Madison consistently gave pluralities to every Democratic presidential candidate. Even Abraham Lincoln lost in Madison both in the 1860 and 1864 elections.[38]

The most exuberant political expressions during this period were reserved for presidential elections. When word was received in Madison that Lincoln had been nominated, Republicans fired off a one-hundred-gun salute at the Capitol Park.[39] When word was received that Lincoln had been elected, a cannon was fired in the Capitol Park every minute for three hours, beginning about eight o'clock, and a bonfire that illuminated an entire block was kindled on Pinckney Street.[40] Both parties held huge rallies in the Capitol Park during the summer and fall and brought in famous speakers to arouse the people. No polling was done but a close count of the number of torches (often cattails from Madison marshes dipped in kerosene) carried at night-time political rallies was thought to accurately reflect political sentiment. The Democrats usually won the torch count, but the Republicans claimed that this was because each torch carrier was given a glass of beer at the end of the parade.[41] If the torch count didn't prove favorable, a wagon count was used.[42]

Toward the end of the Civil War partisan feelings became strained, and epithets were hurled back and forth. The Republicans called Democrats "Copperheads," meaning disloyal or traitorous, and the Democrats called the Republicans "miscegenationists."[43] Soldiers from Camp Randall were allowed—the Democrats said directed—to attend and sometimes break up Democratic po-litical meetings to make sure that "harangues against Lincoln and Lincoln's war" did not go unanswered. Members of the "Copperhead Free Speech and Free Press Party," a strong antiwar offshoot of the Democratic party, tore down posters announcing a meeting of the "loyal Democrats."[44] At a Democratic political rally at the Capitol on October 3, 1864, five thousand Democrats were harrassed by squads of rowdy abolitionists, including soldiers who tried to start disturbances on the edge of the crowd. Speakers were frequently interrupted by cries of "you lie, you lie!," "traitor," and "copperhead." During the torchlight procession around the Square, several torch carriers were knocked unconscious by stones thrown at them by persons hiding in the many areas not illuminated by street lights. Later, amidst jeers, howls, and threats, the speaker's stand was showered by stones, some as large as hen's eggs. Prominent among the disrupters were soldiers, presumably from Camp Randall.[45] A few days later, when the Republicans held a Lincoln rally, the Democrats reciprocated in kind by pelting Republican torch carriers with rocks and eggs.[46]

The War on Roving Animals

One of the most irritating problems endured by early Madisonians were the depredations of roving animals. Indeed it was in direct response to this matter that the second law passed by the

Common Council after receiving its 1856 charter was an ordinance to restrain roaming dogs. Dogs ran in large packs, sometimes attacked citizens, and from time to time transmitted the dread disease rabies. Nor was it any accident that just three weeks later, hogs, sheep, cattle, pigs, and goats were also prohibited from running at large. Farmers buying supplies at the stores around the Capital Square quickly learned that if they left their wagons unattended for ten minutes, nimble, opportunistic bovines would help themselves to feed and groceries. Droves of pigs looking for tender roots would kill young trees planted around homes.

But having the laws on the books was one thing; enforcing them was something else. In practice the laws were enforced only when animal depredations reached relatively high levels. One of those times was the spring of 1859 when the most extensive crackdown ever was begun.[47]

The anti-animal campaign got off to a brisk start when roaming animals were unceremoniously shot by law officers, and a few weeks later the Common Council got a bill for burying "47 dead dogs, 11 dead cats and 12 dead hogs."[48]

Less successful was the attempt to set up the public pound. Unfortunately the city's financial straits made even a one-hundred-dollar appropriation for a pound enclosure out of the question, so the city hired a poundmaster who agreed to rent his own enclosure. At first the job seemed promising. There were hundreds of animals out there to impound, and under the Madison ordinance the poundmaster was entitled to get fifty cents for each animal impounded plus expenses. During the first two days of business the city's first animal control officer impounded at least seventy hogs "without fear or favor," yielding a theoretical profit of thirty-five dollars—not bad in an era when the going wage was a dollar a day.[49]

After two days on the job the poundmaster realized his profession was perilous. Citizens did not like the idea of having their livestock hauled off and having to pay fines and expenses to get them back. The poundmaster on the other hand had

his duty. After three days on the job, the poundmaster got into a fight with the owner of a recently apprehended pig. The council upheld the pig owner, and the poundmaster quit in disgust.[50] Two days after the resignation, the poundmaster's landlord refused to let his property be used as a pound any longer, fearing that irate citizens would set fire to it.[51] With the city without a pound and poundmaster, the *Daily Patriot* observed: "This is sad for a civilized community, but good for the hogs."[52]

A few days later another poundmaster was found, but he, too, ran into problems. An inspection of the fine print in the ordinance establishing the animal pound showed that the pound was intended to service only the east side of town. When this fact was discovered by west side hog owners, they demanded their animals and got them. And so the west side hogs were released, grunting defiance at their captors. Once again the streets of the city were infested by hogs—but this time only the west side hogs.[53]

About this time Mayor Smith realized that the pound operation was not a big vote-getter among the city's many animal owners. Owning hogs was a widespread and commonly accepted method of making a little extra money. Hogs required virtually no attention, since they found plenty of garbage to eat around the city. Keeping milk cows was also a widespread practice. They, too, were easy enough to keep and, best of all, were exempt from the animal constraint laws *providing* they were kept enclosed at night. During the day the city cows would form a herd, amble down to one of the city's many marshy areas to graze and return home punctually at 5:00 P.M. Many cow owners, however, did not put their cows in the stable at night. Consequently, people walking along streets and sidewalks on a moonless night were frequently "prostrated by falling on the soft body of an unperturbed cow."[54]

During the rest of his regime, Mayor Smith decided that the better part of valor was to forget about the pound business. However, when several children died of rabies in September 1859, Smith was in an awkward position of not wanting to kill pets and yet wanting to get rid of rabid dogs.

While Smith procrastinated eight men, two from each ward, resolved to go dog shooting every night until every loose dog was dead.[55] The canine vigilantes provoked the city to place large posters around the city announcing the intent of police to "Kill All Mad Dogs." Mayor Smith astutely recognized that the electorate would only support systematic dog killing when under threat of a rabies scare.

The following year pleas from "the most influential citizens praying that hogs not be allowed to run at large within the limits of the City" forced action on the issue.[56] It was dutifully shuttled from committee to committee until finally the Pound Committee came out in favor of freedom for hogs on the grounds they were the "cheapest and best scavengers" the city could have. In support of this controversial contention, the committee noted that during the brief period when the pound was in operation in 1859, garbage accumulated around the city and became a source of a great stench. "Therefore," the committee concluded, "it is for the best interests and general health of the city to let the hogs roam at large."[57] The conclusions of the report, however, were so controversial that the report was sent back to the Pound Committee—significantly without instructions or comment—where it died.

Another concerted and effective attempt to enforce the animal restraint ordinances occurred under Mayor Levi B. Vilas. The incoming mayor pleaded with aldermen in his inaugural address on April 10, 1861, to "protect . . . the farmers and teamsters who come to our city from the depredations of animals that prey upon their forage and loads and annoy their teams. The trade and prosperity of our city are dependent upon farmers around us, and to invite them here for our benefit and then allow animals to destroy their loads and eat up their forage . . . is without . . . excuse." Moreover, Vilas continued, "I would also suggest that . . . city authorities are duty bound . . . not to suffer animals to run at large which will injure or destroy the trees or render the sidewalks unfit to use."[58] Vilas, backed by eighty-three percent of the voters in the last election, had the attention of the Council. The Council began by electing a defeated mayoral candidate as poundmaster, a "deserved compliment" according to one paper.[59] Several days later the chief of police was seen riding through the streets "armed with two large hard looking revolvers" looking for unlicensed dogs to shoot.[60]

Animal control proponents were delighted. The new poundmaster found he could increase the number of impounded animals by giving a few small boys a percentage of his fee. Consequently, a small army of eager chasers quickly cleaned up city streets. Unfortunately, a few of the small boys became greedy and began letting cattle out of their pens so they could take them to the pound too.[61] The pound, located in a vacant lot near the courthouse, was filled to overflowing with animals whose mooing, oinking, barking, and quacking and stench became intolerable to those who lived nearby.[62]

Meanwhile, things were not going too well for police and constables, who had been directed by the mayor to kill dogs on sight. At first the council went on record as saying it would demand their resignations if the officials did not perform.[63] When the deputized dog slayers failed to do their duty, the council gave them twenty-four hours to start killing dogs or get fired.[64] Even this didn't get results, so the council passed a resolution that said the officers would be fined for every twenty-four hours that went by without dead dogs.[65] Some officers paid fines rather than kill pets.[66] Not until a rabies outbreak in December did the officers start to work in earnest and wagonloads of dead dogs, fifteen to the load, lumbered through the streets. After several days of systematic killing by the police and constables, the streets, for the first time in Madison's history, were free of unlicensed and unmuzzled dogs.[67]

When Vilas ran for reelection in the spring of 1862, he discovered that his animal control policies had not endeared him to the body politic.[68] At the citywide nominating convention, a recent immigrant stood up and said he had come to this country for the "enjoyment of Freedom" but that "during the past year his cow had been put into

the pound six times and that he could not take her out of the yard to milk her without having her taken away by some police officer."[69] According to the *Daily Patriot,* dog owners came to view Vilas with the same feeling Israeli mothers had for Herod.[70] When the votes were counted, only four out of ten persons voted for the incumbent mayor; whereas more than eight out of ten had voted for him the preceeding year. Vilas was bitter about his defeat but proud of his accomplishments. In a swan song during his last few minutes in office, Vilas vowed his intent to "never, without making every manly and lawful resistance, surrender the possession of the city to be overrun by horses, cattle, swine, and geese; nor its government to those whose highest idea of freedom is to pasture their hogs in their neighbor's garden and roost their geese upon our sidewalks."[71]

Irritants: Rowdy Shenanigans, Sabbath Breaking and the Sad Street Conditions

Every city at every period of its history contains conditions that greatly irritate its residents. Like a hangnail or a boil these irritants are never completely disabling, but they can make life miserable. Irritants are usually highly visible, often at the wrong time; all are theoretically correctable, yet they frequently exhibit the exasperating ability to elude solutions. They parade by the historian's viewing stand, rag-tag reminders that they can seldom be entirely eliminated. Still, their changing forms constitute a lively and instructive commentary on every period. For Madison during this turbulent period of prosperity, depression, and war, five irritants stand out: roaming animals (see above); soldier misbehavior (treated earlier); Sabbath breaking; rowdy shenanigans; and the sad, sad condition of the streets.

Regarding how one should spend the Sabbath, the *Wisconsin State Journal* had some straightforward advice: "Either go to church or go out of town."[72] Always the proponent for the Yankee, pietistic point of view, its editors never tired of

criticizing "the degeneracy into which we are rapidly falling." Instead of being a day of "quiet and decorous enjoyment," The Sabbath had become a time for drinking, card playing, loafing, and dancing, the *Journal* said. Even boys coasting down the Pinckney Street hill were berated for their "open violation" of the Sabbath.[73] Certainly one of the more interesting expressions of this point of view came from three-term Mayor William T. Leitch (1862–1865). A devout Episcopalian, he abruptly left a Saturday evening Common Council meeting at midnight without formal adjournment rather than conduct city business on the Sabbath.[74]

If an award were given for imaginative expressions of rowdyism, juveniles of this period would surely have gotten high honors. One group who went swimming in Lake Monona after dark amused themselves by capsizing boats and knocking planks out of the bottoms.[75] Another group ran up and down the back stairs at theaters, making it impossible to hear the actors. Still others indulged in systematic stamping in the gallery at inopportune times during performances.[76] Several young men from the better families in town became notorious for putting on "beastly and obscene exhibitions" at the public bathing house. Jerking pickets off fences was popular for many years after this type of inclosure came into fashion. To this repertoire were the more conventional—one might say the classic—forms of rowdyism, such as spitting tobacco juice on ladies' gowns, making obscene comments to female passers-by, crying fire in theaters, rattling tin pans, and throwing stones.[77]

And, finally, there were Madison's streets. No city budget item was harder hit by depression cutbacks than streets. By 1860 street improvement expenditures had dropped to a miniscule six percent of 1856–57 levels.[78] Between 1858 and 1865 street repairs were not entirely abandoned, but they were kept far below a level required to maintain their utility.

That little could be done when the city was in such severe financial straits did not stop complaints about the dirt, the mud, and the stench.

Dry weather and wind sometimes combined forces to raise "one vast cloud of dust," which was "driven across the lake and prairies to the north east, darkening the air for miles. In the streets, one encountered not only dust, but pebbles the size of peas . . . blown with a violence that was anything but pleasant."[79] Heavy rains and the inability of the city to keep adding annual gravel toppings to build up a hard surface produced deep ruts, small ponds, and impassable conditions.[80] Wagon drivers refused to force their teams through the deeply rutted streets to pick up or deliver items at residences.[81] One account described a situation where a dog swam across the street and shook itself free of mud and dirty water on pedestrians.[82] In one instance, however, the condition of the streets proved to be a lifesaver when a man was violently thrown from his horse, but landed in deep soft mud.[83] More irritating than the mud and dust were the reeking piles of "fetid ooze"[84] consisting of horse manure, slops from chamber pots, decaying meat, rotting vegetables, and a few dead animals. The intersection of Main and Pinckney was so bad that for years it was called "barnyard corner."[85]

Being mayor during this period of no money and unrelenting complaints required a long, damp fuse just to maintain sanity much less effectiveness. In his inaugural address to the council marking his third and final term, Mayor Leitch laid it on the line when he said he simply had to "disregard the cavilings of those who disturb the public ear with crapulous complaints about frivolous matters."[86] What modern mayor would not find this line useful from time to time?

Barnyard Corner: Description of South Pinckney Street between East Main and East Doty Streets

If the plague, cholera, yellow fever, black tongue, and other known and unknown varieties of pestilence do not break out in that section of Pinckney Street lying between the corner of Fairchild's Block and the Post Office, then is there no efficacy in malaria and stink.

Probably no prominent and frequented street in any civilized and Christian city ever smote the olfactories with such rank and stifling smells as the one in question. The prevailing odor, the key-note in this mighty gamut of stench, is a compound of barnyard and hog-pen. This is heightened, and varied, and made pungent by a host of spicy auxiliaries, which play the part of skirmishers and scouts to the main body of odors and filth there encamped. Prominent among these are the scents arising from bits of decaying meat, from rotting vegetables and fruits, the slops thrown out of an eating-house and lager bier establishment, and the putrifying remains of dead cats and dogs, thinly covered over with the street dirt, accumulated last winter. Then there are most malodorous whiffs from a dark and reeking alley between Pyncheon's Auction Room and Fairchild's Block.

To add to the general effect the keepers of the eating house before mentioned, emptied a whole barrel of swill into the gutter in front of their establishment on Saturday last. The scalding sun shone full upon it. A number of luxurious swine—those dainty animals which throng in every thorough fare of the city—immediately took possession of the little pond thus created, and by keeping it in agitation developed all its latent rankness. Such is the condition of one of the most frequented streets in the city, a street through which nearly every citizen passes to reach the post-office—reeking with all the odors of a barn-yard, a hog-pen, a slaughter-house, and a filthy kitchen sewer!

We shall not now inquire who is responsible for this state of things. One thing, however, is certain. If the city would avoid pestilence, it must be corrected at once. It will not do to tolerate it long, with the thermometer varying from 84° to 96° in the shade, day after day. In the first place, the street wants a thorough cleaning. Next the occupants of some of the establishments upon it must be put under bonds, if necessary, to observe some of the more common rules of cleanliness. They must be instructed that the public street is not the place for emptying the receptacles of slop and ordure, especially at this season of the year. If this is done, with a plentiful application of disinfectants to the gutters and alleys generally, the plague may yet be averted.

Wisconsin State Journal
July 18, 1859

Leisure-Time Activities

What Madisonians did in their leisure time depended to a large degree on the state of the local economy, one's relative wealth, personal taste, and the season. Before the depression became severe, boating was an obvious favorite. "One would think if one were to visit the shores of our lakes today that Madison is a great maritime town in a small way," said one report in May 1857. "Everybody owns a boat or a share in a boat. In a few days the waters of Monona will be decked with all sorts of boats from the handsome yacht to the awkward dugout and dotted with all sorts of sails from the flap of an old shirt to the neatly cut and tautly trimmed canvas of the queen of pleasure boats."[87] One entrepreneur made money hand over fist by taking people to a saloon he had set up on Picnic Point on his large steam yacht whose staterooms were fitted with "gorgeous silver and gold trimmings."[88]

During the 1857–1860 depression inexpensive pastimes such as coasting were widely enjoyed. Bascom Hill was a great favorite among University of Wisconsin students who improvised sleds

FIGURE 3.13. 1858 STATE FAIR. The November 20, 1858, issue of *Frank Leslie's Illustrated Newspaper* carried this gala scene of the first state fair in Madison in September of that year. The octagonal building in the upper left is the Fine Arts Hall, one of several semipermanent buildings. The cattle sheds shown around the perimeter of the grounds were later used as barracks by Camp Randall soldiers. Large tents sheltered field and garden projects, floral displays, and other similar purposes. Especially popular was the competition between fire companies shown in the foreground to see which could throw water the greatest distance and climb rope ladders most quickly. In addition to the regular competitions and events, participants enjoyed side shows, minstrel performances, and theatrical programs.

Because it was never possible for the city hotels to house the thousands of fair visitors, special arrangements had to be made to put up the people in private homes. Even the wealthy took in temporary roomers. For example, four leading citizens with large homes on "Mansion Hill" managed to put up ninety guests.

In 1860 Madison leaders persuaded the legislature to allow the city to levy a tax of one thousand dollars during the years 1860 and 1861 so that the fairground could be improved. Thus the state fair—always considered a plum worth seeking by rival host cities—once again returned to Madison in 1860. Had not the Civil War intervened in 1861, the fair would have been in Madison. However, in 1861 the state fair grounds, now much improved with Madison taxpayer dollars, were converted to Camp Randall and the cattle sheds shown around the perimeter of the grounds were converted to soldier barracks. (SHSW WHi(X31)17435) from barrel staves and old chairs.[89] The great American game of baseball first appeared in Madison in 1860 when the high school "scholars" organized a club, and men from all social stratas played every Friday afternoon on a vacant lot bounded by Wisconsin Avenue and Gorham Street.[90] Crude homemade iceboats first appeared on the Madison lakes in 1859.[91] For those who could afford horses, horseback riding was very popular among both men and women, especially on warm summer nights.[92] Some UW students found watching the legislature satisfying, inexpensive entertainment.[93] Almost all UW students who could afford the price rented rowboats so they could visit the new state insane asylum and "marvel at such evidences of secular progress as the water closets. . . ."[94] For the first time in Madison history the Common Council reversed the long-held position about the immorality of public bathing and granted a franchise for a bathing pier at the foot of South Pinckney Street where hot, dirty citizens could come clean in crystal clear water for just a dime a dip.[95] The bathers were enclosed in a temporary wood structure and thus not visible to the public.

Several cruel animal "sports" enjoyed a strong resurgence in 1860. In one version, sportsmen attached razor sharp two-inch steel spurs to the legs of fighting cocks who then proceeded to kill each other for the edification of gambling spectators. Another form pitted dogs against twenty to thirty rats in a specially constructed arena; the dog that killed the rats in the shortest period of time was declared the winner. Sometimes dog-rat "fights" and cock fights were combined into a single evening of entertainment and further enlivened "between rounds" by ordinary dog fights.[96]

The Civil War and the resumption of better economic times brought back to Madison the perennially popular circuses and other traveling companies and exhibitions such as General Tom Thumb, Commodore Nutt, and their "elfin ladies."[97] Plays resumed predepression levels, as did masquerades, balls, benefits, and other gala festivities. Indeed, if it were not for the presence of uniformed soldiers, a visitor would scarcely have been aware that a civil war was in progress.

Winter Night on Lake Monona

Last night was charming. What with the bright moon, the blue sky, the silvery stars and the ice on Lake Monona, a scene was afforded such as could not be excelled by the most fairy like picture. The temperature was fresh without being unpleasantly cold, and when we stood on the ice of Lake Monona, we found ourselves surrounded by the life and activity of the city. There were troops of "young Americans" gliding along and expressing their satisfaction in joyous shouts. There were young men skating ahead and propelling before them "sleds" upon which were seated sisters, wives and sweethearts, and it was a treat to hear the stimulating remarks that these dear creatures made, such as "Oh, Charles, how splendid this is!" "Oh, Harry, do you think the ice will be good all winter?" There were also more venturesome ladies, who with a laudable ambition had donned skates, and passed on the glistening ice apparently as easily and gracefully as if on a ball room floor.

There were business men who were skating with all the vivacity of youthful days, and from the exercise receiving a buoyancy of spirits that gave a romance to the jog trot thoughts of every day, more exquisite and beneficial than the glow bestowed by a successful venture or lucky speculation; and there were quiet groups of sly young men, who stood and enjoyed the sport of young ladies having sudden tosses from sleds, and never failed to greet such lucky accidents with eyes that glistened with merry twinkles for a minute or two after every toss. Of course no man with swift blood in his veins could stand still long in such a scene, and we lost no time in getting to the well stocked hardware store of GLEASON & Bro., and got suited by the younger of those wholesouled brothers to a pair of skates that enabled us to skim over the ice like a "thing of power and speed," and placed within our reach a night's enjoyment.

Daily Patriot
December 10, 1859

An Era Ends

The news of Lee's surrender at Appomattox reached Madisonians Sunday evening between 9:00 and 10:00 P.M., April 9, 1865, four years after word about Sumter's fall had reached the city. Immediately the governor ordered a salute to be fired in the Capitol Park; soon the church and city hall bells joined the cacophony. A huge bonfire was speedily kindled at the intersection of Monona Avenue and Main Street. As the crowd gathered, speeches were made and the "city was uproarious with the noise of the rejoicing till late in the night."[1] Those who gathered at the telegraph office to get the latest dispatches sang spirited versions of the "Star Spangled Banner," "John Brown's Body," "When Johnny Comes Marching Home," and "Praise God from Whom All Blessings Flow." Students, too, rejoiced with a large bonfire and other demonstrations. All trains entering the city were gaily decorated with flags.[2]

Just five days after receiving the joyous news of Appomattox and before the celebration had subsided, word reached Madison that President Lincoln had been assassinated. (Interestingly, his assassin, John Booth, had once appeared in the City Hall auditorium.[3]) The Common Council immediately met to pass a resolution whose very words were "too feeble to suitably express" their "abhorrence of the atrocious crime . . . a crime . . . which stands unparalledled in the history of civilized man. . . ." Two weeks later forty-six leading citizens represented Madison at the funeral ceremonies in Chicago.[4] For one-hundred days all the flags in the city were flown at half mast.

In June and July 1865, train load after train load of returning soldiers rolled into town to muster out. In one twenty-four-hour period in mid-July, two thousand soldiers landed at the depot. Many were treated to a sumptuous hero's dinner, compliments of the state. Then came the march uptown, the bands, the ringing of bells, and the

FIGURE 3.14. CAMP RANDALL MEMORIAL ARCH.   Nearly fifty years passed before Camp Randall was commemorated in any enduring form and then the effort was marred by controversy. "Stop It" read the headline over an artist's drawing of the proposed memorial archway appearing in the *Wisconsin State Journal* on November 22, 1911. Crusading *Journal* editor Richard Lloyd Jones had just received a terse note from the National Art Club of New York City asking if "it was possible that this thing could be imposed upon the City of Madison." Enclosed with the letter was a clipping from a tombstone cutters' trade journal describing the archway. The following week Jones made an appearance before the Madison Women's Club and said the three memorial commissioners had not gone about the work in the proper way. Instead of soliciting proposals from architects or sculptors, the commissioners put a want ad in the *Wisconsin State Journal* and the *Milwaukee Journal* asking for bids. Artists, sculptors, and architects, Jones argued, don't look for work in the want ads of such papers, but tombstone cutters do, and that was exactly what happened. Consequently the Woodbury Granite Company, the same company supplying granite for the new capitol, had been given the job of designing the monument and supplying the stone.

Jones escalated the campaign with a hard-hitting editorial headlined "Save our Soldiers from Ridicule." The editor then triumphantly paraded before readers indignant letters from nationally famous artists, sculptors, and architects. He even provided a convenient tear-off petition so readers could more easily register their indignation. Finally after a meeting with Governor McGovern, the stunned commissioners were persuaded to halt work until nationally known artists could review the now controversial project. For two months the commissioners listened to gratuitous artistic advice from all over the country. To quiet the storm, the commissioners hired local architect Lew Porter, the superintendent in charge of capitol construction, who redesigned the arch and satisfied the self-styled arbiters of monument design.

Not surprisingly, the artistic debate among the local opinion makers didn't appear very interesting to the old soldiers, relatives and friends who gathered for the dedication ceremonies on a gorgeous June day in 1912. One old soldier, writing to his company comrades who could not attend, described the grizzled old veterans, their silver-haired dames, children, and grandchildren who gathered for the event. "Boys and girls came off the streets. Automobiles brought load after load of people from uptown until the hill looked much as it did on a pleasant afternoon when folks used to come out from the city to see us on dress parade. But the real highlight," he said, "was a huge bonfire at 8 in the evening. . . . You should have heard the singing that night as done by the great crowd. It was truly inspiring. None of us who were there can easily forget it. . . . I wish you could have been there to breathe in the spell of the occasion. It was a time to be pleasantly remembered all along our remaining march. And so," he concluded, "our Camp Randall Memorial Arch was most happily dedicated. Long may it stand, a silent teacher of patriotism." (SHSW WHi(X3)34400)

firing of cannon. At the capitol there were speeches by the governor, the mayor, various judges, and other town dignitaries. Eager Madisonians greeted the trains and cheered the men as they marched to the capitol.[5]

All the out-of-town men were eager to get home, but many faced delays in mustering out at Camp Randall. Some passed the time by taking trips on the steam boat all the way to Picnic Point, the Water Cure, and other cool spots around the lakes. The Madison soldiers, of course, had an advantage. They were already home and they lost no time catching up on the local news, getting reacquainted with loved ones, and making plans to resume interrupted lives.

By October Madison had lost nearly all reminders of its role as a military camp town and was quickly resuming its traditional prewar roles as capital, home of the university, and commercial emporium. Nearly all the Camp Randall buildings had been torn down and sold for scrap lumber.[6] Gone was the much-talked-about Camp Randall "liveliness," the colorful dress parades and drills, spine tingling martial band music, the patriotic speeches, and the tearful departures. Gone, too, were the soldier depredations, the assaults, murders, rapes, drunken brawls, thievery, swearing, and general boisterous behavior. On balance it was a liveliness that most of the townfolk were happy to have behind them.[7]

4 Dis ppointment nd Dull Times: 1866–1879

Disputing Madison's Destiny, Round 1

During the Farwell Boom, Madison leaders revelled in an exciting statistic produced by the 1855 state census: Madison had become the second largest city in the state next to Milwaukee. No other statistic could have been more satisfying because size was uncritically accepted as the best single indicator of a city's power, prestige, and success, even a goal to be sought for its own sake. Just ten years later, however, at the close of the Civil War, the state census contained some very disappointing but not unexpected news: Madison had fallen into a disgraceful fourth place behind Milwaukee, Fond du Lac, and Oshkosh.[1] This fact evoked a question that greatly perplexed Madison leaders during the post-Civil War years: How can we get this town growing again?

Madisonians expressed pride in being the home of the university, the state capital, and the commercial center for Dane County. But Madison leaders were hardly content to be merely a center of learning, laws, and merchant trade. All agreed that getting additional railroad lines into the city was essential for any kind of growth and expansion. Some talked about making Madison an exclusive summer tourist resort. Others felt that factories were the answer. Although community leaders were divided on which alternative offered the greatest promise, all agreed that some new element was needed to get the city growing again.

Overview of Local Economy

Getting Madison moving again proved to be an extremely difficult task for two reasons. First, there was the heavy burden of paying off the bonded debt incurred during the 1856–1857 spending spree. Even at the compromised levels worked out with bondholders in 1864, nearly one out of every three dollars levied for city purposes between 1865 and 1880 had to be earmarked for interest and principal on the debt. The problem was exacerbated by spending limits placed upon the city by the state beginning in 1858, which remained in effect during the post-Civil War period. This heavy on-going debt service coupled with state-imposed spending limits meant that the city had no discretionary funds available for any economy-boosting schemes *unless* such schemes were specifically approved by the legislature.[2]

Second, there was a depression or a recession for eleven out of the fifteen years following the Civil War. Two of the four good years came right after the war. Returning soldiers with bonus pay in their pockets eagerly bought lots and built homes.[3] Between 1865 and 1868 the equalized value of real and personal property rose nearly thirty-eight percent.[4] Merchants reported booming sales. One Madison merchant sold such large volumes that he began importing his stock directly from New York.[5] Mayor Elisha Keyes (pronounced Kīze) described the period as one of "unexampled prosperity."[6]

From late 1867 until early 1871 the Madison economy fell into a recession. Equalized value of real and personal property dropped sixteen percent; Madison bank loans dropped seven percent.[7] The *Madison Democrat* pleaded for advertisers, merchants issued circulars telling people to pay their bills, and doomsayers urged Madisonians to "prepare for the worst."[8] The newly formed Young Men's Christian Association (YMCA) conducted Madison's first poverty survey and organized the city into districts so that food and financial relief could be more equitably and efficiently distributed.[9]

By the spring of 1871, however, the pendulum of economic activity swung toward prosperity and stayed there until late 1873. Headlining this prosperous era was a "building fever"[10] that between 1871 and 1873 produced an impressive one million dollars worth of new buildings and a two-hundred-fourteen percent increase in bank loans.[11] The newly established farmers' market on East Washington Avenue between Pinckney and Webster did a brisk business. One reporter counted one hundred wagons loaded with hay, wood, pork, beef, and other commodities in December 1872.[12]

Then, in September 1873, several large prestigious New York banking firms stopped paying out money to account holders, sending the eastern financial market into a panic and the country into a full-fledged depression—the worst of American history up to that time and second only to the Great Depression of 1929.[13] As late as 1880 Madison bank loans were just sixty percent of 1873 levels, and total bank assets *declined* by thirty-five percent between 1873 and 1878.[14] Between 1873 and 1880 annual construction activity rarely amounted to one hundred thousand dollars per year and in most years fell below that amount.[15] Money in Madison became very scarce and many sales were transacted by swapping.[16] A realtor said "it was almost impossible to sell real estate at any price . . ." [between 1877 and 1880].[17] Businessmen declared that their trade was "unsatisfactory and unremunerative, . . .

absolutely dull—almost dead"[18] and were happy if they were able to avert bankruptcy.[19] The Park Hotel, built at a cost of $125,000 in 1871, was sold in 1877 for $54,000 below its cost.[20] The state government began huge staff layoffs in 1874 and cut its budget by more than twenty-five percent.[21] Clearly, this was the most shattering depression ever experienced by Madisonians.

These fiscal and economic conditions constitute a backdrop against which the actions of Madison leaders in the post-Civil War years must be viewed.

Six Railroad Lines into the Center of the World

No map issued in Madison was more etched in public memory than the 1854 railroad map showing nine railroads entering the city like spokes to a hub.[22] At the close of the Civil War only three of the nine lines had been completed, and thoughts once again turned to building the six uncompleted lines. People still remembered the disastrous one-hundred-thousand-dollar loan to the Madison and Watertown Railroad in 1857,

which was supposed to have given Madison a second and much needed competing line to Milwaukee. Unfortunately, the railroad went bankrupt during the 1857 depression and the line was completed only to Sun Prairie—a tantalizing twelve miles from Madison. Even fresher in the memories of Madisonians was fifteen thousand dollars in outright grants given to the Madison and Portage line in 1862, largely on the representations of its president, Simeon Mills, that this amount would be sufficient to complete this important thirty-three mile link to northern Wisconsin.

Again the railroad promise fell short; the money was only sufficient for grading about two-thirds of the roadbed.[23]

As early as July 1865, however, the editor of the *Wisconsin State Journal* said Madisonians had overcome their disgust from these fiascos, pocketed their losses, and were once again willing to try to get these lines completed.[24] The railroads, too, were eager to complete the lines so they could benefit from the growing Madison freight and passenger business.[25]

In 1866 the Common Council took steps to provide city financial assistance to two railroads.

The first was the twelve-mile track linking Madison with Sun Prairie, then the terminus for a line extending to Milwaukee. The second railroad was a thirty-three-mile-long line to Portage. To approve the two railroad aid measures totalling $55,000, a referendum was scheduled for June 22, 1866. But just six days before the referendum the council held an emergency meeting to cancel the event. In their enthusiasm to secure the new lines, they had forgotten an 1858 charter amendment that prohibited the city from borrowing any money that could not be paid back from current operating revenues. Had the measures passed, the

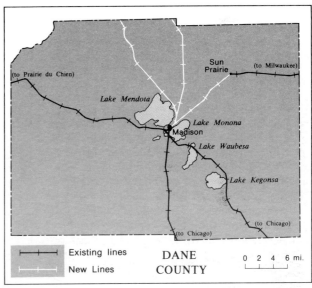

FIGURE 4.1. NEW RAILROAD LINES. The most productive years in Madison's history for new railroad connections were 1869 to 1871. In this three-year period, three new railroads were built into Madison.

The new lines quickly led to the development of two focal points of railroad activity: East Madison (above left) and West Madison (p. 120). Both photographs were taken some time between 1873 and 1879. The small brick building shown in the center of the East Madison photograph just under the capitol dome was the Milwaukee Road East Madison depot built in 1869. Just behind the building on the right was the first North-western Railroad depot built in 1871. The East Madison photo was taken from the 600 block of Williamson Street.

Just behind and to the left of the locomotive was the West Madison depot of the Milwaukee Road. The photograph was taken looking east on West Washington Avenue.

An effort to erect a union depot was made by the Northwestern Railroad in 1864 but was turned down by the Milwaukee Road. (SHSW WHi(X3)32553 and WHi(D31)542 map prepared by the University of Wisconsin Cartography Laboratory)

aldermen would have been in the unenviable position of tripling property taxes—a form of notoriety none apparently desired.[26]

Not until 1868 when local levy limits were increased did the council have the fiscal capacity to entertain railroad requests. Local lawmakers took almost immediate advantage of this new borrowing power to aid the Sun Prairie line but ignored citizens who complained that the measure would increase their taxes by twenty-four percent. When the first train arrived on May 22, 1869, Madison had four railroad lines.[27]

Since the Sun Prairie line used all the extra borrowing capacity then available to Madison, local officials had to find other ways to provide financial aid to railroads. Thus in the summer of 1870, when the Baraboo Airline Railroad, a predecessor of the Northwestern Railroad, asked the city for aid, the only way the city could comply was to get the legislature to increase Madison's debt limit. Unfortunately the legislature was not in session and both city officials and the railroad were eager to proceed. Therefore Mayor David Atwood took the unprecedented step of securing signatures from a majority of property owners who the legislature would later ask to approve the measure. Armed with this near guarantee of referendum passage the railroad began construction. The legislature subsequently approved the request and the line was completed. The first train arrived on July 26, 1871.[28]

By the time the next railroad aid request came in, this one from the Madison and Portage line, a predecessor of the Milwaukee Road, citizen resistance had stiffened due to tax increases stemming from the last two railroad aid measures. But once again official eagerness to get another railroad triumphed over legal formality and gave local meaning to the Americanism, "railroaded through." To raise the money demanded by the Portage line, the council had no choice but go back to the legislature and ask them to raise the city debt limit once again. And since the legislature was not in session, the council once again proceeded without their approval. First aldermen

passed the necessary right-of-way ordinance and then promised to give the railroad the negotiated financial payment *after* the legislature approved the debt increase—assuming of course that they would. Satisfied that the city and the legislature would deliver, the railroad officials began construction. On January 9, 1871, the first train on the new line steamed into town. However, the legislature had not yet approved the debt increase and citizens were demanding a referendum so they could deny the request. Such talk made railroad officials nervous because they had borrowed the money to build the line. The legislature finally passed Madison's request but subject to a citizen referendum, a move which set the stage for a confrontation between railroad supporters and hold-the-line taxpayers. For the first time in Madison's history, a railroad referendum faced substantial opposition. Finally in June 1871, six months after the line was completed, voters approved the measure, but an unprecedented forty-three percent opposed it.[29]

Madison leaders lost few opportunities to brag about the three new railroad lines and speculate on the extent to which they would stimulate the local economy and population growth. In fact there was so much talk about such things one wag decided to comment on all the commentary. Now that the railroads have run six lines into the city, he began, " . . . everyone can get here from everywhere. Nobody desires to get away except on business and means to come home again before they start for heaven. Madison," he concluded, "is surely the home of the Gods and the center of the world."[30]

Satire aside, the new railroads *were* important to the city. In 1870 the Milwaukee Road established Madison as a division point because it lay half way between Milwaukee and Prairie du Chien and erected a huge twenty-four-engine roundhouse on West Washington Avenue.[31] Taken together, the railroads were large employers. The Baraboo Line proved very popular among southern tourists because it made the Dells just an hour's train ride from Madison. The new lines effectively ended efforts to move the capital

somewhere else on the grounds that Madison was not accessible. Not surprisingly, the increase in construction activity in 1871 was labelled "railroad prosperity."[32]

But most of all the new railroad lines established a fresh confidence in Madison's future. Of the nine lines projected on the 1854 railroad map, six were actually built, three in just three years. In January 1873, Madison became a stop on the mainline of the Chicago Northwestern Railroad linking Chicago and Minneapolis-St. Paul. Some leaders confidently predicted that this line would soon be connected with the Minneapolis branch of the Northern Pacific Railroad, placing Madison on the "shortest and most feasible route between the two oceans."[33]

The Music of Clanking Machinery: The Factory Imperative

The 1866 city directory put it kindly when it said "manufacturing interests of Madison are, as yet not very extensive".[34] There was a flouring mill, a woolen factory, a steam planing mill, an iron foundry, and very little else.[35] To be sure, the city's modest manufacturing achievements at the close of the Civil War reflected no widespread animus against factories. It was rather a situation where the promotional energies of city leaders had been preoccupied with developing the town as a commercial center, securing railroads, keeping the coveted capital in Madison (and out of Milwaukee), building municipal services and facilities, enduring depressions, and promoting the fledgling university.

After the Civil War, however, manufacturing emerged as a distinct and exciting new direction for Madison. Madison leaders, like their counterparts around the state and country, were no longer content with just buying and selling somebody else's wares; they wanted to *make* things. To its proponents, manufacturing was Madison's only hope for restoring Madison to the position it once enjoyed as the second largest city in the state.

FIGURE 4.2. ELLSWORTH BLOCK. Shown here in about 1875, the large ornate Ellsworth
Block was an example of a modern commercial building of that era. This block has been
sensitively renovated and is known as The Atrium. (SHSW WHi(X3)6245)

Mayor David Atwood struck the keynote for the post-Civil War interest in manufacturing in his April 1868 inaugural address. "Manufacturing interests have been much too neglected," argued Atwood. Atwood believed that only factories would increase "population and wealth . . . and plant a city upon a solid and enduring basis."[36]

Atwood's point evoked a positive response from the *Wisconsin State Journal*. "We are pleased to note . . .," said an editorial in May 1868, "that there is a growing feeling among our people in favor of encouraging the introduction of manufacturing establishments into our city. The subject is freely discussed among our most substantial businessmen. . . . There is no good reason, in fact, why Madison should not become a manufacturing town equal at least to Rockford, Illinois, if the right measures are taken to induce it. . . . We trust agitation on the subject will . . . continue with increased ardor . . . until Madison shall be filled with mechanical establishments that will double its population and wealth in the next two years."[37] A letter to the editor of the *Wisconsin State Journal* applauded Atwood's efforts to "wake up our long slumbering capitalists and infuse a little . . . excitability into the public nerves. Let us see the smoke from the factory chimneys, let us hear the music of rattling machinery and thrift and prosperity will reverberate through every street in this now quiet peninsula," the letter writer asserted.[38]

Judging from the prompt, warm support of the *Journal,* the reader might conclude that profactory sentiment would soon become epidemic in Madison. In fact, however, *Journal* support reflected an extraordinary circumstance that will cause modern Madison mayors to gasp in envy. At the time Atwood became mayor of Madison, he was also editor and publisher of the *Wisconsin State Journal!* Wearing his mayor's hat he could push certain public policies and then, wearing his publisher's hat, print supportive editorials and letters to the editor. And that is exactly what Atwood did, untroubled by any qualms about conflict of interest. Making Atwood's situation even

more remarkable was the fact that when he took office, there was no rival daily newspaper in Madison. Just one month after taking office, however, Atwood's *Pravda*-like union between newspaper publishing and public policy ended. A new daily newspaper, *The Madison Democrat,* made its appearance and immediately began to provide vigorous partisan opposition to the Republican *Journal*. Very significantly for factory backers, however, in its very first issue *The Democrat* came out four-square for manufacturing.[39] Moreover, the *Democrat* continued its strong support for manufacturing over the years.[40]

Three years after Atwood's "keynote" inaugural, his successor, J. B. Bowen (1871–72) used his inaugural address to express his intense impatience with those who expected the city to grow and prosper "simply on the purity of its atmosphere and the surpassing beauty of its scenery" or upon the "extraordinary educational facilities it hopes to enjoy at no distant day. Like Atwood, Bowen firmly believed that a "few factories" would "infuse into our population a new life . . . to which we are now almost total strangers" and "furnish full and remunerative employment to hundreds of our half idle population. . . ." Best of all, Bowen concluded, factories would "convert Madison from a delightful hum drum retreat to a thriving and prosperous city that would be felt as a positive and beneficient power in the Northwest."[41]

In spite of the profactory cheerleading from both daily newspapers and the exhortations of two very popular Madison mayors, community support proved to be quite limited. Scoffers argued that Madison could never become a manufacturing center because it had no coal or water power. Factory proponents admitted that the water power needed to be improved but insisted that the vast water power of Lake Mendota had never been more than "half employed."[42] But they insisted that it was not essential for Madison to become a manufacturing city. Racine, Fond du Lac, Oshkosh, La Crosse, and Green Bay didn't have an ounce of water power and they all had become factory cities.[43] Manufacturing proponents also

conceded that Madison had no coal but noted that the cost of that commodity had dropped to a point where it was cheap enough to displace wood as the principal home heating fuel. One scheme called for making the Yahara and Rock Rivers navigable all the way to Lake Mendota so that coal-laden steamships from the lower Mississippi could dock there.[44] Most businessmen expected the price of coal to drop further in the near future so that the commodity would be cost-competitive for manufacturing as well as home heating.[45]

Even if coal did not become cheap enough for manufacturing, Madison factory advocates felt that they had a reliable alternative in peat, a black vegetable material found in old lake beds. Though wet and spongy when taken from the ground, when cut into blocks and exposed to the air it quickly hardened and like coal produced a hot flame. Large peat beds had been found in the Madison area prior to the Civil War but had been found unsatisfactory because of their high sand content. After the war, however, new beds were discovered that proved both deep and pure. One experiment showed that peat from these new beds could produce steam for one-third the cost of wood or coal.[46] Madison businessmen moved quickly to exploit these new deposits by forming two processing and distribution companies.[47]

Encouraged by the vigorous postwar local and statewide economy, the promise of peat, and the prospect of new railroads, Madison factory advocates began looking for products that could be made in Madison and easily sold. Nearly all agreed that agricultural implements were most likely to lead the city into the lush pastures of local manufacturing. Under the most conservative scenario, Madison implement factories could supply the large growing Dane County market. Not only did Dane County have large amounts of rich soil, but it was being extensively farmed. The 1870 census showed that the value of farm products and the number of horses were greater in Dane County than in any other county in the state.[48] But most convincing of all was the fact that sales and distribution (but not manufacture) of agriculture implements had become the largest single business in post-Civil War Madison.[49]

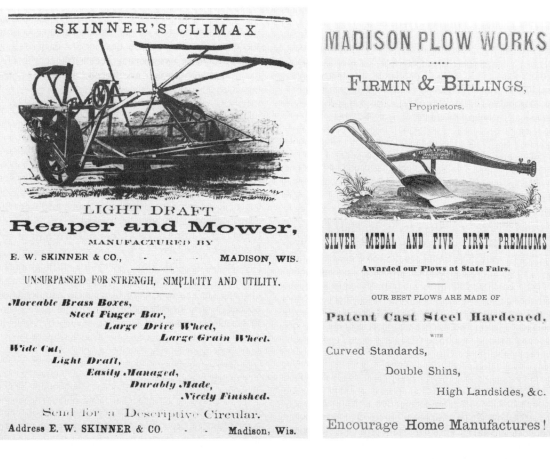

FIGURE 4.3. AGRICULTURAL IMPLEMENT ADS. Many Madisonians expected The Madison Plow Works and the E. W. Skinner Company to become the nucleus of a large and rapidly growing agricultural implement manufacturing industry. The advertisement for the Skinner Climax Reaper and Mower was one of many that appeared in local papers in the late 1860s. The Madison Plow Works advertisement appeared in the 1871–72 Madison city directory. A common theme of these ads was the exhortation to "Encourage Home Manufactures."

Madison journalists calculated that between eight hundred thousand dollars and one million dollars worth of implements were sold each year in Madison, but that only sixty thousand dollars of that total was actually manufactured in the city.[50] It was this type of statistic that allowed David Atwood during his term as mayor to credibly claim that if all implements sold in Madison were *made*

in Madison, that business and population would double in a year.[51]

Fortunately the case for implement manufacturing did not lie on theory alone. The most exciting success story in the brief annals of Madison manufacturing history was the Mendota Agricultural Works, sometimes known as the E. W. Skinner Company, located at the intersection of

Lake Street and Lake Mendota. The factory specialized in sorghum mills and saw its output grow from one mill in 1861 to five hundred in 1865. In 1866 the plant employed fifty men and even had a staff of salesmen combing the Midwest.[52] When the sorghum industry stopped, the firm shifted to reaper and mower production. In 1868 it employed sixty men and produced four hundred reapers. Together with the Carmin and Billings Plow Works, Madison's other implement manufacturer, these firms were seen as a nucleus of a vigorous new manufacturing specialty in agricultural implements.

Between 1868 and 1870 Madison business leaders pushed and pleaded for new agricultural implement factories, but none appeared. Eager to make Madison at least a regional implement manufacturer but frustrated that no one accepted their invitation, a group of prominent Madison capitalists decided that they would start a factory themselves. Known as the Madison Manufacturing Company, the firm began in early 1870, boasting a blue ribbon group of backers and ample capital.[53]

In 1871, momentum behind agricultural implement manufacturers seemed to be growing when Mr. J. H. Garnhart agreed to locate a large implement factory in Madison. Known as the Garnhart Reaper Works, the firm was expected to assemble four hundred "Madison Reapers" and employ fifty people. Even before the firm arrived, business leaders began talking about a "new era in manufacturing" for the city. Getting the factory was not without a price, however. To provide the firm with a sufficient incentive to locate in Madison, citizens had to donate an entire block for the factory site and five thousand dollars to boot. The block selected was bounded by the Yahara River, East Washington Avenue, and Mifflin and Dickinson Streets.[54]

Just when agricultural implement factories had secured a beachhead in Madison, the 1873 depression swept across the country, leaving a rich harvest of new enterprises in its wake. The once promising Garnhart Reaper Works was one such casualty.[55] Madison's three other implements managed to limp through the depression making sorghum mills, fixing plows, and casting cistern covers.[56] By 1874, however, it was clear to the most inveterate factory advocate that Madison—at least for the foreseeable future—was not going to be a city of smoke stacks and clanking machinery.

A Madison writer no doubt spoke for many when he wistfully concluded his 1874 history of Madison with these words: "Ours may never be a city remarkable for . . . manufacturers . . . and the busy life that characterized a metropolis."[57] Indeed, what else could he have said? For the moment manufacturing was "the lost cause of Madison."[58]

Though the 1873 depression was the proximate cause of the failure of Madison to become a leading implement manufacturing town, it was hardly the whole story. Four other factors suggest that even if the depression had not occurred, Madison implement manufacturing may not have established more than a precarious beachhead during this period.

First, the number of business and civic leaders actively promoting factories was relatively small. Only two mayors between 1865 and 1880, Atwood and Bowen, both Republicans, made factory promotion a part of their administrations. Second, during the period when manufacturing was being promoted, many argued that factories would detract from Madison's beauty and attract "grimy workers."[59] Third, inability of investors to make high-quality peat available in substantial quantities and at a competitive price was another deterrent to manufacturers. Had peat been available at $3.50 per ton, as was hoped, at the same time that coal was selling for $10.00 to $12.00 per ton, the outcome might have been quite different. Finally, the effect of three new railroad lines between 1869 and 1873 was not as substantial as expected. Theoretically, the railroads would unite coal from Illinois with iron from

northern Wisconsin in a factory-filled Madison, but the simple existence of the railroads was far from a guarantee that this would happen. Not only did the new lines arrive after the manufacturing boomlet had spent itself, but when the lines did arrive, their freight rates proved to be too high to support transportation-dependent enterprises.

The Rise of the Madison Resort Industry

In the spring and early summer of 1866 Madison developers George Delaplaine and Elisha Burdick invested eighteen thousand dollars in improving a large, four-story frame building located in the center of what is today Olin Park. The two men had built the structure in 1854 at a cost of forty-five thousand dollars and had owned the building since that time. Originally built as the Water Cure, the combination hospital–spa offered various forms of hydrotherapy for guests. After failing to make the institution a financial success, the owners closed it down in 1857. With the exception of a three-month period in the summer of 1859, the building had been standing vacant for nine years.[60]

Delaplaine and Burdick were confident that the handsome structure could be profitably recycled as a summer resort hotel. Still, the venture was hardly without risk. No resort had ever succeeded in Madison before. During the Farwell boom some predicted that Madison would become the Saratoga of the West, but this dream proved elusive because Madison was not easily accessible by rail and also because few thought of the Northwest as a resort area at that time.[61] However, by 1866 Madison became directly accessible by rail from Chicago for the first time, the economy was generally good, and many residents from southern cities were seeking northern resorts where they could escape cholera, yellow fever, and other diseases common in southern cities at that time. The two developers felt they could appeal to this market and were particularly confident about their ability to attract St. Louis residents.[62]

Lying amidst a finely wooded thirty-acre tract with a panoramic view of the Madison skyline, Lakeside House, as the developers called their new enterprise, was easily accessible to the city by road or steamboat and offered guests the choice between country quiet and city bustle. The structure was easily adapted to a resort hotel since it already had sixty guest rooms, a large formal dining room, a concert and promenade hall, a gracious wrap-around piazza, and a complete kitchen. Unlike most buildings of the period, it had hot and cold running water and bathtubs for guests, a remnant of its previous life as a Water Cure. The investors did, however, add several outbuildings calculated to appeal to the summer tourist, including a two-table billiard hall, a refreshment pavilion, a small ice house to keep the refreshments cold, and a generous stable. In late June the building was freshly painted inside and out and the coolers were filled with hundreds of bottles of the finest beer. To manage the enterprise, Delaplaine and Burdick hired two experienced hotel keepers, one of whom had previously managed one of the posh, well-known eastern seaside resorts.[63]

On Monday morning July 2, 1866, the doors of the refurbished facility were opened to the public. Soon guests began arriving, and for the remainder of the summer local newspapers were full of articles describing the arrival of people from New Orleans, St. Louis, and other southern places. While at Lakeside they whiled away the hours playing billiards, sipping cold beer or lemonade, listening to band music, swinging in the long rope swings, rowing, swimming, and reading. Special dances called "hops" were scheduled for the teen-agers. Guests could rent horses and carriages for a drive into the country. Or they could board Captain Barnes' steamer with that unpronounceable name "Scutanawbequon" and go into town. Lakeside House became Madison's first successful resort hotel.[64]

By April 1867, southerners were already writing the Lakeside House and the better hotels in town for summer reservations. One estimate showed that not less than three thousand persons

FIGURE 4.4. LAKESIDE HOUSE, 1866 to 1877.   Lakeside House was Madison's most successful resort hotel. During its eleven-year history, it was probably visited by more people each summer than any point near Madison. The handsome cream-colored building featured a promontory at the top center that offered outstanding views of the surrounding country. During ten of its eleven years the hotel was owned and managed by St. Louis men, which accounts for its large St. Louis trade. The building was ninety-two feet long and forty-two feet deep, not counting kitchen and bathrooms attached on the rear. The hotel burned to the ground on August 21, 1877, and was not rebuilt. The picture appeared in the Madison *Wisconsin State Journal* in July 1875.

from St. Louis alone would spend the summer in Madison *if* they could obtain satisfactory accommodations.[65] That summer the hotels were full of southern visitors and from that time until 1874 the number of tourists pushed the capacity of local hotels.[66] Most came from large southern cities, predominantly St. Louis, but Memphis and New Orleans were well represented.

Madison, along with many other resorts in the state, was benefitting from a growing awareness among affluent residents of the lower Mississippi Valley that there were attractive alternatives to the eastern seaside resorts that then dominated the recreational world.[67] Many had grown tired of the emphasis at the eastern establishments on high fashion, dissipation, display, luxury, elegant cuisine, and pomp. Madison offered a chance to get away from all that. In the words of a *New Orleans Republic* correspondent, Madison offered "quiet, cleanliness, cool pure air and water and fine swimming, rest, health and good society."[68] A Madison man put it a little differently when he said the city offered tourists a place to "worship God out of doors, and go 'a fishing,' a place where the man can unbutton his shirt collar and the woman (can) loosen her corsets and it is nobody's business."[69]

If distinguished guests were any measure of success, Madison scored early and impressively. During that first 1866 season at Lakeside, guests included the well-known St. Louis brewers Adolphus Busch and Everhard Anheuser.[70] Famed Civil War General William T. Sherman arrived in July 1867 and spent that summer in Madison.[71] Robert T. Lincoln, son of the late president, and his wife stayed at Lakeside during August 1870.[72] Some prominent southerners even bought homes in Madison. Mr. D. R. Garrison, vice-president of a forerunner of the Missouri and Pacific Railroad, bought the elegant mansion, now a Madison landmark, at 104 East Gilman for use as his family's summer residence.[73]

Madison enjoyed very favorable treatment in big city newspapers and important periodicals. Superlative-laden feature articles on Madison as a resort appeared in the *Chicago Times* (1870), the *New Orleans Republic* (1872), the *St. Louis Post Dispatch* (1873), the *Chicago Post* (1874), the *Chicago Tribune* (1874), and the *Nashville American* (1877). Influential trade journals such as the *Hotel World* (1877) and the *National Hotel Reporter* (1877) carried feature stories on Madison. The Chicago Northwestern Railroad gave Madison generous and sympathetic treatment in its *Tourist's Manual of the Health and Pleasure Resorts of the Golden Northwest* (1879–1880).[74]

Madisonians quickly accepted their new industry and began to refer with pride and even a little smugness to "the season"—the period between July and September when rich southern tourists streamed into the city to spend their money and mingle with the town folk. However, during the first few years of the tourist business, some Madisonians could not understand why there were so many summer parties reported in the newspapers. Normally such social events were reserved for the colder months. "But this query," said the *Democrat,* "is very easy of reply. Madison, like Newport and Saratoga, is a watering place and all such places have a continuous round of gaieties during the summer season."[75]

Madison's relatively rapid success as a northern resort occurred just in time to make tourism the major alternative to manufacturing as a means of increasing city population and getting the local economy moving again. Although some argued that only factories could provide permanent population growth and economic growth,[76] most Madisonians, however, appear to have agreed with D. K. Tenney, who offered this build-on-strength advice: "Stop talking about manufactories, confine that branch to making and mending your boots and breeches and bet your money on what you are sure of—your natural beauty and your public educational facilities. . . . Madison and its surroundings are the handsomest on the face of God's green earth. This is our capital and should be turned to probable account. No other place in the West possesses it."[77] By 1877 many accepted as a "settled fact" that Madison would never be a manufacturing town and that its "natural advantages would make it one of the most attractive summer resorts in the country."[78] Tenney argued—and many seemed persuaded—that five to ten thousand tourists could be induced to visit Madison each season, each staying long enough to spend an average of two hundred dollars for a total of from one to two million dollars a season.[79]

What a shiny and attractive future tourism offered! No soot-belching chimneys, no noisy factories, and no rowdy workers. To be a nationally famous northern resort, a center of culture, learning and legislation, a city of fine homes, and the commercial emporium for Dane County—this was the dominant vision of what most Madisonians wanted their city to become during the fifteen years after the Civil War.

Improving Madison for Tourism

The growing realization in the late 1860s that Madison could become a preeminent northern resort was accompanied by a growing recognition that this aspiration would not become a reality without a lot of hard work and a concerted action. Those who studied the city as a resort identified six areas where specific action was needed: (1) new hotels, (2) more effective advertising, (3) improved fishing, (4) more tourist activities, (5) mineral water, and (6) several changes to make the city cleaner and more beautiful. None of these needs were offered as a part of a master plan; rather each was pursued because of its perceived connection with the exciting new tourist business.

More and Better Tourist Hotels

Madison's inadequate hotel inventory was evident as early as the season of 1867.[80] During the first five years of the tourist boom, Madison's leading hotels, in order of desirability, were the Lakeside House (120 guests), the Vilas House at Monona and E. Main (100 guests), the Rasdall House on King Street (100 guests), enough for only 320 guests. There were other hotels in town, but they were spartan farmer hotels entirely unsuited for the relatively well-heeled tourists.[81] In 1870 a group of Chicago investors purchased and cleared a sixty-acre tract in what is now Maple Bluff with the intent of building summer residences and an exclusive resort hotel called Eagle's Nest. To enable Chicagoans to get to and from Madison easily, the investors planned to run a fast train out of Chicago every Saturday afternoon.[82] A group of southerners reportedly planned to build a summer hotel at the corner of East Washington Avenue and Butler.[83] Neither of these plans reached fruition, probably because the Park Hotel, in response to another attempt to move the capital, preempted the premium hotel market.[84] From the day it opened the Park Hotel

played a large role in the tourist trade, offering outstanding accommodations to luxury-conscious southern tourists. But even with the addition of the Park Hotel, Madison's better hotels could only accommodate four hundred tourists at a time—small perhaps in contrast to the theoretical demand.

Investors were exhorted to build resort hotels at choice spots around the lakes and chided when they failed to do so. However, summer-only income was not a sufficient return on investment to justify the risks. With the exception of an addition to Lakeside House in 1873, no additional resort hotels were constructed in Madison until 1879.[85]

Effective Advertising

More effective advertising was another quickly perceived need. Depending on big-city newspaper features was not deemed adequate. Madison maestros wanted to blow their own promotional horns. The first locally produced promotion tract was the *Park Hotel Travelers Guide for 1872.* Ten thousand copies of the tiny three-inch by four-inch booklet were distributed. Naturally the features of the Park Hotel were emphasized. Unfortunately, the booklet was marred by ads for rat poison, bed bug powder, coffins, and hearses—not the sort of products designed to leave a favorable impression on the prospective tourist.[86]

The largest and most impressive advertising ever done for Madison as a northern resort was published by the *Wisconsin State Journal* in 1877 as a supplement in newspaper format. Some twenty thousand copies were distributed over the Mississippi Valley and Gulf states. Authors of the well-illustrated piece made unabashed claims for Madison. The climate was "bracing," the women "the handsomest in the West" and the town the "prettiest, the healthiest, the jauntiest of all western resorts," and the hotel accommodations "unsurpassed." Railroad facilities were "unexcelled" and city administration took great pride in the "scrupulous clean lines of the public streets." Believe it or not, fishermen could haul in one hundred fifty pounds of fish at one sitting—big ones, too. Then there were the thrilling excursion trips to Devil's Lake, the "Switzerland of the West." If the thirty thousand-word tract wouldn't entice the prospective tourist to come to Madison, nothing would.[87]

To supplement these pieces and those appearing in big city newspapers, the manager of the Park Hotel sometimes made forays throughout the south, where he tried to persuade tourists to come to Madison.[88]

D. K. Tenney urged the hiring of a jaunty, well-paid correspondent to write quips for the large city dailies. The emphasis, he said, should be upon the "Honorables, the Generals, the Reverends, Doctors and their cultivated ladies. Go lively on the young ladies and their wardrobes, not omitting their coquettery and their flirtations. Be particular to report on the scandals in high life and if there are none, have them invented." There is no indication this was done, but the formula was time honored and usually effective.[89]

Better Fishing

Several steps were taken to make fishing easier and more exciting. Bait suppliers worked out arrangements with the better hotels so that guests could order their fishing worms while having breakfast in the hotel dining rooms. The worms could then be picked up on the way out of the hotel.[90] In 1873 and 1874 the Common Council appropriated funds to introduce ten thousand Lake Michigan lake trout and seven thousand California salmon into the Madison lakes. To enable the city to better enforce fishing laws on Mendota and Monona, the 1870 legislature placed both lakes within city boundaries.[91]

More Tourist Activities

In response to complaints that Madison was dull, various efforts were made to liven things up. The proprietor of the Lakeside House engaged a band to play for his guests two nights a week,[92] and concerts in the Capitol Park were begun. Rowing and sailing regattas were actively encouraged,[93] and efforts were made to get theatrical and minstrel companies to stop at Madison in the summer.[94] The opening of the railroad to Baraboo in 1873 made the Dells a very popular excursion for Madison tourists.[95] Some argued that lakeshore drives especially to Maple Bluff and to Picnic Point were indispensable because they would give people some place to ride horses or drive carriages. The Picnic Point drive came within five hundred dollars of being built during the summer of 1877. All property owners along the route agreed to give an easement at no cost and the stakes were driven for grading, but then one of the property owners reneged and demanded five hundred dollars. The promoters refused to pay and the idea died.[96]

Artesian Mineral Water

At the time of Madison's rise in popularity as a northern resort, nearly all the older, more famous resorts offered guests invigorating and health-restoring mineral water. Though springs were numerous around the Madison lakes, none had been bottled and promoted. This deficiency was finally corrected in 1873 when an artesian well on the capitol lawn began producing.[97] A careful analysis of the water showed that its properties were very similar to the most famous mineral spring in Wisconsin at that time, the Bethesda Spring at Waukesha, also the location of the state's most prestigious resort.[98] Persons associated with the Madison resort business lost no time in publicizing this boon. One promotional tract said the water was a "tonic for the weak," that it would "eradicate . . . chronic diseases" and

even "restore . . . manhood."[99] The Park Hotel kept the valuable water on tap for its guests, who drank twenty-four gallons each day.[100]

Making Madison Cleaner, More Sanitary, and More Beautiful

Several important improvements begun or completed during this period were launched in part to make Madison more attractive to summer tourists.[101] Because nearly all of the tourists were coming to Madison to escape the dirt and disease of their cities, Madison officials recognized the enormous importance of cleanliness and good sanitation—hence the importance of doing a better job picking up trash, getting rid of sewage, and draining the smelly, stagnant marshes on the east and west sides of town. Those close to the tourist business also recognized that cows wandering around the downtown streets were not apt to produce repeat visits from wealthy southern tourists. Then, too, there were things Madison could do to make the city more beautiful and attractive to summer tourists, such as planting street trees and creating parks.

Though a compelling argument can be made that these improvements would have been started without the influence of tourism, the intensity of sentiment behind these improvements cannot be fully explained without reference to tourism. Each of these improvements is treated elsewhere in this chapter.

Decline of the Tourist Business

The eight years between 1866 and 1874 were the glory years for Madison's resort industry. Each year during that period newspaper accounts described the tourist business as greater than the preceding year. But then in 1875, newspaper accounts in that year described the 1875 tourists as "coming in slowly."[102] In 1876 and 1877 the

Steamers "Scutanawbequons,"

Make half-hourly trips on Lake Monona during the summer months, to all points of interest on the Lake, from foot of Carroll street, Angleworm Station, Madison, Wis.   *Capt. F. BARNES, Prop'r.*

FIGURE 4.5. THE STEAMBOAT ERA. In the summer of 1864 Madisonians struggled mightily to pronounce the name of a five-syllable Indian word, "Scutanabequon." The name had been affixed to a twenty-eight-foot-long steamboat launched in Lake Monona on July 21 of that year. According to the owner, the name meant "fire canoe"—a translation many wished had been selected instead of Scuta. . . . Scut nob . . . well, the word itself. Folks soon overcame the pronunciation problem by calling the boat the "Scut." The Scut was the first of a long dynasty of successful commercial steamboats on the Madison Lakes.

Proprietor of the Scut was Captain Frank Barnes, a descendent of a Rhode Island seafaring family. For more than a quarter of a century the fun-loving proprietor landed his boats at Angleworm Station at the foot of South Carroll Street shown *(left).* The name of the popular local institution was based upon a spirited oration Barnes gave

each Fourth of July on how civilization was dependent upon the lowly earthworm. Barnes gradually added steamers to his fleet and all were given nearly unpronounceable Indian names such as Ninniagwanishkota and Katanagarah.

The sleek little Scut appears to have been an immediate success. In 1866 Barnes launched a second steamer the Scut II, a handsome fifty-foot-long side-wheeler featuring cushioned seats, a refreshment cabin, and a covered promenade deck. (The craft appears just offshore to the left of Angleworm Station.) For nearly a decade the Scut II, with its white hull, black smokestack, red trim, and polished brass engine, was the flagship of Barnes' little line of lake steamers.

Lake Monona dominated lake and resort activities through the 1870s. The Monona hegemony was finally broken by a Boston man, Captain E. H. Freeman, who came to Madison for a hunting and fishing expedition. He became enchanted with the city, decided to stay, and

opened a steamer service on Lake Mendota. Freeman commissioned a noted eastern marine architect who designed the largest and fastest steam yacht ever seen in Madison. Christened the Mendota the handsome craft was sixty-five feet long, could carry one hundred fifty passengers on her two decks, and featured a steam calliope. The Mendota ran to Pheasant Branch, Picnic Point, the university, the Insane Asylum, McBride's Point, and elsewhere upon request. Home pier for the Mendota was between Hancock and Franklin Streets in what is now James Madison Park.

By the summer of 1867 four steamers were needed on Lake Monona to transport the growing number of vacationers to Winnequah, Schuetzen Park, and the Lakeside House. Two steamers were operated by Barnes and two by competitors. The steam yacht Mendota maintained its monopoly on Lake Mendota throughout the 1870s. (SHSW WHi(D31)547) and WHi(D31)583)

The Steam·Yacht Mendota

Makes Regular Trips to the Insane Asylum and McBride's Point,

(*HUBBARD, HOSMER & CO. Picnic Ground.*)

Trips Around the Lake Each Day and Sunday Excursion Trips.

Sail, Row and Fishing Boats furnished at all times, and Light Row Boats especially for ladies
.*. TELEPHONE COMMUNICATION. For further particulars see daily papers and time cards.
☞ Boat Yard and Office—408 E. Gorham. **HUBBARD, HOSMER & CO.**

question of how to get tourists back again was a subject of intense speculation and debate. In 1878 the throng of tourists simply "failed to appear in Madison."[103] Dozens of reasons were offered in an atmosphere of buck passing and recrimination. Advertising was criticized as being too little, not directed at the right people, and not containing the right information and too infrequent.[104] The failure to build new resort hotels similar to Lakeside at various points around the lakes was criticized. Madison was said to be too dull. Then, too, there was the absence of lake drives, the condition of the streets, the stagnant marshes, dust in the air, and irregular sidewalks. Certainly there was no shortage of reasons.[105] When Lakeside House burned in August 1877, it came as a severe blow because it left Madison without any lakeside resort hotels.[106] Curiously, none of the commentators attributed the decline to the depression of 1873, the second most severe in American history. Whatever the reasons, the decline was most disquieting to Madisonians, who held high hopes for the tourist business.

The commitment to reestablish Madison's reputation as a resort community during the 1873–1879 decline led to several impressive efforts. Indeed, some of the most aggressive promotional efforts and extensive improvements were not taken until after the business had begun to decline. It was during this period that the Madison hotel managers traveled to selected southern cities trying to arrange feature stories about Madison in southern daily newspapers, when the most ambitious promotional efforts were made, when a number of local improvements were most vigorously pushed. Though resourceful and energetic, these efforts failed to revive the declining business. Madison's resort boom had turned into a bust.

FIGURE 4.6. PARK HOTEL, 1871. In mid-February 1870, a group of enterprising Milwaukeans began still another effort to secure a long-sought prize for their city—the state capital. On behalf of the Milwaukee County Board and Common Council, Cream City legislators introduced bills into both assembly and senate in which the costly Milwaukee County Courthouse, then under construction, was offered at no charge to the State of Wisconsin.

Legislative committees to whom the bill was immediately referred recommended that the bills be opposed. Senate committee members noted that the state had already spent a half million dollars on the Madison new capitol and that abandoning the building "would be supreme folly." Just because Milwaukee was larger and wealthier than Madison was not a sufficient basis to move the capital, they argued. "Almost every state in the country has thought it impolitic to locate its seat of government at its principal commercial town." "The wealth of a people should not be allowed to control its political power," they added. Then the senate committee got down to the often-heard criticism of Madison's modest hotels. Again the committee sided with Madison interests when they said that most legislators came to Madison "to attend to business" and not to stay in fancy hotels. The Assembly Committee on State Affairs submitted a very similar analysis.

Although the committee recommendations against moving the capital were reassuring, Madison leaders took the bills very seriously. Madison and Milwaukee forces met on March 9 on the assembly floor where, after a long and exciting debate, the bill was indefinitely postponed by a vote of fifty-five to thirty-one.

Madison leaders lost no time in erecting a first class hotel and thereby removing this cause for criticism. Just nine days after the vote to postpone, several Madison capitalists received legislative approval to form a Park Hotel Corporation. Twenty days after the vote, fifty to sixty wealthy Madison businessmen met to buy stock in the corporation. Near the end of June, construction began with completion scheduled for December 15—just in time for the 1871–72 legislative session. Unfortunately, the contractors failed to complete their work until eight months after the target completion date and then at a cost nearly double initial estimates.

When completed the Park Hotel was a source of great local pride. The building contained 118 sleeping rooms, including twelve with attached parlors so that legislators and others who brought their families could enjoy more homelike settings. Unlike many hotels of the day, the first floor was not usurped by stores and shops but devoted instead to generously proportioned lobbies, dining rooms, sitting rooms, reception rooms, and even a ball room. The basement contained the kitchens, an elegant bar, and billiard room for the gentlemen. Interior furnishings included finely finished black walnut woodwork, Brussels carpets, walnut marble topped furniture, spring beds, and hair mattresses. The exterior treatment featured Milwaukee pressed brick, Madison sandstone, a mansard roof, and a gracious verandah. (SHSW WHi(X3)38300)

Exporting the Obvious: Growth of the Ice Trade

In 1868, some thrity years after the proposal was first advanced, Madison promoters again urged that the Rock and Yahara Rivers be made navigable all the way to Lake Mendota. Promoters envisioned steamboats docked in Lake Mendota full of cheap coal and other commodities needed to make Madison a great manufacturing city. The thought of steamboats from New Orleans, Memphis, and Minneapolis naturally thrilled town boosters, but the improvement of the waterway also had another major benefit. It would allow Madison to become a major exporter of ice—a resource nature had provided in great abundance and purity, a commodity as ordinary as it was obvious. From Mendota, ice could be shipped down the Yahara, Rock, and Mississippi Rivers to New Orleans and even to the West Indies, where the frozen commodity was in great demand. Best of all, the ice could be shipped on barges constructed of Wisconsin pine so that after the ice had been unloaded into a southern ice house, the barge could be disassembled and sold for lumber—an ingenious twist that allowed not only the commodity to be sold but also its container.[107] Although the improvements in the Yahara and Rock Rivers were never made, Madison did become a major exporter of ice, but not until several years later and under different conditions.

Ice had been harvested and stored in Madison for domestic purposes for many years. The ice box became a common appliance in Madison homes by 1860 and several men made a living cutting, storing, and distributing the cold commodity.[108] The biggest single user of ice in Madison were its five breweries, which required hundreds of tons a year to chill the beer during the aging process and then keep it cold at the tap.[109]

Substantial exporting began in 1875 and continued every year for nearly thirty years.[110] Four factors converged to make Madison a substantial exporter. First, the rapidly growing packing and brewing industries in Chicago and Milwaukee could not supply their needs from local ponds, flooded quarries, rivers, and marshes. Not only was the amount inadequate, but many of these sources were becoming polluted. These factors caused the packers and brewers to turn to the glacial lakes in northern Indiana, northern Illinois, and southern Wisconsin. Not only were they clean, but they were all within one day by rail so that shipping costs and melting in transit could be kept to a minimum. Secondly, Americans were passionately fond of iced drinks and therefore needed a reliable source of ice. In February, 1878, for example, one Madison ice cutter shipped one hundred cars of ice to Nashville, Tennessee, where Lake Monona ice probably cooled Jack Daniel's bourbon and other southern favorites.[111] Furthermore, the expanding railroad network favored cities like Madison with direct routes to large cities such as Chicago and Milwaukee. Finally, warm winters in 1877–8 and 1879–80 all but destroyed the ice crop around Milwaukee and Chicago. For these reasons, Madison—and especially Lake Monona—with a railroad track along its shore leading to the major metropolitan ice markets was in an excellent position to exploit this rapidly growing demand.[112]

The rapid growth of the ice business surprised many Madisonians. In February, 1876, the *Madison Democrat* said that "not one-third of the inhabitants of our city have the least idea of what a big thing our ice trade is." The reporter described the operation at the foot of Pinckney Street alongside the Chicago Northwestern track, where one ice harvester had six runways leading directly from Lake Monona to railroad box cars. With the help of eighty men and fifteen horses, a box car could be loaded in just eleven minutes. At the end of an eighteen-hour day, one hundred railroad cars were on their way South.[113] The *Journal* joined the *Democrat* in urging citizens to witness the amazing cutting and loading process.[114] At night torches illuminated work areas far out on the lake, and to the observer on shore, the spectacle resembled a disorganized torchlight parade.

Madison and Rome

Madison and superlatives have long enjoyed a warm symbiotic relationship. But seldom in the rich literature of praise did the genre become so exalted yet strained as the period during the 1870s when Madison was promoting itself as a *nonpareil* northern resort. The citation below was written in 1876 by Colonel W. B. Slaughter, for a contest designed to evoke the best description of Madison as a tourist resort. Slaughter's essay was not selected by the judges, but it was published in an 1876 tourist manual. *(Madison, Wisconsin, Its Attractions as a Resort for Summer Tourists.*)

Like ancient Rome, it is built on seven hills, and resembles her in other particulars. Rome had her Tiber, Madison has her Yahara; Rome had her Mars Hill in honor of the God of War; Madison has her University Hill dedicated to science, literature and the arts of peace. Rome had her Gladiatorial exhibitions in which the physical prevailed over the intellectual power; Madison has her commencements in which superior intellectual *di-Gladiation* bears off the palm of victory. Rome had her legions for conquest, Madison has her citizen soldiery for defense. Rome had her chariot races in which victory was the prize and the reward; Madison has her drives, meandering to the hilltops and . . . winding around the shores of the lakes in which pleasure is the prize and health the reward. Rome had temples dedicated to 30,000 gods; Madison has churches consecrated to the worship of the Triune God. The people of Rome belong to the government, the government of Madison belongs to the people.

By 1880 the ice trade had grown so large that Madisonians began talking about the "ice boom." Ice harvesters hired more men and teams to increase daily volume to one hundred fifty box cars a day. Both railroads used every available car and then had to send for more to satisfy the demand. In one three-day stretch in February 1880, five hundred cars were shipped out of Madison on the CNWRR alone, and by the end of the season that railroad had shipped 2,621 cars south. Car counts for the Milwaukee Road are not available, but they may have been as large. Some said that all of Lake Monona could have been harvested if cars had been available to haul the ice away.[115]

In many ways the ice business was an ideal industry for Madison. Although not an industry in the esteemed big smokestack, clanking machinery sense of that word, it was nevertheless big business. Moreover, it employed workmen during the slack winter season and grew during the depression of the 1870s after the great expectations of both factories and resorts had failed to be realized.

New Public Policies

Patchwork or Permanence: The Streets
of Madison, 1865–1880

Until 1866 nearly all the streets in Madison were dirt and therefore subject to seasonal maladies.[1] During rainy periods the poorly drained streets became muddy and sometimes impassible quagmires. Heavy rains gouged huge gullies and ditches, making travel hazardous. During hot, dry periods, dust and grit filled the air. Perhaps the best season for Madison roads was winter when cutters and sleds could glide along the smooth frozen surface.

Dirt street maintenance followed a time-honored pattern. Each year the street superintendent hired dozens of men to fill ruts, gullies, and mud puddles with dirt, sand, and sometimes a little gravel. Each time it rained, the process was repeated. Not only was this practice expensive, but it also provided no *permanent* street improvements. However, the practice was good for laborers who depended on the city for work and who voted for aldermen and mayors who provided jobs.

This patchwork policy came to an abrupt though temporary halt after the Civil War under the vigorous leadership of Madison's first Republican mayor, Elisha B. Keyes. Swept into office by the strong Civil War pro-Union sentiment, Keyes sounded a popular note in his April 1865 inaugural address that became a frame of reference for city policy from that point forward. "It must be apparent to you and every citizen that the period has arrived in our history when it is the imperative duty of the city authorities to inaugurate more . . . permanent city improvements." Specifically, Keyes said the "paving of our principal business streets" was an "absolute necessity." What happened to the six thousand dollars spent on streets last year? Keyes asked; "I have looked in vain over the length and breadth of our city to find the place or places where this really large sum was put down, but I cannot find it."[2] Indeed, Keyes' point was tough to refute and his timing was excellent. After four years of austere Civil War budgets, Madison streets were probably in the worst condition ever. The council was eager to act.

The entire question was referred to the Streets Committee, which agreed that the patchwork policy was "radically wrong"[3] and said that until a different course was adopted the streets "will continue to be a shame and reproach to our beautiful city. . . ."[4] After studying Keyes' suggestion the committee recommended, as a first step, an extensive system of permanent stone gutters so that run-off water would be carried off without taking half of the street surface with it.

Simultaneously, the Street Committee explored a new type of patented wooden pavement strongly recommended by Mayor Keyes in his inaugural. Called the Nicholson pavement after the patent holder, the paving utilized pine blocks three inches square and six inches long that had been dried and then pressure impregnated by a preservative. To provide a solid foundation for the blocks, a two- to three-inch bed of sand was covered by a platform of one-inch-thick tar-covered boards. The blocks were then laid on this foundation with the grain vertical; each row of blocks was separated from the adjoining row by a one inch spacer at the bottom. The interstices were then filled up with a mixture of gravel and hot coal tar and topped by a tar-sand mixture.[5] Though not cheap to install, Nicholson pavement was supposed to last from twenty to twenty-five years and was therefore much cheaper than dirt roads in the long run.[6] In June 1865, the council decided to install the wooden pavement of Main Street between Monona Avenue and Pinckney Street with the cost to be apportioned among the city, the state, and the abutting property owners.[7] When it was learned that the state would not pay for its portion of the street, the Common Council decided to pave just the half of the street next to the Capitol Square stores.[8] The state's refusal to pay was most unfortunate, for it meant that only one-half of one quadrant of the square was paved. Still, it was a giant step forward in Madison's effort to find a more permanent paving surface. Work on the Nicholson paving was begun in October 1865 and completed in October 1866.[9]

The extremely high cost of the Nicholson paving forced decision makers to recognize that neither the city nor property owners, or some combination of the two, could afford to extend the novel wooden pavement around the Square—even on the business side of the square. Some other solution had to be found. The Streets Committee investigated alternatives in early 1866 and reported that "macadam," a technique developed by a Scotsman, John L. McAdam, was Madison's best hope.[10] The committee described macadam as "nothing more than manufactured gravel," that is, "hard stone broken into small pieces about the size of a pigeon's egg" and laid over dry earth to a depth of seven to ten inches. Gradually the passage of wagons would compact the stone into a dense mass. If suitable hard stones could be found in nearby quarries, macadamized roads would be the cheapest permanent method.

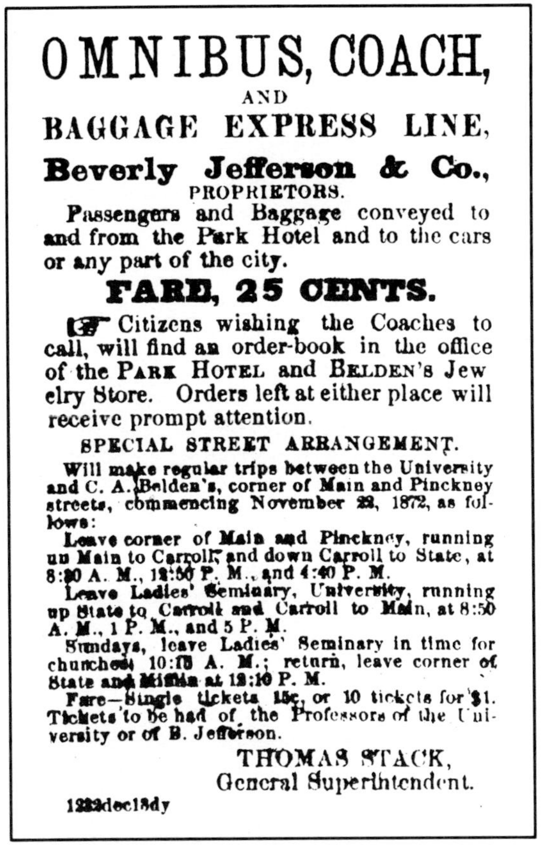

OMNIBUS, COACH,
AND
BAGGAGE EXPRESS LINE,
Beverly Jefferson & Co.,
PROPRIETORS.

Passengers and Baggage conveyed to
and from the Park Hotel and to the cars
or any part of the city.

FARE, 25 CENTS.

☞ Citizens wishing the Coaches to
call, will find an order-book in the office
of the Park Hotel and Belden's Jewelry Store. Orders left at either place will
receive prompt attention.

SPECIAL STREET ARRANGEMENT.

Will make regular trips between the University
and C. A. Belden's, corner of Main and Pinckney
streets, commencing November 22, 1872, as follows:

Leave corner of Main and Pinckney, running
up Main to Carroll, and down Carroll to State, at
8:30 A. M., 12:50 P. M., and 4:40 P. M.

Leave Ladies' Seminary, University, running
up State to Carroll and Carroll to Main, at 8:50
A. M., 1 P. M., and 5 P. M.

Sundays, leave Ladies' Seminary in time for
churches 10:15 A. M.; return, leave corner of
State and Mifflin at 12:10 P. M.

Fare—Single tickets 15c, or 10 tickets for $1.
Tickets to be had of the Professors of the University or of B. Jefferson.

THOMAS STACK,
General Superintendent.

1222dec13dy

FIGURE 4.7. GETTING AROUND: 1865–1880. A resident of Madison during the 1870s had four choices for
getting around: (1) walking (most common and convenient since the city was relatively compact); (2) riding a
horse (expensive); (3) riding in a buggy or carriage (very
expensive); or (4) taking the only form of public transportation, the omnibus (moderately expensive). The omnibus resembled a stretched-body stage coach and came
in many sizes and degrees of luxury. Guests of Madison's more expensive hotels enjoyed the largest and most
finely finished omnibuses.

Beginning in 1872 Madisonians were treated to regularly scheduled service with one omnibus company
servicing the west side of town and another the east.
Schedules, fares, and destinations contained in these
advertisements dated May 29, 1873, reveal the travel
habits of Madisonians of that era.

One estimate showed that a macadam road could
be built for just one twenty-fifth the cost of Nicholson pavement.[11]

In its eagerness to permanently improve the
streets, the Council under Keyes' leadership
passed an unprecedented number of stone gutter
and paving ordinances and spent more money on
streets between 1865 and 1867 than had been
spent on streets during the preceding nine years.[12]
In the process the council ignored the eight thousand dollars spending limit then in effect for general city expenses. In 1866, for example, the city
spent $24,551 on streets alone. This meant that
the next council was stuck with the debt and had
to pay it off before any other expenses could be
incurred. Since this was virtually impossible, several successive councils overspent and passed
along an overrun to the next council. This form
of fiscal kiting was practiced for six years until
the legislature put a stop to the procedure in
1873.[13]

The "permanent" paving programs begun
under Keyes were not without problems. The first
to surface was the fact that the vaunted Nicholson pavement wore out in 1873, just seven years
after it was laid—far short of the twenty to
twenty-five year life expectancy. In the summer
of 1875, the pavement was completely removed[14]
and, ironically, used as fuel in a steam-powered
rock crusher that made gravel to replace the
wooden pavement.[15] Nor was macadam free of
problems. Rather than using hard rock such as
granite as McAdam recommended, a much soft-
er local limestone was used. After being subjected to extended wagon traffic, the top layer
deteriorated into a fine powder which, in dry,
windy weather settled on irritating places like
backyard laundry, store shelves, and front porch
furniture.

Then there were the politics of where the new
pavement ought to go and even how it ought to
be applied. The latter became an explosive issue
in 1878, when State Street was being macadamized. One group of aldermen said that stone for
the job should be broken in the street by City of
Madison laborers, whereas another said the
breaking should be done by machine at the quarry

and hauled to the site. The former alternative
produced lots of jobs for the politically faithful,
whereas the latter alternative cost less and produced better stone. Eight aldermen resigned in
early August to protest a Streets Committee decision to have the rock broken at the quarry. Since
the council consisted of fifteen members at the
time, the eight resigned members constituted a
majority. Thus there wasn't a quorum and no
business could be conducted, including the calling of new elections to replace resigned aldermen
or pay the city workmen who were doing the controversial job. Meanwhile, the newspapers, the
public and the workmen criticized the resigned
aldermen for their "almost criminal obstin-
acy."[16] Finally, after seven weeks of refusing to
attend any council meetings, the resigned aldermen unofficially withdrew their resignations,
swallowed their pride, and joined the other aldermen at a special meeting to approve street worker
wages.[17]

Unfortunately the relatively high cost of even
macadam paving prevented permanent paving
from being continued. Although superior and
cheaper in the long run, more permanent pavements were much more expensive in the short run.
And since Madison was prevented by the legislature from borrowing money until the huge
1856–57 debt load was paid off, Madison had to
pay for all new streets out of current funds. Since
those funds were extremely limited, most mayors
after Keyes reverted to the cheaper expedient of
annually patching streets with dirt, sand and
gravel.[18]

Though followed only intermittently at first,
the permanent paving policy was not without enduring results. By 1879 about four miles of stone
gutters and three miles of gravel pavement had
been laid along Madison streets, including all
streets around Capitol Square, State Street, King
Street, and West Main all the way to the depot.[19]
In one sense the achievement was very modest,
yet when the stringent times and Madison's
budgetary limitations were taken into account,
the seven miles of paving and gutters look more
impressive.

FIGURE 4.8. 1867 RUGER BIRDSEYE. Until the advent of aerial photography, a re-markable group of artists traveled around the country doing what were called "bird-seye" views of communities. Shown above is the first of three birdseyes done for Madison. (the 1908 birdseye on the jacket is the only one done in color.) The artist, A. Ruger, first sketched each of the block faces and then combined them into a composite view using artistic perspective techniques. A study of this and other birdseyes will show that the artists were surprisingly thorough in their attention to detail.

The map vividly portrays several land use problems Madison faced at the time. The barren area bounded by West Washington Avenue, Broom, Lake, and Johnson Streets was a cattail marsh. An even larger area on the east isthmus bounded by Williamson,

East Johnson, Blair, and the Yahara River, though criss-crossed by tree-lined streets, was actually another cattail marsh penetrated by only a handful of streets only some of which had trees.

Note the two belching smokestacks along the Mendota shoreline. The smokestack at the intersection of Lake and Langdon belonged to the foundry of the E. W. Skinner Company, an agricultural implement factory. The smokestack at the foot of North Hamilton Street belonged to a steam planing mill. Unlike more settled communities, Madison still mixed factories and homes.

The large building in the foreground was Lakeside House, then just beginning its rise to fame as a tourist resort. (SHSW WHi(X3)33282)

Better Fiscal Management

Even after ten years under the city charter (1856–1866), Madison officials had a lot to learn about managing municipal finances. Additions were often made to approved city budgets. Inadequate accounting techniques kept aldermen in the dark about what was really happening with city money. Mid-year special assessments were commonplace. During the decade following the Civil War, however, Madison implemented several long overdue changes in the area of fiscal management.

The backdrop against which these improvements must be evaluated were the spending limits imposed by the state immediately after the city ran itself almost hopelessly into debt in 1856–57. From 1858 until 1868 the legislature kept the lid on Madison spending by placing a fixed limit on what the city could spend for general city purposes. From 1868 through 1880 the city was limited to a small percentage of its assessed valuation.[20] The idea was to keep Madison spending on a pay-as-you-go basis and to require legislative approval for any exceptions. From 1858 until 1881, the city did not issue a single additional bond that could not be paid out of current funds.

To the consternation of state legislators and Madison fiscal conservatives, Madison city officials did not take the state spending very seriously. From 1868 to 1873 Madison exceeded the state imposed limits by an average of fifty-two percent,[21] partly because close tabs were not kept on spending, but there was another reason, too. During the recession in the late 1860s, a substantial number of property owners could not afford to pay their taxes. Some of the "overruns" were therefore earmarked to cover delinquent taxes.

The overruns created a dilemma for city policymakers. Since the city could not borrow any money it could not pay back out of current revenues, city officials had only two alternatives. One was to send out a second tax bill to taxpayers in the middle of the year—hardly a popular alternative, but one used from time to time.[22] The other

alternative was to call the budget overrun the "floating debt," borrow the money from a local bank and pay it back either that year with a special assessment or the following year under the general levy. Finally, in 1872, the state cracked down and put a limit of five hundred dollars per month as the amount the city could pay out for short term loans to cover budget overruns.[23] With this loophole closed, the city officials had no alternative but to terminate this practice.

Even before the 1872 crackdown, Madison officials moved to correct some of the causes such as the antiquated accounting system that failed to give interested parties a clear picture of exactly where the city stood in its various budget categories. To correct this problem, a double entry bookkeeping system was implemented in 1869. Unfortunately this system was more complicated than the system then in effect and evoked criticism from some aldermen. D. K. Tenney, for example, demanded that all financial statements be prepared in "plain English . . . without the obscurity to common minds of double entry bookkeeping phrases."[24] In spite of Tenney's complaint, the double entry system prevailed, but it did require some time for the aldermen to become familiar with it and use it effectively.

Madison elected officials had a very compelling reason to get the "floating debt" problem under control. Under the terms of the 1864 state approval plan for compromising the 1866–67 bonds, the city was required to set up a sinking fund to begin paying off the principal on the bonds by 1870. Beginning in that year and continuing until 1878, the city made large annual payments averaging over thirteen thousand dollars a year for a total of $106,000. In addition the city was paying twelve to fifteen thousand dollars per year just for interest on the compromised bonds. Although the debt retirement payments were a large and heavy burden on the city, the city persisted and made impressive progress in reducing its outstanding debt. By 1877 the capital bonds had been paid off. In 1879 the city refinanced the remaining bonded indebtedness at a rate it could easily

carry.[25] Madison was not out of debt, but the city had reduced its once huge debt to a manageable size, and it had done this during a serious depression.

Toward a Larger Public Role

During the first ten years as a city, Madison limited its services to the bare necessities. Included were opening and maintaining roads, building and repairing sidewalks, providing a few street lights, paying for teachers and school houses, providing police and fire services, and very little else. Gradually, however, the public interest required the city to become involved in certain functions heretofore considered inappropriate. City intervention took many forms including takeover of the library, direct management of the fire companies, and supplementation of private efforts in areas of trash removal, parks, and tree planting.

City Takeover of the Library

In 1853, just one year after Boston opened the first free public library in the country, a private library for gentlemen was opened in Madison. Known as the Madison Institute, it was chartered to provide a reading room, literary and scientific lectures, and other means of moral and intellectual improvement.[26] For years it fulfilled the imperatives of its charter, but like many other organizations, it fell into a period of quiescence during the Civil War. In 1866 John F. Ford, a Madison lawyer and educator, infused new vitality into the old organization by getting one hundred fifty new members, increasing its library size, and talking Mayor Keyes into letting the institute use the city treasurer's office for its library. The last action was the first of a series of steps that eight years later led to the establishment of the Free Public Library.[27]

In 1873, just one year after the state had given communities blanket authority to start libraries, Madison Institute members urged the Common Council to exercise that option using the institute's library as a nucleus. Council members considered the request but concluded that expenses for the fire department and an iron bridge across the Catfish River were higher priorities.[28] The following spring S. U. Pinney, in his inaugural address, urged the council to establish a library that year. This time the council complied by passing the enabling ordinance in November 1874 and a fifteen hundred dollar annual operating appropriation as well. Start-up procedures delayed the official opening until May 31, 1875, when Madison became the second community in the state to open a free public library.[29] The Madison Free Library, as it was known, held over thirty-five hundred volumes in its card file on opening day for the use of any Madison resident over fifteen years of age. During the first year of operation, the librarian reported that thirty-five percent of the nearly thirty thousand book checkouts were "of an instructive character," meaning treatises on science, philosophy, and history, whereas sixty-five percent were "works of fiction and children's book."[30] By 1877 the collection had grown to nearly five thousand volumes and boasted good range and balance.[31]

Getting Control of the Fire Department

During the first decade under the City Charter (1856–1866), the City of Madison played a small, almost passive, role in fire suppression: it purchased fire-fighting equipment and then turned it over to independent volunteer companies. However, during the second decade under the city charter, the need for improved fire protection services forced the city to dramatically expand its control.

One justification for city intervention was the simultaneous need to secure better firefighting equipment and to cut back on the cost of the "volunteer" firemen. After ten years of using the two hand-operated pumpers, the limits of these machines were evident to all. Manning the pumps was grueling work and therefore took dozens of men working in shifts to keep up the pressure. Even under optimum conditions, the hand pumpers were incapable of producing a stream of water sufficient to reach the top stories of Madison's highest buildings, then four and five stories tall.[32]

Experts said the solution was the steam-powered pumper, which could pump as much water as four hand-operated machines and send it five stories high. Interestingly, Madison's Fire Chief, W. H. Holt, was not impressed by these vaunted new machines—at least not for Madison at that time. He argued that initial cost was too high and that they were more expensive to operate because they required coal for the engine, hay and feed for horses to pull the heavier engines, and larger engine houses. Secondly, Madison's fire water supply was limited to relatively small capacity—five-thousand-gallon cisterns that even the hand pumpers could empty very quickly. Finally, the steamers weighed two to three tons and could require eighty men and more to pull them through Madison's muddy streets.[33]

Compelling though these arguments may have been to the outspoken fire chief, they were not persuasive to Mayor Elisha Keyes. In his 1866 inaugural, Keyes noted that Madison should "follow the lead of nearly every other city in the Union and add to our department a steam fire engine." "The cost of such a machine has been urged as a reason why the city should not procure one. That seems to me to be very poor reason indeed. If it is necessary in order to save our property from destruction by fire . . . , then I say let it be done at once."[34]

The council sided with the mayor on the need for a steamer, but, in deference to the fire chief the council decided to buy a less expensive used machine and a lighter weight model that fifty men could pull through the deepest mud.[35] The steamer arrived in December 1866, and, in the custom of the period, was named the E. W. Keyes.[36]

The machine performed so well that in 1870 the council decided to buy a second steam pumper, this time a much larger and heavier engine which had to be pulled by horses. As long as the new fire engine had to be pulled by horses, the council decided to get a second team to pull the smaller, older engine, too.[37] The decision to use horses instead of men to pull the pumpers forced the council to make a tough decision about what to do with all the men who had swelled the rolls of the hand pumper companies. Clearly, large numbers of men were no longer needed to pull the machines. Nor were they needed at fires because the pumper companies were supplemented by three fully staffed, specialized companies. A hose company brought and laid all the hose, a hook and ladder company brought the two elements its name implied, and a sack company prevented looting of burning buildings.[38]

The need to cut back on the number of firemen was also required because the fire companies had become an enormous drain on the treasury. An 1866 state law entitled every fireman to five-hundred-dollar exemption in local property taxes, which the Madison council had converted to an annual cash payment. Regardless of which method of payment was used, the firemen were requiring more money than the city could afford.[39]

Armed with financial and technical justifications, the council, in April 1870, cut back the fire companies from an authorized maximum of two-hundred-twenty men to just sixty men plus officers.[40]

In March 1871, less than one year after the fireman cut-back, the council decided to take an additional step to make the independent, private fire companies more responsive to city direction. That object was secured through a charter amendment that authorized that council to elect the fire chief and his two assistants.[41] Previously leadership of the independent fire companies had been elected directly by the firefighters.

The move was sensible from a management perspective, but was highly unpopular with the men who chafed at the loss of independence. As the city began to assert control, the department became "inharmonious" and two steamer companies eventually disbanded rather than submit to city control.[42] However, their places were quickly filled with firefighters who did not find city control odious.

The same charter amendment which empowered the city to elect the fire department leadership also gave the council power to designate a fire warden or inspector for each ward and marked the beginning of a much greater emphasis upon fire prevention. Among measures adopted were the expansion of the area near the Square, where all buildings had to be built of noncombustible materials, and the adoption of ordinances that regulated the storage of combustible materials such as straw, hay, and kerosene.[43]

In spite of better equipment and greater council control, fire department capability was found wanting. In one instance two houses burned down just two blocks from the State Street engine house. Unfortunately the team normally kept at the station had been commandeered by city street crews who were removing rubbish from streets over one mile from the station. By the time the team was driven back to the firehouse, hitched up to the fire engine, and driven to the flaming homes, it was too late. To add insult to injury, someone had forgotten to put fuel in the engine boiler so that when the engine arrived bystanders were forced to scrounge for kindling and fire wood and then wait another ten to fifteen minutes before steam was produced.

The incident led to a full-scale investigation. The *Wisconsin State Journal* said the city was liable because of the "mulish imbecility" of the firemen and that the city should pay the homeowners every penny of the loss. Some urged the establishment of a full-time fire department, but the council decided to make do by getting an extra team and stopping its practice of allowing other city departments to use them.[44]

Although the fire department was sometimes subjected to serious criticisms, most of the time its members basked in citizen admiration. Fire company members were consistently described as "the best citizens of our city," "heavy taxpayers" and "able and reliable."[45] Just about every little boy wanted to be a brave fireman some day. Citizens loved the annual parade and field trails put on each May on the Capitol Square. First the mayor, aldermen and other dignitaries inspected the polished apparatus and the fire companies resplendent in their bright uniforms and glistening brass trumpets. Then, accompanied by the Lake City Cornet Band, the men and spectators moved to a nearby trial area, where the host company impressed spectators by laying and connecting five hundred feet of hose in four minutes flat, and where the companies competed to see which could get steam up the fastest and shoot water the farthest. Spectators eagerly waited for an opportunity to take a turn working the old hand pumper. At the conclusion of the trials the mayor declared the fire department to be in excellent condition, the band struck up a stirring number, and the men marched back to their stations "feeling in high glee."[46]

Supplementing Private Efforts: Trash Pickup

Householders had nearly total responsibility for disposing of a bewildering array of kitchen waste, rubbish, ashes, and human excrement. Most Madisonians took very little active interest in sanitary disposal practices and utilized every possible do-it-yourself expedient. The problem was not a shortage of dumps, for there were plenty of lot owners who solicited fill material. The problem was that the dumps were too far away and hence inconvenient for many. Besides, a wagon was needed to haul the stuff there, and many either did not have a wagon or money to pay someone to do the hauling. Consequently, backyards, streets and nearby vacant lots were extensively used, depending on the time of year and type of waste.

Most householders viewed the streets as legitimate receptacles for filth and rubbish in spite of strong ordinances to the contrary. Many householders felt they had done their duty by putting the winter's accumulation of garbage, boxes, and debris in great piles in the street and setting them on fire. In nearly all cases the smelly concoction would smolder for days, forcing neighbors to close doors and windows. Onc indignant letter to the editor written in April 1875 said every street in the city was full of rubbish and smelly, smoldering fires. When the fire went out, an unburned residue of old brooms, fragmentary boots, and broken crockery remained to be kicked about the street all year.[47] Few householders felt it was their responsibility to pick up the remaining debris.

Kitchen slops were a particular problem. Contemporary accounts show that many people simply threw wastes into a pile in the backyard. This system worked well in the winter, when it was covered by a blanket of snow and freezing temperatures temporarily arrested the smell. Interest in household waste disposal practices always peaked during the first warm days of spring and evoked predictable editorials and letters to the editor. Because the spring thaw often coincided with the commencement of a new city administration, mayoral inaugurals frequently contained expressions of indignation about "scandalous" householder practices and promises to rigorously enforce the laws.[48]

The first mayor who did more than talk about it was S. U. Pinney (1874–1876). Along with many other Madison leaders, Pinney correctly recognized that tourists would stop coming to Madison if they found the city dirty and unattractive. He also recognized that garbage in the streets could lead to disease and that even a *perception* of unhealthfulness by Madison's southern summer visitors could destroy the tourist trade. After all, one of the major reasons they were coming to Madison was to escape the epidemics and diseases so common to southern cities at the time.

In his first inaugural in April 1874, Pinney warned householders that the city would clean up debris and charge them for it if they did not do

the work.[49] When Madison property owners failed to heed the mayor's warning, they found, for the first time in Madison history, city teams in front of their homes doing just what the mayor said. And a short time later they received bills from the city for the work. After a second year of Pinney's get-tough-on-trash policy, householders began to be a little more fastidious about trash— at least in the spring of the year.[50] Judging from some Madison descriptions penned by out-of-town travel correspondents, at least some of the campaigns must have worked. A writer for the *Chicago Tribune* who visited Madison in August 1874, at the peak of the tourist boom, extolled Madison's cleanliness—a quality she said was "akin to Godliness. The streets, sidewalks, the buildings, even the trees and grass," she reported, "are neatly and precisely clean."[51] What a different account might have been written had she seen the city in April!

Mayor Pinney's spring crusades against trash in the streets, though intended to force householders to perform that function themselves, marked the reluctant beginning of a city takeover of this function. Like so many other services eventually taken over by the city, trash removal began as a last resort, but soon grew, in part by repetition and familiarity, to be viewed as a necessary city service supported by all taxpayers.[52]

Supplementing Private Efforts: Starting Parks and Planting Trees

At the close of the Civil War, Madison had no parks of its own, but few seemed bothered by this fact. Not only did the city have generous amounts of vacant land scattered around the city, but it also had the fourteen-acre state-owned and maintained Capitol Park, without a doubt Madison's most heavily-used park.[53]

If there was a need for additional recreational space, most felt it would be supplied by the private sector. Indeed, there was ample basis for this feeling. The fifteen years following the Civil War were the hey-day of the private park. First to develop such a park were the owners of Lakeside House, a tourist hotel which occupied the land where Olin Park is today located. On this site, the proprietors provided such amenities as paths, swings, picnic tables, piers, and benches so their guests could pleasantly pass the time. Captain Frank Barnes, steamboat operator on Lake Monona, was the first to see that the demand for such facilities was not limited to rich southern tourists—Madisonians wanted them, too, and would pay for them. In response to this need, Barnes built Winnequah in 1870, a tremendously popular resort on the southern shore of Lake Monona. Others quickly followed his example and built Schuetzen Park on Lake Monona and Rodermund's Woods on Lake Mendota.[54]

In spite of the dominance and great popularity of private parks during the fifteen years after the Civil War, a few Madison leaders saw the need for *city*-owned parks and successfully pushed for their creation. Their work produced three success stories:[55] a 132-foot-wide unsightly, clifflife street end at the foot of Monona Avenue; a "public square" on Lake Mendota bounded by Franklin, Hancock, and Gorham Streets, originally designated by Doty as the spot where a manmade canal was to pierce the isthmus; and a block bounded by Rutledge, Spaight, Few, and Ingersoll Streets, once used as the village cemetery.[56] Today these parks are known as Olin Terrace, James Madison Park, and Orton Park, respectively. If these sites had not been owned by the city, if the cost of converting them to parks had not been paid at private expense, and if dedicated citizens had not lobbied long and hard for conversion, it seems that the city would have stayed away from the park business entirely. At this stage of Madison's history, parks were hardly a priority item among the local elected officials.[57]

The post-Civil War period marked the beginning of a city commitment to planting street trees. First mentioned in Mayor Keyes' 1866 inaugural, the idea was picked up by the Madison Horticultural Society in 1868.[58] After several meetings the society formulated an ordinance that required property owners to plant trees in their terraces and that authorized the city to plant them if the property owner failed to do so. Though the ordinance was passed unanimously by the council, Mayor Alden S. Sanborn found a legal flaw in its form and vetoed the measure.[59] A much less ambitious but legally binding ordinance was passed in 1873 that required property owners along State Street, Gilman Street, and University Avenue to plant trees. In these areas only, the city was empowered to plant the trees and charge property owners if property owners failed to plant them.[60]

Society and Leisure

Codfish Aristocracy

When Henry Ward Beecher came to Madison in 1877 for a lecture, he said some very nice things about Madison's physical setting. But he reserved his highest compliment for its people. "The whole region," he announced smugly, "is full of New Englandmen."[1] Beecher could easily have gone on to trumpet the achievements of Madison's refugees from New England's stony hills. Once the largest single population group in the city, by the late 1870s they had become a minority of twenty to twenty-five percent.[2] Yet in spite of their dwindling numbers, New Englanders controlled a disproportionate share of local resources and power and in some areas even dominated the city. A local paper called this elite group of Yankees, Madison's "codfish aristocracy."[3]

The codfish aristocracy lived in the best neighborhoods, then located in the vicinity of what is now called Mansion Hill, along Langdon Street, on Monona and Wisconsin Avenues and along Wilson Street on Capitol Hill. At one time there were so many bankers living along Johnson Street near Wisconsin Avenue that someone suggested that its name be changed to Wall Street.[4] Their homes were finely finished with walnut wainscoting, frescoed ceilings, stained glass windows,

and ornate brick and iron work. Most had bathtubs and some even had water closets connected to private sewers that led down to the lakes. Most had new heating systems that warmed rooms with hot air registers or steam radiators, producing what had heretofore been a rarity, namely, comfortably heated homes.[5] The most prestigious row of homes during the 1870s was probably the Mendota side of Langdon Street. Nearly all homes had either a separate billiard hall or a billiard room, summer cottages on the lakeshore with piers and boathouses for private steam launches, plus a coachhouse for carriages, horses and, of course, coachmen.[6]

New Englanders dominated the better paying proprietor, professional, and white collar positions. Immigrants, by contrast, tended to hold jobs in the lower paying skilled, semiskilled, unskilled, and small business categories.[7] The codfish aristocracy maintained a tight grip on the mayor's office. Of the twelve mayors between 1865 and 1880, four were actually born in New England and another five were born in New York of New England parents.[8]

By virtue of their positions, many Yankees were recipients of coveted railroad passes that enabled them to travel at no charge to Milwaukee or Chicago to shop, conduct business, or be entertained.[9]

The New England emigres took an active role in fostering community intellectual life. They led efforts to establish a free public library and brought in prominent lecturers such as Julia Ward Howe, Horace Greeley, Henry Ward Beecher, and Robert G. Ingersoll.[10] In 1878 they founded the exclusive Madison Literary Club whose membership was limited to fifty persons with "acknowledged literary taste." Founder of the Madison group, Dr. Joseph Hobbins, M. D., patterned the constitution very closely after a similar society in Brookline, Massachusetts, with which he was familiar. Programs consisted of papers prepared and read by members on Chaucer, Shakespeare, Darwin, modern fiction, Buddha, and dozens of other topics.[11]

Ole Bull

During the 1870s Madison was the American home for internationally famous Norwegian violinist Ole Bull. For thirty years prior to his Madison interlude, Bull had been lionized by royalty and applauded by critical audiences all over Europe. The popular musician made extended concert tours to the United States in the 1840s, 1850s, and 1860s. By the 1870s Bull was probably the greatest single attraction on the American concert stage.

An appearance in Madison in January 1868 reflected Bull's popularity. His train was met by one hundred torch-carrying Norwegians who formed a welcoming procession with Bull at the head and marched up West Washington Avenue to the accompaniment of Roman candles and jingling sleigh bells. Bull's January 20 concert at the City Hall auditorium was the most successful concert ever given in Madison, more than tripling the earlier box office record for receipts. Tickets to the nine-hundred-seat auditorium were so much in demand that some went for ten dollars through scalpers. In a day when persons holding responsible professional positions made one and one-half to two dollars a day, that was a lot of money. Bull also gave two concerts in Madison in the 1850s.

The most important event of the triumphal Madison stop was not the concert but something that occurred at a reception for Bull attended by Madison's elite. There he was introduced to eighteen-year-old Sara Thorp by Rasmus Anderson, a Norwegian instructor at the University of Wisconsin. Sara, shown here in her early twenties, though not a ravishing beauty, was bright, passionately fond of music, a talented pianist, and a vivacious conversationalist. Thanks to her domineering and protective mother, she was ignorant of young men her own age. Sara was enchanted by Bull's violin virtuosity and seemed to be unable to separate the playing from the man. Though fifty-eight years old at the time, Bull was erect, handsome, distinguished, and looked far younger than his years. Sara was obviously smitten by the man. But so were most other women whose fans fluttered in his presence. Henry Wadsworth Longfellow, a close friend of Bull, claimed that whenever Bull spoke to a woman "you would think he was presenting her with a bouquet."

Sara's father, a wealthy former lumberman from Eau Claire, was horrified at his daughter's infatuation with Bull. His conventional standards would not allow him to accept the forty-year age difference and Bull's "bohemianism." Sara's mother, by contrast, was delighted at the romantic turn of events. An ambitious, intelligent, and imperious woman, Amelia Chapman Thorp had persuaded her husband to buy one of the fanciest homes in Madison in 1867, one year after her husband was elected to a two-year term in the State Senate from Eau Claire. (Thorp served from 1866–1867 and again from 1872–1873) Located at 130 East Gilman, the home later served as the Governor's mansion and is now owned by the University of Wisconsin. Ensconced in her elegantly furnished house and transported about town in a fancy carriage driven by a black coachman, Mrs. Thorp began her reign as society grand dame.

When Bull returned to Madison in March 1870 for a concert, Mrs. Thorp arranged for the famous musician to stay at their Gilman Street residence. During this stay Mrs. Thorp created opportunities for Ole and Sara to be alone and then hovered discretely in the background. The ploy worked. Ole, whose first wife had died eight years earlier, was very attentive to Sara. Before he left Madison, Bull suggested that Mrs. Thorp and Sara accompany him on the trip to Norway that summer. Mr. Thorp declined on behalf of the family, but his decision was soon overridden by his strong-willed wife. A few days after leaving Madison, Bull began sending Sara florid love letters, which, significantly, were sent to Mrs. Thorp so they would not be opened by her husband. Mrs. Thorp realized that the time had come for action. Brushing aside her husband's strong objections to Bull, she and Sara set off for New York, where they joined Bull for the return trip to Norway. After spending an idyllic two weeks riding horses, walking, and sailing around the islands outside Bergen and playing duets together in the evening, Ole and Sara were secretly married in June 1870. Mrs. Thorp had achieved her goal. Her daughter had married very well.

When the couple returned to Madison in September 1870, they were remarried at a small but elegant evening ceremony at the Thorp home by the local Congregational minister. Wedding announcements were sent out to one thousand prominent people all over the country and Europe, producing a stream of elegant and unusual gifts. A Chicago caterer delighted guests with eye-appealing food served on a thirty-thousand-dollar set of silver dishes. Guests danced to the strains of a well-known Chicago orchestra.

Sara, a twenty-year-old small-town Midwestern girl and Ole, the sixty-year-old worldly, unconventional artist might have quickly adjusted their differences if it had not been for Mrs. Thorp. She was immensely proud of the fact that her daughter had married an internationally prominent lion; she therefore expected him to roar upon command. But Bull proved singularly unresponsive to his mother-in-law, whom he quickly came to despise. On several occasions, Mrs. Thorp made elaborate preparations for parties where Bull was to be the

featured attraction. But Ole had other plans. Instead of gracing his mother-in-law's party, he would sneak off to the lower State Street home of his good friend, Professor Rasmus Anderson, to eat whole anchovies and discuss Norse mythology—one of Bull's favorite subjects. Not until after midnight—after the last guest had departed—would Ole return to the Thorp mansion.

For the next nine years the Bulls lived in Madison—that is, whenever Bull was not giving concert tours, fighting with his in-laws, or summering on his six-hundred-fifty-acre island estate twenty miles south of Bergen in the North Sea. During the Madison interlude, Bull put on several benefit concerts to raise money to buy books for Professor Anderson's new Scandinavian studies program at the University of Wisconsin and to prove that Norsemen discovered America four hundred years before Columbus. Bull even found ways to combine his passionate love of billiards with his equally passionate dislike of his mother-in-law by building a billiard house in the backyard of the Gilman Street home. There he could indulge in his favorite pastime with his cronies and get away from his mother-in-law.

Bull left Madison for the last time in 1879 and spent the remaining few months of his life in Boston and Norway. Bull died on August 17, 1880, at his Norwegian island estate with Sara at his side. Sara lived in Cambridge, Massachusetts until 1911, she established a well-known salon attended by leading lights of the day including Julia Ward Howe, Gertrude Stein, William James, Jane Addams, Josiah Royce, and many others. (SHSW, WHi(X3)28544 and the American Scandanavian Foundation)

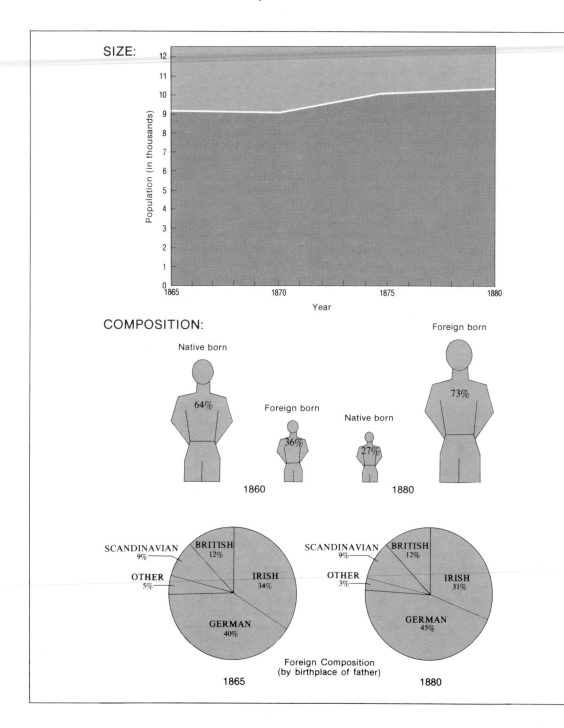

SIZE:

Population (in thousands)

Year

COMPOSITION:

Native born

Foreign born

64%

Foreign born

36%

Native born

27%

73%

1860

1880

SCANDINAVIAN
9%

BRITISH
12%

OTHER
5%

IRISH
34%

GERMAN
40%

1865

SCANDINAVIAN
9%

BRITISH
12%

OTHER
3%

IRISH
31%

GERMAN
45%

1880

Foreign Composition
(by birthplace of father)

FIGURE 4.10. 1865–1880 DEMOGRAPHICS. This fifteen-year period was hardly a boom time for Madison. From 1865 to 1870 population actually declined by eighteen persons and from 1875 to 1880 population increased by only forty-eight persons a year. The only exception to this stagnant pattern was 1870 to 1875 when Madison's population increased by 10 percent, or 2.5 percent per year. Indeed, by 1880 Madison's population had probably not even reached the 1857 peak.

The year 1880 was notable, however, as the year when the size of the foreign population peaked. In that year more than seven out of ten Madisonians were either born in a foreign country or born in the U.S. of foreign parents.

Most of the codfish aristocracy worshipped at the large expensive Congregational, Episcopal, and Presbyterian Churches. When completed in 1874, the First Congregational Church on West Washington Avenue was probably the fanciest in town and had the richest membership. Designed by a prominent Chicago church architect, the edifice could seat seven hundred persons and featured elegant stained glass windows, rich dark red carpeting, sumptuously upholstered pews, tasteful frescoing, and one of the finest organs in the state.[12]

During this period a rich but restrained social life grew up among the New England descendants, featuring balls, masquerades, dinners, and receptions. Other customs added a veneer of gracious gentility. On New Year's Day socially prominent women held open houses so that socially prominent men could make the rounds. Liquor was prohibited but coffee and delicacies were plentiful.[13]

Looking back on this period, some viewed it as an era of great men and cultured women—a time "when such families as the Atwoods, the Fairchilds, the Smiths, Gregorys, Vilases, Bascoms, Mains, Morrises, and Hopkins were active in professional and cultural leadership; when the bearded lions of the bar declaimed on Burke; and when social functions were marked by old school civilities."[14] But to the majority of Madisonians standing outside the Yankee power structure, a very different perception no doubt prevailed. To them Madison "society" appeared smug, clam-tight, and cliquish.[15]

Ethnic Influences

Between 1850 and 1860 a demographic revolution occurred in Madison. In 1850 native-born Americans outnumbered the foreign born by a sixty to forty ratio but by 1860, that ratio was reversed. Foreigners constituted sixty-four percent of the total population, leaving the native born with just thirty-six percent. Between 1860 and 1880 the size of the first and second generation foreign element continued to grow until it reached seventy-three percent of Madison's total population. Thus in 1880, more than seven out of ten Madisonians were either born in a foreign country or were the children of parents who were.[16]

As the size of the foreign population grew, so did its influence. The largest foreign group were the Germans, followed by the Irish and the Norwegians. Not only were the Germans the largest segment of the foreign population, but they exercised the largest and in many ways a disproportionate influence in the areas of religion, education, business, politics and play.[17]

Germans established St. Paul's German Presbyterian Church, the German-Methodist Church, St. Johann's Lutheran Church, the German Evangelical Church, Holy Redeemer Catholic Church, and the Shaare Schomaim Synagogue. In 1866 German-speaking congregations constituted six out of the eleven Madison Churches.[18] Germans began Madison's first kindergarten program in 1879.[19] Germans owned all of Madison's breweries.[20] Germans heavily contributed to huge Democratic political majorities. So eager were Republicans to woo the German vote, they began a partisan version of the popular Turnverein called the Republican Gymnastic and Singing Society.[21] Although no German held the mayor's chair during this period, many were elected to the Common Council.[22]

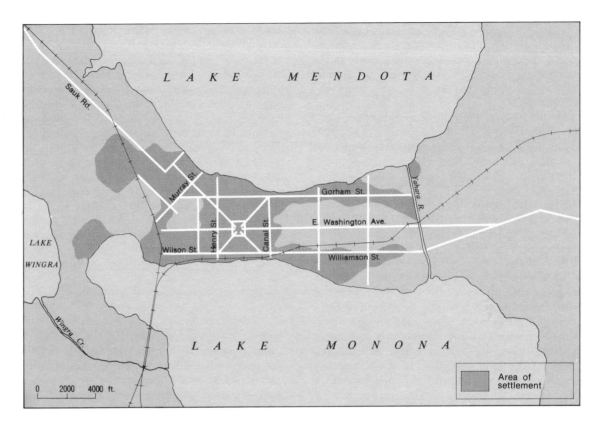

FIGURE 4.11. 1872 SETTLEMENT PATTERNS. By 1872 when a detailed map was prepared by the Milwaukee firm of Taylor and Willits, the boundaries of the urbanized area continued to be confined to the more easily settled and desirable ridges. Indeed, by 1872 the West Marsh had been surrounded by urbanized development and the Great Central Marsh on the eastern end of the isthmus had been nearly surrounded.

Popular appreciation of classical music was attributable in part to concerts of the Maennerchor, and the Liederkranz Society, a men's choir and mixed chorus respectively. German band music became an integral and widely accepted form of community entertainment. Enjoyment of German and European drama was fostered by the Apollo Dramatic Club, later made a section of the Madison Turnverein. Turnverein gymnastics and acrobatics programs introduced Madisonians to the importance of exercise and physical culture.[23]

Though few in numbers, the Norwegians left a significant legacy of institutions and cultural contributions. From 1876 to 1886 Madison had the principal seminary for the Norwegian Lutheran Synod, consisting of sixty-five thousand communicants.[24] Housed in the old Farwell mansion on Spaight Street, the seminary might have remained longer had not a fierce doctrinal fight split the synod into two groups, thereby destroying its financial support. A Norwegian high school was contemporaneous with the seminary.[25] Nearly all Lutherans were members of the Norwegian Lutheran Church, which grew rapidly during this period.

During the mid-1870s Norwegians began celebrating Syttende Mai, the Norwegian independence day, with a parade through town and a party at Winnequah.[26] The Norwegian community also made a vigorous effort to erect a ten-thousand-dollar statue in Capitol Park in honor of Leif Ericsson, who, the Norwegians believed, discovered America in the year A.D. 1000. Though the necessary amount of money was not raised, attendance at benefit concerts showed non-Norwegian elements of the city to be very supportive of their goal.[27]

The Irish imprint was visible through the group activities sponsored by St. Raphael's Catholic Church and in the beginning of St. Patrick's Day celebrations.[28] The latter was widely enjoyed by many non-Irish.

The growth in the size and influence of the German community set the stage for a series of running battles on how one should spend Sundays. To the German, a summer Sunday was a time to be spent with the family in a cool shady garden, sipping ice-cold lager beer, enjoying the week of Virginia, listening to band concerts, playing ten pins, and enjoying good fellowship with friends. Hot coffee and tea were served for the ladies and entertainment for the children was provided too. However, this "continental" concept was utterly contrary to the Yankee notion of how the "Lord's Day" should be observed. To the New England emigres, Sundays should be spent going to church, then going home to reflect upon the scripture. To play or enjoy oneself on Sunday was felt to be a serious violation of the scriptural injunction to remember the Sabbath and keep it holy.

In 1859, without much fanfare, the Wisconsin Legislature had passed a series of "blue" laws, which gave strong legal sanction to the Yankee concept. More specifically, the law prohibited any person from "doing any manner of labor or business or work . . ." on the "Lord's Day, commonly called Sunday." The only exception the laws allowed were works of necessity and charity. The same law made it illegal even to be present at any dancing, or any public diversion, show or entertainment or to take part in any sport, game or plan . . ." on the Lord's Day. Another part of the law specifically forbade the sale of liquor on Sunday.[29] These blue laws coupled with scriptural injunctions put Madison Yankees in a strong legal position.

Until 1870 the state blue laws were quietly ignored in Madison. Given the growing political power of the German community who favored wet, fun-filled Sundays, Madison aldermen were understandably reluctant to enforce these laws or any local ordinances patterned after then. In 1870, however, tolerance ceased to be a virtue. Indeed, tolerance might have prevailed had not a group of rowdies consistently insulted codfish

---

Paper Carrier Tips.

Madison newspaper carriers of the 1870s did not ask their customers for Christmas tips. Instead, during the last week of December they left attractively engraved cards or even small pamphlets containing entertaining and sometimes inspirational verse. The example shown below was circulated by *Wisconsin State Journal* carriers in late 1878.

Cast off the many cares of life,
Forget its petty pains,
The graceless son, the scolding wife,
Hard work and little gains.

Forget ambition's shining lure,
Forget your grocer's bill,
Forget the rich, forget the poor,
Forget what'ere you will,

Yet don't forget one small demand
Mid your forgetful joy,
But drop a quarter in the hand,
Of your poor carrier boy.

---

aristocrats on their way to church. At that time nearly all the churches were very close to the Capitol Square and most church goers walked—at least on nice days. The problem was not the distance one had to walk, but rather the open saloons one had to pass along the way. There churchgoers were subjected to a gauntlet of profanity, obscene gestures, and drunken behavior that was simply too much to tolerate. The problem was especially bad for U.W. coeds who lived at Chadbourne Hall, because they had to pass all the State Street saloons.[30]

After enduring these conditions for years, a coalition of sabbatarians and prohibitionists began to work together to reestablish the sanctity of the Lord's Day. The power of this elite coalition was evident in an ordinance passed in April 1870, which prohibited anyone from playing billiards or ten pins or any other game whatsoever on Sunday.[31] Reaction was strong and swift in coming, especially from Germans, who were accustomed to spending Sundays doing something besides reading the Bible and contemplating. To this influential ethnic group, nothing less than repeal was acceptable. The Committee on Licenses, to whom the repeal request was sent, agreed, saying that such an ordinance "was unnecessary for the public peace and quiet and oppressive to the laboring classes . . . who observe Sunday not only as a day of rest, but as a day of enjoyment and relaxation." Surely, the committee continued, the "time has not yet arrived when the Christian religion requires the law to promote its growth. . . ." Our people, the committee concluded, "should be permitted to spend Sunday in whatever way they may deem proper providing that they do not prevent or disturb others from enjoying the same privilege."[32] Just two months after the restrictive ordinance was passed, the council made games on Sunday legal once again—at least under Madison law.[33]

Defeated on the Sunday game front, the vanquished coalition was quiet for a little more than a year, but then, beginning in 1872, began to mobilize their forces for another battle—this time in a tougher arena. Instead of banning billiards and ten pins, they decided to ban "King Alcohol"

FIGURE 4.12. 1876 CENTENNIAL CELEBRATION. For several days prior to July 4, 1876, the weather had been cool, cloudy, and wet, making the prospect of clear skies for the nation's centennial discouraging indeed. But at 4:00 A.M. on that eventful day a slice of blue sky appeared on the western horizon, and by the time the sun rose, hot and bright, the sky was "one great vault of blue." The people in the photograph above were delighted. Many had been awakened at 6:00 A.M. and subjected to twenty minutes of cannonading, bell ringing, steam-whistle blowing, and firecracker blasting. Soon farm folks were pouring into Madison on wagons to enjoy the Great Centennial Day. By the breakfast hour a lively mass of humanity mingled in the streets enjoying the festive atmosphere. One report said the whole city had been literally wrapped in red, white, and blue flags, pennants, and bunting.

At 10:00 A.M. bands, veterans, the mayor, the governor, the fire department, the Turnverein, civic societies, and citizens paraded around the square. About 10:30 the procession returned to the main viewing stand (see photograph) where the military companies presented themselves.

At noon, following a thirty-eight-gun salute, small groups gathered around picnic baskets for lunch on the capitol lawn. Foot races, trapeze performances, marching competition, sailing and rowing regattas, and cannon firing crowded the afternoon with activities, and a fireworks display capped the day.

Reporters were critical about parts of the program. The fireworks were called "humbug," the specially constructed gateways were declared to be worth about forty-five cents and the artillerymen failed to hit the platform set about a mile out in Lake Mendota after forty-eight tries. But even with the disappointments, it was a glorious day—sunny, fun-filled, exciting—a time to reflect upon the nation's first one hundred years and a good time to forget the severe depression that held the nation in its grip. (SHSW WHi(X3)17892) himself. Few, they reasoned, would play billiards, ten pins, or other such games without lager beer and schnaps. Newspapers reported a cavalcade of prohibitionists, each of whom dispensed an inspirational speech, lecture, or sermon.[34]

After a year of antialcohol rallies, a huge meeting was held on May 4, 1873, in the Assembly Chambers that focused on how to achieve that limited but critically important objective. In a unanimously passed resolution, the participants called upon the mayor and Common Council to enforce the 1859 state law prohibiting drinking on the Sabbath. Proponents did not ignore Madison's pluralistic population, whose elements were imbued with "different notions and customs" about drinking on the Sabbath, but, as one of the speakers said, "When in Rome, do as the Romans do."[35]

The council was anything but eager to deal with the resolution and did not act on the citizen request until June 1873, one month later, and then voted seven to two to indefinitely postpone any further action. Mayor J. C. Gregory, however, in a rare act of mayoral contravention of council will, ordered all the sabbath laws enforced.[36] Perhaps his order was a sop to the prohibitionists because the police did nothing to enforce the law. Then in early August, Mayor Gregory left town on business and Alderman Chandler P. Chapman, one of the two aldermen who had voted against postponement of any action of the citizen petition, became acting mayor. He immediately issued a decree forbidding the saloons to open on Sunday, beginning August 3, 1873. With just two exceptions, all saloons complied and newspapers reported that the Sabbath was more quiet than usual . . . there being a noticeable lack of brawls and disturbances by the boys. . . ." Perhaps that was because most of the boys left town on the steamers and went to Winnequah or out to Schuetzen Park, where the nut brown liquid could still be enjoyed outside the city limits.[37]

Handbills that circulated about the city the following Monday afternoon showed that some residents were not going to take the acting mayor's unilateral enforcement of the Sunday laws lying down. Written in German, the handbills urged all Republicans, Democrats, Liberals, Conservatives, and the Free Men of America—anyone concerned with personal and constitutional freedom—to gather at Turner Hall that evening to "curb the aggressive tendencies of temperance and Sunday fanatics."[38] The *Wisconsin State Journal* took a different view of the invitees, saying they were "brewers, liquor dealers, Turners, sharpshooters, free thinkers, free singers, free drinkers, and free lovers of lager."[39] Nearly two hundred jammed the hall to vent their frustration about the unwarranted intrusion into their lives. All agreed that if a man wanted to drink a glass of beer with his family on a Sunday afternoon, he had a perfect right to do so. What made many mad was that the mayor had promised *before* the election not to "meddle with the Sunday closing question."[40] Those present passed a resolution charging the administration with selective enforcement of the Sunday closing laws and said it was not fair to close down saloons and then allow steamboats, omnibuses, livery stables, clothing stores, tobacco shops, ice cream parlors, and many other businesses to remain open on Sunday. They also told Acting Mayor Chapman that to be consistent and fair, he must issue an order closing *all* businesses on Sunday and gave him until Friday, August 8, to do so. When Friday passed without any such order from Chapman, the Turner Hall group, now calling themselves the Constitutional Union, held another meeting to plan their comments at the "senseless and obsolete Sunday closing laws," arguing that if they were enforced statewide, "one half of the people of this state would be before the courts every Monday morning. . . ." Chapman's actions were portrayed as "vindictive and intolerant toward certain classes of our population . . . particularly the German born."[41] A Committee of Twenty was appointed to walk around town the following day to get the names of all businesses which remained open in violation of the Sunday closing law.

To the delight of Constitutional Union members, fifty Madison businesses, not counting works of necessity or charity, were found to be flagrantly violating the state law. Observers recorded the necessary details so they could issue charges and testify if necessary. Armed with this legally incontrovertible evidence, Constitutional Union members called on Mayor Gregory soon after he returned to Madison from his business trip. Mayor Gregory quickly worked out an acceptable compromise with the pressure group effective Sunday, August 31, 1873. The compromise required saloons to stay closed until 2:00 P.M. and then remain open only until 9 o'clock in the evening.[42] This gave churchgoers time to get back home from church without having to pass any open saloons. But of course the arrangement was illegal.

The *Wisconsin State Journal* ridiculed this mayoral capitulation to the German counter-crusade on grounds that as a lawyer, if not as a mayor, Gregory knew better than to "tell men they are only required to conform to the laws half the time. . . ."[43] Clearly the mayor's interpretation of the law was pure pragmatism; significantly, the Common Council supported the mayor by taking no further action. The *Journal* charged that the council "weakened" when several merchant aldermen were threatened by a German boycott.[44]

Undaunted by another defeat the coalition of sabbatarians and prohibitionists tried another tactic, which the saloonists called "Female Praying Bands." Under the auspices of Methodist and Congregational women, the Ladies Temperance Alliance held thrice-weekly meetings during February 1874 to lay plans for their invasion of Madison's seventy-four grog shops. Under this scheme tipplers were to be subjected to prayers and songs—all designed to persuade men to put down their steins and be saved. Predictably, the *Journal* applauded this "band of earnest Christian ladies," while the *Democrat* said the whole idea of the saloons begin visited by bands of praying ladies was "extremely ridiculous and sacrilegious" besides. Unfortunately, the female saloon invasions were very poorly reported, but it appears that the women became discouraged and abandoned the tactic after visiting four or five of Madison's saloons.[45]

Still not defeated, the highly motivated temperance people persisted. Having failed at outlawing billiards, ten pins, other games and Sunday drinking—and having found no converts to prohibition in the saloons—several coalition members dedicced to enter the political arena and pursue their remedies there. Here failure was quick and merciful. The whole idea collapsed when the majority present at a huge meeting rejected the idea on the grounds that politics would defile their cause. Except for a few scattered lectures and sermons for the faithful, prohibitionist and sabbatarian sentiments were scarcely evident in Madison during the last half of the 1870s.[46]

Local Politics, 1865–1879

Political expression continued to be unabashedly partisan in Madison. Only once between 1865 and 1879—and then in deference to the 1876 centennial—did political parties drop their labels. Even that act was a sham because both candidates ran on partisan platforms; one candidate was even a former mayor whose political label was widely known.[47] The existence of two daily newspapers on opposite sides of the political fence assured Madisonians of vigorous partisan treatment of most local issues. A casual reader of newspapers of this period, however, might easily have concluded that the partisan combat was not between Democrats and Republicans but rather between Copperheads and the Radicals, so frequently and consistently did the papers use those pejorative terms for their partisan rivals.

Although the Democrats easily dominated Madison partisan offices, the Republicans made significant advances. Capitalizing on a ground swell of pro-Union sentiment at the close of the Civil War and later on the personal popularity of certain candidates, Republicans held office for one-third of the years between 1865 and 1879.[48] Of the 168 aldermen elected during this period, two out of three were Democrats.[49] With the exception of just three years when there were an equal number of Democrats and Republicans on the council, Republicans were helplessly outnumbered, sometimes by as much as a five-to-one margin.[50] Democratic strength was heavily concentrated in the first and third wards, where between 1865 and 1879, seventy-four Democrats and just ten Republicans were elected.[51] In the Second and Fourth Wards, by contrast, Democrats elected thirty-eight aldermen whereas the Republicans elected forty-six. When it came to electing presidents and congressmen, Madisonians gave the Democrats a clean sweep.[52]

The Republicans might have done better had they fielded more candidates. For seven of the fifteen years, they did not even nominate a mayoral candidate.[53] The *Journal* complained about the "fashionable aloofness of propertied men who ought to take a lively concern in the prosperity of the city" and urged the election of "good practical common sense businessmen."[54] Perhaps the "aloofness" was because the job of mayor was a "thankless one" requiring the incumbent to "perform a large amount of unpleasant work for which he is likely to receive few thanks and many curses."[55] But if so, the Democrats did not seem bothered by an ungrateful public.

During this period the mayor's chair was consistently occupied by socially prominent, financially comfortable, well-established New England descendents. All were professionals or proprietors: seven were lawyers, three were bank presidents, two were merchants, and one was a newspaper publisher.[56]

Local elections were taken quite seriously in the sense that saloons, the municipal court, and the public library were all closed on election day.[57] Political victory celebrations continued to be boisterous and unrestrained. A typical celebration involved a huge bonfire in the middle of one of the downtown streets, speeches, fife and drum music, and much whiskey.[58]

In his 1877 inaugural address, Mayor Harlow S. Orton expressed pride in the fact that in an era of widespread city corruption, Madison was free of "rings and conspiracies for the benefit of favorites and for plunder and other corrupt purposes."[59] But an outspoken and tart-tongued alderman from the Third Ward, William Welch, disagreed. From 1875 until 1877, Welch launched a one-man crusade against the long-standing practice of mayors and aldermen selling merchandise to the city and then voting their own pay. He charged that the public offices were often sought by men who merely desired to secure the city as a customer.[60] The East-side alderman took great delight in exploiting the numerous instances where he encountered this abuse. Though hardly on the scale or scope of Tammany Hall, the practice was clearly unlawful.[61]

Alderman Welch also attempted to fire a former mayor who had been given the job of city assessor because in that latter capacity he had failed to report twenty thousand dollars in personal property held by his daughter. After investigation the council required the assessor to pay the back taxes, but did not assess any fine.[62] Welch even tried to bring to justice certain persons associated with the 1857 one-hundred-thousand-dollar city loan scandal and to force all of Madison's first aldermen to give back gold-headed canes they awarded themselves.[63] In neither case was he successful.

Welch's vitriolic tactics quickly made him the council pariah and prompted that body to pass an unprecedented resolution declaring Welch to be "the biggest nuisance that ever graced the Council Chamber."[64] The same resolution pleaded with his constituents in the Third Ward to never "impose his presence on any of us at any future period." These attacks only seemed to steel the resolve of the eastside alderman, who persisted in his exposures. In desperation, one of Welch's favorite aldermanic targets got his fellow council members to pass a resolution saying that Welch was "insane and dangerous to the public" and referred it to the Committee on Health. That committee acquitted Welch of these charges and even had the record expunged of the entire transaction.[65] After leaving the council, Welch continued his attacks through a small weekly newspaper that he published, but he failed to persuade the council or the public that the objectionable practices should be discontinued.[66]

FIGURE 4.13. 1866 KEYES-NOLAND MAYORAL ELECTION. On Thursday evening, March 29, 1866, Madison Democrats met in city caucus to select their mayoral standard bearer for the local election the following Tuesday. Wealthy bank president and Madison promoter Simeon Mills won near unanimous support but, unfortunately for the Democrats, Mills decided not to accept the nomination. This left Elisha E. Keyes (right) unopposed for second term as Mayor. Keyes, a prominent and powerful Republican leader, had just been reappointed the previous year as Madison postmaster by President Andrew Johnson. From this strategically located vantage point in the political hub of the state, Keyes was able to exercise control over a large number of patronage positions.

On Friday, March 30, 1866, just three days before the election, the Wisconsin Supreme Court in a landmark decision unanimously held that blacks in Wisconsin had the right to vote and that they had had this right since 1849 when a state referendum on the topic passed. The court decision overruled an earlier interpretation by the State Board of Canvassers who said the 1849 referendum was invalid because too few citizens voted on the measure to satisfy Constitutional conditions.

The following Monday, April 2, 1866, William H. Noland, a forty-six-year-old black businessman (left), was walking past the corner of East Main and King Streets when a large crowd approached him and asked him to go to the office of G. W. Hyer, the editor of the *Wisconsin Daily Democrat.*

Soon after arriving in Madison in 1850 Noland established a reputation as a successful and well-patronized barber. His long and variegated occupational odyssey included grocer, ice cream maker, baker, maker of hominy and rye coffee, law clerk, saloon keeper, dyer and cleaner of clothing, a veterinarian, and even chiropodist. Noland was perhaps most appreciated as a musician and bandmaster. In 1864 an unusual special benefit for the talented black musician, billed as "the ball of the season," was held so that citizens could express their appreciation for his thirteen years of sweet, dependable music.

When Noland arrived at the newspaper office, Hyer urged Noland to run for mayor as an independent candidate. Noland immediately diagnosed the joke. While ostensibly an independent, he would receive the support of Democrats who wanted to embarrass Keyes by giving him a political close call. In a strongly Democratic town, the ploy was plausible, although it seems likely that Keyes, riding atop a crest of pro-union Republican sentiment, would still win.

Noland rejected the offer, citing the anti-black history of the Democratic party, which he interpreted as unsupportive of any black rights except "to labor under the taskmaster's whip." Noland quickly added his strong intention not "to soil his fair fame and his new birth into the rights of citizenship by voluntarily lending himself to their purposes."

In spite of Noland's refusal, his name was added to the ballot at the request of the Democrats. Noland even issued a dignified election statement declaring that he was a Republican and was therefore voting for Keyes.

On Tuesday, April 3, 1866 Keyes beat Noland 961 (76%) to 298 (24%). Between ten and fifteen "Americans of African descent" as the *Journal* described them, voted for the first time in Madison and without obstacles.

The election naturally evoked statewide reaction. The *Wisconsin Daily Capitol* said Noland's vote reflected the strength of the fanatical Republicans. The *Chicago Times* saw the election as a contrived test of black equality. A more likely interpretation is that nearly all Noland's votes came from Democrats who wanted to cast a protest vote against Keyes and that few if any votes came from Madison blacks or Republicans.

A case can be made, but not a very strong one, that the Civil War improved the condition of the black in Madison. Thirty-eight percent of Madisonians voted for Negro suffrage in 1865 compared to twenty three percent in 1857. Though an increase of fifteen percent, Madisonians remained overwhelmingly opposed to black suffrage and would no doubt have continued to vote that way for decades had the Supreme Court decision not intervened. Within Republican circles the black enjoyed *nominal* respect. When Frederick Douglass lectured in Madison in 1866, he was described by the *Wisconsin State Journal* as a "distinguished African." At a Grant-for-President rally involving a march around the Capitol Square, the *Journal* described the assemblage as consisting of Yankees, Irish, Germans, Scandinavians, English, and *American citizens of African descent.*"

Outside Republican circles, however, strong anti-black attitudes were prevalent. Indeed, during the 1868 Capitol Square march for Grant, cries of "nigger, nigger" were hurled at the black marchers. A Madison hotel owner charged with assaulting a woman strenuously resisted having "niggers" on his jury. Newspapers reported numerous incidents where blacks received abuse and indignities. (WHi(X3)1776 WHi(X3)31169)

FIGURE 4.14. SOLDIER'S ORPHANS' HOME Few blocks in Madison have a more interesting history than the block bounded by Brearly, Spaight, and Lake Monona. Originally the site of the extraordinarily elegant home of one of the state's wealthiest and best known men, Leonard J. Farwell, the home lay vacant for five years after Farwell's bankruptcy in 1857. In 1862 the receivers rented the building to the U.S. government for use as a hospital for wounded northern soldiers. Just six months after the soldiers left at the close of the Civil War, the home was recycled for the third time as the Soldiers' Orphans' Home for the State of Wisconsin. The engraving shown above shows the home as it appeared in 1868 after the completion of an adjoining school building.

Opened in 1866, the unusual institution accepted children between four and fourteen years of age whose fathers had been killed or incapacitated in the war and whose mothers had either died or could not care for their children. For nine years the school flourished, providing a home for a total of 683 children. Each child was required to do chores. The boys cut wood, hauled coal, milked cows, fed hogs, cultivated gardens, and mended shoes, and the girls helped with the cooking and sewing. Patriotic mottos in classrooms such as "Fatherless but not forsaken" and "We will love and honor the state which has adopted us" reminded the youngsters of their special circumstances. Every effort was made to give the children a good education. The school on the left was built by the state for the exclusive use of orphans in 1868. Twenty of the children were sent to State normal (teacher's) schools and one young man was sent to the Naval Academy at Annapolis.

The idea for the home came from Benjamin Hopkins, a prominent Madison businessman, who urged Mrs. Cordelia Harvey, the former governor's widow, to pursue the plan. With her characteristic enthusiasm and effectiveness, she raised the necessary money and got the legislature to pass a bill establishing the home and providing for its operation.

After the home was closed in 1874, the legislature transferred title to the University of Wisconsin Regents, directing that the buildings be used as a medical school. A committee investigated the idea but concluded a medical school was not practical. The Regents sold the property in 1876 to the Norwegian synod of the Lutheran Church, which used the property to house two institutions: a Norwegian Lutheran seminary and the Monona Academy. The former, a theological seminary, emphasized the practical duties of the ministry as opposed to the conventional classical course; the latter was a coeducational high school for wealthy Norwegians who desired a strong religious orientation for their progeny. The Lutheran use of these facilities continued until a doctrinal fight in 1886 split the synod and destroyed its financial support. However, the synod kept the property and in 1889 reopened the facility as a Norwegian orphanage known as the Martin Luther Orphan's home. A fire in 1893 led to the transfer of the home to Stoughton, where it remains to this day.

During the 1880–81 term the math teacher at the Academy was Thorstein Veblen, then twenty-three years old and just out of college. In later years he wrote several trenchant criticisms of America, including the classic *Theory of the Leisure Class* (1899), from which came the term "conspicuous consumption," now almost a household word.

In 1894 the Lutherans sold the property to several Madison investors who razed the historic structure in March 1895. In 1908 the block was subdivided into eleven lots. Today a pedestrian walking by the 900 block of Spaight would never know the history of this block except for two reminders. In the replat the developers named one of the new streets Harvey Terrace in memory of Cordelia Harvey, who persuaded Lincoln to turn the mansion into a hospital. A second reminder is a small piece of red marble looking much like a tombstone and lying in the terrace of the Brearly-Spaight corner.

Religion 1866–1880

Although the economy between 1866 and 1879 was far from buoyant, several denominations took advantage of brief economic upturns to erect "larger and more splendid" churches or improve existing structures. The Congregationalists and the Methodists, for example, began costly new churches in June 1872 and September 1873, respectively. Holy Redeemer began its new church in 1867 and the German Lutherans, the predecessor to St. John's Lutheran, in the same year. St. Raphael's began its impressive steeple in 1866.[67]

While the major denominations were building fancy downtown churches, the Congregationalists, the Presbyterians, and the Episcopalians were competing to see which church could boast the biggest bell with the lowest note. Until 1873 the Presbyterians were ahead with a nine-hundred-pound bell whose tone was lower G sharp. But in late 1873 the Congregationalists installed a one-thousand pounder, which hit lower F.[68] The Congregational victory lasted less than a year when the Episcopalians installed an enormous 2,531 pound "Bishop's Bell," putting that church in a class by itself and leaving the two other competitors to trill the upper part of the lower octaves.[69] Soon after the installation of the Bishop's Bell, someone wrote a letter to the editor complaining that the once vaunted Congregational bell sounded "like a demolished brass kettle" and that it annoyed other parishioners when it was rung at noon on Sunday.[70] One cannot help wondering if the anonymous letter writer may not have been an Episcopalian gloating over the incomparable Bishop's Bell.

During this period churches conducted business as usual, with Sunday morning and evening services punctuated from time to time by a spirited revival. In January 1876, for example, two unordained young revivalists with the unlikely names of Bliss and Whittle secured the active involvement of U. W. President Bascom, several university professors, plus the local clergy, and packed in the people during a week long program.[71]

Isaac Smith, P. M.

The job of keeping the city free of livestock was the responsibility of the poundmaster, sometimes called the P.M., one of the most important, yet least appreciated city jobs. The more he succeeded, the more he was hated. Children threw stones at him, women taunted him, and men assaulted him. In exchange for taking all this abuse, the poundmaster was given an exclusive franchise to capture all unpenned animals and receive half of all fines collected. The animal owner also had to pay a daily fee for feed, water, and other expenses of keeping animals in a pound.

Madison's most conscientious and therefore most disliked poundmaster was probably Isaac Smith, who did more than any other person to free the streets of livestock. The story of his eventful one-year term is chronicled in the following newspaper articles and 1873 annual report:

May 2, 1873 *Madison Democrat*	Poundmaster Smith says that most of the owners of cows have from 3 to 7 dogs—in many cases yellow curs trained to tackle poundmasters. Yesterday Mr. Smith attempted to defend himself from these domestic pets with a huge club but being aged, Mr. S. was unable to chase them all at once so today he has armed himself with a revolver in his right hand, a club in the other and expects to be at about 7 this evening up to his waist in blood.
May 6, 1873 *Madison Democrat*	Poundmaster Smith went after 19 cows yesterday and killed 9.
June 2, 1873 *Madison Democrat*	Isaac Smith, poundmaster, was arrested yesterday afternoon and charged with shooting William Salmon. Circumstances of the case are: Mr. Salmon was sitting down in the grass a short distance from his house . . . letting his horse graze along the road. Mr. Smith happened to come along . . . and saw the horse eating. He drove over to where Mr. Salmon was and demanded that the horse be taken to the pound claiming he was violating the cattle ordinance by allowing his horse to be eating along the public highway. A few words ensued and Mr. Smith picked up a stick and commenced to drive the horse off when at the same time Mr. Salmon commenced driving off Mr. Smith's horse. Mr. Smith then turned around, drew his revolver and fired two shots both of which took effect in his left leg inflicting a slight flesh wound.
June 11, 1873 *Madison Democrat*	Mr. Smith was trying to get a bull to the pound and instead the bull chased him and his horse into the Catfish river.
June 18, 1873 *Madison Democrat*	Yesterday Isaac Smith stretched out on the grass on the outskirts of the city for a short nap when about 18 or 19 youngsters came by, unhitched his horse and took it to the pound.

July 3, 1873 *Madison Democrat*	The fiercest battle since the cow and goose law went into force was fought yesterday between Smith and 19 women and as many children. The contest was a long and sanguinary one commencing soon after daylight and ending at twilight. At 6 Smith's enemies received reinforcements and the hottest fight raged resulting in the complete rout of the poundmaster. At dead of night, however, Smith gathered himself and allies of policemen and a revolver and renewed the attack. The suprise was overwhelming and the latter won. The geese are in the pound.
July 11, 1873 *Wisconsin State Journal*	Poundmaster Smith with his little whip is on the lookout early and late for stray cows, pigs, geese, Indians, mules, and any other animals that walk on two or six legs. Any of which happen to fall in Smith's way are sure to find their way to the pound. Smith discharges his official duties very acceptably to citizens interested in seeing the streets of Madison free of cattle but he don't like the Irish. He says he can't reason with them, as they bring forth too many strong arguments in the shape of bricks, stones, and shillelaghs for him. He says the Irish have recently abandoned their former mode of resisting the poundmaster and have resorted to using arsenic, but, says Smith, "I ain't dead yet." He is the bravest poundmaster that ever straddled a mustang poney, Smith is.
July 22, 1873 *Madison Democrat*	Poundmaster Smith has been complaining that he is having a hard time enforcing the animal control ordinance as the city officials aren't backing him up. They are worried about reelection.
July 31, 1873 *Madison Democrat*	Isaac Smith, our very efficient poundmaster, has been out in the country for the past few days harvesting and when he returned last night he said he found the city in a deplorable condition. The geese and pigs were running at large, their owners impudent and saucy. After riding through the city and surveying all its realm, he spied a flock of geese on forbidden grounds in the western limits. He immediately assumed the look of one in authority, took up his official whip and was soon marching through the city with his captives before him, and half a million urchins more or less following behind, not withstanding the jeers he was objected to, the bones and stones that were hurled at him, and the eloquent pleading of women. He turned a deaf ear to all and executed the authority imposed on him and safely lodged his prisoners in the pound.
August 4, 1873 *Madison Democrat* Poundmaster's Report	A note to the Common Council: "I hereby tender my sincere thanks to the honorable common council for electing me to the office of Poundmaster . . . in acknowledgement of my ability to cope with the cow, the goose and the goat, powers for which I feel duly thankful."

Smith, though a very conscientious poundmaster, was not reappointed by the 1874 Council. Perhaps the politicians felt he had been a little too conscientious in the pursuit of his duties.

Perhaps the most significant new development within Madison churches was the beginning of Sunday schools. By the mid-1870s Sunday schools had been started in nearly all Protestant denominations. Systematic exposure to Bible lessons gradually developed a cadre of dedicated lay leaders, some of whom saw the Sunday schools as a means to reach the unchurched. The earliest known effort of this kind in Madison, the Bethany Mission School, was launched in early 1876 by the Presbyterians for children and young people in the Williamson Street area.[72]

Irritants

Cows

In 1882 a seemingly unimportant newspaper article announced that Madisonians were gradually removing fences around their property—a change that signalled the end of a thirty-year period when just about every property owner had one.[73] Madisonians were removing fences not because they had fallen out of style or because they were tedious to paint, but because the time-honored practice of free-roaming livestock had at last been effectively curtailed.

Both Village of Madison and City of Madison ordinances made it illegal for horses, cattle, sheep, goats, swine, and geese to run at large within the populated area of the city. However, at the close of the Civil War these ordinances were generally ignored and few elected officials had the courage to crack down—at least for long.[74]

By 1870, however, conditions once again favored a crackdown, especially on the cow—long the recipient of most favored status in the Madison ordinances. From earliest times milk cows had been exempted from the prohibition against running at large *providing* owners penned up the animals at night. But this practice was based upon the availability of large pastures on the edge of town. The most widely used areas were the lush lowlands on the near east and near west sides.

Beginning in the late 1850s, however, the water table in these areas rose and cattails displaced the pasture grasses. Finding replacement pastures was complicated by the fact that the built-up area of the city had continued to grow, thereby reducing the number of potential pasture sites. Consequently, many cow owners adopted the expedient of simply turning Bessie out to fend for herself. Few people complained so long as cows grazed on vacant lots, but many cows soon learned that vegetable gardens and young trees and shrubs were much tastier than vacant lot grass. In September 1869, for example, several cunning cows found their way into Mayor Proudfit's yard through an open gate and in two minutes nearly destroyed his shrubbery. The following day someone counted twenty-five cows suspiciously loitering around his now closed gate.[75] The same cows who found gardens and bushes tasty, also learned that farmers' wagons often contained bags full of fresh feed, which could be sampled with impunity if the farmer was not around.[76] Some cow owners even seem to have ignored the requirement that cows be penned up at night, leading to another cow-related problem. Said one irritated taxpayer, "the tinkling of cowbells in the Alps of Switzerland may be very enchanting, but in the city people who like to sleep do not much appreciate the ding, ding all night in front of their windows."[77] As if the case against the cow was insufficient to evoke outrage, every now and then a "mad cow" would trample a child.[78]

Fed up by the inconsiderate cow owners who viewed the city as a convenient free pasture, three-hundred citizens petitioned the Common Council in July 1870 for an end to the open grazing system. The council responded by hiring a pound-master whose job it was to corral all roaming animals. This was the beginning of an unusually consistent and ultimately effective ten-year effort to get livestock out of the city.[79]

Backed by growing public sentiment, the Common Council took a bold step in April 1873

in making it illegal for a cow to be outside an owner-provided enclosure.[80] This ordinance set the stage for a tense confrontation between cow owners who belonged to the open grazing school and other citizens who were tired of livestock deprarations (see section on Isaac Smith).

In 1874 the Common Council rejected ten to two an ordinance that would have returned to the pre-1873 policy of allowing milk cows to graze in unfenced pastures during the daytime.[81] In May 1879, the council extended the so-called "cow limits," farther into the country making it even harder to raise or keep a cow in the city.[82] The *coup de grace* for the cow came in 1886 when keeping a cow in the city was made illegal.[83] Perhaps there were some who mourned the passage of this bucolic quality, but, if there were, they were neither numerous nor vocal.

Dogs

Dog packs during the 1870s continued to be a problem. In July 1874, the *Democrat* reported there were so many "homely good for nothing dogs" on the street that "police officers, health commissioners, ministers, and manure gatherers cannot walk the streets without being bitten. . . ."[84] In July 1876, someone complained that "it was impossible to drive around town of an evening without having at least one hundred worthless curs in different localities rush out and attack your horse."[85] Dogs running in packs would nip at the horse's legs, often causing the horse to flee in terror and forcing the rider or buggy driver to hang on for dear life until the horse could be calmed and stopped.

Some suggested that the prohibition against discharging firearms in the city should be amended so that a few good marksmen could drive around the city for a week and abate the nuisance. Others suggested a mad dog scare would give people the justification they all wanted to kill the stray dogs.[86] Under such public pressure the police would sometimes be ordered to ride around

meting out the highest penalty the law allowed, namely, death.[87] At other times citizens would take the law into their own hands. In one instance, four farm boys armed with Colt revolvers drove around town in a wagon shooting dogs who tried to bite their horses' legs. Their work met the hearty approbation of the *Democrat* editor: "We thank those boys for their act of kindness and cordially invite them to repeat their experiment till none of these horrid, hideous howling brutes are left to disturb our evening slumbers."[88] No objective observer could say these dog skirmishes had been entirely successful, but they considerably reduced the stray dog population.

Teen-Aged Toughs

Gangs of teen-aged toughs found a wide range of techniques to entertain themselves and irritate their elders. Their repertory included racing horses up and down State Street, shooting slingshots, insulting persons going to and from church, singing obscene songs, carrying on in the capitol park, enhancing the anatomical details of showgirls featured on posters, seducing country girls, and barricading store doors. The boys especially enjoyed throwing spit balls and peanuts at public performances.[89]

The same boys were also responsible for a series of incidents we would today call "crime in the streets." Their affronts ranged from throwing rocks and watermelons at pedestrians to assault, battery, and stabbings.[90] Focal points for many of their depredations were lower State Street and several popular corners around the Square. During the summer of 1873 hardly a night passed without some kind of incident on State Street.[91] Said the *Wisconsin State Journal* in 1873, "Few cities of its size have a larger portion of worthless, idle, dissolute young fellows ready for any scrape . . . as has Madison."[92]

The Common Council quickly passed several ordinances that made loitering illegal at all the spots frequented by the toughs.[93] But these measures did not have the satisfactory effects some

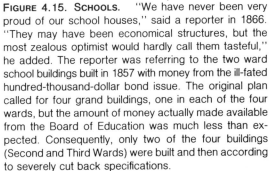

FIGURE 4.15. SCHOOLS. "We have never been very proud of our school houses," said a reporter in 1866. "They may have been economical structures, but the most zealous optimist would hardly call them tasteful," he added. The reporter was referring to the two ward school buildings built in 1857 with money from the ill-fated hundred-thousand-dollar bond issue. The original plan called for four grand buildings, one in each of the four wards, but the amount of money actually made available from the Board of Education was much less than expected. Consequently, only two of the four buildings (Second and Third Wards) were built and then according to severely cut back specifications.

Not until after the Civil War did the public schools enjoy a strong, consistent financial commitment. Between 1865 and 1880 more than one out of every four dollars levied for city purposes were earmarked by the Common Council for school operations and new school houses. The result was a school building boom. Three combination elementary-middle schools were built in just four years (1866–1870). This construction boom is particularly impressive when the continuing state prohibition against borrowing is taken into account. This meant that the cost of the new schools had to be paid in cash and in a single payment from annual budgets. In 1857 school expenses accounted for a whopping forty-nine percent of the city budget.

The 1867 Second Ward School (shown left) was one of several schools built during this period. Designed by the well-known Chicago architect, G. P. Randall, on the same site as the present day Lincoln School, the building featured cream-colored Edgerton brick, a tower with a six-hundred-pound bell, Italianate style, and an indoor "water closet" that could be flushed with cistern water. In an era when all other schools had privies, the last item was cause for considerable comment. Its companion, the Fourth Ward School, constructed in 1866, was described by the State Superintendent of Instruction as the "best arranged school building in the state." Such accolades immensely pleased Madisonians who were eager to make their schools an "ornament to the city." The third of the three new schools was built in 1870 at the intersection of University Avenue and Lake Street to accommodate growth in the university area.

The completion of the ward school buildings allowed Madison educators to begin planning for the long dreamed-about capstone of the educational system—a high school. Actually Madison was among the first cities in the state to have a high school, but the school was run discontinuously in a small, converted private academy, which in an era of rapidly rising expectations was considered "unsightly, badly arranged and wholly unworthy of the city." Thus the construction in 1873 of the

elaborate twenty-five-thousand-dollar high school (shown right) was a source of unfettered pride.

The school building boom caused school capacity to more than double between 1866 and 1873 and for the first time in Madison history, schools could boast a few more seats than enrolled pupils. Liberal financial support for schools also produced other improvements. Pupil-teacher ratios dropped from 97:1 in 1866 to 45:1 in 1876—an obvious boon for the beleaguered classroom teacher. The graded system begun under Kilgore prior to the Civil War was refined, art, music and penmanship were added, and meager teacher salaries were increased. Also during this period, students began using pencils and paper instead of slates. Increased financial support did not, however, solve several enduring problems such as "disobedience, idleness and the various disturbances caused by mischievous boys and girls found in all schools." In spite of classroom discipline problems, the Madison schools decided to spare the rod. Corporal punishment was severely curtailed in 1869 when the Board of Education required any teacher using the rod to submit a detailed written report to the superintendent explaining circumstances and justifying its use. (SHSW WHi(X3)32023)

155

had hoped, largely because of the weak Madison police system. At the time the police force consisted of a part-time chief of police (the only salaried member of the force) and four ward policemen. Only on election days were patrolmen allowed to receive per diem pay of one dollar per day, and then only if it was approved in advance by the council. An examination of city budget records showed that not a single police per diem was paid between 1870 and 1877.[94] The rest of the time ward policemen were paid nothing at all except for fees they received from convictions. Although the system kept police costs down, it also insured that police effectiveness was minimal because very few patrolmen saw any incentive to take on a bunch of hoodlums for tiny or even nonexistent fees. In the words of Mayor S. U. Pinney in a special message to the Common Council in 1877, "I do not know of any faithful or competent person who is willing to do patrol duty nights without a regular stated compensation, and any expectation that . . . police services can be secured under such a law . . . is unreasonable and unfounded."[95] As if this fee system was not enough of a problem, mayors never knew whether to go ahead and appoint a special policeman at the rate of one dollar per day because the Common Council would not always approve the policeman's pay. This further lowered the credibility of the mayor and the willingness of policemen to take considerable risks.[96]

Police were also hampered by the fact that the street lights (only seventy in 1870) were turned off at 11:00 P. M. each night, leaving the streets in darkness—a circumstance that greatly favored the teen age hoodlums.[97]

Tramps

The deepening of the depression in the latter 1870s brought a substantial increase in numbers of tramps wandering around the country looking for food and sometimes work. Madisonians hated the tramps because they loafed about on the streets, begged food, pilfered merchandise, stole chickens, and frightened women and children.[98]

Attitudes toward Law Breakers

Madisonians attitudes toward malefactors, whether they were teen-aged toughs or tramps, were remarkably harsh. An 1878 *Journal* article noted approvingly that "one of the rowdies was very properly shot at and winged. . . . The only pity was the rest of the gang were not similarly treated to a dose of lead and aim taken higher up. A few funerals among the ruffianly gang of the capital city would be highly conducive to the cause of law and order." The *Democrat* encouraged the police to "hunt game."[99] As for the tramps, "no measure is too harsh . . ." said a writer to the *Wisconsin State Journal*. "Sentimentalism will but increase the danger. The solution is to put them to work with ball and chain upon the public streets in the hot sun and after a day or two of this treatment give them a chance to run away."[100] The local Congregational minister also came down in favor of harsh treatment of tramps, quoting the Bible verse: "an idle soul shall suffer hunger and if any would not work neither shall he eat."[101] When two black men got into a fight, the *Madison Democrat* said that such behavior should be punished by "flogging until all stripes show blood."[102]

Bleeding Horses and Hissing Locomotives

In addition to cows, curs, tramps, and teen age toughs, there were plenty of other irritants about which Madisonians complained. Farmers, believing they could purge their horses of bad blood, would bleed their horses on the streets around the Capitol Square. The horse stood "deep in a great pool of his own gore half crazed by the black clouds of flies attracted by the fresh offal."[103] These pools of blood were hardly popular with city residents who had to look at them after the farmer drove off in his wagon behind his purged but weakened horse. Then there were groups of uncouth males who munched peaches and threw the skins and pits on the sidewalks.[104] Slaughter

FIGURE 4.16. UNIVERSITY OF WISCONSIN, 1865-1880. The years 1865–1880 were critical formative years for the University of Wisconsin. In 1867 the state began giving direct financial assistance to the university. Previously the university had been forced to live off proceeds from the sale of federal lands given to the state. One result of this financial commitment was a series of new buildings built between 1870 and 1880, shown in the above illustrations. Among the major new buildings were Chadbourne Hall (1871), Science Hall (1875), and Assembly Hall (1879). Washburn Observatory was built with a gift from wealthy Governor Cadwallander Washburn in 1878. Under the strong support of President John H. Twombly (1871–1874), and John Bascom (1874–1887), coeducation was firmly established. Ironically, Chadbourne Hall, erected in 1871, was named after President Paul A. Chadbourne (1867–1870) who strongly opposed coeducation.

Throughout this era, Madison students and regents continued to be over-represented relative to the state's total population. Although Madison had less than one percent of the state population, Madisonians constituted twenty percent of the total U.W. students. A similar situation prevailed on the Board of Regents. Of an average of twelve members, twenty-five percent were Madisonians.

Although students and professors constituted only four percent of the total Madison population, the influence of the university community on Madison was nevertheless large. University faculty and their wives were lionized in Madison social circles because they represented culture and learning. The development of close town-gown social relationships was greatly enhanced when a scheme proposed by President Chadbourne requiring all faculty members to live in a cluster of houses on Observatory Hill was abandoned. But the faculty strongly opposed the plan, arguing that the university derived its spirit from its host community and that any division between town and gown was detrimental to both. Chadbourne's successor, President Twombly, put this idea into action by moving out of the President's house on Observatory Hill into a home at 110 State Street. The move was applauded by the *Wisconsin State Journal* on the grounds that the president would be more "accessible to the friends of the university." The paper urged the regents to buy a president's residence somewhere in town. When President Bascom began his tenure, he moved back to the house on the hill, but by that time the practice of faculty in-town living had been firmly established.

U.W. presidents were nearly always able to command attention through formal lectures, baccalaurate

sermons, articles, and books. On at least one occasion John Bascom gave the sermon at the First Congregational Church because the regular minister had a cold. Through these forums U.W. presidents served as transmitters and sometimes reconcilers of new ideas. President Chadbourne, a nationally known scientist, was one of several academicians who earned reknown by offering a satisfying reconciliation between science and religion posed by Darwin's 1871 blockbuster, *The Descent of Man.* President Bascom spoke persuasively on *avant guard* topics such as unions and strikes, the control of large corporations, income redistribution, women's liberation, and much more.

The immensely popular debates between the prestigious U.W. student debating societies also exposed Madisonians to new ideas. Beginning in 1867 when the debates became annual events, Madisonians jammed the Assembly Chamber to hear spirited exchanges on prohibition, railroad regulation, labor organizations, and other topics. (SHSW, WHi(X3)2318)

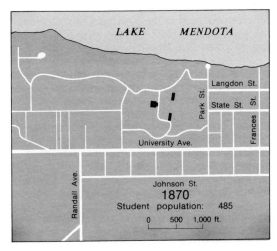

LAKE MENDOTA

Langdon St.
State St.
Park St.
Frances St.
University Ave.
Randall Ave.
Johnson St.

1870

Student population: 485

0   500   1,000 ft.

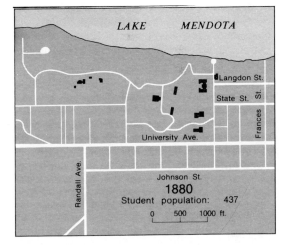

LAKE MENDOTA

Langdon St.
State St.
Frances St.
University Ave.
Randall Ave.
Johnson St.

1880

Student population: 437

0   500   1000 ft.

houses emitted such a fierce stench few could even walk in the vicinity.[105] Prisoners in the Dane County jail (located where the Dane County ramp is located today) yelled out obscenities through the window bars at women passing on the Main Street sidewalk.[106] The exasperating city hall clock sported four clock faces and four different times.[107] Hired boys walked around banging triangles and ringing cow bells to drum up business and tempted some men in their downtown offices to commit mayhem. Other Madisonians were angry about the excessive locomotive whistling and the "terrible" hissing of locomotives letting off steam.[108] Finally, Madisonians were deeply embarrassed by the fact that President Hayes during his visit in September, 1878, could count twenty-nine pig pens in the back yards of one of Madison's main streets—not exactly the image of a cultured city they wished to convey.[109]

Leisure-Time Activities

Lake-Related Activities

One of the great paradoxes of Madison history is that Madisonians paid so little attention to the recreational value of their lakes for so long. During the first thirty years of Madison history, sailboats and iceboats were rare and rather primitive, swimming was actively discouraged, and no lakeside resort enjoyed enough patronage to be successful. Madison's almost *laissez faire* attitude toward the lakes changed quickly after the Civil War, partly in response to the influx of summer tourists who, ironically, not only saw the recreational value of the lakes more clearly, but who also were in a position to "demand" that they be more fully used for summer resort activities.

In July 1870, four little sailing boats, barely more than specially rigged rowboats, competed in the first regatta held in Madison since the Farwell boom. Interest in the event was so great that four other regattas were held later that summer with up to fourteen boats competing.[110] The

Madison Yacht Club (MYC), a direct outgrowth of renewed interest in this "manly sport,"[111] was incorporated in 1871—the first yacht club to be incorporated by the legislature in the state.[112] MYC members confidently predicted that Madison would soon boast "one of the handsomest and liveliest little pleasure navies to be found in the Northwest."[113] Though its members seemed indisputably prosperous with their New York-style commodore jackets, luxurious club room, and high social status, the organization was never strong financially, especially after the 1873 depression.[114] Nevertheless, the MYC managed to hold several regattas each summer during most of the 1870s. Perhaps the best indicator of their success was that Madison, a tiny inland town of nine to ten thousand people during this period, was able to provide remunerative employment to a sailmaker.[115]

Rowing, like sailing, made a sudden, dramatic entrance onto the Madison sporting scene in 1870—partly in response to the famous Harvard-Oxford race of 1869, which sent a wave of interest across the country.[116] Madison leaders saw no reason why two rowing clubs could not be supported, one composed of university men and one composed of city men so that a keen rivalry could be established. The university failed to organize a club, but a Monona Rowing Club was formed in the spring of 1870.[117] The rowing club bought both a fifty-foot eight-oared cedar shell and a forty-foot four-oared paper shell and began regular practice sessions. Oarsmen wore special uniforms of dark blue shirts and white linen pants.[118] After practicing regularly during the early summer, the club issued challenges to the Chicago and Milwaukee clubs. The resulting races attracted great interest. The entire Monona shoreline between Fauerbach's Brewery and the railroad causeway was reportedly one solid mass of people. Unfortunately the Monona Rowing Club lost both races. "But it must be remembered that our crew is composed of rawhands," explained a Madison commentator. "Give them another season's practice and the crack clubs had better not tackle them too loosely."[119] After a

strong start in 1870 and 1871, interest in rowing declined. Only two other regattas were held during the 1870s, one in 1875 and another in 1877. Then in 1879 the club declared bankruptcy and efforts to form a new club failed.[120]

The rapid growth in the number of steamboats on the Madison lakes made the lakeshores accessible to large numbers of people for the first time. Captain Frank Barnes, Madison's first successful commercial steamboat operator, correctly recognized that wealthy summer tourists were not the only ones who wanted and would pay for lakeside recreational facilities. Madisonians would, too. In the spring of 1870 Barnes bought ten acres of land on which he constructed a dance pavilion, billiard hall, bowling alley, a refreshment stand, croquet grounds,[121] a spectacular one-hundred-foot high observatory and a thrilling swing that swooped out over the lake on forty-two-foot long ropes. At first the colorful steamboat operator called the place "Swing Point," but in 1866 he selected an Indian name, "Winnequah," which he said meant "good water." Winnequah—and Barnes' little fleet of steamers—were very well patronized by Madisonians and led others to copy his idea.[122]

In 1871 the Germans bought twenty-six acres of land on the near east side, just east of the Yahara River, which they called "Schuetzen Park." There Germans could enjoy their traditional continental Sunday sipping lager beer, listening to band music, playing ten pins, shooting their rifles, and having a good time without any disapproving looks from Yankees who felt all this fun on Sundays was a terrible sin.[123]

The establishment of regular steamboat service on Lake Mendota in 1877 opened up other popular spots like Picnic Point and Rodermund's Woods just east of the Yahara River. The latter was improved with gravel walks and picnic tables.[124]

All of the private pleasure parks that grew up around the lakes in the 1870s offered cool, shady groves where relief from the summer heat could be found—a place where people could get away

FIGURE 4.17. SCHUETZEN PARK. One of many elements in the cultural baggage of Madison's Germans was a fondness for riflery. The widespread enjoyment of this sport among the German community led to the formation of Madison Schuetzen (Shooting) Club and the acquisition of a twenty-six-acre site just outside city limits to the east of the Yahara River. There German riflemen built targets and shooting ranges for the enjoyment of their sport and from time to time held statewide marksmanship contests called Schuetzenfests. During these two-day contests, shooting continued for ten hours a day and averaged twenty-two shots a minute. Each rifleman had to furnish his own gun and ammunition and could take as many shots as he could afford at a nickel a shot. No telescopic sights were permitted for the targets which lay 660 feet from the shooting building. Members who hit the bullseye twelve times had a silver medal pinned on their coat by the president at an impressive ceremony.

For nearly every year of its existence, Schuetzen Park was the scene of a turkey shoot. From seventy-five to one hundred birds were chained to a stake where they were shot by riflemen one thousand feet away. From this distance most riflemen missed, but since there were so many hunters, the turkeys were eventually killed. Each hunter paid a dime for the opportunity to take a shot. The hunter who hit the bird took it home. This popular event provided cheap Thanksgiving turkeys for many families and at the same time made money for the Schuetzen Club.

The austere Yankee view on how one should spend the Lord's Day (go to church and go home) led to the transformation of the park from a mere rifle range to a Teutonic preserve where Germans could enjoy Sundays in the Continental tradition listening to a coronet band, sipping lager beer, playing ten pins, shooting billiards—in short, having fun and enjoying warm fellowship. The long Schuetzen Park pier shown above were located roughly where Dunning Street end is today.

Schuetzen Park was sold in 1902 due to financial pressures and subdivided into ninety-six lots. Today the approximate location of this ethnic landmark is recalled by two streets: Schiller Court and Schurz Avenue. (SHSW WHi(C73)92)

FIGURE 4.18. CAMPING ON MAPLE BLUFF. Shown here is a group of campers somewhere on Maple Bluff during the 1870s. These couples are a reflection of the growing popularity of lakeshore camping during this period. (SHSW WHi(D31)592)

from it all. The lakeshore resorts were also popular for another compelling reason: In-city picnics at which liquor was served were banned by an 1878 ordinance.[125] Though relatively close to the city as the crow flew, the long steamboat ride magnified the feeling of distance. And getting there on the spritely vessels was always half the fun.

With the lakeshores now accessible by steamboat, camping became popular. With few exceptions the lakeshores were open, and few, if any, property owners seem to have had any objection to people camping on their land. Livesey's Springs, Merrill's Springs, and McBride's Point (now Maple Bluff) were the favorite spots on Lake Mendota, while Mills Woods held that distinction on Lake Monona.[126] Evening trips of the steamer Mendota kept the campers in contact with the "outside world." To the campers the arrival of the steamer was the great event of the day. The craft would go in as close to shore as possible and then wait to be surrounded by camper rowboats. Chaos reigned supreme. First there would be "rapid and anxious inquiries for freight and visitors, for news from home, for the day's packet of mail from town, shaking of hands over the bulwarks . . ., the passage of quips and pinafore jokes and camping puns and phrases. Then . . . the spurting rush of escaping steam . . . the ear piercing whistle and the cries of 'cast off there.' " Then with a noisy clang of the engine bell, "the surging splash of the screw and the lusty cheers from shore and cries of 'goodbye, come over tomorrow,' 'send us some provisions by the next boat,' " the steamer tripped over the light blue sea to town again."[127]

Swimming was finally legalized in Madison in 1879 after twenty-eight years of bans, restrictions, and arrests. In 1851 the Village of Madison banned bathing and swimming in Lake Monona between Henry and Patterson Streets and in Lake Mendota between Francis and Livingston Streets,[128] between the hours of 5:00 A. M. and 9:00 P. M. or anywhere else within public view. Almost immediately after its formation in 1856 the City of Madison adopted similar ordinances except that it expanded the shoreline anywhere where swimming was prohibited and defined "public view" as anywhere within one mile from the shore.[129]

This prohibition was not terribly popular among little boys on hot days—or for that matter among a lot of others. The first crack in this form of repression occurred in 1873, when the council allowed swimming in places deemed sufficiently secluded by the chief of police.[130] An enduring solution to this old problem finally came in July 1879, soon after several little boys were arrested for skinny dipping. At last the council relented and legalized swimming *providing* that bathing dress "covered the person from the neck to the knee."[131] From this point on the city concentrated on how much the person should be covered rather than trying to banish a very popular summer pastime.

To the Madisonian of the mid-1870s Lake Mendota was not merely a place to swim, sail, row, fish, and hunt—it was also something to walk around. U. W. classics professor J. D. Butler, who seems to have popularized the walk-around-Lake Mendota craze, argued that Americans walked too little and rode too much. The reason, he said, was that Americans had too many horses. In 1875 there were twenty-two and one-half horses for every one hundred persons, but in England the figure was seven and one-half and in France eight.[132] Actually in Dane County in 1875 there were thirty-four horses for every one hundred persons.[133] Once Madison men found they could cover the twenty-five-mile distance without much difficulty, women began successfully making the trek too. Butler recommended the trek whenever anyone "felt slightly in need of exercise."[134]

Baseball

Organized baseball clubs sprang up in Madison immediately after the Civil War. The game satisfied a growing need for healthy outdoor exercise. Unlike rowing, sailing, or horse-racing, baseball did not require wealth to play. All one needed was an open field, a bat, and a ball. At first no one wore gloves. Underhand pitching made baseball a hitter's game and produced amazingly high scores such as one hundred to thirty-two, fifty-eight to thirty-two and forty-eight to fifteen.[135] According to one early sports reporter, "the playing was rather wild on both sides and there is considerable chance for improvement."[136] The wild playing however, didn't prevent the Madison teams from challenging out-of-town teams including Milwaukee, Chicago, New York, Beloit College, Appleton, Oshkosh, Rockford, Janesville, and many others.[137] For the five years after the Civil War baseball bordered on a mania, then died down for several years only to become extremely popular again in the middle and later seventies.[138]

Theatrical Entertainment

The quality and quantity of theatrical entertainment changed considerably during this period, not so much because tastes changed but rather because theatrical facilities were markedly improved. The need for a better hall had long been obvious. Until 1871 performers had only three halls from which to choose: the City Hall auditorium; Van Bergan Hall; and Turner Hall. The City Hall auditorium, with its dirty flat floor, poor ventilation, dilapidated scenery, and rough lumber dressing rooms on either side of the stage, embarrassed theater-goers.[139] Van Bergan Hall was little better. Hewed out of a converted office building on the corner of Doty and Pinckney Streets, the hall seated eight-hundred but the seats were not cushioned, the stoves were incapable of heating the hall during the winter and the building was structurally unsound—so much so that companies refused to play there as early as 1862. Turner Hall had a modest auditorium, but it was a private theater that catered to German-speaking audiences. In 1868 the *Journal* pleaded for "some public spirited citizen . . . to immortalize himself" with the creation of an opera house.[140]

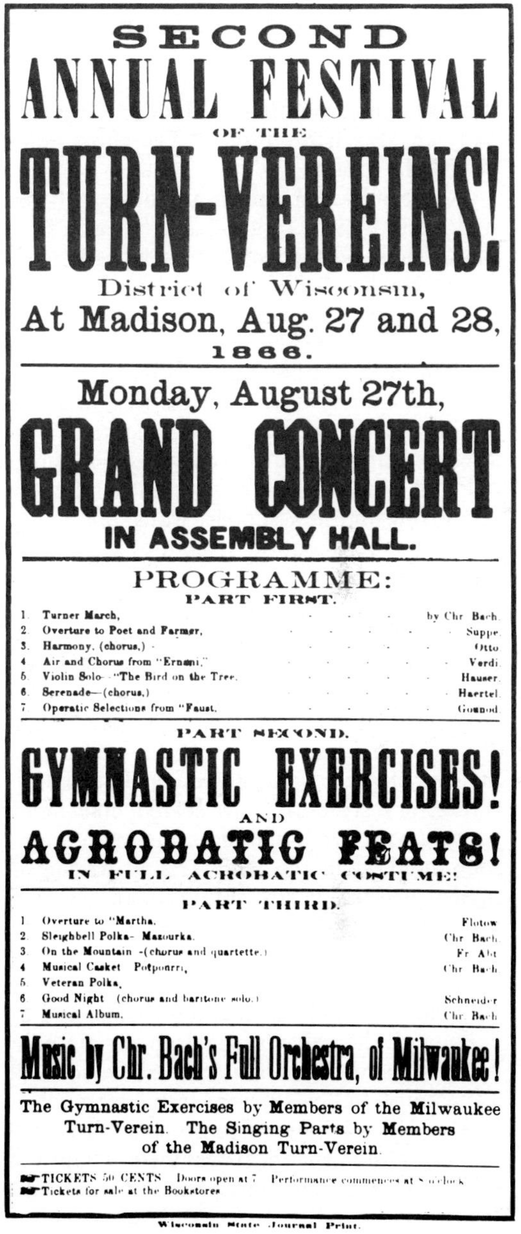

SECOND

ANNUAL FESTIVAL

OF THE

TURN-VEREINS!

District of Wisconsin,

At Madison, Aug. 27 and 28,

1866.

Monday, August 27th,

GRAND CONCERT

IN ASSEMBLY HALL.

PROGRAMME:

PART FIRST.

1.	Turner March,	by Chr. Bach.
2.	Overture to Poet and Farmer,	Suppe.
3.	Harmony, (chorus,)	Otto.
4.	Air and Chorus from "Ernani,"	Verdi.
5.	Violin Solo—"The Bird on the Tree.	Hauser.
6.	Serenade—(chorus,)	Haertel.
7.	Operatic Selections from "Faust.	Gounod.

PART SECOND.

GYMNASTIC EXERCISES!

AND

AGROBATIC FEATS!

IN FULL ACROBATIC COSTUME!

PART THIRD.

1.	Overture to "Martha.	Flotow.
2.	Sleighbell Polka—Mazourka.	Chr. Bach.
3.	On the Mountain—(chorus and quartette.)	Fr. Abt.
4.	Musical Casket Potpourri,	Chr. Bach.
5.	Veteran Polka,	
6.	Good Night (chorus and baritone solo.)	Schneider.
7.	Musical Album.	Chr. Bach.

Music by Chr. Bach's Full Orchestra, of Milwaukee!

The Gymnastic Exercises by Members of the Milwaukee Turn-Verein. The Singing Parts by Members of the Madison Turn-Verein.

TICKETS 50 CENTS. Doors open at 7. Performance commences at 8 o'clock.
Tickets for sale at the Bookstores.

Wisconsin State Journal Print.

FIGURE 4.19. TURNVEREIN. One of the most impressive organizations in Madison history was the Turnverein. The organization was founded in 1855 by German immigrants to provide balanced physical and mental development. Physical development was achieved through gymnastics and acrobatics whereas mental development was cultivated through a reading room and a lecture series. In 1863 the organization built a handsome hall to house its gymnasium and theater. Though composed entirely of Germans, the Turnverein required all of its members to be either naturalized American citizens or to have filed a declaration of intent.

In addition to its charter-declared purpose, the Turnverein functioned as a richly supportive cultural home for the German community. Local German vocal musical groups including the Maennerchor and the Liederkranz Club gave their concerts there. Sometimes statewide "Saengerfests" were held in Madison. At other times two Turnvereins such as Milwaukee and Madison would get together for a festival. Such a meeting was described in the quarter-page advertisement (right) which appeared in the *Wisconsin State Journal* on August 22, 1866.

Eventually most of Madison's German organizations were absorbed by the Turnverein. For example, in 1868 the Maennerchor became the Turnverein Singing Section and the Apollo Dramatic Club became the Turnverein Dramatic Section. In 1880 the Turnverein became the owner of Schuetzen Park when the Madison Schuetzen Club was merged with the Turnverein.

The first attempt to provide a better hall was made by a group of gentlemen of "musical taste and business character" who persuaded the legislature to incorporate the Madison Opera Company on March 27, 1868.[141] The effort failed to get off the ground.

A second—and this time successful—effort was made by real estate dealer George B. Burrows, who in 1870 persuaded a Chicago man, Mr. R. W. Hooley, to buy the old Van Bergan Hall and improve it as an opera house with the former acting as agent.[142] Hooley was a nationally famous minstrel impressario, formerly a member of the popular Christy Minstrels and subsequently a leader of his own national touring minstrel company.[143] Under Hooley's supervision, the old Van Bergan block was virtually rebuilt with a new interior, new support walls, and new roof so that doubts about the structural inadequacy of the building were forever removed.

The Hooley Opera House opened on February 22, 1871, with a musical and oratorical benefit, the proceeds of which went to the theater owner to "richly embellish the hall"—a rather novel way to pay for those little extras that cost so much, yet were so admired.[144] Everyone seemed enormously pleased with the remodelled hall. The three-story structure now seated nine hundred persons with five hundred on the main floor and four hundred in the wrap-around balcony featuring private boxes. Madisonians were impressed with a wood-fired furnace that actually heated the hall to comfortable temperatures during the winter, with the carpeted aisles and halls, with the commodious dressing rooms, and especially with the scene on the drop curtain painted by a famous London artist. At last Madison had a theater with "no superior in the state."[145]

The Hooley Opera House constituted a watershed in Madison theatrical history. Until 1871 stock and repertory companies dominated the theatrical playbills; after that date the one-night stand traveling company took over.[146] The transition from a stock company town to a well-established road company town was completed by

FIGURE 4.20. HAUSMANN BREWERY. Breweries were the most visible business manifestations of the growing number of Germans in Madison during the Civil War period. From 1866 until 1873 Madison beer drinkers supported five breweries: the Fauerbach Brewery at the intersection of Blount and Williamson; the Rodermund Brewery near the point where the Tenney Park lock is today located; the Hausmann (Capital) Brewery shown in this 1879 photograph above at the intersection of Gorham and State; the Breckheimer Brewery on King Street next to the old Frautschi Furniture Store; and Mautz-Hess Brewery at the corner of State and Gilman Streets.

Madisonians appear to have been loyal to the local brands, especially when Milwaukee beers were introduced. In the mid-1870s, it was the custom whenever someone found the beer to be a little sour to ask, "Is this Milwaukee beer?"

Taking a page from the marketing strategy of the large Milwaukee brewers, The Rodermund Brewery, Madison's largest in the early 1870s, built a large addition, had a sidetrack brought in and began shipping sizable quantities of the nut-brown liquid to Chicago. Unfortunately, the ambitious plan never got off the ground; the brewery burned to the ground in the fall of 1873 and was never rebuilt.

With the burning of the Rodermund Brewery, the Hausmann's Capital Brewery became Madison's largest. Just inside the corner door, behind the employees shown in the photograph, was a popular saloon where sauerkraut, sausages, cheese, bread, and radishes could be enjoyed at no charge, providing a nickel beer was purchased. The spot was particularly popular with students on meager allowances and was recalled fondly by student reminiscences. The site of the brewery corner building shown above is now occupied by shops and offices. (SHSW WHi(D31)586) the late 1870s. With the road companies came "stars" whose presence served "to refine the critical tastes of Madison theater goers."[147] Drama, comedy, and musicals rose in popularity while farce and tragedy declined.[148] So many shows came to Madison during the 1870s that some expressed concern that the supply was larger than the demand and that partly filled halls would injure the city's reputation as a good show-town.[149] Indeed, by 1877 it was admitted that the Hooley Opera House was not a paying proposition.[150] This fact forced theater managers to tailor their playbills to those types of performances the public would best support.

Newspaper accounts portrayed Madison as a city with "a large and highly cultured audience" for opera, drama, and classical music.[151] The Hooley gave this component of the theater audience more "cultured" theatrical entertainment than ever before. Probably the most popular dramas were the Shakespeare plays *Richard II, Hamlet,* and *Romeo and Juliet.* Classical music groups such as the Boston Philharmonic Club also appeared, as did many small vocal and instrumental groups. Significantly, no formal opera played at the Hooley. A two-night performance of *Faust* in 1868 at the old City Hall Auditorium was so poorly patronized that no theater owner tried opera again for many years.[152] However, Hooley managers quickly learned that Madisonians would patronize comic operas such as Gilbert and Sullivan's *H.M.S. Pinafore.*[153] Although performances in the Turner Hall were not well reported in Madison's English dailies, the few squibs they did provide suggest that the Germans may have patronized more "high culture" performances than their Yankee counterparts.[154]

Though contrary to the image many socially prominent Madisonians would like to have conveyed, most of the time the Hooley provided "popular" entertainment for the average man. Appearances from "stars" like Wild Bill Cody (Buffalo Bill) and Professor J. M. McAllister, World's Greatest Wizard, were nearly always well attended.[155] But the largest crowds were reserved for the Mme. Genevieve's Can Can Troupe. All nine hundred seats at the Hooley were full for their performances and two hundred men and boys crowded around the depot when the troupe got off the train, straining to get a glimpse of the girls. This simply did not happen with other kinds of entertainers. The more affluent men bought out the seats down in front, forcing the boys to witness the spectacle from the less expensive but less exciting balcony. One reporter who astutely decided to watch the audience instead of the performance noted that church members and legislators went to amazing lengths to avoid being seen by friends but still not avoid missing anything on stage. The reporter evidently took a glimpse or two himself, because he described the scenes as "so disgusting the pen fails to give a description, so sickening were the sights." The only consolation he could find in the whole affair was that not a single female attended the performance.[156]

Next to the can can, the most popular type of performance was the minstrel show, which offered slap stick comedy, foot-stomping music, fast-paced humor, and lots of crowd-performer interactions. Ethnic humor played a very large role, with the Chinese and blacks taking the brunt of the jokes. Most of the companies managed to get a little sex into their performance with slightly off-color jokes and busty women wearing tights. Minstrelsy was so popular that two local groups were able to make a living in between the travelling companies.[157]

On Dullness and Journalism

A reporter for the *Wisconsin State Journal* returned to his desk after a walk about the city in July 1868 and wrote that he "found local items extremely scarce. Our merchants and clerks have abundant leisure for there is very little trading doing. The lawyers have had their cases in the police court adjourned so there are no items to be gathered there. The Barnum show is gone and the minstrels have not come so that altogether a man about town finds it very quiet and dull."[158]

Throughout the post-Civil War period Madison newspaper reporters complained bitterly and openly about how tough it was to come up with local news items. Consequently the local columns were sprinkled with such descriptions of Madison as "very quiet and dull",[159] and "almost dead."[160] The editor of the *Madison Democrat* even pleaded for some poor unfortunate fellow to drown himself in the lake. "We are terribly in want of an item," he explained.[161] Another time he expressed disappointment that no one committed suicide on a "dismal, dreary, damp December 5th—what they call a suicidal day in London."[162]

Was Madison really this dull? The answer is both "yes" and "no." Part of Madison's "dullness" was seasonal and related to agricultural and legislative activities. As a commercial emporium for Dane County, Madison was profoundly dependent upon the annual rhythm of farmer activities. Not long after the meadowlarks returned from their sojourn in the south, the farmers would stream into Madison for what the merchants called the "spring trade." Then in the fall after the crops were harvested, the fall farmer trade would delight Madison merchants. Between the fall farmer trade and the annual session of the legislature in January, though, business was dull. During these periods Madisonians read a lot about the weather, melting snow, and caterpillars in maple trees. But then in January the lobbies of the Park and Vilas Hotels would be jammed with the buzzing voices of legislators attending the annual legislative session, and reporters breathed a sigh of relief.

Part of Madison's dullness was due to the size of the city. In a community with just nine to ten thousand persons, tedium and triviality were formidable adversaries to the reporter in search of a lead item. Consequently reporters found the municipal court one of the most exciting news sources. There they found infrequent but satisfying action, suspense, violence, and scandal. Yet there were times when even this source was "bought to very verge of extinction."[163] The rise of sports such as baseball offered another exciting oasis in an otherwise arid news environment.

FIGURE 4.21. ICE BOATING AND ICE SKATING, 1877.   "Do you want the buttons of your vest and coat all torn off and your shirt collar ripped away from its moorings? If you do, get on an ice boat on a windy day. . . ." This recommendation was included in one of several articles that appeared in Madison newspapers during the ice boat fever of 1876–1877. The sudden popularity of the sport was attributed to an iceboat built by a Poughkeepsie, New York, man and exhibited at the 1876 Centennial Exposition in Philadelphia. The boat caught the eye of several Madison men who were attending the exposition. When they returned to Madison, they sent for plans and built an enlarged version of the design. The result was the famous "Git," probably the largest ice boat ever built in Madison. The craft could seat twenty persons comfortably and carried 1,575 square feet of sail. Her speed, clocked in excess of ninety miles per hour, awed Madisonians of that era and led to a boom in ice boat construction. About two dozen owners competed for the coveted distinction of having the "fleetest and neatest" machine and kept Lake Monona dotted with white sails from morning until late into moonlit nights.

The engraving shown above appeared in the well-known *Harper's Weekly* on March 9, 1878, after Madison had become a national center of ice-boating. All the ice boats shown reflect the new design based upon the Poughkeepsie model. The design was superior to those previously in use in Madison because the runners all pivoted, thereby taking the jolting out of ice boating—a factor that previously had limited its popularity.

Ice boats had been built and used by Madisonians since 1855, but had been very primitive three-cornered platforms set upon runners made of plow-share steel. Only the steering runner pivoted on its mounting; the other two runners were rigid. One iceboater said a trip across the lake was like "riding rapidly over a poor corduroy road on the back axle of a wagon."

The ice boat fascinated Madisonians. Many stood along the Monona shore listening to the scrape and rumble of the runners, the swoop and flutter of wind-whipped canvas, and the wild shouts and cheery laughter of passengers and crews. The more daring accepted invitations to dart about the smooth ice at the breathtaking speed of a mile a minute or even more.

Ice skating, too, was popular, though most had the good sense not to ice skate amidst a pack of ice boats, as shown in the engraving. During most winters Captain Barnes or some other enterprising group would scrape clean an area for ice skaters about two acres in size in front of his Carroll Street pier. Sometimes Captain Barnes would hire a band and dispense hot coffee and oysters to the skaters. (SHSW WHi(X3)30301)

SPECIAL ATTRACTIONS.

Grand Balloon Ascension!

—AND—

RUNNING RACES,

—DURING THE—

WISCONSIN STATE FAIR,

At Madison, Wis.

Prof. GILBERT, of Cincinnati, in his *Monster* Balloon, will make a __nd Ascension, filling his Balloon from the Gas Main that supplies the consin State University and going far up beyond the clouds and of sight, on

Tuesday, September 9th, at 2:30 P. M.

After the Balloon Ascension there will be a Running Race of a mile and a half with a whole field of Horses, which is destined to be

THE GREATEST RUNNING RACE

Ever Held in the West.

Old Camp Randall is one of the *most delightful Fair Grounds in the World*. Everybody should go to the Farmer's Show at Camp Randall, Madison, Wis.,

September 8th to 12th, 1879.

"AMERICA."

Holding 60,000 ft. of Gas, and capable of carrying five persons.

HOOLEY OPERA HOUSE.

THREE NIGHTS ONLY.

Monday, Tuesday & Wednesday,
January 25, 26, 27.

IDA CERITO'S

Female

Minstrels,

AND

M'DLE GENEVIEVE'S

FRENCH CAN-CAN

DANCERS.

A fac simile of the original as produced at Jardin Mabile, Paris, Alhambra, London, and Grand House, New York.

20 BEAUTIFUL LADIES 20

in addition to a

Variety & Pantomime Company

OF

30 Specialty Artists.

Admission 75 and 50 cents; Reserved Seats, $1.00, which can be secured without extra charge at McConnell & Smith's Bookstore.

71jan21d3t

FIGURE 4.23. CAN CAN DANCERS. Never in Madison's history had so many Madison males been given the opportunity to see so many scantily clad women as by the popular double feature described above.

FIGURE 4.22. STATE FAIRS. Madison hosted the Wisconsin State Fair in 1867, 1868, 1878, and 1879. Like the circus, the state fair drew huge crowds, but for slightly different reasons. Posters featuring the "Great Balloon Ascension" were just one gimmick used by fair promoters to add excitement to the farm machinery exhibits, food contests, and produce displays. (SHSW Pamphlet Collection)

Not surprisingly, reporters described every inning in excruciating detail. Society weddings received extremely thorough treatment, including a complete list of all wedding gifts and of course, the color, cut, and special features of the bride's dress.[164]

The editor of the *Madison Democrat* found sexual gossip and incidents especially interesting and printed all the items he could find. For example, when the nineteenth wife of Mormon leader Brigham Young stopped in Madison for a lecture on the evils of polygamy, the *Democrat* ran stories about a conversation between her and her lover that someone overheard through the drawn curtains of their Pullman car. Local equivalents received generous coverage.[165] The *Wisconsin State Journal,* by contrast, downplayed such items but did a good job in reporting the demise of "disorderly houses."[166]

Another part of Madison's dullness was attributable to the economy. While the economy was buoyant stories could be run on new businesses coming into town, new railroad lines, even whole new industries. However, the depression beginning in 1874 reduced story possibilities in this area to an intermittant trickle.

Some of Madison's "dullness" was a result of the perception that a newspaper was first a partisan organ and then a diary of community life. The fundamental purpose behind the founding of the *Madison Democrat* in 1868 was to give an active voice to the Democratic party in Madison. During campaigns the newspapers began to hum with excitement and carried highly colored partisan interpretations of national, state, and even local events. Although interesting from a political perspective, this practice displaced more informative local news stories.

Finally, dullness was caused by reporters and editors who could not see the news going on in front of them. They ignored the demographic revolution in Madison and what was happening in the German, Norwegian, and Irish communities. Indians, though still present in relatively large numbers, were never interviewed about their earlier lives, value systems, or why they kept coming back to Madison. The rise of the tourist industry was reported in a casual and haphazard way. No one covered the story of the hunters who shot eagles at Eagle Heights sometime in the late 1860s.[167] Coverage of potentially fascinating events, including exorcisms,[168] glossolia,[169] and giant eels in Lake Mendota was superficial.[170] Even a vivid reader description of "a luminous disk" over Lake Monona was not pursued.[171] What a rich tapestry early-day reporters might have left had they perceived their job differently.

5 The Entrepreneurial Spirit: 1880–1899

"Madison with all its natural charms has some drawbacks," said a *Wisconsin State Journal* writer in 1880, "and one of them is the fact that . . . a portion of our population like to collect around grocery stoves on winter evenings and grumble because there is no enterprise in this town. . . . We have noticed," continued the writer, "that the majority of the people who make these sage remarks belong to that class of energetic citizens who if they should fall on the sidewalk would remain there where they dropped until someone came along and picked them up."[1]

The frustration this writer was expressing was shared by Madison leaders, who during the fifteen years following the Civil War had failed to find a way to infuse much life into Madison's economy—at least nothing that allowed the city to grow rapidly, or, as they said at the time, "to boom." By 1880 Madison's population had not even reached the level it had been in 1857 at the peak of the Farwell boom. Nearly everyone agreed that at least one effective economic and growth generator had to be found; but what that something should be proved elusive indeed. Not only did Madison's economy need a massive infusion of new life, but many other things needed attention too. The city needed parks, better roads, government reforms, a waterworks, a telephone system, streetcars, and fewer saloons—at least according to the prohibitionists.

Very significantly, however, Madison leaders in 1880 were anything but resigned to a continuation of the status quo—a scenario that would have doomed Madison to a disgraceful also-ran category. Perhaps it was because Madison leaders were confident in their ability to improve the city and cause it to grow. Perhaps it was because they did not feel they had the luxury of allowing their special city to succumb to mediocrity. Perhaps it was the new confidence engendered by a resurgent economy evident in early 1880. Perhaps it was the new resolve that comes with the beginning of a new decade. Whatever the reasons, during the last two decades of the nineteenth century, Madison leaders displayed a yeasty blend of commitment and resourcefulness not seen since the palmy days of the Farwell boom.

Although some leadership came from individual businessmen, much energy was channeled through a dense network of organizations whose goals were to boost and better the city. The Madison Business Club developed schemes to attract new factories. The Madison Park and Pleasure Drive Association sought better recreational facilities. The Civic Federation tried to reform local government. The Church Alliance worked to improve the community moral climate. Each of these organizations and many others left their mark on Madison. Their members were the people who cared enough to get involved. What they achieved during this period was a monument to their dynamic and systematic promotion of their respective goals.[2]

During this two-decade period Madison nearly doubled its population and density—a development that triggered an era of ambitious suburban development. Madison became a mature regional commercial center, a noteworthy manufacturer of farm implements and machine tools, the home of a prestigious and rapidly growing university, and the largest chautauqua in the state. An impressive pleasure drive organization made its debut. Good government advocates fomented a conservative reform movement that ended decades of Democratic dominance of Madison politics. Madisonians also established a full spectrum of utilities including an unusually large telephone system, a nationally known water utility (the city's "first venture into business") a splendid streetcar system, and a sophisticated sewage purification plant. Cumulatively these were impressive changes that gave this two-decade period of distinguishing entrepreneurial spirit.

Disputing Madison's Destiny: Round 2

Introduction

To Madison businessmen, the quickening pulse of the economy in late 1880 was like a warm, sunny day after a siege of cold rainy weather. Merchants reported the best sales since the 1873 depression. Architects strained to keep ahead of

FIGURE 5.1. 1885 NORRIS AND WELLGE BIRDSEYE. This 1885 birdseye view of Madison shows a city where construction had occurred on most city lots not requiring drainage or filling. The large undeveloped areas on both ends of the isthmus area were in fact cattail marshes and the streets shown by the artist in these areas were in most cases nonexistent. The undeveloped area straddling West Washington Avenue, to the right of the railroad yards was a ten-foot-deep pond filled with muskrat houses "thicker than shocks of grain in a grain field at harvest time. . . ." "Boats skipped over the water and the fisherman and the duck hunter were then happy." Settlers who knew the area in the early 1880s were "seized with wonder" when they saw the area in the late 1890s when it was rapidly being filled and used for homes. A similar situation existed for the even larger Great Central Marsh on the East Side..

This outstanding "birdseye" view was done by the Norris, Wellge and Company, Milwaukee, as a promotional item for S. L. Sheldon, a large Madison agricultural implement dealer. The work was commissioned at a time when Madison was straining to develop manufacturing as a growth generator and exploit its excellent railroad network. Consequently, the artist made plumes of black smoke—the symbol of enterprise and bustle—prominent parts of his work. Only two other birdseye views of Madison were done: one in 1867 and another in 1908. The 1908 one, the only one done in color, appears on the jacket of the book. The "birdseye" view was a popular and highly effective early method of making the city coherent and comprehensible. (SHSW WHi(X32)5867) demand for new construction projects scheduled for the spring of 1881. Bankers began to loan money at a rapid and confidence-raising clip.[1]

Encouraging as this upward turn of the economic indicators was, few Madison businessmen were persuaded that these conditions were sufficient to really cause Madison to *grow,* a deeply felt and continuously sought goal among the movers and shakers. To many members of Madison's business elite, Madison needed a surefire growth generator—something that would enable the city to go beyond being a mere "political boarding house"[2] and quiet college town, something that would bring in large numbers of new, permanent residents, money, and jobs. Madison leaders were embarrassed by the near stagnation of the city's population in the years after the Civil War. From 1870 to 1880, Madison's annual population growth rate barely exceeded one percent a year. The 1880 census showed that Madison had fallen to sixth place among Wisconsin cities, behind Milwaukee, Racine, Oshkosh, LaCrosse, and Fond du Lac—a far cry from the number two position it enjoyed during the Farwell boom. Something was needed, and quickly, before Madison was pushed farther down in the population rankings by her more enterprising sister cities.

Four "nominations" for major growth generators were quick in coming but hardly novel: (1) resorts; (2) wholesale and retail trade; (3) factories; and (4) education. All had been pushed in varying degrees of intensity since the Farwell boom of the 1850s. Yet in the last two decades of the nineteenth century, the debate became more strident, shrill, and often ideological in tone. At bottom there was a sense of do or die, that Madison must make its move or forever lose the opportunity. But even this sense of urgency does not fully explain the intensity of the debate. At stake was the destiny of what nearly everyone agreed was one of the most beautiful cities in America. Not surprisingly, the debate evoked strong emotions and very different values. Among other things, the debate turned up a surprisingly large group of opinion leaders who liked Madison the way it was—that is, as a capital and college

town. This group favored growth only if it meant enhancing Madison's reputation as the intellectual and literary center of the state. Proponents of this alternative future were quite content to bask in the flattering cerebral shadow of the University of Wisconsin. It is for these reasons that this spirited controversy on how to exploit Madison's great potential and yet preserve its special qualities is so revealing.

Backdrop for the Debate: A Roller Coaster Economy

For no less than twelve of the last twenty years of the nineteenth century, the American economy was either in a recession or depression.[3] The most serious was the 1892 to 1894 depression, which according to economists was the third worst in American history next to the Great Depression of the 1930s and the depression of the 1870s. This economic downturn settled with frightful quickness in the summer of 1893. In June fearful depositors lined up to withdraw their money from Madison banks.[4] First National Bank had to ship in $175,000 in gold in the middle of the night to keep ahead of withdrawals.[5] Fortunately, those withdrawing their money were the smaller depositors. The wealthier citizens of Madison not only decided to leave their money in local banks but, as an expression of their confidence, they lined up to deposit their money.[6] Had this not happened, Madison banks might have failed at the same high rate as their counterparts around the country.[7] In June 1893 Gisholt discharged half of their workers[8] and in August, Fuller and Johnson, Madison's largest employer, closed their huge shops.[9] The Northwestern Railway laid off many of its Madison-based engineers and firemen, and the St. Paul Railroad cut employee wages by ten percent.[10] Madison bank loan levels dropped nearly thirty percent between 1893 and 1894[11] and new construction dropped to such low levels that the newspapers didn't even run their annual year-end construction summaries. Even

the U. W. student population, then in a period of rapid growth, suffered a decline during the school year of 1893–94.[12]

Fortunately, the effects of the 1892–1894 depression were much less serious in Madison than elsewhere around the country. Madison's relatively small dependence upon manufacturing was the major reason.[13] Moreover crops in the rich agricultural land around Madison were good in both years and the dairy industry did very well.[14] Madison real estate therefore held its value, though speculative purchasing disappeared.[15] The relative strength of the agricultural sector allowed the Fuller and Johnson firm to reopen in October 1893 after being closed for only three months, although only half its employees were recalled.[16]

By 1895 a strong resumption was under way and the Madison economy made rapid and large advances.[17] Until 1896, Madison economy showed a quick resumption to predepression levels. However, a mild recession in 1896 led to some bankruptcies, reduced the rate of new construction, and slowed bank deposit growth.[18] By 1898 wages of Madison's major employers had been restored to predepression levels and some had even increased ten to forty percent about that point.[19] Good times had returned and workers were in short supply.

Madison as a Northern Resort

July 9, 1879 was a special day for Madisonians. Beginning about 2 P. M. on that sunny Wednesday afternoon, carriages and steamboats began converging on a forty-acre wooded grove on the south side of Lake Monona. The well-dressed passengers were in a festive mood and well they should have been because their purpose was to celebrate the official opening of a large new resort hotel—the first ever built expressly for that purpose. To the 200 prominent guests, the event was full of promise and excitement because it embodied fervently held hopes that Madison would become a prestigious, nationally famous resort.[20]

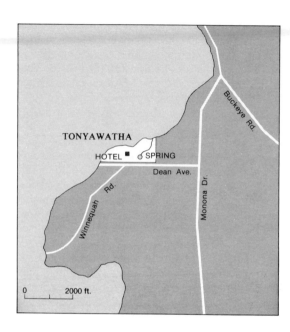

FIGURE 5.2. TOURIST LIFE AT TONYAWATHA. These drawings portray the restful and idyllic life of Tonyawatha tourists. Newspapers supplemented such graphics with their own vivid accounts. One reporter visited the resort in 1884 and made this report: "Row boats were lazily drifting about the bay; the verandas were filled with gentlemen enjoying their cigars in the coolness and quiet; in the billiard and bowling rooms, the click of the ivories and the rumble of the balls showed that the visitors were not altogether occupied by lying in the shade and the picturesque view of the city beyond." The location of Tonyawatha in relation to current roads is shown in the inset. (SHSW WHi(X3)36315 and WHi(X3)36316)

Following the burning of Lakeside House in 1876, efforts to attract rich southern visitors to the city had failed but the vision of Madison as a great northern resort was not abandoned. Its logic was powerful, persuasive, and persistent. Madison offered excellent railroad connections, charming scenery, and ample tourists activities. In theory, Madison could compete with any resort in the country. Nevertheless, seemingly endless editorial exhortations failed to persuade anyone to risk the large outlay necessary to build a summer resort hotel. Finally, in 1879, Dr. William Jacobs, the wealthy owner of the Park Hotel, decided to take that risk, build a resort hotel, and run it as an adjunct to the Park. Jacobs named the hotel Tonyawatha, an Indian name meaning "healing waters" applied to a spring on the grounds from which prized mineral water flowed. The resort provided accommodations for one hundred guests, a billiard hall, a bowling alley, rowboats to rent, croquet, swings, fishing, and paths through the oak woods. In the words of contemporary accounts the Hotel was "elegantly furnished," a "delightful summer idling place," and an "embryo Saratoga."[21]

For the first six years of its operation the Tonyawatha apparently was a financial success, and guests streamed in from the south, mostly New Orleans, at such a rate that in 1880 an addition was added which doubled the capacity of the hotel to two hundred guests. Then in the summer of 1883 still another wing was added giving the Tonyawatha a capacity of three hundred guests. Professional resort managers brought in by the owners promoted the enterprise by bottling and selling the spring water and sponsoring regattas. Few efforts were spared to provide guests with activities and entertainment. In 1886 after six successful years of operation, the *Wisconsin State Journal* editor concluded that Madison had "already grown into a summer resort and the time is not far distant when it will rival (Lake) Geneva and Waukesha."

That claim, however, proved premature. There was *talk* of building an expensive resort hotel at Maple Bluff, but no one followed the example of

Tonyawatha. It stood alone, a flagship without a fleet.[22] Beginning in 1887 patronage declined. At the peak of the 1890 season, a local reporter described the resort as nearly deserted. Its silence, he said was "broken only by the wild song of some bird and the toot of a steamer whistle in the distance." The following year the Town of Blooming Grove, in whose jurisdiction the hotel lay, administered the *coup de grace* to the struggling enterprise by denying the hotel's liquor license. In the words of the bitter Tonyawatha hotel owner, you can't run a successful summer resort "on cold water and pop." For four years, the hotel did not open its doors.[23]

The same year that the Town of Blooming Grove denied Tonyawatha's liquor license, a sharp-eyed development corporation, the Madison Lakes Improvement Company, decided to buy the forty-acre Tonyawatha tract and subdivide it for cottages. The company also owned land at Elmside, which it intended to sell to Chicagoans for fancy vacation homes. By selling lots to summer tourists, company officials were confident they could make Madison "the saratoga of the West." The boom also brought to Madison the general passenger agent for the Illinois Central Railroad, who was interested in generating business for that line. After a tour of the city the agent concluded there was no reason why Madison could not be made "the greatest summer resort in the West. . . . If the Tonyawatha Hotel can be enlarged or if a new one built," he concluded, "I am not afraid to guarantee that from three to five thousand visitors will be here next summer (1892)." In 1891 as a contribution to that goal, the Illinois Central Passenger Department published a handsome twenty-page pamphlet, *Beautiful Madison,* designed to titilate the tourist trade and of course sell passenger tickets. In the spring of 1892 the manager of the Park Hotel travelled through Louisiana, Tennessee, and Mississippi to drum up business for his hotel and came back with promises of visits for that summer.[24]

Before the promised summer tourists descended on Madison, however, a serious and sharp depression descended upon the entire country.

The Madison Lakes Improvement Company was a victim of that bust, and the Tonyawatha was sold by a receiver for the bankrupt development company to a Boston financier on the steps of the Dane County courthouse in June 1893. Not until 1895 did Madison's tiny tourist industry again stir to life. In June of that year the new Boston owner reopened Tonyawatha for the first time in four years, hired an experienced manager, and began to promote the resort. Once again, southern tourists began to trickle in. Unfortunately about 8:00 P. M. on the evening of July 31, just two months after opening day, a fire broke out in the large frame building. By 10:00 P. M., the Tonyawatha lay in ruins, a glowing mass of coals.[25]

Without a summer hotel, Madison no longer had any basis for the ego-soothing claims to being even an "embryo Saratoga." Explanations for this frustrating failure were hardly in short supply. Some argued that Tonyawatha was poorly located on the hot side of the lake (the afternoon sun shown on the veranda), had too many poor managers, and that Madison was too big a city to attract tourists. Such reasons, however, cannot bear much weight. The major reason was at once more substantive and in some ways more obvious. Building summer resort hotels in the Madison area during the 1880s and 1890s was a risky business. A three-month season was little time indeed to recover large initial outlays. With the exception of the first five or six years, the Tonyawatha record hardly buoyed prospective investor confidence. And where was the evidence that tourists would stream into town if only aggressive advertising were done? The resort hotel business was highly developed and highly competitive business in the Northwest at the time. A new resort hotel, however meritorious, faced great odds in becoming known and patronized on a regular basis. And where was the support of leading citizens? A cursory glance would convince even the most sanguine that with the exception of a few interested parties—the hotel owners, the land developers, the railroads, several merchants and newspaper editors—local interest in tourism was extremely thin. Some actually opposed the idea.

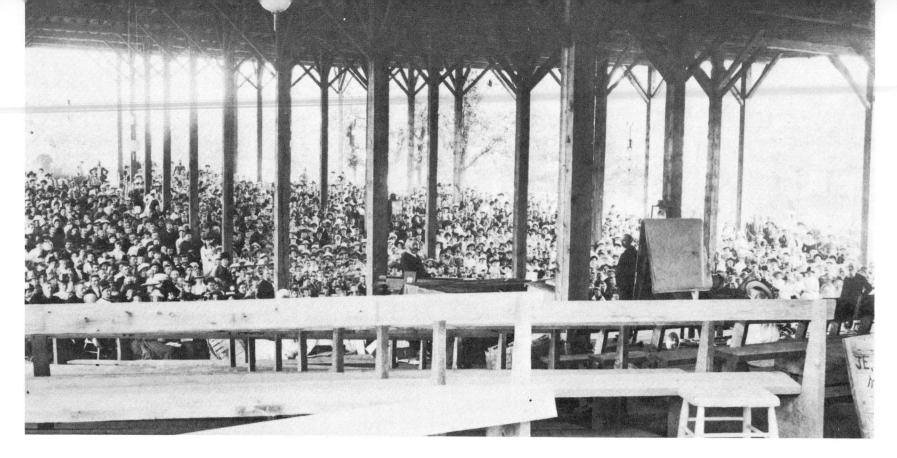

FIGURE 5.3. ICE CREAM, LAKE BREEZES, AND WILLIAM JENNINGS BRYAN: THE WISCONSIN SUNDAY SCHOOL ASSEMBLY. On Sunday evening, April 10, 1881, the sanctuary of the Congregational Church on West Washington Avenue was packed with people all of whom were eager to make Madison the permanent home of the Wisconsin Sunday School Assembly—an organization whose purpose was to train teachers for the Sunday Schools that were then being rapidly established in churches all over the state. The concept that assembly leaders were striving to realize was the highly successful outdoor summertime format developed in the 1870s at Chautauqua, a picturesque lake-oriented community in southwestern New York. Although the primary purpose of the original Chautauqua was to train Sunday School teachers, its leaders quickly learned that religion mixed with recreation worked better than religion alone.

The very prospect of a Madison Chautauqua excited those in attendance that evening, but not simply because the effort would produce more effective Sunday School teachers. A speaker said the New York Chautauqua sometimes attracted twenty thousand persons and that Madison could easily attract three thousand persons a day. To Madison leaders, eager to boom the town, this large number of summer visitors could not help but enhance the city's reputation as a summer resort. Then appealing to the cupidity of his audience, the same speaker noted that Chautauqua caused property values to soar in the small New York community because wealthy persons sought nearby land for elegant summer residences. If the Madisonians sitting on the hard pews that evening were not convinced when they came, they were after hearing the speakers. Madison, they concluded, *must* be the home of the "Chautauqua of the West."

After several months of preparation, twenty-five hundred persons attended the first ten-day session of the Wisconsin Sunday School Assembly in August, 1881, on the grounds of the old Lakeside House, now Olin Park. Managers had converted the Lakeside House pavillion into a dining hall, and the bowling alley into a kitchen and had lined its newly laid out rectilinear "streets" with dozens of white canvas tents. Focal point of the grounds was a huge tent seating three thousand persons. There Sunday School teachers from all over the state heard lectures on topics ranging from the practical ("How to prepare a lesson") to the patriotic ("Our Country for Christ") to the profound ("Christianity and Civilization"). Mixed in with this essentially spiritual curriculum were a few courses on secular subjects such as "micro-organisms" and alternative economic systems.

Over the years program managers gave more attention to secular subjects and allowed more time for rowing, swimming, fishing, sailing, and just plain relaxing. This helped make the event more attractive to families who often came year after year. In the words of one observer, the Monona Lake Assembly was "not a Christian Church, but a summer resort of the highest order whose brains, culture and religion are its chief adornments." Like the original Chautauqua, the Wisconsin Sunday School Assembly, or the Monona Lake Assembly as it was often known, exposed its participants to an impressive array of nationally famous thinkers. For example, in 1895 campers heard William Jennings Bryan orate on the merits of free silver.

In 1882 the Assembly bought the twenty-eight-acre parcel and began to make a number of improvements including the ice cream pavilion shown above and a huge circular five-thousand-seat pavilion (left), the largest room for popular gatherings in the state. The pavilion contractor was J. H. Findorff, founder of today's firm of the same name.

Much of the credit for the success of the Wisconsin Sunday School Assembly must go to its Madison manager, J. E. Mosely, who became one of the best known Chautauqua managers in the country. In 1902 his fellow managers elected him president of the International Chautauqua Alliance.

From 1881 until 1904 the assembly crowds were large and gate receipts more than covered expenses. In that year, however, attendance particularly from Madisonians who constituted the largest single patron group, began to slide. Free lectures at the U. W. summer school drew away some persons, the increased popularity of private camping caused defections and fast-paced, cheap vaudeville attracted still others. But the biggest single factor in the attendance drop was the decline in popularity of the assembly program itself. After nearly three successful decades the staid lectures-classes-and-concert formula had lost its appeal. In December 1908 things came to a head after several highly publicized acrimonious meetings of assembly stockholders. A group of minority stockholders led by MPPDA President John M. Olin urged that this beautiful piece of land never be allowed to fall into the hands of "rapacious speculators" who wanted to turn the choice piece of lakefront real estate into a prime subdivision. Olin and others also offered a variety of imaginative schemes to keep the assembly going.

But the majority stockholders decided to sell the parcel, pay off the debts, divide up the profits, and end the enterprise. Seldom in Madison history was a private corporate decision so soundly condemned.

The minority stockholders immediately took the majority stockholders to court charging that the conditions under which the land had been purchased required that it always remain in the public domain. After losing the first round in a Dane County Circuit Court, minority stockholders appealed to the Wisconsin Supreme Court. Finally in 1911 in the midst of the legal battle, the City of Madison interceded with an unprecedented step. They issued bonds yielding forty thousand dollars and bought the entire parcel—the first park completely purchased with city money. Previously all city money had been used to *supplement* MPPDA Association subscriptions. Justification for the park purchase was that the city needed better summer convention facilities and that the assembly buildings including the five-thousand-seat auditorium, the large dining room, several cottages, and other buildings were ideal for this purpose. Also the parcel provided the only public place on all of Lake Monona where owners of row boats and launches could go for rest and relaxation.

The assembly grounds were known as Monona Park until 1923 when the Common Council decided to change its name to Olin Park in honor of the instrumental role John Olin, then seventy-two years old, had played in getting the city to buy the park, but also to honor his incomparable work as Father of Madison's park system. Olin gratefully accepted the honor. He died just one year later. (SHSW WHi(X3)36003 and WHi(X3)36001)

FIGURE 5.4a. NEW RAILROAD LINES. In addition to providing the usual depot facilities, both this depot and its Northwestern counterpart at East Madison contained small second floor hotels for the convenience of passengers. Such facilities were then common across the country because Pullman cars had not yet come into widespread use. (SHSW, WHi(X3)35545)

FIGURE 5.4b. This 1895 photograph shows a coal-burning locomotive stopped beside the Chicago, Milwaukee and St. Paul Railroad Madison depot on West Washington Avenue. The frame depot shown in the background was the predecessor of the present brick structure. (SHSW, WHi(X3)1472)

FIGURE 5.4c. Ever since 1854 Madisonians dreamed of the day when nine railroads would enter the city like a giant steel spider web. Finally, in 1887, thirty-three years after this map first appeared in the Madison newspapers, the dream became a reality. In that year the Illinois Central, then known as the Chicago, Madison and Northern Railroad Company, steamed into town for the first time. This new line plus a new, direct Northwestern line to Milwaukee and a Northwestern extension to Montfort completed the nine-track configuration. The three new lines are shown in the map on the left.

The new lines coming into Madison made the depots and the switching yards among the liveliest spots in town. In 1882 the newspapers reported that forty passenger trains passed into and out of the city each day. By 1899 a similar count showed that 148 passenger and freight trains passed in and out of town each day, or an average of six each hour.

Although the busy switchyards and depots were welcome developments to Madisonians, complaints were not long in coming about trains blocking railroad crossings. To relieve this problem the Common Council passed an ordinance in 1883 that fined engineers from ten to one hundred dollars if their trains blocked a Madison street for more than five minutes. Not until after the ordinance was passed did the city discover it had no powers to regulate a railroad—a problem city leaders solved by going directly to the legislature and getting a charter amendment. To avoid being harrassed by Madison officials armed with this new power, the Northwestern Road in 1895 brought 192 acres east of the Yahara River and moved their switching operations there.

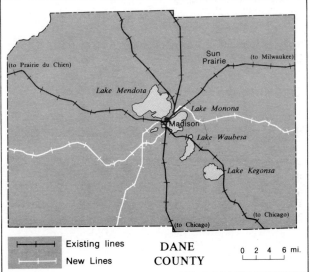

Existing lines
New Lines
DANE COUNTY
0 2 4 6 mi.

That tourists commonly got the cold shoulder from Madison "society" was common knowledge. The fact was few Madisonians saw a compelling need to promote tourism.[26]

A variety of steps *might* have been taken to reduce this risk and improve the investment climate. For example, the private sector could have formed a "welcome club" so that each tourist was made to feel a part of the community. The city might have paid for an extensive and sustained advertising campaign as it had done during the Farwell boom and several other times. Local capitalists could have joined forces to offer a resort developer a financial incentive as was done for some cultural facilities and factories. Yet none of these steps were ever taken. In summary, Madison might have catapulated itself into prominence as a national resort, but its proponents failed to understand the risky realities of the resort business, overestimated the efficacy of advertising, and greatly underestimated the apathy of Madisonians toward tourism.

Madison as a Regional Commercial Center

Among the first to notice the quickening pulse of the economy in the early 1880s, were Madison merchants. Regarding their 1880–1881 winter trade, they were "quite unanimous" that it had been the best they had experienced since the Civil War.[27] Though local editors acknowledged that an increase in business was being seen all over the country, they appear to have been justified in claiming that Madison was getting more than the national average. The *Wisconsin State Journal* agreed, "Madison is now upon an upgrade in a business point of view, and our merchants deserve great credit for assisting in the elevation."[28] A happy confluence of more stores, better merchandising, more competitive prices and better access were responsible.

Between 1880 and 1885, the number of businesses fronting on Capitol Square increased by forty percent—from 89 to 124—a clear indication that the area had become a mature regional shopping center. Never before or again would the Capitol Square have so many stores.[29] A shopper walking around the Square in 1885 would have found one furniture store; two hardware stores and book dealers; three restaurants; four china stores and tobacco shops; five bakeries; six drug stores; seven candy stores and grocery stores; eight women's clothing shops and jewelry stores; nine shoe stores, and no less than ten saloons. Even if a shopper had visited all fifty-five of these stores there would still have been sixty-nine more scattered around the Square area.[30] This large number of stores drew shoppers to the Square area for the same reasons shopping centers draw customers today: convenience, completeness, and compactness. (For comparison, East Towne has about 100 stores and West Towne 75.)

To the great relief of the opinion leaders, more and more Madison merchants were discontinuing the "country" practice of moving a large portion of their stock out onto the sidewalks each day.[31] Selection was more complete and goods were being more attractively displayed.[32] Volume buying and more competitive prices caused more of the "city trade" to shop in Madison rather than to go to Milwaukee or Chicago. Newspapers published special supplements to boom the town, and merchants went all out to decorate their stores.[33] Merchants also got behind efforts to push Madison as a convention town, as a tourist center, as a location for the state fair, and as a horse trading market because these things would increase their trade.[34]

A major factor in the commercial boom that began in the early 1880s was greater merchant exploitation of the superb railroad network serving the city. Here their most significant action was getting the railroads—whose self-interest made them willing allies—to adjust their schedules to better accommodate the "country trade" in Madison's "tributary areas." The revised schedules allowed shoppers to arrive in Madison no later than midmorning, shop the better part of the day, leave late in the afternoon and still be home before eight or nine o'clock at night. On Saturday, December 18, 1880, a *Democrat* reporter said there "were people from nearly every railroad village within a radius of forty miles shopping in Madison."[35] Some said the merchants went too far in promoting business. For example, citizens complained when merchants united to prevent a farmers' market from developing in the city—a facility many felt would lower the prices in the stores. In another instance Madison merchants thwarted an effort by a Milwaukee shoe merchant to undersell Madison stores by slapping him with a prohibitively expensive transient license.[36]

FIGURE 5.5. HORSE MARKET/WATER TOWER. In spite of many efforts of the Madison Businessmen's Club to increase merchants trade, only one was a conspicuous success: the monthly horse market. A Chicago horse buyer said it was "one of the best horse markets in the country," and that he nearly always went back to Chicago with a railroad car full of fine Madison horses. Begun in May, 1890, it was held regularly for many years on the first Wednesday of each month. This photograph was probably taken on November 5, 1890, a cool, but sunny afternoon. To get this picture, the photographer stood on the roof of the building now occupied by the American Exchange Bank and pointed his camera eastward. The market was located on East Washington Avenue between Pinckney and Webster Streets.

The handsome structure in the center of the photograph was a 125-foot-high water tower built in 1889. The weight of sixty thousand gallons of water in a tank at the top of the structure kept water pressure in Madison water mains at a high level. Just seven years after it was built, however, its pressure-maintaining function was replaced by a steam-powered pump. Once touted as an engineering marvel, the water tower was soon criticized for its "unsightliness" and said to be "an impertinence" because it marred the view of the Capitol. A 1903 engineering study showed that the structure suffered from some potentially dangerous structural defects. Finally, after a crescendo of criticism, the tower succumbed to the wrecker's bar and hammer, not so much for its alleged structural weaknesses, but more because it was an eyesore. Although its loss was not mourned by many Madisonians, there are many contemporary residents who wish it had remained. Though not as ornate as the Chicago water tower, Madison's tower might also have become a treasured landmark and the heart of a fashionable shopping area. (SHSW WHi(X3)28461)

At the same time as Capitol Square merchants were building up their businesses, a group of equally enterprising wholesale and retail implement distributors were doing the same thing for their line. The completion of the nine-line Madison railroad network and its connections with the rapidly opening prairies and plains to the west placed the city in an attractive position to a very rapidly growing and lucrative market. By 1883 one such dealer-distributor, the S. L. Sheldon Company, had grown quite large and was reputed to have had a larger stock and greater variety of machines than any other firm in the west, including Chicago and St. Louis. His carriage display room on East Wilson Street, for example, held one hundred buggies and carriages at one time.[37] But it was not until the 1890s that Madison became an important regional implement distribution center. Whole trainloads of implements flowed into the city to supply the growing number of dealers.[38] A conservative 1896 estimate showed that Madison's thirty implement dealers had sold $1.5 million worth of goods in that year.[39] By 1899 Madison was described as being second only to Minneapolis among northwestern cities with annual implement sales exceeding $3.5 million.[40] Many manufacturers built their own factory outlets and concentrated them in an area called "Implement Row."

As a result of their promotional efforts, Madison merchants enjoyed their share of citizen adulation. To many Madisonians it was only their kind of push and pluck that would cause the city to be something beyond a "dull college town" or a mere political and educational center.[41] In this respect they were major contributors to the entrepreneurial spirit that dominated the last two decades of the nineteenth century.

Manufactures: The Ascendent Star

"I call your special attention," said Mayor Phillip Spooner in his 1880 inaugural address, "to the subject of manufacturing concerning which so much has been said, but so little accomplished. . . . While the location of the capital here is a desirable thing and that of the state university still more desirable, it is doubtless true that the location and building up of manufacturing establishments is the only thing which will cause our city to grow much beyond its present proportions. I suggest that you take some steps to investigate and agitate the matter, that the advantages of Madison as a manufacturing center may be brought to the attention of manufacturers and capitalists."[42] With these words Spooner fired a fusillade in the episodic battle to made Madison a factory town. Like his earlier counterparts, Spooner's profactory message remained virtually the same: if Madison was ever to enjoy a large degree of prosperity, grow substantially in population, and become a truly great city, it must be based upon manufacturing. No other economic generator—not tourism, not the university, not wholesale and retail trade, not politics—could do for Madison what manufacturing could.[43]

Factory proponents had little patience for those who did not share their vision of the city. One taxpayer in an 1880 letter to the *Wisconsin State Journal* editor ridiculed as "romantic" those who wanted to make Madison "the flower garden of the state" or keep it a mere "political boarding house." If Madison is to traffic only in its beauty or politics, few can afford to live in the city, he insisted. Workingmen need jobs and jobs come from factories. And what, he asked, would really be lost if "the smoke from factories should mar the beauties of the . . . setting sun?" At least men would have jobs! The angry taxpayer closed his letter by reminding those "who disliked the bustle and turmoil of progress . . . will find no law on the statute books prohibiting his departure aboard one of the many trains that leave Madison each day.[44]

The primary responsibility for attracting factories to Madison fell to several organizations whose members constituted the business elite of the city. The first was the Madison Business Board, formed in 1882 to aid and encourage business enterprises. It made several efforts but accomplished nothing and became a social club instead. Next came the Madison Club. Though formed in 1886, primarily for social purposes, a business promotion clause was added to its charter in 1889. However, like its predecessor, its work was episodic and failed to produce any new factories. The third and most promising organization that was active during this period was the Madison Businessmen's Association, formed in 1888. Its most active period came during the early 1890s when a crest of confidence about Madison's future surged through the minds of Madison's leaders. An enthusiastic meeting of its prominent membership in early 1890 produced an agreement that an industrial promotion company should be formed with one hundred thousand dollars in assets so that its bonds could be transferred to worthy companies as an incentive to locate in Madison. At the same meeting, businessmen decided that they would raise five thousand dollars so that fifty thousand promotional pamphlets could be broadcast around the country. There was even talk of sending a private railroad car full of prominent Madison businessmen to the principal cities of the country to try to persuade industrialists to locate their factories in Madison.[45]

To the chagrin of its prominent and very capable members, this early enthusiasm failed to produce a single factory. Painfully aware of this fact and the long record of failure of such efforts, the organization met once again in May 1891 to formulate a more realistic and effective factory promotion program. They recognized that "spasms of life at semi-occasional meetings will not build a city nor inspire faith in the future."[46] This time the goal was to create a small central power whose work was continuous and oriented toward results. The committee urged that a full-time executive director be hired, "practically a paid attorney employed to act on behalf of our business interests," and placed under the supervision of a nine-person blue ribbon board of directors headed by Civil War hero and former governor Lucius Fairchild. The executive director's jobs were: (1) to watch the movements of industries and try to get them to come to Madison; (2) to attract state and national conventions; (3) to advertise Madison as a summer resort; and

FIGURE 5.6 1880s FAUERBACH BEER ADVERTISEMENT. Sometime in the late 1880s Fauerbach Brewery officials had copies of this chromolithograph advertisement distributed to saloons that sold their beer. The brewery, Madison's first, was begun by Peter Sprecher in 1848 and purchased by Peter Fauerbach in 1868. The demure barmaid with a beer pitcher in one hand and daisies in the other somehow managed to look sexy and proper at the same time—just the kind of young woman every saloon patron dreamed of meeting. To give the impression of bustle and success, the artist filled his drawing with fifty people, twelve wagons, seven belching smokestacks, and one horse drawn streetcar. (SHWS WHi(X3)38099)

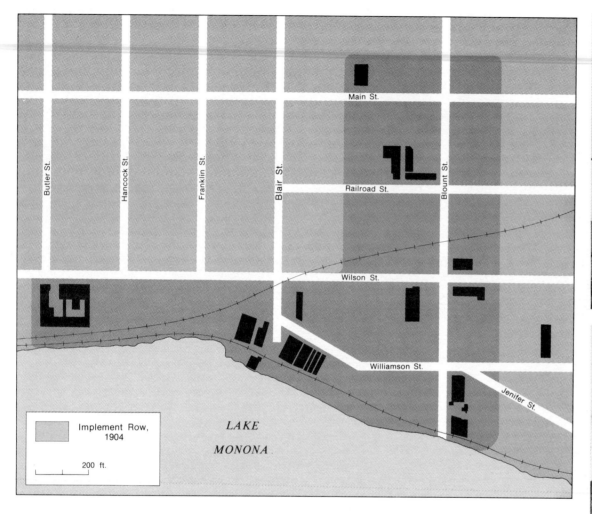

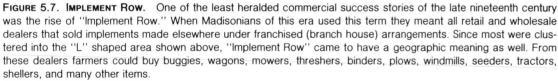

FIGURE 5.7. IMPLEMENT ROW. One of the least heralded commercial success stories of the late nineteenth century was the rise of "Implement Row." When Madisonians of this era used this term they meant all retail and wholesale dealers that sold implements made elsewhere under franchised (branch house) arrangements. Since most were clustered into the "L" shaped area shown above, "Implement Row" came to have a geographic meaning as well. From these dealers farmers could buy buggies, wagons, mowers, threshers, binders, plows, windmills, seeders, tractors, shellers, and many other items.

A few implement dealers located in Madison during the 1850s, but not until the 1890s following the completion of the nine-track Madison-centered railroad network did the number of implement dealers begin to grow rapidly. In 1890 just ten implement dealers were located in Madison but in 1904 thirty dealers were doing business.

Some of the larger manufacturers built their own buildings. One example was the McCormick Company, which erected the building shown at top right at 301 South Blount in 1895. Other dealers such as the Advance Thresher Company, 601 Williamson, shown at bottom right, rented space. So many implement dealers located in this half block long building that it became known as "Machinery Row." The handsome 1898 building was made a Madison landmark in 1982. (SHSW, WHi(X3)38283)

(4) to secure lower freight rates for railroads serving Madison. Money to underwrite these activities was to come from a five-thousand-dollar Madison Advancement Fund raised from the community's wealthier citizens.

Once again these plans came to naught. In fact, the critically important five-thousand-dollar Madison Advancement Fund was abandoned just days after it was announced. Only two subscriptions were taken.[47] These failures aside, the Madison Businessmen's Association continued to meet from time to time and hold annual banquets for several years where bravado and bold plans always received warm applause. Still the results of the Madison Businessmen's Association like its predecessors was disappointingly anemic. They purchased a clubhouse, a fine setting for highly valued cameraderie, entertained legislators on steamboats, and even gave money to the poor. Their most enduring accomplishment was the monthly horse market begun in 1890 on East Washington Avenue as a ploy to get farmers into town to shop.[48]

Madison's Pride: The Story of the Fuller & Johnson Manufacturing Company

Fortunately Madison's industrial future was not entirely dependent upon the sporadic clamor for factories from the city's leading lights. While industrial promotional organizations were getting the headlines, a corporate union between thirty-seven-year-old Norwegian immigrant, John A. Johnson, and a fifty-nine-year-old established Yankee businessman, Morris E. Fuller, was getting results. In January 1880, the two men signed corporate papers, issued thirty-five thousand dollars in stock and bought a small, local thirty-four-year-old plow manufacturing company named Firmin, Billings and Company. The two renamed their enterprise the Madison Plow Company, increased their stock to one hundred thousand dollars, bought a long-vacant factory at the intersection of Dickinson and East Washington

FIGURE 5.8. EARLY SUBURBAN COMMERCIAL DEVELOPMENTS. One of the reasons why the number of stores around the capital square declined after 1880 was because increasing amounts of residential development were occurring one to two miles away from the square. Merchants were quick to exploit these opportunities and began to set up stores along major streets in what were even then called the "suburbs." The Breitenbach Grocery Store and Saloon shown in this 1895 photo, located at the intersection of Williamson and Patterson Streets, just three-quarters of a mile from the Capitol Square, was an example of this retailing trend. Not only could the Breitenbachs more easily capture the rapidly growing trade from the immediate neighborhood, but they could also intercept the lucrative farmer trade before they reached the Square. This handsome old building still stands but has been converted to another use. By 1900 Williamson Street was described as a "lively business street" and on Saturdays, a traditionally heavy farmer shopping day, a *Wisconsin State Journal* reporter said "it was almost impossible for people driving for pleasure to get through the jams of farmers' teams here and there at various corners." (Courtesy of Otto Breitenbach)

Avenue, and began manufacturing a line of plows and cultivators.[49] In 1882 John A. Johnson was elected President (a position he was to hold for almost twenty years), the company's stock was increased to two hundred thousand dollars, and the name of the company was changed to The Fuller and Johnson Manufacturing Company. Just three years after it was formed, Fuller and Johnson became "Madison's pride" because, in the words of the *Madison Democrat,* it was ". . . the largest and most conspicuously commercial enterprise of the city and the one that will compare favorably with any in the West."[50] Indeed, there can be no doubt that Fuller and Johnson Manufacturing Company was Madison's most successful industrial growth story of the nineteenth century.[51]

The early 1880s was an auspicious time to begin the manufacture of farm implements. Liberal government policies had opened up the prairies and plains to settlers, who poured in to claim the land and extract its riches. In the last thirty years of the nineteenth century 430,000,000 acres of the West were settled and 225,000,000 were plowed. Homesteading reached its high point in the Dakota's, Nebraska, Kansas, and in Colorado in 1880. Regional specialties became established with winter wheat in Kansas, corn in Iowa, and spring wheat in Minnesota and the Dakotas. Railroads criss-crossed this new agricultural heartland and linked it to the Atlantic and Pacific. The opening of this vast tract of farmland created a pressing need for farm machinery. There was simply too much work to be done with muscles alone. Farm implement manufacturers rushed in to satisfy this need.[52]

Still, the Fuller and Johnson enterprise was not without its risks. Freight rates placed Madison at a disadvantage to places like Chicago, competition was intense and bill collectors were dependent upon the weather and the economic conditions. Fortunately, both Johnson and Fuller were well equipped to enter the fray. M. E. Fuller had been the principal behind the spectacularly successful Madison implement distributorship, known as Fuller and Williams. For eleven years,

beginning in 1869, John A. Johnson traveled the Midwest plus the upper plains states, Colorado, and Nevada selling implements for Fuller and Williams. Johnson came to intimately know farmers' needs and implement marketing problems and opportunities. Based on their analysis of this opportunity, both men were eager to begin manufacturing what they sold.

One of Johnson's first moves after becoming president of Fuller and Johnson was to open a sales and distribution branch house in Minneapolis to better serve the rapidly expanding needs of the opening prairie lands to the west. Then in rapid succession, the firm opened branch houses in Iowa, Illinois, North and South Dakota, and later in Michigan, at Kansas City, Denver, Helena, Montana, and Los Angeles. The company built its reputation on a prairie sod-breaking plow known as the "Bonanza Prairie Breaker," but they also manufactured a large line of horse-drawn plows, cultivators, harrows, mowers, and sulky rakes. The firm deliberately avoided the well-established wheat-harvesting market. As a mark of their rapid success, the Fuller and Williams Company sent an entire trainload of its implements (twelve cars) to San Francisco in 1888, the largest single purchase made by a western implement dealer up to that time. The following year similar trainloads of Fuller and Johnson implements were sent to other Californian destinations, plus Oregon and Washington. Naturally these developments thrilled Madison factory promoters who watched the number of dealers selling Fuller and Johnson products jump from one thousand in 1894 to two thousand in 1897.[53]

Johnson's years of direct sales work made him a shrewd merchandiser. He knew what to write and how to present implement features effectively. Eye-catching graphics and mind-convincing testimonials embellished his advertising copy, all of which he wrote himself. He concentrated advertising in midwestern newspapers and magazines with special emphasis on Scandinavian newspapers and the *Farm Implement News,* a leading trade journal. Johnson also set up attractive displays at shows, fairs, and exhibitions where

he could expose his line of products to thousands of people and place his implements in competition with other firms. For example, at the 1893 Columbian exhibition in Chicago, the Fuller and Johnson display featured elegant gold lettering, brass railings, luxurious carpeting and specially made show implements resplendently finished in nickel plating and built with cherry and walnut. However, the fine showing at the Columbian Exhibition was not based on showmanship but rather on good engineering. Against national and international competition Fuller and Johnson won two major awards. The resourceful Norwegian chief executive officer took a strong, active role in the design of his company's products, always striving for tough design, easy maintenance, and simple repairs. Between 1888 and 1899 the Fuller and Johnson Company received no less than thirty-two patents.

With few exceptions, Fuller and Johnson sales increased each year during the 1880s, but tough times lay ahead during the recession and depression-ridden 1890s. Collections were very slow, sales declined during several years, and yet the capital needs of the company went up. Money was needed to secure new products, improve old ones, and expand into new markets. Fortunately, Johnson was able to raise his needed capital from wealthy local businessmen. But even with this capital infusion, it was not until 1896 that company sales began showing a strong upward trend. By 1899, annual sales topped one million dollars. Company stock stood at $1.5 million and products from the East Washington Avenue factory were being shipped not only throughout the Midwest and West but also to England, Germany, France, Russia, Scandinavia, South America, and even Australia.

When John A. Johnson died in November 1901 after nearly twenty years as chief executive officer of the Fuller and Johnson Manufacturing Company, he left an impressive legacy. During this time sales rose from less than one hundred thousand dollars a year to over one million, stock was increased from thirty-five thousand dollars to over $1.5 million. The number of employees rose from a mere handful to more than four hundred, and the factory grew from twenty thousand to two hundred thousand square feet. The Fuller and Johnson Manufacturing Company was Madison's first big and important industry and conferred upon the city the heretofore elusive attribute of industrial respectability.

The Gisholt Story

In 1885 just five years after Johnson formed the predecessor company of Fuller and Johnson, he began thinking about the possibility of making machine tools, that is, machines that manufacture parts for other machines. Such a business, Johnson reasoned, would be immediately useful to the Fuller and Johnson Company. After all, the machine tools for making implement parts had to be acquired somewhere. Johnson was also thinking about his sons, then twenty-two, fifteen, twelve, and nine years of age. Although his oldest son, Frederick, was then employed as a salesman for Fuller and Johnson, Johnson recognized there would only be a limited number of positions available in that company for his other sons. And there was still another reason: Johnson saw the limitations of the farm implement business. As early as August 1890, Johnson was confident that Gisholt was "destined in time" to be larger than Fuller and Johnson.[54] In almost every other industry, big corporations had gobbled up smaller ones, often forming huge combines that spelled near certain death for those left "out in the cold." Johnson first tried to persuade his inactive Fuller and Johnson partner, Morris E. Fuller, into devoting a portion of their shops to the production of machine tools. Johnson even offered to pay the rent and reimburse the company for power during the experimental period. The insightful Norwegian believed that the machine tool business was a golden opportunity, but his conservative partner-stockholder did not agree.[55]

Johnson persisted and two years later got Fuller to allow a limited amount of shop space for this purpose. Meanwhile, Johnson had hired an engineer named Conrad M. Conradson away from the E. P. Allis Company in Milwaukee to design the machinery Johnson wanted to produce. Conradson had graduated from the University of Wisconsin in 1881 with a masters degree in mechanical engineering and was later called one of America's six mechanical geniuses. Johnson had known him as a young inventor and was sufficiently impressed by the young man to have underwritten the cost of several of his inventions. Unfortunately the machinery then available to Conradson in the Fuller and Johnson shops was woefully inadequate for prototype fabrication, so much of the work had to be done in Milwaukee. In 1888 while working in Milwaukee, Conradson conceived the idea of building a heavy-duty turret lathe capable of grinding eighteen-inch to twenty-four-inch castings. Such a machine, he noted, was nowhere else available and would therefore enjoy a large market. Johnson agreed and upon this perception a company was formed.

In January 1889, Johnson took out articles of incorporation for the new enterprise. For the name of the company, Johnson, then fifty-seven, went back to his childhood in Norway and the many pleasant summers he has spent at Gisholt, the farm of his paternal aunt. He called the new business the Gisholt Machine Company. Johnson singlehandedly underwrote the cost of the new enterprise, forty-one thousand dollars in cash, every dollar of which was prudently spent. To maximize dollars available for critically important machinery, Johnson took every step to keep physical plant costs down. In the summer of 1889 Johnson put his three oldest sons to work building the frame factory and literally got them into the business on the ground floor. By the end of the summer two small inexpensive buildings were completed, and in early 1890 a handful of workers moved in. Everything was strictly utilitarian. The offices consisted of nothing more than a twelve-foot-by-twelve-foot room in one corner of

the shop, barely large enough for Conradson, who served as shop superintendent and vice president, and Frederick, secretary-treasurer. Both men sat at makeshift desks on Fuller and Johnson corn planter seats with wooden legs attached. Power for the plant was borrowed via a rope belt from the Fuller and Johnson Company just across Mifflin Street. The arrangement worked well in dry weather, but rain, even a brief shower, would cause the rope to shrink and break and give the workers an unscheduled vacation. It was in this small east-side factory that Conradson labored over his 12-foot-long drawing board making full-scale drawings for the big, heavy duty turret lathes the company planned to produce. The major use for the large lathes was in the manufacture of steam engines, principally locomotives.[56]

The fledgling company faced several problems in its early years. Although the big turret lathes were available from no other manufacturer, sales during the first few years were slow, and some of the first models did not work properly. Soon after Conradson completed the initial design of the new line of turret lathes, the brilliant engineer lost interest in the product and began spending company time on his own interests, namely, electric motors. Ultimately Johnson was forced to fire Conradson, but the job was difficult because of Conradson's patent rights and financial involvement in the company. The recession of 1890–91 and then the depression of 1893–94 further damaged sales of the young company. For six consecutive years the Gisholt Machine Company lost money, and Johnson was required to kick in another seventy-nine thousand dollars in cash. Though all these things were deeply discouraging, he doggedly persisted, confident that the company would soon show a profit.

Meanwhile, there were some positive signs. The company had displayed its new line of turret lathes at the 1893 Columbian Exhibition in Chicago and in head-to-head competition with big, established companies such as Pratt and Whitney, Gisholt won a bronze medal for good design.

SHSW WHi(X3)22202

John A. Johnson: Immigrant Industrialist

When twelve-year-old John A. Johnson, his parents, and three brothers and sisters left Norway in 1844 to emigrate to the United States, they all had one goal: to better their condition. For several years John's parents had run an inn at a small crossroads village on the edge of a picturesque Norwegian lake about seventy-five miles southeast of Oslo. Still, they only leased the inn and their future was far from bright. Norway was overpopulated, and economic opportunities for young people were dismal indeed. Because there was little to do in the

village, John spent much of his time at an uncle's farm, a place called Gisholt. For months the family debated whether they should move to the United States—a land extolled in letters from village acquaintances. The prospect was at once frightening because of the many unknowns and yet exhilarating because of the many opportunities. In the midst of their deliberations, their leased inn burned down. The die was cast. They sold everything they had, borrowed money from a relative, and booked passage on a sailing ship that landed in New York on July 4, 1844, after a six-week voyage.

America was providential to the Johnson family but particularly to John. Never in his dreams—even when he was allowed to climb to the top of the mast of the sailing ship as it neared Ellis Island—could he have imagined that in America he would be a farmer, a bartender, a state and local legislator, a journalist, an insurance executive, an educator, a philanthropist, a leader among his Norwegian countrymen, and a wealthy industrialist. Yet, in the brief compass of forty-four years, he became all these things and more.

The family had enough money to pay for a trip up the Erie Canal and across the Great Lakes in a steamer to Milwaukee. There the money ran out and they walked forty-five miles to Heart Prairie near Whitewater, Wisconsin, where they joined two families who had left Norway the previous year. To pay off their debt and get some money ahead, John's father helped build houses, his mother took in washing, and John hired out to an American family to work for his room and board. During this period, John attended an American country school where he had the good fortune to have concerned and capable teachers one of whom taught him to speak English without a trace of an accent. Although his schooling was limited to six winter terms, he proved himself an apt pupil. At the age of eighteen John graduated from a small high school in Fort Atkinson and for a short time taught in a country school. During summers he worked at various jobs including a six-week stint as a bartender in a rough saloon in Mineral Point, an experience that caused him to abstain from liquor all his life.

In 1854 at the age of twenty-two John struck out on his own and made a down payment on a 140-acre farm in southwestern Dane County in the Town of Pleasant Springs. The year 1856 was a major milestone in the life of the Norwegian immigrant. In that year, he became an American citizen, married a girl who had crossed the Atlantic on the same ship with him, was elected clerk of Pleasant Springs Township, and joined the Republican party. Already his fine mind and bilingual forcefulness marked him as a leader among fellow township residents. In rapid succession he was elected town assessor, justice of the peace, and finally town chairman, a job that entitled him to be a member of the Dane County board. In 1857 he was elected to the Wisconsin State Assembly by a two to one margin. While the ambitious young man was not serving in the legislature, or farming, he taught school and even sold implements on the side. By 1860 at the age of twenty-nine he owned a debt-free, productive Dane County farm. In that same year John was elected clerk of Dane County, an event that required him to move to Madison, where he stayed for the rest of his life.

But then, just when his career was looking very bright, tragedy struck: first his wife died leaving him with a six-month old child and then three months later the child died. Johnson compensated for his misfortune by throwing himself into his work as Dane County clerk, often working from seven-thirty in the morning to eleven at night. He read voraciously from the classics, the Bible, and contemporary periodicals. Seeing the large German element in Madison and knowing the enormous advantages of linguistic proficiency, he taught himself German during this period.

For some reason John A. Johnson never enlisted in the Civil War. Perhaps it was because he was engaged to be married (he remarried on October 31, 1861) or because he thought he could help the cause in other ways. Whatever the reason, John played a large role on the home front. He called the meeting that led to the formation of the famous Scandinavian Regiment headed by

Colonel Hans Christian Heg (Heg's statue now stands at the east corner of the Capitol) and at the end of the war Johnson wrote their regimental history. During the war he wrote articles in the Scandinavian press urging his countrymen to fight for the abolition of slavery.

In 1869 after eight years as Dane County clerk Johnson decided to start a new career. He thought about entering law. As county clerk he had come to know the best legal minds in the state and had become an expert in tax law, titles, and contracts. But the possibility of farming was also attractive to Johnson. He still owned his farm in the Town of Pleasant Springs and could easily have gone back into business there. But then a third opportunity presented itself. In 1869 Johnson was offered a position as salesman in the well established Madison implement company of Fuller and Williams. The offer was hardly an effort to reward a diligent public servant. Johnson had established an outstanding reputation among Madison circles, for his attention to detail, his legal acumen, and his skills as a writer and speaker. No doubt the firm felt that Johnson's bilingualism would enable him to sell implements to Norwegian immigrants, then flooding into their market area. And that is exactly what Johnson, then thirty-seven did. As he travelled through Iowa, the Dakotas, Colorado, Nevada, and Minnesota, he established a spectacularly successful sales record. Among Johnson's choice accounts was one of the 75,000-acre bonanza wheat farms in the Red River Valley. Johnson's thorough knowledge of his product, his concern for quality, his unimpeachable integrity, his sincerity, and his genuine concern for his Norwegian countrymen caused his sales to soar beyond the expectations of his Yankee employers. In 1873 the Norwegian immigrant was admitted to the old-line Yankee firm as a full partner. To reflect this development the name was changed to Johnson, Fuller and Company.

At the same time Johnson was selling implements he was building business beachheads in newspaper publishing and insurance. In 1872 he became part owner of the largest and most influential Norwegian newspaper in America, at first called *Amerika* but whose name was changed just one year later to *Skandinaven*. The editorial policy of the Chicago-based newspaper reflected Johnson's intense opposition to slavery, an equally intense support for American public schools as the best institution for Americanizing Norwegians, and his love for freedom, equality, and religious tolerance. Until he sold his ownership interests in 1876, Johnson not only supported the newspaper financially, but he also was a frequent contributor of articles, especially on the cause of the common school, which he believed to be the major safeguard of democracy. Also, as he travelled over the Northwest selling implements, he embodied his careful observations in articles designed to help Norwegians find good economic opportunities. Not surprisingly, Johnson found the pages of *Skandinaven* a prime medium for Fuller and Williams advertising—a fact that naturally enhanced his effectiveness as an implement salesman.

In 1871, Johnson took a leading part in establishing the Hekla Fire Insurance Company, a Madison-based firm founded to better serve the Norwegian market. For seven years, from 1873 to 1880, Johnson was president and guided the firm through the panic of 1873 and the succeeding depression years. Under his leadership the company flourished.

Even these forays into newspapers and insurance did not fully occupy Johnson's talents nor satisfy his eclectic interests. Johnson's interest in public affairs had caused him to run for a seat in the assembly in the fall of 1868 but he had been defeated. Four years later he decided to run for the Senate in a district that included Madison. Johnson's victory catapulted him into the most pressing issue of the day, namely, railroad regulation. Just one week after the Senate convened, Johnson had authored a bill that called for a three-man railroad commission to investigate abuses and establish freight and passenger rates. Though his was a thoughtful and fair solution, no railroad regulation bill was passed that session. Stymied on the railroad front, Johnson introduced a bill that allowed married women to transact business and own property—then a very progressive bill that reflected his life-time commitment to equality for women. That bill was enacted into law. At the beginning of the 1874 session, Johnson once again introduced a tough but thoughtful and fair railroad regulation bill, but another measure known as the Potter bill was enacted into law. Interestingly, defects in the Potter law caused its eventual repeal whereas Johnson's bill appears to have been the model for the Illinois Railroad Law (passed in 1873) and the landmark Wisconsin Railroad Law of 1904. Senator Johnson also introduced legislation that gave bank depositers reasonable assurance that they were dealing with banks whose deposits were properly secured. Once again, no action was taken, but Johnson had the satisfaction several years later of seeing a bill enacted embodying most of his features. Johnson might have gone much higher in Wisconsin politics, indeed even become governor, but he chose to get out of politics and even declined the Republican lieutenant governor nomination in 1877.

Two other areas in which the versatile Norwegian actively sought involvement were religion and education. Soon after moving to Madison Johnson became embroiled in a debate between conservative Norwegian Synod forces that insisted that Norwegian children attend Lutheran schools where the Lutheran catechism and the Norwegian language was taught, and the liberal forces that argued that Norwegian children should go to American public schools and get their religion in church. Predictably, Johnson sided with the liberals. The controversy became so heated that he quit the conservative Norwegian Lutheran Synod and in 1870 helped establish the Evangelical Lutheran Immanuel Church to reflect the new liberal theology and social philosophy. Today that church is known as the Bethel Lutheran Church and is the second largest Lutheran church in the U.S.

Throughout his life Johnson maintained a strong interest in education. One of the most enduring monuments to Johnson's educational interests is the University of Wisconsin Department of Scandinavian Studies. That department owes its beginning to an 1869 letter sent to U.W. President Paul A. Chadbourne in which Johnson urged that courses in Scandinavian languages be offered and that Rasmus Anderson, then an instructor at Albion Academy, should be considered to head the new department. A few days later Chadbourne replied on behalf of the Regents saying that the idea would be implemented. In 1870 Johnson's protege, Rasmus Anderson, became the first instructor of Norwegian at an institution of higher learning in the United States. Johnson then raised money to stock the U.W. library with Norwegian books for the new program. Later in his life Johnson set up one of the first scholarship programs available to women at the U.W. and made his factory dining room available to a kindergarten teacher so that employee and neighborhood children could benefit from this new form of education. All four of his children received U.W. degrees.

Johnson's two greatest business achievements were the Fuller and Johnson Manufacturing Company and the Gisholt Machine Tool Company. Both stories are told in the text of this chapter.

Johnson's experience in running these two enterprises earned him a reputation as a model employer. During his nearly twenty years at the helm of both Fuller and Johnson and Gisholt, he never had a strike. Unlike most of his fellow industrialists, Johnson said that workers deserved higher wages and better working conditions. In 1881 he even sided with workers in the Eau Claire saw mill strike. To Johnson, the workers, mostly Norwegians, were being exploited by rich factory owners. Though he abhorred strikes as wasteful, he defended the workers right to strike: "If manufacturers and railroads can meet to determine their prices, so can labor," he concluded. Johnson was alone among Madison employers in providing cheap rental housing for his employees.

When Johnson implemented an employee profit-sharing plan in 1895, he may have been the third employer in the country to do so. Though limited to supervisors it was a radical proposal at the time and reflected Johnson's belief that workers had to have a larger stake in the business. When the new Gisholt factory was built in 1899 Johnson incorporated worker-oriented procedures and facilities rarely found at the time. For example, workers were encouraged to submit written suggestions to management. The plant had a library, a lunch room, locker rooms with hot and cold running water, and an auditorium for employee entertainment and educational events. That Johnson enjoyed excellent rapport with his men was hardly surprising.

From the 1880s until his death in 1901, Johnson continued his intense early interest in public policy questions, though in these last two decades his interests shifted to foreign and economic policy. Through major U.S. daily newspapers, periodical articles, speeches and pamphlets, Johnson forcefully expressed his concerns about such issues as cheap Sumatran tobacco, the tariff, gold backing for paper currency, the Philippines, relations with South America, and a subsidized merchant marine. Johnson was instrumental in founding the National Association of Agricultural Implement and Vehicle Manufacturers of the United States of America— an industry lobbying organization. In his 1897 presidential address to that organization, he eloquently stated his belief that Americans were destined to be the greatest manufacturing people in history.

When Johnson died on November 10, 1901, following his failure to recover from the removal of his ulcerated stomach at the Mayo Clinic, he was widely mourned. The versatile Norwegian immigrant left a rich legacy of achievements. But above all else it was John A. Johnson who made manufacturing a significant component of Madison's economy. When he died his two factories on East Washington Avenue employed more than six hundred men, easily the largest employer in the city, and their products were known not only in the United States but in many parts of the world.

But more important was the unusually good publicity the company received from trade periodicals. From this exposure several sizable orders had come in from European companies. Heartened by these developments, Johnson boldly established franchise sales agencies in Boston, New York, Pittsburgh, and Leipzig, Germany. Finally in 1895 the company showed a profit for the first time. In 1897, Johnson sent Frederick to Berlin to open the first European branch office. As the orders began pouring in in the late 1890s, the little belt-powered factory proved utterly inadequate. In 1899 Madisonians watched a large new seventy-five thousand dollar factory go up in the 1200 block of East Washington Avenue. Then in 1900 at the World's Fair in Paris, Gisholt lathes won a coveted gold medal against the best machine tool companies in the world. Probably no award in his distinguished career meant more to John A. Johnson. Not only was the gold medal an affirmation of his high standards and his long cherished belief in the "rightness" of the machine tool business, but also a virtual assurance that his sons would have a flourishing business they could carry on in his absence. Indeed, Johnson's failing health prevented him from being at Paris to receive the award, but his sons were. Johnson died fifteen months after his sons had accepted the gold medal on his behalf.

Problems, Opposition, and Apathy: The Perils of Factory Building in Madison

The success of the Fuller and Johnson and Gisholt companies is even more impressive when high freight rates, local business conservatism, city opposition, and a shortage of skilled labor are taken into account. "The interstate law," said John A. Johnson in 1890, "has crippled all our inland manufacturers. They cannot compete with lake-board cities like Chicago and Milwaukee. In the great item of freight, there is a discrimination that works immensely to the disadvantage of cities like Madison. Then there are the items of coal and lumber. Milwaukee gets all her coal by the

FIGURE 5.9. FULLER AND JOHNSON PLANT. This lithograph shows the Fuller and Johnson Manufacturing Company about 1902. The small building in the foreground is the main office at the intersection of East Washington and North Dickinson. It still stands and is now used as a restaurant. With few exceptions, all of the other Fuller and Johnson factory buildings have been torn down and replaced with newer buildings. Curiously the artist showed a train running *along* East Washington Avenue when he should have shown the tracks crossing East Washington Avenue. In the left foreground are two single-story buildings with clerestory roofs that once housed the fledgling Gisholt Machine Company factory. The rope power train described in the text, ran from the Gisholt building nearest North Dickinson Street (foreground) to the very long building immediately across from it. The railroad boxcars shown between the old Gisholt buildings and the Fuller and Johnson complex ran along East Mifflin Street although that street was never extended beyond North Dickinson. At the time of this lithograph, the factory covered about twenty acres of land, had about 400,000 square feet under roof, and provided work for about four hundred employees.

Shop visitors were impressed by the sight of molten metal being poured into a hundred forms, thick steel being bent, punched, pressed, bored, planed and polished and stubborn oak being coaxed almost into right angles for plow handles. (SHSW, WHi(X3)35540)

way of the lakes, also her lumber. Our lumber reached Milwaukee by water, then we have to pay high railroad freight rates to this point. The same is true with our iron and coal. We are almost swamped by these freight rates," he told a reporter.[57] A Fuller and Johnson insider said that Madison freight rates amounted to a tax of three percent of its products, which did not have to be paid by Milwaukee manufacturers.[58]

Johnson was also very critical of the apathy and even opposition of Madison leaders to industry. In the spring of 1889 just after the Norwegian industrialist had incorporated the Gisholt Machine Company, he asked the Madison Businessmen's Club to give his fledgling company five thousand dollars as a start-up bonus and another five thousand for each twenty-five thousand dollars of new annual business the company generated up to one hundred thousand dollars. The

club, composed of Madison's wealthiest men, did not even bother to appoint a committee to look into the matter. This slight naturally angered Johnson, who then proceeded to finance the venture entirely on his own. It was just such "sneers and flings . . . from members of the Businessmen's Club that has a sort of wet blanket effect on the establishment of manufacturing enterprises here," said Johnson not long afterward.[59] Johnson noted that such bonuses were very common among the more wide-awake cities elsewhere in the country but not in Madison.[60]

Behind the "conservatism" of Madison's business leaders so criticized by Johnson was a very strong current of outright opposition to factories, particularly from members of Madison's professional and educational communities. Though such sentiments rarely found their way into Madison's daily newspapers because both editors were pro-factory, there can be no doubt that an 1889 description of Madison appearing in *Harper's Weekly* reflected the sentiments of a large influential group of opinion makers. "Like every Western town possessed of unusual railroad facilities," the author began, "Madison is at intervals seized with the wish to become a great manufacturing center. To my mind this is a mistake. Any town that has railroads and pluck and enterprise . . . can grow into a manufacturing center; few towns, however, can become beautiful and learned, or can achieve social distinction. . . . Madison can of course darken her skies with the smoke of countless furnaces, and cover her vacant lots with long rows of tenement houses, if she so wills it. . . . It would be a great pity if she did so, however, for the industrial West can ill afford to sacrifice those shining qualities that have made Madison famous for the paltry sake of a larger census return and the sale of a few acres of vacant land. Madison ought to be content as well as proud of her present. She is rich and prosperous and cultured; let her exist for the sake of being beautiful," he concluded.[61]

A third very serious problem Johnson faced was an inadequate supply of skilled labor. The shortage forced Johnson to develop a sophisticated apprentice program—almost a trade

Plant of
Northern Electrical Mfg Co.
MADISON, WIS.
U.S.A.

FIGURE 5.10. NORTHERN ELECTRICAL MANUFACTURING COMPANY. In 1895 Conrad M. Conradson, the mechanical genius who designed the highly successful Gisholt turret lathes, lost interest in that type of machinery and began working on electric motors. Fuller and Johnson president, John A. Johnson, reluctantly but wisely decided to let the talented Conradson go. Immediately after leaving the employ of Fuller and Johnson, Conradson plus three other men, William F. Vilas, A.O. Fox and D. Jackson, formed a new corporation known as the Northern Electrical Manufacturing Company with a capital stock of $50,000. With the proceeds they bought an entire block of low marshy land bounded by East Wilson, South Dickinson, Railroad Street and Thornton Avenue. After filling in the block the owners erected a factory, shown above in the birdseye view of their plant as it appeared in 1902. Most of the buildings are still standing but are now used for another purpose. The large residential-looking building on the right, once a well-known mansion, still stands but a commercial building has been squeezed between it and the intersection. The street in the foreground is South Dickinson; the train on the right is running along what would be East Wilson Street.

By 1902 the Northern Electrical Manufacturing Company was providing employment for 350 employees and doing over one million dollars in volume each year. Many of their workers bought or rented housing along Williamson, Jenifer, and Spaight Streets, in what now is known as the Marquette area.

school—and even place ads for experienced machinists in Norwegian and German newspapers.[62]

Given all these problems, Johnson could easily have decided to leave Madison, but he did not do this for several reasons.[63] Johnson loved his adopted city and was intensely loyal of it.[64] He liked its size, the stimulating university influence, and the Madison lakes probably reminded him of Lake Norsjø where he had grown up. Johnson had planted deep roots in Madison; by 1890 he had lived in the city for twenty-three years and had raised his children there. On the business side of the ledger, an excellent railroad network linked his factory to all his markets, even if the rates were high. Finally, Johnson had spent considerable time and money developing a good, dependable, nonunionized labor force.

The Legacy of John A. Johnson

The growth of John A. Johnson's two large factories had two very important enduring effects upon Madison. First, the location of his factories established a land use pattern that prevailed until the middle of the twentieth century, namely the use of The Great Central Marsh for manufacturing. An 1883 *Wisconsin State Journal* editorial could not have made the point more plainly when it argued that ". . . the (east) marsh is the natural seat for manufacturing industries . . . for land is cheap and plenty there for railroad, warehouse and factory purposes."[65] From this time forward, there appears to have been a strong consensus—indeed it was almost a foregone conclusion—that this area would become "the factory district." Most Madisonians seem to have believed that smokestacks would soon displace the cattails.[66]

Second, Johnson's factories attracted a highly skilled and therefore well-paid labor force. An 1888 analysis of wages paid in Wisconsin cities and villages showed that of the fifteen largest cities in Wisconsin at that time, Madison had the highest per capita wages. The State Commissioner on Labor Statistics attributed this to the large number of persons in the Madison workforce employed in high-paying industries such as machine shops and agricultural implement factories, the steadiness of employment at such establishments, and the fact that just ten percent of the total work force were more poorly paid women. Relatively well-paid printers and railroad workers, each constituting a sizable part of the Madison labor force, also boosted the citywide averages, according to the commissioner.[67]

Other Industries

Although the factories out on Great Central Marsh started by John A. Johnson or his former employees were without a doubt the largest and most glamorous manufacturing enterprises, smaller Madison factories produced corsets, bicycles, cigars, beer, flour, soap, lumber, printing presses, socks and underwear, meat, telephones, harnesses, and horse collars.[68]

In addition to these minor manufacturing enterprises, there were two processing businesses that provided relatively large numbers of jobs: tobacco and ice. From the time statistics were begun in 1874 until the 1940s, Dane County was the largest producer of tobacco in the state. Between 1874 and 1884 tobacco acreage in the state increased almost eleven times.[69] Yet Madison failed to become a major center for tobacco processing. Smaller communities such as Edgerton in the center of the tobacco-growing area quickly assumed dominance in the tobacco processing industry while Milwaukee became the major manufacturer of cigars, the principal use for Wisconsin tobacco at that time. These developments occurred just when Madison became the centering point for nine railroad lines and naturally led to queries about why Madison wouldn't get its fair share of the tobacco trade.

Although Madison never came close to dominating this specialty crop, several Madison entrepreneurs quickly found ways to profit by it. One

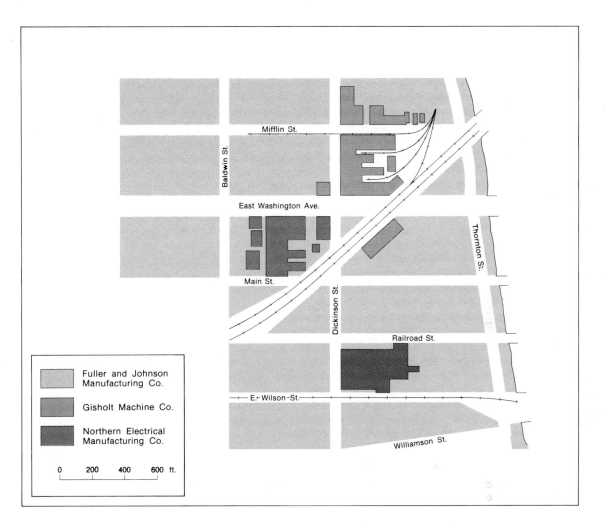

FIGURE 5.11. THE 1900 FACTORY DISTRICT. This map shows the "big three" manufacturing establishments, which in the late 1890s constituted the nucleus of Madison's "Factory District." The three firms were the Fuller and Johnson Manufacturing Company, the Gisholt Machine Company, and the Northern Electric Company. Around the turn of the century, these three factories occupied about 650,000 square feet under roof and provided employment for about nine hundred workers.

Between 1890 and 1910 these factories were a major factor in the rapid growth in population of the Second and Sixth Wards, now the Second and Sixth Districts.

The Sixth Ward was a particularly attractive residential area for factory workers who between 1885 and 1900 were largely responsible for that area growing twice as fast as the city at large.

group of entrepreneurs started tobacco sorting warehouses, the first opening in 1880. By 1885 the number of tobacco sorting warehouses had risen to three and by 1893 as much as one-eighth of the total Wisconsin crop was handled in Madison through warehouses employing two hundred persons.[70] Another group started cigar factories. By 1892 seven such factories were turning out the then popular short, black cigars.[71] Rapid and impressive though the rise of tobacco growing, processing, and manufacturing were in the nineteenth century, the industry was destined to grow even more rapidly in the early years of the twentieth century.

Commercial ice harvesting in Madison began in the later 1870s and matured into a large and well-established business in the 1880s and 1890s. In many ways it was an ideal industry for Madison since it provided work at precisely that time of year when many were out of work.[72] Weather conditions caused the ice harvest to vary substantially from year to year, but even in slow years hundreds of men could get a well-paying job during the four- to six-week harvesting season. During boom years such as 1890, fifteen hundred men were employed on Lake Mendota alone. In that year three hundred thousand tons of ice were cut from the Madison lakes. About half was shipped out immediately to Chicago, New Orleans, and many smaller cities whereas the other half was placed in nine local ice houses for summer export.[73]

From the time the private sewers began discharging their contents into the lakes in any quantity, ice quality suffered. In December 1886, the Common Council passed an ordinance prohibiting the cutting of ice closer than thirteen hundred feet from the outfall of the sewers. Since most of the city's sewage went into Lake Monona, Madisonians quickly refused to buy ice from that lake, referring to it as "that horrid stuff." Consequently ice dealers sent it to Chicago where it was nearly always accepted.[74]

Labor Unions: 1880–1900

With the exception of a few brief bursts of activity, Madison manifested very little unionism during the last two decades of the nineteenth century. Still, what began during that period had enduring effects. The year 1893 marked the beginning of a widespread, organized labor movement in Madison. In that year Milwaukee union organizers formed the Federated Trades Council (the forerunner of the Madison Federation of Labor), organized heretofore unorganized trades, and celebrated the first labor day.[75]

Soon after the formation of the Federated Trades Council, two of Madison's twelve unions decided to go on strike—the printers in January and the carpenters in May. Unfortunately for union organizers, the union cause was strongly opposed by both the Republican-oriented *Wisconsin State Journal* and the Democratically aligned *Madison Democrat*. The *Journal* denounced "the movement of the trades in Madison toward organization with demands for higher wages," and said it was the "logical and natural outgrowth of the doctrine and preaching [of] tonguey Democratic demagogues" during the 1892 election.[76] Conservative *Democrat* editor O. D. Brandenburg had a more difficult problem. His Democratic politics prevented him from opposing unionization on doctrinal grounds. Instead he isolated certain union demands for his fierce attacks. For example, Brandenburg maligned the closed shop as "the embodiment of arrogance," and "an insult to intelligence, a slap at progress and an outrage on decency. . . ."[77] His problem was compounded by the fact that the printers' strike was against his own Democrat Printing Company. However, Brandenburg solved the problem in a then common and straightforward way: he brought in another set of "union" workers from Nebraska and gave them all jobs for two years.[78] The carpenters' strike "fizzled out" after just one week when faced with one hundred eager strike breakers and a rapidly deteriorating economy in the summer of 1893. Indeed the depression that set in very quickly in that summer created pressures that caused many of the newly formed and even older, well-established unions to disintegrate.

The brief flurry of union activity in 1893 and then again in 1895 was not without enduring results. The Federation of Labor prevailed but was limited to providing guidance and encouragement to Madison's small and still weak unions. But it was not until after the turn of the century that the power of the Madison Federation of Labor and its component unions became a force with which to be reckoned.

Athens of the West: Madison as an Educational Center

"We are having a great boom on the hill just now," observed U.W. President Thomas C. Chamberlin at the beginning of the 1889 fall term.[79] Chamberlin was understandably elated by the rapid increase in the number of students who began flocking to the university under his leadership and by legislative passage of several key bills that gave the ambitious administrator the power to establish four separate colleges (letters and science, mechanics and engineering, agriculture, and law, plus any others he or his successors might from time to time find necessary). The bills were an expression of confidence in the new president, but also a reflection of the people's commitment to the university.[80]

Before assuming the U.W. presidency in 1887, Chamberlin had headed the Wisconsin Geological Survey and was a nationally recognized expert on glaciers. Some said his personality was as icy as his subject specialty, yet it was not his coolness or aloofness for which he was remembered. Rather it was the single-minded skill and speed with which he converted a small liberal arts college into a true university. Chamberlin also enjoyed great success in the academic marketplace and was particularly effective in hiring the finest scholars in the country—glittering academic stars—to serve on the U.W. faculty.[81]

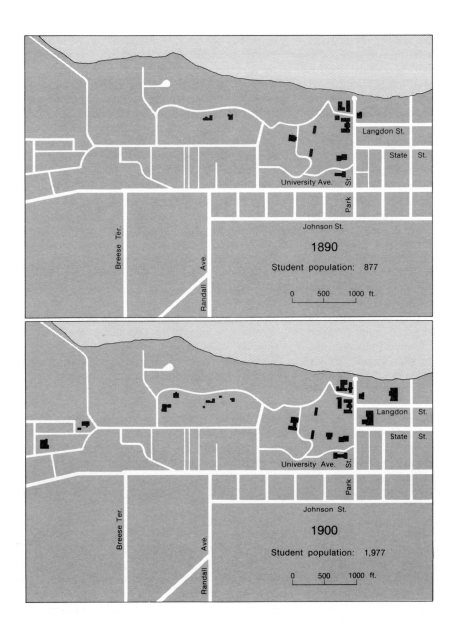

1890

Student population: 877

0   500   1000 ft.

1900

Student population: 1,977

0   500   1000 ft.

FIGURE 5.12. U.W. GROWTH.   Between 1865 and 1885 the size of the University of Wisconsin fluctuated between three hundred and five hundred students. But between 1887 and 1900 the number of U.W. students quadrupled from five hundred to two thousand. To provide facilities for this rapidly expanding student body, a major building program was undertaken. The two maps show the large amount of new construction during 1890–1900 decade.

Among the buildings erected between 1887 and 1900 were: Science Hall, 550 North Park (1887); Hiram Smith Hall, 1545 Observatory Drive, (1891); Old Law School, Bascom Hill (1893); Old Red Gym, 716 Langdon Street (1894); the Camp Randall grandstand (1896); the Dairy Barn, 1915 Linden Drive (1897); the Horse Barn (1897); 520 Elm Drive (1899); the Education Building, 1000 Bascom Mall (1899); and the State Historical Society of Wisconsin-UW Library (1900). Cost of U.W. buildings built between 1887 and 1900 exceeded $1.7 million dollars. Relatively large portions of this total were made during the 1893-5 depression, which helped keep building trades workers busy and the affects of the depression more mild than it otherwise would have been. Also during this period the University bought a one-hundred-sixty-acre farm from H. H. Hill for $13,000. The farm was later plotted for the Hillfarm Subdivision and the Hilldale Shopping Center.

Very significantly, there was one type of building that was deliberately not included in the ambitious new building program: student dormitories. With the exception of Chadbourne (Ladies) Hall built in 1870, the University of Wisconsin built no dormitories for its students until the 1930s. This policy was established largely by President Chamberlin who believed that large groups of young men living under the same roof encouraged those "peculiar rowdy practices which characterized—and perhaps it is not too strong to say—disgrace college life." Moreover, Chamberlin, Adams, and their successors did not feel they could get money from the legislators for both dormitories and instructional facilities. Therefore, all U.W. students with the exception of the small number of whom lived in Ladies Hall lived off campus. Most lived in rooming houses but beginning in 1888 fraternity and sorority members—for the most part the wealthier students—began to build their own chapter houses. By 1894, ten of the thirteen Greek organizations had their own chapter houses. Thus during this period, students began to dominate the area around the university, then called the Fifth Ward, now the Fifth District, and the area became known as the "Latin Quarter." Students were largely responsible for the Fifth Ward growing twice as fast as the city at large.

What Chamberlin began, his successor, Charles Kendall Adams (1892–1903), continued. Like Chamberlin, Adams was highly successful in coaxing large amounts of money from the legislature. Under Adams, the University of Wisconsin probably became the most generously funded state university anywhere in the Midwest.[82]

During the Chamberlin-Adams era the University of Wisconsin grew very rapidly. Between 1887 and 1896 the faculty grew from 40 to 113. Between 1887 and 1900 the student population quadrupled, zooming from five hundred to two thousand. By 1900 nearly one out of ten persons in Madison was either a U.W. student or a faculty member.[83]

With this growth in size, the university began to exert a greater community influence. For the first time the university, long a source of intense community pride, had demonstrated its ability to become a significant and possibly the major growth generator for the city. Although nearly everyone agreed that the university would play the lead role in making Madison an educational center, most recognized that other institutions such as the Washburn Observatory, the State Law Library, and the Historical Society would also contribute. In addition, there were summer educational programs such as the Monona Sunday School Assembly, a local chataqua, and the Columbian Catholic Summer School, its Catholic counterpart. It was this cluster of institutions that prompted some to start calling Madison the "Athens of the West," and some still hoped that Madison would develop as "The Oxford of America."[84]

To many persons, particularly those in the professional and educational communities, this elite, intellectual image was infinitely more flattering and distinctive than being a factory town, full of "grimy workers." That this image of Madison was a "great educational center"[85] was the preferred future among many Madison opinion makers is clear from dozens of sources.[86] U.W. President Charles Kendall Adams placed the full weight of his office behind this image when he said that Madison was "not a business city and should not be boomed in a business direction."[87] Former governor and Civil War hero Lucius Fairchild said he wanted Madison to "boom" but not as a result of factories. In his words: "Give me the University rather than forty factories."[88] Ironically, Athens of the West proponents were in the enviable position of doing little and yet watching the university balloon before their eyes.

Among the many influences of the U.W. during this period was an intensification of a community ethos that emphasized intellectual, cultural, and literary values. Student debates, professors' papers, and visiting lecturers gave Madison what one resident of the period called "the hum of culture" and what others called "cosmopolitan" flavor.[89] To get in step with this brisk cerebral cadence, churches sought ministers whose intellect and speaking ability caused them to be viewed as peers by Madisonians of achievement.[90] Each established neighborhood and each new suburb that desired to increase its stature had at least one literary society.[91] Public school superintendents tailored the curriculum of the Madison high school so that its graduates could excel at the university.[92]

The presence of the university caused certain values, such as a strong strain of antimaterialism and a deep appreciation for intellectual achievement and beauty, to be much stronger than they otherwise would have been. "Nowhere have I seen less respect shown for the Almighty Dollar as in Madison," said an astute faculty wife who moved to Madison in 1896. "When our only rich heiress married a poor man with brains," she continued, "it was considered eminently suitable; not so when a member of one of the honored old families married a rich man without any intellectual distinction."[93] U.W. President C. K. Adams applauded the fact that Madison's "material interests" were "sacrificed so the city could become a place of culture."[94] This same strain of antimaterialism was often expressed as opposition to factories.[95] Such sentiments were not based on antimaterialism alone. They were also based upon a love of beauty and a feeling that Madison could not be both a factory town and beautiful at the same time. In the words of one observer, Madisonians "loved the town and did not want it spoiled for the sake of Big Business."[96] One must wonder whether in the absence of such university-nurtured values Madison would have become a conventional factory town as did many other state capitals well served by a railway network.

As the number of students and faculty increased, so did the economic impact of the university on the community. As early as 1890 a community leader boasted that each year the presence of the university caused a half million dollars to be pumped into the city's economy.[97] At first many Madisonians were skeptical about the relative contribution of student spending to this amount, but their understanding harkened back to a time when many university students were poor almost by definition. During the 1890s, however, U.W. President Adams made a conscious and ultimately successful effort to attract wealthier students to the university.[98] Consequently more and more students spent their money for fancy goods and services. For example, by 1899 the *Journal* could document the fact that Madison was the "best dressed" city in the state and had more tailors than any other city except Milwaukee—a development they attributed almost solely to the fifteen hundred young gentlemen from the best families in the state who demanded the "most fashionable and well-made clothes."[99]

City policies and politics clearly reflected the influence of the university officials. In the mid 1880s President Bascom's outspoken belief that Madison's "saloon influence" made the city an unfit place for young men to get a college education added great impetus to efforts to close the saloons on Sunday and ultimately led to an 1897 ordinance the eliminated saloons in the immediate vicinity of the university.[100] Madison's first successful sewerage treatment plant was a direct result of a professor's eleventh-hour intervention—an initiative which constituted an early and significant expression of the Wisconsin Idea.[101] Direct student voting power was evident in local elections as early as 1888. From that early year on, students held the balance of power in the Fifth

Ward, although they did not always choose to vote.[102] Efforts to reform municipal government structure and operation received strong support from university officials including President Adams.[103] Partly in response to local reform initiatives, university professors ran for alderman and ultimately served on the council. Though the number of professors in local politics were few, they played a large role in key policy decisions,

---

A New York Reporter's View
of Madison, 1887

Madison is a town well calculated for the weary travellers to find some rest in. Like most capital cities, it has no business and can boast only of its pretty situation among half a dozen sheets of water. It is a little country town, pure and simple. Its good folks dine at midday and read the newspapers only as a source for fault-finding and general scandal. In the principal streets of the town, which have not changed their appearance in years, the people pass by slowly, quietly and sedately. There is no sign of hurry nor thought of change. To count the flagstones or the bricks in the sidewalks seems their whole duty. The storekeepers dawdle and yawn before their open stores. The old houses have the air of being bored. Nobody troubles himself about the time of day. If the town clock were to stop the citizens of Madison would never know the difference. Such is the city and the surroundings among which Postmaster-General Vilas was reared and to which he has invited the President.

This disapproving description, which appeared in the *New York Tribune* on October 7, 1887, was written during President Grover Cleveland's visit to Madison. While in the city, the president stayed at the home of his Postmaster General, William Freeman Vilas.

---

especially on matters involving technical expertise.[104] University officials and professors also played a leading role on the Madison Park and Pleasure Drive Association, an organization that was almost single-handedly responsible for Madison's outstanding early park system.[105] A final effect of university presence in the community was its dominant role in providing spectator sports. Following the rise of organized athletics in the 1890s, Madisonians had their choice of following several sports. Clearly, football drew the biggest crowds, followed at a distance by baseball, basketball, track, tennis, and crew.[106]

By the turn of the century some began to complain that university influence had reached undue proportions. Most, however, felt that university influence was beneficent and were therefore not bothered by its relative size.[107] In many ways the more important point was the relative ease with which university influence permeated so many aspects of community affairs. In many small college towns, sharp dividing lines separated town and gown, but for several reasons this schism did not develop in Madison. First, Madison's leaders, specially those with New England roots, put great weight on the value of education generally and the prestigious university in particular. Second, the presence of a dense network of clubs and organizations brought the two communities together on a regular, friendly, and often purposeful basis. Finally, a disproportionate number of U.W. students came from Madison homes. In 1895, for example, Madison had less than one percent of the state's population, yet supplied twenty percent of all U.W. students.[108]

Booming and Building: The Growth
of Methodical Madison

Population and Density Changes

"Madison never booms," said a *Wisconsin State Journal* reporter in summarizing the developments for the year 1885. "It simply pushes steadily forward in a safe conservative way. . . ."[1]

Such statements were common throughout the 1880s, particularly after federal and state census counts had been completed. Clearly there was nothing in the 1880, 1885, 1890, or 1895 census to get anyone excited. The 1880 census had shown that Madison's population had grown to 10,761, roughly the same population the city enjoyed at the peak of the Farwell boom in 1857. Between 1880 and 1890 an average of only 310 persons were added to Madison's population for an annual average growth rate of 3.1%. The average annual growth rate between 1890 and 1895 was little better: just 3.2%. Not until the 1895–1900 period did the growth rate begin to satisfy those who wished to boom the city. During this five-year period the average annual growth rate rose to 4.6%. By 1900, "methodical Madison"[2] had reached a population of 19,164, an increase of 23% in just five years and an increase of 86% in twenty years.[3]

Since the land area within the incorporated city limits remained at 4.7 square miles throughout the last two decades of the nineteenth century, the increase in population meant a substantial increase in density from 2197 persons per square mile in 1880 to 4077 persons per square mile in 1900, an increase of 86%. Thus in twenty years, both population and density nearly doubled. These facts coupled with social and economic developments were responsible for several very significant land use changes.[4]

The Suburban Boom

"Upon nearly every street in the city, the cheerful clatter of the builders has been noticeable throughout the season just drawn to a close," noted a *Wisconsin State Journal* reporter in December 1883. "Many a gap in desirable blocks has been filled up, many a new street opened to a colony of new dwellings, many a new pioneer residence has been planted in the heretofore-deserted thoroughfares in the outskirts; everywhere there are new houses."[5] This observation, though

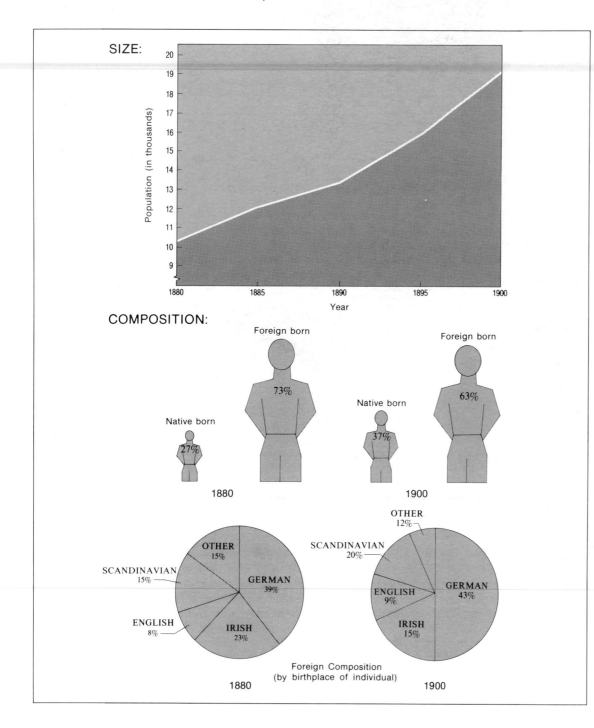

SIZE:

COMPOSITION:

Foreign born 73%

Native born 27%

1880

Native born 37%

Foreign born 63%

1900

OTHER 15%

SCANDINAVIAN 15%

GERMAN 39%

ENGLISH 8%

IRISH 23%

1880

OTHER 12%

SCANDINAVIAN 20%

GERMAN 43%

ENGLISH 9%

IRISH 15%

Foreign Composition
(by birthplace of individual)

1900

FIGURE 5.13. 1880 to 1900 DEMOGRAPHICS. During this two-decade period Madison population showed a moderately fast growth rate averaging 3.4% per year. The slowest growth rate occurred between 1885 and 1900 with an average annual rate of 2.3%; the fastest growth occurred between 1895 and 1900 with an average annual rate of 4.1%. In population composition, the number of foreign born and native born declined only slightly and the Germans continued to be the largest nationality.

limited to 1883 was in fact characteristic of Madison's new residential construction during most of the 1880s. With the exception of a slight dip in new construction in 1884, new construction between 1880 and 1887 remained remarkably constant, averaging about one-half million dollars each year.[6] New homes were being built out along Fourth Lake Ridge on East Johnson and East Dayton Streets. The removal of the slaughterhouses near the intersection of Jenifer Street and the Yahara River in 1888 and the conversion of the old village cemetery to Orton Park in 1887 opened up Third Lake Ridge for residential development.[7] Two factories at the intersection of Lake Street and Lake Mendota closed, launching an era when lower Langdon and State Streets could become as prestigious as its upper counterparts.[8] Elegant homes were added to the fancy neighborhoods along the Monona Avenue-Wilson Street area, Gilman and Langdon Streets, and at many other points around the city. As early as 1887 marshland that extended into residential areas was being filled to create more buildable lots.[9]

Gradually, however, after years of new residential construction, the number of desirable city residential lots declined. Increasingly "inside" city lots available at attractive prices were near factories, marshes, and railroad tracks, and the remaining desirable "inside" lots tended to be expensive. Madison had reached a critical juncture in its history.

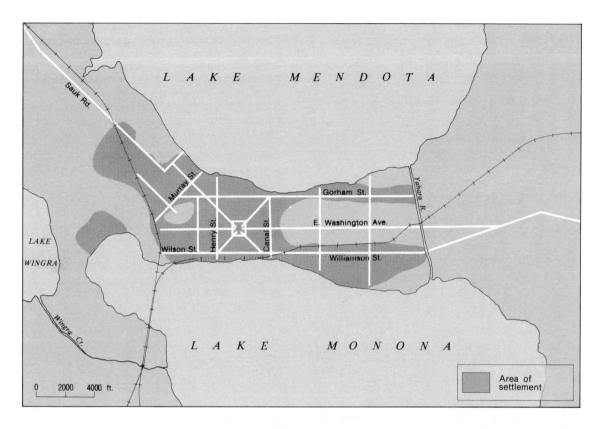

FIGURE 5.14. 1889 SETTLEMENT PATTERNS.   By 1889 Madison had grown about as much as it could without filling in marshes and lakeshores and moving out to suburban land. This map shows settlement patterns as reflected by a very detailed Angell and Hastreiter map published in 1889. As noted in the section on "Booming and Building," Madison developers began extensive marsh filling and suburban platting during the 1890s.

In the nineteen-year period between 1870 and 1889 only one new suburban plat had been recorded. Then in 1889 six Madison developers suddenly opened up new suburban plats. These developers recognized what soon became evident to many other Madisonians: the city was getting built up to the point where growing numbers of homebuyers were looking for a cheaper, better alternative to "inside lots" as lots within the incorporated limits were then called. What encouraged these developers was that between 1880 and 1887 the number of new housing starts had

been high and demand was apparently running ahead of supply.

One of the developers to open a suburban subdivision in 1889 was Madison realtor W. T. Fish, who bought a 104-acre farm on the west end of town. Three months later he was advertising "cheap lots" in a new suburb called "Wingra Park." Unfortunately, just as Fish opened up his 380-lot subdivision for sales, the national economy began to sag. The slumping economy coupled with the lack of streetcar service kept lot sales at very low levels for nearly ten years.[10] Fish and the other developers who opened subdivisions in

1889 were all caught in circumstances over which they had limited control. Still, apart from timing, they were fundamentally correct in their assessment of the market trends: Madisonians would eventually start buying lots outside city limits.

Just two years after Fish placed his Wingra Park subdivision on the market, another developer began a series of bold moves. In February 1891 a letter appeared in the Madison newspapers from a local realtor, John Lamont, secretary of the then unknown Madison Lakes Improvement Company. Lamont coolly announced the intent of his company to make Madison the Saratoga of the West.[11] The Madison Lakes Improvement Company was backed by a very wealthy syndicate allegedly worth "millions of dollars" consisting of capitalists from Chicago, St. Paul, and New England. Madisonians also learned that these men were not speculating on property sight unseen. Company representatives had been in Madison in the fall of 1890 and had concluded that the city had an exciting future as a great summer resort. In early 1891 for twenty thousand dollars the company obtained an option to buy a forty-two-acre parcel on the north shore of Lake Monona later known as Elmside. Less than a year before, the same parcel had been purchased by local investors for sixteen thousand dollars. Also in early 1891 the company obtained options on four other parcels around Lake Monona including the Tonyawatha Hotel. Having secured these options, company officials then left for Chicago, Louisville, St. Louis, New Orleans, and Jacksonville to interest investors in the exciting future of Madison and sell them stock in the company.[12]

Editors of both the *Madison Democrat* and the *Wisconsin State Journal* found the acquisitions of this mysterious company "almost too good to be true." Said the *Journal* on March 10, 1891: "The boom for Madison real estate due to the work of the Madison Lakes Improvement Company is evidently on . . . and it should be kept at white heat until the fame of these beautiful lakes is known throughout the country, and the shores of the lakes are dotted with beautiful homes."[13]

CHEAP HOMES!
WINGRA PARK

A few minutes' walk from the State University lies the beautiful tract of land now platted and known as WINGRA PARK. From this gently rolling upland there is a fine view of the University and City on the north and east, and of Lake Wingra on the south. Vacant resident lots in the city of Madison have increased in value nearly ten-fold within a few years past, and yet our citizens have been sending their money to St. Paul, Kansas City and other cities for investment. The city of Madison is growing rapidly in every direction, and room must be given for cheaper homes. To supply this demand, a limited number of lots in WINGRA PARK are now placed upon the market, at

Low Prices and on Easy Terms.
INQUIRE OF
WILLIAM T. FISH.

FIGURE 5.15. WINGRA PARK. In the summer of 1889 a Madison realtor, William T. Fish, bought a 108-acre farm on the west end of the city and on October 15 of that year this advertisement appeared in the *Wisconsin State Journal*. Fish divided the farm up into nearly four hundred lots, most of which were sixty-by-one hundred twenty feet in size. At first sales were slow, impeded by the fact that the plat was not served by street car and therefore required a thirty-minute walk from the capitol—not an unreasonable distance, but not yet that attractive compared to the relatively large number of closer-in lots available at competitive prices. The extension of the streetcar line out to Camp Randall in 1892 helped sales but it was not until the completion of the Wingra-Park Cemetery line in 1897 that the suburb really began to "boom." By the fall of 1898 residents were getting their mail delivered to their homes once a day, just like uptown.

Fish soon abandoned the "cheap home" emphasis in favor of a more elegant image. In 1891 he advertised Wingra Park as "Madison's fashionable suburb" and place for "elegant residences." Besides, Fish's advertising copy continued, "it is calculated that this property will double in value in three years; probably much sooner." Perhaps it was the new image, perhaps it was Fish's good timing—whatever the reason, by 1892 the *Wisconsin State Journal* said Wingra Park had become "the leading and most popular" suburb. According to that newspaper, its perfect drainage, pure air, and most excellent water attracted "some of our best citizens" who were building "costly residences."

In 1893 Fish sold his remaining lots to three new developers who formed the Wingra Park Advancement Association for the purpose of beautifying and improving the suburb. The association built a hall for members' social use and pushed for the installation of electric lights, city water, and the extension of the street car line.

HAVE YOU SEEN **ELMSIDE?**

YOU CAN SEE IT!
YOU MUST SEE IT! AND
YOU OUGHT TO SEE IT NOW!

YOU can go there by steamboat and see the prettiest lake property that has ever been platted in Wisconsin.

YOU can drive there in twelve minutes from the Capitol and it is the cheapest place to buy a summer home you ever saw

YOU can walk there in a short time along shaded streets and enjoy the exercise.

YOU can have M S ROWLEY, ADAMS & VERNON or G C ATCHISON, the agents of the Company, take you out there

And inside of a year you and all of your friends can go there on an

Electric Street Car Line

that will do business twelve months in a year

We do not wish to take a page of this paper to describe the beauties of Elmside, but have secured it for the purpose of inviting you to go and see for yourself.

HAVE YOU EVER THOUGHT that Two Railroads run near this property and that in the near future there will be two stations within hailing distance?

DID YOU KNOW that there will be a Summer Hotel at Elmside next season and that the plans are already drawn?

DID YOU KNOW that Elmside lots are offered at one-third price of lots of other summer resorts of inferior beauty?

DID YOU KNOW that Madison people are awake and buying them right along?

DID YOU KNOW **TONYAWATHA** Had been sold and will be managed by this Company and **OPENED NEXT MONTH**

DO NOT FORGET that Elmside borders on a lake that fairly swarms with fish and that there is no fishing ground in the state better than that afforded by the Madison lake

DO YOU KNOW that the tide of travel is coming this way in a perfect flood during the next two years.

DO YOU KNOW that the Madison Lakes Improvement Company has worked faithfully for a year upon a comprehensive scheme of lake improvement that will make the city and its surroundings a paradise when completed

WILL THE CITIZENS OF MADISON buy lake property that is worth more than its price, and while helping themselves, give the stimulus to a movement which has for its object the enlargement of their city and the adornment of its surroundings?

WE KNOW that every word on this page from top to bottom is absolutely true.

MADISON LAKES IMPROVEMENT CO.

FIGURE 5.16. ELMSIDE. Shown above is a June 1891, *Wisconsin State Journal* advertisement for Elmside, the first and most aggressively marketed subdivision of the Madison Lakes Improvement Company. During the summer of 1891 real estate dealers were reportedly kept busy all day long driving interested parties out to see the forty-two-acre suburb. Unfortunately, the suburb never really took off as developers had hoped and plans to build a large resort hotel were scrapped. Even the arrival of the electric streetcar at Elmside in October 1892, failed to generate lot sales. The advertisement is a superb example of "booming" in the early 1890s.

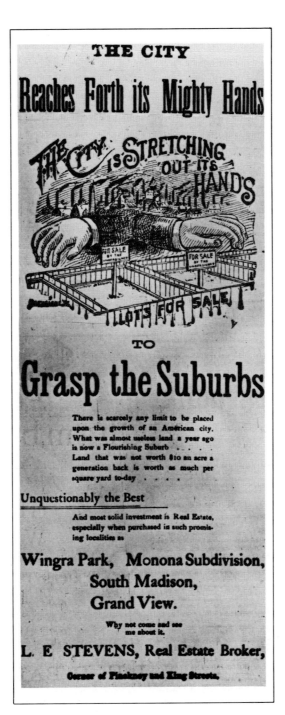

FIGURE 5.17. THE CITY REACHES FORTH ITS MIGHTY HANDS. This dramatic 1892 advertisement for suburban land contained an early version of the "escape" theme.

Many Madisonians, long accustomed to such booming tactics, were unconvinced and declared the whole thing a "fake." Perhaps this was true, responded the *Wisconsin State Journal,* but if so, we need "more such fakes in the city."

If the Madison Lakes Improvement Company was a fake, they were putting on a pretty good show. In May they sent surveyors to work marking off streets and lots. All summer long company officials drove prospective customers around the city in carriages to show them their properties. More Chicago and Milwaukee investors came to Madison that summer than informed observers had ever seen. When the company had their first annual meeting at Tonyawatha in August 1891, stockholders heard a flattering account of lot sales and company activities. By this time one-third of the stock was held by Madisonians who had become believers in the new enterprise whereas the rest was held by out-of-town investors.[14] By August 1891 a Madison realtor observed that suburban real estate was selling much more rapidly than property in the city and that more property was being sold outside the city than inside.[15] Never before in Madison's history had this been true.

In the wake of the apparent success of the Madison Lakes Improvement Company, local Madison investors decided that they, too, could develop suburban land and went on the biggest farm-buying binge in Madison's history up to that point. Between 1891 and 1899, 728 acres—more than half as much land as the original plat of 1360 acres—was platted and put on the market, giving Madison lot buyers a choice of 2204 lots.[16] For these small farms adjacent to Madison developers paid very high prices. For example, developers paid $476 per acre for Elmside, $1000 an acre for University Heights, and $2000 per acre for Willow Park.[17]

FIGURE 5.18. UNIVERSITY HEIGHTS. When a group of wealthy Madison men headed by W. T. Fish, the developer of Wingra Park, paid $106,000 for 106 acres of land just west of Camp Randall, then the Fairgrounds, in April 1893, Madisonians gasped in disbelief. Not only was the transaction one of the largest land sales in Madison's history, but the one-thousand-dollar per acre price was being eagerly paid by some of the most sober and conservative Madison businessmen. Yet these men and many others like them were confident in their ability to recover their investment. In just five years (1887–1892) University of Wisconsin student enrollment had risen from five hundred to one thousand and in 1892 the new electric streetcar line began running cars to within one block of their land. The men quickly formed the University Heights Company, had the site platted into 440 lots, and on Monday, May 22, 1893, opened for business. By close of business the following day, nearly one-third of their lots had been sold and by the end of the first week, one-half of the lots had new owners.

The developers were very fortunate in timing their entry into the market at the peak of the 1890-1893 suburban boom. Had they waited until the following year, or even later in 1893, lot sales at their new subdivision might have been much slower. As the 1893–94 depression edged into the city's economic life, lot sales slowed and nearly stopped. Between May 1893 and May 1895, only forty lots were sold.

At the bottom of the depression in 1894 Charles E. Buell, a local attorney, built the first home in the Heights, a large, modified Queen Ann design. That home, now a Madison landmark, is just barely visible at the top center of this 1898 photograph taken from the southwest corner of the Bascom Hall roof.

The street running along the base of the photograph was then known as Mary Street but was later changed to Charter Street. The street running diagonally on the lower right is Linden Drive. The diagonal street, which begins on the extreme left about half way between top and bottom and which runs along Camp Randall Stadium (then located where the Engineering Building was later built), is University Avenue. In this photograph, Breese Terrace (marked by a row of trees) appears to lie about halfway between the Camp Randall Board fence and the homes in the Heights. All of the homes in the foreground were removed in the 1920s to make room for the University Hospital complex.

By 1902 University Heights had a population of just seventy-five adults and sixty children. In that year, the suburb was described by residents as a place for "those who wish room for their children to romp and room to have a garden, lawn and shrubbery, and who love a wide prospect and a large sky." Its inhabitants were "sometimes surprised by this undeserved pity of friends who sympathized with their remoteness from the city. . . ." But, replied the resident, "electric cars reach the university in six minutes and church or theater in twelve, and the telephone brings near both markets and city friends."

University Heights was the first residential plat to use the curvilinear street layout, popularized by Frederick Law Olmstead's 1869 "romantic" Chicago suburb, Riverside. Unlike Olmstead's suburb, however, University Heights developers did not provide residents with a single park. Contrary to popular belief, University Heights was not the first plat in Madison to incorporate the curvilinear concept. That distinction went to a suburb for the dead, Forest Hill Cemetery, laid out in 1857. (SHSW WHi(X3)8612)

Several "push" and "pull" factors were responsible for this early wave of subdivision development. A growing number of Madisonians wanted large lots and, with most of the subdivisions of this period, got them. Already the practice of splitting a standard sixty-six-foot wide lot into two thirty-three-foot wide lots was common, leaving very small yards and eavetrough-to-eavetrough development. Madisonians wanted to avoid living next to the marshes, which were believed to breed malaria. Some Madisonians—especially the middle and upper income groups—were seeking neighborhoods where people were more like themselves. Suburbs offered more homogeneous enclaves of professionals and professors plus the greater prestige associated therewith. The very large amounts of suburban land placed on the market in a short period of time helped keep the suburban prices low. These factors coupled with rising prices for increasingly scarce but desirable "inside" property made suburban lots very cost competitive. The old problem of suburban inaccessibility had been solved in many cases by the establishment in 1892 of electric streetcar service. Finally, there was another very powerful "pull" factor—namely, the convenience and prestige of living beside one of Madison's lakes. For sixty years remarkably few had taken advantage of lakeshore living and then suddenly, in the 1890s, Madisonians discovered the joys of lakeside living.[18] In short, the suburbs offered larger lots far from malarial marshes and soot-belching locomotives, very competitive lot prices, the possibility of lakeshore living, and the prestige of socially and economically stratified neighborhoods.

In the words of an 1892 *Madison Democrat* editorial, "the city has at last put on its booming clothes and everyone will have to hustle to keep up with the pace."[19] Construction workers and building contractors had more business than they could handle and construction materials were in short supply.[20] Although the very serious depression of 1893–94 slowed and then entirely stopped platting activity, the recovering economy in 1895 brought a quick resurgence to Madison suburban development in the late 1890s.[21] Banks loaned money in larger quantities than ever before in Madison history. In 1900 new construction, a growing amount of which was in the suburbs, topped one million dollars for the first time in history, an increase of fifty-two percent over the 1899 rate and 111% over the 1898 rate.[22] Madisonians agreed, this was a pleasing way to finish the nineteenth century and begin the twentieth.

The availability of suburban land did not, as one might expect, kill the market for inside lots. On the contrary, the sale of inside lots, particularly in certain areas and for certain types of houses, seem to have enjoyed a boom of their own. Not everyone could afford a suburban lot and not everyone wanted to live "out there" even if they could. By the mid-nineties, vacant inside property was described as "very scarce."[23] Lots and existing homes in the prestigious and well-established areas increased rapidly in price.[24] Demand for rental housing was strong and housing stock for this market was in very short supply. One realtor said he could rent one hundred houses if they were available.[25]

The Streetcar as an Urban Sculptor

Until the streetcar arrived, Madison was a walking city. Only about twelve percent of Madisonians owned carriages and few others had enough money to keep their own horses.[26] Consequently, just about everybody walked everywhere. The only exceptions were persons who patronized hacks, cabs, and omnibuses, all of which were quite expensive and out of reach of the average worker for regular use.

The addition of the mule cars had virtually no effect on Madison as a walking city. During its last two years of operation (1891–92) only about four percent of Madison's population patronized the cars.[27] Not only was the mule car service infrequent and unreliable, but it was also slow—a fact that meant most persons could walk to their destinations faster than they could take the mule cars.

The electric streetcars, however, were in an entirely different league. Even the early models could go thirty miles per hour and could *accelerate* on the King Street hill. Their twelve- to sixteen-minute headways, reliable schedules, and line extensions meant that one could live much farther out and spend less time traveling to work. In fact, the electric streetcar was more than just a way to get around the city—it was also a powerful sculptor of urban shape and texture. Simultaneously it dispersed, concentrated, and stratified people.[28]

The 1892 Elmside and 1897 Cemetery line extensions showed the power of electric streetcar lines to open up large amounts of land to suburban development and disburse people. The end of the Elmside line was 2.5 miles from the Capitol Square, almost a mile beyond the outermost point of the old mule cars; yet a person living at this then very far-out location could ride to the Square on an electric trolley in just twelve to fifteen minutes.[29] The extension of the Elmside line meant that 1093 acres of land that lay up to four blocks away from the track were suddenly accessible and hence attractive for homesites.[30]

The 1.5-mile extension of the streetcar line in 1897 from the intersection of University Avenue and Park Street to the Forest Hill Cemetery also had profound land use implications. Counting the land four blocks on either side of the track extension, the cemetery line opened up 722 additional acres of prime land for development. The new line was a boon for already platted suburbs of Wingra Park and University Heights and sparked the beginning of extensive construction in both places. The *Madison Democrat* estimated that the streetcar line immediately enhanced the value of nearby property by ten to forty-five percent.[31]

Thus the combination of the Elmside and Cemetery line extensions opened up 1815 acres prime plattable land and launched an era of streetcar suburbs for the city. No longer did workers have to live within walking distance of their factory, shop, or office. The trolley changed

FIGURE 5.19. MADISON'S MULE CARS. Shown above is an 1884 photograph of one of Madison's first narrow gauge streetcars. Powered by two mules, the cars were fourteen feet long and seated twenty passengers in seats along the sides. Though not evident in this photograph the cars were "double enders," that is, the front and rear were identical so that when the driver reached the end of the line, all he had to do was unhitch the mules, attach them to the other end, and go back the other way. This simple system eliminated the need for expensive turntables. Unfortunately, these curvacious wooden cars proved too heavy for two mules to pull up the King Street hill, and so they had to be replaced by lighter ten-foot-long cars seating just fifteen persons. But even the ten-foot cars were very difficult for two mules to pull up the King Street hill and so a third mule would be added at the bottom of the hill. At the Capitol Square the driver would unhitch the third mule who would then walk back down the hill sometimes stopping along the way to nibble the weeds. But he would always be on time for the next car.

Although the cars were a problem on steep hills, they were remarkably nimble on level ground. Sometimes a frustrated streetcar driver would get stuck behind a slow-moving hay wagon whose driver refused to pull over. In those situations, the driver would pull his mules sharply to one side, which would throw the car off the track. The streetcar would then rumble down the gravel streets past the hay wagon whereupon the driver would maneuver the car back on the track again.

The man with the reins in his hands is probably Tom Shipway, who prior to being hired by Madison Street Railway Company was a stagecoach driver between Baraboo and the Wisconsin Dells, then called Kilbourn. Apparently Shipway and his fellow drivers were sometimes not very good at spotting passengers on side streets. The *Wisconsin State Journal* received numerous complaints from ladies who though yelling and running frantically toward the car waving handkerchiefs and parasols were ignored by the drivers who seemed more interested in snapping flies off their horses' backs with their whips. On other occasions, however, the drivers accommodated their passengers by running into a nearby store to get change. (SHSW WHi(X3)25110)

all that. For a dime a day (a nickel each way) a worker could live in the country and take the trolley to work. In short the street car helped Madisonians to get over their "rustic longing to be within three minutes walk of church and post office. People are beginning to realize," said a *Journal* article, "that they can exist out of shouting distance from the Square. . . .[32]

At the same time the streetcars were dispersing people across the countryside, they were causing an increasingly dense settlement of the downtown and close-in areas. The convergence of streetcar tracks on the Capitol Square virtually assured that this area would remain the dominant commercial area. No place in Madison was so easy to reach so cheaply. Between 1897 and 1899 two to three thousand Madisonians, most of whom were headed downtown, dropped their nickels in the fare box each day. The combination of streetcar passengers, the rural trade, and pedestrian traffic led to an intensified and expanded business district in the Capitol Square area. By 1901 the last vacant lot on Capitol Square was filled with a store—a monument in many ways to the business-generating power of the trolley.[33]

Although the primary commercial effect of the streetcar was in the central business district, trolleys also allowed and even encouraged *secondary* business centers. For example, it was not long after people learned that they could rely on the streetcars that commercial activity began to creep down State Street and at certain outlying points such as Schenks Corners.

The third and final effect of the streetcar was to stratify people. The large amount of suburban land that was placed on the market in a relatively short period of time allowed developers to sell lots to nearly every socio-economic group. At first many Madisonians felt that the suburbs would be a force in reforming society by opening up home ownership opportunities for the poor who could not afford costly "inside" lots.[34] These hopes, however, were quickly dashed when suburban lot prices rose in response to strong suburban demand fed in turn by the streetcar extensions. The same developer who boasted "cheap lots" in Wingra Park *before* the trolley arrived, changed his advertising tune after the trolley and began appealing to the middle class professional market. University Heights developers sold their lots for even loftier prices to upper income owners. The differences between Wingra Park and University Heights were clearly reflected in the cost of homes built in each. For example in the 1890s, homes between one thousand and fourteen hundred dollars were common in Wingra Park, whereas homes in the five- to nine-thousand dollar range were considered commonplace for University Heights.[35] In between these two suburbs were many others offering an almost exasperating array of prices and locations.

Most of the suburban lot buyers were seeking a similar product. They wanted a larger lot providing more privacy and prestige than they could buy in the city. They wanted a neighborhood where people were more like themselves, that is, much more stratified along socio-economic lines. In many cases the suburbs offered the happy combination of larger lots and more homogeneity at prices only slightly higher or, in some cases, even lower than inside lots. Again, it was the cheap, reliable streetcar that made all this possible.

Although the primary effect of the streetcar on suburban development was on the "pull" side, there was one sense in which the streetcar was a "push" factor. Soon after the streetcar became a familiar feature of Madison, people learned that streetcars were very noisy. Their motors and gears whined, their steel wheels thumped and clanked as they rolled over the steel rails, and their bells clanged. Consequently property along the streetcar lines became less desirable to the middle and upper end of the market. This in turn led to the construction of relatively inexpensive homes and apartments along these lines and encouraged the conversion of large homes into smaller units. In this sense, the streetcar pushed some to seek suburban alternatives.[36]

Figure 5.20a. Electric Streetcar Composite.   The car shown above was built in 1892 and then purchased by the Madison Traction Company in 1901. Although this photograph was taken in 1905, the car was typical of those in use immediately after the electric streetcars were installed in 1892. Cars of that vintage had the famous wine/glass cross-sections, clerestory roof windows, coal burning stoves (see stack immediately in front of the telephone pole), fancy wooden coachwork, and two-tone paint schemes with elegant pin-striping. This car was 28½ feet long, 8 feet wide and 10 feet tall and could seat twenty-four persons. It was used on the Wingra Park to Elmside line until 1917. Standing in front of the car are Superintendent George Holcomb and Conductor Charlie Kramer.

Though the new electric cars were the pride of the city, they were not without problems. Because their wheels were so close to the center of the car, a large number of people congregating at one end would actually cause the other end to go up in the air and derail the car. This was a favorite prank of University of Wisconsin students. Also city dogs, long accustomed to the lumbering mule cars, underestimated the speed of the fast electric cars—a fact that led to a sharp increase in the number of trolley-killed dogs during their first year of operation. (SHSW WHi(X3)35548)

FIGURE 5.20b.   Shown above is one of about ten open summer cars placed in service during the 1890s. This car is passing over the Harrison Street viaduct on the Wingra Park line not long after the line opened in 1897. The line served the growing suburbs of University Heights, Oakland Heights, and Wingra Park. This car had ten bench seats running across the car and was rated as a fifty-passenger car. During periods of peak demand, a similar motorless car would be attached to the rear giving a capacity of nearly one hundred persons. Such cars were extensively used for transporting huge crowds back and forth to the circus grounds and for refreshing summer rides.

The Age of Utilities, 1879–1899

Introduction

In an 1897 letter to the editor, a Madison man recalled his first sixteen years in the city. "Sixteen years ago I landed in Madison with my family," he began. "There were no waterworks, no electric lights, no streetcars, no standard telephones, (and) no sewerage. . . . The next year after my arrival the question of building waterworks was agitated and soon adopted, and after that step followed all the other improvements. Madisonians," he concluded, are possessed ". . . by the spirit of improvement and what the next 16 years shall bring about staggers the imagination. . . ."[1] The man had reason to be impressed for in the brief compass of two decades all of Madison's utility systems with the exception of the telegraph and gas works were built and developed. The Wisconsin Telephone Company opened its doors for business in 1879, the Madison City Waterworks began pumping in 1882, mule-powered street cars appeared in 1884 and electric trolleys in 1892, the Madison Electric Company started their generators in 1889, and a sewerage purification system got under way in 1899. Clearly, this was Madison's age of utilities.

Are You There, Charlie? The Telephone Reaches Madison

On August 17, 1877, just seventeen months after the famous conversation between Alexander Graham Bell and Thomas A. Watson ("Mr. Watson, come here, I want you"), Madison had its first telephone line installed. For the test, one telephone was set up at the Northwestern Telegraph Company offices, just opposite the Park Hotel on West Main Street, and another at the home of Mr. Charles Bross, telegraph manager, at 16 West Gorham. Present at the telegraph office were several local dignitaries and members of the press. First to test the equipment was a Professor Lovell who asked, "Are you there,

Those Amazing New Phones

One of the first businesses in Madison to install a telephone was the Kenzler Livery Stable (107-111 East Doty). Its owner, Andrew Kenzler, recognized that the presence of the new invention would be a great convenience to those who wanted to order horses. On the day the contrivance was first hooked up, a good friend happened to be in Kenzler's office and heard the liveryman complain that he had eaten too much sauerkraut. A short time later Kenzler's friend walked into the office of the Park Hotel manager, Phil Parsons. During their meeting Parsons had to place an order for a Kenzler horse for a hotel guest. That gave Kenzler's friend a great idea for a practical joke which the hotel manager agreed to carry out. Parsons called Kenzler, ordered the horse and then after Kenzler replied that he would have it ready and confirmed the arrangements, Parsons reprimanded Kenzler because his breath smelled of sauerkraut. Moments later an angry Kenzler called Charles Bross, the manager of the new telephone system and asked, "Why didn't you tell me your damned machine would carry a man's breath as well as his voice!" Bross reportedly had a very difficult time persuading Kenzler that only sound could be transmitted over the amazing contrivance.

Charlie?" to which Mr. Bross promptly answered, "Yes, all right."[2]

Few new inventions were so quickly and eagerly accepted as the telephone. By May 1879 the Bell Telephone Exchange, the predecessor of the Bell Company, began operation with just thirty subscribers. Since there were only five lines, each customer had from one to six rings.[3] By the end of the first year of operation Madison boasted about one hundred subscribers and long-distance connections with Eau Claire and Whitewater.[4]

Madisonians were thrilled by the telephone and described it as the "wonder of the age."[5] In the article describing the initial demonstration in

1877 the editor of the *Madison Democrat* happily contemplated people sitting in their homes on Sunday mornings getting sermons over the telephone. "This will do away with the expense of erecting churches, and save a great deal of dressing and fixing up. We can have the same mode of communication with the opera house. Make way for the telephone," he concluded.[6] Just imagine, said another editorial, "(omni) buses can be ordered from the bus barns, livery rigs, groceries, . . . dry goods, and in fact everything that is desired can be ordered through the telephone."[7] Indeed, that is just what happened, although at first only rich individuals and businesses could afford the twenty-five-dollar annual cost.[8] By October 1879 "all the principal business houses, depots, hotels, doctors' offices and residences, livery stables . . . were all reported connected with the central office and the benefits of having a telephone in one's house were described as "incalculable.'"[9] But the benefits of having a telephone went far beyond mere business communications. A customer could leave word with the operator to be awakened in the morning by the ringing of the telephone bell. Since very little telephone business was done on Sunday, the telephone company even connected lines between Madison, Whitewater, and Eau Claire so customers could hear a concert through their telephones.[10] The only problem with the Sunday telephone concerts was that only one person could listen to the headphone at a time. Fortunately this limitation was soon overcome by the newly patented Edison phonograph, which was first exhibited in Madison in 1878.

First to get a formal telephone franchise in Madison was the Wisconsin Telephone Company, an affiliate of the Bell System, in December 1882.[11] For thirteen years it had the field to itself, but, like many monopolies, the Wisconsin Telephone Company treated people badly. Rates were increased and any one who lived more than a mile from the business district had to pay a large hook-up charge. Protestations about poor service received a curt take-it-or-leave-it response.[12] Consequently, the company had grown slowly; by 1895 it had only 236 Madison subscribers.[13]

But then in 1894 the basic telephone patents held by the American Telephone Company (the Bell System) expired and the manufacture of telephone equipment and the operation of telephone systems were thrown open to competition. A small group of Madisonians saw the expiration of the Bell patents and the poor service of the Wisconsin Telephone Company as an exciting business opportunity. So, in 1895, they bought the majority stock in a small Minneapolis firm, the Standard Telephone and Electric Company, and transferred its operations to Madison. At the time the company was a manufacturer of oak-backed, wall-hung, crank-operated telephones, but the Madison investors had additional plans. Immediately after moving the company to Madison they formed the Dane County Telephone Company as a subsidiary of Standard Telephone and Electric Company. The idea was very simple: Standard Telephone would make the equipment, both for their new operating company and other telephone companies as well, while Dane County Telephone would begin head-to-head competition with Wisconsin Telephone Company.[14]

The new company cut Bell service charges in half and abandoned the extra charge for outlying customers so that the new suburbs of Wingra Park, South Madison, and Elmside could receive service at the same rate as those living in the central area. On the first day the Dane County Telephone Company offered its services to the public, eighty subscribers signed up. By January 1896, just seven months after it opened for business, the Dane County Telephone Company had four hundred subscribers, one hundred fifty more than the Wisconsin Telephone Company had signed up in thirteen years.[15]

The Wisconsin Telephone Company responded to this invasion of its territory by offering free telephone service to the mayor and many business and professional men.[16] But even these blandishments were insufficient to stem the tide of defections to the Dane County Telephone Company. Each year the new local company added hundreds of subscribers until by 1900 they

had eleven hundred fifty, whereas the Wisconsin Telephone Company had stagnated at just two hundred fifty.[17]

Madison daily papers almost fell over one another trying to say the nastiest things about the Wisconsin Telephone Company and the nicest things about the Dane County Company. It was a classic struggle between a big, outside monopoly and a small, local company.[18]

Finally in 1900 the Wisconsin Telephone Company decided to make its move and began a new round of rate cutting. In that year it began offering residential service for just twelve dollars a year, six dollars under Dane County Telephone Company rate. The Dane Company immediately got out a circular to subscribers reminding them that this was just a trick to kill the local company, after which they would resume their ruinous monopolistic rates.[19]

Still, even the *Wisconsin State Journal* had to admit, "this city no more needs two telephone plants than it needs two sets of water works or parallel driveways to Merrill Springs."[20] In the first place it forced Madisonians to select the Bell Company and talk to two hundred fifty subscribers, or select the Dane County system and talk to eleven hundred fifty persons. Few except the largest businesses and doctors could afford both.

Then there was a second problem, namely where to string all of the telephone wires. At first the Wisconsin Telephone Company strung its lines from housetop to housetop but this system was quickly abandoned in favor of a conventional curbside pole system.[21] In 1880 Madisonians thought telephone poles along residential streets were improvements that gave a street "quite a metropolitan air."[22] But once the telephone companies *and* the electric companies *and* the telegraph companies began to erect their own poles, Madison streets became a mass of drooping lines, and street edges became a battleground for utility company pole sites. Finally after much debate a comprehensive pole ordinance was passed in December 1897, which required wires to be hung minimum heights above the ground and required companies to share poles. This move got rid of

about six hundred poles throughout the city and eliminated the need for them on both sides of the streets.[23]

This rational solution worked well in residential areas but it did not solve the problem in the business district, where twenty to thirty wires were draped across the front of buildings around the Capitol Square, making it impossible for firemen to get ladders next to buildings to fight fires. Moreover the wires were an eyesore. These problems led to Madison's first underground utility conduit around the Square in 1899. Unfortunately, each utility insisted on building their *own* underground conduit, a decision that simply moved the battle for space underground. This system had the perverse consequence of keeping downtown streets torn up for years.[24]

Although the pole ordinances and underground conduits alleviated the visual and safety aspects of the problem, it hardly solved the underlying problem: too many telephone companies. Curiously, the two-telephone-company problem was not solved until 1907 when the Wisconsin Railroad Commission was given permission to regulate these utilities. Among other things the law required utilities to open their books to public scrutiny. This policy was the beginning of the end of utility competition because each company then knew what the other was doing and, of course, so did everyone else. Armed with its superior long-distance capabilities and ability to lower its rates below cost and keep them there, the Wisconsin Telephone Company began to make inroads against its competitor. The *coup de grace* came in January 1909 when a severe ice storm extensively damaged the lines of the independent company. Lacking the financial resources to repair the damage, the Dane County Telephone Company was forced to sell its assets to the Wisconsin Telephone Company. Madison had become a one telephone town.[25]

In 1915 the *Bell Telephone News,* a national news magazine of Bell affiliates, carried an article that credited Madison with having more telephones per capita than any other city in the country (about three out of ten persons had a

FIGURE 5.21. LOOKING NORTH ON SOUTH PINCKNEY STREET, 1885–1890. This quiet springtime street scene shows the elegant Capitol cast iron fence, which surrounded the Capitol grounds from 1872 to 1899. A portion of this fence now surrounds the Executive Residence in Maple Bluff. All buildings along the blockface on the immediate right have been replaced by the First Wisconsin Plaza. Just beyond the Pinckney-East Washington Avenue intersection is the handsome old sandstone building now occupied by the American Exchange Bank, then occupied by the First National Bank, the predecessor of the First Wisconsin Bank. (SHSW WHi(X3)35999)

phone at that time).[26] Ironically, this achievement was more a tribute to the Dane County Telephone Company than the Bell System, for it was the former company whose feisty competition with a national giant caused Madison telephone rates to be unusually low and the number of customers unusually high.

Madison Water Works: The City's First
Venture into Business

"No words can exaggerate the terrible condition of a large number of our wells, nor the evils that are likely to come on the place in the future from faulty drainage and vitiated water supply," asserted U.W. Geology Professor Roland Irving in an 1880 *Wisconsin State Journal* article.[27] Irving based his statement on a paper just completed by

his student, a brilliant but late-blooming twenty-six-year-old Norwegian-born senior, Magnus Swenson. Swenson had tested fifty two wells in the "unhealthy" part of the city and learned that eighty-seven percent were contaminated by sewage to one degree or another. Swenson had concluded that contaminated water was the cause of the unusually high incidence of typhoid fever, scarlet fever, and diphtheria in those areas. The

FIGURE 5.22. LOOKING EAST FROM THE CAPITOL DOME IN THE 1880S. This exceptionally clear photograph of South Pinckney Street between East Washington Avenue (left) and King Street (right) also shows an entire quadrant of the isthmus. Visible in the center rear is the residential area then known as Third Lake Ridge and now known as the Marquette Neighborhood. The large building in this area whose cupola rises above the others is the Farwell mansion. Notice the expanse of undeveloped area on both sides of East Washington Avenue beginning about Blount Street. This was the Great Central Marsh discussed throughout the book. The light-colored areas on either side of the avenue are water filled ditches. Finally, note the farmers wagons parked on East Washington Avenue between Pinckney and Webster Streets. This "parking lot" was a response to a prohibition on horse hitching around the Square following the installation of the capitol iron fence in 1872. (SHSW WHi(X3)18578)

young chemist noted that Madison had about one thousand backyard wells and that most of them were separated from privies by just ten to twenty feet of porous soil—conditions that sooner or later allowed the contents to mix.[28] So shocking was this scientific revelation that the Common Council hired Swenson at five dollars a day and set him up in a basement room at the capitol to run purity tests on other Madison wells. Nearly one hundred citizens brought in quart jars of well water only to have Swenson tell them they were nearly all polluted. The only exceptions, he said, were the artesian wells.[29]

Swenson's findings, however, were immediately challenged. The germ theory had only recently been announced by Pasteur and Koch and did not yet enjoy the approval of the scientific community, much less the public. In Madison a prominent physician, Dr. J. J. Brown, described Swenson's conclusions as "simply absurd and ridiculous." He argued that most well impurities such as toads, mice, rats, cats, and angle worms, fell in *from the top* and that even if there were "communication" between privies and wells, the earth would filter them out. "Clean out your wells," concluded Dr. Brown, "and don't let people scare you into building a waterworks." In this highly charged atmosphere, some householders resisted Swenson's attempts to even gather samples. Some threw bricks and bottles at him and others allowed dogs to chase him. Finally, Swenson had to get two Madison policemen to escort him around town on well-sampling excursions.[30]

For the moment Dr. Brown's advice carried the day, but it was Swenson's scientific analysis that Madisonians ultimately found more convincing. On May 5, 1881, a Milwaukee firm offered to build a water system for the City of

FIGURE 5.23. LOOKING SOUTH FROM THE CAPITOL DOME ABOUT 1890.   By the time this photograph was taken showing West Main Street between South Hamilton (right) and Monona Avenue (left), most of the Square was surrounded by "metropolitan" buildings. The buildings in the left foreground have since been replaced by the M&I Bank of Madison and the posh neighborhood between West Doty and Wilson Streets have since given way to city and state office buildings. (SHSW WHi(X3)25534)

Madison in exchange for a twenty-year franchise and found Madison leaders eager to accept. Just one day after hearing the proposal for the first time, a group of Madison's leading businessmen urged acceptance of the Milwaukee firm's proposition. However, after hearing about the Madison franchise opportunity, the agent of a New Jersey competitor met with several Madison leaders and argued that his firm should also have the opportunity to submit a bid for the franchise. This led to another meeting at which several of

Madison's leading lights protested giving a contract to the Milwaukee firm without first securing other competitive bids.[31]

Just one month after the Milwaukee and New Jersey firms had expressed their interest, a group of Madison businessmen decided that a waterworks franchise was a pretty good thing—certainly too good to give to some out-of-town firm. These businessmen were shrewd enough to know that the Common Council would prefer a good solid home-town proposal, but they also recognized that they didn't know beans about waterworks and that time was of the essence. Therefore

they forged an alliance with the New Jersey Company in which the Madison men agreed to handle the financing and the politics while the New Jersey firm would be responsible for the design, construction, and operation of the system. The new entity was known as the Madison City Waterworks Company.[32]

This flurry of interest in the Madison waterworks franchise quickly raised public policy questions that went far beyond which firm should get the prize. For example, should the water be

FIGURE 5.24. LOOKING SOUTHWEST FROM THE CAPITOL DOME ABOUT 1888. This photograph showing South Carroll Street bounded by West Washington Avenue (right) and South Hamilton (left) shows four landmarks of that era: the Park Hotel; to its right the First Baptist Church; behind the Park Hotel the ornate Dane County Courthouse, now the site of the Dane County Parking Ramp; and the towering spire of St. Raphael's Cathedral. At the far end of West Washington Avenue is another large marshy undeveloped area, one of several such areas in the original plat. This view also shows the "x" railroad crossing in Lake Monona. According to Ripley's "Believe It or Not" column, Madison is the only place in the world where two railroad tracks cross in the middle of a lake. (SHSW WHi(X3)6242)

drawn from artesian wells or from Lake Mendota and should the waterworks be owned by the city or by a private corporation?[33]

In the midst of this discussion, Madison's Democratic Caucus nominated against his will John B. Heim, a foreman in a local book bindery, to be alderman of the Second Ward, a predominantly middle to upper income area extending along the Fourth Lake Ridge. Heim dutifully accepted and sat back to await the results. In that election a powerful Democratic surge swept out every Republican who ran. Heim was on the council. Few expected this son of German immigrants to do much on the council except beef up the German wing and assure enough votes for the continuation of the city laissez faire policy on Sunday saloon closings. After all, at age thirty-two, Heim was not only the youngest alderman but a first termer as well. To nearly everyone's surprise, however, Heim immediately launched a crusade to municipalize Madison's water supply.

He began by forging an alliance with five like-minded aldermen and then getting the council at its first regular meeting in May 1881 to oppose the private franchise proposed by the Milwaukee group.[34] Heim proposed a referendum on the question of public ownership, but this plan went nowhere when the city attorney declared that the city did not have the power in its charter to grant a waterworks franchise. Upon hearing this Heim went to work and got the council to unanimously pass a resolution saying that *only* the city could

FIGURE 5.25 LOOKING WEST FROM THE CAPITOL DOME BETWEEN 1895 AND 1900   Moving from right to left this marvelous panorama reveals dozens of familiar buildings. Most easily recognized is the Holy Redeemer Church flanked by Holy Redeemer School. To the rear of the school are the turreted towers of the Red Gym and the massive red brick facade of Science Hall. Behind and to the rear of Science Hall is Bascom Hall flanked by North and South Halls. The barren hillside at the left rear is University Heights. Note, too, the forest of utility poles on the left side of the street. (SHSW WHi(X3)18574)

own and operate the waterworks.[35] The same solution established a committee of three to prepare the necessary charter amendments. Heim was appointed to that committee and from that time forward called the shots. A bill empowering the city to run its own waterworks was passed by the legislature on May 6, 1882.

From this point, events moved quickly. Heim was then appointed to a three-man committee to supervise the entire waterworks project. The question of where the water would come from was resolved when Heim's committee accepted the recommendation of a consulting engineer that the water be taken from artesian wells. In May 1882, the contracts were let and by October the new waterworks pumping station and twelve miles of mains were ready for testing. Not a single pipe leaked and there was enough pressure at the Capitol Square to throw a stream of water from a one-inch hose 115 feet high. Continuous service to water takers was begun on December 7, 1882.[36] Madisonians were highly pleased with this new civic achievement. In the words of the *Madison* *Democrat,* "Madison in its whole history never did a wiser thing. . . ." Upon taking office just one year later, Mayor Breese Stevens said the "people of our city may well be congratulated upon the success which has attended the city's first venture into business."[37] On October 10, 1882, just before the official test of the new waterworks, the council rewarded Heim for his leadership by electing him to the new post of waterworks superintendent. With the exception of an interlude between 1889 and 1890, Heim was reelected to the job each year from 1882 until 1911 when he was elected mayor of Madison.

As Heim quickly discovered, the early years of municipal ownership were fraught with problems. As the number of users attached to the city mains increased rapidly in the early years, it was necessary to drill six additional wells by 1887 to provide enough water to satisfy demand. Yet, even with all these new wells, demand nearly outran supply. The problem was particularly acute in very warm and very cold weather. On hot summer days so many householders watered their lawns with sprinklers and hoses that pressure dropped to dangerously low levels. In cold weather householders kept faucets running to prevent pipes from freezing. Like a hose full of tiny leaks, both practices jeopardized the city's fire-fighting ability by reducing pressure at the hydrant to the point where water from a fire hose could not even reach the second story of buildings on the Capitol Square.[38]

To combat this problem, Heim prohibited lawn sprinkling and sent inspectors around to fine those who failed to comply. Unfortunately preventing householders from running water all day in the winter time to prevent pipes from freezing proved nearly impossible. Water takers simply shut off the tap when the water inspectors called.[39]

Faced by this dilemma, Heim had just three alternatives. A connection to Lake Mendota would have given the system the substantial capacity it needed in case of fire during peak water use, but this idea was strenuously opposed by those who thought Lake Mendota water was contaminated.[40] A dual water system, one system serving fire hydrants and another general purpose consumption, was ruled out as too costly.

Heim's third alternative was the water meter—a solution intensely disliked by Madisonians. Many felt the meters would not accurately measure the water used and that they were an insidious form of governmental oppression. To overcome this problem, Heim made the citizens of Madison an offer they could not refuse. First, he installed the meters at no charge, an extraordinary move at the time. Second, he lowered the rates so that even if citizens were underpaying under the flat rate system, they would not have to pay any more with a water meter. Third, if a meter was ever found to be defective during a free test, the householder would get free water for six months. Fourth, the Water Commission made the water meters mandatory.[41]

The first meters were installed in May 1888 with amazing results. After only ten percent of Madison households were equipped with meters, consumption dropped twenty-eight percent during the peak month of August. By 1893 with only forty-three percent of water users on meters, total consumption dropped an incredible fifty-five percent. Average annual daily household consumption dropped from 816 gallons in 1885 before the water system was begun to 384 gallons in 1890.[42] By 1900 ninety-four percent of all Madison water users were equipped with water meters. It was this success story told and retold at various national meetings that made Madison a model of municipal ownership and Heim a nationally regarded leader.[43]

Fireflies and the Summer Sun: Electricity Comes to Madison

Beginning on a cool July evening in 1855, most of Madison's streets and many of its homes had been lit by flickering coal-gas flames. At first these gas lights were considered "brilliant," "radiant," and even said to have a "glare."[44] But then in just a three-year period several developments made gas lighting obsolete. By 1879 large electrical generators had been perfected to a point where they were commercially available. In that same year Thomas Edison discovered a filament that made the incandescent light bulb a practical alternative to gas for residential and office lighting. Even before the incandescent bulb, other inventors had developed an ingenious and simple device called the arc light. When focused by reflectors and lenses such lights were capable of producing a very bright light over a large area and were ideal for street lighting.[45] In September 1882, Edison brought all these inventions together for the first time in the world at the famous New York Pearl Street demonstration. Here in embryo form was the technology eventually installed in nearly every American city.[46]

So intrinsically exciting was this new phenomenon that traveling circuses and shows immediately made electricity a part of their crowd-gathering attractions. It was in this way that most Madisonians saw this amazing new technology for the first time. In June 1879, the Great London Show came to town with one of the new electricity generators hooked up to a high-speed steam engine. With just one cord of wood the steam engine would turn the generator for six hours, which in turn powered thirteen arc-lights—each of which produced as much light as two hundred candles.[47]

Electricity generation and lighting quickly moved from circus novelty to main-street reality. In the months following Edison's New York demonstration, entrepreneurs raced to form corporations that would generate and sell this remarkable new commodity. Just twenty-four days after the New York demonstration, three Madison men formed the Madison Electric Light and Power Company. In an interview with a *Wisconsin State Journal* reporter, the men confidently predicted that in a few short years electricity would be lighting most Madison homes and powering sewing machines, wringers, and other household machinery. Though these men had the satisfaction of being correct in their predictions, they made the mistake of being too early. In an era where technological breakthroughs were almost a daily occurrence, there were exasperating questions of what kind of electrical equipment to buy. Then, too, there were serious questions about the size of the market for electricity. Would people really use it? These problems prevented the first corporation from attracting enough capital to get off the ground.[48]

During the decade following the Pearl Street demonstration, the initiative for starting many city electrical systems came from salesmen representing electrical equipment manufacturers.

These salesmen quickly learned that nothing was so persuasive as an actual demonstration. Since city-sized electrical generating equipment was too heavy and bulky to be moved from city to city for demonstrations, they carried small generators and hooked them up to local steam engines.

One such team of representatives from the large Chicago-based Van Depoele Electrical Company came to Madison in December 1883, attached their generator to a steam engine at a laundry located where Penney's is today, and then ran wires to six arc lights that they placed along that block and along what is now the First Wisconsin block. On the evening of December 5, 1883, the switch was thrown. Madisonians were dazzled by the brilliant light the six arc lamps produced. Said the *Madison Democrat:* the "stars went out and the moon, gazing for a moment, dropped behind a cloud; the 'man in the moon' muttered 'What in blazes are they doing this evening down on earth?' When the cloud passed, the poor old moon seemed rayless and lifeless. It seemed to have no duty to perform. Like the gas lamps, it appeared with no more brilliancy than a lightning bug . . . compared with the bright rays of the summer sun."[49] In the midst of this smashing successful demonstration, the Van Depoele salesman told Madison leaders they had a choice: either they could continue to light some Madison streets with dim gas flames until 11:00 P. M. for four thousand dollars a year, or they could hire his company to light every street in the city all night long for sixty-eight hundred dollars! That was a sobering seventy percent increase. Still, to have every street brilliantly illuminated—and all night long at that—well . . . maybe it was worth it. Madisonians were clearly interested but needed time to think about it.[50]

For months following the Van Depoele demonstration, Madison newspapers were full of articles on electricity and particularly on the question of street illumination, the first large-scale use of electricity in the U.S.[51] One month after the Van Depoele demonstration, the Common Council set up a committee to investigate the prospect of electric lights for Madison. For three months its members met regularly, solicited estimates from equipment suppliers, and even travelled to some cities to inspect lighting plants. Unfortunately, for electric light enthusiasts the special committee ended when the incoming mayor, Breese Stevens, decided not to reappoint the committee. The mayor's motives were suspect indeed, for at the time he was director of the Madison Gas Light and Coke Company.[52]

Not until 1888—five years after the Van Depoele demonstration—did electricity reappear as a public issue in Madison. In April of that year the council granted a nonexclusive franchise to the Madison Electric Light Company and on June 10 the switch was thrown, sending electricity coursing through wires along Madison streets for the first time. Just a few days later the company completed its installation of arc lights and thereby became a major provider of street lighting.[53]

For the first time in thirty-three years, the Madison Gas Light and Coke Company had a serious competitor—a circumstance it did not relish and tried to change. The first of several gas company efforts to restore its former dominant position came just six weeks after the Madison Electric Light Company started producing power at its central generating station. The Madison Gas Light and Coke Company asked the Common Council for a franchise so that it, too, could produce electricity. On behalf of the gas company, N. B. Van Slyke argued that competition was needed between electrical companies and that many gas companies in the U.S. had added electricity to their product line. Electric light company representatives agreed (tongue in cheek) that the idea of competition was fine *providing* that the gas company would concede that it would have welcomed a competitor in the gas business when it first began. More to the point was the argument that the city could not support two electrical companies and that if two franchises were issued, the better financed gas company would quickly drive out the new electric company and restore its monopolistic position. And why, added the electric company representative, hadn't the gas company entered the electrical business earlier if it really believed the business was as lucrative as it said it was? These were telling arguments that caused the Common Council to reject the opportunistic and poorly timed gas company franchise request.[54]

Just twenty months later the Common Council inflicted additional damage to the Madison Gas Light and Coke Company by sharply reducing the number of gas lights and increasing the number of arc lamps—a clear expression of satisfaction with the new method of street lighting.[55] To the gas company the handwriting was on the wall: Electricity was here to stay and in the area of street lighting had clear advantages.

A second technique used by Madison Gas Light and Coke Company officials to eliminate their new electrical competitor was to reduce the price on its gas. Just one month after the Van Depoele demonstration, a time when interest in the new commodity was very high, the gas company dropped the price of gas from $3.00 to $2.50 per cubic foot, a move expected to make the new arc light replacements of gas lights unjustifiably expensive.[56] Then in June 1888, one month before the city rejected the gas company plea to add electricity to its franchise, the price of gas was lowered from $2.50 to $1.00 per cubic foot. Thus in just four years the gas company had cut the cost of its product by an extraordinary sixty-six percent.[57]

Having failed to get electricity added to their own franchise and having failed to drive the electric company out of business by cutting the price of gas, the gas company tried still another technique. In 1892, gas company officials decided to get into the electricity generation and distribution business by supplying power for the new electric streetcars. Elsewhere in the country the streetcar was proving a boon to electric utilities because it provided a huge *daytime* power consumer at a time when night-time electric street lights were the principal use for the new commodity. Apparently their plan was to get into the power generation business by supplying electricity for streetcars and then, with this beachhead established, try to capture the electric street lighting contract.[58]

Thus, in 1892 major stockholders of the Madison Gas Light and Coke Company formed the Four Lakes Light and Power Company. At first the Common Council rejected the franchise request,[59] but then two weeks later were forced to reverse themselves. An event on August 25 gave the council no choice. On that date the Four Lakes Light and Power Company bought the Madison Electric Light Company. Curiously just one year before the council had removed a provision in the light company's charter that prevented its owners from selling the company to anyone but the city.[60]

At first efforts appear to have been made to disguise Madison Gas Light and Coke Company control of the Four Lakes Company. But then on September 3 the *Wisconsin State Journal* ran an article noting that the president of the new franchise was Napoleon Bonaparte Van Slyke, a director of the gas company. Four Lakes officials denied that Madison Gas and Coke Company officials were behind the new enterprise. At the huge banquet on October 1 to celebrate the opening of Madison's electric streetcar line, an official of the Thomas-Houston Company, the supplier of Four Lakes generating equipment, said that only three of the five-hundred shares of the new company of Four Lakes stock were owned by Madison men.[61]

However, such protestations did not convince Common Council members. One week after hearing about the gas company takeover of the Four Lakes Company, they willingly approved another nonexclusive electrical franchise for the Capital City Electric Company—a brand new company incorporated by several Madison men with no gas company connections. So negative was council sentiment toward the gas company that it gave the Capital City Electric Company the city's annual street lighting contract in spite of the fact that the new company didn't have a single piece of electrical generating equipment. To the embarrassment of its many council backers, the new company failed to build its plant as expected, which left the Four Lakes Light and Power Company as the sole provider of electricity for Madison.[62]

FIGURE 5.26 MATTHEW J. HOVEN, BUTCHER AND MAYOR.   Shown in front of his butcher shop is Matthew J. Hoven, three-term Democratic mayor of Madison (1897-8, 1899-1900 and 1900-1901). Hoven ran for a second consecutive term in the spring of 1898 but was beaten by just eleven votes by a reform-oriented Republican, Charles E. Whelan, who apparently convinced voters that he would be tougher on saloons than the German butcher. However, in the next election, Hoven beat Whelan. Thus both men had the dubious and rare distinction of being an incumbent mayor and losing reelection. Hoven was the first German and Catholic to be elected mayor of Madison. This 1899 photograph shows Hoven during his second term as mayor.

The building Hoven owned at the corner of North Hamilton and East Mifflin still stands but is today used as a cheese shop. Note the rack on the right front window on which meats were hung for shopper inspection. (SHSW WHi(X3)33755)

The fact that the same people controlled the gas company and the electric company did not endear either of these companies to their users. Long-standing antipathy toward the monopolistic Gas Light and Coke Company was now extended to the Four Lakes Light and Power Company. After several years, people began complaining about the deteriorating quality (the street lights were too dim) and the increasing cost of electricity.

These two problems were sufficiently irritating to cause the Common Council to take a far-reaching step. In January 1896, a five-man committee was formed to investigate municipal ownership. Both newspapers supported the idea and approvingly printed articles favorable to city takeover. For example, the *Wisconsin State Journal* quoted a nationally prominent sociologist, Professor Albion W. Small as saying: "The town which does not own or control its gas, electric light, water supply and street railway lines is presumably a town of low-grade economic intelligence and virtue.[63] The special committee hired an expert who prepared estimates for a city-owned plant which the city clerk put out for bids. Twenty-two bids were received including several *under* the expert's estimates. Municipal ownership proponents had reason to be hopeful.

Then in April 1896, in the midst of plans to build a municipal plant, a New York utility syndicate headed by Emerson McMillin bought the Madison Gas Light and Coke Company, the Madison *City* Gas Light & Coke Company, a newly established gas company, and Four Lakes Light and Power Company and formed the Madison Gas and Electric Company (M. G. & E.). At the time Emerson McMillin bought the Madison plant, he owned eighteen plants around the country including the Milwaukee Gas Company. Unlike some rapacious syndicate owners, he adopted wise long-term management practices including profit sharing for all his employees. Madisonians who held stock in the Madison Gas Light and Coke Company and the Four Lakes Company apparently kept their stock in the new

firm and in some cases were given management positions. N. B. Van Slyke, for instance, was made vice-president of M. G. & E. McMillin brought in as general manager Henry L. Doherty, an experienced utility executive,[64] who quickly became involved in the municipal–private ownership debate. In appearances before the Common Council he said that municipal ownership had been a failure and that people had an inflated view of utility profits.[65]

Meanwhile, many citizens were having second thoughts about the timing of the twenty-four-thousand-dollar outlay for a city-owned electrical plant. They forcefully reminded Madisonians that in just eight years (1904) $152,000 in bonds had to be paid off and that no provision had been made to do this.[66] This debt load coupled with other bonding issues meant that the city was perilously close to its maximum legal debt limit. On top of this, nearly all decision makers in the city at that time had concluded that a sewage treatment system was the number one priority and that any remaining bonding capacity should be reserved for this large project—then estimated at seventy-five to one hundred thousand dollars. As if their arguments were not persuasive enough, the new Madison Gas and Electric Company astutely offered the city a very low rate schedule, which the council on October 23, 1896, unanimously accepted.[67] With this council action, the idea of municipal ownership was effectively killed. Not until 1903 did it reappear in any vigorous form.[68]

With the threat of municipal ownership effectively behind him, General Manager Doherty concentrated on the rapid expansion and improvement of the utility systems, particularly gas. With the aid of Madison Gas and Electric financial assistance, the Madison Cooking School was begun to teach women the culinary arts—on a gas stove of course. At the time the gas stove was viewed as an extraordinary improvement over wood stoves. Programs reminded women that the gas stove being used in the class was available for just thirteen dollars and that it could be connected in their home in a matter of days. With

this highly effective merchandising system and nearly daily newspaper ads during the late 1890s, Doherty could boast in 1898 that over half the women in Madison were "cooking with gas."[69]

From Mules to Harnessed Lightning: Madison Street Railways

The Mule Line

On Thursday morning October 30, 1884, twenty white Texas mules were unloaded at the East Madison depot. These braying animals were a part of an exciting plan launched in January by a group of wealthy Madison businessmen to provide Madison with an unmistakable form of civic progress in the form of a street railway. At the time a street railway was a car pulled by horses or mules along a track. Horse railways, as they were commonly known, were viewed as a breakthrough in urban transportation—a great advance over omnibuses, which had to struggle with muddy, rutted roads. Because flanged steel wheels moving along steel rails offered so little resistance, a horse railway allowed twice as many passengers to be pulled at increased speeds and gave passengers a much smoother ride besides.[70]

Almost from the beginning Madison's street railway was beset by problems. For a variety of reasons the original incorporators were unable to raise the necessary money in Madison to build the line. The incorporators finally found several Chicago investors who were willing to buy stock but only if the local men would take a minority stock position. Consequently only one of the original Madison incorporators remained in the enterprise, and Chicago investors took over. Apparently the Madison men were good salesmen because the new Chicago owners were confident that Madison, though then a town of less then twelve thousand, would more than triple its population by 1894.[71]

What happened on November 16, 1884, the day of the maiden voyage of the mule-powered streetcar was symptomatic of what happened during its eight-year life. At eight o'clock that evening, each of the cars were hitched to two large white mules at the temporary car barns in the 600 block of Williamson Street for the first trip over the two-mile-long line. People lined the streets along the route and cheered for this "latest evidence of Madison's progressiveness." The maiden voyage was anything but successful, however. No sooner had the dignitaries boarded the first car when they had to get off because the mules couldn't make the steep King Street hill. Even more irritating were dozens of small boys who "swarmed over the cars, pushed past the drivers, climbed into the windows, usurped the platform, clung to the sides, and mounted the roof, yelling in the meantime like a troup of wild Arabs." As if this behavior were not enough, the young rowdies derailed the cars dozens of times by putting rocks on the tracks. So persistent were these early-day delinquents that the cars had to be returned to the car barns immediately after their maiden voyage. On top of these problems, the hastily constructed track proved extremely rough and the mules balked and snorted. Indeed, reporters had to strain to be charitable about the new ten-thousand-dollar facility. Nevertheless, this was the beginning of a fifty-year era when rumbling wheels and clanging bells were familiar features of Madison streets.[72]

During the first few months the owners worked diligently to get the bugs out of the system. After a week of trying without success to get the heavy but tiny fourteen-foot cars up the King Street hill, the Chicago owners ordered two smaller cars, barely ten feet long, which were placed in service in December 1884. Curves were fixed so that the cars didn't go off the track, a semblance of a schedule (a car every half hour) was worked out, and a law was passed making it illegal to put rocks on street car tracks.[73]

By the summer of 1885 the line was being remarkably well patronized—at least so it seemed to D. K. Tenney, who with several other Madison investors bought the Madison Street Car Railway Company in August 1885. What Tenney and his fellow local investors did not realize was that

the shrewd Chicago owners had instructed their superintendent to put extra nickels into the fare boxes each day, giving the impression of profitable operation.[74] Based upon this contrived but promising revenue, Tenney added three other cars to the line to provide shorter headways and better service, extended the line from Park and State Streets out to Mills and University Avenue as a means of better serving persons going to the state fairgrounds (formerly Camp Randall), and replaced the slow mules with faster horses.[75]

It didn't take long for Tenney and his fellow investors to learn that patronage had mysteriously fallen off after they bought the line. To save money Tenney directed his superintendent to run all four cars with a single horse except on the King Street hill, where an extra horse was hooked up, but the line still lost money.[76] In May 1886, after a year of operation, Tenney begged Madisonians to patronize the cars and said that although each passenger dropped a nickel in the fare box, it cost him nine cents per passenger to pay expenses.[77] After nearly two years of operation in the red, Tenney appeared before the Common Council and told them "the road ought never to have been constructed" and asked for a series of franchise changes that would help the company reduce its costs. But the council was in no mood to comply.[78] In a second plea a few months later Tenney said that if the council was not willing to maintain the street between and on both sides of the streetcar track, the company would be forced to take up its track and go out of business.[79] That was just fine with the council who at their next meeting ordered the city attorney to get the company to repair the streets on either side and in the center of its tracks or revoke the franchise.

Tenney and his Madison investors decided to throw in the sponge, and the company was sold at auction. For every dollar they had invested, the Madison owners got back seventy-five cents at the time of sale.[80] Two other out-of-town owners tried to make the Madison mule-powered streetcar line a success but failed to do so. It was slow, bumpy, unreliable, crowded, stuffy, and barely faster than walking. Nearly everyone agreed the mule line had to go.[81]

Breaking the Lightning to Harness: The Beginning of Madison's Electric Streetcar Line

"Conspicuous among the many subjects for the reform of this city, is the so-called Madison Street Railway," said Mayor William H. Rogers in his inaugural address in April 1892. "In its present condition, it is a great encumbrance of our streets and of little or no service to the public. . . . I believe it is the duty of this Council to take immediate action in compelling the proprietor . . . to give the public the service his franchise . . . implies, or to tear up his track and give the right of way back to the natives." In the event that such legal remedies failed, Rogers even urged Madisonians to boycott the line.[82]

Rogers could afford to be bold and provocative. He new that the citizens of Madison were fed up with the poor mule-car service.[83] He knew that electric streetcar and equipment manufacturers viewed Madison as a plum, ripe for the picking. And he knew that electric streetcar technology had made rapid strides in recent years and that hundreds of cities across the country had installed electric car systems.[84]

Rogers was hardly the first to suggest an electric car line. In 1885 after successful tests of electric powered cars, D. K. Tenney considered converting his mule line to electricity.[85] In 1888 the salesman for the company that supplied the city with its electric power generating equipment requested a franchise, but was ignored.[86]

However, not until the representatives of the Madison Lakes Improvement Company swept into town in 1890 and started booming Madison as a summer resort did Madison leaders begin to seriously consider the idea of electric streetcar lines. These suburban land developers quickly recognized that their extensive tracts of land around Lake Monona, which they had either bought or optioned, would become valuable only if they could be more accessible by some other means than carriage or steamboat. In September 1890, the well-financed syndicate officials announced their intention of buying the Madison

Street Railway franchise and converting it to an electric line.[87]

Glowing portraits of what the new electric line would do for Madison began appearing in the newspapers. "Smokeless, odorless and noiseless" electric motors would power huge cars up the steepest grades,[88] said one. Spacious cars would pass each corner on the line every seven minutes.[89] said another. Apparently such visions were compelling because conservative Madison investors complained that the syndicate owners had kept them out of this opportunity.[90]

Unfortunately for these suburban land developers, the deal they had apparently worked out with the Chicago franchise holder of the Madison Streetcar Company fell through, and their dream of an electric streetcar line encircling Lake Monona was dashed.

Not until Mayor Rogers threw down the gauntlet in April 1892 did the city once again gain the initiative in the effort to control its street railway destiny. By that time, the arrogance of the Chicago owner had been made unmistakably clear. Rogers had accurately judged the mood of the council and the people they represented. At their first meeting following his inaugural call to action, the council took steps leading to a revocation of the mule-line franchise and the formulation of a new electric car franchise.[91]

Meanwhile the Thomson-Houston Company, the supplier of the electrical generating equipment installed by the Madison Electric Company in 1889, and a subsidiary of the General Electric Company, had been keeping a sharp eye on the city for another big sale, viz, an electric streetcar system. Less than one month after his inaugural address, Mayor Rogers called the citizens of Madison to a meeting to hear a "rapid transit" proposal from the company.[92] If the citizens of Madison would contribute twenty-five thousand dollars in stock, the Thomson-Houston Company said it would install a $125,000, 5½-mile system with the best cars. At the suggestion of company officials, a visiting committee of businessmen was formed to inspect electric railway systems the company had recently put in nearby states.[93] The

men returned in a few days completely sold on what they had seen. A second committee was immediately formed to sell twenty-five thousand dollars in stock to interested Madisonians.[94] Soon after the new franchise was approved in June 1892, work on the track began.

Finally on Saturday, October 1, 1892, the line was ready for its first trial. At 2:00 P. M. three handsome twenty-foot cars were lined up in front of the Park Hotel where a large crowd of a thousand people had gathered to watch. Moments after city officials, reporters, bondholders, and other dignitaries boarded the cars to inspect the line, motormen shoved the power controls forward and the cars bounded down Carroll Street followed by most of the children in town. Everywhere people lined the track to wave handkerchiefs and applaud this great new marvel of technology. On the East Johnson Street line the chief electrician said "let her out" and the car whizzed along at thirty miles an hour. So powerful were the motors that the cars paid no attention to hills—even the steep King Street hill, the bane of the mules. To cap the day a huge banquet replete with champagne, black bass, and cigars was held that evening at the Park Hotel to celebrate "the burial of the mules and the birth of the trolley." In toast after toast and speech after speech the electric wizardry of the Thomson-Houston Company was applauded—work that many probably did not really understand. In the words of the Madison congressman who spoke that evening, these men had "tamed the wild and forked lightning and broken it to harness to drive over our streets."[95]

Unlike the old mule line, the new Madison City Railway Company built the line with care, bought first-rate equipment and offered fast, frequent, and reliable service. During the first two years of operation, twelve- to sixteen-minute headways were offered on all lines and by 1896 headways on some lines were down to nine minutes. If you missed one car you were simply early for the next! Rolling stock was upgraded in 1896 with six elegant, thirty-one-foot-long, fifty-passenger cars— nearly three times longer than the old mule cars.

The interiors were finished with cherry, maple, and oak and trimmed with solid bronze. Thanks to the diligence of an able superintendent, complaints were rare and the patronage grew rapidly. During the first years of service about one thousand passengers dropped their nickels in the fare box each day. But by 1899 that number had risen to three thousand per day or one million nickels a year! For a nickel you could ride for 10¼ miles, the same price as the old mule cars, and yet go three times as fast! Just about everybody rode the streetcars at one time or another.[96]

Extensions to the electric car line were not long in coming. In 1892 officials of the Madison Lakes Improvement Company worked out an arrangement with the Madison City Railway Company to extend service to their east side suburb, Elmside. The extension did not come without a cost, however. Since a streetcar line requires relatively dense development along its track to show a profit, the Elmside developers had a problem. They were asking the streetcar owners to send a track out into the country with only a hope that in the not too distant future, enough people would live at Elmside and elsewhere along the line to make the line a paying proposition. The astute owners of the electric streetcar franchise wisely recognized that they would be foolish to build the line unless suburban land owners would heavily subsidize the high initial costs for laying the track and the power lines. However, the Elmside owners, recognizing that electric streetcar service was a prerequisite for lot sales, eagerly agreed to pay the sudsidy. In exchange the streetcar company agreed to send a car to Elmside every twenty minutes for forty years.[97] A second line extension came in 1897, when the developers of Wingra Park and University Heights and the residents of those suburbs agreed to pay the Madison City Railway Company a ten-thousand-dollar cash bonus. This meant the trolley company only had to pay two thousand of the twelve thousand dollars for track construction costs.[98]

FIGURE 5.27. SPANISH AMERICAN WAR. Almost exactly thirty-seven years after the first two companies left the city for the Civil War, another company of soldiers left Madison for another war. This time the goal was overthrowing Spanish rule in Cuba, Puerto Rico, and the Philippines.

Never before had the nation geared up for war so quickly. Just four days after President McKinley declared war on Spain on April 24, 1898, one full company (101 men) known as the Governor's Guard, a nucleus for a regimental band, left the city to the cheers of a huge crowd aboard a special Northwestern train. So quickly did mobilization occur that doctors were giving volunteers physical examinations up to minutes before the train left. In Madison and throughout the nation this ''splendid little war'' as it was later called was enormously popular. The day before the company left, thirty faculty and alumni members including the well-known economist Richard T. Ely formed a drill team to hone their military skills in case they would be needed. Nearly all the leading professors including Frederick Jackson Turner strongly supported the war with stirring speeches the day the soldiers left. In the frenzied patriotic mood surrounding the soldiers' departure, the university, public, and parochial schools and most businesses shut their doors so that everybody could turn out to see the boys off.

In contrast to the sendoff the boys received, however, the role Madison soldiers played from that point forward was dull indeed. At Milwaukee they were put on a troop train, where with other Wisconsin men they were sent to Jacksonville, Florida, where they spent the rest of the war. There they played baseball, tennis, grew mustaches, got vaccinated, and were even invited to join the local country club. Their primary mission in Jacksonville was to guard the city water works and watch out for Spanish spies. The treaty ending the Spanish American War was signed on August 12, less than four months after war was declared. On September 10 the Governor's Guards had returned to Madison where they were immediately treated to a huge dinner consisting of chicken, liquor-laced eggnog, and cigars.

Though the Madison Company never got into combat, two of its members died of typhoid fever and many others contracted dysentery, yellow fever, and malaria while in their Florida camp.

To celebrate the conclusion of the war, and particularly Admiral George Dewey's dazzling destruction of the Spanish fleet in Manila Harbor, the arch shown above was erected at the head of State Street. (SHSW WHi(B82)1615)

Although the new electric line was dramatically different from the old mule car line in equipment and service, there was one area where the two companies were similar. Both experienced financial difficulties. By December 1893, in spite of good patronage, some lines were not covering the relatively high fixed costs needed to repay the initial investment. In July 1894, following the company's failure to pay their huge electricity bill and the interest due on their bonds, the company went into receivership where it stayed for three-and-one-half years. At the end of this period bondholders were forced to accept sixty-four cents for every dollar they had invested.[99] However, even during these financial difficulties, the receivers continued to provide remarkably good service, reasoning that a cutback could start a downward spiral whose consequences would ultimately cause the bondholders an even greater loss. Fortunately, after the settlement of financial problems and the sale of the company in late 1897, the Madison Electric Railway Company found sound financial footing and paid a profit to its owners.[100]

Privies, Pollution, and Purification: The Early History of Madison's Sewerage System

Private Sewers and Water Closets: An Alternative to Privies, Cesspools, and Chamberpots

In May 1866, the *Wisconsin State Journal* printed a small story about the demolition of the fancy red brick outhouse on the west capitol lawn. Since its construction in 1844 the small, ornate structure had reliably served the purpose for which it was intended. But now it was being replaced by an indoor water closet, a device whose appearance, design, and operation was remarkably similar to today's fixtures. Four years later the owners of the Park Hotel decided to equip their new hotel with this extraordinary contrivance. Then in the early 1870s wealthy citizens in the Mansion Hill area began to install these expensive devices in their homes.[101] These seemingly unimportant events marked the beginning of a major transformation of Madison.

Water closets were a dramatic breakthrough in domestic hygiene and convenience. Just a pull of the chain and everything went away! Elsewhere in Madison household waste disposal technology was primitive indeed. The only other homes in Madison that had "indoor plumbing" were those using chamber pots, little more than china pails kept in the bedroom at night and emptied in the morning. More than half of Madison householders dumped their chamberpots on the ground or even in the street gutters near their homes. In the winter, freezing weather and snow storms concealed the filth and arrested its smell, but when the spring thaw came, the stinking and unsightly piles of filth filled the air with "seeds of death" and "foul vapors." The summer sun made walks through many parts of the city intensely disagreeable. Such gutter deposits were illegal, but with so few policemen, householders soon learned they could use street gutters with near impunity—especially under cover of darkness. The only real alternatives to street gutters were cesspools, which had to be periodically emptied by scavengers. Because Madisonians considered cesspools to be "an outrage on humanity," few of these smelly containers were built in Madison. Homes not equipped with chamberpots and cesspools had the even more primitive backyard privy—the number one health nuisance during the last two decades of the nineteenth century and probably before. No wonder so many householders were eager to install water closets.[102]

In order to install the coveted water closets householders had to solve two problems. The first was keeping water in the flushing tank above the stool. Before 1884 and the availability of the pressurized city water system, householders had to fill the tanks by hand pumping after each use. After 1884, however, city water pressure did the work, making water closets cheaper to install and easier to operate. The second problem was how to get rid of the waterborne wastes. To solve this problem, early water closet owners built private sewers.[103] At first costs were high, but by joining together with neighbors the cost per home could be reduced. Once the capitol, downtown businesses, and wealthy homeowners had shown the way, the number of private sewers increased rapidly. During the late 1870s and early 1880s few Common Council meetings went by without several new private sewers being approved.

Even though all the private sewers emptied their contents into the lakes, few had reservations about the wisdom of this decision. In fact when the wealthy Mansion Hill residents built their private sewer in 1874, the *Wisconsin State Journal* congratulated these "worthy citizens" for their initiative[104] and expressed the hope others would follow their fine example. Then popular theories reassured Madisonians that the lakes were so large and the amount of sewage so small that it could not possibly taint their waters. The reasoning went something like this: If Paris, then a city of 1,900,000 people could dump all of its raw sewage into the Seine, a small river just four hundred fifty feet wide, without any harmful effects on the water, then surely Madison could dump its tiny amount of sewage into the much larger Madison lakes without any harmful effects.[105]

Emergence of a Public-Private Partnership: The 1885 District Sewer System

After more than a decade of continuous private sewer building (1874 to 1884) the limitations of this strategy had become evident. First, because of high initial costs, only a very small part of the city was actually served by the private sewers, namely the homes of wealthy persons living on hilltops and near the lakes. Consequently only a portion of the hilltops and nearly all of the lower sections of the city were undrained.[106]

Second, Madison physicians warned that the continued use of the Great Central Marsh as a popular dumping ground for cesspool contents would cause outbreaks of scarlet fever, cholera, and other diseases. At the time physicians believed that these diseases were transmitted by the stench emanating from such dumping grounds, not by specific germs. However, this incorrect etiology did not matter. People accepted this interpretation and were indignant that East-siders were subjected to this bad air.[107]

Third, a strong division of opinion had developed about the wisdom of dumping raw sewage in the lakes. This practice, argued some, would pollute the lakes, destroy their beauty and drive away tourists. For the moment, however, the technical argument of the sanitary experts and the clamor for sewers that would free neighborhoods from the stench and filth of human excrement prevailed. As late as 1884 even the State Board of Health said a system of sewers emptying into Lake Monona would not affect its purity.[108]

Finally, in the summer of 1884 Common Council members recognized that a more enduring solution to this problem required city intervention. In July 1884, a sewer construction code was passed that required private sewer contractors to meet certain design standards.[109]

In the same month U. W. Professor Allan D. Conover proposed the first integrated total sewage treatment system. Under Conover's plan, raw sewage would be collected and piped to a sixty-acre sewage farm just east of the Yahara River where it would be discharged on the ground and used as fertilizer for raising crops. Although thorough and effective, Professor Conover's plan had a serious flaw: a price tag of one hundred thirty thousand dollars.[110] At the time the city had used up nearly all its bonding capacity and was therefore in no position to even contemplate such an expensive scheme. City Engineer John Nader was therefore commissioned to do a more realistic plan. In September 1884, Nader announced what he called his "district" plan—really little more than twenty-six separate sewer districts all

draining into the lakes. Because of natural drainage patterns, eighty percent of the sewage would drain directly into Lake Monona and twenty percent into Lake Mendota. Some time in the future Nader planned to run a big pipe along the lakeshores to intercept the sewage before it went in the lake and pump it to a sewage purification plant. The most attractive feature of the Nader plan was its price tag—just twenty-five thousand dollars.[111]

Unfortunately for those desiring quick action on the smelly problem, the technical merits of the Nader and Conover plans confused council members. Public clamor for action on the sewage question forced council members to realize that the question was no longer a question of which technique was cheapest and easiest. The question was what was "the cheapest, the best . . . the safest and the most flexible" system[112]—not easy criteria during the very early days of sanitary engineering.

The Sewage Committee proposed that a national expert be hired to evaluate the two plans and make recommendations, but the council deferred action on the grounds that the city couldn't afford a three-hundred-dollar consultant. Finally after two more months of inaction, Mayor Breese Stevens told the council that the sewage disposal question matter was "by far the most important" matter before them and urged them to hire an outside expert even if they had to pay him later. The council acquiesced and hired Samuel L. Gray, city engineer for Providence, Rhode Island. Gray had recently gained national prominence after his analysis of Europe's most advanced sewage disposal systems.[113]

While Gray was studying the Nader and Conover plans, Madison leaders were working with state legislators to modify the city charter so that the city would have the power to build and operate a sewer system. This limitation had been uncovered soon after the Nader plan was announced. The legislature gave this power to the city in March 1885.[114]

Finally, in April 1885, with the help of their consulting engineer, the Common Council adopted a modified version of Nader's district

plan. However, because of the city's financial limitations, the Common Council decided to build only those portions that were directly assessable to adjacent property owners and to defer until a later date the construction of the expensive lakeshore interceptor and purification plant.[115] Though the decision meant the city would have only a partial sewage system, the decision was nevertheless significant. After nearly fifty years of placing the responsibility for sewage disposal on the householder's shoulders, the city finally became an active participant in solving the problem.

The district sewage plan was a giant step forward. Not long after the sewers were laid in the streets, back yard privies and cesspools were removed and bedroom chamber pots were happily put away. The sewers literally purified neighborhoods through which they passed. Thanks to city water, a city sewage plan, and private money, the water closet—once affordable only by the rich—became a reality for many more Madison homes. The exchange, however, was not entirely benign because the lakeshores began to bristle with concrete pipes disgourging raw sewage directly into the lakes.[116] In effect the district sewer system had transferred the problem from backyards and streets to the lake.

Failure of the District Sewer System

By 1892 serious deficiencies of the district sewer system had become evident to many. The *Wisconsin State Journal* reported that Lake Monona, the recipient of nearly eighty percent of the district sewers was rapidly becoming a "pool of filth" and on warm days emitted a "sickening stench."[117] Also many of the district sewers were constructed without the proper downward angle, which caused them to become easily clogged. Consequently, sewage backed up into basements and sent a growing number of householders scurrying to City Hall to file damage claims. This problem put city officials in a lose-lose situation.

If they didn't flush out the sewers, damage claims ballooned. If they did, lakeshore residents found their shorelines littered with foul-smelling fecal matter.[118]

Mounting problems and complaints prompted the council in August 1893 to solicit plans from engineers for a better sewage disposal system. Ideally, the council wanted a collection system that would send the sewage to a central point where it could be purified. If such a system proved too costly, the council wanted a central collection system that would discharge the raw sewage at some point far away from the densely populated areas of the city. This was far preferable, they reasoned, to dozens of district sewer pipes then disgourging sewage into the lake. Local and non-local engineers prepared four proposals for Council consideration, but unfortunately, all proved to be more expensive than what the council could afford and the plans had to be abandoned.[119] However this exercise was not entirely without enduring *policy* significance. All the engineers felt the Great Central Marsh on the near east side was the logical drainage area for the city. Therefore all engineers proposed to run their main sewage line through this low area so they could either discharge it directly into the Yahara or cross the river to a proposed sewage plant. In either case, the Yahara River was to be the discharge point. Since this seemed to be the clear direction for any future sewage plans, the council authorized the purchase of a site just east of the Yahara River near East Washington Avenue (where the Fiore Shopping Center is now located) as the future site for a "sewage purification works."[120]

Worsening conditions in 1894 and 1895 caused nearly all Madisonians to conclude that the district sewer system had to go. In the first place, residents living in low-lying areas around Johnson and Williamson Streets were demanding sewers. Unfortunately, they could not be serviced by the gravity-operated district sewer system. Second, the causal connections between a stinking Lake Monona and raw sewage had been established beyond any reasonable doubt.[121]

Some of the most compelling testimony for getting sewage out of the lakes came from several Madison physicians who on behalf of the local medical society conducted an investigation of city sanitary conditions and reported the "sights seen and the smells endured" to the Common Council in June 1894. They described most of the Monona shoreline and parts of the Mendota shoreline covered with fecal matter in varying stages of decay, the water "filthy and slimy," and the lakeshore bottom near sewage outlets veneered with grease. The doctors said these conditions were the best possible disease-breeding conditions and were unanimous in their insistence that the sewage should be removed from the lakes.[122] In a petition to the Common Council on June 8, 1894, the most influential women in Madison, all members of the Women's Club, added their weight to the movement to find a safer means of treating the city's sewage.

Great weight was also given to the testimony of persons who had closely observed the Madison lakes for many years. One man who had made a habit of walking or riding along a portion of the Monona shoreline each day since 1854 said the thick green scum and the unbearable stench arising from the lake began when the city started emptying sewage into the lakes. A man who had piloted steamboats on Lake Monona since 1878 agreed: the scum, the thick weeds, and the stench were caused by the city sewage.[123]

Prevailing summer westerly winds caused the problem to be particularly severe along the Monona shoreline between Blount and Brearly Streets and produced two lawsuits from irate lake property owners.[124] Immediately after the first of the two lawsuits were filed, the mayor sent a force of men to this area to try to alleviate the problem. After donning rubber hip boots, the men bravely waded into the smelling mass of sewage that had accumulated along that shoreline. At first they tried to push the debris up onto the shore with boards but the sewage eluded capture by flowing around the ends. Finally the men discovered that they could surround the sewage with a long piece of canvas and pull it to shore as if they were netting fish.[125] To remove the weeds that trapped the sewage, several men swung scythes under water while others tugged a harrow out into the water and then had it pulled in to shore by horses. The work was hardly pleasant and one man had to quit because he could not stand the smell.[126] After a few days a great mass of sewage three feet high lay festering along the entire shoreline between Blount and Livingston Streets. Even with the sewage removed the water near shore was "a turgid, filthy, murky mass, thick and strong enough to support quite heavy weights." So abundant was the supply of sewage that workmen would no sooner pile the sewage onto barges for burial at the east end of the lake than the prevailing breezes would blow in a fresh batch.[127] Finally, the wind shifted and a front page *Wisconsin State Journal* headline informed readers that the wind had carried the fetid mass across the lake. Naturally this made Town of Blooming Grove residents angry, and they threatened to sue the city for damages.[128]

In focusing public attention on the sewage problem and fomenting a decision, the influential role of the *Wisconsin State Journal* cannot be underestimated. Almost immediately after he arrived as the new editor of the *Journal* in June 1894, Amos P. Wilder launched a journalistic crusade to get the sewage out of the lakes. In late summer and early fall of 1895 Wilder even resorted to publishing sections of a British textbook on sewage treatment. Day after day he published opinions of doctors, lawyers, and merchant chiefs, nearly all of whom demanded immediate cessation of the district sewer system. Not until city officials committed themselves to a corrective solution did Wilder stop his vivid and sometimes revolting coverage of the sewage issue. The *Madison Democrat*, by contrast, was slow to acknowledge the connection between sewage and lake pollution and refrained from the sensationalism of Wilder's coverage. So strong and sustained was Wilder's sewage crusade that conservative businessmen such as Elisha Keyes asked for a "rest" because he feared property values in Madison would be damaged.[129]

Yet the matter had to be faced. Madison could not maintain its image as a beautiful, healthy city on the one hand and have sewage-fed stinking lakes on the other. Just imagine, suggested one citizen, a tourist from Chicago coming to Madison because he heard it was beautiful. "He rises as the sun does, goes down to Lake Monona, casts his eye along the edge nearest him and wonders whether he is in Madison or in the sheep pens of the Chicago stockyard. A gentle southeast wind is blowing and an insufferable smell, the likes of which he has never known before, fills his nostrils and he begins to believe he *is* in the stockyards."[130] Rare was the Madison opinion leader who felt that Madison could keep dumping sewage in the lakes and expect Madison to maintain its vaunted image as a "professional beauty."[131]

The Search for Sewage Purification Solutions

The rapidly deteriorating conditions of the lakes persuaded Madison opinion leaders that something should be done about it. The unresolved and controversial question was how and at what cost. The *Madison Democrat,* several local engineers, a few influential citizens, and several aldermen argued that the weeds and scum that appeared in 1894–45 were caused not by the amount of sewage dumped into the lake but rather by the improper *method* sewage was being sent into the lake. The most forceful spokesman for this point of view was D. K. Tenney, lawyer, long-time activist, and Madison's favorite curmudgeon.[132] Tenney said the solution was not to allow the sewage to dribble into the water near the shoreline, but rather to extend the pipes out at least two hundred feet into the lake where the sewage could be discharged in no less than ten feet of water. At that depth Tenney's arithmetic showed that one million parts of water could attack one part of sewage and reduce it to its elemental and inoffensive particles before it could cause smelly problems. Tenney asserted that this solution

would satisfy all but the "old maids of the masculine gender," which all communities must tolerate.[133]

Madison leaders were also divided on the wisdom of going to the extreme limits of the city's bonding power to pay for a new sewage system. Tenney and his allies thought any cost above eight thousand dollars—the amount needed to extend the sewers deeper into the lakes—was unjustified and a waste of money. On the other hand there were a growing number of prominent businessmen like piano merchant W. W. Warner who said that to be "up to the gunwales in debt" was the "normal condition of every ultra-American city" and that "nothing would contribute more to our prosperity than removing the foul sewers from our lakes."[134]

By 1894, after months of sustained controversy, Madisonians realized the sewer issue was incredibly technical. To participate in sewerage discussions required a whole new vocabulary with words like "effluent," "sulfate of alum," "oxygen absorption," "nitrates," "intermediate filtration," and knowledge of strange new substance called "sludge." Most troubling of all, local engineers couldn't agree on how sewage should be purified. Even more disconcerting was that very few others in the entire country knew much about the new but rapidly growing science of sewage treatment. In 1894 only thirty cities in the entire country had actually installed sewage systems. Then in the summer of 1894 the Madison Common Council, to their great credit, hired the most famous sanitary consulting engineer in the country, George E. Waring, to lead them out of the arcane wilderness of sewage purification.[135]

After spending a week in Madison, Waring presented his solution to the problem at a public meeting in July 1894. More than two hundred people attended the "largest sewerage meeting" the sixty-one-year-old engineer had ever attended.[136] Waring urged the city to abandon the poorly designed lake polluting district sewer system in favor of a new seventy-five-thousand-dollar system that would deposit the sewerage on a one-hundred-acre sewage farm just east of the

Yahara River. At the time land disposal was widely considered to be the most feasible and reliable method of sewage purification. Do not, he cautioned, use a purification system based upon chemical precipitation because it will leave fertilizers in the effluent that will stimulate weed and algae growth in the lakes and destroy this most attractive feature of a beautiful city. As to the price tag, Waring took the offensive. After noting that he had repeatedly been told to bear in mind limited municipal finances, Waring said he was struck as he walked through the community by the "evidence of wealth so general, evidences of comfort so universal, and evidences of poverty so lacking. . . ." He concluded that Madison could "well afford" the best possible sewage disposal system.[137]

Unfortunately for those trying to clean up the lakes, Waring did not persuade the council to act on his recommendations. In fact, in direct contradiction to his recommendations, the council voted just two days after hearing his plan to allow another huge district sewer to dump its raw sewage into Lake Monona. Council members were skeptical about the whole idea of land disposal and too few were willing to authorize the large bond issue needed to build the sewage system that he had recommended.[138]

The sewage matter might easily have languished in a limbo state—the victim of bonding limits and a babble of confusing solutions—had not the two residents living along that portion of the Lake Monona shoreline most heavily impacted by sewage accumulation decided to sue the city. Faced by this lawsuit and the strong prospect of many more, none of which the city could afford, the council concluded it could temporize no longer. Eight days after the lawsuit was filed, the council appointed a committee of aldermen, physicians, and engineers to recommend the best sewerage plan for the city.[139] On October 16, 1895, city engineer McClellan Dodge and former city engineer John Nader on behalf of the committee recommended a fifty-seven-thousand-dollar plan that combined chemical precipitation with filtration. This time, after a summer of unprecedented lake pollution and public furor, the council was in a mood to act. Immediately after hearing the Dodge-Nader plan the council approved the issuance of up to sixty thousand dollars in bonds to build the plant.[140] The city attorney reported that the cost could just barely be borne by a combination of borrowing and current expenditures.

To avoid mistakes and learn from the few communities that had already built sewage treatment plants, the Common Council decided to send the mayor, the city engineer, the city attorney and the chairman of the Sewage Committee to inspect sewage plants located in nine cities in Ohio, Pennsylvania, New Jersey, and Massachusetts. Committee members returned convinced the city was on the right track with the chemical-filtration plan they had adopted.[141]

Then at the beginning of the 1896 building season when construction of the new chemical treatment plant was to have begun, a group of University of Wisconsin professors asked for and received an opportunity to plead for the land disposal technique. First came N. O. Whitney, professor of engineering, who presented calculations showing that a land filtration system was cheaper to build and operate than a chemical plant and that ground application would work in the winter. Then came Charles S. Slichter, professor of mathematics, who said the proposed chemical filtration plant would cause twice as much fertilizer to flow into Lake Monona, making that lake much worse than its present condition.[142] Finally came Charles R. Van Hise, professor of geology, who argued that all of the world's leading authorities strongly preferred land treatment. On behalf of his colleagues Van Hise urged the council to get bids on both types of plants so that cost-effectiveness comparisons could be made.[143]

The council did exactly what the professors requested. A committee was set up to compare the two systems. The majority of the committee urged land disposal whereas the minority urged

chemical treatment. The most persuasive arguments, however, were found in the report's cost section, which showed that land treatment plants would cost over one hundred thousand dollars whereas the chemical plant was just eighty thousand dollars. The Common Council adopted the *minority* version of the committee.[144]

In many cities this would have ended the matter, but not in Madison. The completion of the plans and specifications for the chemical treatment plant in late February 1897 proved to be little more than a bell announcing another round of fierce fighting between proponents of the land and chemical sewage treatment systems. The *Democrat* welcomed the fight but the *Journal* seemingly exhausted from its earlier crusade said "Give us a rest. We don't know now, and never expect to know anything about sewerage. In regard to the systems proposed here, we have read articles from expert engineers, learned professors, and listened with tolerable patience to dissertations from all sorts of people. As to who is right or wrong, we don't pretend to know and are afraid that life is too short to find out."[145] Other citizens were apparently not yet tired of the controversy. For two nights in early March partisans of the respective systems jammed the City Hall auditorium to hear the professors ridicule the city engineers and the city attorney tweak the professors. Although the meetings produced little new knowledge, the majority clearly favored land treatment and expressed displeasure with the Common Council decision to build a chemical plant.[146]

However, once again the professors prevailed and the council set up a committee of experts to see if there were enough of the right kind of acreage for land treatment within four miles of the sewage treatment works.[147] Finally in July 1897, after boring 440 holes in the countryside just east of the Yahara River, the committee reported that only about twenty-five suitable acres were available, much less than what land disposal proponents desired. Engineers estimated this was enough land for twelve to fifteen years

and that at the end of this period the city would have to go to chemical precipitation. To buy the land and build the plant would cost about fifty-five to sixty thousand dollars—depending of course on what farmers would take for their land. To land disposal proponents the report was disappointing indeed. Having taken all reasonable steps to hear out the land disposal advocates, the council at its meeting on August 13, 1897, directed the engineers to proceed with the chemical plant without delay.[148]

The International System

Then, in early October 1897, a man no one had ever seen before came to Madison and convinced Madison decision makers to let him build the city disposal works for just thirty-seven thousand dollars. The name of this remarkable salesman was John MacDougall, managing director of the American Sanitary Engineering Company, Detroit, Michigan. How the slightly built Scotsman heard about the Madison situation is not known. What is known is that this distinguished "brisk appearing man" with iron-gray hair, chin whiskers, and drooping mustache, walked up to city engineers Dodge and Nader while they were doing soil borings at the East Washington Avenue site, told them who he was, that his company owned the exclusive patent rights for what he called the "international process" of chemical sewage treatment, and that he was interested in building the plant.[149]

MacDougall proudly explained that the process was being used in England, India, South Africa, and Australia. He said the international process was similar to other chemical treatment techniques except that he had a patented process that in conjunction with two proprietary chemicals "ferozone" and "polarite" caused his plant to be much more efficient than conventional plants. Moreover the clear, tasteless effluent would not smell, decay, or kill fish and was "purer than natural waters of many rivers."[150] In short, a smaller international plant would process twice as much sewage at a competitive or lower cost than a conventional plant. The additional capacity of the international process was particularly attractive to the engineers who were being charged by the university professors with designing an undersized plant. Soon the city engineers and MacDougall sat down to talk price and terms. MacDougall amazed them by saying that his company would guarantee to build the plant for just $37,200 and that it would operate the plant for the first three months at no charge to Madison. True, the price for the plant was below actual cost, but MacDougall needed a "model" United States city where he could install his first international plant and then use it as an advertisement of the new system.[151]

Local engineers eagerly embraced MacDougall's process and recommended that the council do the same. MacDougall presented his scheme to the council for the first time on October 11, 1897. Four days later the council met again to act on a recommendation from the Committee on Sewage. The committee made two important additions to the MacDougall proposal to reduce the risk to the city and assure satisfactory results. First, it required the American Sanitary Engineering Company to post a fifteen-thousand-dollar bond payable to the city if the plant did not perform as specified. Second, the effluent was to be "as pure as Lake Mendota water in 1888." (In that year the city was contemplating using still pure Lake Mendota water as a source of drinking water.) By a vote of thirteen to one the council approved the contract with the American Sanitary Engineering Company including the two additions. The only opposing vote was cast by thirty-three-year-old Professor Charles S. Slichter who got so involved in the sewage debate the preceding year that he decided to run for alderman. Slichter argued that the fancy chemicals being used by the American Sanitary Company worked no better than sand and that the company was going to make a financial killing on the Madison plant. But by this time the fight was over. Madison wanted action.[152]

Well, at least almost everybody! Just hours before the mayor was scheduled to sign the contract with the American Sanitary Engineering Company, Dr. A. R. Law, a resident of the sewage-strewn Monona shoreline, obtained an injunction on the grounds that the new system would increase Lake Monona pollution and cause offensive odors and weed growth. Significantly, the complaint was buttressed by expert testimony from U.W. professors who had fought the chemical system including Slichter and Van Hise.[153]

The *Democrat* supported the suit because it might force the city to return to land disposal, which it favored. But the *Journal,* tired of the fight said, "It is a case where doctors disagree and the average ignorant mortal can hardly be expected to have an intelligent opinion."[154] Finally, in December, 1897, the Law injunction was settled out of court on the condition that the MacDougall performance bond be increased from fifteen to twenty-five thousand dollars and that a panel of well-known Madison physicians, engineers, and scientists be selected to analyze the effluent for compliance with the 1888 Mendota purity levels.[155]

Construction could have begun at that point and would have but it did not. Daniel K. Tenney decided that he wanted to have the last word in the form of another injunction filed just four days after the Law injunction had been settled. Tenney devoutly believed that his eight-thousand-dollar solution—that is discharging the sewage into deeper water—would do just as much good as the thirty-seven-thousand-dollar MacDougall solution.[156] Tenney lost his injunction at the circuit court level in February but appealed the case to the Wisconsin State Supreme Court.

Meanwhile the city had passed all the necessary ordinances and was prepared to act once the injunction had been settled, presumably in the city's favor. Finally, in July 1898, after holding up the construction of the plant for six months, Tenney dropped his suit saying, "If the people of Madison want to be robbed, I will not stand in

the way."[157] Actual plant construction began late in the fall of 1898 and was completed in June of 1899.

At first the MacDougall plant seemed to be fulfilling its promise to convert sewage to drinking water. Several Canadian visitors who were considering building a similar plant in their city actually drank the clear effluent and said it was "good" tasting. Even city engineer McClellen Dodge drank the effluent with no apparent ill effects.[158] But then during the ninety-day trial period when the American Sanitary Company operated the plant, a number of problems became evident. The plant started giving off a horrid odor, sludge was being produced in such prodigious quantities that it could not be properly handled, and the costs of operating the plant were two to three times higher than anticipated. Chemical analysis showed the effluent to have four to twelve times as many impurities as the 1888 sample of Lake Mendota water. The two proprietary chemicals sold by the American Sanitary Engineering Company, the mysterious and powerful precipitant, "ferozone", and the marvelous deodorizer, "polarite", were apparently not performing as MacDougall had said.[159]

The city refrained from taking over the plant at the end of the ninety-day period. Finally in January 1900, after operating the plant for six months, the American Sanitary Engineering Company "abandoned" the plant. The city reluctantly took over, assigned several of its employees to operate the plant, declared the twenty-five-thousand-dollar bond forfeited, and began legal procedures to recover this amount. For one year city plant operators made resourceful efforts to make the facility work.[160]

None however, was successful and so in January 1901, the city also abandoned the plant. Consequently each day six hundred thousand gallons of four-smelling, nutrient-rich, black, virtually untreated effluent was disgourged into the Yahara River just one block north of the Steenland (East Washington Avenue) Bridge.[161] Not

FIGURE 5.28. EAST GILMAN NEIGHBORHOOD.   If you had stood at the corner of East Gilman and Pinckney Streets on the morning of August 2, 1889, and looked east, you would have seen this view of one of Madison's most prestigious neighborhoods. Homes had large barns and carriage houses in the rear. Stand at this corner today and notice the changes! (SHSW WHi(X3)30436)

FIGURE 5.29. MONONA-WILSON AREA.   This 1890 photograph, taken at the foot of Monona Avenue looking northwest toward the Capitol, shows the home of General Simeon Mills, one of Madison's most prominent citizens, in the left foreground. Between Mills house and Lake Monona was the mansion of Governor Lucius Fairchild. Until the early twentieth century this was one of Madison's prestige neighborhoods. Today the City County Building occupies the entire block of which the Mills' mansion was a part. (SHSW WHi(X3)23409)

until July 1901, six months later, was the city able to construct a new sewage treatment facility (see chap. 6, pp. 390–391). And not until February 1902 did the long-awaited legal confrontation take place. After a spirited but terribly technical trial, the jury ruled against MacDougall on every count. The city not only received proceeds from the twenty-five-thousand-dollar bond, but damages and costs as well, for a total of forty-two thousand dollars.[162]

Summary

Collecting and purifying sewage was probably the most exasperating problem confronting Madison officials during the last two decades of the nineteenth century. The sewage problem was technical, political, and economic; and each aspect was connected to the others in new and frustrating ways. What must not be forgotten is that when Madison began to grapple with its sewage disposal problem, the science of sanitary engineering was in its infancy. Rare indeed were the communities that Madison leaders could visit that had actually built sewage purification plants.[163] Faced by these difficulties, Madison officials did their homework relatively well. They hired the best experts in the country (although they disregarded their recommendations) and they sent city officials all over the country to inspect the best systems and talk to the most authoritative leaders in the rapidly changing world of sewage disposal. And they enlisted the aid of University of Wisconsin experts, thereby writing a very early chapter in what later became known as the "Wisconsin Idea."

Very significantly, the way the sewage question was resolved established a pattern that would later be followed for many complex public issues. The deeply caring few—led by articulate, self-styled, and credentialled experts, armed by opposing newspapers, and aided by the courts—engaged in bitter, highly technical, and often intractable combat over the correct public policy.

Varieties of Local Government Reform: 1880–1900

In the fall of 1892, the city attorney drafted three amendments to the Madison charter designed to expand the scope and power of city government. Nothing about this process was in any way unusual. Under its state-granted charter, the city could do only those things specifically authorized by that document. Therefore if the city wanted to do something *not* specifically mentioned, a charter amendment had to be created. In this case the Common Council was seeking power to do three things: (1) sprinkle its dusty streets; (2) issue bonds to acquire its own municipal lighting plant; and (3) issue bonds to make street repairs and improvements. Over the years dozens of such charter amendments had been requested and routinely approved.[1]

To Wisconsin legislators, however, this business of issuing special charters for every municipality and then countless amendments thereto was tedious, time-consuming, and unnecessary work. Thus in 1889 the Wisconsin legislature began a series of steps designed to get it entirely out of the charter and charter revision business. In that year it issued a general city charter to replace all special city charters.[2] In 1892 Wisconsin voters approved a constitutional amendment that *prohibited* the legislature from enacting any special laws for city incorporation.[3] These steps got the legislature out of the special charter business, but they created a dilemma for Madison and other cities around the state that had special charters. The Madison city attorney ruled that this constitutional amendment also prohibited legislators from amending Madison's existing special charter. This meant the city could either abandon its often modified special charter, so laboriously worked out over the years, or it could adopt the new 1889 general charter. Unfortunately the new general charter, although more inclusive in some ways than Madison's special charter, did not allow the city to do the three things it was requesting in the fall of 1892.

This dilemma convinced many Madison opinion makers that the state framers of the general charter had no appreciation of the need for enlarged local government powers. However, according to a thoughtful 1892 *Wisconsin State Journal* editorial, the problem lay with an earlier concept that dominated the minds of Wisconsin constitution writers and that had been uncritically accepted by the 1889 general charter framers. That idea was the "old 'let alone' (*laissez faire*) policy of government . . . that people left alone to their own inclinations, left free to engage without restrictions in those enterprises that supply the wants of the people, would give better results than could the collective efforts of people acting as the 'government.' " This concept was viable, the editorial concluded, when the role of local government was much smaller, but not in an era when Madison municipal government had become "a great business corporation."[4]

In effect, the *Wisconsin State Journal* editor was attacking the old *laissez faire* notion of government on the grounds that it was inefficient and irresponsible. This was one of the first expressions in Madison of what later became known as Progressivism and which was then becoming popular among reformers all over the country.[5]

Significantly, other cities in the state were also discovering the limitations of the new general charter and had conveyed those concerns to Madison Mayor William H. Rogers (1891–1893). As mayor of the state's capital city, Rogers was in a convenient position to play a leadership role. Rogers called his fellow mayors to a meeting in January 1893 and was appointed chairman of a committee to secure more power for cities by adding numerous powers to the new general charter. In effect Wisconsin city officials adopted the Madison "platform." Although the effort failed to persuade the legislature, it constituted the beginning of a long and important battle that culminated in the 1925 "home rule" statute, which for the first time in Wisconsin history, gave municipalities broad powers to govern their affairs.[6]

Following their defeat at the hands of the legislature, Madison reformers simply redirected their zeal for change to other areas. This time instead of picking goals that involved relatively esoteric questions of local government structure and powers, reformers picked goals that had much broader voter appeal and launched a conservative reform notable both for the speed and the degree of change it wrought.

The first goal set forth by the reformers was how to get "the more intelligent class of voters," "the businessmen and principal taxpayers," and the "good men" involved in local politics. By the mid-1890s this was a strongly felt need of Madison's Yankee elite. Local politics were dominated by the Democratic Party, which in turn was run by ward caucuses—a system that gave party activists great power. For example, a Fifth Ward Democratic caucus during this period was repeatedly attended by "twelve to fifteen young men and boys, two or three old men, two saloon keepers and a professional ward politician." An indignant citizen complained that there was not "one university or professional man or prominent businessman" in attendance that evening. In effect, Madison's generally Republican business and professional elite had lost control of city government and desired to regain its old hegemony.[7]

Perhaps, reasoned the reformers, the "good men" would become reinvolved in the local political process if politics could somehow be made respectable. To the reformers the change most likely to lure this group back into the local political process was the elimination of "partyism" whose application to local government was a source of growing contempt to many. Said one critic, "There is no such thing as a Republican system of macadamizing (gravelling), a Democratic system of lighting the city, or any other party system of municipal improvement on any line."[8]

Getting good men back into local government and getting partyism out constituted the platform of a reform organization that first called itself the Madison Municipal League but then changed its name to the Madison Civic Federation. Its first meeting was called in January 1895 by a group of university, religious, and business leaders including the president of the University of Wisconsin, Charles K. Adams, the owner of Madison's largest factory, John A. Johnson, and the priest of St. Patrick's Catholic Church, Father P. B. Knox. Nearly all Civic Federation leaders leavened their exhortatory speeches that evening with strong moral justifications for pursuing reform goals. For example, Johnson predicted that if the principal taxpayers of the community would take back the reins of city government, "gambling and disorderly dens would disappear like chaff before the winds."[9] It was this promise to elevate community moral standards that allowed the Civic Federation to attract the sizable number of voters most of whom supported prohibition, the elimination of the stall saloon, and greater respect for the Sabbath. The same high-minded moralism was appealing to disaffected Democrats who reluctantly admitted that their party seemed to always be on the side of the "bum and tough, the law-breaker and the prostitute."[10]

Auspicious though the first meeting was, Civic Federation leaders recognized the need to aggressively seek members. For one year they held well-attended meetings and sponsored lectures, all of which were generously covered and backed by both newspapers. Throughout this period federation leaders trumpeted the virtues of what they called a "business-like administration"—the highest accolade the organization could confer. Among other things, being "business like" meant electing city officials and hiring city employees based on "merit," not on political qualifications;[11] paying the mayor and city officials a reasonable salary;[12] establishing a budget and sticking to it;[13] extending the mayoral term from one to two or three years;[14] giving the mayor more power, especially the power to appoint city officials so that a clear voter accountability could be established;[15] abandoning the razzmatazz torchlight parades and brass band style of campaigning in favor of rational issue-oriented discussions;[16] hiring experts to advise city officials;[17] and, finally, acknowledging that city government had become a "science."[18]

After more than a year of meetings on these topics, the Civic Federation decided that the time had come to enter its own mayoral candidate. Into the ring went the hat of W. W. Warner, vice-president of the Civic Federation, a respected local business leader and bicycle manufacturer. To back their crusader, the Civic Federation even published their own newspaper, the *Non Partisan*.[19] Seldom in Madison's history had the local political cauldron "been so full of bubble, toil and trouble," as one newspaper put it.[20]

When the record number of votes were counted, Civic Federation members were profoundly disappointed. Their mayoral candidate had polled just ten percent of the votes. However, the Republican candidate, Dr. Albert A. Dye, won the election by fifty-two votes over a Democratic incumbent! Rarely in Madison did Republican candidates win, and when they did, it signalled either a strong dissatisfaction with the status quo or support for a particular man in spite of his Republican affiliation. Dye's victory was an example of the former; people wanted a change, but they wanted change *within* the two-party system.[21]

Although the Civic Federation failed to wear voters from their familiar two-party system, they were clearly instrumental in ending nearly forty years of overwhelming Democratic Party dominance of the mayor's office. Between 1880 and 1895 thirteen of fifteen mayors were Democrats and they enjoyed an average plurality of thirty-five percent, not counting the four times Democrats won elections without opposition. By contrast, between 1895 and 1900, mayoral winners enjoyed an average plurality of just two percent, and in two of these five years (1896 and 1898) Republicans were elected mayor.[22] This transformation was probably due to more "good men" voting in local elections than ever before and to Democrats crossing over and voting Republican in the interests of "reform." Thus, for the first time since the close of the Civil War in Madison, Republicans had a good chance of winning mayoral races. Republicans were also successful in electing enough Common Council members to equal the Democrats.[23]

FIGURE 5.30. 1893 SIXTH WARD SCHOOLHOUSE. Today the largest building in the 1200 block of Williamson Street is the Eagles Club. But in 1893 the site now occupied by the Eagles Club boasted the fanciest schoolhouse in nineteenth century Madison. The above photograph shows that building known as the "Sixth Ward School." The elegant five-turreted $33,000 school, easily the most expensive ever built in the city in the nineteenth century, was designed by the well-known local architectural firm of Conover and Porter. The exterior of the building was done in Ashland brown stone and cream brick. The tip of its main turret stood nine stories above the ground. Later it was renamed Marquette School.

The Sixth Ward School was one of several schools and school additions built between 1880 and 1900 to keep ahead of growing school enrollments—a period when the number of children who attended public schools increased by 150 percent. Because Madison's special charter limited the amount the city could levy each year for school purposes, a variety of cost saving efforts were necessary. Unfortunately much of the burden fell on the classroom teacher who had an average of forty-five students in each class during this two-decade period.

Superintendents naturally took great pride in providing statistics that portrayed the Madison school system in a favorable light. In the 1895 *Annual Report of the Board of Education,* for example, Superintendent R. B. Dudgeon noted that of the children in the United States attending school, only one out of fifty-three school-aged children was enrolled in high school. In Madison, by contrast, that figure was one out of every six children. Most superintendents were also candid enough to admit shortcomings. In 1881, for example, a survey showed that of all boys from elementary age through high school, 22 1/3 percent used tobacco. (SHSW WHi(X3)36016)

Just one year after the failure of the Madison Civic Federation to get their reform candidate elected, the state legislature enacted a law that gave to reformers in Madison and all over the state the option of implementing one of their long-sought nonpartisan goals.[24] The law authorized the establishment of a police and fire commission and empowered its three commissioners to hire and fire members of the police force and fire department. Up to that time the Common Council had that power. That system was established in Madison in 1897 and made members of the police and fire departments subject to a civil service system. From this point forward Madison police received salaries instead of fees and commissions. The only power left to the Common Council was the establishment of salaries.[25]

In summary, the Civic Federation left an impressive legacy of good government reforms. Clearly, the most important was their restoration of a viable two-party system at the mayoral level. While federation leaders would clearly have preferred to have elected their own nonpartisan candidates, they quickly recognized the merit of using the Republican party as a reform vehicle. Other important legacies included the nonpartisan police and fire commission, the much more common use of the term "businesslike" as it applied to candidates of *both* parties, more widespread agreement that votes should be cast for the "best" qualified candidates with less emphasis upon party labels, and the idea that local government should have more power over local affairs.

The City Beautiful: The Movement Begins

In January, 1893, one of Madison's most influential citizens, First National Bank president, Napoleon Bonaparte Van Slyke, wrote a letter to the *Wisconsin State Journal* editor in which he insisted that Madisonians had depended too much and too long on the natural beauty of the city and had failed to pay enough attention to its man-made beauty. "Not only have we been negligent to improve our appearance and convenience," he continued, "but we have about destroyed the original beauty and the approaches to our lake borders by allowing encroachments—nuisances—as unsightly as unlawful, and this to a shameful degree. . . . Could the distinguished men for whom our principal streets were named but rise and look upon the unfortunate change wrought by ourselves, destroying nature's loveliness, they would exclaim, 'Twas bright, 'twas heavenly bright, but 'tis past.'"[1]

These were strong words and carried great weight, but not merely because they were uttered by Van Slyke. In fact such sentiments had become almost epidemic among Madison leaders during 1892. Prominent businessmen and politicians urged elimination of shanty-like boathouses then marring the shoreline and the creation of handsome little parks at junk-filled street ends. Some even urged that lakeshore land be purchased for public access. Never before had so many staid businessmen been so strongly in favor of flowers, fountains, boulevards, trees, lawnmowers and public lake access. It was the year beautification became popular in Madison.[2]

To carry out these beautification programs, several prominent Madisonians urged the formation of an "improvement society" but it was not until January, 1893, that several members of the Madison Business Club formed a separate organization known as the Madison Improvement Association (MIA) "to improve and beautify the City of Madison and Dane County."[3] Public response to the new organization surpassed even the most sanguine expectations of its leaders. After just two weeks, over eleven thousand dollars in private subscriptions was pledged to the new organization, in spite of the fact that MIA leaders had no more than a vague idea of how they would spend the money.[4]

Directors of the Madison Improvement Association quickly translated this strong but general expression of support into several specific projects. A Chicago landscape architect, Olaf Bensen, was hired to design street-end parks, boulevards for Monona and Wisconsin Avenues, and a series of walks and fountains for Orton Park. A Chicago architect and "former Madison boy," Frank Lloyd Wright, was hired to do two large boathouses, one at the foot of North Carroll Street on Lake Mendota and another at the foot of South Hancock on Lake Monona, both of which were intended to replace dozens of individual rag-tag structures that then cluttered the shoreline.[5] The Streets Committee of the MIA made street trees available to homeowners at cost and even prepared pamphlets on how to plant and maintain them.[6]

Then, almost as quickly as it had begun, association momentum ground to a halt. Strong resident opposition to the plans to boulevard Monona and Wisconsin Avenues forced association officials to scrap these improvements. Then came the sudden, severe 1893 depression, which prevented many businessmen from making their second and last pledge payment. Before closing their official doors, however, the association completed the Frank Lloyd Wright boathouse at North Carroll Street and laid a sidewalk in Orton Park. All other plans, including the larger and more badly needed boathouse on Lake Monona were shelved.[7]

Fortunately, the demise of the MIA did not mean the end of beautification. Indeed, the same community enthusiasm that gathered a head of steam in 1892 also inspired three men to spearhead the construction of a twelve-mile pleasure drive on the west side of town, a large portion of which lay along picturesque Lake Mendota. The project was destined to have great impact upon Madison history.

The idea for the drive came from forty-two-year-old U.W. French Professor, real estate speculator, and nature lover, Edward T. Owen, who in 1892 bought a fourteen-acre tract of woodland along and over a "commanding height"[8] about a mile south of Lake Mendota and three miles west of the Capitol Square. Owen saw his tract, now known as Owen Drive, as a part of a larger scheme. More specifically, he wanted to

John M. Olin: Citizen Extraordinare, Father of Madison Park System

SHSW WHi(X3) 18058

In 1894 Amos Wilder, the new editor of the *Wisconsin State Journal,* wrote an editorial in which he said a "park crank" was the "most valuable citizen" a city could have. Unlike most citizens who are preoccupied earning a living and cannot think more than ten years ahead, Wilder said the "park crank" "spans fifty years and dreams of the city as it shall be when the lisping child of today is infirm with age." For Madison that "park crank" was John Myers Olin.

Olin arrived in Madison in August, 1874, just twenty-three years old, following an invitation from U.W. President John Bascom to become an instructor of oratory and rhetoric. Olin had studied under Bascom at Williams College and had impressed the future college president with his commencement address and general ability. Olin remained at the university post for four years, but then decided to enter the U.W. Law School. Olin completed the two-year program in one year and opened a solo law office in 1879. Then in December, 1885, after establishing a respected practice, he was named professor in the law school. The years between 1885 and 1893 were busy years for Olin. In addition to teaching in the Law School and attending his growing law practice, he became active in the Prohibition party and even ran for governor on its ticket in 1886.

But it was not for his magnificent flashes of oratory, his brilliant legal mind, his distinguished appearance, or even his prohibition principles that

caused John Meyers Olin to be remembered by Madisonians. It was his unstinting love for his adopted city and particularly his leadership on park development. From 1894 until 1909, Olin was the president and driving force behind the Madison Park and Pleasure Drive Association (MPPDA). When he began in 1894, the city had just 3 ½ acres in parkland (Orton Park) and no park commission. When he turned over the reins to others in 1909, the MPPDA had 269 acres of parkland, a park commission, and a nationally known private park-building organization. At that point Olin had coaxed Madisonians to voluntarily contribute nearly a quarter of a million dollars for the purchase, development, and maintenance of parks—a clear tribute to his leadership and vision.

So industrious was Olin in pursuing parks and pleasure drives that some Madisonians began to think he was making large amounts of money by securing advance options on lands and other means. These baseless charges angered the scrupulously honest park leader. Said Olin: "I believe there is such a thing as the rendering of disinterested service to the public, however difficult it may be for certain people to comprehend the idea."

When Olin died in 1924 at the age of seventy-three, Michael Olbrich, one of Olin's admirers and a respected Association leader, said: "In the very forefront of heroes that I am to tell my boys about is John M. Olin. . . ." Indeed, he was that kind of man. It was Olin whose inspiration, unflagging effort, and almost magical results caused his colleagues to view him as the "Father of Madison's park system and a man without peers."

create a west-side rural pleasure drive that would link his park to a curvy road through the university grounds now known as Observatory Drive, and then to a spectacularly beautiful two-and-one-half-mile road along the shore of Lake Mendota in Eagle Heights. The Eagle Heights road, then known as Raymer Road, had become an instant hit as a pleasure drive when it was opened to the public in 1888 by its public-spirited owner, George Raymer. Unfortunately, Raymer Road could only be reached by a single road, which was often muddy and impassible.[9]

Working with Professor Owen were a forty-one-year-old lawyer and U.W. law school professor, John M. Olin, and a forty-five-year-old livestock farmer and large Dane County landholder, Edward E. Hammersley. Owen donated his fourteen acres of land as a park through which a drive was to be constructed, Hammersley contributed an easement across his property, and Olin worked out easements through the remaining portions of the drive and helped raise money for the construction of a causeway, now Willow Drive, across University Bay.[10]

When the drive was officially opened in October 1892, seventy carriages made the three-hour drive. All returned ecstatic about the extraordinary scenery and views these public spirited men had made available to the public.[11] In the enthusiasm of the moment, someone said the drive was the beginning of a "new era" in Madison.[12] And indeed it was.

At first the enterprise was known as the Lake Mendota Pleasure Drive Association, but in July 1894, in the midst of the serious business depression, a citywide organization was formed known as the Madison Park and Pleasure Drive Association (MPPDA) under the capable leadership of John M. Olin. Their goal was to open, extend and improve rustic roadways through picturesque scenery in and about Madison. Association members saw the drives as an effective and welcome method to escape the frenzied pace, noise, and dirt of the city, an opportunity to "breathe God's purest air," savor nature and refresh the spirit.[13]

Few achievements brought greater pleasure to Madisonians or evoked more compliments from out-of-town visitors than the Lake Mendota Drive. Its success laid the ground work for a second major pleasure drive in 1897, which extended around the eastern end of Lake Mendota, between today's Burrows Park and the state hospital.[14] When Olin announced the plan in March, 1897, over four hundred Madisonians eagerly contributed more than ten thousand dollars for the construction of a 5½-mile lakeshore pleasure drive. After some controversy, the new drive was named after Leonard J. Farwell who had done so much for Madison in the early 1850s and who for a time lived just behind the state hospital, the drive's terminus.[15]

Not to be outdone, the people around the shore of Lake Monona insisted that the MPPDA commence a pleasure drive encircling "their" lake, to be called "Monona Drive." Said E. W. Keyes, who volunteered a right of way for the drive through his subdivision along the northeastern Monona shore: "The people on the shore of Monona will not be content that the great Mendota shall have a monopoly of this pleasure drive business. It is too good a thing to be enjoyed only by the Mendotans."[16] In January, 1899, the association responded and sent an open letter to both daily papers asking Lake Monona property owners to come forward and dedicate a road in perpetuity across their property.[17] Thus began the idea that ultimately produced the parks and drives around a large portion of Lake Monona.

Buoyed by its great promise and impressive successes of the two Lake Mendota drives, the Association grew from just twenty-six members in 1894 to nearly four hundred in 1899.[18] Association members tended to be the movers and shakers of their day. They included the captains of Madison's industries, the president of the university and many of its senior professors, newspaper publishers, people who if they put their collective will behind something, could make it a reality. They were the top slice of Madison's pyramid of wealth, persons who could afford buggies and horses and who merchants then called "the carriage trade."[19]

FIGURE 5.31. FRANK LLOYD WRIGHT. Shown at right in this 1880 or 1881 photograph are the pupils of the seventh and eighth grade teacher at the Second Ward School. The school stood on the same site later occupied by the Madison Art Center (1964–1980), formerly the Lincoln School.

The young man in the top right of the photograph with the fancy belted coat, bow tie, and hat is Frank Lloyd Wright, then twelve or thirteen years old. Wright had moved to Madison in 1880 sometime during the year this photograph was taken. After going through seventh and eighth grades at the Second Ward School, he entered Madison High School in about 1882. There he failed algebra, got grades ranging from good to poor in other subjects, and probably never graduated. In January 1886, at the age of eighteen, Wright entered the University of Wisconsin as a special student. For no more than two years Wright took "scientific courses," attended classes desultorily and joined the Phi Delta Theta fraternity. To earn money for his fraternity bills and his financially pinched family, he worked for Allan D. Conover, professor of engineering at the University of Wisconsin. His most important task as a Conover assistant was performing minor supervisory work on the construction of Science Hall. Wright left Madison in 1887 just before his twentieth birthday without graduating from the University of Wisconsin to take a job in Chicago where he began his professional achitectural career.

This picture was graciously provided by former Madison Mayor Henry Reynolds whose father Edward S. Reynolds, then about fourteen years old, is the first boy on the left in the third row. (Courtesy of Mrs. Henry Reynolds)

The rapid growth of the MPPDA was not, however, achieved without difficulty. At first some thought the pleasure drives were clever schemes designed to line the pockets of real estate speculators but such accusations were quickly shown to be baseless.[20] Then there were those who felt the association was elitist in purpose and membership. This change could hardly be denied. Its first board of directors was a calculated mixture of judges, former mayors, leading businessmen, developers, professors, the minister of the largest and most prestigious church, and even the president of the University of Wisconsin. The association's product, pleasure drives, were primarily

enjoyed by only about twenty-five percent of Madisonians who could afford to own or rent horses.[21] Moreover, all the pleasure drives lay outside the city and were therefore not easily accessible to poorer citizens.

Impressive as its first years were, the golden years of this extraordinary organization did not occur until the twentieth century when the Madison Park and Pleasure Drive Association became a national leader in open space development. That story will be told in the next chapter.

Society and Leisure

The Upper Crust

In 1895 Wisconsin's foremost author, Hamlin Garland, published a novel about Rose Dutcher, a girl who grew up in the coulees of western Wisconsin. To this shy but alert farmgirl, Madison represented something "great and beautiful and heroic. . . ." One of her school teachers had been from Madison, a fact that in itself yielded great distinction. Her father's newspaper came from Madison. The governor lived there. It was the center of "art and society and literature."

When she was eighteen she traveled to Madison for the first time and stayed with a prominent family who lived near the university. Madison was everything Rose imagined and more. She was particularly impressed by the way society women lived. Looking out the window of her elegant new Madison hostess' home, "she saw two ladies come out of a large house . . . and walk down toward the carriage which waited at the gate. The ladies held their dresses with a dainty action of their gloved hands as they stood for a moment in consultation. (How graceful their hats were!) Then they entered their carriage." To Rose these ladies wrapped in soft robes were a "revelation of elegance and grace."[1]

The ladies that Garland described, though appearing in a novel, were hardly a fiction. Three years prior to its publication Garland had spent

a month in Madison where he closely observed the city and its people. The ladies of Garland's novel were members of Madison's elite, which in 1895 were clustered into three cliques on three hills. There was "Aristocratic Hill," today called "Mansion Hill," known by "the rustle of silk and satin." It boasted the Vilas mansion, the home of the governor and many prominent business leaders. There was the "fashionable, wealthy, pretty and learned" university clique in the lower Langdon-Gilman area. Finally there was the Monona clique aligned along Wilson Street near Monona Avenue. There lived former governors, judges, wealthy lawyers, newspaper publishers and others. Most of the residents of these neighborhoods had roots in New England, and all three claimed to be "regular, foreordained, predestined, gilt-edged, all wool and a yard wide," societies.[2]

To those who lived in this favored but "clam tight"[3] circle, life was pleasant indeed. A prominent society woman recalled: "Our houses were wainscoted in walnut and in them we had a lovely time. . . . Of course we knew everyone. Afternoons we sent for our carriages, took our white gloves and card cases and went calling. We were very formal and dressy at formal teas and dinners. . . ."[4] Most entertained in their own homes. Recalling the period around 1896, a faculty wife said "it was very pleasant to have the best of music in your own house before the fireplace, or to go to a neighbor's to see a superb collection of etchings, or a Japanese print, or china or glass, or antique Persian rugs or the rarest edition of Shakespeare while you drink your tea or mint juleps."[5] For people in this group foreign travel was almost routine and elegant country homes were viewed as *de rigour*.[6] House parties with two hundred guests or weddings with one thousand guests were not uncommon.[7] As if the extensive coverage afforded society doings in the two daily papers were not enough, a "bright gossipy" weekly called *The Critic,* which catered to persons of "good breeding," appeared in 1897.[8]

Madison's upper crust viewed themselves as worldly, learned, cosmopolitan, and cultured; and in many ways they were. Yet they were naive

about certain aspects of Madison that did not quite fit into the charm, comfort, and security of their world. For example, few residents of Langdon Street seemed to know that Madison periodically had a small-scale tenderloin district at the foot of East Wilson Street known as the "Midway." Indeed it was an understandable form of blindness. After all, they had their travel, literary clubs, fine homes, teas, and churches and many more pleasant things to engross their attention.[9]

The Melting Pot

In spite of the fact that the foreign born and the native born of foreign parents outnumbered the native born of native parents, by a three-to-one margin, the native born and particularly the Yankee element continued to constitute what sociologists call the "power elite" and the "opinion makers." They owned most of the banks, held the most property, occupied the better-paying jobs, and were the focal point of Madison "society." The primary reason for this continued dominance lay in the fact that they had a considerable time advantage, that is, they had been established in Madison for decades and therefore had time to develop businesses, acquire property, and establish social norms. The foreign born by contrast had a more difficult time creating an economic niche for themselves and consequently tended to be more mobile and took lower-paying, lower-status, and lower-security jobs.

Some very important changes were taking place, however, during the last two decades of the nineteenth century—changes that altered the power structure of the community. Most of the foreign groups were sending their children to public schools where they learned to speak English and developed strong loyalties to their adopted country—a fact that did not go unnoticed by the native born. More and more immigrants established their own businesses, embraced the all important set of "business values" and thereby became a part of the business community. Symbolizing this trend was the decision

FIGURE 5.32. NATIVE AMERICANS: A LINGERING PRESENCE. Although the Winnebagos had been officially banished by treaty from southern Wisconsin after June 1, 1833, some managed a fugitive existence in and around the Madison area for many decades. The two shots showing George Goodvillage and his squaw on King Street in 1892 (shown below) and the Winnebago wigwam in Wingra Woods in 1895 (shown above) provide visual reminders of this fact. During the latter part of the nineteenth century the favorite Indian campsites were Mills Woods (now the Elmside Boulevard area), Fullers Woods, Frost Woods, and the Arboretum. There they ate boiled lily bulbs, muskrats, and fish and lived in wigwams similar to the one shown at left. To make money they trapped mink and speared muskrat in Madison's many marshes. When enough pelts had been collected, they sold them to Capitol Square fur buyers for ten cents apiece.

During this period most Madisonians mustered a kind of strained tolerance for the Indians. Ironically the Indian was most welcome as the subject of scholarly papers especially on the "prehistoric period." Perhaps the greatest tolerance was exhibited for enterprising Indian boys who brought their small hickory bows and blunt arrows to the Capitol Park. There they would insert a two-foot-long stick into the lawn and try to persuade passersby to place a penny in a slot at the top of the stick. Then the boys would back up about thirty feet and take aim at the penny. If they hit it, they would keep the penny; if not, it would be returned to the donor. (University of Wisconsin Archives and SHSW WHi(X3)38333) made in 1885 by John J. Suhr to change the name of his bank from the Deutsche Bank to the German-American Bank.[10] (During World War I the name was changed once again to the American Exchange Bank, by which it is still known today.) Ironically the biggest success of all, indeed the most impressive Horatio Alger story in Madison history was reserved for Norwegian-born John A. Johnson, whose Fuller and Johnson Company became the largest employer in Madison and a source of immense pride among Madison leaders.

Madison's "foreign" element also enjoyed several notable successes in local politics. In 1897 Madison voters elected Matthew Hoven, a German Catholic, as mayor—the first time either a Catholic or a German had ever been elected to that office. Interestingly, his opponent was a long-established merchant who happened to be a Republican German Jew. That Hoven was elected on the heels of the intense agitation by prohibitionists and sabbatarians was hardly coincidental. Many Germans—and for that matter non-Germans too—were tired of this moralistic Yankee interference with their "personal liberty" and no doubt saw Hoven as a man who would enforce the "best" laws and ignore the rest. Long before Hoven became the first German to occupy the mayor's chair, many other foreign-born and first generation Americans were participating in the political process and electing growing numbers of their countrymen to the Common Council.[11] There they supported cetain policies favoring "personal liberty" such as the tacit agreement to keep the saloons open on Sunday. Another clear demonstration of "foreign" power were positions the Common Council took from time to time on European developments. For example in 1886 the Common Council adopted a strong and stirring statement supporting a free Ireland and an independent parliament. As if this were not enough, they directed Mayor Keyes, a card-carrying member of the Yankee elite, to convey this resolution to British Prime Minister Gladstone, which of course he did.[12] And foreign voter blocs

were not above threatening to bolt the Democratic Party and vote for a Republican if they felt they were not getting their fair share of patronage positions and street work.[13]

The growing power of the foreign element in Madison politics and business threatened members of Madison's native born "establishment" and produced a variety of friction points. For example in 1897, several young men belonging to the "best" Yankee families got into a brawl at a lower State Street saloon when they decided it was uproariously funny to yell: "To hell with the Pope." Unfortunately for the boys, a Catholic society had just dropped into the saloon for a nightcap. In the melee that followed, one of the native-born boys had two teeth knocked out and another had his ear nearly ripped off.[14] The same intense reaction was provoked during an effort to enforce the saloon closing laws. Someone wrote an anonymous letter to the *Democrat* editor telling the liberty-loving Germans they ought to go back to Germany where they could have "free beer and tyranny." This time the letter writer had the good sense not to sign his or her name—an act of cowardice that further enraged the German community.[15]

Little progress was made in the treatment of blacks and Chinese, long the occupants of the bottom rung on the Madison social ladder. Newspapers usually reported meetings of black organizations but often with condescending remarks about the "beaming faces of pickaninnies" and the like.[16] Evidence of strong antiblack sentiment was reflected by the fact that few Madison building owners were willing to allow black organizations to hold meetings on their property.[17] After many years of running laundries in Madison, the Chinese were begrudgingly acknowledged by most people to be "harmless, law abiding and industrious," but the *Madison Democrat* said they were "nevertheless a fungoid growth on our constitutions" and a "barnacle on the ship of American progress" because they demonstrated "no inclinations to become American citizens."[18]

Teetotalers, Tomatoes, and East-Side Missions: The Role of Religion

In 1888 writers for the *Wisconsin State Journal* prepared and extensively distributed a special supplement that described Madison's many advantages as a manufacturing center. Its purpose was to induce factory owners to move their factories to Madison. In addition to describing Madison's superb railroad network, proximity to markets and minerals, and other data of interest to a factory owner, *Journal* writers provided a rich narrative portrait of the city itself. In the section on the role of religion in Madison, the *Journal* spoke proudly about the great cathedrals clustered very near the Square, boasted that the people of Madison were "notably religious in the true sense of that term," and that "bigotry, narrowness and exclusiveness are not tolerated. . . ."[19] No doubt such words were reassuring, but in fact beneath these ripple-free descriptions lay tempestuous issues and a very different story.

The last two decades of the nineteenth century were a period of transition for Madison church people. Like their counterparts all over the country, they were becoming much less meditative about their religion and much more concerned about doing something about certain problems then becoming evident in cities. Later this "social gospel" movement produced demands for fundamental social and economic change, but in the late nineteenth century in Madison, this interventionist impulse had two more limited goals: (1) to eradicate certain pernicious forms of evil, notably alcohol, the saloon, and violations of the Sabbath; and (2) to reach the growing numbers of unchurched people in the city.[20]

Saloons and Prostitution

Nowhere was the power of church people more evident than in the effort to close Madison saloons and shut down the liquor traffic. The history of these efforts to make Madison dry might have discouraged some, but not the highly motivated prohibitionists. Theirs was a righteous and noble cause. If anything, they derived strength from the fact that they were few and sinners legion.

As in earlier years, much of the prohibition work was done by women most of whom were re-energized by a visit in January 1880 of Frances E. Willard, national president of the Women's Christian Temperance Union. Miss Willard convinced several Madison women to form a state and local chapter of the W. C. T. U. and don the white ribbon symbolizing total abstinence. At first the women contented themselves with passing out pledge cards, distributing literature and running a game room for boys under sixteen years of age. However, they quickly enlisted the aid of community leaders like U. W. President John Bascom. Getting Bascom's involvement was hardly difficult; he was a devout teetotaler and his wife Emma was an officer in the Madison W. C. T. U.[21]

Bascom was apparently eager to get into the fray. He made his most dramatic impact in March 1884 when he wrote a long and forceful letter to the *Wisconsin State Journal* in which he said: "Madison is not as safe a place as it . . . ought to be for young men," because they are "met at every turn by saloons." This was a great problem said Bascom because "the last days of boyhood and the first days of manhood are days of strong impulses, narrow experience and little prudence." In a second letter several days later, Bascom said that two-thirds of U. W. students were minors but that in spite of this fact Madison saloons sold liquor "illegally and uninterruptedly" to them.[22] Bascom insisted the problem was exacerbated because Madison authorities allowed saloons to openly violate the state Sunday closing law. Bascom concluded by saying the city should "remove these unnecessary temptations from the young men gathered here for instruction." Bascom's remarks on Madison's unsuitability as the home for the state university created a state-wide furor and helped build support for a concerted effort to force the saloons to close on

Sunday in conformity with the existing but widely ignored state law.[23]

Prohibitionists recognized that they could not force Madison to go completely dry, but that they could invoke the state Sunday closing law and mobilize community sabbatarian sentiment. At the time it was common for Madison churches to adopt creeds on Sabbath desecration. For example, members of the First Congregational Church promised to arrange their lives so that they never had to travel, go to the post office, read a newspaper, go on picnics, or visit friends on Sunday.[24]

To give form and substance to the Sunday closing movement, Bascom and others established the Law and Order League in the spring of 1884. To combat what they viewed as a nativistic and puritanical attack, saloon owners formed their own organization known as the Personal Liberty League. At a hurriedly called meeting they shrewdly decided the better part of valor was to shut down on Sunday at least until the moral fervor subsided. However, after a few weeks, the saloons reopened. The Law and Order League retaliated by hiring two detectives—the Personal Liberty League called them "spies"—who went around one Sunday gathering evidence for formal legal actions. Altogether sixty of Madison's sixty-two saloons were caught and taken to court, and fifty were convicted of selling liquor on Sunday. The judge, however, was entirely sympathetic with the saloon owners and let them off with the minimum five-dollar fine. Nevertheless, angry members of the Personal Liberty League held another meeting and agreed to close down until the situation seemed safe again.[25]

Unable to establish more than a temporary victory on the Sunday closing front, prohibitionists decided to try a new state law passed in 1885, that gave them the power to substantially increase the cost of saloon licenses. The law required a municipality to hold an election to increase the cost for saloon licenses if just twelve voters signed a petition. After receiving such a petition from the prohibitionists, the city clerk

scheduled a special election for September 1885 that gave voters the choice between what was called a "low" license of two hundred dollars, a medium license of "three hundred fifty dollars," and a high license of "five hundred dollars." At the time saloon licenses in Madison were just seventy-five dollars. After a spirited debate, sixty-four percent of all Madisonians voted for the "low" license. This meant an immediate increase in the cost of saloon license from seventy-five to two hundred dollars and caused fourteen of Madison's sixty-two (nearly twenty percent) saloons to go out of business. One saloon owner calculated that he had to sell four thousand glasses of beer at a nickel each just to pay the higher license. Temporary victories on the Sunday closing front and their success in increasing liquor license fees persuaded several prohibitionists that the time had come to run for office. Here results were downright discouraging. In April 1888, only four percent voted for a man who ran for mayor of Madison on the prohibition ticket.[26] Results were better when prohibitionists sought the much more limited goal of forcing saloons to close at midnight rather than two or three in the morning.[27]

Meanwhile saloonists quickly adjusted to the higher license fees and the number of saloons rose from fifty-eight in 1886 to ninety-five in 1891. Prohibition leaders decided the time had come for another referendum on license fees. Their hope was to increase the saloon license fee to three hundred fifty dollars or even five hundred dollars and thus cut back on the number of saloons. Unfortunately for the dry forces, the overwhelming majority (sixty percent) who turned out for the special September 1891 election were not interested in any action that might increase the price of a glass of beer.[28]

But the arsenal of weapons available to the prohibitionists was hardly exhausted. In 1889 the state legislature passed a binding referendum law that was far more supportive of total prohibitionists than the 1885 high-low license law. Instead of merely establishing the conditions under which liquor was to be sold, that is, with a high or low license fee, the new law posed a more fundamental either/or question: Shall the community be wet or dry? Prohibitionists were delighted to have the opportunity to vote for prohibition in its pure form, the long-sought goal of the W. C. T. U. members, and they launched an aggressive campaign in the spring of 1894 to test community sentiment. Predictably prohibitionists insisted that drinking was sinful and that no man-made law could make drinking right. But the wets mustered some impressive arguments too; uppermost among them was the fact that going dry would lead to the city's bankruptcy. Twenty-five percent of the revenue for the city's general purpose budget in 1894 was derived from liquor licenses. Thus to go dry meant a very dramatic cut in services or a very large property tax increase, neither of which was attractive. When the votes were counted fifty-nine percent cast ballots to keep Madison wet and forty-one percent voted the other way.[29]

Though Madison voters had overwhelmingly rejected a dry Madison, prohibitionists were anything but dejected. On the contrary, they were elated that four out of ten voters had supported their cause. Dry forces were particularly pleased that fifty-three percent of the voters in the Fifth Ward encompassing the area around the University of Wisconsin campus had voted to go dry. Naturally, members of the "God and morality movement" as one Madison mayor called prohibitionists were eager to find ways to exploit this strength.

They decided to keep active in the political arena but in a different way. Instead of fielding their own mayoral candidate, they got behind a Republican hopeful, Dr. Albert A. Dye, who courted the prohibitionists. Dye won by just forty-eight votes and became the first Republican mayor in ten years and the second in sixteen years. Soon after taking office Dye issued an edict directing policemen to enforce the Sunday closing law, which closed up the town. However, what Dye did not realize was that by closing down

Madison he opened up Middleton. Madison Sunday drinkers rode their horses or bicycles to Middleton, where they caused such a turmoil that Middleton officials concluded that it, too, should enforce the Sunday closing law. Unfortunately for Dye and his prohibitionist backers, this Sunday closing campaign ended very much as had its predecessors. As soon as the heat subsided, saloonists began leaving their back doors open for the convenience of patrons and then finally opened their front doors for business as usual. However, the Dye administration (1896–97) was not without an enduring victory for the dry forces. In January 1897, the Common Council acceded to a plan—quite possibly a *quid pro quo* for no more Sunday harassment of Sunday saloons—which outlawed saloons in the immediate vicinity of the university.[30]

Buoyed by such victories, the prohibitionists decided to test the waters one more time with an April 1898 wet-dry referendum. Once again the city rejected prohibition on a sixty-forty basis, but an even larger majority of Fifth Ward voters (fifty-six percent) supported the dry cause than had done so in 1894. Armed with a clear majority, prohibitionists moved immediately to capitalize on this limited show of support by trying to get the Common Council to outlaw *all* saloons in the Fifth Ward, not just those nearest the university. Toward this end, they got the regents to issue a statement saying that student "idleness and dissipation" were increased by Fifth Ward saloons. They mustered an impressive petition bearing the names of the university president C. K. Adams, university deans W. A. Henry and Edward A. Birge, Professors Frederick Jackson Turner, Charles R. Van Hise, and many others. They even sent W. A. Henry, Dean of the College of Agriculture, to tell the Common Council License Committee that the bad reputation of Madison saloons made it particularly difficult for him to secure students. But the Common Council was unmoved. By a vote of eleven to five they rejected the move to make all of the Fifth Ward dry.[31]

The last major reform initiative undertaken by the prohibitionists in the nineteenth century was done in conjunction with a broad coalition of citizens whose membership went far beyond conventional prohibition circles. The target was the "stall saloon," an innovation in saloon design first noted in a June 1896 *Journal* article which described the stalls as a series of "back rooms which provided a quiet retreat for parties who enjoy private conversation while indulging in liquid refreshment."[32] That, of course, was the polite way of describing them. In reality they were little more than houses of assignation. Many of them were concentrated in the 600 block of East Wilson Street, a lively part of town called the "Midway," across the street from the Northwestern Railway depot.

From the time the stall saloons were "discovered" in 1896 a coalition of prohibitionists, members of the newly formed Church Alliance, and other "God and morality" types made their elimination a *cause célèbre*. Very significantly the stall saloons had been tolerated for years by the authorities. In fact it was not until the girls decided to leave their stalls and solicit on the streets that "businessmen entered a virtuous protest and the mayor and police department leaped to their duty. . . ." Police in a token effort exported a dozen ladies of the evening and gave the coalition a modest victory. But a much more telling commentary on where the real power lay was the Common Council refusal in September 1897 to pass an ordinance that would have made the stall saloons illegal. Thus by the spring of 1898, the girls were back and the stall saloons were doing a good business. Church alliance members made this fact a major mayoral campaign issue in the spring of 1898. A Presbyterian minister told voters through a letter to the editor that there were at least six whore houses in the Sixth Ward and that the town was overrun with one hundred loose women.[33] So strong was sentiment against the stall saloon that a two-term incumbent Democratic mayor was beaten by a Republican—a rare event in Madison's history—albeit by just eleven votes, the smallest margin ever up to that time.[34] Just two months after taking office the Common Council passed an ordinance making it illegal for prostitutes to visit *public* places,—the presumption being that prostitutes in a private place were perfectly all right.[35] However, this "victory" was diluted if not obviated when the council turned around and granted licenses to the stall saloons. It was this type of action that caused many to complain that the Common Council was being governed by the saloon interests.

Looking back on their record during the last two decades of the nineteenth century, the pure prohibitionists, those who insisted on the absolute elimination of alcohol, could only be frustrated. But the pragmatic prohibitionists could reflect with some pride on their record. They had caused the cost of saloon licenses to nearly triple, thereby reducing the number of saloons far below what would otherwise have existed; they had twice demonstrated that four out of ten Madison voters favored prohibition; they caused that part of Madison nearest the university campus to go dry; they forced saloons to close at midnight instead of staying open until two or three in the morning; and they learned to make alliances with other "God and morality" forces to elect Republican mayors. In short, they had learned, as one critic commented, that prohibition could only be achieved by "votes and not by the prayers of unhappy women."[36]

Nevertheless saloons prevailed in spite of persistent and sometimes resourceful attacks by the "rosewater reformers" as the saloon owners called them. Saloon interests continued to be protected by a large majority of Democratic aldermen. It was this continued numerical superiority of the Democratic Party on the Common Council, coupled with the inability of women to vote, that enabled Mayor John Corscott to say with confidence in 1894, "if I live to see this city without saloons, I will go into the angel wing and harp business."[37]

Reaching the Unchurched

In the early 1890s all but one of Madison's churches were concentrated very close to the Square. Many were opulent houses of worship that catered to the wealthier members of the community and were led by ministers whose erudition and forceful delivery kept the pews full of university and business people. But Madison was growing and the downtown churches were not getting new members in proportion to this growth. Reasoning like merchants who at that time were setting up stores in outlying areas to better serve this growing population, several denominations concluded they could get better results if they would take their churches to the people instead of making the people come to uptown churches. Besides, concluded leaders of these denominations, many of the unchurched people were wage-earners who would have felt out of place sitting in the elegant uptown sanctuaries.

Among those who started "suburban" churches during this period were the Congregationalists who selected the rapidly growing Sixth District, now known as the Marquette Neighborhood. In 1894 the church bought an old frame schoolhouse, which stood at the corner of Brearly and Jenifer Streets, and remodeled it into the Sixth Ward Chapel.[38] By 1896 a *Wisconsin State Journal* article said the chapel was proving to be a "storm center of good influence in the Sixth Ward." Chapel leaders sought new adult male members through a men's literary and mutual improvement society "where current questions and other branches of church work could be discussed."[39] For the women there was the familiar ladies aid society.

Hot on the heels of the Congregationalists were the Methodists, who also felt that the Sixth Ward was a likely spot for proselytizing. In 1895, true to their frontier tradition, the Methodists set up a huge tent seating up to five hundred persons near the intersection of Williamson and Baldwin Streets and proceeded to hold revivals during the summer. Gathering a rich harvest of converts, the

Methodists replaced their tent with a permanent chapel in the summer of 1896.[40]

The Congregationalists and Methodists quickly learned that they were not the only groups with designs on the unchurched. The Salvation Army was also interested. With their crowd-gathering trumpets, drums, tambourines, and catchy songs, they took their portable church all over the city seeking street corner converts. Conservative Madisonian church people were incensed by what they viewed as a vulgar and ridiculous brand of religion and got authorities to arrest the Salvationists on the pretext that they were blocking sidewalks. But the authorities were not the only source of harassment for these highly committed and motivated persons. In September 1898, for example, when the Salvationists gathered at the corner of Gorham and State Streets for a routine outdoor service, small boys threw rocks at the drums, older rowdies threw eggs and tomatoes, and recent converts were cruelly tormented. All this was hardly in keeping with a description of just a few years earlier that Madisonians were "notably religious in the true sense of that term." Not until many years later did Madisonians change their mind about the acceptability of the Salvation Army and their methods.[41]

Charity Gets Organized

During the 1890s, the methods of dispensing charity underwent a very significant change. For years most charity had been dispensed by individuals; essentially, the people with a bit extra helped the needy. Giving turkeys or beef roasts to poor families at Christmas time—the most common form of relief—had much to commend it. It was direct, infrequent, and allowed donors to feel they were doing their Christian duty. A second very common but less popular form of providing charity was at the front door of one's home. Poor persons, often vagabonds, regularly knocked on doors in the better sections of town

GENERAL PRINCIPLES OF POOR RELIEF.

1st—Promiscuous almgiving fosters pauperism and ought to be stopped.

2d—In all benevolent work the open eye must accompany the helping hand.

3d—What the poor need as a general rule, is not alms, but a friend who encourages thrift and provides work.

4th—Real destitution and suffering must be relieved promptly with tact and tenderness.

5th—We must remove the cause of distress, and help the poor to help themselves.

6th—Sufficient and prompt help which places a family or individual in a position to take care of himself, is far better than a repeated dole which destroys self respect, induces idleness, and in the end produces beggary.

7th—It is of supreme importance that any family when reduced to want for the first time, be so treated that the spirit of independence shall be preserved and self-support secured as soon as possible.

8th—The two chief evils to be removed and prevented are: (a) Neglect of the deserving poor who suffer in silence because too self-respecting to beg, and who must be sought out. (b) Excess of gifts bestowed upon certain families by sympathetic persons, each of whom is unaware that any one else is giving and all of whom give without personal investigation. In this way families are often given far more than they need, and the result commonly is pauperism. The only remedy is a more systematic benevolence. The public should stop its careless giving and relief must be given only upon thorough investigation.

FIGURE 5.33. GENERAL PRINCIPLES OF POOR RELIEF. These principles of poor relief were promulgated in 1887 by the Madison Benevolent Society.

asking for food, fuel, and money. This practice was as annoying as it was inefficient. The third method of dispensing charity was through organizations including church societies, fraternal lodges, factories, and even the W. C. T. U. The idea was that each association would set up a fund to which nearly every member would contribute, which would then be used to help a member in need.[42]

The limitations of individual and association methods of dispensing charity led to the rise of single-purpose charity organizations in the late 1880s. The first of this new breed of organization was the Madison Benevolent Society, which opened its doors in 1887. Its central purpose was to systematize poor relief and prevent "promiscuous alms giving." It limited its aid to food, fuel, clothing, and medicine for the "deserving poor" defined as widows, old people, dependent children, and sick but normally employed persons. Great emphasis was placed on *temporary* relief; anyone requiring long-term support was automatically turned over to the County Poor Commissioner. Wherever possible the Madison Benevolent Society tried to find a job for the unemployed, encourage industry, thrift and self-dependence, and avoid "red tapism." A cardinal rule was never to give assistance without a careful investigation to verify need.[43]

A second influential charity organization founded during this period was the Attic Angels. In 1889 Elva Bryant, the teenage daughter of the socially and professionally prominent General E. E. Bryant heard that twins had been born into a family so poor they had no money to buy clothing or even the barest necessities. She immediately enlisted the aid of her sister, Mary, and a number of their close friends, all young ladies from socially prominent families, to provide the needed clothing and supplies. The young ladies

This full-page ad for the great Barnum and London Show, a predecessor of the even greater Barnum
and Bailey Circus, appeared in the *Wisconsin State Journal* in June 1883. Madisonians loved the Barnum circus
and nearly always packed its performances. However,
there were other circuses eager for Madisonians' circus
money. One such circus was the W. W. Coles Colossal
Shows, which scheduled a show for June 15, 1883. This
created a problem for Barnum's circus because it was
not scheduled to appear in Madison until September.
Therefore Barnum's publicity people issued this full-page
"wait" announcement in newspapers on June 7 and 13.
This was the first time in Madison that one circus had
used a "wait" notice against another. Apparently the wait
notice worked because fifteen thousand people attended the Barnum show and were awed by Jumbo.

Between 1880 and 1894 the Barnum Circus appeared in Madison about every three years. During this
period Barnum and other circuses set up their tents at
Camp Randall or at a vacant block between Jenifer and
Williamson Streets now occupied in part by the Eagles
Club. The tent enclosing the three-ring circus was itself
an object of awe covering nearly three acres—half again
larger than the block now occupied by the First Wisconsin Plaza and Tenney Building.

quickly discovered that the older children in these
poor families had little to wear and in many cases
were kept home from school for that reason. They
began to ransack their respective attics and found
them to be bounteous providers of clothing for
poor children. One day General Bryant saw the
girls descending the attic stairs at his home at 504
West Wilson, their arms laden with clothing destined for their poor charges, and called them
"attic angels," a name the girls enthusiastically
adopted. At first the girls limited their number to
twelve, allowing a replacement member only if a
member married or resigned. Gradually they expanded their child-care services to include making clothing, bathing infants, and even lecturing
to families on the evils of too many children—a
bit of advice that was rarely accepted. To raise
money, the girls held charity balls and sold cook-
books.[44]

The Circus Parade

During one of the Ringling circus parades, Amos Wilder, editor of the *Wisconsin State Journal,* wrote a moving, almost poetic editorial about a simple incident he witnessed in which a barefoot country boy gave a water lily to a beautiful circus woman.

> Somewhere on the lake shore in Dane County tonight is a boy to whom a hayfield will never seem quite the same. A lady from the marvel world smiled at him and took his modest gift, and her gentle voice thanked him. And somewhere in the confusion of wagon wheels and ghostly mountains of canvas and gilt and gold that look best from a distance . . . is a woman whose heart quickened today because a barefoot boy was to toss her a water lily, and because its fragrance wafted into her dusty, tired life memories of some quiet spot where she dreamed and perhaps loved, and where there was no thread of elephants, nor noisy blare of bands, but only green trees and a brook, and the sweet memory of wind through the grass.

By the late 1890s the experiences of the Madison Benevolent Society and the Attic Angels revealed serious limits of private, volunteer-run charity organizations. As the city's population grew and awareness of poverty increased (due in part to the effectiveness of charity organizations), case loads grew rapidly. Cries for a "trained expert" who would staff a full-time central office were forcefully made but ignored. The first casualty was the Attic Angels, who in 1900 decided to get out of their "unsystematic benevolence" and turn their energies to sewing schools, playgrounds, hospitals, and assisting *public* relief associations. Clearly the handwriting was on the wall, private sector volunteers could not perform the job they had set forth for their organizations.

A much stronger and more centralized system of poor relief was needed, but its actual implementation did not appear until after the turn of the century.[45]

Enduring Irritants

Like their predecessors of earlier eras, persons who lived in Madison during the last two decades of the nineteenth century had no shortage of irritants about which to complain. Judging from newspaper accounts, town rowdies and college men caused the most consternation with their remarkable repertoire of antics. Town boys threw firecrackers into church vestibules during Sunday services, killed squirrels and birds in the Capitol Park with slingshots, vandalized lake cottages, scribbled indecent graffiti everywhere, made obscene gestures to young ladies and spat tobacco juice on their skirts as they passed. Many found the private boathouses that lined the lakeshores convenient to play poker, drink, and deprive young girls of their innocence. Twelve- to fifteen-year-old boys incensed their elders by smoking cigarettes, unaware as a *Journal* editor put it, that this would create "morbid and abnormal passions" and render them "dull, stupid and sluggish."[46]

A favorite university student pastime was throwing spit balls and passing bottles of beer around at Opera House performances. One student discovered that by sawing off the end of a conch shell, then a common porch or lawn decoration, a muted trumpetlike din could be produced. Soon thereafter the conch shell nearly disappeared as a decorative item and became instead the favorite college student noise-making device. The practice became so widespread in 1882 that the Common Council had to pass an ordinance against it. Soon after the trolleys were introduced in 1886, U. W. students learned that if eight or ten passengers would suddenly move to the back of the car, the front end would fly up in the air and cause the car to go off the track.

Sometimes the men would innocently confess, "Oh dear, we didn't realize the car would go off the track" and help return it to the rails. But other times they would flee to the accompaniment of conductor curses. On Halloween night, 1899, several hundred students took to the streets clad only in nightshirts. When they tried to enter Ladies Hall (Chadbourne) they were momentarily rebuffed by the janitor wielding a bludgeon and by young ladies throwing pails of water. But the resourceful men soon found an open basement window and got into the laundry where they found a large assortment of women's undergarments. Moments later they donned this new-found apparel and marched up State Street, quite possibly unaware that they were participating in the first panty raid in U. W. history.[47]

Two animals received the opprobrium of many Madisonians during this period. The first was the stray, savage dog that chased pedestrians and horses. After trying just about every technique from muzzles to dog pounds—all with limited and temporary success, the Common Council finally adopted an ordinance in November 1896 that required every dog in town to have a license by April 1, 1897, or be shot. Apparently the technique worked because dog owners rushed to the city clerk's office to buy the little brass tags, particularly after a huge pile of dead dogs accumulated at the city dump, then at the intersection of East Washington Avenue and First Street.[48]

The second member of the animal kingdom that greatly irritated Madisonians of this era was the sparrow, about ninety million "of whom" made their homes in building nooks and rolled-up store awnings. The feathered plague began in 1877 when fourteen pairs of English sparrows were imported from New York and released. At first the perky little birds were viewed as welcome additions to the city. They ate obnoxious insects, provided a great source of amusement with their feisty, fun-filled antics, stayed through the winter when the native birds left, and could be easily tamed and fed. Unfortunately for the sparrow, several native birds began to disappear from Madison about the time the sparrows began to proliferate causing some to conclude the sparrows were responsible. One charge led to another. Their song was "a harsh musical twitter," their nests were messy, and they ate "dirty food." Soon the English sparrow was viewed as a "bird of the street" with all the stern Victorian connotations of that phrase. In 1895 a newspaper reporter with tongue only slightly in cheek refused to give the name of the only man still in town who had released the original batch of birds for fear he would be killed. Another newspaper article explained how to kill the sparrows by soaking bread crumbs in arsenic. But, as history will attest, such measures had no enduring effect. The sparrows prevailed.[49]

If nothing else the sparrow might have provided an object lesson in the perils of introducing new species into an ecological system. But they did not. Sometime around 1886, another group of persons made the same mistake by introducing carp into the Madison lakes.[50]

Finally there were two noises that grated the sensitivities of those who felt the night was for sleeping. The first was caused by railroad locomotive engineers who sometimes blew their shrieking whistles from the time they entered the city until they reached the depot. Many engineers became regular virtuosos on multitone whistles then in commonplace use, sometimes even playing a secret tune for wives or sweethearts. The other nocturnal disturbance, which at least one crotchety old man complained about, was the sound of "unceasing thumping that can now be heard on every pleasant night until long after everybody ought to be abed and asleep." He was referring to the sound of pianos "suffering under the merciless fingers of 1500 would-be Paderewsky's." What a contrast, he noted, with an earlier era when there were only three pianos in Madison . . . and we could go to sleep with the chickens."[51]

Recreation and Leisure Time-Activities: New Developments and Old Favorites

The last two decades of the nineteenth century witnessed the takeoff period for organized athletics at the University of Wisconsin—a development in which Madisonians played a large supportive role. Measured in crowd size and its rapid rise in popularity, no sport could match University of Wisconsin football. First introduced in 1890, it grew quickly following the U. W. purchase of Camp Randall and the hiring of its first football coach in 1893. By 1894 Camp Randall games had become the major spectator sport for Madisonians. Take the game Wisconsin played with Minnesota in November 1894. A U. W. student in a letter to his parents described the memorable day. Early in the morning students took to the streets blowing tin horns and shouting college cheers. About noon thousands of spectators began to converge on Camp Randall, most on foot, some riding streetcars and a few riding in magnificent carriages. The stands and the edge of the playing field were so crowded that rooftops of surrounding homes became impromptu bleachers. From the time the game began until it was over, the crowd became noisier and noisier. When Wisconsin won six to zero, everybody went crazy, explained the student. "Professors forgot their dignity, and students their reverence. They all danced, shook hands, howled, shouted, screeched, blew, yelled, jumped, ran, and everything else they could do. Processions of course soon formed and the crowd went around town. "That was not all," the student continued. "In the evening a bonfire was built . . . and another procession got underway. First they took (U. W.) President Adam's house by storm, and the president had to make a speech. Then they went uptown and escorted the vanquished Minnesota men to the depot."[52]

For the rest of the 1890's Madison's obsession with U. W. football only got worse. Some of the games were witnessed by ten thousand people.[53] Local newspapers devoted their front pages to

huge banner headlines and blow-by-blow accounts of the game. A *Wisconsin State Journal* reporter said that so many Madison stores and homes were decorated for the Camp Randall games with cardinal bunting, ribbon, and flags that a stranger might easily conclude that "a reign of anarchy had been inaugurated . . . or that the Salvation Army had taken complete possession of the city."[54] So avid was football interest among Madisonians that when the team played games on the road, the Wisconsin Telephone Company hired a person to broadcast the game over the telephone, where it could be heard by a privileged group in Madison wearing earsets. One of the major reasons for this lusty new love affair was the almost unbelievable winning record of the team. Between 1894 and 1900 Wisconsin coaches piled up fifty-one victories and only eight defeats![55]

Though overshadowed by football, other university sports made their debut during this period. They included tennis, introduced about 1887, track and field, which caught on in the mid-1890s, and basketball, viewed as an off-season alternative to football, introduced in 1897.[56] University baseball continued to be a popular crowd sport. Together with football, these sports became the unquestioned focal point of Madison spectator sports. Madisonians were obviously proud of "their boys" and turned out in great numbers to cheer them on.

The fashionable Scottish game of golf secured a tenuous yet promising toehold in Madison in the late 1890s. For three consecutive years a new nine-hole golf course was set up in Madison. In 1897 links were laid out at Maple Bluff; in 1898 at a farm near Picnic Point; in 1899 in the undeveloped area of Wingra Park. There enthusiasts, mostly professionals, businessmen, and professors struggled to learn the exasperating new vocabulary of brassies, bulgers, caddies, tees and greens, and the difficult skill of driving the little white balls with the curious sticks. The only golf organization was the one hundred-member University Golf Club, which in spite of its name consisted of both town and gown members.[57]

COLUMBIA BICYCLE,

H. G. KRONCKE, Agent,

State Street,

FIGURE 5.35. VELOCIPEDES, HIGH WHEELERS, AND SAFETY WHEELS. During the late nineteenth century, bicycles were the object of great interest among Madisonians. The first form to capture public attention was the French velocipede in 1869. This contrivance was similar to the modern bicycle except that the front wheel was larger than the rear (about forty inches to thirty-five inches) and the pedals were mounted on the front wheel. Unfortunately their 150-pound cast iron and wooden frames made them hard to balance, their front wheel mounted pedals made them hard to turn, and their springless frame and seats caused riders to call them "boneshakers." In spite of these limitations, several Madisonians bought the expensive curiosities in 1869 and even raced them at the Dane County Fair that year.

The next version of the bicycle to appear in Madison was the elegant high wheel shown above in this 1883 city directory advertisement. These elegant and prestigious machines first appeared on Madison streets in the spring of 1881 where they reminded residents of huge spiders as they glided silently around the Capitol Square. These machines had front wheels which ranged in size from forty to sixty inches (the bigger the faster), boasted hard rubber tires, weighed thirty to sixty pounds, and were much easier to maneuvenur than the velocipede. However, like the velocipede they had serious limitations. The first was their three-hundred-dollar cost and the second was the great danger they posed to their riders. Since the rider's center of gravity was only slightly behind the large front wheel, a small obstruction in the road or a quick application of the brakes would cause riders to be thrown head first onto the road. These common accidents were known as "headers." If anything these characteristics only enhanced the prestige of high wheel riders several of whom formed the Madison Bicycle Club in 1882 and rode around the Square two or four abreast, proudly clad in mouse-colored corduroy knee britches with matching stockings, tight-fitting navy blue shirts, and straw helmets. Like the velocipedes, the high wheelers turned out to be a fad and were seldom seen on Madison streets after the 1880s.

Beginning in the early 1890s a third form of the bicycle known as the safety "wheel" made its appearance in Madison. Technically, the safety wheel was superior to its predecessors in every way. It had good brakes, soft pneumatic tires, ball bearings, chain drive, weighed just fifty pounds, and could be ridden by women. The only real disadvantage of the safeties was their price, which in the early 1890s was about one hundred dollars. This meant that only the upper income groups or, as a Madison society journal put it, "the fashionable people" could afford them.

Those who first tried the machines could hardly believe that it was possible to sit erect and glide along at such speeds with so little effort. Some described the sensation as the "next thing to flying." The safety bicycle launched Madisonians on an unprecedented debauch of speed and freedom. In 1891 devotees of the new bicycle formed the Madison Cycling Club and sponsored races that drew great crowds from the Madison area and riders as far away as Chicago and Milwaukee.

By the mid 1890s when the price of these machines had come down to a more affordable fifty to seventy-five-dollar range, bicycles went from a craze to an epidemic. As a mark of great distinction, newspapers listed the ministers, professors, doctors, big businessmen, newspaper editors, judges, mayoral aspirants, and women who rode the amazing machines. Bicycling quickly became the most popular outdoor sport that could be enjoyed by both men and women. During the warmer months, rides along the Lake Mendota Drive and around Lake Monona were very popular. The above picture shows four cyclists enjoying such a ride sometime during the 1890s bicycle mania. For several years Madison even had its own bicycle factory which turned out about between two and five thousand bicycles a year.

By 1899 the bicycle craze began to subside. Madison bicycle sales dropped, at least one bicycle dealer went bankrupt, and bicycle races were discontinued. By 1900 the bicycle had fallen from its once fashionable pedastal as the sporting device of the well-to-do to a more lowly station, namely, providing working men and women with reliable transportation to and from work. (SHSW WHi(X3)29664)

FIGURE 5.36. WINTER SCENE, WISCONSIN AVENUE 1898.   This delightful winter vista was captured by a photographer who placed his camera at the intersection of Gilman Street and Wisconsin Avenue sometime during the winter of 1898. (SHSW WHi(X3)35544)

Madisonians made surprisingly little use of the lakes during the last two decades of the nineteenth century. The city did not provide a single swimming facility for its residents, nor for that matter did enterpreneurs. Swimming was limited largely to children who were fond of bathing *au natural*—save a wad of cotton in both ears. Of course, the heavy discharge of sewage into Lake Monona made much of the lake unacceptable for swimming most of the time. Efforts to revive sailing in the mid-1880s failed and the sport nearly died out. Those who had earlier owned sailboats seemed to have exchanged them for faster, more reliable steam launches. The large commercial steam boats continued to ply the waters of both lakes but the demise of the tourist business meant more limited demand.[58]

The major recreational uses of the lakes were rowing (both ordinary rowboats and the graceful eight-oared crew boats), ice skating, horse racing on the ice, and above all else ice yachting on Lake Mendota. Perhaps it was the grating, lion-like snarl of the ice boat blades as they raced across the ice three times faster than the wind. Perhaps it was the fact that these elegant collections of canvas, wood, and steel were the fastest vehicles on earth. Whatever the reason, ice boating enjoyed a great resurgence during the 1890s. By 1897 Madison had the largest fleet of ice yachts and the largest ice yacht club west of the Hudson River. Each week during the season the young owners whose sleek machines brandished names like "Meteor," "Stilletto," "Crystal Slipper," and the "Hot Tamale" competed against wind and the clock for the distinction of being the fastest.[59]

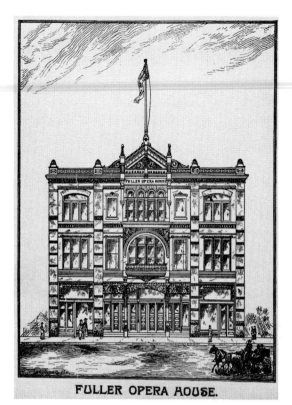

FULLER OPERA HOUSE.

FIGURE 5.37. THE FULLER OPERA HOUSE. To a community that viewed itself as the center of law, legislation, and learning, a capacious, well-appointed theater was a prerequisite of cultural respectability. But the task of providing a theater adequate for Madison's growing size and sophistication was no easy task. From 1870 until 1885 the Hooley Opera House was Madison's fanciest theater. But then in 1885 leaking water pipes from a Turkish bath establishment next door so weakened a foundation wall, the Hooley had to be closed. The only remaining structure even remotely suitable was Turner Hall, a relatively small, poorly ventilated flat floor facility with six hundred uncomfortable seats. Its name was quickly changed to the Turner Opera House, but this hardly solved the problem of inadequate facilities. Beginning in 1886 opera and theatrical companies avoided Madison, leaving the city with an impoverished entertainment "menu" and its leaders with apologies for this embarrassing condition.

For a time it appeared that a stock company incorporated by Madison business and professional men and led by Mayor Elisha Keyes would rescue the city from this situation by erecting a $50,000 facility. Vigorous efforts were made to secure pledges from "the servant girl, the mechanic, the merchant, the lawyer, the student, and the millionaire," but after one year the drive produced barely more than half the needed amount. Leaders then tried to persuade several Chicago theater owners to build an opera house providing that Madisonians would give a cash bonus amounting to about twenty-five percent of total construction costs. Several Chicago people nibbled at the bait, but none would bite. Having failed to raise the money with these two techniques, civic leaders then tried to get the state legislature to pass a charter amendment that would authorize the city to raise the necessary bonus money from tax revenues. For a time this looked promising because city leaders saw the bill as an opportunity to replace the increasingly inadequate City Hall with a grand new city hall-opera house combination. But then

several sober citizens correctly noted that the huge outlay for such a facility, estimated at nearly $100,000, would exceed the city's statutory bonding limit. Such arguments were apparently persuasive to state legislators who rejected the city's request to provide the bonus and gave them instead the right to make the opera house tax exempt. Thus, four years and three resourceful attempts later, Madison's coveted opera house seemed "as far away as the millenium." However, as one Madison newspaper hopefully suggested during the last few days of 1888, perhaps "some enterprising citizen" will give the city an opera house during the coming year.

Indeed, that is just what happened. Two of Madison's "staunchest, wealthiest, largest and most enterprising citizens," Morris F. Fuller and Edward M. Fuller, offered to build a $60,000 opera house on land they had just purchased fronting on the Capitol Square immediately next to the City Hall (then located at the intersection of West Mifflin and Wisconsin Avenue) *providing* that a bonus of fifteen thousand dollars was provided. Elated Madison civic leaders quickly raised the necessary money and ground was broken in August 1889.

When completed in April 1890, the building was finer than anyone expected. The Fuller's New York theater architects produced a tastefully designed facility offering twelve hundred seats on a main floor, a second level balcony, a third level "gallery," and ten private boxes. Interestingly the architect had designed the foyers and stairtowers so that persons who could only afford the hard benches high up in the gallery could reach their seats without mingling with the status conscious ticket holders on the main floor, balcony, and boxes. The five-story high facade shown here was finished in grey pressed brick, trimmed in putty-colored Bedford stone, and featured oiled oak doors and stained glass windows. Inside (see above) theater goers found parquet floors, five hundred gas and electric lights, gold gilt and amber walls, and frescoed ceilings. Chairs on the first floor and balcony were the new design folding opera chairs, and the seats in the private boxes were sumptuously upholstered in dark red velvet and surrounded by brass rails. The huge 36-foot deep, 60-foot wide and 50-foot tall stage boasted five drop curtains, sixteen sets of scenery, and three working traps. One trap was exclusively designed to allow the witches in MacBeth to appear and reappear with the proper dramatic flourish. Behind the stage were twenty dressing rooms. Like almost everybody else, the *Journal* was awed by what they saw on opening day. In the words of their reporter, the Fuller was a "simply faultless . . . temple of culture."

The Fuller launched a new era for Madison's history by bringing to the city a rich spectrum of entertainment ranging from vaudeville to symphony orchestras. During each season of the 1890s, the Fuller Opera House offered a minimum of forty one-night productions and many more multi-night stands. Eight to ten productions each month were not uncommon during the September through May season. The ability of Fuller managers to attract one of the finest theatrical agendas in the Midwest was enhanced by the fact that Madison lay between Milwaukee and Chicago and the Twin Cities. It was during the Fuller era that Madisonians developed a reputation for being a demanding and sophisticated audience. Sometime during this period, someone hung a sign backstage at a Chicago vaudeville theater which said: "If you think you're good, wait until you get to Madison."

The Fuller was later remodelled into a movie house and renamed the Park Theater. The elegant old structure continued as a movie theater until it was torn down to make way for a variety store. (SHSW WHi(X3)34468 and WHi (X3)35645)

The development of pleasure drives, the completion of the electric streetcar system, and the widespread availability of the new safety bicycles made the cry "let's go for a ride" a frequently heard and heeded suggestion. Those who could afford carriages, buggies, horses, and "wheels" made extensive use of Lake Mendota Drive, Farwell Drive, and the roads around Lake Monona. Less affluent persons found rides on the open summer streetcars (see fig. 5.20) a refreshing treat and an excellent buy. For a nickel an adult could ride for fourteen miles, enjoy cooling breezes and some fine scenery as well. Families often took picnic lunches to the ends of the line where they would walk to a favorite picnic spot. For those who wanted the excitement of the streetcar but privacy as well, the streetcar company bought an elegant party car whose interior was finished in polished natural woods and crimson upholstery. The car was rented to up to twenty-six guests who would be driven wherever they liked—but they nearly always ended the trip at the Palace of Sweets, a popular ice cream and candy emporium on the Square where the host or hostess would treat guests to a confection of their choice.[60]

Old favorites such as baseball, billiards, and of course the circus (see fig. 5.34) continued to rank high in popularity among Madisonians. Band concerts continued especially popular among Germans. Each summertime Sunday, weather permitting, crowds consisting mostly of working people would flock to Schuetzen Park where from one to four bands would play. In addition to band concerts there were the usual "nine pins," target shooting, throwing balls at figurines, pole climbing, and striking the strength-testing machines.[61] Beer and popcorn stands were heavily patronized. Picnics continued immensely popular. Many picnickers took the commercial steamers to various private resorts around the lakes; others rented rowboats and helped themselves to inviting spots along the shoreline, then almost completely devoid of homes outside city limits.

If anything, hunting and horseracing—longtime favorites among Madison men—grew in popularity. During the fall migrating season Madison men would take vantage points along the Yahara River between Lake Monona and Mendota, along the railroad trestle crossing Monona Bay and on the hills around Lake Wingra. Getting several dozen ducks in the early morning hours was a common experience for hunters of this era in these locations. Wealthier men bought or leased two huge private hunting preserves, one where the Yahara River flows into Lake Mendota, the other at the outlet of Lake Monona, and even used armed guards to keep trespassers out of these choice areas.[62] Owners of fast horses continued the practice of winter races on the ice along the Monona shoreline. During warmer months horse racers sought out newly gravelled roads such as East Washington Avenue between Blount and Baldwin Streets. At the time there was just one house on this entire one mile stretch. Best of all, at least to the followers of this exciting sport, the Puritanical odium that had once been attached to this activity had nearly gone and horseracing was accorded a place of "honor, character and dignity."[63]

And the children? How did they play? They played marbles "generally for keeps,"[64] hopscotch[65] and of course baseball. In the winter they raced down Madison's many hills on coasting sleds. But the greatest thrill of all was a magnificent toboggan slide where Carroll Street terminated at Lake Monona. There a tower was built forty feet high and one hundred sixty feet long right over the railroad tracks. The slide boasted three separate tracks and sent youngsters on a thrilling one-thousand-foot ride out onto Lake Monona ice.[66]

FIGURE 5.38. ELLA WHEELER WILCOX.   "Laugh and the world laughs with you, cry and you cry alone" are familiar words to many Madisonians and indeed to many Americans. But what most Madisonians don't realize is that they were written in 1882 by a thirty-two-year-old Westport poet, Ella Wheeler, while she was a house guest of Madison Municipal Judge A. B. Braley and his wife, 422 North Henry Street. Their ornate Victorian multi-gabled home shown below is now a Madison Landmark. The photograph of Miss Wheeler was taken when she was in her twenties.

Miss Wheeler was inspired to write the poem as a direct result of an experience she had soon after boarding a late morning train at Westport in February 1882 for the ten-mile trip to Madison where she planned to be a guest of the Braleys and to attend the inaugural ball that evening for Governor Jeremiah M. Rusk. Miss Wheeler boarded the train in high spirits but then as she took her seat, Miss Wheeler saw a friend dressed in black, her body shaking with sobs she was unable to suppress. The last time Miss Wheeler had seen her friend, she was a radiant bride. But now she was a widow. Miss Wheeler sat beside the sobbing young woman and tried to console her, but found that instead of cheering up the friend, she was enveloped in her friend's sorrow.

When Miss Wheeler arrived in Madison she was greeted by the vivacious Mrs. Braley who excitedly told her about their plans for the late afternoon and evening. Immediately she was swept into another world of laughter and happiness and as the day passed the plight of her recently widowed friend completely passed from her mind. However, as she stood before the mirror that evening in Judge Braley's home preparing for the gala ball, a vision of her mourning friend came rushing back and she realized how quickly she had forgotten her sorrow. She contrasted the joy of her situation with the dark shadows her friend must have brought into the home she was visiting. It was at that moment that Miss Wheeler conceived those famous lines, "laugh and the world laughs with you, cry and you cry alone." The following morning at breakfast she recited these lines and several additional stanzas to the Braleys. The judge who was a Shakespearean scholar told her that if she finished the poem at the same high standard at which she had begun, it would be a "literary gem." Two nights later she finished the poem. It was first published by the *New York Sun* on February 21, 1883, and in May 1883 was published as a part of another collection of poetry entitled *Poems of Passion,* which sold 60,000 copies.

Just one year after she wrote these famous lines she married Robert Wilcox and henceforth published under the name Ella Wheeler Wilcox. Until she married she lived with her parents on a prairie farm about five miles from Westport. By the age of nine she had written a novel on scraps of wallpaper; when she was fourteen she had her first poem published by a national magazine. Gradually people from Madison, Milwaukee, and Chicago sought out the country girl with the inspired pen. (SHSW WHi(X3)36317 and WHi(X3)25106)

6 All But Metropolis: 1900–1920

The year 1900 was of course the beginning of a new century but to most Madison leaders this event had no grand connotations. It did not appear to be the beginning of a new era or a new stage of development or even the end of some identifiable phase. The more thoughtful and committed Madison leaders were simply frustrated by "the endless number of things to be done in Madison"[1] and by the general apathy and opposition of the people.

There was, however, a constructive side to this frustration and that was a growing resolve among Madison leaders to build a great city in spite of apathy and opposition and to form organizations designed to give power and direction to those who shared this resolve. Indeed as these leaders came together in such organizations, some of their frustration turned to excitement as they dreamed and planned for a metropolitan Madison. Soon they were talking about a time when the entire Capitol Square would be flanked by "truly metropolitan walls of buildings," a time when bright "metropolitan" electric lights would turn the streets into great white ways, a time when volumes of smoke rolling from mammoth factory smoke stacks and countless locomotives would give the city an undeniable "metropolitan" stamp.[2]

As it turned out the work done by various organizations during the first two decades of the new century produced an extraordinary harvest of progress and change. Population doubled, density increased, suburban sprawl began, the auto began to dominate transportation patterns and high rises appeared around the Square. The progressive era in Madison left the city with rich legacies including an extensive park system, the enfranchisement of women, the discovery of planning and zoning, the prohibition of alcohol, the virtual elimination of vice and corruption, the construction of modern hospitals, the formation of neighborhood associations, and much more.

Thus, it was with good reason that Madisonians of 1920 felt they were passing out of the formative years as a city and into a truly metropolitan state of development.

Disputing Madison's Destiny, Round 3

Many of Madison's business and civic leaders never really got over the city's drop in the population ratings. During the Farwell boom, Madison was the second largest city next to Milwaukee, the unchallenged leader. But then relative to other cities, Madison's population either grew slowly or in two instances even declined. By 1895 Madison had fallen to ninth place behind Green Bay, Eau Claire, Sheboygan, Racine, Superior, Oshkosh, LaCrosse, and of course Milwaukee.

To a large number of business and civic leaders, this slide was a source of intense embarrassment because they believed that size was power and bigger was better. A bigger Madison meant better railroad transportation, better streetcar service, better theaters, better baseball—more of all the good things associated with cities of metropolitan proportions.[1]

Consequently as the new century opened, the lust for bigness and its fraternal twin, power, were the reigning secular values that agitated a broad cross-section of community leaders. This was not to say that these values had not been present earlier in Madison's history for indeed they had. What was different at the dawn of a new century was the development of a kind of "pent up demand" for a much bigger and more powerful "metropolitan city." Never before had so many embraced this goal so tightly.

It was precisely in this context that business and civic leaders concluded that an effective business and population boosting organization was essential, something capable of concentrating the energy of the business community and making Madison a large, bustling and therefore respectable city.

FIGURE 6.1. 1908 KITE AERIAL. CENTRAL BUSINESS DISTRICT. In March 1908 a gentleman representing the Chicago-based George R. Lawrence Company checked into the Park Hotel and set up a display of extraordinary photographs that his company had taken. The Chicago firm had refined a technique that allowed it to take the nation's first aerial photographs. A large-plate camera equipped with a wide-angle lens and suspended from either a helium-filled balloon or "birdlike" "string of kites" was tethered to the ground by a thin wire cable. When the apparatus reached the proper altitude and angle, the photographer triggered the camera shutter by sending an electrical impulse through the wire. Included in the many technically impressive photographs in the Park Hotel display were the famous aerial shots of San Francisco showing that city soon after the devastating fire and earthquake in 1906.

Members of Madison's Forty Thousand Club who viewed the display were told by the Lawrence Company representative that no other city in the country could produce a more superb "airship" photo than Madison. Apparently the members of the promotional organization were convinced, for soon thereafter they signed a contract with the Chicago firm to do several shots of Madison. The photographs on this page and the next were the result. The curvature of streets in the foreground was a distortion caused by the wide-angle lens.

When this picture was taken about noon on Saturday, May 9, 1908, at an altitude of one thousand feet, a small group of spectators had gathered at the foot of Monona Avenue where the photographers had launched and tethered their unusual apparatus. The trees were beginning to leaf out and the warm sun and gentle breezes blowing that day had nearly dried the laundry hanging in the lakeside yards of fancy homes that stood along the high Monona bank. Some of the city's finest homes stood on the block now occupied by the City-County building. The famous Fairchild home occupied the entire block where the State Office Building (1 West Wilson) now stands. Some of Madison's first automobiles are driving along the streets, many of which were lined by new cement curbs, gutters, and sidewalks. The fire-damaged capitol was still standing but work on the west wing of the new (present) capitol was nearing completion.

The rich detail of this photograph is so extraordinary that it can easily transport the willing viewer into another time. At the very least it can provide many moments of pleasant viewing. Many of the buildings still stand, but many have succumbed to the ravages of time. (SHSW Whi (X31)17446)

FIGURE 6.2. 1908 KITE AERIAL, WEST MADISON. The second 1908 aerial photograph taken by the George R. Lawrence Company was taken about one thousand feet over the point where the two railroad tracks criss-crossed Monona Bay. The camera is pointed in a northwesterly direction.

The unusual photograph clearly shows the large amount of lake shore filling that took place under the direction of the Madison Park and Pleasure Drive Association. In the front left, a dredge is sending sandy fill material around the edges of Monona Bay and creating what is today Brittingham Park. The turnaround then jutting out into the say is today the site of the Brittingham shelter house. The large light-colored rectangular area in the lower left was a fill area just completed by the dredge, which soon became the site for homes and apartments. A similar fill operation is visible in the lower right where the original shoreline has been moved out several hundred feet. Today North Shore

Drive meanders along this fill area, and the landmark Brittingham boat house stands at the foot of Bedford Street, the prominent white-appearing street just to the right of the railroad yard area. Note the large amounts of standing water bounded by West Washington Avenue, West Main, and Proudfit Streets. Extensive fill operations had also just begun at Vilas Park on the shore of Lake Wingra, just visible on the extreme upper left.

The fairly dense cluster of homes just to the right of Lake Wingra is Wingra Park, then at the height of its popularity. Large tobacco warehouses dominate the center front of the photograph. (SHSW WHi (X31)17447)

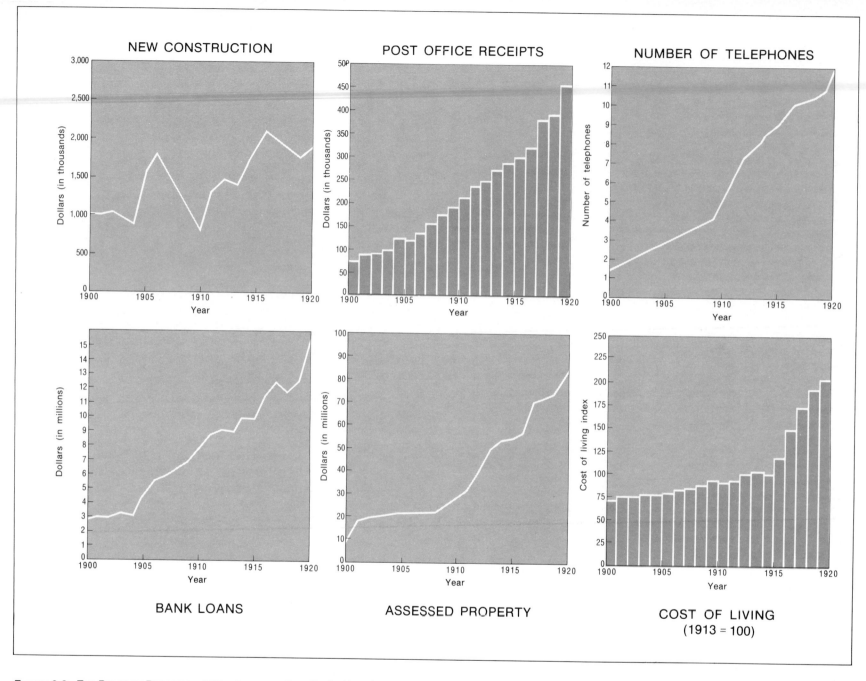

FIGURE 6.3. THE PULSE OF BUSINESS. With a few exceptions the first two decades of the twentieth century were good years for business and real estate in Madison. New construction activity maintained a solid and respectable pace except during an economic downturn between 1907 and 1909 and during World War I (1918). Between 1904 and 1920 bank loans quintupled; between 1906 and 1920 post office receipts quadrupled; between 1909 and 1920 the number of telephones in use nearly tripled; and between 1907 and 1920 property values, as determined by the city assessor, nearly quadrupled. Tempering these increases was a near doubling in the cost of living index between 1916 and 1920.

All these gains were recorded in spite of fluctuations in the nation's economy including two mild recessions (1903–1904 and 1910–1911), one serious recession (1913–1915), and one mild depression (1907–1908).

The Pushers: The Evolution and Ascent of the Commercial Club

"Wake up, Madison, wake up" read the headline over a January, 1899 *Wisconsin State Journal* editorial. In the copy that followed, *Journal* editor Amos P. Wilder told Madisonians that money was plentiful and that capitalists were looking for good investments, and yet "slow" "conservative" Madison did nothing to attract this capital. Other cities including tiny Menominee, Wisconsin, (population five thousand) are forming "advancement associations" to promote their city but not Madison, complained Wilder. "Our people are too self-satisfied" to promote the "business, social, and educational advantages" of the city. "What do you say citizens to making an attempt for an advancement association?" asked Wilder. Wouldn't one of our "enterprising brethren" take this important initiative on this? he pleaded.[2]

Wilder's plea was hardly the first for an advancement association. Three such organizations had been started in the 1880s but none lasted very long or produced much "advancement." All succumbed to apathy, opposition, leader burnout, and a tendency to hold cheerleading banquets, the product of which was bravado and chicken bones but few new businesses. The last such organization had ceased operation in the early 1890s.

This fact was terribly frustrating to Wilder for two reasons. First, he was very much aware of the large role such advancement associations often known as commercial clubs had played in the growth and development in other cities around the country. For example, representatives of Milwaukee's Merchants and Manufacturers Association could point to an impressive list of new businesses as a direct result of their business development work.

Given the crucial role commercial clubs were playing in other cities, the question became: what organization would push *Madison* business interests and its close ally, population growth? The answer, Wilder concluded, was none for Madison had no such organization. In an era that glorified enterprise and entrepreneurial effort, to have no commercial club was downright embarrassing, particularly since many reformers of the era felt that businessmen were the best qualified civic leaders. They were realists who knew how the world operated, and their no-nonsense approach to problems stood in vivid contrast to politicians who puffed and postured. And yet in spite of their vaunted qualities, Madison businessmen had failed to assert themselves.

The second reason Wilder was frustrated by the absence of a commercial club was because it gave credence to those who believed that Madison was merely a college and government town. Because the university and the legislature so dominated "outside" perception of Madison, many concluded that the city lacked enterprising businessmen; that its private sector was small, insignificant, or even dead; that it was dominated by antibusiness attitudes; and that it was populated by salaried types who were primarily interested in cerebral pursuits. These impressions notwithstanding, the fact was Madison had a large, complete collection of retail stores, a rapidly growing wholesale and jobbing sector, and a relatively small but growing group of factories, some of which were internationally known. Part of the problem then was that few outside Madison knew this.

The 1899 Wilder "wake up" editorial was the beginning of an exciting new chapter in Madison's development when enduring and effective commercial clubs were not only established but became a major conduit for much of the city's energy and esprit. But as so often happens, a commercial club did not spring immediately into life. Although a growing number of businessmen recognized the importance of such an organization, they could not agree on just what form it should take. What they *did* agree on was that Madison's image as a college and government town was so deeply engrained that something very big, dramatic, and convincing was necessary. Their solution was an altogether extraordinary extravaganza called a "street carnival," an event utterly unlike anything ever seen in Madison and for that matter in Wisconsin. To pull off this event, businessmen formed the Carnival Association led by go-getter piano merchant, J. W. Groves. For four days in October 1900, Groves' organization offered a glittering array of events and entertainment all designed to prove that the city many regarded "as the most conservative in the commonwealth" was in fact a *bustling business and commercial city* with great future. Although some folks grumbled about the "revolting tent shows" and the extracurricular gambling, nearly everyone agreed the street carnival was a great success. Newspaper publicity in over one hundred state papers and several Chicago papers produced an estimated seventy-five thousand visitors. But perhaps the most important part of this success was that it proved that Madison businessmen working *together* could accomplish great things.[3]

Buoyed by the great carnival success, businessmen held a series of meetings with the idea of forming a permanent organization. The leader of this movement was Dr. Clarke Gapen, a local surgeon who had written an ardent reply to Wilder's 1899 "wake up" editorial, which was printed days later in the *Journal*. The result of Gapen's behind-the-scenes work was an announcement in January 1901 of Madison's first "advancement" association since the ill-fated 1888 Madison Businessmen's Association.

Gapen's catchy name for the new organization was based upon Wisconsin's classification of cities for charter purposes. At the time, Madison had only enough population to be a "second class" city, a term full of reproachful, inferior connotations. To be a first class city, Madison had to have forty thousand "prosperous and progressive" people noted Gapen.[4] Thus the goal he suggested for the new organization was to cause Madison to have forty thousand persons by the 1910 federal census. Gapen's associates enthusiastically embraced the idea and so the new advancement association was named "The Forty Thousand Club."

WISCONSIN'S
GREATEST CARNIVAL
AND STREET FAIR

OCTOBER 15, 16, 17, 18 and 19, 1900,
AT MADISON, WISCONSIN.

## A GREAT $10,000 SHOW.	## TWO POLITICAL DAYS!
One Hundred Free Street Performances Daily,	REPUBLICAN DAY--Monday, October 15--
Introducing Vaudeville by the Best Artists, Acrobats, Jugglers, Dancers, Magicians, Trapeze Performers, Balloon Ascensions and a Balloon Race.	**Senator Mark Hanna, of Ohio,**
Mammoth Mystic Midway.	AND
Solid blocks of popular attractions, best money could procure, best features of all the fairs of the Northwest.	**Senator W. P. Frye, of Maine,**
Spectacular Parades Every Day.	Will Speak in the Evening. Grand Demonstration and Torchlight Procession
Military parade of Eight Militia Companies A Trade's Pageant of 100 Floats Floral Parade of Sixty Gorgeously Decorated Carriages Civic Parade of Secret and Fraternal Societies	
PHINNEY'S CELEBRATED U. S. BAND	DEMOCRATIC DAY--Wednesday October 17
Of Forty Men has been engaged for the entire week Three concerts daily	**George Fred Williams, of Boston,**
Grand Band Concerts Every Hour of Each Day!	AND
Ten of the Best Brass Bands in the state of Wisconsin will discourse music at every street corner	**John F. Finerty, of Chicago,**
	Will Speak Afternoon and Evening. Grand Demonstration and Torchlight Procession

GRAND CARDINAL ILLUMINATION.

The entire city will be decorated in the university colors from the railroad depots to the dome of the capitol. Over 5,000 incandescent electric lights and several hundred extra arc lights are to be used in illuminating the principal streets, so that the main part of the city shall be as light as day. **THE GREAT WHITE DOME** of the capitol building is to be STUDDED WITH 1,000 ELECTRIC LIGHTS, a sight worth going miles to see Then there are to be 64 ELECTRIC ARCHES. All in all, this will be THE GREATEST ILLUMINATION EVER SEEN IN THE NORTHWEST, with the Single exception of the Administration Building at the World's Fair.

500 BOXES OF RED FIRE.

In addition to the blaze of electric lights the committee has provided an ELABORATE PYROTECHNICAL DISPLAY for each evening in which 500 boxes of Greek fire will be used at one time. This is the CARDINAL ILLUMINATION.

Grand Mardi Gras and Masked Carnival Friday Night, Oct. 19.

GREAT FIRE RUN EVERY DAY AT NOON.

Washburn Observatory, the New Engineering Building, the Wisconsin Experiment Station, and Other University Buildings, will be open every day to the public.

HALF RATES ON ALL RAILROADS.

Let Everybody Come We Can House and Feed 100,000 People.

FIGURE 6.4. THE 1900 STREET CARNIVAL ADVERTISEMENT. Never in Madison's history up to that time had the general public been treated to such a "free" extravaganza. Of course, the extravagance was not really free; it cost business sponsors nearly ten thousand dollars but to them it was worth it because it brought nearly seventy-five thousand visitors to Madison during the gala four-day period in October 1900. The event was the first of several such major fall promotional events designed to bring shoppers to Madison from the "tributary areas" and convince them that Madison was a hustling *business* city, not merely the state capital and college town.

FIGURE 6.5. THE SUGAR CASTLE. In October 1906 a rather remarkable factory opened on what was then called the "East End" of Madison. The $600,000, two hundred thousand-square-foot facility shown here was the largest factory ever erected in Madison up to that time. Even more remarkable than its size and cost was the intent of its owners to run the plant just three months a year and still make a profit. Impetus for the plant's construction was the fact that a relatively high tariff kept cheap Caribbean sugar out of the country and that U.S.-produced can sugar could not keep up with demand. This circumstance set the stage for the sugar beet—a homely plant whose fleshy gray root contained up to twelve percent sugar.

When the castlelike plant was completed, it became the fourth sugar beet processing plant in Wisconsin. The others were in Janesville, Menomonie Falls, and Chippewa Falls. The Madison plant was almost an exact copy

of the Janesville plant and was first promoted in Madison by the Janesville plant owners. However, a group of Madison investors soon became involved. Prominent among them was Magnus Swenson, first president of the Madison-based U.S. Sugar Company and holder of several sugar processing equipment patents. The plant was actively promoted by the Forty thousand Club and must rank as one of their most notable achievements.

To get farmers to raise the beets, the owners of the United States Sugar Beet Company took out ads in area newspapers. The ads guaranteed Madison area farmers five dollars for every ton of beets they delivered to the plant *and* choice four-month jobs in the sugar factory as well. Other farmer-oriented literature emphasized the ease with which the beets could be raised, particularly in contrast to tobacco, and how the beets were not subject to the same exasperating price fluctuations.

Apparently the ads worked because when the plant opened, workers were plentiful and farmers from as far away as Prairie du Chien brought forty thousand tons of sugar beets to the factory for processing. Nine hours after being washed, chopped, pulverized, pressed, evaporated, and granulated, the bulbous beet roots were converted to pure white sugar, identical in chemistry and appearance to cane sugar. From October 1 through January, the plant ran twenty-four hours a day, seven days a week, provided employment to about two hundred persons and turned out about one hundred thousand pounds (fifty tons) of sugar each day. At the end of the first season the plant had produced an incredible nine million pounds of sugar. Nearly all Madison stores carried the product, but most of the sugar was shipped to Chicago where some was consumed and the rest was distributed around the country.

For six years the plant conducted its frenetic fall "campaign." But then in 1912, the U.S. Congress responded to demands to lower the cost of living by removing the protective sugar tariff, a decision that gave the cheaper imported sugar a clear advantage over the more expensive sugar beet. Consequently the plant was closed for the 1913 and 1914 seasons. Gradually, however, growing sugar shortages and new tariffs caused the plant to reopen in 1915. During World War I, the production of sugar beets reached new highs and the Madison plant flourished.

Although the plant's large payroll was a welcome addition to Madison's economy, there was one aspect of the plant's operation that was not at all welcome and that was the handling of large amounts of fluid and fibrous by-products. During their first year of operation the U.S. Sugar Company dumped these wastes into Starkweather Creek, which in turn flowed into Lake Monona about a block away. The fluids discolored the lake, and the fibrous materials accumulated several feet thick near the point where the creek flowed into Lake Monona. Pollution was so bad that the Knickerbocker Ice Company, which had a large ice house at the intersection of Atwood and Lakeland Avenues, had to close down because no one would buy their brownish-yellow ice. To correct this problem, the sugar company in 1907 installed its own sewage treatment plant and holding ponds and even found a way to make cattle feed out of beet toppings. Unfortunately, these waste disposal facilities were capable of handling only a fraction of the total plant wastes—a circumstance that led to the dumping of an average of fifty thousand tons of refuse into the lake each year. These organic wastes so exacerbated Lake Monona pollution that in 1919 the city had to drag the north end of Lake Monona to remove the decaying wastes.

The final solution to the pollution problem did not come until 1924 when a combination of circumstances forced plant owners to file for bankruptcy and close its doors. In 1926 the handsome old structure was sold to the Garver Feed and Supply Company whose owners unfortunately removed the top two stories and the elegant Richardsonian turret. Today the old factory at the foot of Sugar Avenue just north of Olbrich Park is still used as a feed and grain warehouse, but to Madison old-timers, it is still affectionately remembered as "the Sugar Beet." (SHSW WHi(X3)35543)

The new name was a gutsy act of defiance, for it contained a built in unambiguous performance measure from which there could be no retreat. Either Madison's population would be forty thousand in 1910 or it wouldn't. Significantly the Forty Thousand Club members did not see any risk in such a name because they were cocksure it would be attained and even surpassed.[5] Much of their confidence came from their feeling that the powerful hand of geographical destiny was pulling the same oar with them. After all, Madison lay at the center of "the richest tributary country . . . of any Western city"[6] and was served by a magnificent nine-track railroad network. Gapen and his colleagues also took heart in the fact that they represented a new generation of community leaders and that the older "ultra-conservative" leaders were dying off and losing power.[7]

Initial community response was marked by skepticism and scoffing. After all, Madison's 1900 population was only 19,164; therefore Forty Thousand Clubbers would have to cause the population to double in less than a decade—a feat never achieved since the heady Farwell boom in the 1850s.

To accomplish this difficult task Forty Thousand Club leaders proposed to use every legal and effective means to attract "manufacturing establishments," to publicize the city as a place of residence, as a summer resort, as a convention city, and to secure the patronage of "the tributary trade" by retail promotions and by making the city a major processing and distribution point for agricultural products, particularly milk, meat, and tobacco.[8]

At first many businessmen dismissed the Forty Thousand Club and their work as "mere agitation"[9] but the visions of Gapen and the new Forty Thousand Club president, J. W. Groves, of "greater factories, taller buildings and a mightier university" soon won adherents. Within a few weeks of Gapen's initial club announcement about sixty "energetic," relatively young community leaders had become members.[10]

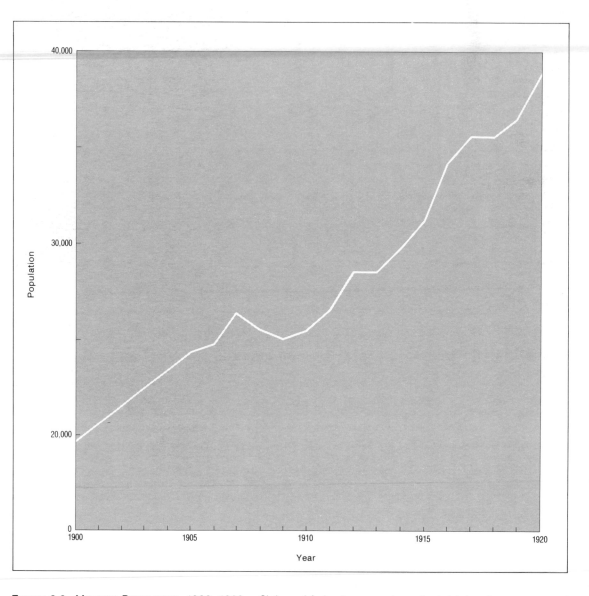

FIGURE 6.6. MADISON POPULATION, 1900–1920.   State and federal censes showed a brisk twenty-seven percent increase between 1900 and 1905, a very sluggish five percent increase between 1905 and 1910, and then a strong fifty percent increase between 1910 and 1920. The graph is based upon official census data *supplemented* by correlations with annual surveys done by the Madison Public Schools to determine school-aged youngsters. The addition of this inferential data provides a much more detailed portrait of population changes including a surprising drop in population between 1907 and 1908. During this period Madison was affected by a nationwide "mild depression," which among other things caused two out of three workers at such major factories as the Fuller and Johnson Company to be laid off.

We Want a Slogan for Madison

"All live, growing, buzzing, hustling cities have slogans," said Richard Lloyd Jones in the space normally reserved for headlines on the front page of the *Wisconsin State Journal* on April 6, 1912. "You have seen them on stationery coming from live energetic businessmen in live energetic towns," he explained. We need something "catchy and famous," he suggested, such as "Walla Walla Wants You." With this introduction Jones announced a contest for the best boosting slogan and a reward of twenty dollars for the winner. Madison, it turned out, had a lot of latent sloganeers because just six days after the content announcement, Jones had received 1,354 entries.

Shown below are fifteen examples Jones received including the winning entry. The winning slogan is noted below.

Madison, Healthy, Wealthy, Wise, and Witty
Madison, the Ideal City
Madison, Pretty, Proud, and Progressive
Make Madison Magnificent
Boost Bob's Beautiful Burg
Brains, Business, and Beauty Make Madison Move
Madison, Wisconsin, the Home of Progressivism
Madison, the Jewel of the Badger State
Madison Now and Always
Magnetic Madison
It's Madison for Me
Madison Makes the Heart Grow Fonder
Madison Maintains Many Magnificent Mansions
Make Your Millions in Madison
Madison Men Make Money
Madison, a Modern Mecca

Winning entry in slogan contest: Its Madison for Me.

Almost immediately the Forty Thousand Club members began writing letters to businesses that might be interested in locating in Madison, dispatching committees to negotiate better railroad passenger schedules and freight rates, endorsing stock offerings of new or relocating enterprises, giving carriage tours of the city to visiting prospective factory owners, and much more.[11]

After barely more than one full year of operation the Forty Thousand Club could point to several impressive victories. Its members had elected their first president, J. W. Groves, as mayor. The victory was a landmark because Groves, a Republican, had beaten a Democrat *incumbent,* Storm Bull, a U. W. professor who represented a more conservative block of voters who had little interest in the rip-roaring go-getter Forty Thousand Club plans for their city.[12] They had attracted a twenty-five-man factory, the Madison-Kipp Corporation, then known as the Mason-Kipp Company, by getting wealthy citizens to buy ten thousand dollars worth of stock.[13] Their catchy name produced national media attention, and their membership roster was filling up with talented and committed businessmen.[14]

Unlike all previous advancement associations the Forty Thousand Club demonstrated gritty staying power. Its members continued to work until 1910 and the day of reckoning. During this period they enjoyed additional victories including getting the huge U. W. Sugar Company plant, securing better railroad passenger schedules, and landing several major conventions. At the same time club members learned to accept the stubborn fact that the success rate in the smokestack chasing and civic improvement business was very low. A free site and large stock purchases, the standard demand of many mobile, mercenary corporations, could not be provided to more than a few companies. Consequently dozens of factories never came. Club members also learned to endure the "gibes and jeers of carping detractors." For example, at one point club members suggested that all Madison businessmen wear a uniform consisting of a blue blazer and white duck trousers so that tourists could spot natives and be welcomed by them. This idea was quickly dropped following widespread community ridicule.[15]

Then came the results of the 1910 federal census. Madison had grown from only 19,000 to 25,531 in 1910, far short of the 40,000 goal. To Forty Thousand Club members the announcement was disappointing but not unexpected. Throughout their nine-year history the goal of the club and the principal means by which they hoped to advance it—industrialization—was opposed by a powerful clique of professors, bureaucrats, and lawyers. Moreover the membership of the club never reached the full complement of one hundred persons even after its leaders changed the format from "solemn, dreary" weekly meetings to a more festive monthly banquet. Consequently the work of the club had to be performed by a tiny band of men whose dedication and enthusiasm could hardly compensate for the lack of a broad-based "live-wire" membership.[16]

Even in failure the achievements of the Forty Thousand Club were noteworthy. No other Madison commercial club had ever lasted so long or accomplished so much. It caused a surge of galvanizing energy to flow through the business community and proved beyond a doubt that a commercial club could cause important things to happen. But of all the things the Forty Thousand Club had accomplished, probably none had more long-term significance than the new community concensus it forged on the role of industry in Madison. A full discussion of this "Madison compromise" is found in the next section.

The failure of the Forty Thousand Club left Madison without any business promotion club—but not for long. In early 1910 Forty Thousand Club leaders formed a committee to make recommendations on a replacement organization. The work of this committee was the subject of intense and widespread interest among the business and civic leaders because they now saw more clearly than ever before the critically important role a business boosting organization could play.

Good Boosters and Bad Boosters

"A booster is a good thing, an excellent thing and we are willing for him to feed at any time of day or night that his doctor will let him. That is, a real booster is a good thing, a man who has more brains than brag, and more elbow grease than gas, a fellow who readily does things and gets things done that are worth doing.

But every town has some professional boosters; hustlers who never let grass grow under their feet nor ideas in their head. These fellows are always wanting the citizens who pay their bills and saw wood to put up $74,000 to hire a sugar mill on a millet ridge, or locate an ax handle factory in the middle of the prairie. They are always yamming along some impossible project by the main strength of their jaws; and their one big service to the town is their annual fall feed creates a temporary market for fried chickens and 10¢ cigars.

Here in Madison as everywhere we have both kinds of boosters—the doers and the talkers. Lets give the doers their full chance."

Richard Lloyd Jones
Wisconsin State Journal
October 1914

The committee recommended that the Forty Thousand Club replacement be known as the Commercial Club, that it should have a much more representative membership and more committees and that its board should have tighter control of committee actions. A great surge of interest greeted this recommendation for a "more verile organization." Just three months after its founding, its membership rolls had grown to 342, more than five times larger than the Forty Thousand Club at its peak. But then following this impressive achievement, the president resigned, the vice-president refused to take over, no meetings were called, membership plummeted, and the organization was never heard from again. Al-

though the causes of the Commercial Club's demise were disputed, it appeared to be primarily attributable to the volatile and divisive issue of industrial growth. At the very moment the new club was being organized the Gisholt Company requested the vacation of several streets so that it could make a substantial plant expansion. The new Commercial Club not only strongly supported this factory expansion but got so swept up by this single issue that the club's purpose was changed from a general purpose business and civic promotion organization to an industry-above-all-else organization. This shift in purpose alienated many members.[17]

And so for the third time in ten years, Madison was again without any commercial club. This time, however, behind-the-scenes preparations for the next incarnation of a commercial club were destined to produce a permanent organization. The new organization, known as the Board of Commerce, was announced in April 1913 and was modelled after a new type of commercial club sometimes known as Associations of Commerce and Chambers of Commerce.

Like its predecessors the Madison Board of Commerce sought to make Madison "a better, bigger and busier community."[18] But there the resemblance stopped and six important differences began.

First the mission of the Board was based "along broad community lines." By this the organizers meant that the Board was not just a population-boosting organization as the name of the Forty Thousand Club implied nor a shill for industrialists, an attribute which killed the Commercial Club. In contrast to these earlier efforts, the Board of Commerce set for itself the goal of improving the economic, environmental, and social conditions of the city. In casting the mission statement this broadly, organizers were acknowledging that one did not conduct business in a vacuum—one did business in a *community* whose overall qualities had a profound impact upon commerce. A community that had poor streets, inadequate police protection, insufficient water and sewer facilities or an improperly equipped fire department could hardly be called a good place in which to do business. But the argument for a

broadly conceived mission statement went far beyond these "primary" needs. Madison Board of Commerce organizers had a vision of an *ideal community* whose qualities included parks and playgrounds, good housing, well-organized charities, enlightened health and safety regulations, wholesome recreation and even abstractions such as justice, equity and beauty. Since local government had the greatest power to make these qualities a reality, Board organizers placed a great emphasis upon working with local government. This in brief was why "commerce" *and* "civics" were heavily stressed. This characteristic is important because there is no organization in Madison today quite like the old Board of Commerce. To create an organization with the same scope one would have to combine the Chamber of Commerce (business), the League of Women Voters (good government), Capital Community Citizens (environment) and even some elements of United Way (charity).[19]

Second, the first time in Madison commercial club history, the board had a full-time paid professional executive director, a seemingly small and yet very important difference because it overcame one of the most serious problems of earlier clubs, namely the inability of harried businessmen to promote commerce and at the same time run demanding businesses. The presence of a fulltime staff director marked the long overdue end to the "amateur hour" stage of business promotion, an era marked by erratic last minute effort and wild swinging lungest at economic development.

Third, the board established a commodious and sophisticated committee structure reflecting all major components of the economy. This meant that all members could get involved in meaningful ways if they chose to do so.

In a related move, the board retained tight control over its committees and divisions. This feature effectively ended the time when members and committees could speak for the organization without prior clearance or undertake projects without prior approval.[20]

Fourth, the board attracted members from *all* sectors of Madison's economy. For the first time bankers joined and played a large role both organizationally and financially. Even merchants in the then developing suburbs became members. Very significantly a large contingent of high ranking city, county and state government employees, university professors and ministers joined. In 1914 following the initial membership drive, nearly one out of seven Board members were on public or church payrolls.[21]

Fifth, Board of Commerce planners insisted and got a three year financial pledge from all its new members, a move which virtually guaranteed the organization's financial success during the first difficult years.

A final difference was the size of the new board. After the first week of the board membership drive, one thousand businessmen, professionals, government officials, and professors joined, almost three times more than had joined the Commercial Club just three years earlier![22]

Following the completion of its initial organizational chores, the Board of Commerce resembled a dog just let outside after a day of confinement in the house. It seemed to run everywhere at once. In 1914 the board began publication of a monthly newsletter distributed four major publications: an elegant "image" pamphlet portraying Madison's many virtues, a pocket-sized visitor guidebook, a fact-filled industrial prospectus, and a promotional tract on the new board.[23] The Board sponsored an impressive display of products made in Madison, actively recruited new and lobbied to keep existing businesses, sponsored lectures on timely business topics, helped raise money for a professional baseball team, issued pro-Madison press releases, laid plans for a consumer credit rating bureau, studied and made recommendations on roads, hospitals, and schools and much more.

This explosion of activity and membership contained two clear messages: (1) a well-organized, well-funded, and professionally staffed organization could accomplish almost amazing feats; and (2) Madison was at last eager to support such an organization. By the end of 1915 the Board of Commerce had become the largest and one of the most powerful organizations in the city, rivalled in overall influence only by the much older and more narrowly focused Madison Park and

FIGURE 6.7. ROOSEVELT AT THE MADISON CLUB OPENING. "When the picture arrives, I will gladly autograph it," said former President Theodore Roosevelt in a letter dated December 7, 1918, to Stanley Hanks, then president of the Madison Club. The photograph to which Roosevelt was referring was the one shown above where the former president is hoisting the flag at the opening of the Madison Club on May 28, 1918. Just a few hours after the flag-raising ceremony Roosevelt delivered a stirring war-inspired patriotic speech (sponsored by the National Security League) to six thousand wildly cheering persons at the Stock Pavillion. The former president stayed at the Madison Club that evening.

The 1918 visit was Roosevelt's seventh to Madison. In the 1890s he journeyed to the city on two occasions to do research at the State Historical Society of Wisconsin for his four-volume work, *The Winning of the West.* While in Madison for his second visit in late January 1893, Robert and Belle LaFollette gave a gala reception for Roosevelt, then a member of the U.S. Civil Service Commission, at their home at 405 West Wilson. At the same time Roosevelt also delivered the biennial address of the State Historical Society. During this period Roosevelt became a close friend of Reuben Gold Thwaites, librarian of the society, and corresponded with Lyman Draper, the first secretary of the society, and Frederick Jackson Turner, the University of Wisconsin professor who in 1893 delivered his famous lecture that called attention to the profound extent to which American character and history were shaped by the presence of the western frontier. During these early visits Roosevelt was very much taken by the beauty of Madison and regretted that he did not have time to go fishing on Lake Monona. His fourth visit came in April 1903 while he was president, and his fifth in September 1910. Roosevelt's sixth visit came in October 1912 while he was seeking the presidential limelight once again, but this time under the aegis of the Progressive party.

As history would have it Roosevelt never did sign the Madison Club photograph. In July 1918, just two months after Roosevelt's last visit to Madison, his youngest son Quentin, a combat aviator, was shot down and killed in France. The death of Quentin was a crushing blow from which the former President never recovered. Roosevelt died in his sleep on January 6, 1919, just one month after sending this letter to Hanks. (Courtesy of the Madison Club)

Pleasure Drive Association. Probably never before in Madison's history had a new organization grown so dominant so quickly.[24]

Although the upsurge of interest in commercial clubs as evidenced by the Forty Thousand Club, the Commercial Club, and the Board of Commerce comprised the center arena of commercial club activity during the first twenty years of the twentieth century, there were several other organizations that made a significant contribution to Madison's business development. In 1909 a group of the "most prominent business and professional men" formed the Madison Club to discuss topics of mutual interest, especially "municipal topics," and to socialize. The club modelled after similar clubs in larger cities, limited its membership to an elite one hundred fifty men. The club proved to be "a great success from the start," a fact that caused its members to build a handsome clubhouse at the foot of Monona Avenue in 1917. Although the club never took stands on issues as the mainline commercial clubs did, it provided an elegant sanctuary where members and guests could conduct business in an atmosphere of boardroom civility. Indeed, according to William T. Evjue, publisher of the *Capital Times,* the Madison Club was merely the Board of Commerce "sitting down for lunch."[25]

A second type of organization founded during this period was the men's service club. The service club was a twentieth century response to certain conditions of American urbanism and business life. More specifically businessmen sought an organization that could help them cope with the impersonalism of the city and the increasingly specialized, dog-eat-dog business world. Service clubs were also a response to a shift in civic leadership then underway from lawyers, doctors, ministers, and professors to businessmen. Madison and most other cities had very few organizations whose composition reflected this shift.

Getting businessmen and professionals together during the regular working day was no easy task, however. The only real possibility was the noon lunch. As more and more Madison businessmen moved to Nakoma, Maple Bluff, Shorewood, University Heights, and other suburbs, many stopped going home for lunch and decided to eat downtown instead. In Madison this pattern developed very quickly during the teens led to a great increase in the number of downtown restaurants and made the business lunch an institution.

Into an extended seventy-five-minute noon hour, weekly service club luncheons offered their members convivial first-name fellowship, a respite from the hectic pace of business, an informative and sometimes entertaining speaker, a chance to gather business intelligence, a feeling of self worth and importance—and of course a good meal.

Madison businessmen were quick to secure charters for these new service clubs. Local Rotarians, now the Downtown Rotary Club, received their charter in 1913 making them the first Madison service club and the seventy-first in the nation. Similarly the first charter for Madison Kiwanis Club was received in 1917, placing them among the first fifty such clubs in the country. Both Rotarians and Kiwanians limited membership to high-ranking executives, business owners, and professionals. Both organizations stressed high business ethics and community service.[26]

The Magic Touch of Enterprise

If there was a single theme which flowed through the pusher organizations, it was the notion that Madison could only become a great city if leaders were willing and able to mount an intense, sustained bootstrap effort. Dr. Clarke Gapen, the articulate founder of the Forty Thousand Club called this "the magic touch of enterprise."[27] These words became the watchword and rallying cry for a whole generation of business leaders who sought to apply this "magic touch" to those sections of the local economy which they believed would yield the greatest results.

The New Industrialism

Around the turn of the century a confluence of factors caused Madison's industrial prospects to brighten. First of course there was the old litany of locational and transportational advantages: Madison lay at the center of a large, rich agricultural region; nine railroad tracks entered the city from almost all cardinal points of the compass; it lay halfway between southern Illinois coal and northern Wisconsin iron.

Second, even Madison's relatively small size—once a liability—came to be viewed as an asset to many factory owners. Historically the larger cities well served by relatively cheap transportation and great pools of labor had been favored. However, following the rise of industrial unions and the epochal strife that sometimes accompanied the movement, factory owners had second thoughts. Smaller cities that offered good transportation facilities, access to markets, and a reasonable supply of nonunionized labor suddenly became very attractive. Such cities rarely experienced labor turmoil and provided superior quality housing and schools for workers. All this meant lower production costs and steadier output.[28]

Adding impetus to these arguments was the tremendous mystique of manufacturing that grew up in America in the late nineteenth century. The complex transformation of raw material into finished products attended by screaming steel drills, spectacular displays of sparks, and fiery-orange fluid iron obediently conforming to molds, evoked the same respect and even awe once reserved for alchemy. To be a manufacturer was to transform matter from one state to another, to have great power, to be a creator, a status far more prestigious than mere retailing or wholesaling or even processing. To be a manufacturer was to be a primary producer of wealth. Therefore in the world of business, manufacturing was very "macho."

The fourth factor was the desire among many businessmen to dispel the longstanding and widespread impression among persons around the state that Madison was merely a pretty government and educational town. The capital city, businessmen insisted, was also an industrial city! Admittedly the size of the city's industrial sector was modest (the 1901 industrial census ranked Madison seventh in population and seventeenth in industrial assets) but it did not follow that Madison had *no* industry! Indeed in an era that glorified

MEN WANTED
AT ONCE
FOR
CUTTING ICE
CONKLIN & SONS

FIGURE 6.8. ICE HARVESTING, 1900–1920. Shown above are employees of the Conklin & Sons Company, Madison's largest domestic supplier, bringing ice into the company's big storage house in 1912. The faded red ice house was one hundred fifty feet long, one hundred seventy feet deep, and forty feet high and stood at the intersection of North Butler, North Hamilton, and East Gorham Streets in what is now James Madison Park. Shown in the right background is the steel frame of the capitol dome, then under construction. The Conklin ice house burned to the ground in a spectacular June 1915 fire and was rebuilt but then torn down in 1939. In 1939 the city acquired the land whereupon it was known as Conklin Park.

In an age before the development of modern insulation materials, the ice houses were a marvel of thermal engineering. Even after a hot summer, only the top two feet of ice in a thirty-foot pile would melt. One engineer estimated that the two-foot thick, sawdust-filled walls had an "R" rating of fifty-three, the equivalent of seventeen inches of fiberglass insulation. Today the optimum insulation standard for residential walls is widely considered to be R-19 for walls and R-38 for ceilings.

During the first decade of the twentieth century about a dozen ice houses stood around the shores of Madison lakes. The larger houses were located in the middle of what is now the Village of Maple Bluff, where the toboggan slide is set up at Olbrich Park on Monona Drive, where the East Side Businessmen's Association clubhouse is now located and on Lake Wingra, roughly at the foot of Knickerbocker Avenue. Smaller houses owned by local breweries, butchers, and ice suppliers and by railroads serving Madison were scattered around the city.

The cutting season generally ran from January 15 to February 15 and required hundreds of men, only some of whom could be obtained in Madison. Even with the help of large newspaper ads like the one shown here, which ran in January 1910, the ice companies had to bring in outside men, most often seasonally unemployed Norwegian sailors wintering in Chicago. For a time the ice companies paid their laborers in checks or orders that could only be cashed at certain saloons, sometimes at a discount of twenty-five percent. The men would then spend the money at the saloons and a few days later would be found begging in the streets.

Cutting ice was both physically demanding and dangerous. Loading the huge ice blocks sometimes weighing five hundred pounds onto the steam conveyor was so taxing that the men would only work in fifteen-minute shifts. The job of handsawing the ice into blocks was also grueling, but was relieved when horse drawn power saws were brought into use around 1906. The men worked eleven-hour shifts and two shifts were usually used. Many of the men received serious cuts and even had eyes put out from pike pole accidents. The men in the left side of the channel of the above picture are using pike poles to slide the blocks to the conveyor. The men in the right foreground are using their U-shaped tools to split partially sawed ice blocks away from the main ice mass.

Beginning about 1910 butchers and other ice-dependent businesses began to buy mechanical refrigeration equipment, which eliminated their need to buy ice. One butcher who used the new equipment even boasted that his meat was cheaper because he didn't have to buy natural ice. The increasing use of mechanical refrigeration equipment coupled with Prohibition, which overnight eliminated the relatively large brewery ice demand, led to a rapid decline in the ice harvesting industry in Madison after World War I. (SHSW WHi (X3) 786) manufacturing and the entrepreneurial virtues, the impression that Madison had no factories suggested that Madison businessmen had no zip and energy—an impression most self-respecting members of the city's business community were eager to refute.[29]

The fifth reason for the great allure of industry was the growing realization among business and civic leaders that factories were the most certain and rapid producers of population growth. Retailing and wholesaling by contrast could only grow if the number of shoppers increased. In this respect the growth of the retailing and wholesaling were largely dependent upon the number of university students and state bureaucrats, and these two growth generators in turn were primarily dependent upon budgets and programs approved by the legislature over which city leaders had little control. But factories on the other hand were also primary population generators and, best of all, were responsive to the actions of Madison's movers and shakers. It was for this reason that many businessmen felt they controlled a powerful lever affecting Madison's size and destiny.

The final reason for the growing infatuation with factories was their ability to produce large amounts of tax revenue. As Madison leaders surveyed the municipal horizon and saw the need for expensive parks, paved streets, sewers, street lights, and dozens of other improvements, they recognized that the city could not afford to break into the metropolitan ranks without either a large tax increase or a new or expanded revenue source. Under the property tax system, factories with their relatively expensive plants (real property) and huge inventories (personal property) seemed to provide the only realistic revenue source for these expensive improvements. The persuasiveness of this argument increased dramatically after 1912 when the state passed the nation's first state income tax and gave seventy percent of its relatively large yield back to the municipalities.[30]

The convergence of these six factors during the first decade of the new century sent some of the city's most prominent business and civic leaders parading through the streets, as if it were, thumping the drum of industrial growth. Among the most active industrial drummers were the Commercial Clubs. Forty Thousand Club members gave stirring speeches at banquets, wrote letters to factory owners who might be willing to move to Madison, and provided incentives to relocate in the form of "bonuses" and stock purchases.[31] During their short but eventful life, Commercial Club (1910–1911) members vigorously supported a major factory expansion. The Board of Commerce worked to make Madison a "busy, hustling, industrial city . . ." by preparing and distributing a well-executed industrial prospectus, sponsoring a huge display of products made in Madison[32] and by working through the state railroad commission to reduce freight rates.[33] To provide an adequate pool of risk capital so critically important to new and expanding industries, the Board of Commerce formed a two-hundred-thousand-dollar "development fund." These funds were then used to buy securities of companies that had been approved by a committee of experienced Madison businessmen. The development fund not only reduced the risk to Madison investors since any losses incurred by approved companies would be shared by all investors, but it also eliminated the earlier "method of soliciting personal subscriptions of capital stock or bonds without sufficient investigation. . . ."[34]

The *Wisconsin State Journal* and the *Madison Democrat* were the second source of industrial cheerleading. Although both ran stories highlighting Madison's growing industry, wrote favorable editorials, and gave front page treatment to commercial club activities, the *Journal* and Richard Lloyd Jones in particular was easily the most eloquent and outspoken on the subject. For example in a 1915 five-article profactory series he scolded Madisonians for their "indifference" to industry, the city's "most important asset," a malady he once termed "Langdon lethargy."[35] In the same series he urged citizens to wage war on those who were "contented with Madison the Peaceful," that is, a city devoid of industry. "Who said we want more peace and quiet?" he snarled. "Let people who want to go to bed at 8:30 go somewhere else." Madison's goal was to get bigger and better and to do this "industrially."[36]

Several East Side developers whose subdivisions were served by railroad tracks also assisted Madison's industrialization through various schemes. For example, owners of Fair Oaks and Madison Square subdivisions gave factory owners free or reduced cost sites because the factory would then increase the demand and value for adjoining lots.[37]

The fourth source of industrial promotion was the factory owner who learned to work both independently and with commercial clubs to achieve their ends. In 1906, for example, Carl A. Johnson, president of the Gisholt Company, one of Madison's largest employers, asked the city to vacate Few Street between East Washington and East Main Street so he could expand his plant. The request angered some citizens who felt they would be inconvenienced by the vacation of this street and forced the city to confront the issue of industrial growth versus public convenience. A few businessmen gathered signatures in support of the vacation but no one else rallied to Johnson's side, not even the Forty Thousand Club. The council subsequently denied the request.[38]

Very significantly Johnson did not try again until 1910—*after* the Commercial Club had been formed. Quite probably Johnson saw the large, newly energized club in the same way a football running back sees a wall of big downfield blockers. The Commercial Club made the Gisholt street vacation request a *cause célèbre* and supported it with a vigor seldom manifested by Madison's business community. In addition to their invaluable support, Johnson also enlisted merchants and professional men, both of whom submitted long petitions. Even Governor Davidson sent a letter to the Common Council urging approval, an action no doubt engineered by Johnson. This time the Council approved the request, thirteen to five, an event that signalled the beginning of an era when the Common Council became a friend of industrial growth.[39]

Immediately after this victory Johnson shrewdly decided to express his appreciation to the city and his backers, give them a preview of the kind of factory their action would soon produce in Madison, and lay the groundwork for any future requests he might have to make. Toward this end he rented a plush railroad parlor car and invited Commercial Club leaders, the mayor, the aldermen, several other city officials, and the editors of both papers to be his guests on a trip to Chicago where he planned to show them a factory similar to the one that he would soon erect. Not long after the train left Madison Johnson made a presentation to his thirty guests, at that point an eager and captive audience, on the importance of city-business cooperation in industrial growth. Following Johnson's presentation the mayor and aldermen decided that since a quorum was present they might as well have a formal council meeting to conduct some routine business, which they did. The event was of course highly unusual. Never before or since has the Common Council held an official meeting aboard a train, much less a plush parlor car provided by a local industrial magnate who sought their favor. When the train arrived in Chicago everyone was whisked out to the plant in automobiles, given a red carnation, fed in the plant cafeteria, and given a tour. After the tour they were driven downtown to the Chicago Athletic Club for cocktails and hors d'oeuvres. The newspaper editors reported that everyone in the party returned to Madison convinced that the plant would be a fine addition to Madison.[40]

The Madison Compromise: Factories and Faculty Too

In February 1901, an after dinner speaker told members of Madison's Forty Thousand Club that "prejudice against making the city a manufacturing center has disappeared."[41] Although that statement was the fervent hope of businessmen gathered that evening at the banquet hall, it was not an accurate assessment of city opinion leader sentiment. The fact was, a relatively large and influential group of Madisonians had for years actively opposed industrial growth and even growth in general, and neither the intensity nor the size of the group had diminished. The anti-industry clique was composed of salaried univer-

sity professors and capital employees, a group of doctors and lawyers, and several others—the same classes that constituted the backbone of Madison's rather intellectual, professional, and salaried "society."[42] This influential group liked Madison the way it was—that is, as a sophisticated, quiet, clean, beautiful college town and state capital.[43] They derived great pride from the fact that Madison had more persons listed in *Who's Who* than Milwaukee had with ten times the population.[44]

This powerful clique rejected as a "profanation" the fundamental premise on which the industrialists based their claims, that is, the concept that bigger was better and growth was good. To them this lust for growth was not a sign of vitality at all, but rather a "disease" called "megalomania," a malady they perceived to be sweeping the world. Madison, they insisted, did not need a single new citizen, especially if it meant bringing in factories.[45] Moreover, they rejected the argument so dear to industrialists that more factories would mean lower taxes for everyone.[46]

One of the greatest fears of Madison's antigrowth and antifactory clique was that growth in general and industrial growth in particular would destroy Madison's magnificent beauty. Would it really be progress if the lakeshores were lined by homes and cottages asked one gentleman. "I want to see trees there, not houses. . . . There are too many buildings here already," he protested.[47] And what would be gained, asked others, if the Forty Thousand Club was successful in building a municipal coal dock on Lake Monona at the foot of South Blair so that soft Illinois coal could be cheaply transported up the Mississippi, Rock, and Yahara Rivers and deposited in the heart of Madison? True, this would be a boon for factories but what about the city as a whole?[48] Do we really want to encourage factories to come here knowing that their smoking chimneys will make our skies leaden and our lakes a depository for their wastes? Is a smoky, dirty, ugly city worth the extra money such factories would bring in? "Reflect gentlemen," warned one writer representing this point of view, "how many places there are which can be made big and how few places there are which God has made beautiful."[49]

The last reason for opposing factories was that it meant a great influx of grimy workers many of whom would be "ignorant, poverty-crushed foreigners,"[50] a prospect that deeply worried and even threatened the Langdon cliques. Father P. B. Knox, priest of the St. Patrick's Catholic Church, no doubt spoke for many when he said such an influx would lower the city's intellectual and moral standards. He reasoned that since workers didn't place the same emphasis upon education and upon improving one's mind as the present population that the quality of schools might and indeed the city's entire intellectual life decline. Father Knox also believed that more workers would mean an increase in drinking, saloons, gambling and houses of ill-repute and immorality of all kinds.[51]

Against a backdrop of American history, Madison's relatively large and effective antifactory and antigrowth sentiment was downright rare. On the other hand Madison with its state "endowments" of the capital and the university was one of very few American cities whose citizens had the luxury of sitting back, doing nothing, prospering, and even growing slowly *without industry*. Indeed throughout the late nineteenth century when the rest of the country was marching to the brassy din of industrialization, Madison opinion leaders were listening to stringed sounds of beauty, scholarship, and culture and for the most part delighting in being out of step with the rest of the nation on this matter.

Thus the crescendo of profactory and progrowth sentiment, which gathered momentum with the founding of the Forty Thousand Club in 1901 and which was sustained by the Commercial Club and the Board of Commerce, set the stage for a great confrontation on the factory-growth issue. The collision of these two points of view produced a fascinating result. Both sides recognized that the pure version of their dream was politically out of the question since each side had enough power to thwart the other. After the first few confrontations, however, both factions could see that each could make certain concessions, "win" great gains, and save face.

FIGURE 6.9. THE UNIVERSITY OF WISCONSIN, A 1907 BIRDSEYE VIEW. By 1907 when this high-quality birdseye campus view was commissioned, the university had come to have many different meanings to Madisonians. To most opinion leaders it represented erudition, culture, refinement, the cutting edge of science, progressivism, hope, youth, and optimism. To Madison's boardinghouse keepers, livery stable and garage owners, florists, confectioners, clothing merchants, and many other businessmen, the university meant lots of money. To more conservative residents the university was "that hotbed of radicalism." To Madison police it was a reliable producer of mischief, misdemeanors, and periodic riots. To an unusually large number of Madisonians it was the place where their sons and daughters went to school. In 1919, for example, Madison had only 1.4 percent of the state's population and yet Madison students made up 16 percent of the student body. Even Milwaukee whose population at that time was twelve times greater than Madison's sent only half as many students to the university as did the capital city. (SHSW WHi(X3)2319)

Industrialists were quick to see the folly of pushing "the ruder kinds of factories" such as steel mills and went out of their way to secure "high grade" factories.[52] In support of this important and anxiety-reducing distinction, the Board of Commerce rejected twenty-two of the first twenty-three industries that expressed interest in locating in Madison in the 1914–1915 era.[53] The insistence upon "high grade" industries also had important implications on the quality of workman the factories would attract. Industrialists insisted and anti-industrialists agreed that high grade factories meant highly skilled, highly paid artisans who owned their own homes and who sent their children to the university, not the "bad" kind of workmen feared by Father Knox. Here the industrialists found that they could win an easy victory by pointing to the very high quality workman the Fuller and Johnson, Gisholt, and Northern Electric factories had already been able to attract.[54]

By the same token the antifactory group found a whole new rationale, which enabled them to accept factories. They conceded that all classes of people were required to make a city work, "people with the dinner bucket and the people wearing the purple." Therefore it was "no more [than] common justice to desire to give to as many (laboring men) as possible the advantages . . . a city like Madison has to offer."[55]

The only remaining question was *where* the factories should be located and where factory workers should live. According to one West Side attorney, John C. Fehlandt, Madison was "especially favored by her topography to be *both* a city of homes and of factories. What made this

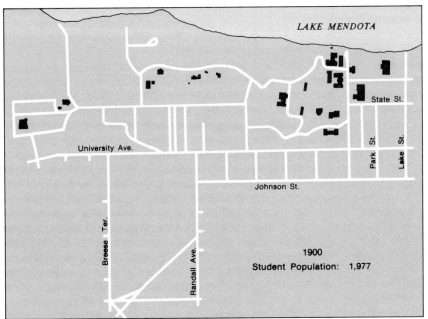

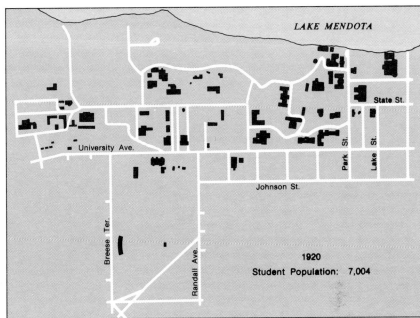

FIGURE 6.10. UNIVERSITY OF WISCONSIN GROWTH, 1900 TO 1920. The first two decades of the twentieth century were years of steady and impressive growth for the University of Wisconsin. With the exception of a sharp dip and then an even sharper rise during and immediately after World War I, student enrollment advanced steadily. When the era ended, enrollment had zoomed from just under two thousand to over seven thousand students. Because the student body grew more rapidly than the city population, the ratio between students and nonstudents rose from one in ten in 1900 to one in six in 1920.

To remain abreast of this relatively rapid growth university officials erected forty-six new buildings and increased campus size from 479 acres to 1,017 acres.

coexistence possible was Capitol Hill, which hygenically separated the East Side "factory district" from the West Side "residence district." The fact that the East Side was also a residence district including several large established prestigious neighborhoods was blithely ignored, condemned as it were to industrial perdition. There was of course a basis for this self-serving and highly elitist distinction. All their profactory rhetoric to the contrary, many Madisonians including Attorney Fehlandt, 638 Langdon Street, wanted very much to keep their neighborhoods free of factories and workers. By encouraging factories in the "factory district," Fehlandt and others could be reasonably sure that workers would live on the East Side since nearly all workers preferred to live near their place of employment.[56]

And so based upon these tacit agreements between industrialists and anti-industrialists, the "Madison compromise" was framed. Only "high grade" factories employing highly skilled and highly paid workers would be encouraged to come to Madison and the factories were to be located "over there"—in the East Side factory district. The capital city would have both factories and faculty, lunch buckets and brief cases, East Side and West Side. It was a comfortable world of cozy compartments separated by a socio-economic fault line that even today sends tremors through discussions of municipal problems.

Consequences of the Compromise

By about 1910 the "Madison compromise" had been accepted by most opinion leaders and began to produce large and relatively rapid results. Between 1910 and 1920 when the city population increased by fifty percent the value of Madison factory output increased by 274% and the number of factory workers increased by 283%. Measured in payroll size and number of employees, manufacturing became the single largest sector in the Madison economy no later than 1915 and probably several years earlier.[57]

Since this very rapid expansion of manufacturing was heavily concentrated in the factory district, it caused the East Side to boom. Between

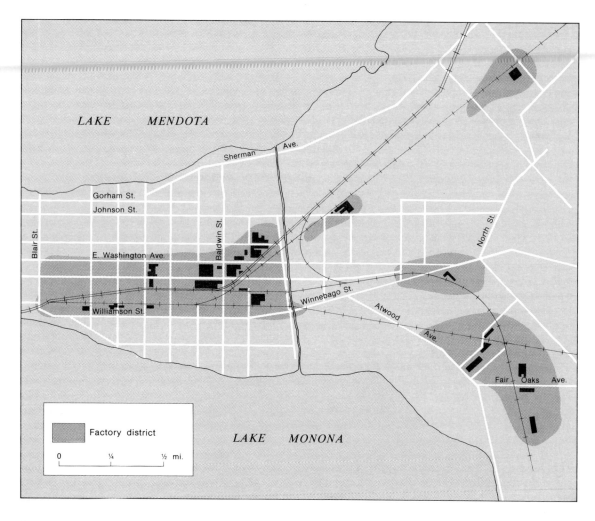

FIGURE 6.11. MADISON'S FACTORY DISTRICT, 1920. Between 1900 and 1920 Madison's East Side factory district
grew rapidly. Nearly all factories were concentrated adjacent to railroad facilities on Madison's east side.

1910 and 1920 when the city population grew by
fifty percent, the East Side grew by seventy percent, while the West Side lagged behind at forty-
four percent.[58]

The rapid increase in the size and number of
factories also caused a strong resurgence of union
activity. In 1902 Madison had just seventeen
union locals and a "well earned reputation of
being a nonunion city." However, between 1912
and 1916 the number of union members more
than doubled and the number of locals rose to
nearly one hundred. A 1916 reorganization of the
local central labor organization produced the
Madison Federation of Labor and marked the
beginning of a period when labor movement received much stronger and more astute leadership. One very significant result of this new
central leadership was the decision in 1916 to endorse political candidates for the first time. Consequently a union member was elected to the
Common Council and another was appointed to
the school board. The 1900–1916 era was a relatively peaceful period with very few strikes and
virtually no violence. Nevertheless the eight-hour
day (but still six days a week) became the standard in the building trades, paychecks were distributed weekly or biweekly rather than monthly,
and hourly wage rates were increased.[59]

The combination of the Madison compromise
plus good management and favorable business
conditions allowed the city's major industries to
grow and prosper. In 1911 officials at the Fuller
and Johnson Company, Madison's oldest and
largest factory, responded to soaring demand for
a small reliable gasoline engine popular on farms
for pumping water and a variety of other applications by exclusively devoting its large plant at
the intersection of East Washington and North
Baldwin to its production. Fuller and Johnson officials then sold the right to make their regular
line of plows, harrows, cultivators, and planters
to a group of Madison investors who formed the
Madison Plow Company and took over a large
vacant factory at 2301 Fair Oaks Avenue. But
even after devoting its entire original factory to

the production of the small engines and running the plant around the clock, the company could not keep up with demand. Therefore in 1919 company officers decided to raze the old plant and built a larger and more efficient facility on the East Washington Avenue site. This building still stands but has been converted to an office building and renamed Washington Square.[60]

The first twenty years of the twentieth century were also boom years for the Gisholt Company. Rapidly growing demand for their high quality turret lathes, vertical boring mills, and tool grinders caused company officials to greatly expand their production facilities from one to five square blocks and the number of their employees from two hundred in 1900 to about sixteen hundred in 1920.[61] By 1916 Gisholt had grown so large that it paid the second highest state corporate income tax outside Milwaukee.[62]

A final consequence of Madison's new industrialism was the birth and very rapid development of whole new types of industry including meat processing, dry batteries, machine lubricators, and hospital equipment.

Meat Processing

"Within a radius of sixty miles of Madison there are more than two and one-half million hogs, cattle, and sheep." "High meat costs for the consumer and unconscionably low prices for the farmer are caused by the greed of the Chicago beef trusts." These and many similar claims appeared in a series of newspaper advertisements in April 1915, urging the construction of a packing plant in Madison. The ads had been placed by the Farmers' Cooperative Packing Company, a ten-month-old organization formed under a new strongly worded Wisconsin law intended to encourage the growth of cooperatives.[63]

That Madison area farmers thought that a cooperative packing plant would increase their profits and inflict financial injury to the despised Chicago packers was reflected by the alacrity with which five thousand farmers bought nearly

$600,000 of stock in the new enterprise.[64] Only two other farm-owned cooperative packing plants had been built in the entire country, both in Wisconsin (La Crosse and Wausau), and both utilized the state's new cooperative law. In this respect the Madison plant was a part of a "brave experiment" of nationwide interest to see whether farmers could recapture control over their financial destiny from the great "octopus" corporations.[65]

As it turned out raising money for this new venture was relatively easy. The thorny question was where the plant should be located, or, as *Journal* editor Richard Lloyd Jones so deftly put it, "where shall we kill the pig?"[66] At the time packing plants were widely considered to be one of the worst possible "neighbors." People especially hated the screams hogs let out as they were killed and stench of drying hair and fertilizer.[67]

The site desired by coop officials lay just north of the Madison-Kipp plant near the intersection of Atwood Avenue and Fair Oaks Avenue in what was then the Village of Fair Oaks. But that location provoked intense opposition from factory owners, residents, and many others. Even the fiercely proindustry board of commerce refused to endorse the site, but it did work behind the scenes to locate an alternative site. They recommended that it be put right next to the new sewage treatment plant. There the noises and smells of a packing plant could hardly be offensive since they would be far removed from the city and in an area that would never be attractive for homes. The Common Council unanimously approved the idea, sold the cooperative twenty acres of city-owned land (originally purchased for sewage plant expansion) and authorized the use of the new sewage plant and city water. The *quid pro quo* was that the site would be annexed to the city so that the city would get the local "rebate" from any state income tax the plant would pay. The cooperative accepted. Foundation work got underway in June 1916 and the plant opened in May 1917, just one month after war was declared on the Axis powers.[68]

After little more than a year, however, problems of inadequate working capital and militant labor began to cast a pall over the future of the fledgling packing plant. For patriotic and selfish reasons workers agreed to stay on the job during the war at what they regarded as low wages. But in January 1919, during the great labor unrest which followed the war, the workers went on strike forcing the plant to be shut down one month later.[69]

Faced by militant labor, mounting operating losses, and no real prospect of getting any new capital from their stockholders, cooperative directors were forced to make a painful decision. Naturally they despised the thought of abandoning their dream and yet they had no real choice. The plant was put up for sale.

To their chagrin no one wanted to buy it. The only nibble they had was from a Chicago lard processor who was willing to *lease* the plant. Lacking any other option the directors called a stockholders meeting at the plant for Tuesday, June 17, 1919, where they planned to urge their members to approve the lease.

Just a few days before the fateful stockholder's meeting Oscar G. Mayer, the thirty-year-old secretary and general manager of the Chicago firm, Oscar F. Mayer and Brother Company, loaded his wife, Elsa, and two sons, Oscar G. Jr., age five, and Harold, age two, into their big V-12 touring car and headed for Madison where they planned to spend a few days as guests of Mr. and Mrs. Fred Suhr, Sr. Mrs. Suhr was Mrs. Mayer's sister and Mr. Suhr was president of the American Exchange Bank. For several summers the spacious Suhr lakeshore home at 512 East Gorham had been a popular meeting place for the two families.[70]

Using the Suhr's home as their base of operation, the Mayers had attempted a trip to Mount Horeb but the roads were so muddy they decided to return to Madison and the comforts of the Suhr porch. Later that day, Fred Suhr turned to his brother-in-law and said, "Oscar, there's this little packing house . . . and its up for auction."

"Gosh that's right," replied Oscar recalling hearing about the plant shut-down through trade circles. "Can we get out there?" The two men jumped in the car and drove out to the plant.

Mayer could hardly believe what he found. For several years Mayer had been "obsessed"—as he later put it—with the idea of establishing a "country slaughtering plant," that is, a rural source for his Chicago processed meat plant. Although the concept inverted the prevailing industry practice of centralizing all operations at a single plant, Mayer was confident that a country slaughtering plant was the best solution for his company. Such a plant he reasoned would eliminate waste inherent in shipping cattle long distances and could also assure a higher quality meat source. And here in Madison was just such a plant—nearly new, well constructed, and thoroughly modern in layout.

The brief plant inspection so excited Mayer that he could hardly wait to get back to the Suhr home where Mayer called his father, Oscar F. Mayer, the founder of the company. The senior Mayer, then sixty, was less than excited by the prospect of running a slaughtering operation or dealing with shippers, neither of which the company had never done before. Nevertheless the senior Mayer respected his son's judgment and suggested that he do what he thought best.

The following day the young Chicago meat processing executive returned to the plant for the scheduled stockholder's meeting. Workers had built a crude platform across one of the livestock holding pens so that officials could be seen and heard when they urged acceptance of the lease proposal. The coop president made a brief speech urging acceptance of the lease and, after discussion, someone moved to approve the deal. Mayer's moment had come. He moved quickly from the rear of the crowd to the base of the wooden platform and tugged at the coat of the coop attorney who was standing near the edge. Mayer introduced himself to the attorney and said he might be interested in *buying* the property, but that he would require several days to get an expert appraisal, arrange financing, and the like.

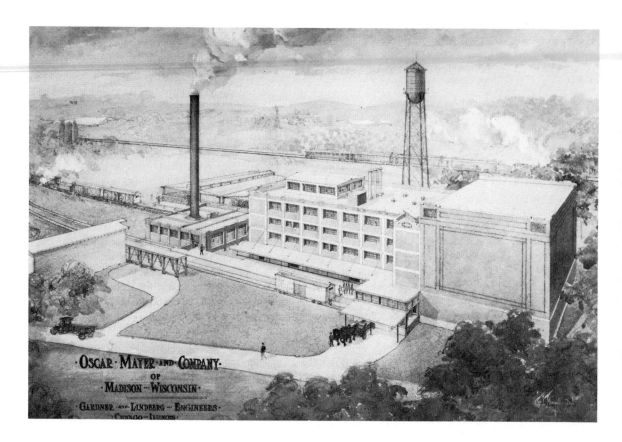

FIGURE 6.12. THE OSCAR MAYER COMPANY. This artist's rendering showing the Oscar Mayer and Company plant was originally done for the Farmers' Cooperative Packing Company in 1916. Apparently the artist merely added a new legend at the request of Oscar Mayer officials. The three-hundred-thousand-dollar brick and poured concrete building was touted as one of the most modern packing plants in the United States.

The large square structure on the right was the cold storage room. The four-story structure in the center contained the offices and all meat processing operations. The one-story building at the base of the large smokestack was the central power plant. The animal holding pens lay behind the power plant and the ice house and car-icing ramp lay in front. (Courtesy of the Oscar Mayer Food Company)

The attorney conferred with the president and other officials on the platform who decided to place the matter before the stockholders. A great murmur went up from the crowd and more questions were asked. They agreed to give Mayer time to get his deal together.

After getting an expert appraisal and securing commitments from bankers, Mayer offered Coop officials three hundred thousand dollars for the plant, very close to its cost. On July 15, the coop directors decided to accept and set July 29 as a stockholder's ratification meeting. Mayer had won the support of the influential directors, but now in the three weeks remaining he had a more difficult task: convincing five thousand skeptical farmer-owners scattered all over south central Wisconsin to accept the offer. For this task Mayer dispatched the trusted and talented Chicago attorney George L. Schein, who spent the hectic two-week period driving from meeting to meeting. Everywhere he went he stressed the fact that the Oscar Mayer Company was a strong independent meat processor—utterly unconnected to Chicago trusts, that the company's products were known far and wide as being very high quality, and that the Mayers individually and as businessmen were unimpeachably honest and fair. The work paid off because on July 29 the members voted 1911 to 168 to accept the offer. Oscar G. Mayer had his country slaughtering plant and, equally important, the good will of area farmers. Local newspapers gave front-page headline treatment to the acquisition, calling it "the most important industrial acquisition of the decade."

A twenty-six-year-old former army aviator and employee of the Chicago plant, Adolph C. Bolz, was sent to Madison to get the plant running in the shortest possible time. Skilled workers were recruited wherever they could be found. One Oscar Mayer recruiter, a Polish-born butcher, made a sweep of Milwaukee's Polish saloons during the Cudahy strike then in progress and came back to Madison with a caravan of cars carrying fifty experienced meat cutters. After a frenzied four-month effort, the plant reopened on November 24, 1919.

From the beginning the Mayer's made an aggressive effort to maintain the trust of farmers and the loyalty of their employees. Although their contract to purchase the plant gave them five years to pay off coop shareholders, the Mayers paid the entire amount barely one month after the deal was approved. They always paid fair cash prices for livestock brought to the plant. Each Tuesday Oscar F. Mayer would come to Madison, change into a pair of old pants, high leather boots, and a well-worn sweater with a hole in the sleeve, and spend the morning in the stock pens. There he would help move and weigh cattle and get to know farmers and buyers on a first-name basis. Positioned by the scales he would instruct the weighers to "give the boys a good price" but then turning to the farmers he would wink and add, "but don't forget Oscar." During plant visits the senior Mayer would often hand out flowers to the office girls and dispense good cigars to plant workers.

Corporate citizenship was another area where the Mayer's moved quickly and won widespread approval. When the plant opened, Madison was in the midst of a serious postwar economic slump. Homes to rent were extremely scarce and very few new homes were being built. Rather than throw their employees into an impossibly tight market, the Mayers contracted to have fifty affordable homes built for their workers. Another problem the company faced was getting their employees to work. F. W. Montgomery, owner of the streetcar company, refused to extend his track to the plant without assurance from Mayer company officials that they would reimburse him for any operational losses the line might incur. Mayer's decision to pay any such losses caused the North Street line to be built.

These early efforts paid off and by 1920 the Madison plant had become the fifth largest packing plant in the country with an annual volume of eleven million dollars. Oscar G. Mayer lived to see his "little country slaughtering plant" become the company headquarters and his son, Oscar G. Mayer, Jr., who at age five stood beside his father on that fateful day in June, 1919, became company president and oversaw an operation whose national and international sales exceeded one billion dollars a year.

The Dry Battery Industry

In December 1905, thirty-five-year-old James B. Ramsay had never heard of a dry cell. But then he got an excited call from a friend, P. W. Strong, extolling its extraordinary but as yet unexploited commercial potential. The call came at a propitious time in Ramsay's career because he had just sold a successful land and lumber business in northern Wisconsin, had returned to Madison where he had graduated from the U. W. fourteen years earlier, and was looking for a new challenge. Ramsay did some quick market research and concluded that there was indeed a growing demand for dry cells in telephones, automobiles, and possibly in a novelty item known as a "flashlight."[71]

In January 1906, just one month after they discussed the dry cell business venture for the first time, Ramsay and Strong found themselves in the Chicago loft-factory of a mysterious Frenchman, Alfred Landau, who professed to know the "secret process" for making dry cells. In fact for some time Landau had been making dry cells by hand in his loft and selling them to Chicago retailers. At that time the standard battery was two and one-half inches in diameter and six inches high, and most commonly used to power telephones. Ramsay, Strong, and Landau discussed the possibility of setting up a company for the large-scale manufacture of dry cells. Landau agreed to cooperate but only under three conditions: that he be made president and general manager of the new business; that he receive fifty dollars per week for twenty-five years, and that he never be asked to reveal his "secret process," even to his partners. Ramsay and Strong agreed, made themselves vice-president and treasurer and secretary respectively, and then turned to the question of a

FIGURE 6.13. FRENCH BATTERY AND CARBON COMPANY.   This photograph taken about 1920 shows employees wrapping flashlight batteries at the Winnebago plant. The large number of female employees was an increasingly common phenomenon in Madison factories at this time.

that had always been done by Landau according to his "secret formula." In desperation Ramsay turned to Dr. C. F. Burgess, the founder of the University of Wisconsin Department of Chemical Engineering. Burgess assured Ramsay that battery making involved nothing more than mixing a few chemicals together in certain proportions. Before giving them too much free advice, however, he expressed an interest in becoming associated with the company, a request to which the directors quickly acceded by making Burgess a board member and the head of the company's engineering department. Under Burgess' leadership battery production resumed and in 1910 the company made a profit for the first time.

Meanwhile Burgess began experimenting with smaller, lighter batteries for "flashlights," so-called because the batteries then available were quickly drained if turned on for more than a few seconds at a time. Burgess' work led to what is now known as the standard "D" cell. Some say that the size of these batteries was established because he wrapped his first battery casings around his wife's mop handle, which just happened to be 1¼ inches in diameter. Not long after Burgess perfected the "D" cell, he designed an attractive new tubular flashlight case.

Significantly both the flashlight batteries and cases had been designed by Burgess in his own research and development facility known as the Northern Chemical and Engineering Laboratory. At the time such enterprises were common among professors and even encouraged by university authorities providing that they did not interfere with teaching. Burgess' laboratory was also completely independent of the French Battery Company.

When the commercial possibilities of Burgess' flashlight specialties became evident, a special arrangement was worked out whereby French Battery Company officials allowed the flashlight batteries to be made in their factory and sold through their rapidly growing sales network. As a marketing gimmick French directors adopted the now famous "french flasher" logo, a symbol which gave their product distinctive appeal and

corporate name. In deference to the French origin of Landau, they agreed to call it the French Battery Company.

For two months the company made its batteries in Landau's Chicago loft-factory and then rising production forced the fledgling company to seek larger quarters. In March 1906 they moved the operation to an old building (no longer standing) at the intersection of East Main and South Blair Streets. There some twenty-four employees using kitchen egg beaters and other rudimentary equipment manufactured batteries. This time the company stayed just four months before rising production forced the company to move to a still larger building at 615 Regent Street. In spite of three moves during their first year of operation,

the French Battery Company turned out thirty-seven thousand batteries.

Then beginning in 1907, the company's second year, Landau fomented a life-threatening crisis for the new enterprise by ordering huge quantities of carbon and other supplies from Paris, for which the company had budgeted no funds, and by producing seventeen thousand "junk" batteries. Company directors, by this time supplemented by several Madison businessmen, fired Landau and directed Ramsay, who had persuaded them to invest in the enterprise in the first place, to get them out of this mess.

Ramsay was both capable and willing but he and other directors labored under a serious disadvantage. Not one of them had the vaguest idea how to mix the ingredients for their dry cells since fame. By 1915 the number of Burgess' flashlight batteries made under contract by French Battery Company had grown to the point where they rivalled the output of their historic mainstay product, the six-inch-high model.

But then the French Battery Company suffered a serious loss. A fire totally destroyed their rented factory just when orders for their products were soaring. In the investigation that followed, harsh feelings developed between Burgess and Ramsay about whose carelessness had caused the fire. Ramsay insisted that the fire had begun in that part of the factory "leased" to Burgess for flashlight battery production. This disagreement ended the close and productive relationship between the two men and caused two battery companies to emerge from the ashes of this devastating fire.

In 1916 the French Battery Company built a huge new plant at 2317 Winnebago, and Professor Burgess—after severing all connections with French—decided to build his own large plant bounded by East Washington Avenue, East Main Street and South Brearly Street. Its office building at 1015 East Washington Avenue is now the headquarters building for Research Products Corporation. The primary Burgess production facility occupied the rear of the block fronting on East Main Street. Thus by 1917 Madison had two large battery factories, the ten-year-old French Battery Company and the one-year-old Burgess Battery Company.

By 1920 the French Battery Company had developed a national sales and distribution network with branches in New York, Chicago, Atlanta, Dallas, Kansas City, Minneapolis, and Denver and had opened a second factory in Newark, New Jersey. After just three years the Burgess Battery Company had established an aggressive sales and distribution network in eight midwestern states with branches in Chicago and Kansas City. Thus, by 1920 Madison had become one of the largest producers of flashlight batteries in the country. The growth of this business also demonstrated the tremendous synergistic potential of university-industry collaboration. Indeed the dry cell business, an early version of high technology industry,

stands as the first large, successful example in Madison of the many fruits a yeasty marriage between industry and university can produce.

In 1934 the French Battery Company changed its name to Ray-o-vac, a vacuum tube radio era outgrowth of the flashlight-era Ray-o-Lite trade name. In spite of the fact that Ray-o-vac was subsequently bought by outside firms and made a part of several corporate conglomorates, its headquarters remain in Madison.

Unlike Ray-o-vac, the Burgess Battery Company did not stay in the city. In 1938 the company moved all its facilities to Freeport, Illinois.

Machine Lubricators

In December 1901 two Madison men, Albert A. Stelting and Burton J. Larkin, both of whom sold farm machinery for the J. I. Case Harvesting Company, decided to sever their relationship with the large Racine corporation and go into business for themselves. As veteran salesmen in southern Wisconsin they were thoroughly familiar with the farm machinery business and therefore with the limitations of then available equipment. One limitation apparent on steam tractors was the failure of various oiling devices to keep valves and joints properly lubricated. It was for this reason that Stelting and Larkin were intrigued by a new patented automatic oil injector invented by a Mr. Mason. They recognized that if this device could be commercially produced, it would constitute a great breakthrough in reliability, machine life, and ease of maintenance. Therefore Stelting and Larkin began to negotiate for Mason's patent rights. Following Mason's agreement to sell, the two implement salesmen filed incorporation papers for the Mason Lubricator Company in December 1901. Soon thereafter stockholders made Stelting general manager of the new enterprise.[72]

Just four months later Stelting opened a factory at 621 Williamson, now a Madison landmark known as "Machinery Row." Barely had production gotten underway at the Williamson plant when growing orders forced Stelting to move to a slightly larger facility at 523 East Main Street. So successful was the company in its first

year that the company declared a ten percent dividend for its stockholders.

Meanwhile Stelting was eyeing a small firm in Rochelle, Illinois, known as the O. G. Kipp Company, which held several valuable patents in the lubricator field. Stelting's plan was to merge the two companies so that a single company controlled the most promising new lubricator patents. The result was the Mason-Kipp Manufacturing Company formed in September 1902.

Following the merger Stelting had to find a larger factory. Although he received tempting offers from LaCrosse and Milwaukee to move the factory there, he received his best offer from the Fair Oaks Land Company, which offered him a "sung bonus and a free site." According to the *Madison Democrat,* this action secured "an important addition to the dinner pail brigade and industrial wealth of the capital city." In the fall of 1903 officers of the merged firms broke ground for a large new factory on Waubesa Street, a short street running north from the 2800 block of Atwood Avenue.

From this point forward growth was very rapid for the new company. By 1917 following another major plant expansion the Mason-Kipp Corporation had become the world's largest manufacturer of machine lubricators and controlled sixty percent of the U.S. market. Two-thirds of all steam and gasoline farm tractors made in the U.S. were "Kipp-Equipt" and some of the largest tractor manufacturers including J. I. Case and International Harvester used the Kipp line exclusively. By 1920, following a second major plant expansion in 1919, the company had four hundred employees, a burgeoning foreign trade, and a reputation for dependability and high quality. By this time the company had acquired the name by which it is well known throughout the city today: The Madison-Kipp Corporation.

Hospital Equipment

A person driving by the beautiful new factory and national headquarters of Ohio Medical Products on Airco Drive might well wonder why a company with a name like that would have their headquarters in Madison. The answer goes back to S. Gwyn Scanlon, a Chicago medical instrument salesman, and Thomas Sherman Morris, then the business manager for the *Wisconsin State Journal*. These two men teamed up to form the Scanlon-Morris Company in 1904 to manufacture a line of hospital supplies. Morris supplied the money, Scanlon supplied the sales contacts, and a relative of Scanlon's, W. R. Grady, supplied several valuable patents on hospital equipment and an inventive mind. The company began production at 623 Williamson ("Machinery Row"). On his first sales trip after forming the company Scanlon sold $40,000 worth of equipment to the Mayo brothers in Rochester, Minnesota. With orders like this the company flourished and in 1907 moved the plant to a much larger factory at the intersection of First and East Johnson Streets. By 1910 Scanlon-Morris officials had set up a nearly national sales and distribution system. The company gained a solid reputation producing what they called the "white line," a group of porcelain products ranging from bedpans to operating tables.

During the 1920s the Scanlon Morris plant was once again enlarged to produce supplies for a national market. In 1946 Scanlon Morris merged with Ohio Medical Products and the operations of the two companies were centralized in Madison.[73]

The Growth of Retailing

Turn-of-the-century Madison retail business was not bad but it was not good either. Sales were growing but at a sluggish, disappointing rate. Merchants saw themselves at a critical juncture: to get more business they had to find more customers, and to get more customers required the pursuit of four simultaneous strategies.

First, they vigorously supported efforts to bring more factory workers, tourists, and conventioneers to Madison because all meant larger cash register receipts. It was for this reason that the Forty Thousand Club had a very large contingent of retailers.

Second, retailers tried to curb the habit wealthy Madisonians had developed of getting on the train and shopping in Milwaukee and Chicago where larger selections and fancier merchandise were available. To counter this practice merchants used a buy-local, civic-duty appeal.[74]

Third, a few bold retailers recognized the need to take their merchandise to the people rather than insist that people come to them. This strategy was particularly designed to capture the growing suburban market and is discussed later.

The fourth and the most promising strategy was the one over which they felt they had the greatest control. Retailers were referring to sales to farmers and small town residents who lived within fifty to one hundred miles of Madison. Historically sales to this market segment, called the "tributary trade," had been large, but for several years this "profit center" had been declining. It was in this context that older merchants recalled the period during the Farwell boom (1846–1857) and particularly after the first railroad arrived in Madison in 1854 when Madison was the economic hub of southcentral Wisconsin and the merchant was king. Because the railroad terminus was here, farmers for miles around sold their wheat to grain buyers located near the West Washington Avenue depot. During this period so many wheat-laden farmer wagons came to Madison that they were forced to form a line up West Main Street to within one block of the square waiting their turn to unload their grain. While in Madison farm families usually went on a great shopping binge and paid cash to boot. Never before or since did merchant sales compare with these palmy times.[75]

But then between 1859 and 1887 eight other Madison-centered railroad lines were built and each outlying community along these new lines built its own depot and stores. Consequently the farmer trade, which once thronged to Madison, was intercepted by this new satellite network of trade centers. From a Madison merchant's point of view, these small towns lying astride that magnificent nine-track Madison-centered railroad network had skimmed off the once large and lucrative farmer trade. It was simply too easy for

farmers to drive over to "the corners" after supper for their sugar, coffee, and calico. There farmers could get good quality merchandise at relatively low prices. Or they could fill out a form in the Sears Roebuck catalog and shop by mail.

Merchants recognized that Madison would never again achieve the nearly exclusive status it enjoyed during the Farwell boom, but they refused to abandon their "tributary trade." In fact they fervently believed that their location at the center of a rich agricultural area served by a nine-track railroad made the receipt of this trade *geographically inevitable.*

Not until after the turn of the century, however, when commercial interests were enjoying a great resurgence of energy and organization, did anyone come up with a viable new definition of this much discussed but seldom defined tributary trade. A Madison wholesale grocer, Paul Findlay, suggested that Madison merchants should *accept* the fact that farmers would continue to buy convenience and some staple items at "the corners," and that city shop owners should instead go after product lines where the crossroads stores could not compete. More specifically Findlay suggested "high line" merchandise—or as he put it, "the finest products of the loom, refinery and workshop." Findlay emphasized that this "new tributary trade" was no tiny slice of a diminishing overall pie. On the contrary, it was a part of a large and growing multicounty market containing more people than Milwaukee![76] The trick of course was to find a way to get this new tributary trade into Madison.[77]

One promising technique was the major fall spectacle. Pioneered by a group of "live-wire" Madison merchants in 1900, it was first called a "street carnival" but later, following the prohibition of girlie shows, became a more dignified "fall festival" or a "homecoming." Each was a major production involving precise coordination, extensive advertising, and large amounts of free entertainment. For some of these festivals merchants even offered customers free railroad transportation from their home to Madison and back if they bought a predefined amount of merchandise.[78]

FIGURE 6.14. NORTH PINCKNEY STREET, 1905. North Pinckney Street at the Capitol Square is here shown in the summer of 1905 when workmen were building a double streetcar track around the Square. The store called "The Fair" just to the right of the steeple was torn down to make way for the Belmont Hotel, now the YWCA, but the three buildings to its right still stand. The first is occupied by the popular Perfume Shop (and the L'Etoile Restaurant above); the second is now a mix of stores and offices known as the Atrium, and the third is an annex to the Atrium. Note the oversize awnings, then common around the Square and along State Street. (SHSW WHi(X3)35547)

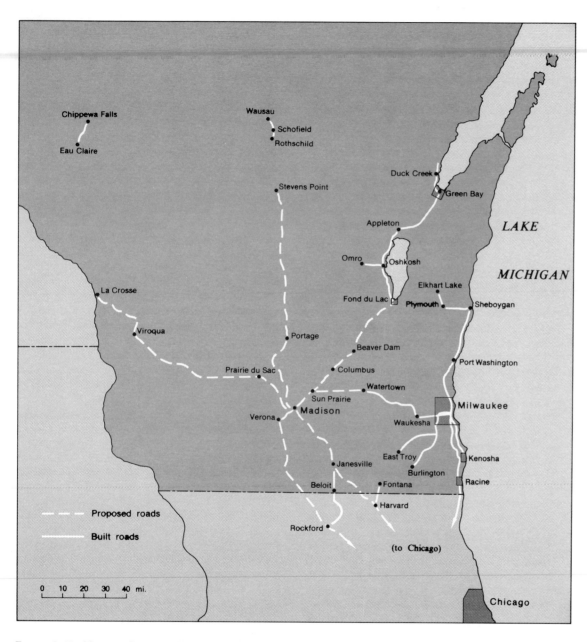

LAKE

MICHIGAN

Chippewa Falls

Eau Claire

Wausau
Schofield
Rothschild

Stevens Point

Duck Creek
Green Bay

Appleton

La Crosse

Omro   Oshkosh

Viroqua

Elkhart Lake

Fond du Lac   Plymouth   Sheboygan

Portage

Prairie du Sac

Beaver Dam

Columbus

Port Washington

Watertown

Sun Prairie

Milwaukee

Verona   Madison

Waukesha

East Troy

Kenosha

Janesville

Burlington

Beloit   Fontana   Racine

Harvard

- - - -   Proposed roads

———   Built roads

Rockford

(to Chicago)

0   10   20   30   40 mi.

Chicago

FIGURE 6.15. MADISON-CENTERED INTERURBAN SYSTEM. No one could accuse Madison interurban promoters of being conservative in their plans. If all the proposed lines Madison-centered had actually been built, the city would have been the center of a network whose tracks would have stretched about 478 miles. In spite of aggressive efforts, however, none were ever built.

Shown here are the 383 miles of interurban trackage actually built in Wisconsin. About one-third of this network was constructed between 1895 and 1900 and the balance later. The last Wisconsin interurban line was completed in 1909.

Although the fall festival enjoyed broad support within the retail community, it suffered from one major defect, viz., it only got customers to Madison once a year, and merchants wanted something that delivered the tributary trade more frequently. In 1902 grocer Findlay in a carefully prepared address to a distinguished group of businessmen said he had the solution: the interurban. Interurbans were forty- to fifty-passenger cars whose powerful electric motors provided very rapid acceleration and cruising speeds of forty to sixty miles per hour, characteristics that allowed interurbans to turn in much higher average speeds than steam-powered trains. Best of all, the interurban offered cheaper fares than the steam railroads and *hourly* service, a great contrast with twice-a-day train service common to many outlying communities.[79]

Just think, said Findlay, what an interurban would do for Madison retailers. From almost anywhere in Dane County a farmer and/or his wife could leave home at nine in the morning, spend two hours shopping in Madison and be home in time for lunch! Or a farmer could do his chores in the morning, leave for Madison after lunch and be home in time for dinner, again with two full hours of shopping time in Madison. No more sixteen- to eighteen-hour days plodding along behind a team and freezing in the winter. Instead farmers would be whisked along at sixty miles per hour in snug, well-appointed cars.[80]

If the interurban had been little more than a shopper express, it would not have won such widespread support among Madison business leaders. An exciting aspect of the interurban was that it had so many other applications. Rural and small-town residents could use the interurban to take advantage of Madison's "refining influences," that is, to take courses at the university, use its libraries, participate in legislative hearings, attend concerts, and much more. Suburbanites could use the interurban to commute. If interurban lines were built about the lakes, they would stimulate a great wave of fine home construction and even a rebirth of tourism, said interurban boosters. Best of all, some of the people the interurban would bring to Madison would be so impressed with its loveliness that they would decide to live here. Therefore many expected the interurban to be a major factor in causing Madison to become a city of forty thousand people, the goal of the city's leading commercial club.[81]

Findlay summarized his speech by saying that the interurban was an "epoch making advance" that would cure sagging sales and sluggish population growth, restore the once booming tourist industry, and knit farm and city together as never before. It was for these reasons that getting an interurban became a near obsession with Madison leaders soon after the turn of the century.[82]

The first promoter to try to make the interurban a reality for Madison was Phillip L. Spooner, a quiet, wealthy, public-spirited bachelor who at fifty-three had purchased the streetcar company, the Madison Traction Company, in February 1901. In July 1901, just five months after he purchased the line, Spooner announced that he would build an interurban to Janesville and that its construction was "assured" by December 31, 1902. However, by July 1903 the line was not built and Spooner was lamenting the extremely high costs of initial construction estimated at twenty-five thousand dollars per mile, and particularly the extra costs of grading swamps and building a bridge across the Rock River. These factors coupled with updated revenue projections caused Spooner to quietly abandon the project.[83]

The next to try was F. W. Montgomery, the wealthy New York capitalist who bought the company from Spooner in March 1905. Just six months later he, too, announced his intent to build an interurban line, but this time a scaled-down version of the Spooner line going only as far as Stoughton. Soon thereafter the Common Council unanimously passed an interurban franchise but failed to secure Montgomery's agreement on key elements. The resulting Montgomery–Council deadlock set the stage for a spirited public debate in which the civic leaders tried to secure almost *any* acceptable compromise. Before one critical test vote the *Wisconsin State Journal* ran a banner headline on its front page saying: "If You Want an Interurban, Call Your Alderman." The

time for conventional editorials had passed but, as it happened, so had this franchise opportunity. Neither Montgomery nor the council would budge from their hardened positions.[84]

The decision by two successive Madison traction magnates to foresake interurbans—the great flanged wheel hope—had a sobering effect upon the almost frenzied excitement that had grown up between 1901 and 1907 among merchants. Forty Thousand Club members, tourism backers, and others who believed the line would bestow huge benefits upon the city. After all, if the wealthy knowledgeable owners of Madison's long-term, exclusive streetcar franchise could not see their way clear to build and operate interurbans, then who could?

Not until 1910, three years after Montgomery's rejection, did anyone make another serious attempt. This time the leader of the initiative was J. E. Jones of Portage who formed the Chicago and Wisconsin Valley Railroad Company to build lines to Portage, LaCrosse, Janesville, Watertown, and even a line around Lake Monona. The council offered Jones a new model franchise, the product of considerable research following the Montgomery franchise battles, and Jones accepted. The historic first spike in the Madison-Portage line was driven at North Street East Washington Avenue on April 12, 1911, an event that caused many to conclude that the long years of talk and no action were at last at an end. But in fact just the opposite was the case. Jones ran into a variety of problems that required him to secure an extension to his franchise. The council granted the extension only to have Jones later tell them that still other problems prevented him from meeting the terms of the extension. Finally in 1915 the company was reorganized and refinanced and in December 1916 built another two miles of track on East Washington Avenue. Then all work ceased.[85]

Meanwhile in 1914 a rival interurban company known as the Janesville and Madison Traction Company incorporated to build a line between the two points in its name. Some of the money for this enterprise came from owners of

lakeshore subdivision lots lying between Monona Drive and Dean Avenue who expected that an interurban line would vastly increase the value of their real estate. The remaining risk capital came from Wisconsin hydroelectric power interests plus Madison and Chicago investors. In 1915 the company received a franchise from the City of Madison but was denied a much more important permit granted by the state railroad commission. Undaunted by the state turn-down, company officials decided to go ahead and start building the line anyway. Therefore in April 1915 it laid two miles of track on Atwood Avenue and Monona Drive. Later the company even had two "interurbans" placed on this section of track. But as it turned out all this bustle belied serious financial problems, which caused these interurban officials to disappear into the night leaving behind two miles of track, two interurban cars, and a large unpaid rent bill in a downtown office building.[86]

Under many circumstances the inability of these interurban companies to complete their lines would have been sufficient cause for bitterness and disappointment among business and civic leaders. But that emphatically was not the case with interurbans. They were conceived and promoted in an atmosphere of unwrinkled optimism almost incomprehensible to the somewhat cynical modern mind. Indeed a prominent Madison attorney in a 1916 speech to a group of merchants received wild applause when he confidently predicted that in spite of the setbacks of the Jones company that the "dirt will fly" within a week on four of his projected lines, that they would all be completed in 1919, and that when completed they would be the "greatest single factor in the development of Madison in the history of the city."[87] Even a conservative Chicago banker, asked to testify to the financial wherewithall of the Jones group, told the Common Council in October 1916 that this promoter's plans were "one of the best interurban propositions ever presented" and that to him it seemed "almost incredible" that this lucrative interurban system had not been developed earlier.[88]

Unfortunately the applause and the Chicago banker endorsement had little meaning. The more important fact was the growing military confrontation in Europe, which caused interest rates to go up and the availability of money to go down, a quiet but inexorable process that starved Madison's capital hungry interurban promoters.

The last but as it turned out brief chapter in the interurban interlude began eight months after the armistice, when J. E. Jones, the interurban promoter who had already received two franchises and two extensions and who had failed to deliver on either, appeared once again before the Common Council to ask for still another franchise. But this time instead of expressing a willingness to cooperate in any reasonable way, the council responded with a contemptuous yawn. Aldermen were tired of all the huffing and puffing, the "absolute assurances," the maps, the plans, the rash promises, and dashed high hopes. Consequently by indefinite postponement the council tossed Jones' measure into the parliamentary wastebasket and then appropriated city money to tear up all remaining interurban tracks and restore the streets to their prior condition. An era had ended.[89]

In spite of nearly twenty years of interurban promotion, Madison could muster precious few tangible results. Instead of being the center of a five-hundred-mile multicounty, multimillion dollar, five-track interurban network whose sleek cars hourly brought farmers, tourists, salesmen, and suburbanites to work, shop, and play, Madison had only three miles of track within the city limits, another two miles in the Town of Blooming Grove, and two run-down, worn-out Chicago streetcars represented as "interurbans." Not a ticket was ever sold, not a passenger was ever carried, and no electric current every coursed through its suspended copper trolley wires. Madison became the only major city bound by the Mississippi and Ohio Rivers, the Great Lakes, and the Atlantic Ocean that was never served by interurban line.[90]

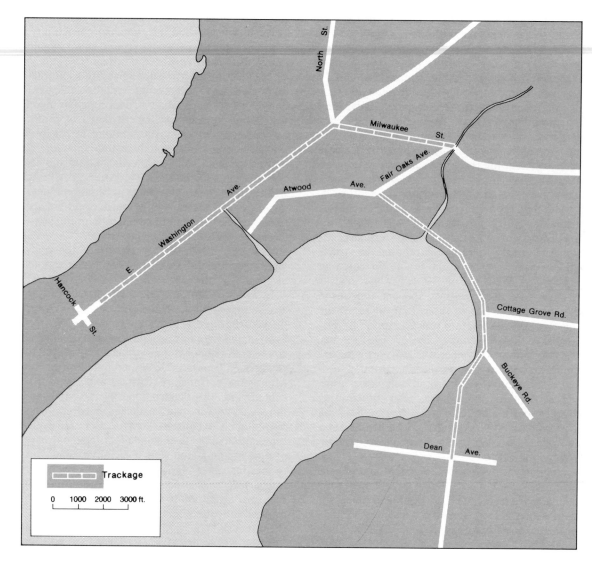

FIGURE 6.16. MADISON INTERURBAN TRACKAGE.   Shown above is the location of Madison's interurban trackage. Track along East Washington Avenue and Milwaukee Street was laid by the Chicago and Wisconsin Valley Railroad Company in 1911 and 1916. Track along Atwood Avenue and Monona Drive was laid in 1915 by the Janesville and Madison Traction Company.

FIGURE 6.17. THE MADISON INTERURBAN CARS. When these bright green cars with red roofs were hauled into Madison in October 1916 by the Janesville and Madison Traction Company, they generated great excitement because they augured the beginning of the much talked about interurban era. But a closer inspection of the cars caused some to conclude that a bad joke was being perpetrated. In fact, the cars were nothing more than run-down, worn-out Chicago street cars complete with old-fashioned coalstoves.

This photograph shows the "interurbans" parked on a stretch of track running along Monona Drive near the intersection of Buckeye Road about November 1916. Promises of the Janesville and Madison Traction Company officials to the contrary, the cars were never placed in service; in 1920 they were hauled away and the track torn up. The cars were not entirely without value, however. During the four years they were parked, they were very popular with children who loved to ring the bell and play streetcar.

The gentleman standing on the platform was Mr. D. J. Leigh, the father of Merrilyn Leigh Hartridge. Mr. Leigh was Madison city treasurer from 1937 to 1954. (Courtesy of Merrilyn Leigh Hartridge)

Very significantly the council's peremptory rejection of the 1919 Jones initiative provoked no expressions of dismay or outrage from Madison retailers. By this time retailers had found an infinitely superior way to get the tributary trade into Madison. It was the cheap automobile, epitomized by the Model T Ford. Once a toy for the rich, Henry Ford and others had found ways to make it a mover of the masses.

As early as 1916 Madison retailers were hedging their bets on which mode would "win." At the same time they were cheering for interurbans, they were running major twice-a-month sales called "Suburban Days" designed to bring in the Ford class of farmers.[91] Not surprisingly this was the take-off era for good roads in the Madison area, the time when the Madison Board of Commerce formed a separate lobby organization known as the Auto Good Roads Club to make it easier for Tin Lizzies to get into town. Retail salvation it turned out lay not with the fixed route, flanged wheel vehicle but rather the go-anywhere rubber-tired automobile. This fact posed the great irony of the long battle to regain the tributary trade. The railroad, touted for decades as the mode that would make inevitable Madison's greatness as a retail center, actually had the opposite effect. In fact it was the railroad that made farmers a stranger to Madison and the automobile that made him a regular citizen.

The Expanding Retail Plant

The combination of growing population, the increase of convention business (see pp. 286) and the return of the "tributary trade" sparked major changes in the size, composition, and location of Madison's retail facilities. These changes were particularly apparent on the Capitol Square where pressure for more retail space set the stage for the passage of two important milestones. In 1901 a store was built on the last vacant lot and by 1907 the last vacant store was rented.[92] From this point forward for many years, Square frontage was full, surrounded by a "metropolitan" wall of buildings.[93] Some businesses left the square, some new ones arrived, and some expanded.

FIGURE 6.18. 200 BLOCK STATE STREET, c. 1910.   This is the north side of the 200 block of State Street about 1910. Most people traversing State Street during this period preferred to walk down this side of the street because in 1907 the legislature passed a bill banning saloons within one-half mile of Bascom Hall or to the intersection of State and Gorham.

When the saloons relocated in the one hundred to three hundred blocks of State Street, nearly all of them chose the south side of the street. Consequently, it became known as the "saloon side."

Many of the buildings shown in the photograph still stand but of course house different businesses. The corner store on the right corner of Henry and State is now occupied by a convenience grocery store. (SHSW WHi(X3)19591)

FIGURE 6.19. SCHENK'S CORNERS, 1900. This photograph taken about 1900 shows the nucleus of Schenk's Corners at the intersection of Atwood Avenue and Winnebago Street. The sign "Schenk's Corners" is partly visible just over the door of the corner store. The "Corners" was ideally located to attract business from incoming farmers and from the surrounding residential area, then growing very rapidly in response to new and expanded factories. (Courtesy of Mr. Robert Huegel)

FIGURE 6.20. SCHENK GENERAL STORE, 1909. Had you walked into the Schenk General Store, 2009 Winnebago Street in about 1909, this is what you would have seen. On the east side of the store, shown above, were groceries, housewares, general merchandise, and cigars; on the west side of the store was a line of ready-to-wear clothing.

The woman behind the cash register was Matilda Schenk the daughter of Fred Schenk whose enterprises gave this intersection its name.

Interestingly the direct descendent of this store, the Schenk-Huegel Company owned by Robert Huegel, is still in business at this location. The firm specializes in uniforms and work apparel. (Courtesy of Robert Huegel)

FIGURE 6.21. UNIVERSITY AVENUE, 1915. Another outlying commercial area that grew up during this period was University Avenue. During the summer of 1915 a photographer took the 600 block photo (top) and 700 block photo (bottom). (University of Wisconsin Archives)

were nearly solid stores.[95] Some thought this transformation from residential to commercial had "wonderfully changed" the street but others thought the commercial tide surging down State Street to the very doorstep of the university had destroyed the beauty of this important link between capitol and campus. In 1915 the Wisconsin legislature was so concerned about this "blight" that it passed a joint resolution pleading with the city to provide better supervision over State Street development.[96]

In spite of such protests, the commercialization of State Street continued. By 1917 State Street had eighty-six stores, almost exactly the number of businesses then on the Capitol Square. Thus on the eve of World War I, the number of businesses around the Square and along State Street had grown to 176 giving Madisonians an extraordinarily rich and varied collection of merchandise and services.[97]

In addition to expanding onto side streets around the Square and down State Street, "live wire" merchants found other choice opportunities in Madison's growing suburbs. This trend began in the late nineteenth century with corner neighborhood grocery stores, but in the early twentieth century several outlying areas became bustling enclaves of commercial activity.

At first most Madison businessmen thought the decisions of these merchants to leave the sanctuary of the Square and set up shop in some cases two miles away was nothing less than "business suicide."[98] But it turned out that these merchants were not as foolhardy as they appeared. It was true that the Square was the number one retail address, but it was also true, and for this reason, that rents were higher there than anywhere else. Outlying merchants delighted in reminding their customers that the Square was the "dearest" place to shop (meaning the most expensive) whereas their outlying locations meant lower overhead and lower prices.[99]

By 1916 enough stores had been established at several outlying locations to cause the formation of separate merchants' associations and cooperative newspaper advertising. For example, the

Nearly all grocery stores and bakeries moved out to be closer to their customers and saloons entirely disappeared, victims of national prohibition. Banks and restaurants moved into some of this vacated space, and merchants used the opportunity to expand their floor areas. The net result was a decrease in the number of stores from ninety-nine in 1900 to seventy-five in 1920. But even with this reduction and change of composition, the Square compared favorably with a large contemporary shopping center. (East Towne has about one hundred stores and West Towne has about seventy-five.) A person shopping on the Square between 1900 and 1920 would have had a choice of about twenty clothing stores, seven shoe stores, seven drug stores, five candy stores, four hardware stores, and many others.[94]

Growing pressure for prime retail space caused some merchants to open shops on the side blocks immediately around the Square and then down State Street. In 1900 State Street was almost entirely residential, but by 1914 the first six blocks

Schenk's Corners area (intersection of Atwood Avenue and Winnebago Streets) boasted a butcher, a grocer, a clothier, a paint and hardware dealer, a milliner, a jeweler, a movie theater, a Rennebohm drug store, and a saloon. In Madison the outlying shopping center was a pre-World War I—not a post-World War II—development.[100]

The Hospitality Industry: Old Dreams and New Realities

The old dreams did not die easily. According to Amos Wilder, writing in a 1901 *Journal* editorial, it was "only a matter of time" before wealthy tourists would come to Madison to enjoy its lakes, stores, libraries, and spring water. That such a beautiful city so well served by railroads would *not* become a premier resort was almost inconceivable to those who nurtured this great dream.[101] At the same time Wilder recognized that the old version of the resort concept, that is, a series of summer hotels scattered around the lakes, would never become a reality. That dream had died in 1895 with the ashes of the Tonyawatha fire. Even before the conflagration it was clear that a resort hotel could not make money on a three-month season.

There were, however, several new ideas that could attract the same well-heeled clientele and in the process reestablish the resort industry. One idea was to build a new type of sanitarium that gave harried men and women a place to unwind, go on a controlled diet, get a massage, enjoy hydrotherapy, attend lectures on a more healthy lifestyle, and much more. More specifically, backers wanted a sanitarium similar to the famous Battle Creek, Michigan institution developed by Dr. J. H. Kellogg.[102] Another concept was to create a new multicounty park district with powers to tax, build roads, acquire and develop parks, and maintain scenic vistas. Dr. Clarke

Gapen, the prime mover behind this concept, believed that the Four Lakes area could be to Chicago what the Berkshires were to Philadelphia, namely a huge beautiful accessible playground.[103] A third new twist of the resort concept was to create conditions that would cause Chicago millionaires to build mansions around the Madison lakes just as they were then doing in Lake Geneva and Lake Delevan. Those who backed this concept held that the only thing needed to make this idea a reality was an interurban line around the lakes.[104]

The last resort building concept was to build a first-class hotel in downtown Madison. Here backers envisioned a high-rise, fireproof structure with electric elevators, a roof garden, elegantly furnished lobbies, restaurants with linen tablecloths, crystal and cut flowers, and 125–250 rooms equipped with a full bath, electricity, and telephones. Such a hotel, backers insisted, could be used as a base of operations by summer tourists and the rest of the year by luxury-seeking business travellers. Thus, instead of a three-month season, the hotel would have year-round business.

In spite of vigorous pushing from newspaper editors, the Forty Thousand Club, hotel owners, and many others, the scorecard for these ideas showed very few results. A sanitarium based upon the Battle Creek model was built on a spacious lakeshore setting where the Medical Society of Wisconsin is now located, but it appealed more to a local clientele than the silk-stockinged Chicago crowd.[105] Nothing else succeeded. Gapen failed to ignite any widespread interest with his park district concept. No interurban line was ever built around the lake. Four luxury hotel proposals on choice sites all failed to receive the necessary local financial backing or encountered other difficulties. With these failures the great dream of Madison as a northern resort was quietly dropped. What was once thought to be "destiny" turned out to be merely another unworkable idea.

At the same time hope for reestablishing the resort business was being abandoned, prospects for the convention business took a promising turn. When the Forty Thousand Club was formed, their leaders vowed to make Madison a convention city for state and national associations. The first juicy plum that club leaders were able to pluck was the 1902 Wisconsin GOP Convention. The warm and thoughtful hospitality orchestrated by the club sent a good many GOP representatives back to their homes praising Madison's convention hosting prowess. The construction of a variety of new hotels such as The Trumpf (1906) and The Cardinal (1908) plus major additions to the Fess (1907), the Capital Hotel (1908), and the Park Hotel (1914), gave convention planners a relatively large inventory of hotel rooms, although as noted in the inset, sometimes at the expense of business travellers. As early as 1910 a Milwaukee newspaper acknowledged that Madison had become the primary Wisconsin convention city.[106] The convention business received a great boost from the formation of the board of commerce in 1913. The board adopted the theme "Ideal Convention City of the West" and directed their new full-time executive director to function as a one man convention bureau.[107]

Then in the summer of 1919 Madison's young hospitality industry received a great surprise. Thousands of tourists began pouring into town in automobiles. This phenomenon was in turn a product of two developments. The first was the rapid increase in the popularity of the automobile. At the same time mass production brought car costs down to the point where middle income groups could afford them, technological refinements markedly increased their comfort and reliability. The second development was the relatively rapid construction of highways. Not until after 1911, when the state began to assume responsibility for building and paying for highways, was any real progress made. In that year the state authorized and partly funded a five-thousand-mile highway network. At first about sixty percent of these roads were dirt and another twenty percent gravel, but it was the beginning

FIGURE 6.22. THE GOOD ROADS MOVEMENT IN MADISON. This unimportant looking 1916 photograph looking northeast from the 2000 block of Sherman Avenue was in fact a picture of a great achievement about which Madisonians were terribly proud—the concrete road. Today such roads are taken for granted, but not then. Then such roads were viewed as triumphs over mud and isolation, and as a great boon for business.

Paved roads were slow in coming to Madison. Prior to 1866 nearly all roads were earthen and therefore subject to the seasonal maladies of mud in the spring and dust in the summer. Beginning in 1866, however, Madison began applying gravel to its roads, and by 1900 about half of all opened city streets were topped by this material. Though gravel was a great improvement over mud, it was not without its own problems. The relatively high speed of autos and then low-slung bodies meant that this stirred up much more dust than horse-drawn vehicles and led to complaints from housekeepers that they could not hang their laundry outside anymore or even use their front porches, unless of course they were willing to put up with the dust deposited by these mechanical whirlwinds. City officials tried oiling the gravel but this helped only temporarily.

The search for something better than gravel began in 1899 when the state removed an ornate iron fence around the Capitol Square. Since the fence extended eight feet into the roadway, its removal was welcomed because it meant that the streets around the Sqaure could be widened by that amount. Thus the question became: With what material shall the Square be surfaced? The state, the city and most businessmen con-cluded that asphalt would be best and so they got cost estimates for its application. This set the stage for a classic Madison donnybrook over what proportion of costs should be paid by the city, the adjoining property owner, the state and the streetcar company. Horse owners meanwhile opposed the whole idea of asphalting the Square because they believed their horses could not stand on it when it was icy much less pull a vehicle. Finally in 1905 after six years of squabbling, the parties compromised and the Square was asphalted. The material proved satisfactory except in warm weather when it softened to the point where wagons left tracks on it.

Then in relatively quick succession Madison officials began to experiment with two other paving materials. In 1907 the city laid its first two blocks of vitrified brick paving on East Main between Pinckney and South Blair Streets. About 1910 concrete made its debut.

All of the new hard surface paving materials were very expensive and so for many years had to be limited to the most heavily trafficked business streets and major city entrances.

By 1918, however, Madison had made considerable progress. A full-page advertisement placed in the *Saturday Evening Post* by an asphalt supplier portrayed Madison as the "town that believes in good roads." By this time the city had nearly forty miles of "dustless, mudless and bumpless" asphalt roads and several more miles of brick and concrete pavement. (SHSW WHi(X3)34458)

FIGURE 6.23. THE GOOD ROADS MOVEMENT IN DANE COUNTY.   The year 1916 was an important watershed in the history of Dane County highways. In that year the county board wrested control of highway development from the towns. Shown above are county highways in 1916 showing the piecemeal character of town board decisions. After 1916, however, the development of an integrated highway system was very rapid because the county board concentrated state and federal road aids on a three-hundred-mile county trunk network. The results are evident just six years later (below). Before 1916 town boards had been spending state money on a seven-hundred-mile network. The most powerful highway lobby organization in Dane County was the Madison Auto Good Roads Club, a group created by the Board of Commerce in 1914 for the sole purpose of pushing better highways.

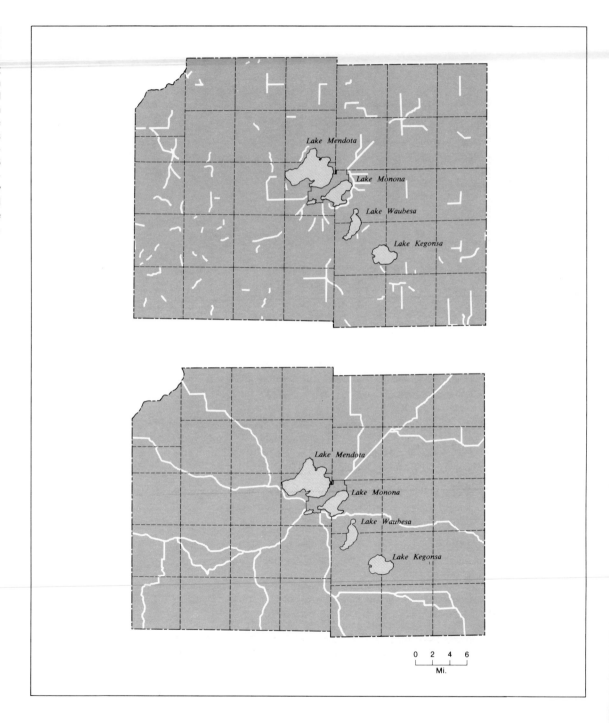

FIGURE 6.24. THE GRAND HOTELS THAT MIGHT HAVE BEEN. During the first few years of the new century, civic leaders sought to build several large downtown luxury hotels. The Park Hotel, then about thirty years old and the best in the city, was no longer a first-class hotel because it was not fireproof, was not built with electricity in mind and did not have bathrooms in each of the rooms.

The hotel (at the top) was proposed by a group of Chicago investors in 1901 for the site just east of Olin Terrace, now occupied by the Madison Club. To take the best advantage of this location the hotel architect located the kitchen and dining room on the top floor. The building was to have been five stories high on Wilson Street side, seven on the lake side, and built of brick and stone. Working through the Forty Thousand Club the Chicago developers required the city to grant them riparian rights (so their guests could have unrestricted use of the lake), and to improve the lake end of Monona Avenue with a circular drive. The success of the project also required that the city work with the railroad and the developers to establish a small railroad station at track level so hotel guests could arrive directly by train and to build an covered walkway over the tracks. Finally the developers required Madisonians to buy twenty-five percent of the capital stock needed by build the hotel.

The Metropolitan Hotel (bottom) proposed in 1902 by a group of Madison investors to replace the Park Hotel on its site. The ornate and architecturally interesting building was designed to incorporate "the thirty-third degree of hotel excellence." Each room was to have hot and cold running water, electric lights, and a telephone. The fireproof eight-story structure featured a delightful "roof garden" offering diners the marvelous panoramic view now enjoyed by Inn on the Park eighth floor restaurant patrons. The success of this hotel required that Madison investors buy the hotel capital stock and that the owners of the Park Hotel lease would sell the lease to the hotel corporation.

Financial and legal problems combined to stymie both hotel proposals.

of a state highway *system*. This five-thousand-mile system included five highways that passed through Madison including the fore-runners of Highways 12, 14, and 51. Another important step came in 1916 when the federal government began pumping money into state road construction. And finally in May 1918, Wisconsin adopted its numbered highway designation system—a technique later copied by every state in the Union. Thus by the summer of 1919 Wisconsin's relatively good network of numbered roads and thousands of privately owned cars combined to produce the largest influx of tourists ever witnessed in Madison.[108]

The onslaught of auto tourism caught everyone napping in the summer of 1919, but by the summer of 1920 they were prepared. The board of commerce opened a tourist information booth that provided facts on road conditions and hotel accommodations, dispensed maps and sightseeing brochures, and even arranged for the weekly rental of two hundred fifty lakeshore cottages.[109] The Rotarians erected billboards to welcome tourists, to tell them what to see while in Madison and then, on the way out of town, to say "goodbye and come again."[110] Some thirty to forty thousand auto tourists visited Madison in the summer of 1920. Between three hundred and five hundred persons toured the capitol each day and in one three-day period in August, five hundred cars from twenty-five states including New York and California were seen parked on the Capitol Square.[111]

In a single season the automobile probably brought more tourists to Madison than all the trains ever brought during those years when the city had some basis to call itself a northern resort. The auto delivered to Madison's doorstep what decades of hotel, railroad, and city promotion had failed to provide—namely, a large influx of summer visitors and elevated tourism from an anemic affectation to a genuine industry.

A Cot in the Hallway

"I was on a train bound for Madison, Wis., and it was three hours behind the schedule. I was tired, cold and hungry, and my imagination was reveling in what I would do to a large, juicy steak, with accompaniments, when I reached the college town. I also had visions of a nice warm bath and a good night's rest in a comfortable bed.

"The train finally reached Madison and I repaired to a certain hotel. After registering I told the clerk I would like a room with a bath.

" 'Nothing doing, son,' said he. 'A cot in the hallway is the best we have left. There are two conventions in town and every room is occupied.'

"I have been up against the cot-in-the-hallway stunt before, and, believe me, it doesn't appeal to one who wants to enjoy a quiet rest. Every late-comer who passes through the corridor either tries to kick a leg off your couch or pushes his hands into your face. After inquiry by telephone and other ways, however, I found the cot was the best I could do; there wasn't a vacant room in town—not even in a private house."

During the first week in March, 1912, the *Chicago Evening Post* carried this story from a disgruntled traveller who found Madison hotel accommodations less than adequate.

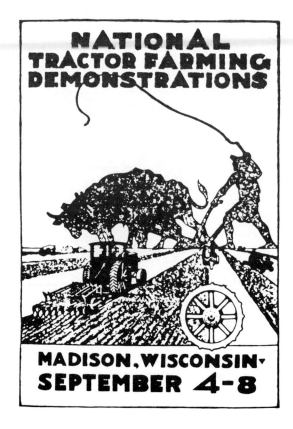

FIGURE 6.25. NATIONAL TRACTOR FARMING DEMONSTRATIONS. The first two decades of the twentieth century witnessed the beginnings of a revolution on the farm when motive power shifted from muscles and steam to gasoline engines. The new tractors allowed almost incredible increases in productivity and at the same time they reduced the length of the work day. At the Frank Allis farm, the site of the demonstrations, farmers watched these new mechanical marvels plow four hundred acres in less than ten hours and inspected about 175 tractors worth $225,000. Getting out to the farm four miles from the Square required every streetcar plus three hundred jitneys and eighteen passenger boats. The event was billed at the "biggest educational event ever staged for progressive farmers."

Wanted—10,000 Rooms

Madison expects to entertain between 25,000 and 100,000 out-of-town visitors during the tractor demonstration Sept. 4 to 8. This, of course, is many thousands more than the hotels can take care of. The Housing Committee of the Tractor Demonstration is making an appeal to Madison people to turn open their homes for the accommodation of these visitors. The visitors will be made up of up-to-date farmers, bankers and business men from all parts of this and adjoining states. They will be people you will like to have in your homes.

The Housing Committee wants 10,000 rooms a night for three nights and IS WILLING TO SEE THAT THE HOUSEOWNERS ARE PAID WELL FOR THEM. The Housing Committee has arranged to have all of the accompanying coupons sent to the board of commerce where the directory will be made up.

If you have one room, two rooms or a dozen which you will rent for these three days fill out the coupon below and send it to the Board of Commerce.

Send This Coupon to the Board of Commerce

Name ....

Address ....

Telephone No. ....

No. of Single Rooms ....

No. of Double Rooms ....

I agree to rent these rooms at $...... per person per night

FIGURE 6.26. WANTED: TEN THOUSAND ROOMS. How could a city with only seven hundred hotel rooms and about sixty-eight hundred dwelling units expect to accommodate seventy-five to one hundred thousand out-of-town visitors for four days? That was the sobering question confronting promoters of the regional meeting of the National Tractor Demonstrations scheduled in Madison for September 4–8, 1916 (see fig. 6.25). Significantly, however, Board of Commerce promoters were anything but paralyzed by the prospect. They simply issued the "invitation" noted above asking householders to rent rooms to incoming farmers. Incredibly, just four days after these forms appeared in the newspaper, four thousand coupons were returned and more were received later. Although promoters never did get the ten thousand rooms they wanted, neither did they get one hundred thousand people. As it turned out, five thousand private rooms in conjunction with Madison hotels and then-empty fraternities and sororities were sufficient to accommodate the fifty thousand farmers who journeyed to Madison to witness this event. Even so, the audacity of promoters to think that Madison could accommodate such a large event and the willingness of so many Madisonians to rent rooms to incoming farmers stands as a high-water mark for civic zeal. To see the enormity of this achievement, one need only multiply Madison's current population by 1.5 and then find rooms for the product!

Other Industries

Madison of course had many other businesses but they tended to get relatively little attention. Nevertheless these "quiet" industries constituted relatively large components of Madison's economy. One such component was the implement distribution industry, which continued to grow very rapidly following its mushroomlike emergence in the late nineteenth century. By 1902 Madison had thirty implement dealers, more than any other city in the state, and these dealers were receiving twelve hundred implement-laden railroad cars each year at their docks. Another thirteen hundred railroad carloads of implements were sold by Madison firms but shipped directly to dealers mostly in western Wisconsin and northern Illinois. The total value of implements totalled about two million dollars. During this period about six hundred implement dealers would come to Madison each year to buy their goods from Madison wholesalers. Until about 1916 the value of implements handled by Madison dealers reportedly exceeded Milwaukee's. Throughout this period the implement business was considered the most powerful illustration of Madison's possibilities as a major distribution point for various products, providing of course that businessmen would only recognize that the city was a "ready to wear" railroad center that required aggressive promoting.[112]

Another industry that enjoyed rapid growth in the early twentieth century was tobacco processing and manufacturing. By 1906 about one thousand men and women were employed in Madison tobacco warehouses processing about one-third of the state crop. However, by 1915 the rapid increase in nationwide popularity of the cigarette spelled the eventual doom of local tobacco industries since nearly all of Wisconsin's crop was used as cigar wrappers. Among the first to feel this shift were Madison's cigarmakers, whose numbers by 1916 dwindled to the point where their union was almost forced to close its doors.[113]

The railroads were still another quiet but large Madison industry. By 1920 their payrolls reached twelve hundred persons.[114]

Tribute to the Commercial Traveler

"If there is such a personage as the 'typical American' he is the American commercial traveler. Restlessly energetic, resourceful, full of optimism and full of self-confidence, with that last extra drop of electric fluid in his nerves that puts him over the line just ahead of the other fellows—there is no class of American so thoroughly typical of the genius of the nation as our commercial travelers."

Wisconsin State Journal
June, 1909
On the occasion of United
Travelers' Association
Meeting

Toward a Bigger, Better, and Busier Madison

During the 1920s, well-known American authors such as Sinclair Lewis, H. L. Mencken, and others took almost impish delight in lampooning businessmen and business culture. Businessmen, they suggested, were vacuous, money-grubbing conformers, and booster organizations were vainglorious expressions of provincialism.[115] Such characterizations were of course entertaining and contained a tincture of truth. On the other hand if we are to understand the true role that businessmen and commercial clubs played in Madison, especially during the first twenty years of the twentieth century, we must put these caricatures aside. The fact is that the organized business community in Madison demonstrated perspicacity and left a legacy of achievements and values quite different from what one would expect from the engaging but very misleading Lewis-Mencken accounts. In support of this alternative view, consider the following evidence.

With a few exceptions the organized Madison business community concentrated its resources in those areas where the yield was likely to be greatest and that probably would not have occurred without its intervention. In this regard Madison business leaders made decisions much the same way a battlefield medic decides who should receive ministrations. Some "futures" such as the university, state government, and the implement distribution business would continue to grow without any local boosting. Therefore there was no point in pushing these. By the same token other futures such as making Madison a posh northern resort complete with huge hotels in sylvan lakeshore settings seemed destined to die even if heroic measures were taken to reintroduce them. Thus there was little point in pushing these. There were, however, still other areas including manufacturing, retailing, milk and tobacco processing, and possibly some new form of the hospitality industry that had great potential to increase population and that would atrophy or die if they did not receive prompt and vigorous pushing. To the credit of organized business leaders, this was where they elected to concentrate their resources.

Consider, too, the many legacies of the organized business community of this era. Often overlooked was the fact that they developed a tremendously appealing and effective new type of commercial club. The Board of Commerce with its broadly conceived business *and* civic goals, professional full-time staff, ample funding, and tight organizational accountability quickly made the board the largest and most powerful organization in the city and gave Madisonians their first glimpse of a modern lobbying instrument. From this new organization came a new elite of civic leaders composed of businessmen and professionals who displaced the older academic-professional group. No mean accomplishments these—particularly when one takes into account the individualism, the cliquishness, and the distrust that had heretofore kept businessmen from working together on a sustained basis.

FIGURE 6.27. THE NEW 1911 NORTHWESTERN DEPOT.   When nearly everybody went everywhere by train, a railroad depot was a terribly important statement about a community because it told arriving passengers how big, how rich, and how important a city was. As the capital city of a growing and progressive commonwealth and the home of the state university, Madisonians felt they were entitled to something better than the small, obsolete 1885 depot. Therefore when the Chicago & Northwestern Railroad informed city officials that it wanted to erect a large, elegant half-million-dollar depot, something that would be "a credit to the city," Madisonian leaders were elated. Unfortunately several persons who owned property or had businesses in the area strenuously objected to this grand new edifice because its long, covered passenger platform required Blount Street to be closed. The objectors said they would be inconvenienced. The council passed the necessary ordinance in spite of these "kicks" but then lawyers for the inconvenienced property owners found a defect in the transaction that required that the whole complicated approval process be repeated. Railroad officials threw up their arms in disgust and abandoned the project.

Not until five years later did railroad officials decide to try again. The result was this scaled down quarter-million-dollar version built in 1910 but shown here in a photograph taken about 1915. It, too, was "a credit to the city" but a mere echo of what might have been. The building still stands but has been adapted to another use by its owners, the Madison Gas and Electric Company. The Freight station shown on the right has also been preserved by the company and sensitively incorporated into a new office complex.

At the time this photograph was taken, the depot was a bustling, buzzing, exciting hub of activity. Each day Northwestern ticket agents sold one thousand tickets and the stationmaster had to accommodate fifty trains. (No wonder residents of the adjoining Sixth District complained that the Blair-Williamson intersection, the major gateway to their neighborhood, was constantly blocked by trains.) Tantalizing aromas drifted out into the streets from the busy depot restaurant. Newsboys hawked papers from Chicago, Milwaukee, and Madison. And if small boys were very good, they could sometimes persuade their fathers to take them to the depot so that they could watch the trains glide to a stop beside the curved canopy and marvel at how the giant engine wheels dwarfed the engineer as he walked around the hissing behemoth appeasing its joints with a long-snouted oil can. (SHSW)

FIGURE 6.28. THE CITY MARKET. Ever since 1872 the block of East Washington Avenue between Pinckney and Webster Streets had been Madison's unofficial outdoor market—a place where farmers could sell hay, straw, cordwood, young pigs, and vegetables; where gypsies told fortunes and sold horses; and where quack doctors peddled medicine, pulled teeth, and pared corns. As the market grew in popularity so too did the number of saloons that made the block a magnet for toughs, idlers, drunks, and degraded women. In addition to being the "farmer's market" and a center of low life, the block was the only one where farmers were allowed to hitch their horses while shopping, a practice that gave the block a nose-wrenching barnyard quality.

Before 1872 farmers generally parked their wagons across the street from the store at which they were shopping. Indeed, they were encouraged to do this by state-provided hitching posts, which surrounded the inside of the Square. To shopping farmers the practice could hardly have been more convenient. However, in 1872 state officials, eager to end the "barnyard" that surrounded the just-completed new capitol building, removed the hitching posts, replaced them with an elegant iron fence, and then passed a law preventing anyone from tieing up horses to the inside of the Square. This meant that farmers had a parking problem since Square merchants were less than enthusiastic about the prospect of this "barnyard" moving from the inside of the Square to in front of their stores. It was in response to this dilemma that the "farmers market" became the unofficial parking lot for shopping farmers.

During the first few years of the twentieth century a group of civic boosters and businessmen joined forces to banish this offensive vestige of the frontier era. Instead of a private open air, unofficial, unregulated, saloon-infested, obscenity-laced, dirty, filthy, farmer's market, Madison should have a clean, enclosed, sanitary, well-designed, well-regulated municipal market. Small fees charged to stall owners would make the market

self-sustaining and would pay the salary of a full-time market manager. A city market would provide a place where producer and consumer could come together to beat the high cost of living. This was their dream in search of a location.

In 1908 the Common Council after considerable debate bought a two-acre "cattail patch" bounded by North Blount, East Main, and Livingston Streets because it was the cheapest site closest to the Square and yet far enough from railroad tracks so as not to frighten horses. The City then hired a local architect, R. L. Wright to design the very pleasantly proportioned Prairie-style building shown here.

On November 2, 1910, the new public market was opened with a flourish seldom seen in Madison. Some four thousand elegant brochures were sent to area farmers. The mayor closed City Hall and stores by declaring opening day an official holiday. A large orchestra played light operatic music. The city not only provided free sandwiches, pickles, and coffee to all guests but it commandeered its highest officials to man the serving tables. In spite of cloudy, cold weather that degenerated into a raging snowstorm, five thousand persons inspected the sparkling new $55,000 market described by some to be "the finest in the state."

The public market was one enterprise where its backers did not have to wait long before they got the verdict of its patrons. It was an almost instant flop! Farmers deeply resented being relegated "down on the marsh" and stayed away in droves, causing the facility to lose money beginning with its first month of operation. An official city investigation just four months after the grand opening as to the causes of this failure cited its terribly inconvenient location five blocks from the square and the existence of what they called "modern business methods," meaning the ease with which shoppers could pick up the phone, order merchandise on credit, and then have it delivered to their door. (SHSW WHi(X3)29348)

293

This new elite operating through this new type of commercial club played a large and many ways extraordinary role in shaping modern Madison. Perhaps their most important achievement was forging a new profactory community concensus, the "Madison compromise." The Madison compromise in turn was responsible for the rapid development of industry, accelerated population growth, and a net increase in the size of the private sector economy. It was during this period that manufacturing, long the brash and unpopular stepchild in a quiet sophisticated campus town, came to be accepted as a major component of the economy on a par with the university.

To the delight of organized business leaders, the maturation of Madison's private sector during this period had a salutary effect upon Madison's rankings relative to other Wisconsin cities. In population Madison rose from a low of ninth place among state cities in 1895 to fifth place in 1920. And in several nonpopulation categories Madison enjoyed an even higher ranking. As early as 1916 Madison ranked second in the state in per capita ownership of telephones, bank resources, building construction, and in bond, automobile, and farm implement sales.[116] By 1920 the products of Madison's factories including machine tools, dry batteries, processed meat, hospital equipment, machine lubricators, and gasoline engines were being sold in regional, national, and even international markets. Indeed against the backdrop of Madison history, these changes might well be called "the new Madison."

From this new type of organization and new elite came a strong new civic consciousness and community service ethic. Board of Commerce members believed that Madison was special, that it had a unique destiny, and that with hard work (no salvation by grace here!) the organized business community could cause this destiny to be realized. It was in this context that they derived

FIGURE 6.29. THE 1915 MADISON CREED. The "Madison Creed" adopted by the Board of Commerce in 1915 was surely written by Richard Lloyd Jones, one of the most talented and prolific Madison publicists. Though to the contemporary reader its prose gets a little bubbly at times, it nevertheless remains a grand period piece that evokes the intense devotion to civic duty that arose in business promotion circles during this period. To best savor its meaning and rhythm, try reading it aloud.

great strength from similarities they perceived between Madison in 1914 and Athens during the fifth century B.C. The greatness of Athens, they concluded, lay in the fact that its citizens willingly bound themselves by a common oath "to fight for the ideals and sacred things of the city."[117] With only slightly different language this was what the Board of Commerce sought to do for Madison. This new civic consciousness meant much more than giving lip service to a "bigger better and busier" Madison.[118] To fight for the highest Madison ideals meant that businessmen had certain *duties* they must perform. A businessman should do more for his community than merely extract a living. He must practice the Golden Rule in all his personal and business dealings. He should contribute his time, money, and expertise. It was for this reason that board members put great emphasis upon *community service* and particularly that which would yield a demonstrable *public good*. So important was this new civic consciousness to Board of Commerce leaders that they embodied these values in "the Madison Creed." Taken together these values were a bright and hopeful business expression of the progressive ferment then evident in Wisconsin and throughout the nation. Indeed it was the application by businessmen of this new civic consciousness and community service ethic that was responsible for many reforms and improvements made in Madison the first two decades of the twentieth century. It is to this subject we now turn.

The Madison Creed

Adopted by the Board of Commerce

I BELIEVE in Madison,— The Four Lake City.

I BELIEVE in her PAST achievement—in the men and women who created and conserved that I might produce and earn, enabling me to buy and pay,—in the courage of her pioneers whose wisdom and foresight built between these lakes a well planned organic city, every foot of whose ground is worth in gold its market value because the brain and brawn of man has added wealth to nature's own endowment.

I BELIEVE in the reality of her PRESENT,—a present that combines the push and friendliness of the newer West with the reflection and poise of the older East, a present which makes her the distributing center of one of the most productive agricultural sections of America, the heart of the richest dairy region of the world, the location of going industry and commerce, and the focus point of miles of railroad trackage, that converges into this hub like the spokes of a wheel from nine directions,—a present that makes her the seat of government for forward Wisconsin, the home of a state university that spells freedom and utility, and the birthplace of so powerful an influence for the well-being of humanity that thousands are attracted annually to this center of achievement in democracy.

I BELIEVE in her ability to become in the FUTURE a city of even greater influence and power,—a city destined to become the abode of one hundred thousand people, where the poor shall be less unhappy, the rich less self-satisfied, for the one shall have a more intelligent understanding of the other; where jails shall be empty of prisoners, streets clear of beggars and neither shall the aged in want be cast upon the charity of strangers; a city where friends shall be true friends; neighbors real neighbors; a city where the strong shall really sympathize with the weak; where there shall be even more respect for those who have traveled the longer road; and even more hopeful confidence in the promise of glowing youth; a city where progress shall be the result of retaining the good of the old and accepting the tried of the new, where co-operative competition shall be the ideal in trade, live and let live the slogan of business, serve others well to successfully serve self the policy of industry and commerce; and finally, where each and every citizen shall be a community builder in fact, as now in name.

AND I PLEDGE TO MY CITY a more complete understanding of her problems, a more liberal conception of her limitations, a more hopeful attitude toward her possibilities, a more generous contribution to her needs, and a more active participation in the broader functions of her citizenship in order that my city may become a greater credit to herself, to Wisconsin, to America and to God because of my having lived in Madison,— "The Four Lake City."

The Progressive Attack on City Problems

During the late nineteenth and early twentieth centuries the United States simultaneously became urbanized and industrialized. Between 1860 and 1910, while the nation's population grew nearly three hundred percent, the number of persons living in cities grew by seven hundred percent. This unprecedented urban influx fueled by millions of immigrants, the exodus from American farms, and natural increase forced the poor, especially in the larger cities, to live in squalid disease and crime-ridden tenements. The heterogeneity of the urban population coupled with the speed and size of the urban growth thwarted efforts to provide adequate water, sewer, and transportation much less safe, sanitary housing. These conditions in turn made the administration of cities almost impossible and led to notorious "boss" rule.

At the same time the nation was moving to the city, the availability of cheap, unorganized labor, the development of integrated transportation and communication networks, and the discovery of vast mineral deposits created an almost ideal environment for the rapid growth of factories and poor working conditions for factory workers. Twelve-hour days, low pay, danger, noise, and child labor were common. As the number and size of factories increased, the *ownership* of these factories was concentrated into gigantic trusts with unprecedented power. The formation of the United States Steel Corporation in 1901, the first one-billion-dollar corporation, was just one expression of this trend.[1]

According to an influential group of social philosophers this concentration of fabulous wealth in the hands of a few industrialists was both healthy and natural. In their view this trend was nothing more than the socio-economic equivalent of a process evident in nature known as "survival of the fittest." It was the process of "natural selection" working in the "struggle for survival."

This "social Darwinism" sometimes called "the Gospel of Wealth" had several widely accepted corrollaries: (1) "that the American economy was controlled for the benefit of all by a natural aristocracy, and that these leaders were brought to the top by a competitive struggle that weeded out the weak, the incompetent, and the unfit and selected the strong, the able and the wise; (2) that the state should confine itself to police activities of protecting property and maintaining order, and that if it interfered with economic affairs it would upset the beneficient effect of natural selection; and (3) that slums and poverty were the unfortunate but inevitable result of the competitive struggle. . . ."[2]

Just after the turn of the century the condition of the nation's cities, the ominous concentration of wealth, the exploitation of factory workers and the justification of all these things by "social Darwinism" produced a powerful reaction known as "progressivism." This reaction was led by doctors, lawyers, accountants, managers, professors, ministers, and businessmen who constituted America's new middle class. Between 1860 and 1910 the size of this group increased by eight hundred percent, more than twice as fast as overall population and faster than the rapid urban growth rate. To this largely urban, well educated, protestant, and Republican group, the problems stemming from rapid urbanization and industrialization were very serious. The concentration of wealth and power and the corruption and bribery that accompanied these trends threatened the very foundations of democracy and augured far-reaching and deep-seated changes to American life. Suddenly it seemed as if the American dream wasn't working.[3]

In reaction to conditions that accompanied this great burst of nineteenth century material progress, the progressives raised fundamental questions. How can capitalism be revitalized? How can democracy be restored? What are the responsibilities of wealth? What are the responsibilities of government? The answers came quickly from progressive economists, sociologists, political scientists, and theologians.

Progressive economists rejected social Darwinism because it sanctified an economic system that glorified greed and oppressed workers. Economics should not be used to justify the status quo but rather to ask what *ought* to be and then to devise an economic system to cause the "ought" to become reality. Very significantly, however, this new "ethical" school did not reject capitalism in favor of socialism but rather sought to reform capitalism to give real meaning once again to the "free" in free enterprise. Their answer, sometimes called "the new individualism" or "progressive individualism," lay half way between socialism and *laissez faire*. Progressive economists believed that government was the only force in society capable of controlling the great aggregations of wealth and power spawned by the industrial revolution and that government powers should therefore be fully harnessed toward that end. This large and aggressive new concept of government included both "negative" and "positive" roles. "Negative" roles included the regulation of "trusts" and utilities; "positive" functions included a new array of government services such as health inspections, safety standards, recreation programs, and charity dispensation. Instead of protecting property and wealth, government should seek to implement the *public* interest, the *common* good, and the *popular* will. Although these new regulatory and service functions were exasperatingly difficult, progressive economists remained serenely confident that experts, special bureaus, and commissions could compensate for their complexities.

Progressive sociologists grabbed social Darwinism by the horns, wrestled it to the ground as it were, and did not let it up again until it had been transformed. The new school sociologists agreed that environment played a large role in human affairs but that it did not work as the social Darwinists said. According to the new school, human beings evolved and changed *in response to* the environment. Put human beings in slums, they said, and you will get criminals. Put the same human beings in a good environment and you will get good citizens. This, baldly stated, was "reform Darwinism"—a school that necessarily placed all its chips on environment as a societal change agent. One particularly important application of reform Darwinism was that the poor were no longer *ipso facto* weaklings, i.e., losers in the survival of the fittest, but rather a group waiting to be led out of the tenements by settlement house social workers.

Progressive political scientists urged adoption of the direct primary, the initiative, the referendum, and the recall to make government accessible once again to the people. They also suggested a variety of ways to remove or reduce the influence of special privilege.

Theologians developed a new brand of religion called the "Social Gospel" emphasizing cooperation and brotherly love rather than acquisitiveness and unbridled individualism. Church members, they said, should abandon their plush sanctuaries and heavy emphasis upon individual salvation and go out into society to do what they could to improve it.

This swirling maelstrom of economics, sociology, political science, and theology in the hands of high-minded, highly motivated progressives proved to be a powerful antidote to social Darwinism, rugged individualism, and indeed to the entire old order. Between 1900 and 1920 progressives succeeded in implementing a long list of reforms designed to revitalize capitalism and restore democracy.

No state was more often or more flatteringly associated with the new progressive movement than Wisconsin. A veritable parade of journalists and reformers flocked to the state to interview progressive leaders and see for themselves the "Wisconsin idea" and the "laboratory of democracy." The history of these two well-known attractions is properly traced to John Bascom, a universal scholar who as president of the university (1864–1887) worked to make the institution a great "influence on the state." His well-known agricultural short courses were just one manifestation of this concept. Bascom also taught his

students to have "a proper attitude toward public affairs" and to "devote themselves to . . . the public welfare." Although there was tremendous power in these seminal ideas, it was never fully realized by Bascom. That achievement awaited Bascom's two most famous students, Robert Marion LaFollette and Charles R. Van Hise.[4]

Following his graduation from the U.W. Law School in 1880, LaFollette was elected Dane County district attorney. After four years as district attorney, he represented Madison for six years in the U.S. Congress. Upon his return to Madison in 1891, he practiced law and gained a reputation as a reformer. In 1900 following a vigorous campaign, the five-foot five-inch attorney was elected governor. During his three terms LaFollette made Wisconsin the first state in the nation to implement the direct primary and got the legislature to pass other reform measures including a railroad regulatory system and several bills to reduce the influence of special interests. One of LaFollette's greatest achievements was the creation of a "brain trust" using University of Wisconsin professors. Following the appointment of his former classmate, Charles Van Hise to the U.W. presidency in 1903, LaFollette began meeting with university professors each Saturday for what he called his "lunch club." At the time the U.W. had several nationally famous economists and sociologists on its payroll. These included economists Richard T. Ely and John R. Commons and sociologist Edward R. Ross. Each had pioneered in the development of ethical economics and reform Darwinism—the philosophies which powered the progressive movement—and at the time were considered quite liberal or even radical. In spite of such taint, LaFollette made each of these men his personal advisor. The informal Saturday lunch club link between capitol and campus had the full support of Van Hise who felt it was a splendid way for the University to serve the state.

When LaFollette resigned in 1906 to go to the Senate, some said the capitol-campus link would atrophy. This fear proved to be unfounded. By 1912 thirty-seven faculty members were serving

at various posts in state government. The extensive use of University specialists gave tremendous power to LaFollette and to his successors and played a major role in the development and implementation of the initiative, the referendum, the corrupt practices act, the civil service law, Wisconsin's panoply of regulatory commissions, worker's compensation, and many other progressive reforms. Indeed it was the harnessing of university resources in this way that became the central component of the famous "Wisconsin idea."

The intense national attention enjoyed by Wisconsin for its pioneering progressivism raises an intriguing question. If Wisconsin was the "laboratory of democracy," then what about Madison, its capital city? To what extent and in what ways was it a laboratory for the progressive movement? That is the question the next section will answer.

The Emergence of Crusading Journalism

The first twenty years of the twentieth century were tumultuous times for Madison daily newspapers. One daily, the *Madison Democrat,* expired after fifty-three years as a city institution, one entirely new daily—the *Capital Times*—appeared, and a third, the *Wisconsin State Journal*, was transformed by four successive publishers. These changes were largely the result of bold new views of what a newspaper could be. During much of the nineteenth century, one of the major reasons for owning a newspaper was to advance partisan politics. Beginning in the 1890s, however, Madison editors began to see themselves as more than shrill partisan trumpets and instead placed their journalistic power behind a fiesty array of social, economic, and political reforms. Local news was one of the big gainers from this new reform-oriented journalism. Instead of being routinely relegated to the back page, important local news appeared on the front page with international, national, and state news.

The Rise of the Wisconsin State Journal

As the century opened, two long-time rivals battled for Madison subscribers: the afternoon *Wisconsin State Journal* and the morning *Madison Democrat*. Sketchy circulation data shows that in the early 1880s the *Democrat* had nearly four subscribers for each *Journal* subscriber. This situation was hardly surprising since the *Democrats* was a fiercely Democratic organ and Madison voters gave almost unflinching support to Democrats. By 1900, however, the two papers were nearly neck and neck in the number of subscribers. This dramatic change in competitive position was caused in part by certain weaknesses of the *Democrat*. The *Democrat* suffered from being an "adjunct" of a much larger business, the Democrat Printing Company, one of Madison's largest employers and one of the state's largest job printers. Since the owners of the printing company made their money from printing and not from the newspaper, their interest in the newspaper was primarily political, that is, in maintaining a strong Democratic voice at the state capital. Although some efforts were made during the 1890s to enliven the *Democrat,* they were unsuccessful, certainly insofar as that success was measured by circulation figures.[5]

The rapid increase in *Journal* circulation was largely attributable to the arrival in 1894 of a tremendously talented new editor, Amos Parker Wilder. When the thirty-two-year-old Wilder arrived in Madison in 1894 with his black Alpaca suit, high clerical collar, and black tie, he looked more like a university professor than a newspaperman—an understandable impression since he had just received a Ph.D. from Yale University six years earlier. Interestingly, he had written his dissertation on municipal reform in New Haven, Connecticut. Like many New England emigres, Wilder possessed a missionarylike zeal to bring Eastern sophistication to the Midwest. At the same time, he was eager to do something important, or in his words, to "influence the history of the times." The new editor was a man of great intellect and wit and a captivating public speaker.

FIGURE 6.30. AMOS PARKER WILDER. (SHSW WHi(X3)2371)

Some said he was the second best after-dinner speaker in the country. His writing was as facile as his speech, and his editorials still rank as outstanding pieces of prose.[6]

Compared to his *Democrat* counterpart, Wilder had a much more activist and aggressive view of what a newspaper should be. Instead of waiting for something to turn up, Wilder sent his talented staff of newly recruited reporters out into the community to dig out local news and write local feature stories. Even so, Wilder found he could not satisfy some firebrands who felt that just about every community problem could be

solved *if* the newspapers would only concentrate their attention on it. Faced with such criticisms, Wilder acknowledged that the paper was indeed a "strong lever at his hand," but that a newspaper editor did "differ from the Almighty at a number of points." Wilder insisted that a newspaper should not be made "a sacrificial goat for the apathy of citizens" or a substitute for committed and enthusiastic leadership. In short, Wilder wanted his paper to be the "handmaiden" but not the instigator of change. To many Madisonians the distinction was probably lost because once Wilder got behind something such as the new high school, a city hospital, better garbage collection, and a more efficient city government, he generally pursued such goals with bulldog tenacity—providing that citizen leaders remained "out front."[7]

The combination of Wilder's more activist role for his paper, his nose for news, his high writing standards, and even his large personal involvement in community affairs, all worked to infuse the venerable *Journal* with a new vitality and make it the city's liberal journalistic voice. These factors caused its circulation to nearly double in just ten years (1894–1904) and for the first time placed the *Journal* circulation well in front of the duller, more conservative but long-dominant *Democrat* in the all important circulation war.

After ten years of editing a small Midwestern daily, however, Wilder became impatient with his role and began looking for a more prominent position from which he could be a "factor in events." In May 1906 Wilder got his chance when President Theodore Roosevelt appointed the *Journal* editor to the position of U.S. Consul at Hong Kong.[8]

Wilder retained majority ownership of the paper but turned editorial reins over to his trusted business manager, August Roden. Roden had graduated at the top of his U.W. class in 1898 and had worked his way through the *Journal* ranks from a three-dollar-a-week reporter to business manager with a part interest in the newspaper.[9] It is doubtful that Wilder expected

BETWEEN THIS DATE AND MAY 1, 1907

The STATE JOURNAL Will Give FREE to One of Its Subscribers a

$1,000 AUTOMOBILE

The plan on which this will be done will be simple, definite, [...] It will be as follows:

Every subscriber who pays six months in [...]ance will be given a re[...] WHICH WILL BE NUMBERED from No. 1 upward. The [...]ffice will g [...]ve duplicat[...] of all such re[...]ceipts issued. On or before May 1, [...]7, these duplicate receipts, in [...] d box, will be turned over to a committee of three responsible business men who will [...] the seal and DRAW FROM THE BOX ONE RECEIPT, at an hour and in a public p[...] be previously announced.

The subscriber who holds the original receipt which will bear the cor[...]ding number WILL DRAW THE AUTOMOBILE.

This is the Automobile.

WORTH $1,000.

A Standard Machine Bought at the Hokanson Garage in This City.

FIGURE 6.31. WIN A CADILLAC. Madison's most flamboyant newspaper subscription offer was no doubt this win-a-Cadillac contest announced in early March 1907. However, no one ever won the car because the contest was withdrawn about two weeks after it was announced. In explaining the reasons for this decision Editor Roden made cryptic reference to the "views of esteemed friends," "fairness," and "things the paper believes to be right."

or wanted more than a knowledgeable and sensible person to manage his paper, but as it turned out, Wilder and Madison got much more than a journalistic custodian.

Roden soon demonstrated that he had very different ideas on how the *Journal* should be run than his well-known predecessor. Although Wilder gave increased attention to local news, his strong personal interest was always state and national news. Roden, by contrast, had an intense personal interest in local news. Moreover Roden had a bolder, more crusading view of the newspaper than Wilder. In Roden's words the *Journal* should dare "to be a real newspaper," "fearless, aggressive and progressive. . . ." Roden moved quickly to build up *Journal* circulation by offering audacious prizes like a one-thousand-dollar 1907 Cadillac touring car, a technique without precedent in Madison.[10]

Although the contests obviously helped Roden expand the *Journal* subscription lists at the expense of the *Democrat*, it was the content and tone of the *Journal* that sent subscription lists on a steady upward swing. Roden was the first Madison editor to use what President Theodore Roosevelt in an angry 1906 speech called "muckraking." Roosevelt was referring to a small but influential group of writers who were bent on exposing corruption and injustice, men and women who named names, respected neither wealth nor status, and documented their charges. To Roosevelt they were unnecessarily revelling in the seamy side of private and public life and pandering to poor taste. But Roosevelt only glimpsed a small part of a much larger picture with his pejorative new label. Muckraking was all the president said it was, but it was much more. Muckrakers were the scouts who located enemy forces and determined their weakness so that larger bodies of reform forces could then surround and eradicate the evil. It was for this reason that muckrakers quickly became an integral, constructive, and popular part of the Progressive movement.[11]

The initial and primary carrier of the muckraker message at the national level were several cheap, large-circulation magazines such as *Colliers, McClure's,* and *Cosmopolitan.* But in Madison the most effective carriers of the muckraking bacillus were the *Wisconsin State Journal* and later the *Capital Times.* It was in these papers that the citizens of Madison read about the ills and injustices caused by local corporate greed and special privilege.

Among early local muckraking efforts, August Roden's attack on the Madison Gas and Electric Company beginning in 1906 was probably the most successful. Cooking and lighting gas provided by MG&E had long been described as "very inferior" although its price was shown to be twenty-five percent above all other cities in the state and twenty-one percent higher than the U.S. average.[12] In spite of these complaints, no one—not even the Common Council—had been able to get any satisfaction when they tried to get MG&E to respond to these charges.[13]

In 1903, for example, when the council requested certain data they needed to determine whether the rates were being fairly calculated, the company refused to cooperate. However the council persisted, hired two attorneys, and took the company to court. The three-year-long legal battle to lower rates ended at the Wisconsin Supreme Court where the city lost on procedural grounds.[14]

Here the matter might have rested had not the university regents hired a professor to test MG&E gas quality at several points on campus. The professor found that twenty percent of the gas was nothing more than an inert element, nitrogen, which provided no light or heat, but which caused the meters to whirl just the same. This study, prominently reported by the *Journal,* caused a wave of indignation to flow through the community. Roden called the presence of nitrogen "fraudulent" and said it was no different than putting oleomargarine in butter, sawdust in cereal, and ashes in coal.[15]

This shocking revelation was quickly followed by a study commissioned for Progressive Governor James O. Davidson (1906–1911) who wanted to demonstrate the need for state regulation of gas and electric companies. Davidson's data confirmed what Madisonians had long suspected: that MG&E rates were based not upon actual production costs plus a "fair return," but rather on the basis of all the traffic could bear.[16]

Armed with what he felt was an irrefutable case, Roden opened his muckraking crusade in March 1907 with a lead story charging the New York-based McMillan syndicate, which owned MG&E, with overcharging its customers forty-seven thousand dollars each year and giving customers a product that fell below state minimum standards.[17] From that point forward, the *Journal* ran almost daily stories deepening, expanding, and documenting these charges. Roden described stock-watering schemes, expensive experiments with untried technology on an unwitting city and, most damaging of all, a heretofore unpublicized MG&E offer to reduce the price of gas by fifty-three percent. The price cut had been offered by the company to stave off a municipal take-over attempt in 1903. Roden also charged that prominent Madison men who served on MG&E's board of directors with complicity with the McMillan syndicate. Although the company never deigned to reply directly to these charges, the resignation of two Madison directors over alleged "differences" with company policy showed that Roden's crusade was taking its toll.[18]

Roden's carefully crafted and timed crusade while the state legislature was in session may well have been the impetus for changing the ambiguous utility-oriented state law, a move greatly feared by MG&E officials who viewed the law as their best ally. Indeed the earlier Common Council court case had forcefully demonstrated that state law provided no workable procedure for the fair calculation of gas rates. To correct this problem, several Progressive state legislators hired U.W. Professor John Commons to draft a new public utilities regulation law, the forerunner of the Wisconsin Public Service Commission.[19]

Then came Roden's *coup de grace.* In July 1907, immediately after passage of the new legislation, the *Journal* hired a highly respected local attorney, Emerson Ela, to file a formal complaint against MG&E, the first such charge ever brought before the railroad commission after it was empowered to regulate gas and electric companies. The case was nationally significant in that it determined the all-important but highly technical question of which assets a utility could include for rate calculation purposes. Was it to include the so-called watered stock or was it to be an actual replacement value (a much smaller number)? There were the questions with which the commissioners wrestled. So complicated was the decision that the commission took two years to gather more evidence and deliberate.

Finally in March, 1910 the commission vindicated the *State Journal* initiative by rolling back gas and electric rates nearly ten percent—an all-important precedent that in the next decade produced three other rate rollbacks for Madison consumers.[20]

With his anti-MG&E crusade, Roden not only wrote a new chapter in Madison's journalistic history, but he also established a crusading investigative tradition that has prevailed—indeed, one is inclined to say "flourished"—from that day to this. At the very least Roden's work was a warning to executives whose actions affected the public. As demonstrated by the resignation of several MG&E directors during Roden's crusade, the mere threat of exposure injected a new blend of caution and conscience among Madison corporate decision makers.

For his work as Madison's pioneer and investigative reporter, Roden deserves a much larger and higher place in Madison's history than he has received. Certainly earlier interpretations that protrayed him as a caretaker editor between two better-known and credentialled editors do a great disservice to Roden and need revision. There is even a sense in which Roden's work is nationally important. Unlike nearly all of his muckraking

editor counterparts who merely exposed injustice, Roden went a step further and *prosecuted* his own case through the courts.

To this new assessment of Roden's importance, one final point must be made: Roden did his muckraking from a position of relative strength. He knew that the price he would pay for attacking a disliked local corporation was the loss of the sizable MG&E advertising account. On the other hand he was confident that this loss would be more than offset by new revenues from new subscribers who supported his attack on corporate misbehavior. In fact, during the MG&E crusade, although not entirely for this reason, *Wisconsin State Journal* circulation nearly doubled. In short, Roden demonstrated a happy truth not lost on his successors: Muckraking could be profitable and progressive too.[21]

On July 29, 1911, a front-page story told readers of the *Wisconsin State Journal* that the thirty-eight-year-old Richard Lloyd Jones had bought their paper. Though unknown to all but a handful of Madisonians at the time, he had attended the University of Wisconsin from 1893 to 1894 and then went immediately into newspaper and magazine work in the East where he could practice a craft he did so well, namely, social criticism. Jones wrote editorials for the *Washington* (D.C.) *Times* and the *Stanford* (Connecticut) *Telegram* and then became an editor with *Cosmopolitan* and *Colliers Weekly* during the period when they were among the nation's leading muckraking journals. As a magazine editor, Jones had frequent personal contact with some of the nation's most famous muckrakers such as Ida Tarbell, who had written a scathing expose on the ruthless practices of Standard Oil, Lincoln Steffans who had written a series of articles on municipal graft and corruption, and Samuel Hopkins Adams, a pure food crusader.[22] Jones was particularly proud of the work he had done at *Colliers* in putting public above private interest. But Jones wanted to be his own man, and so he began to look for opportunities.

FIGURE 6.32. RICHARD LLOYD JONES. (Courtesy of Jenkin Lloyd Jones)

Somehow Jones heard that Wilder was willing to sell the *Wisconsin State Journal*—a thought that greatly excited Jones. Immediately he envisioned the *Journal* as the leading Progressive paper in Wisconsin, a mouthpiece for the less articulate masses yearning for a better life. Senator Robert Marion LaFollette was also strongly interested in this prospect because the senator wanted a powerful Progressive daily newspaper at Wisconsin's capital—something to complement his recently launched *LaFollette's Weekly Magazine,* the medium he selected to advance his

political philosophy on a national level. One observer said the two men formed a "mutual admiration society" whereby Jones would spread the word on a daily basis and the LaFollette magazine on a weekly basis. In fact, LaFollette was so interested in Jones becoming *Journal* editor that he prevailed upon several of his rich Progressive friends to loan Jones eighty-five of the one hundred thousand dollars needed to buy the paper.[23]

Between July 1911, and June 1919, Dick Jones's "verile pen and militant personality"[24] made the *Journal* a powerful voice for the Progressive movement in Madison and throughout the state. In 1912 it carried LaFollette's presidential banner. Naturally Jones pushed LaFollette ideals including labor legislation, academic freedom, women's suffrage, black rights, and decried child labor, big business, and corruption in government. In 1913 the *Journal* was selected as the official state paper. Significantly Jones did not limit his attention to state and national issues. He was also a person who deeply loved Madison not so much as it was but rather for what it could become. Through the pages of the *Journal* Jones took bold and uncompromising positions in favor of municipal utility ownership, commission government, and against liquor interests, vice, sewage in the lakes, and even on aesthetic questions such as what kind of statues should embellish the Camp Randall memorial arch.

Jones brought big city journalism to Madison. Soon after arriving, he hired an unusually large staff to report and investigate the news, changed the format of the paper, and began the popular thick Sunday morning edition complete with an eight-page magazine, a pink sports section, and colored comics.[25]

During his strenuous editorship Jones wrote often and well. His impatience, coupled with his fervent desire to cause change *now*, meant that his strident editorial voice was rarely tainted with objectivity. Unlike many journalists who gave both sides of an issue so that readers could draw their own conclusions, Jones *told* his readers what

was right and never let them forget it. Jones was seldom content merely reporting the news: he wanted to make news. His crusade for commission government in Madison is just one case in point. No Madison newspaper editor had written quite the way Richard Lloyd Jones did. His style was agreeably pungent, provocative, colorful, and above all else, fun to read. The *Madison Democrat* accused Jones of "yellow journalism,"[26] but Madisonians apparently did not think it was. Just a few months after taking over, *Journal* circulation shot up nearly thirty percent. After little more than a year with his new paper, Jones *Journal* circulation doubled and by 1916 audited circulation data showed that the *Journal* enjoyed a two-to-one advantage in subscribers over the once dominant *Madison Democrat*.[27] Clearly, Madisonians liked the lively news and the forceful editorials they found in Jones' newspaper.

Jones explained his remarkably rapid increase in circulation in this way: "The *State Journal* has tried to give Madison a honest up-to-date newsy paper which will compare favorably with any of the metropolitan dailies. The *State Journal* has printed the news without fear or favor. It has not been dominated by any interest or interests, it has taken the side of the people as against the side of big business, it has not allowed itself to be bound by narrow party lines but has supported men who stand for the best things in the city, state and nation."[28]

Jones of course was delighted by the rapid ascent of his newspaper during his eight-year stint as editor of the *Journal* and, as noted elsewhere in this chapter, exploited nearly every opportunity to mold Madison into a model capital of a model commonwealth.

Rise of the Capital Times

The first person Jones hired after he took over the *Journal* in the summer of 1911 was William T. Evjue, the twenty-nine-year-old son of Norwegian immigrants. Evjue was no stranger to Madison nor to the newspaper business. He had attended the University of Wisconsin from 1902 to 1905 during which he had worked for the *Wisconsin State Journal*. Following his recovery from a painful eye infection that required Evjue to drop out of the university, he decided to get a job rather than finish college. Evjue then spent five years as a reporter for the *Milwaukee Sentinel* and several months as a reporter for the Chicago *Record Herald*.[29]

One beastly hot, humid August day on his way to work at the *Record Herald*, Evjue decided to stop in at the LaSalle Hotel bar for a glass of cold beer. The decision altered the course of his life. On his way out the door someone yelled, "Well there's my old friend Bill Evjue." The call came from a former university classmate who had become managing editor of the newly launched *LaFollette's Weekly Magazine*. The classmate told Evjue that Richard Lloyd Jones had just bought the *Journal* and that he was looking for a managing editor. The news could not have fallen on more eager ears for Evjue was most unhappy with his job at the *Herald* and welcomed the idea of returning to Wisconsin, particularly to Madison. And to work for such a well-known crusading Progressive like Jones truly excited Evjue. Immediately after arriving at his office, he called Jones long distance and the following day he took the train back to Madison. That evening with a beautiful moon overhead and a gentle breeze blowing off Lake Mendota the two men sat on the front porch of the Phi Gamma Delta fraternity house, 521 North Henry, where Jones was temporarily staying. There they talked far into the night about Jones' plans for a hard-hitting crusading newspaper that would put public above private interest. Jones was impressed by Evjue's experience and personal philosophy, sensed a kindred spirit in the intense young man and offered him the job of city editor that very evening. Evjue became Jones' protege and for six years played a major role in the *Journal's* revitalization.[30]

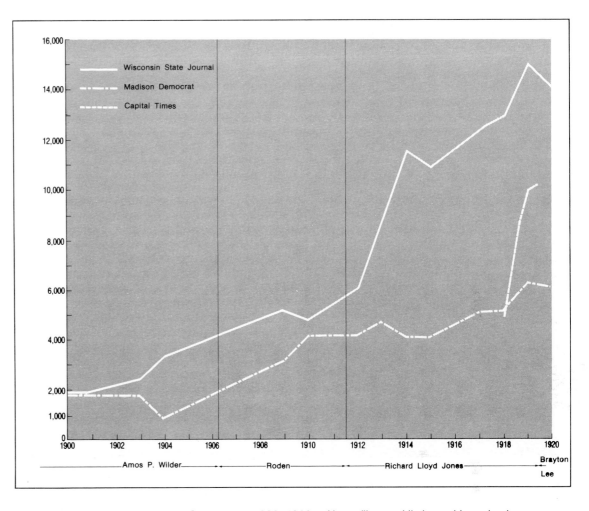

FIGURE 6.33. MADISON NEWSPAPER CIRCULATION, 1900–1920. New editors and their new ideas about newspapers greatly affected the circulation of Madison's dailies during the first two decades of the twentieth century. Wilder's elegance and sophistication lifted *Journal* circulation from a distant second to front runner in less than a decade. His successor, August Roden, used muckraking and investigative reporting to keep the *Journal* ahead in the circulation war in spite of a vigorous challenge from the *Democrat*. Then came Richard Lloyd Jones whose appealing big city journalism so increased *Journal* subscribers that the *Democrat* was almost relegated to an "also ran" category. What Jones did not expect but got was competition from an upstart third daily. In spite of almost stupendous odds, the *Capital Times* succeeded and William T. Evjue, a former colleague of Jones, had the satisfaction of seeing the circulation for his fledgling paper skyrocket from 5,000 to nearly 11,000 in just two years.

Successive *Journal* editors are shown along the baseline of the graph. Editor of the *Madison Democrat* during this entire period was O. D. Brandenburg.

As they waxed rhapsodic that August evening about their plans to create a great state paper, slay the forces of privilege, and carry the banner of progressivism, neither realized that a few years later Evjue would be editing a rival newspaper and that they would become implacable enemies. After an amicable six-year working relationship, the break between the two men came relatively quickly in 1917. The reason for their separation was the same as their reason for joining forces, namely, the ideas of Robert Marion LaFollette.

As the war in Europe became a raging torrent, the United States, like so many other countries before it, was swept into its swirling, turbulent waters. Nearly all Americans heartily endorsed President Wilson's declaration of war but there were a few, led by men like Senator LaFollette, who strenuously opposed American entrance into the conflict. For six staunch years Jones had trumpeted the virtues of LaFollette in whose principles he believed so deeply, but LaFollette's opposition to American involvement in the war was too much for Jones to swallow. Jones not only strongly disagreed with LaFollette, but questioned his integrity as well. Although Evjue could accept Jones' criticism of LaFollette, he refused to brook any questioning of LaFollette's veracity.[31] Deeply angered by Jones' accusation, Evjue resigned from the *Journal* in September 1917 and on the afternoon of December 13, 1917, just three months later, the first issue of the *Capital Times* hit the streets, printed in a run-down former ice cream parlor at 106 King Street.

Evjue could not have picked a more difficult time to introduce a new newspaper in Madison—certainly a liberal LaFollette-tinged paper of the type the testy young Norwegian was contemplating. Amidst war-inspired hysteria, almost anything that anyone called "pro-German" was in trouble. Predictably Jones accused Evjue and the *Capital Times* of being pro-German. Newsboys were harassed as they tried to sell the paper on the streets. Evjue was burned in effigy on the U.W. campus. Rumors were started saying that the *Times* was a thinly disguised LaFollette organ and that it was subsidized by Milwaukee Germans. The newspaper was denied membership into the influential Madison Board of Commerce.[32] So successful was this scare campaign that in January 1918 only one advertiser dared to buy space in the new newspaper.[33]

But the gritty thirty-seven-year-old editor mustered facts and arguments to rebut the rumors and allegations. Evjue placed the *Capital Times* unequivocally behind the war effort, not for the sake of posturing but because Evjue believed this was the right thing to do even if it meant disagreeing with LaFollette, his mentor.

In vivid style sharply reminiscent of his protege, Richard Lloyd Jones, Evjue printed convincing, well-documented stories about big business profiteering involving the streetcar company, Gisholt, Fuller and Johnson, and several others. He boasted no ties, loans, or advertising obligations to influence his news, an obvious reference to Jones whose then shaky financial condition forced him to mute his otherwise frontal attacks for fear that local bankers would call in his notes. Through these efforts Evjue succeeded in persuading Madisonians that the *Capital Times* was "a paper of the common folks," a distinction once claimed by Jones for his paper.[34]

Gradually, Evjue's fortunes began to look up. He got two large printing contracts including *LaFollette's Weekly* magazine previously printed by the *Wisconsin State Journal*. The trained business executives that Evjue had taken with him from the *Journal* worked long and hard for small wages and put out a consistently high-quality product. Evjue was also aided by several tactical errors Jones had made. For example, Jones had gone so far in criticizing LaFollette that the Senator sued for libel and forced Jones to retract his charges. Then Jones denounced the University of Wisconsin because its president, Charles Van Hise, refused to denounce LaFollette. Many people, especially the old line Progressives, resented this. Jones started rumors about the *Times* disloyalty but was forced to retract this charge when a U.S. government official investigated and found no basis whatsoever for the charge. Jones also angered Madison Germans by his intense, shrill antisaloon crusade whose tempo picked up during the war. Finally, Jones was silent on big business profiteering. Instead he attacked a handful of small grocers.[35]

Just ninety days after the first issue hit the streets, *Capital Times* circulation swelled to fifty-two hundred subscribers, more than the *Madison Democrat* had accumulated after more than fifty years.[36] And this without premiums, prizes, or contests. Even more amazing, the paper and its allied printing business began to show a profit in its third month.[37] Evjue was elated. His fragile new enterprise that most said would never survive had already become Madison's second largest newspaper. Once more Madison had a strong Progressive voice, a distinction once appropriately applied to Jones' *Wisconsin State Journal.*

The two years following World War I were eventful years for Madison daily newspapers. In June 1919, Jones was forced to sell his financially troubled paper. This time the buyer was not an individual, but a rapidly growing Iowa-based corporation known as the Lee Newspaper Syndicate. Overnight the tone and temper of the *Journal* changed. Gone was the crusading quality, the lively prose, and the alert reporting always evident under Jones. In its place were bland, dull, and equivocal editorials, and, as if to compensate, a heavily beefed up sports page. The Lee-edited newspaper was the journalistic equivalent of a salt and spice-free diet. On the other hand, it was more restrained and objective.[38]

Then in February 1921 came the announcement that the *Madison Democrat* was going out of business after more than a half-century of service. The *Democrat* had been severely pinched by rising paper and labor costs during and immediately after World War I, factors that forced its editors to reduce the paper's size and raise its price. But the major reason for the paper's demise was the fact that it was not as profitable as the printing business of the parent organization, the Democrat Printing Company. Thus, by February, 1921 the *Wisconsin State Journal* and the *Capital Times* had the journalistic playing field all to themselves.[39]

The City Efficient: The Search for Cheaper and Better Local Government

On the evening of February 25, 1901, one hundred fifty of Madison's most influential leaders assembled at a banquet hall for a monthly meeting of the Six O'Clock Club, an organization whose purpose was to provide good fellowship and a forum for the discussion of current issues. Since the founding of the club in 1899 nearly all of the Six O'Clock Club meetings had concentrated on national and international issues. But this time the subject was Madison. As the members of the prestigious club puffed their after-dinner cigars, they heard glowing speeches about Madison as a resort, as a manufacturing center, as a wholesaling area, and on the important contributions of the University of Wisconsin. Then came Charles N. Brown, a well-known local lawyer and a reform-minded member of the Madison Common Council who represented the affluent Mansion Hill area. "I must strike a jarring note in the discussion of the evening," began Brown, "but what I will say needs to be said and must be . . . acted on by businessmen of the city. . . . With other cities, Madison has experienced poor government," Brown announced.[40] The following day Brown's well-reported criticisms of Madison government set the town buzzing.

Brown was one of a small group of Madison reformers who were concerned about money, morality, and power. Money was an issue in the sense that reformers were convinced that tax dollars were being wasted by inept politicians. Morality was an issue because government officials tolerated saloons, sluts, and slot machines. Power was an issue in the sense that the reformers did not have it.

Madison did not have a notorious Tammany Hall gang but city government was controlled by Democrat party activists who believed in live-and-let-live so long as individual freedom and personal safety were not adversely affected. This permissive political philosophy gave rise not long after the turn of the century to a group of aldermen known as "the bunch" who became a principal target for reformers. The bunch voted again and again to reissue liquor licenses to saloons that offered gambling devices and tolerated loose women. In their private capacities, bunch members accepted contracts with the city and then in their public capacity voted on them in spite of direct conflicts of interest. Once bunch members went dancing at the Elks Club to escape having to attend a council meeting and vote on a controversial matter. During this period mayors complained that they could not get the police to perform their duty and lamented the Common Council practice of exhausting the city treasury long before the end of the year on pet projects and then levying a burdensome catch-up tax.[41]

In many other cities around the country the desire to heighten efficiency, reduce immorality, empower the better elements, and extinguish special privilege produced single-purpose reform organizations. During the first twenty years of the twentieth century in Madison, however, just one such organization appeared. Formed in 1905 the Civic Union was composed of business, professional, and religious leaders and was modelled after similar reform organizations in Boston and Chicago. Like their large city counterparts, Madison Civic Union members vowed to enforce the laws, especially those related to saloon evils, to work for the election of "good" municipal officers and to establish efficient city government.[42] In spite of an auspicious start, the organization lasted barely two months. One year later local luminaries, this time led by prominent clerics, told citizens who turned out for a "good government" mass meeting that Madison needed a mayor that "can rouse us to a white glow of enthusiasm in the cause of civic righteousness."[43] Unfortunately for the reform cause, no mayor induced the desired "white glow" and the effort came to naught.

Madison's failure to develop a viable reform organization did not mean the city was devoid of the reform impulse. Rather it meant that reform was pursued by other means. Late nineteenth and early twentieth century experience had taught Madison reformers that exhortations and educational efforts, then the most common techniques, had disappointingly small results. To a growing number of Madisonians who desired "good government," enduring results could only be achieved *through the state legislature.* And for this group of reformers, the time could not have been more auspicious. Robert Marion LaFollette was ensconced in the statehouse and his vigorous progressive reforms were attracting national attention. Although local government was not the primary focus of most state Progressive leaders, many Progressive programs were directly applicable to the local level, and some were developed in direct response to local government needs.

The progressive prescription for municipal ills was clean, accountable, nonpartisan, and responsive local government run by experts. In support of this prescription the Wisconsin legislature passed bill after bill between 1901 and 1912 that taken together became the backbone of municipal reform in Madison and throughout the state.

A very early focal point of progressive municipal reform was the mayor's office. Under the weak mayor–strong council system then used by Madison and many other cities around the state, the mayor had too little power to be effective. For Madison's chief executive officer, for example, the only positions the mayor could approve without council concurrence were such positions as lifeguards, weed inspectors, and the city veterinarian. The mayor's most powerful weapons were the rarely used veto and the frequently used "message"—little more than a special plea to the council. The real power lay with the aldermen. Through their committees, they developed the budget, approved all expenditures, passed local legislation, and established city policies.

In the late nineteenth century many reformers thought that a strong businessman could overcome the inherent deficiencies of this weak mayor system. After all, they reasoned, only businessmen really understood what it meant to be "businesslike"—a word intended to be a contrast with waste, inefficiency, and politics. In that word lay the hopes, the strategies, and techniques of many municipal reformers. Experience with Madison mayors, however, caused some Madison reformers to reject this long-cherished notion. For example, reform-alderman Charles Brown flatly stated that, "businessmen make poor mayors. They fear to denounce wrong as wrong because they fear that they will injure their business."[44]

Brown's point emphasized the need to make changes to the system and not just the man. One such change in this direction was approved by the legislature in 1901, namely a mandatory extension of the mayor's term from one to two years. In theory, this extra year allowed the mayor to become more familiar with city government and therefore become more effective. The new state law went into effect in April 1902, and from that day to this, mayors have been elected for a two-year term.[45]

Soon after the two-year term went into effect Madison reformers began pushing for a mayoral salary. If you want good executive talent, you must pay for it, they said. Naturally the proposal met with staunch resistance. "It is pregnant with evil" and "would promote grafting . . ." said the *Madison Democrat*. "The honor of the trust, the gratitude of the public is altogether the best and most flattering remuneration that may be returned," its editor concluded.[46] But this civic duty sentiment, once almost universally held among Madisonians, was losing its appeal among the new breed of reformers. The job of mayor was becoming increasingly complex and time-consuming with each passing year. Mayor John D. Groves (1902–1904), for example, was forced to spend so much time on city business that his piano business suffered irreparable damage, and he went bankrupt soon after he left office. Finally, after several years of debate on the matter, Madison began paying its mayor one thousand dollars a year beginning in April 1908. The pay was roughly a half-time salary for a mid-management position—much lower than the reformers wanted but all the council would approve. At the same time, the council agreed to pay the mayor, they agreed to pay themselves three hundred dollars per month.[47]

To the more impatient and radical reformers, however, the mayoral term extension and salary were little more than tinkering. This group of reformers insisted that "poor" local government was a consequence of the weak mayor-strong council *system* and that this entire system therefore had

to go. They charged that mayors had the responsibility but not commensurate authority to govern and could therefore not be held accountable for what happened. Moreover the system encouraged wasteful aldermanic scheming ("I'll vote for your street light if you'll vote for mine") with little real interest in citywide public policies. Even more to the point was the fact that, try as they might, reformers were rarely able to get more than a minority of "their kind" on the Common Council.

Radical reformers argued that the problem was "structure" and that the answer lay in an entirely different system known as commission government. Commission government was first tried in Galveston, Texas, not as a carefully developed scheme to strengthen local government, but rather as a response to a catastrophe. In September 1900 a hurricane and tidal wave devastated the city. The Common Council could not cope with the disaster and so they resigned. A group of businessmen and bankers rose to the occasion and devised a five-man commission, two of whom were elected by the city at large and three of whom were appointed by the governor. Each of the men headed a major city department thus combining both the executive and legislative functions in a single five-man body. In just three years the Galveston commissioners rebuilt their bankrupt and devastated city and at the same time introduced new procedures and practices that dramatically reduced the cost of municipal government. When the achievement of the commissioners became known, reformers all over the country stood in awe. They had seen the future of local government. In one fell swoop it abolished ward politics, partisan machines, inefficiency, lack of coordination, all the things reformers had been trying to do through the mayor-council system—but with very limited success.[48]

John M. Olin, the highly respected head of Madison Park and Pleasure Drive Association, was the first to suggest commission government for Madison in a major speech to community leaders at the pro-planning citizens banquet in January 1909. In his speech, Olin urged adoption of what he called a modified Washington, D.C., type of commission government where three commissioners would be elected at large by Madison citizens and two would be appointed by the governor and confirmed by the senate. Olin argued that since the state had invested five million dollars on the west end of State Street in the form of University of Wisconsin and was about to spend seven million dollars on the east end for the new capitol, the state should have a hand in governing Madison, that is, in "making Madison a model state capital, a model home for the university and a model city."[49]

However, for Olin's form of commission government to become a reality, the state constitution had to be amended since it prohibited the state from being directly involved in municipal government. During the 1909 session, Olin got the legislature to take the first of several steps needed to amend the constitution, but there the momentum stopped. At the same session the legislature also passed a much less radical form of commission government, which did not include state-appointed commissioners and which therefore did not require a constitutional amendment.[50]

Madison commission-backers lost little time pushing for the adoption of this more moderate form of commission government. Meanwhile John Olin and others gave speeches on the impossibility of good local government under the present system.[51]

A few months later commission backers began efforts to get the question on the ballot for a binding referendum. Mayor Joseph Schubert, an early passenger on the commission bandwagon, opened this part of the campaign with an upbeat, kick-off statement. According to the popular three-term mayor, the time had long passed when twenty randomly selected, part-time aldermen could effectively run a one-million-dollar corporation (the amount of the 1911 city budget). Schubert said that commission government centralized authority and responsibility in a more businesslike and economical way and that commission government, in conjunction with the initiative, referendum and recall was true

representative democracy.[52] So went the official justification. In a statement issued nine months earlier, however, Schubert had been more candid. "Popular government is all right," said the mayor, "but popular government such as in in vogue now costs a lost of money."[53] This earlier statement clearly reflected the serious doubts many Madison progressives had about "popular" government and their strong preference for government by experts—a preference based upon the greater control progressives felt they could exert with fewer commissioners elected at large.

Not until early December 1911, however, when backers staged a mass meeting did the drive for commission government generate real momentum. Flyers and handbills distributed by both sides heightened interest and packed the assembly chambers. After hearing a parade of prominent leaders, participants heartily endorsed commission government and authorized the establishment of a Committee of one hundred to direct the referendum campaign. The mass meeting obviously thrilled Richard Lloyd Jones, the new progressive editor of the *Wisconsin State Journal,* who in an editorial the following day unabashedly announced "the mass meeting last night was one of the most important meetings ever held in the history of Madison . . ." and the beginning of "the new Madison. . . . Speed the commission government," said Jones.[54]

Following the mass meeting the publicity campaign went into high gear. Copies of the commission law were distributed to all residents. More meetings were held. By early January 1912, commission backers had almost two thousand more petition signatures than the required fourteen hundred for a binding referendum.[55]

Not until January 30 was established as the referendum date were commission opponents provoked into action. Prominent among opponents were German-Americans who held a well-attended meeting and heard speakers argue that Madison's mayor-council system was basically sound but that several changes would improve it.[56] Commission opponents correctly noted that the new form of government would radically alter access and participation in Madison government.

Though the German-Americans studiously avoided saying so, they clearly feared that commissioners would take a hard line on Sunday saloon closings and generally would be much less responsive to liquor interests than twenty aldermen.[57]

As the January 30 referendum neared, the campaign grew in intensity. The *Journal* made commission government a *cause célèbre* while the *Democrat* acknowledged both good and bad features. But then came the day of reckoning and a disappointing day it was for the reformers. In spite of the skillful promotional campaign, in spite of the hype and the hyperbole, in spite of frenetic support from the *State Journal,* in spite of testimonials from Madison's leading citizens, of those who went to the polls, only forty-five percent voted for commission government.[58]

Commission proponents were quite bitter about their loss and charged that "Tammany methods" had been used to prevent four hundred commission supporters from voting.[59] William T. Evjue, then business manager at the *Wisconsin State Journal* and later the founder of the *Capital Times,* reported that he was prevented from voting by a "trick question" from an election clerk.[60] Such poll irregularities no doubt contributed to the defeat of the commission government referenda, but not nearly so much as the prospect widely circulated by saloon owners that commission government meant no Sunday saloons, Sunday baseball, or much of anything else on Sunday that was fun.[61] The majority of voters wanted familiar, tolerant, ward-centered, part-time aldermanic government rather than the austere efficiency and city-wide objectivity of full-time commissioners. In the end the voters preferred democracy to efficiency.[62]

Two years later structural reformers tried once again to get commission government enacted, but by this time the progressive Wisconsin legislature had passed an impressive array of bills, which strengthened the weak-mayor strong-council form of local government to the point where structural change lost its glitter.[63]

One such bill was the 1911 Corrupt Practices Act.[64] From the time Madison became a city in 1856, dependable but often indifferent voters were plied with beer, euphemistically reported as "refreshments," handed cigars, and transported to the polls in elegant carriages, all compliments of the party who provided these blandishments. A study of local election expenses from 1906 to 1913 showed that beer, cigars, and carriage and/or auto rentals were the three largest expense categories reported by aldermanic and mayoral candidates.[65] Local elections also meant that voters had to pass through a gauntlet of poll workers who were allowed to cluster around voting places dispensing political brochures and slips of paper bearing only candidate's names.[66] The Corrupt Practices Act put an abrupt halt to these time-honored traditions.

The second progressive state law that had great impact upon Madison government was the 1912 Non-Partisan Act,[67] which, as the name implied, required all local elections to be devoid of any partisan element. The law was first applied to Madison aldermanic elections in the spring of 1913 and to mayoral elections in the spring of 1914. Of all the progressive legislation affecting local governments, the Non-Partisan Act was probably the most difficult for local politicos to accept. The intensity of the partisan mind that suffused local elections was forcefully illustrated by a development of the 1902 mayoral campaign. Contrary to its usual policy the *Wisconsin State Journal* decided to endorse Democratic mayoral incumbant, U.W. Professor Storm Bull, rather than his businessman-Republican challenger John W. Groves. Doctrinaire Republicans felt so strongly about the *Journal* disaffection that they published their own newspaper for the duration of the campaign known as the *Evening Republican* and peppered the *Journal* editor with tart letters. Said one of the "loyal" Republicans in a letter to the *Journal* editor: "I confess that Mayor Bull has made a first-class mayor, but what of it? He is a Democrat and you have no business in the paper to say any good about him. . . . It is your

duty to abuse him."[68] The Non-Partisan Act also made mandatory a trend that had been evident in Madison even before the turn of the century, namely, the substitution of rational platforms for emotional partisan appeals. At first candidates found such platforms unnecessary and degrading. For example, in his 1906 mayoral campaign brochure, Joseph Schubert complained that in winning four aldermanic terms, his constituents had never once demanded a platform. "Evidently they had sufficient confidence in my actions and judgment to act intelligently upon the various questions as they might arise," concluded Schubert indignantly.[69] But times were changing. Voters were no longer satisfied with mere party endorsement and personal testimonials.[70]

The combination of the 1903 Direct Primary Act,[71] the 1911 Initiative Act, the Referendum Act, and the 1913 Recall Act also worked to make local government more responsive to Madison voters. The direct primary, first used in Madison in 1905, was a direct assault on the inner sanctum of partisan power—the party caucus—which had heretofore handpicked all local candidates. Under the direct primary system the candidate had to get fellow voters to sign nomination papers. The other measures—the initiative, referendum and recall—were used infrequently.[72]

Of all the progressive reforms adopted by Madison during the first twenty years of the twentieth century, probably none had less glamour and yet had more enduring significance to good government than the adoption of a more sophisticated budget system. From the time Madison became a city, alderman members of the Finance Committee had prepared city budgets for the coming calendar year. But what they called budgets were little more than estimates lumped in loosely defined categories. The combination of the weak-mayor strong-council system of government coupled with the loose budgeting system not only encouraged aldermanic raids on the city treasury, but diluted accountability as well. Particularly vulnerable were the general and street improvement funds. Naturally each alderman tried to get as much for his ward as he could and no one kept track of how much had been spent.

Since very few city projects were agreed upon in advance, capital improvement decisions were typically made by aldermanic initiative, logrolling, and friendly agreements. Inefficiency and waste were the result. The more aggressive aldermen tended to get the most for their wards and left their less aggressive counterparts wondering what happened to the money. Ultimately this aldermanic scramble exhausted the city treasury—sometimes as early as August.[73] Usually, but not always, this meant the game was over. The incoming council would then have to levy a catch-up tax to pay for their predecessor's profligacy.

Reform of this system came in two stages. First came Mayor Storm Bull, the first Madison mayor who really understood the intimate connection between city budgets and good government. At Bull's urging, the council approved a new budgetary procedure that required a three-quarters council vote to spend money for *any other purpose* than that for which it was budgeted or to spend funds *in excess* of the adopted budget.[74]

The second stage came in 1911 when the state passed and Madison took advantage of the new Uniform Municipal Accounting Act.[75] This law required local governments to submit detailed annual reports of monies received and expended, empowered the state to audit local government books and, for a fee, to assist local governments in establishing a uniform system of municipal accounting. The law was stern top-down medicine designed to correct chaotic conditions the Wisconsin Tax Commission discovered at the local level.[76] In effect the law gave a municipality the choice of implementing a much more sophisticated budgetary system on their own or hiring a Wisconsin Tax Commission specialist to do the job. Madison became the second city in the state to hire a state expert to set up the new system.[77] With the help of this expert, all receipts and disbursements were grouped into standard categories such as "recreation," "sanitation," "parks," and "protection of property." Under the old line-item system, labor costs for several of these programs might be grouped under "general labor" and material cost in still other places.

The adoption of the new program budget transformed the way city business was conducted. No longer could the Finance Committee throw together an annual city budget in a few hours. Instead city budget preparation became a very time-consuming and painstaking affair with a heavy premium on planning. For the first time city department heads could be held accountable for expenditures under their control. Aldermanic raids on the city treasury were effectively stopped by a revealing monthly summary prepared by the city clerk and distributed to aldermen. Like an automobile instrument panel the new system gave a clear, complete and up-to-date picture of city finances. Of its many beneficient results, perhaps the most dramatic came in 1915, when the city treasury for the first time in Madison history showed a *balance* at the end of the fiscal year![78]

The Municipal Solution

In addition to making structural, administrative, and fiscal changes, Madison progressives sought to reduce the cost and improve the quality of local services through municipal ownership and regulation. The primary targets for this technique were the public utilities, the so-called "natural monopolies."[79]

Like their counterparts around the country, Madison progressives usually preferred regulation to ownership as a means to achieve these goods. Regulation was in keeping with the progressive acceptance of the capitalistic system and their simultaneous belief that social and economic justice required more governmental intervention.[80] But municipal ownership was recognized as the most extreme form of intervention and was therefore reserved for special situations. In fact, during the progressive era in Madison, municipal ownership was seriously pursued in just two situations: the generation of municipal electrical power and the operation of streetcars. The first was popular and "safe," the second an act of frustration, a remedy of last resort.

Impetus for a municipal power plant lay in the need to sign a new contract with Madison Gas and Electric effective October 1, 1902. Ever since Madison got electricity, city government, like private users, had consumed more and more power. By 1902 schools, street lights, the water works, police and fire stations, and the library were consuming very large amounts of electricity, so much that the electric bill became one of the largest items in the city budget. Traditionally the contract renewal process had been a ritualistic mating dance, with the city striving for the lowest rate and shortest term and MG&E striving for the highest rate and the longest term. But by early summer 1902 when the negotiators got serious, MG&E officials discovered a new militance among council members about their contract. MG&E wanted a five-year contract, but the city was only willing to give them one. This position was the conclusion reached by an aldermanic committee that had surveyed many cities across the country and found that communities that had their own lighting plants were "happier and more contented."[81] The committee also reported that municipal plants could produce power more cheaply than a private plant. The cheaper power rates were of course welcome, but not simply because they would save the city money. Municipalitization would stop the "immense . . . tribute" MG&E was collecting for their "non-resident millionaire owners."[82] Such comments were a reflection of the then strong and prevalent animus toward huge corporations and trusts. Consequently, MG&E got only a one-year contract.

The City then used that year to have a group of University of Wisconsin professors prepare plans and estimates for a municipal lighting plant to be located at the Sewage Treatment Plant, now the Fiore Shopping Center.[83] So attractive was their professional proposal the council placed their plans before the voters in an advisory referendum in 1903 where fifty-four percent approved it.[84] In anticipation of winning the referendum, Madison aldermen unanimously requested the state legislature to remove the last roadblock to municipality by changing the city charter so that the city

could own its own power plant. Unfortunately for reformers the usually progressive legislature refused to even hold a hearing on the bill and forced the council in 1903 to approve another five-year lighting contract with MG&E, effectively ending serious efforts for a municipal lighting plant. From that point forward a confluence of factors including the rising initial cost of buying the municipal generating plant, the gradual reduction in MG&E rates, and the absence of a state legislative charter change all combined to prevent further serious efforts to establish a municipal lighting plant.

The immediate impetus for the most aggressive effort to buy and operate the streetcars came when the company boosted fares from five to six cents in November 1918. However, the push to buy the company following the one-cent fare increase was really the culmination of years of bitter and protracted battles with F. W. Montgomery, a New York capitalist who bought the line in May 1905.[85] Almost from the day he bought the company, the heavily whiskered Montgomery was the center of controversy. Though a man of modest stature, his wealth, appearance, behavior, and above all else his control of the city's most important transportation system on which nearly everyone was dependent caused Montgomery to cut a broad swath in community affairs. At first his massive investment in new cars and new tracks, his illegal but popular removal of the hated streetcar power poles on the Square, and the extension of a streetcar line to South Madison gave Montgomery an almost heroic quality. But gradually, these actions were superceded by others and Montgomery the Beneficient became Montgomery the Arrogant.

Montgomery's personality was such that he gave Madisonians two things to dislike: both himself and his streetcar service. The perverse consequence of this fact was that even when streetcar service was acceptable, as indeed it was much of the time, people could still berate Montgomery the man. Even during the honeymoon stage soon after he bought the line and was making extensive improvements, Montgomery did

FIGURE 6.35. F. W. MONTGOMERY: STREETCAR MAG-
NATE. Not long after buying the Madison Street Railroad Company, flat spots on streetcar wheels, a problem
nearly universal to the streetcar business at the time,
produced a new name for the new owner, F. W. Montgomery. Flat wheels were produced whenever the motorman was required to stop a car quickly; the brake
would cause the wheels to lock, but the momentum of
the car would keep the car moving forward, thereby
grinding a flat spot where the steel wheel slid along the
track. Not only did these flat spots produce a jolting ride
for passengers, but they also made a terrible "pounding" noise that had to be endured by persons who lived
along the streetcar lines. One wag felt the problem was
so much associated with Mr. Montgomery that it should
be a part of his name and that henceforth his initials,
"F. W." should stand for "Flat Wheel" Montgomery. The
suggestion was an instant success and quickly became
the household appellation for the streetcar magnate.
(Courtesy of Mrs. John Lobb)

Magazine Editor Says Streetcar Treats Passengers Like Hogs in a "Side Door Pullman"

Appearing below is one of the earliest complaints about Montgomery's management of the streetcar line.
The letter writer was B. B. Clarke, well-known editor of a nationally distributed magazine printed in Madison
known as the *American Thresherman*. Though the letter was sent to the Wisconsin Railroad Commission,
the predecessor of the Public Service Commission, it was not a formal complaint; rather it was an effort to
procure relief by subjecting the company to the power of public opinion via newspaper exposure. The letter
appeared in the *Wisconsin State Journal* on December 29, 1908.

— Gentlemen—I desire to lodge a complaint against the City street railway of Madison in behalf of
a few thousand residents of the Sixth Ward, who have selected me to be the goat in this matter, a service
which I assume with some reluctance, but with the grim satisfaction of trying to better a condition which
has reached a point where forbearance has ceased to be a virtue, and which if allowed to go on indefinitely will engender a feeling of resentment against the management which should not exist.

The inadequate service now furnished the Sixth warders may be from lack of knowledge of the facts,
but the cars in the evenings and mornings are crowded beyond circus day limits, and especially in the
evenings, our wives, sweethearts, sisters and grandmothers are treated little better than hogs on a double decked side door pullman. Cars are crowded until men and boys have to cling to the edges and
sides like chimney swallows, endangering their lives often. Women have to be crowded, jostled and
embarrassed by climbing in and out between a line of smokers, sometimes a jug or two—which I am
sorry to say occurs once in a while in our end of the burg.

— I have talked with every conductor and motorman on the line about this service and I have held
indignation meetings on the cars with everybody from Attorney General Gilbert to my own Barrister, who
resides in the "Bloody Sixth," (it will be bloody unless something is done) and all are ready to read the
riot act in seven languages and have it set to music if necessary.

— If the company have in view immediate relief in the shape of big street cars like a city of the size
of Madison deserves, then give it a chance, but tell us when. If not, then see to it that the company
scares out as many cars as necessary to carry the people in some degree of comfort. They can and
do it on circus days; why not all the time? The street car company loses more than enough patronage
every day by people walking home rather than being jammed in a street car like fattening hogs for market,
to more than pay for the extra service, and every conductor and every motorman on the line knows it
to be true. If their superiors don't know it, it's time they did. Mr. Montgomery has done many good things
for Madison, and we all appreciate it, but he is going lame on this matter, and we are waving the storn
signal at him. I have tried to get the company's ear about this once before, but the hint never reached
the spot. Now, I am acting for my neighbors, and as I have agreed to be the "goat," I'll butt and bleat
until something is done. Here endeth the first lesson.

(Signed) B. B. Clarke

things to alienate the public. He bought one of Madison's fanciest homes, spoke with a pronounced Eastern accent, wore a plug hat, swallow tail coat, and white spats. No one wore spats in Madison! So notorious were Montgomery's spats that years later a *Wisconsin State Journal* editorial seriously suggested that the public's anticompany attitudes were directly related to the despised patrician spats.[86] Then, from time to time, Montgomery would imperiously stop streetcars, wave the motorman away, and drive the cars himself as if they were a grand toy. It was almost as if Montgomery were sitting for a cartoonist's portrait of the fat-cat capitalist.[87]

For about two years following his purchase of the company, Madisonians were quite restrained in their comments about streetcar service. But beginning in 1907 a steady rain of criticism began. At first there were just a few well-placed drops such as B. B. Clarke's barbed letter to the editor, but gradually those drops became a deluge. As noted in "The City Well Housed," Madison leaders complained bitterly about Montgomery's refusal to extend service to rapidly growing suburban areas.[88] Passengers complained about many cars coming by at one time rather than at regularly spaced intervals and crowding (124 persons in a forty-two-passenger car) during rush hours. Passengers also complained about cold, poorly ventilated, dirty cars, improperly trained employees, and flat spots on the wheels. Finally they complained about slow speeds. In 1909 a jogging U.W. student actually beat a streetcar from the Jenifer-Baldwin intersection on the Near East Side to the U.W. campus.[89]

If Montgomery could have persuaded Madisonians that he had a sincere interest in trying to deal with these problems, people might have been more generous in their treatment of the streetcar company. Montgomery's early efforts begining in 1910 to tell the public his side of the story through newspaper ads, though factual and logical, probably persuaded very few.[90] Montgomery's actions and inactions always seemed to speak more loudly than his advertisements. For

example, Montgomery nearly always refused to pay his share of the cost of making street improvements—a practice that effectively held up paving projects, water main repairs and sewer laying, and usually forced the city to go to court to secure payment. And he almost always had to be prodded to heat his cars to the mandatory forty degrees even after November 10 when the ordinance required the cars to be heated.[91] Then there were certain rules that Montgomery inflicted on his riders such as the 1911 prohibition against mothers bringing folded baby buggies onto streetcars *unless* they were wrapped in a paper or cloth sack. If Montgomery had attacked motherhood itself, it is doubtful that he would have received more furious and indignant community protest.[92]

The "exasperating, money grasping, stupid"[93] baby carriage rule coupled with the failure of numerous public pressure tactics provoked angry passengers to take their grievances to the Wisconsin Railroad Commission, the popular new progressive state regulatory agency whose jursidiction included streetcars. Each time Montgomery was brought before the railroad commission, Montgomery lost. In decision after decision the commission ruled against Montgomery and in favor of better service *without* a fare increase. In December 1911, the railroad commission directed Montgomery to abandon the wrapped baby carriage rule.[94] In 1912, following another formal complaint on poor service, the commission required Montgomery to provide five-minute

> # How long could a merchant of this city do business, if he was knocked as continually as the street railway company?
>
> MADISON RAILWAYS COMPANY

FIGURE 6.36. KNOCKING A BUSINESS. Like human beings everywhere else, Madisonians were fond of complaining. They complained about dusty streets, soft asphalt, noisy automobiles, and smelly lakes, to name just a few. But of all the things about which Madisonians complained, none was more popular than the streetcar company. People said motormen failed to see potential passengers racing after a car, the conductors were rude, and that the cars were too cold, too stuffy, too early, too late, too small, too dangerous, and too expensive. This ad, which appeared in February 1920, might well have been run anytime after 1907 when Montgomery's company was being peppered by complaints. This advertisement was one of several used to gain public sympathy during the 1920 city effort to buy the company.

headways on some lines.[95] In 1913 in a series of rulings, the commission required Montgomery to provide service until after midnight, construct a double track along more of its lines, and to establish minimum ten-minute headways on all lines.[96] In 1914 the commission required Montgomery to pay his share of street repairs and build more double tracks.[97] Madison progressives were naturally elated by their regulatory successes and the commission's consistent passenger-oriented rulings.

But to Montgomery, these were stunning, expensive losses and forced him, quite contrary to his aristocratic tendencies, to intensity public relations efforts. Montgomery recognized that he had to try to win the support of his riding public by telling his side of the story and at least *appear* to be responsive to passenger complaints. For this purpose he established what he called a "Passenger Department" in January 1915, essentially a public relations body then common only in much bigger cities.[98] In a series of large newspaper advertisements Montgomery's Passenger Department detailed the many company efforts to improve service since 1905, alerted customers to temporary changes in service due to track construction, explained why there were no streetcars to pick up concert goers on a particular rainy night, and even described company efforts to cure the nettlesome flat wheel problem.[99] Indeed, the combination of the Public Relations Department coupled with the threat of still other Wisconsin Railroad Commission rulings produced a three-year respite from the recrimination which had characterized the first decade of Montgomery's management.

But then in June 1918, following Montgomery's request, the Wisconsin Railroad Commission approved the famous one-penny fare increase, boosting fares from five to six cents and the *rapproachment* ended. Montgomery attributed the request to rapidly rising, war-fueled inflationary costs. Whatever the reasoning, the decision set off a firestorm of indignation in Madison. Days after the decision was announced the council directed the city attorney to fight the increase.

The railroad commission held another hearing and the city attorney made an impassioned plea to roll-back the fare increase.[100] Finally in November 1918 the commission announced their decision. The six-cent fare would stand.[101] The decision was particularly infuriating to City Attorney William Ryan who had forcefully presented evidence showing that the fare increase was caused by old-fashioned stock watering, that is, issuing stock in excess of the market value of the line. Ironically, the commission agreed with Ryan, noting that the streetcar stock had been "shamefully inflated" to five times the actual replacement cost of the streetcar line.[102] Still, according to the complicated rules by which the commission operated, they allowed the increase.

The decision was particularly devastating to Madison progressives who, heretofore had been elated by the effectiveness of regulation. But now, the Progressives who once praised the railroad commission, were nearly unanimous in damning it. According to William T. Evjue, editor of the eleven-month-old *Capital Times,* the pro-Montgomery decision and others like it around the state made a "mockery of the theory that members of the railroad commission are servants of the people. They have descended to the plane of chair warmers asleep at the toll gates of the special interests," he said. Reluctantly Evjue concluded that "state regulation in Wisconsin has gone the way of regulation of other states. Sooner or later wealth and privilege get the pole with these commissions. The people's side is crowded out."[103]

To many city leaders the fare increase decision dramatized the need for a remedy more effective than mere regulation. Private ownership of the streetcar company had failed to provide good service at a fair price, and public regulation of the private company had failed to uphold the public interest. The only alternative, they said, was city ownership. Seventeen of Madison's twenty aldermen agreed with this interpretation and to Mayor George Sayle, the only question regarding municipal ownership was "procedure and finances."[104]

What Sayle and many others failed to realize, however, was that "procedure and finance" constituted a tangled skein of nearly insoluble problems. For example, in 1918 when Sayle made his remarks, the city could buy the company only if it issued general obligation bonds behind which stood the full faith and credit of the city. By 1919, however, Madison Railways Company assets including the "watered" securities stood at $1.7 million, an amount that far exceeded what Madison could legally borrow. In 1919 the Wisconsin legislature provided a solution to this problem with a bill that allowed cities to purchase streetcar companies using revenue bonds, that is, bonds whose collateral was the value of the streetcar company assets and not the full faith and credit of the city.[105] This bill removed the major procedural and one of the financial obstacles to municipal ownership but it did not resolve the even more complicated questions of what price the city should pay for the streetcar company or what it would cost the city to run the enterprise.

Such questions would have deterred most lawyers and many experts but they did not deter City Attorney Ryan. Angered by his rebuff before the railroad commission and backed by a council resolution, Ryan eagerly plunged into the arcane wilderness of streetcar finance. What he learned was anything but encouraging. The streetcar company had exceeded their borrowing capacity and were therefore financially incapable of providing expensive track extensions into the rapidly developing suburbs, much less paying smaller expenses such as paving between their tracks. Moreover their revenues were going down and the options for reducing espenses were not attractive.[106] If there was anything consoling in this sorry spectacle, it was the fact that a comprehensive and respected national survey had shown that most other streetcar companies in the country were victims of the same problems. Experts blamed the automobile and rising costs. The national survey even went so far as to conclude that the streetcar was "dead as a money-making enterprise and that the future problem was one of getting service at all."[107] In spite of this apparently dismal financial prognosis, Ryan learned that the Montgomerys had found a way to earn a sixteen to seventeen percent return on their actual investment. To Ryan and many other Madisonians, it looked like Montgomery was milking the line while lining his pockets with fare increases.

Finally in February 1920 after a year of analysis, the council followed Ryan's advice and formed a committee to investigate municipal ownership. However, the action quickly shifted from the aldermanic committee to mayoral candidates then battling for attention in the 1920 spring primary. A spirited three-way primary produced a rather extraordinary result: Frank C. Blied, a candidate who had based his campaign almost solely on his advocacy of municipal streetcar takeover won forty-four percent of the vote while another candidate who was almost silent on the issue received thirty-four percent and the incumbant mayor received just twenty percent.[108] Madison voters apparently agreed with Blied that the streetcar company was a "financial parasite" on the city and that it was responsible for Madison "becoming a city of tenants instead of a city with homes."[109] At their first meeting after the primary the council decided the issue was so important that a referendum on municipal streetcar ownership should be held on April 6, 1920—a decision that allowed citizens to vote on the issue for the first time in Madison's history.

The fifteen days between the primary and general spring election in 1920 produced a torrent of ink and oratory seldom seen in Madison. Like few other issues, municipal ownership of the streetcar company gripped the city, dominated newspapers, and produced a campaign notable for the light and not just the heat it generated. Could the city find bond buyers if the only security were watered streetcar assets and not the city treasury? At what point would the streetcar give way to autobuses and would that change the city's ability to recover its investment? Would not the city have to pay just as much as a private company to extend tracks to the suburbs? Where would this money come from? What assurances were there that services could be improved, much

less hold the line on fares? These were just a few of the tough and troubling questions posed during the campaign. Proponents argued that the choice was between private ownership with a subsidy or public ownership with a subsidy, but a subsidy in either case, and that so long as a subsidy was needed, the city should run the streetcars. Opponents of municipal ownership did not find this logic very convincing and pointed to the huge drain on the city treasury the move would require. Toward the end of the campaign activists on both sides lapsed into such highly technical charges and countercharges that average voters walked away shaking their heads in befuddlement.

When the smoke had cleared and the ballots were counted sixty percent had voted *against* municipal ownership of the streetcar company.[110] The result was not entirely surprising to municipal ownership proponents. The fact was, the light produced by the campaign revealed some very compelling reasons for *not* buying the company, not the least of which was the likelihood that the city would be forced by the new municipal streetcar acquisition program to pay for the so-called watered stock in addition to the company's actual assets. Under these conditions, even the municipal purchase proponents could not justify the move. Proponents also failed to demonstrate that the city could provide the large amounts of capital to make needed line extensions without a large annual drain on the treasury.

The ironic and unanticipated consequence of the campaign was that it generated understanding and even sympathy for the serious problems confronting streetcar company management.[111] The campaign showed that running a streetcar company was a very difficult, risky and thankless job—a job the majority of voters said should best be left in Montgomery's hands, even if the price was poorer service on existing lines and no streetcar service to the suburbs, and particularly if better service meant a large annual drain on the city treasury.

In the final analysis the streetcar referendum proved to be still another set-back for those who hoped to achieve the City Efficient through municipal ownership. A fervent progressive hope had been dashed.

The City Virtuous: The Attack on Slot Machines, Sluts, and Saloons

Though Madison was never a Midwestern Gomorrah, it seldom attained the degree of moral purity many reformers desired. Consequently from 1841 when a group of indignant Madison women blamed irresolute legislators for local sin, a long list of citizens and organizations tried to improve Madison's moral climate. Although they worked hard, their efforts were episodic and often ineffective. Not until the twentieth century when a new generation of leaders exploited new conditions and utilized new tactics to forge a new moral majority did these crusaders for the City Virtuous enjoy enduring success.

The Moderate Crusade, 1900–1907

As the new century opened, the focal point for enemies of local iniquity continued to be the SALOON. Like a secular sanctuary, the saloon sheltered the "devil's trinity," namely, alcohol, commercial sex, and gambling. It was the place where girls lost their innocence, men their wages, and boys their fathers. Like a fortress the saloon taunted and then repulsed reformers who sought to make Madison a bastion of virtue.

During most of the nineteenth century, prohibitionists and their close cousins, the sabbatarians, had taken the lead in combatting the saloon. Most were pious church women of New England descent who wore white ribbons denoting purity, signed abstinence pledges, joined the Women's Christian Temperance Union, and held prayer vigils for saloon patrons. To these high-minded

FIGURE 6.37. THE SALOON.   The saloon was a curious contradiction. At the same time it was Madison's most popular *and* most reviled institution. For some students and many working men, the saloon was a congenial place to eat, drink, talk, and play. For a nickel you could buy a tall glass of cold lager and get a free but somewhat salty, thirsty-inducing lunch consisting of sausage, luncheon meats, crackers, and even some delicacies. For example, during the spring of the year young boys would wade into Madison's many marshes and catch thousands of miniature lobsters called crayfish. They would then be cleaned, picked, and served up as tasty tidbits. Saloons also offered music in the form of player pianos and victrolas equipped with morning glory horns. For the more sporting types saloons offered card tables, dice, and for a time even slot machines and roulette wheels. To help their customers while away the hours many saloons provided billiard tables and newspapers. One observer said the saloon was the "church of the poor," a place where one could get consolation and escape from

the world. The saloon was also the most democratic of institutions. There were no creeds to embrace and no memberships to sign. Indeed one did not even have to have respectability to enter. It was for these reasons that throughout the nineteenth century Madison had an average of one saloon for every thirty-eight adult males.

But this flattering portrait was only part of the story. To prohibitionists and progressives the saloon was the enemy of family and frugality and the breeding place for crime, prostitution, gambling, and drunkenness. Saloons were places where men could swear, spit, and fight with relative impunity. Saloons were dark, dingy, and dirty, and reeked of stale beer and cigar smoke. Most were a refuge for beat-up furniture and the home of fly-specked mirrors, unclean glasses, and offensive sanitary facilities.

Saloons were also centers for the sale and consumption of nickel cigars and chewing tobacco, both of which made spitting a biological necessity. This fact in turn required saloon operators to strategically position spittoons along the bar where they would hopefully coincide with the trajectories of expectorating patrons.

However, as the dark stains on the floor just to the right of the column reveal, drinkers were not known for their accuracy. The removal and emptying of these wide-mouthed pails was a most unpleasant task for bartenders who typically walked out the front door and dumped them in the gutter. To this chronic problem there was one magnificent exception and that was the bar at the Fauerbach Brewery. Instead of brass spittoons, the Fauerbach had a large granite trough that ran the length of the bar and that from time to time the bartender could flush with water merely by turning a valve.

This rare interior saloon photograph was taken in the Schenk Saloon at 2006 Atwood Avenue in early 1900. The portly gentleman leaning on the brass rail on the right was the saloon owner, Fred Schenk, whose various businesses in the vicinity of Atwood Avenue and Winnebago Streets caused this area to be known as "Schenk's Corners." (Courtesy of Robert Huegel) crusaders the only pure and legitimate goal was total elimination of the saloon. Anything less than elimination was compromise and compromise with evil was blasphemy.

Though these "purists" were resolute and devoted to their cause, their "red fire and rabid personality" type of campaigns[112] produced more ridicule than results. Two referenda held during the 1890s on the wet/dry question provided wets with a comfortable twenty percent plurality. In another referendum on the wet/dry question in April, 1901, the wet plurality shot up to twenty-eight percent. Seldom could would-be saloon slayers even get officials to shut down the despised institutions on Sundays as the law required. Moreover the saloon growth rate exceeded that of the general population in part because saloons were at this point finding choice locations in the heretofore undefiled suburbs. Bitter pill though it was to swallow, hard-core prohibitionists were forced to conclude that they were losing strength. Indeed to saloon owners prohibitionists were like mosquitoes in summer—one of those irritants in life which simply had to be endured but which caused no serious problems.[113]

Confronted by this discouraging situation, leaders of the Madison Temperance Board, a confederation of church representatives, made a major change in their fundamental purpose: they abandoned their long insistence upon prohibition in favor of a more moderate, proximate goal, namely, *the reduction and regulation of saloons.* Better to soften the goal and infuse new life in the temperance cause they reasoned than to remain ineffective.[114]

Very significantly, however, this goal shift was not merely a response to their relatively unsuccessful recent efforts. It was also a conscious attempt to emulate a highly successful national organization known as the Anti-Saloon League. The basic plan of the Anti-Saloon League was to dry up the nation in stages, first localities, then the states and finally, the nation. From the beginning they worked "to extricate the dry cause from its bondage to an obscure third party and a

FIGURE 6.38. THE GROWTH OF PROHIBITORY DISTRICTS. Prohibition did not descend upon Madison in one fell swoop. Rather it arrived piecemeal over many years. One of the most effective tactics ever developed by dry leaders was the establishment of what were called "prohibitory districts," that is, dry islands where no liquor could be manufactured or sold. Between 1897 and 1907 the Common Council created four such dry districts, three in the university area and another in what was called "industrial Madison." In addition to the four dry districts created by the city, a fifth was created by the state legislature. The locations of these dry districts and when they were created are shown above. Notice the relation between the state-imposed one-half mile *cordon sanitaire* and the Hausmann Brewery.

vast regiment of unenfranchised women."[115] Although they never lost sight of their goal of absolute prohibition, Anti-Saloon League leaders were master schemers. They believed in getting what they could when they could and were therefore willing to compromise along the way. They knew that they could only reach their goal in tiny increments and that if they had had to spend time in the wilderness of saloon regulation and suppression, it was because it was the only effective path to prohibition. This was the highly tactical logic that Madison drys borrowed from the Anti-Saloon League.[116]

Armed with their new moderate goal of saloon reduction Madison drys fomented a referendum in September 1901, but this time instead of asking voters if they wouldn't want to eliminate the saloon, they asked voters if they wouldn't want to cut down on the *number* of saloons by increasing liquor license fees. At the time Madison saloons had to pay two hundred dollars for a liquor license, but voters could increase the amount to five hundred dollars through the referendum. The drys expected the higher five-hundred-dollar fee would eliminate about one out of five Madison saloons.[117] Though the drys lost the election, they were pleased with the results. In April 1901 an eighteen percent plurality had voted to keep Madison wet, but in the September 1901 "high license" election, only a nine percent plurality separated drys from victory, a fifty percent reduction in the number of voters who would have to be won over.

Since state law limited local referenda on the low-high saloon license fee to once every three years, the next election could not be held until 1904. Meanwhile the drys needed an issue to attract support to their cause. They astutely decided to exploit the association between saloons, prostitution, and gambling because community opposition to these evils was much greater than opposition to alcohol. That saloons were vulnerable to such an attack was at no time in dispute. Half of Madison's saloons were equipped with small back rooms or "stalls" where "women of evil name and fame" could ply their vocation.

Also Madison saloons boasted hundreds of slot machines and some even had roulette wheels. Both devices were completely illegal, but Madison police were notoriously casual about enforcing the law. Indeed the Common Council routinely issued liquor licenses to saloons that had such gambling equipment.[118]

As the dry reformers began to apply the heat with the hope that the Council would see the light, they quickly learned that prostitution was not just limited to saloons. The fact was Madison had old fashioned openly operated whore houses. Madison's most famous and possibly its fanciest bordello was called "The House on the Marsh" by reformers and "The Blue Goose" among town sports. Located at 911 East Main Street just west of today's Greyhound Bus Depot, the popular house was conveniently located in the middle of what was then known as "The Great Central Marsh"—an area criss-crossed by little used roads and surrounded by tall waving cattails. This happy coincidence of geography and nature allowed patrons to come and go with relative anonymity. Built in 1898 expressly as a bordello, it was insured, appropriately enough, as a "girls rooming house." Its "girls" came from Chicago and were especially popular among Madison's young men who enjoyed "respectable parentage" but also by older men who arrived in expensive carriages.[119]

Periodic police raids on such houses failed to provide permanent results, though they did give the impression of official diligence. No sooner would police raid one house and run the girls out of town than another bordello would open up somewhere else. However, as enforcement increased in Madison, some operators decided the better part of valor was to set up business outside city limits. One operator, for example, rented cottages to prostitutes on a picturesque oak covered shoreline in the 4800 block of Tonyawatha Trail.[120] Access to this popular "resort" known as "Oak Park" was via electric launches, which departed from the foot of South Blair Street.[121]

Gradually, the dry fomented raids on centers of prostitution and gambling began to pay off. In 1903 the council finally outlawed the back room stalls.[122] Then in April 1904 Madison voters elected Dexter Curtis, a reform-minded businessman, as mayor and under whose aggressive and sustained attacks, prostitution and gambling were virtually eliminated. Also in 1904 the drys petitioned and got another referendum on the low-high liquor license question and came within two percentage points of winning the high five-hundred-dollar license.[123] To reformers the forces of virtue at last appeared to be on the ascendency in Madison.

The new dry leaders, however, were not content to purge saloons of prostitutes and slot machines. Their goal was fewer saloons. In 1906 Leslie B. Rowley, a dry Republican mayoral candidate, championed the cause by running for mayor on a platform that Madison was run by saloon interests. The claim was not dry hyperbole. Just a few months prior to the election, the Common Council, following its long time policy of "justice, mercy and business"[124] had supinely granted a saloon license to a notorious operator who had been convicted of various liquor law violations.[125] Rowley skillfully exploited these policies by pitting saloons against students. "Is the University with its three or four thousand students of more importance to this community than ninety saloons and a few breweries?" asked Rowley. "Is this town to be run largely for the profit of the latter rather than popularizing and safeguarding the former? The greater the liquor dominance," continued Rowley, "the greater the injury to an institution which conspicuously is the basis of Madison's prosperity. Citizens, what do you think of this question?"[126]

As it turned out, Rowely lost the election but his defeat in Madison was only the beginning of a larger though delayed success. What many saloonists forgot was that Rowley's message was inherently newsworthy, particularly to present and prospective parents of U.W. students who were intensely interested in the conditions under which their children would receive their higher

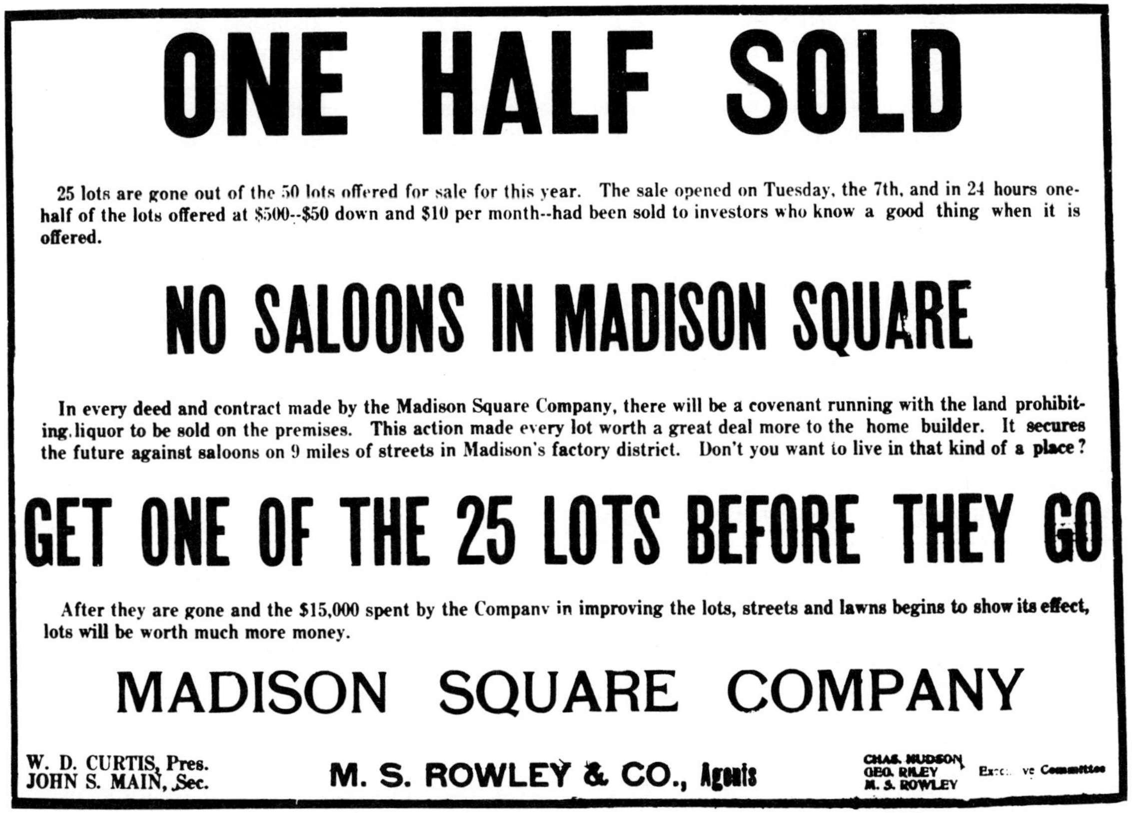

ONE HALF SOLD

25 lots are gone out of the 50 lots offered for sale for this year. The sale opened on Tuesday, the 7th, and in 24 hours one-half of the lots offered at $500--$50 down and $10 per month--had been sold to investors who know a good thing when it is offered.

NO SALOONS IN MADISON SQUARE

In every deed and contract made by the Madison Square Company, there will be a covenant running with the land prohibiting liquor to be sold on the premises. This action made every lot worth a great deal more to the home builder. It secures the future against saloons on 9 miles of streets in Madison's factory district. Don't you want to live in that kind of a place?

GET ONE OF THE 25 LOTS BEFORE THEY GO

After they are gone and the $15,000 spent by the Company in improving the lots, streets and lawns begins to show its effect, lots will be worth much more money.

MADISON SQUARE COMPANY

W. D. CURTIS, Pres.
JOHN S. MAIN, Sec.

M. S. ROWLEY & CO., Agents

CHAS. HUDSON
GEO. RILEY
M. S. ROWLEY
Executive Committee

FIGURE 6.39. NO SALOONS IN MADISON SQUARE. Just as Methodist preachers followed pioneer camp fires westward across the continent, so too did saloon owners follow Madison developers into the suburbs. To prohibitionists it seemed like the corner saloons opened their doors the day after developers pounded their "lots for sale, buy now" signs into the earth. This pattern posed a problem to some developers who strived to make their subdivisions distinctly unlike the saloon-filled central city. Some responded by incorporating deed restrictions that banned saloons. One such subdivision was Madison Square, whose May 1907 advertisement is shown above. Madison Square was bounded by East Johnson, Pennsylvania and North Streets, and Commercial Avenue. Other subdivisions that flaunted their dryness were University Heights and West Lawn.

Some suburbs such as Wingra Park refused to be annexed for many years for fear that this action would bring with it "saloon control."

education. The image of the university campus surrounded by saloons had a chilling effect on student enrollments. In the fall of 1906 student enrollment increased by just thirty-two students over the previous year, an increase of just .01%—a sharp contrast with an average annual increase of 7.4% during the preceding five years. U.W. President Van Hise correctly recognized that if he could not advertise the university as being free from saloon influence, his ability to secure large and growing state appropriations would be jeopardized. Van Hise also recognized that the only convincing way to refute the saloon control image and to get the needed corrective legislation was for a *majority* of Madison citizens to demand a tough new policy.

Van Hise began by affixing his name to the top of a petition urging the expansion of the 1897 U.W. dry district. This district covered just eleven blocks, mostly to the east of the campus, but left University Avenue, the area south of the campus and the area of Frances Street untouched. At the time of the Van Hise initiative both the Common Council and the state legislature had proposals before them to expand the dry district, but neither had acted upon them.[127] The petition was circulated among property owners in the Fifth Ward and quickly accumulated a glittering list of professors, doctors, reverends, and leading businessmen. Next Van Hise worked with Madison ministers to make the Red Gym available and to organize a mass meeting. Van Hise agreed to make the Red Gym available and the ministers agreed to cancel their usual Sunday evening services so that their members could all go to the Red Gym rally.

Never before had so many Madisonians turned out to support an antiliquor measure. Some four thousand citizens jammed the Red Gym on Sunday evening, April 14, 1907, for what was called a "monster mass meeting." For two hours the crowd cheered as legislators, regents, ministers, and aldermen demanded that the saloon—"these guilded signs of hell that line our best streets and lead young men down the crooked path"—be banned within the university area.[128] Public indignation was heightened by the fact that the Common Council just three months earlier had not only defeated an ordinance making Sunday saloon closing mandatory, but it also refused to allow a referenda on the issue.[129]

Just two days after the monster meeting the U.W. regents unanimously endorsed a state bill that established a one-half-mile dry zone centered around Bascom Hall, and Madison aldermen, most of whom had heretofore been utterly unsympathetic to dry sentiment, unanimously doubled the size of the dry district.[130]

Significantly this new council support was not based purely on the size of the crowd but also upon its composition. Aldermen were quick to see the large number of businessmen in the crowd, men who heretofore had been supporters of a "business administration," a political code word implying among other things tolerance for saloons. The presence of so many businessmen was a milestone of great importance in the development of a winning dry coalition and was in turn a product of a rapidly changing perception of the university. From the time the university was founded until the mid-1890s, most businessmen had viewed the institution as a prestigious community ornament. However, following its relatively rapid growth in the 1890s, businessmen began to see the U.W. as a powerful generator of city economic and population growth. Thus the presence of campus saloons was retarding growth not only of the U.W. but the entire city. Therefore the saloons had to go.

Among proponents of a saloon free campus, the Common Council creation of the doubled U.W. dry zone earned high marks for its responsiveness, but not for permanency or size. They recognized that any Common Council action could and (given its long prosaloon track record) probably would be later rescinded once the furor had subsided. A state law, by contrast, would supercede any local ordinance and would be much more difficult to repeal. Moreover, proponents were eager to emulate other universities such as

Purdue, Chicago, and Northwestern, which had established alcohol free zones with radii of three-quarters, one and four miles respectively.

Prospects did not look good for Madison saloon and brewer interests. Even a bill with just a one and one-half mile radius would wipe out all three of Madison's breweries (The Hausmann, the Fauerbach and the Breckheimer) and ninety percent of the city's saloons. It was for this reason that Madison's three breweries united behind a moderate bill calling for a half-mile radius, which would allow all three to continue and require only a handful of saloons to close. Very significantly the brewers recognized the tremendous power legislators possessed and even agreed that a one-half mile *cordon sanitaire* was desirable.

Faced by the prospect of a much larger, legislatively imposed saloon-free district, the Common Council in June 1907—almost in desperation—quadrupled the size of the dry zone over what it had been just three months earlier. But this extraordinary pre-emptive action failed to persuade state legislators who as a result of intense lobbying by Madison breweries passed a bill in June 1907 establishing a .5 mile radius around Bascom Hall.[131]

The new enlarged U.W. dry district was an important and satisfying achievement for the new moderate dry coalition comprised of old school prohibitionists who had learned to accept proximate instead of absolute goals, businessmen who were eager to remove any obstacle to Madison's growth, and progressives who saw saloons as a threat to the development and integrity of the University of Wisconsin. But coalition leaders sensed they could ride their unprecedented surge of dry sentiment to still another victory if they fomented another referendum on the low-high liquor license question in September 1907. Dry leaders therefore secured the necessary signatures to require a special election. Saloon owners were understandably concerned about this crest of dry sentiment surging through the city and immediately launched a counter crusade. Saloon patrons were told that if the high license were approved the then extremely popular free lunch

would have to be abolished and that they would get much less beer for their nickel. In spite of such efforts, the new dry coalition prevailed and the five-hundred-dollar high license was approved by a handsome thirteen percent plurality.[132]

Looking back over the period between 1900 to 1907 the moderate crusade had produced impressive results: commercial prostitution and gambling had been virtually eliminated in the city; the area where the sale and manufacture of intoxicating beverages was forbidden had increased from 44 acres to 163 acres; and as a result of the imposition of the five-hundred-dollar liquor license fee and the one-half mile U.W. dry zone, sixteen of Madison's ninety-nine saloons had been forced to close their doors.

The Quiet Interlude, 1908–1912

This new dry power did not go unnoticed by the saloon lobby. Gone were the days when Madison citizens and state legislators would tolerate the wide-open, look-the-other-way law enforcement that had earlier prevailed. For the first time saloon owners recognized that if they failed to police their own actions angry Madisonians and indignant legislators were capable of inflicting great damage. No longer were their adversaries pious church ladies who eschewed the hurley burley of local politics. During the moderate crusade they had been replaced by savy business and professional men and even paid lobbyists who knew how to mobilize public opionion and implement new laws.

Indeed it was the saloon owners' keen awareness that their operations were being watched by the new dry forces that caused the period between 1908 and 1912 to be a relatively quiet interlude. This is not to say that the wet/dry forces did not skirmish. In 1910 the *Wisconsin State Journal* fomented another vote on the wet or dry issue, the first since 1901, and were pleased to see the wet plurality drop from eighteen to seven percent. Meanwhile in the state legislature, saloon

A Temper-
ance
Education

"*True modesty lies in the entire absence of thought upon the
subject.*" T. H. Lewin, in
"*Wild Races of Southeastern
India.*"

Hausmann's Beer

THE TEMPERANCE DRINK

HAUSMANN BREWING CO.   Phone 33

**FIGURE 6.40. HAUSMANN'S BEER, THE TEMPERANCE
DRINK.** This delightful advertisement by the Hausmann
Brewing Company, which appeared in the *Madison Democrat* in September 1912, was the beginning of an attempt to distinguish "wholesome" beer and temperance
from growing sentiment against hard liquor and prohibition. The *Wisconsin State Journal* refused to carry any
advertisements for alcoholic beverages.

lobbyists were able to beat back efforts to increase the radius of the U.W. dry district from
one-half mile to one or five miles and even an attempt to require the Madison chief of police to
inspect all incoming student luggage for liquor.[133]

Also during this interlude old line prohibitionists took one last crack at achieving their goal
through partisan politics. Frustrated by the new
regulate-rather-than-eliminate philosophy, they
formed the Madison Prohibition party in 1912
and fielded a mayoral candidate.[134] Though the

candidate attracted twenty-four percent of the
vote, the effect of his candidacy was to take votes
away from the law and order Republican and insure the election of a wet Democrat. However,
the prohibitionist initiative was significant in one
important respect. Its "prohibition" platform was
studded with thoroughly progressive planks demanding such things as a strong regulatory role
of local government, more efficient less expensive
government through civil service, the commission
form of government and even public ownership
of utilities—reflections of the increasing overlap
between the two reform impulses. Indeed the
connection between the two was anything but obscure. The saloon was a source of great power in
Madison, capable of turning out impressive numbers of old soaks on election day to keep the city
"tolerant" of prostitution, gambling, and liquor
law violations. "Progressive" reform of the political and social system therefore required the saloon to go.[135]

A final development during this quiet interlude was the resumption of rapid University of
Wisconsin growth following the imposition of the
one-half mile limit. During the five years following its creation (1907–1912), student enrollment
increased fifty percent. Apparently most parents
around the state felt that Madison was once again
safe for their sons and daughters.[136]

The New Militance, 1913–1916

Then in 1913 after four years of relative quiet on
the wet/dry front, three events produced a sharp
new militance among drys and another wave of
confrontations. First, a jury acquitted a Madison
saloon owner charged with what many thought
was an open and shut case of selling liquor to a
minor. Second, the Common Council had in deference to the saloon lobby, increased the number
of saloon licenses until Madison was once again
about to become a one-hundred-saloon city. Finally, Madison's highest officials refused to force
saloons to close on Sunday as required by both

city ordinances and state statutes. A wave of indignation swept through the dry community. The
time had come they concluded to launch another
offensive and to attack the wets on the Sunday
closing issue. But this time the outcome was destined to be different. Indeed, it was the beginning
of the end of saloons in Madison.

To give themselves maximum legal muscle,
the drys joined hands with Robert Nelson, the
Dane County district attorney who accused
Mayor John B. Heim and Chief of Police Thomas
J. Shaughnessy of "brazen defiance of law and
order," told them that he would issue criminal
charges against them if saloons were not closed
on Sunday. Nelson then sat back to watch them
squirm.[137]

The dilemma was excruciating for both men.
Mayor Heim, a beer drinker, the son of German
immigrants and city water superintendent until
he was elected mayor, was very much a believer
in the Continental Sunday concept. His thoroughly Irish chief of police was also not known
for his abstemiousness. Furthermore the chief had
a brother who owned a popular saloon. Both officials were therefore strong believers in "tolerance" when it came to Sunday closings.

At first Heim and Shaughnessy decided to ignore the challenge with the hope the D.A.'s ardor
would subside. When a protemperance *Journal*
reporter called to ask Heim if he planned to close
the saloons, the mayor hung up.[138] When the same
reporter asked the chief whether he had read the
D.A.'s fifteen-line statement, Shaughnessy replied, "part of it."[139] From that point on the two
men ducked reporters altogether. Heim left town
in his car for destinations unknown and the chief
left the station in search of a lost dog.

The official brushoff strategy, however, hardly
deterred the district attorney who pressed his case.
Though the mayor and the chief were backed by
a popular and Common Council majority in their
pragmatic interpretation of the Sunday closing
law, Nelson's legal position left them no choice.
Chief Shaughnessy therefore issued a terse order
to saloon owners to shut down on Sunday or face
arrest.[140]

POINT: The Pragmatic Case against Sunday Saloon Closings

To my mind no greater number of people in the City of Madison today than in the past years are desirous of having the puritanic Massachusetts Blue Laws enforced. My predecessor in office (Mayor Joseph C. Schubert, 1906–1912) was twice reelected mayor of the city when it was well known that neither he nor the majority of aldermen elected with him were in favor of enforcement of the "Blue Laws. . . ." Your honorable body has refused to adopt any ordinances looking towards any unnecessary restriction upon the personal liberty of the people upon Sunday or any other day.

Much has been said recently about the duty of officials under their oath of office and of my violation of my oath as mayor, and that by people who themselves were and are openly violating the law, for the statutes of this state prohibit any person from keeping open his shop, warehouse, or work on Sunday without any exceptions whatever, and also prohibit the doing of any labor, any business or any work, except work of necessity and charity. They also prohibit any dancing or public diversion, any show or entertainment and prohibit any person from taking part in any sport, game or play on Sunday. These statutes make unlawful the publication, circulation and sale of newspapers on Sunday and makes theatrical performances and other amusement illegal as well. It seems to me that the law should be enforced by the officers elected by the people in such a manner as will work the greatest good for the greatest number of people and not be guided in the performance of their duties by those who only see the mote in their brothers' eyes and fail to note the beam in their own.

If I understand correctly the attitude of others who are now clamoring for the so-called law enforcement, it is not that all of the laws should be enforced, but only such laws as those self-appointed guardians of the people desire to have enforced. It does not mean that beer and whiskey cannot be obtained hereafter on Sunday, but it means that it cannot be obtained by the ordinary laboring man, while anyone with a college degree back of his name, or of sufficient means to be a member of the University Club, the Madison Club, the Elks Club or any other similar club can secure beer and whiskey on Sunday to any extent he desires.

I shall not be a party to any movement that seeks to enforce certain laws of the state relating to Sunday and at the same time shut my eyes to the violation of other Sunday laws. If those Sunday laws are to be enforced upon the people of Madison at this time, they should all

FIGURE 6.41. JOHN B. HEIM. (SHSW WHi(X3)37936)

be enforced upon all alike. It is hypocrisy of the worst kind to enforce one law of the state on the plea that it is the sworn duty of officials to enforce the law, and at the same time ignore other laws that are being violated. It is still worse where a violator of the law himself urges the enforcement of the law as to certain classes and openly argues that others including himself should be permitted to violate the law because he thinks that such a course is proper.

. . . It is unfortunate that this disturbance amongst our people had to be engendered. Our city was in a quiet, peaceful, progressive spirit, we were conducting the city in a business like manner, there was no occasion for this intermeddling with the administration, but the evil spirit has no rest for peace. Brother rises against brother and we cannot forsee what hatred this incipient, probably well-meant law enforcement may bring forth. Let us control our heated passion, ignore these meddlesome, would-be world reformers, and the brotherly spirit will again prevail."

From a statement made to the Madison Common Council on July 11, 1913, by Major John B. Heim.

COUNTERPOINT: The Legal Case for Sunday Saloon Closure

Oath Taken by Mayor Heim at His Inauguration

I, John B. Heim, do solemnly swear that I will support the constitution of the United States, the constitution of the State of Wisconsin, and the charter of the city of Madison and will perform the duties of mayor in and for the city of Madison to the best of my ability, so help me God.

Wisconsin Blue Laws

Section 4595: Any person who shall keep open his shop, warehouse or workhouse or shall do any manner of labor, business, or work except only work of necessity and charity, or be present at any dancing or public diversion, show or entertainment, or take part in any sport, game, or play on the first day of the week, shall be punished by a fine not exceeding ten dollars. . . .

State Law Pertaining to Saloons

Section 1564: If any tavern keeper or other person shall sell, give away or barter any intoxicating liquors on the first day of the week commonly called Sunday, . . . such . . . person so offending shall be punished by a fine of not less than five nor more than twenty-five dollars or by imprisonment in the county jail not to exceed thirty days. . . .

The Sunday shutdown naturally delighted the drys and their sabbatarian allies, but greatly irritated Madison's still wet majority. After a month of enforcing the unpopular law, taking flack from his constituents and dodging reporters, Heim decided to confront his tormentors. In a July 1913 statement to the Common Council, Heim delivered a stinging rebuke to drys—easily the most forceful and eloquent defense of the time-honored policy of selective enforcement.[141]

However, like all Sunday crackdowns before it, its effectiveness depended upon the diligence of the enforcing organization, in this case the Sunday Rest Association whose volunteer members soon grew tired of their Sunday morning saloon inspections. By late summer saloon owners began opening their back doors, and by fall their front doors for business as usual.

But Heim and his wet constituency were in for a rude surprise. When he ran for a second term in the spring of 1914, he was beaten by Adolf Kayser, a lumber dealer who promised tougher and more consistent enforcement of the Sunday closing laws. Seldom in Madison's history had an incumbent been beaten, much less a wet Democrat by a dry Republican! (Kayser beat Heim by a plurality of eight percent.)

Heim's stunning upset did not just happen. It was directly attributable to the presence of a savy militant new organization known as the Madison Dry League. Their single purpose was to *eliminate* the saloon, not suppress or regulate it. Toward that end they launched and sustained a campaign notable for its persistence, flair and cunning.[142]

In addition to turning out Heim, Madison Dry League officials caused a simultaneous referendum on this question: Shall Madison go dry?—and came within an eyelash of winning.[143] Now at last the drys could smell victory. For the first time in Madison's history, the drys stood on the threshhold of having a *political majority*—a dramatic new development.

Eager for what they hoped would be the final and decisive battle, five hundred "determined" members of the Madison Dry League decided to engage their arch-enemy, the Madison Business Protective League, the high-sounding saloon lobby organization, in another wet/dry referendum in April 1915. Through an intense multimedia campaign involving newspaper ads, flyers, tracts, billboards, and tent rallies, drys hammered away on the theme that a saloon-free city would mean a "BETTER, BIGGER AND MORE PROSPEROUS MADISON." Wets countered by saying that if Madison would go dry, it would kill the large and growing convention business and cause an infestation of "blind pigs,"

the term then used for unlicensed saloons. Both wets and drys claimed to have "morality" on their side.[144]

Once again, however, a combination of events prevented drys from making the kill. Following the near dry victory in the 1914 referenda, saloon owners saw the time had come for a strategic retreat and in September 1914 begrudgingly but wisely agreed to a Common Council elimination of fifteen saloons. This cutback plus tough saloon enforcement under Mayor Kayser reduced community indignation just enough to prevent a majority of voters from declaring Madison dry.

What Is the Matter with Madison?

What is the matter with Madison? The answer is clear. We have no united effort. There is too much desire to experiment. We live too much in the shadow of the "Wisconsin Idea," which seems to be—if you think something ought to be reformed, pass a law.

Does anyone think for a minute that the adoption of no license is going to make Madison dry with Middleton seven miles away? Does anyone think that the adoption of no license is going to help this city—is going to make it any better? What is all this hullabaloo about? The grand jury says the city is all right. The records of the court show that the law is being observed. Detectives brought here . . . can find no one selling whiskey on Sunday except drug stores. All this agitation and howl has accomplished is to please a lot of rabid prohibitionists and to give the town a black eye.

We support a Board of Commerce to boost the town and then we have an evening paper pounding the place as a 'sink-hole of iniquity.' The Vice Commission of this state made a report and the evening paper in large black type announced that we had twenty-one places of ill-repute. Where are they? The paid detectives could not find them. Then the Vice Commission says that they count in our public parks. Why don't the prohibitionists abolish the parks? The no-license people tell you that if the eighty-one places of business now occupied by saloons are vacated that these places will immediately be occupied. They forget to tell you about the eight places where license was refused last July have no occupants today except sparrows.

What this city wants is to be let alone. Give the city a chance. You cannot expect a kitten to grow if you keep handling it all the time and you cannot expect the city to thrive if somebody tinkers with the machinery all the time. It wants a little less yellow journalism and a little less riding of a hobby. It wants more truth and the whole truth, more boosting and less knocking. . . . This town needs more getting together along practical business lines. It wants less laws and more enforcement, less selfishness and more effort for the general good. See something good in the other fellow even if he doesn't agree with you on the liquor traffic. . . . We want less canting hypocrisy and more honesty. Then we want everybody to put their shoulder to the wheel and boost and we will have a city that will go forward. Go to the polls and put in a vote for license and continuation of the growth of Madison."

(From a paid announcement by the Madison Business Protective League, Wisconsin State Journal, April 5, 1915, the day before the 1915 no-license election.)

Indeed, the wet victory margin in 1915 went up slightly to 1.44%. Nevertheless for the second consecutive time Madison had come within a handful of votes of going dry. The once arrogant saloon lobby now seemed almost eager to make concessions to stem this gush of dry sentiment. Saloon owners now generally agreed that survival required tough self-regulation and elimination of trouble-making saloons. Consequently for the second year, they went along with another Common Council saloon cutback. Of all the saloons in business just two years before, one out of four had been eliminated. Indeed, some saloon owners were sufficiently concerned about their survival that they started making the distinction between beer-only saloons and the full service hard liquor saloon. If the saloon was about to sink, the beer sellers hoped to be on a different boat.[145]

Meanwhile around the nation dry sentiment was growing very rapidly, largely in response to the astute political maneuvering of the Anti-Saloon League. Indeed by December 1916, eighty-seven percent of all U.S. counties had voted themselves dry under various state and local-option laws although cities generally stayed wet.[146] Equally impressive was the almost unbelievable progress drys had made in the November 1916 congressional elections. According to some observers, enough drys were elected to vote in national prohibition.

Drys also made great strides in the nation's statehouses. In Wisconsin, one of these new drys was William T. Evjue, then business manager and part-time reporter for the *Wisconsin State Journal*. The popular Norwegian and later protege of Senator Robert LaFollette waged a vigorous dry campaign on the Republican ticket in which he portrayed the liquor industry as a pernicious special interest group that had been "double crossing labor for years." His constituents, nearly all Madisonians, gave Evjue a nine percent plurality, the largest ever received by a First District assemblyman.[147] Soon after being seated, he introduced a bill that provided for a *statewide* referendum on the wet/dry question. The bill passed both houses by large majorities but was vetoed

by Governor Emanuel Philipp on the grounds that it would throw fifteen thousand state brewery workers out on the street.

Also in its spring 1916 session, the Wisconsin legislature, responding to growing statewide dry strength, had enacted a law limiting saloons in municipalities to no more than one for every five hundred persons.[148] This bill forced the Madison Common Council to make a cutback on the number of city saloons for the third consecutive year. Following this cut Madison had just sixty-four saloons, the lowest since 1888. On a per capita basis Madison now had only one-third as many saloons as it had during the nineteenth century.[149]

Because of this sharp cutback Madison Dry League members wisely decided not to hold a wet/dry referendum in 1916. They recognized that this latest saloon cutback would reduce antisaloon clamor. Unlike their predecessors who put their chin down and charged for the sake of principle, the Dry League leaders were much more calculating, disciplined and tactical. They did not believe in engaging the enemy if success was not likely.

Victory, 1917–1920

The decision to not hold a wet/dry referendum in the fall of 1916 proved very wise indeed though the reason did not become apparent until early 1917. In January of that year members of the Madison Dry League unanimously concluded that "conditions were never so favorable" for achieving their long sought goal of a dry Madison. They therefore voted to hold another wet/dry referendum during the upcoming April local election.[150] They made their decision largely on the basis of a powerful surge of dry sentiment then sweeping across the country and on the hope of adding organized labor to their list of supporters. What they did not realize was the profound impetus the rapidly deteriorating situation in Europe was about to give to their cause.

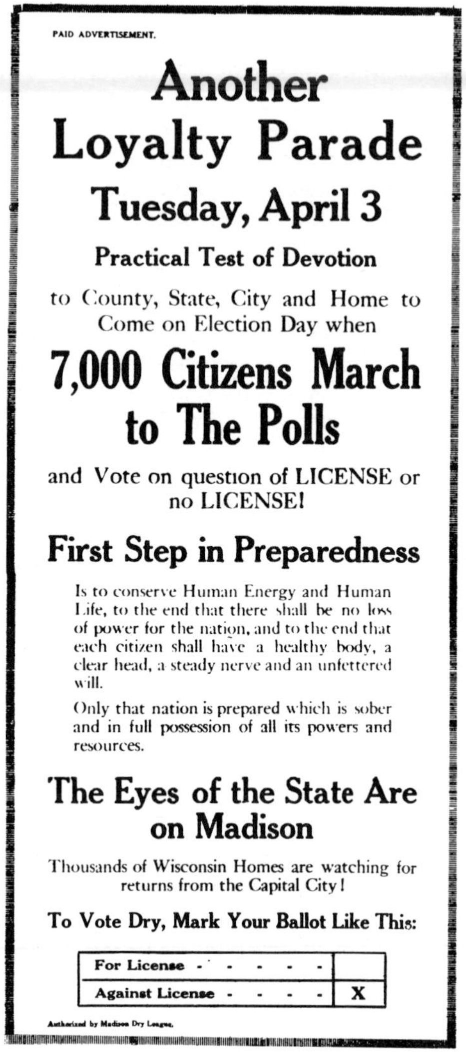

FIGURE 6.42. BE LOYAL: VOTE DRY, THE CRUSADE WITHIN A CRUSADE. As the sound of European war drums grew louder, members of the Madison Dry League jumped on the preparedness bandwagon. The "loyalty" parade described in this newspaper advertisement was scheduled for April 3, 1917, the day Madisonians voted themselves dry and just three days before Wilson declared war on Germany. Clearly preparedness helped make prohibition popular.

In the fall of 1916 Wilson had won reelection on the platform "he kept us out of war." Unfortunately the three-year-old policy of American neutrality toward the European conflict became increasingly untenable in early 1917. In January Germany announced its plan to resume submarine warfare against any American ships in the European war zone in response to which Wilson broke off diplomatic relations with Germany. This event—in conjunction with a simmering sense of outrage at the German invasion of Belgium, the alleged atrocities, U-boats sinking passenger ships, and several other developments—caused American opinion to become much more bellicose.

This new belligerence was quickly evident in Madison. Fanned by strong patriotic winds, "loyalty" and "sacrifice" took on a new meaning. Although the magnitude and nature of American involvement in the war was anything but clear, the need for America to enter the war at least as a major supplier of food and war material seemed increasingly inevitable as the weeks went by.

Leaders of the Madison Dry League were quick to see the ease with which this war fever could be exploited to enlarge the local dry vote. After all with the Allies in grave need of supplies, who could justify the continued flow of grains and coal into something so obviously unnecessary as beverage alcohol? Patriotism therefore became the bugle call to woo wavering wets into the dry camp.

With the election just days away officials of the Madison Dry League were hopeful but anxious. So were their counterparts in the Madison Business Protective Association. So great was interest in this confrontation that the Madison Gas and Electric Company developed an ingenious technique to instantly communicate the results of the election to nearly every household in Madison—at least those with electricity. If the wets won the election, MG&E officials would turn out the lights for a second and then turn them back on again. If the drys won, they would turn out the lights twice in succession. Never before in Madison's history had households been able to get election data so quickly.[151]

After a day of aggressive electioneering on both sides, voters went home to await the signal. They did not have to wait long. At 9:00 P.M., just one hour after the polls closed, the electric lights in Madison homes blinked twice. After decades of fighting, the drys had finally won! The following day Richard Lloyd Jones, *Journal* editor, rushed into print with a panegyric. Said the flamboyant editor: "THE LONG FIGHT IS WON. Madison has at last glorified herself. She stands before the world a strong clean decent community, a city fit to welcome the youth of a great American commonwealth, a city in which the state may be justly proud. . . ."[152]

Casualties of the referenda were the remaining sixty-four Madison saloons, which closed their doors at midnight June 30, 1917, and the small financially ailing Breckheimer Brewery, which closed its doors a few days before.[153]

Newspapers reported that the saloons did a big business on their last day and some patrons bought so much booze that their basements began to look like "wholesale liquor stores."[154] Very significantly, however, Madison's two remaining breweries, the Fauerbach and the Hausmann kept right on making beer. Although the law prevented them from selling any beer directly to Madison outlets or individuals, there was nothing in the law that prevented them from selling their product *outside* Madison. Using this loophole both breweries set up warehouses in the Town of Middleton from which point their beer could be purchased by thirsty Madisonians. The obliging breweries even set up "express companies" known as the Madison and Middleton Express Company and the Middleton Express companies to provide convenient home delivery to customers.[155]

Saloon interests were anything but resigned to their fate and vowed to restore Madison to the wet category at the earliest opportunity. That opportunity came during still another wet/dry referendum in April 1918, following the submittal of a petition this time bearing the names of presumably thirsty former saloon customers who

found the Middleton Express Company a much less convenient way to get their beer than the corner saloon. But once again on election night the lights in Madison homes blinked twice signalling another victory by the drys. This time, however, the victory margin was a razor-thin thirty-six votes out of 8004 cast. Both sides charged fraud and began legal actions to secure a recount. Eight months later the adjusted official count showed that Madison had stayed dry by just one astounding vote—the closest election in city history.[156]

The exciting pitched battles between Madison wets and drys in 1917 and 1918 though engrossing the energies of combatants on both sides were in one important sense utterly irrelevant. The arena that mattered was not localities or even states but rather what was happening at the national level. Just three days after Madison had voted itself dry on April 3, 1917, President Wilson declared war on Germany. In December 1917, the dryest congress ever elected and the proud product of the years of Anti-Saloon League lobbying approved the eighteenth constitutional amendment making illegal the manufacture and sale of any "intoxicating" beverages. On January 16, 1919, just one year and one month after Congress acted, the thirty-sixth state ratified the amendment. Under the terms of the amendment, the nation would therefore go dry one year later, that is, at 12:00 A.M., January 16, 1920.[157]

Meanwhile in September 1918, Wilson using his wartime powers established a stringent food conservation program, which required the nation's breweries to shut their doors beginning December 1, 1918. Logic for the program was compelling and straightforward! Vast amounts of coal and grain used to brew beer were needed for the war effort.[158]

In accord with Wilson's order Madison's two remaining breweries were forced to close their doors on December 1, 1918. The only hope for Madison brewers and saloons—indeed for all the nation's alcohol beverage business—lay in the definition of the word "intoxicating." Nearly everyone recognized that the continued manufacture of regular beer containing twelve percent

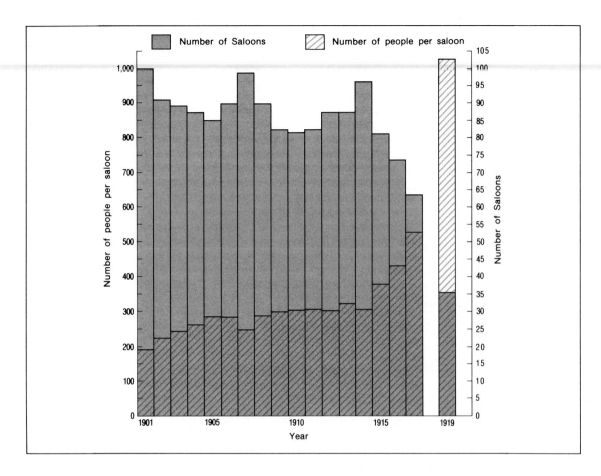

FIGURE 6.43. THE PROGRESSIVE DEMISE OF THE SALOON IN MADISON. From the time Madison became a city in 1856 until 1900 the number of saloons averaged one for every 151 people or one for every thirty-eight adult males. As noted in the above graph, the period from 1900 to 1920 produced a dramatic change of these ratios. Although the number of saloons nearly hit one hundred three times, growing population meant fewer saloons per capita. Before being shut down by national Prohibition the ratio of saloons to people rose to over one thousand.

of alcohol by weight would be outlawed by the eighteenth amendment, but many believed that the manufacture and sale of "near beer" containing just 2½% of alcohol by weight would escape the federal definition of "intoxicating." However, even under this scenario three things would have to happen to allow the resumption of Madison beer brewing. First, the state would have to authorize production of near beer; second, the

voters of Madison would have to restore the city to the wet column through another referendum; and third, the Common Council would have to grant licenses to brewers and saloon owners.

Madison's wets launched this unlikely offensive by successfully petitioning for another referendum in April 1919. This time, however, Madison political chemistry favored the wets. Following the Armistice the drys lost one of their

most persuasive arguments, namely, the stern lash of wartime sacrifice. Indeed if the signatures of twenty-five hundred persons on the referenda petition was any indication, a new mood of indulgence had swept over the city. This time Madisonians voted wet by a decisive five-to-four ratio.[159] Next to act was the state legislature, which in June 1919 passed a bill allowing the production and sale of near beer subject of course to any federal rulings.[160] Then in August 1919 the Common Council granted near beer licenses to both the Fauerbach and Hausmann breweries and to thirty-six saloons.[161] And so once again Madison brewers filled their vats with fermenting though weak lager and saloon patrons passed back and forth through the swinging doors.

Meanwhile, however, at the national level, the Anti-Saloon League had found a way to force the nation to go dry *before* the beginning of constitutional prohibition in January 1920. To do this they got Congress to *extend* wartime conservation measures saying that the war was not really over until the country was "fully demobilized." This lame logic was then incorporated in the National Prohibition Enforcement Bill better known as the Volstead Act. The Volstead Act also provided the critical long-awaited definition of "intoxicating" as any beverage containing more than one-half percent of alcohol by weight.[162]

Under the terms of the Volstead Act the one-half percent definition went into effect in October 1919. Thus, after a two-month near beer interlude, Madison breweries and saloons were forced to close their doors again.

This left the Madison Common Council with the mechanical but unpleasant task of making local ordinances conform to the nation's laws. So unpopular was this task that only eleven of Madison's twenty aldermen, a bare majority, even showed up to vote in the new dry regime.[163] Clearly, it was the end of an era. No more Middleton Express Companies. No more near beer. The Volstead Act had even banished the word "saloon." The entire nation had gone dry.

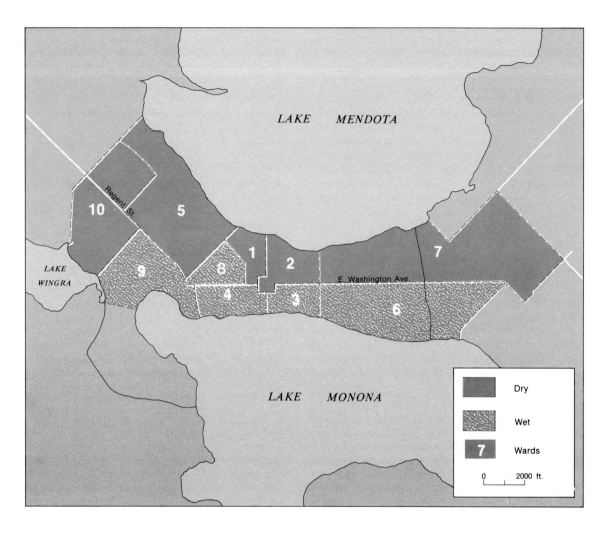

FIGURE 6.44. THE DEMOGRAPHICS AND GEOGRAPHY OF WET/DRY SENTIMENT.

FIGURE 6.44. THE DEMOGRAPHICS AND GEOGRAPHY OF WET/DRY SENTIMENT. Between 1901 and 1919 Madison voters went to the polls ten times to register their views on alcohol. Three times (1901, 1904, and 1907) Madisonians voted on the amount of the liquor license fee and seven times (1901, 1910, 1914, 1915, 1917, 1918, and 1919) they voted on prohibition. A study of these ten elections showed that wet/dry sentiment in Madison was remarkably stable. As noted in the map, there was a kind of Mason-Dixon line on the issue; wards fronting on Mendota voted dry whereas wards fronting on Monona voted wet.

The most fervent and consistent supporters of the dry crusade were concentrated in an arc extending from "Mansion Hill" to lower Langdon to University Heights to Wingra Park. On the ten liquor-related referenda, two out of three voters from these areas supported the dry side of the issue. The hotbed of wet sentiment came from the Eighth Ward between West Washington and State Street, the Third Ward representing the King Street area, and the Ninth Ward representing the area around Monona Bay. On the same ten liquor-related referenda, two out of three voters from these areas voted wet.

The number shown beside the ward designation is a weighted index reflecting both intensity and the persistence of the wet/dry vote.

Wet/dry sentiment was closely correlated with ward population composition. Generally speaking, the wards that had the most white collar native-born protestants registered the most intense and consistent prohibition votes. Conversely, wards with the highest blue collar, foreign-born Catholics registered the strongest and most consistent wet sentiment.

Like their counterparts around the nation, Madison prohibitionists tended to be antiforeign (nativist) in their outlook. They saw Madison's large German population as the principal carriers and transmitters of the wet bacillus. After all Madison's breweries were not named the Bradshaw, the Fuller, and the Hancock but rather the Breckheimer, the Fauerbach, and the Hausmann.

Popularizing prohibition in Madison proved to be a very difficult task. Credit for transforming Madison's almost irretrievable wetness into a new dry majority must go to the new dry leadership, which took over the languishing crusade around the turn of the century. Much of their success was attributable to their painstaking assembly of a majority coalition consisting of hard core prohibitionists who agreed to swallow their purist principles and support saloon regulation, progressives who saw saloons as a source of corruption and unnecesssary social cost, businessmen who blamed saloons for cessation of student enrollment growth at the University of Wisconsin, Madison's largest industry, and finally, patriots who voted for what they believed to be temporary prohibition to help the nation save scarce resources. Much credit must also be given to their brilliant tactics, which allowed the drys, almost always a political minority, to choose the time and place where the greatest force could be applied to the weakest point. This gave the drys the enormous advantage of keeping the wets on the defensive during nearly all of this two-decade period.

Much credit must go to their tremendous skill in merchandising their point of view. Indeed there were moral arguments, economic arguments, patriotic arguments—an argument for everyone. And when it came to techniques the drys were true virtuosos. They held tent rallies, passed out informative tracts, brought in big name, high credibility speakers, sent flatbed trucks through city streets carrying changing lantern slide shows, and even sponsored huge children's parades.[164]

Impressive as dry coalition building, tactics, and merchandising were, these skills and techniques do not explain dry intensity and persistence. These key qualities can only be understood by acknowledging the mainspring of prohibition, the force that powered the crusade throughout its life, namely, a strong, even stern moral connection between the saloon and alcohol. Alcohol after all corrupted the body, the temple of God, stirred up lust, removed inhibitions, and debilitated human reason. Drinking alcohol was therefore an individual sin with dire social consequences. This

was why Richard Lloyd Jones in a spirited 1914 editorial demanded a mayor who exercised a "strong MORAL FORCE" in municipal improvement, who considered ethics just as important as asphalt roads, and who would give battle to the saloons "as would a CHRISTIAN SOLDIER"[165] Prohibitionists stood for all that was sweet, light, and pure whereas the saloon attracted the dark, evil, and bitter side of human nature. This was why Prohibition became a one-dimensional theory of individual and social salvation, indeed the most compelling Protestant crusade of the early twentieth century.

Though claims were made to the contrary, this stern morality was not entirely benign. In practice it proved to be paternalistic, intolerant, and elitist and therefore a source of friction between Catholics, foreigners, and workers who constituted Madison's saloon patrons and the Yankee, white collar, Protestant middle to upper income groups who most fervently supported prohibition. This same stern morality, which gave the dry cause cohesion and direction, was also a source of other shortcomings. Because the drys were preoccupied by the evil of saloons, they failed to see the social function the institution played, particularly for workers and immigrants, and therefore paid scant attention to the need for alternatives. The harsh moral spotlight used by the prohibitionists caused them to see saloons more as a cause than a symptom. They blithely assumed that if the saloon were banished, all the problems from poverty to promiscuity would be banished also. Unfortunately this illusion would soon be shattered by the very dry regime they worked so hard to establish.[166]

Ultimately then the drys succeeded in inflicting their morality upon the masses. Their success, however, was not merely the result of dry efforts. Indeed the wets played a major role in their own defeat by failing to see that their own excesses made them extremely vulnerable to dry attacks. Indeed if they had caught the reform virus then sweeping the city and nation, they might have averted a local dry takeover altogether. But

among Madison saloon owners the old patterns did not die easily. They continued to send their smelly saloon regulars to the polls until the very end. They tried to do business as usual, but discovered, much too late, that times had changed and they had not changed with them.

The City Beautiful: The Movement Matures

By 1899, the Madison Park and Pleasure Drive Association (MPPDA) had become a highly respected organization whose preeminence in the acquisition, development, and maintenance of pleasure drives was unquestioned. Indeed, the new organization so ably led by John M. Olin might well have continued to concentrate all its attentions on the construction and maintenance of rustic carriage drives had not several land owners in the spring of 1899 offered to sell fourteen acres of land near the Lake Mendota outlet to the city as a park. The parcel was easily worth eight thousand dollars but the asking price was just fifteen hundred. Association directors immediately passed a resolution urging the city to buy and develop this land and turn it into an "exceedingly beautiful" park.[167] But then just one week after the association directors took this action—and before the city could respond—Daniel K. Tenney, long time Madison activist and association supporter, intervened with an offer which forever altered the purpose of the association and the history of Madison. Tenney offered to buy the land for fifteen hundred dollars and to give another twenty-five hundred for its development as a park *providing:* (1) that the association would hold the land in trust for the city; (2) that the association would develop and maintain the park; and (3) that another twenty-five hundred would be raised for park development from other sources.[168]

Tenney's offer posed several difficult questions about the purpose of the association and its relationship with the city of Madison. Olin and his

FIGURE 6.45. TWO BOYS AND A SUMMER DAY. Too much playing on a summer day may well have tired out these two boys who fell asleep beside a Tenney Park lagoon. The lagoon behind the boys was dredged in 1900 as a part of the original Tenney Park plan but was filled and planted in 1910 as a part of a park enlargement plan prepared by John Nolen. Shown in the rear is the Sherman Avenue bridge and the malt house owned by the Hausmann Brewery. (SHSW WHi(X3)29646)

association directors knew that Madison density and population had nearly doubled between 1880 and 1899 and that the Capitol Park, the university grounds and Orton Park were hardly adequate any more as recreational spaces. Indeed, throughout the 1890s Olin and a few other opinion leaders gained converts with their notion that parks were no longer frills but rather "the lungs of the city" and "necessary breathing space."[169] Olin also recognized that the limited voluntary subscription resources of his association would have to be earmarked for the maintenance of the drive system *outside* the city where a general tax could not be imposed.[170] On this basis the popular association head concluded that the acquisition, development, and maintenance of *in-city* parks,

such as the fourteen acres to be purchased with the Tenney grant, was preeminently a *City of Madison* responsibility.

Nevertheless the city manifested very little interest in parks. Some of its reluctance was financial. A series of very large one-time outlays for a water system, a sewerage treatment system, plus ongoing outlays for streets and other matters, put the city very near the limit of its statutory borrowing power. Consequently, the city spent very few of its dollars on parks. During its first six years (1894–1900) the association outspent the city by a twelve-to-one ratio. Another source of city reluctance was "political" in the sense that the majority of council members did not feel that parks were a municipal responsibility. Even a new 1897

state law that authorized Madison to *own* parkland, but with no obligation to maintain or improve them, was ignored by the city Common Council.[171]

Given the city's reluctance to accept responsibility for parks, Olin urged the MPPDA board of directors to accept Tenney's four-thousand-dollar gift and to begin raising the required twenty-five hundred dollars. Association directors got their own members to contribute one thousand dollars of this amount and persuaded the Common Council to contribute the remaining fifteen hundred.[172] Meanwhile the city council dubbed the new facility Tenney Park in honor of its benefactor. Actual development of the park began in 1900.

FIGURE 6.46. MADISON'S FIRST PARK PHILANTHROPISTS.   These four remarkable men— a lumber dealer, two lawyers, and a realtor—though differing markedly in temperamer and careers, shared much in common. All had English ancestors and New England roots, all were brainy, diligent, resourceful, successful, and wealthy. But most important of all for the history of Madison, they all deeply loved the city and gave generously to make it a better place to live. In a span of just ten years (1899–1909), these four rich men gave nearly $110,000 for the purchase and development of 146 acres of parks that today bear their name.

DANIEL KENT TENNEY (1834–1915)

During the 1850s many families left New York state for greener pastures in the great developing west. One such family was headed by Daniel Tenney who with his wife and ten children struck out for Green Bay, Wisconsin, in 1850. However, an illness forced the family to stop their westward trek and settle in a small community near Cleveland. It was in this small community where Daniel Kent Tenney, the youngest child of the Tenney family, attended school. At age sixteen young Daniel found that he could bear no longer the arbitrary rule then common in classrooms, and so he decided to join his older brothers who had settled in Wisconsin a few years earlier. At first he worked for his brother Horace, the editor of the Madison *Wisconsin Argus,* but then upon the advice of his brother Henry, a Portage lawyer, Daniel decided to study law. He was admitted to the bar in 1855, just two weeks before he turned twenty-one, and immediately formed partnership with one of Madison's leading lawyers.

At first he concentrated on developing his practice but soon got involved in civic affairs. In 1860 Tenney was elected to the Madison Common Council. At age twenty-six he was not only the youngest man to ever serve on that body up to that time, but he was also its only Republican—and a firebrand warhawk at that. Following the

Civil War Tenney forcefully argued that Madison's brightest future lay in attracting Southern tourists and not factories as many others believed.

But then in 1870, apparently tiring of small town law and politics, Tenney pulled up his Madison stakes and established a law firm in Chicago where he quickly won national acclaim for winning cases against insurance companies who refused to pay damage claims following the disastrous 1871 Chicago fire. Significantly, Tenney did not forget Madison. In fact, he subscribed to its newspapers, returned to the city frequently, and even got involved in major improvement projects. In 1885, for example, he and a handful of other investors bought the Madison Street Railway Company.

Finally in 1897 after twenty-seven years in Chicago, the sixty-three-year-old Tenney returned to his home town where he once again plunged into civic affairs with a vengeance. It was during this period that he made his fateful offer to buy the land near the Mendota outlet, an offer that forced the Madison Park and Pleasure Drive Association to become a semiprivate parks department, triggered an extraordinary era of park philanthropy, and made his name a household word among Madisonians. (SHSW WHi(X3)37754)

THOMAS E. BRITTINGHAM (1860-1924)

When Thomas E. Brittingham died on May 2, 1924 at the age of sixty-four, he was reportedly Madison's richest man. His assets—including 126 lumber yards, thousands of acres of standing timber all over the country, oil wells, and large interests in financial institutions—were valued at between ten to fifteen million dollars.

Brittingham, the son of Dr. and Mrs. Irvin Baird Brittingham, was born in Hannibal, Missouri, where he attended private schools and Hannibal College. At the age of twenty he went to Colorado and California where he engaged in various mercantile businesses. But he did not find his fortune in the West and in 1885 at the age of twenty-five returned to McFarland, Wisconsin, where he opened his first lumber yard. In 1888 he moved to Madison where he spent the rest of his life actively engaged in business, philanthropy, and civic affairs.

Though he is probably most remembered for his $19,500 contribution, which transformed a stinking slough into the beauty spot that now bears his name, Brittingham donated generously to many other local causes including the first Neighborhood House now located at 29 South Mills, Madison General Hospital, the first U.W. student infirmary and the famous Weinmann statue of Lincoln that stands in front of Bascom Hall.

Brittingham's service to the city, state, and university included terms as chairman of the Forest Hills Cemetery Commission (1907–1912), curator for the Wisconsin State Historical Society (1907–1913), chairman of the State Park Board, a predecessor of the Department of Natural Resources (1909–1918), and U.W. regent and chairman of the Executive Committee (1910–1912).

From the turn of the century to about 1915 Brittingham lived in a large home at 640 North Henry Street, but in 1916 when fraternity noise and crowding began to encroach upon his privacy, he bought fourteen acres in the Highlands and built a four-thousand-square-foot home. He whimsically named the home "Dunmuvin" to signify that this was his last home and that he was indeed "done movin'." Under the terms of Brittingham's will, the university became owner of this elegant country estate. Today it serves as the official home of the university presidents.

Significantly, Brittingham's philanthropy did not cease when he died; in fact, it increased. He left two foundations, one designed to benefit the university and the other to benefit the city. Over the years these foundations have assisted hundreds of worthy causes.

GEORGE B. BURROWS (1832-1909)

Unlike other members of the first group of major park philanthropists, George B. Burrows waited until he died in 1909 to make his major gift to future generations—his twelve-acre family estate then valued at fifteen thousand dollars laying between Lake Mendota and North Sherman Avenue. In accord with his will the parcel, which boasted 550 feet of prime Mendota frontage, was named Burrows Park. At the time the park lay outside the city but was accepted on the grounds that the city would grow around it as indeed it did.

Burrows was born and raised in Vermont but went to New York City when he was twenty-one to pursue a business career. Five years later he moved to Sauk City, Wisconsin, where he conducted a bank. Then in 1865 at the age of thirty-three, he bought a well-known local real estate agency in Madison and settled in the city. Although Burrows expanded the business from a local to a truly statewide agency, it did not occupy all his time

nor did it satisfy his desire to serve his city. In 1870 the rising young real estate dealer endeared himself to Madisonians by persuading a well-known Chicago theater operator to convert a second-class theater into a first-class facility capable of attracting the best touring companies. From 1878 to 1882 he represented Madison in the Wisconsin senate and in 1895 he represented the city in the assembly. Burrows also took an active part in Madison's New England Society and in various fraternal organizations.

But of all his civic interests probably none was stronger than the interest he manifested in the Madison Park and Pleasure Drive Association. As a realtor in a rapidly developing city, he knew the importance of securing park land for future generations and therefore became an active member of that organization from the time it was founded until he died. (SHSW WHi(X3)37688)

FIGURE 6.46—Continued

WILLIAM FREEMAN VILAS (1840-1908)

William Freeman Vilas was one of those men who because he was born into such favorable circumstances, might well have spent his entire life quietly sipping the family fortune. But his father, Levi Vilas, a wealthy lawyer, sagacious real estate investor, and member of the Vermont legislature, had more ambitious plans for his eldest son and indeed for his entire family. In 1851 when William was just ten years old, Levi sold the elegant brick family home in the village of Chelsea, Vermont, and moved to Madison, Wisconsin, a city that by virtue of its selection as the permanent state capital three years earlier seemed like an attractive place to settle. Soon after his arrival the senior Vilas built a huge home at the corner of Langdon and North Henry, invested heavily in area real estate, helped start the predecessor of the First Wisconsin Bank, and even served a term as Madison mayor (1861-1862).

Young William attended the University of Wisconsin Preparatory School and at age thirteen entered the university proper. He graduated first in his class in 1858 and promptly entered the Albany (New York) Law School from which he graduated in 1860. Following his return to Madison he formed a law firm and presented his first case before the Wisconsin Supreme Court before he was twenty-one. When the Civil War broke out he enlisted, formed his own company, was commissioned a captain, and went on to fight valiantly in the Battle of Vicksburg.

Following the war Vilas married Anna Fox, the daughter of a prominent Madison physician, and resumed the practice of law. He quickly established a reputation as a brilliant attorney. Blessed by an awesome memory, outstanding judgment, a capacity for hard work, and a drive to excel, his reputation grew, and he began attracting large corporate clients including the Chicago Northwestern Railroad. In addition to practicing law, he taught in the U.W. Law School, engaged in a variety of business ventures, served a term in the Wisconsin assembly (1885 Session), and a term as a U.W. regent (1881-1885) where he spearheaded a major building expansion program and the creation of the now famous agricultural "short course." His astute mind and superlative oratorical abilities caused prominent politicos to offer him a seat of the Wisconsin Supreme Court and an opportunity to run for governor, but Vilas declined them both.

His national political career was launched when he gave a magnificent eulogy to General Grant at the 1879 Democratic National Committee. At this convention Vilas backed Grover Cleveland and stumped Wisconsin for his election. Following Cleveland's victory in November, 1884, the new president appointed Vilas as his postmaster general.

As Postmaster Vilas earned a reputation as a tough-minded reformer who pursued his duties with great energy and effectiveness. Moreover, he became a very close personal friend of President Cleveland's—much closer in fact than any other cabinet official. From time to time the president would even drop in at Vilas's Washington home provided he could be assured "a good cool glass or two of beer. . . ." Vilas' wife Annie was widely recognized as the closest Washington friend of President Cleveland's winsome wife, Frances. Thus when Cleveland visited Madison in the fall of 1887 while on a tour of the Midwest, he stayed, to no one's surprise, at the palatial home of his close friend at 12 East Gilman. After a three-year stint as postmaster general, Vilas agreed to become secretary of the Department of the Interior, a post he held for one year until Cleveland was ousted in the 1888 election.

In 1890 Vilas ran for and won one of Wisconsin's two senate seats. When Cleveland won his second term in 1892, Vilas once again became a confidant and advisor to the president. However, in 1896 when his term expired, he found a Republican rip tide rampaging through the land, a strong reaction to the serious depression the country suffered in 1893–94. Vilas therefore found himself, at age fifty-six, politically unemployed. Not only were the Republicans very much in charge nationally and in Wisconsin, but Vilas' conservative brand of Democracy was on the ropes.

Vilas took advantage of his political retirement to plunge into business ventures with characteristic vigor. In addition to investing in bank securities, he bought huge tracts of the "noble pine" in Wisconsin, Michigan, and Washington and formed the Nekoosa-Edwards Paper Company. These actions caused his fortune to grow from an estimated three hundred thousand dollars just before his service as a cabinet officer to well over two million dollars before his death.

Political retirement also gave Vilas an opportunity to enjoy leisure time and domestic activities. He travelled, played tennis with his neighbor and arch-political rival, Phil Spooner (letting out a loud war whoop each time he won a point), joined the elite Town and Gown Club for their monthly discussions on timely topics, and fished in Lake Mendota. In 1902 he transformed his already large and comfortable home into a Victorian mansion of unrestrained splendor by adding new library and kitchen wings, installing white marble fireplaces, Tiffany windows, oriental carpeting, and rare hardwoods—all with the thought of deeding the home to the university for use as the official president's residence. But as fate would have it, this sterling idea wasn't ever realized and Madison's fanciest home was razed in 1963. Today the site is occupied by National Guardian Life Insurance Company.

Of his various civic commitments the Madison Park and Pleasure Drive Association was probably his favorite. In addition to giving unprecedently large amounts for the purchase and development of Madison Park, he also presided at their prestigious annual meetings, made his home available for park acquisition strategy sessions, and gave generously of his counsel.

Vilas died on August 27, 1908, following a brain hemorrhage five weeks earlier. In his extraordinary will, he decreed that most of his estate be left to the University of Wisconsin until it reached the sum of thirty million dollars, at which time it was to be spent. Vilas Communications Hall, the handsome radio, television, and classroom complex at the intersection of Park Street and University Avenue was the result. (SHSW WHi(X28)1179)

The acquisition and development of Tenney Park was a major milestone in the history of Madison open space—the unwitting beginning of a brilliant period of Madison park development. Although Tenney Park was not the first park to which the association received title (Owen Park had that distinction), it was the first *in-city* park of the association and the first Madison park providing public lake access.[173] The park also marked the beginning of a more "democratic" orientation for the association. Before Tenney Park, it had been in the exclusive business of providing drives *outside* the city for relatively wealthy carriage and buggy owners. Beginning with Tenney Park, however, the association expanded its focus to include in-city parks for the less affluent. This change reflected Olin's belief that the "laboring portion of our City" needed "a place of rest and recreation" too, and that the location of Tenney Park near the "factory district" made it ideally suited to serve this need. It was a conscious acknowledgement that one could never get many people out to the country but that with parks like Tenney, you could bring the country to the people. In a related move, Olin broadened his membership base by reducing the annual membership fee from twenty-five dollars to just five dollars.[174]

But of all the precedents established by the Tenney gift, none was more important than the provision that the association hold the land in trust for the city. It was this detail in the fine print of Tenney's offer that provided the legal basis for the rise of a powerful, quasi-private Madison "Parks Department," whose legacy to the city was so extraordinary.[175]

During the three years following the Tenney grant, Olin became increasingly disturbed by the city's failure to take the initiative and buy parks for its citizens. Hoping to prod the city into what he thought was their legitimate role, Olin told association members at their 1902 annual meeting that Madison should have one acre of park for every two hundred inhabitants or one hundred acres more than the seventeen acres the city then had and that the city should be spending twelve thousand dollars a year for park purposes, quite

a contrast, he noted, from the five hundred fifty per year it was then spending.[176] In spite of these exhortations from one of Madison's most respected citizens, city officials refused to pick up the gauntlet.

Finally in early 1903 Olin decided the time had come for a bold initiative. On January 9, 1903, Olin assembled thirty of Madison's most influential citizens in the palatial home of Senator William F. Vilas, and proceeded to outline what even he admitted was an "exceedingly visionary" plan. His plan called for deepening and widening of the Yahara between Mendota and Monona creating a parkway along both sides, raising all eight bridges across the Yahara so that boats would have at least eight feet clearance, and constructing a lock at the Mendota outlet.[177]

For two weeks after the meeting at the Vilas home, local papers gave the concept extensive and favorable coverage. But the idea was immediately attacked by—of all people—D. K. Tenney, Madison's noisiest conservative. Tenney railed against the project on the grounds that the primary beneficiaries would be wealthy launch owners, that no more than one launch would go through the proposed locks on a given day, that there would never be more than one hundred launches on both lakes, that not a penny of city money should be spent on the project because taxes were too high already and, finally, because there were more pressing needs for private money.[178]

Fortunately Olin had some powerful chips on his side of the board. The rapidly growing numbers of gasoline and electric launch owners, most of whom were association members, found the idea very appealing because their sleek crafts could then travel back and forth between both lakes.[179] Property owners in the vicinity of the Yahara were naturally pleased at the prospect of their real estate increasing in value. Park advocates were excited by the prospect of twenty more acres of park land and seventy-two hundred more feet of water frontage. And town boosters were elated at the prospect of transforming the banks of the river from a "dumping place for defunct horses, cats and dogs" to a beauty spot for all.[180]

The speed with which the project proceeded was almost breathtaking. Three weeks after the meeting in the Vilas home, Senator Vilas met with the presidents of both the Northwestern and Milwaukee Railroads and secured their approval to cooperate in raising their four railroad bridges across the Yahara. Just in case the railroads proved obstinate, Olin got a bill through the legislature before the end of March 1903 that would *force* the railroads to do the work! Meanwhile at a special Common Council meeting, he secured city endorsement of the project. By April, Olin was able to announce that nearly five hundred persons had subscribed $20,600 for the project— five thousand more than the goal—and that nearly all the necessary land had been *donated* to the city for the project! By June the dredges began their work. Thus, in just six months, the Yahara River Project had gone from concept to construction.[181]

The Yahara River Parkway placed beyond question Olin's reputation as the *impressario extraordinaire*. To get the legislature to pass a special bill in less than two months, to raise $20,600 in just three months, to dispatch one of the most influential men in the state to lobby railroad presidents, to complete the project in just three construction seasons, and to get numerous public-minded citizens to *donate* their Yahara water frontage, were all truly impressive accomplishments and signalled the rise of a very powerful but benevolent force in Madison politics.

To Olin's great delight, the Yahara Parkway project primed the pump for the golden era of park-oriented philanthropy in Madison. In 1904, just one year after the beginning of the parkway, William F. Vilas gave the association $18,000 to create a 63-acre park on the shores of Lake Wingra in honor of his deceased son, Henry. Then in 1905 came a check for $8,000 from Thomas E. Brittingham for a 27-acre park bearing his name around Monona Bay. An excited association official concluded "the park spirit had become contagious."[182] Moreover, these huge contributions were just the beginning of large additional gifts from Vilas, Brittingham and Tenney.[183] Other

FIGURE 6.47. MONONA BAY. In May 1904, a traveling salesman who made his home in Madison gave a talk at the prestigious annual meeting and banquet of the Madison Park and Pleasure Drive Association. Speaking as a traveling man, he reminded his gilt-edged audience that ninety percent of all persons entered the city by train and got their first impression of ''beautiful Madison'' from the scene shown above. Of course, the scene was anything but beautiful. The water was covered with a green and yellow slimy scum, and the shores were covered with dead fish, kitchen garbage, and winter ashes. And the smell was anything but pleasant. On a hot day with the wind from the south, persons walking along West Washington Avenue said the stench from the bay almost took your breath away. Former Mayor Elisha Keyes thought the bay so hopeless that he urged that the entire area be filled.

This photograph shows the unappetizing Monona Bay scene sometime during the summer of 1904 near the point where East Wilson Street intersected with the lake. It was precisely this type of situation that made MPPDA members and nearly all city officials eager to create a more esthetic, crisply defined shoreline, devoid of disease-breeding slime, flies, and mosquitos—something that would impress, not repel, Madison visitors.

Having subjected his audience to what he described as an ''uncouth'' description, the earnest traveling salesman unveiled his dream for this area—a grand shoreline-hugging city park featuring rose gardens, a public boathouse, and rustic benches. Such talks did much to galvanize support for the move to transform this ancient eyesore to a beauty spot. Indeed, it may have been this talk which motivated Thomas E. Brittingham to make his first contribution for the park that bore his name. (SHSW WHi(X3)23443)

FIGURE 6.48. EARLY BRITTINGHAM PARK. Real momentum behind the idea of a park around Monona Bay actually began in 1903 when the city acquired by gift and acquisition three blocks of land fronting on the bay. Unfortunately, this fourteen-hundred-foot stretch was just a small part of the total frontage that MPPDA officials wanted and no money was available to either buy or improve the remaining shoreline. Once again, a generous patron, Thomas E. Brittingham, came to the rescue. Between 1905 and 1908 this generous gentleman gave $24,500 for the improvement of this area. O. C. Simonds, the trusted MPPDA landscape architect, prepared plans for the park and work got underway in 1906.

This 1906 photograph shows a part of the park shortly after it had been filled in by the sand dredge. The shot was taken from the railroad trestle and looks northeasterly across the triangle-shaped part of the bay. The Brittingham boathouse was built just beyond the pool of water in the left center of the photograph.

To create Brittingham Park an extraordinary amount of fill material was required. Nearly all of it, the equivalent of 41,666 large dump truck loads, was sucked from the bottom of the bay by a sand dredge. This process also deepened the bay so that bottom-growing weeds would not become a problem. (SHSW WHi(X3)27368) large gifts were received from George B. Burrows and A. H. Hollister (see p. 327). Between 1899 and 1917 these large donors gave more than $133,000 to the association.

The Vilas, Brittingham, Tenney gifts coupled with the subscriber-funded Yahara River Parkway caused a veritable explosion in the amount of Madison parkland. In fact by 1905 Madison-owned park acreage jumped from a modest four acres (Orton Park) and no public water frontage to 154 acres and 4.6 miles of public water access frontage! Using the same parkland standard Olin had used in 1902 to demonstrate parkland deficiency, Madison in 1905 had thirty percent *more* parkland than it needed![184] Probably no other city of its size in Wisconsin and few in the nation were better provided with parks and open spaces.[185]

Noteworthy as the record of major benefactors was, the record established by all remaining association contributors was in some ways even more impressive. The most striking characteristic of this group was the large number of small annual gifts from those of more moderate means. Between 1902 and 1909 an average of 765 Madisonians, about one household in ten, voluntarily contributed money for the acquisition, development, and maintenance of parks. About sixty percent of all pledges were just five dollars, the minimum amount needed for association membership. Moreover, these small grants were solicited through what was called "the postcard system"—a fund-raising procedure that astounded civic leaders around the country for its simplicity and effectiveness. Each year beginning in 1901 Olin sent a printed form-letter to all MPPDA members reminding them of the continuing need to underwrite park development. Enclosed with that letter was a penny postcard on which members approved a particular pledge amount (nearly always suggested by the association directors) and then mailed to the association. The postcard system quickly became the financial backbone of the association, providing enough money to maintain the pleasure drives *and* do a limited amount of park improvement besides.[186]

In spite of Olin's extraordinary success in raising private sector funds for park development, he never wavered in his belief that the primary responsibility for park development lay with the City of Madison. In 1905 Olin scored a major victory when he persuaded the Common Council to hire a park superintendent to oversee the day-to-day operation and development of association parks—a move that removed this crushing burden from Olin who had previously done much of this himself. Very significantly the city ordinance authorizing the new position required the incumbant to be selected by the association and to work under its exclusive direction. The only things the city had to do was to confirm the association's superintendent nomination and pay his salary. The unusual private-public sector partnership reflected the extraordinary degree of confidence the MPPDA enjoyed among Madison decision makers.[187]

At the same time Olin kept pushing the city to shoulder the primary *financial* responsibility of Madison park development. Voluntary contributions, Olin argued, were by their very nature uncertain and inadequate, a vivid contrast to the high yield and reliability of city taxation. Quite aside from the logic of Olin's claims, however, the actual prospect of city takeover looked bleak indeed. Up to 1902 the city had spent only one thousand dollars buying parks (Tenney) though it had contributed miniscule amounts for park maintenance, nearly all for Orton Park; in effect, the MPPDA had outspent the city in park development by the twenty-five-to-one ratio. Gradually, however, Olin had built up a deep, broad propark constituency among influential community leaders. Thus when association directors petitioned the council to buy certain parklands in 1902, the city, after a year of deliberation, voted unanimously to issue its first bonds for park development. Olin was also probably responsible for getting Vilas and Brittingham to make their large gifts contingent upon getting relatively large city contributions—a ploy that resulted in another second large city bond issue for park development in 1905. Today such gifts are called "challenge grants."

Through these efforts Olin established the all important precedent of *periodic* city financial park support. However, the purchase and development of Tenney, Vilas, and Brittingham Parks and the Yahara Parkway, largely with private sector money, rapidly increased the need for *annual* maintenance funds—a burden that fell heavily upon the MPPDA. Olin therefore escalated his pleas for a permanent and regular city commitment to park funding through an annual park tax. In this context he seldom tired of reminding city officials that his association had outspent the city by a huge ratio, obviously trying to embarrass the council into regular giving.

At first council members saw little reason to start annual taxing for parks—certainly not in the face of such a spectacularly successful record of private support. Most council members continued to see parks as pretty places to look at and walk in, but hardly necessities.[188] Finally, in 1909 Olin got a reluctant city council to pass a one-half-mill park tax—a breakthrough for which Olin had fought so long and which must rank as one of his greatest achievements. Very significantly, however, nearly every penny of the city half-mill park tax was turned over to the association for expenditure—another commentary on the high esteem the organization enjoyed in the community. In short, the association maintained nearly absolute control of how park tax dollars were spent.[189]

The new half-mill park tax signalled the beginning of still another era in Madison park history. Not long after the city tax was imposed—and not surprisingly—the yield from the postcard system that once approached nine thousand dollars per year dropped to less than three thousand per year and the number of association members which once nearly reached one thousand dropped to less than three hundred. Conversely, the yield from the half-mill tax averaged nearly fifty thousand dollars per year between 1912 and 1920, more than twenty-eight thousand *above* average annual association contributions during its peak years between 1901 and 1911.[190]

FIGURE 6.49. 1901 TO 1909: THE ERA OF THE DREDGE.   The years between 1901 and 1909 were the Era of the Dredge in Madison history. During this period dredges sucked up hundreds of thousands of cubic yards of lake bottom sand and dumped it in nearby marshes to create new land for parks and residential building lots. New land created by dredges included the Willow Park subdivision along Lake Mendota between Tenney Park and Brearly Street, a series of subdivisions near the point where the Yahara flowed into Lake Monona, and Vilas, Brittingham and Tenney Parks. Dredges also took out the last kink in the Yahara River just before it entered Lake Monona and created a straighter channel for Murphy's Creek. Other major dredge projects included the drainage of about three thousand acres around Starkweather Creek in 1911 and work undertaken by the Lake Forest Land Company around Lake Wingra in 1917.

Shown above is a steam-powered sand pump dredge anchored in Monona Bay about 1907 spewing out sand for the future Brittingham Park. These dredges were so powerful they could suck twenty-five-pound rocks up a fifteen-foot high pick-up tube. On a typical day the dredge would deposit several thousand cubic feet of sand at the mouth of its pipe.

The picture shows Brittingham Park in 1908, just after the dredges had finished their work. The picture was taken from the railroad track south of the site of the Brittingham boat house. A top dressing of black soil was then added to the sand base and planted with trees and grass. (SHSW WHi(X3)8107)

FIGURE 6.50. THE HENRY VILAS PARK. In the spring or early summer of 1903, the developer of Wingra Park, H. C. Adams, then a Madison congressman, and a Madison physician, Edward Kremers, suggested that the land on the north side of Lake Wingra be secured for a park. At the time the idea seemed wildly unrealistic since the land would cost about twenty thousand dollars—an amount far in excess of what the Madison Park and Pleasure Drive Association (MPPDA) could raise and more than the city was willing to commit. Bold though this idea was, it hardly deterred John Olin, the resourceful and energetic president of the MPPDA. To Olin it simply meant finding a generous benefactor.

One likely prospect was sixty-three-year-old William Freeman Vilas, who among other things in his life had been a Civil War colonel, a Wisconsin legislator, a U.S. Senator, postmaster general and Secretary of the Interior under President Grover Cleveland, a U.S. regent and a millionaire lumberman. Not only did Vilas have the money, but he also had been a member and active supporter of the MPPDA for years and a devout Madison lover nearly all his life. When first approached, Vilas said he *might* be interested but would not make a decision until he returned from Europe in the fall of 1903. Meanwhile, he told Olin to secure options on the properties in question—a very encouraging sign.

Finally in the spring of 1904 after a series of discussions, Vilas decided to buy the land providing that others would raise ten thousand dollars for improving the park and

straightening and dredging Wingra Creek. Vilas also said he would be "pleased" if the park were named after his only son Henry who had died of diabetes at the age of twenty-seven in 1899. Naturally, the MPPDA and the city accepted Vilas' generous offer—the largest ever made by a single individual up to that time. The required local contribution of ten thousand dollars was raised from persons who lived in the Wingra area. Vilas' contribution proved to be just the first of several "princely gifts" the family ultimately bestowed upon the park. By 1920 their gifts totalled an astounding $82,500.

Work on the sixty-three-acre tract got underway in 1905 following the completion of a plan done by O. C. Simonds, the well-known Chicago landscape architect who had recently designed Tenney Park. When work began, only twenty-five acres were high and dry; the rest was a bog covered by an average of one foot of water. By 1914 the equivalent of seventeen thousand large dump truck loads had been deposited on the marshy are largely from a dredge operation and caused the park to take the first contours of Simond's plans.

Beginning in 1914 free band concerts were held in Vilas Park on summer Sundays. The concerts were paid for by proceeds from the MPPDA refreshment tent. The above picture shows hundreds of Madisonians enjoying such a Sunday in the city's premier park. Some lounged under shade trees, some listened to the concerts, some strolled over the grounds, and a few energetic young men played baseball. With a little effort, one can almost imagine being there.

Contrary to what one might expect, association officials were anything but alarmed by the decline in membership and contributions. In fact, the large sudden influx of city park money *relieved* the association of the heretofore heavy financial burden of park acquisition and development and allowed its budget to be primarily used, as it once was, to maintain the twenty-three-mile pleasure drive system—a task it could easily do with fewer members and lower annual budgets.

No sooner had Tenney, Vilas and Brittingham made their generous grants to the association when a great but simmering debate began among decision makers about how they should be used. Association officials believed that Tenney Park would do for the masses what the country drives did for the rich, that is, put people back in touch with nature. If the masses couldn't get to the country, then the association would bring the country to the city. According to the then popular theory, contact with nature was intrinsically desirable because it transported people from artificial city life to the natural environment in which humans had evolved. With the help of serpentine lagoons, rolling meadows, clusters of trees and flowering shrubs, all, of course, artfully positioned by some of the nation's leading landscape architects, harried working people could restore frazzled urban nerves and reset their compasses with a true and timeless reality.[191]

To the great surprise of MPPDA officials, however, this passive, aesthetic interpretation of parks didn't sell very well. The masses for whom these parks were built, stayed away in droves.[192] But once again, the MPPDA demonstrated great resourcefulness and flexibility. Like a merchant with a slow-moving product, the association tried a few gimmicks to get people to use the parks, the most successful of which was the blare of the brass band. The people flocked to free Sunday afternoon concerts, and they came back again and

again whenever they were offered. Of course the musicians had to be paid, and here again the association hit upon an ingenious solution. It opened refreshment stands that sold up to twenty-seven hundred ice cream cones on a single Sunday. The result was plenty of money, more concerts, and still another reason to come to the parks.[193]

Then came the next step. While the adults were listening to Sousa marches, *Daisy, Daisy . . .* and other favorites, groups of young people started playing baseball. Soon Sunday afternoons in the park became a popular tradition in Madison. To some Madisonians, however, band concerts and baseball were violations of the aesthetic and pensive purposes for which the parks were designed. This passive interpretation of parks quickly gave way to a progressive, people-oriented, activist interpretation. Parks were pretty places to relax, but they were also places to play and be entertained. According to this new interpretation, the picnic basket, the baseball bat, the band leader's baton, and the swimming suit were *all* welcome in Madison parks. By 1911 the association had taken down its keep-off-the-grass signs, had learned to tolerate damaged turf, and its employees "cheerfully" picked up litter on Monday mornings after the weekend throngs.[194]

The next milestone in Madison recreational history was the playground—a response to a variety of forces then shoving their way into the public spotlight. Madison was growing and, as a *Journal* editorial put it, "growth tightens up a town; vacant lots become preempted by brick and concrete structures and the play spaces go."[195] At the same time a growing number of Madison leaders became concerned about the disappearance of vacant lots, they came to recognize the legitimacy and the importance of play in the development of young people. Indeed, next to poverty, some felt the greatest problem of the twentieth century was how to use growing amounts of leisure time.[196] For these persons the playground was a conscious effort to mold society by altering the human physical environment, an admission that *laissez faire* recreation was a failure. Great emphasis was placed upon helping the

poor and underprivileged children, particularly those who were forced to live in Madison's congested neighborhoods. Playgrounds were touted as a means of overcoming the effects of crowding and congestion then becoming so obvious to Madison. Playgrounds became tools for combatting juvenile delinquency, building character, instilling patriotism and even for "saving . . . modern society."[197] To achieve these pressing and difficult goals, playground promoters abandoned the earlier emphasis on natural surroundings in favor of flat fields, play equipment, and an organized recreation program.

Enduring results from these early prorecreation forces were substantial. Between 1910 and 1917 organized outdoor recreational programs for children were established at most Madison schools and funded by the board of education. Madison's first comprehensive recreational survey was conducted in 1915 (one of the most fascinating documents on Madison ever produced) and led to a much greater emphasis upon *adult* recreation. Certainly one of the most important consequences of this early recreation movement was the extent to which it reinforced the park work which had been and was then being done by the MPPDA. Indeed, the organized recreation movement became one of its most valuable allies the park movement could have had.

As a result of its work, the association fast acquired an enviable local, state, national, and even international reputation. It enjoyed the best possible local press coverage; editors almost fell over one another praising the organization. Association officers were asked to address annual meetings of the League of Wisconsin Municipalities, the leading state professional organization for city officials. Other association leaders were asked to speak to city improvement and state beautification organizations around the Midwest and to a variety of national organizations such as the American Civic Association, then the leading national civic improvement group, and even to the prestigious American Academy of Political and

FIGURE 6.51. BURR JONES PLAYGROUND. The young men and women who posed in the summer of 1909 for this photograph at Burr Jones Playground (intersection of East Washington Avenue and North Livingston Street) were beneficiaries of one of Madison's first publicly funded, organized outdoor recreation programs. The playground was opened in 1907, a gift of Burr W. Jones and was an early expression of the idea that Madison had an obligation to provide recreational opportunities for its young people. The playground featured swings, slides, a basketball standard, and a merry-go-round, but also provided such activities as hiking and track and field events. Soon playgrounds like this one were built at many of the school grounds around the city and became a fixture of Madison summers.

Those who followed the work of the association could hardly believe what this remarkable organization had accomplished. To receive five major parks (Owen Parkway, Tenney, Vilas, Brittingham, and Burrows) as outright gifts from citizens and then in some cases to receive additional large gifts from their donors for their development was almost unheard of. Many larger cities considered themselves lucky if they received just one park from a prominent citizen. People marvelled at the ease with which large one-time subscriptions were raised for major projects such as the Yahara River Parkway. The same people who were impressed when they heard about the thousands of dollars that were raised year after year through voluntary contributions, were awed when they learned that these funds were raised, seemingly effortlessly, through the simple but highly impersonal postcard solicitation. Is it possible, they asked in 1909, that the association raised a quarter of a million voluntary dollars for park work in a city with fewer than twenty-five thousand people? The president of Denver's park commission no doubt spoke for many who sought to learn from the Madison experience. After conducting extensive research of local park systems around the country, he said, "I have yet to learn of a single city where in proportion to the population, so much enterprise and public spirit has been shown as by the citizens of Madison in beautifying their park and boulevard system."[199]

Not surprisingly, nearly all attention the association received from *outside* the City of Madison was focussed on the organization *per se* or upon the organization and its remarkably supportive community. Even among Madisonians it was commonplace to say that the association had "contributed more to the city's good than any other single institution which the citizens of Madison have developed."[200]

However, to Madisonians active in community affairs, the real credit belonged not with the association or even its directors but rather to John Meyers Olin, its founder and first president. Indeed from 1892 when he took the concept of a

Social Science. Influential newspapers such as the *Christian Science Monitor* and the Sunday *New York Herald* carried feature articles on the MPPDA. City officials from other states came to Madison to inspect the handiworks of the association and dozens more wrote asking for information. Annual association reports were avidly read by nationally prominent architects, educators, and civic leaders. Boston and Seattle city officials requested and got a portable pictorial exhibit so they could show their citizens what Madisonians had done. Even the mayor of Wellington, New Zealand, in his 1910 inaugural address described work by the Madison Park and Pleasure Drive Association in very flattering terms, and French and Swedish officials asked for copies of association annual reports so that they could learn how Madison accomplished so much with volunteer contributions.[198]

picturesque pleasure drive along the shore of Lake Mendota and made it into a smashingly successful reality, until 1909 when he relinquished his post, the MPPDA *was* John M. Olin. He was the "master spirit" who provided its inspiration, vitality, direction and "dominating optimism."[201] "He had charge of the subscription list, doing a great part of the solicitation himself. He looked after the details of the work, purchased supplies, made contracts for dredging, for right-of-ways, for the conveyance of lands. He staked out driveways, planned for planting, drew voluminous reports, prepared communications to the council, to the newspapers, to railway officials, trimmed trees, prepared monthly statements of payments, made elaborate financial estimates, interviewed aldermen, made trips to consult with railway officials, and in a hundred other ways gave unstintingly of his time and energy." And, one must hasten to add, Olin did all this while he maintained an exceptionally active law practice![202]

Olin's intense commitment to Madison flowed from his fervent belief that Madison was a very special city that deserved very special treatment. To the lawyer turned citizen activist, Madison was a city upon a hill that could and should become the proud centerpiece of the state and a model for the nation. It was for this reason that Olin insisted upon getting the best possible designers. For example, to lay out Tenney, Vilas, and Brittingham Parks, Olin hired the very highly regarded Chicago landscape architect, Ossian Cole Simonds, who founded the "prairie school" of landscape architecture. When the time came to hire a park superintendent, Olin picked Emil T. Mische who for eight years had worked in New York for Frederick Law Olmstead among whose many famous commissions was New York's Central Park.[203] Rarely would Olin allow local sentiment to override the design judgment of his professionals. Once Olin worked behind the scenes to get the council to reject a grant from D. K. Tenney for a very utilitarian "stock steel bridge," which the philanthropist insisted was "nice" but which Olin thought was an "absurd proposition"

and which would make Madison the "laughing stock" among persons who appreciate good design. Olin prevailed and the graceful arched pedestrian bridge leading to the play area in the center of the Tenney Park lagoons was the result.[204]

John Olin was a born leader. When he talked, Madisonians listened. Like many leaders, Olin wisely recognized that his single most important contribution was to get Madison opinion leaders to embrace certain far-sighted principles and values. In his words his job was the "creation of an intelligent public sentiment and the promotion of correct opinions. . . ."[205]

The mainspring of Olin's "correct opinions" was his belief that city residents needed regular contact with nature but that opportunities to experience nature in a rapidly growing city were quickly declining. Madison businessmen immersed in the pecuniary life, were inclined to forget this important need, argued Olin. Though he hardly viewed parks as a one-dimensional theory of salvation, he did argue that for many Madisonians, parks provided the only convenient and accessible place to play and commune with nature—activities whose therapeutic ability to refresh the sagging spirit were well-demonstrated. Therefore if the people were denied parks, a tragic form of impoverishment would forever afflict Madison residents. It was for this reason that Olin told businessmen that they must devote time and money to park development and that beauty was just as important as business.

From this belief flowed the basic principle in which guided Olin's crusade: *public parks for the masses are a municipal responsibility requiring higher taxes and a much larger local governmental role.* Closely related to this was his view that public ownership of water frontage must be expanded. At the time he began his crusade these principles were very progressive, certainly far to the left of conservative Madison citizen sentiment. Moreover they had never before been embraced in such a coherent way by such a forceful leader.

As a promoter Olin exhibited great style and flair—all fine-tuned for his constituency. His annual meetings were major social, gustatory, and intellectual events of the year for which Olin would rent the largest, finest halls and cater in a splendid repast. After the banquet, the men would puff aromatic Cuban cigars and hear a stimulating battery of speakers challenge members and guests to cause the New Madison to be greener, cleaner, more beautiful, and more functional. To add glitter and prestige to these gala affairs, Olin invited major business leaders. In 1910 he got the presidents of *both* the Milwaukee and Northwestern Railroads to attend—an extraordinary *coup.*[206] His heavily illustrated, artfully assembled, and well-written annual reports exhuded elegance and professionalism—characteristics that marked nearly all his efforts. But here and in many other instances, Olin found ways to get extra mileage from these documents. Ostensibly they were annual reports to his "stock-holders," but they were also his advertising *piece de resistance.* During some years he sent out over one thousand copies to key people all over the country. In fact, it was responses to these reports that furnished the cheerleading grist for that portion of Olin's annual talk where he informed his members of the interest prominent persons around the country had lavished on the association. Olin was very much aware that such flattering comments would heighten local pride and giving. No wonder he told his members that "no money expended by the association has brought better returns." "They advertised," he explained, "without seeming to."[207]

Certainly one of the most compelling reflections of Olin's leadership skills was the organization he founded. Indeed for its persistence, commitment, foresight, selfless public service, and above all else for its achievements, it is unparalleled in Madison history. No other organization in the city before or since brought together under one roof such an impressive assemblage of talent and such a broad cross-section of Madison leaders spanning the commercial, manufacturing, university, and governmental communities.

Although it never had more than four percent of the city's population in its membership, it was, relatively speaking, a very large organization. To be comparable today (1980) an organization would have to have about seven thousand members. No civic organization even comes close.[208]

Perhaps the ultimate test of Olin's leadership was his ability to attract financial support for his cause. Indeed when it came to raising money, Olin was the unchallenged grand master. During the eighteen years he was the guiding force of the association, he fostered a habit of giving and coaxed a quarter of a million dollars in voluntary contributions from Madison residents. It was a glorious era in Madison's history when the richest families gave princely gifts for people's parks, when the subscription system was developed to a point never before seen in Madison and rarely seen elsewhere in the country, and when those who could not afford to give money gave land or their time. Impressive as this private record was, Olin's success in 1908 in getting the city to earmark a one-half-mill park tax produced even larger amounts and quickly eclipsed private contributions. By 1920, just a decade after Olin stepped down as association president, the volunteer and tax-supported financial engines, both of which Olin had built and started, had produced nearly one million dollars for Madison parks development.[209]

During his eighteen years as association president Olin's capacity for hard, sustained, and selfless work became legendary. His profession was law, but parks, beauty, and order were his passion. In the end it was his passion that strained his exceptionally sturdy constitution and led to the breakdown in Olin's health in the summer of 1909. In September of that year Olin submitted his resignation as president of the association.[210]

Olin's brilliant administration was an impossibly hard act to follow. First came Joseph C. Schubert, who at the time was mayor of Madison and a veteran MPPDA director. He was followed by Ernest N. Warner who led the organization from 1912 until 1930 when he was killed in an auto accident. Then came Frank W. Cantwell who served until 1938 when the association turned over all its parks to the city and closed its operation. Dedicated and competent though these men were, they were pale shadows of their predecessor, custodians rather than builders. On the other hand, Olin's achievements were so substantial that the association could afford to coast. By 1910 Madison had twenty-six percent more park acreage than it needed using Olin's one acre per two hundred people standard. Indeed, between 1910 and 1925, much association work focused on the development of the relatively large inventory of parks acquired under Olin's leadership.[211]

Although Olin's park crusade was very popular in Madison, his work did not escape local criticism. So industrious was Olin in pursuing parks and drives that some Madisonians concluded that he and other real estate speculators were making huge profits by securing advance options on the lands. These charges deeply angered the scrupulously honest park leader and provoked him to write a long rebuttal in the *Wisconsin State Journal,* which he concluded by saying: "I believe there is such a thing as the rendering of disinterested service to the public, however difficult it may be for certain people to comprehend this idea."[212] Others criticized Olin's association for its elitism. After all, said these critics, its principal early product, pleasure drives, lay outside the city and could only be used by persons in the top twenty-five percent of Madison's economic pyramid who could afford to own or rent horses and carriages.[213] Moreover, Olin considered these charges valid and took corrective measures to democratize the association. In 1899 he got his directors to change the association bylaws so that persons giving just five dollars (rather than the previous twenty-five dollars) could become voting members and took the pivotal step of committing association resources for Tenney Park so that pleasant outdoor recreational opportunities could be made more accessible to "wage earners" and "pedestrians."[214]

Others took delight in criticizing park design. In connection with Tenney Park, for example, many people including D. K. Tenney ridiculed Simond's design for the lagoon system. "What do you want with more lagoons?," these persons asked, "Is not Lake Mendota enough?"[215] But here and in nearly every other instance of park design criticism, Olin stood by his talented park designers.

Still another criticism came in response to his outstanding success in raising money for his projects. Olin made parks Madison's favorite charity but some resented this because it made raising money for other purposes more difficult. There was some truth to this charge but the far more compelling point made by Olin and others was that Madison was an extraordinarily generous community that simultaneously supported fundraising drives for hospitals, the Women's Building, YWCA's, "shirt waist strikers in Chicago," and even "famine sufferers in China."[216]

However serious these criticisms were, against the backdrop of association history, they were mere rifle fire in contrast to the heavy artillery that began soon after Olin succeeded in getting the Common Council to impose a one-half-mill park tax in 1908. Timing of this new tax was unfortunate because it coincided with a 1½-mill tax increase over the previous year—an increase many Madisonians thought was fully attributable to the MPPDA. Resentment against the association and its presumed profligacy surfaced once again during the 1909 budget development process. Olin and his colleagues descended upon the council chambers and prevailed, but this time it was clear to Olin that some kind persuasive study was needed to convince the public that direct taxation for parks should be continued. Just days after the council passed the 1909 budget with the park tax in it, Olin launched a major countercrusade. Working behind the scenes, he got the council to appoint a blue ribbon committee including the president of the Madison Commercial Club, a Wisconsin supreme court justice, and a member of the Wisconsin tax commission to prove once and for all that park spending paid. After careful deliberation, the committee concluded that ten to fifteen percent of Madison's relatively rapid recent increase in property values was directly attributable to Madison's outstanding parks. This conclusion allowed Olin to take the *offensive* in the park tax spending controversy: because the city was spending on parks only half of what parks actually generated in taxes, Olin could argue that parks were *subsidizing* other city expenses. In other words, Madison's parks reduced, not increased, taxes. And best of all, the report gave park backers hard-nosed "business" reasons for continuing direct taxation and reduced the need to use the more controversial aesthetic, social, and recreational justifications.[217]

Unfortunately, the report's fine-grained logic and complex statistics failed to stem the tide of reaction to growing MPPDA power and spending. So strong was this opposition that in 1910 Mayor Joseph Schubert, a long-time friend and backer of the association, found himself opposed in the 1910 primary by a challenger who ran on an antipark platform. If elected the challenger boasted he would work to "undo" the work of the association. For a time during the vigorous campaign, the direct park tax and indeed the power of the MPPDA appeared as if it would be successfully challenged. But when election day came, Olin breathed a sigh of relief. The antipark candidate got just forty-two percent of the vote in the Democratic primary and Schubert breezed into a third two-year term over token Republican opposition. From this time forward, the direct park tax was never challenged, although there were some years when park budgets were cut back.[218]

In addition to these criticisms of Olin's work, there were several areas where the park leader failed to achieve his goals. For example, Olin's magnificent plan to extend Capitol Park to Lake Monona and to create a five-acre park near the intersection of South Mills and Vilas Avenue (Bowen Park) never became realities. Then, too, there were Olin's vigorous attempts to build a pleasure drive around Lake Monona (Monona Drive), which failed because Monona frontage had already been subdivided into relatively small

FIGURE 6.52. BRITTINGHAM BEACH.   From the day it opened in 1910 the Brittingham Park Bath House was one of the most popular places in Madison. During its first season, an estimated fifty thousand persons, some of whom are shown in the above photograph, enjoyed its cool waters, sandy beaches, and its thrilling water slide. Although the association purchased three hundred suits to rent to swimmers, the demand was so great that there was almost always a line waiting to take the wet suits as soon as the wearers came out of the water. One official doubted if the bathing suits were ever dry during that entire busy summer. The two older boys on the water slide were indulging in a very popular feat of derringdo, namely, *running* down the water slide and then doing a flip into the water.

tracts and many of its owners strenuously opposed the idea. Some property owners, in fact, were so enraged by the mere suggestion of a drive through their property that they drove association officials from their premises with axes. This was just one of several situations where, because the association lacked the power of condemnation, a few property owners could stymie an effort—and did.[219]

In fact it was the failure to build Monona Drive that prompted the visionary leader to adopt a goal toward which he spent a good portion of his life as it turned out unsuccessfully, namely, developing a more powerful municipal replacement for the MPPDA. His first effort came in 1897 when he got the legislature to pass a bill authorizing the City of Madison to *own* parkland outside its corporate limits. The city, however, declined to take advantage of the law on the grounds that the association was doing quite well on its own. But Olin was not one to let such an important matter drop. In 1905 he got the legislature to pass an even stronger bill giving cities the right to *own and condemn* land outside its corporate limits. When Governor LaFollette vetoed the bill, Olin tried again in 1907. This time he ran into a buzz saw of opposition from suburban property owners who feared its municipal condemnation powers. Olin tried a third time. Working behind the scenes five years after he resigned as association president, Olin spearheaded a drive in 1914 that culminated in the Park District Law of 1915. This far-reaching piece of legislation would have enabled the City of Madison to take over all association operations, to condemn lands outside its boundaries, and to use taxation for their development. But here, as before, Olin and his colleagues failed to persuade the Madison Common Council to utilize this far-reaching piece of legislation. His failure to persuade Madison to assume the work of his association and to use its full powers to acquire, develop, and maintain parkland was one of Olin's greatest disappointments during his long and distinguished career as a civic activist.[220]

However important these criticisms and failures, they must be placed in their proper context. No one can play such a large role in building a community and not be the target of criticism. Nor can one set forth so many ambitious goals and realize them all. The far more important fact is that Olin was able to do so much in such a short period of time. He persuaded Madison leaders that providing recreational opportunity for the masses was an important and legitimate function of city government, and he left a magnificent inventory of parks for that purpose. In the final analysis Olin will be remembered as a consummate salesman for a product, which at first many Madisonians did not think they needed but which he persuaded them they could not live without.

The City Well Planned

In the fall of 1907 Emil T. Mische, Madison's first park superintendent, asked the city for a three-hundred-dollar raise to his twelve-hundred-dollar annual salary. The new superintendent felt that his work was easily worth the extra remuneration. After all, he had worked eight years for the presitigious New York landscape architecture firm of Olmstead and Olmstead and had the responsibility of developing Madison parks during the floodtide of park philanthropy. The MPPDA urged the city to approve the raise but the council refused. Angered by the rebuff, Mische began looking around for other employers who would be more appreciative of his services. He did not have to wait long. The City of Portland, Oregon, hired him for nearly double his Madison salary and threw in a house to boot.[221]

Olin viewed Mische's departure more as an opportunity than a setback. Although Mische was reliable, competent, and well credentialled, Olin was eager to get someone with more sophisticated design and communication skills, a co-conspirator with whom he could make and execute grand plans. Olin concluded that he could most easily attract this sort of person if the incumbent did not have to do both park design *and* the more

tedious day-to-day supervision of employees who planted trees, mowed grass, and picked up debris. With the blessing of the council and the MPPDA board, Olin therefore separated the foreman from the designer. For the former job Olin hired a long-time association employee and paid his salary from association funds. Theoretically, this left twelve hundred dollars in the city budget that he could use to hire a landscape architect.[222]

Meanwhile Olin began making inquiries: who, he asked, are the most talented landscape architects in the country?—for the moment sidestepping the question of how he would pay such a person. His audacious goal was to get the best designer in the country to work exclusively for Madison, Wisconsin. From this process, Olin obtained the name of John Nolen, a thirty-eight-year-old landscape architect who had established a highly regarded practice in Cambridge, Massachusetts. The more he heard about Nolen, the more convinced Olin became that Nolen was the right man—indeed the only man—for the Madison job. Though he had been in practice for only two years, he already had major contracts with Roanoke, Virginia, Savannah, Georgia, San Diego, California, and Charlotte, North Carolina, and was moving in the fast track of an ambitious new specialty known as city planning.[223]

Now came the real challenge: how to get Nolen to forsake the Boston area and his burgeoning practice to come to a small Midwestern community. The problem was particularly exasperating because Olin knew that the Common Council would refuse to pay a penny more than twelve hundred dollars for the job of landscape architect and that Nolen was making at least three times that amount in private practice.

Olin's solution to the salary gap was to call on his good friend and next door neighbor, University of Wisconsin President Charles Van Hise, and urge him to establish a new department of landscape architecture with Nolen as its first chairman. Van Hise agreed to take the proposition up with the regents and even authorized Olin to ascertain whether such a position would appeal to Nolen.[224]

John Nolen

In 1908 when the City of Madison hired this five-foot eight-inch sandy-haired man with the walrus moustache, probably no one with the possible exception of John Olin realized the stature of the man they were getting. After all, John Nolen, though thirty-eight years old, had been in private practice as a landscape architect for only two years and therefore had relatively little experience behind him. But even with this limited experience he was marked by his peers as a "comer." Nolen delivered on this promise. He went on to cut a broad swath in the early history of American urban planning and long before he died in 1937 was considered the "dean" of the profession.

Nolen spent his entire lifetime in cities. Born in Philadelphia in 1869, he graduated first in his class at the age of fifteen from an elite private Philadelphia high school. There he demonstrated an unusual facility for public speaking, an avid interest in public issues, and a voracious appetite for books. After working at various odd jobs he saved enough money to enter the Wharton School of Business where he took a degree with high honors in economics and public administration. He emerged from his formal education deeply committed to public service and to the educational role the state should play in achieving human progress.

For ten years after graduating from Wharton, Nolen held an administrative post at the University of Pennsylvania where he directed a rapidly growing adult education program known as the "People's University" and where he enjoyed stimulating personal contacts with some of the leading thinkers of the day. During this period he addressed the students of his former high school and told them that the real problems of the day were "not so much national as municipal" and that the true statement were those who worked to make urban ideals a reality.

What he told these high school students in 1897 was more than stirring oratory. In 1904 at the age of thirty-four Nolen resigned his administrative post and set sail for Europe to study its cities. He was particularly impressed with what the Swiss and Germans were doing in the areas of housing, land-use control, and open space, and by the active interventionist roles that municipal governments played in these areas. When he returned in the fall of 1904, he sold his home, moved his family to Cambridge, and enrolled in Harvard to study landscape architecture—one of the very few programs in the country that offered training for persons interested in what we now call urban planning.

Immediately after graduating in 1906 Nolen launched a whirlwind practice that each year required travelling thirty thousand miles and spending six months in the field. Through books, articles, and lectures Nolen emphasized the critical importance of comprehensive city plans. Though his early work emphasized physical planning, he gave unusual emphasis for a planner of his era to social and economic planning. Just three years out of graduate school, he emerged as one of the giants of his fledgling profession. He quickly departed from the then dominant City Beautiful school of design and its preoccupation with aesthetics and led efforts to establish a much more sophisticated approach to city planning, which later became known as the City Functional movement. In 1909 he organized and was a major contributor to the first National Conference on City Planning. In 1910 he became a founder of the National Housing Association. By 1919 his practice was regarded as the "largest and most versatile" in the country. His work ranged from tiny subdivisions to entire regions and included twenty-nine comprehensive city plans, one of which was Madison. (Photo courtesy of John Nolen, Jr.)

FIGURE 6.53. THE NEW CAPITOL.   Whoever installed a gas lamp in a cloak room in the south wing of the capitol put it so high on the wall that its flames blackened the ceiling. This fact was reported to authorities but no action was taken. About 2:45 A.M. on Saturday, February 27, 1904, a watchman smelled smoke and ran immediately to the cloak room where he found the ceiling ablaze. Firemen were called but when they arrived no water would come from the capitol hydrants. By the time firemen hooked their hoses to the city mains, the fire had spread to a large portion of the south wing and was threatening the dome. When the sun rose, about eighty per cent of the grand old building lay in ruins.

The fire surprised everyone but disappointed few. The 1857 building had long been regarded as inadequate and in 1903 the legislature appointed a building commission to plan a new and larger facility. The commission had barely begun when fire struck. Among other things the fire caused the commission to scrap their enlargement plans in favor of a totally new structure. Toward the end of 1905 the building commission offered $10,000 to the architectural firm that in its judgment best met state requirements. Five firms entered the competition but the New York firm of George B. Post and Sons won the unanimous support from the commission. This rendering shows the prize winning Post design.

Ground was broken for the imposing seven-million-dollar building in late 1907 and completed in 1917, but a formal opening was postponed until after the war. The elegant structure was typical of the monumental and formal architecture in fashion during the City Beautiful era.

Madisonians avidly followed work on the huge structure during the ten year construction period and sometimes became embroiled in discussions on how certain details should be done. In 1914, for example, the burning question was: which direction should Miss Forward face? The fifteen-foot, four-inch-high gilded lady had been designed by the celebrated American sculptor, Daniel Chester French, who among other things did the seated Lincoln statue in the Lincoln Memorial in Washington, D.C. Both the sculptor and the architect wisely left the decision of which direction the gold lady should face to the commission. Some said she should face east and the rising sun, an orientation that would symbolize a new day and a new era. Others said she should face the west in deference to the great university at the end of State Street. A few said point her toward Monona Avenue. No one suggested the golden lady should have to face cold northern winds. After hearing all these suggestions the commission concluded the Monona Avenue orientation was best because the lady could then be looking down on Nolen's Grand Mall, which the commissioners expected to be built between the capital and Lake Monona. (SHSW, WHi(X3)3105)

Nolen replied that he was "deeply interested" in the "attractive position."[225] He could be on the faculty of one of the nation's great universities and the first in the U.S. to establish a course in city planning.[226] He could have a hand in shaping the capital of a commonwealth roundly praised as a "laboratory of democracy." He could further the public spirited work of the MPPDA, which he said was "without parallel."[227] For this assignment the rising Boston professional was to receive three thousand dollars for a nine-month, half-time academic position. This meant that he would have generous amounts of discretionary time to pursue his private practice and take contracts in Chicago, Minneapolis—St. Paul, Milwaukee, in numerous small Wisconsin cities, and for various state agencies. Assuming he could make as much money in private practice as he did as a professor, the Madison-based package could have provided Nolen with an annual income of eight thousand dollars per year—not a bad income at all considering that the U.W. President Van Hise was only making $6,500 per year.[228]

But then to Olin's great disappointment, a variety of pressures forced Van Hise to channel the few discretionary budget resources at his disposal into the newly established medical school and to put plans for the school of landscape architecture on the back burner. However, Van Hise was sufficiently impressed by Nolen's credentials to offer him the job, but only if and when the new department were formed. Unfortunately Olin wanted Nolen immediately, not in two or three years.[229]

Instead of giving up as many might have, Olin concocted still another job package—this one a veritable banquet of Nolen opportunities. Working through Van Hise, Olin got the regents to earmark five hundred dollars for three years during which period Nolen would serve as U.W. consulting landscape architect. Then he went to his friends in state government and got the state park commission to earmark an identical amount for three years in exchange for which Nolen would

343

design state parks. Finally he went to see the members of the state board of control, the agency that supervised all state hospitals, prisons, and institutions, and got them to give Nolen a one-thousand-dollar-per-year stipend—again for three years—in exchange for which he would do landscape architecture and site planning. Thus using his rich network of influential friends Olin had assembled a two-thousand-dollar annual fee for a full three years. With the addition of the city money already earmarked for a landscape architect, Olin's new package provided a guaranteed base of thirty-two hundred dollars per year.[230]

But then, once again, Olin suffered a grinding setback. Nolen concluded that Olin's second job package was much less attractive than the first and that it would not be wise for him to move his practice from his prestigious Harvard Square address and make Madison his base of operations as Olin had demanded. Olin countered that Madison was only twenty-four hours from Boston by train and that his presence in Madison was essential to give "permanence, continuity, and efficiency" to the work.[231] Nolen refused to change his mind but he did agree to make Madison what he called a "preferred client," that is, to take no other commissions that would jeopardize his work in Madison,[232] and to cut his per diem charge from fifty dollars to twenty-five dollars per day.

Hamstrung by Nolen's decision to not move to Madison, but with the state funding package still in place, Olin decided to pursue the best compromise and try to get Nolen to do Madison's work as a consultant. However, this required the consent from the toughest funding source of all: the Common Council. Here Olin's challenge was persuading the aldermen that they should pay a man twelve hundred dollars a year to work *part-time* when Mische had worked fulltime for the same amount. Olin regaled the council with Nolen's impeccable national reputation, cited superlative recommendations from past and present clients, and emphasized that landscape architects rarely lived in their clients' communities.

Madison would be exceptionally fortunate, insisted Olin, to get a man of this caliber to do all the city's park, boulevard, and cemetery design work. Furthermore, Madison deserved nothing less. Over the strong objections of several aldermen who groused about the city not getting its money's worth, the council acquiesced and gave Olin his three-year commitment. Olin got his man.[233]

In this first public appearance at the annual meeting of the Park and Pleasure Drive Association, Nolen made an "excellent" impression.[234] After praising Madison's natural beauty, civic spirit, and the extraordinary work done by the MPPDA, Nolen began telling his distinguished audience about city planning, a movement he portrayed as "sweeping the country." Indeed a city plan was the key to Madison's "aesthetic, economic, and sanitary" future. Madison, he said, should begin preparing a city plan immediately.[235]

Most Madisonians had never heard of city planning—hardly surprising in view of the fact that Nolen was among a mere handful of men who were then giving shape and direction to the infant enterprise. When Nolen came to Madison probably no more than one percent of U.S. cities had even begun to plan, and planning was little more than a yeasty but fragile amalgam of forces. One major component, the City Beautiful movement, received much of its power and direction from the 1893 World's Columbian Exposition held in Chicago. When that summer-long event closed its doors, twenty-one million Americans had sauntered through the Great White City, a spectacular melange of imposing classical buildings artfully arranged along broad boulevards and malls. Civic activists were thrilled by this powerful display of architecture and saw the Great White Way as an example of what could happen if a city were designed and built in accord with *aesthetic* principles. To Americans long accustomed to dirty, ugly, poorly laid out, park-deficient cities, the Great White Way was a revelation that fueled rising expectations. American civic leaders returned to their homes eager to secure a

bit of beauty, order, and even grandeur for their communities. (One expression of this impulse was the park and boulevard movement whose impressive achievements in Madison are chronicled in chapter 5.) As the City Beautiful movement matured it emphasized monumental architecture, downtown civic centers, axial street plans, large manicured street trees, boulevards, malls, and outdoor art such as statues and fountains.[236]

Once unleashed, the desire to improve American cities proved to be deep and strong. In 1900 a how-to-do-it book entitled *The Improvement of Cities and the Betterment of Towns* became—to everyone's surprise—a national best seller![237] The formation of two organizations—the National Municipal League in 1894 and the American League of Civic Improvement in 1901—reflected, magnified, and channelled civic improvement excitement across the country.[238]

As the new century opened, the City Beautiful movement hit its full stride. But then another series of developments revealed urban conditions, the solutions to which the movement had little if anything to offer. Big city settlement house workers trying to improve living conditions for the urban poor quickly learned that monumental buildings were not intended to house the poor. Local business elites found the City Beautiful movement offered scant advice on how to encourage population growth and economic development, much less accomplish the more mundane but equally important upgrading of sanitary and transportation systems. Local reform organizations, agitated by muckraking revelations on local government graft and corruption, saw nothing in City Beautiful aesthetic principles to help them institute more efficient, less wasteful local government.

Simultaneously progressives began to question the fundamental values by which American cities had been developed. Why should access to recreational land be limited to those who could afford it? Why should property owners be allowed to build factories next to homes? Or slums? Why shouldn't the common good prevail over the desires of the propertied few? Why should waste and inefficiency in local government be tolerated? To what extent should market forces be allowed to make critical decisions affecting city environmental quality? What indeed were the proper roles for individuals and the collective will in building better cities?

Into this swirling vortex of urban improvement forces came the first city planners who saw their new discipline as a powerful agent of reform. Most were heavily influenced by City Beautiful principles, but a few men, notably John Nolen and Frederick Law Olmstead, the designer of New York's Central Park, launched a new school about 1907, which later became known as the City Functional movement. To this new group of planners a city was an integrated cluster of transportation, housing, recreation, sanitation, and governmental *systems.* How, they asked, can cities be made more livable, not just more beautiful. From this systemic perception of cities flowed the need for community plans that took all urban components into account.[239]

Nolen's first Madison speech in April 1908 was necessarily general. After all, he had spent only two days in the city prior to the talk, so he was hardly in a position to make any informed observations much less any recommendations. Following the talk, however, Nolen spent several weeks in Madison studying his new client city. Then beginning in December 1908, during another visit, Nolen began firing his heavy artillary. He criticized narrow and misaligned State Street, Madison's numerous dangerous at-grade railroad approaches, the lack of public lake frontage, the clutter of boathouses and factories along the lakeshore at East Madison, the congested capitol site, lackadasical attention to street trees, ugly overhead utilities, and the near absence of children's playgrounds. All these things, he said were the product of "haphazard," "accidental" growth methods followed by nearly all American cities.[240]

Many who heard or read Nolen's words found them grimly compelling. Look, said Nolen in effect, if you don't know where you're going, any road will take you there, and right now, Madison

is travelling without a road map. You must understand that haphazard, accidental growth will not provide the urban excellence you desire. If you care about Madison you must seize the future; you must prepare a comprehensive plan.[241]

Among those who heard Nolen's second plea for planning, none was more convinced than John Olin. The time had come, he concluded, to act— and act he did as only Olin could. In January 1909, just one month after Nolen's plea for a comprehensive plan, Olin packed three hundred and fifty of the city's leading lights into the Women's Club Building on Gilman Street for a gala citizens banquet. The meeting was an almost routine Olin triumph. This time the impressario's script included a university professor, the mayor, and a noted Milwaukee architect, all of whom stumped for a city plan. Then came Olin who held his audience spellbound with a one-hour oration in which he described the preparation of a comprehensive city plan not merely as an opportunity, but as an "obligation." He reported that for this purpose twenty-five hundred dollars had been subscribed to cover the cost of publishing the plan *providing* that "representative" citizens gave the enterprise their "hearty" approval. In the cheerleading spirit of the evening, the group unanimously voted to prepare a city plan under the guidance of a Committee of Fifty including Wisconsin Governor James O. Davidson, U.W. President Van Hise, four dozen prominent Madison businessmen, and headed, not surprisingly, by John Olin. No downfield blocker ever did a better job for his following runner than Olin did for Nolen. The banquet guests left the hall greatly excited about the possibility of remaking Madison.[242]

Twenty-one months after the kick-off banquet, in September 1910, the Committee of Fifty approved the plan and released its bittersweet contents of the public. On the bitter side, Nolen sharply criticized James Doty, the developer of Madison's original (1836) plat, for his "mechanical and thoughtless" adaption of the L'Enfant Washington, D.C., plan—a plan Nolen regarded

as the most farsighted and skillful city plan ever prepared. Specifically Nolen criticized Doty's failure to provide any public parks except the capitol grounds, his failure to provide any public lake access except street ends, and for his failure to make street widths reflect their relative importance. In short Nolen declared Doty's attempt to develop a site of "rare distinction" to be a "failure."[243] In addition to these serious initial design errors, Nolen saw a confluence of ominous forces gaining ascendancy in Madison. Lakeshores were being built up without adequate public access, street trees were poorly maintained, ugly utility poles and wires were proliferating, commercial buildings were invading residential areas, homes were being jammed together so tightly that a dog could barely run between them, railroad tracks were cutting Madison asunder, a stinking dump lay just four blocks from the new capitol, skyscrapers were about to mar the skyline, and much more. Most disconcerting of all, Nolen saw no countervailing public policies capable of dealing with this growing array of problems.[244]

In spite of all these trends and conditions, Nolen was not only bullish on Madison—he was downright excited. If Madison successfully exploited its design opportunities, it could "establish" a new standard for city-making in the U.S."[245] and could become a world-class city comparable in flattering ways to Lucerne, Geneva, Weimar, Oxford, Rio de Janiero, and Versailles. Indeed, of all U.S. cities, Nolen declared ". . . Madison has the best opportunity to become . . . a model modern American city."[246] And if this could be accomplished, Nolen concluded, then in the area of city-making Madison would become "the hope of democracy."[247]

Nolen's design strategy was to identify the unique elements of a city. According to the pioneer city planner, Madison had five characteristics that distinguished it from other cities and gave it its personality: its incomparable site, its people who through the MPPDA had established an impressive record of public spirit, its roles as the capital and home of the university and as a city of homes.

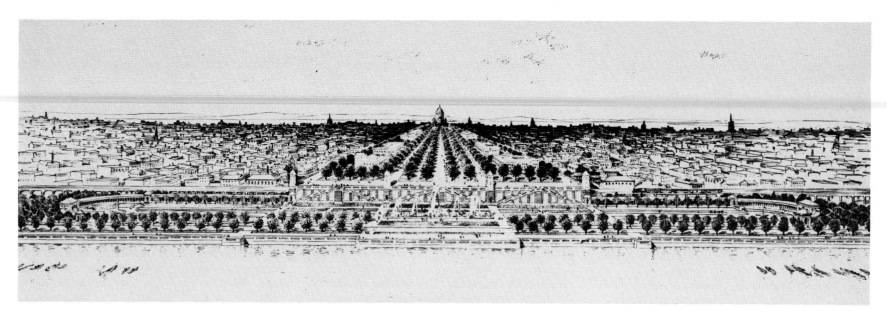

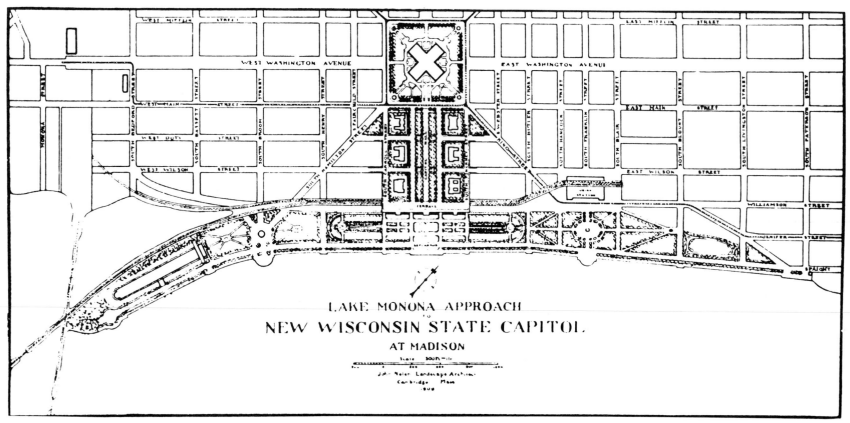

LAKE MONONA APPROACH
to
NEW WISCONSIN STATE CAPITOL
AT MADISON

Scale 300ft.=1in.

John Nolen Landscape Architect
Cambridge Mass
1908

FIGURE 6.54. GRAND MALL AND GREAT ESPLANADE. After seeing plans for the new state capitol Nolen concluded that the fourteen-acre Capitol Square was much too small for such a large building. Should the new capitol be built without expanding its site, it would give the impression, Nolen said, that "the state was too poor . . . to surround the building properly" and that the city was "becoming congested."

His solution was to create an organic link between the capitol and Lake Monona—a link that became the most expensive, most desired, and yet most radical design component of the entire plan. Nolen called the first part of this linkage the "Grand Mall." Nolen envisioned the four-hundred-foot-wide and one-thousand-foot-long mall flanked by government office buildings and reserved the two choice sites at the south end of the mall for a state theater-opera house and a resort hotel. The Grand Mall then cascaded into a one-and-one-half-mile-long "Great Experience" featuring trees, fountains, and sculpture. Sketch plans for these grand concepts are shown here.

Nolen first presented these two concepts to the public at the annual meeting of the Madison Park and Pleasure Drive Association in April 1909. The concept was so radical that Olin, knowing what Nolen was about to unveil, warned his loyal band of supporters that he would not "be surprised if some . . . do not pass out from this room convinced that Mr. Nolen is a visionary dreamer and the reputation of myself and others for conservatism has been severely impaired."

Though neither the mall nor the explanade were ever implemented, they did influence later decision makers. The importance of Monona Avenue was reflected by the location of the U.S. Post Office (1927), the first state office building (1930–1932), and the City-County Building (1954). A token expression of the explanade can be seen in the lakeshore park along John Nolen Drive, but a 1967 version of this concept known as the Monona Basin Plan prepared by William Wesley Peters of the Frank Lloyd Wright Foundation was rejected.

One of the great and bitter ironies of Nolen's work in Madison was the 1967 Common Council decision to name the four-lane expressway built along the lakeshore "John Nolen Drive." To usurp this choice lake frontage for a major transportation artery could not have been more contrary to what Nolen was trying to achieve for his "model city." (Courtesy of Cornell University Archives)

Nolen saw each of these characteristics as great strengths on which to build. Of course he wanted to take advantage of the extraordinary design opportunities that the isthmus site provided. He was particularly hopeful that Madison's relatively large German population would support the same high standard of urban design and management with which they were familiar in their native cities and which Nolen so admired. As the capital of a proud, progressive state, Nolen wanted to give the city "dignity and even some restrained splendor." As the home of the university Nolen expected Madisonians to manifest a much higher degree of concern for "learning, culture, art and nature" than found in other cities.[248] And as a beautiful city of homes Nolen sought to enhance public recreational facilities and make the city more efficient and convenient. Very significantly, Nolen did not want manufacturing or commerce to become a major justification for the city but rather a *leitmotif*.

Nolen's translation of Madison's special characteristics in his plan published as *Madison: A Model City* (Boston, 1911) was audacious, farsighted, and perspicacious, a fascinating blend of older City Beautiful and the newer City Functional concepts. Legacies from the City Beautiful included the Grand Mall and the Great Esplanade, the widening of State Street, the burying of all utilities, the upgrading of major city entrances, the establishment of a strong street tree planting and maintenance program, and the establishment of Capitol Square building height limit to preserve capital views.

Summary of Nolen Recommendations

Nolen's seventeen recommendations of "supreme importance" to Madison were:

1. Limit building height around the capitol.
2. Create an organic link between the capitol and Lake Monona with a Grand Mall and a Great Esplanade.
3. Widen and improve State Street.
4. Improve the appearance and utilize major streets leading into the city.
5. Secure the most important lake frontages.
6. Acquire and fill marshland in and around Madison.
7. Substantially expand the U.W. campus size and range of land-related facilities (arboretum, botanical garden, etc.).
8. Improve railroad approaches to the city and eliminate grade crossings.
9. Adopt a better way of platting streets and subdivisions.
10. Place utility wires underground.
11. Pass an ordinance that assures planting and proper care of street trees.
12. Place Madison parks under the control of the City of Madison.
13. Develop a park system for Madison.
14. Provide children's playgrounds in every neighborhood.
15. Pass a zoning ordinance to control the use and bulk characteristics of all buildings.
16. Provide housing for poor people.
17. Develop financial mechanisms that allow the state and city to share costs of implementing the plan and to keep annual debt service to the lowest possible levels.

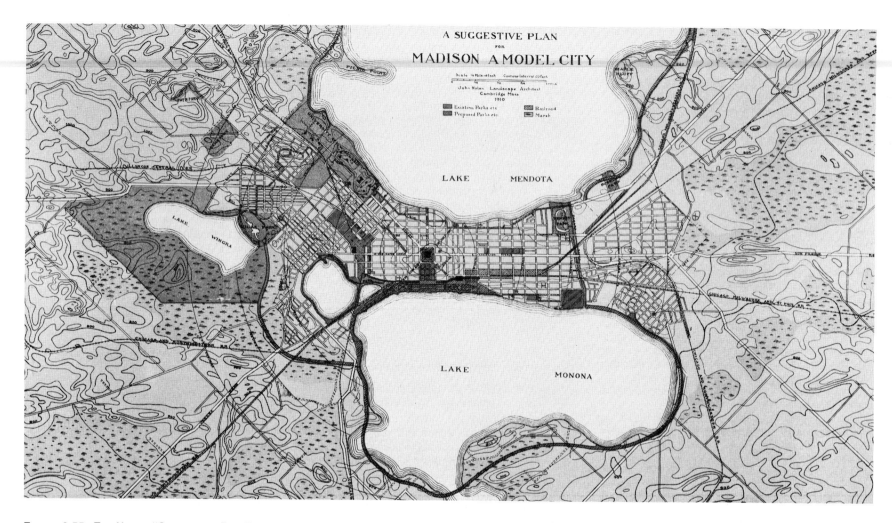

FIGURE 6.55. THE NOLEN "SUGGESTIVE PLAN". Nolen's "suggestive plan," shown here, embodied the concepts he felt Madison must implement to become a model city. The map highlights the "really large" park surrounding Lake Wingra, which eventually became the arboretum, the expanded U.W. campus, the massive Grand Mall and Great Esplanade, and a Tenney Park counterpart at the Yahara River outlet to Lake Monona in what is now the Marquette area. The map is one of one hundred twenty graphics that appear in Nolen's slender, beautifully bound, and well-written book.

The Madison plan like many other Nolen plans emphasized differentiated building zones and streets, improved circulatory systems (note the connection between University Avenue and West Washington Avenue), a continuous park system, a cluster of public and semipublic facilities in a formal civic center, condensed and/or rerouted railroad facilities, waterfront "gateways," and low income housing. Although the Madison plan was not as explicit as some of his later plans, Nolen advocated decentralization as a means of reducing residential "congestion" or what we would today call "high density" living.

Nolen later characterized his 1910 city plan as "elementary and amateurish" and as "largely propaganda and publicity," but these harsh comments must be taken in context. In the first instance, Nolen was saying that city planning had made major strides forward since the Madison plan was done. In the second instance Nolen was saying that to be the first and to be rejected is not to fail but rather to become a necessary stage in the development of public awareness. Nolen didn't get Madisonians to adopt his plan but he got them to think about it. Considering that few Madisonians had even heard about city planning prior to his arrival, this was no minor achievement.

But Nolen also sought to make Madison more humane, convenient and efficient in addition to beautiful, goals that caused Nolen to go beyond aesthetics to housing, recreation, transportation, and land use controls. Nolen asked for low-income housing, a rare emphasis among planners of that era, children's playgrounds in all neighborhoods (at the time Madison had just two), more parks for all, particularly lake frontage, and the elimination of residential congestion then evident in the student housing area near the university, in a festering slum called "the Bush," and near the Square. He also urged Madison officials to reassert control over the railroads whose crisscrossing of the isthmus had been "the most serious factor in Madison's "unmaking."[249]

To achieve these goals Nolen urged Madisonians to concentrate on the "common welfare" by adopting European urban design and management values. Nolen argued that even the poorest Europeans enjoyed advantages and opportunities not available to wealthy Madisonians. These advantages included spacious green plazas, spirit-lifting waterfronts and fountains, enobling statuary, stimulating museums, concert halls and theaters, and convenient and ample parks and playgrounds. It was not that Madison could not afford such amenities; on the contrary it was a city of relatively great private wealth. The problem, said Nolen, was that Madison chose "community poverty." Nevertheless Madison could enjoy the rich spectrum of European urban amenities, but *only* if it were willing to subordinate private to public good, quantity to quality, property rights to people rights, short-term costs to long-term economies, and *laissez faire* to planning. If these values were integrated into public policy, they would, said Nolen, "democratize recreation and art" and ultimately reduce the cost of local government by cutting waste. Nolen even appealed to the commercial expansionists by saying that urban beauty was a profound growth generator.

Significantly, Nolen was not rejecting capitalism but rather, like other progressives, finding

ways to harness its great strengths while minimizing its weaknesses. Nevertheless to Madison's dominant business elite who were challenged by the risks and rewards of speculation, who believed they could do what they liked with their property, who sought urban growth because bigger was better, and who were not terribly bothered by the lack of European amenities, all these new values seemed strange indeed.[250]

In contrast to the hoopla and "hearty support" that the city plan enjoyed when it was commissioned, reaction to the release of the carefully crafted Nolen plan in September 1910, just twenty-one months after it was commissioned, was almost nonexistent. Both daily newspapers did matter-of-fact summary stories and that was it.[251] From that point forward the Nolen plan was virtually ignored. It was almost as if a meteor had crashed in the middle of Lake Monona and left no ripples. Seldom in Madison history had something so potentially important been dropped so quickly. What explained this nonresponse?

First, many key components of the plan had been released to the public over a period of two years. The Grand Mall and Great Esplanade, for example, had been unveiled in detail in April 1909. Thus the contents of the plan could hardly be said to be a surprise.

Second, Nolen was cast in a difficult—indeed one is almost inclined to say "no-win" role—a role not unlike that of a psychiatrist who, as a condition of healing a talented but reluctant client, first had to get the client to acknowledge past and present mistakes. Even though Nolen always phrased his criticisms in a professional way, he was in effect telling Madisonians that they were tight fisted, short sighted, and wrong headed and that present and past policies doomed Madison to ugliness, mediocrity, and waste. Not surprisingly most Madisonians rejected this message in preference for the more charitable view that Madison was Wisconsin's most sophisticated, cerebral, beautiful, and progressive city.

Third, interest in and support for city planning never expanded much beyond the small group of business and professional leaders John

Olin initially assembled. If anything, interest declined during the plan preparation process. It is tempting to attribute this decline to the fact that Olin was forced for health reasons to resign as president of the MPPDA and as leader of the Committee of Fifty in September 1909, just nine months after the plan kick-off banquet and one year before the plan was released. Clearly, Olin's "departure" had a pronounced influence. Had his health remained robust, the Nolen plan *might* have enjoyed a more favorable reception, but the evidence for this speculation is anything but convincing. In June 1909, for example, *before* Olin resigned, the council rejected a Nolen proposal for boulevarding East Washington Avenue and selected instead a more pedestrian proposal by city engineer John Icke. Several other rejections of Nolen's park design work quickly followed. Even more ominous anti-Nolen sentiment surfaced in February 1910 when several aldermen tried to delete Nolen's salary from the budget. Though the action failed, the aldermen came back one year later even *before* the Nolen plan was published and axed his salary. By not renewing Nolen's contract, they had, in effect, fired him. Aldermen said that Nolen was getting paid too much to spend too little time in Madison to do too little work.[252]

The intensity of anti-Nolen sentiment suggests that Olin's influence as a civic leader may well have peaked in 1908 or 1909, not because Olin's esteem in the community declined but because he had taken the community about as far as it was willing to go with planning—even with his extraordinary leadership skills. Indeed, it would appear that much Common Council anti-Nolen sentiment was a backlash to Olin's skillful mobilization of the city's power elite whose collective influence the council could only accommodate by hiring the Boston planner.

Fourth, Nolen's plan required the adoption of major new governmental powers, nearly all of which were viewed by Madison decision makers as major assaults on the rights of private property owners. For example, Nolen said that Madisonians would have to accept new land use controls such as zoning, subdivision regulation, and height limits on Capitol Square buildings.[253] Nolen also sought changes that would have allowed the state to play a much larger role in the governance of Madison such as the control of large amounts of property. Although he did not formally recommend the establishment of commission government dominated by state appointees, he described the system in glowing terms and urged its consideration. At the time, not many Madisonians supported such radical increases in governmental power and loss of local control.

A fifth factor that prevented the Nolen plan from being realized was its huge cost, estimated at between six and ten million dollars. Nolen acknowledged that his plan was expensive and that there was no way that a city of twenty-five thousand people with an annual budget of less than a half million dollars and close to the limit of its legal debt limit could afford his plan. By the same token, Nolen argued, there was no way in the 1870s that the relatively small population of Washington, D.C., could have become a dignified national capital without the substantial financial assistance of the federal government.[254]

Based on this Washington model, Nolen urged a series of constitutional amendments that he believed made his grand plan completely affordable. For example, one amendment increased the state debt limit from one hundred thousand dollars to twenty-five million and another increased the payback period for bonded debt from twenty to fifty years. Nolen argued that these measures would have provided more than enough money to pay for the Nolen plan.[255]

Olin, a superb legislative tactician, decided that these amendments, the early product of his collaboration with Nolen, should be run through the critical first legislative test in 1909, i.e., *before* the plan was completed. All three were approved. This left a second legislative approval in 1911 and a vote by the people to complete the approval process. By 1911, however, the costs of the Nolen plan were available and outstate legislators were inflamed to think that Madisonians

expected the citizens of the state to build a seven-million-dollar showpiece capital and then turn around and lay out another four or five million dollars to pay for various plan components that Nolen said were the state's responsibility. One indignant Milwaukee newspaper editor called it "Madison's money madness."[256]

(Very significantly there was one other element in the 1909 Olin-Nolen legislative package that was approved, namely, a bill making Wisconsin the first state in the nation to authorize its cities to form planning commissions.[257])

Nolen might well have been bitter about the way he was treated in the city he truly believed to be "the hope of democracy." After all, his three-year contract had not been renewed, several plans done under his regular city contract had been brusquely rejected, and his grand city plan into which he had poured his heart and soul had been greeted by a huge yawn. Had he never wanted to hear the name Madison again, he could hardly have been blamed. Very significantly, however, any feelings of rancor that Nolen may have had were quickly replaced by his strong underlying "love for Madison" and high regard for John Olin and that "noble little band" of spirited citizens with whom he worked.[258] Even at the end of his busy career with hundreds of projects around the country to his credit, Madison remained one of his all-time favorite clients. No accident, then, that for twenty-four years (1908–1935) he corresponded with various Madison men.[259]

Still another reason for Nolen's charitable attitude toward Madison was the fact that his work gave him entree to a group of influential Madisonians who in turn provided other opportunities for Wisconsin city planning work. For example, in 1909 Ford H. MacGregor, secretary of the League of Wisconsin Municipalities, invited Nolen to speak at their annual statewide meeting and later printed Nolen's speech in full in the league magazine, *The Municipality,* which went to nearly all mayors and city officials in the state. This superb exposure helped Nolen secure city planning jobs in Milwaukee, LaCrosse, Janesville, and Kenosha.[260]

Fortunately, Madison's decision to ignore the Nolen plan did not mean that none of its recommendations were ever implemented. Indeed, like a peat fire, Nolen's ideas and concepts smouldered underground for years—often with little or no public awareness—and then from time to time they would burst into flame on the surface. Interestingly, the University of Wisconsin was the first to implement one of his recommendations. Under the aggressive leadership of Charles Van Hise, the university expanded the campus size by more than five hundred acres—not the two thousand acres Nolen had recommended, but an impressive start in that direction, nevertheless.[261] Another Nolen recommendation, that the U.W. create an arboretum, became a reality in 1934 after two men who greatly admired Nolen's work, Michael Olbrich, a Madison attorney and U.W. regent, and Joseph Jackson, director of the Madison Board of Commerce, pushed it into being. Very appropriately, Nolen was invited back to Madison for the arboretum opening and gave the dedication address—a task he joyfully accepted.[262] During the Depression years, the university also implemented still another Nolen suggestion, namely, a summer engineering camp on the shores of Lake Mendota.[263]

Eventually even the City of Madison began to implement Nolen's ideas, although not until after a decade when planning was virtually forgotten.[264] Beginning in 1920, however, a combination of circumstances caused planning to surge to the front of public interest. With the War over, Madison decision makers could once again concentrate on the "domestic" agenda, nearly all elements of which had been placed on the back burner during that conflict. For example, fifty percent increase in population between 1910 and 1920 made the cumulative affects of planned growth, especially central city congestion, painfully evident. Rising standards and expectations made decision makers led by the Board of Commerce more eager to try more bold solutions, a development that coincided with a rapid maturation of city planning and a greater acceptance

FIGURE 6.56. MADISON'S FIRST SKYSCRAPER. When the announcement was made in the spring of 1911 that Madison developer Leonard Gay planned to erect an eight-story building on the Capitol Square, a squall line of reaction swept through the city. Among the first to criticize the plan was U.W. professor of philosophy and Madison Art League leader Joseph Jastrow, who said the "innovation" was "very undesirable" since it would "distract from the commanding effect" of Wisconsin's glorious new capitol building, then under construction. The public interest demanded that such skyscrapers be banned, asserted Jastrow. Just a few months earlier John Nolen, Madison's first city planner, placed his full weight behind this antiskyscraper sentiment. In his far-reaching city plan, *Madison, A Model City,* Nolen urged immediate height limitations for all buildings around the square and even suggested an ordinance by which this could be accomplished. In spite of such exhortations, however, the city issued a building permit for the $160,000 Gay Building, as it was subsequently known, and work got underway.

Unsuccessful on the local front, antiskyscraper forces got a bill introduced in the state legislature but were stymied there when the attorney general ruled that the state could only regulate construction on matters of health and safety, not on aesthetic grounds. There the matter stood until 1921 when the legislature passed a bill limiting Capitol Square buildings to ninety feet. However, the Piper brothers who were then planning to erect a hotel on the Square took the law to the Supreme Court. While the law was tied up in the courts Walter Schroeder, a Milwaukee hotel developer, and the Piper brothers moved quickly to construct their hotels, the Lorraine and the Belmont respectively. Finally in 1923 the high court upheld the law and grandfathered the two hotels then under construction. Both hotels were subsequently converted to other uses: the Belmont became the YWCA and the Lorraine was purchased by the state and converted to a state office building. Thus, twelve years after the fight began, one of the city's most important design principles received the sanction of law, still another component in a harvest of progressive legislation.

When the Gay Building, shown here was completed in early 1915, it was subjected to rather harsh reviews. One visiting dignitary said the building was a "crude wall of raw bricks" that stood up "like a sore tooth." "If this town had anything like civic pride," the dignitary harumphed, "it would allow no high building to appear here and mutilate the best capitol square layout in the country."

Although the Gay Building was not a popular addition to the Madison skyline in some circles, it was nevertheless the first of many high-rise buildings and for many years the city's highest building. Designed by Madison architect James R. Law, the Gay Building featured reinforced concrete fireproof construction and plush interior appointments and gave many Madisonians their first experience with the thrilling new high-speed Otis elevators.

In the 1970s the name of the building was changed to the Churchill Building. (SHSW WHi(X3)33757) of it as a legitimate and effective tool. These were circumstances that caused the Madison Common Council to create a City Plan Commission in 1920 using the 1909 state enabling law drafted by Nolen.[265] Gradually, the city adopted other Olin recommendations. In 1923 the supreme court upheld a state law that placed height limitations on Capitol Square buildings. In 1927 the city adopted its first zoning ordinance.[266] In 1931 the city finally formed a full-fledged park commission as Nolen recommended and took over control of all parks from the Madison Park and Pleasure Drive Association.[267] Then in the 1970s the city decided to do something about State Street, Madison's "most important" street, though by this time it was too late to widen the street to the grand proportions that Nolen had recommended. However, the city did accomplish the spirit of his beautification program.[268]

Today it is easy to fault Nolen's work. We can say that he was unrealistic in his expectations, precipitous in his design prescriptions, intolerant in his approach, and preoccupied by City Beautiful concepts. But such criticisms ignore the circumstances under which Nolen worked. There were no tested methodologies for this first wave of planners; there was only instinct, common sense, and exhortation. Nor do such criticisms take into account the buoyant expectations of the era, a time of great national ferment, a time when Progressives like Nolen sensed great momentum swinging to their causes. Indeed for Nolen it must have been terribly exciting. Not only had he staked a claim on a promising new discipline that viewed cities as profoundly malleable, but he had just obtained a new client city comprised of high-grade ore capable of being expressed in a brilliant and exemplary form. For a young man just two years out of graduate school and already a prominent member of his new profession, this was bubbly champagne. These were the reasons why Nolen's plan for Madison was a freer, fuller, and more vital expression of the city's potential than that of any of its successors. All too soon the planning profession was filled with practitioners who believed more in compromise than vision.

In the end Nolen's greatest achievement was to set forth a clear goal, even a burning ideal of what Madison could become and the new values needed to achieve those goals. No plan has ever captured the high destiny of the city so succinctly, eloquently, and convincingly. Indeed even for contemporary readers Nolen's *Madison, A Model City* has a freshness, a clarity of vision, and an effervescence that make it a source of inspiration in spite of seventy intervening years. Madison is still working on the Nolen plan and will continue to do so in the future.

A City Well Housed

During the nineteenth century, Madison leaders actively fostered certain images of their city as a place of great natural beauty, as a center of law and learning, as a posh Northern resort, as a regional emporium, and even as a center of industry. But there was one other flattering attribute Madison leaders sought to exploit: its unusually large number of elegant homes. Each spring Madison newspaper editors, knowing that such things would be read by other newspaper editors around the state, described the latest fine homes planned for construction that season. In addition they ran feature stories throughout the year about the neat gardens, picket fences, spectacular views, and the huge lawns of Madison's homes. Rare was the promotional tract that did not lavish superlatives upon Madison's many distinguished neighborhoods. The public relations effort worked. Madison became known—and not without justification—as a city of beautiful homes.

Densification and Uglification of the Isthmus

Although city publicists did not like to admit it, Madison also had shacks, shanties, and undesirable neighborhoods. Of course they rarely got much attention, and when they did, it usually took the form of denials or boasts. As late as 1902, for

example, Mayor J. W. Groves claimed that Madison had "no slums nor . . . any squalor stricken settlements. . . ."[269] In the sense that Madison did not have big-city teeming tenements, Groves was right. In the sense that Madison did not have a housing problem, he was wrong. From 1902 on, few had much good to say about the prospects of isthmus housing quality.

Among the areas where bad housing was first noticed was the "Latin Quarter," a wilderness of rooming houses, fraternities, and sororities lying roughly between the campus, University Avenue and Henry Street. During the 1880s and 1890s the Latin Quarter had been a quiet and very prestigious neighborhood in which prominent families commonly rented one or two rooms to students. But then between 1900 and 1910 U.W. enrollments jumped from two thousand to four thousand students. This rapid increase, coupled with the long time university refusal to build dormitories for its male students and the absence of city land use controls, caused spacious Langdon lawns to be sold for roominghouses and elegant homes to be converted to fraternity houses. In the scramble for shelter, some students were forced to endure unprecedented conditions.[270] In one instance seventeen men shared a roominghouse without indoor plumbing. In another twenty-two women shared a roominghouse with just one bathtub.[271] Soon the lucrative student roominghouse business became the principal business of the Latin Quarter.

By 1907 a U.W. professor and former resident of the Latin Quarter complained that "parts of Langdon . . . had been spoiled . . ." by the trend. Some houses, he lamented, had been built so close together that one received "the drippings from the eaves of another." By 1910 prominent families had begun their exodus from this area.[272]

No sooner had many Madisonians concluded that the future of the Latin Quarter was imperiled if not ruined by improper development, than another festering neighborhood was thrust into the public limelight. The neighborhood was a part of South Madison known as "Greenbush." An eighty-acre plat bounded by Mills, Regent, Murray, and Erin Streets, Greenbush suffered from a terribly defective birthright. Much of the plat was low and marshy and had to be filled to be usable. During the nineteenth century, scavengers dumped wagonload after wagonload of clinkers and refuse into the marsh until the fill stood just slightly above the water table. There the filling stopped and cheap houses were erected for Madison's poor people.[273] Not only was Greenbush a popular dump for household refuse, but it was also the most popular dumping ground for old houses. Instead of razing small cheaply built homes, they were sold to someone who moved them to another lot where they were either sold or rented. Such hand-me-down, moved, and recycled houses constituted Madison's major source of low-income housing.

Such buildings supplied shelter to a wave of Italian immigrants who came to Madison between 1905 and 1910, most of whom settled in Greenbush. For a time Greenbush therefore became known as "the Italian District," but to most Madisonians it was simply called "the Bush." The area was also popular with Madison's small black population and to newly arrived Russian-Jewish immigrants, both of whom found the modest recycled homes in the Bush all they could afford.[274]

In 1910 Madison club women interested in improving the sanitary condition of city housing publicized the terrible conditions in the Bush. One-third of all homes there had no city water connection, they reported; many residents had to go more than a block for water, and bathtubs were almost unknown. In one home, nine persons slept in one room; in another eighteen people shared five small rooms.[275] Many homes were built so low above the water table that during warm weather they were surrounded by disease-breeding stagnant water and their cellars were always damp if not water filled.

Not until 1916, however, did concern for the Bush reappear as a major issue. In that year Lawrence Veiller, a nationally famous New York housing expert and author of a model tenement and housing law, visited Madison at the request of the Civics Club. Veiller blasted Madisonians for their complacency in the face of such terrible

circumstances. "You've got as bad a slum as any city in the country—worse than the slums of New York and Chicago. The people in Greenbush live in a dump with the most sordid outlook and surroundings I have ever seen except on a garbage dump in Columbus (Ohio)," he told stunned Madisonians. Veiller was probably the first person to advocate urban renewal of Greenbush. In Veiller's words Greenbush was a "civic cancer" on which the "surgeons' knife should be used immediately and liberally."[276] Forty years later city leaders actually did what Veiller recommended. The Bush became Madison's first urban renewal project.

Though some Madisonians tried to persuade themselves that the city's housing problems were limited to the Latin Quarter and the Bush, they found little basis in fact to do so. Two factors converged to cause eave-to-eave construction and high-density living to become increasingly common in nearly all built-up portions of the city. The first was the steady increase in population. The second was the availability of city utilities. Though it is difficult for persons today to realize the importance of now commonplace city utilities, their appeal then was enormous. They were the "great urban advantage." In surrounding Dane County there was a hand pump and a wood-burning stove in the kitchen, a privy out back, and kerosene lamps scattered throughout the house, but in Madison, by contrast, one could have running water and cooking gas merely by turning a handle, electricity by flipping a switch, an inside flushing toilet by pulling a chain, telephone communications by turning a crank, and streetcar transportation by dropping a nickel in the fare box.

The availability of these amenities led to the more intense use of Madison's relatively large 66 × 132 foot standard lots. In the first decade of the twentieth century, the once commonplace single-family dwelling on a 66 × 132 foot lot gave way to two and three flat buildings on 33 × 132 *half*-lots.[277] Then in the second decade of the twentieth century the first generation of apartment buildings made their appearance. Most were built for middle- to upper-income persons and

contained from fifteen to fifty-five units. For example, the Bellevue Apartments, 29 East Wilson Street (1913), featured fireplaces, folding beds, sophisticated on-premises ironing and laundry facilities, and a dumbwaiter system for food and packages.[278] Both the flats and apartment buildings covered very large percentages of their total lot area. Lawns and sideyards, once commonplace amenities in isthmus neighborhoods were sold off as building lots with high yet marketable prices. The closer the lot was to the Capitol Square the more it cost and the smaller it got.

Not only were the new rooming houses, flats, and apartments crowded together, but they were ill-equipped with fire exits. In 1913 a state inspector said that Madison was "without a doubt the worst city in the state in this respect."[279]

City Government Intervenes: Efforts to Solve the Housing Problems

The city's response to the problems of crowded, unsanitary, and unsafe housing came slowly and reluctantly. Gradually, however, officials were forced to respond to the bewildering and frustrating new problem. To call their responses a "housing policy"—at least in the modern sense of a conscious, coordinated strategy—would be a clear exaggeration. In fact, city responses were little more than incremental efforts to cope with this new, yet rapidly intensifying problem. Still, these responses reveal much about the thinking of city decision makers of that era.

The first and in many ways the most dramatic response to the growing housing problem was a popular progressive remedy, namely, governmental regulation. In Madison and in many other cities around the country, the foundation upon which housing regulation was based was the building permit system. First promulgated in Madison in 1910, it was not until 1913 that this system received power and direction from a comprehensive building code covering size, safety, and

FIGURE 6.57. SOUTH MADISON.   Greenbush was the undisputed low rung on the Madison housing ladder. These pictures were taken by a U.W. student whose 1911 thesis on public health showed what happens when you put cheap houses on landfill dump sites just inches above the water table and then fill the modest structures with the poorest people.

The picture above shows the garbage and trash infested corner of Park and Regent Streets. The picture to the right shows a street called Guinnette Court, which was bulldozed in about 1955. The three flat buildings were then inhabited by twelve families whose apartments consisted of two rooms each. (SHSW WHi(X3)36273 and WHi(X3)36275)

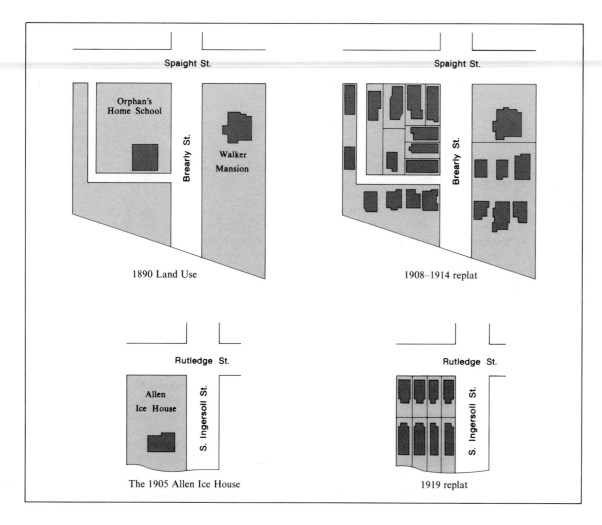

FIGURE 6.58. DENSIFICATION OF THE ISTHMUS TECHNIQUES. Densification of the isthmus took three basic forms: (1) subdividing standard building lots; (2) replatting; and (3) building multi-family housing (flats and apartments). Shown above are several before and after examples of lot subdivisions and replatting.

A 1906 Indictment of Flat Living

"The flat has been rightly named. Existence in it is flat indeed. The oppressive consciousness of another family above or below you can never be escaped. It haunts like an accusing conscious. The family may also be above or beneath you in the social scale, which is a greater calamity still. Often the owner lives in one floor and seeks an opportunity to devour you. Often there is much in common, always stairs, porches, cellars, furnaces, bathrooms, clotheslines. One of the worst indictments against this form of life is that there is usually no yard, front, back or side, with a flat. The thrifty owners spread their great buildings over the entire lot. . . . No room for raising a few vegatables or growing a few flowers. No allowance made for soul expansion; you and your children must be indoors or on the street."

After the turn of the century, high isthmus land costs placed conventional single-family detached housing out of reach for a growing number of Madisonians. Still, the convenience of being near jobs and near streetcar lines and having city sewer, water, gas, electricity, and telephone continued to make isthmus living very attractive. For more and more Madisonians, the answer was the flat, that is, a four- to seven-room apartment occupying an entire floor of a two- or three-level building. Though cheaper than a single-family home, the flat was not without its limitations. On August 28, 1906, the *Wisconsin State Journal* printed this indictment of flat living from one of its readers.

sanitation. Very significantly, it was the 1913 building code that gave Madison its first full-time building inspector with broad powers to condemn, require repairs, and even stop construction. For the first time standards were linked to enforcement. During the first round of inspections, two hundred Madison building owners were required to add fire escapes—a requirement that had been on the books for four years but was seldom enforced. Once the comprehensive code had been passed, the Common Council gradually tightened its requirements and raised its standards.[280]

A second technique used by Madison officials to influence housing quality was annexation. The suburbs had three things Madison leaders badly wanted: (1) more people; (2) more tax base; and (3) higher quality deed-restricted housing stock. Informed Madisonians recognized that all over the country central cities were becoming congested and that the natural reaction of many was to move to the outlying areas. In short, the suburbs were needed to prevent beautiful Madison from becoming a congested ghetto. As one developer put it, Madison needed land for "businessmen and others (who) wanted to get out of the crowded cities and reside in the outskirts."[281]

In its desire to annex the suburbs, the city held some trump cards in the form of city advantages that the suburbs wanted and could not afford. These included water and sewer systems, police and fire protection, and schools. To create these systems from scratch would have been prohibitively expensive for the small suburbs. Madison was also able to get much lower borrowing rates than its small untested, newly incorporated suburbs. Knowing that it enjoyed this strategic high ground Madison officials sometimes deliberately withheld or withdrew certain services to force suburban areas to annex.[282]

Although both city officials and suburban leaders found annexation attractive, the impetus for annexation clearly lay with suburban property owners. To be annexed to Madison one-half of the affected property owners had to petition the city for admission and three-fourths of the Common Council had to approve the petition.[283]

The Siren Song of the Suburbs

These excerpts from suburb ads appeared in the Madison newspapers between 1903 and 1920. Consistent sales themes included space, privacy, quiet, affordability, proximity, accessibility, back to nature, escape to quality, lower taxes, and big profits.

Hillington
"Every lot restricted, No flats, No stores, No unsightly buildings."
July 1920

West Lawn
"WEST LAWN is especially recommended to professional business and university men—to lawyers, doctors, bankers, merchants and professors."
July 1903

University Heights
"My clients are money makers. I advise you to buy, and buy now, some University Heights lots."
April 1903

Shore Acres
"An acre of ground . . . means a place for the children to play and grow, a garden, strawberries, raspberries, gooseberries, apples, cherries and plums; all your own; chickens if you want them. What about the high cost of living then?"
May 1914

The Highlands
"The lots are from 30 to 40 times the size of our city lots, allowing plenty of room for lawn or gardens."
May 1912

Madison Square
"NO SALOONS IN MADISON SQUARE. In every deed and contract made by the Madison Square Company, there will be a covenant running with the land, prohibiting liquor to be sold on the premises. This action made every lot worth a great deal more to the home builder. It secured the future against saloons on 9 miles of streets in Madison's factory district. Don't you want to live in that kind of place?"
May 1907

Nakoma
"If you have a car it is 15 minutes to Nakoma. If you use the bus it is 20 minutes."
July 1916

The Highlands
"It is within a twenty minute ride of Capitol Square at the ordinary speed of an auto."

"The proposed interurban has been surveyed to pass two blocks from the entrance to the Highlands."
May 1912

University Heights	". . . Only five minutes walk from the college buildings."
	June 1903
Madison Square	"5 dollars down, 5 dollars a month, 5 percent interest."
	May 1910
West Lawn	"It lies far back from the factories and the distracting noises of a growing city."
	July 1903
Tenth Ward	"Parents want their homes in the community where boys and girls have no saloon influences. The 10th Ward HAS NEVER HAD A SALOON, and the City Council has no power to grant a license there."
	April 1914
Nakoma	"Invest $500 in one of those beautiful sites and let it sleep for ten years—*then cash in $5,000.00.*"
	July 1915
Highland Park	"What will you leave your family? A stack of worthless rent receipts—or a *Real* Estate."
	April 1916
Wingra and Oakland	"Street cars every 12 minutes."
	April 1903
South Madison	"South Madison lies nearer the capital than Wingra Park or University Heights."
	May 1913
Nakoma	"Taxes in Nakoma are going to be low for many years. The residents of this district will not vote to come into the city when they have almost all the comforts of the city now with the advantages of country life, and, without city taxes."
	July, 1916
Fair Oaks	"Street car line runs along its full length."
	February, 1903
Highland Park	"Get out where you can have a garden plot of your own, where you can sit on the porch in the evening without having the dust roll up in clouds; where in whatever direction your eyes wander, you can see the neat homes and green lawns of your neighbors."
	April, 1916

This mutual attraction between city and suburban property owners produced no less than eleven annexations between 1903 and 1918 and caused nearly eleven hundred acres to be added to the City of Madison tax rolls—an increase in area of thirty-six percent.[284]

The third technique designed to increase housing quality was to open up the suburbs by extending streetcar lines. Between 1910 and 1920 following the "discovery" of congestion, nearly all Madison opinion-makers believed the streetcar—not the auto—was going to be the "great urban decongestant." They noted that before the streetcar, workers were forced to walk to work and therefore lived no more than one or two miles from their jobs—a circumstance that led to crowding and slums. With the advent of the streetcar, however, the age-old tether between job and home was irreversibly loosened. Nearly all workers could afford to drop a dime a day in the fare box and were willing to spend up to an hour a day commuting. For the first time, the streetcar allowed workers to enjoy cheaper, bigger homes and larger backyards, the same amenities previously limited to persons with much larger incomes.[285]

Unfortunately this promising strategy enjoyed a very limited application in Madison. From the time F. W. Montgomery bought the streetcar line in 1905 until the time the streetcars were replaced by motor buses in 1935, only two streetcar line extensions were made. The first was the 1905 track extension to South Madison. Here Montgomery had been persuaded that his line extension would cause the population of this then sparsely settled suburb to boom and that its new residents would fill his fareboxes with their nickels. Unfortunately for Montgomery and others who pinned their South Madison suburban growth hopes on the streetcar, people moved into this area very slowly *in spite* of streetcar availability. The line turned into a money loser and from this point forward, Montgomery refused to lay any new tracks until and unless population was dense enough to justify the large capital outlay. Naturally, this position caused many to blame

West Lawn

Has all City Improvements
such as--

Cement Walks,	**Street Cars,**
Sewerage,	**Water;**
Electric Lights,	**Gas,**

Also shade trees, beautiful view points, pure
breezes and glorious sunlight but

No Saloons

JUST THINK OF IT!
A Great Big Lot, 50x120 ft., for $450 to $650.

WEST LAWN CO.

M. S. ROWLEY,
Sales Agt.. Tenney Blk.
Auto, Carriage or Car Service

E. F. RILEY, Pres.
H. L. RUSSELL, Vice Pres.
A. T. ROGERS, Secy.

FIGURE 6.59. WEST LAWN.   This July 1903 advertisement for West Lawn, a sixty-one-acre, 371-lot subdivision, appeared in the *Wisconsin State Journal* just one day before this suburb, University Heights, Wingra Park and several others were annexed to Madison. However, under the terms of the annexation, no saloons were allowed in any of these suburbs—a feature developers were pleased to flaunt.

him for Madison's congestion and even led to talk that he should be "forced" to extend his tracks into the suburbs and even around the lakes so that large numbers of Madisonians could live in beautiful low-density settings and still be within a thirty-minute, five-cent streetcar ride of the Square.[286]

The only other line extension Montgomery made was in 1919 when he built a one-mile extension out to the large new Oscar Mayer packing plant so that its workers could get back and forth to work. Very significantly, however, Montgomery refused to build the line until the Oscar Mayer Company agreed to pay any operating loss the line might incur and until businessmen agreed to buy thirty thousand dollars worth of stock to pay construction costs.

The fourth element of Madison's response to its housing problem was to encourage the creation of new buildable land in and around the isthmus, by filling in marshes and lake bottoms. Here the initiative lay largely with developers who could dramatically increase the value of their marshy lots simply by filling them in. To assist developers in the process, city officials dumped city refuse in the marshes, praised those who filled their marshy lots, and created docklines out into lakes along the isthmus so that developers could fill in the lake bottom out to these lines.[287]

The fifth weapon in the arsenal of city weapons for dealing with housing problems was planning and zoning. The story of Madison's early dalliance with these tools is told in "The City Well Planned."

The Great Escape: A Private Solution to a Public Problem

The densification of isthmus housing stock and the failure of city officials to effectively deal with deteriorating housing quality ignited an explosion of suburban platting—the greatest in Madison's history up to that time. Between 1900 and 1920 developers subdivided more than three thousand acres (the equivalent of seventy percent of Lake Monona) into more than ten thousand building lots—enough some said for a city of ten thousand.[288]

Shrewd developers offered suburban lot buyers just about everything that Madison refugees could have wanted, beginning with space and privacy. From 1900 to the outbreak of World War I new suburban lots averaged one-third of an acre in size, more than half again larger than the generous 66 × 132 foot lots in the original plat and more than three times larger than the increasingly common 33 × 132 half lots. For those who could afford the price, developers even offered one- to five-acre parcels where one could have huge gardens, orchards, and even livestock. And this was just the beginning of alluring attributes. Developers also offered freedom from city noise, dirt, and high taxes. They offered lake access and curvilinear street plans designed by landscape architects. They appealed to buyer cupidity by promising rapid appreciation. They exploited a rapidly growing back-to-nature movement then sweeping the country by promising verdure and wildlife. They reinforced in almost every conceivable way the real estate industry's popular be-frugal-buy-your-own-home campaign. They offered smug enclaves for status seekers and small lots for worker cottages.[289] And for lot buyers who demanded assurances that no commercial or multifamily structure would be built next door—a very real fear in Madison—developers provided tight deed restrictions that made all but single family homes illegal. Deed restrictions were also used to ban alcohol, privies, billboards, outbuildings, homes over two stories high, and a long list of objectionable characteristics then commonplace in Madison. In short suburban tract developers offered country living with nearly every city advantage. This was the siren song of the suburbs.[290]

HOMES FOR WORKING MEN!

FAIR OAKS Subdivision, on the eastern limits of the city, was opened up, with a total of 322 lots, on Dec. 16, 1901. It was then an empty stretch of field. Today there are in **Fair Oaks** 14 homes and families. New houses will be rushed up with the opening of Spring.

ONLY FIFTY LOTS REMAIN!

These will be closed out during the present month of February. Taxes are low as Fair Oaks is outside the city limit. Where taxes are $5.00 in Madison proper, they are only $1.00 in Fair Oaks.

LAND OFFICE WILL BE OPEN SUNDAY

at Fair Oaks, to accommodate those who cannot get away from their work during the week. Take the street car and look over the field. Some choice lots are left.

JAS. P. CORRY, Exclusive Agent.

Up Town Office over Bank of Wisconsin.   Office open Wednesday and Saturday Evenings

FIGURE 6.60. HOMES FOR WORKINGMEN. One of the most heavily advertised suburbs in the early twentieth century was Fair Oaks, a large suburb on the East End that opened in 1901. So rapid was the development of this area that its residents decided to incorporate as a village in 1906. However, a variety of factors caused the village to vote to come into Madison, and in May 1913 the Common Council voted to accept them.

Gradually the negative "push" factors evident in the increasingly crowded isthmus coupled with the alluring suburban "pull" factors began to take their toll. Between 1900 and 1920 several crowded neighborhoods near the Capitol Square actually lost population for the first time in Madison history. Other close-in areas grew much slower than city wide averages. Meanwhile the big population gainers were the outlying areas then called the East and West "Ends" and the areas beyond the city limits.

But even with powerful push and pull factors operating in their favor, developers of outlying suburbs were confronted by a serious limitation. They had to find ways to get buyers to and from their tracts on a daily basis. Certainly the limited streetcar network could not do it. Madison developers hardly "solved" this problem, but they did take full advantage of a revolutionary new development in transportation—the automobile.

The New Auto-Sculptured City

In the fall of 1899 and spring of 1900 three very brief newspaper articles quietly announced to unsuspecting readers a new era in Madison's history. One article noted that the city library had begun a subscription to *The Automobile Magazine,* a new monthly periodical devoted to the horseless carriage.[291] The other noted that Mr. R. W. Wood, U.W. professor of physics, had just taken delivery of a new auto, the first owned by a Madisonian. The machine carried two persons, used a gasoline burner to heat water for its steam engine and had a top speed of forty miles per hour. In a test run the machine zipped up the Carroll Street hill at an impressive twenty miles per hour.[292]

Yes, there is a war in Europe.
Yes, there is a business depression.
Yes, there is a lot of platted land.
But that doesn't affect NAKOMA.

NAKOMA was placed on sale Monday, July 19th. There were three houses then built and fifteen lots had been sold. They couldn't wait until it was platted. Today there are

42 Lots Sold, Running From 1-4 Acres to 2 Acres Each

14 Houses Under Construction or Contracted to be Built at Once

NAKOMA is the most successful plat in twenty years. WINGRA PARK did not have fourteen houses in three years. UNIVERSITY HEIGHTS had only five houses in four years. OAKLAND HEIGHTS had only six houses in three years. WEST LAWN did not have fourteen houses in two years. HIGHLAND PARK did not have fourteen houses in three years. Neither did they have furnished

Water, Gas, Electricity, Sidewalks, Shade Trees and Transportation

NAKOMA furnishes all of them. It will build up five times as fast and increase in value five times faster than any previous plat.

As an investment a NAKOMA lot at present prices will pay you a big profit.

Watch for our notice of when the sale at present prices will end. IT WILL BE SOON.

SEE NAKOMA. Auto Bus makes hourly trips, week days and Sundays. See one of our salesmen. Our sales force has a representative on the plat. he will show property and give full information.

MADISON REALTY COMPANY

CAPITAL $350,000.00

Office: 119 West Main Street Phone 103 Madison, Wisconsin

FIGURE 6.61. NAKOMA. When Nakoma, a 292-lot, eighty-six-acre subdivision, was placed on the market in July 1915, its owners, the Madison Realty Company, launched one of the most intensive and sustained real estate advertising campaigns ever seen in Madison. At first its ads tried to distinguish the Madison Realty Company from the more typical big splash, fast profit, fly-by-night promoters by emphasizing its unusually high local capitalization ($350,000), its intent to be here "every day for the next ten years," and its value-enhancing installation at the *beginning* of the development of a water system, city gas, electricity, gravel roads, sidewalks, and shade trees. Indeed, the very name "Nakoma," one ad reminded potential buyers, was Chippewa meaning "I do as I promise." Then its ads began to hammer away on Nakoma's country quiet, beauty, sunlight, and fresh air, its city utilities and conveniences, its low Town of Madison taxes, and the rapid appreciation in value the plat was sure to provide for the business and professional men who with their families "had recently bought lots and built homes in the new subdivision."

However, in spite of its charms and prospects, slow first-year sales prompted Madison Realty Company officials, like so many real estate promoters in the city, to use gimmicks to get potential buyers out to the site to see their lots. The company decided on a naming contest for the ten new streets in the plat. Under rules set forth by company officials, contestants were required to pick up a form at the on-site sales office and actually walk over the ground, savor its beauty, enjoy the spectacular views of the city, and to see the natural way the streets circled the knolls and swooped down into the valleys. Each street name winner received a twenty-dollar gold piece. Apparently the contest worked because four thousand nominations were received and reviewed by the judges. The winning names today appear on street signs in Nakoma.

FIGURE 6.62. THE NAKOMA PICNIC. "Isn't the view as beautiful from the ridges of Nakoma as from the top of University Heights Hill?" asked a July 1915 Nakoma ad. The relatively well-heeled Madisonians in this picture obviously agreed, for they had just purchased lots in the prestigious new subdivision. On this sunny but cool Saturday in late October 1915, eighty-five Nakoma lot buyers decided to have an "open-air, housewarming to meet their other neighbors and celebrate the beginning of what was proclaimed as the "ideal residence community." The picnic on this crisp fall afternoon was typical of hundreds of social events sponsored by the Nakoma Community Association. Later events included council fires, house parties, school parties, Christmas parties, serenades, dances, minstrel shows, baseball games, and much more.

Like pioneers in most new subdivisions, Nakoma residents encountered irritants such as cattle from neighboring farms trampling newly raked and seeded lawns. Then there were a few buyers who did not meet community neatness standards. For example, one gentleman allowed an old oilcloth-wrapped wreck of a car to sit in front of his home for months until late one evening a vigilante group disposed of the eyesore. In another instance a man took down his screens and stacked them against the front of his house for the winter. Once again, the aesthetic vigilantes went into action and placed the offending screens in a neighbor's woodshed! (SHSW WHi(X3)9118)

FIGURE 6.63. LAKE FOREST. One of the most extraordinary land developments ever launched in Madison was the 1916 Lake Forest plat shown above. The ambitious plat was the dream child of two experienced Madison men, Leonard Gay, a realtor, and Chandler B. Chapman, a contractor. The two men were confident that one thousand families would buy their lots and enjoy the blend of city and country living their subdivision offered.

On paper they had a very attractive product and maybe the premier subdivision. Unlike most Madison plats, Lake Forest was sensitively laid out by a nationally known city planner and featured a large amount of dedicated park land for its residents on the south shore of Lake Wingra. The circle feature in the center of the plat was to be a civic center, a conveniently located collection of stores, shops, and public buildings. A system of Venetian lagoons meandered through the lower areas of the development.

Almost from the beginning, however, the development was plagued by problems. In 1917 when dredging began, company officials unilaterally lowered the level of Lake Wingra by three feet. The decision to lower the lake was apparently made to facilitate the dredging operation, but it left Wingra residents howling mad. The drop nearly drained the expensive and newly dredged Vilas Park lagoons and exposed large amounts of vegetable matter around the edges of Lake Wingra, which in turn created a terrible stench. Working through the Wisconsin Railroad Commission, Wingra Park residents forced the Lake Forest Land Company to raise the lake to within a foot of its original height.

Although the incident hardly enhanced the image of the subdivision, the developers managed to sell forty-eight lots before World War I broke out and virtually halted lot sales. Not until the spring of 1920, however, did the developers make additional improvements to their sprawling tract and begin aggressive marketing. In that year they built an expensive concrete road (Capitol Avenue) across the marsh, dug an artesian well, brought in electricity, and ran elegant, full-page ads in the Madison newspapers.

Unfortunately for the developers, these activities produced alarmingly few results. By the end of 1920, only sixty-one lots had been sold but only one house had been built. As if lagging sales were not enough, Capitol Avenue began sinking into the marshy ooze. Finally, in 1922 the mortgage loan company that supplied the money to the developers failed—an action that became the opening shot in a long legal skirmish, which sent one man to jail and the developers' net worth plummeting.

Soon aquatic plants choked the half-dredged lagoons, weeds grew through gaping cracks in the tilting concrete roads, and Lake Forest became known as "Lost City"—a term that is still used by old-timers who found the once-promising premier suburb a grand spot to hunt geese, ducks, pheasants, and squirrels.

Ironically, the year the Lake Forest Land Company failed, another group of men under the inspired leadership of Michael Olbrich launched a crusade to turn the entire area into a great public wilderness. Olbrich's group succeeded and the University of Wisconsin Arboretum was the result. (University of Wisconsin Archives)

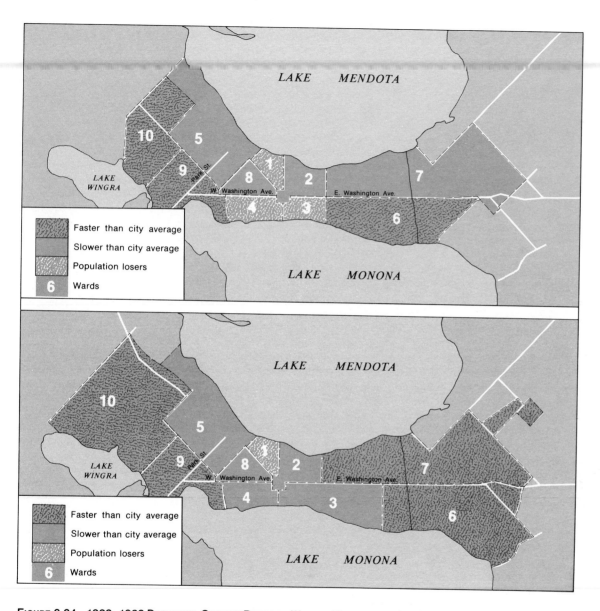

FIGURE 6.64. 1900–1920 DECENNIAL GROWTH RATES BY WARD. These maps showing growth rates by ward by decade reveal the beginning of modern suburbanization trends. The oldest settled areas either lost population or grew at very slow rates while outlying areas experienced very rapid growth rates.

FIGURE 6.65. 1907 FORD RUNABOUT ADVERTISEMENT. Shown above in a 1907 *Wisconsin State Journal* advertisement is Henry Ford's famous contribution to American civilization, the five-hundred-dollar mass-produced Model T Roadster. It was this model that made the automobile affordable to the large middle-income market.

FIGURE 6.66. 1916 CLASSY CLOSED CARS. By 1916 automobiles had gone through a period of rapid refinement. Almost all cars had abandoned the vibrating one- and two-cylinder car engines in favor of smoother and more powerful four-, six-, and even eight-cylinder models. Cold and drafty canvas tops and side curtains had given way to "classy closed cars." While horses were slipping and sliding on ice-glazed city pavements, tires chains allowed automobiles to go through snow drifts and up hills. The all-weather capability of the closed car coupled with the relatively low mass-produced prices made such cars a very practical vehicle for a growing number of Madisonians.

Just a few months later Carl Johnson, vice president and general manager of the Gisholt Company, took delivery of a fragile looking curved-dash Oldsmobile powered by a one-cylinder, four-horsepower gasoline engine and steered by a long curved tiller. Although it was not nearly as fast as Professor Wood's steamer, crowds followed it as it "snorted" along the streets "as though it was a wild animal escaped from the jungle."[293]

Though objects of great curiosity, the auto hardly took Madison by storm. In fact three years after Woods and Johnson bought their machines, Madison only had eight autos. The reasons were not hard to find: the machines were temperamental, unreliable, and exceptionally expensive. At a time when workmen were making around two dollars a day, only the wealthy could afford their price tags of one thousand to eighteen hundred dollars. Early autos therefore tended to be toys for wealthy men who sought speed, novelty, and status.[294]

In spite of their limitations, initial reaction to the auto in Madison was very favorable. At various times during 1900 the *Wisconsin State Journal,* for example, editorialized that the auto would bring relief from smelly stables and filth in the streets, would add to the pleasure of life by allowing people to get together more often and more easily, and would make people much less dependent upon the railroads.[295]

On the other hand, the disadvantages of these curious new contrivances soon became evident. Their most serious sin was that they scared horses, and that fact scared persons in horse-drawn vehicles because it could cause a dangerous runaway situation, a serious accident or even death. The first reaction of policy makers was to ban the automobile from such places as the cemetery, from the eighteen miles of scenic drives owned by the Madison Park and Pleasure Drive Association, and from the Dane County fairgrounds. Some said the bans were a blessing but others said that the auto was an "advance in civilization" and that only the "hysterical will ask that it be suppressed."[296] Fortunately for auto owners, banishment soon gave way to regulation.[297]

At first regulation was the sole province of local government. In 1903 the City Council established a speed limit of twelve miles per hour, made adequate brakes and lights mandatory, and required "autoists" to go slowly or stop in the presence of horses.[298] Just one year later, Madison began its own licensing program for commercial vehicles and lowered the speed limit to five miles per hour in the built-up sections of the city and

ten miles per hour elsewhere.[299] Gradually, however, the state began to pass laws regulating the auto which preempted local government ordinances. For example, in 1905 and 1906 the state established a standard city speed limit of twelve miles per hour, made a state license mandatory, and required all drivers to stop their cars if a horse-driver raised his hand.[300]

As the number of autos in Madison crept up to fifty in 1905, residents were forced to make a difficult judgment about the new machines. Were they a craze like bicycles that would suddenly appear, multiply, and then nearly disappear? Livery stable owners clearly thought so and mustered convincing arguments. The number of horses in the city was still increasing, they noted smugly, and even the folks who bought autos kept their horses just in case their machines had to be towed. Most Madisonians probably believed that horse-drawn vehicles would remain the preferred mode of travel for pleasure driving and general runabout purposes but felt the autos would be preferred for speed and thrills.[301]

But a long list of technical improvements and the advent of mass production soon made this horse-dominated interpretation untenable. By 1907 Madisonians could buy a Model T Ford runabout for five hundred dollars, just one-half or even one-third the price of cars just a few years earlier.[302] At the same time, smoothrunning four-, six-, and even eight-cylinder engines replaced rough one- and two-cylinder types; and good brakes, quiet mufflers, and passenger creature comforts became commonplace.

As reliability and comforts increased and cost decreased, the automobile became more attractive to more and more people. Annual Madison automobile sales rates began to climb about 1907. Between 1900 and 1907 an average of just eleven cars per year had been sold in Madison. However, between 1907 and 1913 the rate began to pick up and Madisonians bought cars at the rate of about eighty per year. Then between 1913 and 1916 that rate skyrocketed to nearly three hundred per year (see Fig. 6.67).[303]

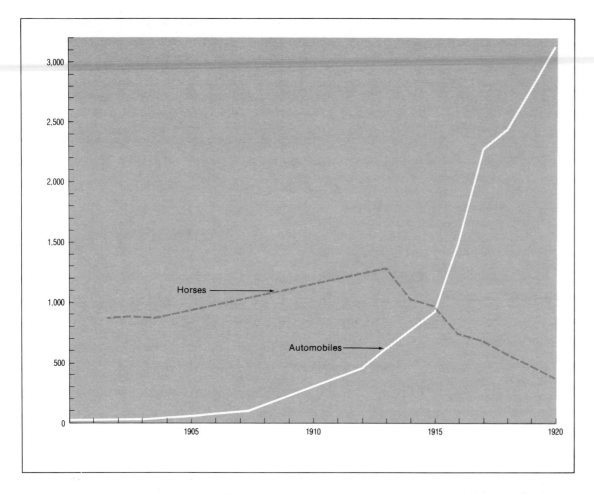

FIGURE 6.67. DECLINE OF THE HORSE AND RISE OF THE AUTO, MADISON, WISCONSIN, 1900 TO 1920. This graph dramatically portrays one of the major developments of the 1900 to 1920 period, namely, the transition of the auto from a speedy toy for the wealthy to a contrivance of great convenience and even necessity for suburbanites, business people, and middle income Madisonians. In the state as a whole the number of horses began to decline in 1916 whereas in Madison the number of decline began in 1913. Note the increase in *both* horses and cars between 1903 and 1913. It was this pattern that caused many to conclude that the auto was little more than a craze.

By 1916 the automobile had become the clear victor in its competition with the horse. In that year for the first time, there were more cars than horses in Madison. In that same year several of the largest livery stables were forced to close.[304] By 1920, just four years after the auto population passed the horse population for the first time, there were ten cars in Madison to every horse!

Gradually the old view of the automobile as a toy for thrill-seeking wealthy men was replaced by the new view that autos were "a necessity" for most businesses and a great convenience to the individual and families.[305] In 1916 even conservative Madison bankers gave tacit support to this view when they began making auto-loans for the first time.[306]

Just about everybody in Madison wanted to own an automobile. Beginning in 1912 Madisonians began flocking to gala annual automobile shows where they could inspect the latest models. At the 1916 Madison auto show, Madison's sixteen auto dealers displayed no less than thirty-nine cars.[307] Between 1914 and 1916 the amount of autos advertising in the *Wisconsin State Journal* doubled[308] and by 1916 Madison had become the second largest auto distributor in the state.[309]

The automobile ushered in a new era in mobility and gave Madisonians an exhilarating new freedom quite unlike anything ever experienced before. Automobile owners could leave when they were ready, stop where they pleased, and go almost anywhere roads would take them. The auto owner could therefore forget streetcar tracks, throw away the streetcar schedule, and live anywhere within convenient auto commuting distance, then generally considered ten to fifteen minutes from work. Since the auto was relatively speedy and did not have to stop all the time for passengers, it could cover more territory in the same period of time as the streetcar. Thus the automobile opened up vast amounts of land for residential purposes.

For the second time in a single generation, city boundaries were shattered and expanded by changing transportation technology, first by the electric streetcar in the 1890s and then by the auto in the early twentieth century. Some persons who fled Madison for streetcar-dependent suburbs moved even farther out to auto-dependent suburbs just a few years later. By allowing greater locational freedom and by making the more widely sought-after suburban amenities available to more people, the auto merely accelerated and made more pervasive what the streetcar had done before.

Though the automobile would ultimately transform the shape and character of the city, its utility to the suburban land developer was much slower in coming than many thought. In 1905 just one household out of one hundred had an auto; by 1910 one in twenty-three and by 1915 one household in eight had one of these remarkable machines. Still, to Madison developers, one family in eight was hardly enough to make their suburban lots accessible to the masses. It was for this reason that between 1912 and 1917 the developers of several silk-stocking subdivisions including Nakoma, Lakewood (now a part of Maple Bluff) and College Hills (a predecessor of Shorewood Hills) compensated for the lack of streetcar service to their plats and the small number of auto-equipped households by providing buses (see fig. 6.68).[310]

Fortunately, for the developers of these subdivisions, the need for these expensive subsidized auto-bus lines was soon obviated by the very rapid rise in the number of autos between 1915 and 1920. Although fifteen years were required for Madisonians to acquire their first one thousand autos, just five years (1916 to 1920) were required for that number to triple to three thousand cars. During this same five year period, the number of Madison households with autos increased from one in eight to one in three. Thus by 1920 the auto had at last created a mass market for suburban lots.[311]

FIGURE 6.68. SURBURBAN BUSES.   Developers of high priced, low density, deed-restricted subdivisions knew they had a product that a sizable segment of Madisonians wanted. However, success required access and therein lay the rub. Though far from the noise, dirt, and crowding of the city, most new subdivisions lay three, four and sometimes five miles from the Capitol Square, and one to three miles from streetcar lines as well. For families with cars, this remoteness was not a problem, but even in 1915 only one household in eight had one. Therefore the developers of such suburbs as Nakoma, Shorewood Hills (College Hills at the time), Lakewood (now a part of Maple Bluff), and Shore Acres (now the north end of Winnequah Trail in Monona) all felt compelled to provide their own transportation and to "absolutely guarantee" its availability. For this purpose they bought twelve to twenty passenger motor buses, which provided hourly service during rush hours. Trip time varied from fifteen minutes to Lakewood to thirty minutes for Nakoma, Shore Acres, and College Hills, whereas fares ranged from 7 ½ cents to 10 cents, 2 ½ to 5 cents more than the existing streetcar fare. Thus, some of Madison's finest neighborhoods began as bus-dependent suburbs. In most cases developer-subsidized bus service was continued for several years. Interestingly, it was this small fleet of buses that demonstrated the reliability and practicality of the motor bus in Madison and that made many Madisonians wary of buying a fixed route streetcar system in 1920.

Shown above is the two-ton twenty-passenger Packard bus placed in service in May 1912 by the developers of the Lakewood subdivision. Although the bus was primarily intended for carless Lakewood homebuyers, it was also made available to the public. The fare was ten cents from the Square to Lakewood and fifteen cents to the Maple Bluff Country Club, the end of the line. (Courtesy of Frank Custer)

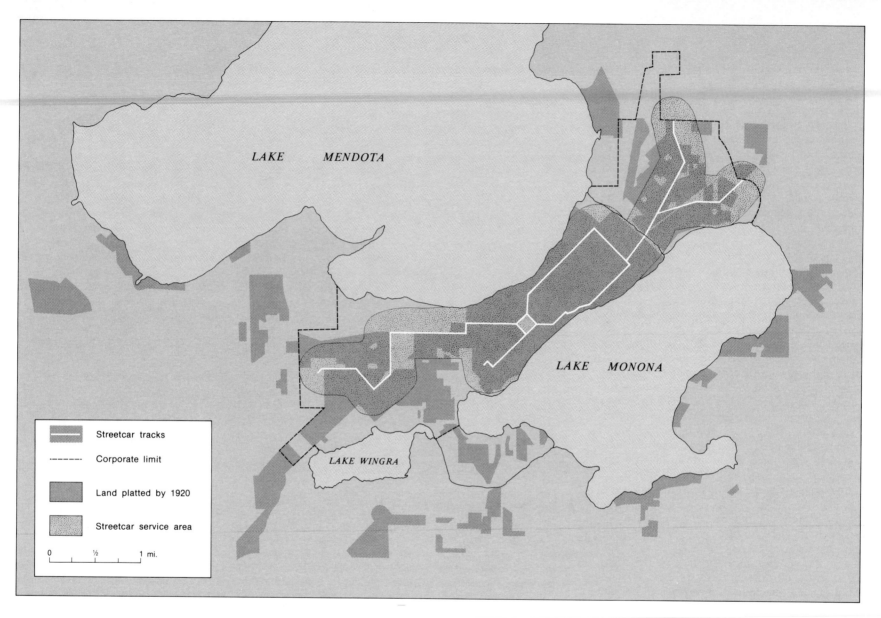

LAKE MENDOTA

LAKE MONONA

LAKE WINGRA

Streetcar tracks

Corporate limit

Land platted by 1920

Streetcar service area

0   ½   1 mi.

FIGURE 6.69. STREETCARS, AUTOMOBILES, AND URBANIZATION. If streetcar operators had been allowed to establish city land use patterns, they would have required everyone to live and work within one-quarter mile of a streetcar line. That was because long experience told them that very few people would walk farther than this to catch a car. This map shows that relative to the 1920 city limits, the streetcar enjoyed excellent coverage of residential areas. However, relative to land that had been *platted* by 1920, the streetcar had fallen very far behind. Moreover deed restrictions on many of these new plats meant that the high densities required to make a streetcar line profitable would probably never be attained. This fact coupled with the very high initial costs of constructing new right of way meant that the likelihood of streetcar service to these newly platted areas was very remote.

Indeed, only the automobile with its relatively greater speed and flexibility was capable of serving such areas. Assuming an average speed of fifteen miles per hour and a driving time of fifteen minutes, a commuter could live anywhere within an arc 3.75 miles from the Square. In other words, one could live in Maple Bluff, or Shorewood Hills, Nakoma, and dozens of other suburbs off limits to the streetcar commuter. The new land falling *within* this arc totalled 14,783 acres even after subtracting the land effectively served by the streetcar! Thus by 1920 the limits of the streetcar were already obvious. It was for this reason that no new streetcar lines were added after 1919, the configuration shown in the above map.

Official City of Madison efforts to improve housing quality during the first two decades of the twentieth century were hardly a smashing success. Probably the most successful city effort was the aggressive annexation policy, but only in the sense that many of the annexed acres that came into the city carried private deed restrictions, which prevented mixing of homes and factories, eave-to-eave construction, multiple buildings on half lots and the like. The next most successful city effort was the 1913 building code and its subsequent revisions. But even this vaunted building code, although making great strides in sanitation and safety, still allowed some of the worst land use abuses such as three-foot sideyards and two buildings on a half lot. City officials felt justified in using their municipal "police" powers to regulate matters of sanitation and safety, but they did not feel comfortable in regulating the more controversial aspects of private property, such as side yard, set back, height, and open space requirements. The early effect of this building code was therefore to make crowding safer and more sanitary.

Other city housing policy elements were even less successful. In the creation of new buildable land, the city was more cheerleader than doer. It praised and cooperated with property owners who wanted to fill marshes. Some of the developments on this former marshland and lake bottom were well conceived but most repeated the same isthmus design sins including tiny lots, eave-to-eave construction and factory-home juxtaposition. With just two exceptions the streetcar company refused city requests to extend its lines out into the country and therefore never became the "great urban decongestant" many had expected. Finally, Madison officials rejected planning and zoning—tools that could have caused a big increase in housing quality.

With the exception of the building code, few City of Madison efforts offered any *immediate* hope of reversing, much less correcting, the serious housing problems evident in the Latin Quarter, Greenbush, and dozens of other parts of the city where crowding had raised its ugly head.

These timid and tardy city responses to Madison's growing housing problems reflected a view then widely held among city decision makers that Madison had messed its nest so badly that the only viable alternative was to look for new trees in the suburbs and try to learn a few lessons from the isthmus experience. Certainly, there was a strong feeling among city aldermen that they should not interfere with property rights beyond insisting on such things as fire escapes and indoor toilets—a consensus that left property owners remarkably free to continue packing rooming houses, flats, and apartments into small lots. In fact, most Madison opinion makers felt that the city role in improving housing quality was very limited indeed. The real action, they believed, lay with the private sector, that is, with those who were platting new subdivisions on the city fringes and building worker cottages on former marshland.

From our smug, contemporary perspective, it is tempting to criticize decision-makers of this era for their failure to take a more resolute interventionist course. However, such criticism ignores the emphasis placed by Madison opinion leaders on the sanctity of private property, the fact that building codes and enforcement systems were in their infancy, and that no U.S. city adopted a zoning code until 1916.[312] Still, in a city like Madison, Wisconsin—the capital of a progressive commonwealth, the home of one of the nation's great universities, a place where so much man-made ugliness could have been prevented—it is disappointing that the deed-restricted suburb and the auto became Madison's major responses to the need for better housing in the early twentieth century.

The City Liberated: The Growing Role of Women

Throughout most of human history, biology and men have defined women's role in society. Hence women have been the child producers, child raisers, sexual gratifiers, food fixers, clothing makers, and home cleaners. These well-developed and widely accepted female "spheres of interest" were not something peculiar to primitive societies. On the contrary, they were accepted by most adult American males in the late nineteenth century.

By the turn of the century, however, urbanization and industrialization began to alter women's situation. One major impact of these two forces was to reduce the amount of time spent on domestic chores. Instead of making time-consuming cornmeal mush, women could throw some Quaker Oats into a pan of boiling water, and—presto—breakfast was ready. Or if that was too much work, they could pour some milk just delivered by the milkman over one of the new dry cereals such as Kellogg's Corn Flakes. Instead of going out to the pump to get water, the woman merely turned the faucet. Instead of cutting and hauling wood, she merely turned on the gas burner. Instead of tending gardens, she bought canned vegetables and instead of slaving over a hot stove she walked down to the bakery and bought her bread there. As for housework, almost all middle income families could afford to have a maid and even a laundress, or they could get one immigrant girl and have her do everything! The availability of cheap domestic sewing machines reduced the time required to make clothes, and the availability of cheap female labor and commercial sewing machines made store-bought clothes an attractive option for many and shopping a way of life for some.

Urbanization and industrialization also forced many men to alter their concept of woman as a household drudge and to substitute an appealing new Victorian interpretation of femininity that placed an exaggerated but elegant emphasis upon home life and a domesticated version of romantic love. According to this new interpretation, home was the true sphere of women, her proper place. Home was a sanctuary where the head of the household could return after a day in the dog-eat-dog workaday urban world, unwind, and be attended by a sensitive and obedient wife clad in a pretty dress. There with his slippered feet comfortably resting on the ottoman, he could survey his domain and admire the efficient domestic management of his wife—a role in which every respectable woman was supposed to find fulfillment. Within this gentile oasis of domestic civility and order man and woman could indulge in the Victorian version of romantic love and man—the active, strong, hard, aggressive worldly breadwinner—could be soothed by his pious, pure, delicate, naive, and submissive chattel. Man was king, superior to women in cognitive skills, physical strength, business ability, and governing. Interestingly, however, men did allow that women, due to their highly developed intuition, refined sensitivities and life-giving powers, were spiritually and morally superior to man. It was for this reason that women were allowed to play a lead role in church and charity.

This was the view of woman held by most Madison men around the turn of the century. But unlike all good fairy tales this interpretation of male-female roles did *not* live happily ever after. Even in the late nineteenth century considerable ferment in the question of women's role was evident in Madison. The 1885 school suffrage law, the establishment of women's clubs, the increase in the number of female university students, the rise in popularity of female exercise, all fomented community discussion and even bold talk about the "new woman." Local response to this new woman concept was chilly. Even Amos Wilder, the relatively liberal *Wisconsin State Journal* editor, could not fully embrace the notion in 1895. Said Wilder: The new woman was "a little too radical, too much of a man and too little of a woman to suit the average taste. There is a freshness and boldness about her that does not add adornment or attractiveness to the sex." According to Wilder women could probably vote without losing "daintiness and delicacy," but he thought the ballot and the sword, that is, "government and its defense" ought to belong to men. Wilder agreed that women who wanted to be "useful" should have the right to seek and secure good jobs—at least in the "lighter employments"—so that they could be liberated from their condition of "helpless dependence."[313]

Shall the Whipping Post be Returned for Wife Beaters?

A rash of wife beating and desertion cases in the summer of 1905 prompted Madison Mayor W. D. Curtis, Chief of Police Henry C. Baker, and Municipal Judge Anthony Donovan to recommend the return of the whipping post. The quote appearing below outlines the Mayor's reason for returning to this punishment.

> "I have always been in favor of the whipping post for such cases. I take this position for various reasons. A jail sentence does not seem to have any good effect on a man who has once suffered the humiliation of being sent to jail. The jail sentence is not much of a punishment for the average criminal. . . . Perhaps some people think the establishment of the whipping post would be a step backward. But it has been tried successfully elsewhere. Personally I know of at least a half dozen men in Madison whom I think it might improve; in fact, I wouldn't mind applying the whip myself in these particular cases. The world has no sympathy for the brute who will lay violent hands on a woman."

In spite of a few "liberals" like Wilder who supported a change in women's status, Madison remained in the late nineteenth and early twentieth century a highly sexist and segregated society. The "little brick" school house had separate playgrounds for boys and girls. At the Vilas Hotel, men could sit on the ground outside on the veranda and watch the passersby but the women were required to sit up on the balcony away from "the world." Private schools were available for boys or girls but not both. And so it went.[314]

During the first two decades of the twentieth century, however, a growing number of women in Madison and across the country made a conscious effort to jump down as it were from this man-created sexist pedestal and demand a more meaningful place in the world. From their demands came the most rapid and dramatic changes in women's place ever witnessed up to that time.[315]

The Modern Civic Agenda

On a sunny but brisk Saturday afternoon in early November 1900, seventy-five well-dressed women gathered in the Guild Hall of the Grace Episcopal Church for the regular monthly meeting of the Women's Club, Madison's most elite women's organization. Nearly all were middle aged, financially comfortable, Protestant, and married to Madison's most prominent business, civic, and educational leaders. By contemporary standards these women were well educated and some even had college degrees, then rare among women. Like other women in the upper socio-economic stratum, they had fewer children than their less-privileged counterparts and therefore spent less time in the child-raising stage. Moreover, most had live-in domestic help to relieve them of household drudgery and lighten the childraising burden. Because social taboos prevented them from entering the workforce, they found themselves with growing amounts of time on their hands. As it were, these talented women were all dressed up but had no place to go.

That was why the Women's Club had been so conspicuously successful. It gave women a place to go and something to do, a potent antidote to boredom. Since its founding in 1893 it had fulfilled its goals of promoting agreeable relations among women, in developing the intellect, and in being a focal point for the study of literature, science, and music. To reach these objectives, clubwomen formed committees, then called "departments" on art, literature, education, music, and history and within these bodies translated Dante, wrote papers on pre-Raphaelite art, and urged the city fathers to establish a children's library. However, by the turn of the century, Women's Club members had grown tired of academic papers and socializing. Dabbling with Dante and sipping tea were nice, and kept two o'clock away from four o'clock, but they failed to satisfy the growing desire of these women to do something more *valuable* with their time. The same frustration applied to the widely accepted female role as charity providers. Taking flowers to the hospital and doing charity work were also nice but came to be viewed as the "lady bountiful" role, after a silly rich lady in an eighteenth century French comedy who spent her time earnestly dispensing charity to the poor.[316]

The speaker that afternoon at Guild Hall was thirty-five-year-old U.W. political science instructor, Dr. Samuel E. Sparling, a man particularly well-suited to address the women on the subject "How May Women Assist in the Government of Our Cities?" In addition to teaching courses in municipal government at the university, Sparling was a Madison alderman (Fifth Ward) and the executive director of the Wisconsin League of Municipalities—an organization he helped found in 1898.

If Madison is ever going to claim to be a modern city, Sparling began, a long list of conditions must be "perfected." "Her schools are crowded, her streets are dirty, her lake shores provide no public baths, her garbage is not systematically collected, her children unattended roam the streets late in the night, no adequate hospital, no kindergartens, no branch libraries." Then came the key message: Because all of these problems are "home questions," Sparling argued that women were the "rightful leaders of public sentiment" in these areas and therefore had an obligation to "develop a wholesome physical and moral environment in the city."[317]

His clear and forceful presentation of what in the women's movement came to be called the "modern civic agenda" proved to be terribly exciting to Women's Club members, the keynote address for a brilliant decade in the history of the Madison Women's Club and indeed for all women throughout the city who sought a larger role in civic affairs.

The Best Club in Madison

This spirited and truculent editorial, which appeared in the *Wisconsin State Journal* on May 27, 1914, was a Richard Lloyd Jones classic. His three purposes in writing it were to express his deep almost uncritical admiration for the Women's Club, to convey his equally strong contempt for Madison's prestigious eat-drink-smoke-talk-and-do-nothing all-male, high-status organizations, and finally, to urge the recently formed Civics Club to emulate the Woman's Club model.

If anybody drove up in a bright brewster brown limousine and asked you what was the best club in town, dollars to doughnuts you'd answer either the University Club or the Madison Club—now wouldn't you? Well is either of them the best club in town? Let's mull it over.

The University is a very nice club. It has a good club house built out to the walk on a residential street, which is run somewhat as a hotel. It has comfortable living rooms, a comfortable place to loaf and read current periodicals. You will find the Atlantic Monthly and The Popular Science Monthly there, in fact almost everything but the Police Gazette,—a very respectable place for mixed high-brow and low-brow recreation. Some of the members violate the spirit of the state dry zone law by keeping liquor in their private lockers,—an inexcusable and shameful example to set before the students of the University.

The Madison Club is another men's club, a good comfortable place to loaf, play billiards, drink booze and eat. Once in a while one of its members gets in touch of public spirit and offers a silver mug,—sometimes called a "Loving cup" which is set up on the mantel with the announcement that it is to go to the winner of a card tournament or a series of Kelley pool.

The annual dues of the University Club are $30.

The annual dues of the Madison Club are $50.

Did you ever hear of the Woman's Club of Madison?

Just women? Yes, I know but looka'. Their annual dues are only $5 a year,—only one sixth of what the University Club costs and only one tenth of what the Madison Club costs and what do they do?

They have their own club house,—they don't own it but some day they may. But these women are not so much concerned about what comfort they can throw about themselves,—what good times they can give themselves as how much good they can do for others.

Here are a few of the things that the Woman's Club of Madison has DONE:

It established the kindergartens in our public schools.

It established the school fund for pictures.

It established a penny provident fund in the schools.

It established both manual training and domestic science in the schools.

It established play grounds in Madison.

It developed the school gardens in vacant lots.

It assisted in establishing and has always assisted in maintaining, the Associated Charities, the visiting nurse fund and the visiting housekeeper.

It brought milk inspection into Madison.

Such garbage collection as we have, the Woman's Club is responsible for.

It started the movement for the Madison General Hospital and collected most of the money which built that benignantly useful institution.

It established inspection in the schools.

It has fought for social centers.

(continued)

It established a detention room for juvenile offenders and young women.

It at all times has made an effort to enforce the curfew law, the smoke ordinance, provide a censor board for moving pictures, enforce the anti-cigarette law, provide protection from flies for food displayed by groceries.

It initiated the fly campaign.

It appointed the committe to assist in municipal house-keeping; it established rubbish boxes throughout the city.

It established a sane and safe Fourth of July.

It has assisted the boys' home of Dousman.

It assisted in establishing a branch library in the sixth ward.

The Woman's Club not only took the initiative in these movements and then brought public opinion to support them, but it assisted these movements generously with money as well.

It's worth five dollars a year to belong to a club with such a record as that.

With all their multiplied membership fee, can the men's clubs point to a civic record like that? Yet we hear members of these men's clubs tell us that in their opinion women are not fit to function as citizens.

Approving all the Woman's Club's splendid expressions of civic interest, we wonder why they limit the privilege of membership to four hundred Madison women. There is no four hundred to any center of democracy. There are at least double that number who would be glad to throw in their $5, even $25 contributions to help carry on such a good and noble work.

But we were speculating on that fellow in the bright brewster brown limousine,—weren't we? Well, if he should drive up and ask us what the best club in Madison tell him to go around and see for himself. We haven't made up our minds.

Best of all, the appeal of Sparling's message was not limited to the women in the Guild Hall that afternoon. His message was no less popular among Madison's male leadership structure. Liberals were delighted by the prospect of a larger role for women in municipal affairs. Conservatives liked the comforting way Sparling hewed out specific spheres of influence for women *without,* it appeared, threatening men's roles. After all, what interest did men have in doing hospital work. Nursing was women's work. Nor did men want much to do with schools; that was child-centered and therefore a woman's preserve. The same logic applied to libraries and municipal housekeeping.

Very significantly, however, there was one characteristic of the new civic agenda that escaped most men but that was immediately evident to astute women leaders and that was the profound elasticity of the fundamental premise on which the modern civic agenda was based. What indeed was a "home question?" And what exactly did women have to do to achieve a "wholesome physical and moral environment" for Madison? To those who thought about these new "spheres of interest" a while, it was clear that women did not just live in a home; they lived in a neighborhood and a city. Therefore neighborhood and city problems were *home* questions. Thus what many perceived to be a fixed-length tether for limiting women's activities was not

really a tether at all but rather a *license* to roam far and wide in municipal affairs.

Women leaders were quick to see the almost mind-boggling expansiveness of their new playing field but equally quick in seeing the wisdom and—yes—the necessity of gradualism and good works. Though it was nice to have ineluctable logic and inevitability on their side, this generation of women leaders were painfully aware of their inherently vulnerable position. They knew that the only way they could ever become meaningful partners in city building was to develop a track record of solid and respectable achievements. It was for this reason that Madison's women leaders resolved to work hard and be patient on the expectation that their good works would be recognized and rewarded.

Armed with this plan, Madison women launched an offensive whose achievements in education, health, housing, aesthetics, morals, recreation, and charity were almost awesome. As one university faculty wife put it, it seemed "impossible for women to congregate without adopting some uplifting cause."[318]

Although all of these achievements were obtained without the ballot, Madison club women proved they were anything but powerless. After all, they were married to the men who ran the city and therefore if they collectively got behind a reform, chances were good they could make that reform a reality by using their trump card, domestic harmony. Another source of their power was, ironically enough, their *absence* from the workaday world. Unlike their businessmen husbands, clubwomen could demand reforms such as clean milk, decent housing, and wholesome entertainment without having to worry about their businesses being boycotted by peers and customers.

In achieving this great harvest for the modern civic agenda, the role of women's organizations cannot be overemphasized. Since with very few exceptions women were barred from membership in men's clubs, women had to form their own.

The Modern Civic Agenda and Madison's Women's Organizations:
A Checklist of Achievements, 1900–1920

Category	Achievement	Lead Organization	Date of Achievement
Education	1. Expansion of kindergartens	Women's Club	1899–1906
	2. Started and sustained the P.T.A. movement	Women's Club	1904–05
	3. Started annual physical examinations of Madison students	Women's Club	1901–02
	4. Started the in-school hot lunch program	Women's Club	1917
	5. Started manual and domestic arts programs	Women's Club	1904–05
	6. Gave cultural-historical names to Madison public schools	Women's Club	1903–04
	7. Successfully campaigned for Central High School bond referendum	Women's Club	1905
	8. Launched a movement that caused the first branch library to be built at 1249 Williamson	Sixth Ward Women	1909
	9. Funded the first children's library	Women's Club	1901
	10. Started Penny Provident Fund, a children's savings program designed to inculcate thrift	Women's Club Women's Christian Temperance Union	1902
Health	11. Started and sustained movement for city garbage pick up	Women's Club	1900
	12. Started and sustained clean milk crusade	Women's Club	1905–1914
	13. Started "war against the fly"	Women's Club	1909–1910
	14. Played pivotal role in Attaining Madison General Hospital	Women's Club Attic Angels	1900–1903
	15. Established free dental clinic for school children	Associated Charities	1915
Housing	16. Brought in nation's leading expert to analyze Madison's housing problems and then with Board of Commerce built six four-room worker cottages as a demonstration of better low income housing	Civics Club	1916
Aesthetics	17. Generated antilitter and clean up crusades	Committee of Eight Women	1900, 1909, 1912
Recreation	18. Raised money for children's playground equipment and adult supervisors	Women's Club Attic Angels	1906–1908
Morality	19. Curtailed immoral entertainment and books, cigarette sales, supported juvenile curfew	Federated Women's Club	1901, 1902, 1908, 1910, 1912
Charity	20. Raised most of the money and managed charity work	Women's Club Sorority Women Attic Angels	1900–1920
	21. Established first well-baby clinic for the poor	Attic Angels	1915
	22. Established and funded free visiting nurse program for the sick poor	Attic Angels	1907

Listed above are some of the many impressive achievements of Madison's women's organizations. Note the concentration of efforts in the 1900–1910 decade. In addition to these achievements, for which primary credit is warranted, there were dozens of others where Madison women joined forces with other organizations to achieve various ends. For example, Madison women's organizations joined their counterparts around the state to secure a factory inspector and tough child labor laws.

A628.   High School, Madison, Wis.

FIGURE 6.70. CENTRAL HIGH: A MONUMENT TO EARLY WOMEN VOTERS. Madison Central High School, here shown in a photograph shortly after its completion, was a monument to Madison women's strong interest in education and the first real hint of local female voting power. Since 1895 Madison school officials had asked that the old three-hundred-student 1873 high school be replaced on the grounds that it was crowded, unsanitary, and unsafe. However, not until 1901 when the old building was jammed with six-hundred students did the Board of Education officially acknowledge its obsolescence. And not until 1904 did the Common Council even select a consulting architect to prepare preliminary specifications. The reason for this delay was the extreme reluctance of the board, the council, and prominent citizens to have to pay out a quarter of a million dollars for a facility capable of accommodating Madison's unusually large number of high school students. "What are we trying to do," asked one prominent citizen, "compete for sublime architecture with ancient Rome and Athens?" Based upon the fear that voters would think they were doing just that, aldermen decided to hold a referendum on the matter in July 1905 and let the people decide. Many astute observers thought Madison voters would reject this "reckless extravagance" but that is not what happened.

Since this was a "school matter," this was an election in which women could participate—and participate they did! And since education had long been a "sphere of interest" in which Madison club women had demonstrated an intense interest, they did everything in their power to mobilize support for the new building. When the vote was tallied the men had mustered a four percent plurality *against* the high school but women swamped this male rejection by a twenty-four percent plurality.

Unfortunately this election did not really settle the matter. Several disgruntled males sought to have the vote declared invalid on the grounds that women did not have the right to vote and on several technical grounds. To the delight of Madison club women, however, both the circuit and the Supreme Courts upheld the validity of the election. With this challenge put aside, ground was finally broken in May 1906 and the building was officially opened in September 1908. Thus this handsome Oxfordian style building designed by nationally famous St. Paul architect, Cass Gilbert, became a lasting tribute to Madison's early women voters. (SHSW, WHi(X3)38056)

Nearly all women's organizations heavily emphasized self-improvement and tended to be strongly problem and action oriented. Simultaneously they served as bootcamps for parliamentary skills, colleges for leadership training, pep rallies for sagging spirits, summit conferences for strategy planning, crash courses for technical knowledge, forums for consciousness raising, and graduate schools in citizenship. By contrast, men's organizations generally followed the lodge model—that is, they concentrated on eating, drinking, smoking, talking a lot and doing little.[319]

The organization most responsible for the rich harvest of achievements in the modern civic agenda was the Women's Club. Its success, prestige, and timely achievements caused leaders of this elite organization to increase their membership limit from one hundred in 1899 to five hundred in 1916 and still they had long waiting lists. The tremendous success of the Women's Club also led to the proliferation of similar organizations. For example, the Civics Club was formed in 1913, the Catholic Women's Club in 1914, and the Girls Civic League, a young women's auxiliary of the Civics Club, in 1918. Each of these organizations in turn experienced the same rapid membership growth as the Women's Club.[320]

As noted elsewhere in this chapter, many other women devoted time and attention to more specialized areas including assistance to working women, prohibition, suffrage, charity, hospitals, and religion.

Women Enter the Work Force

For nearly fifty years a perceptive *Wisconsin State Journal* reporter named Judd Stone roamed Madison's streets in search of local news. In addition to describing the mundane, his many years in Madison allowed him to make fascinating observations on major changes in the city he loved so much. During an early morning walk in May

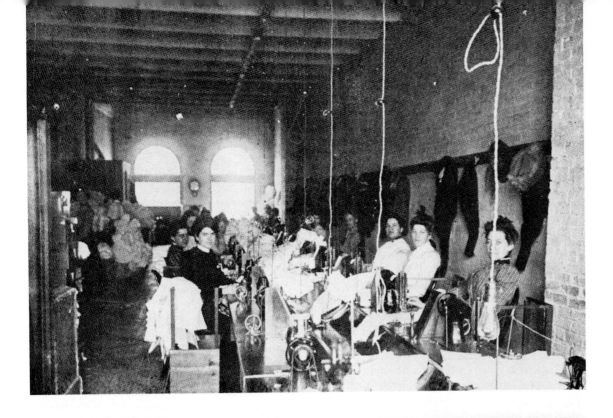

FIGURE 6.71 WOMEN IN THE WORK PLACE: SEWING GIRLS AND TELEPHONE OPERATORS. Although a growing number of Madison women sought work outside the home, the options tended to be proscribed. One option was to become a telephone operator, shown here at the central switchboard tending the city's sixteen hundred telephones. Or one might become a sewing girl, here shown taking a break from their work at the Madison Muslin Underwear Company, 615 Williamson, now a Madison landmark known as Machinery Row. Although the work was steady, pay was relatively low, the hours long, and the work was tedious. Nevertheless such occupations were increasingly preferred to domestic work because one could work fewer hours, enjoy much more time off, and in most cases receive better pay. Both photographs were taken in 1902.

Interestingly, the Madison Muslin Underwear Company located in Madison primarily because the city had a large number of female high school graduates who could find "nothing to do." This labor force assessment proved accurate indeed, for all sixty employees were young single girls who came from "good families" and who lived at home with their parents. Thus to Messers Kessenich, Keeley, and Neckerman, local principals in the firm, these girls provided cheap, reliable, and high quality labor force. Using muslin imported from Massachusetts, embroidery from Switzerland, and lace from France and England, the girls turned out ladies white skirts, nightgowns, drawers, and corset covers.

1901, he was struck by the hundreds of young women walking or pedalling their bicycles to work. "A great change has come upon us," he reported. "Lots of us remember that a girl was scarcely worth bothering about; but now they are getting to the front in fine style."[321]

Certainly insofar as a growing number of women were entering the workforce, Stone's observation was absolutely true. Turn-of-the-century Madison stores, offices, and factories offered a growing number of female job opportunities. Exactly how many Madison women over sixteen worked outside the home in 1900 is not known although inferential data suggests that twenty to twenty-five percent would be reasonable. Almost all Madison working women were between sixteen and twenty-five years of age and single.[322]

By 1920, however, the size and the composition of the Madison female workforce had changed considerably. Now 32.5% of all Madison women over the age of sixteen years worked outside the home, the highest percentage among state cities,[323] and the number of married women in the workforce increased very rapidly. In 1914 only seven percent of all Madison married women worked whereas by 1916 thirty-six percent found themselves receiving salaries and wages.[324] This large influx of married women was a result of a sharp increase in the consumer price index, which doubled between 1915 and 1920—an average annual rate of seventeen percent!

The combination of a relatively large number of women entering the job market in a short time and the control of that job market by males and male values forced most women to work long hours at low-paying, entry-level positions such as seamstresses, office and store clerks, laundresses, maids, and typists. In those few instances such as elementary and high school teaching where men and women took the same jobs, women took home just a fraction of the paychecks of their male counterparts. Not until after World War I when labor became more militant—and, very significantly, *after* women had the vote—did such pay inequities even begin to get addressed.[325]

Because of their meager wages and the high cost of living, most single working women who did not live at home were forced to live in small, often shared rooms. Since almost all rooms lacked kitchen facilities, most young women had to subsist upon convenience foods such as crackers and bologna. To make matters worse, penny-pinching landladies heated the rooms so little that in the wintertime working girls would sometimes go to the railroad station just to keep warm.[326]

The difficulties and conditions encountered by the influx of women in the work force caused a number of women's support institutions to develop. Uppermost among organizations that sought to aid working women was the Women's Exchange. Founded in 1887, its leaders were primarily interested in providing assistance to working women. To fulfill this goal the Women's Exchange set up a day nursery for children of working mothers, an employment bureau to help women find jobs, and a "lunch department" so that visiting and working women could get cheap, wholesome meals without having to go to relatively expensive restaurants or the male-dominated saloons, many of which provided a free lunch with a stein of beer. To assist the young women who were in town looking for work, the Women's Exchange rented a house where they provided cheap, temporary lodging. Later the YWCA became the primary provider of affordable, attractive housing accommodations for single working women. But the most popular institution established by the Women's Exchange was the Women's Exchange itself, that is, a store where married women could bring baked goods and clothing they had made to be sold on consignment. In effect, it was an outlet for "cottage industry" and gave married Madison women a respectable opportunity to earn money *without* leaving the home. Although these programs and organizations could not fully compensate for the low wages, long hours, menial work, and restrictions placed upon female wage earners, they did help women find and keep jobs and live more comfortably.[327]

Well, I had a place on Gorham street and that was a fine place. Also she was a dear to me, with horns, and when she showed me my room, why I was surprised. The finest little room you ever saw; 4′ by 8′ and 6-½″ high, and a window about 18 by 24 inches, and one window at that, right next to the roof. In the summer I would take my bed clothes and lie out in the hall. When it was real warm I could not stand it to dress, but would take part of my clothes and go out in the woodshed and put them on. I had to do all the housework, split wood, clean the sidewalk in the winter and cook three meals a day for six of them, and fix whatever the kids wanted between meals, and, you might say everything but milk the cows and slop the hogs, for the pretty little sum of $4 a week, and I thought I would try someone who would be a little bit easier with me. So I found a place on State street. Well, she was a crank, but I didn't think anything of that because she was old and childish, so I would try and please her. I got $4.50 a week in this place. Wasn't that fine? Well, to make a long story short, I will tell you what cooked my goose here. I did all of the housework and one Monday I had got through with my washing a little early so to be sure that I earned my little $4.50 she asked me if I would just as soon go out and rake the lawn. It looked awfully and I had not thought of making a yard man out of myself, besides doing the housework, for $4.50, so it was up to me to pack my little package and look for new quarters.

Now, remember it costs a girl $1 to get a new place. But I didn't care for money; I had lots of it. Of course, I saved a lot of money. I had nothing to do but work, so, of course, I had no chance to spend it. Well, at last I found the place. And this is what was said. I, of course, rapped on the door and the Mrs. answered the call.

"Why, how do you do; you are the girl Mrs. So and So sent. Well, I am so glad you have come. I just didn't know what to do. You know I cannot do any cooking myself!" She told the truth. Give her credit for that. She said:

"Why, you can come in now and go to work; you needn't wait."

"O, no," I said, "I'll have to go back and get my trunk so that I can change my dress."

"Well, you'll be sure and come back, because I like your looks, and I know you will like the place, so be sure and come."

I suppose she said that because I looked like a big, strong girl and could do lots of work, but I said:

"O, yes, I'll be right back as soon as I can get my trunk here."

And so I came, to my sorrow.

My room was a nice as I would want it, but O, that kitchen! I felt like saying, "excuse me lady, is this the kitchen or the woodshed?" Well, here I went to work, went up to my room, put on my kitchen dress, put water on to heat and then washed the walls and woodwork, told the Mrs. to get me some lime and I would whitewash the walls so that I would not go into the kitchen for wood, mistaking it for the shed. Well, walls were cleaned and whitewashed, dishes were all cleaned up, and the floor was cleaned down as far as I dared to go without going through into the cellar. I did this besides cooking for five, and when night came I was almost ready for my little bed, because I knew it would be the same thing over the next day. But, no, I was not to go to bed yet. When I looked for wood to have by the range to start the fire in the morning I could not find any. So up to the Mrs. I went and asked her where the wood was:

"Why, don't you know where the wood is yet? Right out in the back by the barn and the ax is in the shed. You can break up one of those boxes for kindling."

Well, that was all right. She said I was a fine girl and kept the house so nice, and if I stayed until spring she said she thought she would give me $4.50. Wasn't she nice? Well, I think this is enough for this time, but I could tell a lot more about other places. And now, since I am married, I do the housework and my husband does the man's part of the work. But as for doing housework again, if I had to get out and work, not housework for me any more. Give me a coal wagon or anything else.

Mrs. C. F. L.

PRO

Madison Servant Girl Views

"Force of circumstances has forced me to be a working girl since I was sixteen. Have had two years of high school and like many others, I thought myself too bright to be a "K.M."

Tried telephone work at starvation wages, hard, long tedious hours and nerve wrecking work.

Thought of being a clerk or cashier and looked into the matter, only to find that the wages paid and the hours demanded would not keep me decently dressed. Therefore its 'me back to the kitchen.' Have had two places in three years and here is what I do for $4 per week.

Cook and serve for a family of two, who take many meals out, thereby giving me plenty of extra time.

Have a bright, sunny room, plenty of the best to eat, the choice of any books in the house, with plenty of time to read them.

The result is that I have gained in health, improved in disposition and take pride in having my 'flapjacks' a nice brown, smoking hot for my peoples' breakfast.

A bit of cleaning and dusting occasionally, just enough to keep up the circulation and to keep me from getting overweight.

This I think answers Question No. 1, and for No. 2—My mistress is a perfect 'dear.' I guess that will answer No. 2.

Nos. 3 and 4 are answered in the beginning of this article. In conclusion I wish to say if 'A Madison Working Girl' will cultivate a sunny disposition and cook as good as she writes she will find the lot of a working girl endurable and can even be as proud of her 'profesn' as I am."

—'Queen of the Kitchen'

FIGURE 6.72. THE NEW WOMAN: HOCKEY PLAYER AND HOMEBODY TOO. "Do you know this Madison girl?" asked a December 1916 *Wisconsin State Journal* headline. "She can play nearly every game where man now excels" and yet she "will cook, . . . play the violin and the piano, . . . be a lover of the home, and . . . have all the refined qualities of the ideal woman." This eye-catching introduction accompanied a whole new and in many ways extraordinary section in the *Journal*— a separate sports page for women. To many Madisonians the New Woman concept was unfamiliar and to others it was unacceptable. These interpretations were hardly surprising because the woman athlete was then a very new concept in American life. Indeed in 1913 girls on Madison's supervised playgrounds were limited to folk dancing and ring games. For years most American men had thought of women as fragile creatures who even if capable of athletic feats should refrain from doing so because it would jeopardize their femininity.

All these facts not withstanding, these 1920 vintage photographs below show that many Madison women welcomed the New Woman concept. To be sure U.W. coeds constituted the vanguard of the new movement, but it quickly spread to town women as well when they

realized that they, too, could do these things (this was a major discovery in itself!) and secondly that athletic activities were just plain fun.

Suddenly vigor, sweat, aching muscles, even broken bones and bruises were terribly stylish. To obtain these attributes Madison women swam across Lake Mendota and hiked around it, sailed sloops, paddled canoes, ice skated, tobogganed and skiied down hills, ran in track events, rolled bowling balls, dribbled basketballs, hit baseballs, tennis balls, golf balls, even handballs and hockey pucks. One Madison woman threw a baseball 227 feet and set a new women's world distance record. All these things added credibility to the *Journal's* claim that Madison was "far ahead of other cities in the development of this new phase of women's life."

Though the active woman concept rose to prominence in the early twentieth century, it did not begin then. In Madison its roots went back to the 1880s when young women from the best families organized a "broom brigade" so that they might become proficient in military drill but also to secure vigorous exsrcise. According to one newspaper account, the broom brigade caused the young women's respiratory organs to be "greatly developed" and allowed them to undergo much "more fatigue than formerly." In the late 1890s Madison women made news by establishing and using gymnasiums, not to make them more muscular but rather to make them "more subtle and graceful." Also U.W. coeds rowed the eight-oared shells back and forth across Lake Mendota and made the U.W. the fourth university in the country to establish women's crew.

The new emphasis upon exercise and athletics posed a serious problem for women's fashion since such activities could hardly be done in a full hoop skirt. Here Madison women followed the lead of an American reformer, Amelia Bloomer, who for exercise developed a short skirt with baggy trousers gathered at the knee. The girls shown playing baseball are wearing the new "bloomers."

FIGURE 6.73. NOTHING OUTSIDE THE HOME AFFECTS YOU, LADY.   This cartoon, which appeared in the *Wisconsin State Journal* on September 14, 1912, was one of many attempts by editor Richard Lloyd Jones to ridicule the position then taken by many Madison men who believed that women should not be allowed to participate in municipal offices—except schools.

Only gradually and with great difficulty did a handful of Madison women manage to crack the professional and managerial eschelons. Some positions such as librarian and teacher were accepted female roles whereas others such as doctor, lawyer, and professor required a tremendous act of willpower and ability to succeed. Active male opposition was the rule, a fact illustrated by the development of a new management speciality, hospital administration. Historically, Madison men wanted nothing to do with hospitals and were quite content to let a "matron" run it—that is so long as hospitals were primitive five- or six-bed nursing homes. However, following the construction of Madison General and the need for more intensive management, the matron was replaced by a male administrator. And then, as if to add insult to injury, women who had for years served on the hospital board as trustees were told by a nationally prominent male hospital consultant that they were not qualified to serve on the board. His gratuitous suggestion was that they do volunteer work and nursing.[328]

The Feminization of the Polls

Insofar as women's rights were concerned, Wisconsin's 1848 constitution was quite clear. Women had very few. No women could vote, and married women could not even own property. One of the few areas where constitution writers insisted upon equal treatment for the sexes was that women and men were to be counted in the state dicennial census. This decision was anything but an early burst of liberalism; it was rather an expression of the shopkeeper taking inventory of his goods. Women were viewed as subordinate creatures, wards of their husbands. They were to be counted and yet they did not really count for much.[329]

To the great credit of the 1850 legislature the right of married women to own property was restored though no such happy fate awaited women's suffrage. The fact was, very few women and

even fewer men in nineteenth century Wisconsin advocated female suffrage. Not only was suffrage then an almost blasphemous subject, but its supporters almost always backed the abolition of slavery and temperance too—three reforms hardly calculated to endear one to the body politic of that era. Thus when the Civil War came along, most suffrage backers devoted their energies to the abolition of slavery. But then the war ended and these devoted and high-minded women discovered that the nation was willing to give uneducated black men the right to vote but not white, educated women. This pill was especially bitter to swallow following as it did four years of unstinting service to soldier relief organizations and running farms, shops, offices, and families while the husband was off fighting for the Union.[330]

This setback triggered a boomlet of suffrage sentiment immediately after the war but it produced no new legislation or enduring organizations. Not until the summer and fall of 1882 were suffrage backers even able to establish a permanent organization and that was the result of a bold initiative by two prominent Madison men, General Lucius Fairchild and General E. E. Bryant who issued a call for a statewide convention in Madison. The meeting was keynoted by a brilliant address given by U.W. President John Bascom and chaired by U.W. law school professor and Madison attorney, John M. Olin. The product of this initiative was the Wisconsin Woman's Suffrage Association (WWSA), which quickly became *the* dominant state organization. Significantly its first president was Emma Bascom and its first executive committee chairman was Helen Olin.[331]

After several years of statewide organizing, the WWSA got the 1885 Wisconsin legislature to pass a bill allowing women to vote on school matters.[332] This limited suffrage measure was subsequently approved by fifty-three percent of the state's male voters in November 1886. Madison's men it turned out were much more liberal than their counterparts around the state: some eighty-four percent approved the measure.[333] Unfortunately this milestone had no immediate meaning

for Wisconsin women because the ambiguous meaning of "school matters" was not clarified until after many years of litigation. Not until 1902 were Wisconsin women allowed to participate in school-related *statewide* elections and then only for the position of superintendent of instruction, a race best known for its uninspiring candidates, the absence of clear issues, and anything else which might engender interest or excitement. Sketchy Madison data showing Madison's female turnout for this 1902 election suggest that men outnumbered women by at least a ten-to-one ratio.[334] Had Madison women been allowed to elect *local* school board members, the turnout would doubtless have been much higher, but this possibility was prevented by the Madison city charter, which required that school board members be *appointed* by the Common Council.[335]

With the exception of the limited (school) franchise, the years between 1885 and 1910 were lean in achievements for the WWSA. During this period most women activists devoted their energies to the Women's Christian Temperance Union (WCTU), which by 1910 had two hundred chapters around the state and thousands of members. Although the WCTU'ers felt the evil of drink was much greater than the absence of the franchise, they recognized a direct connection between the two, that is, if women could vote, they could bring all traffic in alcoholic beverages to an abrupt halt. Furthermore the sober vote was a prerequisite for clean politics and all reform. Therefore nearly all WCTU chapters had a committee on the franchise. Wet forces agreed. Giving women the right to vote would surely lead to a prohibition. The perverse consequence of strong and pervasive WCTU interest in *both* prohibition and suffrage was to delay the inauguration of suffrage and to make liquor forces the intractable foe of this reform.[336]

By about 1910, however, a variety of factors led to an upsurge of militance among suffrage backers. The achievements of women's organizations on the modern civic agenda convincingly showed that women were quite capable of improving the quality of urban life and participating in municipal management. This discovery in turn caused many to "graduate" from the ranks of clubwomen, become suffragettes, and assert that "civics and politics are identical."[337] The growing number of female job holders proved that women could hold their own in the roustabout world of commerce. The growing number of women who indulged in athletics showed that females were not the fragile creatures of male mythology and that they did not lose their feminine charm by playing basketball. Still others were swept into the suffrage stream as a part of the growing progressive crusade to correct the ills of society. (Nearly all suffragettes were progressives.)[338]

Finally, there were a series of changes within organizations promoting suffrage. Within the WWSA a new generation of leaders took over who believed the time had come for more aggressive pushing. At the same time the power of the WCTU, though great in membership size and chapter count, had during the first decade of the twentieth century gone through a marked decline as male-dominated secular prohibition organizations assumed leadership of the dry crusade. In summary, more women, especially in the middle- and upper-income ranges had more time and more reasons to jump on the suffrage bandwagon.

Using these new conditions the new WWSA leaders flexed their organizational muscles and got the state legislature to pass a bill calling for a statewide referendum on full female suffrage in November 1912.[339] Once the referendum was set in June 1911, women suffrage proponents lost no time in preparing for battle, nor for that matter did their opponents. The Madison campaign was strangely quiet and orderly for such a momentous issue. The *Wisconsin State Journal* ardently supported female suffrage; although the *Democrat* took no editorial stand, it printed generous amounts of suffrage articles. So committed was *Journal* editor Richard Lloyd Jones that he allowed suffrage leaders to write and edit a special suffrage edition paper. As the campaign heated up, papers carried almost daily suffrage articles and ads from the Dane County Equality League.

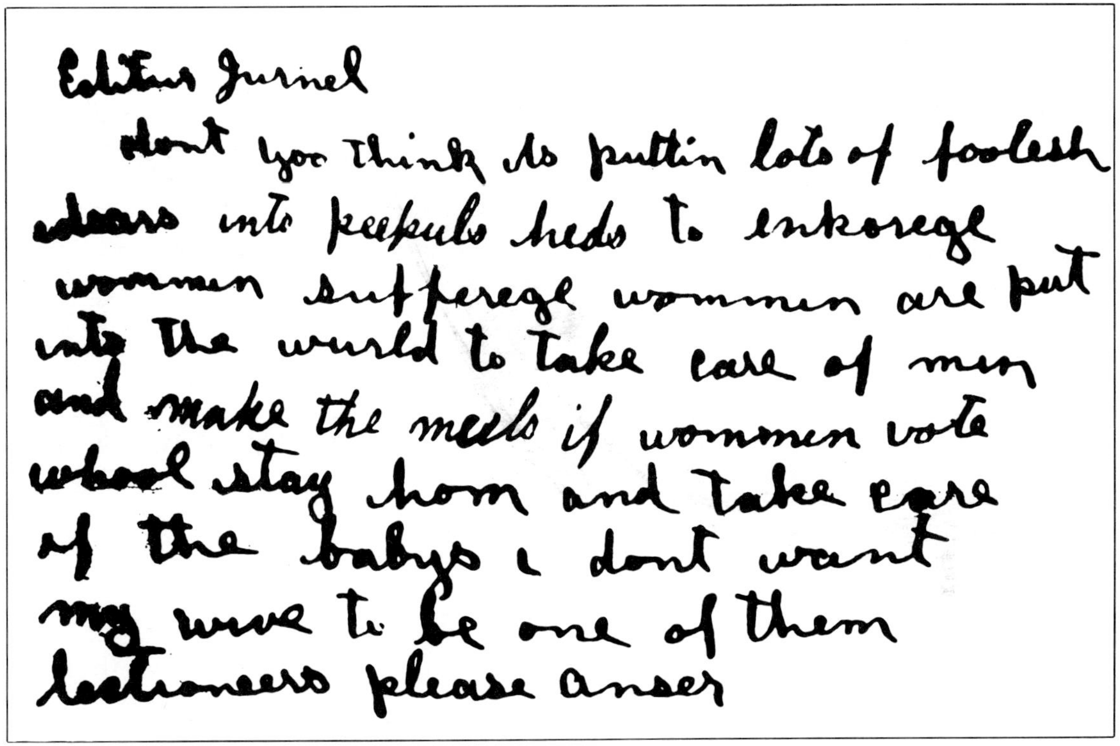

Editers Jurnel
dont you think its puttin lots of foolesh idears into peepuls heds to enkorege womman sufferege wommen are put into the wurld to take care of men and make the meels if wommen vote whool stay hom and take care of the babys i dont want my wive to be one of them lectioneers please anser

FIGURE 6.74. WHOOL STAY HOME AND TAKE CARE OF BABYS? Although the writer of this September 1911 letter to the *Journal* editor could not spell, did not know grammar, and had poor penmanship to boot, he nevertheless voiced a very popular point of view.

Suffragettes brought in big name speakers such as Jane Addams, founder of the famous Chicago Hull House, and distributed flyers. Not very many businessmen would admit that they were going to support suffrage because they feared it might "hurt business" but those who did were given generous play. The most intense confrontation between the two forces was probably the reaction to a decision by the school board to deny the use of Draper School (corner of East Washington Avenue and South Butler Street) for a public discussion of equal suffrage. The board ruled that the topic was "political" and that a schoolhouse could therefore not be used for this purpose. Proponents argued that giving the vote to women would elevate the moral tone of Madison, provide equal justice under the law, give working women (just as it had working men before them) a means to improve their condition, insure the passage of important progressive legislation, eliminate the embarrassment of being classed with idiots, felons, and tribal Indians who were also denied the vote, and finally, that it would cause elected leaders to derive their power as promised by the Declaration of Independence from "the consent of the governed"—including women, who after all were *among* the governed.[340]

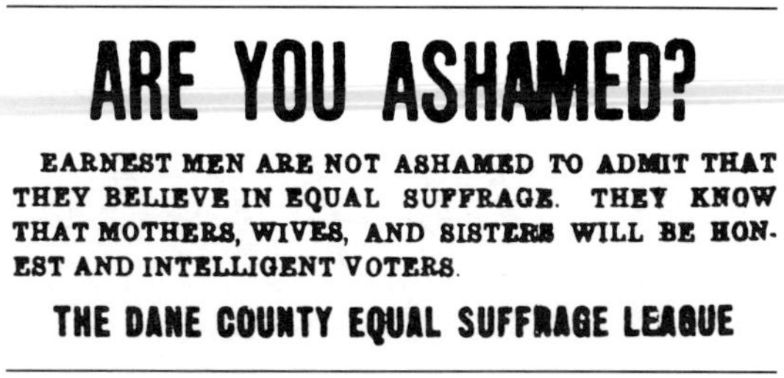

ARE YOU ASHAMED?

EARNEST MEN ARE NOT ASHAMED TO ADMIT THAT THEY BELIEVE IN EQUAL SUFFRAGE. THEY KNOW THAT MOTHERS, WIVES, AND SISTERS WILL BE HONEST AND INTELLIGENT VOTERS.

THE DANE COUNTY EQUAL SUFFRAGE LEAGUE

FIGURE 6.75. ARE YOU ASHAMED? This paid advertisement, which appeared in the *Wisconsin State Journal* in June 1912, was designed to convince Madison area men to vote for women's suffrage in the November 1912 statewide election. And if this message was not convincing, the following variation probably would do the job. "What qualities," suffragettes asked, "should a good voter have that your mothers did not have? Remember your mother when you vote on November 5."

Opponents of suffrage conducted an almost underground campaign. One of the very few overt opponents was a group of prominent Madison women who formed the Madison Association Opposed to the Further Extension of Women Suffrage and who published an expensive pamphlet that said suffrage was totally unnecessary—a frivolous demand by a vocal minority of women. Madison's German brewery interests and retail liquor dealers spread the word through bartenders and others that their votes for women meant no saloons for men. The German Turnverein opposed the measure on the grounds that it would result in a loss of "personal liberty"—a veiled reference to Sunday beer drinking. Father P. B. Knox, pastor of St. Patrick's Catholic Church, feared that if women were given the vote, they would become so free thinking that they would refuse to bring babies into the world and therefore went on record against the measure. Still others argued that women weren't as smart as men, that women would vote on the basis of feeling rather than reason, and that voting was an unnecessary burden upon already busy working girls.[341]

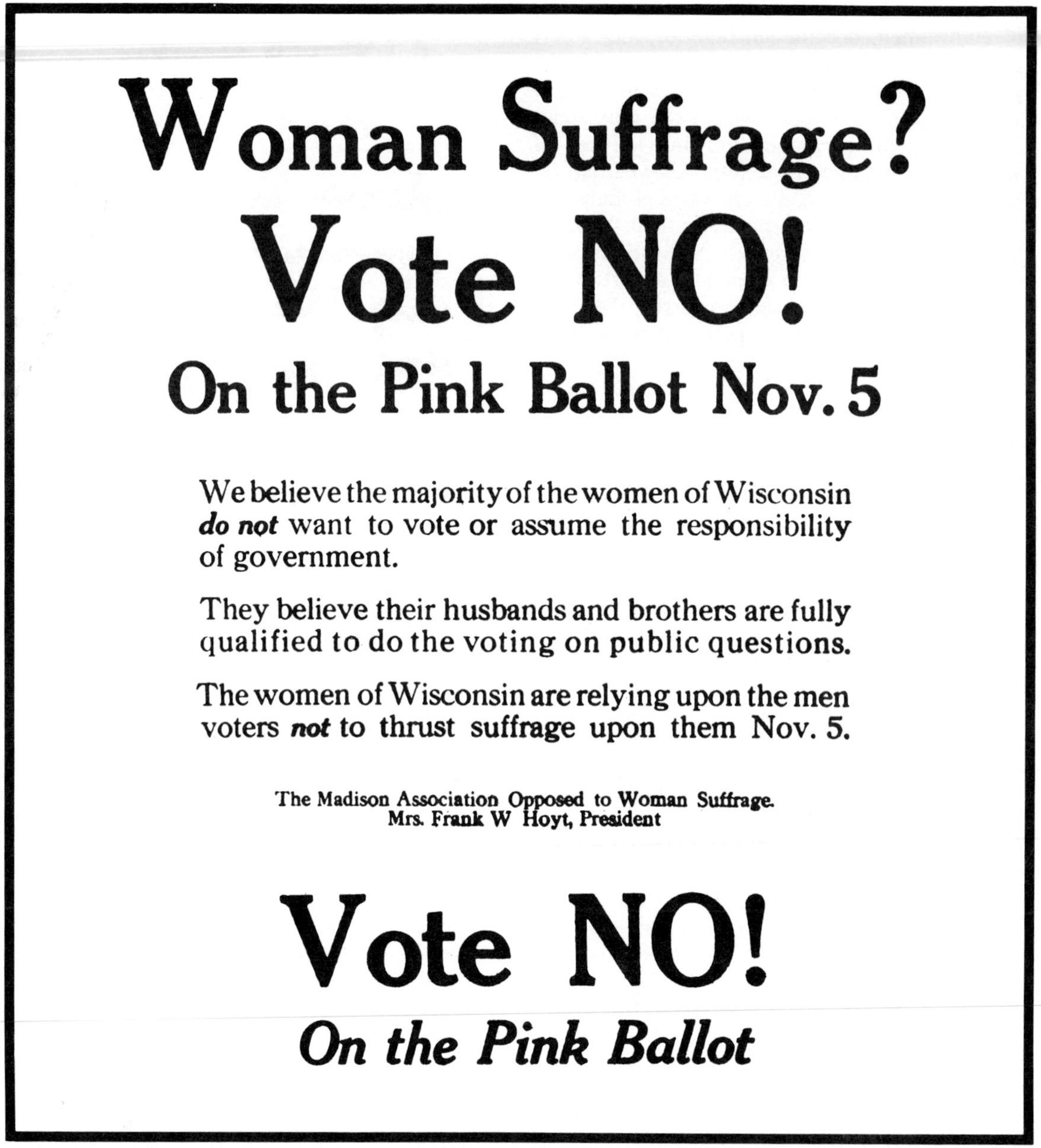

Woman Suffrage?
Vote NO!
On the Pink Ballot Nov. 5

We believe the majority of the women of Wisconsin **do not** want to vote or assume the responsibility of government.

They believe their husbands and brothers are fully qualified to do the voting on public questions.

The women of Wisconsin are relying upon the men voters **not** to thrust suffrage upon them Nov. 5.

The Madison Association Opposed to Woman Suffrage.
Mrs. Frank W Hoyt, President

Vote NO!
On the Pink Ballot

FIGURE 6.76. WOMAN SUFFRAGE? VOTE NO! This advertisement sponsored by the Madison Association Opposed to Woman Suffrage appeared in the *Madison Democrat* just two days before the November 1912 referendum. The *Wisconsin State Journal* refused to carry such ads.

But then came November 4, 1912, the day of reckoning. Madison suffragettes and their allies came close but not close enough. Suffrage carried only the liberal, university-dominated Fifth and Tenth Wards, came close in the wards having a high percentage of affluent Yankees, but lost by sweeping proportions in wards having large German and Irish populations.[342] The defeat showed that Madison men, on balance, still felt that women's place was in the home and that suffrage would destroy this traditional role. The defeat also showed the power of liquor and ethnic special interest groups, the relative apathy among women, and the weakness of suffrage "friends" such as the Progressives and socialists.[343]

Having invested so much time, energy, and money in the referendum, Madison's suffrage proponents were deeply disappointed at the results. On the other hand, they found consolation in the fact that even if Madison had passed suffrage, it would have been hopelessly buried by a nearly two-to-one statewide landslide. Wisconsin with its large German population and huge brewing industry seemed almost irretrievably antisuffrage.

The question facing Madison suffrage leaders was what to do next. Should they wait for another state referendum several years hence and once again jump into the fray, or should they adopt a more proximate and hopefully achievable goal? Madison leaders decided on the latter. Just days after their November 1912 debacle, Women's Club leaders launched a campaign to secure the direct election of Madison's school board members.[344] Despite repeated petitions, it was not until 1916 that the matter was even seriously entertained by the council who, as noted earlier, had the power to appoint school board members. For several years council members played a little game with the women saying that they were in favor of women on the school board, but not if a hard working male member, in effect a good ol' boys club, had to be "fired" to do it. Finally in 1917 a coalition of women's suffrage advocates persuaded the council to petition the legislature to modify the city charter to allow direct election of school board members. In April 1918, the charter revision was placed before the voters in a referendum *including women* since it pertained to school matters. The measure won by a convincing four-to-one margin, even though men voters outnumbered women by about the same ratio. Consequently, one year later, in April 1919, Madison voters—both men and women—went to the polls where for the first time in Madison history they directly elected school board members. Due to female bloc voting, two women, both members of a special nonpartisan citizen slate, received the first and third highest number of votes in a field of fourteen candidates.[345] Thus thirty-four years after the legislature authorized female school suffrage, Madison women sampled the fruit for the first time.[346]

While Madison women were intently pursuing full suffrage on local school matters, national events were moving rapidly and in an encouraging direction. The gradual increase in the number of states that unilaterally extended suffrage to women coupled with intense constant work by national suffrage leaders had produced a terribly exciting prospect, namely, the achievement of women's suffrage by a national constitutional amendment.

Interest in the constitutional amendment was very much a product of growing progressive strength, which between 1910 and 1914 caused seven states to grant the franchise to women. With the two states that had given women the right to vote in the 1890s, this made nine states where women had the complete franchise. This fact coupled with the 1913 constitutional amendment requiring U.S. senators to be elected *directly* by the people meant that eighteen senators were for the first time dependent upon women for their reelection. At last women had the attention of this conservative body! Between 1914 and 1917 the progressive tide continued as other states gave the vote to women and major political party leaders embraced the concept. Then came World War I. In Madison and across the country women's suffrage organizations immediately pledged their full support and went on to compile an extraordinary war service record working for the Red Cross, food conservation, liberty bond drives, citizenship programs for aliens, and much more. That this record hastened the passage of the national amendment is beyond debate. Indeed, it was during the war, in January 1918, that the House of Representatives approved the measure, although the Senate held out until June 1919.[347] The measure was then sent to the states for ratification and Wisconsin, as if to compensate for years of intransigency, won the distinction of being the first state to ratify the amendment on June 10, 1919. Fourteen months later on August 26, 1920, the thirty-sixth state legislature approved the measure and the amendment became law.[348]

With just a little more than two months remaining before the 1920 presidential elections, the spotlight quickly swung away from the work of the National American-Woman Suffrage Association and its Wisconsin affiliate, the WWSA, which for decades had labored to make women's suffrage a reality. Now its carefully designed replacement, the League of Women Voters, sought to harness the new voting power of women to secure additional gains for women's liberation and to assist in the reconstruction of the nation.[349] In Madison the immediate task of the newly formed league chapter was to give instruction to women on registration and voting procedure. From the beginning the league was well known and admired for its high quality, nonpartisan analysis of issues and aggressive interest in "good government." In this respect the league was an extension of the reform and issue orientation of the earlier women's movement.[350]

And so Madison women got the full franchise and Madison government became in the quaint words of a *Wisconsin State Journal* editorial writer "co-educational." "People aren't all agreed that this is wise," the editorial writer continued, "but since it has become a permanent fact, the thing to do is to make the most of it. Best results depend upon welcoming the women with open arms, metaphorically of course. Take them fully

Other Women's Issues: Developing the Bust and Lowering the Cost of Silk Stockings

To conclude that most Madison women were only concerned about the liberation and enfranchisement of their sex would be a grave distortion. For example the members of the prestigious Women's Club known for their civic improvement crusades took time to circulate a petition among their members strongly opposing the 1909 Payne Aldrich tariff on the grounds that it would sharply increase the cost of ostrich feather hats, Italian gloves, silk lingerie, and stockings. Another reflection of this fact was the amount of space Madison newspapers devoted to romance stories, astrology, fashion, and how to improve one's appearance. This how-to-develop-your-bust excerpt from the December 1914 *Wisconsin State Journal* is one delightful example of this less elevated but exceptionally popular genre.

"Stand on the balls of your feet, throw your head and chin up. This will pull up your abdomen and chest. Take a long deep breath and while your lungs are full, bring your hands tightly closed up to your chest. Then push them straight up into the air with a jerk. Hold them there while you empty your filled lungs. Bring your hand down to the first position, fill lungs again, push hands right out in front of you as though you were beating something back, empty your filled lungs.

Now raise your hands over your head, lightly touching the tips of your fingers. Then put them back of you touching the palms.

Now comes the part of the exercise that will probably make your friends think you had suddenly gone insane. Start and sing at the top of your voice the high notes of the scale, holding in your abdomen and keeping your chest high.

Remember no women have finer throats and finer busts than singers."

and gladly into the official family, hear their counsel, employ their effort and resources, share responsibility with them, build cooperation by the spontaneity of the confidence extended to them. Men are largely what their mothers made them, and the stream cannot have risen much higher than its source. We may find in the full flush of manly maturity that the apron strings we clung to in boyhood may still lead us to wisdom in many things." With such gratuitous flourishes, a new era was launched.[351]

Toward the New Woman

The late nineteenth and early twentieth century was a period of extraordinary progress for Madison women. As the new century opened, outside activities of Madison women were by and large limited to church and charity, the lady pious and lady bountiful roles. By the end of 1920, however, five new female roles enjoyed the growing sanction of society: The club woman, the woman worker, the woman athlete, the woman college graduate, and the woman voter. Together with the ongoing traditional roles of wife and mother, these old and new roles flowed together to create *The New Woman.* Although these new roles enriched the lives of most women, they also complicated them. Relatively speaking the changes had come very quickly—particularly considering the depth of prejudice women had to overcome. Therefore time was needed to allow both men and women to become familiar with these new freedoms.

Although the birth of the New Woman was well documented, the obituary for the Traditional Woman could not yet be written. The first two decades of the twentieth century were rather a transitional period marked by an undeniable change in the way Madison men viewed women. More specifically, men began to accept women as more active partners in civic affairs and indeed in life. To be sure the full equality demanded by the radical feminists had not been achieved. And

yet to the more moderate Madison women leaders, progress had been dramatic and tremendously satisfying. Better to have an imperfect new portrait than the old caricature, they reasoned.

The City Healthful: The Rise of Public Health, Personal Hygiene, and Hospitals

Throughout the nineteenth century, most Madison physicians believed that disease was caused by miasma, that is, by poisonous vapors that arose from putrefying animal and vegetable matter. One great advantage of this theory was the ease with which one could find the causes of disease. If it smelled, it probably caused sickness, and the worse it smelled, the more pathogenic it was. The only known remedies for places that generated poisonous and foul-smelling vapors were the use of disinfectants and fumigation. Community cleanliness, and especially spring-time cleanup campaign therefore became the only sure road to public health. However, in an era of privies, private wells, horse power, and careless garbage disposal practices, a clean community was little more than an ideal.[352] To use that delightful expression based upon a carpenter's level, the miasma theory and its emphasis upon environmental sanitation was about "half a bubble off." Cleanliness was important—but not in the way that miasma theorists suspected.

During the last twenty years of the nineteenth century, a group of European scientists led by Louis Pasteur and Robert Koch, working in disciplines that later came to be called bacteriology and epidemiology, developed a whole new theory of disease causation. Disease they said was caused by specific microorganisms or germs. In support of this revolutionary new germ theory, this crack group of scientists identified with almost explosive rapidity the germs that caused typhoid fever and malaria (1880), tuberculosis (1882), cholera (1883), tetanus (1884), diphtheria (1884), botulism (1894), pneumonia (1886), dysentery (1898), and many others. At the same time these scientists revealed the subtle and often incredible ways these organisms were transmitted from person to person and place to place.[353]

The bacteriological and epidemiological work done between the late 1870s and the turn of the century was a dazzling and convincing display of scientific prowess. Seldom in medical history had so few discovered so much with so many tangible and salutary results. It was for this reason that several astute observers around the turn of the century decided that the United States, to borrow a metaphor from its religious history, was on the verge of a Great Sanitary Awakening whose importance was so great that the twentieth century would be known as the "Public Health Century." Even in retrospect these claims compel respect for they accurately anticipated a myriad of changes for U.S. cities and made them the major arena for the development of new public health policies.[354]

Naturally germ theory required a massive reeducation of the public on disease, its control, and transmission. Instead of blaming vague yet very understandable and almost ubiquitous miasma, bacteriologists offered a rogues gallery of tiny but pernicious villains. Some such as the housefly and the mosquito were familiar, but most were strange new microorganisms with even stranger names such as streptococcus.

But the bacteriological revolution required much more than knowing the new cast of villains; it required people to make numerous and substantial changes in the way they lived, worked, and played, and indeed in the relation between individuals and government. The fact was certain types of individual behavior could quickly jeopardize public health. A slovenly dairy farmer could dispense typhoid fever with each dipper of milk, a careless restaurant cook could serve up scarlet fever with his food, and an ignorant parent could condemn an entire class to diphtheria by sending a child to school with certain symptoms. It was for these reasons that germ-theory required public policy and private behavior to be woven together in a skein of unprecedented ways.[355]

Clean Milk, Clean Food, and Pure Water

During the Progressive era a group of journalistic shock troops known as muckrakers decided that a gloves-off, tell-it-like-it-is approach was a sure road to reform. After all, they reasoned, things were bad but if the public didn't know it, there could be no constituency for reform. Using this logic, skilled writers told an incredulous public about unspeakably dirty packing plants, lethal food adulteration schemes, and much more. Although the big name muckrakers concentrated their attention on big cities, journalists and crusaders in Wisconsin's capital city found no shortage of targets.

Just after the turn of the century, scientific studies and local newspaper stories pointed an accusing finger at milk as a major cause of tuberculosis, scarlet fever, and diphtheria. Persons drinking milk from tubercular cattle could contract that dread disease, and Dane County reportedly had one of the highest percentages of tubercular cattle in the state. The same sources showed that dirty dairy barns and the wide-spread practice of ladling out milk to housewives from cans were responsible for outbreaks of typhoid fever in Madison. Still other Madisonians were killed or made ill by the then common practice of adding preservatives such as formaldehyde to milk to keep it from souring. No wonder that a prominent Madison physician said "the cow has killed more people than all the wars."[356]

This was the dismal scene in 1905 that prompted members of Madison's prestigious Women's Club to launch a clean milk crusade. The crusade was a natural for the clubwomen not only because milk purity was viewed as a "domestic" issue (and hence within the purview of women) but more importantly because business*men* feared that their association with the reform would cause farmers to boycott their stores. The women made a hasty but astute and enduring alliance with nationally famous U. W. scientists such as Dr. Harry L. Russell, dean of the College of Agriculture who as a graduate student in Europe had studied under Louis Pasteur and Robert Koch, the two men who founded the science of bacteriology.[357]

The product of this union between clubwomen and U. W. expertise was a tough new ordinance that required all persons who sold milk to Madisonians to have their herds tested annually for tuberculosis. If the tuberculin test was positive, the farmer could sell no more milk from the herd until the diseased animals were removed, cured, or killed. The progress of this ordinance was watched with great interest by dairy and consumer groups around the state because no other city had established *mandatory* tuberculin tests.

Though the risks of drinking milk from tubercular cows were generally recognized, the proposed new ordinance provoked a storm of protest from farmers. At one meeting a farmer stood up and demanded to know "who is going to pay for my cattle if they have tuberculosis?"[358] Farmers threatened to boycott the Madison market but groups of Madisonians responded with a counter-threat to form a municipal dairy and give it the exclusive right to supply the city with clean milk. After two years of haggling over standards and procedures, clean milk proponents got the Common Council to pass the controversial new form of government regulation only to have the mayor veto the ordinance because it was too severe and costly.[359]

This setback only caused Madison clubwomen to escalate their efforts. They made personal visits to aldermen, called them on the telephone, wrote them letters, and carried out an exhaustive house-to-house canvas to educate every housewife to the need for a pure milk ordinance. Naturally they told every housewife to call their aldermen. The pressure tactics paid off. Following a close eleven to eight vote in June 1908, Madison became the first city in the state to require all cows used to supply a city with milk to have an annual tuberculin test. The ordinance also established rudimentary sanitary standards for dairies and farmers, forbade the adulteration of milk, and required skim milk to be plainly labelled.[360]

Meanwhile various scientific tests came into widespread use that revealed the number of bacteria in a unit of milk and for the first time gave consumers a way to measure milk purity. However, what these tests revealed in Madison was anything but encouraging. W. D. Frost, U. W. associate professor of bacteriology, said there were "more bacteria in the city milk than in the city sewage."[361] This statement made before the Civics Club, the other major women's organization, prompted that group to demand an end to "filthy milk."[362]

The city responded with a new ordinance that established more rigorous cleanliness standards extending from the cow to consumer.[363] To give teeth to the new ordinance the city hired a chemist, Fred Rennebohm (the brother of later Governor Oscar Rennebohm), and gave him broad enforcement powers and even a laboratory where sophisticated tests could be performed on all city-bound milk. After just four years of Rennebohm's aggressive inspection and testing program (1913 to 1916) Madison milk quality rose markedly. A milk grading system was established, the use of glass bottles became mandatory for all milk sold at retail in quantities under one gallon (replacing the milkman's can and dipper), and adulteration and skimming were abolished. It was also during this period that the percentage of pasteurized milk rose from thirty-three to about sixty-five percent. This process, which involved the rapid heating and cooling of milk and then delivery in the cool state, virtually eliminated pathogenic microorganisms in the milk.[364]

As a result of these reforms, Madisonians had to pay a little more for a quart of milk delivered to their doors, but in the minds of nearly all, the tradeoff was well worth it. The nutritious and tasty product could now be consumed with reasonable assurance that it would not induce sickness or even death.

Growing knowledge of how disease was transmitted led Madison Board of Health officials and citizens to express concern about unsanitary food preparation and sale practices. However, it was not until the Board of Health conducted a *blitzkrieg* sixty-day inspection of all butcher shops, grocery stores, bakeries, and restaurants in the summer of 1907 that the public became aware of how bad conditions were. Although the front rooms of these establishments tended to be presentable, the back rooms, basements, and food preparation areas were "indescribable" even to hardened health officials. Inspectors found bloated mice laying in front of ice boxes, blood encrusted floors, crawling maggots, rotting meat and vegetables floating in water-filled cellars, equipment covered with grease and grime, and an almost overpowering stench. Moreover these conditions were found in businesses that catered to the "better class of people." Most establishments were given only twenty-four hours to clean up or else be shut down.[365]

This crackdown coupled with unannounced periodic inspections seemed to eliminate the grosser hygenic infractions but left untouched a more subtle but serious disease-producing agent, namely, the ubiquitous housefly. For centuries the housefly had been an integral part of cities and in fact found cities to be a richly supportive environment. Each day in Madison, for example, horses deposited about ten tons of dung in stables and on the streets, an ideal material for nurturing fly eggs. For this reason, Madison's one thousand horses supported a fly population numbering in the millions, and each summer Madison homes would be invaded by the prolific insect. At night, especially in July and August, so many flies would congregate on kitchen ceilings that they would appear almost black. Not until 1898 when an investigation of typhoid fever among American troops in the Spanish American War showed the connection between flies and disease did public health officials understand that this pesky insect was a major cause of disease.[366]

The results of this disturbing discovery were not, however, immediately applied. Not until the Women's Club adopted their "war against the fly" in their 1909–1910 program year did city residents and decision makers understand how pernicuous this little insect was. Their effort culminated in a 1913 ordinance that required garbage to be placed in metal covered cans, windows to be screened during warm months, and produce displays to be covered.[367] Although these ordinances were a step in the right direction, they had little effect on the size of the fly population. The most effective weapon against the fly turned out to be the rapid increase of automobiles, the equally rapid decrease of horses, and the subsequent decline in fly breeding conditions.

Following the development of its public water system in 1882, Madisonians seldom had to worry about the purity of their tap water. A thick layer of sandstone four to eight hundred feet underground penetrated by Madison's growing network of deep artesian wells provided naturally pure, clear water. There was, however, one condition that threatened the quality of this wonderful water and that was hot dry summer weather, which prompted large numbers to water their lawns—so many in fact that hydrant pressure dropped and fire hoses could barely send a stream of water more than ten feet high. It was for this reason that the city water superintendent in 1902 suggested that a connection with Lake Mendota be built so that during peak lawn watering periods it could be drawn into the system to keep up water pressure. But citizens vehemently rejected the proposal on the grounds that Mendota water, though extremely pure compared to the sewage-saturated Lake Monona, was contaminated by decomposing plants, animals, several U. W. students whose drowned bodies never had been recovered, and by raw sewage from the insane asylum. City water utility officials were therefore forced to install expensive new pumps to compensate for heavy seasonal lawn watering.[368]

Not until 1910 was the quality of Madison's wonderful water questioned. In May of that year the state hygiene laboratory conducted tests on water from a campus bubbler and found that it contained human fecal bacteria and duckweed—impurities that experts said could *only* come from Lake Mendota. Madisonians gasped in disbelief. Could the entire city water supply be contaminated with Mendota water? And if so, how?

SPEAKING OF FLIES

Flies are the most dangerous insects known to man.

Flies are the filthiest of all vermin. They are born in filth, live on filth and carry filth around with them. They are maggots before they are flies.

Flies are known to be carriers of millions of death-dealing disease germs. They leave some of these germs wherever they alight.

Flies may infect the food you eat. They come to your kitchen or to your dining table, fresh from the privy vault, from the garbage box, from the manure pile, from the cuspidor, from decaying animal or vegetable matter, or from the contagious sick room with this sort of filth on their feet and in their bodies, and they deposit it on your food, and YOU DO swallow filth from privy vaults, etc., etc., if you eat food that has come in contact with flies.

Flies may infect you with tuberculosis, typhoid fever, scarlet fever, diphtheria, and other infectious diseases. They have the habit of feasting on tuberculosis sputum and other discharges of those sick with infectious diseases, and then going direct to your food, to your drink, to the lips of your sleeping child, or perhaps to a small open wound on your hands or face. When germs are deposited in milk they multiply very fast; therefore milk should never be exposed to flies.

What to Do To Get Rid of Flies.

Screen your windows and doors. Do it early before fly time and keep screens up until snow falls.

Screen all food, especially milk. Do not eat food that has been in contact with flies.

Screen the baby's bed and keep flies away from the baby's bottle, the baby's food and the baby's "comforter".

Keep flies away from the sick, especially those ill with typhoid fever, scarlet fever, diphtheria and tuberculosis. Screen the patient's bed. Kill every fly that enters the sick room. Immediately disinfect and dispose of all discharges.

Catch the flies as fast as they appear. Use liquid poisons, sticky fly papers, and traps.

Place this fly poison in saucers throughout the house: Two teaspoonfuls of formaldehyde in a pint of water, sweetened with sugar.

To quickly clear rooms of flies, burn pyrethrum powder. Sprinkle the powder on live coals carried on a metal shovel. The fumes cause flies to fall in a stunned condition. They must then be swept up and destroyed. Best results are obtained by darkening the room, allowing only ray of light to enter at edge of window shade. Flies, in attempting to escape the fumes, will seek ray of light at windows. This simplifies their collection.

Eliminate the Breeding Places of Flies.

Flies breed in filth.

Allow no filth or decaying matter of any kind to accumulate on or near your premises.

Sprinkle kerosene over garbage and contents of privy vaults. Keep garbage receptacles tightly covered; clean the cans every day, the boxes at least every week. Keep the ground around garbage boxes clean.

Keep manure in screened pit or tightly covered vault. MANURE SHOULD BE REMOVED EVERY WEEK, AT LEAST.

Burn all refuse—such as old bedding, paper, straw, etc.

Pour kerosene into the drains. Keep sewerage system in good order; repair all leaks immediately.

Clean cuspidors every day. Keep 5 per cent solution of carbolic acid in them all the time. Get rid of sawdust boxes used as cuspidors—they're insanitary.

Permit no dirt to accumulate in corners, behind doors, back of radiators, under stoves, etc.

Flies in the Home Indicate a Careless Housekeeper. Remember: No Dirt—No Flies

If there is a nuisance in the neighborhood notify the

DEPARTMENT OF HEALTH, CITY OF MADISON

FIGURE 6.77. SPEAKING OF FLIES. This flyer was distributed throughout the city in 1914 to educate the public on the connection between filth, flies, and disease.

Worried citizens began to boil their water until the mystery was solved. An immediate and thorough investigation by university and city authorities revealed a fascinating fact: in an effort to increase water available for fire-fighting purposes, the university had extended an intake out into Lake Mendota and had then run a system of Mendota water mains around the campus. Campus drinking water, however continued to be provided by the Madison deep well system. Several years later state officials, desirous of increasing fire protection for the capital, decided to tap onto the university supplemental system and therefore extended a ten-inch main carrying Lake Mendota water down State Street. The investigation showed that there were indeed several places on the campus and around the city where the two water systems could be connected merely by turning a valve, a discovery that did little to inspire confidence in the water utility. Happily the investigation showed that the campus bubbler had been polluted by a careless plumber who had hooked up the popular fountain to the Mendota main rather than the Madison artesian main. The bubbler was of course quickly attached to the Madison system. A few months later U. W. and city authorities reported to a greatly relieved public that *all* the interconnections between the two water systems had been severed.[369]

This announcement quelled the storm but only for the moment. In 1915 rapid population growth once again threatened to outstrip the city well capacity and so a group of nonlocal engineers were hired to study the problem. Apparently unaware of the strong local sentiment on this issue, they reopened the debate by urging a Lake Mendota connection. According to the engineers, Lake Mendota water was in fact pure enough to drink and was a much cheaper source of water than drilling more artesian wells. Moreover, Mendota water would give all Madisonians *soft* water and save fifty thousand dollars a year in soap costs alone. But with one thousand persons at Mendota Hospital (the name had recently been changed from the Insane Asylum) and another thousand

lakeshore dwellers dumping raw sewage into the lake, Madisonians were anything but convinced. Richard Lloyd Jones, in one of his stirring and powerful editorials spoke for many when he said, " . . . the engineers tell us that the pure (hard) waters of our artesian wells injure the city commercially; that manufacturers stay away from this town because the water is hard. Everything comes down to the dollar and cents basis! . . . We seem to be going economy mad—eager to put up any kind of a civilization or lack of civilization so long as it does not cost money."[370] Water utility officials decided that it was far, far better to drill more artesian wells—even though they cost much more—than endure the wrath of angry Madisonians. Never again did water officials seriously suggest that Madisonians drink Mendota water.

Sewage Collection and Disposal: The Greening of Lake Monona

During the nineteenth century Madison made impressive progress in removing human wastes from its urbanized areas. The availability of a pressurized city water system, a relatively new contrivance called a water closet, and a network of underground laterals, collectors, and mains caused a growing number of Madisonians to throw away their china bedroom pots, remove privies, fill in cesspools, and for the first time hygenically transport human wastes to a purification plant on the edge of town. But, as noted in chapter 5, collecting sewage and transporting it to the treatment facility, though fraught with problems, proved to be relatively easy compared to making it harmless once it got there. Therefore, effective sewage *treatment* and a variety of refinements to the collection system became the primary challenges for the twentieth century.[371]

Just after the municipal elections in the spring of 1900, the dean of the University of Wisconsin College of Engineering, J. B. Johnson, made the city an exciting proposal that offered a way out of the city's most serious sewage predicament,

namely, the absence of an effective sewage treatment facility. Johnson suggested that Professor F. E. Turneaure, then U. W Professor of sanitary engineering, be made city engineer. If the city would hire Turneaure, Johnson said he would then offer the services of *all* other qualified faculty members who would set up a city engineering department and resolve the sewage mess. Dean Johnson was sincerely interested in helping the city out of the sewage difficulty, but he was also eager to demonstrate the practical value of University-provided knowledge.[372] The *Wisconsin State Journal* thought the idea a good one: "Instead of getting one man, we are getting the whole U. W. faculty . . .," it said.[373]

The offer had particular appeal coming as it did on the heels of the recommendations of Professors Slichter and Van Hise who had warned the city about MacDougall's chemical sewage purification technique. The offer was also appealing because on technical sewage questions, these university professors knew more than anybody else. The council quickly accepted the offer and elected Turneaure city engineer. In the deal came Dean Johnson who prior to coming to Wisconsin was a professor of sanitary engineering at St. Louis, Harry L. Russell, professor of chemistry and bacteriology, Charles Van Hise, professor of geology, and many others all committed to making Turneaure's term the most successful engineering administration the city had ever seen.

Just two weeks after taking office as city engineer, Turneaure and Johnson proposed an entirely new disposal system called "bacterial reduction," which they said was "taking the world by storm." The professors touted the method as revolutionary, cheap, and simple, yet few Madisonians understood what they were talking about. Perhaps a newspaper headline put the concept in its simplest terms when it trumpeted: "Microbes will eat it."[374] Not surprisingly, many were skeptical having just been burned by another experiment in the rapidly changing world of sewage purification. D.K. Tenney, for example, ridiculed this "bugalogical system" as expensive and experimental.[375] In spite of its new and experimental nature, Professor Turneaure boldly staked his reputation and indeed the entire U. W.-city partnership on the septic system—a technique that had been tried in only twenty places in the entire world when he urged Madison to adopt it. The council approved the concept and held its breath for actual operation to begin July 1901. They were not disappointed. Turneaure's "little mites"—469,400 billion of them by someone's count—really did eat the sewage and the new plant built immediately adjacent to the old plant (where the Fiore shopping center is now located) produced a clear effluent.[376]

For several years Professor Turneaure's new septic plant worked well though the location of its eighteen-inch cast iron outfall pipe about one block north of East Washington Avenue caused some to rename the Yahara River, "the Sewage Canal."[377]

The dumping of relatively large amounts of the nutrient-rich effluent in the Yahara River just one block north of the East Washington Avenue bridge so stimulated plant growth that the flow of the river was seriously impeded and shorelines around most of Monona were virtually blocked by weeds. (At the time the reasons for this plant growth were not well understood.) To alleviate this problem, city officials sent an "army" of men armed with scythes into the Yahara River to mow its bottom. However, when it became clear that massed manpower was woefully inadequate for the task, city officials commissioned in 1905 the construction of a barge-mounted, gasoline-powered mechanical cutter. The business end of the aquatic weed cutter resembled a reel-type lawnmower except that it was eleven feet wide; propulsion came from a rear-mounted paddlewheel. The seven-hundred-dollar weed cutter served for only a brief period until a combination of mechanical problems and hundreds of acres of fast growing weeds forced the ingenious contrivance into early retirement—though not without having first earned the probable distinction of being the first mechanical aquatic weed cutter ever built.[378]

Then in 1907, just six years after the new septic plant opened, came bad and very expensive news. During the first few years of the twentieth century so many Madisonians had installed indoor plumbing that the new plant, though four times larger than its precedessor, was already operating above its rated capacity. That meant that the more sewage that came into the plant, the less completely it was purified. Even in 1907 the excess gallonage flowing through the facility had reduced plant efficiency to something like twenty-five percent.[379]

This news, however, did not cause decision makers to rush out and build a bigger plant. Not until several years later when the Board of Health declared the lake a "cess pool," after parents forbade their children to swim in the lake and nearly everyone stopped eating its fish for fear of contracting typhoid fever, did the city get serious about a replacement facility.[380] Not until 1911 did the city even buy the land,[381] not until 1914 did it start construction, and not until January 1, 1917, ten years after the plant exceeded its capacity, did the new plant in the Town of Burke, hence known as the Burke Plant, go into operation (see fig. 6.78).

The decade between the time the old plant became obsolete and the new plant went into operation constitutes one of the sorriest chapters in Lake Monona's history. During this period more than three million gallons of very partially treated sewage were dumped into the lake via the Sewage Canal each day.[382] Consequently, weeds in the Yahara downstream from the outfall grew so thickly that row boats could not traverse it.[383] Summer scum in the lake itself got so dense that power boats could not plow through it and so thick cats could allegedly walk on it.[384] So smelly was the water and scum that some owners washed their boats after each use.[385] Brittingham Beach was closed in the summer of 1915 and was not reopened during the summer of 1916.[386] The lake bottom once brightened by white sand and gravel now lay encased in a tarlike veneer up to six inches thick.[387]

In addition to receiving millions of gallons of partially treated effluent, Lake Monona also had to endure massive quantities of *raw* sewage from thirty-one outfalls around the shoreline. Indeed a single outfall at Bassett Street, a sewer that served the University of Wisconsin, each day vomited one million gallons of the potent pollutant into Brittingham Bay. Unfortunately in spite of a 1903 ordinance[388] forbidding the discharge of any sewage into the lakes, the city was forced to violate its own law because to seal off the outfall would only cause sewage to back up in basements, and to dump it into the existing gravity sewers would overload them and cause problems elsewhere. Not until a new force main was built as a part of the Burke plant project was it possible to intercept and stop this "menace to public health."[389] The remaining thirty outfalls around the lake were either remnants of old common private sewers (see chap. 5) whose locations were never properly recorded and hence forgotten, or individual home and cottage sewers.[390]

During the time the new plant was being discussed and built, city officials were forced by mounting public clamor to DO SOMETHING!—and that meant treating symptoms. To reduce the virulence of pathogens in raw sewage flowing into the lake at the Bassett outfall, for example, city workers doused the foul brown liquid with chlorine.[391] To control population explosions of blue-green algae called "algae blooms" and the resulting stench, public health officials dumped tons of copper sulfate, a toxic algaecide, into the lake beginning in the summer of 1915.[392] Those who complained that fish would be killed by this chemical were silenced by the argument that it was better to kill all the fish in Lake Monona than allow a single human life to be taken by some lake-pollution induced disease.[393] Unfortunately these efforts to control symptoms had little more effect than dabbing perfume on a smelly, unwashed body. In time the perfume lost.

When the half-million dollar Burke plant was opened on January 1, 1917, townspeople breathed an understandable sigh of relief. Most residents

FIGURE 6.78. THE BURKE SEWAGE TREATMENT PLANT. Once the old sewage treatment plant near the intersection of East Washington Avenue and First Street (now the site of the Fiore Shopping Center) became overloaded in 1907, city officials had little choice but to move the plant out into the country. The area around the old plant was rapidly being built up and the site had little room for future expansion. Therefore city officials bought a forty-acre parcel three and one-half miles northwest of the Capitol Square and one and one-half miles northwest of the old plant. At the time the site seemed particularly appropriate because it lay next to another smelly land use, namely, Dr. West's pig farm whose long barracks-looking pig barn is visible in the (*upper left*), background. As noted elsewhere in this chapter, Dr. West had an exclusive contract to pick up city garbage, which he then fed to his pigs.

The new plant provided what is today called primary and secondary treatment. Primary treatment, the separation of liquids and solids, was achieved by allowing the sewage to flow through a one-and-one-half-mile-long concrete maze (above). During this process solids settled to the bottom and eventually were drained off as sludge. Secondary treatment, the removal of smelly and pathological organisms, was achieved by pumping the effluent through the network of pipes and ejecting it as a fountain spray from 910 vertical pipes called "risers" (shown in rows above). This process oxygenated the liquid and accelerated the work of billions of bacteria, which "attacked" the effluent as it dropped through a six-foot-thick gravel bed immediately below the risers. Plant workers then added chlorine to the effluent to kill germs before it was pumped back into the Yahara River. (SHSW WHi(X3) 36265 and WHi(X3) 36267)

realized that time would be required to clean up the lakes and gave the plant the year 1917 as a kind of honeymoon. Besides, the U.S. declaration of war in April of that year preoccupied public attention.[394]

But 1918 was a different story. War or not, the lake still smelled to high heaven; if anything the public thought it was worse than ever before and branded the new plant a "$500,000 lemon."[395] Many opinion makers and ordinary citizens felt they had been duped by sewage treatment experts who implied that the new plant would restore Monona to its pristine state. A kind of lynch mob mentality set in, its members demanding to know who (or what) killed Lake Monona. But the answers they received were anything but satisfying. The sewage plant superintendent said the plant was working just fine and that it produced a clear, odorless, solid-free effluent. The Chicago sanitary engineer who designed the plant was summoned to inspect his handiwork. He, too, protected himself by saying the plant was working in a satisfactory way and that there was no connection between stinking algae and his plant's effluent.[396] Instead he pointed his professional finger at a variety of other causes such as organic debris dumped into Starkweather Creek by the U.S. Sugar Company, street runoff rich in horse manure, and the natural "richness" of Lake Monona.[397]

Nonsense, said the *Capital Times,* in a highly critical series of articles in the summer of 1918. The problem it insisted was *sewage effluent* and anyone who did not believe this and who could see and smell and possessed common sense were invited to visit the plant outfall. In spite of its unsavory qualities, many accepted this "invitation." However, rather than finding a clear, odorless effluent devoid of solids, they found it to be black, foul smelling, and chunky. And why, asked the *Times,* if industrial wastes were responsible for Monona's smell and algae, was the lake polluted *before* the U.S. Sugar Plant opened?

And why if horse manure being washed into the lake from Madison streets was the cause, was Monona pollution increasing when the number of horses was plummeting? And why if smaller, warmer, shallower lakes like Lake Monona are supposed to be so naturally rich and more conducive to algae growth, was Lake Wingra, just ten percent as large as Monona, and much shallower and warmer, full of clear water?[398]

Then came a sensational discovery. Just one month after the Chicago sanitary engineer vindicated his plant an independent investigator discovered that during the construction of the Burke Plant, the contractor had significantly departed from plans and specifications and that part of the plant was therefore operating at only sixty percent of its planned efficiency while another was limping along at just ten percent. Making the optimistic assumption that these defects gave the plant an overall efficiency factor of fifty percent, Lake Monona was receiving the equivalent of raw sewage from eighteen thousand persons, half of the estimated thirty-six thousand persons living in Madison in 1918. But just as indignant citizens readied their ropes for the perpetrator of this crime, the investigator added a sobering disclaimer. *Even if* the departures from plans were remedied, Monona would continue to be green and smelly because a variety of other factors including industrial pollution and urban run off were major contributors to the problem. Therefore no real solution could be attempted until and unless one knew the extent to which *each* was responsible.[399]

City officials quickly voted the money to restore the plant to its original design and hired several consultants to do a definitive study of the lake during the year 1919. Sullen citizens sat back to await the results.[400]

Inexplicably during the summer of 1919 *before* the plant changes were made, Monona was virtually free from algae blooms and odors. This turn of events baffled the new consultants and exasperated citizens eager to find and remedy the problem. Although the team of investigators pushed contemporary knowledge to the limit and

used a sophisticated array of techniques to isolate causes, they found no evidence to link the smell and algae to sewage effluent and even discouraged any effort to remove nutrients from the effluent. The only immediately doable recommendations were applying more copper sulfate and extending the plant outfall twelve hundred feet out into Monona where the effluent would be discharged in twenty feet of water "out of plain sight." Those who had expected the consultants to point the way to salvation could hardly have been more disappointed. Instead of messiahs they turned out to be professional agnostics who suspended judgment and asked for still more studies.[401]

Impatient Madisonians had already sat through what they viewed as the first, second, and third acts of the drama but instead of getting resolution at the end of the third act, a man came out on the stage and announced another intermission. The play, it seemed, was not over. However, when the audience returned to their seats came an event of great dramatic moment. The city engineer told a hushed audience already numbed by twenty years of setbacks and frustration that the Burke plant—a facility designed to handle Madison's sewage until 1950—had just exceeded its rated capacity. This scene occurred in summer of 1920 and came just three and one-half years after the plant had opened and thirty years before its capacity was supposed to be reached.[402]

On this indecisive point another scene in the exasperating and seemingly endless drama closed. And yet the "play" was far from over. The woefully undersized Burke Plant continued to pour increasing quantities of its impartially treated, nutrient-rich effluent into Lake Monona. Not until 1928 when the first unit of the present Nine Springs plant opened did Lake Monona get any relief whatsoever. And not until 1952 when all effluent was removed, was the lake able to begin its long and arduous recovery from its undeserved burden.[403]

FIGURE 6.79. THE GREAT CENTRAL MARSH. These two rare shots of the Great Central Marsh bordering East Washington Avenue were taken sometime between 1909 and 1910 for publication in John Nolan's *Madison; A Model City* (1911). The location of the upper view is unknown. The lower view showing the Kleuter Feed Mill on the right is still standing at 939 East Washington Avenue but has now been incorporated as a part of the Mautz Paint factory and retail outlet at that location. Like so many other Madisonians concerned about the city's image, Noland decried the presence of such ugly scenes occupying the dramatic east approach to the capitol. The tilting telephone poles lay along the north edge of the avenue; the smokestack in the right rear belongs to the giant Gisholt factory at East Washington Avenue and South Baldwin Street.

Nevertheless in 1920 after more than fifty years of trying to find an affordable yet effective collective method of freeing the city from the harmful effects of human waste, Madisonians could point with some pride to the record. Who, after all, could say that a city that had built and placed in operation three sewage treatment plants in just eighteen years (1899, 1901, and 1917) at a cost in excess of $637,000, which increased plant capacity by five thousand percent and which for the first time since 1866 stopped the flow of raw city sewage into Lake Monona through a complex system of laterals, force mains and interceptors, had not made impressive efforts to solve the problem?[404]

And yet despite these efforts Lake Monona remained frightfully polluted. Proximate causes of this circumstance included several unfortunate departures from plans during the construction phase of the Burke plant and a series of engineering miscalculations on plant capacity projections. But the more fundamental reason for this green scum and smell was the limited knowledge of sanitary engineers and limnologists.

The basic but flawed model then used by sewage treatment specialists, was the flowing river and its capacity to dilute and purify relatively large quantities of treated effluent. Unfortunately this model ignored several very important distinctions between rivers and lakes. Rivers by virtue of their constant, one-directional powerful current, contained a marvelous place called "downstream" where sewage effluent disappeared out of sight, out of mind. But Lake Monona by contrast did not have such a current, and "downstream" meant whichever way the wind was blowing. And since the prevailing summer breezes were southwesterly, tons of rotting algae, stimulated into life and then death by the nutrient-rich effluent, were blown back along the Monona shoreline from which the effluent had been expelled—the perilous urban equivalent of urinating into the wind, and fraught with the same predictable consequences. A second flaw inherent in the river model insofar as it applied to Lake Monona was its "flushing time," that is,

the time required to replace existing water with "new" water. The flushing time of a river was measured in minutes but a lake such as Monona in *years*. This longer flushing time meant that Lake Monona would accumulate nutrients much faster than it could flush them out.[405]

In spite of their imposing new technical vocabulary, early-day sanitary engineers and limnologists also failed to understand the intimate and causal connection between phosphorus and nitrogen, the potent nutrients in effluent, and algae blooms. Some suspected the connection but others denied it altogether.[406] Today limnologists know that phosphorus and nitrogen are one thousand times more concentrated in sewage effluent than in waters unaffected by man and that the addition of such effluent to lake water is like turning up the volume control on a powerful amplifier.[407] Even if this relationship had been clearly demonstrated, sanitary engineers had no cost-effective method of removing these nutrients, now called tertiary treatment. At the time the Madison plant and indeed nearly all other plants around the country provided only primary and secondary treatment, that is, the removal of nearly all suspended matter and pathogenic organisms.

Ironically, it was this limited knowledge of sewage treatment and the effect of effluent on a lake that forced Madison officials to become national pioneers in the alleviation of lake pollution symptoms. Lake Monona became the first large body of water in the country to be treated with the algae killer copper sulfate (1915). Also Madison was quite possibly the first to develop and use mechanical weed harvestors (1901).[408]

And so the sewage disposal problem lay in a smelly, unsolved, an ill-understood limbo, an embarrassment to the proud residents of Wisconsin's capital city, a political, technological, and economic hot potato thrown back and forth between citizens who demanded immediate relief and experts who felt they had no choice but to equivocate and demand more studies. Freeing the Madison urban environment and more specifically Lake Monona from the effects of human

waste became the epitome of a complex modern urban problem that strained the understanding of experts, the patience of residents, and the adequacy of the public purse without ever providing enduring and effective relief. Thus Monona, the lake that for years had been the clear favorite among Madisonians for recreation, for residential frontage and as a source of joy and inspiration, continued to be the recipient of the city's sewage, and therefore a universal object of disgust, the lesser lake. Even today its frontage sells for less than Mendota's, an enduring reminder of its sewage stigma.

Garbage Collection and Disposal: The Triumph of Municipal Socialism

Not long after Madison was settled, residents began using a group of highly recommended, experienced garbage collectors. They picked up garbage almost as soon as it was thrown out thereby eliminating the need for garbage cans. They were thorough and what little mess they left could be recycled in the garden. They required no expenditure from the local government treasury and their initial cost was low. Best of all, their garbage collectors were self-perpetuating and could be eaten by their owners. This marvel of sanitary engineering was, of course, none other than the domestic pig.

Unfortunately, in spite of its impressive virtues, the pig was an embarrassment to boosters and boomers who saw them as incontrovertible symbols of sleepy country hamlets. In today's parlance, the pig was bad PR for a growing village with metropolitan aspirations. By the mid 1860s the boosters and boomers prevailed. The pigs were banished and with them went the virtually foolproof daily cheap garbage disposal system they provided.

Finding an effective substitute for foraging pigs proved to be one of the most vexatious problems of the late nineteenth and early twentieth century. The search was complicated by widespread agreement that getting rid of garbage was the *householder's* responsibility—not the city's. After all, went the argument, the household created the garbage and therefore should be responsible for its disposal.

Though this policy was in accord with the American penchant for self-reliance and freedom from government interference, the fact was only a minority of Madisonians were able or willing to make an effort to get rid of their garbage. Some householders burned their garbage in their furnaces, a solution that worked fine in the winter time for those who had furnaces. Some went to the trouble of hiring someone to pick up their garbage, but the typical garbage collector used leaky uncovered wagons for the job, charged as much as the traffic would bear, and came when they pleased.[409] The men who provided this retrograde service were generally farmers who fed the garbage to their pigs. (Ironically, this technique reversed the long standard practice: instead of allowing the pig to go to the garbage, the garbage was collected at a much higher cost and hauled to the pigs who were confined in feedlots on the outskirts of the city.) Still other householders hauled their garbage to the official city dump, that is, *after* the city finally established one in 1894 where Burr Jones Field is located today (East Washington Avenue and the Yahara River).[410] Unfortunately not all householders owned wagons, and even those who did were not eager to use them for the smelly, messy job. Besides, the location of the dump on the east end of the city made it inconvenient for westsiders.[411]

The high cost, poor service, the need for special equipment, and the inconvenience of these methods caused most Madisonians to use another method of garbage disposal, viz., surreptitious dumping. Each evening under cover of darkness householders would sneak out their back doors, pails of kitchen slops in hand. Moments later there would be a muffled splat as the pails were dumped on vacant lots, marshes, street ends, in the lake, and on lake ice just before the spring thaw. Though this surreptitious dumping was completely illegal, it was used by a majority of householders for two very compelling reasons: it was convenient and free.[412]

By the turn of the century, however, a variety of circumstances caused a growing number of opinion makers to become more militant in their demand for a better system. Popular knowledge of bacteriological theory had increased to a point where people were beginning to understand the pathological dangers of decaying organic material. But the immediate and persuasive point was the god awful stench of rotting garbage—sufficient at certain times and places to cause something similar to olfactory arrest.

Finally in 1900 members of the Women's Club launched a campaign for better garbage collection and disposal and were pleased to find other community leaders eager to jump on their band wagon. Contrary to then prevailing views, this small group of opinion makers believed that garbage collection and disposal was a legitimate *city* responsibility. So bold was this thinking that the editor of the *Wisconsin State Journal,* who agreed with their view, confessed that he did not know a single city under fifty thousand in population that assumed this responsibility.[413]

The Common Council responded to this initiative by forming a special committee headed by one of its most distinguished and qualified members, Dr. Samuel Sparling. Sparling who represented the First Ward (Mansion Hill area) from 1900 to 1903 was a highly regarded lecturer in local government and public administration in the U. W. School of Economics, Political Science and History, then enjoying the vigorous progressive administration of Richard T. Ely.[414] Under Sparling's informed leadership the committee conducted an impressive one-hundred-city national survey of garbage collection and disposal systems, the results of which they released in January 1901.[415] The good news in the Sparling Report was that garbage collection in almost all American cities was "primitive and generally unsatisfactory." The bad news was that "conditions in Madison were among the worst and most primitive." But most instructive of all, the committee could not find a single instance where a private system had worked; indeed they were almost "universally condemned." Thus the key question became how the city should do it.[416]

In April 1901, just three months after the Sparling Report had been released, the council incorporated its key elements in a landmark ordinance in which the city for the first time assumed responsibility for collecting and disposing of garbage. Under the ordinance the city was divided into six garbage districts, each served by a specially constructed leak-proof covered garbage wagon manned by city employees. All residents were required to provide their own covered, watertight portable metal garbage cans and to limit their contents to kitchen wastes. The new system began in July 1901 and provided all residential areas with three pick-ups each week. When it came to costs, the city contributed only one-third and the householder two-thirds, but the net cost to the householder was just twenty-five cents a week—just half of the then going private rate. Never before had such good garbage service been available to so many so cheaply.[417]

Although this "innovation in municipal socialism" made Madison a national pioneer in urban hygiene, the system proved to be something less than a raging success.[418] Though the city collection system worked well, the *disposal* systems did not. The private operator of a dump between Fish Hatchery Road and Lake Wingra where much of the city garbage was deposited failed to provide an adequate cover of dirt to mask the smell and thereby provoked an intense protest from people who lived nearby.[419] Other city garbage was hauled to farmers who fed it to their pigs. The problem here was the intense smell of the piggeries and their embarrassing tendency to be located beside major city entrance roads.[420] A second problem was that less than half of all Madison households signed up for the municipal subsidized pick-up and those who subscribed tended to be relatively affluent households that had the most garbage and for whom disposal was therefore the greatest problem.[421] Unfortunately, this left a large number of households practicing the long established unhygenic and unaesthetic do-it-yourself disposal techniques. Third, the costs of Madison's avant guarde garbage program far exceeded projections.[422]

In 1903 the combination of cost overruns, tight budgets, and second thoughts about the legitimacy of a city role in this service area caused the city to retreat from its bold thrust into municipal socialism. In that year the city terminated its thirty-three percent subsidy and reverted to a one hundred percent user fee system, a decision that caused a further decline in the numbers of participants. By 1909 only thirty percent of all households were still paying for "city" garbage service.[423]

Then in 1913 following several deficit-ridden years even under the one hundred percent fee system, Madison abandoned its garbage program altogether and turned the problem over to a veterinarian named Dr. J. P. West who ran a pig farm about one mile north of the city. Dr. West agreed to collect garbage at no charge to the city but for a fee from users of course. By this time city officials were eager to stop the dollar drain that garbage service had caused on the city treasury and at the same time to exchange the necklace of nose-wrenching piggeries that surrounded the city for a single operation far out in the country.[424]

Unfortunately but not unpredictably, the West contract failed for the same reasons all earlier efforts had failed: its user fees meant that it was used by only the more affluent Madison households, which left the masses with the usual unsavory do-it-yourself options. Retrograde equipment and indifferent service further reduced the attractiveness of this West system.[425]

Meanwhile the rapid growth and development of the isthmus between 1900 and 1917 meant the availability of fewer and fewer vacant lots on which do-it-yourselfers could toss their garbage, and those few that remained were nearly always under somebody else's window. This fact and the now widely acknowledged failure of both the private contract system and the subsidized city system were responsible for a new consensus on this long-simmering question.[426]

Finally in April 1917 the council passed another landmark ordinance, which for the first time

made garbage collection and disposal costs *fully* tax funded and staffed by city employees. To prepare for this responsibility, the city once again bought specially constructed garbage wagons and, for the first time, garbage *trucks*. The new service began in the summer of 1917 and had an immediate salutary effect. With the exception of minor problems such as getting people to understand the difference between trash and garbage and keeping ahead of the prodigious debris produced by housewives during the canning season, the system was a great success.[427] Instead of the tried and true surreptitious splat on somebody's vacant lot, householders could now deposit their garbage in metal cans in their own backyards and have the city garbage man haul it away three times a week. And instead of hauling garbage to

smelly pig farms and open dumps, it was taken to the city sewage disposal works at East Washington and the Yahara River where garbage was hygenically *burned* in a large commercial incinerator—one of the first in the country.[428]

And so after nearly sixty years of experimenting and procrastinating, Madison decision makers finally found an enduring and effective alternative to foraging pigs. However, one cannot help but wonder whether Dr. West's pigs whose ancestors had been rounded up and confined to feedlots did not take some grim delight in the difficulty and expense city fathers were forced to go to replace them. After all, the pig is reportedly the most intelligent of all farm animals and therefore just might be capable of such malignant thought.

FIGURE 6.80 EIGHTY YEARS OF FILLING AND LEVELLING. Madison used to have more hills and marshes and larger lakes than it does today. Between the time Madison was selected as territorial capital in 1836 and 1920, Madison residents filled in 3795 acres of marshland, took the tops off hills whose bases covered about 223 acres, and recaptured 223 acres of former lakebed.

Hundreds of thousands of cubic yards of fill material were required for this rather extraordinary transformation. Dredges sucked up tons of sand from lake bottoms and deposited it on nearby marshes. Thousands of wagons disgourged garbage, refuse, and foundation excavation materials. Trains even brought in sand fill from Verona.

This transformation was a product of four forces: (1) physicians who criticized the marshes as disease-breeders; (2) Madison boosters who were embarrassed by the stench and appearance of the marshes; (3) land developers who found they could make handsome profits by filling in lakeshores and marshes and selling them as lots; and (4) civic activists who wanted marshland and lakeshores for parks.

Although few will probably mourn the loss of mosquito-infested marshes, many will lament the loss of several fascinating topographical features. Uppermost among these was a delightful glacial creation known as Dead Lake Ridge. The half-mile-long morainic ridge had steep banks and a serrated top that stood eight stories above the Monona Bay. Its peaks offered spectacular views similar to those afforded by today's Capitol Dome—that is until several businessmen learned that this gift of the glacier was full of sand and gravel, both products in great demand in a growing city. Wagonload after wagonload of this prominent skyline feature was hauled away until by 1920 it was virtually gone. Part of the ridge became fill for Vilas Park, part was dumped in nearby marshes, and much was used for construction.

Charles Brown, an early Indian preservationist and secretary of the State Historical Society of Wisconsin said the destruction of Dead Lake Ridge "was a crime which should never have been perpetrated" because the ridges were honeycombed with Indian graves, campsites, and archeological relics. Clearly, this was a special place to Indians for hundreds and maybe for thousands of years. Unfortunately, this potentially rich archeological harvest was hauled away before it could be properly analyzed.

Dead Lake Ridge was also important because it was from this point that James Duane Doty scanned the beautiful isthmus on his first trip through the area in 1829. What a pity that Madison decision makers believed sand and gravel in this hill was more valuable than the magnificent view from its summit and the archeological treasures within!

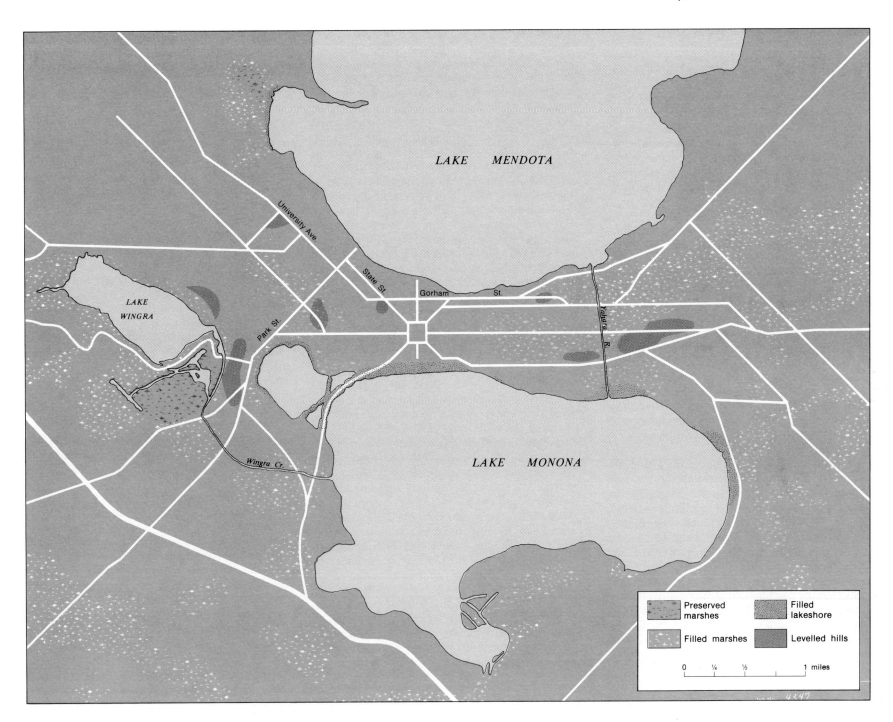

LAKE   MENDOTA

University Ave

State St.

Gorham   St.

Yahara R.

Park St.

LAKE
WINGRA

Wingra Cr.

LAKE   MONONA

| | Preserved marshes | | Filled lakeshore |
| | Filled marshes | | Levelled hills |

0   ¼   ½   1 miles

The Victory over Marshes, A Special Problem

On the printed version of Madison's 1837 plat, Doty's surveyor noted that all land within the plat was "high and dry" except for eight blocks on the east side, which he acknowledged were "wet prairie." This delightful euphemism concealed both the extent and nature of this condition. In fact, seventy-five blocks, more than one-quarter of the total original plat, were a *wet marsh,* memorable to early settlers for quicksand, cattails, muskrats, and good fishing. Two marshy areas bordered the Yahara River, one a thirteen-block area where Tenney Park is now located, and another ten-block area around the point where the river flowed into Lake Monona. Two other marshes lay *inside* the plat nearly surrounded by high dry land. The first, centered around West Washington Avenue and Bedford Street, occupied nine square blocks and contained a pond up to ten feet deep. The second and by far the most troublesome wetland in Madison's history was the "Great Central Marsh," a sprawling 172-acre sea of cattails nearly half as big as Lake Wingra, straddling East Washington Avenue and containing water up to two feet deep. In addition there were many other marshes outside the original plat that the expanding city ultimately encountered.[429]

During the last two decades of the nineteenth century Madison's marshes continued to threaten health, property, and Madison's image. Particularly troublesome were the two inside marshes, which by 1880 had been surrounded by residential and commercial development and which came to be viewed by residents as convenient and therefore very popular places to dump horse manure and garbage. City officials warned citizens that the combination of stagnant water, the summer sun, and rotting organic matter made these marshes into vast "cesspools," "sink holes of pollution" and breeding places for malaria,

yellow fever, typhoid fever, and diphtheria. Periodic floods exacerbated the condition by allowing floating, decaying garbage, and the dissolved contents of inundated privies and piles of horse manure to fill hundreds of cellars and pollute the wells of lowland homes. Property was threatened because nearly every fall after the cattails dried out, some juvenile would set them afire. Depending upon the weather they would smolder and blaze sometimes for weeks and not infrequently cause the destruction of buildings on the edge of the marsh. Finally, the marshes contradicted Madison's city beautiful image because they were the first thing railroad passengers saw—and sometimes smelled—as they entered the city. Said one critic in 1898, "It seems a pity that a city of 15,000 inhabitants and one which has such a beautiful location should allow such a state of affairs to exist."[430]

But getting rid of the disease-breeding, smelly, ugly marshes proved to be as difficult as it was desirable. There were after all just two ways to get the job done: draining or filling, and since filling was fifty times more expensive, draining was strongly preferred. Therefore, during the 1880s and early 1890s officials and interested citizens tried a variety of schemes to drain the marsh by lowering the water level in Lake Monona. Unfortunately after fourteen years of legislation and lawsuits the effort bore no fruit whatsoever. This left only one option and that was filling the marshes—a policy that Madison began in the late 1890s, though not by any formal action. Gradually lot by lot and block by block the marshes were filled. By 1900 the marsh centered around West Washington Avenue and Bedford Street had been filled; by 1905 the Tenney Park marsh, by 1910 the Marquette-Yahara area and by 1920, at long last, the Great Central Marsh, with the exception of a few insolent tufts of cattails, had been obliterated. Thus after nearly forty years of concerted effort, Madison's isthmus marshes were subdued and the lordly bullfrogs that had reigned so long in these boggy kingdoms were heard no more.[431]

Advances in Personal Hygiene: How to Sneeze, Drink, and Use Peashooters

Once bacteriologists had established the existence of an invisible yet real world of microbes and epidemiologists had shown the surprising ways these microbes were transmitted, public health officials had to find ways to make these bewildering scientific advances understandable to the ordinary citizen. Although some key components of the rapidly growing science of personal hygiene was implemented by legislation, notably the 1906 ordinance against spitting (except in spittoons) and the installation of bubbler type fountains,[432] Madison public health officials believed the most effective way to disseminate the new disease preventing techniques was through the public schools where a large, highly receptive, easily accessible audience was available. Best of all, each child had parents most of whom were eager to take reasonable steps to insure the good health of their children and who in turn constituted a bridge to the larger adult community, which ultimately had to understand and adopt the new behavioral code.

Leaders of the new in-school personal hygiene program were an enthusiastic, almost militant, team of health professionals consisting of a school doctor, first hired in 1912, and several visiting nurses, the first of whom was hired during the 1915–1916 school year. This full-time team was a delayed response to the first systematic student physical examinations in the 1909–1910 school year, an event which showed that Madison's youngsters were much less healthy than anyone imagined.[433] Nearly one child in ten had defective hearing, one in three defective vision, and half had defective teeth. Many had diseased tonsils or adenoids, were anemic, and even had dangerous communicable diseases. Only one in three had ever been vaccinated against small pox.[434]

The physical exams also showed students to be woefully ignorant about the rules of personal hygiene—a fact that prompted a special crusade.

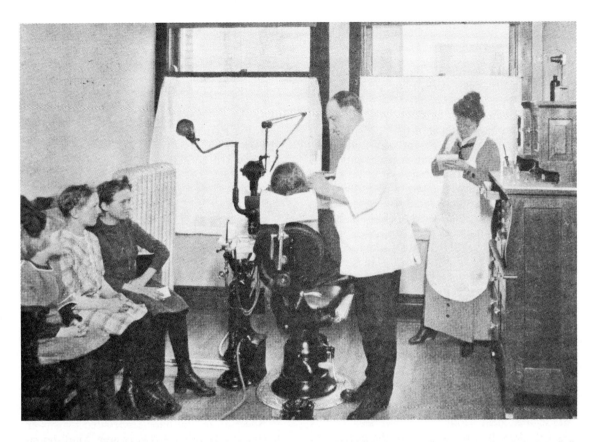

FIGURE 6.81. CHILDREN'S DENTAL CLINIC. The systematic examination of student teeth during the early twentieth century showed that the majority of most children did not brush their teeth or care for them in any way. Some student's teeth were so badly decayed that ordinary chewing was impossible. This shocking discovery caused the Board of Education to establish a free dental clinic shown above in 1915. The clinic was operated by the Associated Charities, the primary provider of charitable services.

Children's Health Rules

One of the most effective methods personal hygiene experts developed to achieve massive, rapid public education were simple health rules. The rules appearing above were designed to prevent diphtheria and were typical of these distributed to Madison school children during this period.

Do not spit if you can help it. Never spit on a slate, floor or sidewalk.

Do not put the fingers into the mouth.

Do not pick the nose or wipe the nose on the hand or sleeve.

Do not wet the finger in the mouth when turning the leaves of books.

Do not put pencils into the mouth or wet them with the lips.

Do not put money into the mouth.

Do not put pins into the mouth.

Do not put anything into the mouth except food and drink.

Do not swap apple cores, candy, chewing gum, half-eaten food, whistles or bean blowers, or anything that is put into the mouth.

Never cough or sneeze in a person's face. Turn your face to one side.

Keep your face and hands clean; wash the hands with soap and water before each meal.

To compensate for the appalling near absence of student tooth care, the school health officer got a local dentist to give stern talks to students on the subject of oral hygiene.[435] To get children to wash and take better care of their bodies, the school doctor developed a powerful talk entitled "Clean Bodies," which he then went from school to school delivering. A variety of other programs on the perils of sneezing or coughing without covering one's mouth, alcohol and tobacco consumption, exchanging peashooters or gum with another person, and how to recognize the symptoms of communicable diseases rounded out the personal hygiene catechism. To make sure this new secular gospel was understood, the school doctor and the visiting nurses met with hundreds of parents in their homes beginning in the 1915–1916 school year. There a special effort was made to persuade parents to stop the "barbarian" practice of sending their children to school with communicable diseases.[436]

During the first two decades of the twentieth century, but particularly during the 1910–1920 period, the school-centered public education strategy produced a rich harvest of results. "Death cups" (common drinking containers) were replaced by the now familiar "bubblers," lavatories were installed in school bathrooms so that children could wash after using the toilet, humidity was added to classrooms to reduce colds and bronchial disorders, and janitors were hired to keep the schools clean and sanitary.[437] Children started brushing their teeth, covering their mouths when they sneezed, and stopped exchanging food with one another. Eventually parents began following their children's example.

The Hospital Crusade

Suppose for a moment that you lived in Madison during the early 1880s and you became ill with some noncontagious ailment. What would you have done? If you were fortunate enough to be a family member, you would have stayed home and had another family member look after your needs. If your illness was serious, a doctor would have been summoned. Not only was the home considered the proper place for a sick person, but the *best possible environment* because of the built-in nursing care it provided. However, if one were a transient or a student or someone outside a conventional family setting, the options for the sick were grim indeed. Those who had money might rent a hotel room; those who did not were sometimes given permission to use the jail. Under these conditions reluctant bellboys and jailers could sometimes be persuaded to bring in food and medicine. But the worst fate of all awaited those who contracted a contagious disease and who had no family to tend them. A cold, vacant Williamson Street warehouse was not an uncommon destination for persons in this category. If none of these options were attractive, and you insisted on going to a hospital—well, you'd have to go to Milwaukee.

This was the inhumane, unenlightened, and unflattering portrait of Madison's treatment of the sick presented in a lecture to a "large and highly intelligent" audience at the Fuller Opera House in December 1880 by Miss Ella Giles, Madison's distinguished librarian, the celebrated author of three novels including the first novel ever published by any Wisconsinite, and a founder of the exclusive Madison Literary Club. Apparently this first public plea for a hospital in Madison's history hit a sensitive nerve because before

leaving the lecture the audience appointed a committee of prominent citizens to erect a hospital, though not a facility with the modern connotations of that word.[438] Today we would call the medical facility they were trying to establish a "hospice," or a "cottage hospital," that is, a small five- to ten-bed facility in a converted residence. Since the primary mission of the "hospital" was to provide nursing care for the poor and unfortunate, it was viewed as a charity to be supported by voluntary citizen contributions. And since the likelihood of recovery for many of its patients was very low, these hospitals were widely viewed as places where poor people went to die—albeit with the dignity of minimal nursing care. Significantly the hospital these 1881 backers wanted to establish was to be devoid of any sectarian taint and available to all doctors regardless of which medical doctrine they embraced, hence the early meaning of the term Madison *General* Hospital.[439]

Madison's little band of hospital backers moved quickly to realize their goal. At their first organizational meeting in January 1881, they decided to ask the city to donate a block of land it owned on the Near East Side, now known as Orton Park, as the hospital site. At the time the site seemed ideal. Until 1877 it had been used as the cemetery, but in that year all the bodies had been disinterred and moved to Forest Hills. Thus the city-owned block stood vacant and presumably available. To Sixth Warders, however, the site was anything but ideal. Why should we allow people with life-threatening contagious diseases to be put in our midst? they asked indignantly.[440]

So fierce was their opposition that the gentle, sensitive and humane persons then promoting the hospital did not venture back into the political area with any new proposals until 1886, five years later. In that year a new group of hospital backers quietly organized another attempt to erect a hospital. However, before the Madison Hospital Association could get underway, a group of Catholic laymen persuaded the Sisters of the Franciscan Order at Milwaukee to set up a hospice in a stone home at 423 North Carroll. Their

first priority was to provide nursing services for the poor although they made their services available to anyone who needed them, regardless of religion.[441]

Thinking the sisters would build a hospital and supply the annual operating funds, the city gave the order a choice site on Lake Mendota just west of North Patterson Street—though not until after the sisters had unwittingly poked a stick into the Sixth Ward hornets nest by first asking for the Orton Park site. Unfortunately Madisonians failed to respond to a fund drive to build a hospital on this city-provided site and so the discouraged sisters closed their two-year old hospice and returned to Milwaukee.[442]

Several years after the Franciscan sisters left town, the city fathers decided that they had to have a steam roller but they had no money and so they sold the hospital lots at the foot of North Patterson Street to raise the cash. Unfortunately this decision forced hospital backers to find a replacement site—a task that enormously increased the difficulty of establishing a hospital in the capital city and very nearly stymied the entire effort.[443]

Following the closing of the Franciscan Hospital, Madison not only had no hospital but no prospect of getting one. Confronted by this embarrassing possibility, two young Madison surgeons, William W. Gill and James N. Boyd, both impatient with years of hospital talk and no action, decided that Madison deserved something more than a mere hospice or nursing home. Their goal was to erect and operate a modern well-designed facility equipped with the latest diagnostic and therapeutic equipment and an operating room, staffed by trained nurses twenty-four hours a day and available to all reputable physicians. Moreover they wanted to radically alter the image of a hospital held by most Madisonians. Instead of being a charitable institution where poor people went to die, Gill and Boyd wanted Madisonians to view a hospital as a place where rich and poor alike could enjoy the benefits of the best and latest medical treatment.

MADISON HOSPITAL

BEST HOSPITAL ACCOMMODATIONS
IN THE STATE.

Dr. J. N. BOYD,   ❋   Dr. W. W. GILL,

PROPRIETORS.

FIGURE 6.82. THE GILL AND BOYD HOSPITAL. Shown above from an 1890 City Directory advertisment is the thirty-five-bed Madison Hospital at 413 South Baldwin, more commonly known as the Gill and Boyd Hospital. Since doctors' credentials had not been refined at this point, it was available to any Madison physicians who behaved like "gentlemen." It was the first structure designed and built as a hospital and the first to offer an operating room and trained nurses. To get design ideas for the hospital, Dr. Gill visited thirty hospitals all over the U.S.

In addition to its advanced equipment and design, the Gill and Boyd Hospital offered a remarkable health insurance program. With the payment of a twelve-dollar annual premium, the doctor-proprietors would issue a certificate that entitled the purchaser to medical and surgical treatment, medicine, and a hospital room up to thirty-six weeks. The only exceptions in the fine print were hospitalizations related to insanity, chronic, contagious or venereal disease or any disease or injury related to fighting or intoxication.

The building stood vacant for many years following its demise as a hospital. In 1905 it was remodeled into a hotel; today it is an apartment building. (SHSW WHi (X3) 35997)

The combination of no hospital and two earnest young physicians with a bold new idea proved to be a winning combination. Following a brief, intense 1889 fund drive, bankers, businessmen, and citizens contributed fifteen thousand dollars for the new enterprise, a very large amount at the time. Doctors Gill and Boyd agreed to run the hospital for three years after which they and their contributors would try to get someone else, hopefully the city, to run it. Still, their initiative was a great gamble because there was no guarantee that another party would pick up the baton and continue the enterprise. Based upon this understanding Gill and Boyd built the largest, fanciest hospital Madisonians had ever seen—a thirty-five-bed facility bristling with the latest design and equipment. For two years the hospital lost money but it broke even in the third year. Nevertheless the city refused to take over the hospital or even grant any tax relief, and no one else stepped forward. Therefore in 1893 after just three years of operation, the Gill and Boyd hospital was regrettably closed. In the minds of Madison decision makers, hospitals had not yet made the transition from private charity to public obligation.[444]

The failure of the Franciscan hospice and the private physician's hospital was a profound setback to local hospital proponents and left the city once again devoid of any nursing or hospital facilities. Not until 1896 was the Madison Hospital Association even able to establish another hospice first known as the Hayes Hospital (9 East Dayton, 1896–1900) and later as the Hicks Hospital (321–323 North Hamilton, 1900–1904) after the dedicated matrons who ran them. Both occupied converted homes and were operated as charities by the Madison Hospital Association.[445]

The failure to establish a modern hospital in the nineteenth century was of course frustrating for backers and unfortunate for the sick. And yet these failures were not surprising so long as nearly all Madisonians believed (1) that the home was the best place for sick people to be and (2) that hospitals were private, charitable, contribution-supported institutions designed to relieve pain and

suffering for those who had no one else to look after them. So long as these concepts dominated public perceptions, a full-service city-run general hospital was hardly possible.

However, the late nineteenth century was a great watershed in the evolution of hospitals and public perceptions of them. The developments that most dramatically altered prevailing views were the discovery of safe, effective anesthetics and the use of antiseptic practices, which in turn allowed a veritable explosion in the use of surgery. Indeed it was surgery and its concomitant need for operating rooms and trained nurses that created the greatest single demand for modern hospitals. This rapid growth of surgery was evident in Madison at the Hays-Hicks Hospital, which was primarily used by convalescing surgery patients. Running a close second were the development and widespread use of new diagnostic and therapeutic tools such as "X"rays and pathology laboratories which because of their cost and complexity tended to be concentrated in hospitals. These developments forced the public to discard the old hospitals-are-for-paupers view and to substitute the idea that a hospital was "the very best place to get well more surely, swiftly, and easily than anywhere else."[446]

The second change in the way the public viewed hospitals revolved around the question: who should operate them? Throughout the United States there was near unanimity that hospitals were a *local* but *private* or *sectarian* responsibility and that local *governments* had a very limited role. Madison's donation of a site for the Franciscan hospital and its periodic contributions to the annual operation of one of the cottage hospitals was then felt to be the limit of local government responsibility toward hospitals.

There was, however, one major exception and that was an obligation that appeared in the 1856 city charter to isolate persons with contagious diseases such as small pox and diphtheria. Not until 1885, however, did the city even appoint a city-wide health officer. And not until 1892, after years of pleading by the new health officer, did the city erect its first isolation facility, officially known as "The Contagious Hospital," but more commonly known as "The Pest House" (short for the Pestilential House). The Pest House was located about one-half mile east of the Yahara River on the extreme eastern edge of the city (1954 East Washington Avenue), then very much out in the country, yet inside the existing city limits. This far-out location was a direct reflection of the miasmatic theory of disease which said that sickness was transmitted through the air and that relatively great distances were therefore necessary to prevent its spread.[447]

Once the Pest House was constructed, it allowed the public to make an important distinction between the "bad" pest house on the one hand where one could contract a deadly disease and a "good" general hospital on the other where one could visit a friend or even have surgery performed in relative safety. This important distinction reduced—though it did not entirely eliminate—the heretofore great fear of having a hospital in or near a residential area.

Thus the question remained: What was the city responsibility toward a *general* hospital? Though there were still those who argued that hospitals were private profit-making enterprises, there was little if any evidence in late nineteenth century Madison that a hospital could operate without subsidies both for initial construction and operation. Meanwhile hospital backers gave a new Progressive twist to their long-used, persuasive humanitarian justification. The city, they argued, had a moral responsibility to provide for the good health of its citizens. And since a modern general hospital could not exist without a subsidy, and since the city was the only realistic and reliable source of this subsidy, Madison should willingly shoulder this burden, just as it paid for sewers, libraries, parks, and fire engines. These, then, were the powerful prohospital arguments that gained force around the turn of the century.[448]

Hoping to take advantage of this new positive hospital image, growing support for a larger city role, and the increasing need for a modern facility, Madison hospital backers in early 1898 launched another major assault on the difficult mountain they had resolved to climb. First came a proposal from a Tomah physician to move his hospital to Madison, but this failed because it was opposed by local physicians.[449] Then came an effort to buy the old Gill and Boyd Hospital with private funds and turn it over to the city providing the city would agree to underwrite up to one hundred dollars per month for its operation. Significantly, the Common Council said the city would pay *something* toward maintenance of a general hospital but certainly not one hundred dollars per month.[450] Then came a proposal from several aldermen that required the city to pay fifty dollars per month toward the maintenance of a hospital. The city refused on a technicality.[451] Then came a group of wealthy citizens who offered to purchase and equip a hospital at a cost of up to ten thousand dollars providing that the city would contribute twenty thousand dollars for a permanent operational endowment. The city refused pleading insufficient funds.[452] Then came a proposal by the Madison General Hospital Association to raise twenty thousand dollars if the city would raise ten thousand. The city refused: same reason.[453] Then came a wealthy physician who offered to build a municipal hospital on land he had just purchased fronting on Lake Monona at the intersection of Spaight and Brearly Streets providing that the Madison General Hospital Association would reimburse him for the price he had paid for the land. The association quickly agreed whereupon nearly everybody in the community jumped on this bandwagon. Unfortunately just after it had developed considerable momentum, the bandwagon came to a screeching and embarrassing halt when someone discovered that the deed prevented this parcel from ever being used as a hospital! And even if this matter had been circumvented, adjoining neighbors

might have killed the project because they objected to smelling ether gas, hearing groaning patients, and seeing corpse-filled hearses roll through their streets.[454] Then almost in desperation the Hospital Association bought several lots along Breese Terrace but by this time six distinct crusades in just thirty months, an average of one every five months (does this pattern sound familiar, reader?), left the once doughty band of hospital backers utterly exhausted, the public confused, and donors demoralized.[455] It was at this exasperating juncture that the *Journal* editor yelped: "For God's sake, let the people of this rich and important city stop talking about a hospital and establish one."[456]

Then on July 4, 1900, Madison newspapers carried a story that gave Madisonians a reason to celebrate something more than the nation's birthday. It was an offer made by Mrs. Wayne Bowen Ramsey, the daughter of a prominent early physician, mayor (1871–2), and banker, Dr. J. B. Bowen, for four and one-half acres at the intersection of Chandler and Mills Streets. At one time Dr. Bowen had owned much of the land in this South Madison area; his large Italianate home still stands at 302 South Mills and is a Madison landmark.

Unlike the other sites that had recently been proposed, this South Madison site was not surrounded by dense development and therefore was not susceptible to the predictable objections from prospective hospital neighbors. However, the site was heavily criticized for being "way out there," one mile from the capitol and the campus. Indeed some physicians felt so intensely about this that they refused to give any money for a hospital on this site and vowed never to send any of their patients there. In spite of this opposition, the Board of the Madison General Hospital Association accepted the site. And so once again, the incredibly resolute and resilient band of hospital backers, inspired by still another site, geared up for what was clearly going to be a difficult twenty-five-thousand-dollar fundraising drive, ten thousand of which had to come from the city.

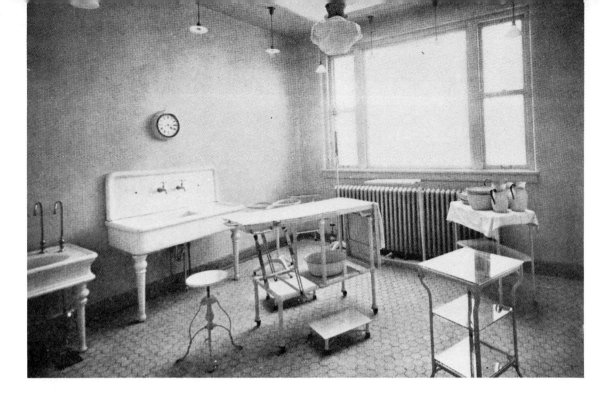

FIGURE 6.83. MADISON GENERAL HOSPITAL: THE PRIDE OF MADISON. The exterior photograph taken sometime in 1906 shows the view one would have seen driving by on Park Street and looking to the west. The handsomely proportioned red brick facility was designed by the talented Madison architects Louis W. Claude and Edward Starck. The kitchen and dining room occupied the basement, wards and doctors rooms the first floor, private rooms and the operating suite the second, and nurses quarters on the third.

Although the building was the best its backers could afford at the time, it was soon viewed by hospital officials as a "small, cheap building." That it was too small was evident from the fact that it reached its design capacity in the first year. By "cheap" officials meant that the hospital was built of frame construction rather than poured concrete fireproof construction. It was torn down in the early 1960s to make way for a much larger facility. Both the ward and operating room shots were taken in 1907. (SHSW, WHi(X3)36289)

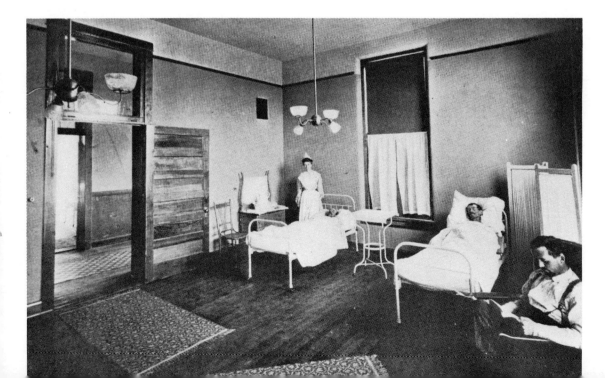

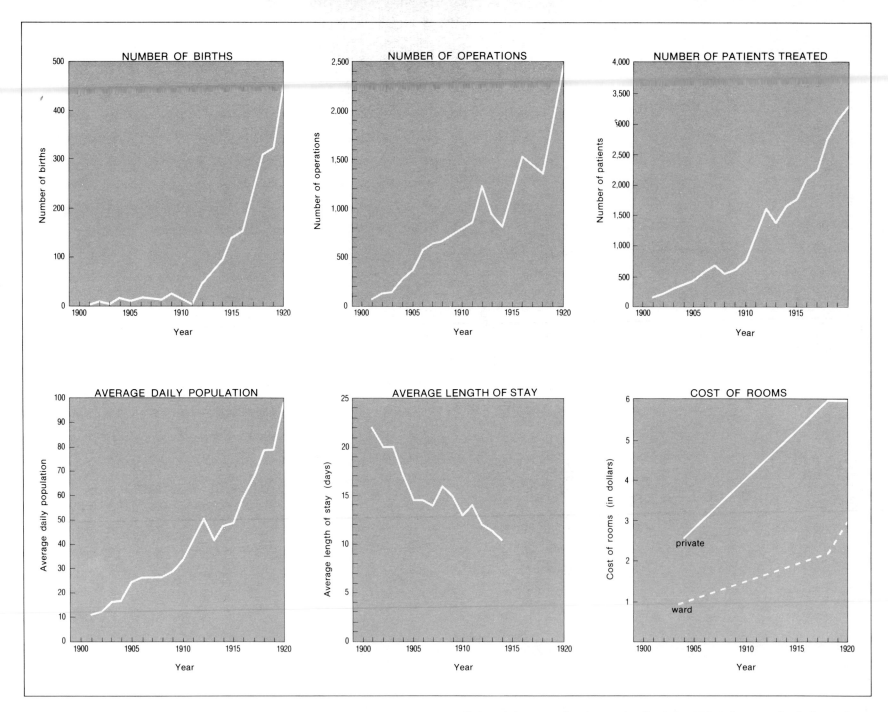

FIGURE 6.84. INCREASE IN HOSPITAL USE. As noted in the above graphs the number of births, operations, patients treated, and average daily populations at Madison General Hospital all showed precipitous increases during the first two decades of the twentieth century. This was the take-off period for the full service modern hospital. As medical standards and the price of living went up, so too did room rates. The only use indicator that went down was the average length of stay. This in turn was due to the decline in the use of the hospital as a nursing care facility (the old perceptions of a hospital), the increase in the use of hospitals for surgery, and the improvement in hospital procedures and sanitation.

But this time instead of sending one of their male officers into the council lion's den to beg for money, the Hospital Association sent Mary Mears Hobbins, the talented wife of American Exchange Bank president Joseph W. Hobbins. In a closely reasoned presentation she blistered aldermen with facts and pummelled them with arguments, all brilliantly organized. Not only did she numb the traditional council reasons for not giving, but she emerged with the full ten thousand dollars she had requested. Perhaps the council members had grown tired from repulsing so many earlier hospital overtures or perhaps they sensed the broad ground swell of community support for the controversial facility and hence the futility of bucking it any longer. But there is one fact that cannot be disputed and that was the singular and salutary role Mary Hobbins played with her virtuoso performance on the evening of March 14, 1902.

Then for an encore to her *tour de force,* Mary Hobbins and a small group of women in the Hospital Auxiliary stormed through the community like soldiers in a fast-paced close-order drill, getting citizen signatures on hospital pledgecards. When they had finished they had raised sixteen thousand dollars, six thousand above the original private sector goal of ten thousand dollars. The increase became necessary when bids for the hospital came in higher than expected. Ground was broken for the long awaited hospital in April 1903.

One might hope that the opening of the Madison General Hospital on October 15, 1903, would have ended the bickering, petty jealousies, intense factionalism, and back biting that for twenty-one years delayed the city hospital. Indeed at the groundbreaking ceremonies Madison General Hospital board president W. A. Henry suggested that all this acrimonious and exasperating chapter of Madison history was "best forgotten." Unfortunately, the record does not permit such a charitable resolution. No sooner had the new hospital opened than a "goodly number" of Madison doctors followed through on their pledge to boycott the new facility and opened a private physicians hospital at 1008 Spaight Street, a location they considered convenient and close-in. But, as it happened, mainline hospital backers did not have to wait long for their vindication. Seven months later the private hospital folded and the grumbling physicians began using the new municipal hospital "way out" in Greenbush.[457]

So great was the demand for the new Madison General Hospital that it reached its capacity less than one year after it opened. This crowding rekindled the desire of local Catholics to establish their own hospital. The Catholics first turned to the Janesville Sisters of Mercy who opened a small temporary fourteen-bed facility at 209 East Mifflin in 1908 until a five-story, one hundred-bed, sixty-thousand-dollar hospital could be built on the ridge overlooking Tenney Park at the intersection of East Johnson and Baldwin Streets. Unfortunately the Tenney Park plan fell through, the temporary hospital was closed, and the sisters returned to Janesville. The job of building a large Catholic hospital then fell to the rector of St. Paul's University Chapel who at first had no success whatsoever. Eighteen religious orders turned him down saying they had too little money or too few people or both. But then one day as the determined rector passed the old Catholic cemetery bounded by South Mills, South Brooks, and Erin Streets, it occurred to him that this two-acre former field of death might be the perfect site for a new house of healing. After all, he reasoned, it was vacant (the bodies had been moved to the Calvary Cemetery, the Catholic section of Forest Hills, in the 1860s and 1870s) and owned free and clear by the diocese. Backed by the local hierarchy and a petition from the men of the nearby St. James parish, the rector convinced the Sisters of Saint Mary headquartered in St. Louis, Missouri, to at least inspect the site. To the delight of the rector and local Catholics, the sisters concluded that this site was superb and that it could be *the* Catholic hospital for a fifty- to one-hundred-mile radius. Ground was broken and in September 1911 the new $157,000 seventy-bed St. Mary's Hospital was opened.[458]

Meanwhile Madison General Hospital officials had raised enough money to construct a $94,000, eighty-five-bed addition, which opened in January 1912, just four months after the St. Mary's Hospital.[459]

At the same time the number of general hospitals was growing, a variety of specialized hospitals were also opened. In 1910 the University of Wisconsin became the second university in the country to provide an infirmary for its students.[460] In 1911 Mary Stoeber, a graduate of a Philadelphia nursing school, founded a maternity hospital in Madison (209 Wisconsin Avenue) where women could for the first time deliver babies under anesthesia, then called "twilight sleep." Miss Stoeber's hospital was largely responsible for getting women in the habit of having babies in hospitals. Prior to its existence, few women in their right minds would have a baby in a hospital because of its connotations of sickness and disease.[461] Following her death in 1918 during the great flu epidemic, the Methodist Church bought and continued her hospital. Then in 1921 the facility was moved to the old St. Regina Convent at 303 West Washington Avenue and expanded to a general hospital.[462] Other specialized facilities begun during the first twenty years of the twentieth century include the Madison Sanitarium (1903) at 330 East Lakeside (today the site of the Dane County Medical Society), which specialized in nervous and digestive disorders, and the Morningside Sanitorium (1918) at a large site near the intersection of Monona Drive and Frost Woods Road, which specialized in tuberculosis.[463]

The year 1919 witnessed the addition of two other medical facilities destined to play important roles in Madison. One was the first teaching hospital connected with the U.W. Medical School known as the Bradley Memorial Hospital and the second was the Jackson Clinic, the first modern physicians' clinic.[464]

Taken together the contrast in Madison health care facilities between 1902 and 1920 could hardly have been greater. In 1902 the city had

FIGURE 6.85. ST. MARY'S HOSPITAL. Madison's St. Mary's Hospital soon after its completion in 1911. (SHSW WHi(X3)37935)

only its twelve-bed Pest House and the twenty-bed Hays-Hicks (cottage type) Hospital. But by 1920 Madison boasted eight hospitals: two owned by the city, two by the university, and four in private hands. Together they provided something in excess of three hundred beds, nearly a ten-fold increase in just eighteen years, whereas population had only doubled.[465]

This rapid expansion and specialization of health care facilities soon provoked talk about Madison becoming a major "hospital center."[466] Then, when the state legislature voted in 1920 to build the first phase of a five-million-dollar medical complex known as the Wisconsin General Hospital (later called University Hospital), newspaper headlines portrayed Madison as a

prospective "*world*" medical center."[467] Though such talk was premature, it reflected the dramatic distance the city had come during the first two decades of the twentieth century when hospitals were thought to be private charities where the poor and unfortunate could go to die.[468]

Summary

During the first two decades of the twentieth century, a succession of crusades for the pure, the clean, and the sanitary caused a phenomenal and unprecedented burst of progress in the quest for the City Healthful. Instead of buying adulterated and sometimes diseased milk from dirty dippers, Madisonians bought pasteurized, bottled milk from licensed dairies and tested herds. Sweeping changes in conditions at hotel and restaurant kitchens, butcher shops, bakeries, and even grocery stores eliminated gross food handling abuses that had been tolerated for years. The development of a comprehensive sewage collection system meant that by 1920 privies had become rare and indoor flush toilets the rule. Universal tax-funded city garbage collection ended a long era of makeshift, unsanitary, and smelly disposal practices. The filling of once extensive city marshes—producers of disease, mosquitoes and nose wrenching smells—ended still another health danger. The plummeting horse population meant the decline of breeding spots for houseflies and the installation of window screens kept the notorious disease carriers away from food. Still other causes of communicable diseases declined as the public began to understand the dangers of unwashed hands, spitting, drinking and eating from common utensils, careless sneezing, and contact with infected persons. And if in spite of all these new and profoundly more hygenic conditions someone did get sick, the contrast between Madison's tiny primitive 1900-vintage nursing homes and the new generation of modern hospitals bristling with laboratories, expensive diagnostic equipment, and surgical suites could hardly have been greater.

There was, however, one notable exception to this impressive display of scientific progress and that was the green, smelly and unhealthy condition of Lake Monona, a victim then and for several decades to come of a debate among experts on the extent to which sewage effluent was the cause of the problem. Today, of course, the dominant role its nutrients played are known and therefore obvious. Yet is is important to remember that we are like the child who just hid the thimble in the game of 'hunt the thimble.' Because we know where we hid it, we cannot understand why the scientific investigators should have been so stupid. To the investigators of that era, however, the solution was anything but obvious.

Credit for these advances in public health must go to various women's organizations, to the new wave of devoted health professionals, and to the University of Wisconsin. The crusade for public health gave American women one of the first opportunities to meaningfully participate in community affairs, an opportunity Madison women used to compile an impressive record. Among their achievements were initiating and sustaining the clean milk crusade, the municipalization of garbage, the "war against the fly," upgrading public school personal hygiene programs, and supporting hospitals. Indeed, according to the Madison health officer "most of the progressive work in preventive medicine on a higher and more scientific level has been done by women."[469] Health professionals including the public health officer, the food and dairy inspector, the school physician, and visiting nurses all played large roles in a difficult, massive, and yet remarkably rapid public education program and in the development of effective enforcement programs. Finally, University of Wisconsin professors made Madison a superb example of the "Wisconsin Idea" by providing technical leadership for the new bacteriological sewage plant, by providing the technical knowledge needed to formulate the tough new clean milk laws, and by researching more hygenic garbage collection practices.

The impressive achievements of the new public health in Madison required a major expansion of local government power and a consequent reduction of individual power. Indeed the case can be made that this substantial shift of the power pendulum from *laissez faire* to government control was inherent in the change from miasma to microbes. The protection and promotion of public health was a long-established function of Madison government and indeed had been set forth in the 1856 charter. And yet from the time of city organization until the early twentieth century, the city did relatively little to safeguard public health except to "sanitize" (almost always after the fact) miasma-producing places. Not until 1883 did the city even appoint its first citywide health officer. And even after he was appointed some physicians refused to report contagious diseases or provide legally required vital statistics.[470] However, after scientists had revealed the wily ways of microbes and specifically the so called "contact points" where communicable diseases were spread via direct contact, indirect contact, air-borne droplets, carriers, and the like, the power and board of health and its principle functionary, the health officer, rose dramatically. Nevertheless the mere knowledge of "contact points" was hardly enough to sustain an aggressive prevention program for such diseases as small pox, diphtheria, typhoid, and scarlet fever, nor for that matter were voluntary citizen cooperation and health official exhortations. Tough citywide standards, procedures, and beefed-up enforcement programs were the only effective and therefore responsible means of sustaining real progress in public health. Consequently Madison health officials backed by influential organizations and individuals got the Common Council to pass dozens of pages of new health-related ordinances. Within those ordinances were authorizations for a new wave of city employees who were empowered to test food and milk, inspect restaurant kitchens, issue orders to shut down privies, correct faulty plumbing, in short, who would march out of city hall each day, regulate citizen lives, and thereby insure their better health.

In Madison and in most cities across the country the new public health movement reached its full stride during the Progressive Era and was both a reflection and reinforcement of this yeasty reform period. Certainly in their emphasis upon government by experts; the eagerness with which they welcomed the expansion of local government to insure better public health through regulation and inspection; in their acceptance of the idea that good health like parks, recreation, and certain other urban goods "can be purchased"[471] with tax dollars; and, finally, in their insistence upon limiting individual freedom and the use of private property to the extent it adversely affected community health, the advocates of the new public health were thoroughly progressive.

The City Democratic: The Quest for Community

In the beginning Madison society was small and simple. Just about everybody in Madison was a direct or indirect refugee from New England and therefore shared many of the same values regarding work, family, religion and leisure. Just about everybody knew everybody else. People worked together, played together, and worshipped together.

However, this blissful picture did not last long. The cumulative affects of immigration and individual differences soon fragmented Madison into dozens of ethnic, economic, religious, and social groups. Madison became pluralistic, impersonal, and complex.

The social consequences of these trends deeply troubled Madison progressives. Two of their most cherished goals were to restore a genuine feeling of community in Madison and to make democracy more than a name. The former was an attempt to eliminate class prejudices and to abolish the mosaic of cliques that prevented the people from "pulling together." The latter was an attempt to substitute the will of the people for government by special interests.

Progressives recognized the intrinsic difficulty of these goals but were confident that with the proper kind of "understanding" among groups they could overcome the effects of fragmentation, stratification and segregation. To achieve the proper kind of understanding required a totally new kind of organization: an utterly inclusive "municipal club" open to rich and poor, black and white, protestant, Catholic, and Jew. Backers believed that to be effective the municipal club must have a clubhouse with a well-furnished reading room, a meeting room, a gymnasium and a swimming pool and a social room for serving refreshments. By working, playing, and socializing together in the municipal club, Progressives thought that the masses could learn something about the classes, the classes about the masses, and that the superficial economic, ethnic, religious, and social differences would melt away leaving only the more important common goals.

In spite of considerable talk about such an organization around 1907, no one came forward to lead it nor did any benefactor appear to provide the "club."[472]

Although the municipal club concept died, the purposes behind it did not. Progressives soon hit upon a new version of the idea known as the "civic center." The civic center movement was led by Edward J. Ward who moved to Madison in about 1910 to direct the civic center movement throughout the state. In 1907 Ward had started the civic center movement in Rochester, New York.[473] His presence in Madison and his organization of the First *National* Conference on Social and Civic Centers in Madison in October 1911 greatly stimulated local interest.

Ward's idea was to turn the public schools into civic centers. After all they were accessible, often had gymnasiums, were seldom used in the evening, and were presumably run by and for the people. Ward suggested that school rooms could be used for debating societies, literary clubs, social organizations, and art clubs and that the school gymnasium could be used for athletic purposes. (Playing together was one of the great levellers, Ward noted.) Although the Madison School Board was not at first in favor of opening up the schools for such purposes, they eventually relented. By 1915 ward schools were being used by a long list of organizations including the Boy Scouts, girls clubs, parent-teacher associations, mothers' clubs, adult musical groups, and several special educational programs for non-English speaking persons.[474] The civic center movement was also the catalyst for the formation of the first neighborhood associations. Beginning in 1910 with the Tenth Ward Association the idea spread quickly. By the end of 1911 all ten city wards had a neighborhood association and so did Fair Oaks and South Madison.[475]

To the great disappointment of its backers, the civic center movement did not last long. Teachers were not eager to have their classrooms used for other purposes and several organizations such as the Boy Scouts moved their charters to neighborhood churches where in many cases they could

have their own rooms. By the end of World War I the civic center idea was little more than a good sounding concept looking for a future.

Interestingly, however, there was one enduring but special form of the civic center idea which not only started during the Progressive era in Madison but which has endured to the present. It was Neighborhood House founded in 1916. Neighborhood House was conceived as a settlement house in the Jane Addams Chicago tradition. Its primary clients were recently arrived Italians who in the judgment of their Yankee-University benefactors needed "Americanizing." This term covered a broad spectrum of humanitarian and patriotic goals. For example, the Attic Angels Visiting Nurse taught American child care and sanitation practices, the Associated Charities Visiting Housekeeper taught American cooking, sewing, housecleaning and shopping and University students and professors taught English, American history and civics.[476]

The search for the City Democratic enjoyed rather limited success in Madison but it did establish goals and ideals that still search for expression.

Madison and Progressivism: A Look at the Record

To those Madisonians who were critically inclined—and it seemed that many were much of the time—turn of the century Madison offered a sweeping panorama of targets. A group of aldermen known as "The Bunch" ran the Common Council and hence the city with a live-and-let-live attitude toward law enforcement. "The Bunch" routinely dispensed dozens of liquor licenses to saloons even though they provided slot machines, served minors, and stayed open on Sunday—all in violation of local law. The Bunch allowed brothels to operate with only periodic interference from police. The Bunch voted themselves city contracts and kept themselves in power by driving "loyal" Democratic voters to the polls in carriages and then rewarding this loyalty with

free beer, cigars, and city street jobs. A huge New York syndicate bought the gas company and then began charging residents dearly for their lighting gas. Madison had just one public park, no playgrounds, and no public lake access in the city except at street ends. In the absence of zoning, factories could be erected in residential sections and four small single-family homes were sometimes jammed onto one city lot. In spite of the rapidly growing use of electricity and indoor plumbing, consumers were protected by the most rudimentary health and safety codes. Milkmen dispensed diseased milk from dippers to housewives, and many restaurants, groceries, and butcher shops were unspeakably filthy. In the summertime Lake Monona turned green with algae and reeked from millions of gallons of partially treated sewage. Garbage was thrown almost anywhere and the only "hospitals" in the city were small primitive cottage-type facilities.

These turn of the century conditions were particularly reprehensible to Madison's Yankee-university elite, a group of middle- to upper-income persons concentrated in neighborhoods such as Mansion Hill, Fourth Lake Ridge, University Heights, and Wingra Park. Although this old line protestant and predominantly Republican Yankee stock had always dominated the cultural and economic life of the community, their political power had been diluted beginning in the 1850s by waves of immigrants, many of whom were Catholic and German, and to a lessor degree, by their own attitude that local politics were "dirty."

Although the Yankee-university elite had lost political power, they had *not* lost their clear, chastened vision of Madison. If anything their concept of the ideal community had matured and brightened during the late nineteenth century when changing demographics forced them to the political sidelines with only periodic appearances in the game.[477]

According to Madison progressives, the ideal city had five characteristics:

(1) *It must be based upon the reign of morality.* According to U. W. Professor Richard T.

Ely, religion must take in municipal reform because every political question was a social question and every social question was a religious question.[478] By this he meant that morality lay at the center of all enduring reform efforts and particularly municipal reform. Vice, corruption, and human degradation cannot, he argued, be driven from the city without the imposition of the highest moral standards. It was in this context that churches were urged to inaugurate the reign of morality by foresaking their then heavy emphasis upon individual salvation and substituting the salvation of society.

(2) *Local governments must recognize that they have a moral responsibility to improve the city.* As noted in the introductory section to the "Progressive Attack on City Problems," Reform Darwinism, the concept that environment shapes people, was almost uncritically accepted by early twentieth century reformers. The application of this concept to cities was both natural and rapid: *cities shaped people.* The stark implication of this doctrine was that poverty and crime were products of urban environment rather than a genetic defect or a product of "social Darwinism." Conversely, a cleaner, healthier, safer, more wholesome, more beautiful city with ample recreational opportunities could produce better people.

(3) *Stronger, more effective, and accountable local government was necessary to meet the growing needs of the city.* Madison progressives were appalled by the waste and inefficiency they saw embodied in the weak mayor-strong council form of government. Government by painters, horseshoers, and bond salesmen, once thought to be the embodiment of democracy, was now seen as woefully inadequate to govern complex cities. Even the once lionized 'Businessman' with his vaunted "business methods" had been overtaken by the city's growing complexity. One prominent Madison progressive writing in 1902 insisted that effective city government required "the sociologist, the economist, the bacteriologist, the chemist, the engineer, the physician, the educator . . ." and above all else, "the administrator trained in municipal management."[479]

(4) *More informed active citizens with greater access to local government.* For too long the Yankee-university elite had contributed to its own political disenfranchisement by their refusal to participate in local government. Finally, around the turn of the century, they realized that reform could only be effected if they adopted a much more aggressive concept of citizenship, one that required diligence, staying informed, and jumping into the political arena to crusade for the good and the true. But even diligence and intervention were not enough; new forms of access were also necessary to counter the tremendous power of the local Democratic caucus, The Bunch and other persons and organizations who controlled the reins of power.

(5) *An intense concern for the public interest.* During the early twentieth century Madison progressives rejected the concept that cities were products of dollar-decision making and individual self-interest; instead they sought a city governed by public policy, social consciousness, and community standards. The city, they were saying in effect, was not just a place to make money, but also a place to live, to play, to be inspired, and much more.

Beginning in the late 1890s and continuing through the first twenty years of the present century Madison's Yankee elite attempted to restore their power and this vision of what the city could become. This attempt is properly called the progressive era in Madison. To be sure it did not arrive in the form of sixteen demands nailed to the city hall door one morning, but rather gradually and with increasing momentum until about 1916, and then in a more attenuated crusading form during and shortly after World War I.

The results of this progressive era in Madison were truly impressive. From the era of crusading journalism led by the *Journal's* August Roden (1906 to 1911), Richard Lloyd Jones (1911–1919), and *Times'* William T. Evjue (1917–1970), three of the strongest progressive voices in the state, came a strong tradition of investigative journalism.

From the City Efficient came a long list of reforms including the two-year mayoral term and salary, the prohibition of various corrupt electoral practices such as giving blandishments to voters, the elimination of partisan politics from local elections, the expansion of the civil service concept, the inauguration of the primary system, the initiative, the binding referendum, and the imposition of a sophisticated budgeting system. Together these reforms, many borrowed directly from the state, made Madison government much more accessible, accountable, democratic, and more issue oriented.

From various efforts to achieve the City Virtuous, progressives created coalitions to conduct a relatively short but successful war on prostitution and gambling and a much longer but ultimately successful war on the saloon.

From the City Beautiful came an intense concern for city aesthetics, a rich tradition of civic beneficence, a magnificent array of public parks purchased for the masses by a few rich men and the acceptance of parks and recreation as a legitimate and important city responsibility.

From the City Well Planned came the first tantalizing glimpse of Madison's extraordinary potential as a model city and, at the same time, the reluctant recognition that *laissez faire* government could not make Madison a beautiful, humane, convenient, and efficient city.

Efforts to achieve the City Well Housed forced progressives to realize that many Madisonians lived in slummy homes and that governmental intervention in the form of building codes and several full-time building inspectors were necessary to insure safer more sanitary conditions.

During the progressive era Madison women achieved major victories in their attempt to escape culturally imposed subordinate roles. Although they were assisted by national events, Madison women were much more than mere beneficiaries of these events. During this period Madison women demonstrated their interest and ability in civic affairs, their ability to hold difficult jobs, to indulge in vigorous exercise without losing their femininity, and to conduct shrewd political campaigns. In Madison the product of the City Liberated was "the New Woman."

Although advances achieved in public health are not often considered a part of the progressive movement, there are compelling reasons in Madison's case, and doubtless in other cities, to view the City Healthful as one of the major achievements of the progressive era. The basis for this contention is straightforward and compelling. As public officials came to understand the way pathological organisms spread from person to person, they recognized that disease prevention and containment strategies required stronger public policies. Therefore the power of public health officials and thus local government rose while certain forms of individual disease spreading behavior were necessarily curtailed. From this interpretation Madison city officials accepted several additional responsibilities including the operation of a general hospital, the deployment of health inspectors, the collection of garbage, the education of public school students, and the promulgation of a rigorous new public health ethic.

From the City Democratic came neighborhood associations, a policy to open up the schools for citizen use and Madison's first settlement house.

In addition to the many changes in each of the specific categories just enumerated, the progressive era in Madison produced three important *general* legacies. The first was big government. From the time Madison incorporated in 1856 until the turn of the century the structure of Madison government remained remarkably constant although the number of employees in the various divisions increased slightly. However, during the first two decades of the twentieth century, in response to demands for more services and higher standards, especially in the areas of education, health, housing, safety, recreation, and consumer protection, city government structure

became more complex and its size increased rapidly. Whole new departments were formed for garbage collection, building inspection, park development and maintenance, auditing, and health. Long lists of new jobs including life guards, garbage teamsters, zookeepers, Yahara lock tenders, reference librarians, park custodians, laboratory technicians, and police matrons and a whole platoon of health, food, dairy, electrical, plumbing, building, and meter inspectors appeared on city payrolls. To support these new employees and functions dozens of stenographers, pages, clerical assistants, typists, and assistants had to be hired. The statistical results of Madison's great growth were particularly dramatic. Between 1900 and 1920 when city population only doubled, the annual City of Madison budget increased seventeen times, the number of city hall employees increased about fifteen times, and the mill rate increased from eleven to twenty.[480] Fortunately for the progressives, their demands came at a time when the city could afford this new liberalism. To pay for this rapid increase in costs, the city shifted from a fractional to a full market valuation system for all real property, received rebates from the new state income tax system, and of course increased property values each year.

A second general result of the progressive era in Madison was the greatly expanded use of experts. During the late nineteenth and early twentieth centuries several of Madison's problems became sufficiently technical and complex to baffle part time city officials and their full time staff. As noted in chapter 5 the first major use of consultants was in the 1880s and early 1890s to help resolve highly technical sewage problems. By the mid-1890s, however, the relatively rapid growth of the University of Wisconsin put that institution in a position where, if called upon to do so, it could have provided considerable technical expertise on the sewage question. Unfortunately a long-standing, deep-seated cultural chasm separated the "practical" alderman from the "theoretical" professors and made the aldermen loathe to ask professors to help them. When the aldermen refused to ask the professors, the professors

asked the aldermen for a chance to present their views. The aldermen gave the professors a chance but ultimately rejected their views in favor of a much riskier system profferred by a high-powered Scottish salesman named MacDougall. This rebuff may well have been a beginning of the "Wisconsin Idea" because in 1900 after the MacDougall sewage treatment system had failed, the University of Wisconsin College of Engineering Dean, J. B. Johnson, urged the council to appoint Dr. F. E. Turneaure, Professor of Sanitary Engineering to the position of city engineer. Johnson was eager to demonstrate the value of the university's tremendous technical resources and promised that if the city appointed Turneaure he would see that the city got not only Turneaure but all other faculty members who had expertise to contribute as well. The city accepted and in the bargain got Turneaure, Harry L. Russell, Professor of Chemistry and Bacteriology, Charles R. Van Hise, Professor of Geology, and several others. This U. W. team designed and supervised the installation of a new bacterial sewage system treatment plant, one of the most sophisticated in the U.S. at the time. The plant opened in July 1901.

While this university team was building the new sewage treatment plant, Dr. Samuel E. Sparling, a U. W. lecturer in municipal government, conducted a survey of garbage collection practices in the U.S. and recommended that the private system of collection be abandoned and that the city assume this responsibility. The city implemented this recommendation in the spring of 1901.

Interestingly these two successful applications of university expertise occurred two years before Van Hise was appointed university president and before LaFollette set up his famous Saturday Lunch Club, often viewed as the first brain trust and a major component of the Wisconsin Idea. Surely to Van Hise these two Madison experiences demonstrated beyond a doubt the value of applying university knowledge to complex urban problems.[481]

A final general legacy of the progressive era in Madison was a heightened sense of *community*. So intense was this new concern that Madison progressives seemed to smother their writings with references to civic virtue, civic welfare, civic patriotism, civic intelligence, civic ideals, civic loyalty, civic responsibility, and civic spirit. Such expressions reflected the belief of Madison progressives that "community" was a transcendent good, a prerequisite of a whole new phase of urban development that could only be achieved by abandoning the heretofore dominant emphasis upon *laissez faire* and individualism. Although the frenzy of the progressive era has long since passed, the ideal of community lives on and is reflected by such phrases as "the *public* interest" and a concern for "*public* policy."

Up to this point we have concentrated upon the "positive" legacies of the progressive era in Madison. However, no survey of this era would be complete without a summary of its blind spots and failures—for it had those too. The relatively well-educated and affluent persons who supported progressive causes in Madison could hardly have been more confident of their abilities to effect reform. In the words of one prominent local attorney, ". . . all things are possible to Progressives."[482] Such statements, though valuable for cheerleading and confidence generating, simply were not true. Madison progressives failed again and again to realize their goals in many areas where they made concerted efforts. Among other things they failed to persuade their fellow Madisonians to adopt the commission form of government, to municipalize Madison Gas and Electric and the streetcar companies, to adopt a city plan, to implement zoning, to alleviate housing problems, to give women the franchise, and to use university experts much after about 1903.

It is tempting for some to shake an accusing finger at these "shortcomings." And yet who can examine the progressive ledger of achievements and failures and not conclude that these failures pale beside their achievements? Surely the far more important and valid conclusion is that a relatively small number of caring, highly motivated

persons were able to form coalitions on a broad array of issues, and that at considerable sacrifice and in spite of sometimes massive opposition and apathy they were able to persevere and prevail so much of the time.

The Great War and Beyond

On Monday evening, June 9, 1913, one hundred members of the Madison Literary Club met in the elegant home of Mrs. Lucius Fairchild to hear a paper by U.W. professor of philosophy E. B. McGilvary. The professor argued that the spread of scientific investigation and national self-interest not only made peace inevitable but made a great war in Europe an impossibility.[1]

In spite of the professor's warm and comforting words, the flames of war spread quickly in Europe. At first the assassination on June 28, 1914 of Archduke Francis Ferdinand, heir to the Austrian throne, provoked only war between Serbia and Austria, but a tangled skein of alliances and events soon engulfed twelve more nations in the conflagration. By the fall of 1914 the belligerent nations of Europe had more than five million men under arms, more than had ever been involved in a war in recorded history.

Although the battles were being fought half a continent and vast ocean away, Madisonians did not stay uninvolved for long. Indeed on August 5, 1914, just one day after Germany invaded Belgium, fifty Madison residents who were still citizens of Germany received notice from the German consul in Chicago to return to Germany at once to bear arms for the Kaiser. Another 450 young German residents who had not yet taken out U.S. citizenship papers waited anxiously for a similar letter.[2] In October, 1914, Madison's two large machine tool manufacturers, the Gisholt Machine Company and Steinle Turret Lathe Company, received large orders from "belligerent countries"—which ones were never revealed—for machines that would make shrapnel and big bore cannons.[3] A little later the French

Battery and Carbon Company received a contract from an undisclosed European nation for six million field telephone batteries.[4] In November 1914, in response to appeals from the Red Cross, Madison residents sent several thousand pounds of cotton to Austria where it was desperately needed for wounded troops.[5]

With some of its residents fighting for Germany and several of its factories making war material, Madisonians had to decide whether to support the Allies (France, England, Belgium, Russia, Italy, Greece, and several Eastern European nations) or the Central Powers (Germany, Austria-Hungary, Turkey, and Bulgaria). Unfortunately the question was easier to pose than resolve. In fact the war was a terribly complex event that the American people had difficulty understanding. The problem was compounded by concerted efforts on both sides to manipulate world opinion with propaganda. To members of Madison's relatively large German-speaking community, some of whom had blood relatives fighting for the Kaiser, the answer seemed obvious enough.

On the other hand, Germany's invasion of Belgium in August 1914 and bloody slaughter of its citizens even after that country had declared its neutrality was a less than inspiring example of German civilization. So, too, was the sinking by a German submarine in May 1915 of the British liner *Lusitania* with one hundred Americans on board. To Americans the incident was a violation of the international rules of war, but to Germany it was one of several efforts to stop the flow of munitions to the Allies. (The German Embassy had duly warned Americans not to travel on the ship because it contained munitions.) Meanwhile the U.S. began supplying increasing amounts of food and machinery to European belligerents, a fact that caused freedom of the seas to be the central ingredient of American policy. Partly in response to President Wilson's demands, Germany stopped submarine warfare in early 1916, a move that improved hopes for "peace and honor."

Throughout these developments almost all Madisonians observed a scrupulous neutrality. Indeed in September 1915, four months *after* the sinking of the *Lusitania,* Madisonians flocked to see gruesome films showing the war from the German perspective, not once clapping when Allied bullets slammed through German skulls.[6] Even in late 1916 the spirit of tolerance and neutrality was evident in news stories reporting that Madison citizens had given generously to the war relief fund of their choice, one for the Allies and one for the German-Austrian troops.[7]

At the same time Madisonians were straining to understand the ominous events in Europe, a revolution in Mexico seemed to pose a much more immediate threat to American sovereignty. There Pancho Villa, a revolutionary leader who controlled northern Mexico, found himself edged out in a power struggle and so he decided to foment war with the U.S., believing that in the resulting turmoil he might regain power. Villa therefore killed seventeen American mining engineers aboard a Mexican train and attacked a small town in New Mexico where he killed sixteen more Americans. In response to these provocations, President Wilson called out the National Guard to patrol the border. One unit called out in this mobilization was Madison's Company "G", whose send-off produced a great patriotic display. On the evening before their departure an estimated twenty thousand persons held a spirited rally on the capitol lawn complete with University of Wisconsin cheerleaders, "On Wisconsin," the "Star Spangled Banner," and a parade of speakers. Not long after the Madison company reached the border, the Mexican incident was peaceably resolved. The men of Company "G" returned to Madison in early January 1917 where fifteen thousand persons were on hand to greet them. Such a welcome was hardly merited by their military contribution but it did reflect a powerful patriotic tide swelling throughout the land.[8]

The return of Company "G" from Mexico allowed Madisonians to concentrate their full attention on deteriorating events in Europe and the North Atlantic. In January 1917 Germany announced its intent to resume submarine warfare; in February an intercepted telegram showed that Germany had worked out an understanding with Mexico whereby Mexico would reclaim its former territories in southwestern U.S. if Germany declared war on the U.S. No longer was the war "over there." In March German "U" boats sank three American ships. Throughout all this the Allies, ill-prepared for a three-year-long war, were rapidly approaching exhaustion. Only American intervention could apparently save Europe from German military power, and American involvement in the world war, a prospect that once seemed impossible, now seemed imminent. Thus when Madisonians picked up their newspapers on April 6, 1917, and saw the words "WAR IS DECLARED," few were surprised.

Just five months earlier Madison voters had elected Wilson to a second term by a sixty-seven percent plurality, the largest ever extended any presidential candidate up to that time, in part because he had kept the U.S. out of war and would hopefully continue to do so. But to Wilson and his advisors, neutrality was no longer a viable option. Prussian legions were threatening to subvert the most precious principles of Western Civilization. This was why Wilson in his declaration of war said that the U.S. must join with the Allies in a great war "to make the world safe for democracy." Greatly moved by this appeal, Madisonians rushed to support their country and their president.[9]

Suddenly everyone in Madison fell into two categories: those who donned a uniform to fight "over there" and those who stayed home to support the boys. Barely one month after war was declared the first one hundred fifty Madison boys marched off to war to the accompaniment of brass bands and huge cheering crowds. Those who stayed home expressed their support for the war by flocking to join the Red Cross and by buying more than one and one half million dollars in Liberty Loan bonds—almost fifty percent *over* Madison's quota.[10]

These actions, however, were nothing more than a modest beginning of what would come. In July 1917 came the first draft call and in October a second Liberty Loan—this one two- and one-half times greater than the first. In April 1918 came the second draft call, in May the third, and then monthly thereafter. The third Liberty Loan was launched in April 1918 and the fourth in September. Counting enlistees and draftees nearly three thousand Madison boys marched off to war and several million Madison dollars flowed into the government war chest through the Liberty Loans.[11]

The need to supply prodigious quantities of war material to the Allies and at the same time field a large army in Europe placed a tremendous strain on the productive capacity of the U.S. economy. This need in turn required Madisonians to cooperate with federal authorities in conserving food and fuel. In order to send more beef, pork, and wheat to the war zone, Madisonians stopped eating beef on Tuesdays, wheat on Wednesdays, and pork on Saturdays. Instead housewives substituted corn, beans, chicken, even frog legs from Madison marshes and carp from Madison lakes. Newspapers cooperated by publishing wheatless, meatless recipes, and city garbage men reported households that threw out hard bread which could be steamed, softened, and eaten. Every home in the city was expected to display a card pledging that household's commitment to participate in the war against food waste. Those who failed to display the sign received a knock on the door from a squadron of women who patrolled the city in forty cars. In addition just about every household planted a "Victory Garden" and canned vegetables. Those whose yards were too small for gardens were given vacant lots by city realtors.[12]

To insure enough coal for priority uses, federal fuel officials had to issue Draconian orders to cut back on coal consumption for domestic heating. In mid-January 1918 all Madison factories were required to close for five days, idling five thousand workers. Then for the next ten consecutive Mondays all factories plus all stores, shops, and theaters were required to close

FIGURE 6.86. OFF FOR FRANCE. This group of draftees was photographed at the Northwestern Depot on May 25, 1918, on their way to basic training and France. (SHSW WHi(X3)36578)

prompting the famous "payless, heatless Mondays." So serious was Madison's coal shortage that the governor had to use his power to send a twenty-car coal train racing for Madison. During this period city residents were forced to substitute the much sootier and smokier soft coal so that the Navy could use the hard smokeless variety. The exchange made ships much more difficult to spot at sea but made Madison a much dirtier city.[13]

To these food and fuel conservation measures the federal government added many others. For example, to insure the availability of building supplies for war-related construction, Madison contractors had to secure a permit directly from Washington to build just about anything. Since these permits were nearly impossible to get, both public and private sector construction in Madison ground to a halt for the duration of the war.[14]

Madison's contributions to the war were hardly limited to resource conservation. Local industries and research facilities made important contributions too. Eleven private corporations received government contracts for the production of machine tools, electrical signalling equipment, batteries, gas masks, and leather goods.[15] The presence in Madison of certain types of machine tool manufacturing expertise was responsible for the construction of two government ordinance plants. The first, the Northwest Ordinance Company, erected a large plant on East Washington Avenue next to the Gisholt Machine Company factory and made 4.7 inch field guns and other armaments.[16] (This plant was recently purchased by the city and remodelled into a bus storage facility.) The other, the Four Lakes Ordinance Company, was incorporated by George A. Steinle, principal of the Steinle Turret Lathe Company, and produced navy guns.[17] After the war this plant fronting on Atwood Avenue was acquired by the Madison Kipp Corporation. In the war research area the Forest Products Laboratory found a way to dramatically reduce drying time for gun stock and airplane woods[18] from three years to fifteen days; Burgess Laboratories did work on gas warfare chemicals;[19] and U.W. faculty members did government research on mineral supplies, submarine detection, chemical warfare, and even helped prepare propaganda.[20]

The departure of nearly three thousand young Madison men and the imperative to produce more put a tremendous strain on local manpower. Part of this manpower problem was solved by a long list of organizations whose volunteer members performed a remarkable array of services. Boy Scouts guarded Victory Gardens, canvassed the city during liberty loan and Red Cross drives, and distributed patriotic literature.[21] Women's organizations started farmers' curbside markets, sold wheat substitutes, and insured compliance with food conservation measures. Board of Commerce members gave patriotic speeches before every movie, organized send offs of the boys, and worked with local businesses to meet production quotas.[22] Even Madison public school children played

FIGURE 6.87. SELLING CORN TO PATRIOTS. Getting Madisonians to substitute corn for wheat sometimes required patriotic merchandising. The woman selling bags of dried corn during the summer of 1918 at the City Market was a Dane County Council of Defense volunteer. (SHSW WHi(X3)32884)

a role. For example, eight- to twelve-year-old boys learned to knit and made afghans for soldiers, high school shop classes made checkerboards and crutches, and still others addressed tons of mail for the government.[23] The other part of the manpower problem was solved by women who streamed into the workforce at an unprecedented rate and scale. Women became streetcar conductors, factory workers, and meter readers. For the first time women were allowed to usher in church and join the Board of Commerce.[24]

The speed with which the U.S. was able to gear up for the war was a truly remarkable feat when one takes into account the lack of preparedness at the time war was declared. Credit for this achievement must go to Americans' perception of the war. In contrast to all earlier wars, this was the "war to end war," a war that would cause democracy to be recognized as the highest form and best form of government. It was a holy war bulging with righteousness and truth.

There were, however, consequences of this interpretation. The same righteousness that inbued Americans with a great commitment to the war also made almost any form of dissent or disagreement a despicable even treasonable act. As if the normal surge of national loyalty following a declaration of war was not enough to insure American support, President Wilson formed the Committee on Public Information to induce almost frenzied loyalty to the war effort.

In Madison loyalty took on a particularly virulent form. Madison was the hometown of U.S. Senator Robert Marion LaFollette, one of six senators who had voted against the declaration of war. From that moment on, the senior Wisconsin Senator was a veritable pariah. Madison was also the home of the liberal "Germanized"—and therefore suspect—University of Wisconsin. Finally, Madison had a large German population. To prove to the state and nation that Madison was impeccably loyal *in spite of these facts,* a crusade began.

A great flood of patriotism inundated the city, making almost anything that appeared to be antiwar or pro-German a target for the local loyalty leagues. Among the first to be attacked for his "disloyalty" was "Fighting" Bob LaFollette who was burned in effigy on the U.W. campus, expelled from the Madison Club, repudiated by the Wisconsin legislature and censured by nearly all U.W. faculty members in a round-robin petition.[25]

Because of its alleged connections to Lafollette and "German money" the *Capital Times,* which first appeared in December 1917, was burned in effigy on the campus, denied membership in the Board of Commerce, and its newsboys were chased away from plant gates where they tried to sell papers.[26]

Another example of the growing hysteria was an incident on March 29, 1918, when about three hundred U.W. students packed Turner Hall, 21 South Butler Street, to throttle a scheduled talk in support of Victor Berger, a Milwaukee Socialist then running for a recently vacated U.S. Senate seat. Speaking on behalf of Berger was Adolph Germer, the national secretary of the Socialist party, who like Berger had expressed his opposition to the war on many occasions. Knowing this the students armed themselves with overripe fruit, a pot of tar, and a sack of feathers and sat down to watch Germer wiggle out of this one. Seeing the hostile audience, Germer decided that the better part of valor was to forsake Berger and the war and give a platitudinous talk on socialism instead. The students allowed the Socialist to give his one-hour exposition, but immediately after he walked off the stage, they took over the meeting. One group of students shoved Germer back on to the stage and ordered him to swear his allegiance to the U.S. Germer knew full well what awaited him if he refused and so he said "Yes, yes, yes!"[27]

FIGURE 6.88. 1918 MEMORIAL DAY PARADE.   During World War I, the square was the principal arena for the largest displays of patriotism, especially parades. The occasion for this parade was Memorial Day, 1918. To get this shot the photographer stood on the balcony of the old Park Hotel. The just completed highrise building in the background is the M&I Bank of Madison. All the buildings in the foreground have been razed. (University of Wisconsin Archives)

FIGURE 6.89. THE BEAST OF BERLIN. One of the lessons taught by World War I was the effectiveness of the moving picture as a means of arousing hatred of the enemy. This film, "The Kaiser, the Beast of Berlin," had Madison movie patrons screaming for blood just like the ad promised.

A New Name for The German-American Bank

Dear Editor:

Within the shadow of our state capitol there is a sign whose bronze face reveals that its company still holds German ahead of American. A bank under the protection of our government operating by the good will of our citizens and thriving under the name of the German-American bank. Apparently its company still holds true to the golden rule of the Kaiser's gospel, Deutschland Deutschland uberalles. . . . Deutschland uberalles—HELL say I hold it there until it is done brown.

Our love for America should not tolerate anything which is German being ahead of anything which is American and we will not tolerate it. The German-American bank should be forced to discontinue business until its company chooses a name which is thoroughly American, purely Democratic and purely PATRIOTIC.

What do you say?
Wisconsin State Journal
January 12, 1918

Just a short time later the bank changed its name to The American Exchange Bank.

Fifteen hundred persons signed a petition demanding the resignation of German-born school board member George Kroncke. The sixteen-year school board member had been angered by a high school assembly at which the principal asked all students to express their loyalty to Wilson and the war by standing and reciting the pledge of allegiance to the flag. The following day Kroncke stormed into the office of the principal and told him to never repeat this action because there were many loyal students who did not agree with Wilson's policies. Although the council refused to respond to this furor, Kroncke was defeated when he stood for his first popular election in April

1919. Even then, six months after the armistice, the *Journal* gloated that "no member of the new school board will be found going about on the highways and public places conversing in the language of the enemy. . . ."[28]

The public distaste for disloyalty was hardly limited to the prominent. Louis B. Nagler, a capitol employee, was sentenced to thirty months at the federal penitentiary at Fort Leavenworth for telling a Red Cross and YMCA fund solicitor "I won't give a cent. The YMCA and the Red Cross (are) a bunch of grafters. Not over ten to fifteen percent of the money collected goes to the soldiers or is used for the purposes for which it is collected." Nagler also allegedly said, "Who is the government? Who is making this war? A bunch of capitalists composed of the steel men and the ammunition makers." Nagler was convicted under the Draconian 1917 Espionage Act.[29]

Another target for loyalty groups was the instruction of German in both Madison public schools and the University of Wisconsin. According to critics, instruction in the "foe tongue" only stimulated a love of German and hatred of all things American. On this premise German was eliminated at the elementary level and reduced from fifteen to two classes at the high school. Leading the attack on German instruction at the university was *Journal* editor Richard Lloyd Jones.[30] Jones insisted that the U.W. was the most *"GERMANIZED UNIVERSITY IN THE WEST"* and was therefore in dire need of *"AMERICANIZING."* Jones based his accusations on the fact that the U.W. with its twenty-seven person faculty probably had the largest German department in the country. Indeed, measured in faculty size it had more instructors than the department of history, the department of philosophy and psychology, and even some of the basic sciences. Although university administration took no action to respond to such charges, students acting under the influence of peer pressure and patriotism dropped German in favor of French. German enrollments plummetted from 1400 in 1917 to 265 in 1918. This reduction in turn reduced faculty size from twenty-seven to

eight and gave the department much smaller influence in overall university curriculum.[31]

A final expression of war-inspired hysteria were two steps taken to prevent local sabotage. Twenty-four-hour guards were placed on all public buildings and most factories. As a second precaution all Madison residents fourteen years of age and who had been born in Germany and who had not yet taken out American citizenship papers were required to register as enemy aliens and to turn over all guns to authorities. All enemy aliens over eighteen were required to carry I.D. cards that prohibited them from going within one-half-mile of the Forest Products Laboratory and the two ordinance plants.[32]

Meanwhile in Europe the massive and relatively sudden arrival of U.S. doughboys in the summer of 1918 allowed the Allies to launch major offenses, which produced the first breakthroughs of the vaunted Hindenburg Line.

Just as the tide of battle began to swing in favor of the Allies, the United States was hit by Spanish influenza, one of the worst epidemics in its history. At first it seemed like any other flu in that its victims experienced dizziness, fever, chills, vomiting, pains, and drowsiness. But there was one very important difference. What seemed like a benign malady sometimes induced pneumonia and death. When the first flu cases appeared in Madison in early October 1918, health authorities denied that they were the dreaded Spanish strain whose death toll elsewhere around the country was rapidly mounting. But then came the first Madison deaths and daily newspaper list of its latest victims, sometimes numbering ten a day. One doctor estimated that one person in ten in Madison had the flu. To reduce its ravages health authorities closed schools and banned nearly all public assemblages including churches, theaters, movies, and even funerals. Not until one month later on Thursday, November 7, 1918, did health authorities feel justified in lifting the ban. When its carnage was totalled, 268 Madisonians died.[33]

Finally on Thursday noon, November 7—the very day the flu ban was lifted—the United Press

International ticker in the newsroom of the *Wisconsin State Journal* announced that the peace had been signed. *Journal* employees immediately called factory officials who in turn ordered their steam whistles opened wide and their employees dismissed. Moments after the factory whistles began, locomotive whistles joined in and then as fast as they could get men to the ropes, church bells added to the festive cacophony whose meaning everyone knew. Stores dismissed their employees and the university dismissed its students. Six hundred university women students marched four abreast up State Street singing victory songs and waving flags and banners. Honking, flag-bedecked cars raced through the streets, their occupants shouting "PEACE" to all within earshot. By prearranged plan everyone headed toward the Square bearing flags and banners. When they arrived, the swelling crowds indulged in an unrestrained release of joy.

But then in the middle of this riotous rejoicing came word that the UPI release was premature and that peace negotiators at Versailles had not yet signed the armistice. The news came as a shock but the crowd took it cheerfully because they knew it was just a matter of time.[34]

At 1:30 A.M. on Monday, November 11, the telegraph chattered the good news to a blurry-eyed group of persons who had maintained a vigil awaiting the announcement. Moments later factory whistles blew, church bells clanged, and honking autos created a jubilant din. This was it: after twenty months of war, this was The Peace and Madisonians knew it. They dressed quickly and walked or drove to the Square where a great mass of humanity assembled in barely thirty minutes. The growing crowd sang "On Wisconsin" and gave spirited responses to university victory cheers. Then, led by U.W. torch carrying coeds dressed in Miss Liberty Bell costumes, almost everyone formed a great victory parade. For three hours the celebrants marched, ran, drove, sang, shouted, hugged each other, cried and cheered. Not until 5:00 A.M. did the crowd begin to disperse for a few hours of sleep before the scheduled celebrations during the great holiday which lay before them. The largest formal celebration began at sunset when about twelve thousand persons gathered at the Square for a march to Camp Randall. Beginning with the roar of cannons celebrants heard a small group of speakers give generous and profoundly hopeful interpretations of The Great War. One speaker said the United States would "reconstruct Germany" in the American image and make it "a land of the people." Another said the war marked the "end of the tyrant and the autocrat." Still another extolled the ninety Madison boys who had given their lives for freedom.[35]

As happy as everyone was to hear that the war had ended, nothing could top the actual return of the brave Madison boys whose exploits in France had been so widely followed through letters and the press. But the return of the boys took time since there were a limited number of ships and over two million men to transport. Not until May 1919, six months after the armistice, did most of the Madison boys return aboard a special troop train. For this event an estimated twenty thousand Madisonians crowded around the Milwaukee Railroad depot to greet these heroes and honor them with a triumphal procession up the Avenue and a capitol ceremony. When the train rolled to a stop and loved ones caught sight of their soldiers, joy knew no bounds. No exuberant abstractions like victory or peace to celebrate here, but rather husbands, sons, fathers, fiances, boyfriends and brothers to kiss and squeeze. The war to end war was truly over. The soldiers were home.

Much as everyone was eager to get back to normal, the war had changed so many things that normal had a whole new meaning. In the first place, the transition from war to peace severely buffeted the economy. The cessation of hostilities caused Washington officials to cut back and even cancel war contracts. Suddenly factories whose productive capacity had been expanded and then

stretched to the limit were idled by the termination of war contracts. This problem was compounded by the decline of non-war related factory orders and led to the dismissal of many additional workers. Within three months of the Armistice hundreds of Madison workers were laid off. What would happen when Madison's soldiers returned was anything but clear. Although local business leaders acknowledged the magnitude of the problem, they were convinced that these events were but momentary aberrations in a readjustment process. Pent up demand for new homes, returning confidence produced by the victory in Europe and the return of lower interest rates would combine to cause "unprecedented building activity" in the spring of 1919 they said. But spring came and so did summer *without* the predicted upturn. Builders refused to build at war-inflated construction costs and then take the risk of having to sell their product at deflated post war prices. Consequently an estimated backlog of 500 homes never got built, rents began to soar and vacancy rates hit new lows. Blue ribbon study committees failed to find solutions and exhortations to build now as a "civic duty" fell on deaf ears. The economy simply did not respond. One of the few bright spots was the decision by city elected leaders to issue $450,000 in bonds, the largest single issue in Madison's history, for a variety of war-delayed projects. Better to have public works they said than have "bread lines" and "soup kitchens."[36]

Returning to normal was also made difficult by an ugly unhealed scar from protracted wartime union-management fights. Although unionization in Madison had enjoyed a period of vigorous prewar growth, this spurt paled beside union growth *during* the war. The almost explosive growth of factories coupled with war-fueled inflation and lagging wages created almost ideal conditions for union organizers. In a single year, 1918, the number of organized machinists increased by four thousand percent, the number of moulders increased by 100 percent, the number of electricians by 50 percent, and a number of new unions were formed. This rapid unionization

was greeted by management with something less than enthusiasm. Indeed they attempted to block unions wherever possible. Wartime conditions, however, placed special constraints on both unions and management. Under normal conditions, workers would have gone on strike but patriotic pressures strongly legislated against this. By the same token management needed every capable body it could get to meet its war contracts and therefore tried to delay a confrontation.

It was against this backdrop that conditions came to a head during the summer of 1918. Under the lash of wartime contracts almost all workers were putting in ten-hour days, six days a week, and some workers were putting in thirteen-hour shifts. In spite of wages whose buying power lagged far behind costs, most workers managed to scrimp on the necessities so that they could still contribute to the Red Cross, the Liberty Loans, and other causes. Soon the war at home took on a drab one-dimensional quality, and that was working, working, working to win the war. In the midst of these stressful conditions the *Capital Times* carried stories about "profiteering" by Madison factory owners. Under the guise of patriotism, factory owners were making millions in profits and paying workers peanuts, said *Capital Times* publisher William T. Evjue. This combination of events convinced desperate workers that in spite of the war and the patriotic need to produce, they had no choice but to strike. However, at the last minute a massive walkout was averted when labor and management agreed to submit their case to a federal government arbitrator working for the War Labor Board, a body created expressly for such purposes.

In February 1919, three months after the armistice and seven months after its intervention, the Labor Board arbitrator directed employers to increase hourly pay rates, instigate the eight-hour day, commence collective bargaining, and make several other changes. Although the ruling represented a complete vindication to the workers, all this was academic because employers immediately exercised their right under the War Labor Board rules and appealed the finding. But in April

1919 the board umpire completely upheld the initial War Labor Board decision, once again a complete worker victory.

These delays greatly angered workers and caused them to begin the "most dramatic and important single event in Madison labor history" up to that time. Insisting that the nine Madison factory owners named in the War Labor Board action had failed to live up to the arbitrated settlement, two thousand union machinists and moulders went out on strike on April 1, 1919. During the same period carpenters, ice haulers, plumbers, and packing plant workers also went on strike. Even the caddies at the Maple Bluff Country Club went out demanding seventy-five cents for eighteen holes.

In the tumult and tension that followed, violence soon erupted. Union members threw bricks through automobile and shop windows, hurled paint at nonunion members' homes, beat up strikers, and issued bomb threats. Amidst increasingly truculent charges and countercharges the strike dragged on for seven weeks. Finally in May 1919 striking unions sent delegates to Washington to appeal for War Labor Board intervention. However, when they arrived, they discovered that the board had been dissolved and that its successor was powerless to enforce the ruling. The delegates returned to Madison and the workers returned to their jobs—that is, if their employers had work and were willing to take them. About seven hundred striking machinists were forced to leave Madison to take work elsewhere. In 1920 the Madison Federation of Labor reported gains of ninety-three members and losses of 930. Not until the mid-twenties was unionism able to recover from this devastating setback.

Society and Leisure

On the surface the first two decades of the twentieth century have a tranquil haze of hard work, progressivism, and simple pleasures about them. To be sure, all of these qualities were a part of the age, but in fact the reality was much more tempestuous. Madison's wealthiest citizens began a gradual exodus from their changing neighborhoods and the struggling poor tended to concentrate in a few slummy areas. Years of clashes between the Yankee-university elite and ethnic groups over what constituted acceptable behavior produced significant changes. The newest immigrant groups created consternation by their different values and reluctance to be quickly "Americanized." Changes in the way people played shocked some but delighted others.

Hill Country, Lakeshores, and Lowland

Through reminiscences, memoirs, letters, articles, and tape recordings members of Madison's Yankee-university elite left a beguiling portrait of their lives. The professors, professionals, manufacturers, faculty wives, and others told of frequent social events with the Governor, visiting professors, and nationally famous guests, ten course dinners on fine china, ubiquitous servants, touring cars, sleek launches, extensive travel (eighteen Madisonians were in Rome during the winter of 1901–1902), men driving wagons through the streets on Sunday mornings selling Chicago and Milwaukee papers, and much more.[1]

Until about 1910 Langdon and Wilson Streets remained the most prestigious and aristocratic addresses. However, the long hegemony of these neighborhoods was jeopardized by increasing population, traffic noise, an expanding business district in the case of Wilson Street, and growing student pressure in the case of Langdon. Many of the upper socio-economic families began to leave for the secluded and deed-restricted purity offered by such areas as University Heights (no saloons, no stores, no apartments), the Highlands with its five-acre lots and architectural controls, the Mendota lakeshore along Sherman Avenue, and Maple Bluff.

At the same time the poor tended to cluster north of King Street, along Williamson Street, in a festering slum known as the "Bush" and in a variety of small quickly built houses on freshly filled marsh lots. Here they tried to scrape together enough money to put a few sticks of furniture in their rooms, second-hand clothing on their backs, and cheap food in their stomachs. Early day social workers blamed the plight of the poor on such things as "inherited racial characteristics," drink, and the absence of social workers and wholesome literature.[2]

Irritants and Immorality

Like their counterparts in every other era of Madison's history, early twentieth century residents found no shortage of things to complain about. For example, they complained about the rise of shoplifting, the discovery of "cocaine fiends," speeding automobiles, noisy motor boats, and the new practice of several Madison businesses of selling their products by phone.[3]

Although these things were all exasperating, most Madisonians were quick to acknowledge that the city had far more fundamental problems that cried out for solutions. At the top of just about everybody's list was the "boy problem." Boys, mostly teenagers, derailed streetcars by putting rocks on the tracks, threw snowballs at persons in sleighs and cars, vandalized lakeshore cottages, made obscene gestures and comments to passing ladies, spat tobacco juice on just about everything within a six-foot radius of where they were standing, and huddled together in boathouses where they smoked cigarettes, read lurid dime novels, and swore.[4]

To control the spread of such youthful depredations the Common Council passed a stiff curfew in 1902 that required all children under sixteen years of age to be at home no later than 8:00 P.M. in the winter and 9:00 P.M. in the summer. The law allowed policemen to disperse boy gangs but it also resulted in several boys being arrested while hunting nightcrawlers after a rainstorm. Also the law was not popular with diligent parents who felt the curfew was an infringement upon their parental rights.[5]

FIGURE 6.90. 1905 GIRLS SEWING CLASS.   The period between 1900 and 1920 was marked by growth and change for Madison Public Schools. The fact that the number of enrolled students doubled caused school officials to spend about $750,000 dollars to build eleven new elementary schools and one new high school. School officials also made aggressive efforts to make school more interesting and relevant. Kindergartens, "domestic arts" (cooking and sewing) for the girls (shown here), manual arts for the boys, and "gym" for everyone were among the changes that became commonplace during this period. Then, to insure that Wisconsin children stayed in these more interesting schools, the legislature passed a law in 1917 (Chapter 285,) Laws 1917 making attendance mandatory. It was in response to this law that Martha K. Riley, Madison's first feared truant officer, was hired in 1917. Other major curriculum changes included special schools for "dull" and handicapped children, technical courses for students not going on to college, and night schools for immigrants.

According to a school of thought then gaining momentum, the only way to solve the boy problem was to acknowledge that boys were endowed with a propensity to destroy property and form gangs. Therefore the only enduring solution was to redirect these tendencies into more socially accepted forms. The idea was not entirely new. Madison prohibitionists had tried creating "reading rooms" where toughs could while away their idle hours by reading uplifting tracts—but such experiments failed quickly. The new twist was to give the boys structure, adventure, and challenge. It was for this reason that a whole spectrum of remedies including the Boy Scouts, the YMCA, and the city organized recreation (playground) program were held in such high regard. And hope! Even churches modified their programs and buildings to accommodate the boy. For example, when Pilgrim Congregational Church, an East Side outpost of the First Congregational Church, was built at the intersection of Brearly and Jenifer Streets in 1914, its basement included a basketball court and showers just for this purpose. This strategy of engaging the boy and then redirecting his energies did not entirely solve the problem but it was more effective than any other program ever tried.[6]

Another problem as serious in its own way as the boy problem was the outbreak of student misbehavior. Often but not always the provocation was a result of student-"townie" enmity. For example, the provocation for a one-thousand-person, three-hour melee in 1908 was a group of university sophomores who threw several high school students into the lake thinking they were "freshies." An even more onerous pattern began in May 1914 when several hundred pajama-clad students marched to the Square, helped themselves to liquor from the Park Hotel bar, and then demanded and got free movies at the Orpheum and the Majestic. That fall the city witnessed its first large student riot. An estimated one thousand rampaging students threw bricks through the police department windows and turned fire

Do You Love Your Wife,

Mother, Sister or Sweetheart?

If so buy her a gas range and don't compel her to stand over a wood stove with the temperature at 90 degrees when you can keep the kitchen at least 20 degrees cooler by using a GAS RANGE. We publish a list of people who have purchased gas ranges during July and do not intend to

···· ROAST ···· THE ···· COOK ····

GAS RANGES SOLD DURING JULY 1903.

Miss Mary Olson, 313 N. Livingston.	Mrs. F. E. Lyne, 420 W. Wilson.	A. P. Landstrom, 410 S. Livingston.
S. D. Griffee, 201 S. Bassett.	Nettie Grady, 708 Langdon.	V. L. Hanchett, 852 E. Johnson.
A. J. Westenhaver, 315 Lake.	Chester Rapp, 834 Williamson.	M. Kalrath, 322 W. Gorham.
G. H. Pengra, 817 W. Johnson.	Sophia Jones, 1344 Jenifer.	B. Severson, 415 N. Baldwin.
S. H. Longfield, 1225 E. Dayton	Mrs. W. H. Gallagher, 1142 Jenifer.	Bell P. Fuller, 709 Madison.
A. Pearson, 438 W. Doty.	Geo. Albright, 649 Williamson	Mary Skelly, 337 W. Main.
Harry Van Wagnen, 17 E. Dayton	Mrs. J. D. Phillips, 113 W. Gorham.	J. J. Connelley, 511 W. Washington Ave.
Mrs. D. Dewark, 224 Brooks.	Jas. Crossen, 1129 Williamson.	Mrs. H. Harnden, 331 W. Main.
Wm. Erickson, o 407 W. Doty.	W. G. Beecroft, 433 Frances.	H. D Clarke, 1148 Spaight.
P. Byrne, 925 W. Dayton.	T. P. Copps, 828 E. Johnson.	Emil O. Seiler, 915 Jenifer.
A. L. Mayers, 412 W. Washington Ave	Wm. C. Peterson, o 1216 Jenifer.	Herman Hanson, 402 W. Doty.
Mrs. A. W. Newman, 2 Langdon.	Mrs. H. C. Pedermoen, 412 E. Wilson.	Miss S. A. Hurd, 1104 W. Johnson.

Madison Gas & Electric Co.,

126 East Main Street. · · ·   Phones: Standard 23; Bell 144.

FIGURE 6.91. DO YOU LOVE YOUR WIFE? Not long after the turn of the century the Madison Gas and Electric Company began an intensive campaign to sell gas stoves. Although they were expensive they were a great leap forward in convenience. Rather than get up an hour early to start a coal or wood fire, the housewife merely turned a valve and struck a match. Furthermore, gas stoves put much less heat into the room than wood or coal stoves—a great advantage in the summer. Apparently the campaign was successful for in 1907 a statewide study showed that Madison had substantially more gas stoves per capita than any other city in the state.

So impressive was this advance in domestic life that it gave rise to the saying, "now you're cookin' with gas" to express a smart new thought or way of doing something.

hoses back upon the firemen who were attempting to disperse the crowd. Not until President Van Hise was roused from his sleep to make an impassioned plea from the steps of the police department was the mob quelled. Police, injuries resulting from the incident so hardened police-student relations that a few years later a student was shot and killed by a policeman for stealing a barber pole. These and numerous but much less serious incidents explain why in annual police department occupational analyses of arrested persons, students always ranked in the top five and why they sometimes placed second just below laborers.[7]

Beyond irritants, the boy problem and the question of how to deal with marauding college students, there was a cultural battleground on which opposing forces had clashed for decades over a variety of value-oriented issues. None of these clashes had been more pitched or persistent than the great dispute over how one ought to spend Sundays. According to the traditional Yankee-university elite—long the self-appointed arbiters of correct conduct—no one should do anything on the Sabbath except go to church, pray, study the Bible, and contemplate God. According to the German's, however, Sunday was a day set aside by God to rest, play, and enjoy one's family. By 1910 the German "Continental Sunday" concept had emerged as the decisive winner of this battle. In that year George C. Hunt, the minister of Christ Presbyterian Church, used a sermon to excoriate the people of Madison for having gone "fun mad" on Sunday.[8] The evidence was everywhere. In nice weather just about everybody went for a walk or a drive on Sunday afternoon, listened to band concerts, ate ice cream cones, rode bicycles, and played golf. Sunday was the busiest day of the week for Madison bowling alleys and movie theaters. One Sunday morning just after the ice froze several hundred children were seen skating even as church bells called citizens to worship. And to assist all this merrymaking, the saloons contrary to state and local laws were often open on Sunday.

The relaxation of tight moral standards was also evident in the treatment of certain aspects of sex. The increasing popularity of swimming after the turn of the century raised the question of female bathing apparel. A local ordinance drawn in 1879, largely to quiet the furor over skinny dipping by little boys, simply said that everything from neck to knee had to be covered. The prospect of a completely nude female foreleg, heretofore covered by dresses and petticoats, therefore raised many eyebrows. One school favored "demure" stockings on the grounds that they would "throw a film of illusion around the stogy ankle" and relieve a "brutal frankness" and "disillusionment" a completely nude foreleg would likely engender. The other school argued that stockings were unnecessary, inconvenient, and uncomfortable.[9] So concerned were Madisonians about nude female forelegs that the Common Council passed an ordinance in 1918 prohibiting anyone from going back and forth to a swimming beach without an outer wrap "to suitably cover the person."[10]

Another aspect of sex came up in 1912 when university students began doing, as the mayor put it, "vulgar and improper" dances such as the tango, the turkey trot, the bunny hug, and the hesitate. So outrageous were these dances, some of which were cheek to cheek, that the Common Council passed a special ordinance making all dances in Madison subject to police inspection.[11] Not long after the college students began doing "vulgar" dances, Madison high school girls began wearing rouge, eyebrow pencil, and mascara, acts that proved about as popular as the "bunny hug" to school authorities.

The increasingly candid treatment of sex in movies, "respectable" novels, and vaudeville drew predictable aspersions from local ministers and moralists.[12] Interestingly, however, a fascinating double standard emerged. In 1909 Isadora Duncan, probably the leading interpretative dancer in the country, gave a performance in Madison

FIGURE 6.92. MADISON'S AVERAGE MAN AND WOMAN, A SARTORIAL SURVEY. From time to time the *Wisconsin State Journal* would send a reporter out into the streets to take detailed notes on the apparel of the first one hundred persons that walked by. The reporter was then instructed to analyze this data and write an article on the findings. According to one such survey done in 1910 the average Madison man was five feet eleven inches tall, was smooth shaven, and wore a soft fedora hat, a blue serge suit, a soft-collared shirt with blank or flowered four-in-hand tie, and high black shoes. All this, said the reporter, was pretty conservative with only a "dash of pep here and there. . . . "

In 1913 a similar expedition produced a portrait of the average Madison woman. According to the reporter, she was five feet five inches tall, had blond hair, wore a close-fitting hat, a tight dress with a low cut neck, silk stockings, and low shoes. When it came to color and style the reporter threw up her hands in despair and suggested that there might be one million color combinations and styles.

FIGURE 6.93. FIRST POLICE CAR, 1912. Shown above is Madison's first police car, a forty-horsepower Oakland Flyer purchased in 1912. The vehicle was one of several efforts to bring the police department into the automobile age. With this car department officials could capture thieves before they got out of town.

The most serious auto-related problem with which Madison police had to contend was speeding or "scorching" as it was then called. Speeding was particularly common in the fall of each year when fraternity men tried to impress pledges with reckless rides in fast cars. But speeding was hardly limited to college boys. Relatively long, flat, recently gravelled streets were an almost irresistable temptation for most motorists. In 1903 Williamson was the favorite speedway; in 1918 the new stretch of Rutledge Street just east of the Yahara River enjoyed that distinction. But there was one street which was favored above all others that was a .7 mile long stretch beside the city cemetery on the west end. Here motorists could "let her out" without fear of arrest. Thus when the street was named, it was called "Speedway."

The first efforts to stop speeding came in 1907 when police were issued stop watches. The stop watches enabled police to time speeders but failed to give the beat policemen holding the watches any way to catch them. Thus in 1914 the department purchased its first motorcycle. The system obviously worked because one year later speeding violations had become the second most common cause of arrest in Madison. At the same time police were cracking down on speeding, the Common Council was passing a tough ordinance on drunk and reckless driving. Then as a number of automobiles increased, the inevitable occurred: In 1915 the council passed its first parking restriction. The highly unpopular ordinance limited parking around the Capitol Square to just fifteen minutes.

to the accompaniment of the New York Philharmonic Orchestra. Before a highly cultured audience she flitted about the stage in a skimpy, diaphanous costume, but no one objected because this was "art." However, had a vaudeville girl bedecked herself in a similar costume and cavorted before a less affluent audience, indignation would surely have followed.

In spite of ordinances and public censure, Madisonians demonstrated increasingly liberal attitudes toward certain behavior once considered sexually inappropriate. Thus, at the swimming beaches, Madison women exposed their forelegs, on the dancefloors, Madison couples stood cheek to cheek and entwined themselves in novel ways, in their living rooms Madisonians read books whose prose would once have been limited to a dime novel, in the movie palaces Madisonians saw films forbidden to any one under sixteen, and in the high school teenage girls wore makeup in complete defiance of the "painted lady" image. In summary, the prim, proper, and prudish Yankee Code was under siege, and cracks were beginning to appear in its once towering walls.

Lumps in the Melting Pot

The first twenty years of the new century were not easy for newly arrived Italians and Jews nor for long-established blacks and Chinese. Ten Italians who arrived in Madison from Chicago about 1900 to work on a railroad section gang formed the basis of what soon became Madison's "Italian Colony." In letters to Italian relatives, the men described jobs, food, and opportunities in Madison as abundant. These conditions were almost beyond belief to the railroad workers' relatives who lived in Sicily, a ten-thousand-square-mile Mediterranian island in the extreme southern part of Italy. At the time this island and most

FIGURE 6.94. THE GROWTH OF THE PUBLIC LIBRARY. From the time the Madison Free Library opened in 1875 it scrimped along with small budgets in a tiny room in the City Hall. Beginning in 1901, however, this much-lauded but underfunded and underhoused "educational cathedral" began a long overdue renaissance. In that year the Library Commission hired their first trained librarian. This new professional began a series of aggressive efforts to get books out to the people. In 1904 Madison received a $75,000 grant from Andrew Carnegie for a new library building. However, as Madisonians are wont to do, they immediately fell into an intense, acrimonious two-year battle on where the facility should be located. The building was finally constructed at the corner of West Dayton and North Carroll now the site of the Dayton Parking ramp. Then in 1913 just seven years after the new main library was completed, a second Andrew Carnegie grant was received. The $15,000 grant was to be used for Madison's first branch library built at 1254 Williamson Street. The handsome result was the building shown above designed by the local architectural firm of Claude and Starck. The branch was located in the Sixth Ward so that it could serve the rapidly growing number of blue collar workers. The first branch library still stands but has been converted to a clubhouse for the Grieg Chorus Club.

The first floor (*above right*) was the main reading room. Judging from the youngsters' coats, the librarian did not have the thermostat turned up very high. The basement of the Oxfordian-Prairie style building was used for lectures and special events (*bottom left*). Today it is a barroom for the Grieg Chorus Club. (Courtesy of the Madison Public Library)

FIGURE 6.95. THE CIGAR STORE. In spite of warnings that smoking was injurious to health, the consumption of cigars by Madisonians was almost legendary. Estimates prepared not long after the turn of the century showed that Madisonians consumed more than four million cigars a year, a rate two to three times higher than other Wisconsin cities of the same size. To satisfy this demand, twelve cigar stores similar to the one shown above plus dozens of saloons, drug, and grocery stores sold the pungent product. Curiously, Madison was a very poor pipe town. Only a few of the larger cigar stores kept pipe tobacco for a "few odd customers." Among adult males, cigar consumption ranged from one a week to a dozen a day with the average being two per day. About eighty percent of all cigars sold were a nickel but some of the finer Havanas ran up to fifty cents. University professors were especially fond of the more expensive brands.

Soon after the turn of the century, however, the cheap cigarette began to gain favor in Madison. For a nickel one could buy a pouch of Bull Durham Tobacco plus a packet of cigarette papers and have perhaps ten smokes for the price of a cheap cigar. Two-thirds of all the boys in the Madison High School were said to be addicted to cigarettes and a large number of university students were too. Some college men allegedly preferred to spend Friday evening with their cigarettes rather than call on the girls at Chadbourne Hall. A Madison judge said that cigarette smoking was a "vicious habit" and that their continued use would "undermine health and character." President Van Hise crusaded against their use by university students. All such efforts failed. The growth of cigarette smoking was particularly rapid in the "teens" when "flying squadrons" of expert Bull Durham demonstrators rolled into town to show the boys the "manly art" of rolling your own—with Bull Durham smoking tobacco of course.

of southern Italy was characterized by disease, poverty, overpopulation, and peasants. Interestingly just when these "American letters" arrived in Sicily, the Italian government adopted a pro-emigration policy as a means of relieving population pressures. The combination of free no-questions-asked passports and nine-dollar trans-Atlantic steamship tickets opened the gates for a massive migration to the United States.

During the first decade of the twentieth century Italians, ninety-nine percent from Sicily, trickled into Madison and settled in the area bounded by Regent, Brooks, and West Washington Avenue. The rapid transition from Italian peasant to American city dweller was difficult for all but particularly for the men who had to make a living for their families in an alien world. Unable to speak more than a few words English, illiterate even in Italian, and unable to offer prospective employers anything except their muscles, the men were forced to take the lowest of jobs. They became Madison's ditch diggers, quarry workers, railroad hands, and hod carriers.

Among the Italian cultural baggage was a great emphasis upon family, honor, macho, the Catholic Church, plus an acceptance of crime and vengeance. The latter characteristics manifested themselves in secret societies such as the Black Hand and caused many Madisonians to view all Italians as criminals.

Almost immediately the Italians formed a tightly knit community with their own stores and shops clustered along Park Street and near the intersection of Milton and West Washington Avenue. Gradually they created their own institutions including the Tripola Italiana Club (1913), an organization for Italian workingmen, and the St. Joseph's Catholic Church (1915). By 1916 "Little Italy" had a population of about eleven hundred persons, and by 1920 Italians had become the third largest foreign-born group in Madison following the Germans and Norwegians.

At almost every turn Italians encountered obstacles on the path to social and economic betterment. Their peasant background, their

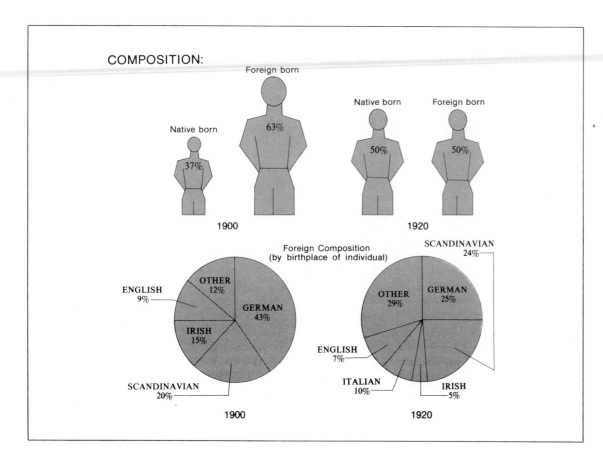

COMPOSITION:

Foreign born

Native born

63%

Native born   Foreign born

37%

50%   50%

1900   1920

Foreign Composition
(by birthplace of individual)

SCANDINAVIAN
24%

ENGLISH
9%

OTHER
12%

GERMAN
43%

IRISH
15%

OTHER
29%

GERMAN
25%

ENGLISH
7%

SCANDINAVIAN
20%

ITALIAN
10%

IRISH
5%

1900   1920

FIGURE 6.96. POPULATION COMPOSITION, 1900–1920. As shown above, Madison's foreign population defined as foreign born and children of foreign born declined relatively quickly between 1900 and 1920. Thus in 1920 for the first time since the 1850s the two categories were about equal. Germans continued to be the largest ethnic group although beginning in 1905 the Norwegians displaced the Irish as the second most numerous ethnic group. Then by 1920 the growing Italian community moved into third place.

inability to speak English, and their Sicilian traditions made them terribly suspect to middle and upper class Madisonians. Even in 1915 only fifteen percent of all Italian workers held "skilled" jobs. Native born Americans and European immigrants of longer tenure could muster little more than condescension for these new residents.[13]

A group of Jews who came to Madison during the early twentieth century to escape Russian anti-Semitism also faced a long uphill battle in their struggle for a better life. They, too, arrived impoverished and settled in the same part of Madison as the Italians because it offered the cheapest housing in town. To make a living they sold brooms, tinware, rags, and junk. Like the Italians they formed a very tight home- and church-oriented community. For twenty-five years the synagogue they erected in 1904 at the intersection of Park and Mound Streets was the center of educational and social activity for this immigrant group.[14]

Madison blacks, long the recipient of the harshest prejudicial feelings took several steps toward bettering their station by creating and then using organizations. The most important was the Free African Methodist Church founded in 1902 by John Turner, a brilliant but illiterate former Kentucky slave who cleaned rugs and boilers for a living. Although the small black congregation could not afford to erect a new church, they bought the Bethel Lutheran Church, then located at the intersection of North Hamilton and North Butler Streets and then moved this small frame structure to a lot Turner owned at the corner of East Dayton and Blount. (Bethel Lutheran then built the brick structure, which still stands at the Butler-Hamilton intersection.) Fortunately, the new congregation was able to attract the services of Reverend Jesse Woods, an ordained minister with a degree from Beloit College and who for ten years was editor of the prestigious *Afro-American Review*. The Church opened its doors in the summer of 1902 with just twenty members. For many years the Free African Methodist church was the center of black community life in Madison.

Give Us Lake Mendota to Swim in Says Afro-Methodist Minister

July 11, 1914

Dear *WSJ* Editor:

I see that there is some complaint about the colored people bathing with the white people at the municpal bathing beaches. I certainly don't see why anybody should fuss over this question. We ought to get credit for the desire to keep clean. As far as the risk incurred by a white man using a suit that a negro has used, I would like to say that soap and water has the same effect on black skin that it has on white.

Of course, if the colored people have been guilty of any impudence at the beaches they should be criticized but that is not the complaint. Any white person that is too exclusvie to rent a suit that a colored man has used should buy his own suit.

I tell you how we can fix it. Why not have the white people take one lake and the colored people the other. That would fix it fine, and there would be no annoyance on either side. I would suggest that the negroes be assigned to Lake Mendota, because the lake is deeper and naturally the waters are ah—a trifle darker.

Signed

Reverend C. H. Thomas
Free African Methodist Church

Let White People Patronize White People

And give them a chance to make a decent living and their premises will always be found in a decent condition.   Who ever knew of a Chinaman to pay out a cent to any white man for labor?   Were the people who patronize Chinese laundries to once walk through them, quite through them, it can safely be said that one thoughful person would ever again allow their shirts, collars or any other articles of wearing apparel to be found in one of them.   Citizens it is for you to say whether you would rather pay two cents for a collar done by this abominable process or pay one cent more to have it done in a cleanly, sanitary manner. What in comparison are a few cents with the comfort and safety that the white (steam) laundry insures for us?   The knowledge that no Chinese spittle is dried and ironed into them is worth the difference.   This presentment of the case may not sound very nice, but plenty of things that are not nice to think and talk about are unfortunately true and this is one of them.

FIGURE 6.97. LET WHITE PEOPLE PATRONIZE WHITE PEOPLE.   This advertisement was placed in the *Wisconsin State Journal* in April 1910 by a confederation of steam laundries.

Just two years later (1904) the all-black Prince Hall Masonic Lodge was chartered and in 1913 a second black religious organization, the Mount Zion Baptist Church, was formed. Less well-known were small self-improvement groups such as the Book Lovers Club, which met to discuss contemporary topics. Together these organizations gave direction and power to black community meliorism.[15]

However, even with the help of such groups, progress was slow and marred by deep-seated anxieties in the white community. For example, Madison dentists refused to treat a suffering black girl.[16] Black basketball players who came to Madison with a Detroit team to play the University of Wisconsin had to stay in a hotel, while their white teammates stayed in a fraternity house. A new minister for the Free African Methodist Church could not find a home to rent after weeks of diligent searching.[17] White Madisonians at public beaches complained about having to wear bathing suits that had previously been rented to blacks.[18] A saloon was refused a liquor license because it was a "loitering place for Negroes." And so it went.

Leisure-Time Activities

Two developments in the early twentieth century contained profound implications for the way Madisonians spent their leisure time. The first was the recognition that exercise was good for the body *and* the brain. Mind and muscles were after all a part of the same machine and could not be "separated" from one another without undesirable consequences. This insight from exercise physiology was understood to apply equally to men and women and was responsible for the sudden popularity of active recreation for women. The second development affecting popular recreation in Madison was the abandonment of the stern sabbatarian code. Once a day of passive, pensive reflection—at least among those steeped in the Yankee tradition—Sunday emerged as Madison's "fun day." The affects of these important changes were evident in the spectrum of recreational activities.

The presence of the magnificent Fuller Opera House, the location of Madison, and its relatively large cultured population made the capital city a great show town. After a run in New York, a show would go directly to Chicago where it might play for two to three days before going to Milwaukee for another several performances. After Chicago or Milwaukee the shows would stop in Madison for a one-night stand before going on to Minneapolis-St. Paul.[19] In addition to getting major New York shows featuring actresses like Ethyl Barrymore and Sarah Bernhardt, this set of circumstances also allowed Madison to secure other forms of "high brow" entertainment such as the New York Philharmonic Orchestra, the Chicago Symphony Orchestra, the incomparable dancer Isadora Duncan, and many others.[20]

Naturally these attractions pleased the more cultured types, but in fact the size of this audience was relatively small, as indeed it had always been. Even the managers of the august Fuller had to limit their booking of serious entertainment in favor of performances that offered the thrill of the sensational, the joy of laughter, or the charm of love. This was epitomized by a musical comedy offered by the Fuller in October 1914 entitled "Don't Lie to Your Wife," a production that promised "three hundred laughs but no blushes."[21] Elsewhere in Madison the most popular form of live entertainment continued to be vaudeville. Interestingly Madison's location between Chicago and Minneapolis meant that the city was also able to get the best New York vaudeville acts on their national tours. During the first decade of the twentieth century Madison

supported two vaudeville theaters and these were booked nearly every night. For a city of Madison's size, this was considered most unusual.[22]

Although Madisonians did not realize it, the days of the big New York dramatic productions and first rate vaudeville acts were numbered. The cause of their demise was a whole new medium that at first seemed terribly unpromising. Beginning in 1897 promoters brought a variety of strange and unlikely looking machines to Madison for demonstrations. When still photographs were run through these machines, they gave viewers the illusion of motion. Hence, they were called "the movies." In 1902 one of these machines was permanently installed in the Fuller Opera House where from time to time reenactments of prize fights and other news events were shown.[23] At first it appeared that the greatest use of the new medium would be peep shows in cheap arcades patronized by teenagers. One such arcade opened in Madison in 1906 where for a penny one could see insipid but racy half-minute productions with titles like "Loving by the Sea Shore" and "Alone in the Woods."[24] However, moviemakers quickly discovered that mass audiences could not be generated by peep shows and reenactments of news events. The big money lay in multi-reel stories adapted to film. Lacking the capability to include sound, producers superimposed succinct "captions" and prepared melodramatic musical scores for piano and drums to be rendered by theater musicians. This kaleidoscope of sound and light was almost too good to be true. At the movies you could be transported to another place and time—it was the ultimate escape. It was, as a local movie advertisement put it, "the difference between the sullen drip from the eaves and the flutter of leaves in a sunny patio beyond Seville . . . , between the monotony of a dull book and the lively creak of saddle leather between your knees . . . , "between the tedium of East Johnson Street and the "sail-shaded deck of an island schooner creaming through the blue" South Seas. And all for a nickel!

By the time Madison's first movie theater, The Grand, 202 State Street, was opened in January

1909, motion picture producers were turning out tremendously appealing films and in Madison they were an instant hit. For the first nine months after The Grand opened, its employees had to turn patrons away at the door every night.[25]

Just four years after the Grand opened its doors Madison had eight theaters exclusively devoted to the movies plus two others that mixed movies with live entertainment. Together these theaters offered enough seats to accommodate twenty percent of Madison's population at once. The equivalent of one out of ten residents attended a movie each day.[26] By 1916 one out of five Madisonians went to the movies each Sunday, and the number of persons who attended movies each week was equivalent to the Madison population.[27] The capstone to this first episode in Madison's love affair with the movies was the construction in 1918 of The Strand, the city's first "movie palace." This opulent fifteen-hundred-seat theater was designed by the nationally famous Chicago theater architects, Rapp and Rapp, the same firm that later designed The Capital, now the Oscar Mayer theater at the Civic Center, The Orpheum, and The Eastwood, now the Cinema.[28]

The effects of the movies upon Madison were large and immediate. The tremendous demand for film "stars" did not quite empty the serious stage, but it left legitimate theater a mere shadow of its once proud self. Instead of getting current Broadway plays on their first national road show, Madison got second rate performers offering five-year-old productions.[29] Even vaudeville, the playhouse of the masses, was devastated by the movies. By 1916 Madison had just one theater that devoted itself exclusively to vaudeville.[30] The ripple effects of the movies, however, extended far beyond the entertainment business. Madison's brightly illuminated movie marquees did something no other entertainment medium had ever been able to do and that was draw large numbers of people to downtown Madison every night. Soon entrepreneurs opened candy and ice cream stores to cater to this new night trade. As a 1920 *Journal* editorial put it, the movie "revolutionized night life."[31]

Varsity Theatre   Saturday, Sunday, Monday

6 Reels Featuring Mary Pickford's Sister, Lottie

This Picture for Adults Only. No one Under 16 Admitted

THE HOUSE OF BONDAGE

Greatest White Slave Picture Ever Made.   It's a Riot of Truth Straight from the Shoulder

Matinee and Night, All Seats 15c.   Continuous Show From 2 to 5 and From 7 to 11 P. M.   Attend the Matinee and Avoid the Evening Crowds

FIGURE 6.98. THE HOUSE OF BONDAGE.   This six-reel blockbuster featuring the sister of Mary Pickford was one of those movies whose content most Madison leaders considered "extremely objectionable." Although its subject, the perils of prostitution, was presented in a moralistic way, no one under sixteen was admitted. In other words it was one of the first "X"-rated movies.

Most Madison leaders felt that on balance, movies had a beneficial effect upon the community. They were cheap, they provided a very appealing substitute for pool halls and other less desirable types of entertainment, and their contents were generally "uplifting." There were, however, exceptions. A careful 1915 study of 110 movies by a citizen committee concluded that only twenty were unnecessarily violent or vulgar.[32]

No sooner had the movies transformed the entertainment habits of Madisonians than a second entirely new medium made its debut. In 1919 Madisonians began buying or making primitive radio receivers known as "crystal sets" so they could pick up the broadcasts of two radio stations, WHA and WIBA, both of which went on the air in that year. WHA is generally credited with being the first radio station in the country to offer scheduled broadcasts.[33]

In the 1890s University of Wisconsin football made big crowd spectator sports a staple in the Madison entertainment diet. Significantly, the football mania of the nineties only got worse after the turn of the century. Up to five thousand persons crowded into Camp Randall stadium to witness the epic contests. No longer were Madisonians content to limit home game decorations to bunting and pennants in store windows. In the spirit of loyal escalation, streetcars were festooned with big red Wisconsin banners and MG&E installed red globes over downtown streetlights. The *Journal* printed its football editions in red ink(!) and relegated national and international news to the inside pages so it could devote page one to the most important news story of the day, viz., a blow-by-blow account of the game. Governor LaFollette addressed a giant pep rally at the Red Gym. Almost no football detail was too unimportant to be omitted. Residents avidly read what the players had for breakfast, why they were taken to the Maple Bluff Country Club to relax, and much more. (The reason they were taken to the Country Club was because they could relax more easily there than in the city.)[34]

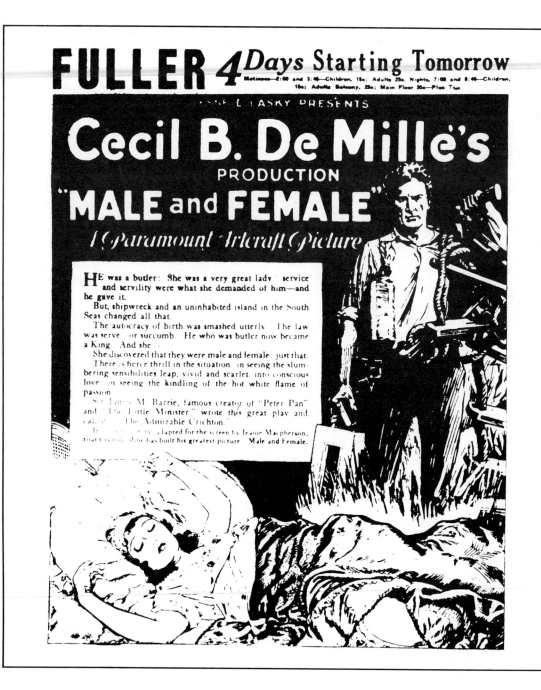

In 1907 a group of local promoters added a decidedly "metropolitan" feature to the sporting scene by fielding Madison's first professional baseball team known as the Senators. The Class D team had winning seasons for several years in competition with teams from other Wisconsin cities and drew large, enthusiastic crowds for its home games. But then several successive losing seasons caused attendance and income to plummet. When various benefits failed to make up the deficit, the franchise was sold in 1914.[35]

The eagerness, for a time, with which Madisonians followed the activities of U.W. football and the Senators was a reflection of a similar phenomenon evident elsewhere in the country. Thus, it was no accident that in 1907 the *Journal* and *Democrat* began to segregate sporting news and shortly thereafter devote whole sections to it.

For the first time in Madison's history residents made extensive use of the lake and the lake shores. The development of the gasoline launch and the outboard motor (see fig. 6.100) turned the lakes into great playgrounds for hundreds of families. The demand for lake property lying outside the city, once relatively low due to its inaccessibility, grew rapidly as the auto and motor boat put such areas just minutes from the city. Consequently nearly all of the Monona shoreline and a large part of Mendota's was platted during this period. Its development, however, was not for year-round homes but rather for summer cottages.[36]

By 1907 the number of new cottages and the continued popularity of lakeshore camping had reached a point where a new rural mail route had to be established. In this case, however, the mailman putted from pier to pier in a boat named the "U.S. Mail." The marine mailman circled Mendota in the morning and Monona in the afternoon.[37] The city decision to run bath houses beginning in 1901 (see fig. 6.101) and then swimming beaches meant that for the first time the

FIGURE 6.99. MALE AND FEMALE. This Cecil B. DeMille film seen by Madisonians in March 1920 was an example of the tremendously appealing movies then being produced by the major studios.

lakes were extensively used for this once illegal purpose. Another development that added liveliness to the lakes was the resurgence of sailing, or "yachting" as it was then called. The catalyst for this comeback was the formation in 1903 of the Mendota Yacht Club and their decision in 1907 to build a handsome club house at the foot of North Blair Street. From this point forward this club sponsored regular regattas and other activities for a growing fleet of class boats.[38] In addition to these new or resurgent activities, the continued popularity of both old and new private parks at various points around the lake created a large business for steamboat fleet owners.[39]

The greater use of the lakes and lakeshores did not imply a reduction of activity in other summer recreational categories. The fact was, Madison's growing population had a growing appetite for leisure time activities. It was for this reason that the circus, the band concert, the picnic, fishing and the Sunday afternoon drive remained very popular, and bicycling, following a slide in popularity from 1897 to 1903, once again captured the public fancy.[40] (See graphics 6.102 and 6.103.)

Complementing these old favorites were several new forms of summer recreation including the zoo and country club (see figs. 6.104 and 6.105) and two new foods that took the city by storm. The first was the five-cent ice cream cone, which made its appearance in 1909. "Have you been coned yet?" Madisonians asked each other until just about everybody had. One vendor estimated that on a hot summer day nearly one out of five Madisonians consumed an ice cream cone. Such statistics, of course, are misleading since they conceal the disproportionate number of cones children licked to destruction.[41] The second food fad was the soft drink or soda. So great was the demand for this liquid confection that in August 1911 one downtown soda fountain owner had to employ twenty-three clerks just to keep ahead of demand.[42]

On Mendota Lake near Varsity Boat House

FIGURE 6.100. THE GASOLINE LAUNCH. When the gasoline launch was first introduced on Madison lakes its advantages were immediately apparent. With a launch anglers could speed to favorite fishing spots in minutes. With a launch the paterfamilias could take his wife and children to a sylvan lakeshore setting for a picnic and return without blisters on his hands. With a launch groups could enjoy cooling lake breezes on a hot day. Moreover gasoline launches were easy to operate and faster than the steamboat. The only real disadvantage of the launch was their extremely high initial cost—a fact that limited ownership around the turn of the century to seventeen of Madison's richest men.

As the number of motor launch owners increased they began to lobby for the boat owners' equivalent of more roads, namely, a way of traveling between Mendota and Monona through the Yahara. Under most circumstances this demand would have been extremely difficult to realize because it required a lock at the Mendota outlet to be built and all the Yahara railroad bridges to be raised. At the time the railroad bridges were so low that a person going under these bridges in a rowboat had to lie down. However, in this case, most of the launch owners were members of the extremely powerful Madison Park and Pleasure Drive Association, and so they used the good offices of the organization to achieve their end. In 1904 the lock was opened for use and the railroad bridges were raised eight feet above the water level. Not long after Mendota and Monona were opened for launch travel, boat owners began to push for improvements that would make Waubesa and Kegonsa accessible. In 1911 the Yahara River Improvement Association dredged the Yahara River between Monona and Mud Lake and in 1916 another group of interested parties worked thru the Railroad Commission to raise the railroad track then blocking launch passage into Lake Waubesa. With these changes the four lakes became a playground for launch owners.

Gradually the cost of motor boats became low enough that the middle class could afford them. This trend was reflected by the number of boats going through the new lock. By 1913 a record 612 boats went through on a single day, and eleven thousand boats went through during the season.

The launch shown above was typical of the relatively large models popular in the 1910 and 1915 era. (SHSW WHi(X3)36288)

FIGURE 6.101. THE OLD BRITTINGHAM SWIMMING HOLE.   Swimming was illegal in Madison until 1879, when aldermen passed an ordinance that allowed swimming, but *only* if the swimmer was covered from "neck to knee." Madison boys however paid little attention to this law and went right on skinny-dipping. This practice produced countless calls to Chief of Police Henry C. Baker from persons living along the lakeshore who were bothered by this form of nudity. Chief Baker, however, being a former boy himself, didn't have the heart to arrest these young citizens and instead went on a three-year crusade to get the city to build bath houses on both lakes. Finally, in 1901 the council responded to Baker's request by voting to locate a bathhouse on Lake Monona at the foot of Hancock Street and another on Lake Mendota at the foot of Wisconsin Avenue. But then just as the contractor unloaded his lumber and supplies at these sites, nearby residents expressed their intense displeasure at the prospect of screaming swimmers at all hours of the day and night. Residents argued that the Monona lake bottom at the end of Hancock was too weedy and full of sewage and that the Mendota lake bottom at Wisconsin Avenue was too weedy and rocky.

This unexpected reaction sent the mayor and an alderman on a rowboat reconnaissance of the shorelines looking for alternative sites. They concluded that the Monona bathhouse should be located at the South Patterson Street end (now the site of B. B. Clarke Beach) and that the Mendota bathhouse should be located at the foot of North

Franklin Street (now a part of James Madison park). Once again the contractor moved his supplies to the new sites and started work. Barely had the staccato of worker hammers begun when adjoining property owners obtained an injunction. By now the summer was two-thirds gone and the "Comedy of the Bath" as residents were already calling it seemed likely to go on indefinitely. Following a hearing the court ruled that the Patterson Street site was quite acceptable but that the Franklin Street site was indeed too close and too visible to adjoining houses. The contractor therefore moved his supplies still another time from Franklin Street to South Park Street. Finally in mid-August the controversial bathhouses opened and Madison got into the towel, swim suit, and lifeguard business for the first time.

Just as Chief Baker predicted, the city-provided bathing spots were an immediate hit. With barely two weeks of summer left, eight thousand swimmers used the facilities. The following year twenty-five thousand patronized the bathhouses and by 1916 the number of swimmers had risen to one hundred eighty thousand during the three month "heated term."

The official city facilities did not, however, completely eliminate the time-honored practice of swimming *au naturel*. The young man clamoring up onto the makeshift diving board in this 1905 photograph of Brittingham Bay was just one case in point. (SHSW WHi (X3)27367)

FIGURE 6.102. THE CIRCUS PARADE. The arrival of a major circus was always a cause for excitement because it meant a colossal free parade. For a few moments the streets would be filled with Arabian Knights, helmeted Roman charioteers, red-uniformed horsemen, spangled women, armor-laden elephants, snarling tigers, roaring lions, the piercing shriek of the steam calliope, the blare of the brass band, and ornate, gilded wagons. It was a form of magic whose power over the people can hardly be imagined today.

Shown above is a clown band tableau as it passed Webster Street on East Washington Avenue late Monday morning August 7, 1916. At this point the wagons were on their way back to the circus grounds near the intersection of East Washington Avenue and Winnebago Streets. The building in the upper left stands at the intersection of North Webster and East Washington Avenue and is now used by Blied Inc.

FIGURE 6.103. THE SUNDAY AFTERNOON DRIVE. During nice weather one of the most popular Sunday afternoon activities was going for a walk or a drive. One of the favorite thoroughfares for these activities was Sherman Avenue. This photograph taken in 1904 at the Sherman Avenue bridge captures some Madisonians strolling across the bridge while another group drives by in one of the new "horseless carriages." (SHSW, WHi(X3)30588)

The early years of the twentieth century were also noteworthy because the city began to provide *winter* recreational facilities for its residents. The city designation and protection of sledding hills and its clearing of ice skating rinks on Lake Monona marked the beginning of this trend. The effort was partially motivated by a resolve to seize winter by the forelock and to provide outside recreation that made this long and most despised season one that could be enjoyed,

not merely endured.[43] In spite of such well-intentioned efforts, however, most adults preferred to peek at winter through the windows of steam-heated rooms. The only question, then, was which forms of recreation would allow inside fun on cold winter nights. The clear favorites for most Madisonians were bowling and billiards. Since the introduction of the "finger ball" in 1899, Madison bowlers grew by leaps and bounds. Between 1899 and 1910 the number of bowling lanes increased

from two to thirty-three and an estimated one out of four Madisonians kept them busy nine months a year.[44] Billiards had once been a popular and respectable game, but had suffered from the taint of the dissolute pool hall. During the early twentieth century, however, billiards once again became respectable. Between 1900 and 1914 the number of city-licensed billiard tables more than doubled, spirited tournaments were held, and national grand masters came to the city for matches.[45]

FIGURE 6.104. THE MADISON ZOO. Sometime during the winter of 1910–1911, Mr. Thomas C. Richmond offered to give the Madison Park and Pleasure Drive Association a herd of five deer, which he had kept on his South Madison estate on Lakeside Street. The association accepted subject to the recommendation of John Nolen on which park the deer should go. Nolen's fateful decision was to place them at Henry Vilas Park. Just days after this almost incidental transaction, Madison opinion leaders began to view the five deer as the nucleus of something much greater, namely, a full-fledged zoological garden. The concept thrilled Madison boosters because zoos were characteristic of "large cities" and because a zoo would expose citizens to the wonderful world of nature.

When the zoo officially opened in 1911 its collection consisted of nine deer, three ground hogs, three woodchucks, two guinea pigs, two rabbits, two white rats, one racoon, one eagle, on squirrel, and one toothless red fox. By 1920 however, the zoo boasted five hundred specimens including an elephant, camels, lions, tigers, a polar bear, leopards, jaguars, alligators—some one hundred species in all. Generous gifts from the Vilas family provided zoo facilities to accommodate the burgeoning collection. By 1920 the Vilas Zoo had become the second largest in the state and was among the listed zoos of the world. Naturally this pleased town boosters and zoo backers, but the most impressive evidence of its success were the huge crowds that milled through its gravelled walks each weekend.

This photograph taken during the summer of 1915 shows a zookeeper feeding one of the California sea lions—one of several animals whose antics seldom failed to please the crowds.

FIGURE 6.105. MAPLE BLUFF COUNTRY CLUB. The incorporation of the Maple Bluff Country Club in December 1899, the first such institution in the city, soon led to the construction of the clubhouse shown here just after it opened in the spring of 1901. Membership was limited to one hundred fifty persons but when this quota was reached in just two weeks, officers raised the limit to two hundred. For a family the initiation fee was $25 and the annual membership fee was another $25. To assist members in getting out to the picturesque facility, the club purchased a steam launch that left a downtown pier at regular times.

The country club was just one of several efforts being made across the country to somehow harmonize the strong American agrarian tradition with the rise of cities. The rapid increase of city parks and pleasure drives, curvilinear (natural) street designs, Boy Scouts, Girl Scouts, children's camps, gardening, nature photography, and indeed the whole suburban movement were all efforts to cause the natural world to remain an integral part of city dwellers' lives.

Epilogue: The Closing of the Formative Years

The year 1920 marked the close of Madison's formative years, a period when the modern contours of the city were shaped. The long simmering sometimes boiling debate over what kind of city Madison was to become had, with a few minor changes, been settled. Madison would be a government town *and* a university town *and* an industrial town but not a northern resort. Conflict between various nationalities had subsided although some marked differences remained. Citizens had abandoned the stand pat get-out-of-the-way-do-little concept of local government for the interventionist progressive model.

By 1920 Madison's appearance had reached a point where it would have been highly recognizable even to persons who moved to the city in the 1980s. The magnificent new white marble capitol stood completed on its glacial pedestal. The first skyscrapers punctuated the skyline and more were under construction. Streetcar motormen clanged their bells to get inattentive drivers to pull over their Buicks, Chevrolets, Fords, Cadillacs, Dodges, and Oldsmobiles. Yellow cabs circled the Square looking for fares. One could attend services at Grace Church, go to the Rotary or Kiwanis Clubs at The Park Hotel, shop at The Hub, Yost-Kessenich's, and Wolff Kubly and Hirsig, bank at American Exchange, First National (now First Wisconsin) or the Bank of Wisconsin (now M & I Bank of Madison). Each day trucks left the post office to haul letters to the airport for scheduled air mail flights. Policemen in squad cars issued tickets to overtime parkers while their counterparts on motorcycles chased speeders. Oscar Mayer and Madison Kipp were running their plants near full capacity as were the predecessor firms of Ohio Medical Products and Rayovac. Women were not only voting but beginning to serve on policy-making boards and commissions. Madison General and St. Mary's offered high quality medical care for their patients.

Even the daily routine would have been familiar. In the morning Madisonians could wash their faces with Ivory or Palmolive soap, brush their teeth with Pepsodent toothpaste, the men might shave with a new Gillette safety razor, and the whole family might sit down to a breakfast of Grape Nuts, Post Toasties or Kellogg's Corn Flakes. During the day one could chew Wrigley's Doublemint, Spearmint or Juicy Fruit gum, smoke Chesterfield or Camel cigarettes, and if things got a little too hectic, there was always Bayer aspirin.

Idle hours could be whiled away in Tenney, Vilas, Brittingham, Orton, Olin, and Lakeside parks. One could go swimming, motorboating, take in a University of Wisconsin football game, or go to the movies at the Majestic or the Strand. For an evening at home one might read the *Wisconsin State Journal* or the *Capital Times* (not many households took both), listen to RCA Victor or Columbia records on a victrola, or adjust a crystal set for a WIBA or WHA broadcast. Young men could join Boy Scouts and the YMCA and their sisters could join Girl Scouts and the YWCA.

Even problems had a familiar ring about them. Large downtown single family homes were being cut up into rooming houses, apartments, and fraternities and sororities. High school boys were smoking cigarettes, the lakes were polluted, the cost of living was going up, and the first trees succumbed to the Dutch Elm disease.[1]

By 1920 even the "personality" of Madison was well established. That term is usually reserved for individuals, but there is a sense in which its application to people living in a city can help reveal certain essential characteristics of that population. Here the term is used to mean those traits produced by the shared experience of living in a city.

At the core of the Madison personality was an intense awareness of the city's extraordinary natural beauty and the honor of being *both* the capital of a great commonwealth and the home of its university. Madison leaders were terribly proud of this distinction and sought to redeem the great promise inherent in these rare circumstances. The challenge of fulfilling the exciting potential of these circumstances brought out the dreamer and the doer in an unusually large number of citizens. It lured people away from their pleasures and duties, made them work for the city's benefit, and take sides in controversies almost against their will. Both as individuals and through a dense network of organizations Madisonians contributed their time, talent, and money for the betterment of their city. This is not to say that Madisonians worked to achieve the *same* goals. In fact, the city's heterogeneous, relatively affluent, and well-educated population were notorious for their alacrity to argue about almost anything. The months and often years needed to reach agreement on many issues were also legendary.

This magnetic city "personality" is not something we read about as an abstract and strange curiosity even though it matured more than sixty years ago. On the contrary, it is alive; it is all around us. We contemporary Madisonians have inherited this city "personality," and in this respect, among many others, the past is a part of Madison's future. Indeed, it is this tension between our declining past and our created future that makes Madison a beautiful, exciting, and very demanding place in which to live. May it never lose these qualities!

Notes

Abbreviations in This Work

CCP   *Common Council Proceedings*
CT   *Capital Times*
MD   *Madison Democrat*
WSJ   *Wisconsin State Journal*
SHSW State Historical Society of Wisconsin

Chapter 1

Paleohistory

1. The story of the capitol well as told by Daniel Steel Durrie in his *History of Madison* (Madison, Wisconsin: Atwood and Culver, 1874), pp. 311, 313, and 358–9, notes the contract for sinking an artesian well in the Capitol Park was signed by J. N. Underwood on May 21, 1866.

2. Governor Fairchild in his message to the legislature on January 9, 1868, noted that up to that time $8,662.70 had been spent on the well (Durrie, p. 313).

For a comment on the geological value of the well, see *WSJ*, September 23, 1867.

3. H. A. Tenney was one who followed the progress of the well drillers and who knew something about the geological history of the drill cores. Said Tenney: "It very clearly reveals the existence of ancient and intense igneous action beneath and proves that our primary is not only below all other mineral ranges, but is equally beneath the deepest borings and the gypsum and slate beds of Michigan and Illinois, the coal regions, and the saline deposits of the great plains, and it is more than suspected that it is the central focus of all the deep drainage of this portion of the Continent" (Durrie, p. 311).

4. One of the most readable, yet reliable, treatments of the glaciers is Gwen Schultz's *Ice Age Lost* (Garden City, N.J.: Doubleday, 1974). See page 117 for an excellent account of how snow is transformed into ice and ice into a glacier.

5. Ibid., p. 173 and following. The rate of speed comes from an unpublished paper by David M. Mickelson.

6. Ibid., p. 62, for ice thickness.

7. See the article by Reid Bryson and David Baerreis, "The Character of Late Glacial and Post Glacial Climatic Changes," in *Pleistocene and Recent Environments of the Central Great Plains*, Wakefield Dort and J. Knox Jones, Jr., eds., (University of Kansas, 1970), pp. 53–76, and Schultz, p. 121, for background on the warming trend and the rate of glacial retreat. David M. Mickelson estimates in an unpublished article that the continental glacier expanded at a rate of one kilometer per year.

8. A map showing thickness of glacial deposits in Wisconsin was prepared by the U.S. Geological Survey and the University Extension by R. G. Borman in 1971. The map was published in David Stephenson's *Wisconsin Ground Water: An Invaluable Resource* (Madison: University of Wisconsin Extension Division, 1974), p. 17.

The gold lump was found in the 4800 block of Tonyawatha Trail by a laborer digging an earthen cellar for Otto Schroeder, the founder of the Schroeder Funeral Home (see *WSJ*, September 30, 1905).

Within the city limits were several hills rich in sand and gravel. The most spectacular was called Dead Lake Ridge, a recessional moraine. Once a dramatic narrow serrated ridge ten stories tall and covered by Indian mounds, its contents were systematically removed from 1870 to 1910. Today all that remains of this once prominent part of the Madison skyline is a low, barely noticeable mound whose high point serves as a foundation for St. Mary's hospital. Mound Street cuts across the once imposing ridge.

Brick kilns in the Madison area include the John George Ott operation in the 1400 block of East Wilson Street, a yard whose clays produced both red and cream colored brick. The brick in the Ott house, at 754 Jenifer, was probably made at this kiln. For a reference on the location of the Ott brick yard, see *WSJ*, September 9, 1905.

The Stevens Brick Yard about two miles west of the university, today the site of the Wisconsin Brick and Block Company, 2840 University Avenue, produced cream-colored brick (*MD*, April 14, 1878). Most brick clays in the Madison area were lacustrine in origin.

9. For a description of what was happening in North America, see Dott and Batten, chapters 13, 16 and 17. Most geologists agree that the land we now call Wisconsin was uplifted around 300 million years ago and that between then and the Ice Age it was subjected to erosion. It would appear that nearly one thousand feet of rock in the Madison area were worn away during this period. See N. H. Fenneman, *Lakes of Southwestern Wisconsin* (Wisconsin and Natural History Survey, 1902), p. 36.

10. Meredith E. Ostrom, "Stratigraphic Relationships of Lower Paleozoic Rocks in Wisconsin," in *Lithostratigraphy, Petrology, and Sedimentology of Late Cambrian-Early Ordovician Rocks Near Madison, Wisconsin* (Madison: Geological and Natural History Survey (UWEX), 1978, is an excellent source for interpretative comments of this period.

The equatorial location was taken from a map showing the late Ordovician period, that is, about 450 million years ago. The map is one of many outstanding graphics appearing in the historical geology text by Robert H. Dott, Jr. and Roger L. Batten, p. 228, cited earlier. During the late Cambrian time, the equator probably lay further west (p. 199).

11. The formation of sedimentary rocks is described in Crowns, pp. 43–48 and 99–103. Actually sedimentary rock was at one time perhaps 1700 feet thick. See N. H. Fenneman, *Lakes of Southeastern Wisconsin* (1902), p. 36.

12. See Crowns, pp. 94–99 and 38–40.

13. Six years after the well drillers left, someone noticed that water had accumulated to within sixty feet of the shaft surface. Governor Cadwallader Washburn (1872–1874) was intrigued by this development. It was true that the drillers never found the hoped-for artesian water source they sought. But that did not mean the well would not be a big producer, Washburn reasoned. To confirm this hypothesis, the governor had workmen extend a pipe to below the water level and then connect it to a steam pump. To everyone's delight, the well produced prodigious quantities of cold, clear water and, best

of all, it replenished itself as fast as it was pumped. The success of this well eventually led to the drilling of an entire network of wells, which proved that the sedimentary rocks underlying the city were outstanding water producers. See Durrie, p. 358–359.

14. Archeologists disagree on when man first entered North America. Some such as Gordon R. Willey, *An Introduction to American Archeology* (Englewood Cliffs, N.J.: Prentice-Hall, 1966), pp. 73–74, believes that a small migration may have occurred between twenty and forty thousand years ago. Others such as Jesse Jennings, *Prehistory of North America* (New York: McGraw Hill, 1974), pp. 47–53, believe the optimum time was between eighteen thousand and ten thousand years ago. Clearly, a range of 25–15,000 B.C. is reasonable.

15. The distinctive fluted points include such types as Clovis and Folsom. For general background on the Paleo-Indian see Jesse Jennings, pp. 71–126, and Thomas Y. Canby, "The Search for the First Americans," *National Geographic,* 156, no. 3 (September 1979), pp. 330–363; and Gordon R. Willey, pp. 37–51.

16. See Philip H. Salkin, "The Paleo-Indian Tradition in Wisconsin," unpublished manuscript, 1974.

17. With the possible exception of the Boaz mastadon, no fluted points have been found in conjunction with bones of extinct mammals in the eastern U.S. All such finds are in the West and Southwest. For background on the Boaz mastadon see Harris A. Palmer and James B. Stoltman, "The Boaz Mastadon: A Possible Association of Man and Mastadon in Wisconsin," *Midcontinent Journal of Archeology* 1, no. 2 (1976), pp. 163.

However, the presence in southern Wisconsin of the mammoth, mastadon, and bison between 10,000 and 7000 B.C. is undisputed. The better documented finds within twenty-five miles of Madison include three mammoths, two woolly mastadons, and one giant beaver. Radiocarbon dates for specimens in this group range from 11,000–7500 B.C. This group only includes specimens found after 1967. See letter dated March 27, 1980, from John Dallmon, Curator of Paleontology, Department of Zoology, University of Wisconsin. Many more specimens were found prior to this time. For example see the *MD,* October 23, 1906, for a mastadon bone discovery in Madison.

18. Support for the 10,000 B.C. data comes from James A. Stoltman, "A Preliminary Study of Wisconsin Fluted Points," *The Wisconsin Archeologist* 50, no. 4, pp. 189–214; George I. Quimby's *Indian Life in the Upper Great Lakes, 11,000 B.C. to A.D. 1800* (Chicago: University of Chicago Press, 1960), pp. 27–33; and Salkin.

19. Postglacial vegetation patterns have been reconstructed from pollen counts taken from bog borings. Bogs preserve plant pollen and allow paleobotanists to determine what percentages various plants represented at a given time. A study of sixty-two such bog borings from the eastern U.S. including several in Wisconsin showed shifts in vegetation patterns from 9000 B.C. to the present. See J. Christopher Bernabo and

Thompson Webb III, "Changing Patterns in the Holocene Pollen Record of Northeastern North America: A Mapped Summary," *Quaternary Research* 8 (1977), pp. 64–96.

The only modern, scientific bog boring done in the Madison area was done in 1974 at Lake Waubesa by U.W. Professor Albert Swain. Swain's unpublished study corroborates the Bernabo and Webb study.

The best source on postglacial climate is the article by Reid Bryson, et al., pp. 53–76.

20. Indians that made this transition are called Late Paleo-Indians by archeologists. The Yahara River-Beltline site was originally known as the airport site because it lay on the east end of the old Royal Airport, Madison's first regularly used airfield. The field is now occupied by a series of commercial buildings including the Wisconsin Physicians Service office building. The site of the Archaic Indian village lay between the Wisconsin Physicians Service office building and the Yahara River. Articles on this site include David A. Baerrais' "The Airport Village Site, Dane County, Wisconsin," *The Wisconsin Archeologist,* 34, no. 3 (September 1953), and a University of Wisconsin bachelors honors thesis by David Huelsbeck, "Salvage and Test Excavation of the Airport Site" (1974). Descriptions of late Paleo-Indian sites in the Madison area include Philip H. Salkin and Thomas E. Emerson, "An Archeological Survey of Phase I of the Dane County E-Way Project," on file at the State Historical Society of Wisconsin, and Robert Nero, "Surface Indications of Possible Early Archaic Camp Site in Wisconsin," *The Wisconsin Archeologist* 36, no. 4 (1955), pp. 128–146.

21. Madison area sites where copper implements have been found include the Outlet and the Dividing Ridge. See C. E. Brown, *Lake Monona* (1922), p. 152, and *Lake Wingra* (1915), p. 89, for two examples.

22. Artifacts diagnostic of the Archaic stage have been found at such sites as Six Mile Creek. See Robert F. Maher in "Six Mile Creek—A Non-Pottery Site on Lake Mendota," *The Wisconsin Archeologist* 40, no. 1 (March 1959).

For a good general treatment of the Archaic period, see Willey, pp. 60–64.

23. For a general treatment of the Woodland culture, see Jennings, pp. 201–265.

24. See David Baerrais, "Early Salvage Excavations in the Madison Area, Dane County, Wisconsin," *The Wisconsin Archeologist,* 47, no. 3 (September 1966), p. 128. Baerrais was referring to the period between 500 B.C. and A.D. 500 with his "flourishing" remark, however, other evidence shows that the Madison area continued to be popular into the historic period.

25. Artifacts diagnostic of Early Woodland period are available from the Airport Village site cited above and perhaps from the "Outlet site." For details on the Outlet site, see Charlotte T. Bakken, "Preliminary Investigations at the Outlet Site," *The Wisconsin Archeologist* 38, no. 1 (1957), pp. 43–70. Also, Philip H. Salkin (U.W.-Whitewater) excavated a site near Lake Waubesa, which he described as "having a large early Woodland component."

The Indian culture centered along the Illinois-Ohio border, which flourished between 300 B.C. and A.D. 400 is known as Hopewellian and occupies the Middle Woodland period.

Artifacts and practices associated with Hopewellian culture have been found at several Madison sites including Frost Woods, Black Hawk Village, Borcher's Beach site, the Burton site, Magnus Swenson site, and the Burkhart site. See Charlotte Bakken, "Preliminary Investigation at the Outlet Site," *The Wisconsin Archeologist* 31, no. 2 (June 1950); David Baerrais, "Black Hawk Village Site, Dane County, Wisconsin," *Journal of Iowa Archeological Society* 2, no. 4 (1953), and Baerrais, "Early Salvage Excavations."

The Hopewellian influence can also be surmised from rectangular burial fire pits found at the Burkhart site, excavated in 1973 by John Halsey but not yet reported in professional journals and on Dead Lake Ridge excavated in 1874 by local investigators. See the article written by J. J. L. Nicodemus *et al.,* "Report of Committee on Exploration of Indian Mounds" in the *Transaction of the Academy of Science, Arts and Letters* 3, pp. 105–109. Both mounds were taller than later effigy mounds in the area, another Hopewellian indicator.

The seashells were found on the north shore of Lake Mendota near Camp Indianola (formerly known as Borchers Beach) and were described in an article by Charles E. Brown, "The Occurrence of Marine Shells at Indian Sites in Wisconsin," *The Wisconsin Archeologist* 12, no. 2 (1912), pp. 55–63. The type of shells found here are indigenous to the Gulf Coast. Another trade item that may have been associated with the Hopewellian was mica. Several mica flakes were found at the Burton site and described in David A. Baerreis' "The Early Salvage Excavations in the Madison Area, Dane County, Wisconsin," *The Wisconsin Archeologist* 47, no. 3 (September 1966), pp. 101–131.

26. The most authoritative sources for general background on the Effigy Mound tradition are William M. Hurley's *An Analysis of Effigy Mound Cultures in Wisconsin* (Ann Arbor, Mich.: University of Michigan, 1975), and Chandler W. Rowe's *The Effigy Mound Culture of Wisconsin* (Milwaukee: Milwaukee Public Museum, 1956). More concise popular treatments can be found in George I. Quimby, *Indian Life in the Upper Great Lakes,* (Chicago: University of Chicago Press, 1960) pp. 85–88, and Robert Ritzenthaler, *The Effigy Mound Builders in Wisconsin* (Milwaukee, Wisconsin: The Milwaukee Public Museum, 1969).

27. Examples of well-known nineteenth century national scholarship on Madison-area mounds include Stephen D. Peet, "Emblematic Mounds and Animal Effigies," in *Prehistoric America, Vol. II* (Chicago: American Antiquarian Office, 1890); F. W. Putnam, (Cambridge, Mass.: Harvard Peabody Museum, 1884); Joseph H. DeHart, "The Mounds and Osteology of the Mound Builders of Wisconsin," *Annual Report* (Washington, D.C.: Board of Regents of the Smithsonian Institution, 1877); and Increase Lapham, "Antiques of Wisconsin," *Smithsonian Contributions to Knowledge* (Washington, D.C.: Smithsonian Institution, 1854).

28. The ninety-eight percent figure came from Robert E. Ritzenthaler, *Prehistoric Indians of Wisconsin,* (Milwaukee, Wisconsin: Milwaukee Public Museum, 1970), p. 22. For the distributions of coded sites and the predominance of Dane County sites, see William M. Hurley, "Codification of Wisconsin Archeological Sites," *Wisconsin Archeologist* 46, no. 2 (June 1965), pp. 148–157. According to David Baerrais' "Early Salvage Excavations," p. 101, Charles E. Brown counted one thousand mounds in the Four Lakes area. In separate studies of mound groupings around the Madison lakes, Brown counted 350 mounds around Mendota, 170 around Monona, and 148 around Wingra. See respectively, *Lake Mendota Indian Legends* (Madison: 1933), p. 5; "Lake Monona," *Wisconsin Archeologist* 1, no. 4 (December 1922), p. 166; and "Lake Wingra," *Wisconsin Archeologist* 14, no. 3 (September 1915), p. 113.

29. See E. G. Dietz, D. A. Baerrais, and Robert Nero, "A Report on the Dietz Site (DA12), Dane County, Wisconsin," *The Wisconsin Archeologist* 37, no. 1 (March 1956). For summaries of subsequent research on lifestyles, see Quimby, Ritzenthaler, Rowe, and Hurley. Radio-carbon dates for the Dietz site come from "Wisconsin Radiocarbon Chronology: A Second Compilation," *The Wisconsin Archeologist* 58, no. 2, pp. 123–124. Another example of an effigy mound tradition village was the Blackhawk Village site. See David A. Baerrais, "Blackhawk Village site (DA 5), Dane County, Wisconsin," *Journal of the Iowa Archeological Society* 2, no. 4, pp. 5–20.

30. The story of the bear mound dedication is found recounted by Charles E. Brown, "Lake Wingra," *The Wisconsin Archeologist* 14, no. 3 (September 1915), p. 98. For theories on why effigy mounds were constructed, see Quimby, Ritzenthaler, Rowe, and Hurley. Perhaps the leading theory on the purpose of the mounds was formulated by Paul Radin in his article, "Some Aspects of Winnebago Archeology," *American Anthropologist* 13, no. 4 (1911), pp. 517–538.

31. Robert L. Hall, *The Archeology of Carcajou Point* 1 (Madison: University of Wisconsin Press, 1962), argues that the Winnebago may be descended from a group of farmer-hunter-gatherers, which archeologists call the Oneota Tradition. Carcajou Point is located on Lake Koshkonong and is one of the very few Oneota sites in the Four Lakes area. This site reflects a people who are undergoing a transition between the Woodland and Winnebago stages.

32. Zachary Gussow, *An Ethnological Report on the Historic Habitat of the Sauk, Fox, and Iowa Indians* (New York: Garland Publishing Inc., 1974). This is a reprint of a 1955 report of the Indian Claims Commission.

33. Descriptions of Winnebago villages can be found in Reuben I. Thwaites, "Narrative of Morgan L. Martin," *Wisconsin Historical Collections II* (1888), pp. 399–402; Brown, *Indian Legends,* and Brown "Lake Wingra," p. 116.

34. For more detail on Indian gardens, see Brown's "Lake Wingra," p. 116, and *Indian Legends.* For a reference on wild rice, see a manuscript written by Ira Hurlburt describing Madison Indians in 1839 and 1840 at the SHSW. The presence of wild rice may have been one of the reasons the Madison area was so attractive for so long.

35. See Hurlburt manuscript and Butterfield, pp. 426–27.

36. Now that the Madison area has been largely urbanized, the likelihood of finding additional sites is limited. Most "new" knowledge will probably come from the application of theories based upon evidence found elsewhere but applied to the Madison area.

For a more complete discussion of the limits of Madison archeological evidence, see David A. Baerrais, "Early Salvage Excavations."

37. About three hundred sites are listed in the Wisconsin Codified Site Files and there are many more described by early settlers' accounts that have never been formally noted by archeologists.

Preparing the Way: Traders, Soldiers, and Surveyors

1. Alice Smith, *From Exploration to Statehood* (Madison: State Historical Society of Wisconsin, 1973), offers excellent general background for this period. For a good discussion of the breakdown of tribal culture caused by the fur trade see Smith, p. 49, and George I. Quimby, *Indian Life,* pp. 146–157. Evidence for the presence of French fur traders in the eighteenth century is limited to several coins found in a Madison garden and a sword found by a boy who was excavating in the bear mound at Vilas circle. Both are open to interpretation. The coins dating back to 1764 are described in footnote #13. The sword story is found in Brown, "Lake Wingra," pp. 99–100.

2. Smith, *Exploration,* p. 22.

3. Ibid., p. 82.

4. Ibid., pp. 57–94.

5. Ibid., pp. 95–121. James D. Butler, in his article "Taycho-be-rah—The Four Lake Country—First White Footprints There," *Wisconsin Historical Collection* 10 (1883–5), p. 71, argues that the military contribution to the settlement of southern Wisconsin had been overlooked. A book that deals with this theme in greater detail and depth is Francis P. Prucha's *Broadaxe and Bayonet: The Role of the United States Army in the Development of the Northwest: 1815–1860* (Madison: State Historical Society, 1953).

6. William Kittle, *The History of the Township and Village of Mazomanie* (Madison: State Journal Printing Company, 1900), p. 58.

7. H. H. T. Jackson, *Mammals of Wisconsin* (Madison: University of Wisconsin Press, 1961). John Jacob Astor, in a letter dated February 14, 1815, to his lieutenant Ramsey Crooks, said he looked forward to a lucrative trade in muskrat pelts. See Smith, *Exploration,* p. 95.

8. Smith, *Exploration,* pp. 130–31.

9. Juliette Kinzie, *Wauban, The Early Days in the Northwest,* Centennial Edition (Menasha, Wisconsin: The National Society of Colonial Dames in Wisconsin, 1948), p. 102.

10. Durrie, p. 24; Butler, p. 76.

11. For information on Rasdall, see Durrie, pp. 24–25, Butler, p. 76, Consul Butterfield (ed.), *History of Dane County* (Chicago: Chicago Western Historical Company, 1880), p. 378, and C. B. Chapman, "Early Events in the Four Lake Country," *Wisconsin Historical Collections* 4 (1857), pp. 343ff.

12. For information on St. Cyr see C. E. Jones, Madison; Its Origins, Institutions and Attractions (Madison: W. J. Park and Co., 1876), p. 18, Butterfield, p. 367, and L. C. Draper, "Michael St. Cyr, An Early Dane County Pioneer," *Wisconsin Historical Collections* 11 (1869–72), pp. 397–400.

13. Durrie said Armel's trading shack was located near the corner of East Johnson and North Butler Streets. An article appearing in *WSJ,* April 26, 1880, however, described the discovery of six coins in the garden located at 23 East Johnson Street near the intersection with Wisconsin Avenue just east of the Methodist Church. Professor J. T. Butler, author of the article, believes the silver, gold and bronze coins may pinpoint the spot where Armel had his trading post. In his Taychoproh article, Butler speculates that the coins were lost by intoxicated soldiers. Butler suggests the older ones dated 1764 and 1771 were surely lost "long ago."

Although Butler does not speculate on this matter, the discovery raises the possibility that a trading post may have been in operation at the site long before Armel's shanty known to have begun by 1832. For general background on Oliver Armel, see Durrie, pp. 23–23, Chapman, p. 347, and Butler, pp. 59–60.

14. Butler, p. 70. Armel's trading shanty was also the site of Madison's first Fourth of July celebration. On that day in 1836, Armel invited seven Four Lakes area fur traders to a party. One man played the fiddle, everyone ate venison, fish, and pork and drank generous amounts of whiskey and coffee.

15. John DeLaRonde, "Personal Narrative," *Wisconsin Historical Collections* 7.

16. One of the few reminders of French presence in Madison is St. Cyr Street, just north of Pheasant Branch Creek, where the trader had his cabin.

Another group, the French *coureurs,* did not stay long in Madison after American settlement began. There were wilderness people whose livelihood was jeopardized by Indian land cessions, sawmills, roads, federal surveys, and farmers. However, the speed with which settlement occurred in the Madison area found several traders caught "behind the lines" of the rapidly moving American frontier.

By 1838 all the *coureurs* who had played bit parts in Madison's early settlement had gone west with the Indians, in most cases following them to their new but temporary hunting grounds in Iowa.

17. H. A. Tenney quoted in *Madison, Dane County and Surrounding Towns* . . . (Madison: Wm. J. Park & Co., 1877), pp. 539–540. According to Tenney, Brigham was a "warm personal friend of Doty" and "probably" was the one who told Doty about the site. Perhaps this explains why Doty made the overland trip in 1829. Brigham had at least two companions with him on the trip, but by the time Tenney wrote his article Brigham had forgotten their names. Eight years later at the Belmont session, Brigham was the only legislator who had actually seen the site of "Madison City."

18. Doty and his companions, Morgan L. Martin, an attorney from Green Bay, and Doty's cousin, Henry Baird, also a Green Bay attorney, thereby became the first Americans to make the trip between Green Bay and Prairie du Chien by land. See Reuben G. Thwaites, "Narrative of Morgan L. Martin," *Wisconsin Historical Collections* 11 (1888), pp. 399–402. The cousin relationship was mentioned in Smith, p. 69. See also Smith, p. 126, for additional facts about this trip.

19. P. L. Scanlan, "Military Record of Jefferson Davis in Wisconsin," *Wisconsin Magazine of History* 24 (December 1940), pp. 172–184.

20. Butler, p. 75.

21. The literature of the Black Hawk War is voluminous. One well-written and researched new account is Cecil Eby's *That Disgraceful Affair* (New York: W. W. Norton, 1973). Much of the background detail for this account is taken from this source. Details on the route followed by Black Hawk have been detailed in William T. Hagen's *Black Hawk's Route Through Wisconsin* (Madison: State Historical Society, 1949).

For specific details, Ellen M. Whitney's (ed.) *The Black Hawk War 1831–32* (Collections of the Illinois Historical Library) is always helpful. Reference to the number of U.S. soldiers who pursued Black Hawk through Dane County is found in vol. 2 in a letter from General Henry Atkinson to Gustavis Loomis dated July 27, 1832, pp. 888–89. Estimates of the number of Indians in Black Hawk's party vary from one to two thousand. A study done by Anthony F. C. Wallace, "Prelude to Disaster: The Course of Indian-White Relations which Lead to the Black Hawk War of 1832," in Ellen M. Whitney's (ed.) *The Black Hawk War*, Vol. 35, pp. 1–51, concludes that one thousand is closer to the truth.

22. Cecil Eby, *That Disgraceful Affair*, (New York: Norton, 1973), pp. 37–90.

23. Brown, *Lake Mendota*, pp. 6–7.

24. Eby, pp. 113 and 163.

25. Brigham's Diary quoted in Butterfield, p. 359.

26. Peter Parkinson, Jr., "Notes on the Black Hawk War," *Wisconsin Historical Collections* 10 (1888), p. 208.

27. J. Gillett Knapp, "Early Reminiscences of Madison," *Wisconsin Historical Collections* 6 (1867–1872), p. 371.)

28. Parkinson, p. 356 (Appendix).

29. Butterfield, p. 359.

30. *History of Grant County, Wisconsin* (Chicago, 1881), p. 431. The quotation comes from Dr. Addison Philleo.

31. Eby, pp. 239–40.

32. Eby, p. 17. Others place the deaths in the 250 range.

33. Charles C. Royce, *Indian Land Cessions in the United States,* (New York: Arno Press, 1971) p. 347.

34. Louise P. Kellogg, "The Removal of the Winnebago," *Transactions of the Wisconsin Academy of Science, Arts and Letters* 21 (1924).

35. Ibid.

36. Ibid.

37. Ibid.

38. Ibid.

39. The Lake Mendota figure comes from Brown, *Lake Mendota: Indian Landmarks and Early History* (Madison: The Wisconsin Archeological Society, 1933), p. 3. The Lake Monona figure comes from Brown, "Lake Monona," p. 126.

40. Kellogg, p. 27.

41. Smith, *Exploration*, p. 144.

42. Kellogg, p. 27.

43. This well-known remark comes from J. A. Wakefield's *History of the Black Hawk War* quoted in Durrie, p. 23.

44. Reuben Thwaites, *The Story of Madison, 1836–1900* (1973 Reprint Edition), p. 3.

45. One of the most interesting documents for students of Madison history are the field notes of the federal surveyors. Bound in tiny leather volumes and filed with the Board of Land Commissioners. The records provide a wealth of detail about plant communities, topography, soil and Indian features.

46. Doty's report on the recommended path of the Military Road is found in the *American State Papers, Vol. 5, Military Affairs,* pp. 512–513. For an account of Doty's work in securing passage of the $5000 Congressional appropriation, see Alice Smith's superb biography, *James Duane Doty: Frontier Promoter* (Madison: State Historical Society, 1954), pp. 126–127. See also Prucha.

Madison City Wins the Territorial Sweepstakes

1. Paul W. Gates, "Frontier Land Business in Wisconsin," *Wisconsin Magazine of History* 52, p. 306.

2. Doty's reason for buying the parcel may have been related to his long-standing scheme to build a canal between the Rock and Wisconsin Rivers via the Yahara. Some time in 1835 he laid out a town at the junction of the Yahara and Rock Rivers called Caramanee. In 1836 Doty laid out the City of the Four Lakes on the north shore of Lake Mendota and Wisconsinapolis on the Wisconsin River at the point where the canal would join the river. With these townsite cards in his hand, no one would benefit more from a Yahara Canal than Doty.

Tillou's Madison area purchase does not appear to be related to Doty's. Like Doty, Tillou was probably concentrating on sites of strategic importance such as dam and mill sites.

3. Smith, *Doty,* p. 195.

4. Smith, *Doty,* p. 195.

5. Ibid., p. 196.

6. Smith, *Exploration,* pp. 239–51.

7. Moses Strong, *History of the Territory of Wisconsin 1836–1848* (Madison: 1885), p. 228.

8. When Doty actually laid out Madison is not at all clear from the record. Most Madison historians base this part of the story upon John V. Suydam's unedited entry in Draper's article, entitled "Naming of Madison and Dane County" (*Wisconsin Historical Collections* 6, pp. 388–396). Written about thirty-five years after the event and laced with errors, there appear to be few accurate elements in Suydam's section. For example, Suydam claims he and Doty left Green Bay on November 2, 1836. Territorial papers and other accounts show they were both present in Belmont by that time! In a letter to Vanderpoel from Green Bay dated October 18, 1836, Doty says he will leave Green Bay in "two days." From this document a departure of October 20 may be surmised.

9. Suydam, p. 392.

10. Phillip Fox, unpublished history of the Brigham-Fox family (copy in the possession of the author).

11. *Journal of the Council of the First Legislative Assembly of Wisconsin,* pp. 45–47.

12. *Journal of the House of Representatives,* pp. 85–86.

13. Moses Strong, who was present at the session, said "Madison town lots in large numbers were freely distributed among members, their friends, and others who were supposed to possess influence with them" (Wisconsin Territory, p. 228). According to Alexander M. Thomson, *A Political History of Wisconsin* (Milwaukee: C. M. Casper Company, 1902), pp. 50–51, Doty may have offered Dodge deeds for several fine lots. This, said Thomson, was probably responsible for the long fierce Doty-Dodge feud.

The notion that *corner* lots were the real prize gained credence from a comment made by Suydam in his article cited above. "Many legislators," said Suydam, "went to their homes the owners of corner lots. . . .," p. 392.

14. Letter to Vanderpoel dated March 27, 1837. Doty said his competitors were "all disappointed and all unite to heap abuse upon the successful rival."

15. This sectional rivalry, so skillfully played by Doty was described in Joseph Schaefer's *The Wisconsin Lead Region* (Madison: SHSW, 1932), pp. 58–73.

16. Ibid. See also Smith, *Exploration,* p. 249. According to Taylor Hawking, "Before and After the Territorial Organization of Iowa," *Annals of Iowa* (January 1871), p. 452, each of the Des Moines County members went home with twelve to forty town lots.

17. Actually Doty might very well have named Madison for the former President's spouse, Dolly. Doty probably never met Madison, but, according to to Butler, p. 86, Doty "knew his widow very well and spoke of her, Madam Dolly, with so much love and admiration that he may be thought to have given Madison its name through a desire to do her honor."

18. The link between L'Enfant's Washington and Doty's Madison was Augustus B. Woodward, a brilliant, eccentric Detroit judge. Woodward owned property in Washington, D.C., when L'Enfant was laying out the Capital. There is some evidence that Woodward performed legal services for him. When Woodward arrived in Detroit just after the disastrous 1805 fire that almost totally destroyed the village, he was given the job of laying out the new Detroit. His plan made extensive use of the baroque radial street concept, but for a variety of reasons, Woodward's plan was formally abandoned in 1818, the year eighteen-year-old Doty arrived in Detroit. Thus, when Doty arrived the "old" Woodward plan may have been a topic of public discussion. Doty had the good fortune, or perhaps arranged to meet, the Michigan attorney general who offered him a law apprenticeship. Two months later he was admitted to the bar and joined the leading attorney in town as a partner.

As a result of his new position, Doty had the opportunity to hob nob with the most prominent people in Detroit, then a tiny village of about seven hundred persons. One with whom he had at least a professional and possibly a social relationship was Judge Woodward. For a time Doty was clerk of the supreme court in Michigan under Woodward. It seems probable that Doty had conversations with Woodward on town planning at this time if not earlier. (See Frank B. Woodford, *Mr. Jefferson's Disciple: A Life of Justice Woodward* (East Lansing, Mich.: Michigan State Press, 1953), Smith, *Doty*, pp. 3–45, and John Reps, *The Making of Urban America* (Princeton, New Jersey: Princeton University Press), pp. 263–275.

19. Doty's isthmus canal was not merely a decoration. It was a part of a grand canal scheme that was to link the Rock with the Wisconsin River. As noted earlier, Doty had been actively anticipating such a route for more than one year with other paper towns. While Doty was concentrating on laying out townsites along the Rock-Yahara route, he was also planning another canal at the Portage so that steamboats could go from the Wisconsin River directly into the Fox River and into the Great Lakes. (See Rudolf Smith's *Observations on the Wisconsin Territory* (Philadelphia: E. L. Carey & A. Hart Company, 1838), p. 194.) Governor Dodge in his inaugural address expressed confidence that the twelve-mile canal between the Yahara and the Rock Rivers was feasible and would be built soon.

20. Thomson, pp. 47–48.

21. Doty had visited Mineral Point, Portage, Helena, Belmont, Koshkongong, Prairie du Chien, and Dubuque. Doty either laid out or had a hand in laying out Fond du Lac, Astor (now Green Bay), Wisconsinapolis, City of the Four Lakes and Madison. The Frontier promoter may also have been in Platteville and Cassville.

22. Hawking, p. 452. According to W. F. Stark, *Ghost Towns of Wisconsin*, Belmont consisted of three lodging houses, one livery stable, one blacksmith's shop, and a half-finished legislative hall.

23. Lot sales were studied by Merle S. Pickford, "The Beginning of Madison, Wisconsin," (Master's thesis, University of Wisconsin, 1902), pp. 19–24 and Appendices A and B.

24. Based on author's analysis of lot sales using 1836 plat. If "choice" meant being on the lakeshore, another eighteen lots can be included in the legislator-purchased list, ten percent of the total number of lots purchased by legislators. It is also instructive to note that some fifty-three legislator-acquired lots (thirty percent of the total) were in marshy areas.

25. Doty wrote the names of lot buyers right on the original plat. It is presumed this is the map Doty had with him at Belmont. See also Smith, *Doty*, pp. 203–204.

26. John P. Bloom (ed.), *Territorial Papers of the U.S.*, Vol. 27, Terr. of Wis. Executive Journals, 1836–1848 and Papers 1836–1839, pp. 875–876.

27. The number of lots was determined from the original Doty plat. Doty also named a street in the plat in honor of Delegate Jones. The street was later changed to Francis Street.

28. *"Vanderpoel Correspondence,"* State Historical Society of Wisconsin.

29. Schaefer, p. 63.

30. Strong, p. 228.

31. The only study of lot sales at Belmont was done by Pickford, pp. 19–24 and Appendices A and B.

Pecks Lead the Way

1. Rosaline Peck, "Reminiscences of the First House and the First Resident Family of Madison," *Wisconsin Historical Collections* 11 (1869–72), p. 348. Interestingly, the gentleman from whom the Pecks purchased their lots for one hundred dollars each, had purchased them just nineteen days before for five dollars a piece. (See Pickford, Appendix B).

2. Peck, p. 349. Wood was assisted by two other *coureurs* named Pelikie and Lavec, who were wintering with a group of Winnebago at the Blue Mound.

3. Ibid.

4. Ibid., p. 350.

5. Ibid.

6. Ibid.

7. *Voyage Up the Minnie-Sotor* (London, 1847). The section of the book dealing with the Madison area was reprinted in "Featherstonaugh in Taychoprah," *Wisconsin Magazine of History* 45 (1961–62), pp. 173–185.

8. Rosaline's rebuttal was published in "Featherstonaugh in Taychoprah" cited above. It was originally published in the *Wisconsin Historical Collections* cited above.

9. Darwin Clark quoted in Butterfield, p. 673. See also I. H. Palmer quoted in Butterfield, p. 426 and William Woodcock quoted in Durrie, pp. 62–65. According to an account written by I. H. Palmer in the *WSJ*, July 13, 1874, all of the persons in capitol construction crews were strangers to one another, poor, and from eastern states.

10. Butterfield, p. 673.

11. Simeon Mills quoted in Butterfield, pp. 680–681.

12. Thwaites, p. 6. See also C. C. Jones, *Madison: Its Origins, Institutions and Attractions . . .* (Madison: William J. Park and Company, 1876), p. 34.

13. Franklin Hathaway, "Surveying in Wisconsin, 1837," *Wisconsin Historical Collections* 15 (1900), pp. 390–397. See also Jones, p. 50.

14. Laura Mae Sandrock, "Frontier Aspects of Early Madison" (Master's thesis, University of Wisconsin, 1919), p. 11.

15. Peck, p. 357.

16. Ibid., p. 358.

17. Durrie, p. 66.

18. Peck, p. 358.

19. Rosaline Peck quoted in Durrie, p. 84.

20. Peck, p. 359.

21. Hathaway, p. 395.

22. I. H. Palmer quoted in Butterfield, p. 426.

23. J. T. Kingston quoted in Durrie, p. 90.

Civilization, Such as It Is, Arrives

1. Willett Main Kempton, *Before Our Day in the Four Lakes Country* (Madison: 1936), p. 21.

2. See J. G. Knapp, "Early Reminiscences of Madison," *Wisconsin Historical Collection* 6, pp. 374–376, for a summary of hotel accommodations. Jones, *History of Madison*, pp. 37, 46–47, and 54–55, offers several additional details.

3. An incident revealing the room size of American hotel rooms is found in Elizabeth Baird, "Reminiscences of Life in Territorial Wisconsin," *Wisconsin Historical Collections* 15 (1900), pp. 256–257.

4. Kempton, p. 21.

5. Knapp, pp. 380 and 383.

6. *Madison Express*, March 14, 1840.

7. Alfred Brunson, *A Western Pioneer: Or, Incidents of the Life and Times of Rev. Alfred Brunson, Embracing a Period of Over Seventy Years* (Cincinnati, 1872–1879), p. 140. Brunson said the prevailing idea seemed to be to "get out of Uncle Sam while we can and let the state take care of itself. One mode of doing this was by appointing as many officers and clerks to the two houses as there were in Congress. This provided places for political friends who had favored and perhaps secured the election of the squandering majority."

There was at least one case of opium addiction. See Chapman quoted in Durrie, pp. 175–176.

8. J. T. Clark quoted in Durrie, p. 187.

9. Ebeneezer Childs, "Childs Recollections," *Wisconsin Historical Collections* 4 (1859) pp. 187–191.

10. Ibid.

11. Announcement that the capitol had been finished appeared in the *Madison Express,* December 5, 1844. For a general account of the capitol scandal, see Alice Smith's *Doty,* pp. 217–218 and 234–237, and Smith's *History of Wisconsin,* pp. 321–322. References to the leaky roof are found in the *Wisconsin Enquirer,* June 15, 1843, and in Robert Lansing quoted in Durrie, p. 155.

12. Knapp, pp. 385–387.

13. Durrie, p. 73.

14. *Wiskonsin Enquirer,* September 2, 1839.

15. C. C. Britt quoted in Durrie, p. 142.

16. This story is told by Simeon Mills in Butterfield, pp. 416–417.

17. Lois M. Craig, *The Role of the Missionary on the Wisconsin Frontier, 1825–1840* (Master's thesis, University of Wisconsin, 1949).

18. *Fifty Years of Church Work: 1840–1890. Fiftieth Anniversary of the First Congregational Church* (Madison: 1890), pp. 9–12.

19. Reverend Gilbert H. Doane, *Grace Episcopal Church: A History of the Parish Commemorating the Centennial Anniversary of the First Service Held in Grace Church* (Madison: Democrat Printing Company, 1958), pp. 11–17.

20. See *Fifty Years of Church Work,* p. 9; George E. Kelsey, *A Century History of the First Methodist Episcopal Church* (Madison, 1937), p. 17; *St. Raphael Souvenir 1848–1903* (Madison, 1903); Doane; and Peter Leo Johnson, *Stuffed Saddlebags: The Life of Martin Kundige, Priest, 1805–1879* (Milwaukee, 1892), p. 224.

21. *Fifty Years of Church Work,* p. 14.

22. Ibid., p. 37.

23. Doane, p. 14.

24. *Fifty Years of Church Work,* p. 12.

25. Ibid.

26. Reuben G. Thwaites, *Historical Sketch of the Public Schools of Madison, Wisconsin* (Madison: Cantwell Printers, 1886), pp. 12–14.

27. Ibid., pp. 15–17.

28. Ibid., pp. 19–21.

29. David Atwood, "The Dane County Press," *Proceedings of the Wisconsin Editorial Convention* (1865), pp. 41–43. See also Butterfield, pp. 589–607.

30. Ibid.

31. A typewritten copy of this September 16, 1837, article is available in the MSS collection of the SHSW.

32. Bishop Jackson Kemper, "A Trip Through Wisconsin in 1838," *Wisconsin Magazine of History* 8 (1877–79), pp. 431–433.

33. Doty letter to Vanderpoel, December 19, 1838.

34. *Madison Express,* August 22, 1840.

35. Tom Benson, Ph.D. dissertation draft, Chapter III, p. 8.

36. Vanderpoel letter, December 19, 1838.

37. Jones, p. 156.

38. Pickford, pp. 29–30.

39. Ibid.

40. For a summary of these transactions see Smith's *Doty,* pp. 219–227, and Keyes, pp. 59–61.

41. *Wisconsin Enquirer,* June 9, 1841.

42. J. M. Peck, *New Guide for Emigrants to the West* (1836), p. 365.

43. Joseph Hobbins, "Health in Wisconsin," in Butterfield, p. 245.

44. Tenney quoted in Durrie, p. 162.

45. Hobbins, p. 245, and R. L. Ream quoted in Durrie, p. 111, and Jones, p. 60.

46. When Eban Peck went blind from inflammation of the eyes he had to go to Fort Winnebago to be treated.

47. Simeon Mills quoted in Butterfield, p. 681.

48. William Woodcock quoted in Durrie, p. 64.

49. Ream quoted in Durrie, p. 105.

50. The hunter story comes from Anonymous, A Merry Briton in Pioneer Wisconsin (Reprinted 1950, SHSW), p. 19. The bishop story is described in Kemper, pp. 431–433.

51. Ream, p. 119.

52. Ibid., p. 120. See also Butterfield, pp. 399–400 and Ira Hurlbert, "Madison Indians in 1839 and 1840" (SHSW).

53. Butterfield, p. 406.

54. Ream, p. 119.

55. H. A. Tenney quoted in Durrie, p. 164; *Wisconsin Argus,* October 31, 1844; George Stoner in an address to the Wisconsin Pioneers (*WSJ,* June 18, 1885) described how prairie fires "swept over the hills around Madison leaving them as clean as a new mown lawn" in the later 1830s.

Another early arrival in Madison told how "prairie fires coming down over the distant hills, on all sides toward the lakes afforded a spectacle for which one could dispense with all the circuses and fat women shows that will ever be sent wandering among us. Twice we witnessed these fires cross the marshes through the woods over the University Hill, and up through the town on the lower ground back of the city hall, firing the marshes on either side as they advanced. Indeed, J. T. Clark, esq. had the timber for his old house twice burnt by these fires before he got it up and . . . made a clearing about it." (*WSJ,* February 4, 1870).

56. Ebeneezer Brigham quoted in Durrie, p. 115.

57. *Wisconsin Enquirer,* April 6, 1839. The territorial papers show that Governor Dodge sent at least two letters in 1838 to Washington officials urging them to do something about the Indian problem. In a letter dated May 23, 1838, Governor Dodge said that eight or ten Indian lodges were camped about the City of the Four Lakes. "I am expecting every day to hear when they have either killed my cattle or stolen my horses" (Vol. 27, *Territorial Papers,*

pp. 1003–1004). On August 16, 1838, Dodge wrote the Superintendent of Indian Affairs for the Wisconsin Territory on behalf of the citizens of Madison. "They complain loudly," he said, "of depredations committed by Winnebago Indians on their property. A short time since these Indians stole two valuable horses within seven or eight miles of my (Dodge's) residence. They were pursued by nineteen riflemen but not overtaken, and the Indians made their escape with the horses" (*Territorial Papers,* Vol. 27, p. 1056).

58. Durrie, p. 149.

59. Reverend Alfred Brunson quoted in Durrie, p. 135.

60. H. A. Tenney quoted in Durrie, p. 161.

61. The prices of eggs, oats, potatoes, and butter comes from the *Wisconsin Enquirer,* May 25, 1839; the price of board, nails, and candles from Jones, 157.

62. Ream quoted in Durrie, p. 111.

63. Ibid., p. 116.

64. *Wiskonsin Enquirer,* May 5, 1841.

65. *Wiskonsin Enquirer,* September 29, 1842.

66. *Wiskonsin Enquirer,* September 1, 1842.

67. Calvin J. Smith, *Western Tourist and Emigrant's Guide* (1839), pp. 166–167.

68. Smith, *Observations* pp. 55–56.

69. *Wiskonsin Enquirer,* July 29, 1840.

70. *Madison City Express,* July 27, 1843.

71. *Wiskonsin Enquirer,* February 18, 1842.

72. *Madison City Express,* March 21, 1844.

73. Mills quoted in Butterfield, pp. 427–428.

74. Ebeneezer Brigham quoted in Butler, p. 73.

75. Jerome R. Brigham quoted in Thwaites, *Story of Madison,* p. 9.

76. See C. B. Chapman quoted in Durrie, pp. 170–172, and H. A. Tenney quoted in Durrie, p. 161, for descriptions of the Capital Hill, Mansion Hill, and University Hill. For a description of vegetation on Third and Fourth Lake Ridges, see Hathaway, p. 395.

77. For comments on the underbrush descriptions see Jerome R. Brigham quoted in Thwaites, p. 9; Ebeneezer Brigham quoted in Butler, p. 73; and Hathaway, p. 395.

78. Thwaites, *Story of Madison,* p. 29.

79. *WSJ,* April 28, 1927.

80. Elisha Keyes, *History,* p. 90.

81. See section on Black Hawk War for a soldier's description of this area.

82. Marsh acreage was calculated from settlement patterns shown on the 1855 Harrison and 1872 Taylor maps. The dimensions of the great east marsh were outlined in the *CCP,* November 21, 1871, in connection with a drainage scheme.

83. J. T. Clark quoted in Durrie, p. 183. The marsh hay reference comes from William N. Seymour, *Madison Directory* (1855), p. 10.

84. Ibid.

85. The *Village Proceedings* contain similar fascinating topographical information.

86. *WSJ*, March 29, 1873, quoting Master Archie Durrie.

87. *WSJ*, February 20, 1900. See also Surveyor Field Notes cited earlier.

88. Thwaites, *Story of Madison*, p. 9. Some early descriptions claim the red cedar grew all around the lakeshore, but this is highly unlikely. Red cedar tend to flourish in rocky soils and steep topography and must be protected from prairie fires. The only parts of Madison offering those characteristics would have been the Maple Bluff and Elmside shorelines.

89. H. A. Tenney quoted in Durrie, p. 163.

90. Ibid.

91. George Stoner, quoted in the *Wisconsin State Journal*, June 6–7, 1895.

92. Peck, p. 354.

93. *Wiskonsin Enquirer*, June 15, 1843.

94. *Madison Express*, September 15, 1844.

95. H. A. Tenney quoted in Durrie, p. 163. In 1849 Winnebago Indians camping near the present day Mendota Hospital fanned out over the countryside north of the lake and drove the deer toward their camp where they were killed. When the "carnage" was over five hundred carcasses had been collected. (Tenney, p. 163.) According to George Stoner (*WSJ*, June 6–7, 1895), wolves would drive deer over the precipice at Maple Bluff where they would fall to their death on the rocks or ice below.

96. Simeon Mills quoted in Butterfield, p. 680.

97. "Darwin Clark Papers" (SHSW).

98. H. A. Tenney quoted in Durrie, pp. 160–161.

99. *MD*, October 29, 1878.

100. Mills quoted in Butterfield, p. 428.

101. Ibid.

102. Ibid.

103. H. A. Tenney quoted in Butterfield, pp. 161–162.

104. Ibid, p. 163.

105. Ibid, p. 164.

106. Butterfield, p. 428.

107. Durrie, p. 75.

108. Ibid, p. 74.

109. Ibid, p. 53.

110. Butterfield, pp. 519–20.

111. Durrie, p. 102.

112. Smith, *Doty*, p. 35.

113. Durrie, p. 97.

114. Butterfield, p. 521.

115. Charles Dickens, *American Notes* (Gloucester, Massachusetts: Peter Smith Reprint, 1968), pp. 268–274. This incident was one of many that helped foster the "wild west" image of the American frontier. For additional background on this event, see Smith, *History of Wisconsin*, p. 353.

116. *Madison Express*, July 7, 1841, and *Wiskonsin Enquirer*, December 14, 1839.

117. *Wisconsin Express*, September 14, 1843.

118. George Stoner Recollections, *WSJ*, June 18, 1885.

119. Ibid.

120. Stoner Recollections, *WSJ*, April 7, 1897.

121. *Merry Briton*, p. 18.

122. Stoner, *WSJ*, April 7, 1897.

123. Catlin quoted in Butterfield, p. 422.

124. Durrie, p. 82.

125. Walter H. Ebbing, "Wisconsin Territorial and State Census," *Transactions of the Wisconsin Academy of Sciences, Arts and Letters*, 55 (1966), p. 48. Rosaline's account (Durrie, p. 43) suggests there were about nine women available as dancers. Assuming a total population of about thirty-five, and the presence of about twelve women—Madison's population fell slightly below the 3:1 ratio elsewhere in the territory.

126. Durrie, p. 82.

127. Stoner Recollections, *WSJ*, June 18, 1885. In this account Stoner recalls the story of how he fell in love with an Indian girl.

128. *Darwin Clark Papers* (SHSW) and the *Wiskonsin Enquirer*, March 4, 1840.

129. Dane County was organized in 1839; between 1836 and 1839 the Madison area was a part of Milwaukee County. For a summary of early Dane County Commissioner actions, see Butterfield, pp. 401–408.

130. *Wisconsin Express*, March 4, 1845.

131. Ibid.

132. See *Charter and Ordinances of the Village of Madison* (Tenney and Carpenter, Printers, 1851).

Chapter 2

Introduction

1. According to one delightful account prairie racers were tall, lean, bristly pigs that were allowed to fend for themselves by their owners. They were said to be so lean that fat had to be added to fry their meat. "That the beast was troublesome is attested by the efforts of pioneers to construct a satisfactory hog-tight fence. And even when (farmers) had it . . . these hogs would put their head through between the second and third rails and root up three rows of potatoes in the adjoining field. . . ." They matured very late, were unconscionable food wasters, and their flesh at best was only tolerable. See Joseph Schaefer, *A History of Agriculture in Wisconsin* (Madison Wisconsin, 1922), pp. 71 and 126–27.

2. Population data sources.

The Farwell Boom

1. See *Dane County Register of Deeds* 7, p. 67.

2. Two publications containing the Farwell flourish are *Statistics of Madison and Dane County with a Business Directory for the Village of Madison* (Madison: Tenney and Carpenter, Printers, 1851) and Lyman Draper's *Madison, The Capital of Wisconsin, Its Growth, Progress, Condition, Wants and Capabilities* (Madison: Conklin and Proudfit Printers, 1857).

Farwell's success in attracting German emigrants was so great that the two Catholic churches in town had to reorganize along nationality lines, with St. Raphael's designated for the Irish and Holy Redeemer for the Germans. See Kate E. Levi's "Geographical Origin of German Immigrants," *Wisconsin Historical Collections* 14 (Madison, Wisconsin, 1898), p. 371.

3. One particularly interesting product of this technique was Dr. J. B. Bowen, a successful physician, prominent businessman and mayor (1871). (*WSJ*, September 12, 1881.)

Another prominent Madisonian who was persuaded to come to Madison by Farwell was John Rodermund, owner of a large local brewery just west of Farwell's Model Mills near the present site of the CUNA Filene House. (*WSJ*, June 23, 1875.)

4. *WSJ*, April 5, 1855. One can speculate that Greeley may have come to Madison in part because he was a "school chum" of David Atwood, the editor of the *Wisconsin State Journal*. According to Atwood's obituary (*WSJ*, December 12, 1889) Greeley and Atwood were "warm friends from the start and maintained a cordial intimacy throughout Greeley's life."

5. See Frederick G. Cassidy's "The Naming of the Four Lakes," *Wisconsin Magazine of History* 29 (Madison: 1945–46), pp. 7–24. All the Indian names were selected for their euphonic, rhythmic characteristics and not because they were actually used by the Indians. Subsequent research by Charles Brown, a local expert, revealed that each of the "Four Lakes" had Winnebago names. They were:

Name of Lake	Winnebago Designation	Meaning
Mendota	Wonk-sheck-ho-mik-la	Where the Indian Lies
Monona	Tchee-ha-be-ke-xa	Tepee Lake
Waubesa	Sa-hoo-cha-te-la	Rushes Lake
Kegonsa	Na-sa-koo-cha-te-la	Maple Grove Lake

Together the Four Lakes were known to the Winnebago as "Taychoprah" (emphasis is on the second syllable). "Tay" meant "lakes," "chope" meant "four," and "rah" the definite article for "the." Nowhere else were there four sizeable lakes in an otherwise lakeless area. For this reason the definite article in *the* four lakes is significant.

6. See Proceedings of the Board of Trustees of the Village of Madison dated July 6, 1846, and February 19, 1847.

7. Other men including some of great ability had tried and failed, prompting skeptics to conclude that water power would never be developed.

8. This unpublished study is in the possession of the author.

9. *Weekly Wisconsin Argus,* January 12, 1849.

10. John Y. Smith, "History of Madison," *Madison City Directory* (Madison, 1866), pp. 22–23.

11. *Wisconsin Express,* February 26, 1850.

12. Durrie, p. 220.

13. Alexander M. Thomson, *A Political History of Wisconsin* (Milwaukee, Wisconsin: C. M. Caspar Company, 1902), p. 77.

14. Ibid., p. 79.

15. *Daily Argus and Democrat,* September 15, 1852. See also Daniel S. Durrie, *A History of Madison, The Capital of Wisconsin: Including the Four Lake Country to July, 1874* (Madison: Atwood and Culver Printers, 1874), p. 229.

16. Durrie, pp. 228, 243.

17. Ibid, p. 245. See also the *Dictionary of Wisconsin Biography* (SHSW), p. 128.

18. *Wisconsin Express,* May 22, 1851.

19. Just how difficult it was to get to Madison from the East prior to the arrival of the railroad was described in a letter from Charles Vilas, brother of Levi Vilas, dated April 27, 1853. "The hardest part and perhaps the most dangerous part I found to be from Whitewater to Madison by stage—a distance of only 42 miles. The road is most of the way about as nature made it—some of the road very dangerous to travel in the night or any other time. . . . The last seven or eight miles we had to perform after dark with no moon and clouds with nine passengers in a four horse coach. But a good team and driver got us there with only a few disturbances." (See the papers of Levi Baker Vilas, Microforms Room, SHSW).

20. *Wisconsin Express,* December 4, 1849.

21. Catlin's letter was included in the Proceedings of the Board of Trustees of the Village of Madison, dated February 11, 1853. Six months after giving the Milwaukee and Mississippi valuable village concessions, the village trustees passed a similar nearly carte blanche resolution for the Beloit and Madison Railroad Company.

22. A ten-year-old boy who was on the train from Milwaukee told a *Wisconsin State Journal* reporter about the trip (see the *WSJ,* June 1, 1924). "The Madison folks set tables clear across the Capitol Park along Main Street and everybody was welcome to eat all they could. There was roast chicken, roast duck and everything that went with it. There were young steers and other animals barbecued in the park. Folks who wanted something to drink could get all they wanted at the best tavern just off the Square."

23. Smith, p. 24, notes that 350 private dwellings were erected in 1854. Data for 1853 or 1852 are not available, but in 1851 only 180 homes were erected.

24. Consul Butterfield (ed.), *History of Dane County* (Chicago: Chicago Western Historical Company, 1880), p. 608. See also *WSJ,* July 25, 1900.

25. *WSJ,* June 15, 1854.

26. These soil boring data are available from a number of local engineering firms.

27. Baltzell, letter dated November 28, 1851.

28. Mrs. John Robinson, Family Papers, May 25, 1854-May 12, 1857 (SHSW).

29. *Daily Argus,* April 28, 1857.

30. Reuben G. Thwaites, *History of the Public Schools of Madison, Wisconsin* (Madison: Cantwell Printers, 1886), p. 39.

31. *WSJ,* May 19, 1853.

32. Elisha Keyes (ed.), *History of Dane County* (Madison: Western Historical Association, 1906), p. 263.

33. The scheduling problem was described in Rev. Gilbert H. Doane's *Grace Church: A History of the Parish Commemorating the Centennial Anniversary of the First Service Held in Grace Church* (Madison: Democrat Printing Company, 1958), p. 22. Source of the "Madison Idol" comment was *Fifty Years of Church Work: 1840–1890: Fiftieth Anniversary of the First Congregational Church* (Madison: 1890), p. 15.

Other sources used for this section were George E. Kelsey's *A Century History of the First Methodist Episcopal Church, Madison, Wisconsin* (Madison: 1937), Daniel Durrie's *Twenty-Fifth Anniversary of the Organization of the Presbyterian Church of Madison, Wisconsin, October 4, 1867* (Madison: 1876) and *St. Raphael Cathedral, Souvenir, 1848–1903* (Madison: 1903). The imperative to build was based to a large degree upon the assumption that shabby church buildings would jeopardize village growth. For this reason editorials of the era commonly referred to this church or that as a "disgrace" or as a "burning shame." (*Wisconsin Express,* June 25, 1850 and *Wisconsin State Journal,* February 25, 1853.)

34. *Wisconsin Argus,* December 7, 1847, May 9, 1848, October 31, 1848; *Wisconsin Express,* June 25, 1850; *Daily Argus and Democrat* November 5, 1853 and the *WSJ,* August 23, 1855.

35. *Wisconsin Daily Democrat,* May 1, 1852.

36. See data provided by Tom Benson for a forthcoming U.W. Ph.D. dissertation.

37. *WSJ,* April 9, 1853. A similar account of Madison's future as a resort was printed in the *Knickerbocker Magazine* (September, 1855) and reprinted in part in the *Daily Patriot,* August 7, 1856. Said author Professor Nobel Butler: "Madison is destined to be a resort for those who wish to retire from the turmoil of business. . . . Those to whom the bustle of Newport and Saratoga gives no recreation, will be delighted to come to such a place as this."

38. References to the steamboat is found in the *WSJ,* April 24, 1854, and July 29, 1854. Apparently the Mendota trade was not too good because in the following year the boat was moved to Monona where it stayed. (See the *Wisconsin State Journal,* July 3, 1855.)

While all contemporary accounts describe lake fishing as excellent, Leonard Farwell, tried to make it even better by introducing both whitefish and brook trout. For years the popular whitefish did quite well, but the trout did not—victims no doubt of marauding pickerel. (See the *WSJ,* May 8, 1874.)

39. *WSJ,* April 28, 1856.

40. C. E. Jones, *Madison, Its Origins, Institutions and Attractions, Persons, Places and Events Graphically Delineated; A Reliable Guide for the Tourist* (Madison: Wm. J. Park and Company, 1876), p. 165.

41. *Daily Democrat,* August 16, 1854. The Crimean War caused wheat to increase in value from thirty-one cents a bushel in May, 1854 to $1.70 per bushel in May, 1855. Few Dane County farmers raised anything but wheat. Prairie land suitable for wheat raising went for as high as twenty dollars an acre so eager were farmers and others to participate in the wheat bonanza. (See Keyes, p. 275.)

42. *WSJ,* May 31, 1856.

43. *Daily Democrat,* October 17, 1855.

44. *Daily Democrat,* May 21, 1855.

45. *Argus and Democrat,* May 7, 1856.

46. *Wisconsin Express,* January 16, 1849.

47. *Daily Democrat,* May 18, 1855.

48. *WSJ,* July 12, 1855.

49. Lyman Draper, p. 16.

Growth Pains: Problems Amidst Prosperity

1. *WSJ,* December 17, 1853.

2. See Reuben Gold Thwaites, *Historical Sketch of Public Schools of Madison, Wisconsin* (Madison: M. J. Cantwell, Printer, 1886), pp. 37–39; the *WSJ,* February 4, 1856; and *Board of Education of the Village of Madison Annual Report,* 1855.

3. Ibid.

4. Thwaites, p. 39.

5. Ibid., p. 34.

6. *WSJ,* December 17, 1853.

7. Ibid.

8. *Daily Argus and Democrat,* December 22, 1852.

9. See Thwaites, *Public Schools,* p. 38.

10. Durrie, p. 170.

11. After 1852 the method of laying out new streets was standardized. Seven "highway districts" were formed in the village under the direction of the Committee on Streets. Upon receiving a petition from property owners "praying" for the opening of certain streets, the trustees, with the recommendation of the Committee on Streets, would direct the village surveyor to lay out the street. From that point on, the actual work of opening the street was left to the citizens themselves. Under the village charter, every male between twenty-one and fifty-five years of age who was not a member of a fire com-

pany was obligated to either work in the streets for one day each year or pay one dollar. Men didn't always show up for work and when they did, they didn't work very hard. Moreover, they did not have good supervision and direction. While good in theory, the system was widely regarded as a "farce."

12. *Statistics of Madison and Dane County with a Business Directory of the Village of Madison* (Madison: Tenney and Carpenter Printers, 1851), p. 7.

13. *Daily Democrat,* May 26, 1855.

14. *Argus and Democrat,* August 2, 1856.

15. *Daily Argus and Democrat,* November 17, 1853.

16. See 1855 Proceedings of the Village Board of Trustees and Elmore Elver's *Financial History of the Village of Madison* (unpublished Master's thesis, University of Wisconsin, 1898).

17. *Wisconsin Argus,* May 11, 1847.

18. See Proceedings of the Village Board, August 6, 1847.

19. *Daily Argus and Democrat,* July 28, 1852. Two excellent articles on malaria and cholera in early Wisconsin were written by Peter T. Harstad and appeared in Vol. 43 (1958–9) of the *Wisconsin Magazine of History.* See "Sickness and Disease on the Wisconsin Frontier: Malaria," pp. 83–97. Dr. Joseph Hobbins penned a brief description of epidemics in Butterfield's *History of Dane County* (1880), p. 245. Like most early descriptions, it glosses over some epidemics.

20. See *Wisconsin Express,* August 28, 1849, and Proceedings of the Village Board during the spring and summer of 1850. On June 3, 1850, the Board of Trustees passed a resolution saying that the health of the village would be promoted by the draining of the marsh or pond southwest of the Capital Square, between King and Morris (Main) Street.

21. *Daily Argus and Democrat,* August 3, 1852.

22. *WSJ,* July 14, 1854. The quarantine house was established "across Lake Monona at a point known as Hoboken." This article reveals that immigrants were a particularly disconcerting problem. "There has been considerable sickness among the German and Norwegian immigrants who have arrived here of late. Several have died at the depot. Strangers in a strange land, poor and homeless, theirs is a sad and pitiable condition."

23. An ordinance dated April 12, 1853, gave the village trustees power to close slaughter houses in just six days. In the summer of 1854 a pond in Block 8 of the University Addition was drained because it was a "health hazard." The pond was at the intersection of State and Lake Streets.

24. See the *WSJ,* November 25, 1853, and August 20, 1856. The problem was compounded by a dropping of the water table beginning 1852. From that time forward, it was necessary to go down sixty to eighty feet, that is, below lake level to be sure of a flowing well.

25. *Daily Argus,* June 17, 1854. Immediately after the 1849 epidemic, one of the village mouthpieces wrote, "The usual good health of our town may be regarded as permanently restored (*AD,* August 10, 1852). A colleague agreed, ". . . in

every respect our citizens were never more healthy. Our doctors are at leisure, and our people are happy (*Wisconsin Express,* September 4, 1849).

26. *Wisconsin Argus,* April 17, 1849.

27. A variety of sources were used for this section including articles in the following papers: *Wisconsin Argus,* September 7, 1847; *Wisconsin Express,* April 17, 1849, and January 15, 1859; and *Daily Argus and Democrat,* September 6, 1853.

28. *Daily Argus and Democrat,* September 6, 1853.

29. The grave robbery incident appeared in the Fitch article cited above.

30. See Proceedings of the Village Board, April 6, 1846.

31. *Argus and Democrat,* April 17, 1856.

32. *WSJ,* May 11, 1853.

33. *WSJ,* November 27, 1853.

34. Sheep and milk cows were not part of animal control ordinances of the village period.

35. See Ordinance dated March 19, 1855.

36. See Ordinance dated March 12, 1855.

37. *Wisconsin Argus,* March 30, 1847. Joseph H. Hobbins, founder of the Madison Horticultural Society, said that in 1854 Madison had only six vegetable gardens and three flower gardens and that the streets were nearly without ornamental trees. (See *WSJ,* March 24, 1874.)

38. Ibid.

39. Ibid.

Village Society: Pluralism, Ruffianism, and Leisure

1. Demographic changes are interpolated from data provided by Richard Roe and from Merle S. Pickford, *The Beginnings of Madison, Wisconsin* (Master's Thesis, University of Wisconsin, 1902), pp. 33–34. Composition of the foreign population is derived from Jacob O. Stampen, *The Norwegian Element in Madison (1850–1900),* Master's thesis, University of Wisconsin, 1965), p. 28.

2. John R. Baltzell, letters dated April 17, 1852.

3. According to Elisha W. Keyes, p. 216, the first Republican convention held in Madison in September 1855, was "largely controlled by a secret political organization, known as the Know-Nothings, although masquerading under the name of Republican. . . ."

4. *WSJ,* June 14, 1853.

5. *WSJ,* May 29, 1854. The nativist dislike of Catholics was based in part upon the fact that by 1853 the Catholic Church had 100,000 members, easily the largest in the state. (See Robert C. Nesbit, *Wisconsin: A History* (Madison: The University of Wisconsin Press, 1973), p. 253.

6. *WSJ,* November 20, 1854.

7. For examples of foreign press involvement, see the *WSJ,* April 2, 1855, and Arlow W. Anderson, "Venturing Into Politics: The Norwegian American Press of the 1850's, "*Wisconsin Magazine of History* 32 (1948–9), p. 38 ff.

The purpose of the St. George Society was to give advice and relief to indigent English immigrants and also to commemorate the annual festival of St. George on the day set apart for that purpose by Englishmen in every part of the world. (See the *WSJ,* August 15, 1856.) The Turnverein provided a place where Germans could come together for gymnastics, singing and discussing social issues. (See Robert Wild, "Chapters on the History of Turners," *Wisconsin Magazine of History* 9 (1925–6), pp. 123–139.)

8. For a description of tactics used to get the Norwegian trade, see E. W. Keyes, p. 266.

The 1854 judgeship election was described in the *WSJ,* September 25, 1854. After the election a spirited victory celebration deteriorated into an old fashioned barroom brawl in which several men were stabbed. Just a few days later citizens gathered at the courthouse to demand that no alcoholic beverages be sold or given away on election day. While the idea was not immediately adopted, it was incorporated in the 1856 city charter.

9. Fredericka Bremer, *Homes in the New World: Impressions of America* (New York: Harper & Brothers, 1853), pp. 630–631.

As noted in the *Wisconsin Express* (October 30, 1847) the same opprobrium normally reserved for Germans was meted out to the governor, a supreme court justice and a few other cronies who on a particular Sabbath morning in 1849 were observed setting off in a boat with "a plentiful supply of excitants, guns and fishing gear." Said the *Express* editor: "It cannot be that good morals and religious inferences can prevail where the Sabbath is so openly violated. . . ."

10. Rev. W. E. Armitage, "The German Sunday," *Transactions of the Wisconsin Academy of Sciences, Arts, and Letters* 1 (Madison: Atwood and Culver, Printers, 1872), p. 68.

11. *Argus and Democrat,* June 2, 1852.

12. *Argus and Democrat,* May 28, 1853.

13. *Argus and Democrat,* June 2, 1852.

14. *Argus and Democrat,* August 14, 1854.

15. The event occurred in 1849 on King Street when a mob tried to hang a black barber for allegedly assaulting a white customer. The story was told by William J. Petherich and was published in the *Home Diary* (April, 1903), p. 9. Negroes were disenfranchised by the village charter. Part I, Section I of the document limited voting to "free and white males."

16. *Daily Democrat,* September 27, 1848.

17. Ibid.

18. *Daily Democrat,* November 2, 1854.

19. *WSJ,* June 5, 1856.

20. *Wisconsin Express,* July 3, 1851. *Argus and Democrat,* July 13, 1852.

21. *Wisconsin Express,* April 17, 1851.

22. John R. Baltzell, letter dated April 7, 1852.

23. *WSJ,* April 2, 1855.

24. Alice E. and Bettina Jackson, p. 9.

25. See Proceedings of the Village Board, 1853.

26. *Daily Democrat,* December 17, 1852.

27. Ibid.

28. *Wisconsin Express,* April 17, 1851.

29. John R. Baltzell, letter dated February 3, 1852.

30. *Argus and Democrat,* May 31, 1853.

31. *WSJ,* May 30, 1853.

32. *Wisconsin Express,* April 17, 1851.

33. *Wisconsin Argus and Democrat,* May 31, 1853.

34. *Wisconsin Daily Democrat,* March 8, 1852.

35. For good general background on this issue see Frank G. Byrnes' "Cold Water Crusade" (Master's thesis, University of Wisconsin, 1951). For details of the Madison situation see the *Wisconsin Democrat,* April 11, July 11, 1846, Proceedings April, 1846.

36. *Argus and Democrat,* August 2, 1856.

37. *Daily Democrat,* March 1, 1855.

38. *Argus and Democrat,* September 17, 1856.

39. F. Garvin Davenport and Lou Datye, "Practicing Medicine in Madison, 1855–1857: Alexander Schue's Letters to Robert Peters," *Wisconsin Magazine of History* (vol. 26, 1942–43), pp. 70–91.

40. *Daily Democrat,* June 5, 1855.

41. Jackson, p. 32.

42. *Daily Argus and Democrat,* July 24, 1854.

43. Ibid.

44. *WSJ,* July 6 and 14, 1856.

45. *WSJ,* December 15, 1854.

46. Davenport and Datye, p. 85.

47. Keyes, pp. 94–5. See also the *WSJ,* January 2, 1877, and December 31, 1878.

48. *WSJ,* May 9, 1855. For an outstanding treatment of Madison Institute, see Janet Ela's *Free and Public: One Hundred Years with the Madison Public Library* (Madison: Friends of Madison Public Library, 1975), Chapter 1, pp. 1–10.

49. Henry C. Youngerman, *Theatrical Activities: Madison, Wisconsin, 1836–1907* (Ph.D. dissertation, University of Wisconsin, 1940), p. 71 and passim; See also the *WSJ,* August 4, 1853.

50. Ibid., pp. 71–73.

51. Ibid., p. 188.

52. *WSJ,* February 15, 1853.

53. Ibid. Per the *Argus and Democrat,* July 14, 1856, the band concert may have been viewed as the closest summer equivalent of the lecture. In this article the band concert was viewed as "innocent" and a "sound public amusement."

A New Charter

1. Elver.

2. Some of these jurisdictional problems were relieved by an Act of the Legislature (Laws of Wisconsin, 1853, p. 452).

3. See Elver, *Argus and Democrat,* December 20, 1852, and Village Proceedings, November 22, 1852.

4. See Proceedings of the Village Board, November 6, 1852 and the *WSJ,* November 18, 1853.

5. Farwell served two terms as trustee, the first in 1851, the second in 1855.

Chapter 3

Great Western Expectations

1. *WSJ,* August 8, 1856.

2. *CCP,* April 6, 1857.

3. *DP,* December 17, 1856, and November 13–14, 1856. *WSJ,* August 20, 1856.

4. *CCP,* April 6, 1856.

5. Ibid.

6. Ibid., April 18, 1856.

7. Board of Education and Superintendent of the Public Schools of Madison, *First Annual Report,* 1855, p. 3.

8. *CCP,* April 7, 1856.

9. *Argus and Democrat,* May 1, 1856.

10. Common Council Committee on Finance, *Report of the Committee on Finance in Relation to the Bonded Debt and Financial Condition of Madison, Wisconsin,* Madison, Wis., 1860, p. 8.

11. *WSJ,* May 1, 1856; *Argus and Democrat,* May 3, 1856.

12. *Argus and Democrat,* May 1, 1856.

13. Nine aldermen were recorded as present at the meeting on May 16, 1856; however, only seven persons voted on the motion.

14. *DP,* November 26, 1856.

15. The possibility of getting the state to underwrite the costs was out of the question because of a state constitutional prohibition against internal improvements.

16. *Madison City Charter,* 1856, p. 19.

17. *Argus and Democrat,* March 6, 1856.

18. *WSJ,* March 7, 1859.

19. *CCP,* December 31, 1856.

20. *DP,* November 24, 1856.

21. *DP,* December 23, 1856.

22. Ibid., *DP,* December 31, 1856, January 10, 1857.

23. *WSJ,* January 12, 1857; *DP,* January 13, 1857.

24. *Madison City Charter,* Ordinance No. 34, 1860.

25. *WSJ,* February 5, 1857.

26. *DP,* April 21, 1857.

27. Ibid., November, 29, 1856.

28. Eric E. Lampard, *The Rise of the Dairy Industry in Wisconsin: A Study in Agricultural Change, 1820–1920* (Madison: The State Historical Society of Wisconsin, 1963), p. 364.

29. *Lippincott's* Magazine, May 1886.

30. Sam Ross, *The Empty Sleeve: A Biography of Lucius Fairchild* (Madison, 1964), pp. 7–21.

31. Madison businessmen who contributed to the Madison and Watertown stock purchase through the mortgage collateral program were included in a subscription list dated July 1856, in Box 66 of the Fairchild papers.

32. See the message printed on page 5 and passim in the 1857 *Senate Journal Appendix.*

33. Wisconsin Assembly, Committee on State Affairs, *Report,* 1857 *Assembly Journal,* p. 169.

34. See *Laws of 1857,* Chapter 26, p. 30.

35. The senate passed the bill on February 23, 1857. Yea votes numbered 22, but nay votes were not recorded. However since there were only members of the senate at the time, there could not have been more than no votes. (See the 1857 *Senate Journal,* p. 393.) The Assembly vote was 54–10. (1857 *Assembly Journal,* p. 569.) The *Milwaukee Sentinel* strongly supported the plan to keep the capital at its unequalled site in Madison. (*Milwaukee Sentinel,* Feb. 25, 1851.)

36. *CCP,* March 5, 1857.

37. Ibid., March 16, 1857.

38. See *CCP,* March 16, 1857. Each successive city loan required more stringent approvals than its predecessor. The $100,000 city loan required only Common Council approval; the railroad loan a referendum of all voters; and the $50,000 capital grant a referendum of property owners.

39. *Milwaukee Sentinel,* June 27, 1857, sec. 2, p. 2.

40. C. E. Jones. *Madison: Its Origins, Institutions and Attractions. Persons, Places and Events Graphically Delineated. A Reliable Guidebook for Tourists* (Madison: William J. Park and Company, 1876), p. 162.

41. *CCP,* April 6, 1857.

42. *WSJ,* July 23, 1856.

43. *CCP,* Jan. 3, 1857.

Disillusionment, Depression, and Reform

1. For articles from which the epithets were taken, see the *DP,* April 24, December 1, 30, and 31, 1857.

2. Details of Van Slyke's life can be found in the *Dane County Biographical Review* (Chicago, 1893), p. 466.

3. *CCP,* August 20, 1856.

4. Ibid.

5. Ibid.

6. *CCP,* September 5, 1856.

7. *CCP,* November 21, 1856.

8. Ibid.

9. *DP,* November 29, December 5, 1856.

10. *Argus and Democrat,* December 22, 1856.

11. Ibid.

12. *DP,* April 25, December 24, 1857.

13. *DP,* March 23, 1857.

14. Ibid.

15. *WSJ,* April 17, 1857.

16. The *Argus* plea was ridiculed in the *WSJ,* of May 9, 1857.

17. *WSJ,* June 11, 1857.

18. *DP,* March 2, 1857.

19. Ibid.

20. *WSJ,* May 22, 1857. On May 13, 1857, the *Journal* made reference to the "present hard times" caused by land speculation.

21. *DP,* July 3, 1857.

22. Ibid.

23. Ibid., June 19, 1856.

24. Ibid.

25. *WSJ,* September 12, 26, 28, and 29, 1857.

26. Ibid., Oct. 22, 1857.

27. Richard N. Current, *The Civil War Era,* The History of Wisconsin Vol. 2 (Madison, State Historical Society of Wisconsin, 1976), p. 237.

28. *WSJ,* November 19, 1857.

29. Still other legal notices appeared in the newspapers in 1858 and 1859. See the *WSJ,* February 9, 1858, November 19, 1859, and January, 1860.

30. Levi B. Vilas, letter dated March 13, 1859, Levi B. Vilas Papers, State Historical Society of Wisconsin, Madison. Some of course managed to glide through the depression without serious financial damage. One such man was Levi Vilas. When asked how he managed to be so tranquil in the depths of a depression, Vilas replied, "because he owed no one any money."

31. See the *WSJ,* September 28, 1859, and Jones, p. 159.

32. *DP,* September 28, 1857.

33. Ibid., December 1, 1857.

34. *WSJ,* October 8, 1857. This drop was between October, 1856, and October, 1857.

35. *Madison: Past and Present,* Wisconsin State Journal Semi-Centennial, 1852–1902 (Madison, 1902), p. 29.

36. *CCP,* April 19, 1860.

37. *Daily Patriot,* October 2, 1859. Several lawsuits against the former President of the line, Mayor Jairus P. Fairchild, were treated leniently in the court of his political ally, Judge Harlow S. Orton. Orton was further disposed to leniency in the settlement of these cases by the fact that Mayor Fairchild's son, Lucius, was Judge Orton's clerk at the time. (See Ross' Fairchild biography, p. 25.)

38. *WSJ,* December 6, 1859.

39. Ibid., November 25, 1857.

40. *DP,* April 30, 1859.

41. *WSJ,* May 12, 1857.

42. *CCP,* April 13, 1857.

43. *DP,* Dec. 29, 1858.

44. *WSJ,* February 23, 1858.

45. *CCP,* April 19, 1858.

46. Margaret Devlin Sennett, "History of Madison, 1850–1875" (Master's thesis, University of Wisconsin, 1918), p. 92.

47. *WSJ,* April 6, 1858.

48. The motion to disband the police force was made on Aug. 10, 1857.

49. Reuben G. Thwaites, *Historical Sketch of the Public Schools of Madison, Wisconsin* (M. J. Cantwell, Madison, 1886), p. 42.

50. *CCP,* April 28, 1860, and January 5, 1861.

51. *CCP,* June 30, 1860, and May 3, 1861; *DP,* Aug. 4, 1860.

52. *CCP,* May 24, 1858.

53. *DP,* December 10, 1860, and June 1, 1860.

54. This period was between June 1858 and March 1859, and comes from an unpublished analysis of ordinances prepared by the author. The Finance Committee even recommended less frequent meetings on the grounds that it would starve out . . . the large number of standing leeches who aim to live out of the taxpayers with little or no labor. . . ." (*CCP,* May 3, 1858).

55. According to one rule of thumb, western cities tended to have one voter for every seven people in presidential elections. In November 1856, 1,524 Madison voters turned out to vote for president. This would imply a population of 10,668. However, one must add to 1,524 a number of voting age adults who were not able to vote because they had not satisfied residency requirements and filed declarations to become citizens, etc. The *WSJ* (November 10, 1856) said this number should be at least 300 and this would produce a population of 12,768.

Another way of estimating population is to apply ratios to city directory census population data. For example, we know the 1855 city directory contained the names of 1,700 persons and that the state census of that year showed 8,664 persons to reside in Madison. Since the 1858 city directory contained the names of 2,200 persons, we can say the implied 1858 population is 11,212. Using the same technique, we can estimate

population by going from 1866 city directory and 1865 census data to 1858 population.

Thus, while the exact number of persons in Madison at its peak in 1857 cannot be known exactly, it seems like that population stood somewhere between 11 and 12,000 persons.

56. *WSJ,* December 21, 1857.

57. Except where noted in separate footnotes, these charges came from the *Taxpayers Committee Report* printed in the Wisconsin State Journal, December 29, 1857.

58. For example, in 1856 twenty thousand dollars had been made available to senior aldermen for street improvements, yet there was virtually no record of how the money was spent, where it was spent, or by whom. Aldermanic "courtesy" made discussion or justification unnecessary.

59. Alderman paid themselves for equalizing assessments, judging elections, and performing the services of street commissioners (*CCP,* December 16, 1857, and March 18, 1858). In some cases the council even passed resolutions specifying their pay rates for functions they were supposed to do for free.

60. One alderman voted for an appropriation that called for his law firm to do legal work for the city. Another voted to appoint himself as city weigher, for which he received half of the fees. The entire council voted funds to give themselves silver-headed canes as emoluments of office (*DP,* January 19, 1857). Even more blatant, of course, was the Van Slyke arrangement to keep city money in his bank, which he could loan out at interest, or Mayor Fairchild's voting one hundred thousand dollars of city credit to the Madison and Watertown Railroad while he was president of the line.

61. For example, Farwell's Mills, said to be worth twenty thousand dollars, were assessed at a modest five thousand dollars. The claim was made that half the personal property in the city was left out of the 1857 tax roll. For examples of unequal assessment stories, see the *WSJ,* December 29, 1856, and June 10, 21, and 25, 1858.

62. This Charter Amendment was published as chapter 4 in the *Private and Local Laws of 1858,* pp. 0–14.

63. Senior aldermen were still allowed to collect and spend the poll tax, amounting to one dollar a year from every resident over twenty-one years of age. The alternative was one day's work in the streets.

64. *CCP,* February 8, 1858.

65. Ibid. Gradually the council implemented additional, seemingly minor, yet very significant reforms. One step taken before the 1858 charter amendment was passed prohibited any money being spent which was not approved by the council *in advance* (*CCP,* August 24, 1857). In 1859 the council directed the city clerk to begin giving it a weekly report on all expenditures by each budgetary category so the policy makers knew where they stood in relation to budgeted amounts *CCP,* April 30, 1859).

66. *CCP,* April 17, 1861.

67. Ibid. April 5, 1862.

68. *CCP*, April 5, 1858.

69. Ibid.

70. Frederich Merk, *The Economic History of Wisconsin during the Civil War Decade* (Madison, Wisconsin: SHSW, 1916), p. 240.

71. *CCP*, April 26, 1858.

72. *CCP*, April 4, 1859.

73. This is based upon the amount of the tax they were able to withhold in a single year ($9,772) compared to the tax level in 1859 for local purposes of $39,360. (See *CCP*, April 4, 1859).

74. The plaintiffs alleged that the city had no power to issue bonds for general city purposes, that it was illegal to sell bonds at below par value as was the case with the city bonds, and to use bonds for current operating expenses. (See the written opinion of Judge Hood published in the *DP*, April 11, 1859.)

75. *DP*, April 11, 1859. The intensity of a "large proportion of Madison citizens determined to never pay a cent on bonds is described in a letter to a Massachusetts bondholder, Josiah L. Hale, dated Jan. 10, 1867. See SHSW Archives under Henry M. Lewis, the letter writer.

76. *WSJ*, July 11, 1860.

77. *CCP*, April 28, 1860.

78. Madison Common Council Committee on Finance, *Report of the Committee on Finance in Relation to the Bonded Debt and Financial Condition of Madison, Wisconsin* (Madison, Wis., 1860), pp. 1–12.

79. *CCP*, March 12, 1862. The state legislature passed an act on April 15, 1862 to authorize the compromise. See Chapter 322, Laws of 1862, p. 351.

80. There were some exceptions, but only minor and inconsequential ones. For example, Mayor Vilas urged the council to do something about the problem. See *WSJ*, January 7, 1862.

81. *CCP*, April 21, 1863.

82. Ibid., Sept. 18, 1863.

83. *CCP*, October 12, 1863. Under the terms of the agreement new bonds would be issued at a rate of seven percent for twenty years.

84. *CCP*, November 27, 1863.

85. State approval was needed before the final agreement was approved. This was done with Chapter 67, Laws of 1864.

86. The 99,000 reduction is accounted for as follows: $30,000 reduced from the city bonds, $66,000 from the railroad bonds and $3,000 from the cemetery bonds. Interest was reduced proportionately.

87. Henry M. Lewis to Josiah L. Hall, January 10, 1867, *Knight Papers*, State Historical Society of Wisconsin, Madison.

88. The Legislatively imposed prohibition on borrowing was by-passed only for a state fairgrounds improvement program in 1868 and again in 1871 for railroad stock acquisition. Not until 1893 did the city start bonding for waterworks, streets, sewers, etc.

89. Governor Randall to Legislature, February 26, 1858, *Assembly Journal*, 1858, p. 20.

90. Wisconsin Legislature, Committee on State Affairs, *Minority Report Relating to the Capitol Extension, Senate Journal Appendix*, 1858, p. 11.

91. Wisconsin Legislature, Committee on State Affairs, *Majority Report Relating to the Capitol Extension, Senate Journal Appendix*, 1858, pp. 3–4.

92. Ibid., p. 6.

93. See *Milwaukee Sentinel*, March 9 and 13, 1858.

94. Ibid., March 13, 1858.

95. *Assembly Journal*, 1858, pp. 1917–1919.

96. Ibid.

97. Laws of Wisconsin, 1858, Chapter 4, p. 10.

98. Committee on State Affairs, *Minority Report*, p. 15.

99. Quoted in the *Milwaukee Sentinel*, May 28, 1858.

100. *WSJ*, April 22, 1858.

101. *Milwaukee Sentinel*, May 17, 1858. See the *DP*, May 15, 19, and 29, 1858, for the Madison stories.

102. *Wisconsin Argus*, May 15, 1858. See also the *Assembly Journal*, 1858, pp. 2015–2019; Daniel S. Durrie, *A History of Madison, the Capital of Wisconsin; including the Four Lake Country* (Atwood and Culver, Madison, 1874), p. 262; Reuben Thwaites, *The Story of Madison 1836–1900* Madison, 1902), p. 27.

103. *Milwaukee Sentinel*, May 17, 1858, Sec. 1, p. 1.

104. *CCP*, June 26, 1858.

105. Still another attempt was made in 1860. In that year a Milwaukee County representative introduced a bill, but it was not taken seriously.

106. See Alice F. and Bettina Jackson, *Three Hundred Years American: The Epic of a Family from the 17th Century New England to 20th Century Midwest* (State Historical Society of Wisconsin, Madison, 1951), p. 296, and the *Wisconsin State Journal*, October 5, 1857. For a description of other construction around the city, see the *DP*, April 30, 1859.

107. Henry C. Youngerman, "Theater Buildings in Madison Wisconsin, 1836–1900," *Wisconsin Magazine of History* 30(1947), pp. 283–284. See also *WSJ*, February 23, 1858.

108. One German and one American in membership *WSJ*, April 4, 1857, and *DP*, April 4, 1857).

109. *CCP*, December 14, 1857.

110. *DP*, August 4, 1857 and April 4, 1857; *WSJ*, April 4, 1857.

111. See pp. 59, 74 for the cemetery story and pp. 106–109 for Madison's educational progress during this period.

112. See *WSJ*, April 2, 1858, and the *DP*, January 17 and March 24, 1859, and November 20 and December 6, 1858.

113. *DP*, May 24, 1859; *WSJ*, June 6, 1859.

114. See the *WSJ*, July 8 and 11, 1857, for the freshly mown hay references and March 27, 1865, for the evocative description of the "waterfall." Nearly every year the papers reported passenger pigeon flights.

115. See the *WSJ*, September 25, 1863, for the references to quails and the *DP*, December 10, 1859, for the reference to ice skating.

The Civil War Era

1. Richard N. Current, *The Civil War Era*, The History of Wisconsin Vol. 2 (Madison: State Historical Society of Wisconsin, 1976), p. 221.

2. *DP*, April 27, 1860.

3. *DP*, July 23, 1856.

4. *The Lee Papers: A Saga of Midwestern Journalism* (Star Courier Press, Kewanee, Ill., 1947), pp. 273–74.

5. For example, see *WSJ* of late July and early August, 1860.

6. *DP*, November 5, 1851.

7. *WSJ*, November 13, 1857; Current, p. 260; *DP*, November 5, 1857.

8. *DP*, January 7, 1861.

9. Ibid.

10. "Minute Men," in Frank H. Bryant *Papers*, State Historical Society of Wisconsin, Miscellaneous Manuscript File.

11. *WSJ*, January 10, 1861.

12. *DP*, January 29, 1861.

13. Ibid., October 3, 1861.

14. See Walter S. Glazer, *Wisconsin Goes to War, April, 1861* (Master's Thesis, University of Wisconsin, 1963).

15. "Minute Men," in Frank Bryant Papers.

16. *WSJ*, April 15, 1861.

17. Ibid.

18. *DP*, April 15, 1861.

19. Ibid.

20. Ibid.; Bryant papers.

21. Current, p. 296.

22. Consul Butterfield (ed.), *History of Dane County, Wisconsin* (Chicago Western Historical Company, Chicago, 1880), p. 635.

23. According to Glazer, pp. 83–84, the Governor's Guard had fallen to thirty-one men and the Madison Guard to forty-two. See also Jerry M. Cooper, "The Wisconsin Militia, 1832–1900" (Master's thesis, University of Wisconsin, 1968).

24. *DP*, April 20, 1861.

25. Glazer, p. 78.

26. *WSJ*, April 17, 1861.

27. *DP*, April 17, 1861. See also Glazer, pp. 83–84.

28. *WSJ*, April 17, 1861.

29. *DP*, April 18, 1861.

30. *WSJ*, April 16, 1861.

31. *DP*, April 19, 1861.

32. Ibid.

33. *DP*, April 18, 1861.

34. *WSJ*, April 19, 1861.

35. Glazer, p. 87.

36. Ibid., p. 77.

37. *WSJ*, Oct. 3, 1876.

38. Glazer, pp. 89–90.

39. A diligent UW student found only one other boy in his geometry class, all the others, including the professor, having gone downtown to see the soldiers off. ("The Diary of Howie Reid: Kept at Madison in the Spring of 1861," *Wisconsin Magazine of History* (1917–18), pp. 35–63).

40. *WSJ*, April 24, 1861.

41. The two best newspaper accounts appeared in the *WSJ*, April 24, 1861, and the *DP* of the same date. The Governor's Guard reference is found in the SHSW Archives.

42. *WSJ*, April 27, 1861.

43. Butterfield p. 616.

44. Wisconsin, *General Laws of the Extra Session of 1861*, Chapter 2. The decision to allow municipalities to use local tax resources for volunteer aid funds was the first of a long series of actions taken by the state during the war which shifted much of the burden onto local units of government. Richard N. Current in his *Civil War Era, 1848–1873*, p. 335, shows that local governments produced $8 million to support the war effort whereas the state provided only $4 million.

45. One hundred sixty-two persons voted in the special election, whereas 1,342 had voted for city officers in April, 1861.

46. See *CCP*, June 18, 1862, and the *WSJ*, June 13, 1865, for details on the volunteer aid fund.

47. Details of the municipal volunteer fund are found in the *CCP*, September 12, 23, and October 5, 1861; the *DP*, and *WSJ*, September 23, 1861; and the Volunteer Aid Fund Record, 1861–64, in the State Historical Society of Wisconsin Archives.

48. *DP*, August 1, 1862.

49. *WSJ*, July 22, 1862.

50. Ibid., August 12, 1862.

51. Ibid. The Militia Act reflected widespread recognition that the old state-controlled militia system had failed and there was need to have legislation strong enough to combat growing public resistance to manpower requests.

52. See the *WSJ*, August 13, 14, and 15, 1862.

53. *DP*, August 28, 1862.

54. *WSJ*, August 29, 1862. This first bounty subscription effort was criticized by the Daily Patriot on the grounds that the wealthy could buy their way out (*Daily Patriot*, July 31, 1862).

55. Wisconsin Draft Records, 1862. See records of August, 1862, pp. 108–111.

56. See the *CCP*, August 26, 1862.

57. It is also possible that the policies and formulae had not been developed until the beginning of the draft (1862). Only then did it become imperative in the interest of equity to accurately apportion and fully credit contributing local jurisdictions.

58. *DP*, October 24, 1862.

59. Ibid.

60. *WSJ*, November 11, 1863; Wisconsin, *Annual Report of the Adjutant General*, Madison, 1863, p. 472.

61. *CCP*, June 13–September 11, 1863.

62. *WSJ*, June 10, 1863.

63. *DP*, September 2, 1863.

64. Ibid., September 5, 1863.

65. See the *WSJ*, November 11 and August 11, 1863.

66. *DP*, November 13, 1863.

67. *WSJ*, November 13, 1863.

68. Several days after the draft, someone discovered that twelve more names than necessary had been drawn. Therefore, the men whose names were the last twelve drawn were restored to civilian status. Horace Rublee, *Journal* editor, was one of them. *Patriot* editors had a field day with the incident! See the *DP*, November 14, 1863.

69. *WSJ*, December 15, 1863.

70. Ibid., December 18, 1863.

71. Many Wisconsin cities passed bounty referenda: Eau Claire, $100; Baraboo, $100; Beloit, $200; Port Washington, $300. Milwaukee did not pass a bounty measure until January 1864 (Lynn I. Schoonover, *A History of the Civil War Draft* in Wisconsin, Master's thesis, University of Wisconsin, 1915, p. 67).

72. *WSJ*, December 21, 1863.

73. *CCP*, December 26, 1863.

74. From November 1863 until the end of the war most new Wisconsin recruits could get a $300 federal bounty while re-enlisting veterans could get a bounty of $402. This was the beginning of the large federal and local bounty phase that continued until the end of the war.

75. *WSJ*, November 19, 1863.

76. Ibid., February 29, 1864.

77. *CCP*, July 19, 1864.

78. Elsewhere around the state communities were having difficulty raising bounty money. Sometimes common councils refused to grant referenda even though most citizens apparently wanted them. The legislature adopted a thoroughly progressive solution in that it took power from government and gave it directly to the people.

79. *DP*, July 22, 1864.

80. *CCP*, August 5, 1864.

81. *DP*, August 17, 1864.

82. Ibid., September 5, 1864.

83. *WSJ*, July 30 and August 3, 1864.

84. Whether these were actually Madison men or men from other parts of the state is not known. See *WSJ*, March 15, 1865.

85. *WSJ*, August 29, 1864; *DP*, August 25, 1864.

86. *WSJ*, January 13–23, 1865.

87. *WSJ*, January 5, 1865.

88. According to the *WSJ* of January 14, 1865, there were probably about 1,000 men left in the draftable pool. Articles in the *Journal* on January 13, 14, and 25 and February 8, 1865, suggest that about 475 actually contributed to the municipal insurance program.

89. Author analysis.

90. See H. A. Tenney papers (SHSW Archives), 1874 Reminiscences.

91. See Ethel A. Hurn, *Wisconsin Women in the War Between the States* (Madison, 1911), pp. 42–45, and the *WSJ*, May 9, 1863, for references to the early version of "victory gardens" and the *WSJ*, April 20, 1863, and Hurn, pp. 22–26 and 67–69, for descriptions of the various organizations and their activities. For a description of the Ladies Union League of Madison see the SHSW Archives.

92. *DP*, July 8, 1863.

93. *WSJ*, December 27, 1864.

94. Hurn, p. 62.

95. *DP*, March 18, 1863.

96. Ibid., August 3, 1864.

97. Madison returns are taken from *WSJ*, November 9, 1864. National returns come from Blum et al., *The National Experience* (New York: Harcourt Brace & World, Inc., 1963), p. 823.

98. See *WSJ*, April 16 and 23, 1860, and "Badger Boys in Blue: Life at Old Camp Randall," *Wisconsin Magazine of History*, 1920–21, p. 210.

99. Thwaites, *Public Schools*, p. 54.

100. *DP*, April 29, 1864.

101. See *WSJ*, April 29, 1863.

102. There are few research tasks as frustrating as trying to precisely determine how many Madison men fought in the Civil War. The 1865 Adjutant General's Report said that 722 Madison men fought in the Civil War.

103. *WSJ*, March 20, 1865.

104. This calculation is based upon an interpretation of 1860 and 1870 census data by Richard Roe for an uncompleted doctoral dissertation. Roe's analysis of manuscript censuses showed that in 1860 twenty two percent of the total population (1,514 men) fell into the 18–44 draftable age bracket. The same analysis in 1870 showed this proportion to be eighteen percent (1,702 men). Assuming that twenty two percent of the 1865 Madison state census were men between the ages

of 18 and 45, about 1,858 men would fall into this draftable age category. Further assuming the *Journal's* 600-man estimate to be accurate, this group would constitute 32 percent of the total men in this age bracket. Thus, sixty-eight percent were no longer in the city.

105. Statistics taken from the 1865 Adjutant General's Report.

106. The Madison figure is calculated on the basis of 722 men credited to Madison in the 1865 *Report of the Adjutant General of the State of Wisconsin* and 171 Madison deaths in Elisha Williams Keyes (ed.), *History of Dane County* (Madison, 1906), pp. 179–185.

107. Keyes, *Ibid.*

108. Daniel S. Durrie, *A History of Madison, the Capital of Wisconsin; including the Four Lake Country* (Atwood and Culver, Madison, 1874), pages 53 and 303.

109. Author analysis.

110. See Horace A. Tenney papers (SHSW Archives). Handwritten volume of reminiscences of the war, written in 1874.

111. Camp capacity after a major expansion program is described in the *WSJ*, March 7, 1864. A detailed site plan dated 1864 may be seen at the Iconography Section of the State Historical Society of Wisconsin.

112. References to the early conversion work are found in Durrie, *History*, p. 276 and in a fine University of Wisconsin Master's thesis by Carolyn Mattern, "Soldiers When They Go" (1968), p. 3. Descriptions of the unfinished camp are found in the *WSJ*, April 23, 1861. Reference to the Randall Guards is found in *WSJ*, April 23, 1861. One of the rare complaints from the first group of volunteers was found in the *DP*, May 6, 1861. That there was so little complaining is remarkable since the spring of 1861 was one of the wettest and coldest on record.

113. Although the camp schedule varied from period to period and even among the regiments, the schedule described by Frank Putney, a member of the 12th Regiment, which came into camp in November 1861 is typical. See his correspondence at the State Historical Society of Wisconsin.

114. An article describing the strong early interest in Camp Randall appears in the *DP*, May 25, 1861. Descriptions of the impressive work done by Madison women are found in the *DP*, November 1, 1861, *WSJ*, December 26, 1862, and in Hurn, pp. 11–12.

115. See "Chauncey Cooke, Badger Boy in Blue: Life at Old Camp Randall," *Wisconsin Magazine of History* 4 (1920–21), p. 208, and Mattern, p. iii.

116. Albert M. Childs Correspondence (SHSW). The letter herein cited was written sometime in 1863.

117. *DP*, May 4, 1861.

118. *WSJ*, May 30, 1861. Throughout the war the *WSJ*, was much more restrained in its criticism of soldier behavior and, for that matter, in all things related to the war than its major competitor, the *DP*. For example, on February 15, 1864, the *Journal* investigated reports that soldiers had been stealing chickens and larger fowls from farmers on the road in the vicinity of the camp. The *Journal* concluded: "We cannot find a soldier who would stoop to take a fowl from its native perch. Nary a one. The report is without foundation."

119. The best account of this incident is in the *DP*, June 11, 1861.

120. Ibid.

121. *WSJ*, June 12, 1861.

122. Mattern, pp. 14–15.

123. The "outrage" was reported in *WSJ*, October 21, 1861, and the *Argus and Democrat*, Oct. 12, 1861 included in Mattern, p. 40. See the *DP*, February 1, 1862, for one of the attempted rape incidents and the same newspaper on October 11, 1861, and January 21, 1862, for typical stealing and assault stories.

124. Religious reform measures were described in Mildred H. Osgood's *A Young Man of that Time: Pages from the Diaries of DeWitt Clinton Salisbury: 19th Century Wisconsin Citizen and Civil War Soldier* (1974), p. 60. Reference to the teetotaler campaign is found in Butterfield, p. 743. Accounts of soldiers being marched uptown to attend Madison churches are found in Mattern, p. 39 and passim. Efforts to provide Christian literature to the men are found in Hurn, pp. 153–4.

125. Supportive citations are found under footnote 114 above. In addition the *WSJ*, (December 26, 1862) said, "Surely no Ladies Aid Society in this State was more generous in the support rendered Randall soldiers." The *DP*, November 1, 1861, described the work of Madison women as "untiring in their displays of kindness and attention to the soldiers." Early in the war, Cordelia Harvey, wife of the governor, was president of the Madison Ladies Aid Society. *WSJ*, December 18, 1861). The soldier comment comes from Mattern, p. 25.

126. This incident and its response were described in both the *WSJ* and the *DP* on January 27, 1862.

127. See Senate Bill 1675 and debate thereon in the *Senate Journal* on February 10–14, 1862. For a more informative account of the debate see the *DP*, February 13, 1862. See also the *Assembly Journal* dated February 14, 15, and 25, 1862 for lower house actions. The soldier's letter was written by Chauncey Cooke January 6, 1863. In the same letter, Cooke explains how some of the boys from his regiment celebrated Christmas and New Years uptown and were thrown in the Madison jail for the exuberance. So angry did the boys back in camp become about the incarceration of their buddies, they formed ranks without officers and swore to storm the city to secure their release. However, the officers intervened and persuaded the men to stop their plan because they would then be mutineers. Thus Madison narrowly avoided a direct and purposeful attack from the Randall soldiers.

The increase in the number of saloon and tavern licenses during the Civil War is derived from Madison liquor license records in the SHSW archives.

During certain portions of Camp Randall history, regimental commanders allowed beer and liquor to be sold *within* Camp Randall. For example, during the period H.A. Tenney was superintending the camp, from 5–12 saloons operated within the camp enclosure. (See Spencer Scott, Master's thesis, "The Financial Effects of the Civil War on the State of Wisconsin" (University of Wisconsin, 1939), p. 16, and Mattern, p. 35.

128. *DP*, February 13, 1862.

129. Mattern, pp. 55–56 and passim. The notion that poisons in bad liquor were responsible for bad behavior appeared to be widely held. In plugging a popular locally distilled whiskey, the *Patriot* noted that the "mild and inspiring article . . . greatly cheer(ed) without inebriating." (December 19, 1861). An interesting distinction!

130. The incident of massive insubordination among Camp Randall soldiers including the twenty-keg incident is found in Robert C. Nesbit's *Wisconsin: A History* (1973), p. 249. Criticism of the new style order giving is found in the *DP*, May 9, 1861.

131. *DP*, October 12, 1861.

132. For examples of complaints about poor camp conditions see Chauncey Cooke, pp. 208 and 216 and the diary of John Buckley Bacon, February 23, 1864, in the SHSW (MSS). The cold snap is described in the *DP*, January 2, 1864.

A partial list of camp riots are as follows: In June 1861 the men destroyed the mess hall to protest the bad food. In September 1861 the cook shack was again burned down to protest the bad food. In 1863 the boys threw some bread loaves through commissary windows. In February 1864 soldiers protested high prices at the camp store by setting fire to the guard house. In September of that year the camp store was burned down supposedly to protest the high prices. Causes of riots and protests were not always apparent or acknowledged. Sometimes a riot would be attributed to "a general splurge by new recruits." *DP*, (September 14, 1864).

133. See the Report of the Joint Select Committee on Camp Randall Conditions in the *Senate Journal*, 1863, pp. 69–70.

134. See Chauncey Cooke's 1863 letter and another letter dated December 25, 1862. See also Scott for various references to waste in Camp Randall.

That Madison men were prominently involved in Camp Randall affairs is not open to debate. In addition to H. A. Tenney's role as superintendent, Simeon Mills was appointed paymaster, William Tredway, quartermaster general, and William A. Mears, assistant quartermaster. Other Madison men formed a coterie of colonels and even generals around Governor Randall. Thus if the food was bad, if the supplies were inadequate and the pay late, there were Madison men to blame. (Butterfield, p. 615.) See also Scott for stories of waste attributed to political motives and H.A. Tenney's role.

Tenney, in his 1874 reminiscences (SHSW archives, Tenney Papers) boasted that "more than a million dollars in money and equipment passed through (his) hands while in this duty and need scarcely say to my children that not a penny wrongfully stayed there."

135. Mattern, pp. 34, 55 and passim, notes the 6th and 8th Regiments were generally regarded as much better behaved than the other units. The 15th Regiment made up of Norwegians was one unit that achieved a notorious reputation among Madisonians for rowdy behavior.

136. See the *DP*, December 9, 1862, for the November 1862 monthly report of the Madison Ladies Aid Society. Not all the newspapers sent to Camp by the ladies were appreciated. One soldier writing in late 1862 asked his family to send him the Milwaukee paper. "We have the Madison *Journal* every day, but it doesn't amount to much," he said. (Frank H. Putney correspondence, SHSW). In 1864 there were complaints from soldiers that Madison's staunch Democratic paper, *Patriot* was not allowed in camp. (See the *DP*, September 6, 1864.

137. Mattern, pp. 108–109.

138. By late April until early May there were three regiments in Camp at Camp Randall, each with one thousand men. The population of Madison in 1865 was 9191. The Leitch initiative is described in the *WSJ*, January 14, 1864. The "marshall law" patrols were reported in both the *WSJ*, and the *DP*, on January 19, 1864. Reference to the "swearing scenes" is found in the *WSJ*, January 18, 1864. The John Muir letter is one of several held by the SHSW. Although it is undated, it was written sometime between 1861 and 1863, the years Muir spent in Madison. DeWitt Salisbury and numerous other soldiers commented on the "vulgarity, profanity and scenes of the most revolting nature" and thanked God for the careful training they had received prior to being sent there.

139. See the John Buckley Bacon diary entry (SHSW) dated February 28, 1864, and Mattern, p. 44. The circus tactic was described in the *DP*, on April 25–26, 1864.

140. *WSJ*, May 14, 1864.

141. The *DP*, June 13, 1864, and August 2, 1864, describe the two murders. The August 8, 1864, *Patriot* contains that newspaper's comments on the "reign of terror."

142. Author analysis of collected data.

143. One of many accounts of assault and battery is in the *DP*, August 27, 1864. Reference to the guard on West Main was included in a letter sent by Sarah Hobbins to a relative in the East. See Alice and Bettina Jackson, p. 278. Prostitute activities are included in articles of the *WSJ*, dated November 22, 1864, and January 6, 1900. The November 22, 1864, *Journal* also contains a delightful story about a group of Madison firemen who had been dispatched to extinguish a fire in a house near Camp Randall. While on the way to the fire they learned that the burning house was a Camp Randall brothel whereupon they "did a turnabout and let the devouring elements do their work." The noisy shouting was recorded in a Salisbury diary entry, p. 37. The girls and chickens quote comes from Nesbit, p. 249. Camp population figures come from the *WSJ*, September 13, 1864.

144. *WSJ*, November 11, 1864.

145. Margaret Walsh, *The Manufacturing Frontier: Pioneer Industry in Antebellum Wisconsin 1830–1860* (Madison, 1972), p. 269.

146. Merk, p. 208.

147. "The Diary of Howie Reid: Kept at Madison in the Spring of 1861," *Wisconsin Magazine of History*, 1917–18, p. 42.

148. *DP*, June 25, 1861.

149. Ibid., June 18, 25, December 6, 1861.

150. See Merk.

151. Joseph Schafer, *A History of Agriculture in Wisconsin* (Madison, 1922), p. 92.

152. Benjamin H. Hibbard, *The History of Agriculture in Dane County, Wisconsin* (Madison, UW Bulletin no. 101, Economics and Political Science Series, vol. 1, no. 2), p. 123.

153. Walter Ebline, Clarence D. Caparoon, Emery C. Wilcox and Cecil W. Estes, *A Century of Wisconsin Agriculture 1848–1948* (Madison: Wisconsin Crop and Livestock Reporting Service, 1948), pp. 13–15.

154. *WSJ*, June 4 and Nov. 12, 1861.

155. Ibid., December 31, 1861; *Wisconsin Argus*, Apr. 22, 1862.

156. *WSJ*, December 31, 1861.

157. Twelve had "refreshment stands," a euphemism for saloons; three were photographers, and one a barber. Others became suppliers of food, lumber, uniforms, and other goods and services. (Mattern, p. 35.)

158. *WSJ*, May 16, 1862.

159. *DP*, May 10, 1862.

160. Ibid.

161. *WSJ*, May 17, 1862.

162. Ibid.

163. Ibid., January 30, 1862.

164. *DP*, May 19 and 24, 1862.

165. *CCP*, January 20, 1863.

166. Ibid.

167. See *CCP*, April 3, 1863, for the council action.

168. See *WSJ*, July 14, 23, August 26, 1858, and October 7, 1899.

169. Ibid., April 25, 1863.

170. Examples include the homes of Timothy Brown, Banker, Gorham, Simeon Mills, Sommers *WSJ*, May 26, 1863; *DP*, July 13, 1863).

171. *WSJ*, August 24 and April 25, 1863.

172. *DP*, March 16, 1864.

173. Ibid., September 17, 1863.

174. Ibid., April 9, 1864.

175. *WSJ*, October 26, 1863. For general references see Mattern, pp. 28–35 passim; Osgood, p. 37; *WSJ*, July 5–8,

1864. The reference to the one thousand horses is found in the *WSJ*, October 26, 1863.

176. Durrie, p. 209. See also Merk, pp. 144–45, and Walsh, pp. 217 and 331.

177. Schafer, p. 88.

178. Merk, p. 20; Hibbard, pp. 146–47.

179. *DP*, June 11, 1863.

180. Durrie, p. 299.

181. John Y. Smith, "History of Madison," *Madison City Directory*, 1866, p. 30.

182. See Hibbard, pp. 146–47, and Merk, pp. 32–34.

183. Smith, p. 30.

184. Merk, p. 34.

185. Hurn, pp. 89–90.

186. A group of upper-middle class Madison women rebuked this group for their "reckless display and extravagance" in a pamphlet entitled "Retrenchment, the Duty of Women of the North," They argued that in a time of national emergency the rich should share their wealth with the less fortunate and not sate their own desires. The pamphlet said the compelling need was to "live cheaper, dress plainer and set the example . . . of doing without." (Hurn, pp. 90–91; see also *WSJ*, May 1, 1863.) The pamphlet enjoyed widespread distribution throughout the state.

187. John Gibbons to Robert Gibbons, Dec. 9, 1864, John Gibbons letters, State Historical Society of Wisconsin, Madison; Jackson, pp. 278–79.

188. Merk, p. 162, and Richard N. Current, *The Civil War Era, 1848–1873* (Madison: State Historical Society, 1976), p. 385.

189. Merk, p. 168.

190. During the boom year 1856 one analysis showed that 1700 acres of timber, about 24,000 cords, had to be cut down each year to satisfy Madison's cooking and heating needs. By 1860 Madison's population decline had reduced this demand to about 1000 acres of timber, but by 1864–65 demand was again up in the 1700 acre range, and quite possibly as high as 2000 acres a year when Camp Randall needs were taken into account. See the *DP*, December 10, 1856, and the *WSJ*, December 20, 1864.

191. *WSJ*, February 20, 1900.

192. *DP*, April 23, 1864.

193. Ibid., December 17, 1863.

194. *WSJ*, January 18, February 15, 1864.

195. Several attempts were made in the 1850s to extract the peat but they proved unsuccessful. The substance provided an adequate amount of heat but in the process of combustion the peat increased in size leaving a piece of slag considerably larger than the original—no small problem for stoves of the day. See the *WSJ*, November 25, 1863. For a description of the new peat extraction equipment, see the *WSJ*, March 8, 1865.

Society and Leisure

1. Thwaites, *Public Schools*, pp. 45–46.

2. Ibid., and *First Annual Report of the Board of Education and the Superintendent of the Public Schools of Madison for the Year 1855*.

3. Thwaites, pp. 46–47.

4. Ibid., p. 48.

5. *Second Annual Report of the Board of Education and the Superintendent of the Public Schools of Madison for the Year 1856*, p. 7.

6. *1855 Annual Report*, p. 6.

7. The visit of Horace Mann is described in the *WSJ*, March 17, 1858, and the formation of the Madison Public School Association in the *WSJ*, November 26, 1858.

8. *1855 Annual Report*, p. 5, and *1857 Annual Report*, p. 10.

9. *1855 Annual Report*, p. 6.

10. Thwaites, p. 46.

11. *1855 Annual Report*, p. 8.

12. *Ibid.*

13. See "General Regulations of the Public Schools" in *1855 Annual Report*, pp. 25–27.

14. *1855 Annual Report*, p. 12.

15. *1856 Annual Report*, p. 9.

16. Thwaites, p. 48.

17. *1855 Annual Report*, p. 10.

18. Ibid., p. 11.

19. Ibid., p. 7.

20. Ibid.

21. Thwaites, p. 46.

22. Ibid., p. 48.

23. Ibid., pp. 43–44. Examples include Greenbush, Farwell's Addition and the Dunning (Northeast) District.

24. Kilgore left Madison to become principal of the Evansville, Wisconsin, seminary. He had a distinguished career, eventually becoming president of the Susquehanna & Delaware River Railroad. (Thwaites, p. 75)

25. See the *Annual Reports of the Board of Education*, 1861–62 and 1863. About 450 attended private schools, leaving one thousand to "grow up in ignorance."

26. See the figure in chap. 2 on the Madison Female Academy.

27. Merle Curti and Vernon Carstenson, *The University of Wisconsin 1848–1925: A History* (Madison: University of Wisconsin Press, 1949), Vol. I, p. 186. The exact percentage was 48 percent.

28. For example, in 1862 the Madison Public Schools Superintendent, Prof. Charles H. Allen, conducted a special preparatory course of UW-bound Madison high school students. (Thwaites, p. 51.)

29. Curti and Carstensen, p. 153.

30. Ibid.

31. *DP*, February 17, 1858.

32. *WSJ*, March 10, 1856.

33. Ibid., February 23, 1858.

34. *DP*, March 29, 1861.

35. See *WSJ*, November 3, 1856.

36. *WSJ*, March 5, 1859.

37. Ibid., March 8, 1858.

38. In 1860, Lincoln lost Madison by 46 votes (*WSJ*, November 11, 1860); in 1864 by 101 votes (Ibid., November 9, 1864). The *Patriot* on May 18, 1860, described Lincoln as the weakest man, intellectually and politically.

39. *WSJ*, May 18, 1860.

40. *DP*, November 8, 1860.

41. *WSJ*, June 25, 1860. For examples of torch count articles, see *WSJ*, July 25, 30, September 13, and November 8, 1860, and *DP*, September 13, 1860.

42. See *DP*, October 25, 1864.

43. Ibid., March 23, 1864.

44. *WSJ*, October 27, 1863. For soldier activities, see *DP*, October 8, 1864, and *WSJ*, March 19, 1863.

45. See *DP*, October 3, 1864.

46. *WSJ*, October 22, 1864.

47. See ordinances #2 and #10 passed on April 16, 1856, and May 9, 1856, respectively. Dog pack stories are found in the *WSJ*, April 14 and April 13, 1857, and the *DP*, Sept. 29 and Oct. 4, 1859. Damage caused by pigs is described in the *DP*, April 27, 1859. See the *WSJ*, March 23, 1859, for an article describing the bovine fondness for morsels found in farmer wagons. Typical rabies scare articles can be seen in the *WSJ*, July 16, 1857, and the *DP*, September 29, 1859.

48. Interestingly, the *WSJ*, severely criticized the editors of the *Wisconsin Daily Argus* for attempting to convince their readers that Madisonians "were nightly in danger of being devoured by small dogs." The reason the *Journal* objected to such articles was that they were a "direct stab at the growth and prosperity of the city. What immigrant—believing as he must, after reading that article—that five or six whole families of our fellow Irish citizens, two or three Hollanders and a Negro are daily devoured by 731½ dogs every morning before breakfast, would think of settling here? What traveler will stop at our depot . . .?" (*WSJ*, April 4, 1857)

49. See the *CCP*, May 23, 1859, and the *DP*, May 27, 1859.

50. *WSJ*, May 30, 1859.

51. *DP*, June 2, 1859; *WSJ*, May 30, 1859.

52. *DP*, June 2, 1859.

53. Ibid., June 28, 1859.

54. Jackson, p. 249.

55. *DP*, September 29, 1859.

56. *WSJ*, April 24, 1860; *DP*, April 19, 1860.

57. *CCP*, June 16, 1880.

58. *DP*, April 11, 1861. Vilas was trying to be supportive to the newly chartered (March 29, 1861) Madison Horticultural Society, whose goal was to plant trees and beautify the city.

59. *DP*, April 28, 1861.

60. Ibid., May 1, 1861.

61. *WSJ*, May 30, 1861.

62. *DP*, December 7, 1861.

63. *CCP*, May 10, 1861.

64. Ibid., August 3, 1861.

65. *WSJ*, October 15–Nov. 12, 1861.

66. *DP*, December 6, 1861.

67. *WSJ*, December 16, 20, 1861; *DP*, December 19, 1861.

68. The *Patriot* noted on Dec. 6, 1861, that Vilas had served "without the least regard to reelection. . . ." It portrayed Vilas suffering from nightmares "in which he groans under piles of murdered dogs and strangled geese as high as huge Olympus."

69. *WSJ*, March 24, 1862.

70. *DP*, December 6, 1861.

71. Ibid., April 10, 1862.

72. *WSJ*, March 28, 1857.

73. See *WSJ*, January 15, 1861, and May 19, 1857, for illustrations of this point of view.

74. *DP*, June 8, 1863.

75. Ibid., July 21, 1859.

76. Ibid., November 4, 1858.

77. See *DP*, August 1, 1859, May 10, 1862, and July 21 and November 4, 1859.

78. Sennett, p. 92.

79. *WSJ*, June 15, 1861.

80. During 1860–61 the city was able to get convicts from the Dane County jail to work on the streets, but this system produced limited results and was discontinued. See the *CCP*, June 30, 1860, and May 3 and 31, 1861, and the *DP*, Aug. 4, 1860.

81. *WSJ*, March 27, 1857.

82. Ibid., March 10, 1859.

83. Ibid., March 17, 1859.

84. Ibid., August 8, 1858.

85. Ibid., June 20, 1859.

86. *CCP*, April 19, 1864.

87. *WSJ*, May 4, 1857.

88. Ibid., May 28, 1858. Business-supported band concerts in Capitol Park were also very popular. (*DP*, August 23, 1856).

89. John Buckley Bacon, Civil War Diary, 1864–65, p. 49. State Historical Society of Wisconsin Archives, Madison. Reminisces of Mrs. Harry Leonard Moseley, an audiotape recorded in 1957 by SHSW.

90. *WSJ*, April 6, 1860.

91. Ibid., March 13, 1861, and December 13, 1859.

92. Ibid., June 21, 1859.

93. "The Diary of Howie Reid: Kept at Madison in the Spring of 1861," *Wisconsin Magazine of History*. See diary entry dated early April, 1861.

94. Curti and Carstensen, p. 195.

95. See *WSJ*, July 8, 14, 16, and August 24, 1857, and *DP*, August 25, 1857, for this story.

96. See the *WSJ*, May 19, 25, 28, 1860, and the *DP*, May 25, 28, 1860.

97. *DP*, Nov. 24, 1863.

An Era Ends

1. *WSJ*, April 10, 1865.

2. Ibid.

3. From a tape recording by Mrs. Lucien M. Hanks, on file at the SHSW.

4. *CCP*, April 28, 1865.

5. *WSJ*, July 8, 15, 1865.

6. *WSJ*, September 1, 1865.

7. The term "liveliness" was popular among latter day local historians. While it clearly denoted a time full of activities and events, the term was used in a euphemistic sense as well—that is, to reflect the bad soldiers' behavior. A good example of this dual use is found in the *WSJ*, January 6, 1900.

Chapter 4

Disputing Madison's Destiny, Round 1

1. Author statistics. Between 1855 and 1865 Madison population had grown just six percent, i.e., from 8664 to 9191.

2. See p. 83 for a more complete explanation of spending limits.

3. *WSJ*, October 10, 1865, and May 10, 1866.

4. In 1865 equalized value stood at $2.9 million; by 1868 this figure had risen to $4.0 million.

5. *WSJ*, November 20, 1865, and March 27, 1866.

6. *CCP*, April 17, 1866.

7. In 1868 equalized value stood at $4,008,545; by 1871 it had fallen to $3,370,000. Bank loans dropped from $392,853 in 1868 to $366,686 in 1870.

8. See *MD*, December 14, 1869, September 14, 1869 and *WSJ*, October 15, 1869, respectively.

9. *WSJ*, December 9, 1867.

10. *WSJ*, May 29, 1871.

11. See *WSJ*, January 3, 1872, for the 1871 summary, the WPA records in the SHSW archives for the 1872 records, and the *WSJ*, January 13, 1874 for the 1873 summary. Much of this new construction was public sector construction such as the post office, the UW Gymnasium, Chadbourne Hall, the Third Ward School, etc. Consequently, much of the construction activity was not reflected in equalized value of real and personal property which went up just 6 percent between 1871 and 1874. In 1870 total Madison bank loans were $366,671; by 1873 loans had grown to $787,357.

12. *WSJ*, December 28, 1872.

13. For a description of the onset of the depression see Samuel Rezneck's *Business Depressions and Financial Panics* (New York: Greenwood Publishing Company, 1968), pp. 129–130. The relative severity of American depressions and recessions was measured in an article by A. Ross Eckler, "A Measure of Severity of Depressions, 1873–1932," *Review of Economic Statistics* 15 (May 1933), pp. 75–81. Eckler showed that economic activity fell 32 percent during the 1873 depression whereas the same indicators dropped 55 percent during the Great Depression.

14. Madison bank loans totaled $787,357 in 1873 but fell to $311,277 in 1880. Bank assets went from a high of $1,452,639 in 1873 to $947,312 in 1878.

15. *WSJ*, January 3, 1876. Madison newspapers clearly favored good economic news. When annual construction totaled $100,000 or more they would provide such information in annual year-end summaries; when the amount fell below this figure, they would say nothing. Annual summaries are available 1875 (*WSJ*, January 3, 1876), 1877 (*WSJ*, October 22, 1877) and 1878 (*MD*, January 1, 1879). The years 1874, 1876 and 1879 were not reported. About $200,000 of construction activity was reported in 1875 and $100,000 in both 1877 and 1878.

16. *WSJ*, August 25, 1876.

17. *Madison Past and Present, Semi-Centennial, 1852–1902* (Madison: Wisconsin State Journal, 1902)., p. 11.

18. *WSJ*, May 9, 1878.

19. *WSJ*, November 21, 1876.

20. *WSJ*, January 31, 1877.

21. "Nineteenth Century Depressions Have Surprising Contemporary Ring," *Wisconsin Then and Now*, (June, 1975), p. 4.

22. See illustration on page 50, Chapter 2.

23. *WSJ*, June 21, 1866.

24. *WSJ*, July 27, 1865.

25. According to the *WSJ*, May 23, 1866, Madison had two passenger trains both ways carrying an average of three hundred passengers and twenty to thirty freight trains each day with an average of twenty-two cars each.

26. The legislature approval for the railroad aid measures were embodied in Chapters 262 and 338, Laws of 1866. For the citation on the referendum cancellation, see the *CCP*, June

16, 1866. Tripling taxes are based upon the following calculations: The 1865–66 levy for city purposes was $31,625. Assuming the 1866–67 levy had remained the same, an additional $79,000 would have been added for the following purposes: (1) $55,000 for railroad aid measures; (2) $15,000 to cover overspending from the previous year and (3) $4,000 for new schools. Thus the 1866–67 levy for city purposes would have been about $105,000 or 333 percent greater than the previous year! In spite of this prospect the *WSJ* supported railroad aid measures. See the *WSJ*, June 14 and 21, 1866.

27. During the years of the absolute levy limits (1858–1867) the city could only spend between $8,000 and $15,000 for general city purposes. In the first year of the levy limits based upon percentages, the city levied a tax for $41,000 for city purposes.

To secure the line a small group of prominent Madisonians visited with Alexander Mitchell, president of the Milwaukee Railroad, Mitchell promised to have trains running in and out of Madison by January 1, 1869 if the city would convey to the railroad free right of way worth about $5,000 and $20,000 in cash. Two weeks later Madisonians approved the measure at a railroad rally. (See the *MD*, June 16, 1868.)

By approving this railroad aid measure taxes jumped from $92,695 to $119,482 in just one year as a result of the railroad aid measure. See the *WSJ*, February 23, 1869, for a description of the taxpayer meeting and the *WSJ*, February 6, 1869, for the withdrawal petition.

28. At a railroad rally on July 22, 1870 (*MD*, July 23, 1870) citizens urged the council to request the legislature for permission to buy $25,000 in railroad stock. For information on Atwood's petition, see the *CCP*, October 1, 1870. Over 1,000 signatures were collected. Legislative approval of this initiative was given with Chapter 287, Private and Local Laws, 1871.

29. For background and early railroad negotiations and difficulties see the *CCP*, June 24 and December 3 and 21, 1870. Legislative approval was extended with Chapter 263, Private and Local Laws of 1871. For referendum results see the *CCP*, July 1, 1871.

30. *WSJ*, July 20, 1871.

31. *WSJ*, between June 4 and 25, 1870.

32. *WSJ*, June 5, 1871.

33. Mayor Bowen's remarks are found in the *CCP*, April 16, 1872. Just one year after the opening of the first transcontinental railroad, Madison merchants began importing tea directly from Japan and China. See the *WSJ*, July 23, 1870.

34. B. W. Suckow, *Madison City Directory* with a "History of Madison," by John Y. Smith (Madison: Atwood and Rublee Printers, 1866), p. 28.

35. C. E. Jones, *Madison: Its Origins, Institutions and Attractions* (Madison: William J. Park Company, 1876), p. 160.

36. *CCP*, April 21, 1868. Atwood's foresquare support for manufacturing was hardly surprising to readers of his newspaper for he had consistently plugged manufacturing during

his ownership of the *Wisconsin State Journal*. On June 9, 1865, in the text of pushing sugar mills, "Manufacturing is just what we need." Again on March 21, 1868, "Manufacturing establishments are essential for the advancement of cities."

37. *WSJ*, May 18, 1868.

38. *WSJ*, May 20, 1868.

39. *MD*, May 21, 1868.

40. *MD*, July 23, 1869, and July 31, 1874.

41. *CCP*, April 18, 1871.

42. Suckow, pp. 28–29.

43. *WSJ*, May 20, 1868.

44. *WSJ*, January 18, 1868. An integral part of this plan called for an enlargement of the water power at the Mendota outlet.

45. The *WSJ*, December 6 and 11, 1867, noted that coal stoves were outselling wood stoves for the first time in Madison history. Moreover, the price of wood had fallen. This drop was all the more promising because it occurred at the same time that the price of wood had dropped from $10 a cord in November 1867 to 1865 to $6 a cord in February, 1866. See the *WSJ*, November 21, 1865 and February 3, 1866.

46. *WSJ*, August 7, 1866.

47. One was the Blooming Grove Peat Company incorporated on April 30, 1867, lead by William R. Taylor, N. W. Dean, Samuel Klauber, Alexander Mitchell, Edwin Buttrick, John W. Cary and Asahel M. Hanchett. Another was organized to exploit a deposit one mile west of Madison on the Mineral Point road. Incorporators here were John N. Jones, John D. Gurnee, James L. Hill, Simeon Mills, John H. Clark and Peter Young. Details on the Blooming Grove corporation can be found in Chapter 548, Laws Private and Local Laws of 1867. On the Mineral Point road deposit see the *Milwaukee Sentinel*, August 23, 1867.

48. *WSJ*, December 17, 1870.

49. *WSJ*, May 16, 1868.

50. *WSJ*, May 20, 1868; *MD*, May 21, 1868.

51. *CCP*, April 21, 1868.

52. Jones, p. 160.

53. Officers included J. M. Bowman, J. M. Hill, banker; a former principal in the E. W. Skinner Co., S. D. Hastings; Timothy Brown, banker, and several others.

54. *WSJ*, September 22, 1871.

55. Only two of the four implement factories managed to survive the 1873 depression. The Madison Manufacturing Company, formerly the Mendota Agricultural Works, and the E. W. Skinner Co.

56. See the *WSJ*, August 7, 1876. In 1887 they quietly closed their books, sold their factory and ended a once promising but ultimately disappointing chapter in Madison's economic history. The Madison Plow Works, sometimes known as the Firmin and Billings Company, was acquired in 1880 by a local

implement distributor, the Fuller and Williams Company, who desired to begin manufacturing their own implements in that year. The Garnhart Reaper Works erected a large factory in block 223 but became a depression casualty. *WSJ*, ibid. For other background on these firms see *Madison Past and Present*, p. 155 and Agnes M. Larson, *John A. Johnson, An Uncommon American* (Northfield, Minnesota: Norwegian American Historical Association, 1969), pp. 62–70 and 128–171.

57. Daniel S. Durrie, *A History of Madison* (Madison Wisconsin, Atwood and Culver Printsrs, 1874), p. 381.

58. *WSJ*, May 20, 1868.

59. This point is more fully treated in the section on tourism.

60. During the summer of 1859 an ambitious young man leased the building to see if he couldn't make a go of it as a summer resort. The enterprise failed, probably a victim of the depression which held the country in its grip at that time. For another view of the structure see the Ruger birdseye map.

61. See Chapter 2, p. 52.

62. There is some evidence to suggest that the two men may have had considerable communication with St. Louis residents and that several influential St. Louians may even have urged Delaplaine and Burdick to open up the old Water Cure. This view is supported by the fact that the property was sold to a St. Louis man, William F. Roos, in July, 1870 (Dane County Title Records). Roos was managing the resort by the season of 1866. The fact that Lakeside was owned or managed by St. Louis men for years explains why so many patrons came from that city. Among articles which describe the dominance of St. Louis guests at Lakeside are *MD*, July 29, 1873.

63. See *WSJ*, June 12, 1866. The two managers were B. Frodham and Henry O. Conover. Conover had earlier managed the famous Seaside Hotel at Long Branch, New Jersey.

64. *WSJ*, July 2, 1866; June 12, 1866.

65. *WSJ*, April 29, 1867.

66. See *WSJ*, August 3, 1872; *MD*, July 17, 1873.

67. *WSJ*, October 4, 1870, quoting an article in the *Chicago Times*. For additional background on U.S. resorts, see Foster Rhea Dulles, *A History of Recreation* 2d. ed. (New York: Appleton-Century-Crofts, 1965) (1865), p. 149 and passim. At the time of Madison as a resort, Saratoga, New York, was the premier inland resort whereas Cape May and Long Branch, New Jersey, and Newport, Rhode Island, were the most popular seaside resorts.

68. *WSJ*, August 3, 1872.

69. *WSJ*, August 24, 1876.

70. *WSJ*, September 25, 1866.

71. *WSJ*, July 22, 1867.

72. *WSJ*, August 3, 1870.

73. *WSJ*, May 4, 1868. D. R. Garrison, was president of the Pacific Railroad of Missouri and the Missouri River Railroad. See *King's Railway Directory*, 1869.

74. All out-of-town newspaper stories and periodical excerpts were reprinted at least in part in either the *WSJ*, or the *MD*. Citations in order listed above are *WSJ*, October 4, 1870; *WSJ*, July 19, 1872; *WSJ*, August 16, 1873; *WSJ*, August 10, 1874; *MD*, July 1, 1874; *WSJ*, May 5, 1877; *MD*, February 18, 1877 and *MD*, July 10, 1877. The Resort Manual was published in Chicago in 1879 and 1880.

75. *MD*, July 9, 1869.

76. *CCP*, April 18, 1871.

77. *WSJ*, August 7, 1876.

78. *MD*, April 16, 1877. See also Durrie's comments at the closing of his book, 1874, p. 381.

79. *MD*, April 16, 1877.

80. *WSJ*, April 29, 1867.

81. Chicago, Milwaukee and St. Paul Railway, *Tourists Manual to the Health and Pleasure Resorts of the Golden Northwest* (Chicago, 1880), pp. 161–2. See also *WSJ*, June 12, 1866.

82. *MD*, October 4, 1870 and *WSJ*, September 14, 1870.

83. *MD*, August 18, 1870.

84. The story of the Park Hotel is found on p. 132.

85. *MD*, July 3, 1873. When the Soldiers' Orphans' Home was sold in 1874 there was some talk about it becoming a tourist hotel but this, too, fell through. See *MD*, September 11, 1874. The prospect for new hotels after the onset of the 1873 depression was especially grim. Even the prestigious and well-patronized Park Hotel was sold at a huge loss in 1877. Built for $125,000 in 1870–71, it was sold in January, 1877 for just $71,000. See *WSJ*, January 31, 1877.

86. *The Park Hotel Travelers' Guide for 1872* (Madison, 1872) and *WSJ*, August 24, 1876. A general promotional tract entitled *Madison, Wisconsin, Its attractions as a Resort for Summer Tourists*, (Atwood Printers) appeared in 1876.

87. The text was printed in the *WSJ*, May 24, 1877; its distributional strategy is described in the *WSJ*, May 12, 1877.

88. *WSJ*, May 8, 1877. The article in the *Nashville Times* described above was a direct result of this effort.

89. *WSJ*, August 7, 1876.

90. *MD*, December 5, 1876.

91. The $100 appropriation for lake trout was passed in November, 1869 (see *CCP*, November 6, 1869), but not actually spent until February, 1873. The fish were introduced in equal numbers in each lake by cutting holes in the ice in March, 1873. (See *WSJ*, February 20, 1873 and March 5, 1873.) One alderman ridiculed the effort to dabble with nature by moving that $100 of city money be spent to stock the University and Capitol Park with Parrots, Birds of Paradise and Turkey Buzzards." His motion lost. *CCP*, November 6, 1869.

The 1874 salmon trout story is found in the *MD*, April 29, 1874, and the *WSJ*, May 1, 1874. The effort to introduce this species was candidly presented as an experiment since no one knew what would happen to their instinct to migrate to the sea when confined to fresh water.

Importation of new fish species was based in part upon the successful introduction of Lake Michigan white fish in 1848 or 1849, by Leonard Farwell. To the great delight of fishermen, these fish had flourished. Farwell also attempted to introduce brook trout, but this effort failed when they were eaten by pickerel. (See *WSJ*, December 13, 1867 and April 16, 1870.)

The desire to dabble with nature also included attempts to introduce bullfrogs and sparrows. In 1873 bullfrogs from Green Bay and Connecticut were placed in Lake Wingra with the hope that "frog steak may eventually be cheap at our market." (See *WSJ*, June 18, 1873 and *MD*, June 18, 1873.) English sparrows were also introduced in 1877. (See *WSJ*, March 28, 1878; *MD*, February 4, 1879.)

Madison jurisdiction over the Mendota and Monona was embodied in Chapter 102, Private and Local Laws of 1870, p. 228. Justification for this action was both to "enact and enforce ordinances or by laws for the preservation of fish" and to maintain water quality in the lakes. Madison remains the only municipal corporation in the state to ever have received control over contiguous waters. This legislative act increased the area within city limits from 4.7 square miles to 25.3 square miles, a five fold increase. Of course, 81 percent of this was water.

92. *MD*, July 8, 1873. Band music in Capitol Park appears to have been provided steadily between 1875 and 1877. In 1877 a bandstand was constructed in the Capitol Park just opposite ths Monona Avenue entrance. For details on this story, see the *WSJ*, August 31, 1875, July 26, 1876, May 25, 1877, May 29, 1877 and August 17, 1877.

93. *WSJ*, May 29, 1877.

94. *MD*, September 8, 1871.

95. Durrie, p. 377.

96. See *WSJ*, August 24, 1876. For details on this story, see *WSJ*, May 2, 30 and June 8 and July 11, 1877 and *MD*, May 8 and 30, 1877. The drive was eventually constructed but not until years later when constructed by the Madison Park and Pleasure Drive Association. See chap. 5.

97. See Durrie, pp. 358–9.

98. *MD*, November 24, 1873.

99. *WSJ*, May 24, 1877.

100. *MD*, January 8, 1874.

101. For examples of this sentiment, see the *WSJ*, March 31, 1874; Atwood's inaugural address, *CCP*, April 21, 1868; *WSJ*, June 6, 1867; *WSJ*, August 16, 1873.

102. *MD*, July 18, 1875.

103. *MD*, July 28, 1878.

104. D. K. Tenney, *WSJ*, August 7, 1876.

105. See *WSJ*, August 10, 1876.

106. *WSJ*, August 21, 1877.

107. *WSJ*, January 18, 1868.

108. The 1858 city directory showed one ice dealer and the 1866 directory two.

109. Although no early figures are available, 1877 brewery consumption was 1675 tons. Another 4,500 tons were consumed by the local market and exported. See *WSJ*, March 14, 1877. No breakdown for domestic or export markets is available for this year.

110. See chap. 5 and 6 for additional elements of the story.

111. *WSJ*, February 18, 1878.

112. Lee E. Lawrence, "The Wisconsin Ice Trade," *Wisconsin Magazine of History* 48 (Summer, 1965), pp. 257–262.

113. *MD*, February 27, 1876.

114. *WSJ*, February 24, 1876.

115. See *WSJ*, January 31 and February 3, 9, 10, and 23, 1880.

New Public Policies

1. The only exception was during the 1850s when Farwell built a plank road along East Washington Avenue.

2. *CCP*, April 18, 1865.

3. *CCP*, July 14, 1865.

4. Ibid.

5. See the *WSJ*, October 21, 1865, and Ellis L. Armstrong (ed.). *History of Public Works in the United States, 1776–1976* (Chicago: American Public Works Association, 1976), pp. 67–8. This paving had been tried with some success in London and Paris and in Boston.

6. *CCP*, May 20, 1865.

7. Ordinance #182, June 9, 1865.

8. Ordinance #227, September 19, 1865.

9. *WSJ*, October 3, 1866.

10. Armstrong, p. 59.

11. See *CCP*, May 25, 1866 and June 1, 1866. A macadamized road would run about 72 cents per frontage foot. Compare this to the *CCP*, May 20, 1866 estimate for Nicholson pavement of about $18 per frontage foot.

12. *CCP*, April 21, 1874.

13. Based on author analysis.

14. *MD*, May 27, 1873.

15. *WSJ*, July 21, 1875.

16. *WSJ*, September 21, 1878.

17. Both the *Democrat* and the *Journal* gave extensive coverage to the issue. See these papers between June and September, 1878.

18. Technically the Legislature did not preclude borrowing. What it said was that any additional debt incurred above 1856–57 load would have to paid from current revenues. While theoretically possible, in practice it was out of the question because the Legislature imposed relatively low levy limits on what the city would spend each year for general city purposes, including streets. That Madison was able to make relatively large one-time payments for the Nicholson and Macadam pavements shows the relative importance Madison leaders placed on improved roads.

After a heavy emphasis upon pavement paving by Keyes and Atwood in the 1865–1870 period, a period of five to six years went by in which streets were allowed to deteriorate. See *MD*, April 18, 1873 for an explanation of the policy changes. Then S. U. Pinney became mayor in 1874. During his two year regime, Pinney strongly pushed the permanent paving program. In his inaugural address in 1875, he was particularly critical of the reversion to the dirtpatch policy. "Over $180,000 have been expended on streets in the city since its organization in 1856," noted Pinney. "How little there is left to show for this great expenditure is a matter of mortification and regret, owing to the wasteful policy of attempting to make streets of dirt and sand." Pinney's push, coupled with a similar push from his successor John N. Jones, was partly responsible for getting State Street paved in 1878. In each instances, a sustained drive by successive mayors produced rather modest results. For example, it took the successive pushing of Pinney (1874–76), Jones (1876–77) and Smith (1877–78) just to get State Street paved in 1878.

19. Author analysis.

20. These limits were as follows:

1858–1865	$8,000
1866	15,000
1867	10,000
1868–1871	1% of assessed value
1872	15,000
1873–1880	1% of assessed value

21. Author analysis.

22. For an example of this, see the *CCP*, April 17, 1867.

23. See Chapter 22, Private and Local Laws of 1872.

24. *CCP*, April 20, 1869.

25. See *CCP*, May 3, 1879, for the refining resolution. For the reduction in the amount of the levy earmarked for debt service see Chapter 160, Laws of Wisconsin, 1873 and Chapter 230, Laws of Wisconsin, 1881.

26. Janet S. Ela, *Free and Public: One Hundred Years with Madison Public Library* (Madison, Friends of the Madison Public Library, 1975), p. 4.

27. Ibid., pp. 1–19.

28. *CCP*, November 22, 1873.

29. Ela, p. 10. Sparta was the first city in the state to open a public library.

30. *CCP*, August 4, 1876.

31. Ela, p. 13.

32. *CCP*, April 2, 1864.

33. *WSJ*, February 19, 1866.

34. *CCP*, April 17, 1866.

35. *CCP*, June 18, 1866.

36. *WSJ*, December 5, 1866.

37. *WSJ*, July 7, 1870.

38. The two pumper companies were known as the E. W. Keyes Company and the Andrew Proudfit Company after the mayors in office at the time they were purchased. Together with the Capital Hook and Ladder Company (founded 1858), the Sack Company (founded in 1858) and the S. U. Pinney Hose Company (added in 1874), these were the major units in the fire department.

39. *CCP*, December 6, 1867; *CCP*, December 16, 1868.

40. *CCP*, April 9, 1870. A special committee of the Common Council directed to look into the spiraling cost of firefighter salaries concluded that a small full time fire department would be cheaper than a large part time department. See *CCP*, April 9, 1870. The Council did not agree with this recommendation.

41. Section 2, Chapter 245, Private and Local Laws of 1871.

42. *CCP*, April 20, 1875, S. U. Pinney inaugural.

43. See Ordinances #616, 617 and 640 for combustible materials. For expanded fire districts see #238, 261, 271, 285, 392, 546, 561, 613, 649, 661.

44. See *CCP*, May 3, 1879 and *CCP*, June 7, 1879; *WSJ*, April 25, May 16, June 9, 1879.

45. *CCP*, February 3, 1877, January 6, 1865, December 7, 1866. Not only did the firemen perform an essential service for which they received a fee, but they also were exempted from jury duty, military service, and from a requirement imposed upon Madison men to work in the streets one day a year.

46. For descriptions of the annual spring fire department parade and field trials, see *MD*, June 20, 1876, and June 16, 1875.

47. *WSJ*, April 23, 1875.

48. *WSJ*, April 20, 1875, for an example of this sentiment.

49. *CCP*, April 21, 1874.

50. See Street Superintendent's Report, *CCP*, May 6, 1876.

51. *WSJ*, August 10, 1874.

52. Madison did not begin picking up garbage on a regular basis until 1917.

53. One of the few who spoke out early in favor of city parks was Mayor Keyes in his April 17, 1866, inaugural address.

54. See pp. 158–160 for additional details.

55. In addition to the serious attempts described in the narrative, an attempt was made to turn Picnic Point into a park. See the *WSJ*, August 13, 1876. An attempt was also made to secure a lakeshore drive from the university grounds to Picnic Point. For details see the *WSJ*, May 2, May 30, June 8 and July 11, 1877, and the *MD*, May 8 and 30, 1877.

56. See *WSJ*, July 10, 1879, and October 9, 1879. In 1873 the cemetery superintendent was directed to remove all bodies from the block so it could be sold and the proceeds invested in the new cemetery (*CCP*, October 18, 1873). When the bodies were finally removed late in 1877 the property was sold for $1,100 allegedly to be used as a beer garden (*WSJ*, December 24, 1877). However, the buyers were unable to come up with the cash and so the city was stuck with the property (Dane County title records). Finally, in 1879 the council passed a resolution directing that the block be cleaned up and designated as Farwell Park (*CCP*, May 3, 1879, and August 2, 1879). Meanwhile, nearby residents wers pushing for the park idea and raising money for its improvement. Work finally began in late 1879 and was continued for nearly ten years using a blend of private and public money.

57. This point is illustrated by the failure of Marsh Park. See the *WSJ*, May 27, 1875, and the *MD*, a day later. For council action on the request, see the *CCP*, September 4, 1875.

58. *CCP*, April 17, 1876. Mayor Keyes' inaugural address appears in the *CCP*, April 17, 1866. See chapter 22 of the Private and Local Laws of 1872 for the state enabling legislation. The tree planting was described in the *WSJ*, May 23, 1876. The city ordinance was signed by Mayor Orton on October 6, 1877, ordinance #738.

59. For details on the ordinance see the *WSJ*, March 7, 1868. Mayor Sanborn's veto is found in the *CCP*, March 18, 1868. Interestingly, the tree planting measure was criticized by the *Journal* because it would create too much shade. "Our people are neither Druids nor fawns," noted its editor. "Unless the Horticultural Society can make some better suggestion than planting trees up and down the center of our streets," continued the *Journal*, "it had better confine its attention to raising cabbage and cauliflowers." *WSJ*, March 13, 1868.

60. See Ordinance #582.

Society and Leisure

1. *WSJ*, May 25, 1877.

2. See demographic section.

3. *WSJ*, March 4, 1870.

4. *MD*, November 24, 1874.

5. *WSJ*, February 4, 1876. See also *Holiday Magazine* (June, 1960), p. 84.

6. J. B. Thornton, letter dated March 21, 1881, Archives and Manuscripts Section, SHSW. Several lived in lavish country estates such as Governor Cadwallader Washburn's "Edgewood Place" and Simeon Mills' home at Elmside. See *MD*, June 5, 1875.

7. Richard Roe, unpublished analysis for forthcoming doctoral dissertation, 1978.

8. See author analysis. Birthplace of the remaining three Madison mayors of this period could not be determined.

9. Rasmus B. Anderson, *Life Story of Rasmus B. Anderson* (Madison: 1915), p. 26. Free railroad passes were also routinely granted to local, county and state officials.

10. References to Howe, Greeley, Beecher, and Ingersoll are found in the *MD*, January 19, 1877, *WSJ*, May 25, 1877 and *WSJ*, May 2, 1877, respectively.

11. *Journal of the Madison Literary Club 1877–1903*, Box 2, Manuscripts Section, SHSW.

12. Durrie, p. 373–375.

13. See the *MD*, January 1, 1875, January 4, 1876, and January 1, 1878, for typical coverage of this practice.

14. Albert C. Barton, "Ole Bull and his Wisconsin Contacts," *Wisconsin Magazine of History* 7 (1923–4), p. 428.

15. Although the Yankee power structure was a closed circle to most Madisonians, there remained numerous opportunities for others to join various organizations such as the Masons, Odd Fellows, Good Templars, the GAR Post, the Brotherhood of Locomotive Engineers, the Druids, the Turnverein, the Dane County Bible Society, the YMCA and half dozen others. According to one Madison historian writing in the 1870s, a person would have to have a "strange intellect" if unable to find anything congenial in the numberless societies that open their circle to the worthy." Jones, pp. 196–7.

16. Author demographics.

17. Author demographics.

18. In 1880 six out of fourteen churches (36%) held services in German.

19. A newspaper clipping given to the author by Merrilyn Leigh Hartridge describes how one of her relatives, Mrs. F. C. (Catherine) Moessner, launched the kindergarten movement in Madison in 1877 by inviting teachers and prominent members of the German community to her home (211 King Street) to discuss the matter. Following several meetings, a Kindergarten Association was opened at Turner Hall. The first teacher was Mrs. Loessner; her pupils sat at a long low table she had specially constructed for this purpose. About twenty years later with the pushing of the Women's Club, the kindergarten program was implemented by the public schools.

20. In 1866 the breweries were the Fauerbach, the Hausman, the Brechheimer, the Rodermund, and the Mautz-Hess.

21. See the *WSJ* in the fall of 1866 for references to this novel organization.

22. A survey of alderman of this era reveals a sizable collection of thoroughly Teutonic names such as Biederstaedt, Schweinem, Hess, Bischoff, Ingman, and others.

23. See graphic 4.19, p. 161.

24. Consul Betterfield (ed.), *History of Dane County, Wisconsin* (Chicago: Chicago Western Historical Company, 1880), p. 513.

25. *WSJ*, February 11, 1886.

26. *MD*, May 18, 1875.

27. *MD*, May 28, 1873. Ole Bull and Rasmus B. Anderson were the major backers of this effort.

28. See *MD*, March 18, 1875.

29. See Chapter 39 and 115, Laws of Wisconsin, 1859, and Chapter 278, Laws of 1861. A journalistic commentary on these laws is found in the *WSJ*, August 5, 1875.

30. References to the drunken Sunday behavior include *MD*, August 4, 1873. See *WSJ*, September 4, 1873, for reference to the coed-State Street problem.

31. Ordinance #452, April 19, 1870.

32. *CCP*, July 2, 1870.

33. Ordinance #480, July 2, 1870.

34. See *MD*, February 18, 1872 and the *WSJ* during all of 1872.

35. *MD*, May 5, 1873.

36. *WSJ*, June 9, 1873.

37. *MD*, August 4, 1873.

38. *WSJ*, August 5, 1873.

39. *WSJ*, August 8, 1873.

40. *WSJ*, August 5, 1873.

41. *MD*, August 9, 1873.

42. *WSJ*, September 1, 1873.

43. *WSJ*, September 4, 1873.

44. *WSJ*, September 1, 1873.

45. *WSJ*, support for the female praying bands is found in March 19, 1874, and *Democrat* criticism is found in March 4, 1874 issue. The number of saloon licenses in the City of Madison License Records, Archives Section, SHSW. Saloon visits of the praying bands are described in *MD*, March 7, 1874.

46. For newspaper coverage of the political strategy, see *MD*, April 7, 1874.

47. *WSJ*, April 3, 1876.

48. The Republican mayors were Elisha Keyes, 1865–67; David Atwood, 1868–69; J. B. Bowen, 1871–72; and J. L. Hill, 1872–73.

49. Data compiled by the author.

50. Author analysis. The three party years were 1866, 1872 and 1873.

51. Author analysis.

52. Data compiled by the author.

53. Democrats ran unopposed in 1869, 1870, 1875, 1876, 1877, and 1878. In 1874 Republicans nominated a temperance candidate who was out of town at the time and who would not have run had he known about his nomination. See the *WSJ*, April 7, 1874.

54. *WSJ*, March 25, 1879.

55. *WSJ*, April 3, 1867.

56. Lawyers included Gregory (D), Finney (D), Orton (D), Smith (D), Baltzell (D), Keyes (R) and Sanborn (R). Bank presidents were Bowen (R), who was also a physician, Hill (R) and Proudfit (D). Merchants were Jones (D) and Leitch (D) and the newspaper publisher was Atwood (R).

57. *WSJ*, April 3, 1877.

58. *WSJ*, April 3, 1867.

59. *CCP*, April 17, 1877.

60. *WSJ*, July 12, 1877.

61. See the *Home Diary*, February, 1904, p. 11 and *CCP*, July 1, 1876.

62. *CCP*, June 5, June 26, and July 10, 1875.

63. See *CCP*, June 5, 1875 and May 5, 1875.

64. *CCP*, April 7, 1877.

65. *CCP*, August 4, 1877.

66. Welch's paper called the *Home Diary* was published from 1866 until about 1904.

67. Reference to the "larger and more splendid" churches is found in Durrie, p. 353. For detail on the new Congregational Church see the *WSJ*, May 2 and May 5, 1874, and Durrie, pp. 372–374. Accounts of the new Methodist church can be found in George E. Kelsey, *A Century History of the First Methodist Episcopal Church* (Madison, 1937). The Congregationalists moved into their elegant $50,000 building in 1874, but the Methodists, plagued by serious financial problems, could not afford to finish their church until 1887. For detail on St. Raphael's, see *WSJ*, October 29, 1866. For background on Holy Redeemer see *WSJ*, May 29, 1866, and June 14, 1869. Accounts of the German Lutheran Church can be found in Durrie, p. 321.

68. *WSJ*, November 4, 1873; *MD*, November 21, 1873.

69. *WSJ*, April 1, 1874.

70. *MD*, July 3, 1875.

71. See *MD*, January 11, 18, 20, 1876.

72. For background on this movement see Daniel Durrie's *Twenty fifth Anniversary of the Organization of the Presbyterian Church of Madison Wisconsin* (Madison, 1876), 14–15.

73. *WSJ*, July 25, 1862.

74. See the Vilas story as an example of what happened to a mayor who did.

75. *MD*, September 24, 1869.

76. *MD*, April 14, 1870.

77. *WSJ*, July 7, 1870.

78. *MD*, June 23, 1868.

79. *CCP*, July 8, 1870.

80. City Ordinance #583, April 15, 1873.

81. *CCP*, May 2, 1874.

82. See Ordinance #768, May 3, 1879.

83. Ordinance #7 897, June 11, 1886.

84. *MD*, July 11, 1874.

85. *WSJ*, July 27, 1876; see also *WSJ*, September 1, 1875.

86. *WSJ*, July 27, 1876.

87. *MD*, June 13, 1871.

88. *MD*, August 9, 1873.

89. Descriptions of the behavior can be found in *MD*, June 23, 1870; *MD*, January 14, May 31, July 19, October 17, 1874; and May 8, 1875, and the *WSJ*, August 24, 1874.

90. Descriptions of several more serious incidents are found in *MD*, September 24, 1874 and *WSJ*, August 24, 1874.

91. *MD*, July 31, 1873.

92. *WSJ*, July 6, 1873.

93. See Madison ordinances #614, April 4, 1874 and #625, June 6, 1874.

94. Author budget analysis.

95. *CCP*, October 3, 1877. Significantly, the Council merely placed the measure on file.

96. During much of the 1870s any per diem pay for policemen (except elections) had to be by three-quarter vote of the Common Council. The possibility of council refusal to pay per diems *after* they had been incurred by mayoral initiative seriously jeopardized the ability of the mayor to respond promptly and effectively to an emergency.

The no-per-diem-fee-only system was a reaction to a series of abuses under the old system whereby the politically faithful were able to garner police jobs and the comfortable $1 per diem with very little work.

97. See the *CCP*, January 7, 1870, and the Madison Democrat, December 10, 1879.

98. See *MD*, July 12, 1878. For the story of the "great tramp invasion" of 1878 see the *WSJ*, July 10, 1878.

99. *WSJ*, July 6, 1878; *MD*, May 8, 1875, and May 24, 1874.

100. *WSJ*, July 28, 1877.

101. *MD*, July 20, 1878.

102. *MD*, April 11, 1878.

103. *WSJ*, July 28, 1880.

104. *WSJ*, August 30, 1875.

105. *WSJ*, August 4, 1879.

106. *MD*, March 3, 1878.

107. *WSJ*, March 8, 1880.

108. See *CCP*, September 2, 1876; *CCP*, July 5, 1879; and *WSJ*, August 12, 1876.

109. *MD*, September 4, 1878.

110. See the *WSJ*, September 16, July 21, August 17 and the *MD*, September 16, August 9, 10, 20, 1870.

111. *Minutes of the Madison Yacht Club, 1871–1876*, Archives Section, SHSW. See entry dated July 5, 1875.

112. Ibid., summer, 1871 entries.

113. Ibid., see 1871 year-end summary. See also Durrie, p. 345 and the *MD*, April 16, 1874 for additional background on the growth of the Madison Yacht Club.

114. Ibid., see also the *MD*, September 14, 1870, April 16, 1874.

115. *MD*, July 5, 1873.

116. *WSJ*, April 17, 1871.

117. *WSJ*, April 1, 1870. An effort was made to establish rowing during the Farwell boom, but it failed when "sailing fever seized her owners" and the rowboat was converted to a sailboat. *WSJ*, April 17, 1871.

118. *WSJ*, April 17, 1871, and September 19, 1870. See also the 1873 city directory for details on the club equipment.

119. *MD*, September 22, 1870. Descriptions on the races can be found in the *WSJ*, August 22, 1870, September 19–20, 1870.

120. *WSJ*, April 16, 1879. Accounts of the 1871 activity is found in the *MD*, August 5 and 23, 1871; for accounts of the 1875 activity see the *WSJ*, August 26 and *MD*, May 23, 1875; for 1877 activity see *WSJ*, August 22 and *MD*, the same date. According to Durrie, p. 345, the Monona Rowing Club was replaced in 1873 by the Madison Rowing Club.

121. During the 1870's croquet was extremely popular in Madison. According to the *WSJ*, May 14, 1877 "every well regulated family is discussing the relative merits of 4-, 6- and 8-ball games." More important than such fine points was the fact that croquet was the first outdoor sport that males and females could play together. See Foster Rhea Dulles, *A History of Recreation: America Learns to Play* (New York: Appleton-Century Crofts, 1965), p. 191.

122. Descriptions of Winnequah are found in the *WSJ*, June 4 and August 4, 1870, August 24, 1875, May 15, 1876 and May 12, 1877; *MD*, May 12, 1870 and June 22, 1875.

123. See caption for graphics.

124. *WSJ*, May 8, 1877.

125. *WSJ*, August 3, 1878.

126. *WSJ*, August 5, 1878.

127. *WSJ*, August 5, 1879.

128. *Charter and Ordinances of the Village of Madison, Wisconsin* (Madison: Carpenter and Tenney Printers, 1851), p. 23.

129. See Ordinance #22, June 19, 1856.

130. See Ordinance #591, July 5, 1873.

131. Ordinance #772, July 15, 1879; see also *WSJ*, June 27, 1879.

132. *WSJ*, April 25, 1875.

133. Benjamin H. Hibbard, *The History of Agriculture in Dane County, Wisconsin* (Madison: 1904), p. 211.

134. *MD*, October 5, 1875.

135. *WSJ*, July 26, 1866.

136. *WSJ*, July 14, 1865.

137. See *WSJ*, Summer 1868.

138. During the later 1870s baseball became so popular people began complaining not about the number of young lads playing, but rather where they played. For some reason vacant lots were seldom used, but the streets were very popular and pedestrians were sometimes hit by balls. (*WSJ*, May 18, 1871). People also complained when baseball was played on Sundays.

139. See *WSJ*, January 22, 1868. The painted drop curtain was considered especially bad. According to one account the scenes were painted "in a great hurry by a blind kalsominer who must have had at least one hand tied behind him during the process of painting. There is only one reason we can imag-

ine," said the *MD*, "why this scenery should be retained and (that is to) prevent a beggar covered with rags from going naked." *MD*, February 9, 1870.

140. *WSJ*, January 22, 1868.

141. Initial incorporators though billed as men of business character were not men of substance. Incorporators were William Lohmillar, a bookkeeper, E. D. Davis, a printer, C. F. Krems, a clerk and F. B. Bruns, a clerk. See bill #1455. According to the *WSJ*, February 12, 1868 a second bill, 207S, providing for a musical hall was also passed. Unfortunately, this bill has been lost.

142. *WSJ*, February 3, 1871. Actually the deal was slightly more complicated. Mr. Hooley was to give title on the improved theater to a Mr. L. B. Bryan, Chicago, as partial payment for an opera house in Chicago Hooley was then buying. Since Mr. Hooley had planned the improvements, the hall was given Hooley's name.

143. *WSJ*, February 23, 1871.

144. *MD*, February 17, 1871.

145. *MD*, February 8, 1871. For details on the interior see the *WSJ*, February 23, 1871, or the *MD*, of the same date.

146. Henry C. Youngerman, "Theatrical Activities: Madison Wisconsin, 1836–1907" (Ph.D. dissertation, University of Wisconsin, 1940), p. 187.

147. Ibid., pp. 61–62.

148. Ibid., p. 190.

149. *WSJ*, November 2, 1877.

150. *WSJ*, October 2, 1877.

151. See the *MD*, June 12, 1878, for one expression of this sentiment.

152. *WSJ*, October 14, 1867.

153. Author analysis of Hooley programs.

154. See *MD*, December 21, 1875, for an example.

155. *Partial Listing of Hooley Opera House Programs, 1877–1881*, Manuscripts Section, SHSW.

156. *MD*, January 26, 1875, and January 28, 1875.

157. See Robert C. Toll, *Blacking Up: The Minstrel Show in Nineteenth Century America* (New York: Oxford University Press, 1974) for general background on ministrelry. For specific comments on ministrelry in Madison see Youngerman, p. 65 and passim.

158. *WSJ*, July 24, 1868.

159. *WSJ*, July 24, 1868.

160. *WSJ*, May 9, 1878.

161. *MD*, January 7, 1870.

162. *MD*, December 6, 1874.

163. *CCP*, April 16, 1872.

164. See *MD*, June 16, 1876, September 25, 1878, and October 11, 1876 for examples of this genre.

165. *MD*, February 20, 1874. For an example see the *MD*, August 7–8, 1874.

166. *WSJ*, August 13, 1868.

167. Mrs. W. F. Allen, "The University of Wisconsin After the Civil War," *Wisconsin Magazine of History* 7 (1923), p. 25.

168. *WSJ*, November 29, 1869.

169. *MD*, September 25, 1872.

170. *WSJ*, June 22, 1883.

171. *WSJ*, October 8, 1872. The problem was compounded by what would have to be called reportial laziness. For example, on January 1, 1875, the *Democrat* carried a story about two children eaten by wolves in the Town of Dane. The Madison Sportsman Club immediately held a meeting to plan a massive wolf hunt. No one bothered to check out the story. Then four days later the editors discovered the whole story was a joke and had to issue an apology. See *MD*, January 15, 16, 17, and 19, 1875.

Chapter 5

1. *WSJ*, May 17, 1880.

2. Charles N. Glaab in his article "Historical Perspective on Urban Development Schemes," Leo Schnore (ed.), *Social Science and the City: A Survey of Urban Research* (New York: Praeger, 1968), p. 219, makes the often-forgotten point about the tendency to view boosters as narrow-minded, provincial and vainglorious Babbitt type characters. Glaab rightly argues that the proper way to portray the boosters is as a dynamic and vital force in city development.

Disputing Madison's Destiny: Round 2

1. See author's statistics, banking records and annual construction summaries cited in next section.

2. *WSJ*, September 3, 1880.

3. There was the "mild" depression between 1882 to 1885, then a recession between 1890 and 1891, and a "serious" depression between 1892 and 1894.

See A. Ross Eckler, "A Measure of the Severity of Depressions, 1873–1932," *Review of Economic Statistics and Supplements*, Vol. 15–17, III, 1933–35, pp. 75–81.

4. *MD*, June 6–7, 1893.

5. *MD*, June 8, 1893.

6. *MD*, December 31, 1893.

7. Hoffman, p. 58.

8. *MD*, June 29, 1893.

9. *MD*, August 3, 1893.

10. *MD*, August 3, 1893; *WSJ*, August 29, 1893.

11. Statistics compiled by the author; $1,695,000 in 1893 to $1,227,000 in 1894.

12. Statistics compiled by the author.

13. *WSJ*, May 9, 1895. One reflection of the serious conditions elsewhere around the country was a division of Coxey's Army, which passed through Madison in the summer of 1894. Coxey's Army consisted of seventeen divisions of unemployed workmen who descended upon Washington, D.C., as a "petition in boots" to protest the economic conditions. The division that passed through Madison consisted of Montana workmen. They were treated unsympathetically and quickly shunted out of town. See the *WSJ*, May 25–26, 1894, for details.

14. *WSJ*, May 9, 1895.

15. Ibid.

16. *WSJ*, August 8, 1894; *MD*, October 17, 1893.

17. *WSJ*, May 9, 1895.

18. Examples of articles on Madison bankruptcies, see *MD*, January 7, 1896 and April 16, 1896. Bank deposit information from author-compiled data.

19. *WSJ*, November 2, 1898.

20. For the opening day account see the *MD*, July 10, 1879. A summary of construction done in 1879 (*MD*, January 1, 1880) noted that Tonyawatha was designed by local architect David R. Jones and that the cost was $5,500.

21. For an example of the widespread presumption that capitalists had a duty to build resort hotels, see the *WSJ*, April 22, 1887.

The *MD*, July 10, 1879, the *WSJ*, August 14, 1884, and many other accounts describe the hotel facilities. The 1880 *Tourists Manual of the Health, Pleasure and Scenic Resort of the Golden Northwest* published by the Chicago, Milwaukee and St. Paul Railway described the hotel as "elegantly furnished." Butterfield's 1880 *History of Dane County* used the term "a delightful summer idling place," p. 929, and the "embryo Saratoga" comment comes from an 1891 pamphlet published by the Passenger Department of the Illinois Central Railroad, *Beautiful Madison*, p. 14.

22. Indications of successful operation appeared in the *WSJ* on September 18, 1880, July 14, 1882, August 7, 1883, and August 14, 1884. Expansions were described in the *WSJ*, July, 1880, and in A. N. Hanson's *Beautiful Madison* (Passenger Department, Illinois Central Railroad, 1891), p. 14. Professional manager credentials were outlined in the *WSJ*, April 12, 1882, May 10, 1883, and May 22, 1895. For details on manager promotional efforts, see the *WSJ*, June 7, 1883, August 7, 1883, and August 14, 1884. The editorial conclusion regarding Madison's role as a northern resort appeared on August 2, 1886.

23. See the *MD*, August 26, 1887, for an early article on the growing financial problems, and the same paper on August 14, 1890, for the descriptions of its lack of patronage. The owners response to the withdrawals of the liquor license was printed in the *MD*, May 16, 1891.

24. For background on the activities of the Madison Lakes Development Improvement Company, see the *WSJ*, February 3, 1891, and June 19, 1891. An informative article on the Illinois Central agent visit appeared in the *WSJ*, June 24, 1891. Its promotional tract, *Beautiful Madison*, is described above. For background on the Park Hotel managers visit, see the *WSJ*, March 8, 1892.

25. The bankruptcy proceeding is described in the *WSJ* on May 5 and June 20, 1893. The final reopening of the Tonyawatha is sketched in the *WSJ*, May 23, 1895. The fire accounts were printed in both the *MD* and the *WSJ* on August 1, 1895.

26. For the reference to the hot side of the lake, see the *WSJ*, August 11, 1895. For an example of the "poor manager" theory, see the *WSJ*, April 7, 1883. According to the *WSJ*, June 29, 1894, "These summer tourists want to go to a small town, where they can have things their own way."

One of the best references on the Wisconsin tourism industry in the 1880s is the *Tourist Manual* . . . (1880: Chicago, Milwaukee and St. Paul Railway) noted earlier. The volume provides a myriad of detail for each resort, including its features, costs, capacity and much more.

Examples of outright opposition to tourism were rare since both daily editors supported tourism. One of the best examples appeared in the *WSJ*, on June 21, 1899. "We are all very apt to complain that our lakeshores are not studded with costly and grand residences like the shores of Lake Geneva," said Jud Stone, a columnist for the *Journal*. "But let us stop to think the matter over for a moment. Should the millionaires of Chicago and other cities come here and gobble up the beauty spots on the shores of Lakes Monona and Mendota and build fancy houses, what would we poor creatures do? There wouldn't be a place left for a common old fashioned picnic. Let us keep still and hold onto the favors now left to us. The shores of our lakes are now in the hands of nature, and belong to 'us common people.' If we behave ourselves, the owners of these beauty spots . . . will give us a chance to be merry on any of these grounds."

The cold shoulder was lamented in numerous articles. For examples see the *MD*, June 16, 1887, and April 10, 1898, and the *WSJ*, March 29, 1898.

27. *WSJ*, December 29, 1880.

28. Ibid.

29. In 1865 there were only 68 businesses; in 1875 the number had risen to 89. By 1915 only 75 stores remained on the Square. See Alfred H. Jensen, "A Study of the Succession of Uses of Property on the Capitol Square" (Master's thesis, University of Wisconsin, 1923).

30. Ibid.

31. *WSJ*, May 3, 1892.

32. *WSJ*, December 29, 1880.

33. *WSJ*, July 15, 1884.

34. The largest convention ever held in Madison up to this time was held in July, 1884 when the National Council of Education held their annual meeting in Madison. Over 6000 of their members came and this number at a time when the Madison population stood at just 12,000. Theoretically every other family in town had to take in a guest. Elaborate arrangements were made to accomplish this and even to the point of aligning visitors with families of similar ethnic and religious background.

35. *MD*, December 19, 1880.

36. *MD*, May 29–30, 1895.

37. *MD*, June 10, 1883.

38. *WSJ*, May 6, 1896.

39. Ibid.

40. Madison, *Wisconsin and Its Points of Interest*, Madison, Wisconsin, 1899, pp. 2–3.

41. Ibid.

42. *CCP*, April 20, 1880.

43. Those who were pushing to make Madison a great manufacturing city could hardly have been more confident. Consider the case for Madison factories which appeared in a special manufacturing supplement to the *WSJ*, published September 1, 1888.

44. *WSJ*, September 13, 1880.

45. A general summary of all business promotion organizations was in the newspaper description of the Madison Club in the *WSJ*, March 26, 1886, March 25, 1887, November 20, 1889, December 18, 1889, February 3, 1896, and the *MD*, January 19, 1890. Sources for the Madison Businessmen's Club come from the *WSJ*, March 5, 1890.

46. *WSJ*, May 5, 1891, and May 8, 1891.

47. *WSJ*, May 25, 1891.

48. See the *MD*, June 29, 1892, May 13, 1893, and December 6, 1893.

49. *WSJ*, November 29, 1881.

50. *MD*, June 10, 1883.

51. Unless otherwise specified this account is based upon Agnes M. Larson's, *John A. Johnson: An Uncommon American* (Northfield, Minnesota: The Norwegian American Historical Association, 1969).

52. Ibid., pp. 128–171. The value of manufactured farm implements ballooned from seven million dollars in 1850 to fifty million dollars in 1870.

53. *WSJ*, August 2, 1894; *MD*, December 12, 1897.

54. *WSJ*, August 13, 1890.

55. Larson, pp. 173–74.

56. *MD*, August 12, 1890.

57. Ibid.

58. *WSJ*, August 22, 1890.

59. *WSJ*, August 28, 1890.

60. "Here," he noted, "things are different. The people are conservative . . . and are not as a class interested in manufacturing. . . ." (*WSJ*, August 13, 1890.) Other slights bothered Johnson. When he asked the city in 1883 to gravel East Washington Avenue from the square down to the Fuller

and Johnson factory, the city only paved the avenue half way to the plant. For details on this story see *WSJ,* April 21 and 23, 1883, and the *CCP,* May 5, 1883.

61. William Willard Howard, *Harper's Weekly* 33, no. 1684 (March 30, 1889) p. 243.

Evidence is abundant that a large number of persons, mostly in academic and professional communities, liked Madison pretty much the way it was. Reflections of these sentiments were often found in letters to the editor from factory proponents. For example, one letter writer ridiculed Madisonians who allegedly refused to buy stock in a company which wanted to locate its factory in Madison because they did not want to see "the air fill up with smoke and the streets with grimy men." Antifactory sentiment was sometimes found in articles extolling the work of organizations such as the Madison Park and Pleasure Drive Association. In one such article U.W. President Charles Kendall Adams was quoted as saying that "it is not a business city which demands booming in business directions." (*MD,* March 19, 1897.) Still other antifactory references are found in descriptions of Madison as a desirable place to live. One 1899 pamphlet, *Madison, Wisconsin and Its Points of Interest* (Madison, Wisconsin, 1899) said that Madison, unlike many western cities "is not a dreary waste of sandy dusty streets nor smoke begrimed houses; on the contrary the manufactories and the residence portion are widely separated. . . ." (p. 2.)

62. Larson, p. 179.

63. It would appear that he came very close to moving his Gisholt factory to Milwaukee in 1890. In fact representatives from various cities successfully wooed away several Madison factories. For one example see the *WSJ,* January 6, 1891.

64. See *WSJ,* August 13, 22, 28, 1890, and *MD,* August 12, 1890; Larson, p. 157 and passim.

65. *WSJ,* April 21, 1883.

66. *MD,* September 26, 1899. The reader should remember that while the Great Central Marsh was viewed by most to be the factory district, there were still many factories scattered around ths city. For example, at the foot of Lake Street and Lake Mendota, were the foundaries and factories of the Lake City Tool Company and the Madison Manufacturing Company. Gradually areas like this *not* served by railroads became less competitive and were eventually used for other purposes.

67. See Frank A. Flowers, *Annual Report of the Bureau of Labor and Industrial Statistics,* Madison, September 30, 1888, pp. xviii and xix.

68. Reference to bicycles, cigars, breweries are all found in graphic captions in this chapter. Other factories are described in special manufacturing supplements published by the *WSJ* from time to time and in dozens of newspaper articles, too numerous to mention. For a comprehensive summary of factories in 1888, see the *WSJ,* September 1, 1888. Another excellent reference is *Madison: Past and Present.*

69. See Ebling, et al. and "Urban and Rural Immigrants Could Earn Their Grubstake in Wisconsin's Tobacco Industry," *Wisconsin Then and Now* 22, no. 2 (September 1975), p. 4.

70. See Keyes, p. 278; *WSJ,* December 22, 1880, January 7, 1885, and the *WSJ,* January 13, 1893. The last cited article said that Edgerton had 60–70 warehouses, Deerfield 14.

71. *WSJ,* October 5, 1892.

72. An 1890 State Bureau of Labor Statistics analysis of seasonal idleness of the building trades showed that 75% of all building trade laborers were unemployed during January and February, precisely the months when the ice harvest occurred. *WSJ,* February 14, 1891.

73. 1890 sources: *WSJ,* February 11, 1890, February 28, 1890. Although no comprehensive records of the ice industry in Madison are available, regular newspaper accounts allow one to assemble a reasonably accurate activity record of Madison ice houses. The data cited in the text comes from dozens of newspaper sources.

74. In 1888 the city health officer somewhat euphemistically reported that the Madison ice was "as pure as can be expected under the circumstances." In his 1889 report he noted that the ice quality was so poor much of it had to be destroyed.

75. The history of union organizing is told in Harold E. Miner's *History of Madison Labor,* U.S. Works Progress Administration, Federal Writer's Project, (SHSW) p. 10. The account of the first labor day celebration is found in the *MD,* September 6, 1893.

76. *WSJ,* January 31, 1893.

77. *MD,* May 25, 27, 1893.

78. *Trades Council and Labor Union Directory of Madison, Wisconsin* (Madison: Federation of Labor, 1894), pp. 8–9; Roland Strand, *The Story of the Democrat: A History of the Madison Democrat,* A Newspaper Published 1868–1921 (Madison: Webcrafters, Inc., 1948).

79. Merle Curti and Vernon Carstensen, *The University of Wisconsin: 1848 to 1925, A History* (Madison, U.W. Press, 1949), Vol. I, p. 608.

80. What was happening at the University of Wisconsin was also going on at many places around the country. It was beginning as a great boom period for American universities. See "The Emergence of the American University: The Pattern of the New University" by Lawrence R. Veysey, *The Emergence of the American University* (Chicago: The University of Chicago Press, 1965).

81. In 1892 Chamberlin brought economist Richard T. Ely to the university, a controversial professor who prompted the regents to issue their stirring "sifting and winnowing" defense of academic freedom. One year later, Frederick Jackson Turner, a young American historian was wooed away from Johns Hopkins University. Just after his arrival Turner presented his famous paper on the role of the frontier in America—a paper that began a profound reappraisal of American history.

82. Curti and Carstensen, Vol. I, pp. 501–607.

83. Ibid., p. 608, for the reference to the increase in faculty size. Burgeoning student enrollment statistics come from data derived from the University Archives. Because U.W. students were not counted as a part of federal dicennial censuses until 1950, it is necessary to take the 1900–1901 student enrollment data from the U.W. Archives (1977) for a total population of 21,141. Thus U.W. students constituted 9.4% of the total.

84. *MD,* August, 1895.

85. See factory section for citation source and the toleration of soot-belching smoke stacks.

86. Ibid.

87. *MD,* March 19, 1897.

88. *WSJ,* March 10, 1890.

89. Gertrude Slaughter, *Only the Past is Ours, The Life Story of Gertrude Slaughter* (New York: Exposition Press, 1963), p. 111. A student who attended the U.W. during the 1880s said that few lectures were well-attended and that college newspapers had to continually exhort folks to turn out. See Frederick A. Pike, *A Student at Wisconsin Fifty Years Ago* (Madison: Democrat Printing Co.), p. 186.

90. Reuben G. Thwaites, "Madison: The City of the Four Lakes," in *Historic Towns of the Western States* (New York: G. P. Putnam & Sons, 1901), Lyman P. Powell (ed.), p. 260.

91. For examples of this see the *WSJ,* February 20, 1895.

92. See superintendent's annual reports, 1880–1890.

93. Slaughter, p. 112.

94. *WSJ,* March 10, 1898.

95. See Fairchild's comment cited above.

96. Slaughter, p. 110.

97. *WSJ,* March 10, 1890. Also in 1896 Rev. Eugene G. Updike, minister of the First Congregational Church, called his parishioners' attention to the fact that every ten new U.W. students meant another five thousand dollars worth of permanent improvements to the city's prosperity in the form of a new house (*WSJ,* March 23, 1896).

98. Curti and Carstensen, p. 573.

99. *WSJ,* December 5, 1899. A *MD* story that appeared on September 26, 1900, noted that Madison had become a great center for fine clothing and that between 1895 and 1900 Madison clothing stores had doubled their force of tailors.

100. See p. 237.

101. See p. 388.

102. *WSJ,* April 25, 1888.

103. See "Varieties of Local Government Reform" in this chapter.

104. See "Privies, Purification, and Pollution."

105. See section entitled "The City Beautiful: A Movement Begins."

106. See "Society and Leisure."

107. This sentiment surfaced in connection with the appointment of a city engineer in May, 1900, a decision that pitted a university professor against a man without university connections. The larger issue behind this flap was the role the university had played in solving Madison's sewerage mess. See the *MD*, May 2, 12, and 13, 1900.

108. According to Thwaites, pp. 260–61, the most important town-gown clubs were the Town and Gown Club, the Six O'Clock Club and the Madison Literary Club.

In 1895, twenty percent of all U.W. students were Madisonians. This fact explained why so many out-of-state students found it easy to stay with "friends in town," thereby cementing town-gown relations in still another way. Interestingly, in 1895 Madison had less than 1% of the state's population, yet supplied twenty percent of the students.

Booming and Building: The Growth of Methodical Madison

1. *WSJ*, December 31, 1885.

2. *WSJ*, December 27, 1887.

3. Though the fervently sought goal of 20,000 persons was not attained counting "regular" Madisonians, there was one way to reach the goal and that was to add the nine-month U.W. student population—a step the federal census takers did not begin to do until 1950. Counting both "regular" residents and students, Madison's turn of the century population reached 21,141 persons, a 96% increase over the corresponding 1880 figure. If the suburban populations at Wingra Park, University Heights, Elmside, etc., were added, the population of the contegories urbanized area probably doubled between 1880 and 1900.

4. Density rates from author's statistics. Madison density rates were destined to more than double over the 1900 levels to a high of 9102 persons per square mile in 1940 before dropping to much lower levels during the post World War II period.

5. *WSJ*, December 27, 1883.

6. During late December or early January, the Madison newspapers published a summary of new construction completed that year. Data for the 1880–1887 comes from the following sources: 1882, *MD*, December 21, 1882 ($600,000); 1883, *WSJ*, December 27, 1883 ($547,950); 1884, not available; 1885, *WSJ*, December 31, 1885 ($475,000); 1886, *WSJ*, December 1887 ($535,000); 1887, December 1887 ($601,000).

7. For background on the conversion to Orton Park, see p. 141. For background on the removal of slaughterhouses, see the *WSJ*, June 10, 1884, *CCP*, June 13, 1884, August 18, 1884, *WSJ*, July 7, 1887, May 5, 1888.

8. *MD*, July 21, 1888. The two factories at the intersection of Lake Street and Lake Mendota were the Madison Manufacturing Company and the Lake City Tool Company. The latter was established in 1883 (*WSJ*, May 15, 1883) to make a newly patented windmill designed by Conrad M. Conradson.

9. As early as 1887 city lots on the edge of the marshes were being filled in and sold for residential construction. For example, see the *MD*, May 27, 1887, for a description of new homes built on filled land on the north side of East Johnson Street between Blount and Livingston.

10. According to the *WSJ* year end edition, 1887 construction totalled $601,000. 1889 construction by contrast totalled just $340,000, just 56% of the 1887 figure.

11. *MD*, February 1, 1891.

12. Accounts of the Madison Lakes Improvement Company are from the *WSJ*, April 10, 1890, March 9, March 10, April 3, May 4, August 10, August 11, 1891, and the *MD*, February 1 and May 3, 1891.

13. *WSJ*, March 10, 1891.

14. The other properties on which they held options were the Webber and Todd properties platted as Bellevue, Oak Park between Tonyawatha and Winnequah, the Harnden farm between Schuetzen Park and Elmside, the Scott farm near Turville Point, and the Oakley property at the corner of Carroll and West Wilson.

15. *WSJ*, August 13, 1891.

16. Among the many plats entered during this period were Wingra Park, Elmside, West Lawn, Willow Park (the lake side of Sherman Avenue between Brearly Street and Tenney Park), University Heights.

17. Statistics and plat analysis by author.

18. According to the *WSJ*, October 2–8, 1892, in an article entitled "Real Estate Field" the greatest demand was for "outlying lakefronts." Interestingly in many cases these lakefront lots had been intended for wealthy big city buyers, who would build "summer cottages" on them, that is, huge mansion-sized summer homes similar to those being built around Lake Geneva and the nationally known lake-oriented resorts. With few exceptions, however, these lots were bought not by out-of-town millionaires but by Madisonians. One of the few exceptions was E. P. Allis, a Milwaukee millionaire who bought seventy-five acres on Lake Monona. In 1888 he built a large home at 4123 Monona Drive. See *MD*, March 7, 1893.

19. *MD*, August 9, 1892.

20. *MD*, August 20, 1892.

21. Even in 1894, the worst year of the depression, Madison new construction totalled $500,000, a very respectable amount comparable to good years in the 1880s and 1890s.

22. Author records. The number of Madison realtors grew apace with the boom. In 1878 there were only two or three realtors but in 1902 their numbers had risen to over forty *Madison: Past and Present*, p. 11.

23. *WSJ*, May 9, 1895 and *MD*, September 26, 1893.

24. *MD*, January 28, 1892.

25. *WSJ*, October 2–8, 1892.

26. This is based upon a comment made in a July 2, 1897 *MD* article, which said that no more than 3500 out of Madison's 4000 families could visit the cemetery except on rare occasions because they could not afford to hire a carriage. This implies that in 1897 at least 88% of all Madison families did *not* own carriages.

27. According to the *WSJ*, June 6, 1892, the mule cars carried 857 passengers a day. Allowing about seventy-five percent of this number were the same person riding twice (say back and forth to work) that meant that only 556 persons rode the cars each day or about 4% of the total population at the time. Seventy-five percent of 857 is 642 round trippers or 341 individuals. Adding the 341 round-trippers to 215 one-way fares yields for 556 persons riding the mule line each day.

28. See George M. Smerk, "The Streetcar: Shaper of American Cities," *Traffic Quarterly* 21 (October, 1967), pp. 569–584.

29. See *MD*, October 2, 1892. This account of the opening day tour noted that the car ran from the Yahara River to the Square in just 10 minutes.

30. Author analysis.

31. *MD*, August 26, 1897, and author analysis.

32. *WSJ*, July 31, 1903, and author analysis.

33. Author analysis.

34. For examples of this sentiment see the *MD*, May 14, 1892, and May 29, 1897.

35. The best sources for home costs were annual summaries of construction activity that appeared at the beginning of the building season and then again during the last week of December.

36. Smerk, p. 575.

The Age of Utilities, 1879–1899

1. *WSJ*, March 12, 1897.

2. *MD*, August 18, 1877. Lovell was described in the article as a "former resident of Madison."

3. Consul Butterfield (ed.), *History of Dane County Wisconsin* (Chicago: Western Historical Company, 1880), p. 820.

4. Ibid., p. 820, and *WSJ*, November 12, 1879.

5. *WSJ*, November 12, 1879.

6. *MD*, August 8, 1877.

7. *WSJ*, April 5, 1879.

8. Ibid.

9. *WSJ*, October 1, 1879.

10. *MD*, November 25, 1879, for the orchestra story and the *WSJ*, October 1, 1879, for the wake-up service story.

11. See Ordinance #831 passed on December 2, 1882.

12. See an interview with B. B. Clarke in the *WSJ*, March 2, 1896.

13. *WSJ*, December 21, 1895.

14. Principal investors were Phillip L. Spooner, B. B. Clarke, Charles E. Bross and R. M. Lamp. Formation of the new company was described in the *MD* on May 14, 1895. For general background on both Standard Telephone and Dane County Telephone Companies see pp. 217–8 of *Madison Past and Present*, and Harry Barsantei, "The History and Development of the Telephone in Wisconsin," *Wisconsin Magazine of History* 10 (1926), pp. 155–158.

15. *Madison Past and Present*, p. 217. The *MD*, February 26, 1896, noted that the number of subscribers had increased to 509. Private citizens were not the only ones to discard the hated Wisconsin Telephone Company. Following a meeting of the University of Wisconsin regents in April, 1896, even the university ordered all the Bell equipment removed and the Dane system installed. *WSJ*, April 24, 1896.

16. *WSJ*, December 11, 1895.

17. *WSJ*, 1902, pp. 217–18.

18. Said the *WSJ*, "No monopoly in this country has practiced such outrageous extortions as has the Bell telephone monopoly. Its charges have been without the slightest reference to the cost of service rendered. It has robbed the public without conscience or compassion. It has steadfastly refused to make any concessions and brutally denied all petitions for relief. It has no rightful claims upon the public." *WSJ*, December 31, 1895.

19. Dane County Telephone Company, *The Telephone Situation in Madison* (Madison, December 22, 1900).

20. *WSJ*, December 17, 1900.

21. *WSJ*, October 13, 1882.

22. *WSJ*, July 29, 1880.

23. *WSJ*, September 7, 1897.

24. See the *WSJ*, May 20, June 30, 1899, and April 23 and 28, 1900, and the *MD*, August 22, 1899.

25. *WSJ*, February 10, 1909.

26. *WSJ*, March 15, 1915.

27. *WSJ*, April 29, 1880.

28. *WSJ*, June 19, 1880.

29. *WSJ*, July 19, 1880.

30. *WSJ*, July 7, 1880.

31. For newspaper accounts of the early May meetings see the *WSJ*, May 7, 11, 14, 1881. The best single account of the founding of the Madison Waterworks is John Henry Sprecher's "The History and Management of the Waterworks of Madison" (Bachelor's thesis, University of Wisconsin, 1905).

32. Principal backers of the Madison City Waterworks Company were Simeon Mills, John A. Johnson, L. S. Hanks, F. A. Brown, D. K. Tenney, W. F. Vilas, E. W. Keyes and others. See Sprecher, pp. 9–11, and *WSJ*, May 14, 1881.

33. *WSJ*, May 14, 1881.

34. See E. W. Keyes, *History of Dane County* (Madison: Western Historical Association, 1906), Vol. III, Biographical, p. 397. At the time the council was divided into three factions, five who supported municipal ownership led by Heim, five who wanted private ownership led by Dexter Curtis and five who were uncommitted or opposed to waterworks of any kind.

35. See the *CCP*, July 2 and August 6, 1881.

36. Sprecher, pp. 20–21.

37. *MD*, February 15, 1883, *CCP*, April 15, 1884.

38. *WSJ*, February 4, 1889. During one fire in December, 1886, so much water was consumed that the pumps sucked all the water out of the pipes and wells.

39. *WSJ*, January 11, 1888.

40. See the *WSJ*, February 3 and 4, 1888 for examples of the sentiment.

41. See the Water Commission Report for 1888 and a very candid retrospective view by Heim in the *WSJ*, June 11, 1895.

42. 1890 Water Commission Report. See also Sprecher, p. 81, and a paper written by Heim entitled "Our Experience with Water Meters," given at the National Convention of Water Works in New Orleans in 1895 and reprinted in the *WSJ*, June 11, 1895.

Not only did the meters reduce water consumption, but they also dramatically reduced the amount of coal needed to pump the water. Enough money was saved on coal to recapture the initial outlay for "free" meters in just six years.

43. Madison's meter system was the subject of several articles published in industry periodicals such as the *Engineering Record* (1895) and the *Water and Gas Review* (1895) and *Municipal Engineering* (August, 1899). Heim also presented papers at national conventions of the National Convention of Waterworks.

44. *WSJ*, July 12, 1855. Until very near the turn of the century, some Madison streets had oil lamps and many of its homes, especially the more modest ones, relied on cheaper kerosene. However, from the time it was introduced the more expensive homes featured illuminating gas.

45. The light was produced when relatively large amounts of current would "jump" a small gap between two conductors and form an arc.

46. Just one year after the successful Pearl Street experiment the Edison Company threw the switch on the world's first successful *hydroelectric*-powered central generating station in Appleton, Wisconsin.

For an excellent general account of the Wisconsin electrical industry and its national context, see Forest McDonald's *Let There Be Light: The Electric Utility in Wisconsin 1881–1955* (Madison: American History Research Center, 1957), pp. 1–32.

47. *MD*, June 27, 1879.

48. *WSJ*, September 28, 1882. The few accounts which describe the first corporate efforts to distribute and sell electricity to Madison suggest that the Madison Electric Light & Power Company was formed to provide street lighting, the first major use to which electricity was put in the U.S. In July, 1883 another group of investors formed the Madison Electric Light Company apparently to provide power for residential lighting, but it too failed. See the *WSJ*, July 19, 1883.

49. *MD*, December 6, 1883. The Van Depoele Company was started by Charles J. Van Depoele, one of two Americans credited with the invention of the world's first successful commercial traction system. Van Depoele was acquired in 1888 by the Thomas-Houston Company, the firm which ultimately sold two power plant installations in Madison, one alternating current system in 1888 and another direct current system for the traction industry in 1892.

50. Ibid.

51. The question was not so much whether electricity was brighter; nearly everyone conceded that. The question was, whether electricity was cost-effective. *MD*, December 12, 1882. This led to great conundrum, viz: how do you compare candlepower, the unit of measure for electric arc lights, and cubic feet of gas, the unit of measure for gas lights?

52. Breese Stevens later appeared before the Council in 1888 as attorney for the gas company. See *CCP*, April 13, 1888. Nine years later another Madison mayor was accused of having a conflict between public and private interests. On March 23, 1894 the *MD* in an editorial entitled "Serving Two Masters" accused Mayor John Corscott of being guilty of a crime each time he took official action on matters relating to the City contract with the Gas Company. Basis for the *Democrat* charge was the fact that Corscott, in addition to being Mayor, was also a Director/Stockholder of the Madison Gas Light and Coke Company.

53. See *WSJ*, June 11, 1888. Though many other Wisconsin cities began electrical systems before Madison, Madison Electric Light Company incorporators guessed wisely about which kind of equipment to select. In a period of rapid technological change, they had selected alternating current (AC) equipment which became the standard of the industry five years later. In fact, Madison was among the first three AC plants to be set up in the state. (McDonald, p. 75.)

54. *WSJ*, July 20, 1888.

55. *CCP*, February 18, 1890.

56. *WSJ*, January 19, 1884.

57. *WSJ*, June 25, 1888.

58. If successful in supplying power for both street lights and streetcars, the company could of course get more business, but they could also reduce their cost of production since they could run their generators full-time rather than part-time.

59. *CCP*, August 12, 1892.

60. See Ordinance #1019, August 14, 1891.

61. *WSJ*, October 3, 1892.

62. Ironically after securing the exclusive power contract with the Madison City Streetcar Company, that company was unable to pay its electricity bill to the Four Lakes Company. The Four Lakes Light and Power Company then began a se-

ries of legal steps against the Madison City Street Railway Company which forced the streetcar company into receivership in 1893.

63. *WSJ,* February 8, 1896. Interest in the question of municipal ownership was not merely a reaction to the interlocking directorates of the Madison Gas Light and Coke Company and the Four Lakes Light and Power Company. In February, 1893, a debate between university literary and debate societies on the subject of municipal ownership of electric and streetcar utilities drew a huge crowd of 1,300 people. While confrontations between U.W. debate teams were a popular annual event on the town-gown calendar, the crowd attracted for this topic was much greater than normal. See *WSJ,* February 18, 1893.

64. Doherty served as manager until 1903 when he went to Denver to manage another of Emerson's acquisitions. Doherty ultimately bought the Denver company and developed it into the massive City Service empire.

65. See clippings in a scrapbook once owned by Henry L. Doherty, and now in the possession of Madison Gas and Electric Company.

66. This large amount of money represented the principal on the compromised bonds going all the way back to the 1857 spending spree. All these years, the city had only been paying interest on the bonds.

67. *CCP,* October 23, 1896. Reductions ranged from 16–27%.

68. There was one rather remarkable exception to the hiatus on municipalization and that was a proposal by John A. Johnson, owner of Gisholt and Fuller and Johnson Companies, to privately build and operate an electric utility. However, he would share the profits above 3% return on investment with the city. The interesting hybrid of public-private ownership idea went nowhere. For details see the *CCP* and Madison newspapers around December 24, 1897.

69. The 1890s were a period when Madison women were rapidly replacing wood stoves with gasoline and oil stoves. On August 17, 1894, the *WSJ* reported that these new types of stoves were making market wood sales very slow.

70. The five Madison businessmen who incorporated themselves as the Madison Street Railway Company and set off to sell $40,000 in stock were: E. W. Keyes, W. S. Noe, Alexander Gill, Phil Spooner and Dr. Phil Fox. *WSJ,* January 29, 1884.

71. *WSJ,* November 10, 1884.

72. The delightful account of the maiden voyage is found in the *WSJ,* November 17, 1884. For accounts of track laying see the *WSJ,* October 22, 1884. The exclusive franchise was passed on March 8, 1884.

73. *WSJ,* November 19 and 21, 1884, and Ordinance #866 passed June 13, 1885.

74. The delightful story of how Tenney was duped by the Chicago owners was told by Tenney himself in *MD,* October 2, 1892.

75. Pike, pp. 13–14; see the *WSJ,* July 21, 1884.

76. Ibid. Pike quotes Tenney's directive as follows: "Now operating the road in this way (with one horse) will be unpleasant to you as you do not believe in it; it will be unpleasant to the public, unpleasant to the animals, unpleasant to the drivers; all of which is very unpleasant to me; but you will loyally and faithfully execute this direction no matter how unpleasant.

77. *WSJ,* May 29, 1886.

78. See the *CCP,* February 11, 1887, and the *WSJ,* February 12, 1887.

79. *CCP,* September 9, 1887, and the *WSJ,* September 8, 1887.

80. *MD,* August 26, 1892.

81. Even before the line was built, the *Badger,* a U.W. student newspaper predicted that students living near the capital would probably not patronize the streetcars, preferring for reasons of pleasure and speed to walk. See Pike, pp. 12–13.

82. *CCP,* April 19, 1892.

83. An article in the *WSJ,* April 22, 1892, said the track of the mule line was in such poor condition passengers could not tell whether they were on or off the track.

84. The earliest U.S. experiments in electric street railways were conducted by Thomas Edison in 1880 and 1881. Because electricity was primarily used for night time street lighting, Edison was interested in developing a major daytime use for this new form of power. Although he built an electric locomotive at his Menlo Park laboratory, he lost interest in the project and left to others the challenge of perfecting this technology. The difficult problem of transmitting electricity to the motors was solved by the invention of the "troller" (hence the name "trolley"), a spring mounted pole which brought electricity from an overhead wire to the car. Then in rapid succession, a speed regulating device, good brakes and a long list of refinements made the electric streetcar a practical and economic transportation system. The distinction of having the first city-wide trolley system is generally reserved for either Montgomery, Alabama, or Appleton, Wisconsin, both of which were built in 1886.

The period between 1885 and 1892 was a period of intensive competition and consolidation among equipment suppliers. By 1892 when Madison made its purchase, two large firms dominated the market: ths Thomson-Houston Company from whom Madison bought its system and Westinghouse. In 1892, the year Madison bought its system, the Thomson-Houston Company merged with the Edison General Electric Company to form the General Electrical Company (G.E.).

85. *WSJ,* November 25, 1885.

86. CCP, October 12, 1888. A check of *CCP* through April, 1889 revealed no action by the council.

87. *WSJ,* September 29, 1890.

88. *WSJ,* June 29, 1891.

89. The best example of trolley promotion articles—an article which surely came from the talented pens of Madison Lakes Improvement Company publicists—is found in the *WSJ,* October 4, 1890.

90. Madison Lakes Improvement Company officials did not hesitate to give brusque replies to such complaints. Said one: "This opportunity has been lying here for 40 years waiting for someone to take hold of it and no one seemed to care to venture, but now we have found men of energy, of the requisite capital and desired determination to push the city of Madison before the people of the world. . . ." *WSJ,* October 11, 1890.

91. *CCP,* April 27, May 27, and June 10, 1892.

92. *WSJ,* May 14, 1892.

93. *WSJ,* May 16, 1892.

94. *WSJ,* May 24, 1892.

95. *MD,* October 2, 1892. Car speeds were estimated from time and distance data in this article.

96. References to headways, see the *WSJ,* November 30, 1892, October 24, 1894, May 28, 1896. For descriptions of the new cars see *WSJ,* May 28, 1896. For data on ridership increases see the *WSJ,* December 3, 1897 and December 14, 1898, and *Madison Past and Present.* Ridership for the year 1899 was interpolated from 1898 and 1901 data.

97. *WSJ,* July 15, 1892.

98. Efforts to get the streetcar line extended to these suburbs had been made in 1892, 1893, 1895, and 1896 but for a variety of reasons were unsuccessful. See the *WSJ,* September 25, 1893, the *MD,* October 27, 1895, and the *WSJ,* June 11 and November 2, 1896.

99. Actually the company went into receivership twice. The first time was between July 3, 1894 and February 1, 1896. A good year in 1895 allowed the company to pay the back electricity bills and interest on the bonds, but not enough to amortize the principal. Thus, on February 4, 1896 the company went into receivership again until it was sold in December 1897.

100. Exactly how much profit the company made, or whether it was profitable at all, was a subject of fierce debate during the effort to municipalize the streetcar company in 1919. See Chap. 6 for an extended discussion of the subject.

101. The *WSJ,* May 5, 1866, for the removal of the capital outhouse; the *WSJ,* May 2 and 6, 1867, for the Monona Avenue sewer; the *WSJ,* November 1, 1870, for the Park Hotel sewer; and the *WSJ,* August 21, 1874, for Mansion Hill sewer. The wealthy owners were E. W. Keyes, postmaster and attorney, 102 East Gorham, Timothy Brown, Secretary-Treasurer of the Madison Gas Light & Coke Company, 116 East Gorham, M. E. Fuller, implement dealer, 423 North Pinckney, and Attorney J. G. Gurnee, 115 East Gilman Street. The first three homes are now Madison landmarks.

102. The claim that more than half of Madison householders dumped their slops on the ground or even in Madison streets

comes from the *WSJ*, April 18, 1883. The inability of the police force to apprehend householders who dumped slops on the ground was described in the *WSJ*, December 9, 1884. References to the rarity and repugnant qualities of cesspools was found in the *WSJ*, May 6, 1878. This observation is based upon the ranking of the top five nuisances done each year by the city health officer beginning in 1886. In all years except five between 1886 and 1900 when Board of health reports were filed, privies ranked number one; in those years when they did not rank number one, privies were never lower than third. Other nuisances that generally came in second or third were fouled yards and gutters—both common collection points for human excrement.

As Doctor Philip M. Fox noted in his 1895 Board of Health report, the sanitary problem in the lower portions of the city, particularly around the west and east marshes was particularly bad during periods of high water. Under these conditions, water would back up, cover privies and spread their contents about.

103. The state built the first major sewer under Monona Avenue leading to Lake Monona. In 1870 the Park Hotel simply tapped onto the sewer. Wealthy homeowners on Mansion Hill built a sewer down Gorham Street into Lake Mendota.

104. *WSJ*, August 21, 1874.

105. The Paris/Seine-Madison lakes comparison was taken from a letter to the editor of the *WSJ*, May 8, 1878. An article that appeared in that same paper on May 14, 1878 noted that discharging sewage in the lakes was "the thing to be desired, the one thing which science and experience approves. . . ." One of the very few early criticisms of this view appeared in two anonymous articles printed in the *WSJ*, May 14 and 17, 1878. This writer argued that the Madison lakes, unlike the Seine, did not contain *moving* water and therefore could not have the same power of dilution and dispersion.

106. *WSJ*, April 18, 1883.

107. See the *WSJ*, December 9, 1884. This writer also noted that city authorities had not been able to prevent sewage from being dumped on the marsh even though the practice was illegal. Besides, the author argued, even if policemen could have halted the practice there, it would merely cause the problem to reappear somewhere else.

108. For examples of early protestations see the *WSJ*, August 28, 1883, August 25, 1883, and *CCP*, July 5, 1884. For the State Board of Health action, see the *WSJ*, August 11, 1884. One of the first good descriptions of the affects of sewage on the lakes was provided by an article by W. Trelease, "The Working of the Madison Lakes," Wisconsin Academy of Sciences Arts and Letters, *Transactions* (Madison, Vol. 7, pp. 121–129, 1889).

109. See Ordinance #848, signed July 7, 1884.

110. See *CCP*, July 5, 1884.

111. Actually the system cost much more than that, but Nader proposed to cover nearly all costs of each sewer district by assessing property owners. See *CCP*, September 6, 1884.

112. This phrase came from John Nader's charge to Samuel L. Gray in a letter dated December 27, 1884 and printed in Nader's Sewerage of Madison: Report of the City Engineer Transmitting the Report of Samuel M. Gray, Consulting Engineer (1885).

113. See *CCP*, December 6, 10, 17, 1884.

114. See Chapter 195, Laws of Wisconsin, pp. 985–993.

115. *CCP*, April 4 and 18, 1885.

116. The locations of these sewers can be determined from a perusal of the *Common Council Proceedings* of this period.

117. *WSJ*, May 12, 1892.

118. See the *WSJ*, May 17, 1892, April 6, 1893, and the *CCP* during the spring of 1892.

119. *WSJ*, October 27, 1893, and December 18, 1893. Price tag ranged from $50,000 to $120,000 but the city could then only borrow a maximum amount of $48,000 before it exceeded its charter-imposed debt limit. At the time the city charter prevented the city from borrowing more than five percent of the value of its equalized property value.

120. See *WSJ*, October 27, 1893, December 18, 1893, and *CCP* during these months.

121. *CCP*, May 2, 1894; *WSJ*, May 3, 1894, June 8, 1894.

122. *CCP*, June 15, 1894, and *WSJ*, June 16, 1894.

123. WSJ, June 7, 1894.

124. Contemporary newspaper articles describing the first suit initiated by James E. Fisher, 139 West Wilson Street, are found on the *MD*, July 23, 1895, and the *WSJ* of the same date. The second lawsuit was initiated by Stephen C. Baas, 727 Jenifer, in August, 1895. See the *WSJ*, August 28, 1895. Both Fisher and Baas described their once sandy and gravelly lakeshore bottoms in front of their homes as covered by six or eight inches of filth.

125. *WSJ*, August 19, 1895.

126. *MD*, August 21, 1895.

127. *WSJ*, August 24, 1895.

128. *WSJ*, August 31, 1895.

129. However, from the time that Waring recommended land disposal, the *Democrat* became a believer and championed this technique until the septic system had proved its reliability. What it lacked in early vigorous coverage, it made up for in testy support of land disposal. Its editor, O. D. Brandenburg, lost few opportunities to ridicule the MacDougall plan. Keyes comment comes from the *WSJ*, September 30, 1894.

130. *WSJ*, June 28, 1894. See also *WSJ*, September 13, 1899.

131. The term "professional beauty" was used by George E. Waring at the large public meeting on July 28, 1894, and reported in the WSJ, July 30, 1894.

132. Tenney even went so far as to argue that the 1894 and 1895 problems were as "natural to the lakes as the fish" and had been present on and off for years. *WSJ*, September 3, 1895.

133. *WSJ*, September 3, 1895. For another expression of Tenney's views see *WSJ*, June 2, 1894. Support for deep water disposal also came from John Nader, City Engineer, in a letter to the *MD*, July 8, 1894. For the expression of aldermanic support, see *CCP*, June 14, 1894, and the *WSJ*, June 15, 1894. The views of other conservative business who continued to support deep water dilution were described in the *WSJ*, May 28, 1894.

134. *WSJ*, June 19, 1894. On this cost question Warner was vigorously supported by the *Wisconsin State Journal* which editorially observed: "It is amazing . . . how doors of escape open for those who march bravely in the path of discretion and duty." *WSJ*, June 16, 1894.

135. Waring was hired by the Common Council on July 13, 1894. Waring had made a national reputation by his pioneering work in New York City in the 1850s and was probably best known for his sewerage system developed for the city of Memphis, which eliminated the dreaded yellow fever. Waring was also the author of the definitive book on the subject of sewage treatment entitled *Modern Methods of Sewage Disposal.*

136. *WSJ*, July 30, 1894.

137. *CCP*, August 10, 1894.

138. *CCP*, July 30 and September 14, 1894, for details on the acquisition of the Gill sewer and the tie in with the Baldwin Street district.

139. *CCP*, July 12, 1895.

140. *CCP*, October 16, 1895.

141. *CCP*, March 13, 1896.

142. One might reasonably ask what credence a U.W. math professor would have had in a sewage debate. The answer lies in the fact that Slichter was an applied mathematician, not a theoretical mathematician. His most important work was in geology and specifically in the flow of underground water. One must also remember that at the time much less attention ws paid to the barriers between departments than today. See Mark H. Ingram's *Charles Sumner Slichter: The Golden Vector* (Madison: The University of Wisconsin Press, 1972), pp. 55–56.

143. *WSJ*, May 23, 1896. Although his name did not appear among the list of university activists in the sewage question, there seems to be little doubt that Professor F. H. King, the first chairman of the U.W. Soil Science Department, played a large behind-the-scenes role. In the summer of 1895 he had made an extensive tour of European applications of sewage irrigation. His favorable conclusions were reported in the *WSJ*, October 3, 1895.

The appearance before the council on May 22, 1896, was the culmination of a series of letters published by the *WSJ* and the *MD* the preceeding month in which they took strenuous exception to the claims of the city engineers Dodge and Nader. Van Hise, for example, had warned Waring about the efficacy of the chemical precipitation plan. Waring in a return letter to Van Hise called the technique "at best a costly scientific toy." In a letter to the *WSJ* on May 1, 1896, Slichter said the chemical precipitation system would make Lake Monona "the city slop bucket." See *WSJ*, May 1, 1896, May 9, 1896, and *MD*, May 7, 1896.

144. *CCP*, September 22, 1896.

145. *WSJ*, February 20, 1897.

146. See both the *MD* and the *WSJ*, Marcy 6, 1897, and March 10, 1897.

147. *CCP*, March 12, 1897.

148. For a report of this committee see the *WSJ*, July 14, 1897, or *CCP*.

149. Descriptions of MacDougall are found in the *WSJ*, February 3, 1902.

150. *CCP*, October 11, 1897.

151. See Ordinance #1167 passed April 11, 1898.

152. *CCP*, October 15, 1897.

153. See the *WSJ*, October 19, 1897.

154. *WSJ*, October 20, 1897.

155. *WSJ*, December 20, 1897.

156. *WSJ*, December 27 and 31, 1897.

157. *WSJ*, February 26, 1898, and July 22, 1898.

158. The story of the Canadian delegates is found in the *WSJ*, June 16, 1899, whereas the Dodge account did not come out until the 1902 trial. See the *WSJ*, February 5, 1902.

159. Newspaper accounts of the plant shortcomings were frequent. For examples see the *MD*, August 13, September 3, 1899, and the *WSJ*, August 28, September 6, 1899. Chemical tests were not done until just a few days before the expiration of the ninety-day trial period on September 28, 1899. The results of these tests were not made public until October 19, 1899, *WSJ*, but then an error was discovered which prompted council members to hire several others including the state chemist to do the job. See the *CCP*, October 27, 1899.

160. The city ran the sewage plant for one year from January 1900 to January 1901. From January 1901 until July 1901, when the new septic system plant opened, all of Madison's sewage was dumped into the Yahara River at the sewer plant outfall.

161. The effluent so polluted the Yahara River that the Chicago Northwestern Railroad had to move its locomotive water intake point upstream from the sewage outfall. Prior to this move, sewage effluent clogged locomotive boilers and made escaping steam so foul smelling that the engineers and firemen could not tolerate it. See the *WSJ*, September 1, 1901, and February 12, 1902.

162. See the newspapers from February 3–15, 1902, for accounts of the trial.

163. See the *WSJ*, September 19, 1901. See also July 12, 1901. For general background on the slow early progress of sanitary engineering, see the chapter on "Sewage Treatment" in Ellis L. Armstrong's (ed.) *History of Public Works in the United States, 1776–1976* (Chicago: American Public Works Association, 1976).

Varieties of Local Government Reform: 1880–1900

1. Beyond the problem of having to secure legislative approval for each additional power it desired, Madison officials were working to solve a more fundamental problem, namely how to pay for large one-time outlays for capital improvements. Conservative interpreters of Madison's charter argued that it was illegal for the city to contract for any improvement whose costs could not be covered in the annual budget. This meant that capital improvement costs could *not* be financed by bonds and then paid back in low annual installments. Making the problem even more difficult was the existence of the state-imposed levy limits which limited the tax rate to two percent of assessed valuation. In this case, the city was trying to get out from under this problem as it pertained to street improvements. See the *WSJ*, February 3, 1893.

The request to own and operate its own electric lighting plant was a direct response to the very favorable experience the city had in owning and operating its water works.

2. Chapter 326, Laws of 1889.

3. Chapter 362, Laws of 1891.

4. *WSJ*, December 10, 1892.

5. The best study of national developments in this area is Martin J. Schiesl's *The Politics of Efficiency: Municipal Administration and Reform in America, 1800 to 1920* (University of California Press, 1977).

6. For background on the early home rule movement, see James Donaghue's "Local Government in Wisconsin," *1979–1980 Blue Book*, pp. 144–5. For background on the charter problems, see *WSJ*, December 10, 13, and 19, 1892, and January 14, 1893. Rogers invited representatives to Madison from Ashland, LaCrosse, Oshkosh, Racine, Eau Claire, Fond du Lac, Superior, Sheboygan, Appleton, Janesville, Wausau, Green Bay, Chippewa Falls, Kenosha, Watertown, and Marinette. *WSJ*, January 14, 17, and 21, 1893.

7. The term "more intelligent class of voters" was first used by Mayor Rogers in the *WSJ*, March 19, 1894. The term "businessmen and principal taxpayers" came from Mayor Elisha Keyes' inaugural, *CCP*, April 20, 1886. In that address Keyes sharply criticized this group for not taking "a greater interest in the management of city affairs and the general proceedings of the council. "The revenues of the city," added Keyes, "are largely derived from this class of our citizens, and yet it would seem that the general practice among them is to pay but little if any attention to city matters which concern them so much." Significantly, Keyes was also critical of *general apathy.* "A new administration of our city government is this day inaugurated," be began. But it was not, he complained, "an event of much moment by those who should be most deeply interested. This change comes and goes with the years creating scarcely a ripple of general interest." The term "good men" comes from the charter of the Civic Federation quoted in the *WSJ* on March 2, 1895. The description of the Fifth Ward caucus comes from a letter to the *WSJ* editor from a "citizen" published on November 21, 1899, but which described a caucus "a few years back."

8. *WSJ*, March 25, 1896. Until the nonpartisan idea entered the political arena, it was necessary even for reform mayors like William H. Rogers (1801–93) to remind Madison voters that the "Democratic party is entirely in sympathy with public education. . . ." *CCP*, April 21, 1891.

9. *WSJ*, January 22, 1895.

10. *WSJ*, April 1, 1898. This phrase appeared in an open letter to incumbent Mayor Hoven written by Presbyterian minister Joseph W. Cochran. In his letter Rev. Cochran asked Hoven questions like: "Can we purify local democracy by again seating you in the mayoral chair?" and "What pure, exalted, or enterprising element among us do you stand for . . .?" Such questions were typical of those being asked by voters during this period.

11. An early expression of the idea appeared in Keyes inaugural, April 20, 1886. There he urged the council not to treat City Hall as any "alms house where only the incompetent and impoverished need apply." Numerous other expressions of support for the merit principle appeared in citations in this section.

12. "What business corporation," asked former Mayor Rogers, and a leader in the reform movement, "would select a man to disperse $150,000 (then the city's annual budget) and pay him nothing? *WSJ*, March 2, 1895. See also *WSJ*, April 4, 1887, December 13, 1890.

13. Mayor Rogers had recommended an executive budget in 1894 (*WSJ*, March 19, 1894) but the council did not act. Mayor Whelan, four years later (1898), in his inaugural address criticized the failure to set up a sound budgeting system. *CCP*, April 19, 1898.

14. See *WSJ*, February 3, 1885.

15. This was a carryover from the 1892 home rule effort.

16. According to the *WSJ*, November 2, 1892, "the brass band and torchlight campaign has passed away and in its place has come one of quiet but systematic work. It takes persistent and level headed argument to influence voters in these days and the fact is realized by both sides."

17. Mayor Rogers first proposed this idea in April, 1892 (*CCP*, April 19, 1892). Mayor Keyes in his inaugural address clearly viewed businessmen as experts whose "counsel and advice" could greatly benefit the mayor and aldermen. See *CCP*, April 20, 1886. Mayor Rogers in his 1892 inaugural had said the same thing except in broader terms. See *CCP*, April 19, 1892.

18. See the lectures by *Journal* Editor Amos Wilder in *WSJ*, April 23, 27, 29, May 2 and 3, 1895. A similar set of lectures was delivered by Wilder in the spring of 1897. Dr. Amos Wilder was indeed qualified to speak on this subject. His Yale doctoral dissertation entitled "The Municipal Problem" had enjoyed a large circulation after it was printed by the New Haven Chamber of Commerce.

Wilder and numerous others such as U.W. President C. K. Adams strongly championed the German model of municipal government. For Wilder's thought on this see *WSJ*, January 22, 1895. For President Adams views, see the *WSJ*, February 2, 1895. Said Wilder: In an era of "electricity and railroad crossings and tenements . . . microbes and political rings, and with the call for parks and libraries . . ." there was no choice, but to implement "the highest developed municipal government, to consider the mistakes and achievements elsewhere—abroad as well as in this country. . . ."

19. Several issues of this newspaper are available at the SHSW microfilm room. Very significantly the *WSJ* endorsed A. A. Dye, whereas the *Democrat* endorsed the Democratic candidate. *MD*, April 3, 1896.

20. *WSJ*, March 27, 1896.

21. *CCP*, April 10, 1896.

22. Data analysis by the author.

23. In 1895, 1896, 1898, and 1899, the number of Democrats and Republicans was balanced in the Common Council.

24. Laws of 1897.

25. See *MD*, April 18, 20, 21, 1897.

The City Beautiful: A Movement Begins

1. *WSJ*, Jan. 9, 1893.

2. For other examples of probeauty letters from leading businessmen, see W. C. Walker's letter to the *WSJ*, April 10, 1892, and W. R. Bagley's letter to the *WSJ* dated January 12 or 13, 1893, in which he stated: "We are tired of the old song, Nature has done much for Madison . . . let it rather be said, Nature has done much, but man more." Bagley described street ends as the "home of the oyster can ash heap."

3. *WSJ*, January 7, 1893. Wealthy businessman W. G. Walker may have been the first to suggest the formation of an "improvement society" in a letter to the editor of the *Madison Democrat* on April 10, 1892. Walker's suggestion was quickly seconded by Mayor William Rogers in a letter to the *WSJ* on April 30, 1892, who urged high schoolers to form a "Madison Improvement Society" to plant trees. The notion was also pushed by Richard T. Ely, newly arrived professor of economics, in an address to his new faculty members in November 1892. See the *WSJ*, November 19, 1892. The most forceful expression of the idea, however, came from lawyer and U.W. Law School faculty member John M. Olin in October 1892 at the huge banquet celebrating the opening of Madison's electric streetcar line. See the *WSJ* and *MD* dated October 2, 1892.

4. *WSJ*, February 27–28, 1893.

5. See the *WSJ*, April 17 and 28, 1893.

6. *MD*, April 7, 1893.

7. The sixty-boat Frank Lloyd Wright boathouse on the 66-foot-wide street end of North Carroll Street was opened in April, 1894. See the *WSJ*, April 25, 1894. The larger, more ornate and picturesque boathouse on Lake Monona might have been built first had not foundation and footing problems been discovered that required additional money. The *adjoining* railroad pledged this additional amount but then withdrew its offer after the 1893 depression. Anticipating the completion of the large Lake Monona boathouse, the Common Council even passed an ordinance (#1070, August 12, 1893) requiring all persons who had erected boathouses on street ends to remove them ten days *after* the completion of the public boathouse. Since the boathouse was never built, the ordinance never went into effect.

For an excellent summary of the Madison Improvement Association see the *WSJ*, October 22, 1895.

8. *WSJ*, October 25, 1906.

9. For accounts of this early period, see C. N. Brown's speech to the National Civic Society reprinted in the *WSJ*, October 25, 1906, and John M. Olin's President's Report in the 1902 MPPDA Annual Report, pp. 7–8.

The Raymer Road through Eagle Heights was constructed in 1888 following an eventful walk Raymer had taken the previous September with Colonel Elisha W. Keyes. According to an account published by the *WSJ*, *Madison Past and Present*, p. 76, the two men "were amazed and delighted" by the scene that greeted them as they reached the top of Eagle Heights. Mr. Keyes remarked that he had lived in Madison forty years but had never before been up there. Raymer was so taken by the place he bought the 150 acre parcel and the next year constructed a two and one-half mile road to and along the shore of Lake Mendota and circling the heights to the top. This was opened to the public.

10. See *WSJ*, June 17, 1882, Oct. 15, 1892, *MD*, Oct. 16, 1892, and *Madison Past and Present*, p. 6.

11. This first pleasure drive was also significant because it included a fourteen-acre park along what is now Owen Parkway, the land for which was bought and then donated to the public by Owen at a cost of $3,000. This was the first of several such parks that then lay outside the city limits that were ultimately made a part of the Madison park system. See 1902 MPPDA Report, p. 8.

12. *MD*, Oct. 16, 1892.

13. Contrary to what many have thought, the key word in the new organization's name was "drives"; "park" and "pleasure" both modified this word.

The best sources for the early history of the MPPDA are the handwritten Association minutes kept in the Forest Hill vault of the Madison Parks Department and hereinafter called *Minutes* and John M. Olin's "President's Report" in the 1902 *Annual Report*, pp. 7–11. Association reports are available from 1898 to 1929.

Although there was no formal connection between the Madison Park and Pleasure Drive Association and the Madison Improvement Association, half of the 26 MPPDA Board of Directors had been contributing members to the MIA.

The MPPDA was a local expression of a strong back-to-nature movement then beginning throughout the country. For a description of the national back to nature movement, see Peter J. Schmitt's *Back to Nature: The Arcadian Myth in Urban America* (New York: Oxford University Press, 1969). For a representative local expression, see the remarks of General Edwin M. Bryant in the *MPPDA 1903 Annual Report*, p. 52.

14. *WSJ*, March 2, 1897; *MD*, March 3, 1897.

15. See *MD*, July 25, 1897, and *WSJ*, March 18, 1897, for background on the decision to name the Drive after Farwell.

16. 1899 Report, p. 9.

17. See the minutes dated January 27, 1899, p. 45.

18. 1902 MPPDA Annual Report, p. 11.

19. In an article appearing in the 1902 Report, p. 67, John Olin said: ". . . We must remember that seventy-five percent of our population are not the possessors of a single horse and buggy and rarely ever indulge in the luxury of a livery turnout."

20. *WSJ*, March 26, 1895.

21. See footnote 19.

Society and Leisure

1. Details surrounding Hamlin Garland's visit to Madison appeared in C. E. Schorer's "Hamlin Garland of Wisconsin" (*Wisconsin Magazine of History* 37 (1953), pp. 147–148). Citations from the novel come from a 1965 edition reprinted by the AMA Press, Inc., New York, New York, pp. 27, 81, 82, and 87.

2. The description of Madison's society comes from the "Highway and Byway" column, which appeared in the *Chicago Tribune* in July 1890. A summary of that article appeared in the *WSJ*, July 14, 1890. All quotes come from the latter source. "Would you believe it," said the Chicago columnist, "that in a city of 16,000 people, there are three societies . . .?"

3. *WSJ*, August 17, 1899.

4. Being quoted was one of Langdon's grand dames, Mrs. Ada Sumner Mosley, who at the time of the article was eighty-four years old. See June 1960 *Holiday Magazine*, p. 84.

5. Gertrude Slaughter, *Only the Past Is Ours, The Life Story of Gertrude Slaughter* (New York: Exposition Press, 1963), pp. 119–120.

6. *WSJ*, June 12, 1894.

7. See the *MD*, December 31, 1893, for a description of a party held by Dr. and Mrs. George Keenan. See the *MD* during June 1894 for accounts of a large society wedding.

8. See the *Critic*, edited by Alice S. Blount, 1897, and the *MD*, January 10, 1897. Although the *Critic* lasted only six months, it reflected the development of a self-conscious formal society.

9. For insights into this form of blindness see a sharply critical letter to the editor, *WSJ*, November 21, 1899.

10. See "Semi-Annual Bank Reports," SHSW Archives.

11. Author analysis.

12. *CCP*, June 11, 1886. See also *MD*, May 11, 1882, and February 19, 1886, for similar incidents.

13. *MD*, October 8, 1899. For details on the Hoven election see the *WSJ*, September 18, 1896, and both newspapers just prior to the election.

14. This type of incident was rarely reported in the newspapers. This incident in fact was recorded in a Madison society magazine known as *The Critic* 1, no. 29 (July 1897), p. 5.

15. See the *MD*, May 20, 1896.

16. *MD*, August 26, 1898.

17. *MD*, December 26, 1899.

18. *MD*, September 11, 1896.

19. *WSJ*, September 1, 1888.

20. For an outstanding treatment of the national background on these matters, see Sidney E. Ahlstrom's definitive *A Religious History of the American People* (New Haven: Yale University Press, 1972), especially p. VII, pp. 732–872; Aaron I. Abell, *The Urban Impact on American Protestantism, 1865–1900* (Cambridge: Harvard University Press, 1943); Charles R. Hopkins, *The Rise of the Social Gospel in American Protestantism* (New Haven: Yale University Press, 1940).

21. Background on the Willard visit see Butterfield, p. 745. For a general description of W.C.T.U. activities, see *MD*, February 4, 1883. For description of the game room for boys, see *MD*, August 5, 1880, September 17, 1880, January 19, 1882.

John Bascom's early involvement with the W.C.T.U. is told in the *MD*, April 25, 1882. Emma Bascom was particularly active in the 1884 fight to prevent alcoholic beverages from being served at the Dane County Fair. See the *MD*, February 24, 1884.

22. *WSJ*, March 25 and 27, 1884.

23. For the reaction to Bascom's remarks, see a strongly worded *WSJ* indictment printed on March 26, 1884. The *Journal* called Bascom's remarks a "deliberate" attempt to libel the city which it said was as "peaceful as a Methodist camp meeting." Other newspapers around the state and even some out of state papers eventually became embroiled in the question of Madison's immorality.

Once Bascom had stirred up this muck it took many years to settle. Six years after Bascom made his charges an incoming Mayor Robert Bashford felt compelled in his inaugural address to respond to the same basic charge. Said Bashford: "The students in attendance are as a class sober, honest, industrious and well behaved and ambitious for high standing in their studies. As student, instructor and citizen I have a close personal knowledge of University affairs for the last twenty-five years and during that time I have never known an instance of disorderly conduct which properly called for the interference of the police authorities. This is a record of which the friends of the University may well be proud; it speaks volumes for the character and conduct of its students and should serve as one of the strongest inducements to parents to send their children here for higher instruction." *CCP*, April 15, 1890.

24. The creed cited was passed in 1887 but was typical of several such creeds adopted during this period.

25. For articles on the Law and Order League see the *MD*, March 13, 22, 1884, and June 13, 1884. Similar background for the Personal Liberty League can be found in the *WSJ*, March 18, 1884, and for several months thereafter. The use of detectives by the Law and Order League was described in the *WSJ*, June 10 and December 19, 1884.

26. *CCP*, April 7, 1888, noted that W. A. Troy, the prohibitionist candidate, got only ninety votes out of 2481 cast—a mere four percent of the vote. Not even five percent of Madison voters cast ballots for Madison attorney John M. Olin and prominent prohibition leader when he ran for governor on the prohibition ticket in 1886. See *WSJ*, November 3, 1886.

27. An attempt by prohibition forces to force saloons to close at 11 PM had failed in 1886 (*CCP*, August 12, 1886) but a similar effort with a 12 o'clock closing time was passed by the council in 1893. Ordinance #1054, May 12, 1893.

28. For newspaper accounts of the 1885 and 1891 low-high license referenda see the *WSJ* and *MD* during late August and early September. Both the 1885 and the 1891 elections were held on September 15. A leading businessman was quoted as saying that "he was tired of seeing every new building that is erected in the city occupied by a saloon. It is about time that our people were directing their attention to other business affairs than the propagation of saloons." *WSJ*, August 22, 1891.

29. The state law that authorized the wet-dry vote was Chapter 521, Laws of 1889. "Wet" arguments for the 1894 election were artfully and persuasively presented in a circular entitled "License or No License" issued on April 1, 1894, just three days before the election. A copy is available in the SHSW pamphlet collection. Dry arguments were the same as those noted earlier by John M. Olin and John Bascom in the high-law license debates. The twenty-five percent budget figure is derived from the above noted circular and from an analysis of city budgets. Vote results were printed in the *CCP*, April 3, 1894.

Perhaps it was the fact that sixty percent of Madison voters in the 1894 referendum voted against prohibition, that Madison council members felt justified in a January, 1896 ordinance (#1096) that *lowered* the drinking age from eighteen to sixteen years of age. The action was accompanied by virtually no attention in the press. The sixteen-year-old drinking law remained n effect until Prohibition was achieved on a national basis in 1917.

30. For background on the Dye Sunday closing campaign, see the *WSJ*, April 1, April 27, April 29, and May 14, 1896, and *MD*, May 1, 1896.

31. The regents' statement was reported in the *WSJ*, May 26, 1898. The testimony of Dean Henry was reported in the *WSJ*, June 25, 1898. See the *CCP*, June 27, 1898.

32. *WSJ*, June 2, 1896.

33. For the stall saloon see the *WSJ*, June 2, 4, 10, 1897, and the *CCP*, September 10–11, 1897, and June 10, 1898. Newspaper accounts of the failure to deny licenses of the "midway" saloons can be found in the *WSJ*, June 28, 1898, July 8, 14, 15, 22, 1898. The Presbyterian minister letter was printed in the *WSJ*, April 1, 1898.

The Church Alliance composed of committees from each church, was formed in March, 1896 to be a "central advisory and directing head by which the reform focus of the city may be brought to bear with a force of unity. . . ." (*MD*, March 6, 1896.) Its members were active both in the Civic Federation as well as prohibition and prostitution issues.

34. *CCP*, April 14, 1898.

35. Ordinance #1173, June 11, 1898.

36. *WSJ*, November 15, 1897.

37. *WSJ*, December 22, 1894.

38. The Sixth Ward Chapel was an outgrowth of a Sunday School which had been formed after the Civil War for children in the Soldiers' Orphans Home. In 1887 the Christian Endeavor Society of the First Congregational Church formally assumed control of this Sunday School. Funds for the chapel were provided for by several public spirited citizens who required that one hundred children from the immediate neighborhood be enrolled in the Sunday School as a condition of getting the money. The Sixth Ward Chapel was later attached as a wing to the Pilgrim Congregational Church when it was built in 1914–15. The building is now occupied by the Wil-Mar Neighborhood Center. For details on this early history see the Papers of the Pilgrim Congregational Church in the SHSW.

39. *WSJ*, January 8, 1896, and March 18, 1896.

40. See the *WSJ*, August 12, 1895, and October 31, 1896.

41. *WSJ*, September 1, 1888. For background on the Salvation Army see the *WSJ*, June 7, 1894, August 21, 1895, and September 21, 1898, and the *MD*, March 8, 1889, October 24, 1890, May 9, 1895, and August 21, 1895.

42. A typical "warning" against front-door charity was issued by Judge Keyes in the *MD*, December 31, 1891. The practice of sending turkeys and beef roasts to the poor is described in the *MD*, December 30, 1884, and December 27, 1891.

43. For descriptions of the Madison Benevolent Society see the *WSJ*, October 14, 1889, September 26, 1889, October 30, 1895, and November 13, 1896.

44. See Mary S. Foster's "Early History of the Attic Angels Association," an unpublished manuscript in the SHSW dated 1947.

45. Professor Ely's plea for a "trained expert" is found in the *WSJ*, October 30, 1895. The termination of the long-standing child support activities of the Attic Angels were reported in the *MD*, November 4, 1900.

46. This type of behavior was described in the *WSJ*, March 9, 1897, February 10, 1881, April 22, 1890, June 29, 1886, April 13, 1880, June 3, 1890, October 26, 1882, and the *MD*, May 14, 1889, February 12, 1892.

47. Newspaper accounts of this behavior are found in *MD*, September 14, 1887, the *WSJ*, January 14, 1899, May 28, 1886, October 31, 1899, and Ordinance #818, signed into law September 18, 1882.

48. For background, see Ordinance #1133, signed into law on November 13, 1896, and the *WSJ*, June 12, 1888, February 14, 1890, June 18, 25, 30, 1897.

49. For details on this story see the *WSJ*, March 28, 1878, May 10, 1883, July 16, 1886, and December 3, 1895; the *MD*, July 16, 1889. For national context see Schmitt, p. 39.

50. See *WSJ*, November 11, 1886.

51. *WSJ*, August 25, 1900 and October 9, 1888.

52. See a letter by Albert F. Boerner dated November 18, 1894, published in the *Pioneer Village Review* (Ozaukee County Historical Society) 8, No. 1, March, 1979), pp. 3–4.

53. *WSJ*, December 9, 1899.

54. *WSJ*, November 21, 1896.

55. *WSJ*, November 9, 1897. For additional background on football and other sports, see the excellent chapter entitled "The Rise of Collegiate Athletics" in Curti and Carstensen's *The University of Wisconsin: A History*, Vol. 1, pp. 693–710.

56. For newspaper coverage of basketball, see the *WSJ*, November 21, 1895, and the *MD*, November 9, 1900. For a description of an early tennis tournament see the *WSJ*, May 23, 1887. For coverage of track and field events see the *MD*, May, 1892.

57. See the *MD*, August 27, 1897, and April 26, 1899; *WSJ*, September 17, 1898 and April 15, and April 27, 1899.

58. For two good accounts on the absence of swimming facilities see *WSJ*, August 11, 1892, and July 20, 1897. Efforts to revive sailing were chronicled in the *WSJ*, August 14, 1884, and the *MD*, August 22, 1884, the summer of 1885 and July 31, 1888. Commercial steamboat activities were summarized in the late spring or early summer. For examples see *WSJ*, May 30, 1884, and July 5, 1898.

59. Alice S. Blount (ed.), *The Critic* (Vol. 1, No. 2), January, 1897, p. 2.

60. For a description of the party car, see the *WSJ*, October 6, 1896. For an account of a trolley party see the *CT*, March 4, 1931.

61. *WSJ*, July 10, 1899. In addition to Schuetzen Park, there was a Max Gaertner's German Garden located at the intersection of Williamson and Baldwin Streets where a gasoline station is now located. Band concerts were also regularly given here.

62. For background on the Mendota Club see minutes, by-laws, and articles of incorporation in the Andrew Mayer's papers (SHSW) and the *WSJ*, January 7, 1892, March 28, 1892, October 16, 1883, and October 21, 1899.

63. *MD*, April 26, 1892. See also *WSJ*, January 22–31, 1896, and November 26, 1897.

64. *WSJ*, April 29, 1881.

65. *WSJ*, November 26, 1888.

66. *WSJ*, December 22, 1886 and January 11, 1887.

Chapter 6

1. *WSJ*, December 1, 1900.

2. *WSJ*, February 25, 1901, January 27, 1903, October 8, 1905.

Disputing Madison's Destiny, Round 3

1. For an example of this progrowth argument see the *WSJ* account (September 30, 1910) of Carl A. Johnson's pep talk to the initial meeting of the Commercial Club. Johnson was president of the Gisholt Company.

2. *WSJ*, January 28, 1899.

3. See the *MD* and WSJ in October 1900 for details.

4. *WSJ*, October 26, 1901.

5. For example, in a talk before the Six O'Clock Club on March 2, 1902, Paul Findlay said that Madison's "population was as certain to exceed 40,000 in 1910 as the sun is certain to rise on January 1st of that year." *Municipality*, Vol. 2, Nov. 12, April, 1902, p. 254.

6. *WSJ*, February 26, 1901.

7. *WSJ*, April 7, 1905.

8. *WSJ*, January 23, 1901, *Madison Past and Present* (Madison: *WSJ*, 1902), p. 23.

9. *WSJ*, October 26, 1901.

10. Analysis of a 1902 Forty Thousand Club membership list showed that Gapen failed to get the balanced state-university-business representation that he desired. The list included just one state employee (Governor LaFollette), one professor, one postmaster, and forty-six businessmen. Of the businessmen, retailers were the most numerous, followed by manufacturers, wholesalers, and lawyers. See the *Madison Past and Present*, p. 209, and *MD*, February 26, 1901.

11. For examples of these activities, see the *WSJ*, March 13, 20, 27, 1901.

12. *Madison Past and Present*, p. 23.

13. *MD*, December 11, 1901, *WSJ*, September 24, 1902.

14. *Madison Past and Present*, p. 23.

15. *WSJ*, September 7, 1903, August 26, 1910.

16. *WSJ*, October 1, 1901, April 10, November 13, 1907.

17. *WSJ*, September 30, 1910. For accounts of the rapid growth and demise of the Commercial Club, see the *WSJ*, March 1, May 10, July 13, September 24 and 30, 1910, and August 17, 1911, and the *MD*, May 4, 1910.

18. *WSJ*, October 5, 1913.

19. See the early issues of *Community Business*. To be sure, their reasons for pursuing these ends were not entirely altruistic. Board organizers believed that people who lived in a city characterized by these much sought after conditions would be more productive and efficient workers who would not be inclined to squander their money on the degrading things of life. Using the same logic, board organizers recognized that real property located in a community with these properties would have much higher market value and hence would produce more tax dollars to pay for the aforementioned urban "goods." In short, better people living in better cities produced better business conditions. For an example of this reasoning see an essay by O. B. Towne entitled "The Relations between Civics and Commerce," in William G. Bruce's (ed.) *Commercial Organizations, Their Function, Operation and Service* (Milwaukee: The Bruen Publishing Company, 1920), pp. 42–49.

20. *WSJ*, November 3, 1915, June 5, 1913. The board had three major divisions: (1) public affairs, (2) business development, and (3) organization affairs.

In 1915 nearly three hundred board members were serving on various committees, almost as large as the entire membership of the entire 1911 Commercial Club, heretofore the largest commercial club. See *WSJ*, November 3, 1915.

21. *WSJ*, April 19, 1913. *Community Business*, October 7, 1914.

22. Actually some fifteen hundred memberships were sold because bylaws allowed members to purchase more than one membership. Even with multiple memberships, however, a member had only one vote. *WSJ*, May 3, 1913.

23. See *Madison: The Four Lakes City; the Pathfinder, A Guidebook for Madison, Wisconsin, and Vicinity; Industrial and Commercial Madison*, and *What Is the Madison Board of Commerce?* Its monthly periodical was entitled *Community Business*.

24. See *WSJ*, December 13, 1914. For another annual summaries, see January 2, 1916, and *WSJ*, November 5, 1919.

In 1917 the Board of Commerce took under its wing a variety of business organizations, some of which had been spawned by board action. Examples included the Madison Commercial Association, a spin-off of retailers, and Auto Good Roads Club, an organization established by the board to lobby for better highways. To reflect this consolidation of organizations, the board changed its name to the Association of Commerce in 1917. However, to avoid confusion, the term "Board" will be used throughout.

25. *CT*, October 15, 1918. For general background on the origins of the Madison Club, see the *WSJ*, October 21, 1901, November 24, 1916, February 4, 1917, and May 21–22, 1918.

26. For a thoughtful analysis of service clubs in American life seee Charles F. Marden's *Rotary and Its Brothers* (Princeton, New Jersey: Princeton University Press, 1935). Information on local clubs was also provided by club representatives and from contemporary newspaper accounts. See the special Kiwanis edition of *WSJ*, February 23, 1920, and *Silver Anniversary Program, 1913–1938*. Rotary Club.

27. *WSJ*, February 26, 1901.

28. *WSJ*, February 27, 1901, March 2, 1901, and September 30, 1910. The arguments outlined in this section were never made by a single speaker or even by several speakers at a single occasion.They are rather a composite of arguments made between 1900 and 1915.

29. *WSJ*, October 11, 1901, *MD*, October 7, 1906.

30. *WSJ*, July 20, 1915.

31. See *WSJ*, October 26, 1901. One firm that apparently came to Madison at least in part because businessmen were willing to buy its stock was the Madison-Kipp Company, then known as the Mason-Kipp Company. See *MD*, December 11, 1901. For a reference to the letter-writing scheme, see *WSJ*, March 13, 1901.

32. *WSJ*, April 18, 1915.

33. *WSJ*, May 27, 1917.

34. Ibid., *Why and How of a $200,000 Industrial Development Stand for Madison* (Board of Commerce, 1916). According to one expert a one-hundred worker plant required $100,000 worth of capital. See *WSJ*, June 20, July 6, 1916.

35. Norman Weissman "A History of the Wisconsin State Journal Since 1910" (Masters thesis, University of Wisconsin, 1951), p. 77.

36. *WSJ*, June 17, July 9, 20, 25, 31, 1915.

37. According to *WSJ*, April 27, 1905, Fair Oaks Land Company gave $53,700 in cash and free lots to factory owners on the condition that they erect factories on them. The Madison Square Company also offered free industrial sites but only if enough Madison investors would buy nearby residential lots at *above* market prices.This concept, which received the endorsement of the Board of Commerce, was based upon the assumption that *after* a factory was located at the designated "free" site, the value of the residential lots would rise to or above the asking price. The concept was a novel alternative to the more common and more direct practice of buying stock in a new enterprise.For details of this scheme, see *Community Business*, August 15, 1914.

38. For descriptions of the 1906 request, see *CCP*, May 11, July 13, 1906, *MD*, June 16 and June 26, 1906, and *WSJ* June 25, 29, July 14, 1906.

39. For the 1910 episode see *WSJ*, May 17, 18, 19, 21, June 15, 17, 25, July 9, 14, September 10, 1910, and *CCP*, July 8 and September 10, 1910.

40. *WSJ*, October 21, 22, 1910.

41. *WSJ*, February 20, 1901.

42. See comments made by A. L. Burdick in *Madison Past and Present*, p. 28.

43. For a good exposition of this view see the interview with Father P. B. Knox in *WSJ*, March 21, 1907.

44. *WSJ*, July 9, 1908, and July 7, 1910.

45. These views appeared in an editorial in the Milwaukee Sunday *Free Press* as a rebuttal of the basic goal of the recently announced Forty Thousand Club and was reprinted in full in the *WSJ* on July 8, 1901. Since this anti-growth and anti-factory point of view was so contrary to the editorial positions of the *Journal* and the *Democrat*, these papers seldom allowed such sentiment to get into print.

46. One who held this view was Unitarian minister Frank Gilmore, who said that more people would simply mean a larger budget and no net per-capita savings. He even issued a challenge to anyone who could prove that a bigger Madison would in any way reduce taxes. See Frank A. Gilmore, *Madison: Our Home* (Madison: Board of Commerce, 1916). p. 95–96.

47. *WSJ*, April 13, 1913.

48. *WSJ*, January 28, 1903, and December 30, 1911.

49. *WSJ*, July 8, 1901.

50. *WSJ*, July 13, 1906.

51. *WSJ*, March 21, 1907.

52. The "ruder" quote was made by J. W. Groves in *Madison Past and Present*, p. 31, and the "high grade" adjective came from comments made by C. F. Burgess quoted in *WSJ*, January 22, 1914.

53. *WSJ*, September 9, 1915.

54. *Madison Past and Present*, p. 31, and the *WSJ* July 13, 1905, June 20–July 7, 1906, September 30, 1910.

55. *WSJ*, March 14, 1907.

56. Ibid.

57. According to the 1910 census Madison factory output was valued at $5,467,000. The corresponding statistic for 1920, $15,000,000, came from the Board of Commerce newsletter, *Community Business*, January 15, 1920. The 1910 census showed 1792 factory workers in Madison. In 1920 the *WSJ*, December 31, 1920, year-end economic summary reported 5,000 factory workers.

58. Calculations by the author.

59. *MD*, April 23, 1904, *WSJ*, December 31, 1916, and *History of Madison's Trading Area, Economic Development, Labor, and Labor Unions* (Unpublished manuscript prepared by the Federal Writers' Project, U.S. Works Progress Administration, no date). pp. 14–26.

60. *WSJ*, June 26, 1911, August 11, 1919, and December 5, 1920.

61. One of the square blocks they took over during this period was the huge plant built by Northern Electric Company in 1897 at the intersection of South Dickinson and East Wilson Streets. This large locally owned maker of industrial electric motors was purchased by the General Electric Corporation in 1903 and in 1915 moved to Fort Wayne, Indiana, as a part of a major consolidation scheme.

62. See *WSJ*, July 15, 1901, February 18, 1903, September 29, 1906, *MD*, June 10, 1906, and September 15, 1915, for the Northern Electric story; and Agnes Larson, *John A. Johnson: An Uncommon American*, (Northfield,Minn.: Norwegian-American Historical Association, 1969), p. 19, and *WSJ*, November 13, 1916, for the Gisholt story.

63. For examples of the advertisements, see *WSJ*, April 5 and 17, 1915. The new state law was Chapter 368, Laws of 1911.

64. According to *WSJ*, October 30, 1915, $375,000 worth of stock was sold in the new enterprise by that date. On April 4, 1917, *WSJ* reported that $587,927 of capital stock had been issued.

65. *WSJ*, October 8, 1916.

66. *WSJ*, September 22, 1915.

67. *WSJ*, October 6, 1915.

68. For details of this interlude, see *WSJ*, September 5, 7, 14, 16, 17, 20, October 6, 8, 9, 17, 19, 22, 23, 29, 30, 1915, the *CCP*, October 8, 29, 1915, and Ordinances #1731 and 1732.

69. See *WSJ*, June 5, August 2, 3, 5, 9, 1918, and January 30, 31, February 7, 1919.

70. Madison held many fond memories for Oscar G. Mayer. He had journeyed here often when he was courting his wife, the former Elsa Stieglitz; one of his sisters, Louise, had married a Madison lawyer, George Schein; and his youngest sister Elsie attended the University of Wisconsin.

There are four written sources for this early history of the Oscar Mayer Company. The first is an unpublished company history written by Alfred Lief in 1950 and updated by John Guy Faulkes in 1954. The second is also an unpublished company history written in 1958 by Dale Kramer for the company's 75th anniversary. The third is a short article written by James P. Aehl, "The Oscar Mayer Story," *The Journal of Historic Madison, Inc.*, III (1977) pp. 13–20. The fourth is a collection of contemporary newspaper accounts assembled by the author.

Unfortunately, many of the accounts disagree on key points and are not documented. In this interpretation considerable weight has been given to contemporary accounts and then to the other histories to the extent that they are consistent with these sources. These sources were then supplemented with interviews of Oscar G. Mayer, Jr., and Fred C. Suhr.

71. The early growth in the dry cell industry in Madison is artfully chronicled in Kenneth D. Ruble's *The Rayovac Story: The First 75 Years* (North Central Publishing Company, 1981), pp. 1–20. His account was supplemented with contemporary newspaper stories.

72. This account was derived from a variety of sources including city directories, Secretary of State corporate records, the *MD*, Dec. 11, 1901, Oct. 29, 1902, *WSJ*, Sept. 24, 1902, Sept. 16, 1903, Sept. 28, 1903, Jan. 2, 1916, March 8, 1917, Aug. 19, 1917, Nov. 29, 1919, Dec. 31, 1920 and *Community Business*, July 15, 1918.)

73. Sources for this section were an unpublished corporate history prepared by Ohio Medical Products, the *WSJ*, February 12, 1907, an interview with Mrs. Sam Arneson, a relative of one of the early corporate officers, and several early corporate records.

74. For an example of this appeal see an advertisement placed by the Forty Thousand Club in the *WSJ*, August 10, 1908.

75. The compelling Farwell backdrop came from a speech given by Paul Findlay before the Six O'Clock Club on March 2, 1902. It was reprinted in full in *The Municipality* (Vol. II, No. 12), April, 1902, pp. 253–257.

76. In 1900 the seven counties surrounding Dane (Columbia, Dodge, Jefferson, Rock, Green, Iowa, and Sauk) had 242,588 persons. Not counting Madison, Dane County had 50,271. Together these totalled 292,859 persons, whereas Milwaukee's 1900 population stood at 285,315.

77. Findlay correctly saw the core of this market as Dane County but others emphasized that contiguous counties must also be included as transportation technology improved. Per J. W. Groves, *WSJ*, February 26, 1901, 200–300,000 persons lived within "trading distance" of Madison.

78. Such festivals were held in 1902, 1904, 1907, 1912, and in a more watered-down form in the teens.

79. Interurbans required fewer people to operate them and could use lighter, cheaper rails for roadbeds. The best single source for the interurban is John F. Due and George W. Hilton, *The Electric Interurban Railways in America* (Stanford: Stanford University Press, 1960).

80. Ibid.

81. Findlay was one of three speakers who addressed the Six O'Clock Club on the subject of interurban in 1902. The content of other speakers' talks was reported by the *WSJ*, March 4, 1902.

82. Ibid.

83. For articles on the Spooner attempt, see *WSJ*, July 9, 10, 13, August 22, September 2, October 1, November 8, 1901, February 19, March 13, 1902, and July 2, 1903.

84. *WSJ*, December 13, 1906. After this failure Montgomery seemed close to working out an arrangement with a Chicago interurban operator, but this plan, too, fell through. For articles on the Montgomery attempt, see the *WSJ*, September 6, November 29, 1905, *CCP*, December 27, 28, 1905. Ordinance #1396, dated December 28, 1905, *CCP*, February 9, 1906, August 9, 10, 17, 21, 27, September 12, 1906 *CCP*, November 9, 1906, *WSJ*, November 10, 12, 20, 26, 27, December 13, 15, 1906, January 26, March 21, 29, May 2, 4, 31, June 4, 27, September 3, 1907, *CCP*, September 13, 1907, September 28, 1907. Franchise activity was not limited to the Spooner and Montgomery initiatives. In fact a variety of local and out-of-town investors made aggressive attempts to garner this prized territory. For example, see the *WSJ*, August 15, 1901, for a story on a Chicago-based competitor.

85. For articles describing the 1910 Jones interurban activity, see the *WSJ*, April 27, August 5, September 8, *CCP*, September 9, 10, Oct. 6, 7, 14, and December 16, 1910, and Ordinance #1550 dated October 13, 1910. For 1911 development see the *WSJ*, March 2, 4, 23, April 13, June 9, 15, September 10, 22, 27, Ordinance #1577 dated October 5. Development in 1912 was chronicled in the *WSJ*, April 22, October 12, November 10, and the *CCP*, November 8, and in 1913 in the *CCP*, April 15, July 11 and 21, *WSJ*, June 13, July 12, 22, and Ordinance #1648 dated July 21. In 1914 a revealing was letter printed in the *CCP* on May 8th. For work done in 1915 see the *WSJ*, September 24, October 7, 16, and 23, and the *CCP*, October 22. For work done in 1916, see *WSJ*, April 14, 15, September 19, December 10 and 27, *CCP*, April 14, May 8, and Ordinance #1774 dated May 9.

86. For details on the Janesville and Madison Traction Company, see the *WSJ*, February 15, 1914, April 15, 1915, Ordinance #1707, April 19, 1905, April 26, 1915, September 24, 1915, October 2, 1916, March 25, 1917, December 13, 1917.

87. *WSJ*, April 14, 1916.

88. *CCP*, October 22, 1916.

89. *WSJ*, July 26, September 27, October 11, 1919, and Ordinance #1907 dated May 8, 1919.

90. Due and Hilton, p. 41.

91. *WSJ*, June 17, 1916,

92. *WSJ*, July 31, 1903, November 8, 1907.

93. *WSJ*, February 25, 1901.

94. For more information on these changes, see Alfred H. Jensen's unpublished master's thesis, "A Study of Succession of Uses of Property on the Capitol Square" (University of Wisconsin, Madison, 1923) .

95. *WSJ*, August 9, 1914. Homes dropped from seventy-six in 1900 to forty-two in 1921, whereas the number of State Street stores increased from a handful in 1900 to eighty-six in 1917. See Tse T. Yu's "Utilization of Land On State Street, Madison, Wisconsin" (Master's thesis, University of Wisconsin, 1928), p. 19, for statistics of residential decline and Kendall Cady's "The Business Development of State Street." (Master's thesis, University of Wisconsin, 1929).

96. See Joint Resolution No. 16. For a positive interpretation of this commercialism, see *WSJ*, August 9, 1914.

97. Jensen, "Study of Succession," and Cady, "Business Development."

98. *WSJ*, May 1, 1908.

99. *WSJ*, June 7, 1911.

100. For an example of cooperative newspaper advertising, see the *WSJ*, January 24 and February 24, 1916.

101. *WSJ*, April 30, 1901.

102. *WSJ*, July 29, 1904.

103. *WSJ*, February 3, 1899.

104. See interurban materials cited in earlier text.

105. See *Madison Past and Present*, p. 199, and other citations provided in the "hospital crusade" section.

106. This excerpt from the Milwaukee *Free Press* was reprinted in the *WSJ*, April 27, 1910.

107. *Community Business*, a monthly publication of the Board of Commerce, March 27, 1915.

108. M. G. Davis (ed.), *A History of Wisconsin Highway Development, 1835–1945* (Madison: State Highway Commission, 1947), pp. 24–58.

109. *WSJ*, June 27, 1920.

110. *WSJ*, July 18, 1920.

111. Ibid.

112. *Madison Past and Present*, p. 26. *MD*, February 26, 1901, *WSJ*, February 27, March 2, 1901, *WSJ*, December 30, 1911. *WSJ*, 1916 Annual Review.

113. Elisha W. Keyes, Ed., *History of Dane County*, 3 Vols. (Madison: Western Historical Association, 1906) 2:278. *WSJ*, November 15, 1915. For a helpful summary of the Wisconsin Tobacco business, see V. E. Bugton, A. J. Hintzman, and M. R. Goodell's *Wisconsin Tobacco Production and Marketing*, Wisconsin Department of Agriculture (Madison, Wisconsin, Bulletin No. 305, January-February, 1951). A highly readable land yet reliable account of the national tobacco picture is Joseph C. Robert's *The Story of Tobacco in America* (Chapel Hill, North Carolina: The University of North Carolina Press, 1949).

114. *WSJ*, May 17, 1920. The Northwestern Milwaukee Road had five hundred, the Northwestern seven hundred, and the Illinois Central about fifteen.

115. Sinclair Lewis, *Babbitt* (New York: Harcourt Brace & World, Inc., 1922), and *Main Street* (New York: Harcourt Brace & World, Inc., 1920), H. L. Mencken, *A Mencken Chrestomathy* (New York: Alfred A. Knopf, 1967), pp. 13, 178, 299.

116. *WSJ*, December 31, 1916.

117. *Community Business*, May 16, 1914.

118. *WSJ*, October 5, 1913.

The Progressive Attack on City Problems

1. For an excellent treatment of industrialization and urbanization, see Maury Klein and Harvey A. Kantor, *Prisoners of Progress: America's Industrial Cities, 1850–1920* (New York: MacMillan Publishing Co., 1976).

2. C. Vann Woodward, *The National Experience* (New York: Harcourt Brace & World, Inc., 1963), p. 433.

3. Two of the best treatments of this reform period are Richard Hofstadter's *The Age of Reform, From Bryon to F.D.R.* (New York: Random House, Inc., 1955), pp. 131–272, and Eric F. Goldman's *Rendezvous with Destiny, A History of Modern American Reform* (New York: Random House, 1956), pp. 66–179.

4. Probably the best analysis of the University of Wisconsin and the role it and the State of Wisconsin played in the progressive movement is Russel B. Nye's *Midwestern Progressive Politics: A Historical Study of its Origins and Development, 1870–1950* (East Lansing, Michigan: Michigan State College Press, 1951). The above quotations come from pp. 158ff.

5. The "adjunct" comment comes from the *WSJ*, January 4, 1904, and the *MD*, February 26, 1921. Efforts to enliven the *Democrat* were led by O. D. Brandenburg, former business manager of the *Wisconsin State Journal*, who took over as editor in 1890 and added more news and advertising. *Democrat* circulation was also adversely affected by a strong antiunion stand taken by the Democrat Printing Company when its printers went on strike in 1893. For an excellent history of the *Democrat* see Roland Strand's *The Story of the Democrat: A History of the Madison Democrat, A Newspaper Published 1868–1921* (Madison: Webcrafters, Inc., 1948).

6. Norman Weissman, "A History of the Wisconsin State Journal since 1910" (Master's thesis, University of Wisconsin, 1951), pp. 1–7.

7. *WSJ*, December 1, 1900.

8. Weissman, p. 47.

9. Gene Hanson, "A Case Study of Newspaper Muckraking: The Wisconsin State Journal's Crusade for Better and Lower Gas Rates" (Master's thesis, University of Wisconsin, 1966), pp. 9–12.

10. *WSJ*, May 16, December 23, 1907.

11. C. C. Regier, *The Era of Muckrakers* (Chapel Hill: University of North Carolina Press, 1932), p. 199.

12. *WSJ*, August 16, 1904.

13. Both Hanson, p. 5, and Louis Filler, author of one of the best analyses of muckrakers, *Crusaders for American Liberation* (Yellow Springs, Ohio: Antioch Press, 1950), p. 30, argue that newspapers have received too little credit as muckraking agents.

14. For a summary of the early stages of this long and arduous legal battle, see *CCP*, November 9, 1906.

15. Roden used these analogies and many other folksy examples during his crusade. For examples see *WSJ*, February 15, March 20, 1907.

16. *WSJ*, February 27, 1907.

17. *WSJ*, March 16, 1907.

18. During this controversy MG&E transferred all its advertising to the *Madison Democrat*, which maintained a discreet silence on the matter. Hanson, "Newspaper Muckraking," p. 59.

19. Chapter 499, Laws of 1907. See Hanson, p. 45.

20. *WSJ*, March 8, 1910. See the *WSJ*, January 3, 1919. In 1916 Roden's successor, Richard Lloyd Jones, hired an attorney to plead for another rate reduction before the Wisconsin Railroad Commission and won.

21. Circulation during Roden's five-year regime went from 3,800 in 1906 to 7,400 in 1911.

22. William T. Evjue, *A Fighting Editor* (Madison: Wells Printing Company, 1968), p. 167, and Weissman, p. 70ff.

23. Weissman, p. 72, Evjue, p. 163.

24. Weissman, p. 73.

25. *WSJ*, October 29, 1912, August 28, 1913.

26. *MD*, September 16, 1911.

27. *WSJ*, January 2, 1916, October 29, 1912, and Weissman, pp. 80, 87.

28. *WSJ*, October 29, 1912.

29. Evjue, pp. 121–170.

30. Ibid., pp. 162–63.

31. Throughout his lifetime, LaFollette called Evjue "Billie" and began his letters to Evjue with "My dear Billie." Evjue, p. 20.

32. *CT*, December 18, 20, 1917.

33. Evjue, p. 291.

34. *CT*, March 22, 1918.

35. Weissman, pp. 110–113, *The Lee Papers: A Saga of Midwestern Journalism* (Kewanee, Ill.: Star Courier Press, 1947), p. 279.

36. *CT*, March 22, 1918.

37. *CT*, April 2, 1918.

38. For an example of a new style *Wisconsin State Journal* editorial, see the paper on March 22, 1920, on the municipal streetcar ownership.

In 1919 Jones bought the *Tulsa Democrat* and moved to that Oklahoma city, where he spent the rest of his life.

39. Strand, pp. 93–97, 105–106. Today the direct successor of the Democrat Printing Company, Webcrafters Incorporated, has a large plant on Fordem Avenue.

40. *WSJ*, February 26, 1901. Brown's talk was titled "A Cleaner Madison, Wanted: A New Broom."

41. For typical references to the "bunch" see the *MD*, July 16, August 19, and October 18, 1904, March 7, 14, 1905. Mayor W. D. Curtis (1904–1906) was generally credited with breaking the Madison political machine. See *WSJ*, October 7, 1907.

For examples of conflict of interest situations see *MD*, February 27, July 10, 1904. Amidst the high-toned awareness of city official conflicts of interest, J. H. Findorff resigned his aldermanic position so he could build the Sixth Ward School. "Rather than be a city official and classed as a wrong doer," Findorff said he would rather be a private "citizen and carry on his regular business." See *WSJ*, August 12, 1904. To the city's credit the Common Council passed Ordinance #1307 in December 1903, to prevent this kind of problem.

The Elks Club incident was described in the *MD*, November 26, 1904.

42. *MD*, February 2, 1905.

43. *WSJ*, March 19, 1906.

44. *WSJ*, February 26, 1901. Piano dealer John W Groves was one mayor (1902–1904) who many said was soft on saloons and who was unable to get the police to obey his orders.

W. D. Curtis (1904–1906) by contrast, the owner of a worldwide horse collar business with factories in Madison and Birmingham, England, seemed to meet the widest approbation. See *WSJ*, March 28, 1906. Brown's fear was echoed by an alderman-merchant, A. G. Schmedeman. See *WSJ*, March 13, 1907.

45. The new state law was Chapter 443, Laws of 1901. For a discussion of the law see *The Municipality,* Vol. II, No. 2, pp. 39–40.

46. *MD*, January 7, 1904, and February 11, 1906.

47. Serious efforts to approve a salary for the mayor began in 1902 but the ordinance did not pass until February 1904 (see Ordinance #1309). Ironically the ordinance was signed into law by John Groves, who just a few months later went bankrupt. Even with the ordinance on the books, another three years went before the required three-quarter's vote was achieved. Along the way came vigorous discussion on the rate of pay. W. D. Curtis, the last unpaid mayor and a wealthy factory owner, thought the $1,000 salary was a mere "bagatelle" and that a rate of $5,000 would be more in line with the responsibilities. *WSJ*, September 10, 1907. In 1918 the mayor's pay was raised to $2,000.

48. For general background on the commission form of government, see Martin J. Schiesl's *The Politics of Efficiency: Municipal Administration and Reform in America* (University of California Press, 1977), pp. 134–148. The best monograph on the Galveston experience is Bradley R. Rice's "The Galveston Plan of City Government: The Birth of a Progressive Idea," *Southwestern Historical Quarterly,* (78, no. 4, April, 1975), pp. 369–408.

49. Olin's speech was printed in full in *WSJ*, January 27, 1909. Olin felt that each of the commissioners should be paid $5,000 per year.

50. See Joint Resolution 15S. The more conventional form of commission government was Chapter 448, Laws of 1909. The bill provided for three full-time commissioners (not five or six as in most states) who would serve overlapping terms and who would earn between $3,500 to $4,000 per year. Unlike most other commission government plans, the Wisconsin plan did not have the recall or initiative feature. The absence of such features deeply angered several influential Wisconson progressives. For example, *LaFollette's Weekly,* and mouthpiece for Robert LaFollette, said the law should remain a "dead letter" until these defects are corrected. See the June 29, 1909, issue, p. 5.

51. See *WSJ* series beginning March 2, 1910, and the *WSJ,* May 4, 1910, for Olin's talk before the reorganizing Forty Thousand Club.

52. *WSJ*, October 24, 1911.

53. *WSJ*, December 6, 1910.

54. *WSJ*, December 9, 1911.

55. *WSJ*, December 20, 1911, January 6, 1912.

56. *WSJ*, January 20, 1911.

57. *WSJ*, January 17 and 27, 1912. This German opposition to the commission plan provoked a famous editorial from the pen of Richard Lloyd Jones entitled "Let's Make Madison a German-Like Town," *WSJ* December 9, 1911. Six years later when Jones was leading efforts to expunge German influence from Madison, Jones' enemies delighted in reminding the colorful editor about his flip-flop. In the context of the editorial, however, Jones was stating a point then prevalent among municipal reformers that German cities were the best administered in the world and that their system was little more than the commission form with a different name.

58. *WSJ*, January 31, 1912. Elsewhere in the state, reformers were more successful. Eau Claire, Janesville, Appleton, and Superior all adopted the commission system by January 1912. For an example of *MD* editorial sentiment, see December 10, 1911. January 5, 12, 13, 19, 24, 28, and 30, 1912.

59. *WSJ*, January 31, 1912.

60. For his own engaging account of the episode, see *WSJ*, January 31, 1912.

61. *WSJ*, January 31, 1912.

62. Commission government was also opposed by the Madison socialists on the ground that the new system would eliminate party labels. *WSJ*, January 31, 1912. However, their influence was quite small and probably did not exceed one hundred fifty votes. In the 1912 presidential election, Eugene Debs, the Socialist candidate, got just 191 votes in Madison.

63. Compounding the problem of the structural reformers was the fact that they were divided between those who preferred commission government and those who preferred a newer form known as the city manager plan, which many Progressives were touting as the superior form of local government. The city manager plan kept the representative democracy of the common council, but centralized executive functions in a full-time city manager, who, unlike the commissioners, had formal training in city administration. For a forceful presentation of the city manager plan by a prominent Progressive, Charles McCarthy, see *WSJ*, December 4, 1912. For accounts of the failure of the second effort to get commission government, see *WSJ*, February 8, 1912.

64. Chapter 650, Laws of 1911.

65. Statements of Election Expenses, 1906 to 1913, State SHSW Archives. For examples of beer-fueled campaigns, see *WSJ*, March 30, 1904, and April 2, 1906.

66. The law allowed the poll workers to stand no closer than one hundred feet from the polling place, but this law was widely ignored.

67. Chapter 11, Special Session, 1912.

68. *WSJ*, March 29, 1902.

69. Joseph C. Schubert, *1906 Campaign Brochure* (SHSW pamphlet collection).

70. The sudden need for platforms and issue-oriented campaigns eminating from the Non-Partisan Act gave rise in 1914 to the Municipal Voters League, whose purpose was to give voters impartial and unbiased information about candidates. See the *WSJ*, March 14, 1914, and April 2, 1916.

71. Chapter 451, Laws of 1903; Chapter 513, Laws of 1911; and Chapter 710, Laws of 1913 respectively.

72. In Madison the initiative was rarely used, and the referendum seldom used. One of the few times that the referendum was used was to force a council decision on commission government.

73. *WSJ*, August 11, 1906.

74. Ordinance #1242, passed June 17, 1901. In his April 16, 1901, inaugural address, Bull said, "I do not know one person connected with the city government who has any idea what the books of the city will show by the end of the fiscal year." To Bull the only "practical way out of this dilemma was to adopt a budget so that everybody . . . can see who the money which is confided to our trust will be expended for the benefit of the city."

75. Chapter 523, Laws of 1911.

76. The need for this Municipal Accounting Act was heightened by the passage of the Income Tax Law Act (Chapter 658, Laws of 1911), which directed that seventy percent of the proceeds from this new tax be returned to the local government where the income-tax payer lived.

77. *Sixth Biennial Report of the Wisconsin Tax Commission* (Madison: 1912), p. 65.

78. *WSJ*, December 18, 1915. Prior to the installation of the new state system, the city budget could be typed on a single page. By 1914 the budget had ballooned to sixty pages, and by 1917 to one hundred pages. See *WSJ*, October 26, 1914, and December 31, 1916.

Other administrative improvements quickly followed the installation of the new program budget. For example in 1915 a money-saving centralized purchasing system was begun and in 1917 responsibility for all city fiscal matters was centralized in a city auditor. *CCP*, January 26, 1916, and Ordinance #1866 passed December 15, 1917.

79. Municipal ownership was also applied to such things as the municipal market and discussed for such things as a municipal dairy and even a municipal home heating system, an early version of the district heating concept. For efforts to launch the city dairy, see *WSJ*, January 18, 1907; for the heating plant see *WSJ*, December 1, 1918 and January 26, 1919.

80. Schiesl, p. 193.

81. *CCP*, May 9, 1902.

82. *WSJ*, November 6, 1902.

83. The professors were F. E. Turneaure, professor of sanitary engineering, and Storm Bull, professor of steam engineering. They were assisted by B. V. Swenson. The municipal lighting system that the men designed included decorative lighting, underground wiring, and even a garbage incinerator so that garbage could be used as a fuel. See the *CCP*, March 13, 1903.

84. Curiously, although the majority of voters approved the municipal plant, only twenty-eight percent of voters in the spring 1903 election cast ballots on this measure.

85. The 1918–1920 effort to buy the streetcar company, although the most aggressive such effort, was not the only instance where city takeover of the streetcar lines was proposed. Emerson Ela, a Progressive Madison attorney, urged municipal ownership in 1902, (see *WSJ*, December 4–5, 1912), but at that time Madison was not ready for such an extreme move. Most Progressives were still confident that regulation would do the job. A second effort was made by a Madison dentist who ran for mayor in 1914 but who was beaten in the primary. See *WSJ*, March 12, 1914.

86. See *WSJ*, July 31, 1919.

87. This detail was recalled by Jenkin Lloyd Jones in a speech describing his boyhood days given to the Madison Civics Club on November 3, 1979. Jones' father, Richard Lloyd Jones, was the editor of the *Wisconsin State Journal*.

88. Other than the South Madison line extension in 1906, the only other streetcar extension made was the North Street or Oscar Mayer extension in 1919. Significantly, the North Street extension was the last streetcar extension ever made in Madison and required a very substantial subsidy from the new packing company.

89. *WSJ*, January 22, 1909.

90. See *WSJ*, August 5, 9, 1910.

91. See Ordinance #1473, January 1907, and #1620, October, 1912. The former required the cars to be heated between November 10 and April 1; the latter expanded the warm-car days to October 10 and May 1. Both required an average temperature of only forty degrees. Finally the State Railroad Commission required a minimum temperature of sixty degrees in the cars. All streetcars were heated by coal stoves until 1919, when the first batch of electrically heated cars was received.

92. For newspaper reactions to this edict see *WSJ*, July 8, 10, 12, 15, August 25, 1911.

93. *WSJ*, July 8, 1911.

94. *WSJ*, December 6, 1911.

95. *WSJ*, March 13, November 26, 1912.

96. *WSJ*, May 27, October 7, 1913.

97. *WSJ*, March 17, June 24, 1914.

98. *WSJ*, January 20, 1915.

99. For examples of these public relations efforts, see *WSJ*, March 8, 14, May 16, June 21, 1915, and February 24, 1916.

100. For coverage of the hearings see *CT*, July 19, 20, August 9, 10, 1918.

101. *CT*, November 12, 1918.

102. *CT*, June 11, 1918.

103. *CT*, November 13, 1918. In a *Capital Times* editorial on June 11, 1918, Evjue had even suggested that Montgomery had the three railroad commissions in his pocket. In a "Society Note" sarcastically positioned in the middle of the editorial page, Evjue noted that when Mr. Montgomery entertained Theodore Roosevelt for dinner at the Madison Club

in May 1918, his dinner guests included the three railroad commissioners, Carl D. Jackson, John A. Allen, and Harold Geisse.

104. *WSJ,* November 26, 1918.

105. Chapter 492, Laws of 1919.

106. One way to improve the financial situation for the streetcar company was to eliminate two-man cars requiring both a motorman and a conductor and go to a one-man car whose operation and layout was nearly identical to a modern bus. This move would have saved a relatively large amount of money in labor costs. A second method was to inaugurate a zone fare system. Under the method then in use, streetcar fares were a fixed rate regardless of the ride length. It cost the same to go five miles as five blocks. Thus, the central city passengers ended up subsidizing the suburbanities who had cheap fares and long rides. Both the one-man car solution and the zone fare system were rejected by Madisonians. Unfortunately both were viewed as evil plots by Montgomery to extort more money and provide less service.

107. *WSJ,* September 5, 1919. The study was done by the Federal Electric Railway Commission.

108. *WSJ,* March 24, 1920.

109. *WSJ,* March 4, 21, 1920.

110. *WSJ,* April 7, 1920.

111. *WSJ* editorial, April 9, 1920.

112. *WSJ,* September 2, 1907.

113. Official city sources showed that in 1896 Madison had eighty-one saloons, whereas in 1900 that number had crept up to one hundred, an increase of 23.5 percent. During the same period Madison population increased from 16,592 (interpolated from the 1895 state and 1900 federal census) to 19,164, an increase of 15.5 percent.

For a view of Madison through the eyes of nationally famous antiliquor crusader, Carrie Nation, see *WSJ,* July 25, 1903. For an example of the concern for suburban saloons, see *WSJ,* September 11, 1901. Election data were compiled by the author.

114. At the time Madison's prohibitionist activities were coordinated by the Madison Temperance Board, composed of two members from each of the churches, two from the young people's church societies, two from each of the temperance organizations, and two from the YMCA. Neither the Catholics nor Lutherans were members of this board because they preferred to work on their own. Also Madison had a Women's Christian Temperance Union with sixty members and ward branches. see *WSJ,* January 28, 1901.

For a good exposition of the "new moderate" logic among prohibitionists, see Amos Wilder's editorial in the *WSJ,* June 25, 1903. Though the new moderation ultimately prevailed, there were some hard-line prohibitionists who refused to go along. So staunch were their views on the matter that they refused to vote in high-low license elections on the ground that they sanctioned evil. See *WSJ,* August 29, 1901.

115. Sidney Ahlstrom, *A Religious History of the American People* (New Haven, Conn.: Yale University Press, 1972), p. 902.

116. Until about 1906 the league concentrated nearly all of its energy in securing local option legislation and then implementing it wherever possible. Wisconsin's 1889 wet/dry referenda law was an example of such legislation.

For additional background on this remarkable organization and the entire prohibition movement, see Sinclair's *Prohibition: The Era of Excess* (Boston: Little, Brown and Company, 1962), Herbert Asbury's *The Great Illusion: An Informal History of Prohibition* (Garden City, N.Y.: Doubleday & Company, 1950), and delightfully succinct and insightful book by James H. Timberlake, *Prohibition and the Progressive Movement, 1900–1920* (Cambridge, Mass.: Harvard University Press, 1966).

117. *WSJ,* September 1, 1901. Election statistics compiled by the author.

118. Slot machines took Madison by storm in 1903. Between one hundred fifty and five hundred of the devices were reportedly ensconced in Madison saloons, pool halls, and cigar stores. *WSJ,* March 25, 1904. Roulette wheels appealed to the "big game" gamblers who came to Madison during legislative sessions. *WSJ,* January 20, 1903.

119. See *WSJ,* February 11, May 13, 1903, March 30, 1906.

120. See *WSJ,* October 24, 1905.

121. *WSJ,* October 24, 1905.

122. Ordinance #1278 passed February 13, 1903.

123. Statistics compiled by the author. Under Curtis' administration (1904–1906), the council created a second dry zone, a relatively large twenty-five block, 119-acre area centered around the Gisholt and Fuller and Johnson plants on East Washington Avenue. Reformers hoped that the action would keep Madison's factory workers from squandering their wages on booze. (See Ordinance #1333, August 12, 1904.)

Between 1906 and 1914 prostitution arrest stories—always good for newspaper sales—nearly disappeared. In 1914, however, a statewide survey of commercial prostitution, known as the Teasdale Report, said that Madison had twenty-one "immoral places," the third highest in the state after Milwaukee and LaCrosse. This finding was so shocking to city fathers that they hired detectives to make an independent investigation. When the detectives failed to find these "immoral places," citizens began to question the credibility of the Teasdale Report. Teasdale refused to release a list of the twenty-one places but did admit that several public parks were included in the list. A grand jury later concluded that Madison was one of the "morally cleanest" cities in the state. See *WSJ,* June 12, 14, July 17, December 5, 6, 12, 27, 1914, and *CCP,* April 20, 1915. For a revealing prosaloon interpretation of the Teasdale Report, see a paid political advertisement by the Madison Business Protective League, April 5, 1915.

124. *MD,* August 31, 1905.

125. Note: The Common Council later reversed themselves on the license question, but not until forced to do so by a citizen lawsuit. See *MD,* March 10, 1906.

126. *MD,* March 18, 1906. The complaint that university students were surrounded by sinful saloons was not a new issue in Madison. Indeed, U.W. President Bascom had created a statewide furor over the issue in 1884, although not until 1897 were prohibitionists in the Fifth Ward able to dry up the campus area with an eleven-block dry district.

Nor was interest in a dry campus neighborhood limited to the 1906 Rowley campaign. In 1902, for example, regents and residents united to prevent the issuance of a saloon license in the U.W. prohibitory district. In 1903 a Wisconsin supreme court justice and several leading U.W. professors stormed up to the mayor's desk after a council meeting and berated Mayor John Groves (1902–1904) for his refusal to enforce city saloon ordinances in the university area. The cringing mayor lamely replied that he could not get the police to do their duty. See the *WSJ,* April 11, 1903.

127. *WSJ,* April 12, 1907.

128. *WSJ,* April 15, 1907.

129. See the *MD,* January 12, 1907, and the *WSJ,* January 14, 19, 26, and February 22, 1907.

130. Regents' minutes dated April 16, 1907, and the minutes of the executive committee dated May 6, 1907. Also see a letter in the Van Hise correspondence dated May 11, 1907, from Regent W. J. McElroy. The city move was embodied in Ordinance #1439 dated April 16, 1907.

131. The bill actually called for a .6-mile radius but was commonly called the half-mile bill (403S). It was introduced by a Madison Republican Senator, Mr. Albert M. Stondall, whose large home at 901 Spaight Street still stands just east of B. B. Clarke Beach. Another bill, 916A, calling for a three-quarter-mile radius, was defeated. The Madison ordinance, which increased the size of the U. W. dry district from forty-three to ninety-one acres, was #1349, passed April 16, 1907. Then came Ordinance #1444, passed on June 18, 1907, which increased the district to 484 acres. Just a few days after the overriding state law was passed, Madison aldermen repealed both expanded districts with Ordinance #1452.

To get a flavor of the brewers' lobbying, see their *Argument in Favor of Bill 403S and Against Bill 916A* in the SHSW archives.

132. To dramatize this point, saloon owners used cards showing two pilsner glasses, the large low-license glass patrons were then enjoying and the small high-license glass they would soon be getting if the measure passed. For an account of this election, see *WSJ,* September 2, 11, 16, 1907.

133. See *WSJ,* April 20, 1911, and 1911 Assembly Bill 188 and its amendments.

134. *WSJ,* March 28, 1911.

135. Among the many sophisticated Madison progressives who worked hard to close down saloons were Richard Lloyd Jones, William T. Evjue and Emerson Ela. One of many quo-

tations that show the direct connection between prohibition and progressivism appeared in a March 7, 1913, *Wisconsin State Journal* Jones editorial. At the time the Wisconsin legislature was debating a bill to expand the size of the U.W. dry district. Said Jones: "If they (legislators) are progressives, real progressives, they must, first of all stand for moral decency and moral decency demands that nothing less than a five mile dry zone be placed about the campus of the university. . . ."

136. Author's statistics compiled from various records.

137. *WSJ*, June 9, 1913.

138. *WSJ*, June 10, 1913.

139. *WSJ*, June 11, 1913.

140. *WSJ*, July 3, 1913. Also named in the order were pool halls, bowling alleys, and movie theaters. For several weeks the ban proved effective except for six ingenious movie operators, some of whom earmarked ten percent of their profits for charity (hence a work of charity) and some of whom showed films of the life of Christ (hence religious instruction). See *WSJ*, July 21, 27, 1913.

141. *CCP*, July 11, 1913.

142. The Madison Dry League was an affiliate of the Anti-Saloon League.

143. In an identical referendum held in 1901 the wets prevailed by eighteen percent; in 1910 the wets won by 7 percent, but in 1914 the wet victory margin dropped to an incredibly thin .46 percent.

144. Accounts of this campaign appear in Madison dailies beginning February 28, 1915.

Drys made a special effort to enlist the support of those who felt their property tax burdens were too high. The argument went like this: if alcohol were prohibited, high police, jail, and judicial costs would be substantially reduced. Another argment used quite successfully by the drys was a more virulent version of *in loco parentis*. For example, in a spirited *Wisconsin State Journal* editorial on April 3, 1915, Richard Lloyd Jones quoted an outstate parent as saying: "I will never send either my son or daughter to the University of Wisconsin until Madison goes dry." Two years earlier (November 16, 1913) Jones approvingly printed a reader letter which said: it was "puerile to argue that (a student's) character should be strong enough to withstand the temptation (of saloons). Amid strangers, away from the life, love, interest and joys of home and early companions, they are expected to withstand the allurment of the saloon which frequently overwhelms men of maturer years. . . ."

145. For an example of this sentiment, see *WSJ*, April 9, 22, 1915.

146. *WSJ*, December 19, 1916.

147. *WSJ*, November 8, 1916, and Evjue, pp. 257–273.

148. *WSJ*, June 24, 1916. Chapter 453, Laws of 1915.

149. Targets for this third cutback were saloons providing exclusive franchised outlets for Milwaukee breweries. For example, Schlitz-franciced saloons were located in the "flati-

ron" building at the intersection of King and Doty Streets and the brick building at the northeast corner of South Patterson and Williamson Streets. The latter franchise saloon was an obvious attempt to do battle with the Fauerbach Brewery.

150. *WSJ*, January 8, 1917.

151. *WSJ*, April 4, 1917.

152. *WSJ*, April 4, 1917. So great was interest in the wet/dry issue that eighteen percent more people voted in the referendum than voted for aldermen. Madison became the largest city in the state to go dry.

153. Although the *Journal* was eager to celebrate the unemployment of Madison's fifty-five brewery workers, it expressed deep concern for the future of Madison's twenty union cigar makers, about half of whom were expected to lose their jobs when the saloons closed, since so many cigars were purchased and smoked in saloons. "Don't let it be said," editorialized the *Journal*, "that the closing of the saloon has injured legitimate business." At the time Madison cigar makers made a variety of five- and ten-cent cigars including the ElCrispo, the Badger, and the Tenney Park. See *WSJ*, April 23, 1917.

154. *WSJ*, June 28, 1917.

155. *WSJ*, June 30, 1917.

156. See the *WSJ*, April 2, 3, and November 16, 1918, and January 20, 1919, and the *CT*, April 4, 1918.

157. Curiously Nebraska became the thirty-sixth and final state needed to ratify the Eighteenth Amendment just one day after Nebraska's most famous son, William Jennings Bryan, told a cheering crowd at a dry rally in the Red Gym that "booze is on its way to the gallows." Bryan also declared that this would be his last speech on Prohibition. He was right. *WSJ*, January 15, 1919.

158. One statistician calculated that the grain that went into beer was sufficient to make eleven million loaves of bread. Another determined that a pound of coal was needed to brew a pint of beer and that thousands of tons of coal were therefore being wasted.

159. The vote was 4,010 wet votes (fifty-six percent) to 3,199 dry votes (forty-four percent).

160. See *WSJ*, June 25, 1919, and Chapter 556, Laws of 1919.

161. *CCP*, August 23, 27, 1919.

162. One of the most instructive developments in the wet/dry war was the speed with which wet strength returned after the war was over. Indeed in April 1918 *during* the war, Madison came within just one vote of going back to the wet column. The decisive five-to-four wet margin produced by the April 1919 election suggests that without a war-inspired patriotic vote, Madison probably would have stayed wet. But what if national prohibition had not been passed and Madison would have been forced to rely on local referenda to decide the matter? What if another referenda had been held in April 1921 *after* women had been given the vote? Would women have voted Madison dry again or would they have followed the new mood of indulgence so evident after the war? Such are the intriguing questions of which history is made.

163. *CCP*, January 14, 1920. See Ordinance #1930.

164. The fact that prohibitionists enjoyed the support of all three daily papers during this period, the *Journal*, the *Democrat*, and the *Capital Times*, played a significant but not overwhelming role. After all, Madison stayed wet for all but two years of the 1900–1920 period in spite of the newspaper support for prohibition.

165. *WSJ*, October 28, 1914.

166. The "causal" connection between saloon removal and the elimination of saloon-related problems was also a reflection of still another popular idea among prohibitionsts, namely environmentalism. This concept was and is widely accepted throughout the United States. Its appeal, however great, is fraught with perils. Just as family problems proved to be caused by factors beyond alcohol, so did "good" public housing fail to produce better people.

167. *WSJ*, April 11, 1899.

168. For the Tenney Park story see the *WSJ*, April 11, 19, 1899, plus the minutes and reports for 1899, 1900, 1901, and 1902. Although Tenney was the largest contributor, others made significant contributions. The Willow Park Association, the developers of the lake side of Sherman Avenue, the Hausmann Brewing Company, and others either donated their land or sold it far below market rates. Also the city contributed fifteen hundred dollars as required by Tenney's grant.

169. The *WSJ* was one such key convert. See their editorial on June 13, 1894.

170. For example, in his 1902 report to association members, Olin said: "The funds of this Association cannot be used, certainly to any large extent, in securing these parks and playgrounds." 1902 *Annual Report*, p. 58.

171. For details on the twelve-to-one ratio, see the 1902 *Report*, pp. 10–11. The new state law was enacted in Chapter 32, Laws of 1897. According to John Olin (1899 *Report*) the city was not interested in taking title to lands because up to that point they all lay outside the city limits. At the same time, many land owners through whose property pleasure drives had been built strongly preferred to give their easement or title to a *private* organization. Not until the Wisconsin legislature passed a special law for the Madison Park and Pleasure Drive Association in 1899 (Chapter 55, Laws of 1899) was this problem solved. That law gave *both* the city and the MPPDA the power to own, improve, maintain parklands and enforce reasonable laws including lands outside city limits. Once again the city declined the additional financial burden and responsibility.

172. See *WSJ*, July 15, 1899.

173. The only other park under the association's control was Owen Park, which lay astride a portion of the Lake Mendota Drive, three miles west of the capitol. Today the park is known as Owens Parkway.

174. 1899 *Annual Report*.

175. 1929 *Annual Report*, p. 71.

176. 1902 *Annual Report*, p. 54.

177. See MPPDA *Annual Report,* 1903, pp. 21–32, for general background. The "exceedingly visionary" quote comes from p. 58 in the same report.

178. See the *WSJ,* December 23, 1902, and January 22, 1903.

179. Olin later admitted that nearly all the launch owners in the Madison area were members of the MPPDA. This fact was largely responsible for the policy of not charging a toll at the lock as proposed by some as a way to keep costs down.

180. *WSJ,* January 12, 1903.

181. Olin's critics were correct, the project *was* very expensive. When the bills for the project were totalled in 1906, the project came to $81,600, $26,000 *above* anticipated costs and six times more expensive than Tenney Park. Of this amount, however, the city only had to pay $4,300. The rest was paid for by the railroads ($46,800) and from MPPDA subscriptions ($30,500), so few could complain that city taxes were being appreciably affected. The $10,000 that the MPPDA raised above the initial $20,000 subscription was contributed by a wealthy Norwegian businessman, Halle Steensland, for the handsome, broad arched bridge that still spans the Yahara at East Washington Avenue. The bill to compel the railroads to raise these bridges was Chapter 30, Laws of 1903.

182. *WSJ,* October 25, 1906.

183. Large contributions from the Vilas family were received in 1906, 1907, 1910, 1916, and 1917, whereas Brittingham added to his record in 1906, 1907, and 1908. Meanwhile D. K. Tenney made additional grants in 1908, 1909, and 1912 to expand and improve "his" park.

184. With 1905 population at 24,301, Madison only needed 121 acres to satisfy the ratio of one acre to every two hundred people. In that year park acreage stood at 153.5 while water frontage stood at 24,210 feet.

185. This was the considered opinion of John Olin conveyed to his members at their 1906 annual meeting. See MPPDA 1906 *Annual Report,* p. 65.

186. A rare copy of the letter that accompanied the famous postcard is available from the John Nolen Papers, Cornell University Archives, Box 2903.

Household giving statistics were based upon a comparison between the average number of members (765) and the number of residential units in 1905 estimated to be 6075.

187. See Ordinance #1390, dated November 11, 1905.

188. See comments made by Major Joseph Schubert in the *WSJ,* September 7, 1910.

189. From time to time incidents occurred that tested association control of park management. One particularly interesting situation involved the design of a bridge in Tenney Park. D. K. Tenney felt very strongly that a utilitarian steel bridge was all the park needed and gave money for its construction, providing that no public funds would ever be used for the construction of another bridge. A summary of the incident is found in the 1911 *Report,* pp. 26–29.

190. See MPPDA reports for these years.

191. For a discussion of the growing role nature played in the minds of leading thinkers around the turn of the century, see Peter J. Schmidt's *Arcadian Myth in Urban America* (New York: Oxford University Press, 1969), pp. 66–73.

192. See the *WSJ,* November 6, 1907.

193. See MPPDA *Annual Reports,* 1910, p. 37, 1913, pp. 42–43.

194. See MPPDA *Annual Report,* 1911, pp. 37–38, 51.

195. *WSJ,* May 10, 1918. See also *WSJ* editorial, May 12, 1906.

196. See a *WSJ* editorial, October 28, 1915, for one expression of this idea.

197. Board of Commerce, *Madison, The Four Lake City Recreational Survey* (Madison: Board of Commerce, 1915), p. 1.

198. For examples of such MPPDA publicity, see the *WSJ,* October 25, 1906, the *WSJ,* May 11, 1908, the *MD,* March 19, 1905, and the annual reports of the association.

199. For representative expressions of this sentiment, see the MPPDA 1905 *Annual Report,* pp. 69–70, and an editorial from the *Milwaukee Free Press* reprinted in the *WSJ* on July 12, 1909. MPPDA officials were anything but bashful about telling the world about their accomplishments. In 1906 MPPDA secretary, C. N. Brown, gave a speech to the annual convention of the National Civic Association and told them that Madison had more park and pleasure drives as individual gifts than any other city in the U.S. and that no city of 25,000 could match Madison's record for voluntary subscriptions. See the *WSJ,* October 25, 1906.

200. See the *WSJ,* May 10, 1918.

201. MPPDA 1910 *Annual Report,* p. 11.

202. Ibid., pp. 47–49. These strong and highly complimentary words from his directors were seconded by others. In a letter to Olin from John Nolen dated September 20, 1909 (Olin correspondence), Nolen said, "I find it difficult to conceive of the Madison work going forward in an unbroken way without your aid, for I think even you, yourself, do not realize how much it owes to your intelligent, energetic, and painstaking direction." Michael Olbrich in a speech to the Tenth Ward Association in 1916 put the case even more strongly: "There isn't anything in a municipal way that Madison has a right to be particularly proud of as their own achievement except the park and pleasure drive system, *and that is due more to the untiring efforts of one man than to any outburst of civic pride*" (author italics). *WSJ,* April 27, 1916.

203. Ossian Cole Simonds (1855–1931) was first hired by Olin to do Tenney Park in 1900 but later received commissions to do Vilas and Brittingham Parks. In addition Simonds did an early version of what is now known as Olin Terrace, several subdivisions including The Highlands, and a plan for boulevarding East Washington Avenue. Simonds also advised the association on various improvements to the Lake Mendota and Farwell drives. Simonds did no work in Madison while Mische was the city park superintendent or while John Nolen was under contract to the city (1908–1911). However, in 1911 he once again became the landscape designer for the Association and served in that capacity for many years. For a national backgrop on his pioneering work, see Mara Gelbloom's "Ossian Simonds: Prairie Spirit in Landscape Gardening," *Prairie School Review,* Vol. XII, No. 2 (Palos Park, Ill.: The Prairie School Press, Second Quarter, 1975), pp. 5–18.

Emil T. Mische, the city's first full-time landscape architect, served as city park superintendent between 1905 and 1910. He revised Simond's plans for Vilas Park, did other design work as well and supervised the day-to-day park development work.

204. Olin's criticism of the Tenney lagoon bridge came from the MPPDA 1910 *Annual Report,* pp. 64–65, while Tenney's adjectives appear in the *CCP,* April 8, 1910.

Olin was also the principal crusader for the graceful arched bridges that now span the Yahara River at six places. The issue came up in connection with the replacement of an ugly steel truss bridge on Williamson Street in 1904. In that year the council, following the advice of Olin and Mayor Dexter Curtis, voted to build an arched concrete bridge even though its first cost was higher than a utilitarian steel bridge. This set the precedent that Olin never let the city council forget. He and the association were successful in getting the city to build similar concrete arched bridges over the Yahara at Sherman Avenue, East Johnson Street, East Washington Avenue, East Main Street, and Rutledge Street.

205. MPPDA *Annual Report,* 1902, p. 58.

206. An examination of Olin's letters in the WSHS archives showed that Olin tried to get the presidents of the Schlitz Brewing Company, the Patrick Cudahy Paking Plant, and many others.

207. MPPDA *Annual Report,* 1903, p. 35, 1908, p. 72.

208. Association records show that it had 995 members in 1905, whereas the state census of that year showed Madison population to be 24,301. Thus four percent of Madison's population actually contributed the minimum five-dollar amount and were therefore members. The 1980 census showed Madison population to be 168,000. Four percent of this population is 6,800.

209. Olin was always modest about his personal role and typically attributed his achievements to the association. For example, in his 1906 report to members (MPPDA 1906 *Annual Report,* p. 16) Olin said: "There is such a thing as the habit of giving and I think *our Association* (author italics) can justly claim some credit for having very persistently but intelligently cultivated this habit."

Another example of the powerful giving mood fostered by Olin appeared in remarks made by William F. Vilas in a 1903 talk on the Yahara River Parkway. Said Madison's largest park benefactor, "We have in this city of Madison such a universal feeling of generous, contributory and cooperative action on the part of all our citizens, extending to large numbers beyond those who have great means to live, everyone, almost from one end of the city to the other, giving in accordance with his means and power, we have such a fraternity as very few communities that I have ever known of possess. It has always been a matter of boast and pride that I live in such a community." (1903 *Annual Report*, p. 86.)

One example of giving services instead of money occurred during the creation of the Yahara River Parkway. Here fifty-six teamsters donated their labor to haul loads of fill material to the job site. (See the MPPDA *Annual Report*, 1903, p. 27.)

210. *WSJ*, September 21, 1909.

211. MPPDA *Annual Report*, 1925, p. 8.

212. *WSJ*, April 17, 1906. During the work on the Owen Parkway some liverymen, the very persons who stood to gain most from the development of a drive system, refused to contribute because they thought the whole thing was "a scheme of real estate speculators." *MD*, March 25, 1895. For another charge of "crookedness and dishonesty," see the *MD*, Feb. 19, 1904. In his 1908 Annual Report, pp. 60–61, Olin made this statement: ". . . If anyone supposes we have not been criticized, I should be pleased to submit to him some of the official correspondence." What distinguished MPPDA work from so many other public enterprises was the fact that very little MPPDA criticism "got into the public press."

213. In an article in the 1906 *Annual Report*, p. 67, Olin said, ". . . We must remember that 75% of our population are not the possessors of a single horse and buggy and rarely ever indulge in the luxury of a livery turnout."

214. MPPDA *Annual Report*, 1902 p. 67.

215. 1902 *Annual Report*, p. 25.

216. MPPDA *Annual Report*, 1911, p. 21. See also Olin's remarks in the 1906 *Annual Report*, pp. 15–16. Still another nettlesome problem that provoked great criticism of the MPPDA was whether to admit automobiles upon the drives. It was an insoluable problem for which only proximate solutions were possible. For a discussion of this controversy, see the 1912 *Annual Report*, pp. 23–27.

217. For an account of the 1909 budget rescue operation, see the *WSJ*, November 4, 1909.

The key point made in the report—that parks pay—had been made many times before by Olin, but never with statistical justification. For examples of Olin's nonquantified arguments, see the 1905 *Annual Report*, p. 51, and the 1907 *Annual Report* pp. 65–75. The Special Committee Report was printed in the *CCP* on March 12, 1909.

218. For details of the 1910 antipark campaign, see the *WSJ*, March 18, 19, 21, 23, 1910.

219. For details on Bowen Park, see *CCP*, May 8 and September 11, 1903. General opposition to Monona Drive and the ax incident can be found in the MPPDA *Annual Report*, 1912, pp. 27–31. See also MPPDA *Annual Report*, 1914, pp. 20–21.

220. See note #171.

The 1907 law, AB70 and SB74, is described in the *WSJ*, February 4 and 7, 1907. A copy of a card circulated by the committee on suburban property owners is available in the WSHS, pamphlet collection. For details on the 1915 Park District Bill (Chapter 180, Laws of 1915), see *CCP*, June 11, 1915, and August 13, 1915, and April 20, 1915 inaugural address by Mayor Kaiser. See also the *MD*, January 7, 1915, and August 5, 1914. A folder and scrapbook of materials describing this effort is available in the SHSW Archives.

221. Mische's first-year salary was $1,200, of which the city paid $900 and the MPPDA $300. His second-year salary was $1,500, of which the city paid $1,200 and the MPPDA $300. Mische served as landscape architect from January 1, 1906, to March 1, 1908. See 1908 MPPDA *Annual Report*, p. 51. See also Olin's letter to Nolen dated January 14, 1908, in the Olin Papers, SHSW.

222. That Olin was less than enchanted with Mische was evident from a "private" letter he wrote Nolen on March 12, 1908, in which he said he was disturbed by Mische's "unfortunate use of English" and "his difficulty in making a good first impression." For details on splitting the job into "park superintendent" and "landscape architect" functions, see his reports to the Common Council dated February 24 and March 26, 1908.

223. For a summary of Nolen's credentials, see Olin's report to the Common Council, March 13, 1908.

224. The twists and turns of these negotiations can be followed through the Nolen Papers at Cornell University, hereinafter called the *Nolen Papers*.

225. Nolen letter to Olin dated January 28, 1908, *Nolen Papers*.

226. John L. Hancock, *John Nolen and the American City Planning Movement: A History of Culture Change and Community Response, 1900 to 1940* (unpublished University of Pennsylvania PhD dissertation, 1964) p. 201. As it happened, Harvard became the first institution in the U.S. to offer a course in city planning in the fall of 1909.

227. Nolen to Olin, March 11, 1908, *Nolen Papers*.

228. In a very revealing and candid letter from Olin to Nolen dated February 11, 1908, Olin explained that a "regular professor" at the U. W. made $2,500 per year and that a "number of the men get $3,000 and some others a still higher salary." Moreover, the understanding with professors was that they only spent half time on their professional duties during the school year. According to Olin this light load was "the only way that the University can secure the best men in certain lines of work." In addition, all professors had a three-and-one-half-month summer vacation. In effect, Nolen would be getting $3,000 for 4.5 months of work, or a monthly salary of $666. For another 7.5 months of work, Nolen could earn $4,995 for a total of $7,995 per year. The Van Hise salary was listed in the 1910–1911 UW Budget Summary, p. 4.

229. See Olin's letter to Nolen dated March 4, 1908.

230. Olin's friendship network greatly aided in the creation of the second job package. Van Hise had been a student in Olin's U. W. class and was a close friend and neighbor; he knew several of the regents. The chairman of the state park commission was a personal friend and Olin was personally acquainted with all members of the state board of control. See letter from Olin to Nolen dated March 4, 1908.

231. Letter dated March 12, 1908.

232. Nolen letter to Olin, March 11, 1908.

233. The vote was seventeen to two. See the *CCP*, March 30, 1908 and the *WSJ* on that date. Olin wrote Nolen that he was "exceedingly glad" to be able to secure his employment and Nolen, in turn, wrote that he looked forward "with the keenest pleasure and enthusiasm" to the Madison work. See Olin letter dated April 11, 1908, and Nolen's reply dated April 16, 1908.

234. *WSJ*, April 28, 1908.

235. No complete text of Nolen's first address is available, but his remarks were summarized in both the *WSJ* and *MD* on April 28, 1908 and in the 1908 MPPDA *Annual Report*, pp. 75–78.

236. Nolen's biographer, John L. Hancock (p. 161), defines the period between 1907 and 1917 as the take-off period of American planning. It was during this period, he notes, that over one hundred cities undertook comprehensive plans, when the first zoning codes were implemented, when the first municipal planning commissions were established, when the first university urban planning courses were offered, and when national planning organizations were held.

One of the earliest counts of U.S. city plans appeared in a Nolen article entitled "City Making in Wisconsin," which appeared in the May, 1910 (Vol. X, No. 6) issue of *The Municipality*, a periodical of the Wisconsin League of Municipalities. At that time Nolen said that seventy U.S. cities had plans. In 1910 the U.S. Census Bureau said that there were 2,722 communities in the U.S. with over 2,500 persons. Thus in 1910, just 2.6% of all U.S. cities had plans and this was *after* several years of planners' insistance upon plans as the only effective way to guide urban growth. Thus the estimate of one percent does not seem unreasonable for 1908.

For good summaries of the early years of U.S. urban planning, see Mellier G. Scott's *American City Planning Since 1890* (Berkeley, Calif.: University of California Press, 1969) and Hancock's Chap. II, "Origin of a Mission."

237. Charles Mulford Robinson, (New York: Putnam 1900).

238. See Hancock, pp. 137–141.

239. Roy Lubove, *The Progressives and the Slums: Tenement House Reform in New York City* (University Publishing Press, 1962), pp. 217–30, 237–8, 243–5, and Hancock, p. iii.

240. *WSJ*, December 6, 1908.

241. Ibid.

242. *WSJ*, January 27, 1909. Olin's role in Madison was typical of the pattern then being followed around the country for

the introduction of city planning. In a study of one hundred fifty U.S. cities that commissioned city plans by 1916, the impetus came from a "wealthy local citizen, civic commission, art society or commercial club. . . ." (Hancock, pp. 142, 163). Olin was a hybrid, embodying elements of both the wealthy local citizen and a civic commission (MPPDA). Like his counterparts around the country, Olin enjoyed great local power, had discretionary time and a fierce commitment.

243. Nolen, p. 26.

244. Ibid, pp. 89–92.

245. Ibid, p. 16.

246. Ibid, p. 150.

247. Ibid, p. 137. One of the great benefits Madison received from Nolen's work was favorable and relatively extensive national publicity. Madison's decision to do a comprehensive plan coupled with its extraordinary track record in park philanthrophy caused Nolen to use Madison as an example in his articles, papers, and books. For example, in a proplanning paper presented to the prestigious American Civic Association at their November 1908 Pittsburg meeting, Nolen applauded Madison (*WSJ*, November 19, 1908). Such comments peaked the attention of others and produced still other articles such as a feature article in the *Boston Sunday Herald* quoted in the *WSJ*, March 29, 1909. Nolen also plugged Madison in an October 1909 article in *American City* entitled "City Making" Vol. I, no. 1, September 1909, pp. 15–19 (*WSJ* citation, October 14, 1909) and in his book *Replanning Small Cities* (New York: B. W. Huebsch, 1912).

Together with Olin's skillful distribution of MPPDA *Annual Reports*, Nolen's books and articles gave Madison a larger, more favorable national image than it ever enjoyed with the possible exception of a brief period during the Farwell boom when Horace Greeley's visit made Madison the recipient of national attention.

248. Nolen, p. 31.

249. These comments are scattered throughout *Madison: A Model City*. The railroad quote appears on page 90. The full quote is as follows: "The railroads appear to be the most serious factor in Madison's unmaking. Their approaches both in east and west Madison are inconvenient and ugly, their yards are located top near the center of the city, their tracts occupy what was a particularly beautiful stretch of lake front crossing an arm of the lake in South Madison; and they actually run through the grounds of the University."

250. Nolen made these points in his major Madison speeches in 1909 and 1910 (see the *WSJ*, April 29, 1909, and April 27, 1910) *prior* to the release of his plan. The same points were artfully reiterated in the plan.

251. *WSJ* and *MD*, September 6, 1910.

252. In a letter dated May 16, 1921, from John Nolen to Michael Olbricht, Nolen recalled, "In the good old days when the plan was first presented to the public, John M. Olin and a few others stood almost alone in backing the plan. There seemed to be no wide spread interest at the time." Others who

publicly supported planning included Mayor Joseph Schubert, Charles McCarthy and *Wisconsin State Journal* editor Richard Lloyd Jones.

Nolen's hope that Madison's German population would get behind his ideas, many of which were based on German urban design and management, never materialized. For background on the East Washington Boulevard rejection, see *CCP*, June 25, 1909. According to a letter to Olin dated September 8, 1909, this rejection "greatly disheartened" Nolen. It augured "ill for the future of Madison," and brought a note of "despair into the heart of anyone who is trying to believe in American democracy," said Nolen.

In 1910 the council rejected a Nolen plan for extending Brittingham Park (see 1910 MPPDA *Annual Report*, p. 64). Only the aggressive actions of Mayor Schubert got the council to overturn their decision.

Nolen's "regular" work for Madison, i.e., work not directly related to the comprehensive plan, included plans for Brittingham, Vilas, Burrows, and Tenney Parks and of course East Washington Avenue.

For information on the escalating efforts to ax Nolen's salary, see *CCP*, February 11, 1910 and February 10, 1911. As a sop, the council later brought two hundred copies of the Nolen plan. See *CCP*, August 11, 1911.

253. ". . . such regulations must sooner or later prevail in American cities even if they interfere with property rights," said Nolen, *Madison, A Model City*, p. 137.

254. Nolen, ibid., pp. 61–64.

255. The four constitutional amendments that Olin successfully lobbied during the 1909 session were Joint Resolutions 63S, 25S, 32S, and 15S. Two very revealing letters from Olin to Nolen dated May 11, 1909, and June 2, 1909, explain how Olin got these amendments through this session.

256. *Evening Wisconsin*, January 27, 1909.

257. Mellier G. Scott, *American City Planning Since 1890* (Berkeley, University of California Press 1969), p. 243. Wisconsin further distinguished itself when the 1913 legislature passed a bill authorizing cities to establish zoning districts. At the time only two other states, New York and Massachusetts, had passed similar bills, making Wisconsin the third in the nation to enact with this progressive concept. Very significantly, however, the law merely *allowed* cities to enact zoning ordinances; it did not require them to do so.

258. The "noble little band" quote comes from a speech that Nolen delivered on April 27, 1909, at the annual meeting of the MPPDA and reprinted in the 1909 *Annual Report*, p. 95.

259. Per a Nolen letter to Michael Olbrich dated April 14, 1923, Nolen said that he had put his "very best effort" into the Madison plan. When Nolen returned to Madison to give a dedication speech at the Arboretum on June 17, 1934, he confessed his "love for Madison" and his friendship with "scores of fine men including such exceptionally public-spirited leaders as President Charles R. Van Hise, John M. Olin, Frank W. Hoyt, Charles M. Brown, Mayor J. C. Schubert, and many others. . . ." The reference to the special place

Madison always held for Nolen comes from a telephone conversation with his son, John Jr., on February 15, 1981.

260. MacGregor, who later served two terms as a Madison alderman (1912–1913), used his position to actively push city planning in the state through *The Municipality*. Indeed, during the three-year Nolen era, MacGregor ran numerous articles on the subject including a 1909 excerpt from Benjamin Clarke Marsh's classic *An Introduction to City Planning: Democracy's Challenge to America*. This truly seminal book on the subject included a prominent and favorable reference to Madison, Wisconsin, as an example of what smaller American cities could do in city planning. MacGregor also ran in full Olin's "kick-off" speech delivered in January, 1909. See "Looking Ahead to Plan the City Beautiful," *The Municipality* (Vol. IX, No. 5), pp. 222–235. The Nolen speech delivered on July 21, 1909, at Marinette entitled "City Making in Wisconsin" was printed in *The Municipality* in the May, 1910, issue (Vol. X, No. 6), pp. 417–423.

For an excellent discussion of Nolen's other Wisconsin work, see Barbara Jo Long's "John Nolen: The Wisconsin Activities of an American Landscape Architect and Pioneer, 1908 to 1937" (master's thesis, University of Wisconsin, 1978).

261. Nolen had made his recommendation in early February, 1909, in his critique of the 1909 Peabody Campus Plan as a part of his contract with the U.W. as consulting landscape architect. He later incorporated this recommendation and others in the 1910 plan. A copy of his critique of the Peabody plan is available from the Nolen papers. Campus expansion statistics were compiled from a ledger filed with the U. W. Department of Campus Planning, entitled "Land Holdings of the University of Wisconsin Regents."

262. Nolen originally suggested a two-hundred-acre arboretum on land just west of the existing campus (Madison, A Model City, pp. 70, 72), but he also suggested a "really large" park of five hundred to one thousand acres on the south side of Lake Wingra (p. 115). Thus the arboretum location was changed and its size was considerably enlarged over Nolen's original recommendations. Today the arboretum has 1,260 acres, but when it opened in 1934 it had just 500 acres, very close to Nolen's initial suggestion. For general history of the arboretum, consult Nancy G. Sachse, *A Thousand Ages: The University Arboretum* (U.W. Regents, 1965).

263. The camp remained open until the 1950s.

264. The only significant exceptions were a proplanning exhibit that came to Madison in March 1914 (see the *WSJ*, March 20, 1914) and a 1916 civics textbook written for Madison school children that praised planning. See Gilmore, pp. 151–157.

265. The sixteen to three council vote to create a city plan commission reflected the strong support that the concept enjoyed (*CCP*, February 12, 1920). To find out what planning was all about, the city sent its engineer to the City Plan Commission Convention in Cincinnati, and that body sent him back with a glowing report (*CCP*, April 23, 1920). By late summer the council was inviting planners to make presentations and

in 1921 they hired Harland Bartholomew, a nationally known St. Louis-based planner who completed his plan in 1922. Bartholomew took a much more nuts-and-bolts approach to city planning than Nolen, focusing on an integrated street system for easier traffic movement, the elimination of dangerous railroad grade crossings, and the implementation of a zoning ordinance as a way of stopping haphazard and ultimately very expensive growth. For examples of Board of Commerce views, see a series of articles that appeared in the *WSJ*, October 26, November 9, 16, 28, 30, 1919.

266. Nolen and other U. W. Planners got the idea for zoning from German cities, which began implementing the concept in 1900. At first the idea was slow to catch on in the United States in spite of exhortations from Nolen and other planners. New York became the first U.S. city to enact a zoning law in 1916; by 1920 only twenty-five others had followed suit. Not until a 1926 Supreme Court decision (*Euclid* vs. *Amber Realty*) did the concept spread rapidly. One of these cities that did not implement zoning until it was declared safe by the Supreme Court was Madison.

267. James G. Marshall, "The Madison Park System, 1892–1937," *The Journal of Historic Madison, Inc.* (Vol. V), p. 15.

268. In addition to the work done for the city, state, and university, cited above, Nolen also did several jobs for individuals and companies. These included residential landscape plans for John Olin (1909), Carl Johnson (1911), and Professor Scott Goodnight (1911), and several subdivisions including the Fairhaven Land Company (1908), Round Top, now Nob Hill (1910), Lakewood, now Maple Bluff (1909), and a job for John S. Main (1910). See the inventory of Nolen jobs in the Cornell papers.

269. *Madison Past and Present*, p. 31.

270. For an excellent account of this transition, see "X-Rays" in the *WSJ*, July 24, 1903.

271. *WSJ*, September 12, 1915.

272. See the comments of Professor B. H. Meyer in the *WSJ*, March 12, 1907. *WSJ*, June 4, 1910. Representative of people in this exodus was John M. Olin who in 1910 sold his home at 762 Langdon for $55,000 and built a $20,000 home at 130 North Prospect. From 1925 to the late 1960s, this home served as the residence for U.W. presidents. The sale price of Olin's Langdon home was cited in the *Survey of the University of Wisconsin* (State Board of Public Affairs, 1914), p. 48.

273. For the fascinating story of Greenbush see the *WSJ*, November 9, 1916.

274. Per John Valentine, "A Study of Institutional Americanization: The Assimilative History of the Italian-American Community of Madison" (Master's thesis, University of Wisconsin, 1967), p. 110, some sixty-three percent of Italian homes had been moved into Greenbush.

275. *WSJ*, December 13, 1910. See also Valentine, p. 110.

276. See the *WSJ*, May 20, 21, 1916.

277. A nearly full page ad, which ran in the *WSJ* on November 14, 1903, boasted that the lots being advertised were "large—40 × 132—big enough to be cut up into two building lots if purchaser desires."

278. Many of these buildings were sufficiently novel to feature newspaper stories during the teens. In 1919 the Madison city directories began to list apartment houses for the first time.

279. *WSJ*, March 19, 1913.

280. See Ordinance #1520 signed into law on January 31, 1910, for building permit details, and Ordinance #1628, dated April 15, 1913, for details on comprehensive building code and enforcement system.

281. *WSJ*, January 10, 1912.

282. For example, in February, 1908, the Common Council cut off several Fair Oaks water customers to whom the water works superintendent had unilaterally extended service.

283. Basis for annexation law was Chapter 326, Laws of Wisconsin, 1889, as amended by Chapter 214, Laws of 1893, and Chapter 245, Laws of 1895.

284. City of Madison statistics show that Madison jumped from 4.7 square miles in 1900 to 6.4 square miles in 1920. One square mile is equal to 640 acres.

285. For a superb expression of the view that streetcars would break up urban congestion, see Richard Lloyd Jones' editorial in the *WSJ* dated September 13, 1911.

286. For examples of this reasoning, see the *WSJ*, May 24, June 5, and December 31, 1916. The only real force the city could exert would have been to purchase through condemnation. It was precisely this type of reasoning that made lower streetcar fares a burning issue in the 1914 mayoral campaign and to the 1918 municipalization effort.

287. A complete record of docklines established between 1889 and 1911 is available from the author.

288. During this twenty-year period an average of one hundred fifty acres, for 535 lots per year, were platted. From data developed by the author and the real estate summary and article by Stanley Hanks in the *WSJ*, December 31, 1916.

289. Developers also learned that suburban living was not everyone's cup of tea. Even the wife of Shorewood (College) Hills developer had reservations about the prospects of moving to her husband's new subdivision. All she could think of, she said, was "no stores, no delivery service, no transportation, no good school" and the like. What she did not say was that there were no sewers or water service then either. And some pioneer suburban women learned to their great dissatisfaction that Madison maids were not willing to work in suburbs that were not served by streetcars (*WSJ*, February 20, 1917). In short, the new suburbs exerted a powerful appeal but, contrary to what many modern readers might think, that appeal was not like a tug of war where all the men are on one side of the rope.

290. For a particularly good example of this, see the *Rule for the Development and Protection of the Nakoma Homes Company* in the SHSW pamphlet collection.

291. *WSJ*, October 27, 1899.

292. *WSJ*, October 4, 1899.

293. *WSJ*, February 14, 1913.

294. However, there was one sense in which even the expensive machines were affordable at least by the rich. In 1900 a good span of carriage horses cost $500 and a carriage could easily run $500 for a total cost of $1,000. Thus, on the basis of initial cost, a wealthy person could buy one of the lower priced autos for the same price as a span of horses and a carriage. But the real cost difference between the auto and the carriage was in its annual operation. Autos consumed gasoline at a cost of just three cents per mile, whereas the feeding and boarding of a span of carriage horses could easily run $375 per year—the equivalent of 12,750 miles by car (*WSJ*, August 11, 1900). In addition to being cost-competitive with a horse and carriage, autos had another advantage: they were so simple to operate that almost any adult could drive them (*WSJ*, May 19, 1900). For a summary of day labor rates from 1880 to 1914, see *WSJ*, December 6, 1914.

295. *WSJ*, May 19, August 11, 1900.

296. *WSJ*, May 30, 1903.

297. The 1903 ban on autos from the park and pleasure drives, for example, lasted just five months (May to September, 1903). The ban on autos in the Dane County fairgrounds adopted in September, 1902, was rescinded in September, 1903. The driving ban in city cemeteries, however, began later (1905) and lasted longer (1912) and then was reinstated to 1914.

298. Ordinance #1294, signed June 30, 1903.

299. Ordinance #1339 and #1340, both signed into law August 29, 1904.

300. See *WSJ*, June 12, 1905, and August 7, 1906.

301. *WSJ*, October 15, 1903. Although this citation comes from a 1903 source, it prevailed for many years thereafter.

302. *WSJ*, January 26, 1907.

303. These figures are interpolated from the chart on page 366.

304. *WSJ*, October 8, 1916.

305. *WSJ*, January 27, 1917.

306. *WSJ*, January 2, 1916.

307. *WSJ*, January 24, 1917.

308. *WSJ*, January 22, 1917.

309. *WSJ*, January 2, 1916.

310. Details of these early suburban bus lines can be found in newspaper advertisements and articles. For typical examples see the *WSJ*, June 15, 1912, June 11, 1913, and May 20, 1915.

311. *WSJ*, January 2, 1916.

312. Only twenty-five cities implemented zoning before 1920.

313. *WSJ*, June 1, 1895.

314. Mrs. Harry Leonard Moseley, tape recording, January 20, 1957, SHSW; Mrs. Lucien M. Hanks, tape recording. January 15, 1957, SHSW.

315. For descriptions of changing nineteenth century concepts of women, see William Henry Chafe's *The American Woman: Her Changing Social, Economic, and Political Roles, 1920–1970* (New York: Oxford University Press, 1972), pp. 3–22; William L. O'Neill's *Everyone Was Brave: The Rise and Fall of Femininism in America* (Chicago: Quadrangle Books, 1969), pp. 3–48, and Eleanor Flexner's *Century of Struggle: The Women's Rights Movement in the U.S.* (New York: Athenum, 1973). For a vivid yet balanced exposition of women's lives at the bottom, middle, and top of society, see Maury Klein's and Harvey A. Kantor's *Prisoners of Progress, American Industrial Cities, 1850–1920* (New York: Macmillan Publishing Company, Inc., 1976), pp. 204–328. For a spirited selection of original sources, see Aileen Kraditor's (ed.) *Feminism* (Chicago: Quadrangle Books, 1968). The concept of Victorian romantic love is most entertainly explained in Morton M. Hunt's *The Natural History of Love* (London: Hutchinson & Company, 1960), pp. 273–279.

316. Madison's Women's Club was modelled after similar organizations in New York and other large cities. Interestingly, the prototype large urban women's club was New York's Sorosis, founded in 1868 by a well-known female journalist, Jenny Cunningham Croly, who was irked when she was not allowed to attend a dinner for Charles Dickens sponsored by the New York Press Club. She therefore vowed to found a rival organization for women and did so. See O'Neill, p. 84 ff.

The Lady Bountiful concept came from the 1707 Farquhar comedy, *The Beaux Stratagem*.

For newspaper accounts of Women's Club activities, see the *MD*, March 9, 1893, February 2, 1895, April 20, 1895, January 15, November 6, 1897, and October 21, 1899.

317. For accounts of the Sparling talk see the *WSJ*, November 2, 1900 and *MD*, November 3, 1900.

318. Gertrude Slaughter, *Only The Past Is Ours, The Life Story of Gertrude Slaughter* (New York: Exposition Press, 1963), p. 120.

319. A convincing expression of this urge to "do something" was a pamphlet first published by the Education Committee of the Wisconsin Women's Suffrage Association in 1913 called *Social Forces* and continued for several years thereafter. According to the 1915 edition of *Social Forces* (p. 4): "All emotion, all knowledge, which does not result in action is futile. The result of these studies (referring to a list of topics in *Social Forces*) should be evident in the practical civic work carried on by each (women's) club." The authors of *Social Forces* also recognized that such good works were "the best preparation for citizenship and for the ballot, and a very forceful means of convincing others of the need and the practicality of universal suffrage. Hence the frequent appearance in this outline of lists of things to do.

320. For information on the Women's Club see the *WSJ*, May 6, 1911, and Frank A. Gilmore's *The City of Madison, The Capital of Wisconsin*, p. 125. For the Girls Civic League see the *CT*, February 1 and April 15, 1918. For Civics Club see the *WSJ*, November 19 and December 18, 1913. An excellent summary of all women's club work is found in the *WSJ*, December 31, 1916. For the early history of the Catholic Women's Club see Allene M. Rohan's unpublished account, "A Fifty-Two-Year Resume History of the Madison Catholic Women's Club, 1914–1966" (SHSW).

321. *WSJ*, May 8, 1901.

322. Unfortunately the 1900 Madison census data on working women was never compiled and published, although statewide and Milwaukee data are available. Statewide 15.5 percent of all women ten and above were reported gainfully employed, but in Milwaukee the percentage stood at 25.6. Since Madison would more closely approximate the Milwaukee data, something between 20 and 25 percent would therefore seem reasonable. By the same token there is good reason to suppose that the composition of the Madison female workforce was similar to Milwaukee's, where 52 percent of all working women were between sixteen and twenty-five, and 55 percent were single. See Joseph H. Hill's *Women in Gainful Occupations, 1870–1920, Census Monographs*, IX (Washington, D.C.: U.S. Government Printing Office, 1929), Table 156, and the *Abstract of the Twelfth Census of the United States, 1900*, 3rd ed. (Washington, D.C.: U.S. Government Printing Office, 1904), Table 66.

323. Hill, *Gainful Occupations*, p. 286, Table 166, and p. 269, Table 156.

324. *WSJ*, March 4, 1917.

325. For an early plea for the elimination of female-male salary differentials, see the *WSJ*, July 17, 1914. A detailed breakdown of the 1920 Madison workforce showed that 27 percent of all women were office workers such as typists, clerks, and bookkeepers, 16.8 percent fell into the business and commercial category such as store clerks, waitresses, and telephone operators, 16.7 percent were domestics (servants and housekeepers), and 10.7 percent were professionals defined as teachers, musicians, nurses, and librarians. See Hill, *Gainful Occupations*, p. 229, Table 118.

326. *WSJ*, January 14, 1911.

327. The best accounts of the Women's Exchange are its annual reports, which the newspapers usually printed in full. For examples see the *WSJ*, May 5, 1888, May 6, 1889, May 9, 1892, and the *MD*, May 14, 1893, *Madison Past and Present*, p. 96. For a good summary of the YWCA, see the *WSJ*, January 14, 1911, and December 6, 1916.

328. See the 1910 annual report of the Madison General Hospital, p. 18. A similar view pervaded the "progressive" University of Wisconsin on female faculty. For a scathing attack on this problem see Helen R. Olin's article in the *WSJ*, March 31, 1900. The issue then came down to men's perception of women's ability. Except in the minds of suffragettes and a few liberated souls, women were not thought to have

the raw ability for society's more complex positions. Nonsense, said Helen R. Olin, a dedicated Madison suffragette. This "petty spirit of superiority . . . in is reality the last refuge of an inferior nature." *WSJ*, October 20, 1909.

329. The best short source for Wisconsin suffrage history is an article by Theodora W. Youmans, "How Wisconsin Women Won the Ballot," *Wisconsin Magazine of History*, Vol. V (1921–2), pp. 3–32. The most definitive study produced to date is Lawrence L. Graves, "The Wisconsin Woman Suffrage Movement, 1846–1920" (Ph.D. dissertation, University of Wisconsin, 1954).

330. Youmans, p. 7.

331. Ibid., pp. 12–15.

332. Chapter 211, Laws of 1885.

333. Youmans, p. 16, and *WSJ*, November 3, 1886.

334. Only the *Madison Democrat* (November 7, 1902) even gave any poll data at all. In the Eighth Ward, for example, only thirty-five women and 498 men case votes for superintendent of instruction.

335. Youmans, pp. 16–17.

336. The intimate connection between suffrage and prohibition is evident from a study of Madison women who had major leadership roles in the WWSA. For example, Helen R. Olin was statewide WCTU superintendent for the Franchise at the same time she was recording secretary of the WWSA. And Mrs. E. E. Chynoweth, one of the most respected suffragettes was also state treasurer of the WCTU. Later Mrs. Chynoweth became the second women to ever be appointed to the City of Madison polity-making body, the Police and Fire Commission, and one of two women to be first elected to the Madison school board in 1919. This linkage was the basis for the observation that nearly all prohibitionists were suffragettes but not vice versa. See Graves, p. 96–99. Very significantly the Prohibition party was the first major political organization to endorse female suffrage.

The editor of the *Madison Democrat* aptly summarized the mutual exclusivity of suffrage and prohibition when he said in a March 9, 1889, editorial: "It is plain to anyone who is not a hopeless crank that the union of the women's rights movement with the prohibition movement practically ruins the hopes of both."

337. *WSJ*, June 21, 1914. From a hard-hitting book by Zona Gale, well-known Portage author, in a talk before the Women's Club.

338. Just what role the Progressive movement played in the women's movement is debated by scholars. Some like O'Neill argue that the women's movement coincided with the Progressive movement but that it would have greatly advanced around the turn of the century without it (p. 103). But Graves and others take the more plausible view that women leaders were sensitized by progressivism to the evils of society and that in response to this process demanded the opportunity to tackle the job (pp. 338–39).

339. Chapter 227, Laws of 1911.

340. See Graves, pp. 186–217, for good general background on the campaign and the Madison newspapers, particularly during the two months before the election.

341. Graves, pp. 201–206, and Madison newspapers.

342. Statistics compiled by the author. An analysis of the 1912 suffrage and the 1914 wet-dry referendum showed a strong correlation between dry-suffrage and wet-antisuffrage sentiment.

343. Graves, p. 219 passim.

344. Youmans, pp. 21–23; *WSJ*, November 20, 1912.

345. One of the two Madison women first elected to the school board had been very active in women's civic affairs. Mrs. William G. Bleyer (B. A. Wellesley, M. A., Columbia University) had been president of the Dane County Equality Suffrage League and the Women's Club. Little is known about Mrs. Weaver.

346. Even before the first woman was elected by popular vote, the Common Council saw the handwriting on the wall and by council vote elected Mrs. E. Roy Stevens to the board of education. Thus she became the first women to serve on this body and the first ever appointed to a major city policy-making body. *CCP*, December 13, 1918, See also *WSJ*, October 1, 1916, *CCP*, October 13, 1916, *WSJ*, December 9, 1916, and January 13, 1917. See also the *CCP*, April 2, 1918.

347. Significantly Senate approval did not come until five months *after* the Prohibition Amendment had become law on January 29, 1919. Once Prohibition had become law, the power of the liquor lobby, long the arch adversary of suffrage, was neutralized. See also Youmans, pp. 29–30.

348. Ida Husted Harper (ed.), *History of Women Suffrage, 1900 to 1920*, Vol. V (National American Woman Suffrage Association, New York, 1922), pp. 617 and 683–701; Youmans, p. 28. According to Youmans (pp. 26–27), the Wisconsin congressional delegation changed its mind on suffrage between 1915 and 1918. In 1915 the delegation voted against a suffrage bill two to nine, whereas in 1918 the vote was eight to two (one vacant seat). Suffrage lobbying in Madison was carried on in part by the Madison Business Women's Suffrage Club, an organization formed in 1914 and which by 1916 had grown to four hundred members. *WSJ*, December 31, 1916.

349. Harper, ibid.

350. *WSJ*, September 4, 1920. Interestingly, according to the *WSJ*, August 31, 1920, registration lists of Madison women who had voted on school suffrage questions had been lost or discarded by male poll workers.

351. *WSJ*, October 10, 1920. This editorial was, interestingly enough, written in response to a furor arising over the appointment of the first woman, Mrs. E. E. Chynoweth, to the Police and Fire Commission, an action that ultimately causes one misogynist to resign in protest.

352. According to miasma theorists, vegetable matter was more pathogenic than animal matter although putrifying humans were thought to be the most dangerous of all. It was for this reason that city graveyards were relocated, disinterred bodies and all, to rural settings and that corpses were required to be buried a minimum of six feet under. Miasma theorists also believed that night air was more dangerous than day air and therefore shut their windows at night. Sunlight and soil were thought to be the great natural purifiers and lime the best artificial purifier. For general background on miasma theory, see Wilson G. Smillie, *Public Health: Its Promise and the Future: A Chronicle of the Development of Public Health in the United States 1607–1914* (New York: Macmillan Company, 1955).

353. George Rosen, *A History of Public Health* (New York: MD Publications, Inc., 1958), pp. 312–314.

354. James H. Cassedy, *Charles V. Chapin and the Public Health Movement* (Cambridge, Mass.: Harvard University Press, 1962), pp. 142, 172.

355. The classic account of this "new public health" was Charles V. Chapin's *The Sources and Modes of Infection* (New York: John Wiley and Sons, 1910).

356. Evidence for the pervasiveness of tuberculosis in Wisconsin cows comes from many sources. Eric Lampard in his 1963 classic study, *The Rise of the Dairy Industry in Wisconsin* (Madison: State Historical Society of Wisconsin), p. 188, describes a test on the prize-winning University of Wisconsin dairy herd conducted by Professor Harry L. Russell. Of the thirty cows in the herd, twenty-seven had tubercular lesions. For an example of a milk-related typhoid epidemic, see the *WSJ*, November 6, 1908; and for a corresponding story on the results of milk adulteration, see the *WSJ*, October 25, 1905. For an article portraying the cow as killer by Dr. Clarke Gapen, see the *WSJ*, February 3, 1908. Milk was also implicated as a source of scarlet fever, diphtheria, and a serious version of the septic sore throat.

357. Lampard, p. 405.

358. *WSJ*, January 15, 1907.

359. See the *WSJ*, January 18, 19, 22, 23, 1907.

360. For accounts of the clean milk crusade see the *WSJ*, May 6, May 14, June 13, 1908. The ordinance, #1484, was passed on June 12, 1908, but an October amendment (#1496) gave farmers until February 1, 1909, to get their herds in compliance. According to Milwaukee's 1908 Commission of Health report, p. 15, that city's tubercular inspection requirement did not go into effect until April 1, 1909.

361. *WSJ*, March 8, 1914.

362. *WSJ*, April 15, 1914.

363. Ordinance #1700, passed November 17, 1914.

364. For an informative account of Rennebohm's work, see his annual reports bound with the annual Board of Health reports. In spite of its almost unbelievable effectiveness, simplicity, and low cost, pasteurized milk was very slow to catch on in the United States. Though it was discovered and perfected in the 1880s, it was available in only a few of the larger Eastern cities by the late 1890s. Not until 1903 did it appear in Milwaukee, and not until 1913 (Ordinance #1623) did Madison pass its first ordinance *allowing* but not requiring the process. The relatively slow spread of pasteurization elevated the importance of the tuberculin test as a primary defense against disease in raw milk. Interestingly, Madison club women saw pasteurization as a kind of cover up for the dirty milk and therefore urged that the primary goal of Madison public policy be clean milk rather than dirty pasteurized milk. See *WSJ*, April 5, 1914.

365. *WSJ*, May 21, June 20, July 13, 1907.

366. Martin V. Melosi, "Out of Sight, Out of Mind, The Environment and Disposal of Municipal Waste Refuse, 1860–1920" *Historian* 35 (August 1973), p. 2; and Smillie, p. 354. Madison's horse population ranged from about 850 in 1900 to a peak of 1,271 in 1913, hence the average of 1,000 horses during this period.

367. See Ordinance #1649 passed September 12, 1913. These laws were subsequently toughened in Ordinances #1820 and #1822 passed on November 10 and December 15, respectively. For information on the Women's Club campaign against the fly, see the *WSJ*, September 16, 1909, and January 12, 1910.

368. According to miasma theory, putrifying human bodies were thought to be the most serious form of contamination—hence the intense concern that just a handful of bodies in a huge lake evoked in the minds of many people. Though the effort was beaten back on the basis of these arguments, it was not until two years later that opponents enjoyed real vindication. In that year a typhoid epidemic broke out at the Insane Asylum and was traced to its Lake Mendoata drinking water. Yes, the same lake into which they dumped their sewage. See the *WSJ*, July 11, August 8, December 10, 1902, and the *MD*, July 12, 1902, May 8, 1903, June 22 and July 4, 1904.

369. *WSJ*, May 7, 18, 19, 20, 30, and September 14 and 24, 1910, and November 16, 1913.

370. *WSJ*, September 4, 1915. See also September 4 and 9, 1915.

371. From the time this new waste removal technology was available, city health officials waged a veritable war on privies. In 1913 the first city building code (Ordinance #1628) made it illegal to use or have a privy or cesspool *if* a sanitary sewer was available. In other words, the law forced property owners to install indoor plumbing. Probably no statistic in the Board of Health annual report gave more satisfaction to the health officer than the number of outhouses condemned and sewers connected.

The sharp increase in indoor toilets, interestingly enough, focused attention on poor quality, unsanitary plumbing. In response to this problem, the city promulgated its first plumbing code as a part of a comprehensive building code (Ordinance #1628 noted above). The ordinance attempted to eliminate practices that allowed pipes to clog, back up, leak sewer gas, or even liquids, and that made the cleanout of sewer pipes almost impossible.

372. See the *WSJ*, April 28, 1900.

373. *WSJ*, May 11, 1900.

374. *WSJ*, May 23, 1900.

375. *WSJ*, December 7, 1900.

376. See the *WSJ*, September 19 and July 12, 1901. According to Leonard Metcalf and Harrison Eddy, authors of *American Sewerage Practice* 3rd ed. (New York: McGraw-Hill Book Company, Inc., 1935), pp. 18–19, the Madison plant was "one of the earliest sprinkling filters in the U.S. . . ." However unlike later models the liquid was distributed below the surface of the cinder bed to avoid freezing. Later plants including the Burke plant used the sprinkling filter technique. For a good description of this "model" plant, see the *WSJ*, July 20, 1907.

Another reason Madisonians were eager to have the new plant work was that it would put an end to 600,000 gallons of raw sewage that had been discharged into the river each day since the old plant stopped working in January, 1901. Thus for six months the city had no choice but to dump its sewage raw into the lake.

377. *MD*, October 7, 1904.

378. For references to the army of scythe wielders, see the *WSJ*, July 21, August 22, 1900, and July 12, 1902. References to the mechanical weed cutters may be found in the *WSJ*, August 12, 17, and 23, 1905, and February 8, 1911.

379. *WSJ*, July 20, 1907. Assuming the 1907 population to be 25,000, Lake Monona was receiving the equivalent of raw sewage from 18,750 persons!

380. See the *WSJ*, June 10, 1911, July 28, 1914, and August 1, 1915. For typical Board of Health warnings, see their annual reports for the years 1916, 1918, and 1919.

381. *CCP*, March 27, 1911.

382. *WSJ*, August 5, 1915.

383. *WSJ*, August 1, 1915.

384. *CT*, July 12, 1918.

385. *WSJ*, September 3, 1915.

386. See MPPDA, 1917 annual report, p. 10, and *WSJ*, August 1, 1915.

387. *WSJ*, March 31, 1914.

388. Ordinance #1284.

389. *WSJ*, April 2, 1916. The term was from Mayor Sayle's platform.

390. For details regarding the notorious Bassett Sewer, see the *WSJ*, July 28, 1914, and August 5, 1915. For information on the vestigal private sewers, see the *MD*, August 25, 1904, the *WSJ*, June 10, 1910, and September 10, 1915.

391. *WSJ*, August 3, 1915.

392. The first application of copper sulfate occurred in the summer of 1915 (*WSJ*, August 1, 1915). The next application apparently came in the summer of 1918, when 4.2 tons were applied. The purpose was to quell the airborne algae stench created by dead algae. The treatment proved relatively effective in the Brittingham Bay area but not in the rest of Lake Monona. In 1919 the dosage was increased to five tons. From 1918 to 1925, Monona received additional copper sulfate treatments but not on a systematic basis. From 1925 to the 1940s, however, the lake received regular and systematic treatment with the chemical. In the summer of 1925 alone, 500 tons were applied. See John W. Alvord, *Report on the Cause of Offensive Odors from Lake Monona, Madison, Wisconsin* (Chicago: 1920), and Merle Starr Nichols, "Copper in Lake Muds from Lakes of the Madison Area," *Transactions of the Wisconsin Academy of Arts, Science, and Letters* 38 (1946), pp. 333–350.

393. *WSJ*, August 4, 1915.

394. For plant cost details, see the *WSJ*, December 22, 1915.

395. *CT*, August 12, 1918.

396. *CT*, November 20, 1918.

397. Each year City of Madison street sweepers dumped tons of horse manure and other street debris on the ice off the foot of Blair Street, where it was allowed to sink with the spring thaw. It ran into the lake anyway, reasoned city officials, so why not dump on the ice and be done with it. *WSJ*, March 13, 1917.

398. For examples of articles from the *CT* crusade, see the *CT*, July 25, 27, 29, 30, August 2, 5, 9, 12, 30, September 10, 1918.

399. *CCP*, December 13, 1918. This report was prepared by W. A. Kirchoffer, consulting sanitary engineer to the state Board of Health.

400. See *WSJ*, June 14, 1919. The new consultant was John W. Alvord, a highly regarded Chicago sanitary engineer.

401. See Alvord.

402. The forty to fifty-year plant life comes from the *WSJ*, June 20, 1911, and October 31, 1915. For the overcapacity story, see the *WSJ*, July 10, 1920.

403. James J. Flannery, "The Madison Lakes Problem" (Master's thesis, University of Wisconsin, 1949), p. 35.

404. For cost sources on the septic plant, see *WSJ*, June 20, 1911. City budget records show that between 1911 and 1915 the city borrowed $495,000 to expand and improve the city sewage system.

405. To better understand the flushing characteristics of lakes, see John R. Vallentyne, *The Algal Bowl: Lake and Men* (Misc. Spec. Publ #22, Dept. Environment, Fisheries and Marine Service, 1974).

406. According to a 1974 study of cultural eutrophication, limnologists have known since 1920 that the addition of phosphorus and nitrogen would dramatically increase plant growth (John R. Vallentyne, pp. 2–3, 36), but the earliest article cited in a comprehensive bibliographic history of North American limnology (David G. Frey (ed.), *Limnology of North America* (Madison: University of Wisconsin Press, 1963), was an article by B. P. Domogalla (City of Madison biochemist) and E. B. Fred, then U. W. professor of agricultural bacteriology, "Ammonia and Nitrate Studies of Lakes near Madison, Wisconsin," *Journal of the Agricultural Society of Agronomy* (Vol. 18, 1926), pp. 897–911. This article attributes high nitrogen and phosphorus contents of the lakes to natural biological processes, not to sewage. Incredible as it may seem, commissioners of the Madison Metropolitan Sewerage District, as late as 1948, insisted that there was no direct relationship between algal blooms and sewage! (Flannery, p. 261.)

407. According to John R. Vallentyne, (pp. 18–20), the intestines and kidneys of the average person produce 13.4 pounds of phosphorus and nitrogen each year, almost none of which is removed by sewage treatment plants. Tests have shown that these 13.4 pounds of fertilizers, when added to lake water, are enough to create one ton of new living plants. Thus in 1920 the 38,400 persons then living in the city would have caused 38,400 tons of algae and lake plants to grow in Lake Monona, which would otherwise not have been there.

408. Nichols, p. 333.

409. *WSJ*, July 26, 1901.

410. *WSJ*, May 23, 1894.

411. See also *WSJ*, March 17, 1900.

412. For descriptions of the catch-as-catch-can system, see *WSJ*, March 17, 1900, *MD*, January 8, 1905.

413. See the *WSJ*, March 17, 1900, for the Women's Club reference and the annual report of this organization. See the *WSJ*, March 21, 1900, for prompt backing that the notice received from the Contemporary Club. See the *WSJ*, March 24, 1900, for the editor citation.

414. Curti and Carstenson, pp. 637–40.

415. This survey had sufficient merit to be printed in *The Municipality* (Vol. II, No. 1, May 1901), pp. 12–16.

416. *CCP*, January 11, 1901.

417. See Ordinance #1240 and the *WSJ*, July 2, 12, 15, and 23, 1901, for start-up details.

418. *WSJ*, July 26, 1900, and March 6, 1903.

419. *WSJ*, August 1, 1901.

420. See *WSJ*, May 8, 1911, for a good account of offensive pig farm at Cottage Grove Road and Monona Drive. See also *WSJ*, May 12 and July 15, 1911.

421. See *WSJ*, March 24, 1900. According to the *WSJ*, July 23, 1901, the heaviest user of the new system was the Langdon area and the lowest, the Sixth District.

422. *CCP*, February 13, 1903.

423. *CCP*, February 13, 1903, *MD*, June 26, 1903. In 1909 (*WSJ*, September 12–16, 1909) the *WSJ* reported 1,500 households were paying garbage fees and the 1910 report revealed that the city had 5,182 dwelling units. Thus, about thirty percent of all households used the garbage service.

424. See *CCP*, April 15, 1913.

425. *WSJ*, September 25, 1915. See *WSJ*, April 17, 1915. In 1915 the fee was $3.30 per year. Residents of some areas such as Greenbush, whose residents were too poor to have their garbage hauled away, had to endure the odor of decomposing garbage during the warm months.

426. In 1915 for the first time, a city council committee urged the inactment of a mandatory, full-tax funded, city-administered garbage collection and disposal system. *CCP,* March 12, 1915. In 1916, George Sayle used his inaugural to become the first mayor to urge a "compulsory" city system as the "only satisfactory solution to the problem." *CCP,* April 18, 1916.

427. *WSJ,* August 31, 1918.

428. Although garbage incineration advocates touted this method as a breakthrough for scientific and hygenic garbage disposal, an incinerator was not viewed as a good thing to have next door or even in your neighborhood. Two sites provoked fierce opposition before a third won begrudging approval. For details on this battle see the newspapers and Common Council proceedings between April, 1916, and June, 1916. City of Madison health officer, Dr. J. P. Donovan (1905–1917) was a strong local advocate for garbage incineration and municipal collection. In 1912 he read a scientific paper on incineration before a conference of state health officers. *WSJ,* June 12, 1912, September 25, 1914.

429. All calculations of marsh area were done by the author from studies and maps. The term "Great Central Marsh" was first used by city engineer John Nader in a report to the Common Council on September 6, 1884.

430. For examples of official city antimarsh sentiment see the inaugural address of Mayors Keyes and Schubert in the *CCP* on April 20, 1886, and April 17, 1906, respectively, and a special communication to the council from Mayor Keyes reported in the *WSJ,* June 12, 1886. For examples of health officer alarms, see the annual report for 1889, 1906, and 1909, issued by Dr. F. H. Bodenius, Dr. J. P. Donovan, and Gilmore. For a marsh fire account, see the *WSJ,* October 14, 1895. Gregerson's quote comes from L. T. Gregerson and A. L. McCulloch. "The Drainage of Madison Marshes (Bachelor's thesis, University of Wisconsin, 1895), pp. 16–17, who provides a good contemporary analysis of the problem.

431. The years that the marshes were filled in were determined by the author from a variety of maps and other sources.

Cost differentials between draining and filling were done in 1901 by City Engineer Turneaure (*WSJ,* April 2, 1901). He estimated that filling the marsh would cost $250,000, whereas draining it would cost just $5,000. A similar differential probably existed in the 1880s when policy makers elected draining.

One of the reasons why the filling strategy was so expensive was because it required the construction of an elaborate, large-capacity storm sewer to drain the Great Central Marsh. The huge public works project was proposed in 1905 (*CCP,* January 13, 1905) and completed several years later. The storm sewer that empties into Lake Monona at Blount Street drained 112 acres of marshland and another 168 acres of surrounding higher land.

The largest and most significant fill operation in the Great Central Marsh was conducted in 1910 by the Chicago and North Western Railroad, which desired to raise its track one and one-half feet. The mammoth task required nearly three hundred men, six months, and fifteen thousand loads of sand brought in from a Verona sand pit (*WSJ,* July 20 and August 16, 1910).

432. *WSJ,* November 17, 1907, May 7, 31, 1911.

433. Credit for the first student health exams must go to the Women's Club, which conducted a program in 1901–1902. See the *Annual Report of the Public Schools, 1901–02,* p. 48, and the same report for 1911–12, p. 58, and the 1915–16 report, p. 62.

434. See the 1909–1910 annual report, pp. 45–49. The annual medical examinations had great utility in reducing or correcting health-related learning problems such as the addition of corrective eye glasses, for example.

435. *Annual Report of the Public Schools, 1912–13,* p. 83.

436. See *Annual Report of the Public Schools, 1910–11,* p. 41, and the annual report for 1912–13, p. 89.

437. See the annual reports 1910–11, p. 41, 1911–12, pp. 56–57, 1912–13, pp. 49–50, 1913–14, p. 52.

438. Unlike nearly all other local boards of directors, one out of three of the new hospital board members were women and one was elected vice-president—an early reflection of the large role women were distined to play in the hospital crusade.

439. For overviews of Madison hospital history, see the Dr. C. A. Harper's *Efforts by the Citizens of Madison Toward Obtaining Hospital Facilities,* a typed paper available in the SHSW and a summary by F. W. Hall entitled "The City and Hospital," in *Madison Past and Present* (*WSJ,* 1902), p. 54. The best one-volume history of hospitals is Mary Risley's *House of Healing: The Story of the Hospital* (Garden City, New York: Doubleday & Company, Inc., 1961).

For a useful national backdrop on hospitals, see Smillie and Risley.

Giles lecture was reported in the *WSJ* and *MD* on December 1, 1880. For background on Miss Giles, see Ela, p. 18, Butterfield, p. 990, and Hall, pp. 44–45, and Ruth Kohler, *The Story of Wisconsin Women,* The Committee on Wisconsin Women for the 1948 Centennial, p. 76.

The term "medical doctrine" refers to the variety of medical philosophies then in vogue including homeopathic, allopathic, eclectic, etc.

440. See *CCP,* February 5, March 5, and May 7, 1881.

441. For details on the second Madison Hospital Association, see the *WSJ,* January 15, June 10, 1886, *MD,* January 19, 1886.

442. The effort to use the old cemetery caused Sixth Warders to pack the council chamber demanding that ". . . no public or other hospital should for sanitary reasons . . . be located in the city limits" and that no public land should be used for a private purpose (*WSJ,* April 18, 1877).

For other aspects of the Franciscan hospital, see the *WSJ,* June 10, 1886, April 19, 1887, February 18, 20, June 29, 1889, July 14, 1890; the *MD,* June 14, 1887; and the *CCP,* April 12, 1889, and April 15, 1890.

443. The decision to sell the hospital lots was bitterly criticized by John M. Olin on the grounds that the site might have become a park. The same logic pertains to the use of the site as a hospital.

444. For other details on the Gill and Boyd Hospital, see the *WSJ,* April 1, May 3, August 3, and October 28, 1889, April 3 and 18, 1890, June 10, 1893, January 6, 1898, and July 26, 1905, and the *CCP,* April 1892.

445. *WSJ,* November 21, 1896, March 18, 1898, March 25, July 7, July 15, 1899, July 10, 21, 28, and August 10, 1900, and the *MD,* January 22, 1897, July 17, 1900, and Cornelius A. Harper, *Efforts by Citizens of Madison toward Obtaining Hospital Facilities* (Madison, 1949), 6 p.

446. The statement of the new hospital mission was made by Dr. J. A. Jackson, founder of the Jackson Clinic, at the official opening of Madison General Hospital on October 15, 1903, but was reflective of sentiment that took hold years earlier.

The person most responsible for the development of antiseptics was an English surgeon, Joseph Lister. In 1863 he read an article by Pasteur in a French medical journal in which Pasteur said that decay was caused by living organisms. Lister concluded that if this was true, then invisible germs were entering patients' bodies from surgical room air, from scalpels, and even from dressings. In his subsequent studies of bacterial control he learned that carbolic acid had been used to control bacteria in sewage and theorized that the same chemical might kill germs in the surgical suite. To his great satisfaction it worked. The discovery caused Lister's name to be enshrined in the annals of human medicine, but the connection between sewage and surgery has been forgotten. See Risley, pp. 195–206.

Persons who enter hospitals today also owe a great debt to Florence Nightengale who not only elevated nursing to a profession but made a number of important changes in hospital design and administration.

447. For details on the Pest Home, see the *CCP,* April 18, 1865, March 3, 1877, November 4, 1866, February 1, 1867; the *WSJ,* August 31, 1872, October 13, 1891, April 7, 1892, August 18, 1898, October 15, 1901; and the *MD,* March 4, 1877, November 5, December 5, 1878, October 12, 1891, April 9, 1892, April 21, 1893, March 9, 1895, and September 22, 1896.

448. For an example of this sentiment, see Professor Richard T. Ely's "no higher duty" resolution reported in the *WSJ,* May 4, 1898, the *CCP,* June 7, 1906, and Mayor Schubert's inaugural address, April 19, 1910 *(CCP).*

Still another argument for hospitals came from businessmen who said that, all other things being equal, the presence of a modern general hospital in Madison would give the city a competitive edge in the struggle to attract population and generate economic growth.

449. *WSJ,* January 3 and 7 1898.

450. *WSJ,* May 4, June 16, 1898.

451. *CCP,* August 25, 1898.

452. *CCP,* January 13, 1899.

453. Ibid.

454. For details on Dr. Keenan's proposition, see the *WSJ*, March 29, 1899, May 17, June 14, 25, 28, and 29, July 2, 1899, May 20 and June 15, 1900.

455. For accounts of the Randall Park site, see the *WSJ* and *MD* April 13, 1900.

456. *WSJ*, June 25, 1900.

457. For details on the successful hospital, see the *WSJ*, July 4, September 17, 1900, March 11, September 10, 13, 1902, January 8, 1903; *MD*, July 6, 1900, February 8, November 27, 1901, March 8, 15, May 7, November 11, 14, 1902, April 14, 1904; the *CCP*, April 16, 1901, April 19, 1904.

458. For background on the St. Mary's story, see the *WSJ*, August 22, 1908, July 8, 1911, Harper, and a variety of material was obtained by the author. Of the total cost, local Catholics raised $25,000.

459. For background on the expansion of Madison General, see the *WSJ*, February 9, 11, 1911, and January 3, 1912, and the annual reports of the Madison General Hospital Association.

460. Curti and Carstensen, Vol. II, pp. 490–491; and Harper. The completion of the U. W. infirmary reduced but did not eliminate the U. W. need for Madison General. Indeed, hospital officials were eager to make its doors "swing wide" to U. W. students. They continued to feel a strong moral obligation to provide such a facility for the university.

461. Harper.

462. Ibid.

463. *Madison Past and Present*, p. 24, and the *WSJ*, January 12, 1898, and Commerce, Board of *The Pathfinders: A Guide Book to Madison, Wisconsin, and Vicinity* (Madison, 1914), p. 46. July 25, 1908, for background on the Madison Sanitarium, and Harold Holand, "Madison Fights Tuberculosis: A Story of 60 years" (unpublished manuscript, 1970), p. 6, and the *WSJ*, December 6, 1916, for details on the Morningside. The principal remedies for tuberculosis were then fresh air, diet, and rest.

464. Curti and Carstenson, pp. 490–493, for background on the Bradley Hospital and Jackson, p. 325, for the Jackson Clinic.

465. Bed capacities of all hospitals were estimated by the author. Even more remarkable in some ways than the growth rate was the fact that in the seventeen years between 1903 and 1919, thirteen new hospitals and one clinic opened their doors. Some, however, such as Mercy and Lutheran hospitals, did not last long.

466. See Mayor Heim's inaugural address presented on April 15, 1913, in the *CCP*.

467. *WSJ*, October 24, 1920.

468. One of the most intriguing aspects of local history is to speculate on how the city might have developed had today's hospitals been located somewhere else. For example, what would the Marquette neighborhood have been like had Madison General been located in the block bounded by Lake Monona, South Brearly, and Spaight? Or Orton Park? Alternatively, how would the Second District have developed differently had Madison General been located at the foot of North Patterson Street, or had the Sisters of Mercy been successful in building their high-rise hospital on the hill just south of Tenney Park?

469. Hugo Muller, "A Sanitary Survey of Madison" (Master's thesis in public Health, University of Wisconsin, 1916).

470. Many physicians looked down their noses at Madison's first health officers on the grounds that they were not able to maintain an ordinary practice and therefore had to take the city job. See the annual reports for the years 1889 and 1886, and Smillie, pp. 232–233.

471. *WSJ*, September 23, 1915, and 1915 Board of Health, p. 1.

472. See the *WSJ* series entitled "What Madison Needs," March 5, 11, 19, 1907.

473. See the *WSJ*, October 14, 1911, and Charles A. Beard, *American City Government* (New York: The Century Company, 1912), p. 345.

474. See the *School Board Annual Report*, 1915–1916, p. 42.

475. *WSJ*, September 12, 1911, and October 23, 1912.

476. See John Valentine, "A Study of Institutional Americanization: the Assimilative History of the Italian-American Community of Madison" (University of Wisconsin master's thesis, 1967).

477. Central to their vision of the New Madison was a new concept of cities. This point was the central theme of a book published in 1902 by U. W. Professor Richard T. Ely entitled *The Coming City*. Ely noted that contrary to the expectations of Jeffersonian agrarianism, an increasing percentage of the American people were living in cities and that the time would soon come when the majority of U.S. citizens would live in cities. Therefore, he urged his readers to "prepare for the coming domination of the city" (pp. 71–72) by recognizing that the highest ideals of western civilization—religion, art, and learning—had been achieved in cities such as Jerusalem, Athens, Rome, Florence, London, Paris, and Berlin, to name just a few. The challenge facing the United States, he argued, was to formulate new urban ideals for the new urban age then underway.

478. Ely, p. 73.

479. Ely, p. 45.

480. Author statistics.

481. The university also made several other important technical contributions to Madison's development. In 1903 the city hired Professor Turneaure to prepare a cost and feasibility study of a municipal lighting plant. In 1905 Dr. Harry L. Russell, the dean of the college of agriculture, teamed up with several members of the Madison's Woman's Club to develop a tough milk inspection ordinance.

482. See the quote by Emerson Ela in the article on municipal streetcar ownership, *WSJ*, December 4, 1912.

The Great War and Beyond

1. Gertrude Slaughter, *Only the Past Is Ours* (New York: Exposition Press, 1963), pp. 180–181.

2. *WSJ*, August 5, 1914.

3. *WSJ*, October 15, 1914.

4. Kennith D. Ruble, *The Rayovac Story: The First 75 Years* (North Central Publishing Company, 1981), p. 7–8.

5. *WSJ*, November 20, 1914.

6. *WSJ*, September 14, 1915.

7. *WSJ*, December 31, 1916.

8. See *WSJ*, June 18, 20, 22, December 19, 1916, January 20, 1917.

9. Election statistics were compiled by the author.

10. For articles on the Red Cross, see the *WSJ*, May 23, 24, June 18, 19, 1917, the *CT*, December 26, 1917, and the *CT* and *WSJ*, May 25, 1918. For descriptions of the first Liberty Loan drive, see the *WSJ*, May 27, and June 12, 1917.

11. Memorandum to the author dated April 1, 1982, from the Wisconsin Department of Veterans Affairs.

12. For a representative sampling of food conservation efforts, see the *WSJ*, May 11, June 3, July 1, 8, September 8, October 31, November 2, 3, 7, 9, 1917, January 19, February 6, 15, June 20, 21, 1918, and the *CT*, January 22, February 8, 13, 20, May 1, 1918.

13. *CT* and *WSJ*, January 15–22, 1918.

14. *CCP*, April 16, 1918, and *WSJ*, August 6, September 26, 1918. Also, to insure the availability of paper pulp, Madison newspapers were required to reduce the size of the papers.

15. *WSJ*, September 27, October 18, 1918.

16. Agnes M. Larson, *John A. Johnson: An Uncommon American* (Northfield, Minn.: The Norwegian-American Historical Association, 1969), pp. 202–203.

17. *WSJ*, October 24, 1917.

18. *WSJ*, January 21, 1918, and *CT*, January 31, 1918.

19. *WSJ*, December 31, 1918.

20. See Curti and Carstensen, II, p. 119, and *WSJ*, October 22, 1918.

21. *WSJ*, April 27, 1917, *CT*, January 8, 1918, and *WSJ*, October 29, 1918.

22. *WSJ*, October 21, 1918.

23. *WSJ*, January 10, 1918, 1917–1918 Superintendents Annual Report, pp. 61, 73–75.

24. *WSJ*, November 1, 14, 18, 25, 1917, and January 20, 1918. The rapid entry into the workforce produced charges that factory owners were giving men's jobs to women at a fraction of men's pay. For an analysis of this issue see a study of Janet Van Hise published in the *CT*, May 25, 27, 29, 30, 1918.

25. *WSJ*, December 13, 1917, and the *CT*, December 29, 1917, January 15, February 26, and March 6, 1918.

26. See the *CT,* February 13, August 13, 1918.

27. *WSJ,* March 30, 1918.

28. *WSJ,* April 2, 1919. For other sources for the Kroncke incident, see the newspapers from March 24, 1917, to mid-April, 1917.

29. *WSJ,* December 9, 1917, July 31, August 1, 16, 1918.

30. For accounts of this imcident, see the *CT,* June 5, 1918, *WSJ,* June 10, 12, 20, and September 10, 15, 18, 1918.

31. See the *WSJ,* June 22, August 1, and September 26, 1917, and Curti and Carstensen, II, pp. 322–327.

32. *WSJ,* April 27, 1917, and all papers during January 1918.

33. For accounts of the Spanish Influenza, see the newspapers from October 4 to early December, 1918, and health department reports.

34. *WSJ,* November 7, 1918, *CT,* November 8, 1918.

35. *WSJ,* November 12, 1918, *CT* and *WSJ,* November 11, 1918. Casvalty statistics are taken from John D. Gregory, *Wisconsin Gold Star List* (Madison: SHSW, 1925).

36. Information on this turbulent period of Madison's history is found in Harold E. Miner's unpublished manuscript "Madison Labor" in the SHSW. This paper was prepared under the auspices of the U.S. Progress Works Administration during the Great Depression. Two other excellent sources are George. D. Spohn's "The Madison Strike of 1919," and unpublished U. W. master's thesis (1920) and Noah J. Frey's papers collected by the Mayor's Committee on the Strike Situation, SHSW. These sources were supplemented by dozens of contemporary newspaper accounts from December 1918 to July 1919.

Society and Leisure

1. For examples of such recollections, see Gertrude Slaughter's *Only the Past Is Ours* (New York: Exposition Press, 1963), and tape recordings on file at the SHSW by Mrs. Harry Mosely and Mrs. Lucien M. Hanks.

2. This portrait is based upon occupational analyses, county poor records, and a variety of other sources. One particularly revealing though wrong-headed study of Madison's poor was Florence Van Slyke Nelson's 1903 U.S. Bachelor of Letters paper, "Representative Delinquents and Dependents of the City of Madison," available at the SHSW.

3. See *WSJ,* October 1, 1916, January 26, 1907, Ordinance #1525 passed on May 13, 1910, and a letter to the *WSJ* editor by Carl Russell Fisk printed on February 21, 1916.

4. *WSJ,* October 30, 1919, February 17, 1912, May 14, 1906, March 21, 1910, March 25, 1900, November 2, 1907.

5. Ordinance #1253 passed January 11, 1902, *WSJ,* July 23, 1902.

6. For early articles on the Boy Scouts see *WSJ,* December 30, 1910. In a committee report to the Common Council on the new Burr Jones playground on November 27, 1906, members expressed the "candid paternalism" mentioned in the text. A properly administered playground, they reported, "corrects many of the dangerous and perverted tendencies antagonistic to social well being in community life. . . . It is generally conceded that the surplus energies of youth must find an outlet." Either we can harness this energy and direct it toward a "more noble manhood" or we can allow these "perverted and unseeming propensities to go uncontrolled. . . ." This same sentiment was embodied in the outstanding 1915 Board of Commerce *Recreational Survey.*

For articles on Pilgrim Church see the *WSJ,* December 10, 1914, and a pamphlet entitled "The Community and the Sunday School," available in the SHSW Archives under Pilgrim Church.

7. *WSJ,* October 6, 1908, May 31, 1914, October 6, 1914, May 30, 1915, May 29, 1920, and author statistics.

8. *WSJ,* January 10, 1910.

9. *WSJ,* July 6, 1920.

10. Ordinance #1882, passed May 25, 1918.

11. See Ordinance #1638 passed in July 1913, and the *WSJ,* November 24, 1913, and November 21, 1914.

12. See the summary of the sermon by Rev. George Hunt, *WSJ,* January 10, 1910.

13. Sources for Madison's Italian history include an outstanding 1967 University of Wisconsin Master's thesis by John Valentine, "A Study of Institutional Americanization? The Assimilative History of the Italian-American Community of Madison" and articles in the *WSJ,* February 23, 1913, and March 18, 1917.

14. For details on this ethnic group see Leslie H. Goldsmith's article, "German-Jewish and Russian-Jewish Immigration: Assimilation and a Ghetto in Madison," *The Journal of Historic Madison* 3 (Madison, 1977), pp. 28–44, and Manfred Swarsensky's *From Generation to Generation: The Story of the Madison Jewish Community, 1851–1944* (Madison, 1955).

15. For articles on the formation of the Free African Methodist Church, see the *WSJ,* October 8, 1901, the *WSJ,* March 4, April 9, 1902, and the *MD,* February 9 and June 7, 1902. Another useful source is Kim Efird's "A History of the Blacks of Madison," an unpublished 1970 paper prepared for a Carthage College class. Minutes of the Book Lovers Club are available at the SHSW Archives.

16. *WSJ,* April 21, 1909.

17. *WSJ,* October 25, 1911.

18. *WSJ,* July 10, 1914, June 30, 1915.

19. William T. Evjue, *A Fighting Editor* (Madison: Wells Printing Co., 1968), pp. 99–100.

20. *WSJ,* September 17, 1904, *MD,* April 29, 1906, *WSJ,* January 19, 1909, October 16, 1909.

21. *WSJ,* October 13, 1914.

22. *WSJ,* July 17, 1908.

23. Henry Youngerman, "Theatrical Activities, Madison, Wisconsin, 1836–1907" (Ph.D. dissertation, University of Wisconsin, 1940), pp. 73–74.

24. *WSJ,* October 30, 1906, April 30, May 4, 6, 1907.

25. *WSJ,* December 2, 1913.

26. Ibid.

27. Madison Board of Commerce, *Madison, The Four Lake City: Recreational Survey* (Madison: Board of Commerce, 1915), p. 52.

28. *Community Business,* October 16, 1918, and *WSJ,* September 22, 1918.

29. *WSJ,* December 31, 1916.

30. *Recreational Survey,* p. 59.

31. *WSJ,* June 19, 1920.

32. *Recreational Survey,* pp. 55–57.

33. John C. Gregory, *History of Southwestern Wisconsin* (Chicago: S. J. Clark Publishing Co., 1932), Vol. II, p. 787; and Curti and Carstensen, Vol. II, p. 347.

34. See *WSJ,* November 1, 1902, October 30, 1903, October 31, 1912, and Normal Weissman, p. 38, for examples of this frenzy.

35. See *WSJ,* January 16, 26, May 9, 1907, July 31, September 15, 1908, May 6, September 8, 1909, September 9, 1913, July 30, 1914, and November 20, 1914.

36. For descriptions of this trend see *WSJ,* June 26, 1901, July 1, 1903, *MD,* May 14, 1904, *WSJ,* July 19, 1910.

37. *WSJ,* April 12, May 21, 1907.

38. *WSJ,* June 10, 1907.

39. *WSJ,* August 2, 1910.

40. Madison bicycle dealers attributed the doubled number of "wheels" in the city between 1906 and 1909 to a variety of reasons. Following certain technical improvements such as the coaster brake and reliable pneumatic tires, the bicycle was the cheapest, fastest, most convenient and most enjoyable way to get around. *WSJ,* March 29, 1906, and June 9, 1909.

41. *WSJ,* August 17, 1909.

42. *WSJ,* July 5, 1911.

43. *WSJ,* February 10, 1913.

44. *WSJ,* October 18, 1910, November 18, 1899.

45. *WSJ,* February 4, 1916, November 9, 1914.

Epilogue

1. *WSJ,* August 22, 1920.

Index

This index contains the names of people, places and subjects included in the narrative and figure legends (captions). Entries from narrative material will appear in regular type and entries from captions will appear in boldface type.